ENCYCLOPEDIA OF AESTHETICS

ENCYCLOPEDIA OF

AESTHETICS

MICHAEL KELLY

Editor in Chief

Volume 4

OXFORD UNIVERSITY PRESS

New York   1998   Oxford

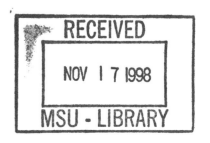

OXFORD UNIVERSITY PRESS

Oxford   New York
Athens   Auckland   Bangkok   Bogotá
Buenos Aires   Calcutta   Cape Town   Chennai
Dar es Salaam   Delhi   Florence   Hong Kong   Istanbul
Karachi   Kuala Lumpur   Madrid   Melbourne   Mexico City
Mumbai   Nairobi   Paris   São Paulo   Singapore
Taipei   Tokyo   Toronto   Warsaw

and associated companies in
Berlin   Ibadan

Published by Oxford University Press, Inc.,
198 Madison Avenue, New York, New York 10016
http://www.oup-usa.org

Oxford is a registered trademark of Oxford University Press

Library of Congress Cataloging-in-Publication Data
Encyclopedia of aesthetics / editor in chief, Michael Kelly.
p.   cm.
Includes bibliographical references and index.
1. Aesthetics—Encyclopedias.   I. Kelly, Michael, 1953–.
BH56.E53   1998   111′.85′03—dc21   98-18741 CIP
ISBN 0-19-511307-1 (set)
ISBN 0-19-512648-3 (vol. 4)

Printing (last digit): 9 8 7 6 5 4 3 2 1

Printed in the United States of America
on acid-free paper

P

CONTINUED

PLEASURE. The concept of pleasure is fundamental to aesthetics as it arose in the eighteenth century as a specific style of philosophical meditation on the nature of art and beauty. Having decided that taste is the central category under which the aesthetic is be thought, taste is in turn conceived of as the capacity for a special and rarefied kind of pleasure taken in the sensuous encounter with—indifferently—art and nature. Eighteenth-century theories that enfranchise the aesthetic as the central category of experience and value in terms of which art and beauty are to be thought, do so in part by attempting to specify what is distinctive about "aesthetic" pleasure. Highly sublimated and even "contemplative" in character, largely (in the case of Immanuel Kant completely) drained of desire and interest, such pleasure does not function to impel a person to get up and act but serves instead as a form of enjoyment that occurs "for its own sake." Self-justifying in essence, the autonomous character of such enjoyment from the stream of life in which it is set is in fact just what serves to justify it. For in accord with the great eighteenth-century idea that persons are autonomous beings who are by natural capacity and right able to form their own "pursuits of happiness," to follow through on their own life plans in accord with their tastes and desires, the exercise of taste (i.e., of this species of pleasure) is conceived of as part of this exercise of personal autonomy, and indeed as a celebration of it. In aesthetic enjoyment—in enjoyment for its own sake—is thus contained the promise of human happiness.

Eighteenth-century aesthetic theory quickly comes to see, however, that it cannot succeed in getting remotely clear on, much less define, taste purely by reference to the kind of pleasure that pertains to it. It must take a dual approach: at once attempting to mark out aesthetic pleasure as a distinctive psychological or metaphysical kind, and attempting to mark out the objects of taste in terms of what is distinctive about them. For pleasure is too diffuse a kind of thing—its domain, range, and vicissitudes are too opaque, its intermediate cases too many—for any definition of the aesthetic to rest entirely on it. We cannot beyond a certain point know what pleasure (or enjoyment or delight) is apart from speaking about the kinds of objects toward which it directs its gaze and which occasion or cause it. Aesthetic pleasure must therefore be characterized not merely in terms of its psychological or "metaphysical" kind but also in terms of the kinds of objects, events, or forms (the sunsets, paintings, performances, colors, shapes, timbres) toward which the "aesthetic attitude" is directed.

Eighteenth-century aesthetic theory may be glossed as having its origins in the writings of David Hume and Kant, who set the two conceptual poles in terms of which taste is thought. Each philosopher takes this dual approach. According to Hume, taste involves the capacity to detect the subtle parts of objects (Hume calls this "delicacy of passion") as it operates in conjunction with the ability to respond vividly to their material and formal qualities (he calls this "strong sense"). Insofar as one is defective in these (and other) characteristics, one's taste is lacking. The pleasure caused by this act of vivid yet delicate perception is of a refined sort (relatively distant from the powerful desires that lead directly to action). Similarly, the unpleasure caused by an equally intense survey of "distasteful" objects is of a refined sort that does not lead to the violent feelings felt about truly repugnant things. Feeling such pleasure (or unpleasure) is itself the judgment of taste (the act of feeling says, "I like it" or "It does not appeal to me"). Therefore, taste is both the capacity to detect properties of objects (their delicate colors, shapes, expressive nuances, narrative intensities, brilliant chiaroscuros, floral aromas) and the actual pleasure caused by this attitude of perception. While pleasure or displeasure (the judgment of taste) is described as a causal effect of the object, it is easy to see that pleasure (in the sense of enjoyment) is also (along with modes of tension and attention) the attitude under which vivid and delicate parts of the object are perceived. Pleasure is a "sliding signifier": it is both a causal state and an attitude of enjoyment directed toward its object. Pleasure suffuses the entire aesthetic event.

By contrast, Kant begins by specifying taste as a metaphysical kind: it is a noncognitive, disinterested (read: free of all interest) delight taken in an "object." Being free of all interest this type of delight does not involve any ordinary experience of psychological "satisfaction." (Similarly, it is unrelated in kind to the unpleasure of dissatisfaction or the frustration felt at the interruption of satisfaction.) This in turn means that the delight is in no way conditioned on properties of the object itself. For were the delight directed toward and caused by the specific properties of the objects of taste, these properties would excite our interest (by virtue of their pleasurable effects), and the perception of them would provide us with "satisfaction." It thus follows, somewhat astoundingly, from the disinterested condition of taste that delight must be unconditioned by the object. What, then, is it directed toward? It can only be directed toward the subject herself. The Kantian twist is that the objects, events, natural scenes, or performances we perceive are the mere occasions for the imagination to construct from them a harmonious play of forms. Kant describes this free play of forms as the "harmonization" of the subject's "faculties." Perhaps the deepest theorist of autonomy in the entire history of aesthetics, Kant is therefore saying that taste is the subject's means of taking pleasure in herself: in her own capacities for autonomous harmonization. Note that even Kant cannot avoid saying something about the "object" of pleasure, and he tells us that the free play of harmonization that is the "object" of delight is characterized by "purposiveness without purpose." All the forms seem to conspire to produce some end, even though they have in actuality no end at all and are "for their own sake." This is important for Kant because it shows that in her experience of delight, the subject is celebrating her own capacity for free and purposive activity: for moral activity. Taste is the celebration of autonomy, not merely (as in Hume) its exercise. [See Hume; and Kant.]

In the history of aesthetics since the eighteenth century, the concept of pleasure has gone through a number of reconceptualizations that have partly freed it from its connection with taste. Two in particular will be noted here, and a third, of special importance, will be noted below. All are part of the legacy of present thinking on pleasure, making our current approaches multiperspectival and highly fragmented. The first major changes in the concept occur in the late nineteenth and early twentieth centuries with the vitalist writing of George Santayana and John Dewey. Writing as they are in the whirl of a modernity whose rhythm and energy appear indomitable, writing also in response to biological theory that preaches the organismic "energy" of the species, these thinkers conceive of art and the aesthetic as experience writ large, experience intensified in all of its energies, vitalized to the point of ecstasy, and characterized by the pleasures of memory, repetition, crisscrossing between art and life, and the transmogrification of fragments into wholes. For Dewey, "having an experience" becomes a theoretical ideal and practical achievement defined by its robustness and wholeness. In a noted phrase, he now thinks of the opposite of the aesthetic not as a state of displeasure but as the an-aesthetic: an "aenesthecized" state in which experience is diminished, habitual to the point of catatonia or anhedonia. In the rich liveliness of "experience," form and content merge organically since form is nothing other than the way content unravels and comes to completion (in a thrust of formal mastery). The distinctiveness of art (its formal pleasure associated with timbres, colors, modeling,

carving, representation, song, and the like) pales into oblivion; what is stressed are the crisscrossings between the arts and the energies of life generally. Everything that happens in art happens because it also happens elsewhere, and vice versa. Simultaneity and interpenetration, two of John Cage's basic ideas for avant-garde art, find their origin here. It is not fortuitous that Dewey is writing out of direct experience of early avant-garde art (the canvases of Henri Matisse, Pablo Picasso, Paul Cézanne, and others that he is privileged to see in the collection of his friend Albert Barnes). [See Dewey; and Santayana.]

It is worth noting that this American immersion of aesthetics into the whirl of modernity has its counterpart in the writing of Charles Baudelaire (who famously inaugurates the aesthetics of modernity with his concept of "the pleasure of the present" half a century earlier than Dewey). Baudelaire is keener to stress the pleasures of the fragmentary than Dewey, who is obsessed with the way the embodied person formulates wholeness out of the blooming, buzzing confusion of experience. Baudelaire's *flâneur* resists the imposition of wholeness, preferring to sample, taste (taste is still important), watch, wait, and purchase from the contingent and modulating spectacle that is Parisian modernity. It is the impression as such, not simply its transmutation into an eternalized form of wholeness (in art); it is the transience of things, not simply their eternalization in Impressionist painting, that counts. What is at stake is reverie as much as formulation.

With Baudelaire pleasure is reconceptualized in another new way: as a poetic mood of the subject that must always be thought in relation to states of pain or "spleen" that give pleasure meaning and shape and that are themselves part of the aesthetic as such. Pleasure is a mode of apprehending the world, a mood of abandonment to its details of transience and reverie at its details, yet this mood is always counterbalanced by attitudes of resentment, anxiety, boredom, and disenchantment that are at once essential to the subject and directed to the "disenchantment" produced by modernity itself. (Again, pleasure and pain are characterized in part in terms of their quality and in part in terms of the object—modernity and the self's being in it—to which they are directed.) If the aesthetic is about the proprioceptive and emotional embodiment of the subject in the world, then pain is now thought to be a fundamental part of the aesthetic rather than the mere interruption or negation of it. [See Baudelaire.]

This second change in how pleasure is thought in relation to the aesthetic is immensely deepened by Sigmund Freud and psychoanalysis. Pleasure (in art and life) is now rethought in terms of a locus of concepts: the unconscious, the principles of association, overdetermination, the ideas of fantasy, wish fulfillment, symptom, and working through, but also in terms of the idea of unconscious conflicts, repressions, anxieties, and, finally, death wishes, that engender the structure of fantasy, repetition, and working through. Freud thinks of pleasure in art in various interrelated ways, and together these provide a rich picture of the complexity of pleasure. The pleasures of art consist in a repetition of earlier pleasures taken in childhood play. Reading across his writings freely, we can see that Freud thinks of childhood games as occurring for a number of reasons, any or all of which may be repeated in the work of art. Games may serve the mere purpose of spontaneous fun. They may have cognitive purposes. Or they may be symbolic ways in which the child acts out, expresses in symptomatic form, or works through unconscious conflict—as in Freud's famous description of his grandchild's game of sending a ball out and uttering "fort!" ("gone!"; "out there!") and then bringing it back and uttering "da!" ("here!"; "here again!"; Freud, 1957). Freud tells us that through this repetitive game the child is symbolically working through the dislocation and anxiety surrounding his separation from the mother. He goes on to tell us that this rhythm of sending the self (the ball) out and then pulling it back in is also the rhythm of mourning: the mourning process repeats the childhood process of separation. In the work of art this and many other such games may be repeated: the pleasure in art (as well as its pain) consisting of the pleasures in this symbolic act of working through unconscious conflicts and requirements of all kinds.

Freud also assimilates the pleasure in art to the (often unconscious) wish fulfillments encoded in fantasies and dreams. In the work of art, formal pleasures "seduce" the viewer to take up an identification with the artist's own unconscious fantasies, which therefore spread the pleasure associated with them from artist to viewer. In art we should find exhibited the wish to be loved, to dominate, to possess the phallic grandiosity of a Don Giovanni or the Oedipal victory of an Electra, and the panoply of pleasures associated with the fulfillment of these desires through the mechanism of fantasy. Indeed, both Freud and the character of Giovanni have shown that the artist (be he a painter or a *Lebenskunstler*) may "win through his art what the neurotic merely wins in fantasy (and, we may add, the viewer wins only through identification with the artist): fame, fortune and the love of beautiful women." This highly gendered remark (which views women as prizes to be won like money or travel) is spoken by Freud but responds to the romanticization of the artist as a person capable of bringing about special pleasures through his sacred and seductive instrument (read: phallus). (Of course, if Giovanni is an example, he will die by the hand of the law of the father in the end. The "Oedipal victory" is short-lived.)

Finally, Freud speaks of the pleasures of art in connection with those of sublimation. Leonardo da Vinci's art is said to allow that painter the pleasure of sublimating his symptomatic "compromise formations" into a new and vital domain where "talent and genius" subsume the neurotic im-

pulse and give it transformed form. That is, the artwork may be understood as itself a symptom: an arena of representation in which desire and its negation are simultaneously expressed, a "compromise formation" in Freud's own language. Again, Freud will tell us that it is the beauty of the work of art's form that will "seduce" the viewer into accepting and even enjoying this symptomatic "content." (We may assume that it is through the sublimation of symptom into form that the fantasy of wish fulfillment is likewise expressed by the artist and "accepted" by the audience, on Freud's account.) Note that Freud's own account of sublimation in art is not adequate to the complexity of the concept he actually introduced, since the pleasures of sublimation will, if deep enough, pass far beyond the mere exhibition of symptoms into a realm of elevation in which desire is given space to be born. No doubt this elevation of desire will also involve the anxieties of the sublime, since an expressive act in which unrepresentable desire is brought to presentation must bring forth terror as well as joy: the fear of obliteration by "the I that is elsewhere [than in myself]," as Jacques Lacan, the deepest theorist of *jouissance* (the sublime), will say. It is well known that the art of the twentieth century contains these depths of expression, making important regions of it an occasion for terror and self-obliteration (whose generic name is "pain"), as well as for the raising up of conflict into its revelatory and communicable forms. It is not by accident that Jackson Pollock was deeply influenced by the field of psychoanalysis.

Nor is Freud's account adequate to ideas that he breached at the end of his life about the "death instinct," alternately phrased as the desire on the part of the organism to attain a total state of null excitation (Dewey's "anaesthetic") and as a masochistic desire for the pleasure inflicted through painful excitations. Whether or not the death instinct is an instinct, or is even coherent as a singular concept (see Laplanche, 1976), it is certain that human "self-destructive" desires do give rise to repetition/compulsion in art, especially in twentieth-century Modernist art, which expresses a planet on the brink of self-annihilation and, more particularly, art on the brink of self-annihilation (see Foster, 1993, and Herwitz, 1995). [*See* Freud.]

Lacan's complex "writing through" of Freud has engendered in his followers a picture of the poetic as an existential and indeed metaphysical state in which the symbolic rule of the father is partly "suspended." Through an amalgamation of psychoanalysis and avant-garde culture, Lacanians associate the poetically amniotic and disruptive values of modernist writing with the capacity for the subject's desire to break through the bounds of law, which have been imposed on it during the moment of the Oedipal conflict. In that psychological moment, "desire is castrated," and law in its most general form (moral, cultural, linguistic, legal, even stylistic) is imposed on the body and person of the subject, thus making him or her into a "person." To be a person is therefore to lack wholeness, which means that the fantasy of wholeness is fundamental to the human condition. The work of art can represent a breakthrough of *jouissance:* the sublime, unrepresentable flow of primordial desire known only by its lack, in which erotic joy, amniotic oneness, and reverie merge and spontaneously recur, thus affording a unique and untranslatable form of enjoyment and renewal (the roots of Lacan in Baudelaire's poetics of reverie are also clear).

The work of Lacan has also given rise to a mode of critiquing practices of enjoyment as they are psychologically constituted. The fantasy of wholeness can lead to regression to the famous "mirror phase," in which the young, childlike Narcissus misrecognizes his own reflection and takes himself to be perfect. This desire for the return to the illusion of perfection, the desire to defeat the recognition that one is forever incomplete, tends, according to Lacan, to be played out visually, since in the earlier mirror phase the sense of perfection is engendered visually (through the "scopophilic" drive). In the light of Lacan's work, visual and plastic art—especially cinema—have undergone a generation of interrogation regarding the extent to which these media inculcate the scopophilic pleasures associated with this fantasy. [*See* Lacan.]

It is a great insight of the twentieth century that the cultivation of practices of enjoyment—like the theorization of enjoyment that arises in conjunction with those practices—can serve to inculcate scopophilic fantasies, forms of fetishization, and, ultimately, styles of domination. One can call this insight the twentieth century's response to the great eighteenth-century Enlightenment thought (again due to Kant but deepened by Friedrich von Schiller) that a culture may achieve a route toward moral perfectionism by developing shared forms of pleasure ("delight"). Kant believes in the need to cultivate a *sensus communis:* a community of taste in which persons will share objects in which delight is taken, thus at once taking pleasure in their shared moral capacities and taking pleasure in the fact that all other members of the community are taking the same pleasure as themselves. This idea finds its first and most trenchant criticisms in the 1880s in the writings of Friedrich Nietzsche, the third and perhaps most overarching innovator in the thinking about pleasure. Nietzsche formulated the thought that enjoyment taken in the moral self must be understood as a cultural construction—the construction of the entire history of the West—which represses the genuine pleasure an individualized and empowered subject might take in the contours of his own life, mortifies the subject into believing that he is guilty (which for Nietzsche means nothing else than that he believes that he has a soul that can "speak the truth about life"), and thus constructs him as a person displaced from his own potential sources of power. The pleasure this disempowered subject is now brought to take in the kind of highly sublimated art, nature, and religion that

Kant praised is for Nietzsche a form of compensatory enjoyment, a form of pleasure in the ascetic rather than the genuine aesthetic. Indeed, for Nietzsche the history of eighteenth-century aesthetics is really part of the history of the ascetic—part of the history by which the subject is mortified. For Kant's delight in the moral is in effect a symptom of the power of desire blocked from its own expression. Kantian delight is an aspirin that makes the subject feel better about her dispossessed (read: moralized) self but in the end does her no more good than Karl Marx's "opiate of the masses" does. Thus, aesthetic enjoyment for Nietzsche, and after him for Michel Foucault, is always to be understood in terms of its modality of power: in terms of how it empowers women, cultures, selves, and the like, or disempowers them through hegemonic practices or symptomatic displacements of desire into "delight."

Indeed, it is not by chance that the category of autonomous aesthetic enjoyment arose historically in conjunction with the institution of the museum in the European capitals of the eighteenth century. For the modern museum also displaces works of art from the sites of their making and the streams of life in which they are set and places them in ordered relations (chronological, regional, by media, and so on) with other artworks—some of which would seem quite unrelated to each other when viewed in situ. Having been displaced from the sites of their enmeshment and turned into sights to be viewed in abstraction by the fascinated and absorbed viewer, artworks are now relegated to the realm of autonomous enjoyment (read: enjoyment abstracted from and oblivious of context, which means of the otherness of the work). This removal of art from the world of its locality, tradition, social commerce, and distinctive cultural conceptualization, this orphaning, prepares the category of the aesthetic by assimilating art to the category of abstract natural beauty, with a work of art "meaning" little more than a sunset or a waterfall. Autonomous enjoyment was for Europeans in part the power to turn the art and culture of the other into a museumized sign, an abstracted, naturalized form for their own gaze. Not to overstate this point, but even Kant's theory of aesthetic autonomy must be understood to arise in conjunction with (and play some role in articulating) practices of enjoyment that license this abstracted gaze: a gaze disinterested in the otherness of colonial art and culture. In this specific sense, eighteenth-century theories of taste license domination through styles of (abstracted) enjoyment. Herein resides the Foucauldian interrogation of enjoyment and its theorization by eighteenth-century aesthetics.

We are now in a position to draw three general consequences about the history of "aesthetic" pleasure.

1. The realm of "aesthetic pleasure" is always conceptualized as a cross section between art and something else. Whether the pleasures of art are assimilated to the realm of taste (which goes beyond art to include nature and, in

Hume's case, whatever we ordinarily have taste in), to the realm of the vitalist (which is everywhere and nowhere), to the realm of fantasies, dreams, and sublimations (which inform all representations), or to the poststructuralist realm of that place where desire is freed from the domination of law (linguistic, Oedipal, moral, cultural, legal), enjoyment in art will always be thought in relation to a set of models, examples or regions of life with which it is seen to have essential relations. As the conceptualization of pleasure changes, so the other regions of life with which enjoyment in art is thought to be essentially connected also change. We thus have a history of these realignments between art and whatever else that is the history of writing about pleasure in art. It is the history of the aesthetic—that always amorphous, always partly articulated, always shifting domain.

2. Pleasure must always be thought of in relation to its opposite (distaste, anhedonia, masochism), which changes and whose aesthetic relevance changes.

3. The history of these theories of pleasure (and unpleasure) must be contextualized in relation to two other histories. It must be understood in relation to the history of art and culture. As the history of art evolves, so modernity brings its changes to the practices of cultural enjoyment, changing their dimension, their quality, and their centrality. The theory of pleasure must thus change accordingly to keep pace. (No doubt the history of art and culture evolves in part by absorbing new concepts of pleasure, making the exchange between these semiautonomous histories a two-way one.) In short, art practices have changed since the eighteenth century from an art of delight (Jean-Antoine Watteau, Joshua Reynolds, the Rococo) and absorption (Jean-Baptiste Greuze, Jean-Baptiste-Siméon Chardin) to an art of twentieth-century avant-garde practices no longer concerned with pleasure primarily but instead with increasingly deep and painful expression (which finds its theoretical voice in the theories of R. G. Collingwood and Benedetto Croce), cultural interruption, the construction of radical futures, with the interrogation of cultural rationality, the defamiliarization of ordinary belief, the destruction of past aesthetics, especially of nature and naturalism, and with the sublime in all of its forms. This history of art has also inaugurated its own critique of pleasure, and this history, from Édouard Manet to contemporary postmodern practices via the route of Marcel Duchamp, is well known and is evidently in alliance with the history of theory. Some would call it a history of theory, although this is to forget that the medium of writing theory (mostly in the academy) is substantially different from that of making it arise through an experimental practice with plastic forms.

The history of pleasure must also be understood in relation to the history of institutions (the growth of the concert hall, the museum, the academy of art, the gallery system), of technologies (mass media and so on), and to the larger socioeconomic setting (the growth of commodity capitalism, etc.) in which art is played out. It is the crisscrossing intersections of these histories that together characterize the history of enjoyment from its inception in the eighteenth century to the present. But in thinking through these crisscrossings, let us not assume that each notion of pleasure renders its predecessor wholly obsolete. No doubt we should not dehistoricize the history of pleasure to the point where we believe that every concept of pleasure applies to every work of art. That would simply be to project onto art a postmodern attitude according to which theories of enjoyment are tried on objects like clothes in a department store. New notions of pleasure do arise historically (for example, in the context of late modernity) that are to some degree irrelevant to past art. New art arises that renders past notions to a degree out of date. But we also need the entire range of what has been thought and practiced in the history of pleasure to stand as potentially available for the interpretation of any art object. We need, for example, the concept of taste to interpret Cézanne's choices of his motifs and even Duchamp's composition of parts into wholes. Similarly, we need the concepts of fantasy, reverie, and "working through" to speak to the elegant and playful art of Watteau with its whiffs of psychologically dark chiaroscuro. Pleasure never comes simple, even if it is spontaneous. Pleasure is overdetermined and must be approached from various perspectives. What pleasure in art does is to confirm for both the artist and the viewer that to be embodied in the world is to participate in this spontaneity of feeling, without which one is not human.

[*See also* Emotions; *and* Taste.]

BIBLIOGRAPHY

Baudelaire, Charles. "The Painter of Modern Life." In *The Painter of Modern Life and Other Essays,* translated by Jonathan Mayne, pp. 1–41. London, 1964.

Collingwood, R. G. *The Principles of Art.* Oxford, 1938.

Croce, Benedetto. *Aesthetic* (1902). Translated by Douglas Ainslie. Rev. ed. Reprint, Boston, 1978.

Croce, Benedetto. *Guide to Aesthetics* (1913). Translated by Patrick Romanell (1965). Indianapolis, 1995.

Dewey, John. *Art as Experience* (1934). Reprint, New York, 1979.

Foster, Hal. *Compulsive Beauty.* Cambridge, Mass., 1993.

Foucault, Michel. *The Order of Things: An Archaeology of the Human Sciences.* New York, 1970.

Freud, Sigmund. "The Relation of the Poet to Day-Dreaming" (1908). Translated by Grant Duff. In *Character and Culture,* edited by Philip Reiff, pp. 34–43. New York, 1963.

Freud, Sigmund. *Leonardo da Vinci and a Memory of His Childhood* (1910). Translated by Alan Tyson. New York, 1964.

Freud, Sigmund. "Mourning and Melancholia" (1917). Translated by Joan Riviere. In *The Standard Edition of the Complete Psychological Works of Sigmund Freud,* edited by James Strachey, vol. 14, pp. 237–258.

Herwitz, Daniel. "Review of Hal Foster, *Compulsive Beauty." Journal of Aesthetics and Art Criticism* 53.4 (Fall 1995): 433–435.

Hume, David. "Of the Standard of Taste." In *Essays: Moral, Political, Literary,* rev. ed., edited by Eugene F. Miller, pp 226–249. Indianapolis, 1987.

Kant, Immanuel. *Critique of Judgment.* Translated by Werner S. Pluhar. Indianapolis, 1987.

Kristeva, Julia. *The Kristeva Reader.* Edited by Toril Moi. New York, 1986.

Lacan, Jacques. *Ecrits: A Selection.* Translated by Alan Sheridan. New York, 1977.

Laplanche, Jean. *Life and Death in Psychoanalysis.* Translated by Jeffrey Mehlman. Baltimore, 1976.

Melville, Stephen. "Psychoanalysis and the Place of *Jouissance*." *Critical Inquiry* 13.2 (Winter 1987): 349–370.

Mulvey, Laura. "Visual Pleasure and Narrative Cinema." In *Narrative, Apparatus, Ideology,* edited by Philip Rosen, pp. 198–209. New York, 1986.

Nietzsche, Friedrich. *The Genealogy of Morals* (with *The Birth of Tragedy*). Translated by Francis Goffling. Garden City, N.Y., 1956.

Santayana, George. *The Sense of Beauty.* New York, 1896.

Santayana, George. *Reason in Art.* New York, 1905.

Wollheim, Richard. *Painting as an Art.* Princeton, N.J., 1987.

Wollheim, Richard. "Freud and the Understanding of Art." In *The Cambridge Companion to Freud,* edited by Jerome Neu, pp. 249–266 Cambridge and New York, 1992.

DANIEL HERWITZ

PLOTINUS (205–270 CE), Roman Neoplatonic philosopher. Art, in the modern sense of fine art, is not a central notion in Plotinus, although it does come up for consideration in his writings. Beauty, however, is a central focus of two treatises: treatise 1.6, and treatise 5.8. In these, Plotinus accounts for beauty within the context of his understanding of the nature of soul and its progress from ignorance to self-knowledge. This larger account of the nature of the soul, its place in the universe, and the course of its development is the subject especially of his treatises 5.1, 4.8, 6.9, 3.8, 5.2, and 2.9. In order to understand Plotinus's doctrine of beauty one must first understand his account of the condition of the soul and, especially, the soul's relationship to intelligence.

According to Plotinus, souls are lost. We find ourselves involved in a changing world without a clear sense of our bearings, which especially means without a clear sense of ourselves. Although involved in this world we remain in a sense alien, strangers. We seek an understanding of ourselves and our situation, and we want to find our proper place, our home. To be a person—to be a soul—is, according to Plotinus, to be in this situation of disorientation and desire to get home.

This desire we have is not a self-conscious wish but is a constitutive drive, more like the innate impulse a plant has to turn and open itself toward the sun. This desire to get to its metaphysical home is experienced by the soul as a longing. Initially, this longing is immature and the object toward which it is directed will not give the soul all of what it wants, but will only advance the soul a single step. Taking this step, however, is the beginning of the soul's education, because from this point the soul's longing can develop to a more sophisticated state. The objects toward which this longing is directed, the things that are immediately attractive to the soul's constitutive drive, are beauties. Objects that are beautiful, *kalon,* act as beacons for the soul, and the soul feels for these beauties a passionate longing, an *erōs.* The development of the soul on its path homeward, the education of its *erōs,* is equally a journey along a path of recognizing progressively more sophisticated—and progressively more beautiful—beauties.

The list of the beauties through which we must advance according to Plotinus is basically taken over from Diotima's speech in Plato's *Symposium.* Plotinus accepts from Diotima that we must develop from initially seeing beauty in body to seeing beauty in soul to seeing beauty in laws and knowledge and ultimately to seeing real beauty itself, that is, the Platonic Form, which is the cause of the beauty in all the particular sensible beauties. In its search for its home, then, the soul must go from lusting after beautiful bodies to engaging in virtuous relations with other souls, and ultimately to understanding its own true nature. Its true nature is that it is a being that participates in the world of intellect and the eternal intelligible truths while struggling to realize and embrace the unity and goodness that govern all reality. On most interpretations of Plotinus, the intelligible vision of beauty itself is the stepping-stone to a mystical experience of "the One," the ultimate principle of Plotinus's universe. It is within the context of this understanding of the condition of the soul that Plotinus's technical doctrines concerning beauty can be understood and his place in the history of philosophy can be delineated.

The specific condition that makes a thing beautiful is the mastering of that thing by its own immanent form: to be beautiful, the thing must exist in a way that supports the full flowering of its defining essence without impediment or intrusion of anything foreign. Form, reality, beauty, and intelligibility are various ways of describing the same thing, according to Plotinus. Consequently, the extent to which a thing is mastered by its form is the extent to which it is real, which is equally the extent to which it is intelligible, the extent to which its existence is given over to the manifestation and realization of the rational principle that is its generative ground. A dwarf corn plant is not as beautiful as a corn plant whose perfected growth has fully expressed its guiding reason. A cancerous body is not as beautiful as a healthy body because the cancerous growth is a material existence acting independently of the definitive organic form. A hedonistic, uneducated criminal is not as beautiful as a soul that has perfected its nature in a virtuous life. A painting that still shows itself to be paint and canvas is not as beautiful as a painting that immediately conveys us to an embrace with the intelligibility it communicates by concealing its own existence as a painting and allowing us to be directly absorbed in its subject matter. Beauty exists when the matter as which a thing is realized is wholly given over to the resistance-free expression of form: beauty is intelligence displaying itself.

It is because beauty is thus the show of intelligence in a thing that beauty can play the role of stimulating the soul's development to self-knowledge. Beauty is attractive to the soul because it is itself like the soul, and because in seeing beauty the soul sees a mirror of its own inner essence as intelligent. It is the soul's inherent kinship to the beautiful that allows beauty to be the privileged route for the soul's ascent.

An understanding of beauty is itself something that can come only through the experience of beauty and cannot be explained to those who have not had the experience, in the same way that one cannot explain color to a blind person. The experience of beauty is thus irreducible to any other form of experience. This experience is also necessary to the soul's experience of intelligence, for it is the recognition of and attraction to beauty that is our most immediate way of acknowledging the presence and value of intelligence. Finally, the experience of beauty itself takes the form of a desire to create something in the presence of the beauty to which one is attracted. This erotic pursuit of beauty thus equally amounts to an activity of self-expression.

Plotinus's philosophy in general is marked by an ambivalence toward the body, and this can also be seen in his account of beauty. In many places throughout his writings, Plotinus seems to regard the body as inherently good, and he interprets embodiment as the soul's natural self-expression. On other occasions he treats the body in a more dualistic way as an alien vessel used by the soul. Although this ambivalence is present in his account of the ascent of the soul through beauty, the dualistic emphasis is the more prevalent tone, and the soul's ascent is described more as a purification of the soul from any alien materiality than as an attraction to the immanent rationality of its own embodiment. This dualistic attitude toward the body is perhaps also visible in Plotinus's claim that beauty is something added to bodies, whereas the beauty in the higher steps on Diotima's ladders is not added to, but is the substance of, the beautiful objects themselves.

Plotinus's philosophy in general and his doctrine of beauty in particular stand at an interesting and ambiguous border between ancient Greek philosophy and medieval Christian philosophy. Plotinus's doctrine of beauty as the route to mystical union with the One became for Saint Augustine a model for the turning of the soul to God. At the hands of Augustine, Plotinus's understanding of the soul's return to its true home simultaneously received legitimacy and was transformed from a pagan, possibly pantheistic, possibly nontheistic metaphysics of the soul into a Christian journey toward personal salvation by God. It is a matter of debate whether Plotinus should be read as a latent Christian or whether Augustine should be read as a misguided Neoplatonist. Analogous questions can be asked regarding the relation of Plato and Plotinus. Plotinus's doctrines clearly synthesize the doctrines of Plato with those of Aristotle and the Stoics, and it is not clear whether this is a development

or a confusion of the Platonic doctrines. With respect to beauty in particular, Plotinus may reveal a Stoic (or generally Hellenistic) inclination toward the self-sufficiency of the single individual that seems at odds with Plato's (and Aristotle's) insistence on the inherently political nature of human existence. Although Plotinus repeats from Diotima the need for the soul's *erōs* to develop to the love of beautiful laws and institutions, Plotinus's writings (and life) as a whole evince no serious interest in politics, and, indeed, he pays no attention to Plato's extensive discussion of the political ambivalence of art.

Plotinus's Neoplatonic doctrine of beauty was extremely influential for artists and art theoreticians of the Italian Renaissance in particular. Much of the debate between competing artistic movements of this period turned on such questions as whether beauty was to be found in intelligible design or sensible color, in idealization of subject matter or in realistic portrayal of earthly things, whether art was an end in itself, or whether its goal was the elevation of the soul, and so on. For artists like Michelangelo and writers like Giovanni Bellori, the Neoplatonic doctrines of the mastery of matter by form and of the soul's striving for intellect provided the basis for their preferred artistic program.

[*See also* Beauty, *article on* Classical Concepts; *and* Plato.]

BIBLIOGRAPHY

Work by Plotinus

Enneads. 7 vols. Translated by A. H. Armstrong. Loeb Classical Library. Cambridge, Mass., 1966–1988. Contains complete Greek text and English translation of Plotinus's writings.

Other Sources

Anton, J. "Plotinus' Refutation of Beauty and Symmetry." *Journal of Aesthetics and Art Criticism* 23 (1964–1965): 273–284.
Anton, J. "Plotinus' Conception of the Functions of the Artist." *Journal of Aesthetics and Art Criticism* 26 (1967–1968): 91–101.
Armstrong, A. H. "Plotinus." In *The Cambridge History of Later Greek and Early Medieval Philosophy,* Corr. ed. Cambridge, 1970.
Armstrong, A. H. "Beauty and the Discovery of Divinity in the Thought of Plotinus." In *Kephalaion: Studies in Greek Philosophy and Its Continuation,* edited by J. Mansfield and L. M. de Rijk. Assen, 1975.
Armstrong, A. H. "The Divine Enhancement of Earthly Beauties: The Hellenic and Platonic Tradition." *Eranos Jahrbuch* 53 (1984): 49–81.
Brown, Jonathan, and Robert Enggass. *Italy and Spain, 1600–1750: Sources and Documents.* Englewood Cliffs, N.J., 1970.
Moreau, J. "Origine et expressions du beau suivant Plotin." In *Neoplatonisme: Mélanges offerts à Jean Trouillard,* pp. 249–263. Cahiers de Fontenay. Fontenay, 1981.
Panofsky, Erwin. *Idea: A Concept in Art Theory.* Translated by Joseph J. S. Peake. Columbia, S. C., 1968.
Rich, Audrey N. M. "Plotinus and the Theory of Artistic Imitation." *Mnemosyne* 13 (1960): 233–250.
Rist, John M. *Plotinus: The Road to Reality.* Cambridge, 1967.
Schwyzer, H.-R. "Plotinos." *Paulys Realencyclopäedie der klassischen Altertumswissenschaft* 21 (1951): 471–592.

JOHN RUSSON

POETICS. In a comment that does not even refer explicitly to poetry, in a book concerned primarily with linguistics and psychology rather than aesthetics, Ludwig Wittgenstein not only succinctly formulates the basic aesthetic question regarding poetry, but also expresses the perpetual fascination with poetry that gives the question its force: "Can anything be more remarkable than this, that the *rhythm* of a sentence should be important for exact understanding of it?" (Wittgenstein, 1980).

Poetics, the attempt to understand, appreciate, explain, and evaluate poetry, asks many questions: What is poetry? What distinguishes poetry from prose? What makes some poetry more beautiful than other poetry? What does poetry do? What social and political value does poetry have? Does poetry convey truth? All those questions, however, bear some relation to the question why the rhythm of a sentence (or, more narrowly, the sounds of words or, more broadly, the poetic elements in an utterance) matters to its meaning.

The first substantial statement of a poetics in the traditional literature of Western philosophy comes from Plato, who in several dialogues, especially the *Ion* and *Republic*, puts into Socrates' mouth negative evaluations of poetry. Many later commentators have attempted to construe Plato's view of poetry as less condemnatory than it appears, on the assumption that no well-intentioned lover of wisdom can reject poetry, least of all Plato, whose writings are themselves so poetic. With or without mitigation, Plato's condemnation of poetry exposes the centrality of the Wittgensteinian question about the importance of the rhythm of a sentence. Plato's poetics centers on the question about poetry's social and political value. He answers the question by excluding poetry from his ideal republic, but he justifies that exclusion on the basis of his answer to a different question, the one about what poetry does: poetry, he says, destroys the rational part of the soul. In turn, that answer depends on his answer to the question about what poetry is: Plato sees it as *mimēsis,* a copying that substitutes a mendacious appearance for a veracious reality. But how does poetry fool its hearers into accepting the pastiche? Plato says that the rhythm of a sentence seduces the *thumos,* the basest part of the soul and the adversary of reason: it "awakens and nourishes this part of the soul, and by strengthening it impairs the reason." Poetry intoxicates, Plato charges, and its musical elements are the inebriants.

Aristotle does not deny Plato's contention that poetry intoxicates, but he does assert, against Plato, that the intoxication has salubrious effects. At least as tragedy, the one type of poetry for which we have extant Aristotle's full exposition, poetry does stimulate irrational states of the soul (pity and fear), but rather than strengthening their grip on the soul, as Plato believes, poetry actually releases us from their domination. Tragedy, Aristotle says, purges us of pity and fear. Because Aristotle disagrees with Plato about what poetry does, he also disagrees about poetry's social and political value, but those two questions, central to Plato's poetics, are secondary in Aristotle's, where the accent falls heavily on clarifying what poetry is.

Following his usual method of investigation, Aristotle first identifies the genus into which poetry fits. Like Plato, Aristotle considers all poetry a mode of imitation, but unlike Plato, who sees imitation as necessarily meretricious, Aristotle considers imitation a healthy part of human nature. We delight actively in imitating, and passively in works produced by imitation; the *Nicomachean Ethics* even makes imitation one of the ways we acquire virtue. After identifying the genus of poetry, Aristotle distinguishes its species: epic, tragedy, comedy, dithyrambic and nomic poetry, and even flute and lyre playing. These species, he notes, differ in their means (the particular combination of rhythm, language, and harmony employed), their objects (what kind of characters they portray), and their manner of imitation (narrative, dramatic, or mixed form).

Aristotle finds in tragedy six formative elements: spectacle, character, plot, diction, melody, and thought. Identifying these elements enables Aristotle to offer more subtle answers than those Plato gives to the various aesthetic questions about poetry. For instance, to the question of what distinguishes poetry from prose, Aristotle specifically discounts the easiest answer, that poetry employs verse. Putting the work of Herodotus into verse, says Aristotle, would not make it poetry. Instead, poetry differs from prose in the nature of its plot. The historian, Aristotle's exemplar of prose writing, narrates what has happened, but the poet narrates "what may happen,—what is possible according to the law of probability or necessity" (Poetics).

Enumeration of poetry's elements grounds not only Aristotle's answers to descriptive questions like what distinguishes poetry from prose, but also his answers to normative questions. The same thing that makes poetry different from prose also makes it better than prose: according to Aristotle, narrating what might be instead of what has been makes poetry's statements universals, unlike the merely singular statements of prose. The historian records, but the poet exemplifies. Pericles is Pericles, but Oedipus is all of us. The elements disclose what makes some poetry better than other poetry. All tragedies produce pity and fear, but one that does so primarily by use of spectacle is inferior to one that does so through its plot. The plot of a good play would arouse pity and fear simply by being told, even without the events being shown; to arouse pity and fear "by the mere spectacle is a less artistic method." Similarly, characters should be good, appropriate, realistic, and consistent; ceteris paribus, a poem with inconsistent characters is weaker than a poem with consistent characters.

Under the influence of Christianity, poetics in and around Europe took as its primary object biblical texts. No figure stands as more representative of this practice than Saint Augustine, who says Scripture does what Aristotle says tragedy does: remove the soul's flaws. But the mechanism Augustine posits differs from Aristotle's. Tragedy, according to Aristotle, cures by catharsis, purging the offending states, pity and fear; Scripture, according to Augustine, cures by displacement, substituting the love of God for the offending state, sin. Whatever the character of its tropes (the poetic elements with which Augustine is preoccupied), a scriptural passage always signifies the love of God. Whoever

> thinks that he understands the divine Scriptures or any part of them so that it does not build the double love of God and our neighbor does not understand it at all. Whoever finds a lesson there useful to the building of charity, even though he has not said what the author may be shown to have intended in that place, has not been deceived, nor is he lying in any way.
> (Augustine, 1958)

In spite of (or because of) Christianity, Aristotle's *Poetics* remained for centuries the definitive anatomy of those poetic elements for which the rhythm of a sentence stands as synecdoche in Wittgenstein's remark, as can be seen by the Aristotelian influence on figures as disparate as Saint Thomas Aquinas and Alexander Pope. Still, the esteem accorded Aristotle's descriptions could not forever prevent others from questioning his evaluations, as the British Romantic poets did at the beginning of the nineteenth century. In his preface to the *Lyrical Ballads,* William Wordsworth contradicts Aristotle on many points. For instance, one part of Aristotle's answer to what makes one poem better than another has to do with the element of character: on his view, tragedy is better than comedy in part because it depicts "persons who are above the common level," or to use Northrop Frye's later Neo-Aristotelian terminology, because it is written in the "high mimetic" mode. To purge us of pity and fear, says Aristotle, a poem needs to depict an unusually good person enduring unusually bad circumstances. In contrast, Wordsworth advocates what Frye would call "low mimetic" poetry, preferring to portray persons who are on the common level, not above it. He depicts "humble and rustic life" in the *Lyrical Ballads* "because, in that condition, the essential passions of the heart find a better soil in which they can attain their maturity, are less under restraint, and speak a plainer and more emphatic language." Could they agree for the sake of argument on Horace's observation that poetry serves a dual function, to delight and to teach, Aristotle and Wordsworth might go on to agree that poetry instructs through the example of its characters; but they would still disagree about what kind of characters provide the best exemplars. Aristotle asks for kings, the men most nearly gods; Wordsworth wants carls, boors, those nearest nature: "such men hourly communicate with the best objects from which the best part of language is originally derived."

Wordsworth shares Aristotle's disdain for spectacle, asserting the inferiority not only of spectacular poems but even of people who demand spectacle: "one being is elevated above another, in proportion as he possesses" the capability "of being excited without the application of gross and violent stimulants." But Wordsworth disagrees with the primacy Aristotle grants to plot. Wordsworth answers the question of what poetry is by calling it "the spontaneous overflow of powerful feelings." By making feeling definitive of poetry, he also gives it precedence over plot: "the feeling therein developed gives importance to the action and situation, and not the action and situation to the feeling."

In Wordsworth, as in Plato and Aristotle, the foregrounded question betrays its immediate connection to the Wittgensteinian question about the importance of the musical elements to understanding. The poet's possession of a larger capacity for feeling than ordinary mortals leads poetry "to produce excitement in co-existence with an overbalance of pleasure." Wordsworth thus agrees with Plato that poetry produces "an unusual and irregular state of the mind; ideas and feelings do not, in that state, succeed each other in accustomed order." But the rhythm of the sentence alleviates the danger of this overstimulated state of mind: "the co-presence of something regular"—namely, the meter of the poem—"cannot but have great efficacy in tempering and restraining the passion."

Less than a quarter century after Wordsworth disputed Aristotle's views on plot and character, Percy Bysshe Shelley in *A Defence of Poetry* seconded Aristotle's asseverations of poetry's truth against Plato's accusations of its falsity. "A poem," Shelley says, "is the image of life expressed in its eternal truth." As with other theorists, Shelley's answer to the question that preoccupies him (whether poetry conveys truth) connects with his answers to the other questions of poetics, in particular the question about the importance of the rhythm of a sentence. Like Aristotle, Shelley refuses as oversimplified the most obvious answer to the question about what distinguishes poetry from prose. Shelley contends that "the popular division into prose and verse is inadmissible in accurate philosophy," and should be replaced by "the distinction between measured and unmeasured language." Doing so, he claims, would clarify that the rhythm of a sentence invokes truth.

Unlike Aristotle, who asserts only a greater potential for truth in the universal statements of poetry than in the singular statements of prose, Shelley insists on the necessity of truth in poetry. For Aristotle, poetry's truth telling is a matter of degree: a poem is capable of more truth than is prose, and presumably capable of more falsehood as well. But for Shelley, poetry's truth is absolute: if it is poetry, it tells the truth. "All the authors of revolutions in opinion" are necessarily poets partly because they are inventors whose "words unveil the permanent analogy of things by images which participate in the life of truth," but mostly because "their periods are harmonious and rhythmical, and contain in themselves the elements of verse; being the echo of the eternal music."

The question about the relation of sound and sense remains central in contemporary poetics, informing all of its various preoccupations. For example, both the philosopher Hans-Georg Gadamer and the poet Louise Glück cite "the rhythm of a sentence" in their own answers to the question whether poetry conveys truth.

That the relation between sound and meaning stands as the crux of poetry's truthfulness appears in Gadamer's writing when he announces that he considers "incontrovertible" the "particular and unique relationship to truth" enjoyed by what he names not poetry but, more specifically, "poetic language." Gadamer argues for poetry's truth-telling character by a genus-and-species definition. Poetry belongs to the genus of "autonomous" texts, along with two other species, religious texts and legal texts. The religious text is a pledge, which can be called on and relied on as binding in ways that mere communication cannot, but only when "acknowledged on the part of the believer" (Gadamer, 1986). The legal text, too, is binding, but only becomes so by declaration and promulgation throughout a community.

Poetry belongs in the category of autonomous texts because, like religious and legal texts, it claims completeness. It "expresses fully what the given state of affairs is." Poetry's specific difference from religious and legal texts, however, lies in its being "self-fulfilling." Religious and legal texts effect their aims only through the complicity of their audience, but poetry "bears witness to itself and does not admit anything that might verify it." Gadamer illustrates his point by appeal to the staircase down which Smerdyakov falls in *The Brothers Karamazov*: every reader knows exactly—and correctly—what the staircase looks like, even though Dostoyevsky himself could not adjudicate an argument between a reader who contends the staircase turns to the right and one who contends it turns to the left. The poet, Gadamer says, "manages to conjure up the self-fulfillment of language." Poetry resembles less an assertion of empirical fact than a performative utterance. It *does* something, and the doing subjects it to coherence rather than correspondence as the criterion for its truth.

But how does poetry assume this disposition? Gadamer's answer should by now be predictable: "in the language of poetry, the dimensions of sound and sense are inextricably interwoven." Because of the sound of its words, the rhythm of its sentences, "the poetic creation does not intend something, but rather is the existence of what it intends." Sound and rhythm, Gadamer says, raise the poem above the need for confirmation by the world, giving it a necessary rather than a contingent connection to truth. A poem is no more subject to empirical validation or invalidation than is a symphony. Or, to use a sentence from Wittgenstein as another avatar of Gadamer's idea, "Do not forget that a poem, even though it is composed in the language of information, is not used in the language game of giving information" (Wittgenstein).

The question whether poetry conveys truth Gadamer answers in one way, by an answer to the question what poetry is; Glück answers the same question in a different way, by an answer to what makes one poem better than another. Glück argues that an artist's success "depends on conscious willingness to distinguish truth from honesty or sincerity" (Glück, 1994). Our customary association of honesty with truth, Glück calls "a form of anxiety." She defines truth as "the embodied vision, illumination, or enduring discovery which is the ideal of art."

Glück argues that honest speech is merely a relief, but true speech a discovery. Like Gadamer, she subjects poetry to a coherence rather than a correspondence standard of truth: "Any attempt to evaluate the honesty of a text must always lead away from that text, and toward intention," but any attempt to evaluate the truth of a text leads into the text, and it does so through the rhythm of the sentences. When Glück sets out to elucidate the truth of her three illustrative works, poems by John Keats, John Milton, and John Berryman, she does so by studying the musical elements of the poems. She connects truth to "distinctive voice," itself inseparable from rhythm. An informed reader can recognize the voice of Keats in the rhythm of his poems no less certainly than one recognizes the voice of a friend or lover by its rhythms. Truth, on Glück's view, is elemental, incapable of change in form without change in substance, and that elementalness derives from and is manifested in the musical elements of the poem.

Like Gadamer's and Glück's accounts of poetry's truth, recent attempts to answer other questions in poetics touch on the relation of sound and sense. The last quarter of the twentieth century saw heated debates over what should be included in the poetic canon (one form of the question what makes one poem better than another). Albert Cook's entry in that debate argues that the criterion for including a poem or body of poetry in the canon should be its wisdom. Wise poetry should be included, unwise poetry excluded. Cook states explicitly his intention not to consider rhythm. "Wisdom," he says, "comes about through a strategic combination of features," namely, thought, image, and story. Cook alludes to Ezra Pound's list of relevant features, melopoeia (charging the words "with some musical property" that directs the "bearing" of their meaning), phanopoeia (imagery), logopoeia ("the dance of the intellect among words"), but what Pound placed first, rhythm, Cook eliminates—or tries to eliminate.

Cook makes wisdom his criterion for canon formation, but rhythm proves to be a component of wisdom. Explaining why *Leaves of Grass* should be canonized, but *Hiawatha* should not, Cook calls Whitman's wisdom "far more complex" than Longfellow's, and attributes that complexity in large part to "the rhythms of *Leaves of Grass*." Not all wisdom is complex, though: some resides "in a radiant simplicity." Still, Cook argues for the generality of the connection between poetry's musical elements and its wisdom, contending that *any* explication of the superiority of one poem's wisdom to that of another poem will appeal to "the particular arrangement of language that brings about so penetrating an utterance."

Even in the apparently paradoxical preoccupation with silence in recent poetics, the Wittgensteinian question about the relation of sound and sense has a place. No ingredient appears more frequently in recent *ars poetica* poems than silence. Archibald MacLeish's "Ars Poetica" avers that a poem should be

> mute
> As a globed fruit,
>
> Dumb
> As old medallions to the thumb,
>
> Silent as the sleeve-worn stone
> Of casement ledges where the moss has grown –
>
> A poem should be wordless
> As the flight of birds.

Heather McHugh begins her volume of selected poems with "What He Thought," in which one of the characters recounts the execution of Giordano Bruno on charges of heresy. Fearing his eloquence, "his captors / placed upon his face / an iron mask," in which they burned him. "That is how / he died," the speaker says, "without a word, in front / of everyone. // And poetry . . . is what // he thought, but did not say." W. S. Merwin describes poetry as "what passes between // us now in a silence / on this side of the flames."

The relation between the silence so often alluded to by poets and "the rhythm of a sentence" receives its explicit formulation in T. S. Eliot's "Four Quartets." After saying that "Words, after speech, reach / Into the silence," Eliot explains how: "Only by the form, the pattern, / Can words or music reach / The stillness." Poets' frequent recourse to silence in their own poetics expresses the fact that a poem cannot be reduced to its propositional content, as if (returning now to Wittgenstein) to modify the Tractarian maxim that "What can be shown, cannot be said," not by reducing language to pictures but by insisting that neither sound nor sense can be separated from the totality that is the poem. The sense of a poem cannot be *ex*tracted because the form cannot be *sub*tracted. In Eliot's formulation, "the sound of a poem is as much an abstraction from the poem as is the sense."

Silence has become a stock poetic metaphor for the inseparability of sound and sense, the untranslatability of poetry, the inevitability of the poem that prevents it from being restated. Sound and sense generate a totality greater than its parts, and that totality prohibits adding anything to the poem by further speech. Thus, contemporary poets make a virtue of the vice Socrates in the *Phaedrus* attributes to writing: writing fails, he says, because, unlike speech, it cannot defend itself from misinterpretation and will not respond when queried. It speaks once, but cannot speak again. Poetry, like Giordano Bruno in Heather McHugh's poem, refuses to defend itself. The frequent appeal to silence in the statements of poetics offered by recent poets means not that poems do not speak, but that they do not speak twice.

To assert the centrality to any poetics of the question of why the rhythm of a sentence should be important for understanding is not to accept the doctrine of formalism, a particular poetics with its roots in Kant and its flowering in critics like Eliot and Cleanth Brooks, but to acknowledge that any question about poetry will include within itself a question about form. "The rhythm of a sentence," the formal aspects of a poem, will not be the entirety of any attempt to understand poetry, but will be a part of every attempt.

[*See also* Aristotle; Baudelaire; Coleridge; Collage, *article on* Collage and Poetry; Dryden; Haiku; Hölderlin; Ibn Rushd; Ibn Sīnā; Mallarmé; Plato; Postmodernism *article on* Postmodern Poetry; Russian Aesthetics, *article on* Russian Formalism; Stein; Symbolism; *and* Wordsworth.]

BIBLIOGRAPHY

Aristotle. *Poetics*. Translated by Stephen Halliwell. Chapel Hill, N.C., 1987.

Augustine. *On Christian Doctrine*. Translated by D. W. Robertson, Jr. Indianapolis, 1958.

Cook, Albert. "The Canon of Poetry and the Wisdom of Poetry." *Journal of Aesthetics and Art Criticism* 49:4 (Fall 1991): 317–329.

Eliot, T. S. "Four Quartets." In *Collected Poems 1909–1962*, pp. 173–209. New York, 1963.

Eliot, T. S. "The Music of Poetry." In *Selected Prose of T. S. Eliot*, edited by Frank Kermode, pp. 107–114. New York, 1975.

Frye, Northrop. *Anatomy of Criticism: Four Essays*. Princeton, N.J., 1957.

Gadamer, Hans-Georg. "On the Contribution of Poetry to the Search for Truth." In *The Relevance of the Beautiful and Other Essays*, edited by Robert Bernasconi, translated by Nicholas Walker, pp. 105–115. Cambridge and New York, 1986.

Glück, Louise. "Against Sincerity." In *Proofs and Theories: Essays on Poetry*, pp. 33–51. Hopewell, N.J., 1994.

Hall, Donald, ed. *Claims for Poetry*. Ann Arbor, 1982.

Handy, William J., and Max Westbrook, eds. *Twentieth Century Criticism: The Major Statements*. New York, 1974.

Kaplan, Charles, ed. *Criticism: The Major Statements*. 2d ed. New York, 1986.

Lilburn, Tim. *Poetry and Knowing: Speculative Essays and Interviews*. Kingston, Ontario, 1995.

MacLeish, Archibald. "Ars Poetica." In *Collected Poems: 1917–1952*, pp. 40–41. Boston, 1952.

McHugh, Heather. "What He Thought." In *Hinge and Sign: Poems, 1968–1993*, pp. 3–4. Hanover, N.H., 1994.

Merwin, W. S. "Cover Note." In *Travels* pp. ix–x. New York, 1992.

Pound, Ezra. "How to Read." In *Literary Essays of Ezra Pound*, edited by T. S. Eliot, pp. 15–40. Reprint, New York, 1968.

Wittgenstein, Ludwig. *Remarks on the Philosophy of Psychology*, vol. 1. Edited by G. E. M. Anscombe and G. H. von Wright, translated by G. E. M. Anscombe. Chicago, 1980.

HARVEY HIX

POLITICS AND AESTHETICS. *To clarify both the politics of art and the ways in which aesthetics has embraced or excluded politics, this entry comprises six essays:*

The first essay is an overview of the many ways art and politics have supported or opposed one another in the history of aesthetics from Plato to the present. The second essay analyzes the role of the concept of culture in debates between liberalism and communitarianism in contemporary political theory. The third essay critically examines how art history and criticism have treated various forms of difference—race, gender, and sexual preference—in contemporary American and European culture. The fourth essay discusses examples of twentieth-century art that have been the subject of political controversy. The fifth essay shifts the focus from politicized art to the aestheticization of politics that occurs under fascism. The final essay analyzes the debate between aestheticism and activism in the contemporary discussions about art and AIDS (Acquired Immune Deficiency Syndrome). For related discussion, see Iconoclasm and Iconophobia; Ideology; Law and Art; Monuments, *article on* Twentieth-Century Countermonuments; Morality and Aesthetics; National Endowment for the Arts; Nietzsche, *article on* Nietzsche on Art and Politics; Obscenity; Postcolonialism; *and* Sociology of Art.]

Historical and Conceptual Overview

Historically, art and politics have been linked for almost as long as there have been political entities. Throughout the civilizations of antiquity, we find poems, statues, and structures commemorating the rulers, warriors, and battles that past peoples believed contributed to the course of history. Moreover, that art still has this practical function for politics can be seen in evidence ranging from lowly postal stamps to the Vietnam War Memorial in Washington, D.C., and to structures projecting the aura of state power, such as the Pentagon. Likewise, philosophically, the nexus between art and politics is long-standing. In Plato's *Republic*—the earliest sustained theoretical treatment of art in the Western tradition—political censorship of the arts is defended for reasons of state.

Because the practical as well as the theoretical linkage between art and politics has been perennial, it should come as no surprise that the range of relationships between art and politics is quite diverse. For the purpose of giving some order to this collection of functions, we can organize our thinking around two primary relationships, namely, support and opposition. This yields four basic (nonexhaustive and not mutually exclusive) categories: art in support of poli-

tics, art in opposition to politics, politics in support of art, and politics in opposition to art. Using these categories, it is possible to organize the most fundamental functional relationships between art and politics.

Art in Support of Politics. If we begin by taking the extension of *politics* narrowly—that is, as pertaining to formal political entities, such as the state, and political organizations, such as political parties—then the first role of art with respect to politics is that of service. Under this category, art explicitly advances the cause of the state, the ruling monarchy, and class or political factions. Art that celebrates military prowess, such as the monuments on Freedom Square in Budapest, is political art in the service of the state. Triumphal arches; victory steles; the paintings of historic lawgivers, generals, civic founders, battle scenes; and epic poems all commemorate the past of a people, often linking present regimes with fondly remembered ones. The imagery on stamps and currency functions this way as well, whereas governments use architecture to erect an appropriate vision of themselves—such as august courthouses and suitably solid, central banking offices. Art can make government buildings feel creditable.

Art in the service of the state often has a legitimating function. Artistic images may correlate a contemporary government with a past regime in order to claim the authority of history for the present. Such was Benito Mussolini's appropriation of the sign of the fasces. For this reason, art in the service of government often trades in idealizations. That is why the workers are so much more muscular in Socialist Realist paintings than they are in actual factories. Artists can also endorse specific political programs, as did those depression artists in the United States who portrayed social welfare as justifiable.

Political regimes and movements require commitments from their citizens and followers. Customarily, art provides the symbols around which solidarity can take root and flourish. Even liberal democracies require allegiance to certain core values, such as equal respect and tolerance. Thus, liberal art generally aspires to promote and to rhapsodize the sentiments of equality.

In the twentieth century, attempts have been made to transform art in the service of politics into a quasi science. This endeavor is called propaganda. The notion of propaganda itself has at least two senses—a pejorative sense and a nonpejorative one. The pejorative sense of propaganda construes propaganda as always a matter of deception. On this account, propaganda is the dissemination of what its creators know to be lies for the purpose of intentionally misleading the public for political ends. Falsely depicting enemy aircraft allegedly strafing civilian populations would be an example here.

Alternatively, the notion of propaganda may simply apply to any explicit attempt to persuade by means of artful rhetoric. Thus the opening shots of Leni Riefenstahl's *Tri-*

umph of the Will, portraying Adolf Hitler as a demigod and savior alighting from the clouds, would count as propaganda in the nonpejorative sense so long as Riefenstahl believed this to be a fair account of Hitler. But, if Riefenstahl thought otherwise and was merely cynically manipulating her audience, then the sequence would count as propaganda in the pejorative sense. Although it is hard to be certain in this matter, nowadays "propaganda" appears to be used most frequently in the pejorative sense.

So far we have been concerned with art in the service of politics narrowly construed. Some critics and theorists, however, think of "politics" more broadly—not in terms of specific political formations (regimes, factions), but in terms of society at large. Art performs a service to society at large, of course, inasmuch as it acts as a conduit for social values and beliefs. Call this the reflection theory of art.

Art presupposes many of the beliefs and values of the society from which it emerges, and readers, listeners, and viewers must fill in these presuppositions in the process of assimilating the artworks in question. In this way, artworks may come not only to reflect but also to reinforce the beliefs and values of the larger culture. Art, for example, may reflect and reinforce prevailing social ideals of leadership even in fictions and pictures not expressly concerned with politics. Many critics, especially since the 1960s, have come to regard the role of art in the transmission of culture as a political function.

Of course, one can take a more circumscribed view than this. One may not find it advisable to suppose that every aspect of art is involved in politics. One might want to focus one's attention on only those artworks that are concerned with disseminating false (or otherwise epistemically defective) thoughts, beliefs, attitudes, emotions, and desires for the purpose of sustaining some practice of social domination. This is to be concerned with the *ideological* function of art.

This approach tracks the service of art to political formations less formally individuated than regimes and parties. It allows one to speak of racist, homophobic, and patriarchal ideologies. At the same time, this approach is more specific than the reflection theory of art, since it does not regard every topic as politically significant. The ideologue also differs from the propagandist (in the pejorative sense) because, although both traffic in deceptions, the propagandist does so intentionally and in the service of an overt political institution, whereas the ideologue need not meet either of these conditions. In this respect, it may be profitable to regard propaganda (in the pejorative sense) as a subcategory of ideology.

Our discussion of the services art performs for politics has emphasized content rather than form. In the twentieth century, however, questions have arisen, not only about the use of art's content to promote political ideas and emotions, but also about the means that art employs to do so. Revolu-tionary movements, such as Soviet Marxism, have spawned artistic fellow travelers who aspire to create new revolutionary forms in order to express appropriately and to emblematize heralded transformations of revolutionary consciousness—hence, Soviet Constructivism. Nevertheless, at the same time, such endeavors have often been denounced as formalist by other political radicals, who defend realism as the proper form of socialist art on the grounds that, though it is admittedly bourgeois in origin, it is what the people understand and, therefore, the politically appropriate means of serving them. Bertolt Brecht and Sergei Eisenstein are famous representatives of the formalist line. György Lukács is a leading theorist of Socialist Realism. In dance, for example, this contrast can be marked by Nikolai Foregger's machine dances, on the one hand, and ballets like *White Haired Girl* and *Red Detachment of Women,* on the other.

Art in Opposition to Politics. Of course, art can oppose foreign regimes and factions, although in this sense of political opposition, opposition to one regime can just as easily be reconceived as political service to another regime. Thus, in considering art in opposition to politics, it is most useful to focus on art's opposition to the political unit with which it is affiliated, as is the case with Bill T. Jones's *Last Supper at Uncle Tom's Cabin/The Promised Land.* In this light, Franscisco José de Goya's *Execution of May 3, 1808* is primarily in the service of Spanish patriotism, while Erich Maria Remarque's *All Quiet on the Western Front* opposes war as a political instrument in general, including the German war machine. Art in opposition to politics can also be referred to as protest art, subversive art, or social criticism.

Art as social criticism may be explicit or implicit, and it may be targeted broadly or narrowly. Social criticism is narrowly targeted where its domain of concern comprises formally individuated entities like states and political parties. It is broadly targeted where it is directed at society or culture at large (or, at least, at substantial portions thereof, such as bourgeoisie culture or patriarchal ideology).

An example of explicit social criticism, targeted narrowly, is a film like *El Norte,* which focuses expressly on U.S. immigration policy and makes its concern with the injustice of that policy evident. Similarly, John Steinbeck's *Grapes of Wrath* explicitly addresses an identifiable social problem. Honoré Daumier's drawing "The Third Class Carriage," on the other hand, while clearly critical, does seems critical, not of isolable social practices, but of the treatment of the poor in general. In a similar vein, the choreographer Kurt Jooss's *Green Table* criticizes war throughout the ages. Likewise, much German Expressionist painting appears to be critical of the existing social world as such rather than of this or that policy of any specific political regime.

Indeed, throughout the twentieth century, many avant-garde artists have come to conceive of art as a form of social criticism. Dada is overtly critical, but of everything (or

POLITICS AND AESTHETICS: Overview. Francisco Goya, *Execution of May 3* (1808), oil on canvas, 266 × 345 cm; Prado Gallery, Madrid. (Courtesy of Alinari/Art Resource, New York.)

everything bourgeois), rather than of anything in particular. Much contemporary art commentary—as well as practice—presumes that art, or, at least, ambitious art, is always subversive social criticism of such large-scale social phenomena as capitalism, racism, sexism, and homophobia. This is not to say that contemporary artists may not focus on criticizing specific policies and identifiable official regimes, but that their conception of the political is frequently much broader than one restricted to particular governments and self-conscious parties. Sometimes artists will attack Senator Jesse Helms—as in Paul Schmidt's play *The Bathtub*—but "Amerika" is a more likely, explicit target for most of them.

Social criticism may also be implicit in art. An artist may reveal the machinations of a society while being unaware that he or she is doing so. Lukács maintains that the conservative Honoré de Balzac actually portrayed French society

in his *Comédie humaine* in a way congenial to socialism. Certain structuralist theorists, such as Pierre Macherey and Louis Althusser, perhaps imitating Claude Lévi-Strauss's analysis of myth, have even argued that it is the role of art to reflect social contradictions, as if art were essentially a Marxist social critic.

Some theorists, like Herbert Marcuse, argue that art itself is essentially (rather than contingently) a form of progressive social criticism, since the artwork, by means of such core art-making structures as fiction and representation, provides alternatives to what exists and, thereby, effectively argues for the possibility of social change (although this argument appears to overlook the possibility that certain artworks may at the same time be in the service of ignoble social alternatives).

Similarly, Theodor W. Adorno allegorizes Modernist art's quest for autonomy as an implied criticism of the tendency in capitalist society to reduce all value to market or instrumental value. Modernist art does not succeed in this quest, but its honorable defeat shows us in microcosm—from a critical perspective—the operation of capitalist society writ large. For Adorno, this is only true for Modernist art. Mass art, on the other hand, is complicit with the marketplace and functions to sustain the political domination of the population by capitalism.

Arguments that suppose that it is of the nature of art to belong to the general species of social criticism err either by being too loose in what they think of as social criticism (e.g., Marcuse) or by speaking of art in an honorific rather than in a classificatory or descriptive sense of the term (Adorno). Art is not essentially social criticism. Too much of it is either critically mute politically or involved in uncritical political advocacy. Nevertheless, social criticism and protest represent one avenue of art, an avenue increasingly traveled since the eighteenth century (as art came to be more independent of religious and political patronage) and one especially popular toward the end of the twentieth century.

Politics in Support of Art. As we have already seen, art making itself can be a form of political activity. Governments hire artists to design stamps, currency, monuments, and uniforms; to compose music; to sing anthems; to play marches; to organize parades and spectacles; and so on. Where governments or official parties pay the bills or otherwise support artistic activity, politics plays the role of employer with respect to art. In the past and across different cultures, many artists were employed by sovereigns, nobles, and churches in this manner. Nevertheless, even in modern times in the industrial world, artists are employed to secure political ends.

Despite being a source of revenue for artists, government commissions can also result in a conflict between the claims of artistic autonomy and claims about the common good. This happened with respect to the publicly financed monument titled *Tilted Arc*, by Richard Serra. Serra's claim to a right to express freely his belief in the oppressiveness of modern life by means of a sculpture that oppressed spectators was challenged by citizens who claimed the right not to be oppressed by a public edifice. After extended court hearings, a judge ordered that *Tilted Arc* be dismantled, indicating that political backing of the arts, insofar as it is political, can be a risky source of support.

Artists are employed by political units when they are commissioned or salaried to produce specifiable artworks for use by political entities (narrowly construed). There is another form of government support of the arts, however. We might call this "patronage" (where this means that artists are given government support to pursue their own ends, rather than the ends of the commonwealth). That is, whereas government employment involves hiring artists to produce specifiable artworks for public use—such as a mayoral seal—patronage involves extending money or ben-

efits, directly or indirectly, to artists so that they can carry out their own aims. Indirect support for the arts involves things like tax benefits to museums, nonprofit accreditation of arts organizations, and federal grants to art schools. Direct support for the arts involves outright cash payments or benefits in kind (land, buildings, etc.) to artists or to arts organizations to produce their own work.

Government patronage of the arts is widespread throughout the industrial world. It is, however, a practice that has recently become controversial in the United States. A particular source of debate concerns monies granted by government organizations, like the National Endowment for the Arts, to individual artists in order to produce original art. The recent furor began over federally funded artworks—like *Piss Christ* by Andres Serrano—that offended the sensibilities of many taxpayers, especially those of a religious and right-wing bent. Nevertheless, the theoretical concerns here are not simply conservative, they cut to the heart of liberalism as well. For if liberalism is the doctrine that the state should be neutral between competing conceptions of the good life, and if there are significant numbers of citizens who doubt whether the pursuit of art is anything but a sectarian perspective on the good, then the question arises whether a liberal state can, on its own terms, legitimately extract taxation on behalf of the art world from nonconsenting citizens.

Political entities, like governments, may also benefit the arts through their licensing and regulatory activities by creating venues for artistic creativity. Government regulatory activities can also, however, impede the autonomous development of art in a number of ways.

Politics in Opposition to Art. Political bodies, whether formally constituted or informal, may oppose the arts through criticism. Public officials, party leaders, and the representatives of social movements may speak out against the political content, putative cultural repercussions, social significance, and alleged moral consequences of artworks. Political entities, such as states, typically, however, have even more powerful levers than criticism for opposing art. They standardly have the prerogative to regulate and, ultimately, to prohibit artworks. That is, formal political entities, like states, have the capacity to censor art. The theoretical grounds for censorship were established long ago by Plato. Censorship rests on the presumption that the function of art is to serve the political ends of the state. Where art fails to advance those ends, or where it even appears to subvert those ends, censorship is apposite.

From the eighteenth century until quite recently, a typical Western response to the Platonic viewpoint was that art is autonomous—it is not an instrument of politics or of anything else. Art, so the story went, has its own ends and functions, irrespective of and independent from those of politics. Art, that is to say, is disinterested. This position, however, has come to sound rather empty by the end of the twentieth century, which is perhaps why the case against political censorship seems more embattled now than at any other time since the 1960s.

Political censorship can be motivated by opposition to the political content of the relevant artworks. Artworks containing explicit or implied criticism of certain sets of political arrangements or of regnant philosophies may be suppressed—as they were in the former Soviet Union. But political censorship can also be motivated by fear of the behavioral consequences of certain types of artworks. This seems to be the direction that movements in favor of censorship have taken recently in the United States.

Violent programming on television and in the movies as well as aggressive song lyrics are opposed on the grounds that they will lead to violent behavior. Pornographic art, likewise, is condemned, and banning it is advocated because it is said to lead to rape or to other sex crimes. These allegations are extremely difficult to test. One obvious reason for this is that any experiments that possessed the potential of causing criminal activity would probably themselves be illegal and would certainly be immoral.

The emphasis on behavioral consequences in American debates about censorship undoubtedly signals a commitment in the United States to the liberal notion of the harm principle. That is, for government censorship to be legitimate, certain burdens of proof must be met. Specifically, the state must show that the artworks in question are likely to cause harm to innocent, nonconsenting bystanders. This desideratum can be met—at least in principle—by claiming that the artworks in question are likely to bring about untoward consequences to the interests of third parties. Whether they do so, however, is in the end an empirical question, one to which no one has yet found a conclusive answer.

BIBLIOGRAPHY

Adorno, Theodor W., and Max Horkheimer. *Dialectic of Enlightenment.* Translated by John Cumming. New York, 1972.
Adorno, Theodor W. *Aesthetic Theory.* Edited by Gretel Adorno and Rolf Tiedemann, translated by Robert Hullot-Kentor. Minneapolis, 1997.
Althusser, Louis. *Lenin and Philosophy and Other Essays.* Translated by Ben Brewster. London, 1971.
Barrell, John. *The Political Theory of Painting from Reynolds to Hazlitt: "The Body of the Public."* New Haven, 1986.
Brecht, Bertolt. *Brecht on Theatre: The Development of an Aesthetic.* Edited and translated by John Willett. New York, 1964.
Carroll, Noël. "Can Government Funding of the Arts Be Justified Theoretically?" *Journal of Aesthetic Education* 21.1 (Spring 1987): 21–35.
Carroll, Noël. *Philosophical Problems of Mass Art.* New York and Oxford, 1998.
Copp, David, and Susan Wendell, eds. *Pornography and Censorship.* Buffalo, N.Y., 1983.
Eagleton, Terry. *Criticism and Ideology: A Study in Marxist Literary Theory.* Atlantic Highlands, N.J., 1976.
Edelman, Murray. *From Art to Politics: How Artistic Creations Shape Political Conceptions.* Chicago, 1995.
Johnson, Pauline. *Marxist Aesthetics: The Foundations within Everyday Life for an Emancipated Consciousness.* London and Boston, 1984.
Lukács, Georg. *Realism in Our Time: Literature and the Class Struggle.* Translated by John Mander and Necke Mander. New York, 1964.
Macherey, Pierre. *A Theory of Literary Production.* Translated by Geoffrey Wall. London and Boston, 1978.
Marcuse, Herbert. *The Aesthetic Dimension: Toward a Critique of Marxist Aesthetics.* Boston, 1978.
National Television Violence Study: Scientific Papers, 1994–1995. Studio City, Calif., 1995.
Plato. *Republic.* Translated by G. M. A. Grube. Indianapolis, 1974.
Sorrell, Tom. "Art, Society and Morality." In *Philosophical Aesthetics,* edited by Oswald Hanfling, pp. 297–347. Oxford and Cambridge, Mass., 1992.
Williams, Raymond. *Marxism and Literature.* Oxford and New York, 1977.

NOËL CARROLL

Culture and Political Theory

Liberal political philosophers have often been charged with failing to recognize the importance of culture in the design of social and political policies and institutions. While the basic liberties guarantee citizens the freedom to pursue their own cultural aims and conceptions of the good, liberalism's advocacy of state neutrality with regard to the value of different ways of life is said to undermine political support for cultural values, encourage an atomistic conception of society, and disregard the role of cultural mechanisms in generating ideological distortions of citizens' preferences.

It has been thought by some that the conception of justice proposed in John Rawls's *Theory of Justice* excludes state support for culture. Rawls develops a "political" or (as he says in more recent publications) "freestanding" conception of justice for what he calls a nearly just, democratic, well-ordered society. Such a society is viewed as a fair system of cooperation between citizens (rather than an involuntary scheme coordinated from above), and principles of justice are to specify the fair terms of cooperation between citizens viewed as free and equal persons. A conception of justice is said to be justified if it would be agreed to by citizens themselves in a suitably specified initial situation.

The original position (Rawls, 1971, section 4) is Rawls's favored interpretation of such an initial situation. Rawls describes the original position as a "device of representation" intended to help us model and introduce order into our considered judgments about justice. Rational individuals are thought of as coming together to choose principles for the basic structure of society, which Rawls describes as "the way in which the major social institutions distribute fundamental rights and duties and determine the division of advantages from social cooperation" (section 2). The basic structure of society is the first subject of justice, and its importance derives in part from the profound and pervasive role it plays in shaping citizens' expectations over a complete lifetime.

The original position represents the parties to this choice of principles as free, equal, mutually disinterested, and rational. In order to rule out the effects of social and natural contingencies on their choice of principles, and in order to exclude unfair bargaining advantages and threats of force, coercion, and fraud, Rawls specifies that the parties are situated behind a veil of ignorance that excludes knowledge of particular contingencies such as their place in society, their class and wealth, gender or race, strength, intelligence, cultural sophistication, talents, or conceptions of the good. In this way, bargaining advantages that normally arise as a result of cumulative historic, social, and natural processes cannot influence the choice of principles.

Rawls argues that, deprived of this knowledge, but rational and aware that they possess two basic powers of moral personality (the capacities for a sense of justice and for a conception of the good), the parties in the original position would vote unanimously for a social scheme that would secure them an adequate share of certain all-purpose primary social goods ("rights and liberties, powers and opportunities, income and wealth and the social bases of self respect") needed for the realization of any plan of life or, as he later emphasizes, for the exercise and development of the basic powers of moral personality. No matter what their eventual starting place in society, they hope, by making their choice of principles under the guidance of this thin theory of the good, to guarantee themselves the basic resources necessary to the pursuit and successful realization of any foreseeable plan of life.

Rawls maintains that in this choice situation the parties would rank his own two principles of justice higher than other well-known conceptions of social justice (including classical and average utilitarianism). Rawls's first principle of justice, which is lexically prior to (i.e., must be satisfied before) his second principle, entitles each citizen to a fully adequate scheme of equal basic liberties compatible with a similar scheme for all (the principle of liberty). The second principle is designed to ensure a roughly equal distribution of primary social goods, with the modification that inequalities are to be permitted to the extent that they improve the position of the least well off representative group in society (the difference principle) and subject to the further condition that opportunities must be open on a fair basis to all (the principle of fair equality of opportunity).

Because they are situated behind a veil of ignorance, the parties to the agreement made in the original position are compelled to avoid choosing principles of justice that might require them to sacrifice their as yet unknown particular conceptions of the good to all-embracing social and cultural ideals such as the maximization of utility or human excellence. In section 50 of *A Theory of Justice*, Rawls argues that the principle of perfection, in both pure and mixed ("as but one standard among several in an intuitionist theory") forms, and other principles advocating a teleologically motivated design of the basic structure of society would therefore be rejected. At the same time, he insists that, in the

well-ordered society of what he calls justice as fairness, the human excellences and perfections could still be pursued by individuals or groups at their own initiative, without government support, within the limits of the principle of free association. Further support for associations dedicated to advancing the arts, sciences, and culture generally would have to come from voluntary contributions or as a "fair return for services rendered" rather than from the state.

Rawls's apparent readiness to abandon support for culture to the "private" sphere and to the activities of individual associations within society has provoked a variety of criticisms. Joseph Raz, for example, has argued that such a policy would undermine the chances of survival of "many cherished aspects of our culture" (Raz, 1986). According to Raz, society as a whole must shoulder the burden of preserving certain basic perfectionistic ideals or risk total cultural impoverishment. Amy Gutmann has argued, in an extensive study of the social and philosophical foundations of democratic education, that the citizens of the well-ordered society paired with Rawls's two principles of justice would be compelled to forgo collective political support for the cultural heritage. She proposes, instead, a form of democratic perfectionism that would secure the place of the most widely accepted cultural values within society while also equalizing the cultural influence of equally interested and able citizens.

Communitarians such as Michael J. Sandel argue that Rawls fails to make allowance for the morally significant role of a common cultural life in enabling individuals to develop values and discover and shape their own identity. Rawls is said to conceive the human self without regard for the constitutive aims and deep human attachments that are bound up with existence in a community founded on solidarity and a shared sense of obligation. Another philosopher sometimes described as a communitarian, Charles Taylor, argues that free and autonomous moral agents can only achieve and maintain their identities in the context of certain institutional "bearers of culture" such as museums, symphony orchestras, universities, laboratories, political parties, courts of law, newspapers, publishing houses, and television stations, which require "stability and continuity and frequently also support from society as a whole" (Taylor, 1985).

But although Rawls rejects perfectionistic justifications for the support of specific cultural associations and enterprises, his theory does allow for culture to be treated as a public good that government may promote in those cases in which, as with the defense of a nation in time of war or the maintenance of public health, the market mechanism breaks down because the desired benefits are indivisible, and must hence be enjoyed by all or none. In such cases, Rawls foresees among the background institutions of government an "exchange branch" (1971, section 43), which is an arrangement designed to discover the most efficient method for providing society with indivisible goods of the kind everyone is likely to want. Where there is a de facto social consensus concerning the desirability of certain cultural goods, Rawls sees no difficulty in making their provision and administration the task of background institutions of government.

Furthermore, Rawls states at the end of section 50 of *A Theory of Justice* that a well-ordered society may devote substantial resources to support "social conditions that secure the equal liberties or advance the long-term interests of the least advantaged." Goods secured or provided by cultural institutions may well figure (although not for perfectionistic reasons) among the primary goods to be distributed under the principles of justice. The equal liberties, inasfar as they are essential conditions for the adequate development and full realization of the moral powers, will play an important role in the protection and promotion of culture. Fair equality of opportunity requires that citizens have equal opportunities of education, and that chances to acquire cultural knowledge and skills not depend on one's class position. Rawls also states, in section 17, that resources for education would be allocated under the difference principle, not merely in the interests of economic efficiency and social welfare but to enable "a person to enjoy the culture of his society and to take part in its affairs." It is thus evident that support for culture and access to cultural resources will indeed play a significant role in the well-ordered society associated with Rawls's two principles of justice.

Although some criticisms of Rawls's views on culture may be accommodated in this way, it might still be argued that he attaches too low a value to the role, character, and significance of cultural institutions in society. To treat culture as a public or primary good is to disregard the fact it is in their noninstrumental character that the real significance of cultural values resides. It is perhaps skepticism in this respect that makes Rawls's perfectionistic and communitarian critics argue that government must take a more active role in determining the character and quality of a society's culture. But such proposals, rarely elaborated in detail, also conjure up the specter of a state perfectionism that liberalism is bound to regard as unworkable in a society of free and autonomous individuals.

One alternative for liberals, therefore, is to look in the direction of primary goods and the thin theory of the good for a deeper understanding of cultural values that is compatible with the basic premises of liberalism, but does not ignore what might be regarded as the distinctive character of cultural values. The concept of culture can be understood in a variety of ways. Traditionally, it has often identified it with a realm of "higher," authentic values and self-contained ends in opposition to a practical and "lower" world of social utility. Social scientists and economists, by contrast, often seek to resolve questions about cultural preferences in the context of the theory of rational choice. According to such

views, no qualitative distinction ought to be made between preferences for "higher" cultural values and other preferences, wants, or needs. What counts is not what people want but how much they want of it.

But the term *culture* may also refer to a more basic kind of context within which value judgments and aesthetic preferences are possible. In this sense, it may be regarded as a background structure that gives meaning to individual choices, rather than as a set of foreground options or alternatives. Considerations such as these have led Ronald Dworkin to distinguish "two kinds of consequences our culture has for us: on the one hand particular paintings, performances, novels . . . and on the other, the structural framework which makes aesthetic values of that sort possible" (Dworkin, 1985).

According to Dworkin, the "cultural structure" of a society is not a particular conception of value or set of values to be secured by direct political intervention in specific cultural transactions, but rather a basic framework within which citizens are able to form and pursue their own cultural preferences. In this sense culture may be compared to a language. Just as a language presents us with the opportunity to say many different things, so the cultural structure of society furnishes the basic context of choice within which individuals can pursue diverse conceptions of the good. The center of the cultural structure of a community, according to Dworkin, is its language, together with "a shared vocabulary of tradition and convention, and the conceptual equipment to find aesthetic value in historical and cultural continuity."

A rich and diverse cultural structure is needed if citizens are to be able to entertain a diversity of different models and ways of life. Since the existence of a cultural structure rich in opportunities must be presupposed if citizens are to be able to pursue any values whatsoever, and since in promoting such a structure it would not be permissible to create or oppose any individual's specific preferences, a government may promote and protect the cultural structure of a society without paternalism or perfectionism.

But what would it mean to protect the cultural structure of a society? If the cultural structure resembles a language, can it be subjected to political influence? How can a government enhance a basic context of choice without promoting or favoring particular kinds of cultural choice? Moreover, what justification is there for thinking that there is just one cultural structure rather than many?

Such considerations have led Will Kymlicka to argue that while Rawls and Dworkin recognize the importance of the cultural structure, they mistakenly assume the political community to be culturally homogeneous and hence take cultural membership to be "a kind of public good, equally available to all." In fact, a modern political community embraces many different cultures, and the good of cultural membership may be enjoyed by different citizens to different degrees. Since participation in a culture, viewed as a context of choice, is essential if the representative citizen is to be able to pursue a meaningful plan of life, access to a cultural community may be a relevant criterion for distributing the burdens and benefits of social cooperation. Hence, there is a strong case for regarding cultural membership as a primary good, an individual's claim to which may be balanced against other primary goods, including the basic liberties.

But while liberal regimes may have good reason to want to protect the existence of specific, perhaps threatened, cultural structures within the larger political community, it remains unclear whether treating membership of a specific culture as a primary good is the most reasonable way of achieving that goal. An alternative view, not so far considered, is that it is not so much access to specific cultural contexts of choice as the ability to develop a relationship to and master different contexts of choice that should be the focus of liberal concern.

Dworkin's and Kymlicka's accounts of the cultural structure might be deepened by invoking the idea of a basic cultural competence. On this view, suggested by applications of Noam Chomsky's linguistic competence theory to a variety of specific areas of culture such as art theory, music, and literature, citizens' capacities to choose and revise particular conceptions of the good and to take advantage of different contexts of choice presuppose a more fundamental mastery of the basic framework within which cultural choices can be made. Like any specific aesthetic or cultural competence, such a basic cultural competence may be assumed to be extremely complex in character, including a variety of temporal, linguistic, cognitive, and aesthetic components.

Unlike a specific competence, however, this more fundamental kind of cultural competence may be taken to involve the basic capacity to have a relation to linguistic, cultural, and historical continuity as such, and not merely to particular kinds of representation, value, tradition, or cultural continuity. On this view, it is not in protecting the cultural structure, or guaranteeing citizens membership of a specific culture, but in the provision of the primary goods necessary to the development of a more basic capacity to have value that the fundamental cultural task of a liberal political regime consists.

[*See also* Cultural Studies.]

BIBLIOGRAPHY

Chomsky, Noam. *Aspects of the Theory of Syntax.* Cambridge, Mass., 1965.
Dworkin, Ronald. "Can a Liberal State Support Art?" In *A Matter of Principle,* pp. 221–233. Cambridge, Mass., 1985.
Gutmann, Amy. *Democratic Education.* Princeton, N.J., 1987.
Kymlicka, Will. *Liberalism, Community, and Culture.* Oxford, 1989.
Kymlicka, Will. *Contemporary Political Philosophy.* Oxford, 1990.
MacIntyre, Alisdair. *After Virtue: A Study in Moral Theory.* 2d ed. Notre Dame, Ind., 1984.
Rawls, John. *A Theory of Justice.* Cambridge, Mass., 1971.
Rawls, John. "The Basic Liberties and Their Priority." In *The Tanner Lectures on Human Values,* edited by S. MacMurrin, vol. 3, pp. 3–87. Salt Lake City, 1982.
Rawls, John. *Political Liberalism.* New York, 1993. Includes revised version of "The Basic Liberties and Their Priority."
Raz, Joseph. *The Morality of Freedom.* Oxford, 1986.
Sandel, Michael J. *Liberalism and the Limits of Justice.* Cambridge and New York, 1982.
Taylor, Charles. *Philosophical Papers,* vol. 2, *Philosophy and the Human Sciences.* Cambridge and New York, 1985.

JOHN STOPFORD

Difference and Culture

In the epilogue to his *Mythologies,* a treatise on modern-day myth, representation, and ideology that helped shape an entire generation of critical thinkers, Roland Barthes wrote about a chance encounter with the image of a black youth in the racially charged Paris of the late 1950s. While waiting in a barbershop for a haircut, Barthes was offered a copy of *Paris-Match.* On the cover was the photograph of a young man of African descent dressed in a French military uniform. His hand was raised to his head in a gesture of salute. His uplifted eyes were fixed on the tricolor, that great symbol of French militarism and civility. The image intrigued Barthes: he searched for the political meaning that lay just below its glossy surface; he speculated on the ideological demands that would sanction its presence on the cover of one of France's leading picture magazines; he analyzed the various semiotic systems that conspired to produce its multiple meanings. While the cover's signifier—a black soldier saluting the French flag—yielded its literal meaning, Barthes argued that it was in the realm of secondary signification, the signified, that one could decipher its intended ideological message: "that France is a great Empire, that all her sons, without any color discrimination, faithfully serve under her flag, and that there is no better answer to the detractors of an alleged colonialism than the zeal shown by this Negro in serving his so-called oppressors" (Barthes, 1972).

Not satisfied with merely articulating the message, Barthes journeyed deeper into interpretation, arriving at the image's purest, and paradoxically most sinister, level of meaning—that plane of content he would refer to as myth. Within the realm of public speech, myth existed to conceal the undesirable, to make bearable the unbearable, to whitewash the contradictions and dissonance that threatened to disrupt the social order. Contemporary myths, Barthes argued, served "not to deny things" but to take the problematic representations of everyday life, depictions fraught with our fears, our intolerance, our bigotry, and make "them innocent . . . give . . . them a natural and eternal justification." It was this "duplicity of the signifier" that determined the special character of myth, allowing it to "henceforth appear . . . both like a notification and like a statement of fact." Following through on this logic, Barthes concluded that *Paris-Match*'s mythic notification—that colonialism was a fiction—existed to assuage anxiety and guilt at a time when France was coming to terms with its own history of brutal racism. Thus, the image further oppressed the black subject even as it offered its bourgeois audience a reassuring alternative to the historically encoded presence of the angry, colonized black body.

More than thirty-five years after Barthes first directed his uncompromising and rigorous eye toward society's myths, social institutions, in an atmosphere of little or no critical resistance, continue to freely perpetuate lies and deceptions. Despite the supposed vigilance of a media-oriented culture that bombards us daily with political exposés and instant polling results, the vast majority of American and European cultural commentators remain blissfully ignorant of the duplicity of visual representation: while critical methodologies have come a long way since the 1950s—one thinks of the advances of a whole range of new critical and historical studies—most writers, out of naïveté, cowardice, or even malice, ignore these mechanisms for exposing our intolerance. Even when such methodologies are employed, there is no guarantee that theoretical critics and historians, who are themselves often lacking the self-awareness that might allow them to see their own bigotry, will not avert their eyes from what they would rather not see.

This map of misreadings and distortions is perhaps most pronounced in the severe methodological deficit of American and European art-historical, museological, and critical practices in the second half of the twentieth century. While the disciplines of art history and art criticism are not interchangeable, either in their methods or motives, they both share a direct relationship to the ideological hierarchies of the art world and, as such, can be understood to embrace similar attitudes toward the issue of art and politics. Ruled by the interests of upper-class white patrons, the art world has long accepted the mythology of its own social removal. The Baudelairean dandy, a hallmark of early modernist conceptions of the role of the artist in society, celebrated his distance from the grimy reality of a new, urbanized Paris by refusing to identify with a specific economic class.

For the critic Clement Greenberg a century later, formalism could serve as a way out of the harsh realities of late industrial society, but only as a negation of social reality—as a metaphysical transcendence from politics and mass culture (or what he called "kitsch"). More recently, art history and criticism rooted in structuralist and poststructuralist methodologies—while considerably more sophisticated than formalism in its analyses of visual representation—most often assume formalism's apolitical stance by refusing to consider cultural artifacts in their broader socioeconomic context. The rise of neo-Marxist methodologies in the 1980s has not been without problems: frequently lacking a rigorous theory of representation, such writing has often settled on a simplistic iconographic approach. All of these methods have preserved a fundamentally conservative and restrictive definition of high culture, one that inevitably embraces the interests of white, upper-class people at the exclusion of others. Greenberg's racist and classist definition of high culture ironically continues to resonate in most art-historical and curatorial circles: "There has always been on one side the minority of the powerful—and therefore the cultivated—and on the other the great mass of the exploited and the poor—and therefore the ignorant," he wrote in 1939. "Formal culture has always belonged to the first, while the last have had to content themselves with folk or rudimentary culture, or kitsch" (Greenberg, 1961).

The world of the art museum is no less politically isolated. In the work of the curator, which fastens on objects, conservation, and elegant installation, a resistance to the flux and chafe of the social sphere (and, most particularly, issues of marginality) may be the path of least resistance. Despite a range of ideologically grounded art-historical methodologies, contemporary curatorial method continually returns to principles established more than half a century ago by Alfred H. Barr, Jr., the first director of the Museum of Modern Art in New York and incontestably the father of Modernist curatorial studies. In many ways, Barr was an extraordinarily innovative curator, sanctioning groundbreaking exhibitions of Latin American modernism or reexamining the physical nature of the exhibition itself and the role of the catalog in elucidating issues beyond the formal. It was his ambition, for example, to provide analyses of modern art that were as scholarly as academic studies of earlier work. But despite his exposure to debates on the nature of social cause in art (particularly during his travels to Soviet Russia), his writing largely overlooked this particular kind of historical specificity. By attending to stylistic concerns above all others, Barr produced what is now commonplace in catalog essays—a curatorial history constructed outside political or social issues. In effect, he retrospectively validated certain sectors of the Modernist aesthetic at the expense of others. While he read the abstract symbolism of Paul Gauguin, for example, as a progenitor of German Expressionism, he omitted from his historical equation the activist realism of Gustave Courbet and Honoré Daumier.

The dualistic modern art that Barr proposed—an art predicated either on abstract, rationalist tendencies or on dreamlike, romantic sensibilities—virtually forced contradictory elements into agreement in broadly defined and vigorously defended dialectical categories and movements. Barr's reading was fundamentally motivated by his belief in the exhaustion of "representational" art and, consequently, in the autonomy of art from social conditions. Ultimately, his hermetic style of organizing exhibitions preempted the notion that one purpose of the art exhibition could be to analyze the relationship between society and the cultural arti-facts it produces and sanctions. What is most problematic about Barr's still-prevalent model is that it rarely considers the audience or the social imperatives for art; it presumes that such issues as patronage and the social temperature at both the art's creation and reception are somehow irrele-vant to the institutional interests of the art world. But the museum is not just a place to preserve beautiful objects; it is also a space where the relics and events of history can be juxtaposed in order to allow access to a range of social and cultural meanings.

Over the past decade, the narrow ideological basis of art history, criticism, and curatorial practice has shown definite signs of expanding. For one, the nature of history writing it-self, the historiography of art history and history in general, has come under intense scrutiny. Such interrogations into the discipline of history—from the French historian Michel Foucault's influential analysis of the relationship between knowledge, ideology, and power to the emergence in the United States of community or identity-based history projects—have served as important catalysts in the trans-gression of traditional historical methodologies. The colo-nized, the working classes, people of color, women, gay men, and lesbians are now writing their own histories, more or less independently of the hierarchies of the academic pat-rimony. Such enterprises as subalternist, gay and lesbian, race, and feminist studies, the history workshop movement in Europe and the United States (which sponsors the publi-cation of local history pamphlets and workshops on the oral history of working-class people), have brought together academics, activists, and workers to change the social agenda of history. Indeed, as Barbara Kruger and Phil Mar-iani have pointed out, it is these projects that have cogently demonstrated the inability of "conventional methods of his-torical analysis—which create polarities or tend to choose the most 'dramatic' movement or end in the typical trajec-tory of linearity—[to] . . . excavate and disentangle all the voices" that constitute any historical moment (Kruger and Mariani, 1989).

The strides made by these critical reevaluations of the historian's practice have, to one degree or another, trickled down to art history. Since the mid-1970s in the United States and Europe, a number of influential cultural journals (e.g., *Block, October, Representations,* and *Screen*) have chal-lenged, mostly through poststructural theoretical methods, the conception of art history and art, film, and literary crit-icism as ideologically neutral disciplines. Yet, the question of difference and who was entitled to speak for whom was less rigorously examined. Building on the innovations and consciousness-raising of feminism and the civil rights movement, however, other art historians and critics (such as Gerald Davis, Ann Gibson, Lucy R. Lippard, Eugene Metcalf, Linda Nochlin, Griselda Pollock, Richard Powell, Abigail Solomon-Godeau, Lisa Tickner, Jonathan Wein-

berg, and Judith Wilson) have attempted over the past three decades to include the possibility of difference—to allow those voices marginalized by official history to speak, to be analyzed, and to be heard.

Visual artists have also helped to create an art-world envi-ronment conducive to recent theoretical advances in femi-nist, gay and lesbian, and race studies. Looking to these the-oretical models as well as to the aesthetic innovations of the 1960s and 1970s—including Pop art, Minimalism, concep-tual art, post-Minimalism, and 1970s feminist art—socially minded conceptual artists such as Hans Haacke, Jenny Holzer, Kruger, Adrian Piper, Carrie Mae Weems, and Fred Wilson have produced radical and theoretically rigorous work that has examined the relationship between culture, politics, and the institutions of culture. Their work has en-gaged questions and strategies central to the recent revi-sionist debates around art-historical, critical, and museolog-ical practices: the relationship between representation and ideology and representation and power; the appropriation of mass-media strategies; the challenging of the white, male, upper-class hegemony of art and art history; the role of community; the validation of gender, sexuality, and race as legitimate issues in art; the deconstruction of patronage; and the conservative institutional values of the museum.

The area of identity politics, in particular, has pushed the envelope of art-historical revisionism. The politics of identity—a subject central to much so-called political art of the past two decades—both magnifies the methodological limitations of art history and suggests important models for transcending these limitations. Because the issue of racial, ethnic, national, and sexual identities stirs up a torrent of emotions about difference, power, and entitlement, ques-tions concerning identity are often charged with feelings of resistance, anxiety, and even outright bigotry. The issue of race is a significant case in point. It is clear that certain as-pects of deconstructive theory have played an important role in elucidating the mechanisms and effects of racism. The recent critiques of "essentialism," for example, have been useful for African-American intellectuals and others concerned with challenging outmoded notions of identity that have imposed, from both the inside and the outside, what bell hooks has called "a narrow, constricting notion of blackness" (hooks, 1990).

But many of prejudices that beset African Americans in the cultural "mainstream," for example, also plague the var-ious disciplines of critical theory: the tendency to ignore cultural producers of color, the impulse to reduce racist be-havior or representations to intellectual abstractions, and most important, the inability to engage in any substantive degree of self-inquiry or to question one's own absolute au-thority to speak. As hooks has observed, in order for "radi-cal postmodernist thinking" to have a transformative im-pact, it must make a critical break with the notion of "'authority' as 'mastery over.'" This break must not simply be a rhetorical device, she argues, but must be reflected in the "habits of being," including styles of writing as well as chosen subject matter. "Third world nationals, elites, and white critics who passively absorb white supremacist thinking," she concludes, "are not likely to produce liberatory theory that will challenge racist domination, or promote a breakdown in traditional ways of seeing and thinking about reality, ways of constructing aesthetic theory and practice."

The art historian and the curator, driven as they are by the ideological and disciplinary need to construct tidy categories and movements, face a significant challenge in meeting this goal of refashioning an aesthetic theory motivated by difference rather than unity and bias. Few curators or art historians challenge the "mythic" nature, to reinscribe Barthes, of their disciplines—the unquestioned ease by which the messy paradoxes of our lives and of our culture are repressed within the art-historical, critical, or curatorial narrative. It is precisely these parodoxes and differences that need to be foregrounded—a methodological exchange, to paraphrase Cornel West, of the monolithic with the diverse, the abstract with the concrete, the universal with the specific—if new and more socially responsible interpretive practices are to emerge. While the need to systematize and homogenize diverse and often disparate objects and ideas can appear to enhance the didactic role of the museum, the art journal, and the art-history professor, such avoidance of difference also distorts meaning, fosters stereotypes, and engenders a false sense of aesthetic and intellectual unity. In an increasingly diverse and global society, it is the challenge of the art historian, critic, and curator to be self-critical as well as to find or create methodologies for exposing the myths of our time and for exploring the meaningful variances that resonate in the interaction between people and culture and culture and politics.

BIBLIOGRAPHY

Barthes, Roland. *Mythologies.* Translated by Annette Lavers. New York, 1972.
Berger, Maurice, ed. *Modern Art and Society: An Anthology of Social and Multicultural Readings.* New York, 1994.
Bhabha, Homi K. *The Location of Culture.* London and New York, 1994.
The Block Reader in Visual Culture. London and New York, 1996.
Clark, T. J. "Clement Greenberg's Theory of Art." In *Pollock and After: The Critical Debate,* edited by Francis Frascina. New York, 1985.
Ferguson, Russell, Martha Gever, Trinh T. Minh-ha, and Cornel West, eds. *Out There: Marginalization and Contemporary Cultures.* Cambridge, Mass., 1990.
Foucault, Michel. *The Archaeology of Knowledge.* Translated by A. M. Sheridan Smith. New York, 1972.
Greenberg, Clement. "Avant-Garde and Kitsch." In *Art and Culture: Critical Essays,* pp. 3–21. Boston, 1961.
hooks, bell. *Yearning: Race, Gender, and Cultural Politics,* Boston, 1990.
Kruger, Barbara, and Phil Mariani, eds. *Remaking History.* Seattle, 1989.
Lippard, Lucy R. *Mixed Blessings: New Art in a Multicultural America.* New York, 1990.
Owens, Craig. *Beyond Recognition: Representation, Power, and Culture.* Edited by Scott Bryson, Barbara Kruger, Lynne Tillman, and Jane Weinstock. Berkeley, 1993.
Rutherford, Jonathan, ed. *Identity: Community, Culture, Difference.* London, 1990.
Wallis, Brian, ed. *Art after Modernism: Rethinking Representation.* New York, 1984.
West, Cornel. "A Matter of Life and Death." *October* 61 (Summer 1992): 20–27.

MAURICE BERGER

Politicized Art

The French public savored a bumper crop of pears throughout the 1830s. The artist and publisher Charles Philipon was largely responsible for this fecundity, through the innumerable caricatures he presented of King Louis-Philippe as a dowdy fruit in the pages of *La caricature* and *Le charivari.* Philipon's most famous spoof appeared in 1831: in a series of four drawings titled *Les Poires,* he metamorphosed the sovereign's face from a solemn, jowly chap into a ridiculous, scowling pear. It was a brilliant artistic turn, and an ingenious linguistic one, too: the appellation was also slang for "simpleton."

This image was an instant hit on the streets, and Philipon's journals kept refining the idea: the persona French liberty sits and frets, her foot clenched in a chain attached to a massive pear; pear trees are irrigated by blood; typographic pears spell out the terms of repressive government edicts; pears are symbolically castrated or guillotined. A particularly robust sign, these permutations considerably rankled the powers that be. Not surprisingly, Philipon was prosecuted six times for publishing various caricatures, and twice convicted.

Philipon was part of an elaborate minuet of regulation and transgression performed between French governmental functionaries on the one hand, and artists and their publishers on the other. Such pas de deux regularly took place from 1820 until 1881—the number of participants overall was immense, including Philipon's renowned colleague Honoré Daumier—because drawings were subject to official censorship at various junctures during this period, whereas words were not. In a largely illiterate society, the power of images was thus duly acknowledged. While the specific partners may change over time and space, the following general principle pertains: whenever and wherever the realms of art and politics intersect, a *danse macabre* of some sort frequently plays out.

In the past, artists' dependence on the patronage of leaders of church and state sometimes led to even more subtle forms of resistance. Consider *Don Manuel Osorio Manrique de Zuñiga* by the court painter Francisco José de Goya (ca. 1788). At first glance, it is the tender portrait of a young boy, the embodiment of innocence. But it contains an ominous quality as well: the boy holds a string that tethers the leg of a magpie, while three wide-eyed cats lurk close by. The child may appear to be guileless, but he is, in fact, complicit. Moreover, the bird holds a card in its beak that bears Goya's name, dramatizing the risks and restrictions of his professional life.

Artists in our own time, at least those in the West, are seldom so indirect. They have adopted a more "in-your-face" attitude as the twentieth century has unfolded, often frankly confronting their leaders and directly addressing political and social issues. The resulting disputes confirm Michel Foucault's observation about "perpetual spirals of power and pleasure" (Foucault, 1980, p. 45): there are thrills to be had both in challenging and in exercising authority, in being either a provocateur or a police officer.

The following discussion will focus primarily on the late nineteenth and the twentieth century. *Art* and *artists* will be construed in the widest possible sense, and examples will be drawn from a variety of creative fields. In many instances, the material in question self-consciously confronts significant social and political questions. But artists' intentions are merely one factor in a complex equation of critical response that includes aspects of production as well as reception. Even those artists who aim to stay above the fray are sometimes swept along with the tide of controversy.

It is not uncommon for contemporary artists to transgress boundaries. They dissipate the distinctions between time-honored categories, melding together what cultural prescriptions traditionally have kept apart. Since the advent of modernism, artists have been blending what anthropologist Mary Douglas designates as "natural categories," binary classifications of experience such as masculine and feminine, public and private, sacred and profane, which every society sustains in some form. In this regard, many artists no longer fit the Marxian view of them as handmaidens of the ruling class, transmitting dominant ideologies and perpetuating systems of economic (or even gender or racial) stratification; they instead commonly disturb the presumptions of everyday life.

When an artist fiddles with revered taxonomies, there is often hell to pay. Jean-Baptiste Carpeaux discovered this when he produced a sculptural group for the facade of the new Paris Opéra. *La Danse* (1865–1869) featured a cluster of frenzied female dancers surrounding a *génie de la danse*. The central figure is sexually ambiguous, bearing the slim body of a male youth capped by a female face. S/he became the lightning rod for a heated controversy that included extensive debate in periodicals of the day, defacement with a bottle of ink, and even an order of banishment issued by Napoleon III.

The sculptor Constantin Brancusi precipitated something similar with *Princess X* (1916). In one respect it resembles the classic pose of a madonna, her enshrouded head tilted reverentially. But it also unmistakably resembles a set of male genitalia, the penis gracefully arched over the scrotum. The salon president had it removed from the Salon des Indépendants in 1920, preempting the possibility of adverse public response or even police action.

All the cast members, along with the producer of the play *The God of Vengeance* (penned by Sholem Asch, 1910), were arrested and charged with obscenity, immorality, and indecency after a New York production in 1922. This is the tale of Yankel, who operates a brothel in the basement while he maintains a "wholesome" atmosphere for his wife and chaste daughter, Rivkele, upstairs. Sacred and profane, public and private are strictly segregated—until Rivkele falls in love with the prostitute Manke.

Today, many artists blur the distinctions between natural categories. The photographer Andres Serrano's notoriety was established by *Piss Christ* (1987), when he placed a plastic crucifix in a jar of his own urine. Whereas many people were repulsed by the idea of mixing sacred and profane, one canny reviewer shifted the figure/ground perspective: instead of the crucifix being despoiled, perhaps more importantly the urine was being sanctified. Nevertheless, politicians condemned Serrano on the floor of the U.S. Congress, he received death threats, and others claimed his work was an example of the inappropriate use of taxpayers' money, channeled through the National Endowment for the Arts (NEA).

The widespread protests against Martin Scorsese's film *The Last Temptation of Christ* (1988) and Salman Rushdie's novel *The Satanic Verses* (1988) have similar origins. In both, major religious figures were demystified by focusing on their humanity alongside their divinity. But to the fundamentalist mind, this was an unbearable assault on received wisdom.

Protection of natural categories, and intolerance of their combination or violation, are at the base of a significant portion of modern-day controversies about art. Feminist performance artists Karen Finley and Annie Sprinkle transgress social expectations of femininity, the self, and the proper display of the body in public: they use "earthy" language, vault from persona to persona, and reveal intimate parts of their bodies and their functions. Each has been roundly condemned, as have many gay and lesbian artists: they elicit criticism by candidly including who they are in their creations, for the mere fact of their choice of partners automatically unnerves people wedded to conventional notions of what is appropriately masculine and feminine. Art makes homosexuality visible and tangible, as with the homoerotic photographs of Robert Mapplethorpe.

An artwork that demonstrates the hazards of boundary crossings was a 1988 portrait of the late Chicago mayor Harold Washington, created by School of the Art Institute of Chicago (SAIC) student David Nelson. Nelson unflatteringly presented Washington seminude, outfitted only in women's underwear. This white art student symbolically emasculated a revered African-American politician, recalling archaic measures of controlling "uppity niggers" such as lynching. In one of the most sensational contemporary bids to quash expression, several Chicago aldermen marched to SAIC and, with the support of police, "arrested" the painting.

Beyond the adverse response to what is, in essence, coloring outside of approved lines, it is clear that addressing certain hot-button issues in practically any manner can provoke controversy. The most important of these topics are race, religion, patriotism, gender, and sex. Because the United States is a complex, heterogeneous society—and one that experiences a great deal of social change—people hold a wide range of opinions on these subjects. Many works of art incorporating them are therefore destined to offend someone.

Race remains, in Gunnar Myrdal's notable 1944 phrase, "an American dilemma," and artistic representations of it an important flash point. Religious depictions also easily inflame passions, as Serrano, Scorsese, Rushdie, and many others can attest. Indeed, religion and politics become the warp and woof of many public conflicts, so that when either spiritual or secular officials feel threatened by what they view or hear, they pull out all the stops to protect both their doctrines and their institutions.

Patriotism may seem passé in many quarters at present, but it can be quickly mobilized when central social values appear to be threatened. Self-named artist-provocateur Dread Scott discovered this when he displayed his mixed-media installation *What Is the Proper Way to Display a U.S. Flag?* in *A/Part of the Whole,* an SAIC-sponsored exhibition showcasing the work of minority students in 1989. The work consisted of three parts: a photocollage of students burning the U.S. flag in various parts of the world; a shelf with a blank book for comments; and a flag on the floor. The piece seemed to invite viewers to step on the flag, although the book could in fact be reached without doing so.

Many people were scandalized and expressed their outrage in a variety of ways. Some entered the gallery, removed the flag from the floor, ceremoniously folded it, and placed it on the shelf, turning this into a truly interactive piece (gallery personnel or supporters of the artist would then restore it to its original position). Thousands more turned out for public rallies, and political opportunists at every level—local, state, and national—sensed the opening to polish up their nationalistic credentials and to enhance their own positions. There was also considerable congressional support for a constitutional amendment to safeguard this symbol. Artworks seldom generate fireworks of such magnitude and luster. But whenever artists skewer the performance or integrity of politicians, they are likely to find their work tossed around in a political game where they are up against more powerful, much more savvy opponents.

Sex and gender are the final hot-button issues. In fact, some observers claim that they are the most important ones, arguing that a "sex panic" has commenced in the late

twentieth century. While there is truth to this assertion, it masks several important points. First, the anxiety over candid depictions of sexuality is long-standing and broadly expressed, from the papal decree that Michelangelo's nudes on the ceiling of the Sistine Chapel be covered with loincloths soon after they were completed, to the similar alterations ordered by cemetery administrators in Paris regarding the male genitalia on Jacob Epstein's sphinxlike memorial to Oscar Wilde (1909–1912).

Second, as we have seen, other issues commonly kindle controversy as well. It is myopic and exclusionary to focus solely on gender and sex. Finally, many of the disputes over culture can only artificially be confined to one category of event. Rushdie was condemned because of his religious transgression, yes, but an additional consideration was that he fictionally characterized the wives of Muḥammad as prostitutes. Nelson's portrait of Harold Washington drew charges of racism, certainly, but some of the monikers attached to the work—including "the African Queen"—also recognize its allusions to transvestism and homosexuality. Few "pure cases" of violation exist.

Having said this, once critics started to sound the alarm over the depiction of sexual issues in the late 1980s, they indeed found it difficult to remove their fingers from the panic button. Feminist, gay, and lesbian artists have become particular targets, especially as they reflect the current debate over sex roles in the United States and elsewhere.

Although the primary emphasis up to this point has been on the artistic content of artworks that have become controversial, more specific attention must be paid to their denouncers. A 1957 study by philosopher Richard McKeon and his associates clarifies a key point: in order for constraints to be placed on expression, not only must there be the sense that values have been violated, but power must also be mobilized to do something about it. Outrage that is not backed up by action subsides into undirected anger; power that is not guided by principles disintegrates into diffuse and arbitrary force.

The concept of moral entrepreneurs, which was developed by sociologist Howard S. Becker to describe individuals who are profoundly unsettled by something and contrive to stamp it out—by legislative measures or other restrictive means—is obviously relevant here. Girolamo Savonarola, who staged "Bonfires of Vanities" in late fifteenth-century Florence, "antifilth" campaigner Anthony Comstock, who attempted to regulate everything from fine-art reproductions to birth control information in late nineteenth-century New York, and a panoply of contemporary crusaders are all examples of ideologues or absolutists who inflexibly embrace conventional rules and understandings, and are unable to abide ideas and representations that challenge them. Those moral crusaders who establish a lasting name for themselves are those who successfully couple values with power in a distinctive fashion.

Donald Wildmon, leader of the American Family Association, has done just that. He has parlayed his anxieties over what he perceives to be "anti-Christian biases" in contemporary culture into a multimillion-dollar industry sustaining radio shows, publications, and direct action. Yet, it is important to note that absolutists exist on the other end of the political spectrum as well. With the evolution of identity politics—people united on the basis of common ancestry or other ascribed characteristics, behaviors, or shared interests—so-called progressive individuals and groups on the political left sometimes also act in a heavy-handed, dictatorial way against cultural forms they feel compromise their sense of themselves and the world. For example, a female writing instructor successfully pressured administrators at a branch of Penn State University in 1991 to remove a reproduction of Goya's classic painting *Naked Maja* from the classroom wall where it had hung for years; she found teaching in the room a form of "sexual harassment."

In many instances such actions are aimed at influencing market or curatorial decisions, not legislation. These groups are typically so disenfranchised, or distrustful of governmental regulation, that they are less likely to view the government as an ally than are some groups on the right. The political waters have recently become so murky, however, that classifications such as "left" and "right" have been drained of much of their meaning. For example, how to classify law professor Catharine MacKinnon and writer Andrea Dworkin? They claim to be working for women's rights, but many other feminists distance themselves from the pair because of their puritanical notions and their attempts to enact laws restricting sexual expression. Rather than a horizontal continuum of political sentiments ranging from right to left, perhaps the measure we should use now is more horseshoe-shaped: the ends contain the absolutists of either stripe, the rounded middle admits of flexible plurality with a greater threshold for difference and change.

Those who hold elected offices have become important players in these battles. The Republican Jesse Helms of North Carolina, one of the most tireless critics of contemporary culture in the U.S. Senate, is clearly an accomplished practitioner of the politics of diversion. Helms targets symbolic issues while his constituents languish under the burden of tangible problems such as high infant mortality rates, low wages, and a seriously deficient educational system.

A related issue is the social construction of acceptability. In other words, work that is tolerated or even venerated in one time and place can be vilified in another. The work itself does not change. But audiences, and the values, experiences, and beliefs they carry with them, vary widely. The range of reactions accorded the Mapplethorpe retrospective *The Perfect Moment*, which toured the United States from 1988 through 1990, is a prime example.

The exhibit was a critical and popular success when it was mounted in Philadelphia and Chicago. It ran aground, however, when it was scheduled to open at Washington, D.C.'s Corcoran Gallery: the director canceled it, fearing that the conjunction of sexually charged images and an overheated congressional debate regarding public support of the arts had made it too hot to handle. It traveled to Hartford and Berkeley with little commotion, but encountered a substantial challenge when it reached Cincinnati. There, long-established moral entrepreneurs and their governmental allies tried to draw a moral line in the sand: in a uniquely vigorous alliance of values and power, they brought obscenity charges against the Cincinnati Contemporary Arts Center and its director (both were subsequently acquitted).

By the time the show reached its conclusion in Boston, public sentiment had changed—or at the very least, its supporters had learned how to become proactive. Neighboring institutions installed a number of "solidarity shows" on the body and censorship; the local public television affiliate broadcast some of Mapplethorpe's most controversial images; and gay and arts activists far outnumbered opposing demonstrators at the opening. Supporters had significantly transformed the context of reception.

In fact, we can talk of cycles of reception: work may fall in and out of favor as social attitudes shift. This lies at the heart of the *Naked Maja* controversy: peering through a late twentieth-century feminist lens, the college instructor shifted the work out of the canon and into the realm of sexist, degrading portrayals of women.

In conclusion, three important preconditions heighten the likelihood for art to become politicized and controversy to erupt. First, controversy is more likely when a community has already become fractured by conflict, public morale is low, and polarization and alienation are high. At these times, art can crystallize problems and present a visible target for people to vent their frustrations on. Second, the probability of conflict over art is enlarged when the legitimacy or effectiveness of governmental leaders is being questioned. Emotions are closer to the surface then, and defenses more likely to be rallied. Third, controversy is common when art is presented in public places or when it is publicly funded. Public display widens the audience and therefore the likelihood that divergent points of view will clash. Government monies always come with the string of accountability attached to them—just ask Goya.

[*See also* Law *and* Art, *article on* Censorship.]

BIBLIOGRAPHY

Becker, Howard S. *Outsiders: Studies in the Sociology of Deviance*. New York, 1963.

Childs, Elizabeth, ed. *Suspended Licenses: Essays in the History of Censorship and the Visual Arts*. Seattle, 1997.

de Grazia, Edward. *Girls Lean Back Everywhere: The Law of Obscenity and the Assault on Genius*. New York, 1992.

Douglas, Mary. *Natural Symbols: Explorations in Cosmology*. New York, 1973.

Dubin, Steven C. *Bureaucratizing the Muse: Public Funds and the Cultural Worker.* Chicago, 1987.

Dubin, Steven C. *Arresting Images: Impolitic Art and Uncivil Actions.* London and New York, 1992.

Dubin, Steven C. "Art's Enemies: Censors to the Right of Me, Censors to the Left of Me." *New Art Examiner* 21 (March 1994): 26–31.

Foucault, Michel. *The History of Sexuality,* vol. 1, *An Introduction.* Translated by Robert Hurley. New York, 1980.

Goldstein, Robert Justin. *Censorship of Political Caricature in Nineteenth-Century France.* Kent, Ohio, 1989.

Jansen, Sue Curry. *Censorship: The Knot That Binds Power and Knowledge.* New York and Oxford, 1991.

MacKinnon, Catharine A. *Only Words.* Cambridge, Mass., 1993.

McKeon, Richard, Robert K. Merton, and Walter Gellhorn. *The Freedom to Read: Perspective and Program.* New York, 1957.

Shikes, Ralph E. *The Indignant Eye: The Artist as Social Critic in Prints and Drawings from the Fifteenth Century to Picasso.* Boston, 1969.

Strossen, Nadine. *Defending Pornography: Free Speech, Sex, and the Fight for Women's Rights.* New York, 1995.

STEVEN C. DUBIN

Aestheticized Politics

Culture can be conceived as a dynamic in modern political systems, and in the case of fascism this relation is magnified. Fascism, which came to dominate Italy following Benito Mussolini's rise to power in 1922, and engulfed Germany with Adolf Hitler's seizure of power in 1933, is a form of politics in which aesthetic issues permeate all aspects of society. Thus, the political, economic, and cultural realms cannot be considered separately when discussing fascist societies. Analyzing the "palingenetic" dimension of fascism, the historian Roger Griffin has demonstrated that fascism's

> thrust towards a *new* type of society means that it builds rhetorically on the cultural achievements attributed to former, more "glorious" or healthy eras in national history only to invoke the regenerative ethos which is the prerequisite for national rebirth, and not to suggest socio-political models to be duplicated in a literal minded restoration of the past.   (Griffin, 1991, p. 47)

The historian Emilio Gentile has reached similar conclusions, claiming that references to ancient Rome in Italian fascist discourses were

> reconciled, without notable contradiction, with other elements of fascism that were more strictly futurist, such as its activism, its cult of youth and sport, the heroic ideal of adventure, and above all the will to experience the new continuity in action projected toward the future, without reactionary nostalgia for an ideal of past perfection to be restored.   (Gentile, 1994)

Thus, fascism's palingenetic, totalitarian, and nationalist aspirations allowed this ideology to address both the past and the future by proclaiming the present to be decadent and therefore in need of regenerative cultural renewal (Sternhell, 1994).

Both Griffin and the historian George L. Mosse (Mosse, 1988) have analyzed fascism's restriction of its critique of modernism to those elements considered to be degenerative, and its palingenetic drive to create a new (hence modern) type of society. Griffin has drawn on this theory to critique those who would describe Nazi ideology and its aesthetics as ultraconservative, restorationist, and antimodern. Indeed, in the period before Hitler's coming to power the Nazi leadership remained divided over whether avant-garde art should be condemned as antithetical to fascism's racial ideals or considered revelatory of an emerging National Socialist ethos. Before Joseph Goebbels took up his position as Reich Minister for Public Enlightenment and Propaganda in 1933, he and Nazi ideologue Alfred Rosenberg waged a pitched battle over the relative merits of the Expressionist painter (and party member) Emile Nolde, the Expressionist sculptor Ernst Barlach, and the architecture of such figures as Walter Gropius. Thus, Goebbels, in his semiautobiographical novel *Michael: Diary of a German Destiny* (1931), condemned the Jews as an "anti-race" and "poisonous bacillus" on the body of the German *Volk* even as he proclaimed the Expressionism of Vincent van Gogh an embodiment of the "Christian Socialist" ideals of "a new Germany" (Goebbels, cited in Griffin, 1995, pp. 119–120). After the Nazi rise to power, Goebbels signaled his continued support of Expressionism by appointing the young Expressionist painter Hans Weidemann as one of his chief aides in the propaganda ministry (Lane, 1968, p. 177). For Goebbels, Weidemann, and their followers, Nolde's art supposedly combined references to Nordic regionalism with an expressive style reflective of the youthful vigor of the new Germany; by contrast, Rosenberg, in the *Völkischer Beobachter* (July 1933), declared Nolde's Expressionist technique "negroid, impious, raw, and lacking in any genuine inner power" (Rosenberg, cited in Berman, 1992, p. 58). To successively overcome contemporary decadence, Rosenberg instructed artists to emulate the "ideal of beauty" created by the Greeks and such "Nordic" artists as Sandro Botticelli and Hans Holbein.

This debate was settled in 1934 when Hitler, speaking at a Nazi party congress, indicated that he did not consider Expressionism in keeping with Nazi ideals; in response, Goebbels initiated the suppression of modern painting that culminated in the inaugural *Entartete Kunst* (Degenerate Art) exhibition in July 1937 (the exhibition circulated throughout Germany and Austria between 1937 and 1941). Organized into nine groups that were listed in the *Guide to the Exhibition of Degenerate Art,* works by Nolde dominated a section representing the art promoted by "Jewish art dealers" to falsely symbolize "German religiosity"; other sections focused on themes of political and artistic "anarchy" (represented by George Grosz and Otto Dix), social decay, loss of "racial consciousness" through endorsement of "Negro" art (Expressionist sculpture), art that celebrated physical and mental deformity, and "the endless supply of Jewish trash" as a prelude to the "height of degeneracy," namely, the nonobjective art of Cubists and German Constructivists (Hinz, 1979, p. 40). The Nazi association of avant-garde art with spiritual and biological degeneracy was indebted to the writings of the architect and racial theorist Paul Schultze-Naumburg, whose 1928 volume *Kunst und Rasse* (Art and Race) juxtaposed examples of Expressionist art with photographs of diseased and deformed people to suggest the models for such pictorial innovations. In short, German Expressionism was now identified with a state of degenerative decay to be overcome by the palingenetic turn to other art forms.

The *Entartete Kunst* exhibit was counterbalanced by the July 1937 opening of the first *Great German Art* exhibition in the newly opened House of German Art, co-designed in a modernized, neoclassical style by architect Paul Ludwig Troost and Hitler. This exhibition—the first of a series of exhibitions from 1937 to 1941—celebrated painting and sculpture patterned after Greek sculpture, eighteenth-century neoclassicism, and nineteenth-century realism. The Nazi counterpart to degenerate avant-gardism was an aestheticized conception of the human body, patterned after those societies and cultures deemed to be morally, hence physically, regenerative (Mosse, 1988, 1991). Sculptural images of the ideal male, such as Arno Breker's *Readiness* (1937), were modeled after works of Greek classical sculpture such as Polykleitos's *Spear Bearer* (450–420 BCE; Mosse, 1991). Whereas the political role of the male as national symbol required dynamic images of nude warriors and contemporaneous soldiers, woman's role as childbearer was emphasized in images of peasant fecundity such as Jürgen Wegener's *Thanksgiving* (*Great German Art* exhibition, 1943; Adam, 1992, pp. 140–155). Resolutely heterosexual, such imagery captured what Mosse has termed the bourgeois ideal of "beauty without sensuality," conducive to the Nazi official emphasis on marriage, the family, chastity, and self-discipline (Mosse, 1991). In the realm of architecture the Nazi aesthetic was much more eclectic, however; every building type alluded to an idealized "Nordic" or "Aryan" past in order to reconnect German society to a healthy cultural precedent that would point the way to a regenerated future. Thus, the modernized neoclassicism of Albert Speer's party congress buildings in Nuremberg, like Clemens Klotz's neo-Romanesque, quasi-military schools at Ordensburgen, or the thatched-roof buildings that served as hotels along the ultramodern autobahn, were meant to suggest the continuity uniting a racially pure German past to modern society under the Nazi dictatorship (Lane, pp. 185–200).

The concept of palingenesis, furthermore, is also germane to the study of Italian fascist aesthetics, and this is especially evident in critical reassessments of Walter Benjamin's evaluation of the relation of Italian Futurism to fascism, as developed in his important essay "The Work of Art in the Age of Mechanical Reproduction" (1936). In this

POLITICS AND AESTHETICS: Fascism. David Alfaro Siqueiros, *Echo of a Scream* (1937), enamel on wood, 48 × 36 in. (121.9 × 91.4 cm); Museum of Modern Art, New York (Gift of Edward M. M. Warburg). (Photograph copyright 1998 by the Museum of Modern Art; used by permission.)

text, Benjamin highlights the fascist championing of the retrograde aesthetics of *l'art pour l'art*, and contrasts that aesthetic model with the emancipatory role signaled by new aesthetic forms such as cinema and montage. By cloaking politics in auratic rituals and aestheticized rhetoric, fascism sought to impose passivity on the working class and simultaneously uphold the bourgeois order that was threatened by the class-based politics of the newly created urban proletariat. Aesthetic notions of an unchanging, organic unity, whose self-referential value transcends the historical circumstances from which it emerged, were transferred to the political realm to justify fascism. Thus, in Benjamin's view, fascism sought to overcome sociopolitical dissension under capitalism by imposing an aestheticized ideology on the fragmented and pluralistic flux of contemporary society. To quote the historian Russell Berman, Benjamin regarded "the closed order of the organic work of art," as "a deception that imposes an enervated passivity on the bourgeois recipient"; in contrast, Benjamin valorized "fragmentary, open genres: the German Trauerspiel of the baroque as well

as the avant-gardist valorisation of montage," whose negation of aesthetic closure precluded any passive response on
the part of what was invariably a collective audience. "In
place of the auratic art work, with its isolated and pacified
recipient lost in contemplation," asserts Berman, Benjamin
proposed "a postauratic model that would convene a collective recipient (the 'masses') endowed with an active
and critical character" (Berman, 1989, pp. 38–39). Thus,
Benjamin valorized those art movements—Dada and
Surrealism—that consciously attacked bourgeois notions of
artistic autonomy, while aligning Futurism with the aestheticized discourse of the Italian fascists (Benjamin, 1969,
p. 254).

Benjamin's analysis of fascist aesthetics has inspired contemporary scholars not only to explore the implications of
his model for an analysis of literary texts written by fascism's apologists, but also to counter that the aestheticization of politics can serve a variety of political positions, and
to question Benjamin's restriction of fascist aestheticization
to nostalgic models of organic unity and completion (Jay,
1993, pp. 71–83). In this regard, fascism's relation to Futurism has undergone revision, for a number of historians have
argued that Futurist aesthetics embraced the very fragmentary, dynamic, and collage-based aesthetic that Benjamin
would associate with antifascism and proletarian emancipation. Thus, the literary historian Andrew Hewitt claims that
Benjamin's relation of fascism's politics to "falsified principles of harmony, organic totality, and unity," serving to
mask a society typified by class conflict and social fragmentation, cannot explain the fascist embrace of Futurism, because that movement trumpeted the very conflict fascism
supposedly sought to cover up (Hewitt, 1993, pp. 134–137).
Turning Benjamin's construct on its head, Hewitt argues
that Futurist proponents of fascism thought contemporary
society was in a condition of ossification, organic closure,
and stasis, and thus in need of rejuvenation through violence. By calling for "the ontologization of struggle as both
an aesthetic and a political principle," the Futurist wished to
reinvigorate a culture subsumed in the very organicist
metaphors Benjamin would identify with the fascist project.
"Whereas a more traditional analysis might stress the occul-
tation and aesthetic resolution of class struggle under fascism," states Hewitt, "it might be more valuable to speak instead of the generation of depotentialized areas of struggle
within the aesthetic," that is, the transference of the dynamism of class conflict to a realm of avant-gardism.

Hewitt's critique of more "traditional" analyses, which, like
Benjamin's, would relate Futurism to "the classical aesthetic
of harmonization" and "the false reconciliation of social conflict," finds an echo in Mosse's essay "The Political Culture
of Futurism" (Mosse, 1993, pp. 91–105). Here, Mosse analyzes two forms of nationalism, one that "apparently slowed
down change and restrained the onslaught of modernity" by
"condemning all that was rootless and that refused to pay re-

spect to ancient and medieval traditions" and "another kind
of nationalism, exemplified by the futurists in their acceptance of modernity." Paradoxically, "while most twentieth-
century nationalism retained its role as an immutable and unchanging force, the repository of eternal and unchanging
truth," Futurism exemplified a "different nationalism" that
exalted violence, condemned the past, and declared modern
technology to be "a vital symbol" of renewed national energies. The human correlate to this cult of violence and technological dynamism was the "so-called new man—symbolic
both of modernity and the power of the nation." Thus, for
Mosse, fascism in Italy embraced two aesthetics, one dynamic and fully accepting of technology, the other more traditional in its desire to anchor nationalism in the organicist
and auratic aestheticism outlined by Benjamin.

Here, Mosse raises a key issue, that is, whether fascism,
though resolutely modern in its aim to create a new society,
nevertheless subsumed the auratic vestiges of past traditions within its aesthetic. In this manner, the organic and
dynamic could coexist within a political aesthetic premised
on regeneration. This Janus-faced aesthetic serves to confirm the palingenetic model developed by Griffin. It also
bears directly on Italian fascist and Nazi approaches to architecture, both of which sought to impose an "auratic" and
"theatrical" experience on the beholder. For instance,
Hitler's favorite architect, Albert Speer, created architectural spaces designed for theatrical events on a scale that
consciously evoked the sublime (Mosse, 1975). "We must
build as large as today's technical possibilities permit," declared Hitler in 1939, for "we must build for eternity" (cited
in Lane, pp. 189–190). To meet Hitler's demands, Speer
constructed a gigantic *Zeppelinfeld* at Nuremberg, designed
to accommodate more than one hundred thousand people
at mass rallies and parades. In order to build for eternity,
Speer developed a "theory of ruin value": the buildings of
the Third Reich were designed so as to ensure that they
would resemble Greek and Roman models after centuries
or even thousands of years had passed (Hinz, p. 197). In effect, Hitler and Speer collapsed the past, present, and future
life of Germany under the Nazis into an image of the monumental and sublime, modeled after their aestheticized experience of the ruins of ancient Rome and Athens.

In Italy itself, Mussolini's aestheticized politics led him to
employ his favorite architect, Marcello Piacentini, in the
creation of a modern Imperial Rome. In his 31 December
1925 address, "La nuòva Róma," Mussolini declared that
Rome must appear "vast, ordered, mighty, as it was in the
days of the first empire of Augustus"; to achieve that goal he
would "open space around the Augusteo [the mausoleum
of Augustus], the Theatre Marcellus, the Campidoglio, the
Pantheon." "Everything from the periods of decadence
must disappear," Mussolini declared, and "the majestic
temples of Christian Rome" would likewise be liberated
from "parasitic and profane constructions," for "the mil-

lenary monuments of our history must tower like giants in a necessary solitude" (Mussolini, cited in Etlin, 1991, pp. 391–392). In short, Mussolini wished to convert architecture into a form of monumental sculpture, isolated for veneration by the masses; moreover, through the creation in 1932 of the vast Vìa dell'Impèro, which connected the Colosseum to the monument to Victor Emmanuel II, Mussolini drew a symbolic connection between Roman imperial glory, the nineteenth-century unification of Italy, and fascism's imperial aspirations.

The use of historical references also has relevance for an evaluation of modernist architecture of the Italian rationalists or Gruppo Sette, composed of architects Adalberto Libera, Luigi Figini, Guido Frette, Sebastiano Larco, Gino Pollini, Carlo Enrico Rava, and Guiseppe Terragni. The historians Diane Ghirardo and Richard Etlin have attributed the conflation of traditionalist and modernist themes in the architecture of the Italian rationalists to Gruppo Sette's wholesale endorsement of fascist ideology. Thus, in contrast to Italian architectural historians who would cite the rationalists' embrace of the modernism of the French architect Le Corbusier as proof of their distance from fascist political aims, Ghirardo and Etlin demonstrate the integral relation of Italian rationalism to a fascist ideology that, in Ghirardo's words, vacillated "between an apparently adventurous modernism and a recalcitrant traditionalism" (Ghirardo, 1989). This conflation of modernist forms with references to Italy's past is even evident in the ground plan for Terragni's Casa del Fàscio in Como (1932–1936), which, according to Ghirardo, resembles that of the Palazzo Farnese in Rome. Ghirardo has also noted the rationalists' assimilation of Le Corbusier's authoritarian pronouncements in *Vers une architecture* (1923) to the fascist imposition of a corporate hierarchy *(gerarchìa)* on Italian society, while Etlin has charted Gruppo Sette's relation of Le Corbusier's stated interest in Greek classicism to the fascist doctrine of *mediterraneità.* By arguing that Le Corbusier was a modernist wedded to Mediterranean culture, the rationalists effectively countered claims that they favored internationalism over an indigenous Italian tradition, reflective of a "Latin" and imperial past. In this manner the rationalists could take their place alongside architectural advocates of *Romanità* and *latinità* in supporting an ideology that laid claim to the cultural legacy of Imperial Rome as a springboard to colonial conquest in Africa. "The cult of Romanness," to quote Emilio Gentile, served to justify "political action" and as such "was celebrated modernistically as a myth of action for the future" (Gentile, 1994).

In Italy, in contrast to the German situation after 1934, fascist aesthetics was heterogeneous in nature; that is, the messages of fascism were articulated across a spectrum of sensibility that ranged from various abstract trends through many versions of historicist and traditionalizing figuration. Nevertheless, a fascist aesthetics can be effectively defined, at a for-

mal level, through the same characteristic structure of polarization that informs our study of fascist ideology. That is to say, fascist aesthetics, although revolutionary and modernist, comprised progressive and traditionalizing currents, and was both elitist and populist in its logic. It is important to note, furthermore, that fascist aesthetics brought together these opposed terms in such a way as to challenge, on the theoretical level, any simple parallelism between progressive aesthetics and utopian and revolutionary ideologies, on the one hand, and reactionary art and authoritarian politics, on the other. Indeed, the study of fascist aesthetics has helped to call into question a central precept in the theory of the avant-garde, according to which the concepts of modernism and fascism were generally seen as mutually exclusive.

BIBLIOGRAPHY

Adam, Peter. *Art of the Third Reich.* New York, 1992.

Adamson, Walter L. *Avant-Garde Florence: From Modernism to Fascism.* Cambridge, Mass., 1993.

Benjamin, Walter. "The Work of Art in the Age of Mechanical Reproduction." In *Illuminations,* edited by Hannah Arendt, translated by Harry Zohn, pp. 219–254. New York, 1969.

Berman, Russell A. *Modern Culture and Critical Theory: Art, Politics, and the Legacy of the Frankfurt School.* Madison, Wis., 1989.

Berman, Russell A. "German Primitivism/Primitive Germany." In *Fascism, Aesthetics, and Culture,* edited by Richard J. Golsan, pp. 56–66. Hanover, N.H., 1992.

Carroll, David. *French Literary Fascism: Nationalism, Anti-Semitism, and the Ideology of Culture.* Princeton, N.J., 1995.

Etlin, Richard A. *Modernism in Italian Architecture, 1890–1940.* Cambridge, Mass., 1991.

Gentile, Emilio. *Il culto del littorio: La sacrilizzazione délla politica nell'Itàlia fascista.* Rome, 1993.

Gentile, Emilio. "The Conquest of Modernity: From Modernist Nationalism to Fascism." *Modernism/Modernity* 1.3 (September 1994): 55–87.

Ghirardo, Diane. *Building New Communities: New Deal America and Fascist Italy.* Princeton, N.J., 1989.

Griffin, Roger. *The Nature of Fascism.* New York, 1991.

Griffin, Roger, ed. *Fascism.* New York and Oxford, 1995.

Hewitt, Andrew. *Fascist Modernism: Aesthetics, Politics, and the Avant-Garde.* Stanford, Calif., 1993.

Hinz, Berthold. *Art in the Third Reich.* Translated by Robert Kimber and Rita Kimber. New York, 1979.

Jay, Martin. *Force Fields: Between Intellectual History and Cultural Critique.* London and New York, 1993.

Lane, Barbara Miller. *Architecture and Politics in Germany, 1918–1945.* Cambridge, Mass., 1968.

Mosse, George L. *The Nationalization of the Masses.* New York, 1975.

Mosse, George L. *Nationalism and Sexuality: Middle-Class Morality and Sexual Norms in Modern Europe* (1985). 2d ed. Madison, Wis., 1988.

Mosse, George L. "Beauty without Sensuality/The Exhibition *Entertete Kunst.*" In *"Degenerate Art": The Fate of the Avant-Garde in Nazi Germany,* edited by Stephanie Barron, pp. 25–31. New York, 1991.

Mosse, George L. *Confronting the Nation: Jewish and Western Nationalism.* Hanover, N.H., 1993.

Sternhell, Zeev. *The Birth of Fascist Ideology: From Cultural Rebellion to Political Revolution* (1989). 2d ed. Translated by David Maisel. Princeton, N.J., 1994.

Mark Antliff

AIDS, Aesthetics, and Activism

In the late 1980s, before the AIDS crisis was a decade old, a debate broke out over the uncertain role of the arts in the mobilization of cultural forces against the epidemic. It was never a formal scholarly debate: its participants were far too engaged (as many still are) in life-and-death struggles with the disease itself to simplify their dialectical moves into an intellectual game. Nevertheless, for the purposes of provocation, a critical distinction was drawn in 1987 between two movements emerging out of the conflicting cultural reactions to the epidemic. The authors of the distinction, gay art critics Douglas Crimp and Simon Watney, defined their movement as "cultural activism" by opposing it to "aestheticism." Cultural activism was not opposed to "aesthetics," however, because Crimp and Watney strove to defend certain philosophical views about the social function of art in accordance with their political theorization of the epidemic as a "crisis of representation." Whereas cultural activism with its revolutionary fervor looked forward to a radical reinvention of art as a social healing force, aestheticism with its transcendental impulse harked back to the "art-for-art's-sake" movement of the Wildean Belle Époque.

Background. In 1987, when the AIDS Coalition to Unleash Power (ACT UP) was formed in New York City, the militant objectives of the activists seemed momentously at odds with the memorializing projects of the aesthetes. Many gay artists and authors "acted up" at the time by producing AIDS-related works that addressed the crisis of representation in terms or images directly influenced by the debate. The debate itself became a subject for artistic meditation in the provocative installation "Let the Record Show . . ." (1987) at New York's New Museum of Contemporary Art. So aggressively did this work attack the political apathy behind the elegiac posturing of America in the "Age of AIDS" that its critical repercussions were soon felt beyond New York. By 1989, similar works were challenging gallerygoers in San Francisco, Los Angeles, Toronto, Montreal, London, Paris, and Berlin.

As the cultural vistas of the epidemic broaden with the increasing incidence of HIV-infection among heterosexual "risk groups"—for example, Hispanic, Asian, and African-American women—the aestheticism-activism debate is bound to resurface in communities far beyond the New York art world and in terms that complicate the oppositions originally experienced by white gay men (for whom the epidemic has tended to sink, of late, into the background of ordinary life). When AIDS educators in Thailand advertise the importance of safer sex to villagers by painting brightly colored condoms on the sides of elephants, is this an example of activist art practice? Should it be judged by the same aesthetic criteria as the cartoon-style condoms painted by New York graffiti artist Keith Haring? Although specific issues raised by the aestheticism-activism debate may not be relevant to all art produced in response to the epidemic, perhaps the international efforts to redefine and resolve the debate as its cultural implications expand will reveal its universal applicability to the problem of defining the social value of art.

Media pronouncements of an "AIDS Apocalypse" provided the background noise to the activism-aestheticism debate, stirring the activists especially to take aggressive stands on basic aesthetic issues ignored or glossed over in journalistic accounts of the epidemic as a "special crisis for the arts." The prejudicial representation of people with AIDS (PWAs) in the mainstream media generated heated discussions on the obligation of artists to become activists. The ancient issue of the truthfulness of images surfaced in an urgent new guise in the critical years 1985–87 when the politics of representation became a major concern for radicalized PWAs who strongly objected to being cast in the passive and intensely moralized role of "AIDS victims."

Certain ethical and epistemological issues long debated in university circles were now raised by plague anxiety to a level of more than academic interest. Is the pedagogical function of art more important than its "purely" aesthetic role? Does any clear criterion exist for distinguishing truthful images of reality from delusional misrepresentations? Can artists know what AIDS really is apart from its cultural metaphors or artistic signs? Should art be valued solely on the basis of its social impact? These were some of the questions that demanded to be addressed whenever the arts were recruited to join the war against AIDS or to create the "AIDS Renaissance" prophesied by the media.

Aestheticism. With the consoling notion of an artistic renaissance resulting from the epidemic came a renewed focus on artist-centered aesthetic issues. "The artist's choice to produce representational work always affects more than a single artist's career, going beyond . . . the walls on which an artist's work is displayed," proclaimed an activist flyer handed out to protest the opening of photographer Nicholas Nixon's "Pictures of People" exhibition at New York's Museum of Modern Art in 1988. The time-lapse design of Nixon's black-and-white portrait series seemed to critics to have the disquieting effect of turning people still living with AIDS into studies for a Still Life with AIDS. Much to his dismay, Nixon found himself figuring in activist diatribes as the archaesthete who had haughtily ignored his critics' counteraesthetic dictum: "Ultimately, representations affect those represented."

Many artists and authors sympathetic with Nixon's memorializing aims preferred not to engage in public disputes over the politics of representation. Their introspective focus was fixed primarily on the agonies of the creative process: how the task of representing AIDS affects those struggling to represent it. Were Nixon's images a painful documentary record of the artist's brave examination of the impact of the virus on the human body? Or was his show simply a high-art version of the "Before and After" diptych endlessly repeated in the media? The Wildean design of the diptych remains all too familiar: a beautiful face or figure on the nostalgic pre-AIDS side helplessly confronts its wrinkled and withered double on the postdiagnostic side—like Oscar Wilde's Dorian Gray confronting the image of his decadent inner self.

No artist-centered issue in the Western aesthetic tradition has provoked more agonized reflection during the AIDS crisis than the difficulty of reconciling two indispensable truisms concerning beauty. The first and no doubt more ancient of these, an idealistic promise that the combined beauties of nature and art may console the living in grievous times, has traditionally justified the creation of beautiful memorials for the dead. The second, its cynical counterdictum, thwarts the desire to memorialize by insisting that art can neither soften nor stop the relentless blows of death because all beauties in this world inevitably "come to dust."

Reflected in the design of the "Before and After" diptych is the teasing opposition of aesthetic idealism and apathetic cynicism always latent in elegy. Why offer beautiful words and music to the dead when death itself cannot hear "what vain art can reply"? This is an issue for all mourners, regardless of race, gender, sexuality, or serostatus. If frail memorials and frantic laments cannot stop death, might they not at least save lives? Should elegiac art not ally itself with epidemiology on the educational front? Or should it act as a polemical fuse, exploding the medical construct of the syndrome as a battle between faceless pathogens and failed immune systems? Medical knowledge has long been subject to aesthetic critique. "Physic himself must fade," as the English elegist Thomas Nashe lamented in 1592, for "All things to end are made."

The elegists of the new plague are haunted by an old Renaissance question: why should a ruinous disease prompt its sufferers (both the infected and the affected) to contemplate beautiful scenes, capture beautiful moments, construct beautiful monuments? To some, aesthetic compensation for loss seems too fragile an explanation for the prodigal expense of artistic spirit that has been lavished on memorializing the AIDS dead—who are no more lost, after all, than those who die of other causes. Even frailer, to others, is the classic pedagogical rationale for elegiac art: its usefulness as a moralizing mirror held up to the vanities of mortal corporeality. However earnestly Nixon may have conceived his photo series as a memento mori for people without AIDS, his critics were quick to point out that the sick and the stricken need no reminding from him (or from his romantic forerunner John Keats) that we all live in a bad ugly world where "Youth grows pale, and spectre-thin, and dies."

Adrienne Rich, in her 1987 elegy "In Memoriam," explains the aestheticization of AIDS as a therapeutic antidote to cynical despair. A PWA of her acquaintance was losing his lifelong delight in flowers, poetry, and music. To him, and to herself as his soul mate, she poses a devastating question about art as therapy: "How will culture cure you?" Despite the difficulty, if not failure, of elegists' efforts to transcend the ugliness and meanness of death, the aestheticizing drive that AIDS simultaneously frustrates and sustains must be gratefully acknowledged by the living as a prophetic yearning for the miraculous. Elegies such as "In Memoriam" ensure at least the preservation (if not the realization) of the dream of a *locus amoenus* where ancient fantasies of purgation and regeneration are mythically recollected.

Countering the cynical attitudes litanized by the media is a transcendental impulse that few AIDS elegists on the aesthetic side of the debate have resisted in their efforts to justify the momentous outpouring of literature and art concerned with the epidemic. Andrew Holleran, for instance, has shown how swiftly the gay male gaze can transform scenes of erotic dejection into visions of ecstatic joy through aesthetic refigurations of memory. Haunted by the shades of men who reveled in the lost world of 1971, he hails their successors at a bathhouse in 1983:

> They were as improbable and beautiful lying in their rooms in their Jockey shorts and towels as the gods Michael [a recently deceased PWA] had painted on his ceiling on Seventh Street—a burst of beauty, fantasy, art—in the midst of a nightmare reality. The thrill of homosexuality is finally an aesthetic thrill.   (1988)

More than an aesthetic thrill in the jaded Dorian Gray sense, this burst of beauty is a prophetic transport beyond the here and now into a Sistine Chapel afterlife where Michael (replacing Michelangelo) has endured martyrdom for the Religion of Art. However ironic its setting, the mystical intensity of Holleran's vision contrasts sharply with the media-hallowed mundanity of another aesthetic thrill: the dubious pleasure afforded by the Silver Lining fantasy that the arts are currently enjoying a miraculous rebirth because of the AIDS crisis.

Even if artists were to declare an end to the AIDS Renaissance, the hope of aesthetic transcendence would surely persist along with the fantasy of resurrection because of the clinical manifestations of the syndrome itself. AIDS does not simply debilitate. It disfigures. Despite the pharmaceutical industry's promise to restore the look of health to PWAs who drink the right "cocktail" of protease inhibitors, the epidemic still stirs up deep-seated religious wishes about the preservation and transfiguration of the flesh.

"The body becomes central," reflected Holleran's friend and fellow apologist for aestheticism, Edmund White, in 1987. "If art is to confront AIDS more honestly than the media have done," he argued, "it must begin in tact, avoid humor, and end in anger." Thus condensed into an Horatian epigram was the neoclassical argument for artistic truthfulness, high seriousness, creative self-restraint, tragic decorum, sensitivity to social proprieties. Horace could not have argued the case more succinctly—even if he had had White's pressing medical motive for doing so. Like the Stoic hero in a Roman tragedy who must face the predicted consequences of his fatal flaw but not give way to unseemly grief or rage, White grimly confessed to feeling "very alone with the disease": the isolation that it imposed on him because of its infectious character (or that he imposed on himself because of his good manners) was consolingly similar to the leave he had long ago taken from ordinary social life to follow the Parnassian route of the "solitary high arts."

It is hard not to hear an epitaph in his epigram. Here lies a gay outsider who began his literary career by turning closety tact into an exquisite prose style; avoided queeny humor and low camp in his lofty pursuit of artistic fame; and would inevitably end his life in anger at the vulgar misrepresentation of himself as just another poor plague victim. A decorous beginning, a serious middle, and a furious end: it is also hard not hear Aristotle's classic formula for the perfect tragic plot behind White's triple prescription for a dignified life with AIDS. Because this formula is also his aesthetic cure for AIDS hysteria, it seems to offer the diminishing arts community he addresses a nobly rational, perhaps even cathartic, way out of the AIDS tragedy chorally lamented by the media. The solitary high arts alone can purge the irrationality clogging up the channels of the popular mind.

In a spiritual sense, the muddle of the plague ceases for the oracular aesthete who can impose a tragic form on its maddening incertitudes. By bravely facing the terrible facts of the plague, White can give the lie to the simplistic myth of divine judgment that "explains" its origin to the masses; then, by heroically rising above his own sufferings, he can see with transfiguring (if not transcendent) clarity the whole design of the crisis from its hidden causes to its catastrophic effects. AIDS truly becomes for him a crisis in a neoclassical sense: a disastrous turning point in the hero's career when his rising action begins to fall, as fall it must, through righteous anger, desperate fury, and helpless rage, down to dusty death.

There is no humor in this solemn patterning of otherwise random agonies. Its form has to be clear because its function is moral clarification. Its appeal to Stoic fatalism has to be strong because its therapeutic strength lies in its demand for aesthetic detachment. But there also lies the tragic dilemma for White: his artistic prescription for a more honest (i.e., honorable as well as true-to-life) representation of AIDS compels him to organize its confusing vastness into a mimetic design that is surely no less fictional—despite tragedy's higher claims to aesthetic sophistication—than the vulgar mythologizations of the epidemic in the media. This design may well help White feel less alone with the disease by granting him the luxury of identification with tragic heroes: but how does it connect him to the multitudes of un-

heroic PWAs? Perhaps a shared appreciation of the moral truths revealed in the terrible beauty born of his tragic engagement with AIDS will bind the prophetic aesthete to the community of artists who share his anagnorisis. Perhaps, if pushed, they would attempt some philosophical defense of Keats's tautology about truth and beauty.

Activism. The activists scorned the neoclassical attitude of Stoic grief. If art is really to confront AIDS more honestly than the media have done, they rejoined, it must begin in anger—not end in it. "What will it take to make you angry?" was playwright Larry Kramer's incendiary refrain after the recitation of Centers for Disease Control statistics at the early meetings of ACT UP. His incessant questioning of the fantasy of the AIDS Renaissance ushered in what might be called the "Activist Reformation," a period of skeptical attack on the prevailing orthodoxies (medical, political, aesthetic) of the official AIDS world that climaxed in 1989 when ACT UP stormed the podium at the opening ceremonies of the Montreal International AIDS Conference. The activist demonstrations and art exhibitions at this critical collision of the AIDS establishment with its unorthodox opponents endeavored to shift concern away from artist-centered aesthetic issues toward the complex system of economic and political power relations in which the epidemic was being constructed to profit the institutions supposedly responsible for controlling or containing it.

The iconography of rage crackled with the satiric humor of ACT UP's graphic arts collective Gran Fury, which took its name not only from the driving emotion behind activist polemics but also from the make of car favored by the New York Police Department. The symbolic engine of heterosexism was wittily "queered" to drive home ACT UP's main political point that AIDS phobia was fueled by homophobia. Gran Fury's wit was a discordant concord of critical theory and street-level politics. "AID$ Now" proclaimed a poster from their 1988 campaign. Behind its forthright demand for more AIDS research funding lies a sly reference to Michel Foucault's theorization of disease as a "discourse" constructed by the financially empowered institutions of dominant culture.

The furiously comic work of Gran Fury ran counter to White's solemn decree that humor should be avoided because it "seems grotesquely inappropriate to the occasion." Why avoid humor when it can be used as a weapon against the false prophets and fascist profiteers of the official AIDS world? As for tact, that was merely a face-saving rhetorical strategy for presidents and belletrists. How could tact spark a revolution against the massive institutional forces mustered by the dominant culture to blame the crisis on already stigmatized minorities? Tact was just another word for closety, complacency, self-censorship. Its consequences were spelled out in the activist slogan "Silence = Death." Fortified with desperate certainties and defiant rallying cries, ACT UP threw tact to the winds as it brashly picketed art openings, stopped rush-hour traffic, "zapped" television stations with surprise on-air protests, and rioted in savvy political overstatement.

If aestheticism was in bad odor among the activists, aesthetics was not. Far from ignoring or downplaying the aesthetic issues raised by their punchy poster campaigns ("demo graphics") or by their militant mourning rites ("die-ins"), the strategists of ACT UP advanced and articulated a counteraesthetics that justified their aggressive reaction to the AIDS Renaissance—which they saw as the self-congratulatory flip side of the AIDS Apocalypse.

Two basic principles of activist art theory may be inferred from the balanced negatives and affirmatives of Crimp's 1987 manifesto: "We don't need a cultural renaissance; we need cultural practices actively participating in the struggle against AIDS. We don't need to transcend the epidemic; we need to end it" (1988). First, the transcendental impulse of aestheticism must be countered by a practical focus on specific medical and social justice issues affecting those who struggle against AIDS in the here and now. Second, the process of activist art making must become primarily collective if it is to meet the enormous social and political challenges of the epidemic: in other words, a demanding "we" must replace the "I" hallowed by the Renaissance tradition of the lone creative genius, even as the preemptive "we" of the official AIDS world (like the "general public" of the media) must defer to the emerging authority of the sick. Implicit in these principles is a recommendation that the value of any AIDS-related cultural work be judged chiefly on the basis of its effectiveness in addressing the urgent needs of PWAs and their caregivers.

A stringent utilitarianism underlies the activist struggle to replace the production of passive "cultural commodities" (e.g., paintings auctioned at a benefit) with vital "cultural practices" that might alter the status quo to benefit the sick (e.g., protesting placebo trials). Activist insistence on "cultural interventions" to help the infected springs from moral outrage at the injustices of a culture hierarchically ordered by race, class, gender, sexuality, and health.

Aesthetic issues, from the activist viewpoint, cannot be divorced from the ethics of civil disobedience or the morality of holy warfare. Like their mortal foes, the televangelists, AIDS activists are inveterate moralists to whom notions such as aesthetic distance or transcendence make no sense. The street is their original pulpit, and the small screen their happy zapping ground. By reversing the homophobic messages of their doctrinal opponents, activist icon makers effectively define their mission as preaching to the perverted, the ritually shamed, the socially excluded. Thus, while activist art is designed to take on the immediate task of saving lives, its ultimate goal is the frankly apocalyptic telos of deliverance from evil. Considered from this angle, the activist critique of aestheticism has an intellectual history that predates the AIDS crisis: its philosophical origins surely lie in

the schism between formalism and contextualism that has deeply divided artists, critics, and aesthetic theorists through much of the twentieth century.

According to the activists, art stored in museums is a passive bourgeois commodity, whereas art storming the battlements of public health is an active force for saving lives and salvaging society. The institutional theory of art expounded by Crimp in his activist manifesto reveals his allegiance to contextualism as a corrective approach to the formalist dismissal of ideological contents and social constraints in the definition and evaluation of art. If the activist drive to champion art or literature that strategically represents PWAs as an oppressed class ripe for insurgency (at least within the panoptical constraints of what Watney has called "the spectacle of AIDS") owes something to the decades-old momentum of the Marxist aesthetic tradition, a brisk current of which surfaced in the "Black is Beautiful" movement of the 1960s before flowing into the gay and women's liberation movements of the 1970s and thence into the angry turbulence of ACT UP. A Marxist contempt for the worship of religious or commercial icons must surely underlie the activist reflex to criticize to the point of excoriation the "ars longa, vita brevis" line spouted by the black-tie organizers of AIDS benefits.

If the Marxist critical impulse to dissolve art objects into the conflictual fluidity of their social contexts had any counterpart on the creative side in the 1980s, it might be found in the subversive disposability of Gran Fury's agitprop—words and images deliberately designed to work only within specific "zaps" or "actions"; to have no meaning apart from their ideological frameworks and political frays; and to mock by their very disappearance after the events that called them into being the formalist admiration for the immutability and autonomy of the artistic masterpiece. Marxist art practices must hasten the revolution. Activist art practices must advance the cure.

Aestheticism and Activism. Are advocates for the aesthetic transcendence of AIDS necessarily noncontextualists in their evaluation of art? Or do they only seem so from the polarizing standpoint of the activists? Have aestheticism and activism been falsely dichotomized in the debates over detachment and engagement? Or have they been pushed toward synthesis by the metamorphic pressures of the epidemic on the medical front? Has the fire of dialectical urgency cleared a middle ground for activists with aesthetic leanings and aesthetes with activist links?

Questions of this sort were left hanging at the end of the first decade of the epidemic. Now, as the possibility of a "magic bullet" cure seems increasingly tenuous, they are being asked again with fresh urgency by artists and critics whose works on AIDS are assessing the progress made on the cultural front following the decline of ACT UP and related groups in the early 1990s. Whether that decline is irreversible remains to be seen: it may be the result of the permanent thinning of the activist ranks as "the plague full swift runs by," or merely to a temporary exhaustion of their reserves of energizing anger.

In any case, the muting of the activist voice in the political arena does not mean that the aesthetes have won the day (or the debate) in the philosophical forum. Although art production on the activist side has noticeably dropped off since the heyday of Gran Fury, the contextualist principles of cultural activism have not been discarded: their academic promulgation has ensured that the repercussions of ACT UP are now felt in cultural contexts far broader and more diverse than the New York art circles that polemically equated silence with death.

Philosophical debates conducted over many years tend to lapse into the silence that equals tedium. So where is the activism-aestheticism debate headed if it is to remain vital and engaging? Will the aesthetes launch a kind of counter-reformation against the activists? Indications from the volatile worlds of the gallery and the theater suggest that aestheticism is indeed returning in the aftermath of ACT UP's war against the indulgences of the AIDS establishment. But it is no longer a simple "et in Arcadia ego" effort to meditate on death in the presence of beauty. The aestheticism of the 1990s has fortified itself against critical attack by absorbing and redeploying activist anger into a new elegiac project: the invention of queer anagoges. Like the saints of the Catholic Counter-Reformation, who float heavenward on clouds of glory in Baroque painting and sculpture, the martyrs of the Aesthetic Counter-Reformation are finding their way up into strange new heavens in dirigible-size AZT capsules, through magic video portals, and on libidinous angel's wings.

If the arts have hitherto failed to synthesize activist fire with aesthetic form, it has not been for lack of trying. The results have been bewildering, at times contradictory. Compare, for instance, the bleakly menacing poster "Enjoy AZT" by Vincent Gagliostro and Avram Finkelstein (1990) with the brightly monumental installation "One Day of AZT" by General Idea (1991). Both works gesture toward the same controversial subject, the therapeutic value of the antiviral drug zidovudine. Both are parodic in design: the poster copies the white wave image of the "Enjoy Coke" logo with the deadpan humor of Andy Warhol; the installation recalls the outsize objects of Pop art in the style of Claes Oldenburg. An academic taste for postmodern archness mixed with political cheek would certainly find satisfaction in both.

Yet, how differently their respective artists treat the same unlikely material—as if they were setting up a textbook contrast between activist engagement and aesthetic detachment. Whereas the poster was published anonymously for distribution at demos during the San Francisco AIDS conference, the installation was launched on a widely publicized tour of major contemporary art galleries in Europe and North America. Whereas the poster shouted its sarcastic slogan ("We Volunteer—They Profiteer") against an enemy establishment, the ruefully ironic installation celebrated the promise of pharmaceutical magic bulletry by displaying five giant AZT capsules on the gallery floor. Once the poster had zapped out its ideological critique, it was stapled over or torn down and trashed. Once the installation had finished its tour, it was bought by the National Gallery of Canada and permanently displayed in a white alcovelike space for meditating on the impact of the epidemic on the arts. Now that two members of General Idea have died of AIDS, their giant capsules look like space-age sarcophagi launched on a shuttle mission to paradise.

No art has been more engaged in the ecumenical project to link the solace of the AIDS Renaissance with the zeal of the ACT UP Reformation than drama, which was also the first art to envision the birth of activism as a mythical rupturing of gay aesthetic culture. That was in 1984, when Larry Kramer's political antimasque *The Normal Heart* opened at the Public Theater in New York. Nine years later, with audiences still reeling from the steady blows of Kramer's rhetoric, the masque of heavenly beauty bursts onto the scene at the climactic end of *Millennium Approaches*, part 1 of Tony Kushner's two-part mystery play *Angels in America*. Along with its sequel, *Perestroika*, which opened on Broadway in 1994, this "Gay Fantasia on National Themes" is at once an aesthete's vast elaboration of the "Before and After" diptych and an activist's visionary explosion of the media fantasy of the AIDS Apocalypse.

The aesthete's urge to impose a unifying structure on the confusing vastness of the plague is expressed early in part 1 by Lou, a burned-out leftie who seeks solace in aesthetic meditation after his lover Prior is diagnosed with AIDS. To Lou's Edmund Whitish argument that "it should be the questions and shape of a life, its total complexity gathered, arranged, and considered, which matters in the end," Prior responds with a sardonic putdown: "I like this; very Zen; it's . . . reassuringly incomprehensible and useless. We who are about to die salute you."

Just when the split between the lovers threatens to divide the play's restless philosophical current into a repudiation of aesthetic solace on Lou's side, and a drift toward activist martyrdom on Prior's, Kushner sends an angel—the ultimate embodiment of the Aesthetic Counter-Reformation—crashing through the ceiling of their old bedroom into the confusion of their debate. The angel comes "with a great blaze of triumphal music" to celebrate what looks like the imminent victory of transcendental aestheticism over the ugliness of the plague. Surely, now the discord between aestheticism and activism will be resolved through divine intervention.

In part 2, however, Prior discovers that the angel cannot cure him with illuminated books, Baroque trumpet concerti, or flaming Michelangelesque tableaux. Ironically, it is the PWA who is summoned into heaven to save the angelic hierarchs from the plague of mortality, the "Virus of Time." By firing Prior up with prophetic zeal, restoring his defunct libido, and liberating him from the mundane prison of the status quo, the angel reveals herself as the driving force behind the sexual revolution in America. Far from floating above the action as a decorative image in a traditional elegiac allegory, she plunges into it with ferocious energy as if she were an ACT UP zapper with wings. She knows how to fan the flames of rage. Prior must wrestle with her (literally) as a flying contradiction *in actu* as well as *in verbo*—a beautiful yet terrible synthesis of activist spunk and aesthetic spirituality—as we must too, it seems, unflinchingly, as long as the old debate over form and context renews itself in our prayers and protests.

[*See also* Gay Aesthetics.]

BIBLIOGRAPHY

Crimp, Douglas. "AIDS: Cultural Analysis/Cultural Activism." In *AIDS: Cultural Analysis/Cultural Activism,* edited by Douglas Crimp, pp. 3–16. Cambridge, Mass., 1988.
Crimp, Douglas. "Mourning and Militancy." *October* 51 (Winter 1989): 3–18.
Crimp, Douglas, and Adam Rolston. *AIDS demo graphics.* Seattle, 1990.
Holleran, Andrew. *Ground Zero.* New York, 1988.
Kramer, Larry. *The Normal Heart.* New York, 1985.
Kramer, Larry. *Reports from the Holocaust.* New York, 1989.
Kushner, Tony. *Angels in America,* part 1, *Millennium Approaches.* London, 1992.
Miller, James, ed. *Fluid Exchanges: Artists and Critics in the AIDS Crisis.* Toronto, 1992.
Miller, James. "Raising Spirits: The Arts Transfigure the AIDS Crisis." In *1995 Medical and Health Annual: Encyclopaedia Britiannica,* pp. 124–149. Chicago, 1995.
Murphy, Timothy, and Suzanne Poirier, eds. *Writing AIDS: Gay Literature, Language, and Analysis.* New York, 1993.
Rich, Adrienne. "In Memoriam." In *Poets for Life: Seventy-Six Poets Respond to AIDS,* edited by Michael Klein, p. 202. New York, 1989.
Watney, Simon. *Policing Desire: Pornography, AIDS, and the Media.* Minneapolis, 1987.
White, Edmund. "Esthetics and Loss." *Artforum* 25.5 (January 1987): 68–71.

JAMES MILLER

POP ART. [*To explore the twentieth-century art movement known as Pop art, this entry comprises two essays:*
An Overview
Aesthetics of Andy Warhol
The first essay explains the general history and legacy of Pop art. The second essay, although focused exclusively on Warhol, examines the philosophical and aesthetic significance of Pop art. For related discussion, see Comics; *and* Popular Culture.]

An Overview

For thirty years scholars have asked, "What is Pop art?" Art historians and theorists pose the question in different voices while addressing many of the same issues. The historian wants to know how the art world initially received Pop art, how Pop artists responded to or rejected the artists who preceded them, what historiographic shape emerged in subsequent years. The theorist conceptualizes Pop as implicated in a larger cultural condition—for many theorists, that of late capitalism. While these two strategies are not mutually exclusive, they are distinct: historians emphasize details of artistic careers and critical responses, whereas theoretical practitioners draw out broad synthetic structures.

One of the shared beliefs of those who identify with modernism is that the public fails to understand the avant-garde of its time; true to form, bewilderment was the primary reaction to Pop art. In 1962, Peter Selz hosted "A Symposium on Pop Art" at the Museum of Modern Art in New York. Selz did not ask his five invited critics "to come up with a definition of Pop art at this stage," but simply "to present prepared papers and engage in a lively discussion." Nonetheless, almost every one of the participants began with the question, "Is it art?," taking the rhetorical opportunity to define art themselves. Curator Henry Geldzahler found the question ridiculous, asserting that Marcel Duchamp had demonstrated that artists define what art is by their actions. Hilton Kramer answered that Pop is art, but only by default, by virtue of not being anything else. Leo Steinberg too answered in the affirmative, reserving the right to adjust his assessment of Pop art in time, but provisionally defining art as whatever produces "a new shudder" in the audience; he determined that Pop art met this requirement.

If Pop art followed certain patterns of Modernist art's introduction to the art world and, eventually, the art-historical canon, it also notably disappointed these expectations, breaking from Modernist art history. In a new twist on the avant-garde posture of the traditional rejection of new objects and forms of expression, the question for these critics was not quite "Is it *good* art?" but "Is it art at all?" This new question centered on Pop's "realism"—not whether artists had ineffectually or insufficiently aestheticized the real object, but whether they had aestheticized it at all. An earlier avant-garde realist painter, such as Gustave Courbet, might be accused of making ugly paintings, but because he took his subjects from live models and natural scenes, there was no possibility of avoiding some kind of translation from three dimensions into two. Pop artists such as Roy Lichtenstein, however, chose two-dimensional subjects from the mass media and depicted them two-dimensionally, often using a technique seemingly borrowed from those same media and from commercial art. The question becomes not good or bad, or beautiful or ugly, but art object or mass-culture object. That is, had the Pop artist failed to adequately "transform" the model? Once the viewers of Pop art decide that even Lichtenstein's paintings of comic book subjects are high art, and not the low culture they superfi-

POP ART: Overview. Jasper Johns, *Painting with Two Balls* (1960), encaustic and collage on canvas with objects (three panels), 65 × 54 in. (165.1 × 137.2 cm); collection of the artist. (Copyright by Jasper Johns/Licensed by VAGA, New York; photograph courtesy of Leo Castelli Gallery, New York; used by permission.)

cially resemble, the question "Is it art?" seemed to be (at least provisionally) answered.

Despite the fact that Pop art holds its own relationship with high and low as constantly shifting, critics and public agreed they could, indeed, exchange the one question for another: "What is Pop art?" The inquiry seemed so pressing in the 1960s that G. H. Swenson used it as the title of the two important interviews he conducted with the leading Pop artists. Seen against contemporary art history, this posing of the question appears ironic. When, in the 1940s, artists such as Willem de Kooning, Jackson Pollock, and Mark Rothko began to work in their well-known styles, art critics immediately recognized that they were making a new kind of art, one that furthered rather than imitated the achievements of European abstraction. Critics basically agreed which artists belonged to this group (although not necessarily who was major or minor) and what they were doing, but not what to call them. In response to a 1945 exhibit, *A Problem for Critics,* prominent art critics were invited to suggest a variety of names for this new American art (one of them being "the New American Art"). But whereas Abstract Expressionism's problem was always to name properly a recognizable artistic phenomenon, the

problem with Pop art was to define the strange thing with a familiar name. It was immediately understood who was a Pop artist, which artworks were Pop; but today one can still look directly at this uncannily familiar art, and yet remain unsure of its meaning: "What is it?" Here, then, is a double irony. Abstract Expressionism, superficially so turgid and murky, so personal and idiosyncratic, has become clearly legible for us—in both form and content, and even in its sociopolitical "subtext." Pop art, almost always crisp and clean formally, apparently public or common in its meaning, so literally legible, is enduringly difficult to read.

The term *Pop art* was invented by an English critic in the late 1950s. Although we commonly think of this movement as emerging around 1962 under the supervision of American artists such as Andy Warhol, the term was first used by Lawrence Alloway in 1957. Alloway initially conceived of Pop art, not as the latest avant-garde art movement, but as a shorthand reference to increasingly dominant modes and monuments of popular culture—television, magazines, film, advertising. He characterized this early usage as Pop's "anthropological" phase. In the hands of British artists such as those in the Independent Group, which met at London's Institute for Contemporary Art in the mid-1950s, *Pop art* came to indicate their art practice as well as their source material. Most notably, the artist Richard Hamilton, who worked in collage and painting, created art with a startlingly banal content: British and American consumer life. His famous collage *What Is It That Makes Today's Homes So Different, So Appealing?* was shocking not only for the images it used—vacuum cleaners, swimsuits, bomb blasts—but also for its cut-and-paste aesthetic, which underlined the art's parodic, rather than sublime, aspirations.

Between 1960 and 1962, in New York City, several young artists seemed to find their signature styles within a few short months of each other, initially appearing in group exhibitions, then having their first solo exhibitions one after the other. The key word for these early group exhibitions of Pop art was *new,* in exhibitions such as *New Forms, New Media* of 1960, and *New Realists* of 1962. Critics were initially shocked by the subject matter of these paintings—in fact, by the fact that they *had* a subject matter. Appearing after approximately fifteen years during which all "serious" American painting was abstract, this new way of painting was defiantly referential, if not representational—hence, their tentative descriptions as the "New Realists." Looking more closely, the content of that newness made itself felt almost immediately: comic books, consumer products, canned soup, hamburgers. Finally, however, the style of the newness came into its own: Pop art took consumer, image-based culture not only as its subject but also as its style. Benday dots, billboard airbrushing, and multiple, collectively produced silkscreens constituted the form as well as the content of Pop art. According to Harold Rosenberg, the public debut of the Pop artists, creating a break in both content and form, hit New York and particularly the Abstract Expressionists "like an earthquake."

By the end of 1962, all of the major Pop figures had held solo exhibitions and begun to establish their positions publicly and in the art world. While it has been debated to what extent the artists were aware of each other's work, it seemed clear from the beginning that their art held something in common. Who were these artists? Retrospectively, the first histories of Pop art in the late 1960s and 1970s used differing criteria to determine membership. Lucy R. Lippard admits to only five truly "hard-core" Pop artists: Warhol, Lichtenstein, Claes Oldenburg, James Rosenquist, and Tom Wesselman. She identifies these artists as sharing a hard-edge, commercial style (with exceptions made for Oldenburg's sensual idiosyncrasies). But this kind of formal approach to Pop art (also taken by Robert Rosenblum) seems primarily designed to insert Pop smoothly into the historical chain of contemporary art, linking Pop art to hard-edge abstraction before and minimalism afterward. As with any approach that places the art-historical end before the individual art object, this feels forced. More commonly, the list of Pop artists included not only the most successful figures listed above, but lesser-known artists from both New York and California ("West Coast Pop") such as Jim Dine, Mel Ramos, George Segal, Robert Indiana, Billy Al Bengston, Ed Ruscha, Joe Goode, Wayne Thiebaud, and Marisol. The list could easily be longer still.

Pop art hit the ground running. During 1960–1962, not only did the major figures find their signature styles and appear in their first gallery shows, they were introduced to a broader public in magazines like *Time* and *Life*. From that point forward, critics and historians have debated endlessly the attitude of Pop art toward popular culture: does high art critique or celebrate mass culture? Regardless of the position one takes, it is clear that Pop art turned the attention of high art (and its audience) toward popular culture. The nature of that attention—aesthetic appreciation, semiotic game playing, or social investigation—often shifted. Conversely, Pop art turned the attention of the mass audience toward high art. That is, Pop art took popular culture as its subject matter, but also engaged the popular more directly in drawing attention from a mass audience, appearing to be predicated, in fact, on notions of career, commercialism, success, attention, fame, celebrity. Two new figures, each a topic of critical debate, were created in the 1960s: the mass audience as art audience and the artist as a combination of movie star and professional.

A 1963 article in *Time* magazine, "Pop Art: Cult of the Commonplace," designed to introduce its broad national readership to Pop art, described its viewers as "decorous teenage girls" from prestigious private schools giggling at the Guggenheim Museum. Similarly, the art critic Max Kozloff, in an early review of Pop art, referred to its supporters as "vulgarians" and "bobby soxers." Obviously, there was

something new about this audience, something at least as seemingly popular as the art. This new audience of high schoolers and bobby soxers was young, much like the audience for movies, Top 40 music, and comic books—the products of popular culture. It was also an audience that cut across class boundaries, including traditional art audiences, the nouveaux riches, and average American consumers. Lichtenstein, Oldenburg, and Warhol discussed this issue in a 1964 interview with Bruce Glaser. The artists disagreed whether Pop appeals to a larger audience—it comes as no surprise that Warhol insisted that it does. Oldenburg argued that the audience, having heard that the art was about Coca-Cola, was often disappointed to find it so much like traditional art. Warhol, in a rare assertive moment, stated that people loved it because the subject matter was familiar: "it looks like something they know and see every day." This contrast reflects a difference in the two artists' work. Although Oldenburg's art is often humorous, his artistic engagement with paint and issues of material sensuality is much less ironic than Warhol's seemingly affectless recreation of flat, commercial art appearances.

In 1965 the critic Sidney Tillim went so far as to characterize the whole of Pop art by its relationship with its audience. Rather than falsely credit the artists with a ponderous social critique, Tillim located the importance of Pop art in its reception. The entire American culture here adheres to the model of the rebellious and perhaps fun-loving adolescent, rather than the more sophisticated adult or the more innocent child: "We are witnessing . . . a release from the conventions, values and consciousness of a culture. . . . grown men and women have thrown off the trappings of 'respectability,' i.e., the serious side of culture, auctioned off their collections of Abstract Expressionism and rolled out the American flag" (Tillim, 1965). Tillim describes a change in a certain group of established art collectors who, together with the "bobby soxers," formed "the new audience."

As Pop art has become the object of art history, by simple virtue of historical distance, a line of inquiry related to the sociologically based criticism of Kozloff, William Seitz, and Tillim has appeared. Economic and social histories by scholars such as Christin J. Mamiya detail not only the reception of Pop art but its context of American consumer society. Mamiya in particular finds that changes in the way the United States did business between 1959 and 1964— the new pervasiveness of mass marketing and a corporate mentality—established a "climate" conducive to the inventions and interests of Pop art. Subsequent art-historical accounts have developed more specific topics, such as the gendered role of the consumer as woman in the 1950s.

The historian William Seitz had made a similar point in 1963, saying of Pop art, "New manifestations now appear with such regularity and rapidity that the professional or collector who wants to remain in style must switch quickly"

(Seitz, 1963). Seitz concentrated on the effects on the rhythm of artistic creation itself rather than on its audience. Even in comparing the relatively recent career development of artist Jasper Johns during the mid-1950s to that of the Pop artists during the early 1960s, Seitz found a tremendous acceleration in both the success and the obsolescence of artists. He was concerned that the notion of the avant-garde or newness itself had been co-opted by advertising and thus rendered invalid for the art world (to which it is nevertheless returned, tainted with the language and expectations of the commercial world). The artist becomes a celebrity marketing a commodity. As Robert Indiana said in 1964, "It isn't the Popster's fault that the A-Ers [Abstract Expressionists] fought and won the bloody Battle of the Public-Press-Pantheon."

Indiana's seemingly flippant statement reveals an important change in American art that began with Abstract Expressionism and was completely realized by Pop art. Many critics noted at the end of the 1950s that the recent market success and public acceptance of Abstract Expressionism invalidated its avant-garde status. As "advanced" art gained critical and public acceptance more and more quickly (almost immediately in the case of Pop art), the time during which it was possible to consider an art movement avant-garde grew shorter and shorter, placing the future viability of any avant-garde in doubt. This concept of the "death of the avant-garde" responds to a change in art's social position. By altering the artist's traditional relationship to society, this "death" creates uncertainty as to the very nature of artists: if they are no longer to act as figures of passionate alienation, what is their new role?

For some, the answer was for the artist to act as a professional. Warhol, Rosenquist, and others were successful commercial artists before becoming fine artists. Warhol claimed he made the switch in part because he realized he could make more money in the latter role; he thus brought his commercial motivation to an area where it had previously been taboo. Although fine artists had often worked in illustration and other fields, for the first time these "day jobs" were not merely despised necessities for artists, but in fact clearly influenced their artistic practices. In a subtle way, Warhol serves as a model for the contemporary artist Barbara Kruger, who proudly displays rather than hides her credential of years spent working at *Mademoiselle* magazine.

If popular culture fascinated the Pop artists, they were equally absorbed by and equally ambivalent toward high art and its history. Most of the Pop artists struggled with and often rejected the very concept of artistic expression, as embodied primarily in Abstract Expressionism, the dominant mode of American painting during the 1940s and 1950s. In large part they addressed the exhausted, even debased, version on public offer toward the end of the 1950s—thousands of second-rate, second-generation Abstract Expressionist "expressive" but unoriginal paintings. Allan Kaprow, who taught with Lichtenstein and was much admired by him, said of these painters that they all threw their inner beings onto the white canvas, but unfortunately the canvases (and by extension their inner beings) appeared to be almost identical. As Warhol facetiously asked Swenson, "How many painters are there? Millions of painters and all pretty good." Warhol may have been alluding to a Stanford Research Institute study (cited by Stanley Kunitz in the 1962 Pop symposium) that found that there were "as many painters in this country as hunters," 50 million altogether (counting the "do it yourself practitioners," as Kunitz calls them). These comments reflect a certain careerist bent, the concept of newly professional artists pressured by a flooding of the market. But they also bespeak another function for art in contemporary America: that of avocation, or even hobby, and a concomitant disgust with the reality of the ideal of individual expression for all, including the most unimaginative.

The Pop artists also critique the possibility of a sustained use of any kind of Expressionist mark, in the sense that it cannot be performed both consistently *and* authentically. Lichtenstein's representations of heroically scaled abstract brushstrokes, carefully crafted from benday dots, make this point. Warhol also developed a critique of the authenticity of expression in his work, as well as in these often-cited remarks: "I think everybody should be a machine . . . you do the same thing every time. You do it over and over again. . . . You should be able to be an Abstract-Expressionist next week, or a Pop artist, or a realist, without feeling that you've given up something." Given a painter's ability to switch from style to style, Warhol questions the need to "mean" even a style of painting that appears to be extremely expressive. Existential anguish becomes simply another pose to adopt and discard. Warhol most famously, but the other Pop artists as well, has the ironic sense that the artist is motivated by self-interest and exterior concerns, rather than helplessly impelled by the need to reveal a coherent, interior identity.

Pop art was heralded as the quintessentially American art, as was Abstract Expressionism only years before: how to reconcile these two positions? A social historian would assert that the difference between the two practices is only the facet of American life that they choose to represent or express. The point can be made that to communicate the idea of impersonality or uniformity, so prevalent in the United States of the 1960s, one must paint in that way, just as to convey the idea of expressive individuality, the hallmark of the 1950s, one must paint in a different way. The counterintuitive swerves into the ridiculous only when we insist that Abstract Expressionism and Pop art are equally expressive. Yet, we would do well to remember that both Lichtenstein and Oldenburg state that their styles merely *seem* impersonal, that what they are painting in fact, is their own "fantasies"—a word that indicates that they work from their private imaginations as much as from parodied stereotypes.

Both of these facets of Pop art—its involvement in popular culture and with the traditional aspirations of high art—share a common ground in the manipulation of a preexisting discourse. We have seen that Pop art plays with the difference between popular culture and fine art, as well as the difference between the sincere, original, or expressive mark, and that which is calculated, imitative, or constructed. Beginning in the early 1970s, a new approach to art history, semiotics, addressed both of these concerns. Semiotics, initially theorized by Charles Sanders Peirce and Ferdinand de Saussure, is a method of understanding the process of representation through linguistic terms such as *signifier* (the representational symbol), *referent* (the thing represented), and *signified* (the meaning, or contextual interpretation).

In the book accompanying his 1974 retrospective of Pop art at the Whitney Museum, Alloway defined the concerns and message of Pop art as lying in four directions. Primary among these concerns is Pop art's function as a sign. This point had first appeared in Swenson's "The New American 'Sign Painters'" (1962). At that time, semiotics was not prevalent as an art-historical method of interpretation; and Swenson, for the most part, speaks of signs in the literal, material sense, largely in reference to Indiana, who painted words and numbers within bold, geometric designs. Nevertheless, Swenson does argue that many Pop art paintings recreate the tension between handmade and mass-produced signs and symbols, an issue previously recognized by earlier twentieth-century artists. Selz also made reference to this tradition by including photographs of gas stations and roadside stores by Walker Evans in the slides shown at the Pop art symposium.

The Culture of Consumption (1970) stands as one of the first works to use semiotic theory deliberately in order to understand Pop art. Jean Baudrillard asserts that by painting numbers, symbols, and labels the Pop artists realize what is important about consumer culture: not the objects, but their trademarks or signs. We are not interested in the Brillo pad inside the Brillo box any more than we are interested in what is "inside" Marilyn Monroe. The traditional hierarchy of signifier and signified is leveled into a play of simulation. Baudrillard takes the familiar idea of resemblance (present in early commentary on Pop art) to an extreme, depicting a complex (yet shallow) culture composed solely of images, or "simulacra"—Guy Debord's famous "society of the spectacle."

Baudrillard's Pop artist (who most resembles Warhol) performs a Duchampian trick: he acts like an artist and therefore he is an artist. He copies or simulates a cultural type—the artist (or, as suggested earlier, the movie star or professional)—rather than occupying the role naturally and without any attendant irony, "feeling" it like earlier avant-garde artists. The artist of late capitalism, like the manufacturer of late capitalism, is not satisfying needs but creating them, producing objects that seemingly answer a new demand, the demand created by the object itself. In a parody of early capitalism and early modernism, these new objects appear to improve an older, obsolescent objects. But for most theorists, the notion of modernist progress lies moribund at this point in history, and Pop art is no more a genuine improvement on Abstract Expressionism than a white telephone is on a black one, or an old detergent (or scouring pad) packaged in a new box. Clement Greenberg, champion of Modernist painting, suggested that despite its rapid canonization, Pop art was at best frivolous, at worst simply bad art; the Pop artists themselves leave us room to wonder, not only about their own status, but about the very logic of modernism itself.

The semiotician and cultural critic Umberto Eco began his 1971 commentary on Pop art with the standard question: "What is pop art?" Eco's argument focuses on the shifting nature of the messages and references running between high and low culture. He asserts that Pop artists borrow from mass-media sources, while the mass media in turn borrow back, and are inflected by both the formal conventions and the knowing tenor of Pop art itself. Eco also touches on an anxiety present in the very earliest commentary on Pop art: the reverse of the implication that Pop art may not be art is that things we do not consider to be art may indeed be Pop art (such as a can of soup). Once Pop imagery begins to circulate between realms of high and low culture, the divisions seem to disappear. In fact, in Alloway's chronology of Pop art, the third and final phase is the co-optation of "Pop art" by common language, and our commensurate ability to see horror movies and romance comics as already being Pop art, or kitsch. Eco ends his essay not by answering his original question but by obviating it, in a sense. He concludes that there is no such thing as purely highbrow or lowbrow culture: all are equally part of the metadiscourse of bourgeois society.

In a 1980 essay, the critic Roland Barthes ends by asking his own particular question: "What do you mean?" Much like Eco, Barthes emphasizes that Pop art upsets the relationship between the signifier (in this case, the art object), the referent (the mass-culture source object), and the signified (the meaning, what is inside or behind). It is the last, he maintains, that Pop art at least pretends to destroy. According to Barthes, Pop art critiques the social and cultural world through the simultaneous "banal conformity" of the image to the thing represented, and a cold distance lying between them. By flatly posing the object to the viewer, Pop art returns the spectator—clueless—to the perennial question of meaning in art.

The closeness between the interpretations of Baudrillard, a sociologist, and Eco and Barthes, language theorists, shows that Pop, more than any other kind of art, has the ca-

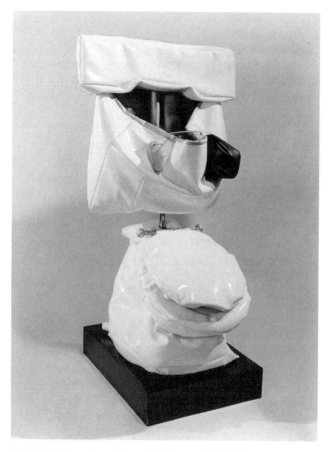

POP ART: Overview. Claes Oldenburg, *Soft Toilet* (1966), vinyl, plexiglass, and kapok on painted wood, overall: 57 1/16 × 27 5/8 × 28 1/16 in. (144.9 × 70.2 × 56.7 cm.); Whitney Museum of American Art, New York (Purchase, with funds from the Howard and Jean Lipman Foundation, Inc. [69.6a-b]). (Copyright 1997 by the Whitney Museum of American Art; used by permission.)

pacity to mediate semiotics and social history, two methodologies usually seen as distant, if not oppositional. Baudrillard is explicit: the logic of consumption can be defined as the manipulation of signs. Looking back from the 1990s, it appears that both semiotics and cultural and social history have defined our approach to Pop more definitively than have other methods.

At the same time artists were inventing Pop art, philosophically inclined academics were moving away from aesthetics and toward ideas about art based on semiotics, general theories of representation, and the study of cultural context. These concerns, as much as the advent of Pop art, gave rise to conclusions about changes in art that went beyond the moment of Pop art itself. In the 1980s a general consensus developed among historians and critics that Pop art marked the beginning of a new kind of art, perhaps even a new period in art history, in which image and idea superseded formal values and authorial presence. Hal Foster in *The Anti-Aesthetic* (Port Townsend, Wash., 1983), and Paul Taylor in

his *Post-Pop Art* (Cambridge, Mass., 1989), premised their anthologies on the given that, beginning with Pop, we have moved toward an art form that cannot be explained by considerations of beauty or even artistic expression; instead, this art develops interpretive strategies, cultural critiques, and finely drawn theoretical points. This shift has often been characterized as the advent of postmodernism.

The philosopher Arthur C. Danto's interest in Pop art intersects at certain points with those of the theorists discussed above. Like Foster, Danto reaches the conclusion that works such as Warhol's *Brillo Boxes* changed the very way we see art, perhaps effecting a break in art history. But unlike proponents of the postmodern, Danto believes that Pop art has revealed the fullest nature of art itself, rather than merely reflecting a historical shift in its social production. Like Baudrillard, Eco, and Barthes, he is concerned with the close relationship between the products of Pop art and the common objects that serve as its models. But Danto eschews specialized, theoretical language, citing John L. Austin's ideas on ordinary language usage rather than semiotic theory. He has long maintained a simple, literal lack of a perceptible difference between art and the commonplace as the center of his argument. Danto's inference is that the status of artworks does not depend on beauty, or appeal to the senses, or visual information of any dimension.

Nevertheless, the Pop artists themselves have often insisted on the unique physical presence of their artwork, its final difference from other objects. Even if one finds that Danto has elided the material and visual differences between a Brillo box and a *Brillo Box* (between the mass-produced household product and the mass-produced art product), it is possible to see that this is beside the point. The 1964 exhibition of Warhol's *Brillo Boxes*, a revelatory experience for Danto, marks an event in his own thinking that ends his career as an aesthetician and begins his career as an art critic. Concomitantly, although Danto believes that Pop represents the end of art (as a visual form of high culture), he also believes that it functions as a new beginning. Rather than closing down the debate on Pop art, or assigning a particular methodological lesson to Pop, he opens up its possible meanings, and the larger possibilities for the nature of art. For Danto, Pop art is fundamentally philosophical in that it not only asks "Is it art?," "What does it mean?," and "What is Pop art?," but returns the viewer to the initial and ultimate question, "What is art?"

Curiously, despite at least twenty years of committed theoretical work on Pop art, the sophistication of the statements by the artists themselves has not been surpassed. (Does Pop level the playing field of intellectuals as well as objects?) The early interviews conducted by Swenson and Glaser with Warhol, Lichtenstein, Oldenburg, and others provide humorous, but also profound, insights into the individual characters of the artists. Additionally, they provide unusually clear but also complex discussions of the relations between individual style, mass culture, personal expression, and artistic technique. If these artists are equal to their critics, they are no less but also no more illuminating on the question of Pop art:

> OLDENBURG: I think we have made a deliberate attempt to explore this area [the line between fine art and popular culture]. . . . But still the motives are not too clear to me as to why I do this.

> LICHTENSTEIN: Nor with me either, nor even why I say I do it.

For the Pop artists, to do and to "say," or to represent that doing, are equal, and equally opaque.

[*See also* Baudrillard; Danto; *and* Eco.]

BIBLIOGRAPHY

Alloway, Lawrence. *American Pop Art.* New York, 1974. Exhibition catalog, Whitney Museum of Art, New York.

Battcock, Gregory, ed. *The New Art: A Critical Anthology.* New rev. ed. New York, 1973.

Baudrillard, Jean. *La societé de consommation.* Paris, 1970.

Coplans, John. "The New Painting of Common Objects." *Artforum* 1.6 (December 1962): 26–29.

Danto, Arthur C. *The Transfiguration of the Commonplace.* Cambridge, Mass., 1981.

Glaser, Bruce. "Oldenburg, Lichtenstein, Warhol: A Discussion." *Artforum* 4.6 (February 1966): 20–24.

Kozloff, Max. "Pop Art, Metaphysical Disgust, and the New Vulgarians." *Art International* 6.2 (1962): 34–36.

Lippard, Lucy R. *Pop Art.* New York, 1966.

Mahsun, Carol Ann. *Pop Art and the Critics.* Ann Arbor, 1987.

Mamiya, Christin J. *Pop Art and Consumer Culture: American Super Market.* Austin, Tex., 1992.

McShine, Kynaston, ed. *Andy Warhol: A Retrospective.* New York, 1989. Exhibition catalog, Museum of Modern Art, New York.

The New Realists. New York, 1962. Exhibition Catalog, Sidney Janis Gallery.

Rose, Barbara. *Claes Oldenburg.* New York, 1970. Exhibition catalog, Museum of Modern Art, New York.

Seitz, William. *What's Happened to Art? An Interview with Marcel Duchamp on Present Consequences of New York's Armory Show.* New York, 1963.

Selz, Peter, et al. "A Symposium on Pop Art." *Arts* 37.7 (April 1963): 36–45.

Swenson, G. H. "The New American 'Sign Painters'." *ArtNews* 61.5 (September 1962): 44–47, 60–62.

Swenson, G. H. "What Is Pop Art? Part I." *ArtNews* 62.7 (November 1963): 24–27, 60–65.

Swenson, G. H. "What Is Pop Art? Part II." *ArtNews* 62.10 (February 1964): 40–43, 62–67.

Taylor, Paul. *Post-Pop Art.* Cambridge, Mass., 1989.

Tillim, Sidney. "Further Observations on the Pop Phenomenon." *Artforum* 4.3 (December 1965): 7.

KATY SIEGEL

Aesthetics of Andy Warhol

Since at least Andy Warhol's exhibition in the spring of 1964 of Brillo (and other) cartons at the Stable Gallery on East Seventy-fourth Street in Manhattan, it is arguable that he possessed a philosophical intelligence of an intoxicatingly high order. He could not touch anything without at the same time touching the very boundaries of thought, at the very least thought about art. The 1975 text *The Philosophy of Andy Warhol: From A to B and Back Again,* and its pendant volume, *POPism: The Warhol 1960s,* sparkle with conceptual observations and wit, put forth in the most piquant aphoristic language ("So full of thorns and secret spices, that you made me sneeze and laugh," Friedrich Nietzsche says of his own "written and painted thoughts" in *Beyond Good and Evil*). But one could refer to the very art that Warhol's critics saw as mindless and meretricious. Indeed, it was among Warhol's chief contributions to the history of art that he brought artistic practice to a level of philosophical self-consciousness never before attained. G. W. F. Hegel had proposed that art and philosophy are two "moments," as he put it, of Absolute Spirit (religion was the third). In a certain sense, if he is right, there must be a basic identity between the two, and Hegel believed that art fulfills its historical and spiritual destiny when its practice is disclosed as a kind of philosophy in action.

That someone as astute as Warhol should have chosen to disguise his depth by what passed as motley in the 1960s has, in its own right, a certain allegorical appropriateness. In any case, we can identify some fragments of the philosophical structure of Warhol's art, while also relating it to certain of its art-historical as well as cultural circumstances. But this interpretation differs from the standard art-historical exercise in that it seeks to identify the importance of Warhol not in terms of the art he influenced (or by which he was influenced) but in terms of the thought he brought to our awareness. Whatever he did, "he did it as a philosopher might," wrote Edmund White in a memorial tribute. Warhol violated every condition thought necessary to something being an artwork, but in so doing he disclosed the essence of art. As White goes on to say, all this was "performed under the guise of humor and self-advancing cynicism, as though a chemist were conducting the most delicate experiments at the target end of a shooting gallery" (see McShine, 1989, p. 441).

These claims about Warhol can be illustrated with an initial example drawn from Warhol's films, which, whatever their standing in the history of cinema may prove to be, have an unparalleled contribution to make in our philosophical understanding of the concept of film. The example is his *Empire* of 1964, which someone might just wander into under the misapprehension that its title promises one of those sagas of colonization or business in which a nation, or a mogul, builds up an empire. It is indeed of epic length, but it is marked by a total absence of incident, and its title is a pun on the Empire State Building, which is its only actor, doing what it always does, namely, nothing.

Imagine that someone, inspired by Warhol, were to make a film titled *Either/Or* "based," as the title promises, on the masterpiece of the celebrated Danish philosopher Søren Kierkegaard. Let the film be just as long as *Empire* (or longer, if you wish), and let it consist of nothing but the title page of the book, because the producer thinks that there might be an internal joke here for someone who is familiar with Kierkegaard's sly aphorisms. These aphorisms allow us to ponder the ambiguity in the concept of books, which exist as physical objects, of a certain color and size and weight, and as objects of meaning, which have a certain content and are in a certain language, and capable, as makes no sense with physical objects, of translation. That ambiguity immediately is transferred to the concept of being based on. Here is one of the aphorisms: "What the philosophers have to say about reality is often as disappointing as a sign you see in a shop window, which reads Pressing Done Here. If you brought your clothes in to be pressed, you would be fooled: for the sign is only for sale."

The two modes of being of a sign, as one might portentously say, are as a rectangle of plywood with paint and ink on its surface, which costs so many kroner at the store where signs are made and sold; and also as an emblem that gives information to potential customers—information, for example, that they can have their clothes pressed in the place where the sign, by convention, means that that is the business of the place where the sign is.

These are also the two modes of being of a book—as something that takes up space and as something dense with wisdom. It is this that makes the film *Either/Or* a kind of joke, or for that matter, makes *Empire* a kind of joke. The ambiguity that generates them, in fact, generates certain of Warhol's paradigmatic works of art such as, for signal example, the *Brillo Box* sculptures, which as works of art have all sorts of rights and privileges mere cartons of Brillo systematically lack, not being art. Here might be two Kierkegaardian-Warholian jokes:

> A man sees what looks like an ordinary soap-pad carton in a shop window and, needing to ship some books, asks the shopkeeper whether he can have it. The shop turns out to be an art gallery and the shopkeeper a dealer who says: "That is a work of art, just now worth thirty thousand dollars."

> A man sees what looks like Warhol's *Brillo Box* in what looks like an art gallery, and asks the dealer, who turns out to be a shopkeeper, how much it is. The latter says the man can have it, he was going to throw it away anyway, it was placed in the window temporarily after it was unpacked.

Perhaps half the visitors to the Stable Gallery were angry that something could be put forward as art that so verged on reality that no interesting perceptual difference distinguished them. Perhaps the other half were exultant that something could be put forward as art that so verged on reality that it was distinguished by no interesting perceptual difference. In the early 1960s it was universally assumed that art must be something exalted and arcane, which put

one in touch with a reality no less arcane and exalted. The reality on which Warhol's art verged was neither arcane nor exalted: it was banal. This was perceived as intoxicating or degrading, depending on where one stood on a number of issues having to do with American commercial reality, the values and virtues of the commonplace, the role and calling of the artist, the point and purpose of art. For me, the interesting feature of the *Brillo Box* was that it appropriated the philosophical question of the relationship between art and reality and incorporated it into the *Brillo Box* and in effect asks why, if it is art, the boxes of Brillo in the supermarket, which differ from it in no interesting perceptual way, are not. At the very least the *Brillo Box* made plain that one cannot any longer think of distinguishing art from reality on perceptual grounds, for those grounds have been cut away.

The *Brillo Box* example helps to explain what makes *Empire* finally so philosophical a film. Philosophers from ancient times down have been concerned with framing definitions—definitions of justice, of truth, of knowledge, of art. This means in effect identifying the essential conditions for something to be an instance of art, of knowledge, of truth, of justice. The first thing that might occur to anyone as obvious in framing a distinction between moving and still pictures is that the former do and the latter do not show things in motion. A still picture (let us restrict ourselves to photography) can show us things we know must be moving, as in a famous image by Henri Cartier-Bresson of a man leaping over a puddle. But it cannot show them in motion. A motion picture of the same scene would show the trajectory the leaping man describes, and with this the hopeful philosopher of film might suppose something had been nailed down. What *Empire* demonstrates is that something can be a moving picture and not show movement. Nothing much in the film changes at all, in fact, even though, since the film was taken over an eight-hour stretch, something did change: a light in a window went on or off, a plane could have passed, the dusk in fact fell. But none of this is essential to the thought that the entire film could have been made in which nothing whatever changed or moved. At once it must become clear that only moving pictures can show stillness, as well as motion.

A photograph by Ansel Adams of the Rockies, paradigmatically immobile to the point of being natural symbols for eternity, is a still picture of a still object. But even so, the photograph, we now realize, no more shows the stillness than Cartier-Bresson's shows the motion. Still pictures show neither stillness nor motion. Think, for comparison, of the difference between black-and-white photography and color photography. A black-and-white photograph may be taken of a black-and-white object—a zebra, say. But it does not show the blackness and the whiteness of that object, it merely shows the difference. For all we can tell from the photograph, what registers as black could be red and what registers as white could be pink. A color photograph of a black-and-white object actually shows the black and the white of the object. Black-and-white photography, like still photography, is essentially more abstract than its counterpart.

Warhol subtracted everything from the moving picture that might be mistaken for an essential property of film. What was left was pure film. What we learn is that in a moving picture it is the film itself that moves and not necessarily its object, which may remain still. Warhol's art, in film and elsewhere, goes immediately to the defining boundaries of the medium, and brings these boundaries to conceptual awareness. What makes him an artist, however, is that he actually makes the art and is not content with imagining it, after the manner of my *Either/Or*. To sit through an entire seance of *Empire*, all eight or so hours of it, in which nothing essentially happens but nothing, may have the collateral effect of making the experience of time palpable, almost as if in a sensory deprivation experiment. We do not become aware of time in ordinary cinema, because too much takes place in time for time itself to become the object of consciousness. Time ordinarily lies outside the experiences with which, as we say, we kill time, seeking distraction. Time is not killed but restored to awareness in *Empire*. Usually, in the ordinary moving picture, the time in the film is a kind of narrative time, so that a century may pass in the course of watching a two-hour film. In *Empire*, narrative time and real time are one. The time in and the time of the film are the same. There is, as with the *Brillo Box* and the cartons of Brillo, no interesting perceptual difference.

Finally, with *Empire*, we become aware of the material properties of film, of the scratches, the grain, the accidental luminosities, and above all the passing before our eyes of the monotonous band. Warhol had an almost mystical attitude toward the world: everything in it had equal weight, it was all equally interesting. Or perhaps it says something about the human mind that under conditions of sensory deprivation it will find interest in the most marginal and unpromising differences. The film is made with the barest equipment, the zero degree of intervention, the null degree of editing. It was concerned, rather, with meaning, material, and, finally, mystery. That the film, like the *Brillo Box* itself—like almost everything to which Warhol put his hand—should have the form of a philosophical joke bears out a conjecture of Ludwig Wittgenstein's that it is conceivable that a philosophical work could be composed consisting solely of jokes. They have to be the right kinds, of course. For one thing, Warhol's jokes are not funny. There was, in my recollection of the Stable Gallery nearly thirty years ago, a spirit of play. But the boxes on display were not made in the spirit of play, Nor was Warhol capable of play. His seriousness seems almost otherworldly.

The deep philosophical bearing of Warhol's central achievement is part of the classical phase of Pop art in the early 1960s. A great many questions must be answered be-

fore we have a full historical understanding of this extraordinary movement, and in particular of what it meant that imagery was appropriated from all across the face of commercial and mass culture. It was often suggested, even by some of the Pop artists themselves at the time, that their intentions were to blur, if not obliterate, the boundaries between high and low art, challenging, with commercial logos or panels from comic strips or advertisements from newspapers and magazines, distinctions assumed and reinforced by the institutions of the art world—the gallery, with especially its decor and the affected styles of its personnel; the collection; the carved and gilded frame; the romanticized myth of the artist.

Even then, differences among Pop artists must be made. In 1962, for example, Roy Lichtenstein painted a work that looked like a monumentalized composition book of the most familiar kind, with black-and-white mottling on the cover, and a label that says "Compositions." Iconographically, it looks as if it goes with the soup cans and the like that Warhol used, but in fact it has a really different meaning altogether. The word *compositions* is something of a pun, for it of course refers to the ways artists arrange forms in pictorial space. And the black-and-white mottling looks like the allover composition for which Jackson Pollock earned high critical praise. The whole work makes a number of sly art-world allusions, and is in every sense a piece of "art about art," as such work came to be known. It is like the painting of large brushstrokes Lichtenstein made, lampooning the veneration of the heavy, looped swirl of paint that emblemized Abstract Expressionism. Mockery is one of the armaments of civilized aggression, and Lichtenstein's work is filled with internal art-world barbs.

Warhol's jokes were of another order altogether and had little to do with insider attacks on the pretensions of the art world. Rather, he was asking where the distinction is to be sited between art high or low on the one side, and reality on the other. This in a way was a question that had driven philosophy from Plato onward, and while it would be preposterous to pretend that Warhol generated the kind of systematic metaphysics that seeks to define the place of art in the totality of things, he did, in a way that one could say had never before been achieved, demonstrate what the form of the philosophical question must be. In doing this he invalidated some two millennia of misdirected investigation. It is the imagery of Pop that enabled him to do this.

There is a famous section of the *Philosophical Investigations* in which Wittgenstein seeks to call into question the idea of philosophical definitions, asking whether they can be achieved and whether there is any point in achieving them. Wittgenstein uses the example of games and asks us to try to imagine what a definition of *game* would look like. He asks us to "look and see," and then, when we have complied, we will see that there are no overarching properties shared by all the games and only the games. Rather, games form a kind of "family," the members of which share some but by no means all properties. Yet, Wittgenstein says, we all know what a game is and have no difficulty in recognizing something as one without benefit of a definition. So what is the point of pursuing it? His followers not long afterward applied this strategy to art, where similar reasoning suggested that artworks form a family rather than a homogeneous class, that there are thus no properties common and peculiar to works of arts, and that anyway we all know which are the works of art without benefit of such a definition. The upshot, these philosophers argued, is that the long search for definitions was misguided.

It is against this background that Warhol's *Brillo Box* seems to have something significant to say. A photograph of Warhol among his boxes looks indiscernible from a photograph of a stockroom clerk among the boxes in the supermarket. With what license can we pretend to tell the work of art from the mere utilitarian object? One is made of plywood, the other of cardboard, but can the difference between art and reality rest on a difference that could have gone the other way? In the end, there seems to be a "family resemblance" far more marked between *Brillo Box* and a Brillo box than between the former and, say, any paradigm work of art you choose—the *Night Watch*, say—which in fact seems to have exactly as many resemblances to the Brillo carton as to *Brillo Box*. After all, experts in the art world at the time were quite ready to consign Warhol's Brillo boxes to some less exalted category than sculpture, making them subject to customs duties when a gallery sought to import them into Canada. The point is that the difference between art and reality is not like the difference between camels and dromedaries, where we can count humps. Something cannot be a camel that looks like a dromedary, but something can be an artwork that looks just like a real thing. What makes the one art may be something quite invisible, perhaps how it arrived in the world and what someone intended it to be.

Brillo Box does for art what *Empire* does for film. It forces reflection on what makes it art, when that is not something that is obvious, just as the film demonstrates how little is required for something to be a film. To see *Empire* as film is to shelve as inessential a lot of what theorists have supposed central to film, all of which Warhol unerringly subtracted.

To be sure, Warhol made his point in a clearly negative way. He did not tell us what art was. But by his framing the question, those whose business it is to provide positive philosophical theories could at last address the subject. It is difficult to pretend that Warhol's intention was to clear the underbrush and make room for a finally adequate theory of art. In some ways it is perhaps inscrutable what his intentions ever were. Warhol's name is associated with frivolity, glamour, publicity, and making it big. The awesomeness of his achievement is that under the guise of the simple son of the fairy tale, seemingly no match for his daunting siblings,

Warhol made the most profound conceptual discoveries, and produced examples of pure art that appear uncannily to look like examples of pure reality.

BIBLIOGRAPHY

Works by Warhol

The Philosophy of Andy Warhol: From A to B and Back Again. New York, 1975.
POPism: The Warhol '60s. In collaboration with Pat Hackett. New York, 1980.

Other Sources

Angell, Callie, et al. *The Andy Warhol Museum.* Pittsburgh, 1994.
Bourdon, David. *Warhol.* New York, 1989.
Colacello, Bob. *Holy Terror: Andy Warhol Close Up.* New York, 1990.
Crow, Thomas. "Saturday Disasters: Trace and Reference in Early Warhol." In *Modern Art in the Common Culture*, pp. 49–65. New Haven, 1996.
Danto, Arthur C. "The Abstract-Expressionist Coca-Cola Bottle." In *Beyond the Brillo Box: The Visual Arts in Post-Historical Perspective,* pp. 131–145. New York, 1992.
Foucault, Michel. *This Is Not a Pipe.* Translated by James Harkness. Berkeley, 1983.
Herwitz, Daniel. "Andy Warhol without Theory." In *Making Theory/Constructing Art: On the Authority of the Avant-Garde,* pp. 232–268. Chicago, 1993.
Krauss, Rosalind. *The Optical Unconscious.* Cambridge, Mass., 1993. See chap. 6.
McShine, Kynaston, ed. *Andy Warhol: A Retrospective.* New York, 1989. Contains a tribute by Edmund White in "A Collective Portrait of Andy Warhol," pp. 423–455, on p. 441.
Swenson, G. R. "What Is Pop Art? Answers from 8 Painters." *ArtNews* 62 (November 1963): 24–27, 60–65; 62 (February 1964): 40–43, 62–67.
Yau, John. *In the Realm of Appearances: The Art of Andy Warhol.* Hopewell, N.J., 1993.

ARTHUR C. DANTO

POPULAR CULTURE. The term *popular culture* can refer broadly to common aesthetic or life practices, in both the statistical and qualitative senses. But theorists have used the term more precisely to designate a particular form of common culture that arises only in the modern period. Popular culture in this account is distinct from both folk culture and high culture: unlike the former, it is mass-produced; unlike the latter, it is mass-consumed.

Throughout the eighteenth and nineteenth centuries, western European societies experienced a particularly intense social reorganization. Vast numbers of the former peasantry now concentrated in dense cities to work in newly developing mass-production industries. Industrialization and the rise of organized capitalism restructured virtually every sphere of life: new concepts of uniform time, the mixing of previously dispersed local cultures, and the dehumanizing life of factory work all contributed to a homogenization of experience, producing a sense of shared fate across wide territories. At the same time, mounting social density and the vastly higher division of labor in capitalism increased social differentiation, giving rise particularly to vibrant middle classes. The demands of complex administration in capitalist industry and in the state contributed to widespread literacy in these new groups. These changes had profound implications for political as well as cultural life.

A decisive shift in the sources of power occurred with the simultaneous concentration and differentiation of society. The notion of the popular as distinct from the folk and elite implies not just large numbers of ordinary people, but large numbers organized as the people. The French Revolution marks the people's emergence as a political and cultural force. Earlier, power flowed down from the heavens through the monarch and its agent, the feudal aristocracy. The French Revolution challenged this ancient order, relocating power in the Third Estate, that protoparliamentary body representing and, for the first time, conceptualizing the people as possessing "interests" that differed from those of the old regime. Where Louis XIV had declared he was the state, the Third Estate declared they were the nation. Modern politics was thus born, in which legitimacy flows from the people, and "citizens" demanded the right to participate in their own governance.

Throughout this period, culture industries arose to meet the aesthetic desires of the newly emerged middle classes just as these groups developed new administrative and governmental forms to represent their political interests. As the ever-growing middle classes became more and more literate, as the efficiencies of mass industry produced often stupendous economies, and as social differentiation gave more people a sense of their own lives as projects filled with possibility, the western European bourgeoisie sought to "cultivate" themselves as more than mere interchangeable workers laboring for existence. The novel, for instance, rose as an expression of and reflection on modern life and its central figure, the subjective individual. The "news" was invented by as well as spread through new media, documenting the accelerated occurrence of history. Entertainment and leisure emerged as new categories of experience and possibility, at first restricted to the high middle classes, later accessible to virtually everyone.

These new cultural interests and practices contributed to, as well as grew from, changes in the social organization of aesthetic production. A court-based system of arts sponsorship in Europe before the nineteenth century had supported a "high" culture not available to ordinary people. Such a system provided necessary insulation for an artistic conception of aesthetic production, allowing producers to pursue aesthetic impulses in the abstract; while they depended on the understanding and support of an elite audience, that audience was cultivated and trained, with the time and energy to contemplate aesthetic products as a separate category of existence. Artists were thus free from the uncultivated judgments of the masses, while through their association with the centers of power they and their work enjoyed high status and official sanction.

With the rise of industrial society, however, these conditions of aesthetic production changed dramatically. The resources and prestige of court patrons declined precipitously at the same time that less insulated and exalted forms of culture began to occupy the public stage. Industry produced culture and leisure products on a mass scale just as it manufactured durable goods. Creators of high culture thus faced the choice of appealing to wider publics by subjecting their work to popular criteria, working in the culture industries as hired hands, or retreating to specialized—often countercultural—settings, contexts in which they produced only for themselves in ever more esoteric forms, creating as well the contemporary ideal of the devoted artist who renounces all worldly goods.

A clear-cut distinction between popular culture and high culture, however, depended not just on the middle classes generally or on the situation of aesthetic production from the point of view of the artist, but on the active work of the upper classes in response to these changed circumstances. Qualitative distinctions do not come only from the intrinsic qualities of works—that is, from their level of abstraction and degree of esotericism—but from the ways various social groups use culture to distinguish themselves socially. In his own time, for instance, William Shakespeare's plays were common entertainment, and the Globe theater included room for all sorts of people, though each group in its separate place. In the mid-nineteenth century, roving theater troupes performed Shakespeare all over the American countryside as popular distraction, and lines from the plays were at the hands not only of specially educated elites but of wide numbers of ordinary people as well, perhaps more so. Music performances included all varieties of composition in one long evening, ranging from what we now call the "classics" to dance and folk music.

In the realm of culture, threatened elites developed qualitative distinctions to dramatize and defend their exalted status. Although the newly emerging middle classes might achieve material equality, there was to be no doubt that they were not true equals of the older establishment, who distinguished themselves through their level of aesthetic and intellectual cultivation. Old elites engaged in processes of cultural entrepreneurship, founding art museums and symphony societies in which to entrench their cultural values and, thereby, defend their social position. In the process, they created conditions for the autonomy of high cultural values, even leading initiatives to educate and enrich the masses; but in practice these arrangements led to even further separation of high art from popular culture, and elites gained even more status from their association with the arts since the criteria of excellence were now objectified in purportedly impartial institutions.

Similar processes were at work in politics as well as culture, and arguments in the two fields are in fact intricately connected. Through the French Revolution, aristocratic elites articulated a political theory to shore up their declining fortunes: democracy—the rule of the people—was inherently debased, nothing more than submission to an undifferentiated and unknowing mob. Early on, this critique focused on the danger *from* the masses, who had no idea of what was good for themselves and whose unfettered passions threatened stability and the proper order of things; later, elite theorists highlighted the dangers *to* the masses, whose essential formlessness left them gullible and susceptible to demagogic manipulation, especially through new media.

As popular culture developed into a powerful category of aesthetic and life practice, there thus arose as well a vibrant tradition of commentary on it. Within such discourse, the concept of popular culture is Janus-faced: with it, we either celebrate or revile the ordinary people. Popular culture refers democratically to the capacities of all human beings, no matter what their social position or level of "cultivation," to produce and consume symbolic products, indeed, to entertain ideas worth attention at all. It refers as well to the baseness of common thinking, the homogenized incapacity of the masses, their danger to the life of aesthetic refinement, their irrelevance, even threat, to thoughtful governance. In politics, we simultaneously embrace democracy and lament its low level. In culture, we encourage general aesthetic expression and bemoan its poverty.

A basic line of division is thus between those who identify popular culture negatively as mass culture—undifferentiated and low—and those who reject the association. The so-called mass culture critics, nevertheless, come from both left and right. Among the most famous of right-wing mass-culture critiques is Matthew Arnold's *Culture and Anarchy.* Arnold argued that the middle classes were uncultured "Philistines," wealthy but lacking proper appreciation of what he called "the best that has been thought and known in the world." Later, Van Wyck Brooks drew a distinction between "highbrow" and "lowbrow" culture. Critics in this tradition saw the battle lines clearly: on the one side, the invading hordes, on the other, that small cultivated elite who alone were able to discern what is of value, on whose judgment and leadership alone the future depends. They often employed analogies to the decline of the Roman Empire, though now the enemy was within—it was the people itself.

Defense of "high" culture against the masses, however, was by no means limited to the right. Theorists in the Western Marxist tradition worried about the effects of mass production and mass media on political as well as cultural life. Members of the so-called Frankfurt School argued that popular culture was "industrial" insofar as it shared the debased features of capitalist society more generally, which included rampant individualism, superficiality, and instru-

mentalism. Given the unique capacities of mass production in all spheres of life, popular culture destroys the foundations for critical reflection, pervading leisure time with entertainment commodities that have a narcotizing effect on the masses. These cultural commodities, like capitalist commodities generally, helped maintain the alienated condition of contemporary society, creating out of atomized individuals a shapeless mass incapable of recognizing its own situation. In contrast, the aesthetic dimension of a "pure" high culture provided a last refuge of critical thinking. Insofar as commodification is an ever-expanding scourge, however, mass culture threatened to extinguish even that remaining realm of hope and critical potential.

In contrast, however, there have been varieties of popular culture theory that reject the identification of popularity with massification and commodification. Theories of this variety criticize mass-culture theorists for objectifying ordinary people, for denigrating their enduring capacities for reflection and subjectivity even in a mass-mediated surround. Herbert J. Gans, for instance, argues for a populist position that appreciates the aesthetic (and, by extension, political) capacities of all people, no matter what their level of "cultivation." Gans argues that differences between high culture and popular culture have been exaggerated, that they are similar in their abilities to express the needs of different people: for every "taste public" there corresponds a "taste culture." Moreover, Gans argues that all taste cultures are of equal value, to be judged not one against the other but in relation to the groups they serve.

Additionally, writers from widely divergent political positions saw some redemptive possibilities in popular culture. Walter Benjamin, for instance, while wary of many aspects of culture in the age of mechanical reproduction, also saw in it a liberating potential: mass-produced works were no longer enthralled to the "aura" of the original, thereby providing an escape from the jargon of authenticity that defined so much work in aesthetic theory. It also allowed more people to approach the "great" works, although such works did face the risk of becoming clichéd and debased through repetition. Edward Shils, as well, argued that the spread of classical music and art through mass production had to some degree "improved" the tastes of the people, though the condescending tone of this argument is apparent.

In the second half of the twentieth century, a new line of (often British) cultural theory known as Cultural Studies has emerged from the tradition of Western Marxism, critically appropriating that school's understanding of commodification, but avoiding its implied low opinion of the people. Cultural Studies theorists agree with the Frankfurt School that the industrial commodification of culture inculcates the masses into a hegemonic ideology that saps them of some critical potential. But writers in this tradition disagree with the Frankfurt School about the totality of ideological domination: ordinary people bring to bear sometimes significant critical capacities in their reception of culture, and oppositional readings are always inscribed in mass-culture texts, even if only through their exclusion.

Theorists in the Cultural Studies tradition redefine popular culture—the culture of the people—in terms of reading and reception as a realm of resistance to dominant culture: popular culture is the culture that arises out of the experiences of ordinary people, experiences that include consuming mass-produced culture but only within contexts that are always more complex than can be controlled by such over-generalized, mass-produced images. Cultural Studies thus involves a shift from a focus on production to a focus on reception.

Writers like E. P. Thompson, Raymond Williams, and Richard Hoggart emphasize the ways in which people use mass-produced culture within the contexts of their everyday lives, pointing out especially the ways in which ordinary people resist the implied messages of that culture. Through continuous selection and interpretation, people resist the totality of mass culture: they act as gatekeepers, rejecting the majority of what is produced; they "read" what is offered through the sometimes quite critical lenses of their own experiences, which are often not those addressed by the products (women, for instance, filter male-addressed media through their lives, as working-class youths respond to middle-class utopias not always in the inscribed manner); consumers often create hidden—and sometimes not-so-hidden—practices of resistance or appropriate images and commodities contrarily to the ways in which these are sold. An important implication of this approach, then, is that meanings are not transcendent, to be uncovered through expert strategies, but are products of social contestation, the result of negotiation among producers, texts, and readers. Pure aesthetics has thus fallen, and sociology replaces philosophy. Distinctions among kinds of culture are matters of social relations, not intrinsic aspects of the works themselves.

Artists as well as cultural theorists have also participated in this "deconstruction" of pure aesthetic distinctions. In the 1960s, Pop art blurred and eventually demolished distinctions between high and low, exalted and ordinary, pure and prosaic. Supportive theorists of this movement dismissed the possibility of distinguishing between highbrow and lowbrow, attacking those who maintain such distinctions as elitist. This so-called new sensibility sought to explode the "canon" of Western civilization's great works, embracing film as well as painting, the Beatles as well as J. S. Bach and Ludwig van Beethoven. Later, this rejection of boundaries contributed to an attack on traditional reading lists in American universities as inscribing an exclusionary program meant to support the dominance of a Eurocentric worldview. Critics sought to make reading lists more "inclusive," reflecting the experiences of people (mainly women and minorities) traditionally excluded from analysis and participation in academic and political discourse. In the wider political context, we refer now to the "culture wars," where the parties argue about the political implications of social and cultural distinctions and about the very possibility of drawing them innocently or objectively.

[*See also* Comics; Cultural Studies; Fashion; Folk Art; Kitsch; Pop Art; Rock Music; *and* Television.]

BIBLIOGRAPHY

Arnold, Matthew. *Culture and Anarchy.* Edited by J. Dover Wilson. Reprint, Cambridge, 1963.

Benjamin, Walter. "The Work of Art in the Age of Mechanical Reproduction." In *Illuminations,* edited by Hannah Arendt, translated by Harry Zohn, pp. 217–251. New York, 1969.

Bourdieu, Pierre. *Distinction: A Social Critique of The Judgement of Taste.* Translated by Richard Nice. Cambridge, Mass., 1984.

Burke, Peter. *Popular Culture in Early Modern Europe.* New York, 1978.

Fiske, John. "British Cultural Studies and Television." In *Channels of Discourse,* edited by Robert C. Allen, pp. 254–289. Chapel Hill, N.C., 1987.

Gans, Herbert J. *Popular Culture and High Culture: An Analysis and Evaluation of Taste.* New York, 1974.

Hall, Stuart. "Cultural Studies: Two Paradigms." In *Media, Culture and Society: A Critical Reader,* edited by Richard Collins. Beverly Hills, Calif., 1986.

Hoggart, Richard. *The Uses of Literacy.* London, 1957.

Horkheimer, Max, and Theodor W. Adorno. "The Culture Industry: Enlightenment as Mass Deception." In *Dialectic of Enlightenment,* translated by John Cumming. New York, 1972.

Mukerji, Chandra, and Michael Schudson, eds. *Rethinking Popular Culture: Contemporary Perspectives in Cultural Studies.* Berkeley, 1991.

Rosenberg, Bernard, and David Manning White, eds. *Mass Culture: The Popular Arts in America.* New York, 1957.

Thompson, E. P. *The Making of the English Working Class.* London, 1963.

Williams, Raymond. *The Long Revolution.* London, 1961.

Williams, Raymond. *Keywords.* Rev. ed. New York, 1985.

JEFFREY K. OLICK

PORNOGRAPHY. *See* Obscenity.

PORTRAITURE. The terms *portraiture,* conventionally defined as "the action or art of portraying," and *to portray* as "to make a picture, image, or figure of" are familiar terms in everyday language. They move between the poles of descriptive delineation in the literal sense and a much more generalized concept of representation, where depiction has a tenuous connection with a palpable object of reference to which some name, some specific identification can be given. In either case, there is an operative assumption that the portrait, the product of portrayal, bears a significant relationship with some being, or entity, in the world that has, or had, both actual existence and some degree of singularity, sufficient for identification. However difficult it may be to portray a specific person, the exclusive subject of "por-

PORTRAITURE. Man Ray, *Gertrude Stein Sitting in Front of Picasso's Portrait of Her* (1922), photograph. (Copyright 1998 by Artists Rights Society, New York/ADAGP/Man Ray Trust, Paris; photograph courtesy of Man Ray Trust; used by permission.)

traiture," however unrecognizable to all but a chosen few, portraying "the face" of someone is an infinitely simpler task than portraying, to quote Christopher Marlowe, the "personage of a wondrous man." The former seemingly provides a tangible, material point of reference, the object of verifiable description, even if disputed by readers, viewers, and other respondents. The latter requires a complex process of interpretive analysis whose goal is to manifest the intangibles of personality, spirit, character, "soul," and the self, the very qualities that, allegedly, fill the corporeal envelope with "being" and make its portrayal of value and interest to others.

Still, visualizing or otherwise representing the self is a task beset with serious obstacles. In his discussion of concepts of identity and their uncertain reliance on the posited continuity of permanence of some defining essence of being, David

Hume observed that he had never seen a self and, by implication, that he was rather skeptical of its existence. Others have challenged the very notion of selfhood, alleging its fictional character as a particular cultural artifact of the now discredited ideology of individualism, the latter deemed a manifestation, perhaps, of the sin of pride, or at the very least of an anticommunitarian sensibility. There are many, moreover, who argue that terms such as *personality, character,* and *self* are themselves transitory concepts, constantly subjected to redefinition and incapable of being indissolubly associated with anyone. Indeed, these very terms, with or without a psychological or philosophical gloss, are ultimately imposed from the outside—by an artist, by a viewer-reader, by all who participate in the social order and are concerned about their place in it—and they serve to establish an effective frame of reference for simplifying the encounter with another. Even self-portraiture may be understood as a form of representation, couched in terms either formulated by others or based knowingly on their expectations: to wit, "I am the person you think I am, or I'm not."

Putting aside the ongoing dispute about the nature of the existence of selfhood, portraiture may be considered a well-tested instrument for differentiating among persons, past and present, and for preserving that difference over time through the medium of art. Portraiture should also be construed as an operative construct, asserting a particular predicate (fictional or not), as a propositional statement of the subject portrayed, in the form, "This is XYZ, who . . ." The act of portrayal can then be compared with the use of personal pronouns in ordinary speech—especially in the third person—but with a permanence that neither speech nor the corporeal being possesses. In this way, portraits serve to extricate individuals from the mass of humanity and provide a lens to focus on the defining "idiosyncracies" of various persons; they also fix such persons in time but are limited neither in their affective authority nor in their reception to the time and conditions of making. Above all, portraits are the products of a conscious intent to portray and of a strong interest in such portrayals. Without this reciprocity, portraits not only fail to function but will be unrecognizable for what they are or purport to be, a "picture, image, or figure of" a particular someone.

But does that someone of whom the portrait is an image have to exist? All of us can recall fictional characters in novels, so completely realized by an author that they leap off the page into our minds and there form vivid mental images of the individuals portrayed. Charles Dickens and many other novelists of the nineteenth and early twentieth centuries created such characters, whose very existence seemed an intrinsic part of life, certainly less circumscribed in their apparent nature and appearance than the depiction of these selfsame characters in the movies. The novelist's art creates such characters from life, but the world they inhabit is fictional, and the only access to them is through the medium of their depiction by an imaginative writer.

Absent the requisite intention to portray an actual figure, the genre of the novel itself categorically stands in the way of the reader taking the author's characters as portraits, however lifelike they may appear. On the other hand, artistic invention alone does not necessarily impugn the claim of these fictional characters to be thought of as "portraits." Visual access to the long dead may exist only through the medium of preserved portraits, whose legitimacy or authenticity has been established by convention rather than by any rational method of historical verification. We readily accept sculpted and painted portraits as being "true" likenesses of actual, living persons, even without identifying labels and, often, in the absence of corroborating evidence. An example of our willingness to suspend doubt, to accept the propositional truth presented by the work of visual art,

occurs in the case of the sculpted busts of Homer, acknowledged to be posthumous inventions, at best. Since antiquity, they have been accepted as portraits of the poet because they satisfied preconceived notions of Homer, the blind master of epic. All Greek portraits of Homer must be considered historical fictions on two counts: as portraits they are pure inventions because Homer preceded the development of portraiture in Greek art, and "Homer" himself may never have existed. The classical "Homer" can be differentiated from Dickens's Fagin, who existed only in fictive time, but they do share many features of inventive characterization. More closely, perhaps, the fictive image of "Homer" resembles those actual personages whose participatory appearance in historical novels imparts an air of veracity, or authenticity, especially in the figures of Napoleon and the Russian generals in Leo Tolstoy's *War and Peace,* Walter Scott's medieval English kings and nobles, and Gore Vidal's nineteenth-century American politicians.

Indeed, such personage-punctuated historical novels occupy an intermediate position between the wholly fictive presentation of lifelike characters and the biographical treatment of historical figures in works ostensibly devoted to that sole purpose. The genre of literary portraiture notoriously tends to blur distinctions between an objective depiction of the subject and the highly confected forms of self-representation assumed, consciously or not, by the same subject, just like portraits painted on commission. Literary portraiture traditionally combines the description of places, persons, and circumstances with the interpretive analysis of behavior patterns and their reception in an attempt to define the whole subject; literary models, narrative conventions, and the codified language of psychological insight offer a much broader repertory to the biographer than is available to the visual artist, although both rely heavily on typologically determined forms to portray the person "in context." Biography establishes its own justification for being in human curiosity, in the desire to explain the actions of distinguished persons as part of something greater than their momentary instantiation. The autobiographer is further preoccupied with self-justification, whether expressed in a confessional mode or with pseudo–third person distance, but has the great advantage of speaking in his or her own voice, however contrived.

What, of course, separates the literary from the visual portrait is the space and time available to the writer, permitting the establishment of the changing contours of the subject's presence over the years and revealing the transformation of body and spirit. In this regard, the literary portrait is surely more rounded, the multivalent interaction between the subject and his or her contemporaries more fully revealed, the author's analysis both grander and more detailed than in the visual portrait. As a result, although the biography may be full of literary symbols and motifs, the visual portrait functions more immediately as a comprehensive sign, collapsing biographical dilation into a single, all-incorporating image, closer then to the actual experience available to us all in the course of an encounter with another.

Alterity energizes the visual and psychological transaction between the beholder and the portrait image, especially when the portrait is presented at human scale, so direct eye contact takes place. This *simulacrum* of the person portrayed thus functions as a surrogate presence, and the intensity of the relationship engages all those faculties that are brought into play in social encounters with friends, relatives, and strangers, sometimes to such a degree of rapport that the artwork becomes invisible. The resulting triumph of the person-sign, materialized in the art object and existing in the viewer's space and in his or her field of vision, may account for the appearance of the visual portrait before the textual, at least in the Western cultural tradition. It is much easier to empathize with the portrait when confronting the visual image of another, even if the viewer is restricted to the immediate perception of the moment. Histories are written in faces, bodies, poses, costumes, settings, and in the conventions of portraiture itself.

Considerations of the visual portrait as an effective surrogate for the original inevitably bring up the question of *likeness,* that much used, or abused, term, imposed for centuries as the standard of achievement by which the success of the portrait was measured. Achieving a good likeness guaranteed continued employment, because verisimilitude was the normative goal of the portraitist, or at least a close approximation to it, subject, of course, to such improvements of the original deemed necessary. The invention of photography in the nineteenth century seemed to preempt the field, because with the photograph it seemed possible to attain such a truthful likeness whose verifiable objectivity denied to the portraitist the opportunity to impose his or her interpretation on the portrait image. The new technology appeared to nullify the distortions, the departures from objective truth that made painted and sculpted portraits so defective as likenesses—even if the photograph itself was small and lacked the color of nature. This illusion of photographic objectivity still informs the documentary use of photographs for purposes of identification, an index of one's existence. It has little to do with portraiture, fundamentally an interpretive art that through depiction reveals the individuality of the subject; and a portrait, whatever its value as a surrogate, does not reproduce the original but, rather, stands apart from that subject, linked to it forever like cause and effect.

Most twentieth-century portraits still resemble the physical appearance of their subjects because recognition/identification remains a desideratum of the genre, and so too its practice of representing the social dimensions of a life, implicit in the depiction of someone as "a someone." Photography, however, liberated modern portraiture from the tyranny of likeness; the authority of an illusory objectivity, derived from the world, weakened before the growing sensitivity to the perceiver's subjectivity as the only authentic source of knowledge about the world and its human inhabitants. The mimetic function of traditional portraiture thus gave way to interpretive strategies, expressed in a formal language of symbolic abstraction, that seek to visualize the particular, salient aspects of the subject's interior life—to go beneath the skin, that accident of nature, to reach the heretofore unrepresented "self" within. Evidently, the modern portraitist's investigative, reactive approach to the subject demonstrates a preference for characterization over description, for the dynamic of response over the stability of presence, sometimes at the price of recognizability. When that happens, the portrait's very reason to exist is compromised, and the fundamental connection between *image* and *of,* essential to portraiture, has been severed.

[*See also* Photography; Realism; *and* Representation.]

BIBLIOGRAPHY

Borgatti, Jean M., and Richard Brilliant. *Likeness and Beyond: Portraits from Africa and the World.* New York, 1990.

Breckenridge, James D. *Likeness: A Conceptual History of Ancient Portraiture.* Evanston, Ill., 1968.

Brilliant, Richard. *Portraiture.* Cambridge, Mass., 1991.

Feldman, Melissa E., and Benjamin H. D. Buchloh. *Face-Off: The Portrait in Recent Art.* Philadelphia, 1994.

Freedman, Luba. *Titian's Portraits through Aretino's Lens.* University Park, Pa., 1995.

Koerner, Joseph Leo. *The Moment of Self-Portraiture in German Renaissance Art.* Chicago, 1993.

Marin, Louis. *Le portrait du roi.* Paris, 1981.

Parfit, Derek. *Reasons and Persons.* Oxford, 1984. See esp. pp. 199–347.

Spiro, Audrey. *Contemplating the Ancients: Aesthetic and Social Issues in Early Chinese Portraiture.* Berkeley, 1990.

Taylor, Charles. *The Sources of the Self: The Making of the Modern Identity.* Cambridge, Mass., 1989.

Wendorf, Richard. *The Elements of Life: Biography and Portrait-Painting in Stuart and Georgian England.* Oxford, 1990.

Zanker, Paul. *Die Maske des Sokrates: Das Bild des Intellektuellen in der antiken Kunst.* Munich, 1995.

RICHARD BRILLIANT

POSTCOLONIALISM. During the 1980s, the term *postcolonialism* emerged as a popular rubric for a certain terrain of discussion within the fields of literary criticism, culture studies, and the humanities in general. There is no simple bundle of theories or ideas that, packaged together, constitute a single, unified entity of postcolonial thought; rather, postcolonial theory is a hotly debated set of conflicting beliefs and interests, with scholars, artists, authors, and critics fiercely advancing and defending opposing views on what postcoloniality is, whether and where it exists, and who is best fit to understand and explain it. In order to provide a framework to make some sense of these debates, this essay will (1) stake out the boundaries of the field's terrain—the frame that sets up a space for coherent discourse between the various voices who speak in these debates; (2) discuss and explain some of the critical terms commonly used by participants in this field; and (3) chart a brief history of the ideas advanced by a small selection of some of the more influential figures in the field: Frantz Fanon, Edward W. Said, Gayatri Chakravorty Spivak, and Homi K. Bhabha.

At the most basic level, postcolonial studies are investigations into the cultural situations of nations or peoples who have formerly been subject to imperialist colonizing territorial control. The field includes critical analyses of the processes of colonization and decolonization, and discussions of how those historical processes are responsible for the present cultural contexts and cultural products of the formerly colonized.

Postcolonial studies are generally based on the idea that the material conditions of colonization and decolonization are determinative elements in shaping the makeup of a culture, and thus in defining the subject identities of all those peoples who are constructed within that cultural system. Postcolonial theory is a response to an interest in the way concrete political and historical cultural interrelations have affected various cultures' internal systems. Within this approach, a culture's aesthetics must be seen both as a tool used in furthering its specific intercultural agenda and as a product of its own political past.

The *post* in *postcolonialism* might seem to imply that the effective period of colonial impact on colonized cultures ends once territorial control has been returned from the imperialistic powers to the indigenous peoples. *Colonialism,* however, is seen as the social assertion of a national identity whose perceived uniqueness and special value justify that nation's acts of interference and control in regards to the peoples and nations outside its own self-designated boundaries. These acts of interference may include political, economic, and cultural dominance as well as raw territorial domination. With this broadened understanding of colonialism, theorists can justify their concern with the ways in which postcolonial societies remain subject to forms of neocolonial domination, despite putative political independence.

In the same way, the seeming polar oppositionality of the terms *colonial* and *postcolonial* might appear to suggest that historical periods of overt territorial colonialism are typified by monolithic one-sided domination of colonized peoples by their colonizers. While the profound inequity of the colonizer-colonized relationships should never be downplayed, colonial discourse theory argues that the domination of the colonizers always calls forth a response of resistance from the colonized. The ways in which colonized subjects subvert their colonizers' tools of cultural control and counter their domination with secret defiance constitute a major topic for analysis in postcolonial studies.

The field is primarily concerned with the cultural history and situation of territories and peoples made "marginal" by the self-positioning of Western societies and cultures as "the center" of the civilized world. At the same time, the field's very privileging of these so-called marginal territories and their cultural products is a tacit acknowledgment of the real historical and present-day power wielded by this Western center. The complex and intricate dynamics of the relationships between marginal and central societies are discussed by many postcolonial theorists.

Postcolonial analysis comes out of an awareness of cultural borders—the imagined separating spaces from which people project the beginnings and endings of their own identities and the identities of those they call Other (the imaginary oppositional subjects whose invention supports the definition of the self). The postcolonial project addresses the construction and projection of identities—of the processes of conformation and repudiation that allow people to position themselves within the realm of the social.

This general interest in the problem of identity is related to other contemporary theories that focus on the difficulties in discussing human agency and subjecthood. Postcolonial theorists, like scholars in other branches of contemporary studies, investigate the ways in which ideology and cultural discourse—specifically the ideologies and discourses of colonialist relations—are responsible for determining individual positions within social systems. The place from which the colonized subject speaks, writes, or projects himself into the social realm is of great interest to postcolonial theorists. Solutions to this problem are widely divergent, ranging from positions that emphasize a need to recover or invent essential discrete cultural or ethnic identities to positions that suggest that colonized subjects can ever project their voices into the common territory of global discourse (see discussions of Fanon and Spivak, below).

The postmodern, poststructural emphasis on text and on the textuality of social discourse has had enormous influence on the approaches used by many postcolonial theorists. As a result, there have been far more investigations of the literary text as a means of cultural domination than of the impact of other forms of aesthetic production. The literary text is often seen as the site within which the identity of the "native" is constructed and affixed by the colonizing culture. Contemporary literary theories have also led postcolonial theorists to emphasize the lapses, omissions, and contradictions that reveal the agenda beneath colonialist literary formulae (see discussion of Said, below).

In addition, the major academic disciplinary ancestor of the postcolonial field is "Commonwealth literature," a subset of British literary studies that took on the (primarily English-language) literary production of the Commonwealth's outlying territories. This has led to much debate over the meaning and consequence of language usage itself. Questions have been raised as to whether the continued use of the colonizers' language in postcolonial culture is a politically justified and forward-looking aesthetic choice, or whether it merely demonstrates a continued submission to one of the major forms of colonial domination.

The ways in which the texts of colonized and formerly colonized peoples "write back" at their colonizers, subverting the cultural forms of their oppressors to create a mode of resistance, are another significant area of postcolonial interest. This area of literary analysis highlights the ways in which a text achieves some sort of double meaning, seeming on the surface to bow to the standards of the dominant culture, yet finding ways to project secondary, oppositional meanings from the same space. Rhetorical forms such as irony, which simultaneously work within an existent discourse and also contest that discourse, are of particular interest here.

Finally, the strangely intimate relationship that exists between colonizing and colonized cultures has led to extensive discussion of the notion of hybridity. A dialectical relationship between cultures is theorized that involves two-way receptions and resistances. The idea of syncretism is often raised, positing a pluralistic notion of cross-cultural interpenetration. Working out the nuances of these sorts of interactions within the grid of the primary relationship of oppression that exists between the two cultures occupies a significant portion of contemporary postcolonial theoretical discussion (see discussion of Bhabha, below).

The scope of postcolonial theory is too broad and too multidisciplinary (spanning sociology, anthropology, philosophy, literary studies, and even mathematics) to condense its major lines of research into a discussion of a few representative theorists. Within the general scope of the field, however, a few writers have had such impact on the thinking of their fellows that their work requires a more specific treatment. Although the case could be made that there are others whose work deserves such treatment, there is no doubt that the works and influence of Fanon, Said, Spivak, and Bhabha justify their inclusion in this category. The following discussions treat only their works that have been broadly influential on the field at large; it would be impossible adequately to treat the full scope of any of these authors' works within the limitations of this space.

Fanon. Frantz Fanon, a French West Indian psychiatrist who trained in France after World War II, came to global prominence through his best-selling texts *Black Skin, White Masks* (1952) and *The Wretched of the Earth* (1961), both of which were originally published in French. Based on his observation of French colonial practices and their consequences for their colonized subjects, Fanon promoted an ideology of resistance through a strategy of national identification.

Although his death in 1961 situates his theories into a historical period preceding the articulated development of postcolonial theory, he has taken a place as a sort of ancestor figure to present-day theorists. His work, which theorizes the enormous complexity of colonial subjectivities, has been particularly influential in considerations of the psychological relations between colonizers and colonized. His focus on the states of marginality and Otherness that are forced on the colonized subject and his prescriptions for resistance prefigure many of the major threads of contemporary postcolonial discussion. In addition, his analysis of the role of nationalism and national cultures in helping to effect the transition from the colonial to postcolonial states has had significant impact on later thinkers and writers.

Fanon's ideas regarding the importance of the ways that the combined forces of nationalism and local culture can act to provide an organizational framework for mounting indigenous opposition to a colonial presence are best articulated in *The Wretched of the Earth*. In the chapter titled "On National Culture," he suggests that the search for a valorous and authentic precolonial local culture is the first necessary step in breaking through a colonized state's psychological dependence on the colonizer.

The intellectual and upper classes in a colonized state have the greatest access to the cultural, economic, and militaristic tools of resistance, and yet, because these groups have achieved their elite positions through successful negotiations of the colonizer's educational and economic systems, they are also the people who have been most thoroughly ideologically formed in the colonizer's mold of the "good native." In order even to contemplate resistance against the colonizing presence, the colonized must find a way to value a heritage separate from that of the colonizer.

Fanon tells us that "for these [cultured] individuals, the demand for a national culture and the affirmation of the existence of such a culture represent a special battle-field. While the politicians situate their action in present-day events, men of culture take their stand in the field of history" (Fanon, 1967, p. 168). For Fanon, one of the primary psychological violences visited on colonized subjects is the mutilation of their past. "By a kind of perverted logic, [colonization] turns to the past of oppressed people, and distorts, disfigures and destroys it" (p. 169). Restoring that sense of past becomes a means by which native intellectuals gather the strength and self-conviction that will enable them to actively oppose their oppressors.

Fanon argues that colonized subjects begin from a state in which they accept the cultural standards of the colonizers as transparent (what is "good writing"? It is writing like a Westerner, in the Western tradition). From this starting point, he theorizes an evolutionary model of rising opposition.

Fanon suggests that the first attempts at countering the cultural domination of the oppressor will come in the form of paeans to a romanticized version of a mythically splendid native past, which still demonstrate formal obedience to the conventions of the oppressor's cultural categories. For example, instead of trying to write novels with Western characters moving through Western scenes, the writer will now produce novels with native character in native scenes—yet the product, a *novel*, will still be judged according to the traditions of the novel, as developed in the West.

The nationalist phase of cultural development comes next, and it is also the first phase of active resistance to the oppressor. This phase is typified by shift in intended audience for a native intellectual's work. No longer written to be read by the oppressors, either in order to please them or to castigate them, the native intellectual's writings are now constructed for consumption by a local readership.

It is at this point, when native writers begin addressing their own people with their texts, that Fanon tells us we can truly speak of a national literature. This is the point when the national culture will become vital and meaningful to the local audience. Cultural products will no longer be met with disinterest, but will become the means of a cohesion among society, coalescing them against their oppressors.

Fanon warns of the dangerous potential contained within the rise of a national consciousness (see "The Pitfalls of National Consciousness" in *The Wretched of the Earth*), as the nationalized middle class who wrest power from the colonial regimes can easily assume the roles held by their former oppressors, creating a state whose class-based system replicates the injustices of the colonial past.

Fanon's influence has led to certain theoretical investments in essentialized ideas of national or racial identity as useful tools for effecting political change. Concepts like negritude (which theorized a discrete cultural identity for black peoples) and movements like the Pan-African political project (which attempted to promote a sense of meta-African shared identity) have roots in Fanon's cultural prescriptions and his pragmatic politics.

Said. Edward W. Said's 1978 text, *Orientalism*, essentially laid the groundwork for postcolonial thinking, introducing an entirely new territory for academic study. This text provides a rigorous analysis of the binary opposition between West and East, or Occident and Orient. Said attacks the white Western ways of thinking about the peoples that they term "Oriental." The basic goal of his text is to demonstrate that the idea—the organizing category—of the "Orient" is a Western invention that, among other things, serves as an Other for the West's construction of its own sense of identity. Crucial to his argument is his insistence that this invented Orient is not purely a thing of the West's imagination: it is an integral part of Western material culture, embedded in Western images, literature, and language. For Said, the aesthetic is essentially a sphere of invented stereotypes that permit one culture to define and thus control another.

Said uses a Foucauldian-based analysis to identify Orientalism as a discourse of domination, allowing and asserting a Western network of power to repress and dominate the peoples and cultures it purports to describe. Following this Foucauldian line, he asserts that, during its period of hege-

mony, the overarching discourse of Orientalism has controlled the products of every Western person writing about, thinking about, or otherwise representing the Orient. At the same time, unlike Michel Foucault, he does acknowledge some "determining imprint of individual writers upon the otherwise anonymous collective body of texts constituting a discursive formation like Orientalism" (Said, 1978, p. 23). His goal in the text is to make some beginning toward unraveling the many interrelated strands of this network of power—to see how they function to determine what the West can (and does) say about the Orient.

This task is one that has subsequently been carried out by many postcolonialist theorists. Said's ideas regarding the manner in which Western discourse has represented the "Orient" in a manner aimed at furthering covert political goals and his desire to uncover the imperialist agenda behind the West's manufacturing of powered knowledge have served as a blueprint for further analyses, most often of literary texts, but also of the visual arts (see Nochlin, 1989).

A significant part of Said's strategic effort to dismantle these modes of Orientalist discourse, however, is to suggest not only that the discourse is flawed insofar as it is a means of oppression, but also that it is flawed because it does not match up to the "brute reality" of the East. This insistent suggestion that the West, in its construction of the "Orient," is failing to see the true cultures and peoples that occupy the nations and spaces of the East becomes the most troubling aspect of his work. How this "truer" vision might be achieved is never spelled out, but its potential existence lurks within the text, serving as an additional justification for condemning the Orientalist construct that Said deplores. Nonetheless, his discussions of the myriad ways in which the West has constructed its relationships with the East, always maintaining the upper hand, are compelling and continue to be useful. In his isolation of the rhetoric and behavior of Western scientific, scholastic, militaristic, religious, and mercantile activities, Said is able to reveal significant patterns of conceptual control.

Said's project is an overtly political one, aimed at undermining what he sees as the West's continuing modes of repressive representation of the East. For Said, following Foucault, knowledge is power, and thus the primary role of the academic, that of accumulating and legitimizing knowledges, is one of secret power. In his essay "Criticism between Culture and System," he contrasts the value of the reading theories advanced by Foucault and Jacques Derrida, in terms of their usefulness for his project.

He describes Foucault and Derrida as having a similar reactions to text, insofar as both see text as duplicitous, as containing more than it makes visible. Derrida, however, Said views as content simply to make these lacks in the text his business—content to show that texts have no link to reality or to meaning. Foucault, on the other hand, identifies texts (and knowledge) with power, and he attacks the invisible, or hidden, moments in the text as a part of his larger scheme to attack and make visible the secret modes of power and repression that control all of social discourse. Said, in essence, prefers Foucault to Derrida because he perceives Foucault as providing a linguistic/critical model that is useful for motivated political activity, whereas he thinks Derrida is too esoteric; he finds that Derrida's linguistic strategy cannot be applied in any larger context. It becomes a general question of power: Said finds the Derridean method useful only for baring the ultimate powerlessness of all textual (social) effort, while he sees Foucault's ideas as having more potential for use in a directed, strategic effort to strip power from the empowered and transfer it to the (currently) powerless.

Ultimately, Said's quarrel with Derrida boils down to Said's impatience with what he sees as Derrida's insistent attack on the hope of making meaning. Said's own agenda is bound up in the need to make knowledge and, indeed, to make that knowledge intentionally, through the application of will and reason. Said believes that Derrida disallows such a possibility, and thus Said finds his method useless. Said wants to target and dismantle "Western thought," and feels this cannot be done so long as "Western thought" remains the abstraction it must be for Derrida.

Because Said sees Foucault as using textual analysis to identify the links between institutional power and textual assumption, he believes Foucault's method will allow him to reveal and thus agitate against this monolithic Western social discourse. Where Derrida concerns himself with texts as locations where the impotence of the writer is constantly revealed, Foucault concerns himself with texts as locations where the potence of social discourse is constantly concealed. Said's project becomes the locating and mapping of these strategies of control as they manifest themselves in text.

Spivak. Gayatri Chakravorty Spivak's greatest influence on postcolonial theory comes out of her various writings that theorize the position of the colonized subject within the cultural space created by their colonizers. She has brought particular attention to bear on the position of the postcolonial female, whose double marginalization within the spheres of patriarchy and colonial control makes her case both particularly difficult and particularly valuable to address.

Spivak's essay "Can the Subaltern Speak?" focused attention on the role of the "subaltern"—the insurgent colonized subject—asking whether the subaltern can inject her voice into the master discourse of dominant culture. Spivak's conclusion is that, in fact, there is no possibility for the subaltern's voice to be heard in this way. In "Subaltern Studies: Deconstructing Historiography," Spivak asserts that "the subaltern is necessarily the absolute limit of the place where history is narrativized into logic" (Spivak, 1987). This conclusion has provoked strong disagreement,

including Benita Parry's criticism that Spivak's work serves to valorize the theorist and silence the colonized subjects, perpetuating the very conditions of colonialism that postcolonial theorists are supposed to be committed to dismantling.

Spivak bases her argument on a combined rejection of the theories proposed by Foucault and an alignment with the work of Derrida. Spivak's criticism of Foucault is based on her belief that later stages of his work claim to grant an expressive subjectivity to the oppressed—a notion that is criticized in earlier stages of his logical construct. In addition, she sees Foucault as having a complicit relationship with Western culture's imperialistic domination of the colonized subject-states. She accuses him of ignoring the international division of labor that locates bourgeois-capitalist control in the industrialist hands of the West and has them exploiting the labor of the colonized non-Western nations. Indeed, she suggests that Foucault's emphasis on the repressed of the West—the mad, children, prisoners—serves as a mask that reemphasizes a Western-centric vision of the world, hiding the greater power relation of repression and domination that ultimately connects West to non-West.

She is especially troubled by what she reads as Foucault's (and also Gilles Deleuze's) expectation that the dominant networks of power/desire/interest can be revealed in the narratives or histories constructed by intellectuals, and further by his belief that the intellectual can (and should) identify and disclose the discourse of society's Other. She feels that Foucault's work supposes that these oppressed subjects know their condition and can speak their condition if permitted. In contrast, she suggests that through the ideological power of the dominant culture, the masses are brought to participate in the imagination of and maintenance of the very system that represses them. Spivak argues that the networks of power/desire/interest are so heterogeneous that they cannot be reduced to useful narrative or text. Further, she sees no possibility for the intellectual, either Western or Eastern, ever to be genuinely able to know and speak (for) the marginalized Other.

Instead, Spivak proposes a political agenda for the intellectual: "the difficult task of rewriting . . . conditions of impossibility as the conditions of its possibility" (Spivak, 1988). Representation, although impossible, is advocated as necessary and useful. She anchors this approach in the methodology of Derrida, seeing his critique of Western humanism's quest for origin as the means that invalidates Foucault's efforts. Derrida having, in her eyes, cleared the field of the obstacles represented by the Western tradition that she sees culminating in the work of Foucault, Spivak sees herself free to proceed with her own project, which is the critique of imperialism.

Her politically motivated interest in representing the status of the subaltern, despite the ultimate impossibility of that task, is made more clear in her discussion of the Subaltern Studies writers, a group of revisionary theorists of India's colonial history and postcolonial state.

While she disagrees with the group's positivistic efforts at providing an account of the "true" Indian subject, she suggests that the group's work uncovers the limits of the poststructuralist critique of humanism. "The radical intellectual in the West is either caught in a deliberate choice of subalternity, granting to the oppressed either that very expressive subjectivity which s/he criticizes or, instead, a total unrepresentability" (1987).

She suggests that (unbeknownst to them) the work of the Subaltern Studies group rests on the idea of the subject consciousness as a moment of individuation constituted on the great semiotic chain of the socius (or the essentially textual web that links people into a social group). Because all historians attempting to discuss such a subject consciousness must themselves also be positioned in the same semiotic chain, their work will always be incontrovertibly compromised. All of the group's works, therefore, are and must be failures.

Spivak suggests, however, that the methodology of deconstruction (specifically of Derrida) can be used to reassess these failures as a practice that denotes its success in the action of disruption rather than in the possibility of making meaning.

The failure inherent in the work of the Subaltern Studies group, as she sees it, would be the failure inherent in making their work of investigating and establishing the subaltern consciousness a positivistic project—making it a project that assumes it can, in fact, uncover or discover some actual, objectively true narrative of reality. She offers this justification for such a seemingly positivistic project, however: it becomes valuable not as an actual project of truth revealing or knowledge making, but instead as a strategic project with a political object. The "truth" or "knowledge" that is found or made should be weighed not against an objective, positive standard of actuality, but instead against the political standard of effectivity. If the knowledge that is "found" or made is useful for achieving the political goals of the group, it does not have to live up to its own professed goal of verity.

She discusses the importance of the group's work in revealing the inadequacy of Western categories of identity for locating the subaltern. Neither the Marxist category of preindustrial (and thus lacking class consciousness) nor the Marxist category of "working class" fits the communal identity asserted by the group for the subaltern. For Spivak, the value to be found in the practices of history writing and literary critique is in the power of such activities to take away the ability of Western master narratives (such as Marxism) to define and thus control their subaltern states and subjects.

Spivak's work has been especially influential in focusing critical attention on the significance of the concept-

metaphor of woman for the practice of postcolonial theory. For Spivak, women become the ultimate subalterns— wholly unvoiced, wholly displaced, stripped of identity within and without. As such, her (woman's) position is one of extreme discursive usefulness. Spivak's construction of histories for such displaced subaltern women has constituted a significant portion of her contribution to the field.

Said and Spivak are tied together, despite their very different reactions to and uses of the work of Derrida and Foucault, by the desire to effect a political goal through their scholarly work. Both Said and Spivak assert overt political agendas, and both evaluate available critical approaches in terms of their usefulness for furthering those political ends.

Bhabha. Homi K. Bhabha's essays, collected in *The Location of Culture*, return to some of the questions raised by Fanon in the 1950s, looking again at the issue of the subjectivity formation of the colonized person. Bhabha's project focuses on an attempt to theorize the ways in which colonized and colonizing subjects are determined by their colonial relationships, and to challenge any notion of simple polar dissimilarity between the two groups. Identity formation and the ways in which it is manifested through representations of Self and Other are his major interests, leading him to question practices of image making and imaginary spatial positioning. This approach incorporates an understanding of the aesthetic as a means of creating identities within social space.

In "Of Mimicry and Man," included in *The Location of Culture*, Bhabha sets out to describe some of the ways that colonial cultures imagine an identity for the cultures that they dominate. Unlike Said and Spivak, whose methods of analysis are essentially textual, Bhabha provides a descriptive narrative highly reliant on the ideas of psychoanalysis, especially those of Jacques Lacan. He sets up the idea of mimicry as one of the fundamental ways in which the colonizer invents a colonial subject who is always both controllable and in need of control. The colonized is put into an identity construct that mimics the colonizer's own identity: the colonized subject is always *almost* but *not quite* like the colonizer.

This complex relationship of sameness and difference informs Bhabha's notion of the essential hybridity of colonized identities. In "Signs Taken for Wonders" (also included in *The Location of Culture*), Bhabha tells us that

> produced through the strategy of disavowal, the *reference* of discrimination is always to a process of splitting as the condition of subjugation: a discrimination between the mother culture and its bastards, the self and its doubles, where the trace of what is disavowed is not repressed but repeated as something *different*—a mutation, a hybrid.

For Bhabha, this ambivalence becomes the heart of the relationship constructed by the colonizer. It provides the ground for colonial control: the colonial subject, insofar as she or he is never precisely like (never as good as, as able as, as civilized as) the colonizer, is in need of the colonizer's guidance and aid. Insofar as the colonized is almost like the colonizer, the colonized can be controlled, which means that she or he is fertile ground for the colonizer's efforts at civilization and social control.

Bhabha suggests that within the constructed thinking of the colonial mind, the native is fixed at the boundaries of civilization, the liminal space from which the white person feels her own presence begin. The colonizer projects the native as almost like (but not quite like) herself. This double (k)not (not different, not the same) that binds the relationship is presented by the colonizer as transparent: yet in order to keep it fixed, it must be constantly repeated. The terms of the colonizer's stereotype threaten one another: "almost" implies the possibility of the native becoming the same as the white man, whereas "not quite" implies that the native could become so wholly Other that the white person might lose the ability to know and thus to control the native. Neither of these changes would permit the continuation of the colonial situation. Thus, the representation of the colonized is couched in terms of eternity—terms that insist on the fundamentally static nature of the colonized culture.

Bhabha's Lacanian foundation becomes apparent in his discussion of the colonizer's controlling gaze. Gaze, which is linked to the exertion of control, is also linked to desire. It is here that the colonizer's construction of a colonized subject elides into a threat. Desire and gaze are associated with lack as well as with control. Bhabha suggests that because the colonizer has imagined a colonized that is not quite like himself, he has constructed for himself a lack that can never be made up: the colonizer will never be able to gaze on this invisible face of the colonized. This unredressable lack threatens the colonizer's feelings of control and well-being.

Bhabha theorizes that the colonizer makes the native an alien in her own land. The realm of the construction of the relationship between colonial and colonized is, in Bhabha's thinking, essentially spatial. Who owns this space? The colonial eye/I makes a representation of the colonized in order to define the space of control. The eye/I that makes this space delights in its control: the eye/I sees the colonized, but the colonized cannot return that gaze. The I/eye surmises that the colonized is unaware of being watched, too innocent, too foolish to feel the eyes on her back. But even as the colonizer asserts dominance over the space of the colonized, with the gaze of secret surveillance, secret fears tear at the core of this construct. The colonizer's fantasy of control, of possession itself, produces a phobia of impotence. The ability to make a representation—to make an image—hinges on the ability of the colonizer to know, to define, to see the colonized.

It is that very need to represent, and to anxiously rehearse and repeat the terms of the representation, that demon-

strates the colonizer's suppressed awareness of the limits of that knowing/defining/seeing. The colonizer's image construct is a product both of power and of lack of power. The colonial construct of the native further complicates this situation. As the native is almost (but not quite) of the same nature as the colonizer, so the native can almost (but not quite) be represented within the framework of the colonial mind. The impossibility of representing the truly other, the wholly alien, eats away at the colonial vision.

The delight that the colonial eye/I took in its illicit possession of the native village/body is tainted by limits imposed by its fixed position. This static viewing position is written into all representations of the colonized—into the stereotypes of the enigmatic Oriental, the lying Indian, the primitive African. The colonizer's paradox goes like this: the only thing more dangerous than a native who lies is one who tells the truth: the only thing more dangerous than the native who cannot be seen is the native who can.

Within the pleasure taken in the colonial eye/I's scopic surveillance of the native, there lives the fear that the native will respond with some scopic surveillance of his/her own. There exists always the fear/the threat of the returned gaze. The colonizing eye prefers to construct an uncomfortably incomplete representation of the native, rather than to construct a representation that would allow the native access to this power. Hence the native is turned away from the gaze of the colonizing eye/I. The colonizer cannot see him or her (or it?)—but only in this way is the colonizing gaze assured of safety from the reciprocal desires manifested in the colonized subject's own gaze.

In Bhabha's work, the making of the colonial representation constructs two subjects: the colonized and the colonizer. The representation exists only in the colonist's mind. In the ambivalent shifting of desire, fear, possession, and lack, the categories of Self and Other are constantly under formation and re-formation. The existence of the two categories depends on their relation and response to one another. In the colonial construction, ultimately both self and other belong within the colonizing consciousness. As the eye/I constructs its oppositional they, the eye/I disappears; and as the eye/I reasserts itself, the they fades away. Ultimately, both eye/I and they must inhabit a tenuous relation of partial presencing in order to allow for and account for the Other.

Modes of analysis such as the ones sketched here are ultimately appealing because, within the sphere of cultural and aesthetic analysis, they enable a recognition of the significant conditions that peculiarly inform postcolonial societies and cultures. The postcolonial condition includes a particularly vital present-day relationship to history: the postcolonial identity is simultaneously constituted by its history and by a need to break with that history and become something entirely new and distinct. For the theorist of culture and cultural products, an understanding of this relationship is crucial.

The very popularity of postcolonial studies breeds a new set of problems, however. The steady broadening of the term's usage threatens to eliminate its specific relation to the historical condition of prior colonization and, instead, generally to assign it a catchall meaning aligned with any condition of marginality. While widening the possibilities for employing the term's attendant theories, this must inevitably weaken the potency of both term and theories, decreasing their usefulness for unraveling specific modes of social discourse.

At the same time, it is worth remembering that postcolonialist theory is predicated on the existence of difference and the dangers of essentialism, or subscribing to monolithic understanding of entire cultures or peoples. Formulations that rely on the existence of some monolithic "postcolonial condition," "postcolonial subject," or "postcolonial discourse" threaten to recreate the colonial situation, in which the postcolonial intellectual's academic discourse serves simply to reconstitute the West-East knowledge/power relationship of ownership and domination. The discussion of postcolonial women is especially problematic, with certain formulations threatening to create an essentialized "third-world Woman" who serves only as a foil for Western feminist intervention.

In other words, as many theorists at work in the field acknowledge, postcolonial theory threatens, at worst, to erase the various, singular words and actions of actual postcolonial peoples in favor of the ideas of an intellectual elite located within the Western academic system. The lived experiences of the colonized and formerly colonized become raw data to be fed into the machinery of postcolonial theory. Once again, East becomes mere fodder for the global theory knowledge-making activities of the West. The theorist becomes the hero of the piece, the one capable of explaining the postcolonial past and present to the very players who lived out that history. As postcolonial theorists square off against one another, debating variations of their conceptual constructs, postcolonial subjects become pawns whose location matters only in terms of institutional one-upmanship.

This leaves Western scholars in the following situation: we can either discuss the postcolonial situation and in doing so, potentially perpetuate it, or we can ignore it entirely, thereby *certainly* perpetuating it. Said's and Spivak's preoccupation with the motivated political aspects of their work must be recognized as crucial to this dilemma. Perhaps it is only when postcolonial theory is deliberately wielded as a political tool, aimed at unsettling the dominant power relationships linking the cultures of center and margin, that it might hope to escape becoming simply another excuse for the production of academic symposia, panel discussions, journal articles, and encyclopedia entries.

[*See also* African Aesthetics; Caribbean Aesthetics; Cultural Studies; Indian Aesthetics; Orientalism; Politics and Aesthetics; *and* Primitivism.]

BIBLIOGRAPHY

Adam, Ian, and Helen Tiffin, eds. *Past the Last Post: Theorizing Postcolonialism and Post-modernism.* Calgary, 1990.
Appiah, Kwame Anthony. "Is the Post- in Postmodern the Post- in Postcolonial?" *Critical Inquiry* 17.2 (Winter 1991): 336–357.
Ashcroft, Bill, Gareth Griffiths, and Helen Tiffin. *The Empire Writes Back: Theory and Practice in Post-colonial Literatures.* London and New York, 1989.
Ashcroft, Bill, Gareth Griffiths, and Helen Tiffin, eds. *The Post-colonial Studies Reader.* London and New York, 1995.
Bhabha, Homi K., ed. *Nation and Narration.* London and New York, 1990.
Bhabha, Homi K. *The Location of Culture.* London and New York, 1994.
Fanon, Frantz. *The Wretched of the Earth.* Translated by Constance Farrington. New York, 1963.
Fanon, Frantz. *Black Skin, White Masks.* Translated by Charles Lam Markmann. New York, 1967.
Hutcheon, Linda. "Circling the Downspout of Empire: Postcolonialism and Postmodernism." *Ariel* 20.4 (October 1989): 149–175.
Mercer, Kobena. "Diaspora Culture and the Dialogic Imagination." In *Blackframes: Critical Perspectives on Black Independent Cinema,* edited by Mbye B. Cham and Claire Andrade-Watkins, pp. 50–61. Cambridge, Mass., 1988.
Nochlin, Linda. "The Imaginary Orient." In *The Politics of Vision: Essays on Nineteenth-Century Art and Society,* pp. 33–59. New York, 1989.
Parry, Benita. "Problems in Current Theories of Colonial Discourse." *Oxford Literary Review* 9.1–2 (1987): 27–58.
Said, Edward W. *Orientalism.* New York, 1978.
Said, Edward W. *The World, the Text, and the Critic.* Cambridge, Mass., 1983.
Said, Edward W. *Culture and Imperialism.* New York, 1993.
Spivak, Gayatri Chakravorty. "Subaltern Studies: Deconstructing Historiography." In *In Other Worlds: Essays in Cultural Politics,* pp. 197–221. New York and London, 1987.
Spivak, Gayatri Chakravorty. "Can the Subaltern Speak?" In *Marxism and the Interpretation of Culture,* edited by Cary Nelson and Lawrence Grossberg, pp. 271–313. Urbana, Ill., 1988.
Spivak, Gayatri Chakravorty. *The Post-colonial Critic: Interviews, Strategies, Dialogues.* Edited by Sarah Harasym. New York and London, 1990.
Tiffin, Chris, and Alan Lawson, eds. *De-scribing Empire: Postcolonialism and Textuality.* London and New York, 1994.
Williams, Patrick, and Laura Chrisman, eds. *Colonial Discourse and Post-colonial Theory: A Reader.* New York, 1994.
Young, Robert. *White Mythologies: Writing History and the West.* London and New York, 1990.
Young, Robert. *Colonial Desire: Hybridity in Theory, Culture, and Race.* London and New York, 1995.

ELIZABETH CORNWELL

POSTMODERNISM. [*To clarify the phenomenon of postmodernism, this entry comprises three essays:*

Historical and Conceptual Overview
Postmodern Dance
Postmodern Poetry

The first essay is examines the meaning, history, and current status of postmodernism as both a historical and an aesthetic concept. This overview is followed by essays that explain what postmodernism has meant in the specific arts of dance and poetry—two areas where postmodernism has been particularly important. While the focus in both essays is on the American context of postmodernism, the broader, international context is also discussed. For a discussion of postmodern architecture, see Architecture; *for postmodern art, see* Contemporary Art. *For related discussion, see* Appropriation; Modernism; *and* Poststructuralism.]

Historical and Conceptual Overview

The more one begins to fathom the plethora of discourses, theories, sociocultural conditions, art objects, stylistic traits and historical events that are called, envisioned, stigmatized, or theorized as postmodern, the less it is clear that there is any clear and coherent object of study to be encompassed by the encyclopedic imagination. Thus at issue in an overview of postmodernism is the question of what an overview ought to look like, granted the diffuse, fragmentary, multi-dimensional, and contestable character of the object of study. The problem is not insuperable, but is indeed one at the very origin of postmodernism itself, which is why we begin with a statement of it. For the epistemological difficulties raised about 1) the coherence of an object of study (here: "postmodernism"), 2) the capacity of a genre (here: the encyclopedia) to provide a coherent narrative of that object of study, and 3) the socio-politics of the "archive" (the storehouse of texts, the fabric of research, the social attitudes) out of which the narrative is composed, are issues at the heart of the postmodern debate. Certain postmodernists throw their hands up in glee over the supposed collapse of the project of rendering the world comprehensible at all—even in "overview" terms, while others seek to expand our sense of how the world is composed (the unity of the object, the structure of the subject), and how our languages capture it: making these terms more elastic, multi-perspectival, and contextual. We should be obliged to keep this issue in mind in what follows.

History of Postmodernism. The history of the postmodern—that is, of a collection of events with roots in modern life, modernism in the arts, and post-war economics and politics,—events which are, some will say, still occurring—is straightforward enough. The term *postmodernism* was first made popular by Ihab Hassan, who used it to characterize emerging trends in the literature in the 1960s. Such writers as John Barth, Donald Barthelme, and, later, Thomas Pynchon, responding to the great stylistic and conceptual breakthrough of James Joyce's *Finnegans Wake* and the work of Samuel Beckett, began to write novels that played with the very idea of the novel—novels whose twists of language, contortions of plot, multiple narrative voices, unclarities of narrative resolution, and stylistic games called into question the claims of the novel to objectivity and authority in characterizing, explaining, and, in general, picturing its subject. Whereas the classic vision of the novel as articulated by Stendhal described the novel as a mirror being carried along a road, as if the novelistic form were nothing but a transparent recording device that presented reality in its deepest form, these novels called attention to their lack of transparent connection to reality—to the fact that they are acts of creative writing that arise out of literary genres. By extension they called attention to the prismatic nature of reality itself. The epistemological self-suspicions voiced by the postmodern novel (suspicions no doubt already present in nascent form in such great modernist works as Joseph Conrad's) may also be found in the early poststructuralist writings of the 1960s. It is as if the postmodern novel were written in tandem with the writing of Jacques Derrida, whose critique of subjectivity, authorship, and truth, whose attention to the artifices, complexities of dissemination, and intertextual nature of writing, whose exposure of the contradictions in its conceptual organization, and whose play with language, are of a piece with these novels. Roland Barthes also spoke of the exhaustion of the novel as a genre, and raised the question in his work of what it means to write in an exhausted art form (the question of the one who comes too late).

These attitudes shared by postmodern novelists and certain poststructuralist writers prepared a later interweaving between postmodernism and poststructuralism. Many theoretical pictures or definitions of the postmodern are provided by poststructuralism, and these definitions—whether adequate or not—enter the fabric of postmodern arts. Postmodern art has continually relied on poststructuralist ideas (about the critique of the unity of the subject, the failure of discourse to contain the world through its conceptual "laws," about the implication of language in the history of power, about the collapse of traditions of philosophical objectivity and historical progress), and in its later phases on feminist and multicultural ideas, in articulating to itself its own concerns and investing its art with theoretical power and perspicuity. This infusion of theory into the practice of the arts is itself a legacy from modern art, which had already relied on its own theories and the theories of others in investing its art with meaning and force, in articulating its artistic experiments and lending it a theoretical and a political voice. Through theory conjoined with artistic experimentalism, art claims to make a statement to the world about life, art, the institutions of art, to speak in a political voice. In turn, poststructuralism formulates its theories partially in response to modern and postmodern art (Marcel Duchamp, René Magritte, Valerio Adami, John Cage, Dada, Surrealism, and so on).

Postmodernism then comes into play in architecture in the late 1960s and early 1970s. It is roughly datable to the writings and architecture of Robert Venturi, whose book *Learning from Las Vegas* claimed that the urges of modern architecture—to impose utopian changes on the lives of

POSTMODERNISM: Overview. Charles Moore, *Piazza d'Italia* (1978). New Orleans. (Photograph courtesy of Michael Kelly.)

everybody through an architecture whose purist principles could be elaborated prior to all actual building contexts—were almost totally wrong. Turning from the high to the low, Venturi stated with admirable cheek that the buildings of Las Vegas could serve as worthy architectural models for the United States in virtue of their intelligent adaptation to the context of the automobile, their inventiveness, and their dramatic elaborations of architectural space. His early buildings from that time sent up modernism by interpolating "wrong" architectural details into essentially modernist structures (cf. his Guild House). (More profoundly disturbational to the concept of art were Cage's riotous interpolations of the sounds of everyday life into the space of music and Merce Cunningham's recasting of dance forms into vernacular [everyday] movements produced in part by chance operations. Cage and Cunningham aimed to overrule those hierarchies according to which art is distinguished from the flow of life itself.)

Architecture could hardly survive indefinitely on a joking style, and it tended to move in a variety of directions in accord with Venturi's injunctions: (1) to build contextually in terms of local vernaculars, in terms of the desires of local patrons, the specific needs of cities, towns, and distinctive populations; (2) to play the game of stylistic juxtaposition and pluralism; and (3) to retain the game of high modernist send up (turning it into a somewhat stale joke). Architecture also continued modernist stylistics in a number of ways, retaining modular construction, open plans, and (in some domains) theory-based architecture.

Architectural pluralism began as free and wonderful aesthetic innovation but all too often degenerated into mere consumerism, with the architect treating the variety of extant styles as mere consumer products locatable in a huge cultural department store called "the global museum" and juxtaposing these for no other reason than to come up with the latest architecturally new "look" for the client to consume. As buildings turned into consumer products, attention to the complex issues surrounding stylistic appropriation and pluralistic context diminished. This degeneration of the artist or architect into a mere consumer and the artwork into something to be valued by its audience as little more than a commodity is a general postmodern tendency, one theorized as the result of late capitalism's colonization of the cultural sphere by Fredric Jameson, David Harvey, and others. Other strands of architecture continued avant-garde norms of theory-based design. Thus, for example, the deconstructionist architecture of Peter Eisenman aims to speak philosophically against architectural totality and determinacy and for the idea of architecture as an event through its "deconstructionist" look. The claim of the postmodern to speak through its spectacular look or theatrical event—itself a legacy of avant-garde shock values—places postmodern art securely within the space of the "society of the spectacle" (Debord, 1967).

Visual arts exhibit a similar trajectory to that of architecture in the 1970s and 1980s. What Arthur C. Danto has called the creative pluralism of the 1970s (in which visual art, like architecture, freed itself from minimalist/modernist canons of purity and discovered the norms of free expression and juxtaposition) gave way (especially in New York) to "the painting of importance" (Danto). This painting arrived with a size, inscrutability, and suggestion of depth guaranteed to impress the viewer who enjoyed being seduced into the illusion of meaningfulness, and who wished to consume and collect greatness as if it were a glamour product available with the immediacy by which television delivers the news. The concept of meaningfulness became replaced by its simulacrum (Jean Baudrillard), as "you invest[ed] in the divinity of the masterpiece" (Barbara Kruger). Paintings by David Salle, Rodney Allen Greenblatt, and Julian Schnabel are often mentioned in this regard, although each of these artists may also be given a counterreading.

Other regions of postmodern art have aimed to voice their suspicions of this commodification of art (even if these artists have sometimes ended up generating their own commodification in the process). These regions have also voiced suspicions about the history of representation and their place in this history. They have done so by theatricalizing art and its history in the manner of Duchamp, creating games played in and around art that aim to expose the practices of art as veils that silently encode attitudes of omnipotence, ideology, gender, and degradation—art practices ironically played out under the guise of the beautiful, the natural, and the sublime. (Again, poststructuralist ideas have informed this art.) At its best, postmodern art also comprehends that power is produced and conveyed (in part) through "visualities": by turning words into white hot images and images into spectacles (Debord, Michel Foucault). Such artists (Hans Haacke, Kruger, Jenny Holzer, Cindy Sherman) simulate the guise of the media (photos, newsprint, ads, signage, etc.) in order to symbolically harness its power and subvert this power to the purpose of critique.

Even those regions of art that cannot bear to live in a state bereft of the artistic voices of their past (Anselm Kiefer) are also deeply suspicious of their inheritances, believing the representational schemes of the past can be resurrected only through a rigorous interrogation of their bleak interconnections with social and political life (as in Kiefer's interrogation—as far as it goes—of connections between the grandiose German Romantic voice and the Nazi atrocity).

Postmodernism and Modern Life. *Postmodernism* quickly came into use as a term in sociology, political science, and other academic disciplines as way of characterizing alterations in the structure not only of the arts but also of the greater processes of life in which the arts are set. If postmodernism in the arts has stood in some ambivalent position toward modernism—on the one hand, desiring clear separation from some region of modern art, while on the other, working within the aesthetic legacies that modernism had set up—postmodernism as an academic philosophical position directs its ambivalence toward modernity (the structures, processes, and myths of modern life). Postmodernism in the academy is thus a debate about the dissolution of modernity or its preservation in transformed form (a debate also extending to the role of art in this). This debate is complicated, however, by the difficulty in producing a clear (much less a complete) list of the elements comprising modern life. Different theorists claim that different aspects of modernity (philosophical, cultural, political, economic, geographical, etc.) have broken up just as different artists write the epitaph for different regions of modern art (and, by extension, modern life).

The locus classicus of the theory of modernity is G. W. F. Hegel, who posited as the central structures of modern life those of the state (the nation), with its three modes of absolute spirit (art, religion, and philosophy), its connections to science, its vision of itself as existing within history, and its boundless capacity for self-reflection, self-reflection that could and had produced, in Hegel's self-adulating idea, continuous historical progress. At the basis of this vision is that of humanity as a singular, universal entity capable of being seen and exemplified in the actions of the particular man, a vision which has allowed the West to claim that its men (above all, Hegel himself) speak in the name of everybody. It is this grandiose self-conception held by the West that Gianni Vattimo takes to be the underlying myth that has characterized its modernity. According to Vattimo, the dissolution of this cultural myth and its powerful employment in the history of the West has in turn prepared the West for a multicultural liberation in which history may be written and society understood as multiplex tapestries inclusive of the stories and concerns of everybody, rather than as singular stories that silence the voices of this multitude. Jean-François Lyotard's vision of justice as the free forging of dialogue between different persons (such that none will be consigned to indignity) imposes on art and culture the goal of witnessing differences between persons, thereby searching (in the absence of pregiven rules) to find and invent ways of their speaking and listening to one another. On this view, those regions of postmodern art that attempt to witness how representational schemes are implicated in processes of victimization (Kiefer) and those that remake representational schemes to articulate the identities of persons not yet listened to by society (Sherman, Nancy Spero) are paramount.

By contrast, Harvey believes the conditions of modern life to be defined in terms of economics and geography. For him, modern Fordist capitalism (the production line) has given way to late or "flexible" capitalism in a world of postmodern "space-time compression," with the results that (1) cultural life is commodified as information processes (computers, global markets, telecommunications, etc.) become the locus of capitalism; and (2) we live in Marshall McLuhan's global village, in a state of overstimulation by the flow of information. For Baudrillard it is the media that have engendered the current "age," a desultory age in which we can no longer tell simulacrum from reality, in which reality has become the object of scopophilic interest, and the autonomy of the self is obliterated by the ecstatic pressures of media(tion).

Theories of the Postmodern. The most famous and influential theory of postmodern (and therefore modern) life is Lyotard's. His *The Postmodern Condition: A Report on Knowledge* assumes that three factors jointly define the postmodern. First and foremost, the postmodern is defined by our age's incredulity toward metanarratives—stories that claim to determine the relations between the subject, humanity, objectivity, and the sociocultural or historical spheres—the stories of Hegel, Karl Marx, Christianity, the avant-gardes, and the like. Old metanarratives of legitimation are no longer viable, granted the pressures of late-capitalist production (which turns information into capital), our suspicions of what our totalizing ideas have wrought in this century, and the vague and multiplex dispersion of language games played over forms of knowledge in our contemporary interglobal world. The world is interdisciplinary, multiperspectival, and shifting, thus denying all the old repertoire of justifications for the forms of knowledge. Nor are any new large-scale pictures of legitimation adequate to the terms of the age. Thus, we are skeptical about all general concepts of legitimation. The contemporary instability of knowledge practices to shift and realign themselves also has, according to Lyotard, its positive side; it provides for the possibility of new and creative modes of knowledge in which disciplines converge and social institutions realign. These new sources of knowledge can only be legitimated contextually: in terms of their specific modes of application.

Lyotard's picture of knowledge as a contextual and pluralistic mode of combining old ideas and conceptual styles in new ways can easily be seen to picture trends in the literature, art, and architecture of the 1970s. Indeed, Lyotard believes that avant-garde art is in fact the underlying model for authentic knowledge in general today, with its experimentalism and its capacity (in Lyotard's rosy picture of it) for resisting bourgeois sedimentation through its free experimentalism. Moreover, the postmodern task of witnessing those who are different and forging dialogue between such persons also cannot rest assured by previous acts of legitimation, since the point is to find and invent modes of listening, speaking, and connection that are, by Lyotard's definition, not captured by existing rules.

In general, the postmodern will look very different depending on whether it is pictured as a moment of new opportunity for the West or (primarily) as a moment of loss, breakdown, and corruption. Thus, on the one hand, one has Baudrillard's bleak vision and, on the other, Vattimo's and Lyotard's rosier one.

Each of these theoretical perspectives relies on some favored set of examples that paradigmatically illustrate (and prove the truth of) its analytic categories. Each of these theories therefore may be read to contain an implicit Hegelian (i.e., modern) assumption that the postmodern is a univocal zeitgeist with an underlying shape capable of being explained in terms of that single analytic category that the theory provides. Thus, Baudrillard's vision of the postmodern as a vast simulacrum depends on the choice of television, the media, and the half-real and half-mythical America of his *America* as definitive (Baudrillard, Kiefer, and Sherman would be old modernists). Jameson's vision of the commodification of art, the loss of the "semi-autonomous cultural sphere," and the empty tiredness of this age of stylistic "pastiche" relies on regions of art and architecture already discussed, and on high-concept Hollywood films. Lyotard's vision adulates Duchamp and Cage and nicely characterizes Kiefer. Note also that all these theorists fall into the Eurocentric mode of theorizing the postmodern (and the modern) to the exclusion of most of the world. Little attention is given to the diversity of (plausibly) postmodern cultures. Indeed, even the various cultures of the United States and Europe exhibit distinctive postmodernist features. For example, Italian postmodern art is closer to traditional aesthetic features of the beautiful and the expressive than its counterparts from New York.

Finally, different theories (and different works of art) negotiate the *post* in *postmodern* differently. Some wish to, hope to, intend to, or claim to produce or theorize a radical break with whatever came before the "post" (the avant-garde, modernism, modern life, the nation-state as the paradigmatic modern institution, modernity as a systematic arrangement of concepts including those of objectivity, subjectivity, historical progress, justice, etc.). Others view their *post* phase as a continuation of the past in a modified form, as a pause from it, or even a sublation of it. There is no one way in which the past is received, negotiated, or theorized, but rather many.

Postmodernism and the Classical Concepts of Aesthetics. The discourses of aesthetics arose in the eighteenth century in conjunction with the culture of the museum, and postmodern art is typically suspicious of both, while also remaining unwilling and unable to pry itself away from its dependence on the museum. Postmodern art, when concerned to expose the dark underside of artistic practices, focuses not only on the social codes inscribed in works of art but also on the modes of voyeuristic omnipotence cultivated in art making and art viewing, and the museum is seen to play a central role in the cultivation of what postmodern art history has called (if not fetishized as) "the gaze." When Édouard Manet and, later, Duchamp attack the gaze, they thereby attack the museum (Manet implicitly and Duchamp explicitly), along with those related institutions of art that have participated in its construction and been a crucial condition of its possibility. The museum (and the museumizing imagination associated with it) fixes the art object independently of its original site and turns it into a sight: an object known independently of its enmeshment in the stream of life and redefined through its artificial placement in the visual space and narrative arrangement. It has traditionally served to rewrite the history of art as part of its national patrimony (Benedict Anderson), thus encoding viewers as agents of the nation who are symbolically allowed to revel in their ownership of these objects and this story. Furthermore, by turning the entire colonial world into a museum without walls—into a timeless space of exotic objects (Edward Said) and endlessly repeated calcifications of life—colonialism bridged the museum and the colonial world, laying claim to unbridled possession of and unchallenged epistemic access to both. Were one to speak in a Foucauldian way about the museum, one would refer to it as an institution whose genealogy derives in part from a heterogeneous pattern of power—national, colonizing, and male—that partially brought it about, and that it serves to articulate. This is to speak in a postmodern way, the other side of the equation being the museum's recent contributions to fostering multicultural presentations of art.

Seen from Foucault's perspective, the eighteenth-century discourses of aesthetics—ironically and in spite of their explicit intentions—also played a role in the articulation of this power. In spite of their emphases on the ideals of artistic autonomy, on art's capacity to engender a free play of the human imagination and its role in inculcating a moral community of persons, aesthetic discourses have served the interests of the museumizing imagination by defining fine art and the beautiful in abstraction from art's role in the stream of cultural life. Thus, these discourses helped to legitimate the transposition of art from specific cultural context to museum, and the sedimentation of the museumizing gaze, a gaze now believed to be "aesthetic" because it is abstracted from particular interests, desires, beliefs, and forms of cultural life. The claim of aesthetics that art is there to give pleasure and delight of a sensuous and formal kind was, moreover, precisely what the museum required when it feminized the object before the prideful and possessive gaze of the nationalist, Western, male viewer. No epistemic (or moral) problem could therefore arise in the viewing and interpretation of artworks since they were meant to be viewed "aesthetically" in abstraction from their streams of life—no question about the viewer's own capacity to know, understand, cognize, perceive, or fathom them, no question about their subjectivity. Therefore, a postmodern approach to the history of aesthetics would render these discourses objects of ambivalence: on the one hand, the propounder of thoughts about art we cannot do without and, on the other, deeply implicated in the history of power. Feminist critiques of aesthetic discourses are of this sort.

A postmodern approach to aesthetics would also abjure universal definitions of art and instead stress the diversity of art objects, the contextual nature of artistic construction and definition, the role of art in the stream of life generally, and the opacities of artistic interpretation. It would also, following the thought of Foucault, find the aesthetic to be a basic dimension of the social construction of bodies, whose systems of pleasure and taste are in part products of the history of power. A corollary would be the retrieval of ancient ideas linking the aesthetic to the erotics of pleasure.

Postmodern Explanation of the Postmodern. We may grant both the failure of modern styles of (Hegelian) explanation to place the complex and diffuse set of events that fall under the name of the postmodern into a single procrustean explanatory framework, and of the extreme postmodernist position that gleefully exclaims that neither object of study nor discourse of analysis can therefore allow for any coherent account or "overview." Perhaps the best sketch of the kind of overview we have indeed given is provided by the work of the philosopher Ludwig Wittgenstein. Wittgenstein's work pictures the identity and integrity of concepts in terms of strands of crisscrossing similarities and organic interconnections that hold them together. A Wittgensteinian approach to the postmodern would think of it as a family of related discourses and events (including events in the history of theory), related not in one way but in myriad ways, the myriad of interrelationships defining the concept of the postmodern—or, the postmodern "world." Postmodernism is an interlocking set of language games, related in numerous ways: nothing more and nothing less. Let us further appropriate a thought from Wittgenstein and state that in different contexts of discussion, different conceptions of the postmodern (and different representative examples of it) will be useful or required. Since we give up the Hegelian assumption that there is an age called the postmodern with a single historical shape that can be theorized in accord with a single analytic category, we are thereby freed to use all theories, to test each for its domain, its range, its contexts of use. All will have some use or other. (The key is to avoid becoming a consumer of theories like the artist or architect who consumes rather than recasts styles, something all too rampant in the academy.) Finally Wittgenstein's contextualist thought that our concepts depend for their integrity and use on a broad and interwoven background context will open us up to the right range of explanatory sources for the postmodern—namely, everything. In this sense, Wittgenstein's monumental writings, like Joyce's in literature, inaugurate the postmodern approach to explanation in philosophy.

[*See also* Baudrillard; *and* Lyotard.]

BIBLIOGRAPHY

Anderson, Benedict. *Imagined Communities: Reflections on the Origin and Spread of Nationalism.* Rev. ed. London and New York, 1991.

Baudrillard, Jean. *Simulations.* Translated by Paul Foss, Paul Patton, and Philip Beitchman. New York, 1983.

Baudrillard, Jean. *America.* Translated by Chris Turner. London and New York, 1988.

Danto, Arthur C. *The Transfiguration of the Commonplace: A Philosophy of Art.* Cambridge, Mass., 1981.

Danto, Arthur C. *Beyond the Brillo Box: The Visual Arts in Post-Historical Perspective.* New York, 1992.

Debord, Guy. *La société du spectacle.* Paris, 1967.

Derrida, Jacques. *Dissemination.* Translated by Barbara Johnson. Chicago, 1981.

Docherty, Thomas, ed. *Postmodernism: A Reader.* New York, 1993.

Ferguson, Russell, et al., eds. *Discourses: Conversations in Postmodern Art and Culture.* Cambridge, Mass., 1990.

Foucault, Michel. *The Order of Things: An Archaeology of the Human Sciences.* New York, 1970.

Foster, Hal, ed. *The Anti-Aesthetic: Essays on Postmodern Culture.* Port Townsend, Wash., 1983.

Harvey, David. *The Condition of Postmodernity: An Enquiry into the Origins of Cultural Change.* Oxford and Cambridge, Mass., 1989.

Hassan, Ihab. *The Postmodern Turn: Essays in Postmodern Theory and Culture.* Columbus, Ohio, 1987.

Jameson, Fredric. *Postmodernism: or, The Cultural Logic of Late Capitalism.* Durham, N.C., 1991.

Jencks, Charles A. *The Language of Post-Modern Architecture.* 6th ed. New York, 1991.

Jencks, Charles. *Post-Modernism: The New Classicism in Art and Architecture.* New York, 1987.

Lyotard, Jean-François. *The Postmodern Condition: A Report on Knowledge.* Translated by Geoff Bennington and Brian Massumi. Minneapolis, 1984.

Lyotard, Jean-François. *The Postmodern Explained: Correspondence, 1982–1985.* Translation edited by Julian Pefanis and Morgan Thomas, translations by Don Barry et al. Minneapolis, 1992.

Perloff, Marjorie, ed. *Postmodern Genres.* Norman, Okla., 1988.

Rorty, Richard. *Contingency, Irony, and Solidarity.* Cambridge and New York, 1989.

Said, Edward W. *Orientalism.* New York, 1978.

Vattimo, Gianni. *The End of Modernity: Nihilism and Hermeneutics in Post Modern Culture.* Translated by Jon R. Snyder. Baltimore, 1988.

Vattimo, Gianni. *The Transparent Society.* Translated by David Webb. Baltimore, 1992.

Venturi, Robert. *Complexity and Contradiction in Architecture.* 2d ed. New York, 1977.

Venturi, Robert, Denise Scott Brown, and Stephen Izenour. *Learning from Las Vegas: The Forgotten Symbolism of Architectural Form.* Rev. ed. Cambridge, Mass., 1977.

Wellmer, Albrecht. *The Persistence of Modernity: Essays on Aesthetics, Ethics, and Postmodernism.* Translated by David Midgley. Cambridge, Mass., 1991.

Wittgenstein, Ludwig. *Philosophical Investigations.* 3d ed. Translated by G. E. M. Anscombe. New York, 1968.

DANIEL HERWITZ

Postmodern Dance

In dance, the term *postmodern* is used differently from its application in the other arts. In the other arts, especially architecture, the visual arts, and literature, the term *postmodern* is used to refer to art that sets itself in opposition to high modernism in various ways: by making allusions to the history of the art form; by eliding "high" and "low" culture in the self-conscious fusion of modernism with the vernacular; and by embracing pleasure and rejecting austerity. Postmodern artworks are thus said to challenge values of originality, authenticity, and the masterpiece by copying, commenting on, or otherwise "deconstructing" modernist artworks, perhaps thereby offering political resistance to dominant Western culture. They reintroduce representation, but by making representations of representations.

Yet, often it has been in the arena of postmodern dance that issues of modernism in the other arts have arisen: for example, the acknowledgment of the medium's materials, the revealing of dance's essential qualities as an art form, the separation of formal elements, the abstraction of forms, and the elimination of external references as subjects. Certain aspects of postmodern dance also fit, however, with current notions of postmodern culture: irony, playfulness, historical reference, the use of vernacular materials, the breakdown of boundaries between art forms and between art and life. Charles Jencks has argued that in architecture, postmodern style has a doubly coded aesthetic that appeals to both popular, untutored audiences and to esoteric specialists (Jencks, 1986). In dance, this definition could be used to categorize the work of such crossover choreographers, straddling modern dance and ballet, as Mark Morris and Twyla Tharp. But to do so would be to ignore the term's use since the 1960s to mean something quite different. That is, there is an ambiguity in the use of the term *postmodern dance*. Using it as a historical term has a certain temporal and geographic specificity. In this sense, it is a historical style marker, like the term *German Expressionism.* But there is also an analogical use of the term that is transhistorical and transgeographic. This article will primarily be concerned with the historical use of the term, since that is the way it was introduced into dance-historical and theoretical discourse and that is its primary reference. The analogical uses of the term will also be briefly discussed.

Yvonne Rainer first used the label "postmodern dance" in the 1960s in a strictly chronological sense, referring to her own generation of American dancers as that which came after historical modern dance. In the modern dance of Martha Graham, Doris Humphrey, José Limón, and others, stylized movements and energy levels, organized in legible (usually musical) structures (such as theme and variations, ABA, and so on) conveyed feeling tones and social messages. With the publication of the postmodern dance issue of the *Drama Review* (1975), the term gained wide currency and began to be used to classify what had by then emerged as a style.

Although postmodern dance continued into the 1980s and 1990s and spread from New York to other parts of the United States and internationally, the term is generally used to refer to the values of the 1960s and 1970s, rooted in the origins of the movement in the work of dancers associated with the Judson Dance Theater in New York City, which had by then become recognized as the world center for modern dance. Sally Banes has referred to the 1960s and 1970s as encompassing two phases of postmodern dance: "breakaway" postmodern dance and "analytic" postmodern dance (Banes, 1987). These two phases are discussed here, tracing the history of the genre in terms of its aesthetic and moral commitments.

The early postmodern choreographers saw as their task the purging and amelioration of historical modern dance, which they felt had made unfulfilled promises in regard to the use of the body and the social and artistic functions of dance. The radical departures of Merce Cunningham's dances and John Cage's theories of music and performance formed an important base from which many of the ideas and actions of the postmodern choreographers sprang, either in opposition or in a spirit of extension.

Perhaps the most important principle, for the dancers of the breakaway years, was the Cageian idea that boundaries between art and life should be broken down. This led them away from Cunningham's virtuosic technique as well as from the theatricality of modern dancers like Graham. Perhaps the most important break with the past was their use of the ordinary body and workaday, nondance actions (parallel to Cage's opening up of music to ordinary, nonmusical sounds). For some, this was simply an aesthetic issue—a way to refresh the exploration of movement qualities by using bodies that were not already constrained by a given dance technique. But for many, this—along with the cooperative structure of the Judson Dance Theater group—stemmed from a political commitment to the democratic ideals of equality and freedom. It was meant to embody equal rights, to level the playing field so that even the nonspecialist could perform, and so that all members of the audience might find something familiar (or at least doable) in the dance spectacle they beheld. Out of this perspective, a communitarian ethos emerged in many of the works.

Thus, in Rainer's *We Shall Run* (1963), a group of twelve adults—dancers and nondancers, in work clothes ranging from suits to sweatpants—runs steadily in shifting patterns that cause them to group and regroup for seven minutes to music by Hector Berlioz. There are no permanent leaders; every time someone seems to head the group for a time, the changing floor plan guarantees that a new facing will produce a new leader—from the back of the flock this time. The temporary leaders are sometimes men, sometimes women; the large group is not factionalized, but harmoniously and with a purposeful mien constantly divides in random groups and then reunites. The image is one of a serious, even heroic, egalitarian collective.

But the incorporation of the ordinary into choreography extended not only to including the nondancers' bodies onstage. It framed ordinary movements and quotidian gestures, even by trained dancers, as worthy of notice in a dance. This was an aspect of democratic leveling that celebrated the mundane, the awkward, and other aspects of movement that, it was felt, had previously been overlooked in both ballet and modern dance, which had privileged special, heightened, theatrical movements.

As well, the postmodern dancers showed that any space could be an appropriate stage. As the dance critics raised their eyebrows, the postmoderns danced in church sanctuaries, gymnasiums, lofts, galleries, outdoors in fields, and in all sorts of other buildings and nontheatrical sites.

Arthur Danto has argued that 1964 was the key year in the history of modern art, because in that year Andy Warhol's *Brillo Boxes* confronted the art world with the possibility that something indiscernible from an ordinary object could be an artwork. In 1963, however, at Judson Dance Theater concerts, postmodern choreographers had already anticipated Warhol's breakthrough in dances like *We Shall Run* and Judith Dunn's *Acapulco*, which included a woman ironing a dress and combing another woman's hair and two women playing cards. These dances raised the question of the difference between dance and ordinary movement. If Warhol leveled the perceptible distance between artworks and real things, Rainer, Dunn, Steve Paxton, and others attempted to put dance on a par with everyday gesture. Undoubtedly, an aspect of this leveling was not merely an exercise in aesthetic experimentation, but political symbolism as well.

And the demotic ideal focused not only on issues of equality but also on aspirations to freedom. In this, the body—with its complex social meanings—served as a potent medium. An unabashed examination of the body and its functions and powers threaded through early postmodern dance. One form it took was relaxation, a deliberate letting go of the tight control that has characterized much Western dance technique (both in ballet and modern dance). This loosening of the body's boundaries metaphorically stood for liberation from cultural restrictions, foreshadowing the many modes of bodily freedom practiced in the late 1960s. Basing dances on children's games and free play also served as a model for escaping adult bodily strictures. Simone Forti explored these in dances such as *See-Saw* (1960) and *Huddle* (1961). Another form of searching for the emancipated body was the use of nudity, as in Robert Morris's *Waterman Switch* (1965), in which he and Rainer appeared totally nude, walking slowly while clinched in an embrace. Many dances espoused liberation from bourgeois codes of propriety by celebrating erotic pleasure, as in Carolee Schneemann's *Meat Joy* (1964), an orgiastic performance in which men and women undressed one another, painted one another's bodies, cavorted with raw fish, chicken, and hot dogs, and generally indulged in making a mess with paper, paint, and other objects. Yet another aspect of the body and its open boundaries was various references to bodily processes, from eating to digestion, as in Paxton's works involving food and plastic inflatable tunnels, reminiscent of digestive tracts.

The years 1968 through 1973 saw more political themes and contexts emerge in postmodern dance, which, like the experimental theater movement, participated in the heightened political activism around the country. Active audience engagement extended the democratic values of the early 1960s even in ostensibly nonpolitical dances, for instance, Trisha Brown's *Rummage Sale and the Floor of the Forest* (1971), in which old clothes were threaded through a rope grid and two dancers worked their way through it, while the audience had to choose between watching them and participating in a genuine rummage sale taking place below. In a gesture of democratic leveling, Brown seemed to put the "special" theater event—the dance performance—on a par with a perfectly ordinary event.

The rise of improvisational groups like the Grand Union advanced the theme of liberation through methods that stood metaphorically for freedom. Many dances, such as Deborah Hay's *Deborah Hay with a Large Group Outdoors* (1969), mobilized large groups as if inspired by the political movements of the late 1960s.

But other dances were more explicitly engaged in anti–Vietnam War, black liberation, or feminist politics. This, too, was part of the democratic project of this generation, for although undemocratic countries also fight wars, these choreographers exercised their right to protest the war, just as millions of demonstrators did. Dances that supported the liberation of African Americans and women fitted with democratic ideals of freedom as well as equal rights. In 1970, Rainer choreographed *WAR* as well as a street protest, and she contributed a dance to the Judson Flag Show, supporting the rights of artists to use the flag in their works. In 1971, the Grand Union gave a benefit performance for the Black Panthers, and a women's improvisation collective, the Natural History of the American Dancer, was formed. Paxton's *Intravenous Lecture* (1970) protested censorship, and his *Collaboration with Wintersoldier* (1971) was an antiwar piece done in collaboration with a Vietnam veterans group. Contact improvisation evolved,

beginning in 1972, as an alternative social network as well as an alternative dance technique and performance format (Novack, 1990).

Although many of the white dancers supported civil rights for African Americans or even the Black Power movement, for complex historical reasons, very few African Americans were involved in the early postmodern dance movement. The aesthetic and political objectives of the black dance movement in the 1960s diverged sharply from the predominantly white postmodern dance. Although at times the broad political goals of the two groups may have coincided, the paths toward those goals were quite separate (with one notable exception in Gus Solomons, Jr.) until the 1980s, when a younger group of African-American choreographers identified themselves as "bicultural" artists—both black and postmodern.

By 1973, a wide range of basic questions about dance had been raised in the arena of postmodern choreography. A new phase of consolidation and analysis began, building on the issues that the experiments of the breakaway years had unearthed. Michael Kirby has defined the genre at this stage:

> In the theory of postmodern dance, the choreographer does not apply visual standards to the work. The view is an interior one: movement is not pre-selected for its characteristics but results from certain decisions, goals, plans, schemes, rules, concepts, or problems. Whatever actual movement occurs during the performance is acceptable as long as the limiting and controlling principles are adhered to. . . . In the discussion of their work, the post-modern dancers do not mention such things as meaning, characterization, mood, or atmosphere. (Kirby, 1975)

Although Kirby does not refer to stylistic features, in fact, the conceptual basis of analytic postmodern dance and its systematic attention to the essential features of dance had given rise to an identifiable style. It was casual, dispassionate, and ascetic. If the watchword of the early 1960s was *play,* that of the seventies was *work*. Postmodern dance no longer participated in an unruly, carnivalesque disruption of social boundaries, or in a mass political movement, but rather, moved into a laboratory to carry out serious investigations into dance, attempting to strip the art form down to its quintessence.

In order to do this, choreographers did away with extra theatrical trappings like music, special lighting, costumes, and props, as well as what Kirby has elsewhere called the theatrical "matrices" of character and place (Kirby, 1969). Or, if they used them, it was to disrupt theatrical illusion and "bare the devices" of the dance. Choreographers used simple movements, often performed with a low-energy, uninflected phrasing, in structures of comparison and contrast that would allow for reflection on the medium of dance itself.

In analytic postmodern dance, movement became objective as it was distanced from personal expression through the use of scores, bodily attitudes that suggested—in a democratic spirit—work and other ordinary daily movements, verbal commentaries, and tasks. These dances called attention to the workings of the body in an almost scientific way. The anti-illusionist approach demanded close viewing and clarified the smallest unit of dance, shifting the emphasis from the phrase to the step or gesture. For instance, in Lucinda Childs's *Particular Reel* (1973), the choreographer walks along twenty-one parallel lines, making her way in silence from one corner of the space to the opposite corner, while rotating and reeling her arms in a three-minute phrase that then reverses and finally repeats in its original order.

Esoteric as these research projects may sound, they nevertheless partook of the democratic project, for as they immersed themselves in the exploration of the dance medium, the postmodern choreographers did so by rejecting virtuosity as well as the specialized symbols and conventions of theatrical dancing. One of the most obvious divergences from modern dance and ballet was the rejection of musicality and rhythmic organization. But also, postmodern choreographers retained the 1960s renunciation of refined bodily techniques. They were no longer necessarily committed to a project of audience accessibility—perhaps they had come to realize that popular audiences found art that broke down boundaries between art and life less, rather than more, accessible than conventional high-art masterpieces—but they nevertheless subscribed to a democratic aesthetic of the ordinary, insisting on the evidence of the senses and getting back to basics.

Although the analytic mode of postmodern dance dominated the mid-1970s, another strand developed out of related sources. The spiritual aspect of the same asceticism that led to the clarification of simple movements led in another way to devotional expression. The appreciation of non-Western dance as an alternative to Western dance techniques led to an interest in the spiritual, religious, healing, and social functions of dance in other cultures. The disciplines of the martial arts forms led to new metaphysical as well as physical techniques. The spinning dances of Laura Dean and Andy deGroat, recalling Sufi dances, fell somewhere between images of private and communal devotion. Related to this metaphysical strand of postmodern dance was a metaphoric style, for instance, in the mythic, theatrical works of Meredith Monk and in Kenneth King's uses of dance as a metaphor for technology, information and power systems, and the mind itself. Metaphoric postmodern dance included the expressive theatrical means and representations analytic postmodern dance had eschewed. But it still differed from modern dance in significant ways. These dances drew on the processes and techniques of postmodern choreography, especially that of radical juxtaposition. They also used ordinary movements and objects; they proposed new relationships between the performer and spectator; they employed pronounced stillness and marked repeti-

tion; and they participated in the distribution system—the lofts, galleries, and downtown theaters—that had become the venues for postmodern dance. Harking back to Cage's zen tenets, the metaphysical and metaphoric postmodern dancers united the quotidian with the spiritual.

For several reasons—among them New York's dominance in the international art world generally after World War II, that city's centrality to the development of American modern dance, and the quiescence of postwar German modern dance—New York was the site where postmodern dance emerged in the 1960s and 1970s. By the 1970s, however, postmodern dance spread throughout the United States and began to be exported abroad through tours of American postmodern dancers as well as an influx of European, Canadian, and Japanese dancers studying and performing in New York. The situation in dance internal to various countries, partly influenced by American postmodern dance, resulted in distinctive national avant-garde movements, including the New Dance movement in Great Britain, *danse actuelle* in Montreal, and *Tanztheater* in Germany. These movements often paralleled, but did not necessarily imitate, the American experience of the 1960s and 1970s. In Japan, the movement known as *butoh*, which correlates in some ways to American postmodern dance, arose during the 1960s and 1970s in reaction to both Japanese traditional dance forms and Western modern dance.

Also, in the 1980s and 1990s, a new movement arose in dance, perhaps most appropriately called postmodern*ist* dance, that was akin to postmodernism in gallery art and architecture. Choreographers of this generation were not necessarily concerned with ordinary movement but, rather, often used virtuosic movement, engaged in theatricality and narrative, made allusions to popular culture, mixed genres of dance from high- and low-art traditions, and raised questions about identity politics, while still taking a critical approach to dance traditions.

[*See also* Dance.]

BIBLIOGRAPHY

Banes, Sally. *Terpsichore in Sneakers: Post-Modern Dance.* 2d ed. Middletown, Conn., 1987.

Banes, Sally. *Democracy's Body: Judson Dance Theater, 1962–1964.* 2d ed. Durham, N.C. 1993.

Banes, Sally. *Greenwich Village 1963: Avant-Garde Performance and the Effervescent Body.* Durham, N.C., 1993.

Carroll, Noël. "Post-Modern Dance and Expression." In *Philosophical Essays on Dance,* edited by Gordon Fancher and Gerald Myers, pp. 95–104. Brooklyn, N.Y., 1981.

Carroll, Noël, and Sally Banes. "Working and Dancing: A Response to Monroe Beardsley's 'What Is Going On in a Dance?'" *Dance Research Journal* 15 (Fall 1982): 37–41.

Copeland, Roger. "Postmodern Dance/Postmodern Architecture/Postmodernism." *Performing Arts Journal* 19 (1983): 27–43.

Danto, Arthur. *After the End of Art: Contemporary Art and the Pale of History.* Princeton, N.J., 1997.

Drama Review 19 (March 1975; T65). Postmodern dance issue.

Febvre, Michèle, ed. *La danse au défi.* Montreal, 1987.

Hoghe, Raimund. *Pina Bausch: Tanztheatergeschichten.* Frankfurt am Main, 1986.

Jencks, Charles. *What Is Post-Modernism?* London and New York, 1986.

Johnston, Jill. "The New American Modern Dance." In *The New American Arts,* edited by Richard Kostelanetz, pp. 162–193. New York, 1965.

Jordan, Stephanie. *Striding Out: Aspects of Contemporary and New Dance in Britain.* London, 1992.

Jowitt, Deborah. *Time and the Dancing Image.* New York, 1988.

Kirby, Michael. Introduction. *Drama Review* 19 (March 1975; T65): 3–4.

Kirby, Michael. "The New Theatre." In *The Art of Time: Essays on the Avant-Garde,* pp. 75–102. New York, 1969.

Kuniyoshi, Kazuko. "Butoh Chronology, 1959–1984." *Drama Review* 30 (Summer 1986): 127–41.

Livet, Anne, ed. *Contemporary Dance.* New York, 1978.

Novack, Cynthia J. *Sharing the Dance: Contact Improvisation and American Culture.* Madison, Wis., 1990.

Rainer, Yvonne. *Work, 1961–1973.* Halifax, 1974.

SALLY BANES

Postmodern Poetry

Describing any aspect of postmodernism is, to a postmodernist, inseparable from enacting it, and hence from partially undoing any truth-value in the description. How can one capture self-reflexively where one actually stands, or what one actually performs, while also trying to bracket one's involvement so as to make testable claims? Problems compound when we turn to contemporary American poetry, since there was a substantial "postmodernism" in the 1950s that is in many ways sharply opposed to contemporary versions, and yet continues to wield considerable influence. There also seem to be in the genre itself certain orientations difficult to reconcile with the versions of postmodernism that now prevail in the art world and in social theory: poetry tends to impose emotional pressures not compatible with relying on the play of simulacra; there is no significant marketplace that poets can ironically manipulate; and poetry makes demands on its audience for close attention to precise articulation and structural intricacy not well suited to immediate consumption and pastiche. Perhaps the only fully postmodern mode for poetry is the poetry slam. Nonetheless, postmodernism remains an important issue for many poets because it provides a rubric for setting "experimental" poetic work in opposition to traditional romantic versions of lyric expression. These oppositions are difficult to fix in any abstract formula, in part because these experiments destabilize the very notion of lyric poetry. It is possible, however, to offer a general definition of contemporary postmodern poetry as a range of efforts to make the condensed space of poetic language responsive to themes and dispositions developed within postmodern theory, such as the celebration of contradiction and heterogeneity, the foregrounding of surfaces, commitments to transgression and marginality, and treatments of the person stressing unstable, decentered, and multiple selves.

The tale of two postmodernisms in poetry begins with the widespread rebellion in the late 1950s against a New Critical establishment that had reduced modernism to a cult of dry, impersonal meditative lyrics intricately balancing passion with ironic distance and suffusing its concern for worldly particulars with an overwhelming sense of mortality. Most of the work that emerged could not be considered postmodern, largely because it turned away from theoretical models of any kind to concentrate on the personal intensities exemplified by Robert Lowell and Sylvia Plath. But Donald Allen's anthology *The New American Poetry, 1945–1960* (1960) would popularize three loose communities of poets that did set themselves the task of directly addressing what seemed changing notions of self, world, and society requiring a distinctively postmodern sensibility. The earliest and most theoretically sophisticated of these emerged from Black Mountain College—preeminently in Charles Olson's writings on poetics and in the poetry of Robert Duncan and Robert Creeley. Olson insisted that the then-dominant concerns for formal balance and closure tied poets to an outmoded metaphysics and psychology: "to take on the post-modern" poets would have to pursue "continuous inquiries into what ways ideality no longer fit modern reality in a form proper to its content." Ideality was problematic because it located the basic values made available by art in the work of formal composition. Hence, the work becomes abstract, something to interpret in terms of how the artist imposed form on experience. This orientation separates the work from the immediate processes of thinking, feeling, and selecting in which the artist's full creative energy might take direct concrete expression. To "restate man" so as to "repossess him of his dynamic," verse had to become "projective": it had to restore a sense of spirit as inseparable from the poet's control of breath as the basis for a rhythm not tied to fixed measure, and it had to make the syllable its cutting edge for the display of intelligence, since there could be no more elemental unit by which to display a selecting intelligence at work. Finally, such unmediated intelligence could establish form in terms of how it gathered "the objects which occur at every given moment of composition (of recognition we can call it)" (ibid.) into a field defined simply by the internal tensions responsible for its intensity. Relying on projective energies does not allow for hypotheses about mysterious inwardness or meditative comprehensiveness. No longer bound to the "lyrical interference of the subject as ego," this poetry could establish "a seriousness" sufficient to cause the thing the poet makes to "take its place alongside the things of nature" (ibid.).

Olson's own poetry has few advocates now, probably because it seems dangerously flat, impersonal, and abstract in its efforts to make concrete descriptions bear large cultural ideals. But Duncan and Creeley opened other possible uses of projectivist concerns for breath and syllable taken up by numerous poets. Duncan transformed Olson's concern for myth into an intricate psychology sustained by a remarkable ear for how syllables might dance together. Creeley used the sense of breath units to bring within the psyche the objectivist techniques of William Carlos Williams, so that his poetry seemed excruciatingly exact and direct in its renderings of personal states. Creeley showed how poetry could build dense lyrical presence by an intelligence at the level of the syllable's refusing any of the trappings of well-made representational artifice.

By the mid-1950s this suspicion of artifice had also become central for the New York art world and the poets who worked within the sense of excitement the art created—first in the action painting of Jackson Pollock, then in the flatbed openness of Robert Rauschenberg and the paradoxical doubling of mediating surfaces in Jasper Johns, and later in the influence of John Cage's elaborate structural ways of freeing the imagination from cultural indoctrination. These models influenced work ranging from the black arts aesthetics of Amiri Baraka to Jackson MacLow's chance operations to the talk poems of David Antin. But for contemporaries, Frank O'Hara's work seems to best represent what that art world made possible for a poetry in rebellion against modernist values. Like the confessional poets, O'Hara is completely personal, but his is a version of the personal thinkable only in relation to the fascination with surfaces and folds emerging in the art world of the 1950s; and his is a mode of taking things lightly sadly lacking in poets who continue to sing the tribulations of the romantic ego. O'Hara's "Steps," for example, offers a love poem based entirely on being able to feel "foolish and free" as he celebrates the simple details of wandering through New York. Rather than offer ideas and idealizations of love, O'Hara defines it simply in terms of the atmosphere it creates and the expansiveness it releases:

> oh god it's wonderful
> to get out of bed
> and drink too much coffee
> and smoke too many cigarettes
> and love you so much.

This love, in fact, can be measured precisely by its capacity to free the self from any need to take itself more seriously, and thereby to lose its openness to its environment. Here O'Hara's fluid urban world finds a corresponding subjectivity capable of thriving on contingency and multiplicity.

On the other coast, in San Francisco, quite different formal experiments seemed necessary for freeing postmodern subjectivities. At the center of the revolution was the New Yorker Allen Ginsberg's *Howl* (1956), with its ecstatic refusal of all decorums and its insistence that poetry had to find ways of addressing public life and popular culture without losing either a critical edge or a commitment to soul making as still a viable lyrical ideal. But West Coast writers had their own versions of the postmodern to elaborate, ranging from Gary Snyder's efforts to recast Western experiences of nature in terms compatible with Zen Buddhist models of attention to Jack Spicer's self-hating internalization of Zen emptiness.

As various discursive versions of postmodernism proliferated, each of these modes of writing underwent severe transformations, but without surrendering the two basic demands distinguishing postmodernist ambitions from more traditional lyric work—its resistance to the formal and thematic closure basic to an ideal of well-made artifacts and its foregrounding aspects of experience that emerge within the very processes of writing and hence cannot be captured as aspects of some illusionistic drama. The most elaborate transformations took place as Olson's projectivism came ultimately to serve as one sponsor for the work published in the $L=A=N=G=U=A=G=E$ anthology edited by Charles Bernstein and Bruce Andrews (1978). Olson himself was far too resolutely a New Englander to satisfy the needs that poets conscious of immigrant traditions like Bernstein had as basic to their sense of America. So these language poets crossed projectivism with the objectivist tradition and with the disjunctive work of Gertrude Stein and Louis Zukofsky, in the process providing radically new understandings of how breath and syllable might address postmodern realities.

This is Bernstein's "Use No Flukes":

> Close to stand
> Glitter with edge
> Clouds, what's but
> Weather of devoid
> Uses unwrapping
> Lower the second
> Gravity for allowing, but
> Slowly, as if
> Backward, falling
> Folded

It would be foolish to attempt to interpret this poem in any traditional way. Rather than postulate an imaginative situation that it portrays or that underlies its speaking, we are better off treating it as a painterly exploration of the texture, weight, and possible harmony among verbal elements, each bearing a range of semantic echoes. Notice first how the sounds actually do fall folded into two basic patterns—one characterized by versions of a long *o*, the other by versions of *a*, with "allowing" bringing both melodies into harmony. This flow of echoes then provides a key for approaching what the poem does semantically. Its opening lines can be read as either imperatives or descriptions, so that the play of possibility between noun and verb in the composition of a visual field becomes a literal "grammar for allowing." What this grammar affords is best defined by the closing lines as they bind the work of words to the drifting clouds. If we let ourselves seem to move backward, by analogy to the clouds, we find ourselves as viewers and as readers reaching through our confusions to a glimpse of harmonious reconciliation in the folds that the scene composes, even though, or perhaps because, the language too drifts and will not allow us to confine it to any one representation. We have enough structure to see how there emerges a kind of stability within passing time and loss, if only we can learn to conform our own reading habits to a world in which there is no need to impose specific determinate structures as mirrors of a will to order.

For Bernstein, Olson's emphasis on breath needs to be redirected: the primary energy within the poem is to be attributed not to the writer but to the readers' coming to a grasp of what occurs as their participation deepens within the sets of forces potential within the poem. Olson's emphasis on syllable now provides a means of understanding how a composing intelligence can find satisfactions while it resists the structure of demands inherent in more imposing syntactic and semantic units. As Cage loved to demonstrate, simple depersonalized structure can develop a "gravity for allowing" that is a worthy antagonist to the will to power—a lesson central to Language poets' experiments in form that extend to Ron Silliman's using a Fibonacci series as the framework for his long poem *Tjanting*.

In their more recent work these Language writers have let cogent syntax and some sense of referentiality return, primarily because they have discovered that their purposes are best served by foregrounding a range of voices, as if voices themselves were the actual building blocks of our semantic universe because they most intensively embody a postmodern sense of how social grammars carry embedded emotions and habits and political orientations. Their elemental approach to language then turns out to be a feasible way of making good on Olson's dreams that poetry could become a means of social research because it could make vital America's most fundamental imaginative orientations. Thus, we find Rosemary Waldrop bringing the voices of Puritan Connecticut into conjunction with contemporary life, and we find Susan Howe teaching us to hear both how women came to bear their oppression and how fully writers like Herman Melville and Rowlandson made that resistance the basis for modes of expression valorizing much of what had to remain marginal in relation to the dominant imperial culture.

Language poetry engages postmodern culture by treating poets' encounters with silences and gaps not as openings into some metaphysical site beyond the powers of understanding but as conditions generated by the overlap and discontinuity among language practices within society. Thus, it lends itself not only to the concerns about gender in Howe and Waldrop, but also to various ways that the logic of what Jean-François Lyotard calls "différends" plays out in all cultural domains. Nathanial Mackey, for example, manages to extend Baraka's insistence on immediate political speech into a concern for "discrepant awarenesses" and dissonances through which we gain access to "an unlikely Other whose inconceivable occupancy glimpses of ocean beg access to." Understanding race in America is largely a matter of what we can hear in what is not said or said obliquely or projected beyond seeing. More generally, the same set of poetic resources provides crucial means for keeping cultural diversity in the foreground without collapsing into an identity politics that claims as new the very idealizations of the romantic expressive ego that postmodern poets have been trying to overcome. In the work of Alfred Arteaga and Myung Mi Kim, ethnicity is less a matter of seeking individual identity than of learning to recognize the constraints on lives and the corollary experience of potential powers that emerge for those living in bilingual societies: the more finely poetry attunes us to the social embeddings carried in our senses of voice and linguistic expression, the better it prepares us for appreciating forces and dangers within a multicultural society that extend far beyond the quite limited languages we have for projecting personal and ethnic identities.

The New York school has followed a very different trajectory, keeping issues of contradiction and multiplicity confined primarily to quasi-philosophical reflection. Yet it has in the person of John Ashbery the contemporary poet most fully connectable to postmodern theoretical discourses (perhaps especially when he is in fact indulging his own version of late nineteenth-century decadence). Ashbery retains Olson's and O'Hara's antiartifactual immediacy of the speaking voice alive to its own compositional activity, but for him this sense of presence finds itself wound into an impenetrable set of social echoes that poetry gets us to hear within our language. If there is to be any satisfying sense of personal speech, it will emerge only in and as the quality of play that the poet sets up within a constant process of displacement:

The clarity of the rules dawned on you for the first time.
They were the players, and we who had struggled at the game
Were merely spectators, though subject to its vicissitudes
And moving with it out of the tearful stadium, born on shoulders,
  at last.

The last line here so fully takes on the space of public fantasy that it allows a strange sense of emotional release. In other poems Ashbery asks us to see how "Underneath the talk lies / the moving and not wanting to be moved, the loose / meaning, untidy and simple like a threshing floor." So while the lyric ego is forced to surrender the sense of "permanent tug that used to be its notion of home," it reemerges in an astonishing range of registers leading us from the sliding functions of the *you*s that the imagination invokes to a sense of something driving desire that resists all our efforts to represent it within a cogent language of motives. Multiple, fragmented, contradictory, and evanescent states of self become his lyric version of O'Hara's habitable urban space.

This Ashberyian poetic space has proved a fertile field for younger poets who only now are fully finding their own ways to develop his interplay of floating surfaces with enigmatic resistance to all our interpretive efforts. Where Kenneth Koch emphasizes the comic side of a flip urban imagination, David Shapiro's latest book, *After a Lost Original*, beautifully brings the resources of lyric intensity to the work of furthering that enigmatic psychology:

> We are the sculptors now making our own doors
> The words remain, but the gods are gone for good

The idea remains but the words are gone like gods. In work that increasingly opens itself to highly charged visible fragments evoking and displacing an intense personal pressure, Ann Lauterbach restores to this painterly poetics some of the sharp edges and collagist formal dignity evocative of modernism at its most ambitious, without losing an Ashberyian commitment to the constant slippage among surfaces that may be the only available locus for imaginative life.

The heritage of the San Francisco Renaissance and Beats is now far more diffuse, perhaps because so much of what the Beats created got consumed by and as popular culture. One still hears in recent work echoes of the most intense, least playful poets from that Renaissance, like Spicer and Duncan, especially in the ways that Robin Blaser has brought their ways of approaching myth and discursivity to the lively writing scene in British Columbia. But Beat values have not had much to offer those contemporary cultures where alienation is just bad economics. The interest in Zen fostered by Snyder and Philip Whalen still has considerable currency, however, although often in ways that adapt it to urban Western lifestyles. One might say that Zen provides for these younger West Coast poets a mode of strangeness analogous to what New York poets get from Surrealism and Rousselian enigma. Leslie Scalapino's work provides the purest example of Zen fused with postmodernist versions of the absences that haunt our efforts to make experience articulate, and Michael Palmer's fascination with echoes and mirrors and traces manages to thicken Zen concerns for emptiness by combining that with a profound engagement in the negative dialectics Palmer finds in French modernist writing. Finally, perhaps the most original of Bay area poets, Lynn Hejinian, adapts this strangeness to distinctively Western intricacies of self-consciousness by always positioning her lyrical intelligence on the margins of anything that counts as knowledge. For her the basic quest of poetry is making palpable the "experiencing of experience." In place of pursuing knowledge and its idealities, she tries to decompose "the unity / of the subjective mind by / dint of

its own introspection." Quotation is necessary here because valuing Hejinian's thinking depends on our registering its capacity both to coexist with and to transform the denotative ambitions basic to received ideals of knowledge. Each line break calls attention to the disruption of habitual unities, and the ensemble defines the powers of mind by its capacity to register complex echoes and variations on pacing and weighing of phrases, so that rhyme becomes something a good deal more than a formal device. In Hejinian's poetry this mind is able to maintain the dignity Olson sought by denying itself any of our typical representational fantasies that serve as mirrors facilitating our struggles to establish stable egos.

Now that postmodernist theory seems no longer capable of producing fresh ideas, and hence rests on the verge of becoming one more layer of history's junk heap, young poets have the task of determining what they can make of this heritage. It may be the case that as the contradictions within the theory become more evident, the poetry discussed here will emerge as more fully contemporary because of how it tried to negotiate what in the theory became forced into dichotomies. But even if this distinction between the poetry and the theoretical environment proves impossible, the past three decades will make it extremely difficult for serious poetry to celebrate those struggles by the romantic ego, unless the egos involved manage to coexist with the various bodies afforded it by its own listening to the language that is its dwelling.

BIBLIOGRAPHY

Primary Sources

Allen, Donald, ed. *The New American Poetry, 1945–1960.* New York, 1960.

Hoover, Paul, ed. *Postmodern American Poetry.* New York, 1994.

Lehman, David, ed. *Ecstatic Occasions, Expedient Forms: Sixty-five Leading Contemporary Poets Select and Comment on Their Own Poems.* New York, 1987.

Messerli, Douglas, ed. *From the Other Side of the Century: A New American Poetry, 1960–1990.* Los Angeles, 1994.

Other Sources

Altieri, Charles. *Enlarging the Temple: New Directions in American Poetry during the 1960's.* Lewisburg, Pa., 1979.

Altieri, Charles. *Self and Sensibility in Contemporary American Poetry.* Cambridge and New York, 1984.

Breslin, James E. B. *From Modern to Contemporary: American Poetry, 1945–1965.* Chicago, 1984.

Conte, Joseph M. *Unending Design: The Forms of Postmodern Poetry.* Ithaca, N.Y., 1991.

DuPlessis, Rachel Blau. *The Pink Guitar: Writing as Feminist Practice.* New York and London, 1990.

Easthope, Antony, and John O. Thompson, eds. *Contemporary Poetry Meets Modern Theory.* New York and London, 1991.

Gardiner, Thomas, ed. *American Poetry of the 1980s.* Special issue of *Contemporary Literature* 33.2 (Summer 1992): 177–413.

Hartley, George. *Textual Politics and the Language Poets.* Bloomington, Ind., 1989.

McGann, Jerome. *Black Riders: The Visible Language of Modernism.* Princeton, N.J., 1993.

Nelson, Cary. *Our Last First Poets: Vision and History in Contemporary American Poetry.* Urbana, 1981.

Perloff, Marjorie. *Poetic License: Essays on Modernist and Postmodernist Lyric.* Evanston, Ill., 1990.

Perloff, Marjorie. *Radical Artifice: Writing Poetry in the Age of Media.* Chicago, 1991.

Quartermain, Peter. *Disjunctive Poetics: From Gertrude Stein and Louis Zukofsky to Susan Howe.* Cambridge and New York, 1992.

Schultz, Susan M., ed. *The Tribe of John: Ashbery and Contemporary Poetry.* Tuscaloosa, Ala., 1995.

Shoptaw, John. *On the Outside Looking Out: John Ashbery's Poetry.* Cambridge, Mass., 1994.

CHARLES ALTIERI

POSTSTRUCTURALISM. Poststructuralism is aptly characterized by Roland Barthes in his 1977 "Inaugural Lecture to the Chair of Literary Semiology at the Collège de France" as "a certain *individual* labor, the adventure of a certain subject," one of whose aims is to bring about a forgetting that "imposes unforeseeable change . . . on the sedimentation of the knowledges, cultures, and beliefs we have traversed." Arising in the mid-1960s and centering on the radical conception of language advanced by Ferdinand de Saussure early in the century, poststructuralism has wrought various changes on the tenets of what is known as structuralism. Saussure developed linguistics as an ahistorical science at a time when the study of language consisted of phonology, the history of the sounds of language. He deemed the proper study of linguistics to be language and language to be a system of signs that signify by virtue of their difference from other signs in the system rather than by their connection with any kind of language-independent meaning. A sign is defined as the indissoluble union of a sound image (signifier) and concept (signified), where concepts are language dependent in being constituted by the same cut in the "ribbon of thought" that breaks the "ribbon of sound" into identifiable units. The arbitrariness of language lies in there being nothing in the flow of sound or thought that necessitates the constituting cuts being made in one place rather than another. Pragmatic criteria, and chance, reign.

The model of language developed by Saussure proved to be a powerful explanatory tool and was responsible for the spread of structuralism across the human sciences. Starting in the 1950s the model was extended to art, film, and literature (Roman Jakobson), kinship systems (Claude Lévi-Strauss), the unconscious mind (Jacques Lacan), the history of knowledge (Michel Foucault), and contemporary culture and its myths (Roland Barthes). It was taken to yield knowledge of the unobservable structure that underlay and determined the nature of the observable world. The original model consisted of two axes, a horizontal string (syntagma) broken into units of signification identified as such by the

possibility of their being occupied by various other units taken from a vertical list (paradigm). For example, the paradigm for "____" in "The ____ is on the mat" has as members *cat, pet, dog, feline creature,* or *feather* if the membership condition is sense or grammaticality, but not if it is truth. If the membership condition is truth and, for example, "The cat is on the mat" is true, then *pet* and *feline creature* belong to the paradigm, while *dog* and *feather* do not.

Two changes made in Saussurean linguistics paved the way for the inauguration of poststructuralism. The first undercut Saussure's belief that language exists for the sake of speech and that, therefore, only signs uttered are present in language, while the indefinitely many signs exchangeable for any sign in an utterance are present only in the minds of the language users but absent from language itself. At a conference in 1956 celebrating the fortieth anniversary of the publication of Saussure's *Course in General Linguistics,* Jakobson argued that members of paradigms of the model of language are fully as much in language as are spoken syntagmas. He went on to assert that it is the resonance in signs actually used of the presence of all the signs exchangeable with them that gives language its peculiar power. Since the primacy accorded to speech by Saussure gave weight to the role of the speaker's intention in selecting signs from among all the possible occupants of a position, once language is thought of as having all the possible occupants already within it, the importance of the choice of the signs actually used fades along with the importance of the distinction between actual and possible occupants of given positions.

Moreover, possible occupants are precisely what the Freudian unconscious has at hand to use as disguises to dupe the conscious mind into letting unconscious contents slip past its censor. This gives rise to the thought that what has been repressed by any mental faculty or social institution or what has simply settled out from everything might return in a guise other than that under which it fell or was pushed out of mind or present time. This in turn gives rise to the thought that the concept of the unconscious can be extended to language and other signifying systems, whose unconscious is what is latent in the manifest system of signs, namely, the signs substitutable for other signs in the system, where this unconscious contributes causally to the system's having developed as it has and being operated as it is. Finally, the idea of the unconscious can be extended as well to social systems and their practice of constituting themselves by excluding myriad others, where the unconscious consists of those put out of sight and hearing but nonetheless there, an energy and a force.

Poststructuralism theorizes not only the ways in which Saussure's linguistic paradigm contributes to the production of meaning but also the ways in which what is repressed by social and cultural institutions contributes to their constitution and functioning. In undermining the sovereignty of the sign (what actually occupies a given site that could be filled by other members of a paradigm), poststructuralism undermines the social institutions whose signs are agents of repression. It does so by disrupting the founding oppositions of such institutions, governed as they are by the law of excluded middle. With this change worked on Saussure, poststructuralism becomes a critique of culture, especially of its modernist conceit that certain things, the visual and narrative arts among them, have finally been got right because "What is *X*?" has been unflinchingly asked and "*X* is . . ." increasingly refined. Poststructuralism contests the modernist belief that the subject can be determined by excluding from its concept whatever is not essential to it. For what particular predicates are essential to *X* is a function of those that are accidental. The accidental turn out to be necessary and cannot have been excluded, but only repressed, whereas *X* is determined precisely by its difference from them.

The second enabling moment of poststructuralism questioned Saussure's prediction of the creation of a science of signs in general, semiology, where a sign is any kind of element that signifies by virtue of its difference from other elements within a system and linguistics is but part of the general science. In the *Elements of Semiology*, published in France in 1965, Barthes reversed the envisioned relation between linguistics and semiology. He noted that nearly fifty years after its existence was predicted there was still no science of semiology because there are only trivial nonlinguistic signifying systems like the highway code. The reason for this, he argued, is that collections of objects or images and instances of behavior are significant only when admixed with language, which "extracts their signifiers (in the form of nomenclature) and names their signifieds (in the forms of usages or reasons)." Semiology needs language both as a model and as a component. The science of language is, then, not part of semiology, but semiology is part of it.

Thanks to this reversal, semiology need not be a science to assure that linguistics is, and indeed semiology ceased to be a science as structuralism ran its course, branching off into poststructuralism. Since science is a social rather than an individual labor that seeks to explain rather than to "impose unforeseeable change" on the status quo formed in part from the deposits of our collective past, the semiology heralded by Barthes is not a science but a playing of signs, albeit an utterly serious play. To the extent that the status quo valorized by the science of signs is determined by such deposits and to the extent that their contribution is unknown, evaluation of the object of the science cannot be objective. Nor can the science itself be objective, for it too is influenced by what Barthes refers to as the residue of "what we have traversed." Semiology as it is practiced by poststructuralism is an art, not a science: it reveals the individual subject's operating the signs of the world, as does the artist in producing and the audience in receiving a work of art.

With this second change, poststructuralism becomes a performance of the deconstruction of the various oppositions between art and its others, a disruption. [*See* Barthes.]

French structuralism was introduced into the United States at a conference in Baltimore in 1966. Even as it arrived in the English-speaking world, however, changes that would issue in poststructuralism were being wrought by such as Foucault's *The Order of Things: An Archaeology of the Human Sciences* and Lacan's *Ecrits: A Selection,* which appeared in 1966 to be followed in 1967 by the first books of Derrida: *Of Grammatology, Writing and Difference,* and *Speech and Phenomena.* May 1968 saw the uprisings in Paris by factor workers and students for whom the political and intellectual status quo was unsatisfactory. They wanted its transformation, not a science of its signs. The idea grew that what was to be sought was not knowledge of the structure of what underlay the manifest world but knowledge of its workings, of what had to have been excluded for the world to be as it is, of what happened to have settled out from the restless workings of instinct, desire, intention, mind, of the myriad overlappings of instincts and intentions, of chance. Barthes, Derrida, Foucault, and Lacan nourished this idea by directing their inquiries to what was murmuring underground. Those engaged in such inquiry must silence the music of the world in order to be able to hear its underground: and what will be heard cannot be foreseen.

Poststructuralism's discoveries are unforeseeable because of the large element of arbitrariness in its objects. While Saussure located the arbitrariness of language in the fact that its units could have been other than they are, poststructuralism locates it in how values get assigned to variables or how signs get selected for positions on either axis of the linguistic model. Because a sign carries with it all the other signs difference from which enables it to signify, what particular sign gets foregrounded barely matters. But to read anything in a productive way, a way that unsettles assignments of meanings that have become fixed, it is necessary to know what are the various series of signs whose difference gives significance to the present manifest signs. Each sign present in a text is a path out of the text to other signs, and there are at least two ways to recover the others and to enter the intertext, the vast open network of language of which a particular work is but a fragment. One way is to make the kind of totally uncensored association of given signs with others that the analysand is called on to make in psychoanalysis. Such associations yield a very small subset of all the possible associations that can be made with any fragment. That there are indefinitely many of them can be seen by thinking of a computer running, for example, through all the items in the six paradigms that intersect each of the positions in "The cat is on the mat," then running through all the syntagmas in which each item in each paradigm can occur, then through all the paradigms in each of these syntagmas, and so on. This strategy is licensed by the belief that there is no principled way to close (to totalize) the set and its corollary that there is no principled way to exclude anything from the set.

The other way to recover signs whose difference from present signs gives them significance is to cruise the past to recover associations of which present signs were or could have been a part. The privilege of the present having waned with the waning of the privilege that structuralism accorded speech, poststructuralism takes the present to be combinations and permutations of the already written and the past to be there in the present as the elements combined and permutated. Where structuralism makes a science of language, poststructuralism makes language the scene of a performance in which the performer is working with the already written or inscribed, combining and permutating readymade signs. Tradition has held that the present and the spoken are privileged because of their presence to consciousness, but the intuition of poststructuralism is precisely that presence and speech are mediated by and constructed out of the past and the written, respectively, as consciousness is constructed out of the unconscious. The potential is prior to the actual, and the actual is the unstable product of the performance of language, of acts of speaking, hearing, writing, reading. Here, as in any performance, the individual and the imaginary reign. Association of sign with sign is limited only by the imagination of the individual language user in so associating them as to make some sort of sense in and for the moment at which the user makes the assignment.

Poststructuralism risks contradiction and radical relativism in order to reconceive certain concepts centering on that of the human subject. The intuition is that both the electronic revolution and breakthroughs in the life sciences have had the effect that extant conceptions of the human subject as the only or primary source of meaning do not do justice to what is already written in the material world, instructions and inscriptions that are not mere records of speech. Should poststructuralism fail, it will stand convicted of having contradicted and relativized the tradition. Should it succeed, it will have imposed an "unforeseeable change . . . on the sedimentation of the knowledges, cultures, and beliefs we have traversed," through its refusal to allow what has been wrought to stay still.

[See also Postmodernism; Semiotics; and Structuralism.]

BIBLIOGRAPHY

Barthes, Roland. *S/Z.* Translated by Richard Miller. New York, 1974.
Barthes, Roland. *The Responsibility of Forms: Critical Essays on Music, Art, and Representation.* Translated by Richard Howard. New York, 1985.
Barthes, Roland. *Elements of Semiology.* Translated by Annette Lavers and Colin Smith. New York, 1967.
Derrida, Jacques. *Of Grammatology.* Translated by Gayatri Chakravorty Spivak. Baltimore, 1976.
Derrida, Jacques. *The Truth in Painting.* Translated by Geoff Bennington and Ian McLeod. Chicago, 1987.
Foucault, Michel. *The Order of Things: An Archaeology of the Human Sciences.* New York, 1970.
Jakobson, Roman, and Morris Halle. *Fundamentals of Language.* The Hague, 1956.
Kristeva, Julia. *Desire in Language: A Semiotic Approach to Literature and Art.* Edited by Leon S. Roudiez, translated by Thomas Gora, Alice Jardine, and Leon S. Roudiez. New York, 1980.
Lacan, Jacques. *Ecrits: A Selection.* Translated by Alan Sheridan. New York, 1977.
Lévi-Strauss, Claude. *Structural Anthropology.* Translated by Claire Jacobson and Brooke Grundfest Schoepf. New York, 1963.
Saussure, Ferdinand de. *Course in General Linguistics.* Edited by Charles Bally and Albert Sechehaye, translated by Wade Baskin. New York, 1959.
Wiseman, Mary Bittner. *The Ecstasies of Roland Barthes.* London and New York, 1989.

MARY WISEMAN

POUSSIN, NICOLAS (1594–1665), French painter. Nicolas Poussin stands at the center of several important turning points in early modern European art. He was born in France, but he worked primarily in Italy, in the Baroque Rome that was the artistic capital of Europe in the seventeenth century. Steeped in the austere classicism of both Roman antiquities and the High Renaissance, Poussin's paintings came to be seen as the foundation of a new French school of painting. French neoclassicism, partly based on the model of Poussin's works, would then dominate the European art world for the next two centuries. Poussin's career thus marks an important shift from the artistic hegemony of Italy to that of France, and from a Renaissance model of classicism to the academic neoclassicism that is the gateway to modernism in the nineteenth century.

The two most important early biographies of the artist—by Giovanni Pietro Bellori and André Félibien—are also important texts in establishing the later theory and practice of neoclassicism. They tell us that Poussin was born in the rural village of Les Andelys in Normandy. Little is said of his early training with provincial painters, nor of his work in Paris before he departed for Rome sometime in 1624. But the biographies document an apparently crucial friendship in Paris, between Poussin and the great Italian poet Giambattista Marino. Bellori's biography notes that Poussin provided drawings to illustrate one of Marino's most famous poems, the *Adone*. However, a set of extant drawings from this early period now in Royal Library at Windsor Castle, known as the Marino drawings, show that the text Poussin illustrated was Ovid's *Metamorphoses*. These rapidly executed, vivid line and wash drawings show an expressive force not previously found in Ovid illustrations, and reveal Poussin's affinity for classical texts and mythology in particular. Marino encouraged the artist to leave the artistic backwater of Paris and travel to Rome.

On Poussin's arrival in Italy, the poet introduced him to the powerful circle around the Barberini pope, Urban VIII.

Eventually it was Cassiano dal Pozzo, the learned secretary to the pope's nephew Francesco Barberini, who championed Poussin and gave him work. Poussin provided drawings for Cassiano's *musèo cartàceo,* or paper museum of antiquities, which gathered together images of all known fragments of ancient Roman arts. His paintings for Cassiano and others at this time were relatively small in scale, many representing subjects from classical mythology and ancient history, often in a highly poetic mode: a representative example from this period would be his *Diana and Endymion,* now in the Detroit Institute of Arts. For Cassiano he painted a series of seven paintings depicting the *Seven Sacraments,* each ritual set in a painstaking re-creation of early Christian antiquity. Poussin thus settled into the rarefied world of erudition and antiquarianism that flourished among intellectuals under the Barberini papacy. For the rest of his career, he would shun the exuberant public art of the Baroque, working instead for a small group of private patrons in Italy and France.

In 1640 the French king Louis XIII called the now prominent Poussin back to Paris to serve as *premier peintre du roi.* The artist reluctantly complied, spending two unhappy years battling court intrigue in Paris and working on the kind of public, decorative projects that he had hitherto avoided. His work on the decoration of the Louvre has since been lost except for drawings. Letters from Paris show that Poussin found some refuge with a few intellectual friends of Cassiano dal Pozzo's who now also found themselves in Paris. These were men like Gabriel Naudé, who later became the librarian of the prime minister Cardinal Mazarin, or Pierre Gassendi, a prominent opponent of Jules René Descartes's, who wrote on natural science and Epicurean philosophy. But Naude and Gassendi are now also well known as the core of the secret group of religious and political skeptics known as *libertins* or *libertins érudits.* Poussin may have shared some of their attitudes, as his later painted allegories seem to be based on *libertin* texts and ideas about the relation between history, natural history, and human morality.

After Poussin fled back to Rome in 1642 he never again traveled. But increasingly his paintings were bought by French patrons, particularly by Paul Fréart de Chantelou, whose friendship and patronage eclipsed the artist's earlier relationship with Cassiano dal Pozzo. For Chantelou, Poussin painted a second set of *Seven Sacraments.* Like the first set done for Cassiano, it depicts each Christian ritual in careful historical context. But the Chantelou version also shows the artist's evolving concern for the play of light and deep shadows, as well as the overall unification of light with pictorial space and action. This series, painted between 1639 and 1647, shows Poussin at the peak of his powers as a history painter.

After 1647, Poussin turned increasingly to landscape painting in addition to historical or religious subjects. Works such as the *Landscape with Diogenes* or the *Landscape with Orpheus,* both from around 1650 and both now in the Louvre, show how the artist transformed the classical landscape format he inherited from earlier artists such as the Carraccis or Domenichino. The landscape is still an idealized, symmetrical container for human narratives. But Poussin found a more perfect union between the portrayal of nature and the depiction of dramatic action. He also explored ways of uniting landscape with the communication of rather abstract ideas, as in his late *Landscape with the Blind Orion,* which E. H. Gombrich showed was an allegorical depiction of a stormcloud's birth.

Poussin's mature paintings were acclaimed as models for serious painting in the following generations. When the Académie Royale de Peinture et de Sculpture was founded in Paris in 1648, it was to foster the ideal of a learned artist after the manner of Poussin, as well as to break with the older guild traditions of training artists in the manner of craftsmen. In the 1660s, when the minister Jean-Baptiste Colbert sponsored official monthly discourses on individual paintings, several of Poussin's works from the royal collection were among the first to be selected. Poussin himself kept his distance from the Académie and never joined forces with it in any way. But the reception of his works by the Académie was crucial to that institution's formation as well as to Poussin's later reputation. Charles Le Brun, the driving force behind the Académie, derived his tenets about the centrality of design over color, and the clear articulation of human expression as the basis of painted narrative, from his discourses on Poussin's *Israelites Gathering Manna* and *Saint Paul in Ecstasy.* Similarly from outside the *Académie,* the critic Roger de Piles grounded his opposition to Le Brun in an opposition to Poussin, holding up the colorism of Peter Paul Rubens against Poussin's emphasis on line. The ensuing quarrel over *dessein* versus *coloris* was also about many other issues—institutional politics, of course, but also the notion of a temporal versus an instantaneous perception of pictures, and the definition of painting as primarily concerned with visual illusion or with the exposition of ideas. The highly simplified understanding of both Rubens and Poussin as they were employed in this battle was only partly based in reality: Rubens was a consummate master of design as well as color, and Poussin's use of color is far richer than this view would allow. But the reception of Poussin in the late seventeenth-century Académie brought about a remarkable reversal in the significance of both painters' works. As Svetlana Alpers has recently remarked, the emphasis on his color transformed the public diplomacy of Rubens's art into a model for private and intimate painting—as in the works of Antoine Watteau. The private, almost arcane art of Poussin became the model for public, state-sponsored history painting, an understanding of his works that would later influence Jacques-Louis David.

POUSSIN. Nicolas Poussin, *The Shepherds in Arcadia* (1650, after restoration), oil on canvas, 85 × 121 cm; Musée du Louvre, Paris. (Photograph courtesy of Giraudon/Art Resource, New York.)

The critical and public reception of Poussin from the eighteenth century to the present has, however, consistently focused on an aspect of his art that would indeed seem to have been crucial to the artist himself: the relation of the painted image to written texts. In a letter, Poussin admonished a patron to "read the story and read the painting." In a conversation recorded by Félibien, the artist spoke of the letters of the alphabet forming words as the depicted expressions in a painting form the story. Poussin's remarks come from the Renaissance tradition of *ut pictura poesis,* or the parallel of painting and poetry. Later generations of critics, even while questioning the validity of the analogy, would turn to Poussin as the best example of its application.

In a 1719 text that forms a prehistory to Gotthold Ephraim Lessing's more famous *Laocoön,* in which the sister arts of painting and poetry are similarly driven apart, the abbé Jean-Baptiste Du Bos would cite Poussin's *Death of Germanicus* as the most extraordinary visualization of a scene of heroic death, in which the painting's vividness would far surpass the ability of a writer to convey the same scene. But not even Poussin, Dubos claimed, could make a

painting that would reveal the interior workings of the soul with the same force as the poet and playwright.

Some of the finest and most important twentieth-century interpretations of Poussin have also focused on word and image in his art. Perhaps the most famous is Erwin Panofsky's seminal essay on Poussin's painting *Et in Arcadia Ego,* also called *The Shepherds in Arcadia,* Panofsky's essay pioneered the study of pastoral literature and art, providing the first cultural history of Arcadia from antiquity through the Renaissance. But the core of the essay is his attempt to link Poussin's image of shepherds encountering a tomb in the midst of a landscape with the textual motto shown engraved on the tomb's side: *et in Arcadia ego.* Later generations understood the motto as Johann Wolfgang van Goethe translated it: "Auch ich in Arkadien," in the nostalgic sense of "I, too, was once in Arcadia." But Panofsky believed the phrase could only be translated accurately as "Even in Arcadia am I," an ominous phrase spoken by an invisible personified Death. In an early version of the painting, the motto seems to emerge, metaphorically, from a death's-head atop the tomb, and the mood of moral urgency is carried through in

the diagonal surge of the composition. The calm, planar stability of the later painting seems to mistranslate the warning
words on the tomb, but in a way that was peculiarly resonant for later viewers. Panofsky did not dwell on the mis-
match between the text and the painting, finding Poussin's
image an appropriate expression of pastoral reverie. But
perhaps now we can see more in it: from an accurate use of
classical Latin in a more Baroque painting, to an incorrect
Latin in a consummately classical composition, Poussin's
two works show the trajectory of a new "classicism" in the
making—one whose genesis begins with a rift between
word and image.

More recently, the later *Et in Arcadia Ego* also inspired the
critic Louis Marin, in various essays that form the core of
Marin's writing on French painting in the "classical age."
Marin relied on the linguist Émile Benveniste's distinction
between *discours* and *récit*, discourse and narration, to analyze the structure of Poussin's painting. He focused not only
on the absent verb in the inscription—so appropriate in
painted narration, where there is no equivalent to the temporal marker of a verb—but also on the absent, undefined
"ego" who speaks the phrase. The eclipse of the speaker is
then the hallmark of this painting's narrative structure, just
as the turn to *récit* in writing makes the narrated events
seem to emerge as if by their own volition on the horizon of
the reader's consciousness. This structure of *récit* then allows Marin to situate Poussin's work as a prime example of
what Michel Foucault defined as "the classical sign."

After the post–World War II burst of scholarship on
Poussin, much of which was iconographic in nature, a new
wave of Poussin scholarship seems to be emerging in the
wake of Marin's writings. The Poussin who was *peintre-
philosophe* or painter-philosopher in the French academic
tradition may take on a similar role for our own fin de siècle,
as the representation of history and the functions of representation itself remain important critical concerns that link
us to the art of this pivotal figure.

[*See also* Classicism; *and* Ut Pictura Poesis.]

BIBLIOGRAPHY

Work by Poussin

Poussin, Nicolas. *La correspondance de Nicolas Poussin.* Edited by C.
    Jouanny. Archives de l'art français, vol. 5. Paris, 1911; reprint, Paris,
    1968.

Other Sources

Batschmann, Oskar. *Nicolas Poussin: Dialectics of Painting.* London,
    1990.
Blunt, Anthony. "The Heroic and the Ideal Landscape in the Work of
    Nicolas Poussin." *Journal of the Warburg and Courtauld Institutes* 2
    (1938–1939): 271–276.
Blunt, Anthony. *Nicolas Poussin.* 2 vols. New York, 1967; reprint, Lon-
    don, 1995.
Carrier, David. *Poussin's Paintings: A Study in Art-Historical Methodol-
    ogy.* University Park, Pa., 1993.
Cropper, Elizabeth, and Charles Dempsey. *Nicolas Poussin: Friendship
    and the Love of Painting.* Princeton, N.J., 1996.
Gombrich, E. H. "The Subject of Poussin's *Orion.*" In *Studies in the Art
    of the Renaissance,* vol. 2, *Symbolic Images,* pp. 119–22. London, 1972.
Marin, Louis. *Détruire la peinture.* Paris, 1977.
McTighe, Sheila. *Nicolas Poussin's Landscape Allegories.* Cambridge and
    New York, 1996.
Pace, Claire. *Félibien's Life of Poussin.* London, 1981.
Panofsky, Erwin. "Et in Arcadia Ego: Poussin and the Elegiac Tradi-
    tion." In *Meaning in the Visual Arts,* pp. 295–320. Garden City, N.Y.,
    1955; reprint, Chicago, 1982.
Rosenberg, Pierre, and Louis-Antoine Prat. *Nicolas Poussin,
    1594–1665.* Paris, 1994.
Teyssèdre, Bernard. *Roger de Piles et les débats sur le coloris au siècle de
    Louis XIV.* Paris, 1957.
Verdi, R. "Poussin's *Eudamidas:* Eighteenth Century Criticism and
    Copies." *Burlington Magazine* 124 (November 1982): 681–685.
Thuillier, Jacques. *Nicolas Poussin.* Paris, 1988.

SHEILA MCTIGHE

PRAGUE SCHOOL. The Prague school is the established name for the international group of scholars in linguistics, literature, theater, folklore, and general aesthetics institutionalized as the Prague Linguistic Circle
(1926–1948). In its origins, the Prague school was in part
indebted to Russian Formalism, especially the Moscow
branch (the Moscow Linguistic Circle) with whom it
shared its name as well as some members (Petr Bogatyrev,
Roman Jakobson). At the same time, the Prague school had
roots in the Czech aesthetic tradition: the nineteenth-
century Herbartian Formalism (Josef Durdík, Otakar
Hostinský), which conceived of the artistic work as a set of
formal relations, and in some post-Herbartian developments in poetics and theater (Otakar Zich). Among other
schools of thought the Prague school was influenced by
Saussurean linguistics, Edmund Husserl's phenomenology,
and Gestalt psychology. Such intellectual affinities were
welcomed by the members of the Prague school because
they perceived their enterprise as the crystallization of the
new scholarly paradigm for the humanities and social sciences that Jakobson in 1929 christened structuralism.

The history of the Prague school can be conveniently divided into three periods. The first begins with the establishment of the circle in 1926 and extends to 1934. During this
time, the research of the structuralists was oriented toward
the internal organization of poetic works, especially their
sound stratum. Jakobson's and Jan Mukařovský's histories
of old and modern Czech metrics are the most representative works of this phase.

The subsequent period (1934–1939) opens with
Mukařovský's study of a little-known Czech poet of the early
nineteenth century, Milota Zdirad Polák, which sparked an
extensive and thoroughgoing discussion about the fundamentals of criticism, and ends with the circle's collective volume devoted to the leading Czech Romantic, Karel Hynek

Mácha. In this period, the Prague school transcended its immanent orientation toward literary history: the semiotic concept of a literary work rendered it a collective entity (i.e., a sign understood by the members of a given society), and, furthermore, it enabled the structuralists to relate the developmental changes in literary history to all other aspects of human culture. Consequently, Prague school scholars extended poetics into aesthetics, shifting from a concern with verbal art alone to a concern with all the arts and with extra-artistic aesthetics as well. Mukařovský's *Aesthetic Function, Norm, and Value as Social Facts* (1936) exemplifies this theoretical shift.

The last period, roughly from 1938 to 1948, is delimited by external interventions. The German invasion forced some members of the group to leave Czechoslovakia (Bogatyrev, Jakobson, René Wellek) and severed the international contacts of the circle; the Communist takeover a decade later effectively banned the structuralist study of art and eventually led to the disbanding of the circle. The first blow, however, was mitigated by an influx of junior members into the group: the literary historian Felix Vodička, the student of dramatic art Jiří Veltruský, and the musicologist Antonín Sychra, among others. During this final stage the research of the Prague school moved toward the subjects involved in artistic process (both the author and the perceiver). Vodička's systematic attempt to elaborate the history of literary reception is among the most promising developments of this last stage.

In the postwar years the intellectual heritage of the group was disseminated around the globe by those members who left Prague. The structuralist revolution of the 1960s in France and the United States was to a considerable degree stimulated by Jakobson, who in the 1940s helped to establish the Linguistic Circle of New York, of which the French anthropologist Claude Lévi-Strauss was a member. Petr Bogatyrev, who returned to the Soviet Union at the outbreak of the war, performed a similar role there. A group of young literary scholars (Miroslav Červenka, Lubomír Doležel, Mojmír Grygar) attempted a resurrection of the school in Czechoslovakia in the 1960s, but the Soviet invasion of 1968 dealt it a final blow.

For the Prague school, structuralism was a dialectic synthesis of the two global paradigms dominating European thought in the nineteenth century: Romanticism and Positivism. "European Romantic scholarship, Jakobson observed in 1935, "was an attempt at a general, *global* conception of the universe. The antithesis of Romantic scholarship was the sacrifice of unity for the opportunity to collect the richest factual material, to gain the most varied *partial truth.*" Structuralism, the Prague scholars argued, would avoid the one-sidedness of its predecessors by being neither a totalizing philosophical system nor a narrow concrete science. As Mukařovský put it in 1941,

> Structuralism is a scholarly attitude that proceeds from the knowledge of the unceasing interaction of science and philosophy. I say "attitude" in order to avoid terms such as "theory" or "method." "Theory" suggests a fixed body of knowledge, "method" an equally homogenized and unchangeable set of working rules. Structuralism is neither—it is an epistemological stance from which particular working rules and knowledge follow, to be sure, but which exists independently of them and is, therefore, capable of development in both these aspects.
>
> (Steiner, ed., 1982)

What characterizes Prague structuralism is its conceptual frame formed by the interplay of three complementary notions—structure, function, and sign.

Structure. The concept of structure, which gave this intellectual matrix its name, requires special attention. In the parlance of the Prague school it referred to what might be seen as two distinct entities. On the one hand, it denoted the holistic organization of a single work as a hierarchical system of dominant and subordinated elements. But in the same way as Ferdinand de Saussure recognized that every concrete utterance *(parole)* is meaningful only against the background of the collectively shared linguistic code *(langue),* the Prague scholars saw every individual work as an implementation of a particular aesthetic code—a set of artistic norms. These they also termed a structure.

There were, however, important differences in how the Swiss linguist and the Prague group conceived of the code (whether linguistic or aesthetic). For Saussure it was a harmonious system, synchronic by its very essence and incapable of changing. Once affected by an external intervention the code was destroyed and replaced by another one. From this perspective the history of language was a random succession of disconnected momentary codes. For the Prague group, on the other hand, the system was a priori diachronic. Its present state, they believed, contained not only the traces of the past but also the seeds of the future. Concerned with literary history, the structuralists advanced three different models accounting for the code's development. The earliest emulated to a considerable degree the immanent orientation of Russian Formalism according to which the literary series develops because of its intrinsic need for deautomatization *(aktualisace).* But the limits of this approach soon became apparent. Poetry does not exist in a social vacuum Mukařovský recognized in 1934: "The developmental series of individual structures changing in time (e.g., political, economic, ideological, literary) do not run parallel to each other without contact. On the contrary, they are elements of a structure of a higher order and this structure of structures has its hierarchy and its dominant (prevailing) series." The immanent study of literary change was thus supplemented by consideration of its external context. The historical trajectory of any art was seen as determined simultaneously by the purely artistic needs and the external impulses stemming from social developments.

Despite their differences, the immanent and extrinsic models of literary change describe history from the same vantage point: that of production. But it is clearly insufficient to explain the becoming of a text solely as a function of the context that generated it, as Vodička observed in 1942: "Only if read does the work achieve its aesthetic realization [and] become an aesthetic object in the reader's consciousness" (Vodička). The history of literary reception proposed by Vodička relativizes significantly the bond between the text and the underlying literary code against the background of which it was written and which allegedly provides it with its identity. Any work can potentially be reconstituted according to reading conventions that did not exist during its inception and, in this way, assume new and unprecedented appearances.

Function. The second key concept and the trademark of Prague structuralism was function. Rooted in a purposive view of human behavior, it designated in Mukařovský's parlance "the active relation between an object and the goal for which this object is used." The Prague group always stressed the social dimension of functionality, the necessary consensus among the members of a collectivity concerning the purpose that an object serves and its utility for such a purpose. From the functional perspective, every individual structure mentioned above (political, economic, artistic, etc.) appeared as a set of social norms regulating the attainment of values in these cultural spheres.

Within the functional typology proposed by the structuralists, the aesthetic function played a special role. Whereas in "practical" functions the telos lies outside the object used, in the aesthetic function the telos is this object. That is to say, in extra-artistic activities functional objects are instruments whose value stems from their suitability for particular purposes. Works of art, on the other hand, as objects of aesthetic function, do not serve any particular goal directly and thus constitute ultimate values in and of themselves.

The structuralists, however, did not believe that an artistic work is completely severed from its social context. The Prague group conceived of an object's functionality in terms of hierarchy rather than mutual exclusivity: the dominance of the aesthetic function does not preclude the presence of other functions. Although unrealized, practical functions do not vanish from the work; they remain there in all their potentiality, merely shifting their corresponding values to a different level. The transformation that extra-aesthetic values undergo in art depends on another component of the structuralist frame of reference—the sign.

Sign. "The problem of the sign," the members of the circle declared in their joint statement inaugurating their new journal, *Slovo a slovesnost,* in 1935, "is one of the most urgent philosophical problems of the cultural re-birth of our time," because, "all of reality, from sensory perception to the most abstract mental constructs, appears to modern man as a vast and complex realm of signs." As mentioned above, the Prague group classified all artifacts according to the functions they serve. Humanmade objects do not, however, merely carry out their functions (i.e., a house protecting us from weather) but also signify them (i.e., a house as a sign of civilization). A conjunction of material vehicle and immaterial meaning, the sign reinscribes in different terms the dual nature of structure—its physical embodiment in individual artifacts and its mental, socially shared existence as a normative code. From a semiotic perspective, then, culture appears as a complex interaction of signs mediating among the members of a particular collectivity.

At this point we might return to extra-aesthetic functions in art whose appurtenant values are not realized because of a dominant aesthetic function. But since an artistic work is also a sign, these unrealized values are transferred from an empirical to a semantic plane. They become partial meanings that contribute to the total semantic structure of the work. Thus, "from the most abstract point of view," Mukařovský concluded in 1936,

> the work of art is nothing but a particular set of extra-aesthetic values. The material components of the artistic artifact and the way they are exploited as formal devices are mere conductors of energy represented by extra-aesthetic values. If at this point we ask ourselves where aesthetic value lies, we find that it has dissolved into individual extra-aesthetic values and is nothing but a general term for the dynamic totality of their interrelations.
> (Mukařovský, 1970)

Poetic Language. Despite the breadth of their research interests, the members of the Prague school devoted most of their attention to the study of literature. Following the path charted by the Russian formalists, they approached verbal art from a linguistic perspective, treating it as a particular functional dialect—poetic language. The circle's "Theses" of 1929 presented such dialects as a series of binary oppositions: internal versus external, intellectual versus emotional, poetic versus communicative (the latter subdivided into practical versus theoretical), and so on. Although in subsequent years the structuralists further elaborated, augmented, and terminologically modified this typology, the basic characteristics of poetic dialect remained the same. As a realization of the aesthetic function in linguistic material, it transforms the verbal sign from an instrument for signifying other, extra-linguistic realities to a self-centered composition.

The most obvious manifestation of the aesthetic function in language is the hypertrophy of the signifier—the striking organization of linguistic sound, especially in poetry. The entire range of phonic features, which in messages governed by other functions serve as an automatized vehicle of meaning, are arranged in poetic language so as to call attention to themselves, turning thus from a means toward something else into their own ends. Consequently, the Prague group investigated closely the problems of sound orchestration, prosody, and intonation in poetic compositions. The distinctive feature of these inquiries was their phonological basis. That is, for the Prague structuralists only those phonic elements of language capable of differentiating cognitive meanings could be exploited poetically. By the same token, they regarded the sound configurations permeating the poetic work (including meter) not as mere formal clusters but as partial semantic structures comprising the overall meaning of the text.

The foregrounding of the *phonē* in a poetic composition disrupts the process of linguistic designation, the matching of signifiers with signifieds to produce meaning, and results in the heightened polysemy of verbal art. To explain this point, we can turn to the Prague model of linguistic designation advanced in 1929 by one of Saussure's students, Sergej Karcevskij.

According to this model, every language use is a struggle between the "psychological" meaning the speaker wishes to express and the "ideological" meaning imposed by the code. Linguistic designation, then, involves two antithetical tendencies. The signifier and the signified can be matched in a way the speaker sees as adequate to the particular context or as adequate to socially shared linguistic conventions. The tension between these two tendencies results in the homonymic/synonymic extension of the word: the asymmetrical dualism of sound and meaning. That is to say, every application of a linguistic sign necessarily implies other possible applications of the same sign in different contexts (homonymity) as well as the existence of applicable, but in this case not applied, alternative signs (synonymity). In Karcevskij's words:

> The signifier (sound) and the signified (function) slide continually on the "slope of reality." Each "overflows" the boundaries assigned to it by the other: the signifier tries to have functions other than its own; the signified tries to be expressed by means other than its sign. They are asymmetrical; coupled, they exist in a state of unstable equilibrium.

The aesthetic manipulation of sound in verbal art intensifies the semantic slippage of linguistic signs. The dissolution of the signifier into its constitutive elements and their regrouping according to a particular phonic prescript (e.g., meter) provide language with a new network of signifying possibilities: a different ground on which sound and meaning can meet. Yet, by problematizing the process of verbal representation, according to the Prague group, poetic language performs a signal role in the linguistic system. In contrast to some other functional accounts that stress the maximal adequacy of signs to what they stand for and strive to obliterate their difference, poetic language underscores the reciprocal inadequacy of the two, their deep-seated nonidentity. But, "why is it necessary to point out that the sign does not merge with the object [it signifies]?" Jakobson asked in 1934 in his probing essay, "What Is Poetry?":

> Because besides the immediate awareness of the identity between the sign and object (A is A_1) we need the immediate awareness of the lack of this identity (A is not A_1). This antinomy is necessary for without contradictions there is no mobility of concepts, no mobility of signs, and the relationship between concept and sign becomes automatized. Activity stops and the awareness of reality dies out.   (Jakobson, 1987)

The extreme extension of signs in verbal art, however, was still an insufficient criterion by which to distinguish poetic language from other functional dialects. Emotive designations (curses, endearments), Mukařovský insisted, demonstrate an equal if not higher tendency toward semantic novelty; yet, their purpose is clearly not aesthetic. The specificity of poetic language vis-à-vis its emotive counterpart, therefore, cannot be sought in the act of designation but in another fundamental linguistic operation: the process of combining signs into higher linguistic units.

The difference between linguistic designation and combination corresponds to another basic semiotic dichotomy discussed by the Prague group, between arbitrary and motivated signs. "Language," Karcevskij paraphrased Saussure in 1927, "always offers the spectacle of battle between lexicology (the tendency toward the arbitrary and phonological sign) and syntagmatics (the tendency toward the 'motivated' and morphological sign)." The possibility of homonymic/synonymic slippage is predicated on the essential arbitrariness of the link between the signifier and signified; anything can be designated by any word, and vice versa. The conventionality of the linguistic system provides this flux with social limits, but in itself is incapable of stopping it because the individual sign users may always violate these limits in the name of "psychological adequacy." Given this fact, it is not surprising that emotive language charged with the task of expressing a speaker's immediate mental state strives toward the pole of lexicological arbitrariness.

Although poetic and emotive languages share a propensity for semantic shifts, they differ in regard to arbitrariness. For the Prague school, verbal art was the prime example of syntagmatically motivated signs. Since the aesthetic function transforms language from an instrument for signifying something else into a self-centered sign, the meaning of poetic designation is a function not of the external context but of the internal contexture of the utterance. This fact results from the complexity and systematic organization of the poetic text at all levels. The series of phonological, morphological, and syntactic parallelism, and the hierarchical correlations among partial signs create what the structuralists termed the work's "semantic gesture"—the grid of formal possibilities that motivates the overall meaning of the literary sign. It is the relational properties of the signifier, the interactions among its partial constituents that create the structure of its signified, the work's semantic universe. Therefore, in transgressing linguistic conventionality, poetic language does not slide toward the pole of arbitrariness. Instead, each work generates from within its own textual conventions, a paradigm of intersubjective expectations that suggest its interpretation.

[*See also* Formalism; Poetics; Russian Aesthetics, *article on* Russian Formalism; Semiotics; *and* Structuralism.]

BIBLIOGRAPHY

Galan, Frank W. *Historic Structures: The Prague School Project, 1928–1946.* Austin, 1985.
Garvin, Paul L., ed., *A Prague School Reader on Esthetics, Literary Structure, and Style.* Washington, D.C., 1964.
Havránek, Bohuslav, and Jan Mukařovský, eds. *Čtení o jazyce a poesii.* Prague, 1942.
Jakobson, Roman. *Verbal Art, Verbal Sign, Verbal Time.* Edited by Krystyna Pomorska and Stephen Rudy. Minneapolis, 1985.
Jakobson, Roman. *Language in Literature.* Edited by Krystyna Pomorska and Stephen Rudy. Cambridge, Mass., 1987.
Matejka, Ladislav, and Irwin R. Titunik, eds. *Semiotics of Art: Prague School Contributions.* Cambridge, Mass., 1976.
Mukařovský, Jan. "Polákova *Vznešenost přírody:* Pokus o rozbor a vývojové zařazení básnické struktury." *Sborník filologický* 10 (1934–1935): 1–68.
Mukařovský, Jan. ed. *Torso a tajemství Máchova díla.* Prague, 1938.
Mukařovský, Jan. *Aesthetic Function, Norm and Value as Social Facts.* Translated by Mark E. Suino. Ann Arbor, 1970.
Mukařovský, Jan. *The Word and Verbal Art.* Edited and translated by John Burbank and Peter Steiner. New Haven, 1977.
Mukařovský, Jan. *Structure, Sign, and Function.* Edited and translated by John Burbank and Peter Steiner. New Haven, 1977.
Rudy, Stephen. *Roman Jakobson, 1896–1982: A Complete Bibliography of His Writings.* Berlin, 1990.
Steiner, Peter, ed. *The Prague School: Selected Writings, 1929–1946.* Translated by John Burbank et al. Austin, 1982.
Striedter, Jurij. *Literary Structure, Evolution, and Value: Russian Formalism and Czech Structuralism Reconsidered.* Cambridge, Mass., 1989.
Vodička, Felix. *Počátky krásné prózy novočeské.* Prague, 1948.

PETER STEINER

PRE-COLUMBIAN AESTHETICS. It has often been said that in archaic societies art is the handmaiden of religion. Concomitant with that is the fact that in such societies there is no word for "art." Yet, these societies have a remarkable amount of formally sophisticated objects that appear to fit the concept of art of those societies that have it. Moreover, despite the apparent emphasis on religion, some of the most sacred objects in archaic societies are not formally exquisite works of art but simple, rough-hewn, or even found objects, like pebbles and feathers in bundles or rock outcrops, indicating that the relationship of art and sacredness is not a simple matter. Artistry is clearly lavished on the dresses, badges, crests, palaces, temples, and images of the social and political world. Although its subjects are often religious, art is, more correctly, the handmaiden of society.

Pre-Columbian concepts of art are coded into the works of art themselves and, hence, implicit. We collectors, curators, scholars, and tourists tease an aesthetic philosophy out of the works, the texts, and other data. It is our creation. The aesthetic does not reside in the object nor in the mind of the viewer, but is a complex relation of the two. Reconstructing the mind of the pre-Columbian viewer in the absence of texts and informants is nearly impossible. Nevertheless, pre-Columbian cultures are particularly instructive for the Western intellectual quest to understand the nature of art. In at least one pre-Columbian society, the Classic Maya (317–889 CE), art appears to have been a somewhat self-conscious enterprise with a glorification of the artist that is closer to the concept of art and artist in the West. Having emerged outside of the Old World traditions, the cultures of ancient America are a fruitful testing ground for theories derived from the development of Western art.

Before attempting a reconstruction of the pre-Columbian concept of art it is useful to note how the West had come to see it as "art" and how it has been fitted into Western schemata of aesthetics. In the sixteenth century, when the Americas were conquered, the only art admired was that of architecture and engineering. The bridges, causeways, and temples of the Aztec and the Inca aroused the admiration of Europeans used to living with monumental architecture. It was a sign of high civilization. The other arts were seen as either heathen images and works of the devil that had to be destroyed or merely as quaint curiosities. There is a famous passage in Albrecht Dürer's notebooks in which he merely admired the Mexican objects taken to the court of Charles V in Brussels for their ingenuity and strangeness, in the same way that he was fascinated by all other oddities he came across on his trip. His language in describing them is not the one he uses for Western art. No one in the sixteenth century admired the "art" of the goldwork enough not to melt it down for the value of the metal. It can be said quite categorically that in Renaissance times, pre-Columbian things were wonderful curiosities, but not "art." Moreover, despite the interest in local European styles, northern and southern, Florentine and Venetian, there is much less a sense that for them exotic objects had a "style" of their own other than a generic strangeness, crudeness, or grotesqueness. (The one foreign artistic tradition the West saw and understood to some extent was that of the Islamic Arab countries, because of their closeness and long intertwined history with the West.) So it is not surprising that in the many books engraved by Théodore de Bry on the Americas there is often no precise knowledge of, or apparent desire for, accurate stylistic depiction. Roman arches form the buildings, and European pitchers and trays are put in the hands of the Inca. Naked Caribbean Indians greet Christopher Columbus with similar Renaissance gold vessels in another de Bry engraving. Such stylistic vagueness is generally true of early illustrated books, such as the *Nuremberg Chronicle* (1493), in which all dress and constructions of various places and epochs are seen as if they were contemporary or purely imaginary.

Recognizably exotic styles emerge in the illustrations of the middle of the seventeenth century as, for example, in the monumental treatise on Egypt written by Athanasius Kircher. Egypt plays the role of the exotic ancient "other" to classical European civilization. Kircher compared Egyptian to all exotic world art known to him, including Chinese, Hindu, and pre-Columbian, and the illustrations indicate a sense of the style of each of these. Their spirit, however, is scientific rather than artistic or aesthetic. To Kircher's mind, all these styles were similar to one another and to the Egyptian and different from that of the West. This attitude in various guises has remained in force until the first half of the twentieth century.

The late eighteenth and early nineteenth centuries were the great sorting ground of the arts and civilizations in Western thought. While on the one hand this is the era of Lord Elgin and the museum enshrinement of the marbles of the Parthenon, of Johann Joachim Winckelmann's glorification of Greek art as the supreme creation of Western man, it is also the time of the creation of the exotic, the non-Western, the archaic and the primitive. The fascination with Greece coincides in time with Napoleon's colossal scientific project regarding the antiquities of Egypt, visits to the ruins of the ancient Near East, and the beginning of the exploration and recording of Maya ruins. The apotheosis of the classical and the delectation of the exotic go hand in hand, and, in fact, define each other. John Lloyd Stevens and Frederick Catherwood both traveled in Greece, Egypt, and the Near East looking at ruins before joining forces and setting out in search of the Maya. Their attitude was thoroughly comparative.

None of this could have been possible without a philosophical concept of aesthetics. It is precisely the separation of the aesthetic aspect of works of art from their functional, social, and religious aspects that made it possible to see alien arts as nonthreatening and nonheretical. While the sixteenth century saw the art of the Americas in religious terms, the eighteenth could see it in two new ways: scientific and aesthetic. These indicate a major change in attitude to which the Kantian concepts of disinterest, detachment, and universal judgment of taste are crucial. Whereas the scientific attitude is detachment for the sake of knowledge, the aesthetic attitude is detachment for the sake of appreciation. The foreign can now be understood and enjoyed without its having to be the same as one's own. There is no heresy involved. The eighteenth-century concept of the sublime also allowed for exotic beauty and grandeur that was not within the canons of Western art, but could include that which was strange, violent, disturbing, or perhaps even ugly. The only element alien to the aesthetic, for Immanuel Kant, was the disgusting.

The Western measure of exotic art was, and to a large extent remains, classical art, and especially the art of the Greeks—what in the mid-twentieth century E. H. Gom-

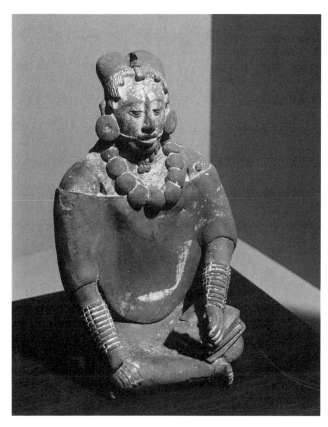

PRE-COLUMBIAN AESTHETICS. *Mayan Figurine of a Woman Writing* (seventh to tenth century CE), terra cotta, Island of Jaina; Museo Nacional de Anthropologia, Mexico City. (Photograph courtesy of Werner Forman/Art Resource, New York.)

brich still considered unique and a "miracle" ("The Miracle of the Greeks"). Idealistic naturalism, characteristic of Greek art, is still therefore the favorite style of the West. Maya sculptures, first brought to Western attention in the late eighteenth century, were immediately fascinating precisely because such "idealistic naturalism" is their hallmark. (Eventually the Maya would be considered the "Greeks of the New World.") When Jean-Frederic Waldeck, the self-proclaimed pupil of the neoclassic painters Jacques-Louis David, Joseph-Marie Vien, and Pierre-Paul Prud'hon depicted the images of Palenque with some enthusiastic inaccuracy, he saw them as approximating neoclassic forms. Actually, Waldeck's original drawings were in the "scientific tradition," much like his sketches of fish and flowers, and quite "exact" in that sense. As he elaborated them into paintings, however, the Maya forms began to look more and more Western and classical, in order to become "beautiful," at the same time that their grotesque features were exaggerated in order to become "sublime." In his finished paintings he enlarged them next to small human figures so as to increase the sense of their awesomeness. (Giambattista Piranesi had already used such changes in scale to make his views of Roman ruins more exotic.) Many modern collectors still appreciate Maya art for the same reasons Waldeck did: because its ideals of beauty are close to that of the classical while it has the added excitement of the exotic features, mysterious hieroglyphics, and barbaric (i.e., violent or sexual) elements that to the West signify the "other." At the end of the twentieth century the most accessible and favorite pre-Columbian style remains that of the Maya.

Most other pre-Columbian styles had to wait for the twentieth-century language of modernism and the appreciation of abstraction and conventionalization to be seen as works of art. While the art of the Maya is lauded for its elegance and naturalism, the arts of Mezcala, Teotihuacán, or Tiahuanaco, are appreciated for their abstraction and compared to Constantin Brancusi, Georges Braque, or Pablo Picasso. Modernism set itself up in opposition to classical values of representation and sought as "authorities" and precursors various "primitive," "archaic," and "medieval" styles. There is no question, however, that Western modes of art wag the tail of pre-Columbian appreciation. Minimalist Earth art of the 1960s, for example, has kindled interest in the famous lines in the desert of the Nazca plateau in Peru. The very language of the appreciation of these pre-Columbian arts is borrowed directly from the formal analysis of modern art, with its preoccupation with lines and shapes and the invention of ingenious abstractions. While modern art in the West has a sizable following, it is still an acquired taste for most people whose preference is for classical forms. There is thus a clear ranking of pre-Columbian arts in the minds of both scholars and the public. These tastes determine the valuation and language of (and even prices paid for) pre-Columbian arts. The rise of any new Western artistic movement may potentially rescue some so far obscure pre-Columbian artistic tradition.

Because of the preference for classical art, since the nineteenth century evolutionist theories generally imagined art to have a stylistic progression from abstraction, which seemed to be "crude and easy," to naturalism, which was seen as "sophisticated and difficult." These concepts derive from a parallel of art and technology, the acquisition of naturalism being compared to the slow accumulation of technical and scientific knowledge. In most of his work, Gombrich is still a proponent of this idea on the basis of the type of "vision" required for naturalism, which, in his view, is a detached, scientific vision in which an attempt is made to match images to the real world rather than to create, through abstractions, alternative worlds. Abstraction is thus associated with "magical" as opposed to "scientific" thinking. His terms for these "visions" are the "conceptual" and the "perceptual." According to the prevalent nineteenth-century art-historical paradigm, the Greeks created a "perceptual" art out of the rigid "conceptual" canons of Egyptian art by gradually "matching" the image to reality. Nineteenth-century anthropologists studying ornament debated endlessly whether designs began in naturalistic forms

and became more abstract as time went on, or the opposite. Such evolutionist theories presupposed gradual, incremental evolution in a single direction (even though neither medieval nor modern art fitted into that schema particularly well). Non-Western arts were condemned often for not fitting into linear evolutionary sequences and thus lacking proper "development" and in any case remaining at a primitive, nonnaturalistic level.

Pre-Columbian art history, as we know it so far through archaeology, does not support the Western evolutionary paradigm of naturalism rising out of abstraction. The earliest art in Mesoamerica, that of the Olmecs, is one of the most naturalistic, three-dimensional, and free in movement (1300–900 BCE). Thereafter the arts are in many ways more constricted in form. Olmec art does not appear to have emerged out of an older more "abstract" tradition, but to have been invented fully in that form. Some centuries later, Classic Maya art undergoes a seven-hundred-year-long history in which for about a hundred and fifty years there is remarkable naturalism in style (650–800 CE). Andean art has its idealized/naturalistic cameo appearance in the Moche style (200 BCE–600 CE), but then becomes progressively more abstract and minimal. Idealized naturalism occurs at various points in pre-Columbian history, but it is more episodic than developmentally determined.

Because the arts of pre-Columbian America emerged entirely separately from the arts of the Old World, they are crucial to the understanding of the evolution of art and of the roles of naturalism and abstraction. It is clear that naturalism and abstraction are cultural choices and potentially always possible, not steps on a ladder, or end points on a scale. Naturalism is neither a specific "vision" nor a technological skill belonging to a particular stage of culture. It has most to do with the social and political requirements of a given context. Moreover, it is also clear that there is not, necessarily, a grand overall development in the arts of an area. Development is restricted largely to the art of individual cultures, such as Olmec, Moche, or Maya. Within individual cultures there are developments that can be described as "formative," "classical," or "baroque," and tendencies either toward or away from naturalism. But, the disjunctions between cultures are great enough to redirect art into any new directions, depending on the given social conditions. The developments of Western art seemed so compelling to art historians such as Heinrich Wölfflin precisely because they were part of a single cultural tradition.

In order to reconstruct pre-Columbian aesthetics one is forced to deal with the context as defined anthropologically. The most immediate issue is the function of art, which is said to be "utilitarian" in traditional societies and "free" in the modern West. Although we can say that as the embodiment of value, status, taste, and intellect, art of all periods has a similar function, there is indeed a difference between implicit and explicit concepts of aesthetics. Pre-Columbian cultures whose arts survived in permanent media were complex hierarchical societies defined as chiefdoms and states. Because these cultures had limited systems of writing, artworks were the most important communicating media. While their means were aesthetic, these were as implicit as the good design of cars or rockets is implicit—indeed, it is not their primary function. (We usually do not ask who designed the lines of a space shuttle.) Any perusal of the few texts available on the arts or the artists of the Aztec, Inca, and Maya indicates a high regard for skill, the ability to understand a commission in terms of the genre required, the imagination to invent something new and different. Curiously, traditional non-Western arts are considered conservative and unchanging (the Egyptian example is usually quoted) and yet extremely varied and ingenious (the vast variety of non-Western styles). The variety of styles existing worldwide and archaeologically makes sense only if the notion of sticking to tradition had to have been very loosely understood in most of these cultures.

Every culture has its concept of the beautiful. Frequently that is evident in an idealized or stylized human figure or face, or in elaborate ornament. Both from contexts and from texts we know that the beautiful, the good, and the powerful were often equated with one another. Characteristic of preindustrial arts of states is a high valuation of technical skill, virtuosity of craft, labor, and time intensiveness—the use of stone tools to carve jade and basalt in Mexico, the painstaking textile techniques of the Andes. There is also evidence that the artist is seen to have a mysterious creative power akin to the supernatural and that some of that power also resides in the work the artist creates.

What most pre-Columbian art did not share with Western art since the Renaissance is a "cult of the aesthetic" and a "cult of the artist." Artists did not sign their works or make images of themselves. The aesthetic features of their works may have been discussed as "better" or "worse" than others, but there was no philosophy of art. This does not make such art "anonymous," since it is likely that these artists were known in their day. But the lack of the glorification of the artist affects the nature of the art created. It gives it a straightforward, self-assured and unself-conscious quality sometimes much admired by aesthetically self-conscious cultures such as ours. Mannerist strivings for effect—or a kind of visual "signature"—are usually lacking.

The Maya are a partial exception to this in the Americas because they appear to have had a cult of the aesthetic. The evidence that the Maya focused specifically on the "aesthetic" as a facet of experience comes from the nature of their art and the inscriptions. Aestheticism among the Maya is generally an aspect of the emphasis on individual rulers and aristocrats. The glorification of individual achievement characterizes much of Maya art, which is concerned with dynastic matters such as accessions and conquest. Rulers are sometimes individualized by portraiture and by inscrip-

tions giving their names, proofs of legitimacy, and exploits. It is this climate of the celebration of individual achievement that appears to be behind the development of individual polity styles in art. Within the short span of Classic Maya art there is a wide variety of regional styles, as each Maya city, like the cities of Renaissance Italy, has its own genres and forms.

Tatiana Proskouriakoff has shown that temporal changes in style affect the art of all the Maya cities, indicating high levels of interaction. As she conceptualizes them, these phases are comparable to the European developmental notions of the formative, classical, and Baroque. It is relatively easy within a given site, like Yaxchilan, to select the work of an individual carver on the basis of style. Advances in hieroglyphic inscriptions have made it possible to see the styles favored and patronized by individual rulers.

Aesthetic preoccupation is also evident in the design of individual monuments in which the elegance of forms and exquisiteness of detail suggest patrons interested in aesthetic matters, and especially clever refinements. All these elements can be read out of the works of art just with a cross-cultural knowledge of art. Recent excavations and finds have brought to light more specific proofs of this aesthetic interest in the form of the sculpture of a deity represented as an artist with a brush in his hands from Copán, and names on pottery that are interpreted by some as the names of the artists who painted them. Most dramatic of all is a carved bone from Tikal that represents the hand of an artist with a brush emerging from the maw of a supernatural creature, in the same way that deities are often shown emerging from supernatural maws. It does not take much imagination to interpret the hand and brush as representing the divine aspect of artistic creation. Various pre-Columbian sources indicate that younger sons of aristocratic families were involved in different sorts of artistic activity and that artistic activity was an integral part of court life, especially among the Maya.

Besides idealistic naturalism, self-conscious aestheticism brings the Maya close to the Western classical ideal of high art. The really interesting question is why explicit aestheticism developed among the Maya only for that relatively brief period of time. One possible answer is that, like the Balinese or Louis XIV, the Maya lords ruled through a form of theatricality of which aesthetics was a significant and distinct component. Aesthetics was separated out because it was in some ways socially useful. As Clifford Geertz noted for Bali, theatrical aesthetic activity may be one way for a state to pretend to have and thus acquire power it is not able to amass in more practical ways. Another possible answer is that with the high development of hieroglyphic writing, images were freed from the necessity of conveying certain sorts of information and were available to communicate ideas about art itself. This does not, however, explain why writing was so much more elaborate among the Maya than

PRE-COLUMBIAN AESTHETICS. *Sculpture of Quetzalcoatl, God of Life and Death* (fourteenth to sixteenth century), Aztec; Museo Nacional de Antropologia, Mexico City. (Photograph courtesy of Giraudon/Art Resource, New York.)

among their neighbors. Writing seems to have been invested with an artistic interest similar to that of calligraphy in Asia. Regardless of cause and effect, the Maya were clearly separating image and text, and it is partly within that separation that explicit aestheticism emerged.

The aesthetic attitude assumes that the raison d'être of art objects is to be visual. That is, they can be examined, decoded, enjoyed, perhaps even feared or hated, but the sensory experience of vision and the intentionality of some visual effect are presumed to be primary. This is indeed the case in Western art since the Renaissance: an invisible work of art is meaningless. (Market value and aesthetic delight assume a human audience. Twentieth-century art has tried to invert this value by creating nonvisual or noncollectible arts.) Archaic societies are neither "visual" nor "antivisual" in this sense. The Aztecs carved the bottom of colossal sculptures with intricate images of the earth, presumably for the visual appreciation of a supernatural audience with human tastes. Many Maya reliefs, such as lintels, were originally embedded in badly lit and difficult-to-see architectural contexts accessible only to the elite. The designs of Nazca lines are mainly visible from the air or partially from

a nearby hill but were invisible to their makers and users the way we see them now. Aestheticism assumes display—in a church, museum, palace, or home in which a work can be present either as "background" ornament or as the focus of attention.

Astheticism emerges in a continuum and not as an absolute stage. It is always involved with display, however, and thus with secular, political power or the pomp and circumstance of religious power. The most sacred objects of many cultures are either natural objects not fashioned by man, such as the rocks of Mecca and Jerusalem, or crude and overtly nonaesthetic objects, such as the boli of the Bamana. In many cultures artworks are destroyed in the process of their use. The "oracle" in the Andean temple of Chavín de Huantar was a crudely carved natural stone, much less finished and "beautiful" than the carvings in the anteroom courtyards. The Aztec patron god Huitzilopochtli had no images and was perhaps a collection of powerful charms in a bundle, or a dough image. The really sacred statue of Athena on the Acropolis was an old wooden one and not the colossal ivory-and-gold masterpiece of Phidias in the Parthenon. In many cultures, natural, crude, or old objects are more venerated than elaborately made new ones.

Magnificent objects buried with the dead in many past cultures also illustrate the point that availability for use and the visibility of an object for the living were not always its main essence in the past. The beautiful and elaborate, when it is meant to be visual, is intended to communicate with a human audience in some social context. In a spectacular funeral there is at least one, final, grand display. Subsequently, the objects communicated functionally and aesthetically with the dead and the gods. Aesthetics in this sense is an immanent rather than transcendent social value. The ultimate powers of the unseen are often felt to be inexpressible, invisible, and unrealizable—beyond the province of the visual arts.

The transcendent aspects of aesthetics, art turned into the expression of the divine in human beings, emerges fully in eighteenth-century European thought, associated with the decline of religious faith. Since the eighteenth century, aesthetics has become a sort of religion, a substitute for the forms of worship of the past, with the museum as its temple. This is not, however, a sudden and total change, nor is it restricted to the West. Various forms of aestheticism existed in Asia and Africa, as well as in pre-Columbian America. Paradoxically, although the aesthetic has always been felt to have something supernatural about it, it is mostly secular and worldly in its manifestations: this, too, it has in common with aspects of religion.

One of the most striking aspects of archaic and exotic arts is the ease with which we recognize them as "arts" and the extent to which we can understand their formal "message," even if their precise cultural meanings are unknown. One of Immanuel Kant's most important observations about aesthetic judgment is that it is "universal"—even if we disagree, the mere fact that we can quarrel about taste means that we have grounds in common. We need not have the same opinions, but we have a similar ability to form judgments. Kant's own taste seems to have run to classical allegories and English gardens, but Maori tattoos, Sumatran pepper gardens, mathematics, and tulips are among the broad range of things that inform his thinking. This eighteenth-century concept of a shared, universal ability to make aesthetic judgments is related to the new ability to see and valorize exotic arts as desirable and pleasurable. Many eighteenth-century scholars and travelers routinely used charts to compare the arts of all of these peoples. The aim of these comparisons was to show the similarities despite the apparent differences between Egyptian, Hindu, Mayan, and other styles. While this attempt seems naive to those of us who are attuned to differences, it underlines the universalizing tendency of the previous century and the process by which the foreign was made available as "art" in Western terms. In the sixteenth century, Huitzilopochtli was represented in European prints as a devil with hooves. To the eighteenth century, pre-Columbian art looks more like Greek art. For the twentieth century, pre-Columbian art outdoes Cubism in abstraction and complexity.

Nevertheless, while pre-Columbian art reveals a great richness and variety of traditions and implicit aesthetics, and while it has been and will be used to justify and authorize Western experiments in art, as Henry Moore once used it, it is a passive body of material on which aesthetic theory can play its games and test its various ideas. Although these aesthetic games have been suspect in the eyes of anthropologically oriented scholars in the business of serious cultural reconstruction, would we expend the energy on excavation and analysis of the Maya if it were not for the great body of extant Maya art and what it means to us? We claim that reason, science, and technology are more central to our culture than art, but we define the peoples and cultures of the past through their art. It matters a great deal who has art and what kind of art it is.

[*See also* Caribbean Aesthetics; *and* Latin American Aesthetics.]

BIBLIOGRAPHY

Baudez, Claude-François. *Jean-Frederic Waldeck, peintre: Le premier explorateur des ruines mayas.* Paris, 1993.
Bennett, Tony. *The Birth of the Museum.* London and New York, 1995.
Boone, Elizabeth H. "Incarnations of the Aztec Supernatural: The Image of Huitzilopochtli in Mexico and Europe." In *Transactions of the American Philosophical Society.* vol. 79, pt. 2. Philadelphia, 1989.
Braun, Barbara. *Pre-Columbian Art and the Post-Columbian World.* New York, 1993.
Burger, Richard L. *Chavin and the Origins of Andean Civilization.* New York, 1992.
Burke, Edmund. *A Philosophical Enquiry into the Origin of Our Ideas of the Sublime and Beautiful* (1757). 2d ed. Edited by James T. Boulton. Notre Dame, Ind., 1968.
Coe, Michael D. *The Maya.* (1966). 5th rev. exp. ed. London, 1993.
Cohodas, Marvin. "The Identification of Workshops, Schools and Hands at Yaxchilan, a Classic Maya Site in Mexico." In *Proceedings of the 42nd International Congress of Americanists,* vol. 7, pp. 301–313. Paris, 1976.
Demarest, Arthur A. "Ideology in Ancient Maya Cultural Evolution: The Dynamics of Galactic Polities." In *Ideology and Pre-Columbian Civilizations,* edited by Arthur A. Demarest and Geoffrey W. Conrad, pp. 135–158. Santa Fe, N. Mex., 1992.
Fash, William L. *Scribes, Warriors and Kings: The City of Copan and the Ancient Maya.* London, 1991.
Geertz, Clifford. *Negara: The Theatre State in Nineteenth-Century Bali.* Princeton, N.J., 1980.
Gombrich, E. H. *The Story of Art.* (1950). 16th exp. ed. London, 1995.
Gombrich, E. H. *Art and Illusion: A Study in the Psychology of Pictorial Representation.* (1960). 2d ed. Reprint, Princeton, N.J., 1969.
Heidegger, Martin. "The Origin of a Work of Art." In *Philosophies of Art and Beauty: Selected Readings in Aesthetics from Plato to Heidegger,* edited by Albert Hofstader and Richard Kuhns, pp. 650–703. Reprint, Chicago, 1976.
Kant, Immanuel. *Critique of Judgment* (1790). Translated by Werner S. Pluhar. Indianapolis, 1987.
Kircher, Athanasius. *Oedipus Aegipticus.* 3 vols. 1652–1655.
Kubler, George. *Studies in Classic Maya Iconography.* New Haven, 1969.
Leon-Portilla, Miguel. *Aztec Thought and Culture.* Norman, Okla., 1963.
Pasztory, Esther. "Shamanism and North American Indian Art." In *Native North American Art History: Selected Readings,* edited by Aldona Jonaitis and Zena Pearlstone Mathews, pp. 7–30. Palo Alto, Calif., 1982.
Pasztory, Esther. *Aztec Art.* New York, 1983.
Pasztory, Esther. "The Function of Art in Mesoamerica." *Archaeology* 37.1 (1984): 18–25.
Pasztory, Esther. "Still Invisible: The Problems of the Aesthetics of Abstraction in Pre-Columbian Art and Its Implications for Other Traditions." *RES* 19/20 (1990–1991): 105–136.
Proskouriakoff, Tatiana. "The Study of Classic Maya Sculpture." *Carnegie Institution of Washington Publication,* no. 593. Washington, D.C., 1950.
Reents-Budet, Dorie. *Painting the Maya Universe: Royal Ceramics of the Classic Period.* Durham, N.C., 1994.
Tate, Carolyn E. *Yaxchilan: The Design of a Maya Ceremonial City.* Austin, Tex., 1992.

ESTHER PASZTORY

PRICE, UVEDALE (1747–1829), English landscape designer. Uvedale Price contributed to the development of the Picturesque way of seeing from 1794 until his death. He did so in theoretical terms, in *Essays on the Picturesque, as compared with the Sublime and the Beautiful; and on the Use of Studying Pictures for the Purpose of Improving Real Landscape* (1794–1801, reprinted in three volumes in 1810), *A Letter to Humphry Repton, Esq., on the Application of the Practice as well as Principles of Landscape-Painting to Landscape-Gardening* (1795), and *A Dialogue on the Distinct Characters of the Picturesque and the Beautiful* (1801). Price argues that the Picturesque is a visual property of landscape that takes its independent place alongside Edmund Burke's categories of the Sublime and the Beautiful; but as the lengthy titles of his works reveal, for Price, much more than for the other major Picturesque theorist, William Gilpin, the Picturesque was a property that could be given practical expression (that could, in short, be designed). Price's main contributions on the practical level were made at his own estate of Foxley (approximately 3,800 acres) in Herefordshire, although he also advised some friends or relations about their estates at Cassiobury Park, Bentley Priory, Beckett, Mongewell, Coleorton Hall, Whitfield, Eywood, Packington Hall, and Guy's Cliffe. Another of his achievements was his enthusiastic recommendation of William Sawrey Gilpin (nephew of William Gilpin) as a garden designer. William Sawrey Gilpin's published ideas on landscape gardening were strongly influenced by Price, and his major work, the garden at Scotney Castle, survives in a very recognizably Picturesque state. The house became the home of Christopher Hussey, whose book *The Picturesque: Studies in a Point of View* (1927) contributed to the twentieth-century resurgence of interest in the Picturesque. Other landscape gardeners, notably J. C. Loudon in Britain and Andrew Jackson Downing in the United States, avowed Price's influence. That the Picturesque idea had become so largely naturalized and widespread in thinking about gardens by the 1840s is in part due to Price: especially in his changing the emphasis away from Picturesque tourism toward active intervention in the landscape.

While the categories Burke was interested in arose from the biological imperatives of self-preservation and reproduction, Price advanced explanations for the Picturesque of a more practical and material kind: he explained the delight we get from Picturesque stimuli (which are greatly characterized by roughness and variety—expressible in the visual texture of foliage, for example) in terms of the "irritation" of the optic nerve, which we experience as a pleasure, and which Price links to "curiosity." Landscapes that displayed smoothness and sameness were therefore less pleasing than rugged and intricate ones, and Price decided that the landscape gardens of Lancelot "Capability" Brown and Repton exemplified the former. With a resonant clashing of military similes, he condemned Brown's work as a "levelling" system that produced boring landscapes of "solitary grandeur."

For Price, picturesqueness is a quality innate in certain scenes and things. His love for broken and textured surfaces led him to celebrate a range of objects, from old mills, shattered oaks, and worn-out cart horses to gypsies and beggars. In contrast to these he rejected the "arts of industry," stating that "in a moral view, the industrious mechanic is a more pleasing object, than the loitering peasant. But in a picturesque light, it is otherwise." His preference for dilapidation often had a historical sense. He explained the joy derived from ruins in national and historically specific terms. Referring to the castles and abbeys that occur frequently in the English countryside, he urged that they should be seen as the nation's pride: "we may glory that the abodes of tyranny and superstition are in ruin." While metaphysical concerns might underlie this attitude, they are buried some levels beneath the surface. Price's vision of landscape rarely reaches a purely formal level devoid of associations. Indeed, one of his chief criteria for a pleasing countryside was a sense of "connection" between social classes. The desire of parvenu landowners to isolate themselves from poorer classes met with disapproval from Price's brand of Toryism. Interest in "connection" led him to embrace farming as able to contribute to picturesqueness, and his own forest management at Foxley became of great importance to him. In his composition of views there, foreground details (gnarled trees, bushes, banks of lanes) became as important as long vistas. For Price, studying paintings was a guide "in our search for the numberless and untouched varieties and beauties of nature."

[*See also* Landscape; *and* Picturesque.]

BIBLIOGRAPHY

Work by Price

Essays on the Picturesque. 3 vols. London, 1810. This contains the *Letter to H. Repton* and the *Dialogue.*

Other Sources

Andrews, Malcolm. *The Search for the Picturesque: Landscape Aesthetics and Tourism in Britain, 1760–1800.* Stanford, Calif., 1989.

Andrews, Malcolm. *The Picturesque: Literary Sources and Documents.* Robertsbridge, Sussex, 1994.

Daniels, Stephen, and Charles Watkins. "Picturesque Landscaping and Estate Management: Uvedale Price and Nathaniel Kent at Foxley." In *The Politics of the Picturesque: Literature, Landscape and Aesthetics since 1770,* edited by Stephen Copley and Peter Garside, pp. 13–41. Cambridge and New York, 1994.

Downing, Andrew Jackson. *A Treatise on the Theory and Practice of Landscape Gardening.* New York, 1841.

Everett, Nigel. *The Tory View of Landscape.* New Haven, 1994.

Gilpin, William Sawrey. *Practical Hints on Landscape Gardening.* London, 1832.

Hunt, John Dixon. *Gardens and the Picturesque: Studies in the History of Landscape Architecture.* Cambridge, Mass., 1992.

Hussey, Christopher. *The Picturesque: Studies in a Point of View.* London, 1927.

Lambin, Denis. "Foxley: The Prices' Estate in Herefordshire." *Journal of Garden History* 7 (1987): 244–270.

Loudon, J. C. *Observations on the Formation and Management of Useful and Ornamental Plantations: On the Theory and Practice of Landscape Gardening; and on Gaining and Embanking Land from Rivers or the Sea.* Edinburgh, 1804.

Repton, Humphrey. *Observations on the Theory and Practice of Landscape Gardening.* London, 1803.

Michael Charlesworth

PRIESTLEY, JOSEPH (1733–1804), English clergyman, chemist, and polymath. In particular, Joseph Priestley was known for sermons and theological writings in defense of a tolerant, Socinian (Unitarian), and rational form of Nonconformist religion. He also had a substantial influence in experimental science; for example, his experiments on the nature of gases and combustion led him to identify oxygen as a separate gas from air. He may have been even more important as a historian of the contemporary scientific movements. At the behest of Benjamin Franklin, Priestley wrote a history of electricity that helped to popularize and codify scientific practice. He followed its success with a later history of theories of vision. Finally, Priestley entered into the philosophical debates of his day, defending associationism and a Lockean view of ideas against the theories of Thomas Reid (1710–1796), James Beattie (1735–1802), James Oswald (d. 1793), and others and taking the side of toleration in ethical and political theory as well as in religious matters. He was honored by the revolutionary movement in France and eventually immigrated to the new United States, where he died in western Pennsylvania.

Priestley wrote his *Lectures on Oratory and Criticism* in 1762 as part of his duties at the Warrenton Academy, one of the dissenting schools that provided an alternative to Anglican and Calvinist education, although the *Lectures* were not published until 1777. Priestly was less concerned with originality than with providing practical advice to potential preachers. He drew heavily on the recently published work of Henry Home (Lord Kames; 1696–1782) and illustrated his points copiously and practically. But Priestley had come under the influence of David Hartley (1705–1757), whose *Observations on Man* established associationist psychology. According to Hartley, simple atomistic ideas combine by association into complex ideas, and that process of associationist combination can be controlled by education and skill. Thus, Priestley's practical and theoretical concerns came together in the areas of rhetoric and criticism and extended the Lockean program along associationist lines.

Priestley advocated a Lockean version of beauty and criticism interpreted in terms of Hartley's associationist mechanics. Priestley explicitly claimed that he wrote to extend and promote Hartley's work. But Priestley's approach was his own, and, perhaps because he saw theories of beauty in relatively pragmatic terms, he gave to them a straightforwardness that they lacked elsewhere. Hartley had a very Newtonian, mechanical interpretation of association, complete with undetectable vibrations in the nervous fluid that served to account for the similarity of ideas. Priestley abandoned that microscopic theory in favor of a more ordinary grouping of ideas that come together as the result of education and accumulated experience. In the process, he also departed from Locke, for whom complex ideas were the passive result of accumulated experience or the reflexive product of the mind's reflection on its own activity. Priestley took the activity of the mind to be combinatory and built his theory on the ways that mental activity may be influenced.

According to Priestley, taste and judgment are both the product of acquiring experience. The operative principles are all traceable to the ways that the mind is acted on by ideas and in turn is actively engaged. The pleasure and effectiveness of oratory and taste arise from mental activity. Thus, there can be no standard of taste independent of one's situation in life (Priestley, 1968, p. 134). Beauty has two sources: it may arise directly from the exercise of the mind, or it may arise from association. The former attributes pleasure, and thus beauty, not to qualities in objects but to the kind of mental activity in which the mind is engaged. The extremes of mental activity are torpor and hyperactivity. Both produce discomfort. But a moderate exercise of one's faculties is experienced as pleasurable and thus as beautiful. Once such expectations have been established either for objects or situations, association also produces pleasure even in the absence of the mental activity itself. Thus, a speech that is too short and easy or too long and confusing will not be beautiful. But one that engages the minds of an audience actively without overwhelming them will be pleasant and a just object of taste. By association, one may then also take pleasure in contemplating such a speech, in anticipating it, and in preparing to give it. A person of taste will have acquired many such associations and will be an able judge of what is good and what is not. Those who have no such extended experience are excluded as fit judges of taste.

Priestley treats the mind as a faculty with an appetite for exercise. For him, no special sense or attitude is required. Arts and sciences alike may exercise the mind. Aesthetic pleasure is no different from the pleasure of a theorem or experiment. Instead, association does the work of sorting ideas and combining them anew. Novelty and the sublime are instances of how mechanical operations of the brain plus associations combine to change simple pleasures into more complex wholes by providing new stimulation and mental activity. Priestley's aesthetic predicates are not expressive metaphors such as *force* and *elegance* but predicates like *novel* that imply degrees of mental activity. Thus, he is eventually led back into his practical discussion of tropes and their effects.

Priestley should not be made into too much of an innovator. Most of his ideas are to be found in other, more theoretically minded writers on taste and the beauty and pleasure of imagination. Had Priestley published his defense of Hartley's associationism in the realm of taste when it was written, it might have had more influence. But even then, it would have been secondary to David Hume's "Of the Standard of Taste" and Edmund Burke's *On the Sublime*. Priestley's efforts in the theory of taste are interesting primarily for their Lockean overtones and their simplification of Hartley. Priestley was a supreme optimist. He believed in the perfectibility of human beings through education and scientific discovery. He carried that optimism over to matters of taste. He was tolerant, hopeful, and rather limited in his vision. After 1762, Priestley turned his attention to what to him were more important matters in science, religion, and politics. His aesthetics remains interesting nevertheless.

[*See also* Beauty; *and* Taste.]

BIBLIOGRAPHY

Works by Priestley

A Course of Lectures on Oratory and Criticism (1777). Menston, England, 1968.
Selections from His Writings. Edited by Ira Brown. University Park, Pa., 1962.
The Scientific Works. 10 vols. Hildesheim, n.d. Facsimile editions prepared by Bernhard Fabian.

Other Sources

McEvoy, J. G., and J. E. McGuire. "God and Nature: Priestley's Way of Rational Dissent." In *Historical Studies in the Physical Sciences: Sixth Annual Volume,* edited by Russell McCormmach, pp. 325–404. Princeton, N.J., 1975.
Schwartz, A. Truman, and John G. McEvoy, eds. *Motion toward Perfection: The Achievement of Joseph Priestley.* Boston, 1990.
Townsend, Dabney. "The Aesthetics of Joseph Priestley." *Journal of Aesthetics and Art Criticism* 51.4 (Fall 1993): 561–571.

DABNEY TOWNSEND

PRIMITIVISM. A particularly succinct definition for the polymorphous and multivalent phenomenon in modern culture known as primitivism might be deliberate regression. Primitivism always involves a going back, a return to, a recovery of some early state of being that is perceived to be simpler or more vital or more innocent; for primitivism always has at its core a sense of loss. Emerging as a cultural force in the Enlightenment and dominating the arts of the twentieth century primitivism was one of the principal directions taken by modern European culture. It was not simply the emulation of so-called primitive or early visual expression; rather it was a search for origins and an attempt to escape the inexorable progress of historical time. Yet, the linkage of *deliberate* with *regression* describes the powerful contradiction within primitivism. Regress is not a simple antonym of progress, but a negative-to-positive relation as well. Regress implies a backward movement that is (unlike progressive movement) without intention.

Conjoined with the contradictions within primitivism is its self-reflexivity, always playing against the insurmountable distance between that which is perceived to be "primitive" and its contemporary emulation. Two phrases coined by Émile Zola (from his daring essay "Une nouvelle manière en peinture: Édouard Manet," 1867): "elegant awkwardness" *(raideurs élégantes)* and "sweet brutality" *(brutalité douce)* offer further critical insight into this phenomenon. *Elegant awkwardness* captures the persistent irony that runs through much of the primitivist aesthetic. Zola is describing qualities in Manet's paintings that were not only objectionable to the general public, but were consistently linked to folk and "primitive" expressions, including brutality or crudeness, awkwardness, rudeness, naïveté. He qualifies each, however, to indicate not only that the brutality and awkwardness are intentional, but that they are pleasurable to the viewer who understands them as such, as a deliberate regression.

In this way, primitivism corresponds closely to the root definition of irony, *eirōnia,* "to dissemble, or to simulate ignorance." Self-aware and ironic are quite the opposite of what primitivism purports to be: instinctive and spontaneous, or raw, physical, even transgressive expression. Irony exists in relationships, one of the most common being when the literal meaning of the thing expressed is the exact contrary of the actual meaning intended. But the intended meaning is only discernible (or visible) to those who know better, those who have the memory or experience that provides the broader context necessary to discern irony in a situation. For example, Paul Gauguin's *Soyez Amoureuses et Vous Serez Heureuses* (1889), a carved and painted wooden relief, exhibits both brutality and awkwardness. The sophisticated discourse of the piece is contradictory to its literal patois and apparent only to the viewer aware of the relationship between academic classicism and Gauguin's deliberate inversion of it. A viewer unaware of this relationship would simply think this was a folk carving. For even the naive viewer, however, context is everything. If the relief were found in an antique or curiosity shop, it would seem indeed to be a folk carving; but if it were exhibited with contemporaneous paintings and sculptures, even an untutored eye would perceive the contradiction held in balance by this image. Someone like Zola, however, would appreciate the Gauguin relief precisely for its ironic relationship to the fine-art tradition. To the naïf, it is brutal. To Zola, it is a sweet brutality, for he understands that Gauguin's regression is deliberate, that while he appears to be falling backward, he is actually moving forward into the vanguard of modern art.

These linkages do not simply illustrate that deliberate regression often creates ironic situations. The relationship is more fundamental: primitivism is irony in a historical and cultural matrix. Put another way, the manifestations of primitivism, however diffuse and various, all draw on the conditions and relations of irony. The inverse: only in reconstructing the historical and cultural contexts of a given example of primitivism does the irony of the relationship become apparent. Yet surprisingly, little research has been done on the eighteenth-century origins and development of primitivism, despite its impact on both modern and contemporary art. Art-historical discussions of primitivism, notably Robert Goldwater's *Primitivism in Modern Art* (1938) and the 1984 Museum of Modern Art exhibition and catalog organized by William Rubin, have until recently been primarily formalist inquiries, defining primitivism as a twentieth-century phenomenon. In this line of thought, primitivism is characterized as stylistic influence from so-called primitive styles, particularly African and Oceanic, leading to the overthrow of the classical hegemony in Western art.

Recent challenges to this view of primitivism, all drawing on the seminal work of Edward W. Said (1978), point out the ethnocentricity and one-sidedness of these histories. These critiques redefine primitivism on what might be described as ideological grounds, challenging the formalist, apolitical representations. Arguing that primitivism encompasses far more than the assimilation of stylistic elements, the postmodern critiques describe this phenomenon in terms of complex cultural exchanges, issues of representation and appropriation, and link visual culture in Europe to imperialist, colonialist political culture. Neither the modernist story nor its postmodern critique attempts to reconstruct the formation of the primitivist aesthetic, although this process began almost two hundred years prior to Pablo Picasso's *Demoiselles d'Avignon* (1907). As a consequence, two of the most vexing problems concerning primitivism remain: (1) identifying what "primitive" art is or was, and (2) explaining why, since primitivism emulates the "primitive," there are so few examples of direct influence.

One of the difficulties facing any study of primitivism is the bewildering array of styles identified and emulated by modern artists as "primitive." In the work of Gauguin alone, the "primitive" encompasses Italian Gothic, Javanese Buddhist, Marquesan, pre-Columbian, Japanese, Egyptian, Tahitian, and medieval. Folk arts and popular arts were frequently included in this mix, although artists in this category, like Henri Rousseau or Grandma Moses, differ from those in Gothic Italy, Benin, or the Marquesas Islands in that they have not been trained in the image tradition of their culture, and therefore might be more accurately described as naive. Compounding the confusion concerning what is "primitive" is the proliferation of primitivisms (consider, for example, the distance between the primitivizing of Dominique Ingres, Paul Klee, and Joseph Beuys). European artists used the term *primitive* loosely and often. Even more problematic than the shifting identity of "primitive" art are the derogatory connotations of the word when it is applied to culture. To identify something as "primitive" is to place it in an early stage of development, an entirely appropriate use of the term when applied to technology: a hoe, a typewriter, a wristwatch. To describe a culture and its symbolic expression as "primitive" assumes a single path of progression and a single definition of civilization, branding that culture as infantile and undeveloped. It is in the latter half of the eighteenth century that archaic Greek and Gothic images were first described as "primitive," and throughout the nineteenth century, other art traditions were included under this rubric. Some historians have drawn a distinction between historical "primitives," the archaic or "court" styles that influenced nineteenth-century artists, and living "primitives," or tribal styles that exerted their full impact only in the twentieth century, in order to claim precedence for Picasso as the fountainhead of primitivism in modern art. The tacit claim made here, however, is that

African, Native American, and Oceanic arts are indeed "primitive," whereas nineteenth-century references to Egyptian, pre-Columbian, or Italian Gothic arts as "primitive" are simply incorrect. The historical sources show that these distinctions were not made by Picasso, Gauguin, or other primitivizing artists. Rather, the interest in "primitive" art began with styles of the historical past that were more readily assimilated and progressed ever outward to the more distant and alien.

Rejecting the idea that any actual tradition is "primitive," the postmodern critique corroborated Said's thesis by arguing that the "primitive," like the "Orient," was located in the eye of the European beholder, and reflects more on the viewer than the object of his or her gaze. This puts us far closer to understanding the relationships involved in primitivism, but this critical stance needs more historical grounding. Without considering the limitations and contingencies of actual, historical circumstances, the beholder's-eye argument implies that definitions of the "primitive" are completely individual and arbitrary, or that cultural constructions are more fantasy than reality. It does not confront the historical reality that European artists and intellectuals of the nineteenth and twentieth centuries consistently used terms like *primitive, savage,* and *art nègre* to identify a wide range of imagery, including African and Oceanic arts as well as Western traditions like Romanesque and archaic Greek. "Primitive" art cannot be defined as either objective reality or subjective eye-of-the beholder; it exists in the relationship between the two.

Another rather surprising aspect of primitivism confronting art historians is that a remarkably small percentage of modern paintings or sculptures contain documentable examples of direct visual borrowing, despite the obvious impact of "primitive" art. Picasso's *Demoiselles d'Avignon,* a pivotal image in any history of primitivism, quotes no specific "primitive" source directly. At the same time, however, this painting is consistent with other primitivizing imagery, demonstrating that there was some agreement as to what "primitive" art was assimilated. [*See* Picasso.] This problem is particularly troublesome to art historians because it poses a real challenge concerning historical process and creative exchange. In fact, one of the principal tasks undertaken by the 1984 Museum of Modern Art exhibition was to attempt to historically ground the phenomenon of primitivism by documenting these "primitive" sources. Goldwater argued that European artists were influenced more by an idea of "primitive" art than by specific visual images. Defining primitivism as an "attitude productive of art," Goldwater reasoned that "primitive art only served as a kind of stimulating focus, a catalytic which, though not in itself used or borrowed from, still helped the artists to formulate their own aims because they could attribute to it the qualities they themselves sought to attain." It is possible to find a common framework of ideas concerning "primitive" expression through a careful reading of period sources from the eighteenth and nineteenth centuries, including voyage accounts, ethnographic studies, missionary reports, and art criticism. It is important to recognize that the ideas concerning the nature of "primitive" expression were established well before "artificial curiosities" were brought back from the South Seas by Captain James Cook or the Comte de Bougainville (c.1770s), Egyptian artifacts were carted from Egypt for display in the Musée Napoléon (c.1800), or African masks and sculptures were featured in the colonial sections of world's fairs (c.1890s).

In the first decades of the eighteenth century the efforts to reconstruct the origins of culture began in earnest; the earliest such enterprise was Giambattista Vico's landmark treatise of 1725, *La sciènza nuòva*, which used as evidence biblical accounts, Homeric poetry, Roman descriptions of ancient Germans, Gauls, and Picts, as well as contemporary reports of New World peoples. The notion of "primitivity" as an infant state of development through which all cultures passed was an invention of Enlightenment universalism (and paradoxically, this universalist notion opened the door for the assimilation of particular ethnic traditions). Through these early cultural studies a diverse collection of art traditions was redefined as "primitive" art. It is not coincidental that art history emerged as a discipline concurrently with these studies of cultural development. Johann Joachim Winckelmann's *Reflections on the Imitation of Greek Works in Painting and Sculpture* (1755) and *History of Ancient Art* (1764) were extremely effective in promoting his conception of classical art as the standard against which all other artistic expressions were measured. Classicism was already established as the official "fine art" taught in the art academies (following the influential French model). Winckelmann's polemical writings elevated the classical tradition to a master narrative, transforming the elements of classical style into universal principles. In the same era that Winckelmann codified an idealist and intellectual classicism as "fine art," an odd grouping of nonclassical styles was categorized as "primitive" art through scholarly debate and ethnographic collections. If "fine art" exemplified the culmination of artistic progress, "primitive art" represented its earliest stages. Classicism functioned as both end point and as center. Not surprisingly, the characteristics of "primitive" art, also thought to be universal, were comprised of visual elements that already existed on the periphery of the classical tradition.

Period sources, including voyage accounts, art criticism, and popular literature, reveal that debates about the nature of "primitive" art were less concerned with specific styles than with these "universal" attributes that Europeans identified and later assimilated as *Urformen*. Although a great deal of nonclassical imagery was routinely identified as "primitive," "savage," "art nègre," and "carib," with little if any care or consistency for actual provenance or use, there was surprising consistency in the visual characteristics ascribed to "primitive" expression. Understanding "primitive" art as a collection of visual attributes goes some distance toward explaining the comparisons made between radically different art traditions. It corroborates Goldwater's observation that the avant-garde emulated the idea of "primitive" imagery more often than specific styles, but goes further to demonstrate that this idea of "primitive" art was far more consistent and complex than previously thought. Although eighteenth- and nineteenth-century characterizations of "primitive" imagery are ethnocentric and inaccurate as descriptions of actual styles, it does not follow that they are without meaning or system. To the contrary, these terms carried specific aesthetic meanings within the classical tradition and fit into a consistent European construction of "primitive" art, however derogatory and misapplied they were as descriptions of actual traditions. The negative connotations of the term *primitive art* have provoked efforts to find neutral substitutes, or to condemn the term altogether, but historical sources show that "primitive art" was an amalgam of visual traits, completely a European construction that had only vague associations with actual styles. The characteristics ascribed to "primitive" art point directly to the classical tradition as the principal framework through which certain images could be assimilated into European verbal and visual discourse as "primitive." These terms, *naive, grotesque, ornament, hieroglyph,* defined "primitive" art by its opposition to classical norms and determined the directions primitivism could and could not take.

These terms also link "primitive" art to visual traits associated with excessive imagination and lack of reason, setting it in contrast to the excessively rational classicism taught in the academies. Without the tools of rationality, "primitives" were immersed in an immediate, physical world, with no way to mediate this experience. They could not impose the abstract systems of illusion and narrative, idealized form and action, that were the foundations of European fine art. Imagine any figure from the Parthenon frieze next to the elaborate carvings of a Maori canoe prow. To the European observer, this "primitive" carving provided indisputable evidence that its maker lacked the rational faculties necessary to impose abstract ideals on random experience. Unlike the slab of Parthenon marble, carved so that the figures seem to have volume and the slab seems to be an illusionistic space continuous with our own, the "primitive" image manipulates line and pattern on a flat two-dimensional surface. Narrative was just as much an abstraction as illusion, isolating a significant moment, such as the Panathenaic procession, and composing it for maximum dramatic and didactic effect. The Maori's submersion of figures within the pattern and the determination of its form by an ornamental scheme seemed to echo the "primitive's" own submersion in unreflective experience. It is also important to recognize the extent to which idealized beauty was synonymous with intellectual rigor and moral purity in Winckelmann's theory and in academic pedagogy. Framed by this standard, a great deal of nonclassical imagery was categorized as caricatured, or if more horrific, as grotesque, and these visual traits carried associations with unreason, passion, and superstition, as well as profane or bestial behavior.

If the classical tradition constructed "primitive" art as its inferior opposite, what then is the relationship of modernism to the classical tradition? The story modernism wrote for itself was that the encounter with "primitive" art was an epiphany, inspiring avant-garde artists to break free from the past, not simply from academic convention but from their cultural patrimony. The assimilation of the "primitive" led to the overthrow of academic classicism.

Or so we are led to believe. This Oedipal drama, like the original, is not what it seems. The historical sources tell quite the opposite story. They show that the "primitive" existed in a dialectical relationship with the classical tradition. If the classical tradition determined the initial construction of "primitive" art, it follows that it also defined the shape of primitivism. Although modernist appropriations of "primitive" art have been heralded as a precocious appreciation of non-Western imagery, historical sources show that the avant-garde borrowed only those elements already identified through the classical tradition as "primitive." Consequently, their primitivism might better be understood as the construction of an anticlassical aesthetic, the antithesis of the classical thesis. The avant-garde did not so much break from the aesthetic norms as turn them upside down, because the center of academic classicism determined the ways in which they rebelled against it. Primitivizing artists did not reinterpret the nature of "primitive" art, nor did they describe "primitive" art with terminology that was in any way different. The critical distinction lay in their embrace of the attributes of the "primitive." Gauguin clearly associated a love of ornament with "primitive" expression, but this was turned to a positive attribute. He observed in *Avant et après* that "one does not seem to suspect in Europe that there exists, among the Maoris of New Zealand, as with the Marquesans, a very advanced decorative art." He characterized his own work as decorative, fully aware that this would offend the sensibilities of his European readers and viewers as much as his stated desire to become a savage. In short, the reasons for admiring "primitive" art were just as culture bound as the reasons for rejecting it. Gauguin, like other primitivizing artists seeking to overthrow academic classicism, nevertheless operated within its system. Another look at his panel, *Soyez amoureuses*, reveals a thorough inversion of the classical standards: with grotesque, crude, and crudely rendered figures, the male (self-portrait?) profile willfully disfigured; with hieroglyphic or emblematic segmentation of the picture plane and inclusion of lettering and seemingly symbolic imagery; and with increased orna-

mentation and pattern at the expense of illusionistic form and space; but, significantly, there is no direct quote from any specific nonclassical tradition. Picasso's *Demoiselles d'Avignon* presents a similar case in which the inversion of the classical/rational is systematic and explains far more about the meaning of this image than attempts to describe its possible affinities with Iberian, Oceanic, or African traditions. Goldwater's argument that borrowing from styles outside the Western tradition signals a breakthrough because it "frees the individual and so makes his desired return to a single underlying intensity that much easier" now reads as the height of irony.

Primitivism is the ultimate in dissembling, then, for it is only within the larger frame of a self-defined "civilized" and "rational" culture that artists can be "primitive" and "irrational." The crude and grotesque figures of Picasso or Jean Dubuffet are frightening yet pleasurable because they, like the primitivism they embody, are framed and controlled by the broader aesthetic norms of "fine art." Herein lies their "sweet brutality." While the driving force behind primitivism was a desire to return art to its vital origins, to reembody it by eschewing the rational and verbal, it is no small irony that these increasingly mute and physical images have generated an extremely sophisticated critical theory to frame them. As Goldwater observed, the more childlike the image, the more subtle and esoteric the argument necessary to distinguish it from the art of a child. Primitivism's progress was as inexorable as it was voracious, moving from those "primitives" close to the classical center to those ever more distant and other, until that which was strange was now familiar. No longer a screen for the projections of a dominant culture, the other now has a voice and a presence that look back at us, like Olympia's gaze. By the 1930s the search for the primal began turning inward, toward the exploration of the subconscious. In the last quarter of the twentieth century, deliberate regression has turned toward Earth art and the environment.

Modernism was so successful in its struggle against a dominant classical tradition that, like all victors, it rewrote its own history. Only when we resituate modernism into its own history are we able to confront its complex and conflicting relationships with non-Western arts and with the classical tradition. It is telling that Westerners have only been able to see the irony in the modernist "discovery" of "primitive" art in recent decades when the voices of those whose cultural expressions were partially assimilated began to be heard in intellectual and artistic discourse.

Examining the course taken by primitivizing artists from the late nineteenth through the twentieth century reveals a fascinating reversal of identities as well. The desire to recover cultural memories and expressions that Europeans presumed to be "universal" led to the rapid assimilation of an extremely diverse range of non-Western styles. This process resulted in a modern style that superseded classicism as the international style. The modern styles shaped by the assimilation of non-Western arts have become (through the dominance of Western culture) the global, universal definition of fine art in the twentieth century, taught in academies around the world and displacing traditional expressions. But whose universal style is it? As we have seen, these "universal" attributes constructed a kind of transcultural style that first obliterated the identity of its influences, stripped away their cultural moorings, and then incorporated them into a new lexicon as "primitive," rude, grotesque, ornamental. In the late twentieth century, the quest for identity has shifted: the concern now is to find ways for postcolonial peoples to recover or retain their identities. In Europe, artists such as Anselm Kiefer have crafted a progressive strategy for the legitimate primitivist desire to reject the dehumanizing elements of modern culture. Kiefer's images reach back into the mythic traditions of Germany, Egypt, and Judaism, but they do so in an attempt to recover historical memory, and in order to confront modern Western history rather than to escape it.

[*See also* Cubism; Modernism, *overview article;* Orientalism; Postcolonialism; *and* Romanticism.]

BIBLIOGRAPHY

Antliff, Mark, and Patricia Leighten. "Primitivism." In *Critical Terms for Art History,* edited by Robert S. Nelson and Richard Shiff, pp. 170–184. Chicago, 1996.
Bhabha, Homi. "Of Mimicry and Man: The Ambivalence of Colonial Discourse." *October* 28 (Spring 1984): 125–133.
Boas, George, and Arthur O. Lovejoy. *Primitivism and Related Ideas in Antiquity.* A Documentary History of Primitivism and Related Ideas, vol. 1. Baltimore, 1935.
Clifford, James. *The Predicament of Culture: Twentieth-Century Ethnography, Literature, and Art.* Cambridge, Mass., 1988.
Connelly, Frances. *The Sleep of Reason: Primitivism in Modern European Art and Aesthetics, 1725–1907.* University Park, Pa., 1995.
Foster, Hal. *Recodings: Art, Spectacle, Cultural Politics.* Port Townsend, Wash., 1985.
Goldwater, Robert. *Primitivism in Modern Art* (1938). Enl. ed. Cambridge, Mass., 1986.
Harbison, Robert. *Deliberate Regression.* New York, 1980.
Hiller, Susan, ed. *The Myth of Primitivism: Perspectives on Art.* London and New York, 1991.
Laude, Jean. *La peinture française, 1905–1914, et l'art nègre.* Paris, 1968.
Leighten, Patricia. "The White Peril and l'Art Nègre: Picasso, Primitivism, and Anticolonialism." *Art Bulletin* 72 (December 1990): 609–630.
Previtali, Giovanni. *La fortuna dei primitivi dal Vasari ai neoclassici.* Turin, 1964.
Rhodes, Colin. *Primitivism and Modern Art.* London and New York, 1994.
Rosenblum, Robert. *Transformations in Late Eighteenth-Century Art.* Princeton, N.J., 1967.
Rubin, William, ed. *Primitivism in 20th Century Art: Affinity of the Tribal and the Modern.* 2 vols. New York, 1984. Exhibition catalog, Museum of Modern Art.
Said, Edward W. *Orientalism.* New York, 1978.
Todorov, Tzvetan. *The Conquest of America: The Question of the Other.* Translated by Richard Howard. New York, 1984.
Torgovnick, Marianna. *Gone Primitive: Savage Intellects, Modern Lives.* Chicago, 1990.

FRANCES S. CONNELLY

PSYCHICAL DISTANCE. *See* Bullough.

PSYCHOANALYTIC THEORIES OF ART. *See* Bachelard; Freud; Irigaray; Klein; Lacan; Marcuse; *and* Winnicott.

PSYCHOLOGY OF ART. All aspects of the human mind have applications to the arts. These aspects can be described under the three main headings of motivation, cognition, and emotion.

Motivation refers to the mind's strivings, the dynamic straining toward certain goals. The most general problem facing the psychologist of art in regard to motivation concerns the question of why art exists. What are the impulses that make human beings create performances and works of art, and what makes people all over the world so eager to receive art? The oldest answer to these questions has asserted that art exists universally because it gives pleasure. The hedonistic approach to motivation derives in Western culture from the Cyrenaic school of Greek philosophy and has been favored as an easy answer through the ages to the present. Psychologists have used it in experimental aesthetics when they confronted their subjects with sets of objects, such as shapes and colors, and asked, "Which one do you like best?" The answers to such questions, however, served at most to ascertain preferences, for instance, in market research; they did not discover the causes of motivational pleasure, and only those causes tell us why art exists.

The most general answer to this question relates the aesthetic impulse to a more general human striving. It is the desire to unfold all potential abilities of mind and body to the fullest extent. The ability to discover, to enjoy, to think, to construct makes for the strong wish to do so. In their more specific realm, artists feel impelled to explore the entire range of human experiences and to clarify their nature by describing and representing them. In particular, the puzzles, the mysteries, and the imperfections of reality challenge not only the philosopher, the scientist, the ruler, and the reformer, but equally the artist, who endeavors to wrestle with the tasks of life in his or her own way. To be sure, to undertake and carry out such tasks generates pleasure, but pleasure is merely the symptom of the motives bringing it about.

One of the most attractive motives of artistic creation is that of conjuring up an ideal state of being. To give shape to perfection, artists use their imagination with all degrees of realism, depending on how well they adapt human wishes to the actual conditions of existence. The fancies of wish fulfilment operate at their least responsible level in cheap literature depicting total fulfillment at the price of neglecting the actual obstacles to be faced in the world. Similar purposes are met by the kitsch images of painting or sculpture, offering embodiments of perfection and harmony. Their lack of realism, however, makes more thoughtful persons ridicule and reject them. Emotional indulgence in music reduces artistic quality by reducing music's more arduous concerns with building structures, dealing with counterforces, and so on that make better music portray the more serious and mature mind facing the tasks of life.

Such differences in artistic value modify the prime products of artistic motivation, which embody beauty and ideals. When traditional theory of aesthetics limits the definition of beauty to perfection and harmony, it really reduces itself to the inferior category of kitsch. Ideals defined in a similarly limited fashion produce—for example, in the literary depictions of utopias—pictures of tedious societies where nobody would care to live. Such one-sided definitions of the most desirable conditions and products imply also an inferior conception of human motivation.

Psychologists have confirmed the harmful consequences of such one-sided motivation. The "Bovary effect" of cheap novels or movies deflects their users from effectively dealing with the problems and offerings of life and from realistically accepting responsibility. The opposite one-sidedness of artistic motivation leads to a similar reduction of quality by limiting itself to the negative aspects of human existence. It distinguishes the depiction of human depravity and inferiority, say, in the etchings of a William Hogarth from the satires of an Honoré Daumier, whose figures display their frailties and distortions to make viewers laugh without depriving them of a melancholy compassion for the human condition.

In the field of social psychology, the position and function of art and artists in society make for a great variety of motivational relations. In early societies, performers and art makers are so closely integrated in the community that their motivational objectives coincide with those of the group. At first, there may be no distinction between those who supply the arts and those who consume them. Performances of dances and other ceremonies are shared by all for a common purpose, and craft work is contributed by everybody. Even when the arts become specialities reserved for certain individuals, there is in early societies no noticeable distinction between the objectives of the artists and those of the community. Only in ages of individualism such as that of the Renaissance in the Western world do artists cease to be employed artisans like bricklayers or shoemakers and develop their own aesthetic values, which must try to cope with those of monarchal and ecclesiastical princes using their services. By the time of Michelangelo, motivational conflicts between providers and customers in the arts re-

flect simply the interplay of antagonistic forces in a modern economy. In the nineteenth century, the artist, detached from the give-and-take of well-functioning social relations, is typified by isolated loners pursuing their own standard and taste, which more often than not are not shared by the public.

In particular, the narrative media of literature or painting mirror the social conditions of the time. They vary from period to period and depict the differences between totalitarian regimes and liberal democracies. Hence the psychological and sociological content analyses of the narrative media, whose ideologies are extracted and theoretically formulated. A world of difference emerges between, say, Voltaire's *Candide* of 1750 and Bertolt Brecht's biting satire of modern society in his *Three Penny Opera* of 1934.

When the discussion moves from motivation to cognition, psychologists ask more generally what the arts contribute to the knowledge and understanding of the world facing the mind. Sensory perception is our only access to that world, and among the senses vision, hearing, and the sensations of touch and kinesthesia are the principal contributors. Only one of the sense modalities, namely, vision, is truly an exteroceptive distance sense in that it provides images of the outer world; and only two are truly proprioceptive: kinesthesia and touch provide information by sensations of the perceiver's body. The others, such as hearing or smell, are intermediate in that they generate experiences not clearly separating the outer from the inner world. These basic differences of the sensory modalities influence their applications to the arts. They determine the ways in which the various media select and represent aspects of reality.

While the sense of vision provides images of the physical world, it is limited to doing so by projections of three-dimensional space on a two-dimensional receptor surface in the eyes. This means that at any moment of time the visual image records the way the world is seen from a particular vantage point; but because the viewer synthesizes a multitude of these momentary perceptions, the resulting image of the world can greatly compensate for the one-sidedness of optical projections. This makes for a basic difference between media such as painting, which must commit themselves to single projections or their combinations, and media that move in time, such as the film. Sculpture and architecture dwell in physical space and allow viewers freely to move around the art objects they are looking at.

Nevertheless, although vision is limited optically to projection, the visual images of painting hardly ever proclaim their worldview as one determined by the individual observer. Object-bound rather than subjective, pictorial images of the three-dimensional world present the world as a hierarchy of powers differing in weight and distinguishing the dominance of what is close and large from what is distant and small. This is particularly obvious in styles ignoring central perspective, such as Western pre-Renaissance paintings or those of classical China. But even central perspective is mostly perceived as offering particular ways of how the world *is*, rather than how it appears to someone's momentary vision.

When a visual medium uses the time dimension, as do the dance or film, it is able to show the interaction of motion and stillness. The world of becoming and changing is presented in counterpoint with that of being, and depending on the mental attitude of the artist, the more fundamental state of the world appears to be either that of timeless persistence or that of restless flux. Visual representation, however, profits not only from naturalistic completeness but equally from a partial selection of perceptual aspects. Architecture, painting, and sculpture use timelessness as an indispensable virtue.

Similarly, the omission of color makes for monochromatic images in which all surface values are fitted to a unitary gray scale. This enhances the compositional unity and simplicity of the image and lets the powerful contrast of light and darkness rule undisturbed. The use of color, while increasing the wealth of complexity and allowing for more naturalistic representation, greatly complicates the artist's task. It increases the number of parameters to be dealt with, dominant among them being the compositional primaries of red, blue, and yellow. Psychologists have studied the number and selection of colors referred to in the languages of various cultures.

Music, like nonrepresentational painting, combines abstractness with strong concreteness. It is abstract by disregarding the world of objects, which is so prominent in representational painting; but it strikes the ears with the unmatched immediacy of auditory expression. It limits itself to describing reality as action, motion, and change, and it thereby serves admirably to accompany and interpret visual events, such as social ceremonies. In the opera, the happenings on the stage and the dynamics of the music complement each other. Film music supplies the action on the screen with all levels of emotion, from the serenity of idylls to the highest pitch of excitement. Experiments have demonstrated how the character of what the eyes see in a film can be changed when a different music accompanies it.

Music takes place essentially in the two dimensions of progression in time and the simultaneity of what may be called musical space. Pure percussion on a single drum limits the performance to the differences of rhythm, from the regular beat to its endless deviations of speed or syncopations. To such rhythmical play, monophonic music adds the variations of high and low tones, of rising and falling in a single melodic line. The mere progression of monophony is enriched, under certain cultural conditions, by polyphony. Here a basic psychological difference is observed between antagonistic actions, as in the voices of counterpoint, and the rich unity of consonant or dissonant chords.

In spite of the differences between the various musical systems, most of them, and perhaps all, rely on some of the basic intervals, such as the octave, the fifth, and the fourth. Their universality has been derived in several theories from physical and physiological factors, reflected in aural experience. The diatonic system of traditional Western music relies on the interplay between the attractive powers of the basic intervals, especially those serving as the tonic, and the gravitational weight governing high and low pitch. The absence of bases of reference in modern atonal or serial music has deprived the system of its clearly centered stability and replaced it with the mutual relations of the individual tones—a symbolical reflection of a social situation devoid of a dominant central power.

Literature, the aesthetic medium of language, differs from the other media by not basing its references to the outer world on the direct perception of either sight or sound. Language is a referential medium, meaning that it has to rely strongly on memory images. Here it needs to be said that, in a much more general sense, memory images are the indirect medium of the mind. Even in the absence of language, memory images are an indispensable component of cognitive behavior. They enable animals or persons to connect past experiences with present ones, to compare and distinguish them. What is more, they also strengthen perceptual concepts, which generalize perceptual experience. All perception is tied to generalization. For example, the knowledge of trees begins with "treeness" in general and is specified only gradually to, say, oaks. From there, perception may be individualized to one's recognizing the oak in one's garden, different from all others.

Perceptual concepts make verbal language possible because language consists of tokens for concepts. Language strengthens the system of concepts most powerfully by naming concepts at all levels of abstraction, from the individual to the general. Because language consists explicitly of concepts, it refers to any percept by calling it by its name: "I am seeing an oak!"

Hence the unique range of the verbal medium. Not only can it rely on the mental images of all sensory modalities in any combination, talking of smell and sound and vision in the same sentence, it also combines all levels of abstraction. When Emily Dickinson writes, "past the houses, past the headlands, into deep eternity," she connects the most concrete with the most abstract concepts, thereby raising her poem to a philosophical level of thought without abandoning concrete presence. This unique virtue of the verbal medium is evident in metaphors, which relate experiences from different realms and thereby raise the comparison to a higher level of abstractness.

Literature, however, is limited like the other media to a selection from the experiential aspects of reality. It is limited to sequences in time, which strengthen its emphasis on action, but make it difficult to describe events occurring simultaneously or objects dwelling in the same space. It must resort to translating synchrony into diachrony.

Even so, psychologists see literature as the most comprehensive of all aesthetic media. It compensates for its remoteness from direct perceptual experience by its unrivaled range of perceptual references at all levels of abstraction. It unites experience and thought in a uniquely human fashion.

Finally, a reference is needed to the third aspect of the human mind, namely, emotion. Emotion is the level of tension or excitement accompanying all acts of motivation and cognition. All motivational strivings for a goal or the escaping from a threat are tinged by the nervous system with some degree of excitement. Similarly, any cognitive recognition or discovery makes for an arousal of tension, which may be slight or powerful. This is as true for the making of art and responses to art as it is for any other human behavior. It adds a particular quality of warmth and involvement to what, by comparison, may be described as the mere functions of existence—the functions of striving toward goals as well as identifying and understanding the world. Emotion is no privilege of the arts, but they would feel dead without it.

[*See also* Arnheim; Color, *article on* Color Science; Creativity; Freud; Gombrich; Imagery; Imagination; Klein; Lacan; Perception, *article on* Psychology of Perception; Perspective; Synaesthesia; *and* Winnicott.]

BIBLIOGRAPHY

Arnheim, Rudolf. *Art and Visual Perception* (1954). New exp. rev. ed. Berkeley, 1974.
Arnheim, Rudolf. *Visual Thinking.* Berkeley, 1969.
Berlin, Brent, and Paul Kay. *Basic Color Terms: Their Universality and Evolution.* Berkeley, 1969.
Berlyne, D. E. *Aesthetics and Psychobiology.* New York, 1971.
De la Motte-Haber, Helga. *Handbuch der Musikpsychologie.* Laaber, 1985.
Freud, Sigmund. *Creativity and the Unconscious.* New York, 1958.
Kobbert, Max J. *Kunstpsychologie.* Darmstadt, 1986.
Kreitler, Hans, and Shulamith Kreitler. *Psychology of the Arts.* Durham, N.C., 1972.
Langfeld, Herbert Sidney. *The Aesthetic Attitude* (1920). Port Washington, N.Y., 1967.
Mitchell, W. J. T. *Iconology: Image, Text, Ideology.* Chicago, 1986.

RUDOLF ARNHEIM

Q-R

QUALITIES, AESTHETIC. Whether a painting has a black square in the middle, or a particular poem is written in French or Italian, is seldom the subject of controversy. If any two people were to disagree over this, the issue could be settled quickly by persons without aesthetic taste; the contested statements are intersubjectively testable by fairly uncontroversial methods. But whether a painting or poem is graceful, unified, melancholic, harmonious, clumsy, or disorganized is something that is often debated. When critics and others disagree over this, it would seem that the issue can only be settled by people with some aesthetic taste; and it is far from obvious that the contested statements are testable by uncontroversial methods. The notions of "aesthetic taste" and "ability to make aesthetic discriminations" are difficult to apply in an uncontroversial way, however; alleged counterexamples may be defined away by arguing that the critic has no aesthetic taste or no ability to make aesthetic discriminations. They are also notoriously difficult to analyze in a coherent and convincing way, and without ending up in a vicious circle or an infinite regress. They are probably as obscure as the notion of an aesthetic quality. Thus, the question arises as to whether there are any alternative but roughly equivalent ways of demarcating and characterizing aesthetic qualities or concepts.

Many theoretical problems are raised by such qualities and the attribution of them to artworks and other objects. The starting point of the discussion can be the terms used to characterize the aesthetic qualities of artworks and other objects. The focus can then be on these terms, or on certain uses of them, or on the qualities they refer to, or on the act of attributing these qualities to objects and actions of different kinds. If focus is on the terms, the methods used are often semantic analyses of how these terms are used by certain critics in a specified context, possibly combined with philosophical analysis and criticism of such uses. If, however, focus is on the qualities, a phenomenological approach suggests itself.

The problems include the relation of aesthetic qualities to qualities and properties of other kinds, the further characterization and definition of these qualities, what methods, if any, could be used to check such attributions, the relativity or objectivity of aesthetic attributions, and the truth claims of aesthetic judgments.

Historical Background. How are aesthetic qualities related to qualities and properties of other kinds? The history of the problems raised by aesthetic qualities can be traced back to the ancient distinction between primary and secondary qualities discussed by Democritus (c.469–370 BCE), a distinction also commented on by Galileo Galilei (1564–1642), René Descartes (1596–1650), and Robert Boyle (1627–1691). But the classical starting point of the contemporary discussion of the distinction between primary qualities (such as solidity and extension) and secondary qualities (such as color and taste) is to be found in John Locke's *Essay concerning Human Understanding* (1690). Locke states the distinction in several ways, and argues for it in several different ways. These passages have been the subject of widely different interpretations and also criticized. The precise way to state the distinction between primary and secondary qualities is still controversial, though there is growing agreement that the distinction is basically sound.

The contemporary discussion of the nature of aesthetic qualities started with Frank Sibley's seminal essay "Aesthetic Concepts" (1959), which gave rise to a lively and intensive exchange of ideas that lasted for decades. It concerned semantic and phenomenological as well as ontological and epistemological issues. For example, is it true, as Peter Kivy (1968) has suggested, that "X is graceful" is synonymous with "Look how graceful X is!"? If so, in what contexts? This semantic problem is clearly different from the ontological question of whether qualities such as "graceful" are part of the fabric of the world, as well as from the epistemic problem of what can be known about such qualities. These problems are not identical with the phenomenological question of how such qualities are experienced, and if, for instance, they are experienced as qualities of objects or as responses in us to objects.

The Characterization of Aesthetic Qualities. Because "aesthetic taste" is probably just as obscure as "aesthetic quality," it is hardly astonishing that attempts have been made to identify a number of conditions, each of which is necessary and jointly sufficient, for qualities to be aesthetic.

The following characteristics, among others, have been proposed as elements of a three-part conjunction:

1. that aesthetic qualities are perceived or perceivable;
2. that aesthetic qualities are value-relevant, that is, relevant as reasons for positive and negative judgments about the aesthetic (but not artistic) value of objects; and

3. that aesthetic qualities are tertiary, supervenient, or emergent, that is, dependent on primary and secondary qualities.

The precise interpretation of these conditions has been much discussed. The second requirement presupposes an analysis of the notion of aesthetic value, which is just as problematic as the notion of aesthetic quality. Also, the analysis of the dependence requirement—(3) above—has been debated in the literature.

Do "This movie is obscene" or "That picture is sacrilegious" attribute or ascribe aesthetic qualities to the works referred to? If not, why not? It seems clear that here the notion of "aesthetic value" plays a crucial role in arguments over answers to these questions. Given a narrow, formalistic conception of artistic value, the answer to the first question will be no. But given a wider notion of aesthetic value, where no sharp distinction between aesthetic and ethical concerns is maintained, the answer will be different. The basic idea underlying the above characterization is that aesthetic qualities (e.g., "is unified") resemble secondary qualities (e.g., "is red") in that both are phenomenal, that is, perceivable and perceived. But they differ from secondary qualities in that they are value-relevant and tertiary.

To say that a particular painting has a blue spot in the upper right corner is not to say or suggest anything about the value of the painting; such a statement is clearly not relevant as grounds for aesthetic praise or blame of that painting. Moreover, one can easily imagine two objects x and y that differ qualitatively only in that one of them is red, the other not—for example, a red and a black billiard ball. But it is not possible for two paintings or sculptures x and y to differ *only* in that one of them is unified, but the other is not. If x is unified but y is not, there must also be other differences between these two works of art, concerning, for example, how the parts are related to the whole or the way colors are spread on the canvas.

The Variety of Aesthetic Qualities. Examples of aesthetic qualities include garishness, tenseness, grace, harmony, gaiety, nervousness, sadness, excitement, somberness, sereneness, solemnity, joy, cheerfulness, boldness, vitality, restraint, sublimity, monumentality, coherence, picturesqueness, mysteriousness, and beauty.

An important obstacle to progress in the discussion of the nature of aesthetic qualities has been the implicit or explicit assumption that these qualities form a homogeneous class. This assumption needs to be examined critically. In other words, it is important to recognize that within the class of qualities thus demarcated, there is a variety of aesthetic qualities that cannot be analyzed in quite the same way. Thus, attempts have been made to distinguish between aesthetic qualities along a number of dimensions: (complexity) simple, complex; (location) internal, external; (value) descriptive, evaluative; (sense) literal, metaphoric. Thus, "sad-

ness" is a simple quality, but "unity" is a complex one in that it presupposes that the parts of the work are related to the whole in a particular way. The quality "melancholy" is internal in that it is experienced as a quality in the work, whereas "excitement" is different. Some aesthetic qualities are more obviously tied to value judgments than are others. For example, to say that a work is disorganized or clumsy is to give an argument for a negative value judgment. (But it does not prove that the work is bad: the work can be good, though it is disorganized or clumsy.) To say that a work is "powerful," that a tune is "cheerful," or that a line is "nervous" is clearly to use these terms in a metaphoric way; living as well as dead metaphors are among the terms used in aesthetic characterizations.

Moreover, some aesthetic qualities ("unity," "balance") behave like gestalt qualities in that the parts of the work are related to each other in such a way that the work would look unified (or balanced, respectively) to anyone contemplating the work under standard conditions and noticing the relation between these parts. Other aesthetic qualities ("joyfulness," "sadness," "melancholy") are perceived emotional qualities in objects, and still others (such as being intriguing, moving, or exciting) are tied to the reactions or responses of the beholders in a way that the previous ones are not. To put some of these differences in a nutshell: a work of art cannot be moving if nobody is moved by it. But a work can be unified or harmonious even if nobody is unified or rendered harmonious by it.

The Relativity of Aesthetic Qualities. Are aesthetic qualities in the objects themselves or in the eye of the beholder? In the latter case, aesthetic attributions could be relative to many things. The basic idea is then simply that an object does not have a particular aesthetic quality A per se, but only relative to a certain tradition, upbringing, culture, frame of reference, and so forth.

In view of the obvious differences between aesthetic characterizations in different cultures, and disagreements between critics in the same culture, relativism would seem to be a tempting and rational choice. But it could also be argued that one needs to distinguish not only between different kinds of relativism (e.g., perceptual, descriptive, normative) but also between whether a particular object x has the (aesthetic or nonaesthetic) quality A and whether, as a matter of fact, certain people discern or discover that x has A.

If it is true that certain people do *not* discern this quality, this may be the result of their upbringing, lack of training, cultural frame of reference, and so forth; but the fact that they do not notice that x has A does not prove that x does not have the quality A. On the contrary, the statement that a particular person does not notice that x has A is clearly compatible with the statement that x has A.

The Existence of Qualities in General. The statement that there are qualities of a certain kind can be interpreted in several ways. To say that there are qualities of a certain sort—let us call them Q's—can be to say or imply that a statement such as "x is Q" is meaningful, can have truth-value, or that one can distinguish between objects exemplifying or having Q and those that do not, or that there are reliable methods by means of which such discriminations can, on the whole, be made.

More important than a general discussion about conditions for the existence of qualities is probably whether there are rational methods, or generally accepted methods, in disciplines such as art history or musicology, by means of which it is possible for art historians and critics to settle conflicting claims concerning aesthetic attributions in particular cases. Such methods are based on some of the arguments below.

A number of arguments have been raised for and against the existence and objectivity of aesthetic qualities. The most important arguments against the existence and objectivity of aesthetic qualities are probably various versions of the arguments of variation and simplicity. According to the former, aesthetic attributions vary with individuals, time, upbringing, and culture. Because there is no unprejudiced way of deciding which of two incompatible qualities attributed to an object is indeed a quality of that object, aesthetic qualities are not qualities of objects. They are, rather, in the eye of the beholder. According to the latter argument, there is no need to introduce aesthetic qualities when one wants to describe, interpret, and explain works of art and one's responses to them; to assume the existence of aesthetic qualities introduces unnecessary complications and violates Occam's razor (that is, the commitment not to introduce unnecessary entities).

The most important arguments for the existence and objectivity of aesthetic qualities are probably the causal, the phenomenological, and public language arguments. According to the core of the causal argument, aesthetic qualities are dependent qualities: if a work of art x has the aesthetic quality A, then it has A because of the presence of the primary or secondary qualities B in x. If A is caused by B, then: if B exists, A also exists. According to the phenomenological argument, there is no fundamental difference between our experiences of a line as red and as graceful; hence, it would be arbitrary to say that in one case but not in the other we are dealing with a quality of an object. Finally, according to the public language argument, critical disagreement presupposes that the contested terms are understood by the disagreeing critics; the terms are mutually understood only if the critics agree on the general conditions of application of these terms—and these conditions define in principle the truth conditions (or the correctness conditions) of aesthetic attributions.

[See also Attitude, article on Aesthetic Attitude; Beauty; and Realism.]

BIBLIOGRAPHY

Beardsley, Monroe C. "What Is an Aesthetic Quality?" *Theoria* 39. 1–3 (1973): 50–70.

Beardsley, Monroe C. "The Descriptivist Account of Aesthetic Attributions." *Revue Internationale de Philosophie* 109.3 (1974): 336–352.
Halldén, Sören. *Emotive propositions.* Stockholm, 1954.
Hermerén, Göran. *The Nature of Aesthetic Qualities.* Lund, 1988.
Hermerén, Göran. "Emotive Properties: The Role of Abstraction, Introspection and Projection." *Theoria* 51 (1993): 80–112.
Kivy, Peter. "Aesthetic Appraisals and Aesthetic Qualities." *Journal of Philosophy* 65.4 (22 February 1968): 85–93.
Kivy, Peter. *Speaking of Art.* The Hague, 1973.
Levinson, Jerrold. "Aesthetic Supervenience." *Southern Journal of Philosophy* suppl. vol. 22 (1983): 93–110.
Margolis, Joseph. *Pragmatism without Foundations: Reconciling Realism and Relativism.* Oxford and New York, 1986.
Mitias, Michael H., ed. *Aesthetic Quality and Aesthetic Experience.* Amsterdam, 1988.
Sibley, Frank. "Objectivity and Aesthetics." *Proceedings of the Aristotelian Society* suppl. vol. 42 (1968): 31–54.
Sibley, Frank. "Aesthetic Concepts." *Philosophical Review* 68.4 (October 1959): 421–450. Reprinted in *Philosophy Looks at the Arts,* edited by Joseph Margolis, 3d ed. (Philadelphia, 1987).
Tormey, Alan. *The Concept of Expression: A Study in Philosophical Psychology and Aesthetics.* Princeton, N.J., 1971.

GÖRAN HERMERÉN

QUINCY, ANTOINE CHRYSOSTOME QUATREMÈRE DE. *See* Originality.

QUINTILIAN, MARCUS FABIUS QUINTILIANUS. *See* Rhetoric; Roman Aesthetics; Sublime, *article on* The Sublime from Longinus to Montesquieu; *and* Text.

RACE AND AESTHETICS. *See* Black Aesthetic; Harlem Renaissance; *and* Locke.

RAPHAEL, MAX (1889–1952), German aesthetician. Max Raphael was born in Schönlanke (West Prussia) and studied art history, philosophy, and political economy at the universities of Berlin and Munich with Heinrich Wölfflin, Georg Simmel, and Gustav von Schmoller. While in Munich he became acquainted with the artistic founders of Expressionism: Paul Klee, Franz Marc, August Macke, and Max Pechstein, who had founded the groups Der Blaue Reiter and Die Brücke. In the course of his encounter with these Expressionists, Raphael developed an interest in French painting. He moved to Paris to study philosophy, where he attended the lectures of Henri Bergson, studied the work of Henri Matisse, and met the young Pablo Picasso. Out of these experiences came his first book, *Von Monet zu Picasso,* based on lectures he gave on Picasso in Munich in 1913.

Raphael moved to Switzerland around the end of 1913, where he studied sociology with the idea of applying sociological theory to art history. There he remained until the outbreak of World War I, in which he served a brief period in the German army. After the war, he returned to Switzerland, where he again became deeply immersed in the world of art. Here he wrote *Idee und Gestalt* in 1919, published in Munich in 1921. More books followed: *Der dorische Tempel* (1930), *Proudhon, Marx, Picasso* (1933), *Zur Erkenntnistheorie der konkreten Dialektik* (1934).

In 1941, during the Nazi occupation of France, he was temporarily detained in the concentration camps at Gurs and Les Milles. After many difficulties, he was able to leave France and emigrate, via Lisbon, to the United States. After he arrived in New York, he studied and wrote on neolithic Egyptian paintings and prehistorical cave art. These studies resulted in the publication of *Prehistoric Cave Paintings* (1945) and *Prehistoric Pottery and Civilization in Egypt* (1947). After the posthumous publication of *The Demands of Art* (1969), there followed the publication in German editions of his unpublished manuscripts in the 1980s and 1990s (see bibliography). Raphael continued to write while in the United States until his death.

Raphael's Method. It was in 1921 that Raphael began to develop his distinctive method. This method he characterized as the taking up of an objective attitude. The "objective attitude," which is preliminary to a more complete analysis, involves taking the artwork as a singular datum and analyzing its constituent elements. This was not meant as a formalist deviation from Marxist social-historical analysis, but a new way, a more dialectical way, toward its fulfillment. It takes "pure" aesthetic inquiry to be prior to the historical sociology of art. Raphael insists that an adequate formal analysis of a work of art will reveal not only the laws of construction of the work itself, but also the causal connections between aesthetic form and the social conditions that give rise to it. This method can be called "inside-out" dialectics. But Raphael's point is that if one deduces the meaning and compositional components of a work of art from social theory, then one has abandoned dialectics for a mechanical method of positivistic sociological description; one has lost the inner dynamic of the work.

Raphael's method was highly original in that he believed that one must know the nature of the object itself before its history and content can be reconstructed and written. His analysis applies the Marxist dialectic to the sociology of art, thus uniting sociology, political economy, art history, and philosophical aesthetics.

In his book *Prehistoric Cave Paintings,* unappreciated by most Marxist aestheticians of the period, Raphael's grasp of the internal compositional elements and total structure of Paleolithic cave drawings allowed him to establish a direct correlation between the mode of production in Paleolithic communities and their artistic production. And as he was to write later, his method

involves the comparative study of works of art from all epochs in the history of all peoples. From this comparative study are abstracted the most general elements, relationships, totalities, and domains of concretization. In this manner, the ideal work of art in its most typical aspects is constituted. . . . Moreover, the laws for the construction of form in the work of art, as well as the laws of connection among various kinds of art, are at the same time the laws of relation and association of production.

Even though the process of mediation between art and material society in modern times is far more complex than in Paleolithic communities, an understanding of this relationship is still possible. Establishing such an understanding was to become Raphael's life's work.

Major Works. *The Demands of Art,* Raphael's most important book, consists of five highly concentrated analyses of individual works of art. These studies are supplemented by an introductory chapter titled "The Struggle to Understand Art" and an extract from Raphael's essay on method, "Toward an Empirical Theory of Art." In these analyses, Raphael seems primarily concerned with understanding the work of art only as a work of art, as a specific aesthetic datum, as autonomous—not as a reflection, not as mediating the relations of production. But these are not purely formal studies. Raphael himself warns in this text against excluding those social and historical conditions that inform the painting. A purely aesthetic and structural analysis leads to empty formalism. On close analysis, however, we can discover Raphael's penetrating dialectical technique at its best; for the historical and social conditions are perceptible in each work, even though contextual detail is absent—the social and the historical impregnate each painting. This is especially true of the chapter on *Guernica,* the sociological details of which were already set out earlier in *Proudhon, Marx, Picasso.* In this work, Raphael begins with an attack on the utopian tendencies of some currents of modernism, specifically the Abstractionist and Surrealist movements. By means of this critique, he is able to show how art functions to mediate contradictions in the forces and relations of production, through an explication of the internal dialectical interaction of form and content in actual works of art.

In demonstrating the manner in which the laws of dialectical materialism operate in art history, Raphael opposes the view attributed to "crude Marxist sociology" that art is a direct reflection of the economic basis of society and that art develops in correspondence with stages of economic development. Here, of course, he can refer to Karl Marx's own, and presumably very similar position, in the introduction to the *Contribution to the Critique of Political Economy:* "certain periods of the highest development of art stand in no direct connection with the general development of society."

Both in this work and in *Arbeiter, Kunst, und Kunstler* (1975), Raphael examines the role of myth in the artistic mediation of material anxiety. With regard to the mediating function of myth, he writes that Marx expressed a view that is usually associated with that form of bourgeois aesthetics found in the art of Richard Wagner, Arnold Böcklin, and Paul Gauguin. The differences are as follows:

1. For Marx, only an indigenous mythology was capable of constructively mediating art, that is, a mythology with the same origins, the same people, the same cultural outlook, and the same economic organization of society that produced the work of art.

2. For Marx, mythology was a cultural product *(Volksprodukt)*. For the (Romantic) artist and aesthetician of the nineteenth century, its attraction lay directly in the personal (and objective) transformation of its *(völkisch)* content.

3. The bourgeois and reactionary artist necessarily sought in mythology—because he wanted to escape the real conditions of his own time and place—an idealistic, metaphysical, symbolic mode with which to conceal the fragmentation and truncated nature of his own composition and construction.

4. For Marx, mythology was a historically conditioned connection or link that would disappear with the ascendancy of natural understanding, so that a demythologized art would be possible in the nineteenth and twentieth centuries.

Myth, he concludes, is a crucial element in the mediation of material society through art. By grasping the role of myth, one is able to specify the lack of proportion between the economic and ideological developments of a society and to account for the attribution of normative status to certain arts whose economic foundations have long since disappeared. Raphael is now in a position to show that only certain ages have been capable of producing works of art that are organically and "naturally" coordinated to prevailing developments in the forces and relations of production. He assumes that communism will represent a stage in which such an integration becomes possible.

In these explications of mediation and organic unity, Raphael believed that he had discovered the key to understanding artistic efflorescence and how the normative values expressed in art are related to material society. Thus, he began to apply his assumptions and methodology to specific problems of modern art. The best statement of his methodology is to be found in "Toward an Empirical Theory of Art," which was published as an appendix to *The Demands of Art.* By *empirical,* Raphael means an approach that makes art an object of scientific cognition. Such a theory would involve empirical analyses of works of art from all periods and all nations. Subjective experiences of works should be eliminated whenever possible and replaced with mathematical techniques. For example, Raphael writes in his studies of Giotto di Bondone:

> Unlike the *Lamentation,* the scheme of the *Death of Saint Francis* is fitted into a rectangular format in the ratio 3:2, i.e., the golden section, the proportion that most closely links the whole with its parts . . . there is no tension between format and compositional

scheme, for the verticals at the left and right extend nearly to the top of the picture.

Raphael was opposed to the traditional analytic procedure in which knowledge is built up from elementary units with no reference to any concept of the whole. Rather, he believed that

> it is more in keeping with the facts of art to start with a more highly structured element whose components are variable . . . I should like to replace an abstract system of concepts, each designating a simple thing with a simple term, with a system of variable elements and variable functions.

In the domain of art, he argues that one must pair the concept of particularity with the concept of totality. A totality that "combines the . . . factors of form, content, and method at a higher level."

It is assumed in this theory that there are laws governing human creative activity and that these laws can be studied theoretically. Such study will show that a composition is rendered in such a way that it makes it possible to discover that universal in the particular. Raphael's approach is, perhaps, best exemplified in studies of Paul Cézanne, Edgar Degas, Giotto, Rembrandt van Rijn, and Picasso in *The Demands of Art.* The comments that follow focus on his study of Picasso, in whose work he had a long-standing fascination.

To criticize Picasso's art, and particularly the political effort that *Guernica* represented, was to go in the face of most, if not all, progressive criticism of the time. Nevertheless, Raphael was compelled by the dialectical logic of his own system to come to grips with this great artist and his work. In the analysis of *Guernica,* Raphael traces the exact relationship between the social, material, and ideological conditions, on the one hand, and the forms in the painting, on the other. He describes Picasso's art as being conditioned by capitalist society. Picasso's fundamental individualism is in conflict with his mathematical, generalized means of composition. In his work, Picasso has resorted to an abstract idealism—this is most evident in *Guernica.*

To say that the painting is antifascist is no more than to reiterate its political purpose. No gain has been made toward an understanding of those forces that mediate the subject and the expressive means employed. Nor is it enough to invoke the political view that capitalism, its technology, and its ideology dominate society and the individual, alienating man from himself and his community, and that his condition is reflected in the work. Indeed, Raphael maintains, the painting shows Picasso's own continued alienation and his inability to abandon bourgeois values. But how does one come to this in the painting? Raphael argues that it is reflected in the composition. Raphael's task is to show that this personal failure is discoverable in the work, and his thesis is that even though Picasso sought a new pictorial form, the form he achieves fails utterly. *Guernica* is a striking contradiction between form and content.

A compact account of Raphael's treatment of the painting exhibits both his political attitude and his analytic approach to most modernist art: The immediate objective of the painting is shock. The assault on the visual senses gives rise to feelings of uncertainty and irritation. Thus, both the visual and the emotional assimilation of expressive elements are precluded. Feelings of isolation and destruction are intensified. Yet, the artist is the only one who knows the road to the picture's inner allegorical and symbolic truth. Still, it is apparent that the painting constitutes the annihilation of traditional expressive forms, just as the bombing signifies the destruction of impotent pleas for peace. Yet, nothing in this picture is synthesized: form and content remain irreconcilable.

> The local movement of lines scans the emotion which has become affect, the end effect, divorced both from its cause and from the process of its emergence. And it is by this choice of the emotional end effect that Picasso brings the line of movement closest to the effect of color [in which the picture is virtually lacking]—the torment of the finite, frozen in its explosion, in the face of an absolutely silent conscious-being, none of whose potentialities are realized. This is a world without hope of salvation; mankind is reduced to a scream. (1968)

What is the pictorial solution to this desperate clash? According to Raphael, the horror and anguish of the psychological content of the work suggest no answer. Perhaps this is the key to an understanding of the fundamental discord between form and content. This discord exhibits a collapse of affect in the painting that corresponds to the rampant violence and destruction in the real world. Here Raphael shows that Picasso has attempted to overcome the horror and panic (which are pictorially superficial precisely because they are restricted to the subjects) by means of a serene execution of colorless lines: "these lines are born of emotion, [but] they are not themselves emotional; rather, they are aloof to the point of academic coolness" (ibid.)

In this work, the total construction is sundered by a contradiction—the willingness to radically destroy established tradition pictorially in opposition to a refusal to come to grips with the brutalization of social reality. For Raphael, this last was an intellectual failure characteristic of the bourgeois, liberal mentality. Hence, all of the elements of content are visually brought to materialization in the work, but they fail to achieve form within the whole. Form is separated from content as bourgeois theory is separated from practice. The possibility of achieving essential artistic unity is foreclosed.

The contradiction is reinforced again, for even though Picasso portrays a historical event in *Guernica* (which none of his other paintings do), he fails to grasp the event pictorially in its historical significance. It appears as an ahistorical his-

torical event, a puzzle, to be illuminated only through that impotent mentality that invokes a plea for reason (reasonableness) symbolized in the lamp questing after lost truth.

But, as Raphael points out, bourgeois appeals to reason and nonintervention were exactly what the fascist barbarization of capitalism thrived on. Reasonableness at this juncture of history was complicity. Picasso imposes his personal allegory of reason, which in turn sanctions and sustains the values of that class that "needs it because it can only talk and talk cannot act, and therefore thinks it understands Picasso, although it misunderstands him" (ibid.). Raphael insists that understanding resides in the contradiction, not in an uncritical acceptance of the impotent ideology that informs the work. Picasso has, in this sense, a limited appeal to literati who dwell in a dreamworld in which his art serves as a fetish for those dreams. The work is politically constrained, naive. It fails to transcend the immediate sense of events. As bourgeois ideology, it cannot resolve the present into a possible future. Helplessly, it appeals to reason.

This ideology in its vacuity was unable to stem the fascist tide. In its false consciousness" we glimpse one of the reasons for the split between line and color and between empirical emotion and [a metaphysical and nonhistorical solution that uses] signs and allegories to bridge the gap" (ibid.).

Against the trend of leftist criticism, Raphael insisted that *Guernica* was a contrived painting and therefore arbitrary. Yet, it is important to recognize the admiration in which Raphael held Picasso. The conclusion reached was the result of a most detailed analysis of the work itself—and this is true of all of Raphael's studies of individual paintings.

What was at stake in the struggle to understand Picasso's art was not whether he was a gifted painter—that must be acknowledged in any event. Rather, it was, in Raphael's words, "the historical fate of the European bourgeoisie" (ibid.). Raphael saw in this study, and also in his analyses of classical art undertaken in his period of American emigration, a continuing struggle against all forms of irrationalism and subjectivism: phenomenology, existentialism, Expressionism, and Surrealism.

Raphael's Legacy. What, then, was Raphael's paradigm for good art? The answer is that it is those works of art that are autonomous, dialectical, and organic in nature. Agreeing with Marx, he concludes that this kind of art is most typically characteristic of classical Greece. Genuine classical art, he says, is dialectical and that is why Marx and many others have remarked on its timeless quality. It is this dialectical and timeless quality that artists must grasp if the art of the future is to be great. Such an art will bear a resemblance to the society that conditions and informs it. In the aesthetic sphere, its dialectical characteristics will be increased integration of form and content. In the social field, it will be a reflection of increased integration of social institutions and individuals, a free and yet collective society devoid of exploitation, that is, a socialist society. Raphael believed that only art that is created in the environment of socialism is capable of overcoming the contradictions inherent in modern art.

Although Raphael's contributions to Marxist aesthetics still remain somewhat unrecognized, it is likely that a Marxist theory of the visual arts must begin with his work, for in this field he has not been surpassed. Before Raphael, many approaches to art had been empirical in the sense that they were limited to a history of artifacts or a "scientific" analysis of the structure of individual artworks (formalism) or philosophical generalizations based on the interpreter's personal sensibility (subjectivism). Raphael's originality lies in an approach to empirical facts that employs a complete theory of the psychology of creative activity within a Marxist framework.

Raphael's influence in the fields of aesthetics, art history, and criticism has been modest at best. There are several reasons for this. Among them, his works were virtually ignored in the socialist countries because they were not compatible with official Socialist Realism. He was read widely in Poland and Bulgaria in the 1970s and 1980s, but no publications appear to have resulted.

In the United States, at the time of the posthumous publication of his major book, *The Demands of Art*, grand systematic theories of art were looked on with suspicion as a result of the analytic movement in aesthetics that followed Morris Weitz's dismissal of theory in "The Role of Theory in Aesthetics" in 1956. Raphael's method was adopted, however, by the art historian Hanna Deinhard in her *Meaning and Expression* (1970).

[*See also* Marxism.]

BIBLIOGRAPHY

Works by Raphael

Von Monet zu Picasso: Grundzüge einer Ästhetik und Entwicklung der modernen Malerei. Munich, 1913.
"Die Wertung des Kunstwerkes." *Deutsche-Französische Rundschau* 36.2 (May 1915): 144–155.
Idee und Gestalt: Ein Führer zum Wesen der Kunst. Munich, 1921.
Der dorische Tempel, dargestellt am Poseidontempel zu Paestum. Augsburg, 1930.
"Zur Kunst Theorie des dialektischen Materialismus." *Philosophische Hefte* 3.3–4 (1932): 313–329.
"C. G. Jung Vergreift sich an Picasso." *Information* 6 (December 1932): 11–18.
Proudhon, Marx, Picasso: Trois études sur la sociologie de l'art. Paris, 1933.
Zur Erkenntnistheorie der konkreten Dialektik. Paris, 1934.
Prehistoric Cave Paintings. Translated by Norbert Guterman. New York, 1945.
Prehistoric Pottery and Civilization in Egypt. Translated by Norbert Guterman. New York, 1947.
The Demands of Art. Translated by Norbert Guterman. Princeton, N.J., 1968.
Arbeiter, Kunst und Kunstler. Frankfurt am Main, 1975.
Marx, Picasso: Die Renaissance des Mythos in der bürgerlichen Gesellschaft. Edited by Klaus Binder. Frankfurt am Main, 1983.
Lebens-Erinnerungen: Briefe, Tagebucher, Skizzen, Essays. Edited by Hans-Jürgen Heinrichs. Frankfurt am Main, 1989.
Das schöpferische Auge, oder, Die Geburt des Expressionismus. Vienna, 1993.

Other Sources

Barrett, Michele. "Max Raphael and the Question of Aesthetics." In *The Politics of Pleasure: Aesthetics and Cultural Theory,* edited by Stephan Regan, pp. 33–58. Buckingham, 1992.
Deinhard, Hanna. *Meaning and Expression: Toward a Sociology of Art.* Boston, 1970.
Heinrichs, H. J. "The Empirical Aesthetics of Max Raphael." *Merkur-Deutsche Zeitschrift für Europäisches Denken* 40.9–10 (1986): 844–851.
Pazura, Stanislaw. "The Concept of Art in the Aesthetics of Max Raphael." *Dialectics and Humanism* 15 (Winter–Spring 1988): 133–136.
Truitt, Willis. "A Marxist Theory of Aesthetic Inquiry: The Contribution of Max Raphael." *Journal of Aesthetic Education* 5.1 (January 1971): 151–161.
Truitt, Willis. "Towards an Empirical Theory of Art: A Retrospective Comment on Max Raphael's Contribution to Marxian Aesthetics." *British Journal of Aesthetics* 11.3 (Summer 1971): 227–236.
Truitt, Willis. "Ideology, Expression, and Mediation." In *For Dirk Struik,* edited by Robert S. Cohen et al., pp. 435–463. Dordrecht, 1974.
Truitt, Willis. *Mainstreams in American Aesthetics: A Marxist Analysis.* New York, 1991. See chap. 3.

WILLIS TRUITT

RASA. An emotive theory of aesthetics first formulated by Bharata in his *Nāṭyaśāstra* (c. second century BCE–second century CE), primarily in the context of the theater, *rasa* later developed into a general poetic principle by Ānandavardhana (ninth century) in his *Dhvanyāloka* and by Abhinavagupta (tenth to eleventh century) in his commentary on Bharata, "Abhinavabhāratī," and on *Dhvanyāloka,* "Locana." Its influence is also seen on the theories of dance, music, painting, and sculpture. Literally, "savor," *rasa* has come to mean "aesthetic relish" generally, and it comprehends two related ideas: the relishable quality of the work, that is, its emotional content, and the relishable experience produced by the work in the reader/spectator—the *rasa* experience, which, for Bharata, was the essence of stage drama. Again, because emotions are many and every work will exhibit a different emotional quality, one may also speak of *rasa*s in the plural and categorize works generically, each according to its *rasa.*

The Sanskrit word for "emotion" is *bhāva,* meaning a mental state. No differentiation is made between emotions, feelings, moods, and other cognate terms, as they are all mental states or affects, ranging from simple sensations to the most complex emotional attitudes, dispositions, and inner tensions of varying intensity and duration. A distinction is made, however, between *bhāva*s or "life emotions" described as undergone by the persons in the poem and *rasa*s or the aesthetically excited emotions that are generalized or departicularized in the reader's apprehension owing to the pressure of the literary context, namely, its phenomenological remoteness from the personal concerns of the reader. But still, these (the *rasa*s) are qualitatively the same as the ordinary emotions, not some anonymous "aesthetic" emotions.

Rasa is generally taken to be a theory of emotional response to artworks. True, but it is equally a theory of the art object. Notwithstanding the spiritualized accounts of *rasa* experience by Abhinavagupta and others, the overriding concern of the *Nāṭyaśāstra* and other critical texts is with objective criteria for identifying and interpreting emotions and with the formal means for presenting them in art; for only the emotions expressed in the work as its meanings are fit for comment. Whether in life or in art, emotions are identified by their (intentional) objects or causes (which may be any emotion-producing object, thought, or event) and by their overt expressions (speech and voluntary and involuntary behavioral reactions). But these situational factors must appear in conjunction, because of the contingent connection between emotion objects and emotion expressions. There can be no objectless emotion—one that cannot be specified in terms of its criteria.

Bharata works out an elaborate typology of emotions, of nearly all the commonly recognized varieties, each with its distinct criteria. Of these, nine—erotic love, humor, grief, rage, heroism, fear, disgust, wonder, and serenity—are the major generic categories and are called the basic emotions (*sthāyin*s), and thirty-three others, such as joy, longing, and agitation, are the transient type (*vyabhicārin*s) because they have no fixed identity of their own and they become meaningful only in the context of one or other of the basic emotions (e.g., the "joy" of victory, of sexual fulfillment). A poem is conceived of as an orchestration of several emotions. But, as a unified discourse, it will establish a single dominant tone—that of a basic emotion. This dominant tone, which colors the whole composition and stamps it as tragic, comic, erotic, and so on, is the focalized mood of the poem, its basic emotion or emergent *rasa*. The *rasa*s, in this sense, are phenomenally objective because they are anchored in the meanings of the work and are not merely qualities ascribed to the work paronymously. They are delivered by the words of the poem. *Rasa*, as a commentator puts it, is the purport of the poetic statement.

The *rasa* theory further holds that the primary end of poetry is "evocation"—not, however, in the perlocutionary sense, but in the sense that the presentation of the emotions in terms of their objects and situational contexts will have the illocutionary act potential of prompting (*bhāvanā*) the reader to contemplate it for its emotional significance, not for its "propositional sense" alone, but for the "propositional attitudes" expressed via the sense. This being the case, the purely cognitive or heuristic values of poetry, although they may still coexist with the evocative value, are subordinated to the primary end of aesthetic gratification.

There were three other, rival theories of poetry in Sanskrit poetics: poetry as figuration or deviant speech (*alaṃkāra, vakrokti*), poetry as style or structured expression (*rīti*), and poetry as suggestion or implied meaning (*dhvani*). The critics of the *dhvani* school, Ānandavardhana and Abhinavagupta, argued for a special poetic semantics, but they were also responsible for restoring Bharata's concept of *rasa* to its former status of essentiality, after its comparative neglect by the figurationists, by assimilating it into the doctrine of suggestion. They maintained that the emotive purport of the sentence describing the objects and expressions is not its literal meaning but another meaning flowing from it through the power of implication. The admissibility of this claim was questioned by other schools of thought. The *dhvani* critics must be given credit, however, for giving the *rasa* concept a firm semantic footing and for establishing the primacy of emotive meaning over figuration and style in determining the aesthetic character of a poem.

Bharata's theater was a composite theater and included not only speech and physical action, but dance and music too as enhancing devices. He uses the term *rasa* to describe the total experience of the stage spectacle. But the question of how *rasa*, understood as a kind of meaning or thematic content, may be applied to dance and music is left ambiguous. On the one hand, Bharata and, following him, Abhinavagupta, maintain that dance as pure rhythmic movement of the limbs of the body serves no expressive need, even when it occurs in the context of the stage drama; it is simply an ornamental addition to drama. Whereas nonrhythmic movements of legs, hands, face, and so on are naturally meaningful as symptomatic expressions of the characters' emotional states, dance steps and dance figures do not stand in any such expresser-expressed relation to the emotive meanings of the literary text or of the action situation of the drama. There is no direct apprehension of a content in them.

But, on the other hand, both Bharata and Abhinavagupta seem to recognize tacitly that there can be an infusion of gestic meaning even in abstract dance when it is introduced in an expression context. Bharata mentions that Śiva's dances were called forth by certain specific emotional situations—which suggests that they were behavioral acts on Śiva's part, performed through dance. Further, Bharata's distinction between the forceful (*tāṇḍava*) and graceful (*lāsya*) modes of dancing—the former being suitable for expressing heroic fervor, ecstasy, and wrath, and the latter for expressing amorous sentiment—is based on the quality of feeling. It implies that even noncontextualized dance movements are capable of exhibiting not only "regional" or "volitional" qualities, such as languidness, grace, and energy, but more specific emotive attitudes, such as amorous, heroic, and angry, associated with those qualities, and (at least some of them) are isomorphically related to expressive human behavior. They do so especially in conjunction with facial expressions that invariably accompany bodily movements and that Bharata regards as vital to stage action. Again, following a long tradition of dance theory, post-Bharata writers, including Abhinavagupta, assign to the various dance actions, movement patterns, group formations, gaits, jumps, pirouettes, and stances, and to rhythm patterns and tempi, described by Bharata, their appropriate expressive uses. The formal distinction between pure dance (*nrtta*) and expressive action (*nātya, abhinaya*) established by Bharata is still maintained in the texts on dance written after Abhinavagupta, but a distinction is set up between pure dance (*nrtta*) and expressive dance (*nrtya*), and greater value attached to the latter. One gathers from Abhinavagupta's account of dance drama varieties that even in the ancient theater pure dance was fused, in varying degrees, with expression. Even in current practice, in its pan-Indian format, one may notice the same fusion: as when expression itself is rendered rhythmically in dance step, or when a rhythmic number is employed to reinforce or prolong the emotive import of a text or action situation, or when it is presented as part of a ritual or some other performance context, thereby giving it a gestic or mimetic import and dramatic motivation. At any rate, it is apparent that Indian dance is heavily influenced by the *rasa* concept.

The relation of *rasa* to music is more problematic. No doubt, Bharata assigns specific emotional or evocative values to musical notes (*svaras*) and melody patterns or tunes (*jātis* or *rāgas*) when they are used in stage presentation for heightening purposes. To each note or tune is assigned its use in the evocation of specific moods, such as love, sorrow, and fear. But neither Bharata nor his commentator, Abhinavagupta, explains how precisely musical sounds are related to the moods and how they can even evoke any definite emotional responses. Sometimes specific musical notes or tunes may seem more fitted than others to the expression of certain moods. But this relation may be purely associational or subjective, not something constant and invariable; for, in practice it can be seen that the same *rāga* or choice of notes may be adapted to different emotional contexts, and it is not always possible to tell the emotion from the *rāga* without a meaning-giving context, such as that of a verbal text or the action situation of a play. Again, Ānandavardhana and Abhinavaguta credit musical sounds with a suggestive property even though they recognize that they have no denotative value. But they do not clarify how a semantic function, which suggestion is claimed to be, can be attributed to sounds that are not meaning-bearing signs. The texts on music too do not clarify the matter. But, following Bharata, they tacitly assume a vague connection between music and emotion. The musical notes, as well as the *rāga*s, are defined affectively, in terms of the delight they cause to the listener's ears.

On the other hand, the application of the *rasa* concept to the theory of portrait painting and sculpture is well established in the Vāstu and Āgama texts. Expressiveness was considered to be the very essence of image making. Portrayal of feelings (*bhāva-vyakti*) and faithful representation of human and animal attitudes, conditions, and actions (*avasthānukrti*) were among the guiding principles of image making, as they were of dancing and stage acting. The *Visnudharmottara* says that image making is an extension of dance pantomime in the sense that both arts seek to depict human actions and feelings, and employ the same expressive devices—eye expressions (*rasa-drṣṭis*), hand gestures (*mudrās*), and body postures (*āsanas* and *sthānas*). Even as one speaks of dramatic emotions (*nātya-rasas*), one can also speak of the *rasa*s expressed in painting and sculpture (*citra-rasas*).

As for temple architecture, the chief concerns of the Āgama and Vāstu texts are either utilitarian or metaphysical. Temples were designed according to certain metaphysical/symbolic formulas and for various ritual and practical uses. There is no suggestion in the texts that the temple structure as such—barring, of course, the reliefs and sculptured images on it—is expressive of any emotion. There is no mention of *rasa* in this connection at all.

Emotive theories run into difficulties when they are applied to all art forms irrespective of the differences in their mediums, as may be seen from discussions in Western aesthetics. For the expression of emotions in art, in terms of *rasa*, two conditions must be presupposed: first, a well-defined emotional situation or attitude, involving sentient beings who are capable of expressing emotions; and second, a medium that is inherently meaningful or self-expressive—that is, either speech (*vācika*) or physical gestures (*āngika*), including involuntary reactions (*sāttvika*). These two are, according to Bharata, the most essential modes of expression (*abinayss*) in stage action. By these criteria, only literature (where expression is effected solely through the verbal medium) and some forms of the visual and performing arts (which use physical gesture in one way or another to express feelings) would be amenable to an explanation in terms of *rasa*. Nonsentient, nonexpressive (*avācaka*) objects—buildings, landscapes, musical sounds—can only be objects of emotion to people, not expressers of it. Hence, emotive characterizations of such objects are necessarily metaphoric, in the sense that the quality of the effect is extended to the cause, as a maxim in Sanskrit has it.

The *rasa* concept cannot therefore serve as a basis for a global theory of art. In fact, the Sanskrit critics do not essay a general philosophy of art in terms of this or any other concept. They are, wisely enough, content to treat the arts separately, each according to its mode of existence, although their mutual affinities and interdependence are also recognized.

[*See also* Abhinavagupta; Indian Aesthetics; Music, *historical overview article;* Poetics; Taste; *and* Theater.]

BIBLIOGRAPHY

Ānandavardhana. *Dhvanyāloka of Ānandavardhana with the Locana of Abhinavagupta.* Translated and edited by Daniel H. H. Ingalls et al. Cambridge, Mass., 1990.

Bharata Muni. *The Nāṭyaśāstra.* 2d rev. ed. 2 vols. Translated by Manomohan Ghosh. Calcutta, 1961–1967.

Chari, V. K. *Sanskrit Criticism.* Honolulu, 1990.

Deutsch, Eliot. "Reflections on Some Aspects of the Theory of *Rasa.*" In *Sanskrit Drama in Performance,* edited by Rachel Van M. Baumer and James R. Brandon, pp. 214–225. Honolulu, 1981.

Gerow, Edwin. "Rasa as a Category of Literary Criticism: What Are the Limits of Its Application?" In *Sanskrit Drama in Performance,* edited by Rachel Van M. Baumer and James R. Brandon, pp. 226–257. Honolulu, 1981.

Gnoli, Raniero, ed. *The Aesthetic Experience according to Abhinavagupta.* 2d rev. enl. ed. Varanasi, 1968.

Masson, J. L., and M. V. Patwardhan. *Aesthetic Rapture: The Rasādhyāya of the Nāṭyaśāstra,* vol. 1, *Text.* Poona, 1970.

Rowland, Benjamin. *The Art and Architecture of India.* Harmondsworth, England, 1953.

Śārṅgadeva. *Saṅgītaratnākara of Śārṅgadeva,* vol. 4, *Chapter on Dancing.* Translated by K. Kunjunni Raja and Radha Burnier. Madras, 1976.

Śārṅgadeva. *Saṅgītaratnākara of Śārṅgadeva* vol. 1. *Text and Translation.* Translated by R. K. Shringy and Prem Lata Sharma. Delhi, 1978.

The Viṣṇudharmottaram (Pt. III): A Treatise on Indian Painting and Image-Making. 2d rev. enl. ed. Translated and edited by Stella Kramrisch. Calcutta, 1928.

V. K. CHARI

READING. *See* Imagery; *and* Reception Aesthetics.

READYMADE. *See* Duchamp.

REALISM. [*To analyze the multiple meanings of the concept of realism, this entry comprises two essays:*
Realism and Aesthetics
Pictorial Realism
The first essay explains the meaning of realism in aesthetics, namely, the belief that aesthetic qualities, such as beauty, are independent of those making judgments about them; it also discusses the views of antirealists who critique this belief. The second essay explains what realism has meant in art history, where it represents a particular type of art as well as an aesthetic concept tied to many art types. For related discussion, see Fiction; Mimesis; Photography, *article on* Catachresis; Qualities, Aesthetic; Representation; *and* Russian Aesthetics, *article on* Socialist Realism.]

Realism and Aesthetics

Realism in aesthetics is the thesis that properties such as grace, beauty, power, unity, or sadness are instantiated in artworks independently of judgments ascribing them and of the values and perceptions underlying these judgments. Such properties are held to ground and explain aesthetic perceptions and judgments. Realism requires a distinction between the ways artworks appear to various audiences and the properties they really have. According to the antirealist, by contrast, aesthetic properties can be analyzed as ways of appearing to perceivers with different aesthetic sensibilities. Realism allows for a broader class of errors in aesthetic judgments.

Realists will generally defend their view on explanatory grounds. According to them, critics will agree that Wolfgang Amadeus Mozart's concertos are graceful and Ludwig van Beethoven's powerful because these judgments are true in the ordinary correspondence sense. These works instantiate grace and power. This explains the perceptions and judgments that they do so, and contrary judgments must result from faulty or nonoptimal perceptions. Realists offer more particular explanations and predictions as well, which include appeal to particular tastes. A certain critic prefers grace to power; hence, she appreciates Mozart more than Beethoven. A certain artist paints as he does in order to create a delicate poignancy in his works; the property aimed at, but not always achieved, explains his technique. Realists will argue that their opponents cannot offer equally plausible explanations for such phenomena.

Antirealists in response will point to disagreements among even educated tastes for which the realist seems to lack an explanation. What one critic finds powerful, another finds strident, grating, or raucous; what one judges to be delicate and poignant, another finds mawkish or maudlin. In both cases, both critics are knowledgeable of the traditions from which the works emerge, and both perceive all the formal properties of the works that prompt these opposing judgments. Antirealists will argue that there is no fact of the matter in such cases as to which property the work has; it is instead simply a matter of different taste or sensibility. The opponent who holds that one of the parties to such a dispute must be mistaken has no non–question begging way to defend that claim.

Can each side to these arguments respond to its opponents? Antirealists will attempt to offer rival explanations for the phenomena to which realists appeal. They will explain agreements in aesthetic judgments by appeal to common aesthetic educations and resultant tastes and sensibilities. Such common training or upbringing will result in similar responses to the same works, hence in agreed judgments. To the other cases cited by the realist, the response will be slightly more complex. Instead of aiming at a real aesthetic property, an artist will actually aim at a certain response from an audience that shares her taste (in a transparent sense of "aim"). This goal will explain the artist's technique. Instead of preferring real grace to real power, a critic will prefer works (or formal properties of them) that prompt ascriptions of grace from those with his sensibility to works that other critics call powerful (but he probably finds raucous or strident). This more complex preference (again, not normally conceived as such) will explain the more particular preference for Mozart over Beethoven.

On the other side, realists, like antirealists, will explain seemingly intractable disagreements in terms of different backgrounds and training. But for realists, training in a particular tradition or style may lead to insensitivity to properties typical of opposed or very different styles. This will in turn explain why certain critics who are otherwise well educated will fail to perceive those properties in certain sorts of works.

This dispute can be brought into sharper focus by examining what both sides can agree on in regard to the nature of aesthetic properties. Both realists and their opponents must admit that ascribing such properties to works expresses a reaction on the part of the subject to the objective structural properties of the works. This reaction typically includes an evaluative component. To call a work powerful or unified is normally to praise it; to call it raucous or monotonous is normally to condemn it. There are nevertheless exceptions: to call a musical work sad may not be to evaluate it one way or the other. But the ascription of sadness still involves a perceptual and normally an affective response to the music (not necessarily the feeling of sadness itself). One can therefore largely assimilate the structure of aesthetic properties to that of secondary qualities of objects. The latter are analyzed in terms of objects being such as to appear certain ways to certain observers, where reference to the appearance or perceptual response is essential to the analysis. Aesthetic properties seem also to be relations of this sort, although they involve higher-order responses, in many cases responses to the secondary qualities and formal relations among them within artworks.

That aesthetic properties are relational in this way and include a subjective component does not in itself defeat the realist, although it might seem otherwise. The analogy to secondary qualities shows this, because debates occur between realists and antirealists regarding them, even though both sides accept the sort of analysis suggested above. In the case of colors, the realist's position depends on our being able to specify a class of ideal or normal perceivers and conditions relative to which colors appear as they are. The perceptions of others in other conditions then prompt errors in regard to real colors, as these conditions directly reveal only misleading appearances. Realists then have the distinction they need. Similarly, if the analogy is sound, an aesthetic realist would need to specify a class of ideal critics and conditions of judgment such that they perceive real aesthetic properties as they are, while others err in their judgments or are misled by false appearances.

The task of isolating such a class is more difficult in the case of aesthetics. To begin with, one cannot find physical defects in those whose aesthetic judgments differ from others whom one might take to set the standards for art criticism at a given time, whereas one can find such defects in those whose color vision deviates sharply from the norm. In the absence of physical differences, one can nevertheless demand that ideal critics, whose judgments in the face of disagreements refer to real aesthetic properties, be educated in the type of work being judged, be capable of perceiving all its relevant formal properties and relations, and be knowledgeable of the tradition from which the work emerges. Thus, one does not trust those who listen mainly to rock music and are untrained in the classical traditions to judge the aesthetic properties of classical works.

But who is to judge the aesthetic properties of rock songs? One answer is those who know and love rock, instead of classical devotees who hear only grating noise when rock lovers hear driving force. The problem with this answer is that further subdivisions can be made within rock music—heavy metal versus disco versus rap, and so on. If one specifies only lovers of each subgenre (who will also tend to be most knowledgeable of each) as critics ideal for perceiving the real aesthetic properties of songs within that style, the outcome of this narrowing process would be that virtually every piece has mainly positive evaluative aesthetic properties (because each will have its devotees). The criterion is too lenient.

The alternative answer is that the perceptions of those with the best overall taste in music, presumably devotees of serious classical music, are to be the gauge of the real aesthetic properties of musical works. (This answer, of course, still requires divisions among arts, because no one has best taste across all the arts. Thus, one would have to justify divisions across but not within artistic media.) This alternative might be held justified by the best overall explanatory theory, in terms of which realism for aesthetic properties is itself justified. But finding the required explanatory asymmetries is not so easy. The claim that the failure of rock lovers to discern positively evaluative and subtle aesthetic properties in classical works can be explained by their lack of musical education can be matched by the claim that most classical devotees lack detailed knowledge of the current rock repertoire. Ultimately, the realist who seeks to identify ideal perceivers of aesthetic properties across styles and genres must defend the thesis that taste can be compared across styles and genres, and that better taste indicates greater ability to discern real aesthetic properties and to distinguish them from mere appearances. Perhaps this can be accomplished by isolating better works (by consensus) within each genre and then showing that the better works in the inferior genres are distinguished by properties (e.g., complexity, subtle nuance, variety) that works in the better genres have to a higher degree.

Even if they can successfully make this case, realists are not yet out of the water. The equally difficult problem for the realist account being considered is that disagreements seem to persist among fully qualified critics within each suitably broadly defined genre. For one music critic, the triumphant final movement of Camille Saint-Saëns's organ symphony is powerfully moving and uplifting; for a second, it is bombastic, banal, and overblown. When such disputes occur, the realist's proposed criterion seems to require assigning incompatible properties to the same works, properties that they cannot simultaneously have. It becomes inconsistent.

In order to avoid this inconsistency, the realist who accepts the relational account of aesthetic properties must find some way to explain away such disagreement. Two options are available, but neither seems very promising. The first is to find some reason why an apparently well-educated and qualified critic would nevertheless err in aesthetic perception in the case at hand. Perhaps some hidden bias deriving from past experience might be postulated. The second option is to maintain that these disagreements among qualified critics occur mainly at the borders of aesthetic concepts or properties. Just as red and orange might be real properties despite vagueness at their borders, so might higher-order aesthetic properties. This option is problematic, however, because disputes do not seem to be confined to the border areas in the case of aesthetic properties. What is a paradigm of a triumphant, uplifting quality to one critic might be a central case of bombastic prententiousness to another.

It might be argued that nonevaluative aesthetic properties on which critics can agree underlie these opposed evaluative judgments and properties. But the two critics mentioned above will appeal only to the objective formal properties of the piece in defending their opposed aesthetic judgments; and this makes it doubtful that there exists a layer of aesthetic properties between the evaluative properties ascribed and the objective properties that prompt those ascriptions. As noted earlier, not all aesthetic properties include an evaluative component. Sadness as ascribed to music or paintings normally does not. But even here, when one attempts to specify more narrowly the property as instantiated in particular works, disagreements will arise. Is the slow movement of Gustav Mahler's Fifth Symphony melancholy, wistful, or tragic?

It might also be objected that the relational account of aesthetic properties is the problem for the realist in the face of educated disagreement. But it is difficult to see how realists can avoid some such account. If secondary qualities must be analyzed in terms of objective properties causing objects to appear in certain ways, or causing certain perceptual responses, then the same must be true of aesthetic properties. The latter are akin to higher-order perceptual properties, often including also affective and evaluative response components.

If realists could give a plausible account of educated disagreement in ascriptions of aesthetic properties, then realism would be the more attractive metaphysical position. This is because realists can offer other explanations that are deeper and/or more economical than their nonrealist counterparts. Whereas nonrealist explanations for aesthetic judgments end in appeals to aesthetic sensibilities that at bottom only summarize sets of such judgments, realists explain these judgments more deeply by appealing to aesthetic properties that prompt them. As noted earlier, the antirealist can appeal to the objective properties on which, according to the realist, the aesthetic properties supervene, but then the realist's explanations are more economical. If different works prompt similar judgments, the antirealist will have to refer to different objective properties in each case. But the realist can unify many such explanations by appealing to the same aesthetic properties as causes of the same judgments. Different formal relations among musical elements in different symphonies will prompt judgments that the works are powerful, but for realists the same property prompts all these judgments. If their framework is not inconsistent, such explanations may be preferable.

In the end, a compromise position might be best. In order to avoid inconsistency in the face of disagreement among ideal critics, one might have to relativize aesthetic judgments to critics who share taste. That the truth of these judgments should be relative in this way contradicts full-blooded realism. But this would not imply that aesthetic properties reduce to the ways artworks appear to whoever happens to be viewing them. Errors in ascribing such properties remain possible. If one is uneducated in the relevant tradition, or inattentive, or biased (on nonaesthetic grounds), then one is likely to miss the aesthetic properties of a work, to ascribe properties that an ideal critic who otherwise shares one's taste would not ascribe. The suggested account also allows for the fact that taste can improve. Those with undeveloped tastes may judge as no ideal critic would.

The conclusion is that aesthetic realism, that is, independence of aesthetic properties from appearances and beliefs about them, is a matter of degree. There may be several viable positions between the extremes of full-blooded realism and antirealism.

[*See also* Qualities, Aesthetic; *and* Representation.]

BIBLIOGRAPHY

Goldman, Alan H. "Realism about Aesthetic Properties." *Journal of Aesthetics and Art Criticism* 51.1 (Winter 1993): 31–37.

Levinson, Jerrold. "Aesthetic Supervenience." In *Music, Art, and Metaphysics: Essays in Philosophical Aesthetics.* Ithaca, N.Y., 1990.

McDowell, John. "Aesthetic Value, Objectivity, and the Fabric of the World." In *Pleasure, Preference and Value: Studies in Philosophical Aesthetics,* edited by Eva Shaper. Cambridge and New York, 1983.

Pettit, Philip. "The Possibility of Aesthetic Realism." In *Pleasure, Preference and Value: Studies in Philosophical Aesthetics,* edited by Eva Shaper. Cambridge and New York, 1983.

Scruton, Roger. *Art and Imagination: A Study in the Philosophy of Mind.* London, 1974.

Sibley, Frank. "Aesthetic Concepts." *Philosophical Review* 68.4 (October 1959): 421–450.
Zangwill, Nick. "Metaphor and Realism in Aesthetics." *Journal of Aesthetics and Art Criticism* 49.1 (Winter 1991): 57–62.
Zemach, Eddy. "Real Beauty." *Midwest Studies in Philosophy* 16 (1991): 249–265.

ALAN GOLDMAN

Pictorial Realism

From Zeuxis's painting of grapes and the dubiously naive birds of which aestheticians are so fond to today's debates about pictorial perception and the politics of representation, the concept of pictorial realism has been central to reflection on the nature of art and its history. What pictorial realism is, however, is not easily answered.

Jean-Baptiste-Siméon Chardin's still-life paintings, James Abbott McNeill Whistler's portraits, and John Constable's landscapes are paradigms of realistic painting. A natural way of explaining this realism—call it a theory of realism as resemblance—is to say that a painting is realistic in virtue of looking like what it is a painting of. A natural objection to this explanation is that even the most realistic painting looks very little like what it depicts: paintings typically have a flat surface, exhibit brushstrokes, and possess edges, whereas subjects of paintings typically do not. Nelson Goodman (1976) argues that the concept of resemblance does not explain any relation among natural objects in the world, and, a fortiori, it does not explain the relation between pictures and the natural objects they depict. He puts the objection stated above this way: a realistic painting resembles another realistic painting more than it resembles what it depicts, thus resemblance cannot be the relevant relation between a realistic work of art and what it represents. Although concise, this seems a weak way of describing the objection because the resemblance view need only be committed to describing a relation in virtue of not all, but only certain, features of a depiction and what it depicts, such as color, shape, and scale, but not felt texture or absolute size. One should add, moreover, that if two pictures resemble each other, it may be in virtue of each painting being the kind of thing that resembles what it depicts.

What does threaten to undermine the resemblance view is the suspicion that there is a circularity involved in the appeal to resemblance as an explanation of realism, that is, a suspicion that the concept of resemblance employed in explaining realism may be itself explicable only with reference to the concept of realism, or concepts that stand in for it, such as verisimilitude, likeness, and so on.

A second kind of theory of pictorial realism—realism as illusionism—dispenses with the need to define the notion of resemblance, and holds that a painting is realistic if, and to the extent that, under appropriate conditions, a viewer of the painting would have a tendency to mistake it for actually being what it only depicts. Richard Wollheim rejects this theory because, he says, no such tendency in a viewer exists: "It is surely quite untrue to suggest that, in looking at the masterpieces of Constable or [Claude] Monet, we have any temptation, even a partial or inhibited temptation, to react towards them in a way similar to that in which we would to the objects they represent" (Wollheim, 1973, p. 277). Wollheim is right in saying that we have no tendency to respond to realistic works as if they succeeded as illusions, but it may be that we have no such tendency to be deceived *in spite of* their potential for illusionistic depiction, say, because we know upon approaching them that they are only representations. Certainly, some kinds of painting, most notably trompe l'oeil, have an illusionistic effect, and this illusionistic effect is affected in great measure by what spectators believe in viewing the paintings; that is, whatever measure of success such works have in appearing to display, for example, real playing cards and dollar bills, that success is immediately diminished when one learns that such paintings belong to a genre of which illusionism is a defining goal. Such illusionism may be strengthened, by contrast, if one comes to believe that the painting in question belongs to a painter who, like a Cubist painter, routinely used the methods of collage in his work. Thus, it is not a strong argument against the view of realism as illusionism to say that a realistic work by Constable or Monet may not be illusionistic to most or all spectators, because this may not be a difference in kind, but only in degree, from such works as trompe l'oeil that do tempt one to respond as one responds to what they depict. Nonetheless, there is still a question as to why one should assume that the tendency of a painting to deceive its viewers is an explanation of the painting's realism; that is, what justifies the assumption that the illusionism of a painting should be identified with its realism? One can know with certainty that a painting is nothing more than a representation and still judge it realistic. If illusionism were essential to, or identical with, realism, this absence of any possibility of a painting's illusionism should not leave its realism uncompromised.

A third account of pictorial realism, often attributed to E. H. Gombrich, is that the realism of a painting is a matter of how much true information can be derived from the painting about what it depicts. Described in this general way, the account is intuitively plausible. It allows one to say that a painting of a bowl of apples is realistic because one can derive from it facts such as that apples are red, somewhat spherical, look like they weigh less than automobiles but more than raisins, and so on; and, in comparing two paintings of apples, one might say that the more realistic painting gives more true information about those apples. The problem with this view is that different paintings can yield different information about an object by representing it in different ways. Information about the shape or color of an apple can be supplied by one painting, information about molecular structure by another. The amount of information in each case could be identical, but only one painting would possess realism in the sense that it is being discussed here. That realism is not a matter of how much true information is supplied by a painting is also suggested by the fact that sometimes the way in which an image offers *false* information can support its realism. In, for example, Andrea Mantegna's foreshortened depiction of the dead Christ laid out on a slab, the feet are reduced in scale compared to the rest of the body. This deliberate distortion in foreshortening is necessary to avoid having the feet seem impossibly large, as they would in "correct" depiction. In this case, the realistic image is a poor guide to the nature of things independent of how they appear. As it happens, the truth or falsity of the information one could derive from a painting is of little consequence in whether the painting appears realistic. Jan Vermeer's *View of Delft* supplies a great amount of information about the place it depicts: the shapes and relative heights of the buildings, the geography of the harbor, the construction of the ships, and so on. But how unimportant it is for this information to be true is demonstrated when one reverses, say, with a slide projector, a reproduction of the painting such that everything that was on the left is now on the right and vice versa. Now, someone else who did not know the proper orientation of the image could derive information about the same kinds of things in the same fashion; but whereas much of this information would be false, it seems to be at no cost to the image's realism.

Returning to the theory of realism as resemblance, Wollheim and other commentators have stressed that the perception of pictures has a twofold nature. One can both attend to the brushstrokes, colors, and surface of a painting and see these aspects of a painting as an image. This capacity to "see in," rather than explaining how a painting can resemble what it depicts, takes it for granted that such resemblance is possible. Still, because one can "see in" a painting, one need not be troubled by the objection to the resemblance theory that features of a painting seen when viewing the painting—the texture of its brushstrokes, the flat array of patches of colors—do not look like whatever object in the world the painting depicts. One refers not to those material features of the work, but to what one "sees in" those features, what image one sees those material features as.

Finally, support for the resemblance view, although not an explanation of pictorial resemblance per se, is found in studies such as Julian Hochberg's demonstration that a child raised to nineteen months in a picture-free environment was able, when confronted with pictures for the first time, to recognize and speak of the objects in the pictures in the same way that he recognized and spoke of the objects themselves. This kind of experiment—and those with chimpanzees, that, after being taught to communicate with objects, are able, without further training, to use pictures of the objects for the same functions—suggest that however

one explains pictorial resemblance, it exists in a form that is not exclusively, although perhaps extensively, a conventional phenomenon.

[*See also* Perception.]

BIBLIOGRAPHY

Bryson, Norman. *Vision and Painting: The Logic of the Gaze*. New Haven, 1983.
Danto, Arthur C. *The Transfiguration of the Commonplace: A Philosophy of Art*. Cambridge, Mass., 1981.
Gombrich, E. H., Julian Hochberg, and Max Black. *Art, Perception, and Reality*. Baltimore, 1972.
Goodman, Nelson. *Languages of Art: An Approach to a Theory of Symbols*. 2d ed. Indianapolis, 1976.
Wollheim, Richard. *On Art and the Mind: Essays and Lectures*. London, 1973; reprint, Cambridge, Mass., 1974.
Wollheim, Richard. *Art and Its Objects* 2d ed. with six supplementary essays. Cambridge and New York, 1980.

JONATHAN GILMORE

REALITY, VIRTUAL. *See* Virtual Reality.

RECEPTION AESTHETICS. Sometimes known as "reception theory," reception aesthetics is commonly used to designate a direction in literary criticism developed by scholars in West Germany, particularly at the University of Constance, during the late 1960s and early 1970s. In general, the members of the "Constance school" advocated turning to the reading and reception of literary texts instead of to traditional methods that emphasize the production of texts or a close examination of texts themselves. Their approach is therefore related to reader-response criticism in the United States, although reception aesthetics for a time was more homogeneous in its theoretical presuppositions and general outlook than its American counterpart. Informed by the Continental traditions of hermeneutics and phenomenology, reception aesthetics dominated literary theory in Germany for about a decade. It was virtually unknown in the English-speaking world until around 1980, when it was made more readily accessible by a number of translations of the most seminal works. Hans Robert Jauss and Wolfgang Iser are the two most original theorists, although several of Jauss's students, among them Rainer Warning, Hans Ulrich Gumbrecht, and Karlheinz Stierle, also made important contributions to this branch of theory. In response to the writings of Jauss and Iser, scholars from the German Democratic Republic such as Robert Weimann, Manfred Naumann, and Rita Schober raised objections to some propositions and suggested Marxist alternatives, and the most productive East–West postwar dialogue in literary theory involved issues of reception and response.

Reception aesthetics arose at a time of great turbulence in West German society. At universities throughout the country, the student movement agitated for educational reform and advocated a basic questioning of traditional methods and educational standards. The impact on literary studies was substantial. During much of the postwar era, criticism had been dominated by close textual analysis, existentially based theory, and other ahistorical methods. Only in the 1960s did the climate gradually change when students, together with younger professors, demanded a reexamination of the canon and insisted on relevance in literary scholarship. The experimental University of Constance, founded in 1967, was at the forefront of general educational reform. Thus, it is not surprising that it fostered an atmosphere in which novel ideas about literary theory and aesthetics flourished as well.

An inaugural address at the University of Constance in April 1967 marked the beginning of reception aesthetics. This lecture was delivered by the newly appointed scholar of Romance languages, Hans Robert Jauss, and the title echoed another famous inaugural essay, one held on the eve of the French Revolution at the University of Jena by the playwright, theorist, and historian Friedrich von Schiller. Schiller had spoken on the topic "What Is and for What Purpose Does One Study Universal History?" Jauss modified this title by substituting the word *literary* for *universal,* but this slight alteration did not diminish the impact in the least. Jauss suggested, as Schiller had in 1789, that the present age needed to restore vital links between the artifacts of the past and the concerns of the present. For literary scholarship and instruction, such a connection could be established only if literary history were no longer relegated to the periphery of the discipline, Jauss maintained. He therefore sought to prod his colleagues into a new era of historical criticism, and the revised title to this lecture, "Literary History as a Provocation to Literary Scholarship," captured the innovative challenge that Jauss sought.

The approach to literary texts that Jauss outlined in his lecture became known as reception aesthetics. It is best understood as an attempt to overcome what Jauss viewed as limitations in two important and putatively opposed literary theories: Russian Formalism and Marxist criticism. In general, Marxism represents for him an outmoded approach to literature, related to an older positivist paradigm. Yet, Jauss also recognizes in this body of criticism, especially in the writings of less orthodox Marxists such as Werner Krauss, Roger Garaudy, and Karel Kosík, a fundamentally correct concern with the historicity of literature. The Formalists, on the other hand, are credited with introducing aesthetic perception as a theoretical tool for exploring literary works. Yet, Jauss also detects in their works the tendency to isolate art from its historical context, a *l'art pour l'art* aesthetics that valorizes the synchronic over the diachronic. The task for a new literary history, therefore, becomes to merge successfully the best qualities of Marxism and Formalism. This can be accomplished by satisfying the Marxist demand for his-

torical mediation while retaining the Formalist advances in the realm of aesthetic perception.

Reception aesthetics proposes to do this by altering the perspective from which literary texts are normally interpreted. Traditional literary histories were composed from the perspective of the producers of texts; Jauss proposes that one can truly understand literature as a process by recognizing the constitutive role of the consuming or reading subject. The interaction between author and public replaces literary biography as the basis for literary historiography. Thus, Jauss meets the Marxist demand for historical mediations by situating literature in the larger continuum of events; he retains the Formalist achievements by placing the perceiving consciousness at the center of his concerns. History and aesthetics, which seemed to be irreconcilable, are united in his theory. The historical significance of a work is not established by qualities of the work or by the genius of its author, but by the chain of receptions from generation to generation. In terms of literary history, Jauss thus envisions a historiography that will play a conscious, mediating role between past and present. The historian of literary reception is called on to rethink continuously the works of the canon in light of how they have affected, and are affected by, current conditions and events. Past meanings are understood as part of the prehistory of present experiencing.

The integration of history and aesthetics is to be accomplished largely by examining what Jauss refers to as the horizon of expectation (*Erwartungshorizont*). This methodological centerpiece of Jauss's theory is an obvious adaptation of the notion of horizon (*Horizont*) found most prominently in the hermeneutic theory of Jauss's teacher Hans-Georg Gadamer. For Gadamer, the horizon is a fundamental tenet for the hermeneutical situation. It refers primarily to our situatedness in the world, our necessarily perspectival and limited purview. [*See* Gadamer.] Jauss's use of the term is slightly different. For him, the horizon denotes an intersubjective system or structure of expectations, a system of references, or a mind-set that a hypothetical individual brings to a given text. All works are read against some horizon of expectation; indeed, certain types of texts—parody, for example—intentionally foreground this horizon. The task of the literary scholar, Jauss suggests, is to "objectify" the horizon, so that one may evaluate the artistic character of the work of art. This is most readily accomplished when the work in question thematizes its horizon. But even works whose horizon is less obvious can be examined with this method. Generic, literary, and linguistic aspects of the work in question can be used to construct a probable horizon of expectation.

After establishing the horizon of expectation, the critic can then proceed to determine the artistic merit of a given work by measuring the distance between the work and the horizon. Basically, Jauss employs a deviationist model: the aesthetic value of a text is seen as a function of its deviation from a given norm. If the expectations of a reader are not "disappointed" or violated, then the text will approach the culinary; if, on the other hand, it breaks through the horizon, then it will be a work of high art. Sometimes a work may break its horizon of expectation and yet remain unrecognized as a great work of art. This case poses no problems for Jauss's theory. The first experience of disrupted expectations will almost invariably evoke strong negative responses from its initial audience, but the original negativity will disappear for later readers. The reason for this is that in a later age the horizon has changed, so that the work in question no longer ruptures expectations. Instead, it may be recognized as a classic, that is, as a work that itself has contributed in an essential way to the establishment of a new horizon of expectation.

Jauss modified his deviationist position in the 1970s, when he reexamined the viability of a model based exclusively on an aesthetics of negativity. Reacting in particular to the posthumous publication of Theodor Adorno's *Aesthetic Theory* (1997), as well as to the aesthetics of the *Tel Quel* group in France, Jauss reconsiders the implications of his own theoretical provocation of the late 1960s. What bothers Jauss about Adorno's view is that it allows a positive social function for art only when the artwork negates the specific society in which it is produced. It therefore leaves no room for an affirmative *and* progressive literature, because literature in general is defined by its opposition to social practices, by its "ascetic" character. Such a theory tends to valorize modernist directions, promoting an elitist, avant-garde concept of art, and scorning communication in literature as anathema to genuine cultural achievement. Jauss therefore recognizes the weakness in his earlier work when he admits the partial nature of his former depiction of aesthetic experience. By excluding a primary and positive aesthetic experience, the reception aesthetics shared an artistic asceticism with other contemplative and self-reflexive modes of speculation; and, by orienting itself on autonomous art, it ignored not only the important role of preautonomous art (pre-Romantic), but also the great variety of functions that art has historically possessed and potentially still possesses. Eventually, Jauss expanded his purview, developing a theory that encompasses a great variety of aesthetic responses, from uncritical identification to critical reflection against ironic negation.

Jauss's historical approach to understanding literary works was complemented by Wolfgang Iser's examination of the interaction between reader and text. Like Jauss, Iser attracted a great deal of attention with his inaugural lecture at Constance, but his theory is perhaps best represented in his book *The Act of Reading* (1976). What has interested Iser from the outset is the question of how and under what conditions a text has meaning for a reader. In contrast to traditional interpretation, which has sought to elucidate a hidden meaning in the text, he wants to see meaning as the result of an interaction between text and reader, as an effect that is experienced, not an objection that must be found. Roman Ingarden's conception of the literary work of art thus provided him with a useful framework for his investigation. According to Ingarden, the aesthetic object is constituted only through an act of cognition on the part of the reader. Adopting this fundamental precept from Ingarden, Iser thus switches focus from the text as an object to the text as a potential, from the results of a reading to the act of reading itself. [*See* Ingarden.]

To examine the interaction between text and reader, Iser looks at those qualities in the text that make it readable or that influence one's reading, and at those features of the reading process that are essential for understanding the text. Particularly in his early work, he adopts the term *implied reader* to encompass both of these functions; it is at once textual structure and structured act. Later, depending more heavily on Ingarden's terminology, he distinguishes between the text, its concretization, and the work of art. The first is the artistic aspect, what is placed there by the author to be read, and it may be conceived best as a potential waiting to be realized. Concretization, by contrast, refers to the product of the reader's own productive activity; it is the realization of the text in the mind of the reader, accomplished by the filling in of blanks or gaps (*Leerstellen*) to eliminate indeterminacy. Finally, the work of art is neither text nor concretization, but something in between. It occurs at the point of convergence of text and reader, a point that can never be completely defined.

The work of art is characterized by its virtual nature and is constituted by various overlapping procedures. One of these involves the dialectic of protention and retention, two terms borrowed from the phenomenological theory of Edmund Husserl. Iser applies them to our activity in reading successive sentences. In confronting a text, we continuously project expectations that may be fulfilled or disappointed; at the same time, our reading is conditioned by preceding sentences and concretizations. Because our reading is determined by this dialectic, it acquires the status of an event and can give us the impression of a real occurrence. If this is so, however, our interaction with texts must compel us to endow our concretizations with a degree of consistency—or at least as much consistency as we admit to reality. This involvement with the text is seen as a type of entanglement in which the foreign is grasped and assimilated. Iser's point is that the reader's activity is similar to actual experience. Although Iser distinguishes between perception (*Wahrnehmung*) and ideation (*Vorstellung*), structurally these two processes are identical. According to Iser, reading therefore temporarily eliminates the traditional subject-object dichotomy. At the same time, however, the subject is compelled to be split into two parts, one that undertakes the concretization and another that merges with the author, or at least the constructed image of the author. Ultimately, the reading process involves a dialectical process of self-realization and change: by filling in the gaps in the text, we simultaneously reconstruct ourselves. Our encounters with literature are part of an enlightenment process in which we come to understand others and ourselves more completely.

Iser's model of reading has been productively supplemented in the work of Karlheinz Stierle, the most incisive second-generation theorist from the Constance school during the 1970s. Stierle proceeds from Iser's contention that the formation of illusions and images is essential for the reading process, and labels this level of reading "quasi-pragmatic," a designation that distinguishes it from the reception of nonfictional texts ("pragmatic reception"). Although Iser seems to remain on this plane in his studies, Stierle suggests that a quasi-pragmatic reading must be supplemented with higher forms of reception capable of doing justice to the peculiarities of fiction. He argues for a pseudoreferential use of language, an application located between its usage in simple reference and its autoreferential function. What distinguishes narrative fiction is this pseudoreferentiality, which may be considered autoreferentiality in the guise of referential forms. Fiction is self-referential, although it appears to be referential. What Stierle suggests, therefore, is an additional reflexive level of understanding in our encounter with literary texts.

The critics of reception aesthetics from the former German Democratic Republic approach its accomplishments from a somewhat different stance. Robert Weimann and Manfred Naumann are not as interested in the reading process outlined by Iser and Stierle as they are in the literary historiography developed by Jauss. Their objections to his theory are threefold. First, they complain of one-sidedness, claiming that reception theory has gone too far in emphasizing the response to a work of art. Although they admit that this is an important aspect—and one that has been downplayed somewhat in the Marxist tradition—Jauss and his colleagues, in positing reception as the sole criterion for a revitalization of literary history, destroy the dialectic of production and reception. Second, Marxist critics detect a danger in the totally subjective apprehension of art and the resultant relativizing of literary history. The problem here is that if one follows Jauss (and Gadamer) in relinquishing all objective notions of the work of art, then one's access to history would seem to be completely arbitrary, because it is ceaselessly changing. Third, these critics argue that reception aesthetics provides scant sociological grounding for the reader, who supposedly stands at the center of its concerns. Scholars from the former German Democratic Republic find a general failure to link literary history with larger concerns. The reader in the reception aesthetics of Jauss and Iser, they claim, is conceived as an idealized individual rather than as a social entity with political and ideological, as well as aesthetic, dimensions.

In the United States, where reception theory had comparatively little impact until the 1980s, the work of Iser provoked the most controversy. Stanley Fish (1981) argued that Iser's theoretical apparatus, when applied to literary works, produces comprehensible interpretations of texts. He denies, however, that Iser's theory identifies elements in a literary work; rather, he asserts that it creates them. The issue for Fish is thus really one of epistemology. Perception, for him, is always a mediated activity; it is never innocent of assumptions. For Iser, on the other hand, there are some things that simply exist and must be grasped by all rational perceivers.

Jauss and Iser defended their positions against these and other objections in polemical rejoinders during the 1970s. They have also corrected and refined theoretical positions based on criticism. But the cost of these modifications has been a loss of the original excitement that surrounded the emergence of reception theory in the late 1960s and early 1970s. Both Jauss and Iser subsequently took directions that depart somewhat from their most influential work. Increasingly, Iser has concerned himself with the notions of the imaginary in fiction and with literary anthropology. Jauss's magnum opus, *Aesthetic Experience and Literary Hermeneutics* (1982), in which he articulated a more differentiated notion of response, was no longer perceived as a provocation to literary scholarship, but as a differentiated scholarly treatise. For this reason, this work evidenced a comparatively smaller impact on critical circles in Germany, and one could argue that reception aesthetics as a coherent and innovative approach to literature had exhausted itself by the early 1980s. Activity around literary theory at Constance, on the other hand, has survived the demise of its most important theoretical product by virtue of the personalities of its members and the biannual scholarly colloquiums held there. The meetings of the group Poetics and Hermeneutics, so important for the advent of reception theory, continue to produce some of the most exciting contributions to literary, cultural, and philosophical criticism in Germany.

[*See also* Hermeneutics; *and* Literature, *article on* Literary Aesthetics.]

BIBLIOGRAPHY

Primary Sources

Adorno, Theodor W. *Ästhetische Theorie.* Edited by Gretel Adorno and Rolf Tiedemann. Frankfurt am Main, 1970. Translated by Robert Hullot-Kentor as *Aesthetic Theory* (Minneapolis, 1997).

Gumbrecht, Hans Ulrich. "Konsequenzen der Rezeptionsästhetik oder Literaturwissenschaft als Kommunikationssoziologie." *Poetica* 7 (1975): 388–413.

Iser, Wolfgang. *Die Appellstruktur der Texte: Unbestimmtheit als Wirkungsbedingung literarischer Prosa.* Constance, 1970. In English as "Indeterminacy and the Reader's Response in Prose Fiction," in *Aspects of Narrative: Selected Papers from the English Institute,* edited by J. Hillis Miller (New York, 1971), pp. 1–45.

Iser, Wolfgang. *Der implizite Leser: Kommunikationsformen des Romans von Bunyan bis Beckett.* Munich, 1972. In English as *The Implied Reader: Patterns of Communication in Prose Fiction from Bunyan to Beckett* (Baltimore, 1974).

Iser, Wolfgang. *Der Akt des Lesens: Theorie ästhetischer Wirkung.* Munich, 1976. In English as *The Act of Reading: A Theory of Aesthetic Response* (Baltimore, 1978).

Iser, Wolfgang. "The Current Situation of Literary Theory: Key Concepts and the Imaginary." *New Literary History* 11 (1979): 1–20.

Jauss, Hans Robert. "Paradigmawechsel in der Literaturwissenschaft." *Linguistische Berichte* 3 (1969): 44–56.

Jauss, Hans Robert. *Literaturgeschichte als Provokation.* Frankfurt am Main, 1970.

Jauss, Hans Robert. *Kleine Apologie der ästhetischer Erfahrung.* Constance, 1972.

Jauss, Hans Robert. *Ästhetische Erfahrung und literarische Hermeneutik.* Frankfurt am Main, 1982.

Jauss, Hans Robert. *Aesthetic Experience and Literary Hermeneutics.* Translated by Michael Shaw. Minneapolis, 1982.

Jauss, Hans Robert. *Toward an Aesthetic of Reception.* Translated by Timothy Bahti. Minneapolis, 1982.

Naumann, Manfred, et al. *Gesellschaft, Literatur, Lesen: Literaturrezeption in theoretischer Sicht.* Weimar, 1973.

Naumann, Manfred. "Das Dilemma der 'Rezeptionsästhetik.'" *Poetica* 8 (1976): 451–466.

Schober, Rita. *Abbild, Sinnbild, Wertung: Aufsätze zur Theorie und Praxis literarischer Kommunikation.* Berlin, 1982.

Stierle, Karlheinz. *Text als Handlung: Perspektiven einer systematischen Literaturwissenschaft.* Munich, 1975.

Stierle, Karlheinz. "Was heisst Rezeption bei fiktionalen Texten?" *Poetica* 7 (1975): 345–387. Abbreviated version in English as "The Reading of Fictional Texts," in *The Reader in the Text: Essays on Audience and Interpretation,* edited by Susan R. Suleiman and Inge Crosman (Princeton, N.J., 1980), pp. 83–105.

Warning, Rainer, ed. *Rezeptionsästhetik: Theorie und Praxis.* Munich, 1975.

Weimann, Robert. "'Rezeptionsästhetik' und die Krise der Literaturgeschichte: Zur Kritik einer neuen Strömung in der bürgerlichen Literaturwissenschaft." *Weimarer Beiträge* 19.8 (1973): 5–33. In English as "'Reception Aesthetics' and the Crisis of Literary History," *Clio* 5 (1975): 3–33.

Weimann, Robert. "'Rezeptionsästhetik' oder das Ungenügen an der bürgerlichen Bildung: Zur Kritik einer Theorie literarischer Kommunikation." In *Kunstensemble und Öffentlichkeit,* edited by Robert Weimann, pp. 85–133. Halle, Germany, 1982.

Weinrich, Harald. "Für eine Literaturgeschichte des Lesers." *Merkur* 21 (1967): 1026–1038.

Other Sources

Bürger, Peter. "Probleme der Rezeptionsforschung." *Poetica* 9 (1977): 446–471.

Fish, Stanley. "Why No One's Afraid of Wolfgang Iser." *Diacritics* 11.1 (1981): 2–13.

Fokkema, D. W., and Elrud Kunne-Ibsch. "The Reception of Literature: Theory and Practice of 'Rezeptionsästhetik.'" In *Theories of Literature in the Twentieth Century,* pp. 136–164. New York, 1977.

Grimm, Gunter. *Rezeptionsgeschichte: Grundlegung einer Theorie.* Munich, 1977.

Hohendahl, Peter Uwe, ed. *Sozialgeschichte und Wirkungsästhetik: Dokumente zur empirischen und marxistischen Rezeptionsforschung.* Frankfurt am Main, 1974.

Holub, Robert C. *Reception Theory: A Critical Introduction.* London and New York, 1984.

Holub, Robert C. *Crossing Borders: Reception Theory, Poststructuralism, Deconstruction.* Madison, Wis., 1992.

Link, Hannelore. "'Die Appellstruktur der Texte' und 'ein Paradigmawechsel in der Literaturwissenschaft.'" *Jarhbuch der deutschen Schillergesellschaft* 17 (1973): 532–583.

Solms, Wilhelm, and Norbert Schöll. "Rezeptionsästhetik." In *Literturwissenschaft heute,* edited by Friedrich Nemec and Wilhelm Solms, pp. 154–196. Munich, 1979.

Zimmermann, Bernhard. *Literturrezeption im historischen Prozess: Zur Theorie einer Rezeptionsgeschichte der Literatur.* Munich, 1977.

ROBERT C. HOLUB

REFERENCE. *See* Perception, *article on* Music Perception; Realism; *and* Representation.

REID, THOMAS (1710–1796), Scottish philosopher and founder of the "commonsense" school of philosophy. Reid was born into a distinguished family of clerics and intellectuals and received his education in theology and philosophy at Marischal College, Aberdeen. From 1736 to 1750, he served as minister of New Machar, where he first read David Hume's *A Treatise of Human Nature.* This work was to have a profound impact on Reid's own philosophy, which is by and large an attempt to refute some of Hume's basic assumptions and thus to avoid the "skeptical" conclusions that he believed Hume was forced to draw concerning humankind's relation to the world. From 1751 to 1764, Reid was professor of philosophy at King's College, Aberdeen, where he wrote his first work, *Inquiry into the Human Mind on the Principles of Common Sense* (1764). In 1764, he succeeded Adam Smith in the chair of moral philosophy at Glasgow, where in 1774 he delivered his *Lectures on the Fine Arts.* He gave up lecturing in 1780 in order to work on the *Essays on the Intellectual Powers of Man,* which was published in 1785. He remained at Glasgow for the next ten years, during which he wrote a number of philosophical papers and the *Essays on the Active Powers of Man* (1788), in which he defends a rationalist theory of ethics.

Reid's "commonsense" philosophy gives an account of the basic powers (practical and intellectual) of the human mind. The account is driven by a conviction that the most universal aspects of human language and practice mirror the basic structures of thought—the first principles of truth and judgment that he takes to be embodied in a "common sense" universal to mankind.

The three following claims capture the most essential and most distinctive features of Reid's aesthetics:

1. Theories that analyze beauty in terms of a subjective state are inadequate because they misdescribe our aesthetic practices.
2. There are intersubjective criteria for justifying claims of taste, and these criteria are based on objective perfections.

3. There are different kinds of beauty and sublimity (e.g., original or derived, natural or artistic) that must be analyzed in different ways.

The most striking feature of Reid's aesthetics is perhaps his claim that objects that are beautiful or sublime must either possess or signify some real perfection. Reid is here reacting to a tendency among empiricist aestheticians "to resolve everything into feelings," to think of beauty as a feeling in our minds rather than a property of objects (Reid, 1973, p. 35). Francis Hutcheson, for example, identifies beauty with a sensible "idea raised in us"—an idea that may, for all we know, carry no resemblance to what caused it—and has to conclude that "were there no mind with a sense of beauty to contemplate these objects, I see not how they could be called beautiful" (An Inquiry Concerning Beauty, Order, Harmony, Design, 1973). Reid thinks people like Hutcheson confuse our response to beauty with that *to which* we are responding. This leads them to misrepresent what we take ourselves to be doing when we make aesthetic judgments—namely, to be making claims about *objects* and not about the mental states they evoke in us (Reid, 1969, pp. 755, 759, 783). In order to capture this fact about our aesthetic experience, Reid insists that objects are beautiful or sublime in virtue of either possessing or expressing some perfection—more specifically, some perfection of mind and its active powers (ibid., 791; 1973, pp. 43–51). In what follows, this claim will be referred to as the "objectivity thesis."

Reid puts forward the objectivity thesis in order to identify a source of value for objects of taste. He thinks that the falsity of locating their value in our affective response to them becomes apparent when we examine our own aesthetic practices and modes of judgment. The structure of our claims of taste shows that "in every operation of taste, there is a judgment implied" (1965, p. 759)—a judgment that does not refer to the mental state of the subject, but rather involves the belief that the object we deem beautiful or sublime has some real value (ibid., p. 807; cf. pp. 759–760). Our aesthetic judgments, in other words, indicate that favorable responses do not supply the source of value that merits those very responses. Because our claims of taste refer to something else than a subjective state, it is misguided to think that the fact that we favor objects of taste is our only basis for deeming them valuable.

Reid thinks that not only our common sense but also our use of language attest to the objectivity thesis. When we argue about matters of taste, we strive to justify our love or admiration for certain objects. In other words, we take the object to have some real merit stemming from a source of value to which we can refer in justifying our aesthetic judgments (ibid., pp. 807–808; cf. p. 758). Because we do dispute about taste, Reid thinks that there exist public criteria—both affective and rational—for defending our claims of taste and that these criteria are veridical (guide us

to the truth) in the sense that they pick out real perfections in the world.

The problem with this argument is that the existence of intersubjective criteria for justifying claims of taste does not imply their veridicality, does not imply that they refer to real (perceiver-independent) perfections in the world. It is possible that the things we deem excellent have no value in themselves but are instead valuable only with regard to our own contingent purposes or to our historically conditioned social and moral codes. If that is the case, it is hard to see how a beautiful or sublime object can have "its excellence from its own constitution, and not from ours" (ibid., p. 770), because its value would then stem entirely from the fact that we (or other perceivers) approve of that particular quality.

Here we need to remind ourselves that Reid's location of beauty in real excellence is a move against empiricist aestheticians' tendency to explain beauty in terms of utility, which in turn reduces to an object's tendency to produce pleasure. Reid believes that the mere fact that we take pleasure in aesthetic objects cannot explain why we value them. Our sentiments must themselves be well grounded, and it is in order to justify those responses that Reid insists that beauty and sublimity must be sought in "the scale of perfection and real excellence"—in particular, in the perfections of mind and its active powers.

All the beauty and sublimity in the material world are then said to "derive" from mental perfection: material objects are beautiful or sublime insofar as they bear the signs or effects of mental excellence—that is, either insofar as they express amiable or admirable mental qualities by resembling the physical expressions or "natural signs" of those qualities, or else insofar as they show a high degree of "design, art, and wise contrivance" by being well adapted to their specific end (ibid., pp. 791–792; 1973, pp. 41–42, 47). Aesthetic objects in the material world are thus connected to mental perfection through expression, and that is what gives them the value that "merits" our favorable response.

Reid emphasizes that there are different kinds of beauty in the world. Because only intelligent creatures can properly be said to possess mental and active perfections, they become the primary objects of taste in Reid's theory—the bearers of what he calls "original" beauty and sublimity. His account of "derived" beauty divides into the following categories:

1. the beauty of organisms and machines (attributable to their adaptedness to a natural end or function);
2. the beauty of things that express or bear the signs of mental excellence (a birch swaying in the breeze is beautiful because it "beckons," reminding us of hospitality);
3. the beauty of things that are analogous to certain kinds of mental excellence (musical harmony and soft colors or shapes are analogous to mental balance and concord).

By connecting aesthetic merit to mental excellence, Reid explains how certain inanimate objects can justly inspire the feelings of love and admiration that we normally think of as reserved for our fellow human beings.

[*See also* Hume; Hutcheson; *and* Taste.]

BIBLIOGRAPHY

Works by Reid

Essays on the Intellectual Powers of Man (1785). Cambridge, Mass., 1969.

Lectures on the Fine Arts. In *Thomas Reid's Lectures on the Fine Arts,* edited by Peter Kivy. The Hague, 1973. An unpublished manuscript transcribed and edited by Kivy.

Other Sources

Cummings, Phillip D. "Reid's Realism." *Journal of the History of Philosophy* 12.4 (October 1974): 317–340.

Dalgarno, Melvin, and Eric Matthews, eds. *The Philosophy of Thomas Reid.* Dordrecht and Boston, 1989.

DeRose, Keith. "Reid's Anti-Sensationalism and His Realism." *Philosophical Review* 158.3 (July 1989): 313–348.

Ferreira, M. Jamie. *Skepticism and Reasonable Doubt: The British Naturalist Tradition in Wilkins, Hume, Reid, Newman.* Oxford, 1986.

Gallie, Roger D. *Thomas Reid and "The Way of Ideas."* Dordrecht and Boston, 1989.

Gracyk, Theodore A. "The Failure of Thomas Reid's Aesthetics." *Monist* 70.4 (October 1987): 465–482.

Jones, Peter. *The "Science of Man" in the Scottish Enlightenment: Hume, Reid and Their Contemporaries.* Edinburgh, 1989.

Kivy, Peter. "Introduction." In *Thomas Reid's Lectures on the Fine Arts,* pp. 1–17. The Hague, 1973.

Kivy, Peter. "The Logic of Taste: Reid and the Second Fifty Years." In *Thomas Reid: Critical Interpretations,* edited by Stephen F. Barker and Tom L. Beauchamp, pp. 118–132.

Lehrer, Keith. "Reid on Primary and Secondary Qualities." *Monist* 61.2 (April 1978): 184–191, esp. pp. 188–189.

Lehrer, Keith. *Thomas Reid.* London and New York, 1989.

Lobkowicz, Erich. *Common Sense und Skeptizismus: Studien zur Philosophie von Thomas Reid und David Hume.* Weinheim, 1986.

Manns, James. "Beauty and Objectivity in Thomas Reid." *British Journal of Aesthetics* 28.2 (Spring 1988): 115–131.

Nauckhoff, Josefine C. "Objectivity and Expression in Thomas Reid's Aesthetics." *Journal of Aesthetics and Art Criticism* 52.2 (Spring 1994): 183–191.

Robbins, D. O. "The Aesthetics of Thomas Reid." *Journal of Aesthetics and Art Criticism* 5 (1942): 37–38.

JOSEFINE NAUCKHOFF

REINHARDT, AD (1913–1967), American painter, critic, and art activist. Coming of age in the United States in the 1930s, Reinhardt saw himself not as an innovator but rather as the uncompromising militant in defense of the "timeless" tradition of radical modern avant-garde art. Abstraction is an ethos that with Reinhardt assumed the standing of a ideological cause. In paintings that at last approached, yet never quite reached, the absolute condition of black, Reinhardt remained an idealist in both his art and his politics, resisting any popular or ingratiating form. His car-

toons of aesthetic and art-political "isms," published from college on into maturity, show Reinhardt early on to have been criticizing the sociologically distracted ideology of abstraction from within.

Reinhardt's assimilation, synthesis, and deliberate reduction of radical abstraction antecedent to his era, and the significance of this artistic process, are symptomatic of the ethos that attaches to abstraction immediately after World War II. If viewed historically, Reinhardt came to be known as the most extreme of those New York school painters whose color field reductions of formal and symbolic content enabled an abstract painting of aesthetic rectitude.

A chronology that Reinhardt himself compiled of his lifeworld in 1966 reveals the narrative the artist wished for himself and art. The year 1913 is miraculous on this account: Reinhardt's birth, coinciding with the fact that "Malevich paints first geometric-abstract painting," announces an implicit design for Reinhardt's future development as an artist. In 1914, Henri Matisse paints *Porte-Fenêtre, Collioure* appears, and "Mondrian begins 'plus-minus' paintings." Reinhardt will later cite Piet Mondrian and Matisse, together with the Cubists, as indispensable to art history.

The significance of this is that, in Reinhardt's constructed narration of his career after the fact, he acknowledged his historical antecedent in the Suprematist icon of nonobjectivity, Kasimir Malevich's *Black Square* of 1913. Liberated from resemblances, the *Black Square* is a radical expression of something like the highest level of mind, an absolute mind in art to which Reinhardt refers in mature work, culminating in his reconceiving the notion of black on black in paintings achieved during the last decade of his life.

Aesthetically, Suprematism and Neoplasticism attain to idealist explanations of a concrete reality, and the concrete realizations of idealist syntheses informing Suprematism and Neoplasticism will in turn inform Reinhardt's aesthetic vocabulary. Malevich's own polemic reflects the changing lexicon of the avant-garde in Soviet Russia. Initially, Malevich speaks of the pure plasticity of Suprematist art as achieving a compound of "utilitarian reason and intuitive reason"; by 1920, he speaks of plastic relationships among lines and planes forming a dynamic "system." The idealist and utopian construal of concrete form similarly holds true in Mondrian's scheme of things, for, having penetrated nature, abstraction has achieved the "expression of relationships" exclusively. Perpendicularity expresses the "one permanent relationship," attaining, as it does, an equilibrium of spirit with matter, active with passive, male with female, truth with beauty. Reinhardt will assume the mantle of this aesthetic. By the late 1940s, he will have adapted a version of Mondrian's late Neoplasticism to a contrapuntal horizontality of planes within a vertical format.

More like annals that pick events of historical significance highly selectively and leave conspicuous gaps, Reinhardt's chronology displays its partisan view of world-historical events as though providing the relevant context for the artist's own life: "1917 October Revolution in Russia. Lenin replaces Kerensky. 1921 Abstract painters have trouble in Russia. 1922 Mexican painters issue anti 'art for art's sake' manifesto. Joyce completes *Ulysses*. 1923 Duchamp gives up painting."

Sampling this chronology brings into focus further cultural constellations of personal significance to Reinhardt. "1929 Museum of Modern Art opens. Stock market crashes. Georgia O'Keeffe paints 'Black Cross, New Mexico'." A nexus of events in Reinhardt's life-world that indicates not only themes but the content of these themes, and the value invested in them.

"1931 Enters Columbia College. 1932 Paints studies of Michelangelo's Sistine Ceiling figures for literature class of Raymond Weaver, who suggests courses with Meyer Schapiro, who suggests joining radical campus groups." This notation is symptomatic of the relation of art to politics and social action in Reinhardt's understanding of things. Schematically put, for Reinhardt there is no contradiction in the phrase "political artist," if it means that an artist is radical in art, and radical in politics without appeasement to the public taste in either activity. One can be a political artist without doing what is popularly construed as political art, the subject matter of which is overtly about politics. Finally, one can be a political artist insofar as commerce is resisted and materialistic values are disdained.

"1943 Tries to talk Thomas Merton out of becoming a Trappist. Refuses to help Arshile Gorky start a camouflage school. Wonders what Adolph Gottlieb and Mark Rothko are up to when they announce, 'There is no such thing as good painting about nothing.' Continues making paintings about nothing." The axiological aetheticism of Reinhardt is in place. It comes in part to his having subscribed to Clive Bell's notion that "all uncompromising belief is religious" (not that Bell urged subscription to religion as such). Reinhardt also responds to Bell's notion that, pictorial content having been dispensed with, certain combinatory relations appear as significant form (Bell, 1914). An aesthetic "disinterestedness" capable of sparking ironies and paradoxes characterizes Reinhardt's attitude toward art. Although Reinhardt had read Søren Kierkegaard and Friedrich Nietzsche in his German literature seminar at Columbia University, the renunciations he professes are those expendable to abstraction in art, including marks of individuality and variety. As Reinhardt sees it, the renunciations are positive choices for the integrity of abstraction. Ethical resistance to journalism and commerce, because they encourage easy choices in art, does not imply withdrawal from the world.

"1944 Liberation of Paris." Reinhardt notes the first show in an art gallery, and in this year and those following World War II other professional events interleave notices of peace, wars, and independence.

The late 1940s brings a crisis of competing modes of abstraction. Alternating between hard-edge and painterly facture, Reinhardt's compositions chromatically calibrate fragmented labyrinthine elements dispersed throughout the visual field. In some works from around 1946 to 1949, small calligraphic gestures disperse across a monochromatic field even as, in other paintings, contrasting or close-valued tesserae of color assume modular form. Then, too, taking into account later Neoplasticism (owing in part to Carl Holty's intervening introduction to Mondrian), by 1951 Reinhardt's restatement will come to systematize a few large tesserae by relating them symmetrically.

Reinhardt's mature style announces itself through entries beginning in 1953: "Gives up principles of asymmetry and irregularity in painting" and "Paints last paintings in bright colors." From 1950 to 1953, Reinhardt concentrates on a counterpoint of optically keyed planes, oriented horizontally within a vertical field. A state of dynamism through "certain magnetic interrelations" of planes in Malevich, or equilibrium in Mondrian (especially those canvases of 1917 in which tonal pinks and tinted blues align with gray in a gridded field), has assumed a singular opticality once Reinhardt, graying his colors, brings close-valued chromatism into privileged cohesiveness (see Bois, 1991).

In the next decade, pictorial dynamism will come to be expressed in forces at rest in the perfect symmetry of Reinhardt's off-black cruciform composition, "at rest yet no less binding after all," as Hermann Weyl puts it when lecturing on symmetry. Meanwhile, however, one observes Reinhardt's concern to establish formal cohesion, and through cohesion, necessity.

A concern with form's structural entailment is culturally pervasive as well. Beyond Weyl's celebrated book *Symmetry*, deriving from a 1951 lecture series, the events and publications that aggregate in evidence also include "Aspects of Form"—a symposium held in conjunction with the exhibition "On Growth and Form" at the Institute of Contemporary Art, London, and published in book form 1951, in homage to D'Arcy Thompson's classic work *On Growth and Form* (1924)—to provide an instance of the reinvigoration of logical and scientific thought after the cataclysmic interruption of World War II. These publications are indicative of cultural concerns for congruent arrangements (a definition of geometry employed by Weyl) in the artistic milieu that Reinhardt found compatible.

The collective wish for stable structures developing into form language are revealed through Reinhardt's own words. Participating in the three-day symposium on art published in *Modern Artists in America* (1951), Reinhardt, at odds with Willem de Kooning, assumes synonymy between geometry and intellectual clarity and is particularly keen on distinguishing geometry in other ways: "An emphasis on geometry is an emphasis on the 'known,' on order and knowledge." He inquires of Hedda Sterne whether her art is, as it suggests, "planned and preconceived." By these comments, Reinhardt reveals his own concern for an abstraction that signifies structure rather than expression. He insists on an art that is "classic" in form.

"1953 Visits Greece. Daughter born. 1954 Cambodia, Laos, Vietnam achieve independence. Macdonald Wright returns to Abstract Art. 1955 Listed in *Fortune* magazine as one of top twelve investments in art market. 1956 Borrows money from bank to travel. Suez crisis. Makes last cartoon, a mandala." From travels to Greece in 1953 and travels to Japan, India, Persia, and Egypt in 1958, and to Turkey, Syria, and Jordan in 1961, there accumulated "hundreds of color slides" (Wittman, 1992). These he presented at the Artists' Club on 10 October 1958 and 23 January 1959, in a two-thousand-slide lecture titled "An Evening of Slides: The Moslem World and India." The lecture, as well as an album of photographs from travels aggregating architectural detail by structural theme, indicate Reinhardt's intentions for an imaginary museum of world art. Clustered by formal motif or structural function are pyramids, arches, windows, lattice ornaments, and crosses, among many forms. Predominantly architectural, the album also collates painting in this personal "museum without walls." The implicit intention would be to derive a universal language of form implicative of necessity in painting.

Ultimately significant is Reinhardt's very choice of travel destinations: traditional and ancient civilizations, the form languages of which are utterly antithetical to the premium on novelty in the West. But this only substantiates Reinhardt's commitment to the tradition of abstraction and gives credence to his belief that form is an expression of thought within art, thought re-created throughout historical time—hence timeless. Notions of progress in art were, therefore, ill conceived in Reinhardt's view of things, and held no sway against the notion of stylistic recurrence. Reinhardt found this attitude shored up through the writing of Henri Focillon, whose *The Life of Form,* originally published in France in 1934 (and translated by George Kubler in 1948), became a "classic" for students of art and literature soon after, and provided the direct inspiration for Kubler's equally revered argument for "a linked succession of prime works with replications," in *The Shape of Time,* published in 1962 and reviewed favorably by Reinhardt.

Meanwhile, Reinhardt has given up publishing cartoons, for instance, those on art-historical lineage whereby the modern trunk is all that remains once the representational limb snaps (1948), and the abstract limb, weighed down by ideology and commerce, comes crashing down (1960). As Lucy Lippard (1981) remarks, Reinhardt engaged in political activity throughout his life, and civil liberties were always very much on his mind; indeed, as his notebooks say, "Painting cannot be the only activity of a mature artist." But by announcing the end of cartooning with a mandala that brings a phase of public chastisement of the art world to a

close, Reinhardt renounces a certain form of applied polemic for an argument conveyed through the internalized polemic of fine art alone. In 1959, he sends a Black Painting to be the hermetic companion of the Trappist Thomas Merton, who already had taken a vow of silence.

"Black as Symbol and Concept," written in 1967, the year of his death, shows Reinhardt continuing to contemplate the meaning of the term to which he had devoted himself since 1955:

> I once organized a talk on black, and I started with black as a symbol, black as a color, and the connotation of black in our culture where our whole system is imposed on us in terms of darkness, lightness, blackness, whiteness. Goodness and badness are associated with black. As an artist I would like to eliminate the symbolic pretty much, for black is interesting not as a color but as a non-color and as the absence of color.

If intentions matter, then this statement reveals Reinhardt's own shift in the nature of "meaningless" art for art's sake over the years. If anything, Reinhardt now chooses to reinforce the positive sense of the once derogatory Stalinist use of meaningless formalism by declaring the irrelevancy of even the traditional symbolic meanings of black in art history and culture. Yet, throughout this talk, Reinhardt in fact continues to accrete, in effect, shades of the symbolism he has just forsworn.

The Black Paintings, then, may be said to embody the conventional cultural symbolism of black newly aestheticized and designated as such. Pragmatically, the Black Paintings remain as they were once for him, a "free, unmanipulated and unmanipulatable, useless, unmarketable, irreducible, unphotographable, unreproducible, inexplicable icon." Epistemologically, the Black Paintings are meant to stand for the epitome of painting even as they resist every Western satisfaction with things identifiably known as paintings. Sometimes considered icons without iconography, these Black Paintings take their (paradoxically) replete meaninglessness from known ideas of spirituality informing traditional religion and culture. Presupposed by Reinhardt is fulfillment of these traditions in the art, art history, and the endless cycle of universally renewed aesthetic ideas that bring forth art through time.

Metaphysically, the spiritual content of traditional cultures informs Reinhardt's own, whether the artist legislates against this meaning or not (Masheck, 1978; Inboden and Kellein, 1985). This includes Christianity, if not its institutions. Friends with Thomas Merton since their days at Columbia, Reinhardt retained respect for religion as being better than any business, for the value placed in principled integrity and the resistance to worldliness. In a postwar ecumenical spirit, Reinhardt further prized the "negative theology" of Buddhism as well as the likes of Meister Eckehart in the West. "The tao is dim and dark," Reinhardt quotes Laozi in his talk "Black as Symbol and Concept." The posi-

REINHARDT. Ad Reinhardt, *Black Paintings* (23 December 1966–15 January 1967), photograph of Ad Reinhardt room; Jewish Museum Exhibition, New York. (Copyright by the Artists Rights Society, New York; photograph courtesy of the Jewish Museum/Art Resource, New York; used by permission.)

tive value of black as a signifier of receptivity may complement the Pietist equilibrium achieved through union of dualistic spiritualist principles.

He was confident in the universal and lawlike nature of painting, and largely impervious to the cultivation of doubt in his humanist contemporaries, insofar as the affirmation of belief also coincides with his assertion of negation set forth in contemporary modes of thought. Yet, a phenomenological existentialism may also be said to inform Reinhardt's writing on art, and in notes to himself, the concept of black as "absence" or "negative presence" coexists alongside "dematerialization, nonbeing" and "the dark of absolute freedom." Thus, by the time Reinhardt delivered his seminar talk "Black as Symbol and Concept," he was intent on emphasizing the entirety of cultural content of black: "I want to emphasize the idea of black as intellectuality and conventionality."

Finally, however, black conventionally signifies the radical principle itself. If, in Alexei Kruchenikh's *Victory over the Sun* (1913), the eclipse of the sun supersedes the world as it is in everyday life, Malevich's blackening square done in backdrop shows—to the extent it symbolizes anything—the sun in eclipse, a metonomy for nature in eclipse. An eclipse of objective for nonobjective art expresses the aesthetic principle in extremis. It is a principle of radical commitment to art as art. Eclipsing nature for culture informs the Black Paintings by Reinhardt, and ultimately identifies painting as a sign for itself.

That black absorbs all pigmented color may be a material fact that Reinhardt exploits to make a point about painting at the limits of its own enterprise, and the synonymy of painting with self-reflexivity. In this sense, Reinhardt's aesthetic meaning differs from that proposed by Malevich in his famous 1918 white-on-white canvas. Reinhardt's messianic utopianism proffers no "futurism." Instead, it signifies an eternal present. Contemplative rather than active, Reinhardt's darkly hued blacks would seek to manifest a certain antithesis of Suprematism in a steady-state dialectic.

"Art-as-art" in Reinhardt's lexicon would then fulfill its prescription for art. The tincture of color that renders black "almost" black is suggestive of an articulation of the absolute situation for painting; or, it is suggestive of the articulation of final painting. Whether art-as-art does not finally suggest the limit of painting (Bois, 1991) rather than nature's extinction is an issue still under discussion.

"1966 One hundred twenty paintings at Jewish Museum." The significance of Reinhardt's art, as with Reinhardt himself, lies with an idea of artistic integrity and purpose. In a more immediate historical sense, it inspired a younger generation of artists (arguably named Minimalists) to imitate an aesthetic of formalism even as it provoked a materialism in reaction. Surface and support determining the quantification of aesthetic result appear in the work of Frank Stella, Robert Ryman, and others, to substantiate through constitutive means the physical nature of painting as object. Despite the competition offered by Pop Art on the one hand, and varieties of conceptual art on the other, the sort of dematerialization embodied in Reinhardt's art remains substantially unchanged in the formal grammar developed from the principles and methods of structuralism emerging thereafter.

At the same time, the consummation of a tradition also implies an exhaustion of that tradition. Cued by Reinhardt's statement that his are the "last paintings one can make," critics have found the work to intend a minimal expressivity and a minimal content (Wollheim, 1965). On this account, not only has the pictorial subject matter been vacated, but the canvas appears vacant, owing to the elimination of only the most necessary differentiation made to render the artifact a work of art.

On other accounts, Reinhardt's art announces a postformalist era, insofar as composition and other creative choices are deemed to be expendable to abstraction as a sign of itself. Whether in Ellsworth Kelly's or Gerhard Richter's canvases showing a mechanistically charted color series in modular extension, or, for that matter, in Andy Warhol's replication of the commercial image and object, the so-called exhaustion of form has been said to emerge in part from the grid that Reinhardt eventually preconceived in lieu of composition. Further rationalizing painting's exhaustion is the metaphor of entropy, as a metaphor derived from the science of natural systems popular in the 1950s and 1960s. Art discourse would then find form exhaustion implicative of some Minimalism and/or dematerialized conceptual art, especially such as that of James Turrell, for which (in analogy with Reinhardt) actual emanating light or its palpable absence tests the limits of phenomenal visibility.

Reinhardt's art has continued to remain paradoxical in the meaning and significance imputed to it. Replete with meaning, yet also meaninglessness; symbolist yet concrete, it has contributed to a history of art in which recurrence rather than progress of formal language is the norm, while bringing art to the point of, if not extinction, then objectlessness.

[See also Abstraction; Malevich; Modernism; and Mondrian.]

BIBLIOGRAPHY

Works by Reinhardt

Art-as-Art: The Selected Writings of Ad Reinhardt. Edited by Barbara Rose. New York, 1975; reprint, Berkeley, 1991.
Modern Artists in America. Edited by Ad Reinhardt, Robert Motherwell, and Bernard Karpel. New York, 1951.

Other Sources

Arnason, H. H. "The Quest for Art-Is-Art." In Ad Reinhardt: Black Paintings, 1951–1967. New York, 1970.
Bell, Clive. Art. New York, 1914.
Bois, Yve-Alain. "The Limit of Almost." In Ad Reinhardt. New York, 1991.
Inboden, Gudrun, and Thomas Kellein. Ad Reinhardt. Stuttgart, 1985.
Kubler, George. The Shape of Time: Remarks on the History of Things. New Haven, 1962.
Lippard, Lucy R. Ad Reinhardt. New York, 1981.
Malevich, Kasimir S. Essays on Art, 1915–1933. 2d ed. Translated by Xenia Glowacki-Prus and Arnold McMillan, edited by Troels Andersen. New York, 1971.
Masheck, Joseph. "Two Sorts of Monk: Reinhardt and Merton." Artforum (December 1978). Reprinted in Historical Present: Essays of the 1970s (Ann Arbor, 1984).
Mondrian, Piet. Natural Reality and Abstract Reality. Translated by Martin S. James. New York, 1995.
Rowell, Margit. Ad Reinhardt and Color. New York, 1986.
Weyl, Hermann. Symmetry. Princeton, N.J., 1952.
Wittman, Walter T. "Ad Reinhardt Collection." Museum of Modern Art Library Bulletin 85 (Fall 1992).
Wollheim, Richard. "Minimal Art." Arts Magazine (January 1965).

MARJORIE WELISH

RELATIVISM. Relativists standardly make two claims: first, with regard to some subject matter, they claim that there is no universal standard for understanding or evaluating it; second, they claim that the correctness of an understanding or evaluation always depends on something local, such as a conceptual scheme, conventions or norms shared within a community, or the reactions of a group or an individual. There are two main subject matters for relativism in aesthetics: relativism about aesthetic value judgments (e.g., "William Shakespeare's *Hamlet* is a great tragedy") and relativism about interpretative judgments or claims ("It is Hamlet's Oedipus complex that causes him to hesitate").

One can be a relativist about the *truth* of these judgments by claiming that this varies with a variation in conceptual scheme, in community norms or conventions, or simply in the actual or hypothetical reactions pro or con of individuals or groups. Such a relativism implies that these judgments are true or false, but not true or false *simpliciter*. Rather, their truth-value is relative to scheme, convention, or individual or group reaction. Hence, not all conjunctions of (nonrelativized) true judgment preserve truth.

One might instead be a relativist about the justification of such judgments, claiming that what would justify them for one group differs from what would justify them for another, depending again on variation in scheme, convention/norm, reaction, or, alternatively, differences in histories or practices. A relativist regarding justification might not be one regarding truth. This might be because one believes these judgments to lack truth-value or because one believes that their truth-value is nonrelative.

Finally (for the purposes of this survey), one may be a relativist about the very meaning of such judgments. Thus, if one believes that one's procedures of justification enter into the meaning of one's aesthetic value judgments, and these procedures vary from group to group, then the meaning of these judgments would also vary from group to group. Two individuals from different groups might say, "Pablo Picasso's *Guernica* is a great painting," but they would be making different statements. An individual from a third group might at first appearance deny the first two judgments by claiming that *Guernica* is not great. But if her standards of justification were different in nature than those of the others, and the assumption holds that these standards enter into the meaning of her judgment, then she says something different from, but not strictly inconsistent with, the others.

Motivations for Relativism. What makes a relativistic position attractive? One of the strongest and most widespread reasons for embracing relativism is the existence of seemingly irresolvable disagreements with regard to both judgments of value (in aesthetics as well as ethics) and interpretative claims. Such disputes appear to continue without closure, and often without mutual agreement on the evidence or considerations that would produce closure. This motivation is epistemic in nature, based on a problem of establishing value judgments and interpretative claims to everyone's satisfaction.

A second reason to accept some form of relativism derives from a sociological or political conception of the origin of aesthetic value judgments and interpretative claims. It is sometimes suggested that these judgments and claims have their basis in supporting the hegemony or legitimacy of a particular class, or group, whether a large social class such as the bourgeoisie or a small academic subdiscipline. Given such a view, it might seem plausible to suppose that such judgments and claims have validity only within the relevant group. If, as suggested in the preceding paragraph, there really were no generally accepted evidential criteria for accepting or rejecting the statements in question, that fact might bolster this view of them.

A third motivation for accepting relativism is that there is a way of conceiving of the world that can provide a reason for doing so. There is no easy way to state this conception, but a simple rendering would be that the world is in part constructed by human cognitive activity (by perceiving, conceiving, theorizing, and interpreting). What is meant is not merely that among the things that exist are artifacts that are in part the result of the cognitive activity of their makers. What is meant is that even "natural objects" are at least in part constructed, and artifacts reconstructed, by our ways of thinking about them. Add now to this idea that this construction of the world varies according to historical period, tradition, society and culture, and language or conceptual scheme, and one has a basis for believing that the truth, justification, and even the meaning of our statements would also vary and be relative. The basis of this relativism, however, is itself a kind of ontological relativism that would be in need of independent justification.

A final motivation is based on an understanding of the appreciation appropriate to art and the role of interpretation in bringing about this appreciation. One appreciates many works of art by interpreting them, and if one can come to interpret them in more than one way, perhaps in many ways, then the possibilities and opportunities for appreciation are enhanced. Hence, the practice of interpretation ought to, and in fact does, allow for multiple interpretations of artworks, even interpretations that often seem to clash. This has suggested to many that some sort of relativism is required by the very nature of art, or the very point of art appreciation, in order to explain how clashing interpretations can all be acceptable. This relativism would carry over to aesthetic value judgments insofar as they are based on interpretations of artworks.

Relativism about Aesthetic Value Judgments. Although all of the motivations just mentioned are influential, it is the first that has been most important in discussions of aesthetic value, whereas the final one has been dominant in discussions of interpretive claims.

The crucial issue regarding aesthetic value judgments was concisely set out by David Hume in his brief but much-discussed essay "Of the Standard of Taste." Everyone recognizes the great variety of tastes that inform evaluative judgments and that creates the disagreements noted earlier. A painting that seems vibrant to one spectator may seem gaudy to another. An avant-garde gesture that seems profound to one spectator may seem respectively gratuitous, banal, and superficial to three others. Some of this diversity in judgment results from defects in the spectator, who may be biased, uninformed, or insufficiently sensitive to the nuances of an art form. Even after judgments defective in these and other ways are disqualified, it is plausible that differences in taste—that is, differences in the way individuals perceive and react to artworks—will result in different evaluations of the same work. This suggest that evaluations are relative to taste, however "taste" is ultimately defined. [*See* Hume.]

Whether one accepts such a relativism depends on at least two issues. The first issue concerns the nature of artistic value. What are the properties that make works valuable as artworks? The relativist claims that these properties are to be defined in part in terms of potentially variable reactions (tastes). Second, even if the relativist is right on this matter, are some tastes (possibly a single taste) better than others? For example, perhaps there are some tendencies to react to artworks that are more likely to deliver more valuable experiences and other things of value than other tendencies. These issues are only beginning to receive the attention they deserve and remain largely unresolved.

Relativism about Interpretation. An obsessive concern with the interpretability of art and literature, along with many other phenomena, has been characteristic of the thought of the twentieth century. To get a proper perspective on the nature and plausibility of a relativistic position about interpretation, it should be distinguished from another doctrine with which it is easily confused. The doctrine is critical pluralism, which claims that, for many works of art and literature, there are multiple, acceptable interpretations that cannot be combined into a single acceptable interpretation. The doctrine with which critical pluralism is usually thought to directly compete is critical monism, the view that there is a single true interpretation of each work of art and literature that captures the meaning of those works. Critical pluralism is widely, though not universally, accepted. The acceptance of critical pluralism is not, however, tantamount to the acceptance of relativism. Relativists are pluralists, but not all pluralists are relativists.

Relativism provides one explanation for the truth of critical pluralism. The standard relativist explanation is that the correctness of an interpretation is not determined simply by its adequacy to the work under interpretation, but by the conventions, assumptions, or norms of a community of interpreters. Correctness is relative to such a community. The correctness of interpretation i of a work w in community c_1 does not imply correctness in any other interpretive community, and hence there is no valid inference from the fact that i is correct in c_1, and j is correct in c_2, to the conclusion that the conjunction of i and j gives a correct interpretation of w. Because this implies that there are acceptable, noncombinable interpretations of w, the truth of critical pluralism is secured by this route.

One of the clearest examples of this standard version of relativism in contemporary thought is provided by the writings of Stanley Fish. Fish not only holds that interpretations of a given work are true only relative to the assumptions of an interpretive community, but that this is so because works acquire meaning only when these assumptions are applied to them. Hence, the very meaning that works possess and the justification for ascribing such meaning to them are also relative to such communities.

An alternative view is advanced by Joseph Margolis under the label "robust relativism." Margolis rejects the standard relativist approach of indexing the truth or warrant of an interpretation, or the meaning of an object of interpretation, to a community. His alternative is to claim that interpretive claims are to be understood within a many-valued logic. On such a logic, interpretative claims can be false, but are never true. Instead, they are affirmed by "truthlike" predicates such as "plausible," "reasonable," and "apt." According to Margolis, this view permits one to affirm (as plausible, reasonable, or apt) interpretations that would be logically inconsistent, that is, incapable of being true together, in a bivalent logic. Such interpretations nevertheless remain "nonconverging" even within the many-valued logical framework. If Margolis is right about all of this, then he offers an alternative route to critical pluralism, because on his view too there are acceptable, noncombinable interpretations.

Robust relativism resembles standard relativism in claiming that the appearance of logical inconsistency between interpretative claims that we accept is illusory, because, when properly understood, both claims make true (or truthlike) claims that nevertheless cannot be conjoined. Hence, although they offer different routes to critical pluralism, they are routes that share a somewhat similar strategy.

There are nonrelativistic ways of establishing pluralism, however. One is to take matters a step further than Margolis and deny that interpretations make claims that are true, false, or even truthlike. On this view, an interpretation's acceptability is determined in other ways, such as its ability to heighten appreciation of a work. Clearly, there can be interpretations that are acceptable because they accomplish this, but are noncombinable because, when yoked together, they fail to enhance appreciation.

There are more conservative strategies that suffice to establish critical pluralism. Suppose one holds the view that interpretations of a work are to be constrained by the conventions in place when it is created (not conventions in place when it is being interpreted, as relativists tend to hold), and only by such conventions. Such a constraint provides a standard of acceptability that applies to all interpretations, but may permit several noncombinable interpretations of the same work. Or suppose one holds the view that interpretations of a work are acceptable if one is justified in believing that they were intended by the creator of the work (whether or not they were really so intended). Again, several different interpretations may satisfy this requirement.

Finally, one can arrive at critical pluralism by recognizing that one interprets with different aims. Sometimes one aims at understanding a work as the product of the historically situated artist. Sometimes one merely looks for *an* understanding of a work, one that makes plausible sense of it in a way that promotes appreciation. Sometimes one aims at maximizing the aesthetic value or intelligibility of a work. Sometimes one is trying to make a work relevant to a particular audience by finding a significance in the work especially appropriate to that group. In the process of pursuing these different aims, one sometimes will offer interpretations that genuinely contradict each other, and hence cannot both be true. Even in this case, both may be acceptable relative to the evidence on hand, which is insufficient to eliminate one of the interpretations. Given the different aims with which one interprets, however, it will often happen that apparently inconsistent interpretations are in fact logically compatible. The assertion that a work can be understood as representing an F is compatible with the assertion that it can be understood as representing not F, but G.

(Grant Wood's *American Gothic* is usually understood as representing a man and his wife, though there is some evidence that it was meant to represent a man and his daughter. It is at least true that it can also be understood in this way.) Although such interpretations are strictly compatible, there may be no point in combining interpretation pursued with different aims (or sometimes the same aim, as in the case just cited).

The last approach also renders compatible critical pluralism with its supposed rival, critical monism. If one interprets with different aims, it is possible that only one of these aims seeks to discover the meaning or core content of a work. It is also possible that there is only one correct interpretation that gives a comprehensive statement of this meaning. This still permits many other acceptable interpretations that aim at something other than identifying work meaning and do not sensibly combine with such a statement. This is not to say that monism is actually true. To establish that would require a great deal of further argument.

Evaluation of Relativism about Interpretation. Sometimes *relativism* is a term used to dismiss a view as being beyond the pale of reason. A universal relativism (e.g., the view that all truth is relative) is sometimes said to be self-refuting because its very assertion implies that at least one truth is not relative (that is, that *all* is relative). The relativisms being examined here, however,—about the interpretation of artworks and aesthetic value judgments—are local rather than universal, and thus could not be criticized in this way.

A limited relativism is not an intrinsically unreasonable doctrine. The question that should be asked is whether the motives for adopting relativism provide sufficient reason to accept it.

It must be said that most of the motivations offered for a relativism about interpretation fail to do this. Of the four reasons for accepting relativism discussed earlier, the first is the apparent irresolvability of interpretative disagreements. Standard relativism explains some of this irresolvability by claiming that many of the disagreements are not real when relativized to different communities. Irresolvability results from the different standards underlying the apparently conflicting interpretative claims. Proponents of this view, however, fail to show that real disagreements within an interpretative community are any more resolvable—as they should be—than merely apparent disagreements among different communities. Robust relativists would claim that interpretations are evaluated as more or less plausible, apt, or reasonable. This process would eliminate some interpretations, while leaving a plurality of others in the field. What a robust relativist is not so clear about is why disagreements should persist beyond this point.

Other approaches offer as good, or better, explanations of interpretative disagreement. The approach that claims that one interprets with different aims would suggest that a cer-tain amount of apparent disagreement arises through unclarity about interpretative aim, through talking at cross-purposes, as it were. The remaining real disagreements have to be handled piecemeal, for resolvability turns on what is actually asserted by an interpretation, and this will vary with aim. Once again, the problem does not require a relativist solution.

A second motivation for relativism is the view that interpretative claims have an underlying social or political basis. Whether or not such a view has plausibility, it supplies the weakest reason to accept relativism—a view about the truth, justification, or meaning of interpretive claims. A political basis for such claims—such as a tendency to help sustain the power of a group—says nothing about the meaning of those claims or whether they are true or justified even within a particular group. Hence, they do not provide a good reason to accept relativism.

A third reason to accept a relativism about interpretive claims derives from an ontological relativism—the idea that what exists is constructed by human cognitive activity and the practices and institutions in which this activity is embedded. This view itself is not easy to understand, and its implications are far from clear. Suppose that it implies that groups with different institutions and practices are interpreting different *Guernica*s and different *Hamlet*s, which are, in part at least, constructed by the cognitive activity of individuals within the respective groups. It would then be true that they would be interpreting objects with different meanings, which would make appropriate different truth claims, but this would be no more surprising than that *Hamlet* and *Twelfth Night* or *Guernica* and *The Man with a Violin* (Picasso, 1912) have different meanings. If one has already established a difference in object of interpretation, one does not need a relativism about meaning or truth to explain differences in interpretative claims.

A final reason for accepting relativism is that the nature of artistic appreciation encourages—perhaps requires—one to accept multiple interpretations of artworks. That, however, merely points to the truth of critical pluralism, and relativism is only one of numerous routes to that doctrine. Hence, this motive provides no compelling argument for relativism.

One can conclude that none of the reasons for accepting relativism about interpretative claims provides compelling reasons to do so. There is a another sort of relativism, however, that does seem compelling. This relativism derives from the view, mentioned earlier, that one interprets works of art with different aims. When one evaluates interpretations, it is plausible that one should bring different standards of acceptability to interpretations with different aims. Thus, it would be wrong to apply the same standard to an interpretation that attempts to recover the intention of the artist and an interpretation that attempts to find significance in a work that would make it relevant to a particular contemporary audience. Success in these two cases involves very different things. Thus, it appears to be true that the acceptability of an interpretation is relative to its aim.

[*See also* Essentialism; Goodman; Historicism; Interpretation; Truth; *and* Universals.]

BIBLIOGRAPHY

Relativism about Aesthetic Value Judgments

Budd, Malcom. *Values of Art: Pictures, Poetry, and Music.* London, 1995.
Goldman, Alan H. *Aesthetic Value.* Boulder, Colo., 1995.
Hume, David. "Of the Standard of Taste." In *Essays: Moral, Political, and Literary,* edited by John W. Lenz, pp. 226–249. Indianapolis, 1987.
Hutcheson, Francis. *An Inquiry into the Original of Our Ideas of Beauty and Virtue* (1725). New York, 1971.
Kant, Immanuel. *Critique of Judgement.* Translated by James Creed Meredith. Oxford, 1952.

Relativism about Interpretation

Carrier, David. *Principles of Art History Writing.* University Park, Pa., 1991.
Fish, Stanley. *Is There a Text in This Class: The Authority of Interpretive Communities.* Cambridge, Mass., 1980.
Iseminger, Gary ed. *Intention and Interpretation.* Philadelphia, 1992.
Krausz, Michael. *Rightness and Reasons: Interpretation in Cultural Practices.* Ithaca, N.Y., 1993.
Margolis, Joseph. *The Truth about Relativism.* Oxford and Cambridge, Mass., 1991.
Margolis, Joseph. "Plain Talk about Interpretation on a Relativistic Model." *Journal of Aesthetics and Art Criticism* 53.2 (Spring 1995): 1–7.
Stecker, Robert. *Artworks: Definition, Meaning, Value.* University Park, Pa., 1997.

ROBERT STECKER

RELIGION AND AESTHETICS. [*To examine the relationship between religion and aesthetics, this entry comprises two essays:*

An Overview
Religion and Art

The first essay explains the relationships between religion and art in the history of aesthetics. The second concerns the relationships between religion and art in the histories of religion and art. For related discussion, see Byzantine Aesthetics; *and* Russian Aesthetic, *article on* Religious Aesthetics.]

An Overview

The religions of humanity and the art of humanity have always been intertwined; neither can be understood without attending to the other. Most religions use music in their rituals and liturgies, and develop architecture to house the performance of their liturgies. Most use poeticized language in their address to God. Most use visual art to keep alive the memory of their founding and defining narrative, and to represent or symbolize the holy and the divine. For

these reasons, and many more, the religions call forth art. Then, subsequently, the art shapes the religion—shapes the affections, the emotions, the beliefs, the memories, the actions, of the religious participant and believer. It all happens so naturally that, even in literate cultures, relatively little about art and religion was written down before the modern era. Abbot Suger wrote down some of his thoughts concerning the church of Saint Denis in Paris, whose construction he supervised; Procopius wrote a bit about Hagia Sophia in Constantinople; the church fathers wrote a bit about iconography; Augustine made some comments about the power of liturgical music; and so forth. But in the West, at least, altogether it does not come to much—no substantial reflections on the positive relation of religion to art.

Things do not always go smoothly between religion and art, however. Religions not only evoke art, they reprimand artists, and try to dismiss and exclude certain forms of art; and artists, rather than laboring faithfully in the cause of one or another religion, sometimes rebel and act subversively. In the Occident, the most substantial writing that exists from the premodern era about the relation of religion and art is polemical writing, evoked by points of tension. The most articulate of such polemical writing is that which emerged from the Byzantine iconoclast controversy that raged from around 725 CE until about 840 CE.

Controversies concerning images have erupted repeatedly in the history of Christendom. The biblical proscription of idols has always played a role in these, often up front, sometimes in the background. In the biblical Book of Exodus the second of the Ten Commandments given by God through Moses to Israel states: "You shall not make for yourself an idol, whether in the form of anything that is in heaven above, or that is on the earth beneath, or that is in the water under the earth. You shall not bow down to them or worship them." But although controversies over images have been common, the Byzantines conducted the debate with a level of sophistication never elsewhere equaled. [*See* Icon.] Let it suffice to say here that though a major point of contention throughout the controversy pertained to the appropriate mode of interacting with an image of a holy person—is it appropriate to kneel before such an image and kiss it—there were also debates concerning the worth, and even the legitimacy, of such images. Quite astonishingly, the Byzantine emperor Leo III developed the argument that images of Christ violated the Christological formulas agreed on in earlier councils, and were accordingly heretical. Whereas the councils had declared that Christ's humanity and divinity are inseparable, an image of Christ is only capable of representing him as human, not as divine.

Although the most substantial body of writing about art and religion from the premodern West is polemical in character, that is not true for the closely related topic of beauty. The topic was placed on the intellectual agenda of the West by the Neoplatonists, Plotinus in particular, with Plato's

Symposium in the background. It was generally agreed that beauty is that which pleases upon being contemplated; and a question regularly considered was which features of entities evoke such delight. The answers given varied somewhat: unity, due proportion, clarity, brightness, perfection. But it was agreed by all parties that there is beauty in things because, and insofar as, those things reflect God. God is primordially beautiful.

To understand modern Western discussions about religion and the arts—of which there are a multitude—one must recall the dramatic changes in the arts, and our characteristic way of thinking about them, that took place in eighteenth-century Europe. A number of related things happened more or less simultaneously. First, and perhaps most important, the concept of the aesthetic emerged. Though the concept was related to the older concept of beauty, it was nonetheless significantly different. Beauty had been understood as a property, or "transcendental"; the aesthetic, by contrast, was understood as a distinct sphere of value. Although the eighteenth-century theorists borrowed from the traditional discussions of beauty by defining "aesthetic delight" as delight in contemplating, they added two important qualifications not found in the medieval discussions of beauty: delight in contemplating, to be aesthetic delight, must be *universal*, in the sense that it is grounded in our shared human nature rather than in particularities of makeup or training; and, even more important, it must be *disinterested.* That is to say, it must be independent of delight experienced in the achievement of purposes or the satisfaction of desires. Second, the conviction emerged that art, along with wilderness, is peculiarly apt for evoking such delight. Third, increasingly it became the case that works of art were created, and made available to the bourgeois public in performance and display, for exactly this purpose. Such works and such performances constitute the "high art" of the modern Western world. Fourth, as Paul Oskar Kristeller argues in his well-known article "The Modern System of the Arts" (1965), the conviction solidified that music, poetry, fiction, painting, and sculpture are to be grouped together as paradigmatically "fine" arts. Finally, the conviction emerged that commerce with the arts and wilderness that is aesthetic in its orientation—thus, contemplative and disinterested—is essential to becoming a member of what Joseph Addison, in a pair of articles in *The Spectator* (19 and 21 June 1712), called "polite people," by which he meant, in present-day vocabulary, cultured people. Aesthetic commerce with the arts is essential to the acquisition of what the Germans came to call *Bildung.*

Almost all modern Western discussions of religion and the arts take for granted the coherence and legitimacy of these developments. For example, they focus their attention on the high art of the modern West, and ask what that art has to do with religion. Liturgical art seldom comes into view; when it does, it is regularly dismissed as art that has not yet come into

its own. So too for memorial art—art meant to keep alive in a religious community the memory of central events and persons in its founding and defining narrative.

The views on art and religion that have been articulated in the modern West do not appear to fall into any natural classification. One theme that emerged already in the eighteenth century was that of the sublime. When discussing art, wilderness, contemplation, and imagination (imaging), the eighteenth-century theorists spoke regularly not only of beauty but also of sublimity—by which they meant the grand, the majestic, the awesome, to which correspond feelings of being overpowered and being overwhelmed. Writers reported experiencing such feelings in the presence of mountains and oceans, but also, early in the nineteenth century, when listening to the music of Ludwig van Beethoven or reading the poetry of William Wordsworth. Feelings of sublimity were, as one might expect, also regarded as prominent among the religious affections. Friedrich Schleiermacher located the origin of religion in one's primordial feeling of dependence; and that feeling, if not exactly the same as what the eighteenth-century theorists had in mind by feelings of sublimity, certainly incorporated such feelings. Thus, sublimity and its feelings were regularly regarded as connecting art and religion. As to the precise mode of connection, there was little consensus, and often not much clarity. The feelings of sublimity that one sometimes experiences when contemplating wilderness or art—are these merely one species of the genus, feelings of sublimity, with another species being the feelings one has when one senses oneself in the presence of God? Or is the connection closer than that? Are the former feelings themselves somehow religious in character? When one contemplates oceans and mountains, when one listens to Beethoven and reads Wordsworth, are the feelings of sublimity experienced themselves *religious* affections? Is one somehow in the presence of the divine? Is the feeling of sublimity, regardless of its phenomenal object, a religious emotion—perhaps the *primordial* religious emotion?

Somewhere in the latter part of the nineteenth century, sublimity fell from fashion, with the consequence that, since then, beauty has more often been seen as the connector between art and religion than sublimity. The book by the bishop of Oxford, Richard Harries, *Art and the Beauty of God* (1993), is a good example of this approach. Harries argues, in classic neo-Plotinian fashion, and with the assistance of a good many neo-Plotinian references, that beauty in "earthly" things is a reflection of the beauty of God. All beauty is, in that way, of "spiritual" significance. Accordingly, Harries calls the religious person to be sensitive to the beauty in earthly things (lack of such sensitivity indicates a deficiency of spirituality), and he calls the person concerned with the arts to ascend from "earthly" to "heavenly" beauty (lack of sensitivity to "heavenly" beauty indicates a deficiency of openness to the full range of beauty).

This same theme, of art as reflecting God, is found in the essays of Dorothy Sayers and a number of her Anglo-Catholic cohorts. Rather than singling out beauty as the point of connection, however, Sayers and her group focus on artistic creation: the religious believer, she argues, and especially the Christian believer, should see in artistic creation a rich and articulate reflection of the creative activity of the Triune God.

In a line of thought articulated with extraordinary eloquence by Clive Bell in his *Art* (1914), it is not sublimity or beauty but the aesthetic attitude itself that is the fundamental connection between art and the aesthetic. Some writers, such as Frank Burch Brown, have argued that the aesthetic attitude is always an informed attitude, and that part of what enters into its formation, for many people anyway, is their religious convictions. What Bell singles out instead is the supposed disinterestedness of the aesthetic attitude. Definitive of art, Bell argues, is that art has "significant form"—by which he means form that evokes aesthetic emotion. He goes on to ask why it is that human beings are moved by the contemplation of pure form. The answer he proposes is that when it is the pure form of an object that evokes emotion, one has set off to the side all of one's purposes and come face to face with reality itself—Reality. Whether it is called God, says Bell, is a matter of indifference. Disinterested contemplation pierces the veil of human purposes and intentions and puts one in touch with the Ultimate—hence the deep feelings.

Quite a different approach from any of these emerged in the early years of Romanticism. The Romantics were the first great critics of modernity. Their fundamental critique—whether of the new science on which they had their eye, or capitalism, or institutional Protestantism, or French revolutionary politics—was that modernity dissolves the organic unities in society, self, and culture that previously characterized human life. In the words of John Keats, it "unweaves the rainbow." It was also the conviction of the Romantics, however, that the genuine work of art constitutes a true, organic unity. Thus, the work of art provides an image of what society and culture would be like if the dynamics of division and alienation were overcome. Some writers have gone farther and suggested that art not only provides an imagistic symbol of a healed humanity, but is itself an agent for bringing about renewal in society and culture. Repeatedly in the modern period, salvific potential has been ascribed to art. The major aesthetician of the Frankfurt School, Theodor Adorno, was on many points a biting critic of Romanticism. On this point, however, he shared their hopes, albeit guardedly; art, and perhaps art alone, has the potential of casting a "messianic light" on a fractured society.

Finally, the enormously influential line of thought that G. W. F. Hegel initiated should be mentioned. It was Hegel's conviction that art, religion, and philosophy represent alternative ways of giving expression to the mentality, the spirit, the *Geist,* of an age. Art does so in a sensuous medium; religion does so imagistically, though without a sensuous medium; philosophy does so neither imagistically nor in a sensuous medium. Hegel clearly regarded philosophy as the most advanced expression of *Geist*. Yet, he did not regard art and religion as simply outmoded. In any case, he regarded all three—art, religion, and philosophy—as fundamentally united in being cultural expressions of the mentality of an age. The writings on art of the Protestant theologian Paul Tillich are a twentieth-century variant on the Hegelian approach.

As these observations suggest, modern discussions on religion and art have been diffuse. In the eighteenth century, something of extraordinary importance happened to Western art, and to Western ways of thinking about art. A form of high art emerged that has nothing directly to do with the church or any other form of institutional religion. Many theologians and theorists of the arts have nonetheless been convinced that this development did not mean a separation of art from religion, nor of religion from art. Surely, they are right about that. The connections are subtle, however; the multiplicity of lines of attack are witness to that.

It should be mentioned, in conclusion, that a few authors have refused, in their reflections on art and religion, to go along with the majority in focusing all attention on the modern Western institution of high art, and have insisted that an accurate understanding of the interaction between art and religion requires the recognition that the modern Western institution of high art represents an idiosyncratic development within the history of humanity's art. It is true that the high art of the modern West has religious significance, and that this art continues to interact in various ways with religion; but the full story of religion and art cannot be told if one focuses just on this high art. The story of religion and art in earlier ages cannot be told; witness the Byzantine iconoclast controversy mentioned earlier. But neither can the full story of religion and art today. Alongside high art, for example, liturgical and memorial art continue to thrive.

[*See also* Beauty; Iconoclasm and Iconophobia; *and* Sublime.]

BIBLIOGRAPHY

Abrams, M. H. *The Mirror and the Lamp: Romantic Theory and the Critical Tradition.* New York and Oxford, 1953.
Abrams, M. H. *Natural Supernaturalism: Tradition and Revolution in Romantic Literature.* New York, 1971.
Adorno, Theodor W. *Minima Moralia: Reflections from Damaged Life.* Translated by E. F. N. Jephcott. London, 1974.
Adorno, Theodor W. *Aesthetic Theory.* Edited by Gretel Adorno and Rolf Tiedemann, translated by Robert Hullot-Kentor. Minneapolis, 1997.
Balthasar, Hans Urs von. *The Glory of the Lord: A Theological Aesthetics.* 7 vols. Various translators. San Francisco, 1982–1989.
Bell, Clive. *Art.* London, 1914.

Brown, Frank Burch. *Religious Aesthetics: A Theological Study of Making and Meaning.* Princeton, N.J., 1989.

Burke, Edmund. *A Philosophical Inquiry into the Origin of Our Ideas of the Sublime and the Beautiful.* London, 1757.

Dillenberger, John. *A Theology of Artistic Sensibilities: The Visual Arts and the Church.* New York, 1986.

Eco, Umberto. *Art and Beauty in the Middle Ages.* Translated by Hugh Bredin. New Haven, 1986.

Eire, Carlos M. N. *War against the Idols: The Reformation of Worship from Erasmus to Calvin.* Cambridge and New York, 1986.

Harries, Richard. *Art and the Beauty of God.* London, 1993.

Hegel, Georg Wilhelm Friedrich. *Aesthetics: Lectures on Fine Art.* 2 vols. Translated by T. M. Knox. Oxford, 1975.

Kant, Immanuel. *Critique of Judgment.* Translated by Werner S. Pluhar. Indianapolis, 1987.

Kristeller, Paul Oskar. "The Modern System of the Arts." In *Renaissance Thought II: Papers on Humanism and the Arts,* pp. 163–227. New York, 1965.

Van der Leeuw, Gerardus. *Sacred and Profane Beauty: The Holy in Art.* Translated by David E. Green. New York, 1963.

Maritain, Jacques. *Art and Scholasticism.* Translated by Joseph W. Evans. New York, 1962.

Maritain, Jacques. *Creative Intuition in Art and Poetry.* Reprint, Princeton, N.J., 1978.

Pelikan, Jaroslav. *Imago Dei: The Byzantine Apologia for Icons.* Princeton, N.J., 1990.

Sayers, Dorothy. *The Mind of the Maker.* London, 1941.

Sayers, Dorothy. *Christian Letters to a Post-Christian World.* Edited by Roderick Jellema. Grand Rapids, Mich., 1969.

Tatarkiewicz, Wladyslaw. *A History of Six Ideas.* Translated by Christopher Kasparek. The Hague, 1980.

Tillich, Paul. *On Art and Architecture.* Edited by John Dillenberger and Jane Dillenberger, translated by Robert P. Scharlemann. New York, 1987.

Wandel, Lee Palmer. *Voracious Idols and Violent Hands: Iconoclasm in Reformation Zurich, Strasbourg, and Basel.* Cambridge and New York, 1995.

Wolterstorff, Nicholas. *Art in Action: Toward a Christian Aesthetic.* Grand Rapids, Mich., 1980.

NICHOLAS WOLTERSTORFF

Religion and Art

The question of the relations between art and religion can be analyzed according to four complementary approaches, at once thematic and chronological:

1. the role of art and the controversies surrounding it in the definition of religious identities;
2. the functions and practices—private and public, orthodox and heterodox, liturgical and devotional—of the religious image;
3. the substitution of the work of art for the cultual (or cultic) image and the modern emergence of an aesthetic posture;
4. the religion of art.

Such an analysis is comprehensive, yet it avoids being a general synthesis and does not privilege an ahistorical history of ideas.

Art and the Definition of Religious Identities. May one see in the place conceded to art a satisfactory criterion for distinguishing different cultures and the forms of religious experience they favor? There is a general consensus here (Baaren, 1962) to oppose, in this respect, magic and religion. In the case of magic, cultual objects are generally realized by those who use them, are not destined to be viewed permanently by a large public, and are tied to the manipulation of natural forces. In the case of religion, the objects refer to supernatural forces and to the acquired distinctions among professional clerics and producers and spectators of artworks, and thus, ultimately, to the need to legitimize these last and to define their usages within the church—that is, to elaborate a theology, a liturgy, and a discipline of images. If one limits oneself to Europe and the figurative arts, one can only note that the attitude of great religions of the Book with regard to images has served to accentuate religious borders and differences.

Even if it is necessary to give up the cliché of radical Jewish and Muslim aniconism (that is, absolute renunciation of religious imagery), as recent works (Sed-Rajna, in Boespflug and Lossky, 1987) and archaeological discoveries (the synagogue of Dura-Europos) show, there is no doubt that in the interval between late antiquity and the Middle Ages, the gap in facts, and above all in mental outlooks, became more pronounced between a Christianity unified by the use of images and by the pilgrimages (Wirth, 1989) and other religions. Countless examples of such a divergence are provided by the religious controversies among Jews, Christians, and Muslims; by the direct confrontations at the time of the Crusades; and by more or less legendary accounts (Jean-Claude Schmitt, in Boespflug and Lossky, 1987).

The parallel history of Greek and Latin Christianities is a testimony as well to the role played by the question of the image in the definition of religious orthodoxies. The iconoclastic crisis of the eighth century and the final success of iconodules had lasting consequences. Not only did the fathers of the Second Council of Nicaea (787) confirm the legitimacy of figurative and anthropomorphic representation, but they made the practice of icon worship obligatory as well. For a long time, they delineated the position of the Greek church in affirming that the icon is the imprint of the prototype, which is, as it were, present in it; it thus takes part in the nature of the prototype and establishes a direct connection between humans and God. John of Damascus affirms also: "I do not venerate matter, but rather the Creator of matter who became matter for me and who deigned to live in matter and perform the work of salvation by matter." The icon is thus a theology of presence, indissociable from the Incarnation. Closely linked with the liturgy that it intensifies and clarifies, the icon will thus be a gospel (Nikephoros). In the preparation of the icon, the artist is only an agent whose conformity with the rules is expected above all. The Frankish church rejected the conclusions of the Second Council of Nicaea and established, notably in the *Libri Carolini,* a via media destined to a long posterity in the West. The Frankish bishops recognized only the pedagogical, memorial, and ornamental functions of images, refusing the idea of the passage of the image to the prototype in religious practices, the notion of an access to the invisible world by visible objects, and above all the idea of the presence of the prototype in the image drawing veneration. The opposition between the Orient, which develops a rich and complex theology of the image, and the Occident, which sustains above all a practice and an aesthetics, is thus shaped since the iconoclastic controversy.

Certainly, from the fifth century onward, the East and the West assumed convergent paths, and the worship of images took on similar aspects on both sides. Despite this rapprochement and the considerable success of the Byzantine icons that flooded the Occident beginning with the Fourth Crusade and the fall of Constantinople—such as the icon of Suffering Christ represented in mosaics around 1300 and transferred from Rome to Santa Croce in Jerusalem in 1380 (Belting, 1990; Os, 1994)—the gap has never been closed. Moreover, as a form of creative liberation, the Renaissance made an effort to break with the techniques and the iconography of the icon. Giorgio Vasari thus recalled the meaning of the innovations of Cimabue, who knew how to surpass his masters who worked not in the Greek manner of Antiquity, but in that of the modern Greeks.

Within the very interior of Latin Christianity, the quarrel over images precipitated the confessional explosion of the sixteenth century and played a decisive role in the makeup of religious boundaries between Catholics, Lutherans, Calvinists, and dissidents. The break between Martin Luther and the radical reform of Andreas Bodenstein von Carlstadt and Thomas Münzer took place in the winter of 1521–1522 in large part as a result of this quarrel. In England and the Netherlands, the internal disputes over Protestant confessions were as lively as those between Protestants and Catholics. The Lutheran via media (the condemnation of idolatry as well as iconoclasm, the retention of certain images for noncultual ends, a simplification of the themes and a predilection for the episodes of the Passion represented with a didactic care) led then to a combat on two fronts between Catholic iconoduly, confirmed by the Tridentine decree of December 1563 concerning the relics of saints and images and Calvinist iconophobia. The efforts to establish a reconciliation between Protestants and Orthodox stumbled as well over the image, following the example of the discussions (1574–1581) between the theologians of Tübingen and the patriarch of Constantinople (Michalski, 1993).

The problem of adaptation partially complicates the analysis with regard to architecture: the utilization in Christian churches of architectural elements taken or copied from Roman monuments, the conversion of churches into mosques or of mosques into churches, and the transformations of Catholic churches into Protestant temples suggest a greater flexibility. In a general manner, art, including music, seemed to have constituted, and to constitute still, an effective religious marker. The scandal raised in autumn 1995 by the destruction of the image of the Virgin of Brazil, relayed by the world press, bears a supplementary proof.

Functions and Practices of the Religious Image. The question of the relationships between art and religion covers three interdependent but distinct problems:

1. the artistic treatment of themes, dogmas, and religious personages: choice and diffusion of subjects, evolution of styles and techniques, innovations and iconographic repetitions
2. the functions of religious art and the immense diversity of usages—orthodox and heterodox, private and public—of the image (Baxandall 1972, 1980)
3. the position of the churches and clerics in regard to figurative arts, architecture, or music

Concerning images in particular, it is not impossible to identify the dominant and recurring arguments. Since the sixth century in the East and the West, one encounters arguments of a didactic type: for example, in a famous letter by Gregory the Great, for whom paintings are the reading of the illiterate. Arguments of a memorial and emotional type also certainly play a role, as in a sermon that appeared in 1492 according to which images were introduced "firstly because of the lack of education of simple peoples; secondly because of our emotional inertia; thirdly because of the precariousness of our memory" (Baxandall, 1972). Most important are the Christological arguments and considerations on the Incarnation as putting an end to the Old Testament taboo on images (Exodus 20), along with arguments indirectly inspired by the Neoplatonic philosophy of Pseudo-Dionysius the Areopagite, in particular in the East, and by anagogic reasoning, which all consider the icon a receptacle of a constant presence of the divine. Theodore of Studious concludes that once that Christ is born of a describable Mother, he naturally has an image corresponding to that of his Mother; and if he could not be represented in art, it would mean that he was born solely of his Father and was thus not incarnate.

Here, it is only a question of an analytic division, which is impossible to retain in the course of the inquiry because the historical phenomena across the three areas can be understood only in their interaction and intersection. The example of the sixteenth-century quarrel over images, familiarity with which was profoundly revived, suffices to illustrate the point. It quickly proves deceptive to confine oneself to theological controversies to explain the conflicts surrounding the image in the sixteenth century and the iconoclasm that affects the greatest part of Europe. The overwhelming majority of the arguments employed by the adversaries were already found in the quarrel of the eighth century and in the thought of Carolingian theologians (Scavizzi, 1992). In a significant manner, Theodore of Studious, John Damascus, the canons of Nicaea II, and the *Libri Carolini* were edited and often translated during the strongest conflicts of the sixteenth century. Iconoclasm itself did not constitute in any way a radical novelty in the Europe of the 1520s: the medieval precedents in the Lollard and Hussite uprisings (Bredekamp, 1975), as well as in the banal situations of the coercion of saints are countless.

The quarrel over images and the iconoclasm of the sixteenth century can be understood, then, as a conjunction of complex and partially autonomous processes:

1. The quantitative and qualitative explosion of images at the end of the Middle Ages, in part under the effect of the activity of mendicant orders, brotherhoods, and certain devout circles, in part also as a function of the technical ease offered by the printing press and wood engraving, which allowed for the reproduction of images at the slightest cost.

2. The concomitant diversification of usages and the expansion of images of devotion *(Andachtsbilder)* next to images invested with liturgical functions (Os, 1994). The question remains controversial, both concerning the existence of a particular type of image linked to the new culture of prayer that established itself at the end of the Middle Ages and concerning what touches on the interpretation of the complex symbolism of art in this epoch of transformation. How, for example, can one distinguish in the Flemish retables of the fourteenth to fifteenth centuries the elements that refer to the strong times of the liturgy from those that attest rather to the personal piety of the donors, to their spiritual experiences, their visions? Does the painting of the Arnolfini couple illustrate the debates about the sacrament of marriage or a precise marriage contract? In a good many cases, we are reduced to hypotheses by the lack of sufficient sources. There is no doubt, however, that between the fourteenth and sixteenth centuries, art expressed more and more the aspirations and personal religious experiences of donors and patrons, religious, and laity, and that, in turn, it played a growing role in their devotions in supporting their prayers and meditations. Of this change, the *Livres d'Heures* bear proof.

3. The stylistic, thematic, and iconographic transformations of the end of the Middle Ages and of the sixteenth century reveal at the same time an affirmation of new genres (portraits, landscapes), the emergence of novel subjects linked to the evolution of religious practices (the interest in the humanity of Christ leads artists and religious people to accord more importance to Joseph, Anne, and the Holy Family), and the increasing use of illusionist or realist processes. These transformations provoked the suspicion of numerous theologians and prelates who were concerned about the confusion that could result for believers between the image and its prototype, the propagation of superstitions linked to the excessive cult of images (notably in the works of Desiderius Erasmus with regard to the cult of Saint Christopher), or the diffusion of indecent apocryphal or heretic subjects (for example, in Saint Anthony of Florence, who condemns the three-headed Trinities.

4. The crisis of the theology of the image and the erosion of the Thomist position—which affirmed that one owes the same veneration to the image of Christ and to Christ himself (*Summa Theologiae,* IIIa, 25, a3)—under the double critique of heterodox movements and the internal dispute of the church. In 1542 again, in the middle of confessional confrontations of the Reform, the theologians Matthew Ory, Ambroglio Catarino, and Martin Perez de Ayala, having remained loyal to the Roman church, could only state their disagreement on the question, however central, of adoration and keep a prudent distance with regard to the Thomist thesis. Until the Council of Trent, Catholicism did not present a united front before Protestant disputes.

In Byzantium, as in the medieval Occident or modern Europe, the legitimacy and function of religious art depends on the interactions between the three aspects distinguished at the beginning of this section in the interest of clarity and on the historically changing configuration of the relationship between artists, patrons/buyers, believers/spectators, clergy, and political authorities. Its status itself thus predisposes the image to be at the same time the stakes, the terrain, and the means of struggle (Bredekamp) for confrontations and complex compromises in which political preoccupations, social aspirations, economic conflicts, and religious rivalries are inextricably intertwined (Cormack, 1985; Warnke, 1973). Lacking consistent works, it is difficult to bring a similar judgment on architecture and music, even if the quarrels of the sixteenth century surrounding religious music, organ music, and canticles in the vernacular provide convincing elements.

Substitution of Art for the Cultural Image. The problem of the transformation of the status and function of the image and of the autonomization of the artistic field around the end of the Middle Ages has become the object of new debates, the stakes of which can be reviewed.

The emergence of collectionism (Groote, 1994) and the aesthetic posture that constitutes the image as a work of art whose value resides above all in its formal qualities opened the way to the transformation of the gaze and the forms of judgment made on artistic creations: "A picture is no longer to be understood in terms of its theme, but as a contribution to the development of art" (Belting, 1994). It leads as well to the formation of places consecrated only for aesthetic pleasure and to the exercise of a judgment of taste: cabinets, galleries (of sovereigns, princes, cardinals, or dealers), salons, and museums. The works that were collected there were invested with a new value, which was largely independent of the political, dynastic, or liturgical functions formerly imparted to the image. In the modern collection, the icon became a work of art, as Victor I. Stoichita shows concerning the garland Madonnas in the cabinets of Antwerp amateurs (in Groote, 1994). Ultimately, the religion of art for art, with its own rites, substituted for Christian practices. Is it any wonder, then, that the traditionalist Pope John Paul II concluded that "art for art's sake which only refers to its author, without establishing a rapport with the divine world, has no place in the Christian conception of the icon" (*Duodecimum Saeculum,* 1987)?

The thesis calls for a few nuances. Allowing for exceptions, the adoption of an aesthetic posture and the new type of relationship to the work of art that it implies was found at first in a limited number of intellectual and social elites and did not touch the immense majority of believers, who continued to maintain more traditional relationships with their images, relationships in which artistic judgment played only a very secondary role. It is in this sense that one can understand the refusal in March 1794 of the Museum of Arts opened by the revolutionary French government to accept a Saint Jerome from Gaspand De Crayer into its collections, for fear that such paintings "would serve only to feed the fanaticism further."

Moreover, certain images produced for precise liturgical, pastoral, or spiritual ends (paintings of missions, popular engravings, ex-votos) lent themselves very badly to the new discourse of aesthetic celebration because they did not comply with the criteria of excellence decreed by the academies. Moreover, the officiants of the new cult of the beautiful did not have strict enough terms to censure the processes and works that seemed to them to be incompatible with the rules in use in the modern artistic field and especially everything that recalled the ancient bonds between the artist, the religious person, and the patron: Charles Perrault at the end of the seventeenth century *(Parallèle des Anciens et des Modernes)* and Stendhal at the beginning of the nineteenth century *(Voyages en Italie)* thus took an ironic stance toward the habits and moral prejudices that called for donors to be present in the paintings that they had done. The discredit that struck the religious images that could not be reduced to aesthetic discourse beginning with the seventeenth century bore proof *a contrario* of their survival and of the permanence of the religious sentiments that they continued to inspire in certain categories of the population at least, as one observes in the scornful judgment passed on the ex-voto in the *Encyclopédie* of Denis Diderot and Jean Le Rond d'Alembert. Finally, the too clear-cut distinction made between the epoch of images-objects of veneration and that of the art object of admiration and pleasure undoubtedly underestimates the medieval aesthetic and the long heritage of Neoplatonic philosophy, from Pseudo-Dionysius to Michelangelo, which favored the development of the arts within Christianity.

From the sixteenth century onward—earlier here, later there—art in the service of religion loses the preponderant place it had held since late antiquity or the High Middle Ages. The rather strict control over images introduced by the Tridentine decree (1563) certainly did not condemn medieval art to a rapid disappearance, as has been at times suggested, but it ultimately drove the church to adopt a position of extreme prudence—indeed, of suspicion—regarding stylistic or iconographic innovations. The attempts that were more or less aimed at the revival of sacred art (pre-Raphaelites, German Nazarenes, the Sacred Art of Father Couturier) did not succeed in reversing this process; it was thereafter outside of the institutional orders of the church, its liturgy, and its dogmas that the most brilliant artistic careers were made and that the modern artistic field was formed.

The appearance of matters of artistic blasphemy (in literature Théophile de Viau and Molière, in painting Gustave Courbet for *The Burial at Ornans,* George Grosz for his *Crucifixion with Gas Mask* at the origin of a series of trials between 1928 and 1931) attests as well to this reciprocal distancing between the religious and artistic fields.

The Religion of Art. The autonomy claimed for the field of art, the affirmation of the aesthetic position with the eighteenth and nineteenth centuries, and Kantian criticism led to new theoretical formalizations and new experiences of the relations between and art and religion that go well beyond the simple substitution of one for the other. One might seek to annul the respective distance between the areas of religion and art, as Father Couturier and the initiators of Sacred Art attempted, by trying to make religious art the site of an avant-garde at once spiritual and aesthetic. Or one might work to invest art with a new sacrality that owes nothing to the institution of the church, or the liturgy, or even the religious subject, strictly speaking, of the artwork. Finally, one might try to escape the strict limits of Christianity to reconcile an intense religious sentiment, enthusiasm for Greco-Roman antiquity, and admiration for Islam.

It is thus that from Gotthold Ephraim Lessing to August Wilhelm von Schlegel and Friedrich Schlegel, and via Johann Wolfgang von Goethe, there is affirmed a will to go beyond Christianity and to find an art acceptable to the three great religions. Despite their divergences and their hesitations, these efforts favor the creation of religious works of which the subject matter is not Christian, and they anticipate the formation, in the nineteenth century, of a secular religion of art, which would have Albrecht Dürer and Raphael for its patron saints. Goethe goes so far as to venture that whoever has science and art, has religion as well; whoever has neither of those two has no religion either.

Inspired originally by Novalis, but taken up and developed by Georg Wilhelm Friedrich Hegel and the Jena Romantics, the concept of art-religion *(Kunstreligion)* defines art as a divine service that is not conceived of as a service rendered to God, for the absolute resides in the person who is capable of the sublime: art itself—at least Greek art—is in itself a religion. The beautiful is an intuition of absolute Spirit; art is invested with an ontological function of revealing transcendental truths in a way inaccessible to profane cognitive activity. From the circles of German Romanticism, these theories, which make art into the privileged place of knowledge, are disseminated in all of Europe, including artistic milieus.

Finally, how is one not to see in the reflection of von Ramdohr about Caspar David Friedrich's *Cross in the Mountains (Tetschen Altar)*—from now on landscape painting wants to climb onto the altars—a penetrating definition of the ambitions of nineteenth-century art?

BIBLIOGRAPHY

Baaren, Theodorus Petrus van. *Bezielend Beelden: Inleiding tot de beeldende Kunst der primitieve Volken.* Amsterdam, 1962.

Baxandall, Michael. *Painting and Experience in Fifteenth Century Italy: A Primer in the Social History of Pictorial Style.* Oxford, 1972.

Baxandall, Michael. *The Limewood Sculptors of Renaissance Germany.* New Haven, 1980.

Belting, Hans. *Bild und Kult: Eine Geschichte des Bildes vor dem Zeitalter der Kunst.* Munich, 1990. Translated by Edmund Jephcott as *Likeness and Presence: A History of the Image before the Era of Art* (Chicago, 1994).

Boespflug, François, and Nicolas Lossky, eds. *Nicée II, 787–1987: douze siècles d'images religieuses.* Paris, 1987.

Bredekamp, Horst. *Kunst als Medium sozialer Konflikte. Bilderkämpfe von der Spätantike bis zur Hussitenrevolution.* Frankfurt am Main, 1975.

Christin, Olivier. *Une révolution symbolique: l'iconoclasme huguenot et la reconstruction catholique.* Paris, 1991.

Cormack, Robin S. *Writing in Gold: Byzantine Society and Its Icons.* London, 1985.

Foucart, Bruno. *Le renouveau de la peinture religieuse en France, 1800–1860.* Paris, 1987.

Freedberg, David. *The Power of Images: Studies in the History and Theory of Response.* Chicago, 1989.

Groote, Andreas, ed. *Macrocosmos in Microcosmo: Die Welt in der Stube: Zur Geschichte des Sammelns, 1450 bis 1800.* Opladen, 1994.

Hofmann, Werner, ed. *Luther und die Folgen für die Kunst.* Munich, 1983.

Michalski, Sergiusz. *The Reformation and the Visual Arts: The Protestant Image Question in Western and Eastern Europe.* London and New York, 1993.

Os, Henk van. *The Art of Devotion in the Late Middle Ages in Europe, 1300–1500.* With Eugene Honee, Hans Niewdorp, Bernhard Ridderbos. Translated by Michael Hoyle. London, 1994.

Scavizzi, Giuseppe. *Arte e architettura sacra.* Rome, 1981.

Scavizzi, Giuseppe. *The Controversy on Images from Calvin to Baronius.* New York, 1992.

Warnke, Martin, ed. *Bildersturm: die Zerstörung des Kunstwerks.* Munich, 1973.

Wirth, Jean. *L'image médiévale: Naissance et développement, VIe–XVe siècles.* Paris, 1989.

OLIVIER CHRISTIN
Translated from French by Terri Gordon

RENAISSANCE ITALIAN AESTHETICS.

It is difficult to speak of Renaissance aesthetics in general terms, as if there were an established doctrine representative of all reflection on art in that period. The large number of works dedicated to artistic topics from the fourteenth to the late sixteenth century actually suggests that attempts to codify principles of artistic creation are as manifold as Renaissance art itself. There is, indeed, a variety of different, more or less elaborated views on art written in Latin or in the vernacular. They take the shape of scientific treatises making much use of perspective studies, or else align themselves in the tradition of erudite humanist dialogues and letters. Both genres, the "scientific" and the humanist, are sometimes united in one and the same text, revealing the writer's competence in both fields. Among the earliest authors of treatises exploring topics devoted to the nature of art are Italian poets of the late thirteenth century. They are soon followed by fourteenth-century humanists who elevated poetry to the rank of liberal art. A new phenomenon appears in fifteenth-century Italy with the artists breaking out of the realm of mere craftsmanship (which medieval culture had assigned to them) and addressing their own reflections on art to fellow artists as well as to the learned public. Finally, philosophers made rich contributions to the Renaissance discussion of art. Although they were initially relegated to the role of observers passively witnessing the discovery of perspective by mathematicians and artists, they soon gave thought to how the geometrization of space and bodies in the arts might affect the perceptional theories of their time and developed concepts supportive of theories of artistic creation. Moreover, they emphasized human inventiveness to the extent that "creativity" became a central theme in their philosophies.

The distinction between poets, humanists, artists, and philosophers is not a strict one, because Renaissance authors typically excelled in more than just one field. In addition, Renaissance dialogues that examine topics related to art offer a vivid picture of intensive discussions across disciplines that were differently demarcated in those days. The philosopher Marsilio Ficino, for instance, appears in Cristoforo Landino's *Disputationes Camaldulenses* (1475), and Landino is himself one of the representatives of humanism in Ficino's *Commentary on Plato's Symposium* (1469). A generation later, the poet Torquato Tasso wrote a dialogue, *Il Ficino, o vero dell'arte*, in which both Landino and Ficino converse on art. Although Ficino occupied a unique position in the intellectual life of the early Renaissance, other examples could be cited to show how freely similar views, opinions, and theories circulated in different fields—making it in some cases difficult to determine precisely the authorship of a single idea or a concept.

Poets and Humanists. The poets' reflections on art—whether incorporated in the classical form of a "poetic" or laid down in treatises, dialogues, or letters—are an indispensable source for an overall appreciation of the Renaissance discussion of art. The poets' theories of inspiration and, more specifically, their claim to truth (and not just

RENAISSANCE ITALIAN AESTHETICS. Jacopo de Barbari, *Portrait of Luca Pacioli* (1495), oil on wood, 99 × 120 cm; Museo Nazionale die Capodimonte, Naples. (Photograph courtesy of Alinari/Art Resource, New York.)

verisimilitude) paved the way for the humanist emancipation of poetry from grammar and rhetoric. Already Albertino Mussato (1261–1329) had conceived of the poet as a *poeta doctus* and an enunciator of "truth," whether dealing with fictional or historical events. As to the poet's relationship to history, Mussato announced proudly that he, for instance, was in ancient Troy "before" the city's founder himself appeared there—implying that his knowledge of past events was rooted in a historical memory accessible to divinely inspired poets like himself. Although Mussato found a severe critic in the Dominican Giovanni di Mantua, who defended the Thomist position according to which truth needs to be anchored ontologically, many later poets and humanists followed in his footsteps. His conviction that poetry represented a *theologia mundi* is echoed in Francesco

Petrarca's and Giovanni Boccaccio's writings with their assertion that the poet's fables have the same origin as the stories of Scripture and therefore harbor a divine message. In line with this view is Pico della Mirandola's (1463–1494) project of a "poetical theology" that aimed at unifying ancient and biblical traditions. Asked about the sense of the *poetica figmenta* that "veil" the true nucleus of their fables, poets and humanists answered that divine wisdom needed to be "protected" from profanation. More significantly, they also pointed out that figurative speech bears the mark of "inventiveness." Authors such as Leonardo Bruni (1377–1444) and Juan Luis Vives (1492–1540) attributed poetic figures to a creative natural disposition, called by Roman poets *ingenium*. This natural disposition uncovers similarities between objects and between words that cannot be detected by reason alone and it translates them, in the field of poetry, into figurative language. Landino (1424–1498) therefore suggested that poetry, being the art of vesting truth with the beauty of metaphoric garments, occupied an intermediary position between unreflected myth and rational philosophy. Other humanists such as Coluccio Salutati (1331–1406) argued, with Mussato, Dante Alighieri, and Petrarca, that poetry, insofar as it embraces all of the liberal arts, is itself philosophy. Salutati also justified poetic speech by emphasizing the salutary effect it has on the recipient, to whom it transmits not only the poet's encyclopedic knowledge but also his inspired state of mind. Salutati is alluding to the Platonic doctrine of *furors*, which was discussed by poets and humanists long before Ficino offered his elaborate version of it. The concept of poetry as an activity unto itself added to the "nobility" of poetical production and provided a basis for the notion of the poet as a creator and as an *alter deus*. Variations on the creator-poet theme can be found in almost all works that emphasize the inventive nature of poetry, most importantly in Pierre de Ronsard's *Abrégé de l'art poétique* (1565), Sir Philip Sidney's *A Defence of Poetry* (1595), and Lope de Vega's *Arte nueva de hacer comedias* (1607). A particularly striking passage is offered in "A Defence of Poetry": "Onely the poet disdeining to be tied to any such subjection, lifted up with the vigor of his own invention, doth grow in effect into *another nature*: a making things either better then nature bringeth foorth, or quite a new, . . . so as he goeth hand in hand with nature" (Sidney, 1973, p. 78).

The other powerful doctrine of the time was Aristotle's theory of imitation and whose *Poetics* became available in the original in the fifteenth century. Although Latin translations followed, it is only after Francesco Robortello's *In librum Aristotelis de Arte Poetica Explicationes* (1548) that many other commentaries began to appear (not all of which promoted an Aristotelian stand). Robortello himself worked within the limits of the ancient author's philosophy, for instance, by conceiving poetry as the product of a natural process of intellection. In a similar vein, Julius Caesar Scaliger, in his *Poetice* (1561), connected poetical theory with Aristotle's psychology when he reflected on the effect of pleasure on the soul.

The Artists. A fruitful connection between humanist studies and art theory is found in the works of Leon Battista Alberti (1404–1472), the only Renaissance artist whose systematic studies included perspective as well as painting, sculpture, architecture, and theory of inspiration. In the dedication of *Della pittura*, Alberti stated to his fellow artist Filippo Brunelleschi that mathematics revealed the emerging of art "from roots within Nature itself" (Alberti, 1972, p. 32), implying that the measures used by painters have their origin in nature's creations. Central to this understanding is the concept of "proportion," which is derived from the observation of physical objects and their relations

to other objects and is then transmitted to works of art through the use of perspective. Related to the notion of proportion are comparisons as a means of accuracy: "There is in comparison a power which enables us to recognize the presence of more or less or just the same" (ibid., p. 53). This power *(vis)* is also needed for conceiving the outlines of a painting, especially if the painting is a *storia* involving many figures whose spatial relations have to be carefully designed. Most remarkably, the theory of composition that Alberti developed in that context also serves as a basis for artistic creativity, which earlier artists such as Cennino Cennini did not think of stimulating. The humanistically well trained Alberti sought help to that effect from two established disciplines, rhetoric and poetry. Although he recommended the reading of poetical works as an essential source for developing the *storia* (a step that in rhetoric corresponds to *inventio*), he used rhetorical schemes as a way to systematize the sequence and variation of figures (equivalent to *ordo*). The strength of his theory of composition lies in his idea of figures that are not to be understood abstractly but always in connection with the *storia* they represent (Kuhn, 1984, p. 163). Composition thus exerts a "double" visual impact on the artist's creative disposition, through the cohesion of narrative and figurative elements and through the mutual correspondence between these elements.

Unlike Alberti, Leonardo da Vinci (1452–1519) rigorously opposed the idea of "ennobling" art by linking it with humanist studies. Although Leonardo owed many insights to his predecessor, he legitimated the high status of painting not by borrowing from liberal arts but by understanding it as a science. As a consequence, he demolished the humanist opposition between "imitators" and "creators" by stating that all who deal solely with "words" condemn themselves to futile mimetic production. For him, a "discoverer" bases himself on "experience" mediating between "artful nature" and humankind (Vinci, 1970, C.A. 85a). The other prerequisite is mathematics, a tool that confers "certitude" on the scientific investigation of nature (W. An. III 241a; G 95b). There has been much debate concerning Leonardo's understanding of mathematics. It appears that for him the real power of mathematics does not lie in its ability to trace back reality to abstract laws, but, on the contrary, in its being instrumental in rendering nature's laws visible. This explains, for instance, the high status of mechanics as "the paradise" in which the fruits of mathematics can be found (E, 8b), or why water currents are being called "visible science" (ibid, 54b). Painting as the discipline par excellence that captures the visible world by the use of mathematics (perspective and geometry) is therefore a science and at the same time an art in that it is creative. Theory of science parallels theory of art, and both disciplines are considered "second creations." Nevertheless, it is only of the painter that Leonardo says that he is the perfecter of nature. The scientist's (i.e., the engineer's) inventions can never compare to nature's creations, "because in her inventions nothing is lacking and nothing is superfluous, and she does not use counterweights, but places there the soul, the composer of the body" (*Leonardo da Vinci: Engineer and Architect*, 1987, p. 109). Not so the painter's work, which, born of nature, as the source of all visible things, can even surpass her finite basic creations by producing infinite new compounds of natural forms. As a consequence, the art of painting is a "grandchild" of nature and also related with God (Ash. I, 15b; 16a).

Most of Michelangelo Buonarroti's (1475–1564) aesthetic views are dispersed throughout his *Rime*—beauty in visual arts being, as it were, expressible through the veil of poetry only. A distinctive feature of his artistic understanding is the rejection of the mathematical expression of reality, particularly in respect to the human body, although he did admit that proportions "please" the eye (and also applied them to the buildings he designed). In contrast to his contemporary Albrecht Dürer (1471–1528), who was aware that beauty ultimately escapes mathematical formulation but still recommended the use of proportions, Michelangelo did not view beauty as a calculable harmonious concord of lines and colors. The actual measure is not performed by the compass in the artist's hand, but by his *intelletto*, a term that for Michelangelo translated Plotinus's *voûs noûs* (reason, intuition) and also had features typically associated with the *ingegno*. Warren Cheney aptly coined the notion of "creative proportion" to characterize Michelangelo's art (Clements, 1961, p. 33). The possession of *intelletto*, however, does not dispense with the process—and torment—of artistic creation. The beauty discerned by the "external eye," explained Michelangelo, penetrates the artist's soul and "grows" therein to a new "shape." Through the artist's technical skills, that new shape (the terms used are *concetto*, *immagine*, and *idea*) will eventually outlive nature's creations. In this respect, "Cause to effect bows and gives way, whence nature is bested by art" (ibid., p. 12). This also justifies why, even though all forms preexist in nature (another Plotinian notion), the sculpted stone is worthier than the untouched rock. Nevertheless, art is ultimately not superior to nature, because it is nature herself that gives art the power to overcome her. This is in harmony with Michelangelo's ideal of an effortlessness, or spontaneous creation, that is modeled after nature's own mode of creation—requiring no preparatory studies, no instruments, and no measurements.

The Philosophers. The advancement of fine arts accompanied by the enhancement of technical skills suggested to many Renaissance philosophers the return of the golden age. They did not, however, develop an actual aesthetics—something that emerged as an independent philosophical discipline only in the eighteenth century. They nevertheless worked with concepts that clearly reveal the impact of artistic themes and procedures. The most visible

expressions of that impact are the many terms they used associated with notions of order, symmetry, and harmony: *ordo, numerus, modus, mensura (immensurabilitas), commensuratio, commensurabilitas, convenientia partium, consonantia, concordia, dispositio, harmonia, proportio, proportionabilitas, forma, species, figura, figuratio, adaequatio, congruitas, pulchritudo, formositas, venustas, elegantia, gratia.* Although not all of these terms refer necessarily to a reflection on art, the concentration of some of them does indicate an interest in aesthetic categories. More significant, of course, are concepts clearly reminiscent of artistic topics or philosophical problems that are encoded in aesthetic terms. Nicholas of Cusa, or Cusanus (1401–1464), for instance, not only employed almost all of the terms above, but also elaborated the philosophical foundation of "proportion," the use of which he strongly recommended for the fine arts. Moreover, the notion of proportion was of major importance because "every inquiry is comparative and uses the means of comparative relation [*proportio*]" (*On Learned Ignorance*, 1981, 1, 1, p. 50). This is a lesson one can learn also from Alberti, with whom Nicholas of Cusa shared some of his mathematical studies. He focused his attention, however, on the presuppositions of a comparative relation. Such a relation does not equalize the terms it relates, but only opens up a perspective under which similarity can be established. On the one hand, because similitude requires a notion of dissimilitude, proportion must be understood as a derivative of sameness and otherness. On the other hand, its substantiation requires that the opposite terms, from which it stems metaphysically, be unified. This is effected by the famous doctrine of the *coincidentia oppositorum*, which, translated into modern terms, represents the condition of the possibility of any opposition. There is only one opposition for which no adequate proportion can be found, and that is the distance between the finite and the infinite. Nicholas of Cusa offered a brilliant solution to this problem in *The Vision of God*, a work that employs a recently discovered technique in portraiture that makes the face appear to be watching observers independently of the position they take. To him, this exemplified the absolute seeing of God as an unmovable "omnivoyant" who "encompasses at one and the same time each and every mode of seeing" (*The Vision of God*, 1985, vol. 2, p. 121), and is thereby present to every individual visual act. Whereas human seeing is "contracted," that is, perspectively determined and thus finite, divine vision is integral and infinite. Although "uncontractible" in itself, absolute vision functions as the "contraction of contractions," meaning the totality of all perspective sights. Whether this subtle speculation on vision has had an impact on the actual practice of painting is difficult to establish, although Leonardo, for instance, was apparently acquainted with Nicholas of Cusa's works, which were discussed in learned Milanese circles (Cassirer, 1963, pp. 48ff.). He could certainly have drawn on the philosopher's view that man is a *secundus deus* be-

RENAISSANCE ITALIAN AESTHETICS. Sandro Botticelli, *Calumny of Apelles* (1495), tempera on wood, 62 × 91 cm; Uffizi, Florence. (Photograph courtesy of Alinari/Art Resource, New York.)

cause he is himself a creator whose mind produces mathematical and rational notions that measure God's creation.

Renaissance scholars are sometimes disappointed to find that Marsilio Ficino (1433–1499), the Florentine friend of Alberti and the brothers Antonio and Piero Pollaiuolo and inspirer of Sandro Botticelli (Cheney, 1985), did not himself attempt to codify principles of aesthetics. But in fact, as André Chastel's (1975) study on the Florentine philosopher shows, Ficino took a deep interest in optics and perspective, reflected on the applicability of the Vitruvian canon, and even developed a scale of colors—not to mention his studies on musical theory. It is true that Ficino did not analyze single works of art. The primary object of his aesthetic investigation was beauty in natural bodies, and in that his approach was no different from an artist's point of view. Ficino distinguished between shape *(figura)* and beauty *(pulchritudo)* of bodies, in terms that echo Vitruvius's definition of *symmetry* and *eurythmy* and also some aspects of Alberti's aesthetic categories *pulchritudo* and *concinnitas* (Alberti, 1988, 9, 5, pp. 302ff.). Whereas shape can be described in terms of agreeable arrangements of parts and

colors, beauty is "act, vitality, and a certain grace shining in itself through the influence of its own Idea" (Ficino, 1985, 5, 6, p. 93). Because beauty is related to vitality, the soul, which gives life to the body, is defined as the artist *(artifex corporis)* fashioning the body from inside. To that effect, the soul predisposes the body for its final shaping by introducing three intelligible components: disposition *(ordo)*, measure *(modus)*, and aspect *(speties)*. Disposition has to do with the distance between the body parts; measure is responsible for the shaping of the parts by using the scale of geometric progression (surface–line–point); aspect provides the accord of light, shadows, and lines (ibid., p. 93f.). Ficino's description of the soul's operations on the body as an artistic process is one that can easily be applied to his understanding of the artist's work. More significantly, it exemplifies a Renaissance mentality that was not content with adorning living space, but also strived to "aestheticize" the world of thought (to the extent that psychology was also conceived in aesthetic terms). The human soul in Ficino's metaphysics eventually "re-forms," that is, reshapes, the face of the universe in the soul's effort to understand it (Albertini, 1997, pp. 130–147)—intellectualizing thus becoming an equivalent of beautifying.

Many more Renaissance authors have aestheticized their philosophies or used features of artistic creation as paradigms for epistemological and metaphysical notions. Charles de Bovelles (1479–1567), Francesco Patrizi (1529–1597), Giordano Bruno (1548–1600), and Tommaso Campanella (1568–1639), for instance, made abundant use of these conceptual transformations. Patrizi, whose work bridges fourteenth-century humanism and early modern science, not only wrote on various humanistic disciplines and the philosophy of nature, but also managed to link the two divergent study fields through the use of geometry. He applied the methodical rigor of geometry to history and rhetoric and took its spatial quality as a basis for the studying of physical bodies. Reflecting on the presuppositions of corporeity, he discovered that space—being at the same time corporeal (three-dimensional) and incorporeal (without the bodily quality of resistance)—is prior to the world of bodies. In *Nova de Universis Philosophia* (1591), Patrizi defines space as what "communicates to them [bodies] all of its points, lines, surfaces, and depths, . . . so that they possess those things that it retains for itself" (Patrizi, 1943, p. 239). He insisted that geometric bodies are not abstracted from physical bodies but are to be thought of as being actualized in nature as their primary space. Interpreted in the context of sixteenth-century art theory, this concept of (absolute) space can be understood as a response to the mathematically constructed space in the artist's shop that still rested on the Aristotelian assumption that space is what is being occupied by a body. The aesthetic dimension of Patrizi's theory of space becomes evident if one considers that space is related to light—also an "incorporeal body"—and that light is the first to "fill" physical space (ibid., p. 244). This dimension has been acknowledged by artists, in particular by El Greco (1541–1614), who held Patrizi's metaphysics in high esteem.

Looking at how artistic categories have been employed in the works of Renaissance philosophers, one understands why no independent aesthetic discipline emerged from their reflections on art. More appealing than the examination of the ontological status of an artistic object, more significant than the analysis of pleasure derived from harmonies and proportions found in artworks, and certainly more urgent than questions related to taste, was the global quest for harmony. It was that quest that gave rise to new metaphysics and new cosmologies, in which the universe itself was considered as an object of "beautification." Not content with mere symmetry and regularity in the planetary order, Johannes Kepler (1571–1630), for instance, searched for the divine *disegno* in the way the cosmos is structured, a scheme that he considered to be governed by rules of artistic disposition. As is well known, Kepler embodied his aesthetically determined vision of the heavenly order in a model of nesting polyhedrons—which has been recently interpreted as an arrangement of "cosmopoetic" figures (Hallyn, 1993, p. 182). The demands of Renaissance art theory, with its ideal of harmonious disposition, which could be codified in many different ways, pervaded philosophical discourse and eventually reached the threshold of modern science.

The contribution of Renaissance philosophers to the refinement of aesthetic categories lies in their elaboration of notions that were basic to the artistic discussions of their time. Their interest in aesthetic principles was, in a sense, an extension of their desire to make their own intellectual work conform to the highest standards of art and beauty.

[*See also* Alberti; Architecture, *article on* Italian Renaissance Aesthetics; Artist; Origins of Aesthetics; Perspective; Rhetoric; *and* Vasari.]

BIBLIOGRAPHY

Primary Sources

Alberti, Leon Battista. *On Painting and On Sculpture.* Edited and translated by Cecil Grayson. London, 1972.

Alberti, Leon Battista. *On the Art of Building in Ten Books.* Translated by Joseph Rykwert, Neil Leach, and Robert Tavernor. Cambridge, Mass., 1988.

Buonarroti, Michelangelo. *Complete Poems and Selected Letters.* Translated by Creighton Gilbert, edited by Robert N. Linscott. Reprint, Princeton, N.J., 1980.

Ficino, Marsilio. *Commentary on Plato's Symposium on Love.* 2d rev. ed. Translated by Sears Jayne. Dallas, 1985.

Hopkins, Jasper. *Nicholas of Cusa on Learned Ignorance: A Translation and an Appraisal of De docta ignorantia.* Minneapolis, 1981.

Hopkins, Jasper. *Nicholas of Cusa's Dialectical Mysticism: Text, Translation, and Interpretative Study of De Visione Dei.* Minneapolis, 1985.

Patrizi, Francesco. "On Physical Space." Translated by Benjamin Brickman. *Journal of the History of Ideas* 4 (1943): 224–245.

Sidney, Philip. "A Defence of Poetry." In *Miscellaneous Prose of Sir Philip Sidney,* edited by Katherine Duncan-Jones and Jan van Dorsten. Oxford, 1973.

Vinci, Leonardo da. *The Notebooks of Leonardo da Vinci.* Compiled and edited by Jean Paul Richter. 2 vols. New York, 1970.

Other Sources

Albertini, Tamara. *Marsilio Ficino. Die Vermittlung von Denken und Welt in einer Metaphysik der Einfachheit.* Munich, 1997.

Barasch, Mosche. *Light and Color in the Italian Renaissance Theory of Art.* New York, 1978.

Baxandall, Michael. *Painting and Experience in Fifteenth Century Italy: A Primer in the Social History of Pictorial Style.* 2d ed. Oxford and New York, 1988.

Burke, Peter. *Culture and Society in Renaissance Italy, 1420–1540.* New York, 1972.

Cassirer, Ernst. *The Individual and the Cosmos in Renaissance Philosophy.* Translated by Mario Domandi. New York, 1963. Originally published as *Individuum und Kosmos in der Philosophie der Renaissance* (Leipzig, 1927).

Chastel, André. *Marsile Ficin et l'art.* 2d ed. Geneva, 1975.

Cheney, Liana. *Quattrocento Neoplatonism and Medici Humanism in Botticelli's Mythological Paintings.* Lanham, Md., 1985.

Clements, Robert John. *Michelangelo's Theory of Art.* New York, 1961.

Elkins, James. *The Poetics of Perspective.* Ithaca, N.Y., 1994.

Greenfield, Concetta Carestia. *Humanist and Scholastic Poetics, 1250–1500.* Lewisburg, Pa., 1981.

Hallyn, Fernand. *The Poetic Structure of the World: Copernicus and Kepler.* Translated by Donald M. Leslie. New York, 1993. Originally published as *La structure poétique du monde: Copernic, Kepler* (Paris, 1987).

Kristeller, Paul Oskar. *Renaissance Thought and the Arts: Collected Essays.* Exp. ed. Princeton, N.J., 1990.

Kuhn, Rudolf. "Alberti's Lehre über die *Komposition* als die Kunst in der Malerei." *Archiv für Begriffsgeschichte* 28 (1984): 123–178.

Leonardo da Vinci: Engineer and Architect. Montreal, 1987.

Panovsky, Erwin. *Studies in Iconology: Humanistic Themes in the Art of the Renaissance.* Reprint, New York, 1962.

Tigerstedt, F. N. "The Poet as Creator. Origins of a Metaphor." *Comparative Literature Studies* 5 (1968).

Weinberg, Bernard. *A History of Literary Criticism in the Italian Renaissance.* 2 vols. Chicago, 1961.

Wind, Edgar. *Pagan Mysteries in the Renaissance.* New Haven, 1958.

TAMARA ALBERTINI

REPRESENTATION. [*To clarify the role of the concept of representation in aesthetics, this entry comprises three essays:*

Conceptual and Historical Overview
Depiction
Resemblance

The first essay is an overview of the general topic of representation as it has been treated in the history of aesthetics. The second essay analyzes two of the main theoretical accounts of pictoral depiction: perceptual theories and symbol theories. The third essay, on resemblance, discusses a topic that has been important in the history of aesthetics but that has been marginalized by various critiques of it since the 1960s. For related discussion, see Fiction; Goodman; Gombrich; Imagery; Mimesis; Perception; Photography, *article on* Catachresis; Portraiture; *and* Realism.]

Conceptual and Historical Overview

Plato gave birth to aesthetics when Socrates claims in book 10 (598b) of *The Republic* that a painting is a representation that aims to reproduce only the appearance or image of an object. In this brief passage, Plato both suggests a criterion for a painting's representing a certain object and begins to raise deep skeptical questions about the value of such representation. The criterion, properly spelled out, stands up remarkably well despite much criticism and many proposals of alternatives in the contemporary literature of aesthetics, and the skeptical questions have proved remarkably difficult to answer.

The criterion for a painting's representing an object, which Plato describes as aiming to reproduce its appearance, might be spelled out as follows: a painting represents a certain object if and only if its artist intends by marking the canvas with paint to create visual experience in viewers that resembles the visual experience they would have of the object. One might add that the intention must be successful

in the sense that the following conditional is true: if the painting is seen in normal conditions, then it will produce visual experience similar to that of the object, such that the intention is recoverable from this experience.

The idea that resemblance could be sufficient for representation has been attacked by Nelson Goodman (1976). Borrowing freely, his counterexamples to this claim are as follows: twins resemble but do not represent each other; reprints of a painting resemble the painting more than it resembles what it represents, yet both the painting and its reprints represent the objects seen in them and not each other; a fabric sample both resembles the fabric and (in a sense broader than that intended to be captured by our criterion) represents it, but it is not a pictorial representation (depiction) of it. Our criterion as spelled out refers to resemblance between visual experiences of a painting and an object and not to resemblance between the objects themselves, but the Goodman's counterexamples are not affected by this difference, because the objects in question will generate similar visual experiences.

The other clauses of the criterion do eliminate such counterexamples, however. These clauses include reference to the intention of the artist and to her marking a canvas with paint as the manner of fulfilling that intention. Twins, fabric samples, and reprints are not created in that way with those intentions behind them. Goodman's counterexamples do show that resemblance is not sufficient for representation, but Plato's criterion does not claim that it is.

Goodman held that resemblance is not necessary and is not an important factor in pictorial representation either. According to him, depiction depends on a conventional symbolic system similar to language in its referential functions but different in the formal structure of its symbolic system. Aesthetic symbols are, for example, syntactically and semantically dense, that is, small differences in them make for different symbols and they pick out small differences in their objects. They typically refer by exemplification, that is, by referring to some of their own properties. These are interesting features of aesthetic representation, but Goodman's main thesis that such representation depends on conventional symbols has been successfully attacked, most notably by Flint Schier (1986).

Schier points out that, in order to recognize represented objects in a painting, one does not require semantic rules to relate its parts to their referents or syntactic rules to relate these parts to each other. Recognition of represented objects normally depends only on one's ability to recognize the real objects represented. One simply assimilates the perceptual experiences of painting and object. Schier proposes a criterion of pictorial representation based on this point. Roughly, something is a picture of an object if one can naturally interpret it visually as such, if this interpretation depends only on one's being able to recognize the object.

This proposal again appears to be an alternative to that which appeals to the intentional creation of resemblances between experienced visual properties. But it also seems upon reflection that the recognitional capacity triggered by a picture of an object can itself be explained by the similarities between visual experiences of picture and object. Thus, Plato's criterion is not only compatible with Schier's, but it seems to be the more deeply explanatory of the two. Furthermore, Schier's criterion fails just when the relevant intention of the artist is not recoverable on the basis of resemblances between experiences alone. If an artist paints a biblical figure that he has never seen, then one's ability to recognize the real person in the closest possible world in which one saw him might not suffice to interpret the painting correctly. The artist here relies on his image of what the figure looked like (or would look like), and viewers might need to rely on knowledge of certain conventional ways of representing the figure in paintings. This example shows that Plato's criterion needs some filling out to cover such cases, but it also shows once more that Schier's criterion depends for its application on the applicability of Plato's. One's interpretation of a picture as being a representation of an object O will be based on ability to recognize O only if there is a resemblance between visual experience of the picture and visual experience of the object.

Another alternative has been advocated by Kendall Walton (1990). He holds that a painting is a representation of an object if it prescribes that one imagine that the experience of looking at it is visual experience of that object. If one is indeed to react to paintings in this way, one remains suspicious that the aptness of this prescription would depend on an antecedent similarity between the visual experience of the painting and that of the object. Without this similarity, the prescription (if it could be communicated in some other way) would be useless and, in any case, would not render the painting a representation of the object. Thus, once more, Plato's criterion seems to be more fundamental.

To complete properly the account implicit in Plato's criterion would require spelling out the ways in which visual experience of a painting must resemble that of its object if the intention of its artist is to be successful. Similarity of shape in the visual field is usually crucial, but not always so. A child's depiction of a leaf may depend more for its success on its bright green color, for example. If this criterion is correct, however, then, because resemblance comes in degrees, being a successful representation falls in a scale somewhere between failure and perfect true-to-lifeness. In addition, a painting will be more true to life the more visual experience of it resembles that of its object.

The question of value raised by Plato—how a representation, an imitation of an appearance of an object, could have value approaching that of the object itself (let alone its Platonic form)—has been addressed far less often in contemporary philosophy. One might imagine three standard sorts of answers, all problematic, to the question of the value of representation in painting. The first would appeal to knowledge of an object gained through perceiving its painted representation, at best knowledge normally not gained by perceiving the object itself. The second appeals to the way that viewing paintings is supposed to alter one's visual experience of objects in the real world. The third emphasizes the exercise of imagination that pictorial representation prompts.

The claim about representation as a source of knowledge of its objects might be most plausible in the cases of portraiture and historical and religious paintings. A good portrait might be claimed to reveal deep or hidden facets of its subject's personality or to reveal her true personal identity. But in fact, most portraits, even very good ones, reveal rather wooden poses, designed to project a certain dignity and social status instead of true inner states. Other genres, such as still life, afford no (propositional) knowledge of their objects worth having at all. Historical and religious paintings might bring to life episodes of which there is prior knowledge, but they cannot teach anything about those events not available in far more detail in written texts.

The latter two examples suggest the second and third answers to the question of value. Still lifes might be said to retrain one's vision, to invite one to appreciate aesthetic qualities of everyday objects that are normally overlooked in everyday practical concerns. This sort of answer—the effect of representational art on ways of perceiving outside the context of art—is again associated with Goodman. Many still lifes provide evidence for it in the way that they distribute sharp focus evenly across the canvas, seemingly directing attention at otherwise unnoticed qualities that they exemplify or refer to. But this thesis assumes a plasticity in viewers' visual systems that they may not have. That visual perception remains normally in the service of practical behavior may be evolutionarily hardwired and therefore not subject to such facile readjustment. It is more plausible that viewing art changes the ways one looks at other art, where practical concerns are suspended, than that they have major effects on one's perceptions in more pressing everyday contexts.

In bringing to life episodes from religious or mythological texts or from history, narrative paintings may have the sort of value suggested by Walton's theory of representation, the value of exercising imagination in fictional games. According to him, representations function as props in games of make-believe. By prescribing certain complex imaginings in common, they prompt viewers to enter imaginatively the worlds of fictional texts and paintings. They therefore allow others to share in the imaginative genius of artists, to enter artists' imaginary worlds, thereby expanding their own emotional capacities, envisaging new possibilities of experience, and sharing these vicarious experiences with others. But does one typically imagine oneself to be in the fictional world of a painting? The thesis seems more at home in the context of literature, but even there it is more likely that one imagines the narrated events occurring than that one imagines oneself witness to them, or even to their narration. Some paintings may encourage the viewer to enter their fictional worlds, as when a subject in a portrait averts her gaze, but others—for example, those that strongly emphasize formal balance or unity—discourage it. The thesis therefore at best provides a very partial answer to Plato's question (Walton never intends otherwise).

An approach at least as promising as any of the three canvased above would focus on the way that representation contributes to or enhances other acknowledged sources of value in painting. It is obvious that representation functions as a means of expression. Despite the somewhat misnomered movement of Abstract Expressionism, there can be little doubt that human events, demeanors, and (not surprisingly) expressions, as well as natural scenes as depicted in paintings, are more expressive than abstract forms and colors. Perhaps less appreciated is the fact that representation enhances the pure sensuous beauty of many paintings and affords the possibility of levels of formal structure beyond those achievable in purely abstract forms. The flesh tones of a Titian or a Renoir are far more sensuously beautiful for being just that—representations of flesh tones.

In regard to form, representations naturally group formal elements into larger units, which can unify otherwise diverse or incomprehensible spaces and can relate into higher-level formal structures. In addition, they create new formal elements: increased depth, movement, weight, and human mental aspects that can create tensions, harmonies, contrasts, unities, and so on. All this can greatly enrich the formal possibilities available to artists beyond those derivable from line and color alone. In a representational painting, such material forms can reinforce expressive aspects or tensions and harmonies on the psychological level, for example, or they can generate new contrasts and tensions.

Thinking thus of the interactions between representation and other sources of aesthetic value makes it easier to answer Plato's question. Returning to the genre of still life, if one thinks of how perceptual and cognitive capacities are challenged and satisfied in grasping the ways that formal elements in the paint create content, which in turn creates and enhances formal structure in a painting, it seems easy to see why such rich perceptual experience is of more value than the visual experience of ordinary real fruit. That the former must resemble the latter in order for representation to succeed at all does not imply, as Plato seemed to think, that it must remain subordinate in value. That we appreciate this more easily when we relate representation to expression and form does not imply that there is not some truth in each of the approaches indicated to answering Plato's challenge.

[*See also* Plato.]

BIBLIOGRAPHY

Gombrich, E. H. *Art and Illusion: A Study in the Psychology of Pictorial Representation* (1960). 2d rev. ed. New York, 1961; reprint, Princeton, N.J., 1969.
Goodman, Nelson. *Languages of Art: An Approach to a Theory of Symbols.* 2d ed. Indianapolis, 1976.
Neander, Karen. "Pictorial Representation: A Matter of Resemblance." *British Journal of Aesthetics* 27.3 (Summer 1987): 213–226.
Peacocke, Christopher. "Depiction." *Philosophical Review* 96.3 (July 1987): 383–410.
Plato. *The Republic.* Translated by Allan Bloom. New York, 1968.
Sartwell, Crispin. "Natural Generativity and Imitation." *British Journal of Aesthetics* 31.1 (January 1991): 58–67.
Schier, Flint. *Deeper into Pictures: An Essay on Pictorial Representation.* Cambridge and New York, 1986.
Walton, Kendall L. *Mimesis as Make-Believe: On the Foundations of the Representational Arts.* Cambridge, Mass., 1990.
Wollheim, Richard. *Painting as an Art.* Princeton, N.J., 1987.

ALAN GOLDMAN

Depiction

Our visual world is awash with pictures representing all kinds of objects and scenes. The ease with which we interpret these pictures, using what seem to be ordinary visual skills, might make it seem as though there can be little mystery to pictorial representation. But three facts about pictures seem to be in conflict and prove difficult to reconcile.

The first fact is that we understand what pictures represent almost without effort. Unlike languages, for example, little or no learning is needed to interpret pictures. This a fact about our *competence* with pictures. The second fact is that when we look at pictures, we seem to see the objects and scenes they represent or purport to represent. All pictures inform us about things by causing us to have visual experiences "as of" those things. This fact about the *phenomenology* of pictures also sets them apart from other representational media such as language. The third fact is that pictures represent their subjects in a remarkable variety of ways. Consider, for example, how a Cubist, a Haida printmaker, and a Byzantine icon painter would portray a face. As already acknowledged, each portrait will evoke an experience as of the face, yet none of these experiences will be much like looking at the face itself. (Picasso's portrait of Kahnweiler evokes an experience that is not at all like looking at the art dealer in the flesh.) This *diversity* gives pictures a history, an anthropology, and a sociology, for how the world is portrayed varies with time, place, and purpose. It suggests that pictures are like languages in their reliance on social conventions.

These three facts are puzzling when taken together. Our competence with pictures and our experiences of them lend support to the widely endorsed view that pictures are perceptual representations. But some philosophers, notably Nelson Goodman, have been so impressed by the fact of pictorial diversity that they have argued that pictures are not perceptual representations but function as symbols whose meaning is determined by social conventions.

Perceptual Theories. The central tenet of perceptual theories is that depiction is applied seeing: the processes employed in interpreting pictures depend on the very processes involved in seeing the real-world objects that are their subjects. Of course, this claim can be, and has been, elaborated in different ways. Different conceptions of vision are apt to inspire different views of the way it figures in depiction.

Mimesis or resemblance. According to one version of the perceptual theory, a picture represents either because it is objectively similar to its subject, sharing visual properties with it, or because it evokes visual experiences that are similar to visual experiences of its subject. Thus, we interpret *Wivenhoe Park,* the painting, by noticing that it looks like Wivenhoe Park, the place. But "looking like" can mean just about anything, so the challenge is to state in some detail what features pictures (or our experiences of them) share with their subjects (or our experiences of them).

Surprisingly, the resemblance theory wins little support from the phenomenology of pictures, provided certain elementary distinctions are drawn. In particular, one must not confuse the marks, shapes, colors, and textures on a picture's surfaces in virtue of which it represents its subject with the visual properties (including properties of shape, color, and texture) it represents its subject as having. Call the former a picture's "design," and the latter its representational "content." It is undeniable that the fact that we experience pictures as of their subjects means that their contents resemble properties of their subjects. But this lends no support to the resemblance theory because it is precisely this content-subject resemblance that we are seeking to explain. The resemblance theory must therefore explain how pictures acquire their contents in terms of similarities between their designs (or experiences of them) and properties of their subjects (or experiences of them).

The resemblance theory loses much of its appeal once it is acknowledged that it posits similarities between a picture's designed but flat surface and the scene it represents. After all, a picture's designed surface usually looks more like the designed surfaces of other pictures than like its typically three-dimensional, animate subject. Moreover, it is doubtful that the kinds of similarities in virtue of which pictures are alleged to represent things are uniform across the spectrum of pictorial styles. The design-subject similarities that obtain in *Wivenhoe Park* and its subject are not of the same kind as those that obtain between Marcel Duchamp's *Nude Descending a Staircase* and its subject. Finally, the resemblance theory must come to terms with pictures that represent things that do not exist. How can a picture of a unicorn resemble a unicorn when there are no unicorns?

Illusion and seeing-in. One might maintain that depiction depends in some way on vision, but without invoking the notion of resemblance. In his groundbreaking discussion of depiction, *Art and Illusion* (1960), E. H. Gombrich explains that pictures exploit "illusion devices," designs that take advantage of the possibility of visual ambiguities and failures in visual discrimination, so as to trigger false or "illusionistic" visual experiences as of objects that are really not there. *Wivenhoe Park* tricks viewers, as it were, into experiencing it as if it were Wivenhoe Park. Likewise, Richard Wollheim (1987), taking a hint from Leonardo da Vinci's notebook on painting, suggests that viewers *see* things *in* pictorial designs, just as they see horses in clouds or landscapes in certain water-stained walls. Both the illusion and seeing-in theories are ultimately concerned with the network of relations between the experience of a picture's designed surface, its content, and the actual objects or scenes that it represents.

As his use of the concept of illusion would suggest, Gombrich claims that an experience of a picture is the kind of experience one might actually have of its subject. An experience of *Wivenhoe Park* is illusionistic because it is the kind of experience one might have while looking at the place itself. This does not mean, as some object, that pictures are necessarily deceptive in the sense of engendering false beliefs ("oh, there is Wivenhoe Park!") but merely that they have the potential to deceive.

Yet, it seems unlikely that the illusion theory either accommodates the diversity of pictures or correctly characterizes all pictorial experiences. Surely, there is little if any chance that Cubist collages, or even line drawings, for instance, cause experiences that might be confused with experiences caused by their subjects themselves. Moreover, the illusion theory implies that when one looks at a picture, one experiences either its designed surface or the scene it represents, but not both at the same time. If an experience of a picture is an experience that its (three-dimensional) subject might cause, then it is not simultaneously an experience as of a flat, designed, inanimate surface. But surely one can simultaneously experience a picture as a flat, colored surface and as representing its subject.

The seeing-in theory takes seriously the possibility—indeed, the desirability—of simultaneous experience of a picture's designed surface and an experience as of its represented subject. Wollheim argues that the distinctive phenomenology of pictorial experience lies in its "twofoldness." Unlike experiences its subject itself might cause, an experience of a picture is always both an experience as of its subject and an experience of a flat, designed surface. This suggests that the seeing-in theory can embrace pictorial diversity. Indeed, line drawings and Cubist collages might deliberately draw attention to their surface features and the way those features support a particular content. If pictorial experience is distinct from ordinary visual experience, however, and if seeing-in is a distinctive kind of seeing, then we need an account of the relationship between seeing-in and just plain seeing. Wollheim speculates that seeing-in comes down to resemblance, but what rules out the possibility that seeing-in depends not on seeing visual resemblances, but on a mastery of symbols, as the symbol theorist claims?

Symbol Theories. Goodman is the most prominent champion of the symbol theory of depiction. Pictures, he argues, do not depict because we first see scenes and objects in them; on the contrary, what we see in pictures is determined by our beliefs, imaginings, or knowledge about what they represent. The notoriety of Goodman's repudiation of perceptual theories of depiction has, unfortunately, overshadowed his more abiding insight that an analysis of pictures can usefully be modeled on an analysis of linguistic expressions and other symbols with which they share certain logical properties. It is useful to separate Goodman's observations about the logic of pictures from his assault on perceptualism.

The logic of pictures. Goodman offers a semantic theory of depiction: pictorial representation involves denotation and predication in a symbol system. Just as a word or sentence in a language refers to an object or a state of affairs, a picture belongs to a pictorial symbol system in which it refers to objects and scenes; and just as some words or phrases in a language function as predicates, pictures in a pictorial symbol system represent what they denote as having properties. The *Mona Lisa* portrays a woman as smiling enigmatically because it belongs to a system in which it denotes a certain person and predicates of her the property "is enigmatic." With predication comes the possibility of misrepresentation and the phenomenon of representation-as. A drawing that represents Winston Churchill as a lion denotes Churchill and predicates a property of him that he does not literally have. The distinctions that Goodman draws among the various representational functions that a picture can perform enable us to rigorously analyze the complex structure of its content.

Denotation and predication always take place in the context of a system whose function is to lay down what any given design denotes or predicates. The systematicity of pictures accommodates their diversity. As already noted, pictures belong to diverse styles or systems, each sufficiently different from the others to frustrate the resemblance theory. These styles have an internal coherence because pictorial competence is system-relative; that is, an ability to interpret some pictures in a style or system entails an ability to interpret readily and correctly other pictures in the same system, but not necessarily an ability to interpret readily and correctly pictures in other styles or systems. Someone versed in the system popularized by Leon Battista Alberti can interpret any number of academic landscapes but may need to learn how to "read" Cubist pictures because they belong to an unfamiliar system.

What systems are familiar varies from one social setting to another. Pictorial systems, like languages, gain footholds in communities whose members have developed the requisite picture-reading skills. The hypothesis that the competence of makers and users of pictures is a social phenomenon is a powerful analytic tool, useful to anybody who studies pictures, for investigating why pictures are made in certain styles at certain times and places.

Although picture systems have the same semantic structure of denotation and predication as linguistic systems, the two media are obviously different. Goodman ascribes this to the formal properties of pictorial symbol systems. Pictures are "analogue," because any difference in a design property makes a difference in what symbol the picture is and what content it has; and pictures are "relatively replete," because more surface properties have representational significance in pictures than in other kinds of symbols.

Antiperceptualism. None of Goodman's observations about the logic of pictures entails antiperceptualism. Assuming a sufficiently fluid conception of vision, there is no reason why the mechanisms of pictorial denotation and predication and the organization of pictures into systems might not turn out to depend on facts about vision. Despite this, Goodman insists that pictorial representation is arbitrary. *Wivenhoe Park,* he proclaims, could represent a pink elephant—it could denote an elephant and attribute to it the property of being pink. The arguments for this are unconvincing. Goodman proceeds with remarkable insouciance from a refutation of the resemblance theory and the observation that pictures denote and predicate to a repudiation of perceptualism. To admit that pictures belong to diverse systems is not to say that any picture may depict any object as having any property.

Moreover, the antiperceptualist version of the symbol theory neglects the obvious candidate for distinguishing pictorial symbol systems from others, namely, their visual phenomenology. This is implicit in the principle that what a picture represents does not depend simply on the look of the individual picture, but on what pictorial symbol system the picture is part of.

The symbol theorist might attribute the distinctive phenomenology of pictures to the way they are embedded in social contexts. In a particular social setting, pictures in familiar symbol systems will typically be taken as setting the standard for what things look like. As Goodman puts it, pictures do not look like nature, they look the way nature is usually painted. The trouble with this, however, is that even a picture in a wholly unfamiliar system is experienced as looking like its subject in some way (though perhaps not in the preferred way). *Nude Descending a Staircase* belongs to an unfamiliar system, yet it looks like its subject (though not in the same way as would a portrayal employing a more familiar system). All pictures are experienced as of their subjects, not just pictures in familiar systems.

Hybrid Theories. One response to the impasse between symbol and perceptual theories is to cobble them together.

According to Gombrich, for example, there is a continuum of pictorial styles, with illusionistic pictures employing purely perceptual means of representation at one extreme and "conceptual" pictures that represent by convention at the other. Like too many attempts at compromise, however, Gombrich's pictorial dualism avoids the disadvantages of neither theory. By separating conceptual pictures (Cubism, the split style) from illusionistic ones (Constable and Company), it privileges the latter as most closely approaching an absolute ideal of visual experience that is insulated from social factors, while simultaneously relinquishing perceptual accounts of so-called conceptual pictures.

A better, nondualistic, hybrid recognizes the contribution that both symbol and perceptual theories can make to a unified theory for all pictures. The symbol theory stresses the advantages of sensitivity to the diversity and systematic organization of pictorial styles, and reminds us that what system of depiction is used depends on who uses it and where it is used. Enjoying these advantages does not commit one to antiperceptualism. The advantage of perceptual theories is that they promise to explain the obvious phenomenological affinities between seeing things in pictures and seeing them in the flesh.

Most perceptual theories are unstable because they rest on too narrow conceptions of vision. Pictorial diversity does not call perceptualism into question, provided one tolerates a fluid and flexible conception of visual processes. It is useful perhaps to think of pictorial diversity as stretching the boundaries of the visual in a number of directions.

Recent years have seen a growing appreciation among philosophers and psychologists of the dynamism of vision. For example, such processes as object recognition cannot be reduced to noticing resemblances, for we are able to recognize objects despite changes in the way they look. We can recognize objects from novel points of view, in distorting mirrors, or when changed over time. We can also recognize objects as they appear in pictures belonging to different styles or systems of representation. These new recognition abilities are learned, though in a special way: once we have learned to recognize some objects whose appearance changed in a particular way, we can recognize any object changed in the same way. Once we can recognize some things upside down, we can recognize anything upside down; once we have learned to recognize a Cubist mandolin, we can recognize a Cubist art dealer. This might explain why there are many styles of depiction, why new ones are acquired as a system following a moderate amount of learning, and why pictures can evoke experiences of objects that do not appear as they do in the flesh.

Hybrid theories have the happy side effect of illuminating the aesthetics of pictures. Not all pictures are works of art, of course, but if aesthetic engagement with pictorial art differs from engagement with other kinds of art, then a theory of depiction should provide a foundation for explanations

of this distinctive pictorial aesthetic. Both the view that pictures merely imitate reality and the view that pictures are merely conventional symbols assimilate experience of pictorial art to a generic aesthetic. One should acknowledge that pictures extend the kinds of visual experiences one can have in novel ways that are responsive to social practices, for herein lies the importance of picture-making not only as a form of communication but also as a medium for artistic expression unlike any other.

BIBLIOGRAPHY

Black, Max. "How Do Pictures Represent?" In *Art, Perception, and Reality,* by E. H. Gombrich, Julian Hochberg, and Max Black, edited by Maurice Mandelbaum. Baltimore, 1972.
Bryson, Norman. "Semiology and Visual Interpretation." In *Visual Theory,* edited by Norman Bryson, Michael Ann Holly, and Keith Moxey. New York, 1991.
Gombrich, E. H. *Art and Illusion: A Study in the Psychology of Pictorial Representation* (1960). 2d rev. ed. Reprint, Princeton, N.J., 1969.
Gombrich, E. H. *The Image and the Eye: Further Studies in the Psychology of Pictorial Representation.* Oxford, 1982.
Goodman, Nelson. *Languages of Art: An Approach to a Theory of Symbols.* 2d ed. Indianapolis, 1976.
Hagen, Margaret A., ed. *The Perception of Pictures.* 2 vols. New York and London, 1980.
Hagen, Margaret A. *Varieties of Realism: Geometries of Representational Art.* Cambridge and New York, 1986.
Lopes, Dominic. *Understanding Pictures.* Oxford, 1996.
Maynard, Patrick. "Depiction, Vision, and Convention." *American Philosophical Quarterly* 9.3 (July 1972): 243–250.
Neander, Karen. "Pictorial Representation: A Matter of Resemblance." *British Journal of Aesthetics* 27.3 (Summer 1987): 213–226.
Novitz, David. "Picturing." *Journal of Aesthetics and Art Criticism* 34.2 (Winter 1975): 144–155.
Peacocke, Christopher. "Depiction." *Philosophical Review* 96.3 (July 1987): 383–410.
Podro, Michael. "Depiction and the Golden Calf." In *Visual Theory,* edited by Norman Bryson, Michael Ann Holly, and Keith Moxey. New York, 1991.
Schier, Flint. *Deeper into Pictures: An Essay on Pictorial Representation.* Cambridge and New York, 1986.
Walton, Kendall L. *Mimesis as Make-Believe: On the Foundations of the Representational Arts.* Cambridge, Mass., 1990.
Wollheim, Richard. "Seeing-As, Seeing-In, and Pictorial Representation." In *Art and Its Objects.* 2d ed., with six supplementary essays. Cambridge and New York, 1980.
Wollheim, Richard. *Painting as an Art.* Princeton, N.J., 1987.

DOMINIC M. McIVER LOPES

Resemblance

One often talks about works of art as resembling what they represent in some respects and to some degree. Paintings, photographs, and sculptures are said to look like the objects they stand for. Some pieces of music are said to sound like their subjects. Actors are sometimes said to move like the people they portray. The issue of interest to philosophers of art is whether these resemblances are significant. Does an artwork represent or refer to an object by virtue of resembling it? Is an artwork a better or more realistic or more pleasing representation the more it resembles the object it stands for? Can one distinguish different forms of representation by the fact that some forms necessarily resemble what they represent and some do not?

Although these are questions about the general relationship between artworks and their subjects, the notion of resemblance in aesthetics is most often introduced in theorizing about the pictorial arts. Most people are inclined to believe that pictures bear some resemblance or likeness to the objects that they depict, and this intuition has led many theorists to claim that it is just this relation of resemblance between a picture and its referent that is the condition of pictorial significance; it is by virtue of a resemblance between pictures and objects in the world that pictures make sense, that one can tell what a picture is of. Thus, a picture of Winston Churchill represents or refers to Churchill and not Napoleon Bonaparte because it resembles or looks like the former and not the latter. In the so-called copy theory of representation, one of the least complicated models adopting this ontological approach, resemblance is taken as natural relation between a picture and referent where the referent is "reality" or "the way things are" or "the way things look." A belief in this privileged relation accounts for the way many art historians and theorists explain elements of realistic depiction. Pictures can be said to be more "realistic" in proportion to the completeness of the resemblance relation. The more the picture of Churchill resembles that man, the more realistic or perhaps more accurate a representation of Churchill it is.

The view that representational works, especially pictures, resemble or mirror or look like things in the world has been a predominant one in Western aesthetics. Its influence is often traced to the development of naturalistic representation in Greek visual art from the sixth and fourth centuries BCE. Historically, Greek naturalism is believed to be important for two reasons: first, because it is believed to have determined the main character of European art in antiquity, and second because the naturalistic tradition was revived in the Renaissance and has retained its influence until this century. The main concern of aesthetic naturalism is to produce convincing facsimiles of the visible appearances of things; the more an artwork looks like the object being represented, the more successful it is as a naturalistic representation of that object. A considerable fund of popular stories about the Greek artists has been preserved, mainly by Pliny, attesting to their fascination with the creation of illusions of nature. Apelles was supposed to have painted a horse so realistically that live horses were deceived and neighed. In a painting competition between Parrhius and Zeuxis, Zeuxis painted grapes so lifelike that birds pecked at them. Parrhius was supposed to have countered by painting a curtain that deceived even Zeuxis into asking to have the curtain drawn so that he could see the picture. Similar stories ap-

pear during the Renaissance. Giorgio Vasari, for example, recounts that Bernazzone painted strawberries that were pecked at by peacocks. Giotto painted a fly on the nose of a portrait that Giovanni Cimabue was working on that was so lifelike that Cimabue took it for a real fly and tried to brush it away.

The conception of artworks as illusions or replicas of reality encourages the view that representational art involves the copying of the external appearances of things. To a great extent, this view was largely taken for granted by many philosophers and historians prior to the twentieth century, and this had a profound effect on the kinds of theoretical questions raised about the arts. One question that concerned both Plato and Aristotle is whether or not artworks have any cognitive value. If one assumes, as both these thinkers do, that the primary purpose of the arts is to duplicate the way the world looks, then one might wonder whether they can teach us anything about the objects that they represent. In the now famous passages of the *Republic* dealing with the mimetic arts, Plato concludes that they cannot. His attack is largely influenced by his ontological commitment to a unique and unvarying realm of Forms. For Plato, any particular sensible object is not wholly a real thing because it comes into being and perishes and is perpetually changing. Sensible objects do embody, however, albeit imperfectly, their respective essential Forms. A picture, because it is merely a two-dimensional representation of the appearance of a solid object seen at a certain angle, is, so to speak, as far as possible from the realm of Forms. One cannot, in other words, gain any knowledge of reality, the Forms, through pictures. Aristotle also assumes that pictorial art is imitative, although he believes that the enjoyment of recognizing likenesses in pictures is specifically the intellectual pleasure involved in learning something new about the objects represented.

The adoption of the resemblance model led to an increasing emphasis being placed on the representational content of artworks and on the skills of the artist in reproducing those likenesses. The work of art becomes, as it were, transparent and one looks through it at what it represents. One does not see a beautiful picture so much as a beautiful body skillfully imitated. Thus, in much of Western art criticism, attention is focused on the scenes and the stories represented as opposed to the artworks themselves, and if the quality of the artwork is to be evaluated, it is usually in respect to how accurately or how cleverly it achieves a semblance of reality. For example, for many theorists, including Aristotle, it is the artist's craftsmanship that explains why one enjoys looking at pictures of ugly or disturbing subjects. The notion of accuracy or craftsmanship of representation is also at the heart of a dominant view in art history that the development of new representational styles and techniques is connected with the progression toward greater and greater verisimilitude.

Clearly, if one assumes that artworks visually resemble the world in some way, then the problem arises about how to deal with works that purport to represent something that cannot be seen. For Plato, the Forms are the kinds of things that could not be understood or approached through the appearances of things. Pictures and poetry, he believes, are misleading or dangerous precisely because they give the impression of reality without affording any access to it. This idea is echoed in the religious debates on idolatry and in the biblical injunction against the production of likenesses of God. Again, the assumption at work here is that certain representations, specifically pictures and sculptures, resemble what they represent. One of the fears with similarity-based representation is that there is the possibility of substitutive error in which the symbol, the idol, ceases to be a representation of God and comes to be seen as God himself or as part of him. If one assumes that God has no image or that no person has ever seen it, then any likeness created of God must necessarily be mistaken. The error involved is in the very act of making a likeness of something that either has no image or of which one has no visual experience.

The ban against the production of likenesses of God is interpreted as a ban specifically on the visual arts and is not typically extended to linguistic descriptions of deities. Representations of the latter sort are not considered prone to the same kind of representational or substitutive errors because they do not purport to resemble the objects they stand for. The idea that pictures and words can be distinguished by the way in which representations or symbols refer gains greater prominence at the start of the twentieth century with the development of semiotics. Charles Sanders Peirce, for example, divided the various kinds of representations into three categories. The first is representation based on resemblance; the second is causal representation; and the third is conventional-based representation. Representation based on similarity means that one thing represents or refers to another in virtue of its being similar to it. In causal representation, the relation between the symbol and the thing symbolized is not a relation of similarity; other relations are involved, such as metonymy, in which a part represents the whole. In conventional representation, the symbol is associated with a thing by conventions or rules. This is taken not to be true of representations based on similarity, where the representation is natural and obvious and not controlled by special rules that must be learned. [See Peirce.]

Although Peirce's taxonomy does not necessarily commit him to placing pictures in one class over another, he nevertheless puts pictures squarely in the class of similarity-based symbols and words in the class of symbols determined by conventions. Like many before him, he assumes that this is the way that pictures work. In the later part of the twentieth century, this assumption comes under greater and greater scrutiny. Partly this is the result of increasing interest in both philosophy and psychology with understanding the formal nature of the relation and the nature of similarity judgments. Also, during this time, there is growing skepticism of the ontological and epistemological assumptions inherent in naturalism that there is one way that the world is or is given to us. In fact, some of the most thorough accounts of pictorial representation in the twentieth century are all predicated on a rejection of a natural connection between pictures and the objects they depict. There is a group of art historians and philosophers who argue that various sorts of resemblance, or naturalist accounts of pictorial representation, cannot be correct. According to these so-called conventionalists, there is no special sort of similarity between a picture and its subject. Instead, one is habituated to certain styles of picturing the world and it is in only virtue of this familiarity that such styles seem so well suited to their representational tasks. For a conventionalist, it is habit that favors or constrains the choice of pictorial styles and the way pictures work within those styles. For the naturalist, on the other hand, there is a real resemblance between picture and pictured. There are facts about us as human beings, and facts about the world, that prompt us to recognize the world in pictures.

The art historian E. H. Gombrich (1960) argues that there is no "innocent eye," no way of perceiving objects free of experience and knowledge, and thus no way to determine the way these objects "really are." Although he does not want to deny that visual skills are perhaps at some deep level automatic and programmed to seek out certain features of the world, Gombrich stresses that perception itself is the product of habit. Elicited by certain clues in the environment, vision is a process of making judgments about meaning or expectations. One does not passively receive information from the world. Instead, one is motivated by specific purposes to look for and find significant features of the world. Representational practices are conventional in that the artist has to invent rules or schemata for laying down clues that can substitute for the information sought when looking at nature. The recent history of art, for Gombrich, is a progressive history in which the artist has sought to invent artificial methods of eliciting these responses. Pictures are realistic not because they mirror or look like the objects they depict but because they can be read or interpreted in the same terms as natural objects. The similarity of a picture with natural objects is not like the relation of a copy to an original but of the kind of mental or visual activities both can arouse. Although Gombrich shifts the relation of resemblance away from the representation and the object to the judgments of viewers and denies the naturalist's epistemological and ontological assumptions that one can get at the way the world actually is, he manages only to postpone and recast the question of a natural or privileged relation between pictures and the world. If a judgment that two things are similar is based on similar uses of visual skills, and if ultimately these skills are anchored in a natural mechanism, then there remains the possibility of explaining depictive practices in terms of this natural basis.

A more radical conventionalist analysis of representation is put forward by Nelson Goodman. According to Goodman, descriptions and pictures are semantically analogous. Both kinds of symbols denote what they represent and denotation is independent of resemblance. That pictures seem to function symbolically is quite important for Goodman. If pictorial systems are symbolic systems, then he thinks that he can fully explain the relation between a picture and what it pictures merely by detailing the formal conditions of these systems. Outlining what these formal conditions are for representational systems makes up a large part of his project in *Languages of Art* (1976). Although Goodman likes to stress the analogy between picturing and describing, he does maintain that pictorial and discursive systems are different. Nevertheless, because both picturing and describing are species of the same mode of symbolization, Goodman believes that the difference between them is not found in the way that symbols are correlated with their referents (as in Peirce's analysis), but in the structure of the systems themselves. In order to know whether or not something is a picture and in order to determine what a picture is of, one need only know the lexicon and formal rules of the actual representational system that the symbol belongs to. Whether a picture depicts Napoleon depends on the rules correlating the picture with that French emperor, in the same way that a series of sentences in French describing the emperor is a function of the rules or the linguistic system of French. Just as one could choose another language—for example, English—to describe the world, one could choose another pictorial system to depict it. Pictures are just as conventional as language.

It should be noted that Goodman's claim that many systems of representation can be constructed does not by itself constitute a threat to the resemblance model of depiction. The possibility of there being many systems may lead one to ask which is the more correct. Proponents of resemblance need not deny the possibility of there being a system of representation in which the symbols stand for objects they in no way resemble. What they do deny is that all systems accurately or truthfully describe the world. Resemblance, therefore, works as a kind a standard of realism or accuracy or truthfulness. The system of representation employed in the Renaissance, for example, can be said to be more realistic than that employed by the Cubists because the pictures produced in accordance with that system more resemble the objects and scenes that they stand for. Given Goodman's own analysis of the pictorial, it should not be surprising that he is committed to showing that resemblance is not a condition for pictorial representation. Much of Goodman's critique of this relation, however, is motivated by doubts of a more general, and perhaps more

damning, nature. Goodman thinks that the notions of resemblance and similarity can play no explanatory role in philosophical analysis. Moreover, and more importantly in his specific attacks against the role of resemblance in the pictorial arts, he thinks that any account that appeals to these relations either to explain the relationship of pictures to the world or to explain their accuracy does so because of what he believes to be misguided ontological assumptions.

One of the major problems that Goodman finds with the notion of similarity is that it cannot be formally defined in a way that can do any explanatory work. If one takes similarity as an unrelativized primitive holding between objects and measured in terms of possession of common features, then one option might be to say that two things are similar if they have only one property in common. The problem with this definition is that any two things have some property in common: any two objects, regardless of what they are, are similar. We advance no further if one specifies that the objects must share all their properties, because no two distinct things have all their properties in common. Defined in this way, the relation turns out to be either vacuous (the claim that an object resembles itself) or false (the claim that there exist no two distinct objects that are similar). This problem is only complicated when one tries to define similarity as a comparative rather than an absolute relation—objects x and y are more similar to one another than objects a and b—for any two things have as many properties in common as any other two. If there are three things in the universe, then any two of them belong exactly in two classes and have exactly two properties in common: the property of belonging to the class of two things and the property of belonging to the class of three things. As the universe gets bigger, the number of shared properties—the classes they belong to—will be larger, but will remain the same for any two things. Every two things will be as similar as any other two things. If resemblance is going to do any explanatory work—for example, if it is to distinguish resembling pairs from nonresembling ones—it has to be defined in a nonvacuous way. As Goodman has shown, a definition of resemblance in terms of quantity of properties shared will not suffice. This puts the burden of proof on the proponent of resemblance to come up with another definition, and most importantly, a definition that functions as a fixed standard for measuring likenesses in all cases.

One might object that, in saying that two objects resemble each other, one has not established any significant relationship between these objects until one specifies the respect in which they are similar, that is, until one specifies what the properties shared are. Goodman argues, however, that once one defines similarity in terms of specified respects, the resemblance relation turns out to be epistemically superfluous, for it is the respects and not some abstract principle of resemblance that conveys the meaning of the relation. Put another way, to say that a set of things is similar in respect to be being green is just to say that all those things are green, and to know this is to undermine the need to ask why they are similar in the first place. Resemblance in terms of respects, for Goodman, is highly dependent on the conceptual systems used to classify features of the world: to say that someone resemble her grandmother in one respect and not in another is a matter of the task, the conceptual system employed, and the appropriateness under that system of applying that predicate to that person and not to her grandmother. It is these conceptual systems (or, in Gombrich's terminology, schemata), that are the force in determining which respects are a relevant or significant feature of an object, not nature. Like Gombrich, Goodman is opposed to the idea that knowledge of the world can be built up of conceptually free perception. All knowledge and perception involves classification and selection for specific purposes. The world does not come ready-made.

As Goodman sees it, the resemblance view of representation is committed both to the idea that pictures mirror the world and to the idea that the world is structured in only one way. It is this latter ontological commitment that Goodman takes to be at the heart of the naturalist's belief that pictures are more or less true, or more or less realistic, in virtue of how well or how poorly they resemble this world. Given this commitment, Goodman argues, the naturalist cannot be satisfied with resemblance in respects because this kind of resemblance is not independent of the representational systems we are accustomed to. What the naturalist needs is a kind of resemblance that will allow her to judge degrees of correlation with reality across representational systems, a kind of similarity that has some sort of epistemically privileged status outside any particular way of conceptualizing the world.

Another common line of attack aimed specifically against resemblance as a requirement of depiction, and one used both by Goodman and Max Black, is that resemblance cannot be a sufficient condition for representation. The claim that resemblance is a sufficient condition for representation amounts to the claim that every case of resemblance is a case of representation, and both Goodman and Black believe that this is fairly easy to disprove. They point out that, unlike representation, resemblance is reflexive. Particular objects resemble themselves to a maximum degree, but rarely represent themselves. Also unlike representation, resemblance is symmetrical. If a portrait resembles its sitter, then it follows that the sitter resembles her portrait. The sitter, however, does not represent her portrait. Many pairs of objects resemble each other to various degrees—a twin looks like his twin and a car of a certain make and model resembles another car of the same make and model—yet not every like pair exhibits a symbolic relation. The success of this attack is dependent on it being the case that resemblance and not representation is both reflexive and symmetrical. Neither Goodman nor Black substantiates this claim.

Nevertheless, it is not hard to see why they believe it to be true. In many cases, what one means when one says that two objects resemble one another is that the objects share properties.

Against this line of argument, critics have replied that when one says that a portrait looks like its sitter, one rarely means that the sitter looks like her picture. The formal properties of the relation are not reflected in the way one makes similarity judgments. Several studies in psychology support this view. Amos Tversky (1977) concludes that resemblance statements are in fact highly directional and never constant. For Tversky, this shows that similarity should not be understood as the matching of properties between two objects but as a process in which a subject, in a particular context, determines which predicates apply to two objects once the choice of primary subject and reference—which variable position the objects fill in the statement "a is similar to b"—has already been given. Similarity judgments are highly dependent on context and tasks. Although Tversky's analysis of similarity judgments takes a lot of the power out of Goodman's and Black's counterexamples, his conclusions do support Goodman's contention that similarity judgments are highly relative to one's purposes. If one assumes that determinations of similarity in pictorial cases are dependent on the systems of representation one is accustomed to, then it is the systems that constrain the fact that a picture looks like its subject. Claiming this is not to deny that pictures resemble their referents, but to deny that they look like them in any fixed or independent way.

Because Goodman's attack on resemblance is primarily an attack on a certain metaphysical picture, it works well against theories of depiction that assume that the relation between pictures and the world is direct and neutral and that measure fidelity in terms of a fixed standard of correspondence between the two. The problem is that Goodman assumes that any account of depiction asserting a correspondence between pictures and objects, be it through the notions of imitation or illusion or "looking like," is guilty of these assumptions. He takes all as saying that there is only one correct way that a picture can look or be like its referent. He rules out the possibility that when one talks about likenesses between pictures and natural objects, one can be employing a notion of resemblance for which standards vary from cases to case.

One of the fundamental problems in saying that a picture represents its subject by virtue of resembling it is that it confuses the problem of how pictures are about their referents with how they are like them. To say that something represents something else is to say that it is about or refers to that object. What is it that gives one the status of a signifier and the other the status of something signified? Suppose one has two Brillo boxes, one by the artist Andy Warhol and the other a "real" Brillo box; one wants to say that the former is a representation of the latter. Apart from the fact that one seems to enter into the history of the other, however, there is no observational criterion for saying that one is the "real" Brillo box and the other a representation of the box. Resemblance cannot establish reference in this case, yet it is clear nonetheless that one signifies the other. One cannot reduce the question of what a picture is about to the question of how it is like what it refers to. The former is one of which objects have semantic significance, and this representational significance has to be determined by the appropriate conventions. On at least this point Goodman seems to be correct.

The question of what it means for pictures to look like or resemble what they depict remains open. The problem is that, as they stand, these notions are too loose to bear any weight. Just what does it mean for a picture to look like its subject? One way of trying to spell out these relations is in terms of shared properties. The weakness with this approach is that resemblance is a matter of degree. Even if one assumes that both Pablo Picasso's portrait of his daughter Paloma and Jacques-Louis David's portrait of Napoleon resemble the people they depict in this way, it does not appear that the properties that the latter shares with the French emperor are exactly the same as those shared by Paloma and her portrait. Nor do the portraits and their sitters seem to share the same number of properties. The likenesses between pictures and their subjects will be have to be accounted for on a case-by-case basis.

Many people have pointed out that the intuition that resemblance is involved in depiction does not amount to the claim that there is similarity of substance. No one expects the physical object that is the painting to resemble the physical object that is its subject. One does think, however, that the picture visually resembles the appearance of its subject. Thus, rather than searching for resemblances between things perceived, perhaps one should search for whether there are significant similarities between the experience or act of seeing a picture and the experience or act of seeing things. One of the benefits of understanding resemblance in this way is that it does not appear, at least initially, to fall prey to the kind of formal critique of the similarity relationship leveled by Goodman and Black, because their attacks are aimed primarily against resemblance theories adopting a shared-property relation explaining the relationship between pictures and their subjects. To say that one should understand the seeming correspondence between pictures and their subjects in terms of a correspondence between kinds of visual experiences, however, is merely the start of an analysis of depiction. The primary work that needs to be done is in characterizing the kind of experience involved in seeing representational pictures as well as in specifying how this particular kind of experience is similar to, as well as different from, visual experiences of natural objects.

One of the earliest proponents for understanding pictorial representation as a kind of perceptual capacity, Richard Wollheim (1980), proposed that there is a specific kind of visual experience of a picture—what he calls "seeing-in"—that is analogous to seeing the object pictured and that accounts for the picture's representational effects. Christopher Peacocke (1987) has taken this kind of approach one step further by arguing that depiction can be understood as a "purely perceptual phenomenon" and can thus be defined exclusively in perceptual terms. For Peacocke, a picture of a cat is related to a cat in that it is presented in a region of the visual field experienced as similar in shape to that in which that cat could be presented. Peacocke's account stands in stark opposition to conventionalist analyses of representation, for, on his view, depiction will turn out to be independent of any representational or referential practices that one might learn and employ: the only thing that makes something a picture of a cat and not of anything else is the special perceptual relation of experienced similarity. Not all theorists ascribing to the idea that the relationship between pictures and their subjects should be understood in terms of a correspondence between seeing a picture and seeing a thing take an anticonventionalist stance. In Kendall Walton's (1985) theory of depiction, pictures are props in games of visual make-believe. Make-believe games are governed by conventions that determine which propositions or activities are fictionally true within that game. According to Walton, in the make-believe game played when looking at pictures, fictional truths about the viewer's visual activities are generated by the viewer's actual visual activities, and it is this correspondence that makes the act of looking at pictures similar to the act of looking at things. Joel Snyder (1980), on the other hand, argues that both representing and seeing are conventional practices governed by constructional rules. One learns to see the "natural" world just as one learns to make pictures, and what explains belief in a special relationship between pictures and their subjects is that the same rules of construction apply to both the seeing of an object and the seeing of a representation of that object.

Although these attempts to understand the relationship between pictures and their subjects come to very different conclusions, all of them suggest that depiction is integrally and importantly connected to certain visual practices or experiences. Moreover, it is just this connection that may be at the heart of the deeply entrenched belief in the arts that pictures, unlike other representations, bear a significant and privileged relationship to objects in the world. Whether this is a relationship of resemblance of some kind, or whether it is natural or conventional, is still a matter of debate.

BIBLIOGRAPHY

Gombrich, E. H. *Art and Illusion: A Study in the Psychology of Pictorial Representation* (1960). 2d. rev. ed. New York, 1961; reprint, Princeton, N.J., 1969.
Gombrich, E. H., Julian Hochberg, and Max Black. *Art, Perception and Reality.* Baltimore, 1972.

Goodman, Nelson. "Seven Strictures on Similarity." In *Problems and Projects,* pp. 437–446. Indianapolis, 1972.

Goodman, Nelson. *Languages of Art: An Approach to a Theory of Symbols.* 2d ed. Indianapolis, 1976.

Goodrich, R. A. "Plato on Poetry and Painting." *British Journal of Aesthetics* 22.1 (Winter 1982): 126–137.

Maynard, Patrick. "Depiction, Vision and Convention." *American Philosophical Quarterly* 9.3 (July 1972): 243–250.

Peacocke, Christopher. "Depiction." *Philosophical Review* 96.3 (July 1987): 383–410.

Podro, Michael. "Depiction and the Golden Calf." In *Visual Theory: Painting and Interpretation,* edited by Norman Bryson, Michael Ann Holly, and Keith Moxey, pp. 163–189. New York, 1991.

Pole, David. "Goodman and the 'Naive' View of Representation." *British Journal of Aesthetics* 14.1 (Winter 1974): 68–80.

Schier, Flint. *Deeper into Pictures: An Essay on Pictorial Representation.* Cambridge and New York, 1986.

Snyder, Joel. "Picturing Vision." In *The Language of Images,* edited by W. J. T. Mitchell, pp. 219–246. Chicago, 1980.

Tversky, Amos. "Features of Similarity." *Psychological Review* 84.3 (July 1977): 322–352.

Walton, Kendall L. "Looking at Pictures and Looking at Things." In *Philosophy and the Visual Arts: Seeing and Abstracting,* edited by Andrew Harrison, pp. 277–300. Dordrecht and Boston, 1985.

Wollheim, Richard. *Art and Its Objects.* 2d ed., with six supplementary essays. Cambridge and New York, 1980.

GABRIELA SAKAMOTO

REYNOLDS, JOSHUA (1723–1792), a British portrait painter and aesthetic theorist. A native of Plympton, Devon, Reynolds trained under the portraitist Thomas Hudson, before embarking on a journey to Italy in 1749. Upon returning in 1752, Reynolds painted his first significant work—a dramatic full-length portrait of his companion on the continental journey, Commodore Augustus Keppel (c.1753–1754; London, National Maritime Museum). Reynolds established his home and studio in Leicester Fields, London, and developed an extraordinarily lucrative portrait practice, with a wide range of patrons that included royalty, writers, actors, nobility, and the gentry. He moved in a variety of social circles, and was a member of the Literary Club and the Society of Dilettanti. When the Royal Academy was established in December 1768, King George III appointed Reynolds the institution's first president. His first of fifteen discourses on art was given at the academy's inaugural annual exhibition of paintings on 2 January 1769 and, three months later, he was knighted. Reynolds's grand style is best typified by the portraits of *Sarah Siddons as the Tragic Muse* (exh. RA 1784; San Marino, Huntington Library and Art Gallery) and *Lord Heathfield* (exh. RA 1788; London, Royal Academy), and the subject pictures *The Infant Hercules* (exh. RA 1788; Saint Petersburg, Hermitage) and *Cymon and Iphigenia* (exh. RA 1789; Royal Collection). Reynolds died having established himself as the most successful portraitist of the era and an artist who attempted to enlarge the subject, scope, and quality of English art, in ad-

dition to elevating the status of artists in society, through his pictures, publications, and teaching.

It was to *The Idler* that Reynolds first offered his ideas on art in the form of three letters published in 1759. These initially appeared in the *Universal Chronicle* on 29 September, 20 October, and 10 November of that year, and were later republished together as "A Letter on Painting" in the 12–14 May 1761 edition of the *London Chronicle*. The letters represent the first indication of the range of Reynolds's literary aspirations prior to the *Discourses*, serving as a prelude to some of the directions he would later pursue. *The Idler* was published by his close friend Dr. Samuel Johnson, an immense presence in English literary society and a man whom Reynolds clearly emulated. Along with Oliver Goldsmith and Edmund Burke, Johnson was a founding member of Reynolds's The Club (later the Literary Club) in 1764, and encouraged the artist's literary pursuits.

The first letter both attacked and challenged wayward critics of painting and connoisseurs who slavishly adhered to restrictive rules. The second letter presented Reynolds's initial concept of the grand style with respect to the art of Italian painters, contrasting their manner to the fine detail and empirical approach of Dutch artists, which Reynolds saw as mechanical simulation—an idea reprised in his later writings: "Painters should go to the Dutch school to learn the art of painting, as they would go to a grammar school to learn languages. They must go to Italy to learn the higher branches of knowledge" (Reynolds, 1851, vol. 2, pp. 205–206). The final letter provides a recognition of beauty, identifying it with the concept of the "central form" as it emerges from nature and as it is relevant in specific cultures. The issue of beauty defined as the "central form" would be an integral aspect of his aesthetic theory as it later emerged in the *Discourses on Art*.

In 1765, five of Reynolds's scholarly notes were published in the final volume of Johnson's edition of Shakespeare. Two other notes were subsequently included in the edition of 1780. Although these works were largely reprises of arguments by Johnson and earlier authors, they also were indicative of the range of Reynolds's interests across the arts and his aspirations as a writer and critic. There is evidence that he preferred his reputation to rest on his scholarly writings, at times over his profession as a painter, as seen in a number of self-portraits (mid-1770s, London, Royal Academy of Arts) and in portraits of him by his friends and peers, such as Angelica Kauffmann's of 1767 (Saltram, The National Trust).

The *Discourses,* which Reynolds referred to as "some instructive observations on the arts" (1975, no. 15), were a series of fifteen lectures delivered from 1769 to 1790 at the Royal Academy's annual distribution of prizes to students. The first seven discourses were published in 1778, and in 1797 the entire series appeared in Edmond Malone's posthumous compilation of Reynolds's works. Reynolds's general aim was to provide words of guidance for a very specific audience consisting primarily of aspiring art students, and ultimately to develop a theory of painting and aesthetics that would promote painting as one of the liberal arts, on a par with poetry, and thus elevate the status of the painter in society. The *Discourses* functioned as the guidelines for the newly formed Royal Academy. After the publication of the first seven lectures in 1778, Reynolds seems to have recognized the expanding audience for his ideas and responded by widening the appeal of his themes. Thus, the early lectures tell students how to go about creating art via a step-by-step process in which the student begins by acquiring a mechanical facility in drawing and using artistic implements. This is followed by a call for rigorous study of the approved forms of past art, including the old masters as typified by sculpture from antiquity, the painters of the High Renaissance, and the Baroque painters of France and Italy. The final stage of artistic learning allows the advanced student to make his own compositions and to begin his professional career by creating works that draw on the knowledge gleaned in the first two stages and attain perfection through the application of the student's intellect and imagination. The later *Discourses* are concerned with what is appropriate for the artist to then attempt in his work.

In Reynolds's theory, the object of art was beauty of a general and intellectual nature, which is an idea derived from the mind itself, and thus dependent on the imagination of the artist. It is the painter's role to objectify this beauty, in order to "raise the thoughts, and extend the views of the spectator," and to become the "means of bestowing on whole nations refinement of taste" (ibid., no. 9). Ultimately, by adhering to this process, art will result in forms of "virtue" that are at once ethical and moral. This forms the end of art. It is a truth not meant to enhance the artist's professional profile, nor the pleasure of art's audience, but for the edification, in a broad moral sense, of the human mind.

Beauty, for Reynolds, was initially derived from the natural world, but throughout the *Discourses* there is a distinction between an artistic approach to nature based on description and specificity, and one that implies generality. "Deception, which is so often recommended by writers on the theory of painting, instead of advancing the art, is in reality carrying it back to its infant state" (Du Fresnoy annotations, in Reynolds, 1851, vol. 2, p. 350). Accordingly, beauty must be attained through a distillation of nature and a thorough grounding in the achievements of past artists, to the extent that the artist is encouraged to look at past art for inspiration and models, and also for specific forms that one may subtly borrow. This theory of beauty "as an idea in the mind abstracted from the bedrock of experience" (Mahoney, 1978, p. 127) is very much of its era, a firm part of the tradition of neoclassical theory dating back to the previous century. Essential in this conception is the importance

of experience via study and awareness. It is this experience that must then be accessed by the artist to inspire his or her creative productions, and then to touch the audience.

Reynolds also presents a simplistic form of reception theory by isolating the importance of the viewer's imagination and response in aesthetic creation, but it is an approach steeped in the rhetoric of association of ideas that was prevalent in the eighteenth century. "The great end of the art is to strike the imagination. . . . the spectator is only to feel the result in his bosom" (*Discourses*, no. 5). This is combined with his concepts of custom and habit, which influence the perception of beauty and essentially the viewer's culturally formed taste. For Reynolds, taste was something aesthetically intuitive and objective—a response to the very nature of an object—yet it also had a spontaneous or subjective dimension, as considered most fully in the seventh discourse. This is just one of the many instances in which Reynolds appears to be presaging the concerns of the next generation of artists in Romanticism, while remaining tethered to the prevailing tradition of the eighteenth century. Implicit and important in these writings is the distinction between art as a mechanical trade and the fine artist, a gentleman schooled in higher knowledge, who pursues one of the liberal arts rather than a craft.

The inspiration for the *Discourses* and Reynolds's other writings on art appears to come from a variety of sources. These include the French and Italian literary traditions arising out of the works of Plato and Aristotle such as the writings of Roland Fréart, whose treatise on painting, *L'idée de la perfection de la peinture* (1662), Reynolds had with him in Italy. Reynolds was also well versed in British writings of the seventeenth and eighteenth centuries, including his contemporaries Johnson, Burke, Goldsmith, and David Hume. In total, the *Discourses* represent "the most eloquent, as well as the last, presentations of the ideas that dominated European art criticism and theory from the mid-fifteenth to the mid-eighteenth century" (Robert R. Wark, in Reynolds, 1959, p. xxiii).

In *A Journey to Flanders and Holland,* the notes of a voyage undertaken in 1781, Reynolds rarely strayed from descriptions of individual pictures and largely confirmed his thoughts in the early *Discourses*. But he occasionally delivered broad pronouncements on general themes, such as the death of history painting (1851, vol. 2, pp. 188–190), its relationship to religious changes, and its exclusion from the productions in English art. This should be seen as part of a continuing protest over Reynolds's failed proposal, together with the artists Benjamin West, Kauffmann, James Barry, and others, to decorate the interior of St. Paul's cathedral, which had been vetoed by the Bishop of London in 1773.

Subsequent publications of Reynolds's theories include annotations added to William Mason's publication of Charles Alphonse du Fresnoy's *The Art of Painting*, appearing in 1783, and his *Ironical Discourse*, published in the *Gen-*

tleman's Magazine of July 1791. In the annotations to du Fresnoy, he reiterates many of his ideas regarding the painting of particulars and generalities in approaches to nature but also acknowledges the limitation of restrictive rules, much as he did in his first letter to *The Idler:*

> What relates to the mind or imagination, such as invention, character, expression, grace, or grandeur, certainly cannot be taught by rules; little more can be done than pointing out where they are to be found; it is a part which belongs to general education, and will operate in proportion to the cultivation of the mind of the artist.   (Du Fresnoy annotations, in ibid., p. 353)

It is also in these annotations that Reynolds writes very practically and usefully about technique, composition, and individual artists. The *Ironical Discourse* largely reprises his previous conceptions in a sarcastic manner. Reynolds's aesthetic theories set the standard for academic artistic practice in England and the Royal Academy through the nineteenth century. His ideas on education were critiqued by Barry in the 1770s, however, although his aesthetic perspectives remained essential. The most sustained and aggressive attack on his pedagogy remains William Blake's notes in the margin of his copy of the *Discourses* that had been published in 1798, providing a Romantic perspective on Reynolds's teachings. Taken individually, Blake's comments read as fiery outbursts focused on individual points, but, when considered comprehensively, they reveal Blake's objections to the substance of Reynolds's ideas. For Blake, who began his marginalia with "This Man was Hired to Depress Art," Reynolds was a paradox who did not practice his prescriptions in his own art, and Blake's own wellspring of creativity—his private visions and imagination, which combined with an awareness of past art to result in minutely realized imagery in watercolors, prints, and tempera on a small and symbolic scale—stood in direct opposition to Reynolds's preaching, the grand style, and use of an oil-based medium. Additionally, Blake's insistence on the workings of genius and the appeal to reason allowed him little sympathy for Reynolds, a man who appeared to stand for the age of reaction, the patronage of the upper classes, and an earlier generation.

The vituperative nature of Blake's criticisms would be picked up in the 1840s by the Pre-Raphaelites, whose pejorative nomenclature for Reynolds, "Sir Sloshua," not only drew attention to the slathering manner of the grand style that they found so repulsive but also to Reynolds's high social position and overarching influence in academic circles. They also clearly deplored his taste in art in their fundamental antipathy toward the post–High Renaissance painters. A more level assessment was provided consistently over the whole of his career by John Ruskin, the most important art critic and theorist of the era. Ruskin found himself moved by Reynolds's art from a young age, and repeatedly cited Reynolds as one of the seven or eight most important artists in history, as well as the artist most representative of the English school. Nonetheless, Ruskin disagreed intensely with Reynolds's denial of empirical accuracy and detail in painting, an essential aspect of Ruskin's own writings and the preferred Pre-Raphaelite practice. Ruskin also was completely opposed to Reynolds's appeal for generality and conception of beauty as the effect of custom. Despite the fact that Ruskin found the artist's teaching fundamentally flawed, he encouraged students to look at Reynolds's paintings for inspiration. He wrote that Reynolds "seems to have been born to teach all error by his precept; but that is because the only errors that were to be found in his precept, were seized upon as its essence by scholars determined to err" (Ruskin, Oxford Lectures 1875, *Works,* vol. 22, p. 494). Later Victorian critics are typified by Frederic George Stephens, formerly a member of the Pre-Raphaelite Brotherhood and later lead critic for the *Athenaeum,* who agreed with Ruskin in recognizing that Reynolds did not practice what he preached, labeling his mythological and subject pictures "laborious mistakes," but still remained enamored of the portraits and the artist's skillful brushwork and composition. Victorian interest in the artist was confirmed by an exhibition of his works at the Grosvenor Gallery in 1883–1884.

Many twentieth-century critics have been attracted to Reynolds's art and theories. Roger Fry republished the *Discourses* in 1905 with an introduction and notes that served to reintroduce the artist to the modern public. Of particular relevance for Fry were Reynolds's practical approach and applied aesthetics, his hands-on manner, and his artist's point of view. He also perceived Reynolds's later writings, especially *A Journey to Flanders and Holland,* as indicative of Reynolds's cutting-edge taste in past art such as Flemish primitives—a predilection for the kind of art that would gain adherents and acclaim in the nineteenth century. Finally, Fry, who was reflecting back on the revolt and individualism of the tumultuous nineteenth century and was ushering in the twentieth century with an eye toward stability and a hope for the resurgence of English art, was drawn by Reynolds's call for an adherence to tradition and an implicitly national community of artists formed around solid principles of instruction.

Scholars of the postwar era have consistently delved into Reynolds's writings and found relevance for his traditional approach in the twentieth century. Wark's republication of the *Discourses* in 1959 and its subsequent reprinting introduced the artist's theories to the second half of the twentieth century. There remains a continuing interest in his art, as demonstrated by the retrospective exhibition of 1986 at the Royal Academy of Arts in London and the Grand Palais in Paris. Moreover, Reynolds's theories figured heavily in John Barrell's *The Political Theory of Painting from Reynolds to Hazlitt* (1986), in which the author interpreted Reynolds's call for a public painting that would create a specific audience for art as part of a pancultural move toward defining a political public in the late eighteenth century. Barrell has been followed by David Solkin, who, in *Painting for Money* (1993), establishes connections between Reynolds's writings in *The Idler* and the *Discourses* and those of Anthony Ashley Cooper, earl of Shaftesbury, and explores Reynolds's conception of the grand style in the construction of a public for art.

The continued importance and relevance of Reynolds's writings are evidenced by a small allegorical portrait by him of "Theory" on the ceiling of the foyer of the Royal Academy of Arts in Burlington House. She is imaged with a pair of dividers symbolizing order, proportion, reason, and judgment—and holding a scroll in her left hand that reads "THEORY is the Knowledge of what is truly NATURE." The portrait is a succinct assessment of Reynolds's ideas, placed for posterity in the institution to which he devoted much of his intellectual and artistic life. He was, however, an artist well aware of the place of his particular theories in history:

> Rules are to be considered . . . as fences placed only where trespass is expected; and are particularly enforced in proportion as peculiar faults or defects are prevalent at the time, or age, in which they are delivered; for what may be proper strongly to recommend or enforce in one age, may not with equal propriety be so much laboured in another, when it may be the fashion for artists to run into the contrary extreme, proceeding from prejudice to a manner adopted by some favorite painter then in vogue.
>
> (Du Fresnoy annotations, in Reynolds, 1851, vol. 2, pp. 353–354)

[*See also* Beauty; Ruskin; *and* Taste.]

BIBLIOGRAPHY

Works by Reynolds

Discourses. Edited by Roger Fry. London, 1905. Edited by Robert R. Wark as *Discourses on Art* (San Marino, Calif., 1959); reprinted including Blake's marginalia (New Haven, 1975).
Letters of Sir Joshua Reynolds. Edited by Frederick Whiley Hilles. Cambridge, 1929.
The Literary Works of Sir Joshua Reynolds. 2 vols. Edited by Henry William Beechey. London, 1851.
Portraits. Edited by Frederick Whiley Hilles. New York, 1952.

Other Sources

Barrell, John. *The Political Theory of Painting from Reynolds to Hazlitt.* New Haven, 1986.
Hilles, Frederick Whiley. *The Literary Career of Sir Joshua Reynolds.* Cambridge, 1936.
Hipple, Walter John, Jr. "General and Particular in the Discourses of Sir Joshua Reynolds: A Study in Method." *Journal of Aesthetics and Art Criticism* 11 (1953): 231–247. Revised in *The Beautiful, and the Sublime, and the Picturesque in Eighteenth-Century British Aesthetic Theory* (Carbondale, Ill., 1957), pp. 133–148.
Mahoney, John L. "Reynolds's 'Discourses on Art': The Delicate Balance of Neoclassic Aesthetics." *British Journal of Aesthetics* 18 (1978): 126–136.
Mitchell, Charles. "Three Phases of Reynolds's Pictorial Method." *Burlington Magazine* 80 (1942): 35–42.
Murray, Roger. "Working Sir Joshua: Blake's Marginalia in Reynolds." *British Journal of Aesthetics* 17 (1977): 82–91.
Olson, Elder. Introduction to *Longinus' On the Sublime and Sir Joshua Reynolds' Discourses on Art.* Chicago, 1945.
Penny, Nicholas, ed. *Reynolds.* London, 1986.
Perini, Giovanna. "Sir Joshua Reynolds and Italian Art and Literature." *Journal of the Warburg and Courtauld Institutes* 51 (1988): 141–168.
Postle, Martin. *Sir Joshua Reynolds: The Subject Pictures.* Cambridge and New York, 1995.
Solkin, David H. *Painting for Money: The Visual Arts and the Public Sphere in Eighteenth-Century England.* New Haven, 1993.
Will, Frederic. "Blake's Quarrel with Reynolds." *Journal of Aesthetics and Art Criticism* 15 (1956–1957): 340–349.

JASON M. ROSENFELD

RHETORIC. [*To treat the relation between rhetoric and aesthetics, this entry comprises two essays:*
    Historical and Conceptual Overview
    Exemplarity
The first essay explains the tradition of rhetoric and its relationship to aesthetics. The second essay explores the topic of exemplarity, that is, the use of examples to persuade somebody of an aesthetic point or to illustrate that same point; exemplarity also serves to mediate between aesthetic theory and practice. For related discussion, see Poetics; *and* Renaissance Italian Aesthetics.]

Historical and Conceptual Overview

The connection of rhetoric and *aisthēsis* (sensation) is originary and strong. Classical rhetoric depended on a classical psychology that predicated a continuum, a series of interactive human faculties and actions, including sensation or *aisthēsis*, imagination *(phantasia),* memory, reason, and the acts of perceiving, self-movement, desire *(orexis),* choice, judgment *(krisis).* This dependence is stipulated by the nature of the rhetorical task. Turning to Aristotle, as compendious of early Greek rhetorical moments and the opposition they generated, one finds rhetoric defined as the art *(technē)* that masters the available means of persuasion in a specific problematic (1991, 1355b). Cicero and Quintilian, who dominated the Latin tradition, divided rhetorical persuasion into three tasks—instructing *(docere),* delighting *(delectare),* and moving *(movere)* (*Cicero, Brutus,* 1952, p. 185). The practice of rhetoric, in short, requires a base in psychological theory, because its focus is not simply on discourse and discursive techniques but on discursive effect on an audience, on doing things with words. Whether one chooses the civic, Aristotelian notion of persuasion or Quintilian's more inclusive claim that rhetoric is the art/science of speaking well ("ars/scientia bene dicendi"; 1921, II,xiv,5;xvii,38), one notes two heavy constraints. First, because the speaker, the audience, and the issue inhabit a domain of the probable, uncertain, the rhetor must always specify (Aristotle, 1991, 1357a). Variety is basic parameter of both issue and mode. Second, the rhetor is obliged to appeal to the entire range of human faculties. To put it briefly, where the Platonic philosopher prefers to address and develop the disembodied mind, the rhetor may not exclude any function of the incarnate soul in his practice.

Thus *aisthēsis*, sensation, which is inevitably accompanied by pleasure and pain, gives rise to desire or avoidance. The rhetor as orator must connect virtue with pleasure and vice with pain in his primary public task of seeking adhesion of spirits to the shared beliefs *(doxa)* of a community. Rhetorical address assumes the centrality of the passions *(pathos* or *adfectus)*. The passions are situated in the map of body *(soma)* and soul *(psyche)* relations, which account for human motive and motion. But because the actions of sensation are enchained with the actions of the imagination in producing, and the memory in storing images, a primary mode of engaging the passions is through vivid imagery *(enargeia* or *illustratio)* (Quintilian, VI,ii.29–32). Quintilian claims that of the three tasks, moving the affects is the quintessential rhetorical competence (ibid., VI,ii,4). The rhetorician, unlike the philosopher, does not have the luxury of dealing only with an educated elite within a rationally delimited discourse. On the contrary, he must at times perturb the audience's feelings, and drag them away from the truth in order to make truth and justice prevail (ibid., V,xiv, 29). The emphasis is on motion: the affects are, and cause, motions of the soul, *(motus animi)*. The passions, according to Aristotle, are the elements that cause changes, movements; in judgment, they are responsible for differences in beliefs (Aristotle, 1991, 1378a). Quintilian's strategic division of affects into mild *(ethos)* and perturbing *(pathos)* is a strong tactic of insisting on emotion as both substance and mode (vol. VI,ii,8f.). The orator functions within a domain of the ethical and pathetic, where he must confront the distances and differences within the community by means of a range of strategies of conciliation and perturbation; the passions, then, are constitutive of politics as the practice of vital negotiations of differences in a community. Thus *aisthēsis* and imagination, pleasure and passion ground rhetoric as a political as well as simply a literary competence. Strong classical theory presumes and presents continuities: between reason and emotions, between argumentation and appeal to affect, and between topic and mode, substance and expression, *res* and *verba;* and there are continuities within the classical and medieval curriculum of the seven liberal arts, where rhetoric shares interests and strategies with grammar and dialectic, the other elements of the liberal trivium, the arts of language.

Canons and Techniques. The premise of psychological continuum grounds the very rich elaboration of canons and techniques in the rhetorical tradition. The tidiness and clarity, and often the brevity and simplicity, of instruction in the wealth of pedagogical manuals of this very long development should not obscure the enduring complexity of the rhetorical project; because the mechanisms of human motive are so various and interconnected, so must be the skills of appeal, of engagement with motive. It is a mistake to stipulate too strong an opposition between, for example, style and argument, between frivolous ornamentation and serious reasoning. If there is a continuous range of faculties, there is, necessarily, a continuous range of modes of appeal to these faculties, a range that includes subtle changes of mood, as well as the coercion of dialectical argument, or passionate arousal.

Yet, there is a single, comprehensive rule: because the rhetor functions in the realm of the probable *(eikos)*, not the certain, the hegemonic canon for argument as well as style is decorum: the orator must at all times seek the appropriate *(to prepon, quid decet)* to time, place, audience. In Greek rhetoric, decorum rules in three genres of oratory: the deliberative, which deals with the politically expedient or useful, the juridical, which defines the just, and epideictic, which engages in praise of the honorable, in blame of the shameful or vicious (Aristotle, 1991, 1358b); to be sure, any one genre may employ a mixture of appeals. The injunction of decorum also gives rise to Cicero's lengthy treatment of *genera dicendi*, types that persist in the tradition: they specify a high style for grave, serious topics, a middle style for quotidian affairs, and a low style for popular use and reception. Decorum requires that of the three sources of skill, exercise *(exercitatio)* is more important than nature *(ingenium)* or art *(doctrina);* imitation *(imitatio)* is the necessary exercise in the appropriation from authoritative texts of the decorous. Even the late-antique development by Longinus of the canon of the sublime as value simply specifies a necessary surpassing of decorum as goal; it delimits a domain of excess as edification.

Although decorum should invest every aspect of rhetorical performance, Cicero's specification of five distinct rhetorical competences endures in the Western textual tradition of rhetoric manuals, and offers an organizational frame for the extraordinary diversity of their technical instructions. Cicero's faculties of invention *(inventio*, the finding of arguments) and disposition *(dispositio*, the arrangement into parts of the—usually juridical—text) address tasks of instruction, *docere*. Yet, disposition, into preface *(exordium)*, narration *(narratio*, or setting out of the case), confirmation and disputation *(confirmatio* and *disputatio*, the positive and negative arguments for the case), and peroration *(peroratio*, conclusion) makes a place for *movere* as well; the *exordium* and *peroratio* offer the great opportunities for moving the affects. In the long tradition, invention and judgment *(judicium)* encompass the skills of finding arguments and critically establishing them as valid. Here Aristotle reveals an archetypical rhetorical complexity. Although it is possible to see Aristotle, in making rhetoric the counterpart *(antistrophe)* of dialectic (1354a), as providing a rationalist account of rhetoric as argument, it is more accurate to see him as proffering a continuum of modes of suasion, ranging from the most rigorous to the most relaxed. He claims that there are three sorts of "proof" or means of establishing belief *(pistis): ethos,* those establishing the speaker's character; *pathos,* those appealing to the audience's deeply held convictions or affects; and *logos,* those establishing the veridical in the text. But, Aristotle calls the *enthymeme,* or rhetorical syllogism, the body *(soma)* of all three proofs; and the concern with audience dominates. Both Quintilian and Aristotle call the enthymeme a defective, because only two-part, syllogism; the enthymeme constrains the audience to supply the defect, the third part, either major or minor premise, or conclusion. Thus, the enthymeme is more powerfully audience-oriented than the logical syllogism because it draws the audience into participation and pleasure (Aristotle, 1991, 1400b). Further, the Aristotelian commonplaces *(koinoi topoi)* have a rich historical development in rhetorical and dialectical manuals. These both map and give access to the intersubjectively held beliefs of audience and speaker. The topics are both the bins or spaces that contain lines of argument ("the more and the less") and the contents (the precepts contained—"virtue exceeds pleasure as goal"). The maxims as content require the example *(paradigma* or *exemplum)* as illustration or instantiation in the rhetorician's inductive appeal to a particular audience. There is a strong relation between rhetorical invention and skeptical inquiry, brought out in Cicero's *Academica.* The argument on both sides of the question *(in utramque partem)* is both primary skeptical tactic, according to Sextus Empiricus, and basic to rhetoric, where it is, again, audience-oriented. In rhetorical training, argument on both sides, deemed immoral by the philosophers, is an exercise in anticipating, countering, and replacing audience beliefs.

Under Cicero's competence of elocution *(elocutio)* are gathered all the skills and elements of what is called style. In modern rhetoric, elocution *is* rhetoric: the prolix lists of tropes and figures of premodernity now constitute a rhetorical epistemology as well as rhetorical technique, heavily elaborated in the *Rhétorique générale* of the Groupe Mu. *Elocutio* is associated with the task of *delectare* and *movere* in Roman rhetoric, but, again, the concept of continuum must be evoked; Quintilian, in his masterly accounts of books 8 and 9, distinguishes between trope and figure, and then between figures of speech and figures of thought. This account, with its plethora of terms, maps in great detail an area of connections and disjunctions, parallelisms and contrasts, that enable the rhetorician to use language in innovative, powerful, and pleasing ways. Repetitions and contrasts of sounds and rhythm, as well as the conjunctions and distinctions of metaphor, metonymy, synecdoche, and irony, and the distinctions and connections of argument, enforce

eloquential power. In a seventeenth-century text, amplification *(amplificatio)* is the rubric for moving the affects, yet it is defined simply as an extension or intensification of argument. The same criterion controls the employment of argumentative example and of stylistic figure: both require vividness, lifelikeness.

Cicero's pronunciation *(pronuntiatio)* is the competence of bodily gesture *(gestus, actio)* as well as oral delivery, and is strongly associated with the goal of *movere.* Once again, psychological continuum motivates: the body represents the soul of the orator, the visage bespeaks his mind. The rhetorical program requires here, too, a discipline of decorum, lest extremes of pride or humility in external signs subvert the verbal performance. In the Renaissance and early modernity, very elaborate treatises detail every minute adjustment of the body and voice; every posture or sound is assigned oratorical meaning, and decorum of gesture and voice is a primary value.

Cicero's skill of memory *(memoria)* is a competence most pertinent to an oral culture, which requires spontaneity and quickness of argumentative and stylistic invention and response. The Renaissance, again, proffers a rich development of treatises on the arts of memory. Excellence in memory is psychologically defined, visually stipulated in the early Latin treatise the *Rhetorica ad Herrenium.* Memory stores and makes available the phantasmata of the imagination, which may be the product of external sensation. Sensible pictures, the visual images of buildings and landscapes, provide the organizational frame for this storage and retrieval.

Rhetoric, Poetics, Criticism. Of course, the figures of rhetoric are important in poetry as well as in prose, and the figures of sound, of repetition and rhythmic emphasis are essential. Quintilian offers a merely technical distinction between poetry and prose: prose is freer, less constrained by patterns of sound and rhythm. Quintilian's metaphor is that of prose eloquence as a broad, free-flowing river, poetry as a channeled stream, controlled by sharply formed banks (V,xiv,33). In Quintilian's encyclopedic education, the early, grammatical stages of the orator's formation include training in *enarratio,* in the critical reading of the great poetic, historical, and moral works in order to distinguish and internalize aesthetic as well as moral value. Indeed, his book 10 prescribes a continuous task of reading and rereading as necessary to the development of a sense of value and goal in private as well as public discursive performance. Rhetoric is an enduring source of moral-aesthetic formulas in criticism; Quintilian's definition of the orator as a good man experienced in speaking ("vir bonus dicendi peritus") (ibid., XII,i,1) roots eloquence, speaking well, in virtuous posture. Most important, however, rhetorical canons and values furnish the basic vocabulary for poetics and for criticism and appreciation of literature and the fine arts through early modernity. Thus, the goal of *enargeia, illustratio,* or vividness in representation, informs visual as well as verbal arts. This rhetorical vocabulary—such as seriousness *(gravitas),* charm *(venustas),* copiousness *(copia)*—persists beyond the Renaissance in treatises on art. It must be stressed that many of these canons of beauty and excellence—harmony *(harmonia),* accord *(convenientia),* the golden mean or moderation *(mediocritas)*—derive from the hegemonic rhetorical canon of decorum.

Continuity and Change in the Rhetorical Tradition. The history of rhetoric is marked not simply by the continuous development of formulas, but by the enduring contestation of its claims to value by philosophy. Whether one follows Cicero's and Aristotle's account of the origins of rhetoric in the instruction in legal pleading of Corax and Tisias after the fall of the Sicilian tyrants or agrees with modern historical narratives that stipulate the advent of Athenian democracy and the ensuing activity in legislative and legal arenas as creating a demand for Sophistic instruction in public discursive performance, the connection between rhetorical competence and civic identity defines rhetoric against philosophy. For Jacqueline de Romilly (1992), Sophistic rhetoric and Plato's antagonist Gorgias are exemplary, engaged in the task of forming civic theory as well as practice; similarly, Eugene Garver (1994) argues that Aristotle's *Rhetoric* is primarily a handbook on discursive action for politicians. This emphasis coheres with Cicero's account in the *Brutus,* which maps the decline of eloquence onto the decline of the Roman republic, and with Quintilian's project, which assumes the absence of political possibility, and designs an encyclopedic education for a Roman elite, still engaged in the public domain of the law but engaged as well, or primarily, in a lifelong task of moral-aesthetic formation and self-fulfillment in discursive as well as intellectual performance. Quintilian illustrates one of the important, but elided, continuities of rhetoric, for the generation of texts and the analysis of texts are not two separate roles, but two sides of a single competence; there is no disjunction between criticism and performance in the rhetorical student or the finished orator. Yet, modern critics must note a nonreciprocity: one may analyze the rhetoric of any text but need not presuppose conscious rhetorical program in generation.

In the Middle Ages, the early patristic, preeminently Augustinian, appropriation of rhetoric for biblical exegesis and ecclesiastical homiletics and apologetics was a striking innovation. John O. Ward (1995) argues that, contrary to modern notions of medieval impoverishment, the Middle Ages was a time of enlargement and elaboration of rhetorical technical instruction in a very wide range of functions: in arts of bureaucratic and commercial communication *(ars dictaminis),* in arts of preaching *(ars predicandi),* in arts of praying *(ars precandi),* and in arts of poetry *(ars poetria).* Because rhetorical theory and practice are organized in specific handbooks for these functions, there is a general diffusion of rhetorical canons and values through a wide range of cultural practices.

In the Renaissance, the Italian humanists of the fourteenth and fifteenth centuries are the first to return to the task of elaborating a Ciceronian and Quintilianesque adult rhetorical formation. In part, this is a strong reaction against the dysfunction of a scholastic formation, an assemblage of university discursive genres and of topics, a formation that the humanists see as ignoring, or impertinent to, both the familiar, intimate moral domain and the political needs of the new Renaissance elites. There is, then, a general revival of rhetoric as the art dominating grammar and dialectic in the trivium, a strong rhetorical defense of poetry, a reconnection of rhetoric and politics in civic humanism, and a rhetorical contribution to the hermeneutical skills of philology. In the sixteenth century, there are strong pedagogical developments for these new elites that consist, by and large, in the rearranging of the relations of dialectic and rhetoric in instructive and investigative modes. A major strategy is to collapse rhetorical and dialectical interests in argument into dialectic, as a simple technical formation; this has the effect of splitting off *elocutio* or style as the primary, even only, rhetorical interest.

In early modernity, this reduction of rhetoric to a concern with style considered as "mere" ornament is abetted by the Cartesian innovations in psychology. The strong intrusion of rationalist and mechanist models, the power of the new psychology that purveys a dualism of mind and body, subverts the classical psychology of continuum, and thus disallows the claims of rhetorical engagement across the board and relegates rhetoric to an inferior, impure realm of frivolous activity. This subversion endures in the modernist account that stipulates rhetoric as a subordinate, merely complicitous, skill.

In part as a continuation of Friedrich Nietzsche's revisionist approach to the classics, however, there are, in the twentieth century, a variety of modes of revival of rhetorical interests and values. The "new rehabilitation of the Sophists" in classical scholarship functions as well as a rehabilitation of rhetoric as competence in civil theory and practice. To some extent, all positive modern initiatives can be seen as acts of retrieval of classical rhetorical problematic. They are not simply retrievals, however. The anti-Cartesianism that informs recent philosophical revision informs rhetorical revision as well, for the new rhetorical theory does not simply restate classical continuum, but is sharply, polemically, antidualist. Thus, Chaim Perelman (1969) attempts to undo the Cartesian subversion of rhetoric, by focusing on epideictic as the central genre, with a task of creating through praise and blame "adhesion of spirits" to the intersubjectively held values that form political and social identity, a goal that transcends mere referential translucence. This moment contests, then, another modern revisionism, that of the Groupe Mu or of Paul de

Man as first, an acceptance and systematization of the late-Renaissance reduction of rhetoric to style, and, indeed, to metaphor, and second, as complicitous with a Cartesian solipsism in epistemology, subversively apolitical. Further, the new rhetorical hermeneutics is more than a Foucauldian effort to restore to the text its character as event, to reconstruct the vital speaker–text–audience relation. Claims for the importance of recognizing rhetorical argumentative and figurative strategies in the texts of inquiry in general are based on the pervasiveness and inclusiveness of rhetorical modes of appeal. When Michel Meyer (1993), a paradigmatic contemporary theorist, asserts that rhetoric flourishes where ideologies fail, he argues that the rhetorical concern with audience reveals a deep commitment to question/response formations as more fundamental than concepts of referentiality in discursive exchange, a commitment that structures political rhetoric. Meyer refers to Martin Heidegger's lectures on Aristotle's *Rhetoric* of 1924, where Heidegger argues that the emotions constitute the social, and passions ground politics. Because the passions constitute difference, the preoccupation with the passions distinguishes rhetorical from philosophical formation; where philosophy seeks identity, intellectual closure in its arguments, rhetoric, committed to movement, emotion, deals with difference. This insistence on rhetoric as preeminently a political skill recalls the originary classical position, but also marks in rhetoric a resistance to systemic closure; rhetoric aims at specific victories, perhaps, but not closure. Finally, Meyer, like all strong rhetorical theorists, explicates and insists on continuities. There is a vital, self-conscious engagement of bodily, sensitive capacities; *aisthēsis* is folded into the account of rhetorical competence. Or, command of the range of discursive techniques associated with rhetoric requires mastery of what Klaus Dockhorn (1966) calls *pathosanthropologie*, an anthropology of the passions.

BIBLIOGRAPHY

Aristotle. *On Rhetoric: A Theory of Civic Discourse.* Translated by George A. Kennedy. New York and Oxford, 1991.

Augustine. *On Christian Doctrine.* Translated by D. W. Robertson, Jr. New York, 1958.

Cicero. *De oratore.* 3 vols. Translated by E. W. Sutton and H. Rackham. Loeb Classical Library. Cambridge, Mass., 1942.

Cicero. *Brutus.* Translated by G. L. Hendrickson. *Orator.* Translated by H. M. Hubbell. Loeb Classical Library. Cambridge, Mass., 1952.

Conley, Thomas M. *Rhetoric in the European Tradition.* Reprint, Chicago, 1994.

Dockhorn, Klaus. Review of Hans-Georg Gadamer, *Wahrheit und Methode. Göttingische Gelehrte Anzeigen* 218.3–4 (1966): 169–206.

Garver, Eugene. *Aristotle's Rhetoric: An Art of Character.* Chicago, 1994.

Groupe Mu. *Rhétorique générale.* Paris, 1970.

Meyer, Michel. *Questions de rhétorique: langage, raison et séduction.* Paris, 1993.

Nietzsche, Friedrich. *Friedrich Nietzsche on Rhetoric and Language.* Edited and translated by Sander L. Gilman, Carole Blair, and David J. Parent. New York and Oxford, 1989.

Ong, Walter J. *Ramus, Method and the Decay of Dialogue: From the Art of Discourse to the Art of Reason.* Cambridge, Mass., 1958.

Perelman, Chaim, and L. Olbrechts-Tyteca. *The New Rhetoric: A Treatise on Argumentation.* Translated by John Wilkinson and Purcell Weaver. Notre Dame, Ind., 1969.

[Pseudo-Cicero]. *Rhetorica ad Herennium.* Translated by Harry Caplan. Loeb Classical Library. Cambridge, Mass., 1989.

Quintilian. *Institutio oratoria.* 4 vols. Translated by H. E. Butler. Loeb Classical Library. Cambridge, Mass., 1921–1922.

Romilly, Jacqueline de. *The Great Sophists in Periclean Athens.* Translated by Janet Lloyd. Oxford, 1992.

Ward, John O. *Ciceronian Rhetoric in Treatise, Scholion, and Commentary.* Turnhout, Belgium, 1995.

NANCY S. STRUEVER

Exemplarity

Exemplarity may be defined as a form of argument and persuasion where a particular instance supports a general conclusion. Although the instance is typically narrative (historical or fictive), it need not be explicitly rendered: allusion to a name or a relevant feature suffices. What constitutes exemplarity is not the case or instance as such but a feature extracted from it, a feature "drawing its meaning from the controlling generality" (Lyons, 1989). In this sense, exemplarity involves not so much a discursive entity to be studied analytically as a hermeneutical practice, a practice that is integral to many kinds of discourse—literary, ethical, juridical, political. In the context of literature, example is not itself a genre but serves as a central component of genres where an aesthetic appeal is interwoven with a pragmatic—parable, fable, novella, *roman à thèse,* essay, sermon.

In rhetorical terms, the goal of example is not proof but persuasion and illustration, the latter in the sense of making visible, showing forth (cf. Latin *evidentia, ex + videre*). The persuasive or didactic use of example is often designed to mask its contingent status by invoking some basis in authority or tradition. But, in another sense, it is this very contingency, the irreducible particularity of example, that contributes to its cognitive capacity. Its intermediate status—both inside and outside the rule or truth exemplified—allows it to serve as a discovery tool, a means of testing the applicability of truth claims.

Whatever is designated as example functions as a nexus for convergent interrogations: What is it an example of? To whom is the example directed? What makes it "exemplary"? Consistent with its etymology (Latin *eximere*), example implies an excision, a sampling cut out of an entity. There is a vector back to a source, the whole from which the example derives. In this sense, example operates in a heuristic manner, opening up a generality and extracting constitutive features. But there is also a vector in the other direction—to an addressee, an agency for whom the example has been prepared. The pragmatic force of the example—its didactic or prescriptive function—has traditionally been associated not so much with the enunciation of truths or rules as with the construction of models to be imitated. Example thus turns into exemplar. One can appreciate from this why, in the system of ancient rhetoric, the function of pictorial realization, *imago,* was closely linked to the structure of exemplum (Barthes, 1985).

From early Greek thought, the offering of examples has been both approved of and disdained. A primary goal of Homeric epic was to provide exemplars, paradigms of experience and judgment, for aristocratic education and culture. Such models from the mythic tradition may have served as a basis for the Ideas or absolute forms of Platonic philosophy, as Werner Jaeger (1945) has suggested, but in the process the status of the exemplar was subject to change. In Plato's *Euthyphro,* Socrates challenges his interlocutor not to list particular cases but "to tell me what is the essential form *[paradeigma]* of holiness which makes all holy actions holy." Aristotle, however, in both his ethics and his rhetorical theory, stressed the inductive function of example, how the gathering and linking of particular instances can bring about a conclusion, whether in the context of judgment or of persuasion. The practical wisdom at the heart of Aristotelian ethics, Martha C. Nussbaum (1990) has argued, involves the distillation of an immensely complex fabric of particulars, a fabric that could not be derived from any rule or generality. In this sense, moral choice requires the kind of "attentiveness to particulars in all their contextual embededness" (Nussbaum, 1990) that, in the modern era, can be found in certain novels, biographies, and other narrative forms.

Whenever an example is invoked as support for a general proposition, what is claimed implicitly is that its validity, its "exemplarity," will be self-evident. But just how is this validation realized? If by way of the example, then it can hardly serve as conclusive support for the general proposition, because the example would be taken primarily on its own terms, as an isolate, singular instance. If, on the other hand, the validation is to be achieved at the level of the generality, this would require an act of stipulation or imposition, which exceeds the logical framework, because the general proposition has not yet been authenticated. "Can any example ever truly fit a general proposition?" Paul de Man asks. "Is not its particularity, to which it owes the illusion of its intelligibility, necessarily a betrayal of the general truth it is supposed to support and convey?" (1984).

Within a relatively homogeneous culture such as that of medieval Christianity, the illustrative function of example will typically tend toward the performative. What might seem to be simply a demonstration of a principle or truth assumes, in such a context, the force of a directive. The medieval exemplum, Larry Scanlon writes,

> illustrates a moral because what it recounts is the enactment of that moral. . . . [It] is not a purely textual exchange between

two discursive genres, the narrative and the interpretive, in which the narrative supports some proverb-like interpretation. In its narrative the exemplum reenacts the actual, historical embodiment of communal value in a protagonist or an event, and then, in its moral, effects the value's reemergence with the obligatory force of moral law.   (1994)

But this does not mean that the form of exemplum in medieval usage followed a single pattern. The invocation of great individuals and notable occurrences *(exempla maiorum)* characteristic of classical (Ciceronian) rhetoric coexisted with a more popular sermonizing style that featured instances typical of the quotidian experience of the congregation. This latter type, labeled "paraestenic Everymanexemplum" by Peter von Moos, was the staple of diverse kinds of popular predication and religious instruction. At the same time, "historical-inductive exempla were always a basic constituent of the culture of aristocratic courts: as a form of diversion, of dynastic self-legitimation, of ethical training for rulers and functionaries, or as pragmatic initiation into worldly practices and strategies" (Moos, 1988).

The authority of historical models in ancient and medieval culture, as expressed in the Ciceronian motto "historia magistra vitae," was based on a conception of history in which criteria of age and established authority far outweighed a modern sense of probability and verifiability.

> In the daily life of the Middle Ages, the past was clearly more directly present and operative than in the modern era; but knowledge about the past was not yet governed, as is the case now, by an underlying conception of evolution and change. The first point can help us understand the extraordinarily vast range of applicability granted to the *historical* example; the second explains why it is so difficult to separate, in terms of a pragmatic perspective, the historical example from the *fictional.*
> (Gumbrecht, 1986)

Within the institution of literature, the example is most readily associated with the fable, the novella, and certain forms of the novel. In the fable, the example is intended to support something like a general truth, often expressed as maxim or *sententia,* whereas in more elaborated genres, such as the novel, one often finds mutually reflective narrative elements where one might be posited as providing the truth factor, the signified, and others then serve as illustrative instances.

The proximity of exemplum to fable—already noted by Aristotle—is instructive. Both fable and exemplum orient a narrative core in terms of a larger, systematic whole. But, as Karlheinz Stierle notes, fable does so by presenting the general *as* a singular instance, thus in a sense allegorizing the instance. In the exemplum, on the other hand, the moral is, as it were, implied *in* the particular, and for this the narrative instance is required. Thus, exemplum

> is a form of expansion and reduction all in one—expansion as regards its underlying maxim, reduction as regards a story from

which is extracted and isolated that which the speech action of the exemplum needs in order to take on a concrete form. . . . [U]nderlying the unity of the whole is the "purpose" of the exemplum, the moral precept.   (Stierle, 1979)

Insofar as the exemplum is in the service of doctrine or ideology, the congruence of narrative and moral conclusion is anticipated and unchallenged. But a narrative may be taken in ways that exceed any single conclusion. "The example, it seems to me," says a character in Johann Wolfgang Goethe's *Die Wahlverwandtschaften* (The Elective Affinities), "doesn't exactly fit our case," and this could be said of any example. The fit of an example is dependent on the mode of extraction or, to draw on the terminology of speech-act theory, its performative force is a function of the uptake.

When the joining of an example with a rule or general principle proves to be questionable, the example, far from serving as validation or illustration, becomes a means of testing or challenging the applicability of any truth claim. This can be evidenced in the uses of *mashal* (signifying both example and parable in the Jewish tradition of midrash [see Boyarin, 1995]) or in various types of fable. In Jean de La Fontaine's *Fables,* one reads:

L'exemple est un dangereux leurre:
Tous les mangeurs de gens ne sont pas grands seigneurs;
Où la guêpe a passé, le moucheron demeure. (Book 2, no. 16)

[The example can be a dangerous bait: Those who would be man-eaters may not be such great personages; where the wasp has slipped through, the flea gets caught.]

In the postmedieval period, the exemplum gives way to diverse forms of exemplarity—in the Renaissance tale and novella (Geoffrey Chaucer, Giovanni Boccaccio, Marguerite de Navarre), in the essay (Michel de Montaigne), in political philosophy (Niccolò Machiavelli). What is common to all these is a problematization of the exemplum model whereby the narrative element comes to occupy an oblique relation to a stated or implied precept.

Machiavelli, Nancy S. Struever writes, "compels the sharing of unwanted knowledge." The reader is drawn into "a hypothetical exchange of dialogic counters, tokens. . . . Each exchange implicates, making the reader complicitous in the handling of the tokens" (1992). For Montaigne, "Le Dire est autre chose que le faire" (saying is quite another thing from doing), and it is in this gap, "the *écart,* or disjunction between the model and recognized norms of human behavior" (Nichols, 1995), that Montaigne engages in the work of exemplification in the *Essays.*

What comes to the fore in these instances is the way that example is capable of entangling the reader, engaging him to account for the discrepancy, the bad fit between particular and universal. Montaigne's "Tout exemple cloche" (Every example limps) is evoked by Thomas Keenan when he writes: "Responsibility begins in the bad example: one could even say that the only good example, the only one worthy of the imitation, interiorization, and identification that the example calls for, is the bad example" (1995). The "bad example" has the effect of foregrounding the mode of address, of interpellation, that inheres in the form. Commenting on Horace's dictum, "mutato nomine de te fabula narratur" (with a change of names, the fable is told about you), Keenan writes, "We are addressed in the fable under what can only be a pseudonym. . . . And the other is, among others, you" (ibid.)

Although exemplarity was conceived primarily in rhetorical terms from antiquity to the Renaissance, in the modern era it has been incorporated in various theoretical constructs, for example, of aesthetics, logic, and language. This is well illustrated in Immanuel Kant's philosophy, which both devalues and revalues exemplarity.

The issue emerges at various points in Kant's philosophy. In the *Critique of Pure Reason,* he distinguishes between the understanding, as the faculty concerned with formulating and grasping rules or principles, and judgment *(Urteilskraft),* whose special function consists in the application of rules, or more precisely, of *subsuming* particular cases under a rule in order to determine "whether a case falls under it in concreto." This is "a particular talent that cannot be studied but only practiced *[geübt]*" (Kant, 1956, p. A133). Kant likens it to a native, ingrained wit, *Mutterwitz.* In a theoretical sense, the status of examples is accessory, prosthetic. Kant refers to them as training wheels, a child's walker for the judgment ("Gängelwagen der Urteilskraft"). A given example in its particularity is replaceable. But it is only by way of examples that general principles can be activated and applied. Examples are thus both secondary and, for heuristic purposes, necessary. There can be no rules for the application of rules, and thus the "singular and great use of examples [is] that they sharpen the judgment" (ibid., p. A134).

In the *Critique of Judgment,* examples assume a primary and irreducible function in justifying the basis of evaluation, of judgment itself. What is at issue is the capacity of judgment "to think the particular as contained under the universal." The realization of the universal rule by way of example does not lead to an abstract, reified sense of a universal, but rather to "the means whereby the rule regulates diverse instances within a circle of possible applications" (Buck, 1967).

Kant's analysis of the work of art—more properly, of the *experience* of art—proceeds by way of a revision of key concepts such as taste, beauty, pleasure *(Wohlgefallen),* and common sense *(sensus communis).* Kant's approach was not to focus on *what* evokes an aesthetic response, but rather to inquire why it cannot be objectified or conceptualized independent of the experience itself. Aesthetic judgment takes its point of departure in the particular case and then needs to find a more general basis for assigning value. The analysis of what makes the judgment reflective—turned on itself and drawing its standard of judgment from the example of its own operation—is designed to demonstrate an outgoing, creative facet of the mind's "response."

This subjective experience, which may at the same time serve as the basis of an act of judgment, is curious: it is not altogether "cognitive" in that it does not operate on the basis of a *theoretical cognition* related to a priori concepts of nature (Kant, 1987, Introduction). Yet, it does "cognize" what it itself feels. This form of cognition operates not in terms of the a priori of nature, but by deriving validation from its own pleasure or displeasure.

Kant conceived the reflective judgment as a way of establishing a form of generality or finality that is neither apodictic (derived from a rule) nor empirical (based on experience), but "only *exemplary*," defining it as "the necessity of the agreement of *all* [men] in a judgment that can be considered as example for a general rule that cannot be stated" (ibid., section 18). Exemplarity here involves a principle of universal validity *(Gemeinsinn)* that serves as a basis for the communicability of cognitive data. The "general rule that cannot be stated" signifies not a hidden or inaccessible truth but the *positing* of such a generality as the condition for predication and communicability. Although the standard invoked here may be "a merely ideal norm" (ibid., section 22), it serves as the necessary bridge between subjective judgments of taste and any general standard of aesthetic value.

This *projection* of a (universal) principle that cannot be stated but only postulated is predicated on "a formalization of the particular" (Lloyd, 1995) Thus, an appeal to common sense is an appeal to example not only specifically (to an instantiation) but generically, to the very structure that underwrites common sense. "This paradoxical demand is rooted in the first place in the problem of a common sense that is at once the a priori foundation of taste *and* its product" (ibid.).

Kant's focus on the structure of judgment is designed to underwrite the continual need to judge even in light of the relative indeterminacy of available criteria, whether at the level of aesthetics ("Is it beautiful?") or of ethics ("Is it right?"). Far from being unconsidered or merely intuitive, the Kantian reflective judgment operates in terms of a projective-reflexive loop, invoking a "general rule that cannot be stated." Exemplarity here assumes a quite different valence than it had in a rhetorical context. In Kant, as in other modern thinkers, the focus is not so much on the modeling function, the example as exemplar, but rather on its paradoxical but indispensable role in an evaluative praxis.

Although the rule or law as such resists formulation, its point (or *pointing*) may be deduced from what has been termed a "symbolization . . . through permutations of instances" (Lyotard, 1991). It is in Ludwig Wittgenstein's *Philosophical Investigations* that one finds a sustained reflec-

tion on the effect of a series, the tendency or "drift" that multiple instances set into motion. "You give him examples,—but he has to guess their drift" (Wittgenstein, 1958). Wittgenstein focuses on practices rather than foundations, rules being taken primarily as "signposts" along a path. They may be limiting but are not mandatory or prohibitive in any absolute sense. One can always not follow a rule, though one may pay for it. At the same time, any instance of a rule in practice can raise questions as to how it is to be taken, what application it has in a given case.

The true test of a rule, for Wittgenstein, is how it is acted on, what practice it gives rise to, but our need to supply cognitive validation, to *know* what the rule means, draws us repeatedly into a mode of interpretation, an effort to formulate how the rule fits the case at hand. What Wittgenstein stresses is the sense of the indetermination of rule in relation to the act of judgment. Example brings together a model and a directive. Nothing guarantees that a reception, an "uptake" in J. L. Austin's (1975) sense, will come out right. Nor need the form of the uptake be precisely calibrated. But as example, the particular is projected beyond itself, not so much toward a formulable rule, a universal, as toward what Wittgenstein termed "a form of life"; and in the process, rules of a kind are repeatedly invoked and displaced.

Lyotard has put forward a conception of postmodern art under the aegis of the sublime that derives from a dialectization of exemplarity in the sense of Theodor W. Adorno's negative dialectics. In order to rescue the example from the universalizing drift of the concept, of speculative thought, Adorno envisaged a kind of "micrological activity" that would give voice to what lay immanent in objects:

> Only a philosophy in fragment form would give their proper place to the monads, those illusory idealistic drafts. They would be conceptions, in the particular, of the totality that is inconceivable as such. . . . The call for binding statements without a system is a call for thought-models *[Denkmodellen]*, and these are not merely monadological in kind. A model covers the specific, and more than the specific, without letting it evaporate in its more general covering concept.
>
> (1973)

Lyotard's postmodern sublime represents an application of Adorno's call for a fragmented, "micrological" mode of thought. What Edmund Burke and Kant identified as the sublime may now be understood, according to Lyotard, as an adumbration of the avant-garde's terror of the void, of the insistent and unanswerable "Is it happening?" ("Arrive-t-il?") that denotes a response to art no longer guided by the aesthetic norms of beauty or taste. What Enlightenment thinkers diagnosed as a breach of those norms, the sublime, "outlined a world of possibilities for artistic experiments in which the avant-gardes would later trace out their paths. . . . The art-object no longer bends itself to models, but tries to present the fact that there is an unpresentable" (Lyotard, 1991).

Lyotard's "presentation of an unpresentable" as a distinguishing feature of postmodern art parallels what Kant analyzed as the failure of the imagination in relation to the sublime, its incapacity to realize by way of representation or figuration experiences of overwhelming magnitude or power, of the sublime. Although for Kant this incapacity served as a kind of negative warrant of an Absolute, Lyotard's "Is it happening?" may be taken as emblematic of the exemplarity of postmodern art, of its insistent, ongoing interrogation of the very possibility of art.

The difficulty of defining or circumscribing the topic of exemplarity is that it is not a formal entity, like a trope or a genre, but rather a constituent of a variety of rhetorical and hermeneutical practices, part of the back-and-forth between part and whole, though never simply an instance of a universal or the application of a rule. It lies not in the particular instance nor in any governing principle but in the oscillation that puts into question, that *imposes* the question of their mutual determination. As illustration, the example is like the *illustrandum* (that which is illustrated), but not altogether, because a sign cannot exemplify itself. Thus, there always needs to be another feature, distinct from illustration, that marks the example, singles it out as emblem of something sought. Exemplarity constitutes a breach in discourse, an opening that exposes an inside to an outside, a particular to a universal, but always with the possibility that the particular will be inassimilable to any universality of meaning.

[*See also* Kant.]

BIBLIOGRAPHY

Adorno, Theodor W. *Negative Dialectics.* Translated by E. B. Ashton. New York, 1973.
Aristotle. *On Rhetoric: A Theory of Civic Discourse.* Translated by George A. Kennedy. New York and Oxford, 1991.
Austin, J. L. *How to Do Things with Words.* Cambridge, Mass., 1975.
Barthes, Roland. "L'ancienne rhétorique." In *L'Aventure sémiologique,* pp. 85–165. Paris, 1985.
Boyarin, Daniel. "Take the Bible for Example: Midrash as Literary Theory." In *Unruly Examples: On the Rhetoric of Exemplarity,* edited by Alexander Gelley, pp. 27–47. Stanford, Calif., 1995.
Buck, Günther. *Lernen und Erfahrung: Zum Begriff der didaktischen Induktion.* Stuttgart, 1967.
de Man, Paul. "Aesthetic Formalization: Kleist's *Über das Marionettentheater.*" In *The Rhetoric of Romanticism,* pp. 263–290. New York, 1984.
Derrida, Jacques. "Parergon." In *The Truth in Painting,* translated by Geoff Bennington and Ian McLeod, pp. 15–147. Chicago, 1987.
Gelley, Alexander. "The Pragmatics of Exemplary Narrative." In *Unruly Examples: On the Rhetoric of Exemplarity,* edited by Alexander Gelley, pp. 142–161. Stanford, Calif., 1995.
Gumbrecht, Hans-Ulrich. "Menschliches Handeln und göttliche Kosmologie: Geschichte als Exempel." In *La littérature historiographique des origines à 1500,* edited by Hans Ulrich Gumbrecht et al., Grundriss der Romanischen Literaturen des Mittelalters, pp. 869–950. Heidelberg, 1986.
Hampton, Timothy. *Writing from History: The Rhetoric of Exemplarity in Renaissance Literature.* Ithaca, N.Y., 1990.
Harvey, Irene. "Derrida and the Issues of Exemplarity." In *Derrida: A Critical Reader,* edited by David Wood, pp. 193–217. Oxford and Cambridge, Mass., 1992.
Jaeger, Werner. *Paideia: The Ideals of Greek Culture.* 3 vols. Translated by Gilbert Highet. 2d ed. New York and Oxford, 1945.
Kant, Immanuel. *Critique of Pure Reason* (1781). Translated by Norman Kemp Smith. Reprint, London, 1956.
Kant, Immanuel. *Critique of Judgment* (1790). Translated by Werner S. Pluhar. Indianapolis, 1987.
Keenan, Thomas. "Fables of Responsibility." In *Unruly Examples: On the Rhetoric of Exemplarity,* edited by Alexander Gelley pp. 121–141. Stanford, Calif., 1995.
Kosolleck, Reinhart. "*Historia Magistra Vitae:* The Dissolution of the Topos into the Perspective of a Modernized Historical Process." In *Futures Past: On the Semantics of Historical Time,* translated by Keith Tribe, pp. 21–38. Cambridge, Mass., 1985.
Lloyd, David. "Kant's Examples." In *Unruly Examples on the Rhetoric of Exemplarity* edited by Alexander Gelley pp. 255–276. Stanford, Calif, 1995.
Lyons, John D. *Exemplum: The Rhetoric of Example in Early Modern France and Italy.* Princeton, N.J., 1989.
Lyotard, Jean-François. *The Postmodern Condition: A Report on Knowledge.* Translated by Geoff Bennington and Brian Massumi. Minneapolis, 1984.
Lyotard, Jean-François. *The Inhuman: Reflections on Time.* Translated by Geoffrey Bennington and Rachel Bowlby. Stanford, Calif., 1991.
Nichols, Stephen G. "Example versus *Historia:* Montaigne, Erigena, and Dante." In *Unruly Examples on the Rhetoric of Exemplarity,* edited by Alexander Gelley, pp. 48–85. Stanford, Calif, 1995.
Nussbaum, Martha C. "The Discernment of Perception: An Aristotelian Conception of Private and Public Rationality." In *Love's Knowledge: Essays on Philosophy and Literature,* pp. 54–105. New York and Oxford, 1990.
"Paradigma." In *Historisches Wörterbuch der Philosophie,* edited by Joachim Ritter et al., vol. 7, col. 74–76. Basel, 1989.
Plato *Euthyphro.* In *The Collected Dialogues,* edited by Edith Hamilton and Huntington Cairns, pp. 170–185. New York, 1961.
Scanlon, Larry. *Narrative, Authority, and Power: The Medieval Exemplum and the Chaucerian Tradition.* Cambridge and New York, 1994.
Stierle, Karlheinz. "Story as Exemplum—Exemplum as Story: On the Pragmatics and Poetics of Narrative Texts." In *New Perspectives in German Literary Criticism,* edited by Richard E. Amacher and Victor Lange, pp. 389–417. Princeton, N.J., 1979.
Struever, Nancy S. *Theory as Practice: Ethical Inquiry in the Renaissance.* Chicago, 1992.
Moos, Peter. *Geschichte als Topik: Das rhetorische Exemplum von der Antike zur Neuzeit und die historiae im "Policraticus" Johanns von Salisbury.* Hildesheim and New York, 1988.
Suleiman, Susan Rubin. "'Exemplary' Narratives." In *Authoritarian Fictions: The Ideological Novel as a Literary Genre,* pp. 25–61. New York, 1983.
Warminski, Andrzej. "Reading for Example: 'Sense-Certainty' in Hegel's *Phenomenology of Spirit.*" In *Readings in Interpretation: Hölderlin, Hegel, Heidegger,* pp. 163–179. Minneapolis, 1987.
Wittgenstein, Ludwig. *Philosophical Investigations.* Translated by G. E. M. Anscombe. 3d ed. New York, 1958.

ALEXANDER GELLEY

RICHARDS, IVOR ARMSTRONG (1893–1979), one of the founders of modern literary criticism. Richards contributed to aesthetics, semantics, literary criticism, the theory of metaphor and translation, elementary reading and second-language training, and world literacy. In the decade following World War, I he published a series of works that ushered the age of analysis into the study of literature.

The third son of a Welsh chemical engineer, Richards was born in Sandbach, Cheshire. He entered Magdalene College, Cambridge, in 1911 and studied moral sciences under J. M. E. McTaggart, W. E. Johnson, and G. E. Moore, who exerted the strongest influence. After winning first-class honors in 1915 Richards succumbed to tuberculosis and spent the war years recuperating in the mountains of Wales, where he took up what became a lifelong sport, high mountaineering. In 1919 he began teaching the theory of criticism and contemporary novels in the new English School at Cambridge. He was appointed Lecturer in English and Moral Science by Magdalene in 1922 and Fellow in 1926, the year in which he was married to Dorothy Eleanor Pilley.

At the outset of his career, Richards rejected nineteenth-century historicism and biography, fin-de-siècle aesthetics, and abstract formalism. He attacked Roger Fry and Benedetto Croce, the one for blurring the distinction between aesthetic and scientific theory and for positing a specifically aesthetic emotion, the other for his idealist premises and his reduction of art to expression. Instead, Richards argued that truth is the "decisive notion" for both art and science, however differing are their modes of verification, and he defined six ways in which emotion enters art. *The Foundations of Aesthetics* (1922; coauthored by C. K. Ogden and James Wood) outlines sixteen theories of beauty ranging from objectivism and imitation to social usefulness and psychological wholeness. His preferred theory is "synaesthesis," which involves a full, disciplined engagement of the self, without a tendency to action. He distinguishes between an end state of equilibrium and harmony (where, in a state of heightened tension, the mind experiences the varied attitudes before it) and a mere oscillation of just two sides, or a deadlock, or an inflexible order.

A vast and many-sided project, *The Meaning of Meaning* (1923; coauthored by Ogden), has been called the best-known book on semantics ever written. Again, Richards performs a "multiple definition," analyzing twenty-two meanings of "meaning" (Richards's favorite book was the dictionary and 250 "multiple definitions" of key words can be found across his writings). Abstractions, universals, and concepts are taken as so much symbolic machinery—some useful as heuristic tools, the rest verbiage or "word magic." Combining American pragmatism and behaviorism with British philosophical psychology, his corrective theory begins with a Triangle of Interpretation, which subsequently became a common item in linguistics textbooks: symbol (e.g., a noun), reference (or thought), and referent. Words carry out jobs or functions; no utterance has its meaning alone, but only in a context, described in physical and psychological terms. One function is referential, the pointing to objective reality; a second is emotive, the conveyance of

feeling; a third, the expression of a sense of relation to an audience; a fourth, the attitude of the speaker to the object under discussion; a fifth, the overall intention of the utterance. Richards later enumerated seven functions, each more or less simultaneously present in a given utterance. At times, however, he spoke simply of two broad uses of language: "referential," exemplified by strict scientific or expository prose; and "emotive," conveying or stimulating feeling and attitude. His early emphasis on the emotive function and poetic form stemmed from his effort to counter an excessively message-oriented approach to literature, but, as the battle was won, his attention went increasingly to referential factors. His semantic theory anticipated developments in logical positivism.

Principles of Literary Criticism (1924) applies a psychological model and theories of value and communication to the analysis of literature. The poet's mind (and its representative, the poem) "outwits the force of habit" and presents "conciliations of impulses which in most minds are still confused, intertrammelled, and conflicting"; it has gone furthest in temporary conciliations—temporary because a fresh reading might result in a newly balanced poise—and exemplifies a central principle: a "growing order is the principle of the mind." In the lesser "poetry of exclusion," a writer eliminates the heterogeneous elements for the sake of a more easily won wholeness and closure. The highly valued "poetry of inclusion" wins its unity by embracing the broadest oppositions within its formal boundaries; contrary attitudes are not scarecrows but menacing alternatives. The poem creates an "equilibrium of opposed impulses." Irony is prized for widening the scope of a poem; it "consists in the bringing in of the opposite, the complementary impulses." Tragedy, greatest of the poetries of inclusion, is Richards's paradigmatic genre because it is "perhaps the most general, all-accepting, all-ordering experience known" and can "take anything into its organisation, modifying it so that it finds a place." Through the mid-1920s, Richards explored the nature of poetic ambiguity, which opens up linguistic complexities in a poem and prevents premature closure.

Often considered his masterpiece, *Practical Criticism* (1929) presents the results of an experiment in which Richards enlisted hundreds of students to interpret thirteen poems of varying quality. Four hundred responses (many as shocking as they are revealing) are examined and ten main obstacles in reading are identified: stock responses, irrelevant associations, doctrinal adhesion, inhibition, sentimentality, and so on. A poem is a blend of many meanings and linguistic functions, categorized under "sense," "feeling," "tone," and "intention." Tone, for example, includes the author and the narrator, their separate attitudes toward each other, toward the audience (real or fictitious), and toward the subject matter. Linguistic structures are broken down into smaller and smaller units, which can then be studied in relation to one another and to the whole. The poem allows for variant readings, while defending itself from misreading by contextual checks and controls. "Close reading" or contextualism, as the method also came to be known, had its precursors, but no one had ever proceeded so systematically with a micrological approach to language, nor endowed the method with such incisive theoretical depth, nor applied it so broadly and with such revolutionary results. One proof of the method was that it could deal with high modernist texts, some of the most difficult literature ever written. In the lecture hall—Richards was a spellbinding lecturer—he championed high modernism, and his influence hastened its acceptance by the academy. William Empson, Richards's pupil at Magdalene, employed the method in his epoch-making *Seven Types of Ambiguity* (1930). Richards also exerted a powerful impact on American New Criticism, of which he is the acknowledged "father," and which dominated the academic study of literature from the 1940s to the 1960s.

Practical Criticism is also concerned with the effects of literature on behavior, as well as the deleterious effects of the new communications media, propaganda, and "bad" art, a strong theme throughout Richards's career. In studies on "doctrine in poetry" and "sincerity," he questions how readers "translate" the import of writers whose beliefs and systems of thought have passed into history. One should not, he argues, suppress the problem by concentrating attention solely on formalist matters or historical reconstruction. Neither is suspension of belief (as commonly understood) a solution—pretending, say, to believe for a moment in Dante's angels, then to drop the belief. What great writers communicate ought to be assimilated by and modify the structure of the mind. Acceptance of the artistic import depends not on the object of belief, which may be disproved or superseded, but on the value of the feelings and attitudes associated with the belief. Although Richards expects preparatory work of "unremitting research and reflection" on a work of art, which in itself may settle the question of value, there remains the "technique" or "ritual" of sincerity and a pragmatic "backwash" effect of the poem over the long term. A supreme virtue of the critic and reader, "sincerity" is the feeling that comes from accepting and speaking truth, the deepening sense of inner coherence and stability.

In the 1930s, Richards elaborated on his theories. *Mencius on the Mind* (1932) contains multiple definitions of key words in Mencius's psychological vocabulary. *Coleridge on Imagination* (1934), reinterpreting a Romantic transcendental metaphysics in terms of applied psychology, refounds studies of Samuel Taylor Coleridge in the modern era. *Interpretation in Teaching* (1938) attempts for expository prose what *Practical Criticism* did for poetry. The most significant and influential work of this period lay in an original theory of metaphor propounded in *The Philosophy of Rhetoric* (1936). Traditionally, the two halves of a metaphor (the "image" and the "idea") were given unequal value: one side was treated as ornamental (often called the "metaphor"); the other contained "the meaning." By contrast, Richards grants parity to the two halves of the metaphoric copula; the metaphor is the whole double unit whose meaning is generated by the interactive process of a *tenor* ("underlying idea" or "principal subject") and a *vehicle* (what the principal subject is compared to, the "figure"); the *ground* is what they share in common. Tenor and vehicle bring their own contexts, not all parts of which become active, to the process that creates a metaphor; more often, what is *not* shared in common determines its effectiveness; and neither tenor nor vehicle go through the process unchanged. Metaphor is "a transaction between contexts."

In 1939, Richards left Cambridge to accept a position at Harvard and the task of developing methods for English language instruction. Teaching in China had convinced him of the potential benefits of audiovisual aids in the teaching of Basic English, an 850-word version of normal English designed by Ogden as an international auxiliary language. With Basic and expanded versions of it, he experimented for two decades applying the media to learning to read a first or second language, beginning with stick-figure drawings, filmstrip, record, tape, and moving on to television, video, cassette, and computer, as they became available. Devised in collaboration with Christine M. Gibson, his *Language through Pictures* series went into seven languages. He also translated such works as Homer's *Iliad* and Plato's *Republic* into expanded Basic so that learners could have invaluable works to read upon entering the new language.

Richards was University Professor at Harvard from 1944 to 1963. In his sixtieth year, he turned to writing poetry and published four collections as well as three verse plays. His humanist testament, *Beyond* (1974), explores relations between central human figures and their gods, from Homer, Plato, and the Book of Job to Dante and Percy Bysshe Shelley.

In 1974, Richards returned to Cambridge, England. In spring 1979, he was lecturing in China on the teaching of English as a second language when he fell seriously ill. He was taken back to Cambridge, where he died on 7 September.

[*See also* Literature, *article on* Literary Aesthetics; New Criticism; *and* Rhetoric.]

BIBLIOGRAPHY

Works by Richards

The Foundations of Aesthetics. Coauthored by C. K. Ogden and James Wood. London, 1922.
The Meaning of Meaning. Coauthored by C. K. Ogden. London, 1923.
Principles of Literary Criticism. London, 1924.
Science and Poetry. London, 1926.
Practical Criticism: A Study of Literary Judgment. London, 1929.

Mencius on the Mind: Experiments in Multiple Definition. London, 1932.
Coleridge on Imagination. London, 1934.
The Philosophy of Rhetoric. New York and Oxford, 1936.
Interpretation in Teaching. New York, 1938.
How to Read a Page. New York, 1942.
The Pocket Book of Basic English: A Self-Teaching Way into English. Coauthored by Christine M. Gibson. New York, 1945.
Speculative Instruments. Chicago, 1955.
So Much Nearer: Essays toward a World English. New York, 1968.
Internal Colloquies: Poems and Plays. New York, 1971.
Beyond. New York, 1973.
Complementarities: Uncollected Essays. Edited by John Paul Russo. Cambridge, Mass., 1976.
New and Selected Poems. Manchester, 1978.

Other Sources

Collini, Stefan. "On Highest Authority: The Literary Critic and Other Aviators in Early Twentieth-Century Britain." In *Modernist Impulses in the Human Sciences, 1870–1930,* edited by Dorothy Ross, pp. 152–169. Baltimore, 1995.
Hotopf, W. H. N. *Language, Thought, and Comprehension: A Case Study of the Writings of I. A. Richards.* London, 1965.
McCallum, Pamela. *Literature and Method: Towards a Critique of I. A. Richards, T. S. Eliot, and F. R. Leavis.* Dublin, 1983.
Needham, John. *"The Completest Mode": I. A. Richards and the Continuity of English Criticism.* Edinburgh, 1982.
Russo, John Paul. "A Bibliography (1919–1973)." In *I. A. Richards: Essays in His Honor,* edited by Reuben A. Brower, Helen Vendler, and John Hollander. New York, 1973.
Russo, John Paul. *I. A. Richards: His Life and Work.* Baltimore, 1989.
Schiller, Jerome P. *I. A. Richards' Theory of Literature.* New Haven, 1969.
Shusterman, Ronald. *Critique et poésie selon I. A. Richards: De la confiance au relativisme naissant.* Bordeaux, 1988.

JOHN PAUL RUSSO

RICHTER, FRIEDRICH. *See* Paul.

RICOEUR, PAUL (b. 1913), French philosopher. The tradition of phenomenological hermeneutics has had two principal representatives: Hans-Georg Gadamer (b. 1900), whose *Truth and Method* (1960) first defined the tradition, and Paul Ricoeur, author of major works extending the scope of the tradition, most notably *Freud and Philosophy: An Essay on Interpretation* (1965), *The Symbolism of Evil* (1960), *The Conflict of Interpretations* (1969), *The Rule of Metaphor* (1975), the three-volume *Time and Narrative* (1983–1985), and *Oneself as Another* (1990). Because the development of Ricoeur's thought has been unusually complex, driven at various points by the powerful influence of a wide array of thinkers—in addition to Gadamer and Martin Heidegger, Gabriel Marcel, Jacques Lacan, Claude Lévi-Strauss, and Jacques Derrida—this article will confine itself to a presentation of a summary account of Ricoeur's theory of interpretation as developed especially in the work of the 1970s and 1980s.

Gadamer's key hermeneutical insight, which distinguishes his position from that of the Romantic hermeneutic tradition, is that all interpretation involves of necessity an act of appropriation in which the object of interpretation is made "one's own" through the reader's endeavor to make sense of the text in the light of her personal experience. Thus, Gadamer insists on the autonomy of the text's meaning—on its freedom from the dictates of the author's intention and its perpetual availability for reinterpretation by new readers—and, by implication, on the legitimacy of varied readings of the same text. Although Ricoeur endorses Gadamer's claim that appropriation is an integral component of the interpretive act, he contends as well that Gadamer, in his eagerness to apply Heidegger's phenomenological insights to the interpretive problems of the human sciences, does not attend seriously enough to the *actual practices* of those disciplines. Thus, in trying to complete Gadamer's project, Ricoeur vows to "keep in contact with the disciplines which seek to practice interpretation in a methodical manner, and . . . resist the temptation to separate *truth,* characteristic of understanding, from the *method* put into operation by [the] disciplines which have sprung from exegesis" (1974, p. 11).

The problem that Ricoeur takes as central, then, is how to reintroduce the possibility of critically distinguishing between correct and incorrect interpretations of a text without sacrificing the Gadamerian insight that interpretation is essentially a matter of making the text "one's own." The first thing to be recognized, Ricoeur claims, is that certain important consequences follow from the text's independent existence as a written communication. Although it is true that the text belongs to us in the sense that it is addressed to us and must be appropriated, it is also true that the text is not ours—that it inevitably stands at a distance from us by virtue of its having a verbal structure that we (as readers) did not produce. This verbal structure establishes, Ricoeur claims, borrowing his terminology from J. L. Austin, the locutionary (or propositional) dimension of the text's meaning. Insofar as the text can be said to have a stable and re-identifiable sense, it is to be found here. But the meaning of the text has dimensions extending beyond the locutionary. These concern the author's intention and the effect that the text produces on its readers, and constitute, respectively, the illocutionary and perlocutionary dimensions of the text's meaning.

These three distinct dimensions of the text's meaning must still be seen as interrelated. What we take to be the author's intention must be consistent with the words that are actually on the page, for these were chosen by the author specifically in order to fulfill her intention. So too, only those personal appropriations—those perlocutions—can be considered correct that do justice to the actual propositional (locutionary) sense of the text; for, as an interpretation of the text in question, the implicit claims made about its meaning in our appropriation of it can be either correct or incorrect.

Corresponding to the three dimensions of textual meaning are three separate stages in the process of interpretation: explanation, understanding, and appropriation. Explanation is concerned with elucidating textual structure, understanding with the clarification of meaning (understood as the author's intention), and appropriation with the establishment of the text's significance for a particular reader. These three stages are passed through in succession, and the success of each depends on the correctness of what has been determined in the earlier stages. Only on the basis of an accurate explanation of textual structure can one hope to arrive at a proper understanding of the author's intention, and only when the author's intention has been correctly identified can one meaningfully appropriate the significance of the text for one's own life.

Given Gadamer's critique of the attempt to re-create the mind of the author, this may seem like a strange position for Ricoeur to adopt. But, in speaking of the "author's intention," he does not mean (quite) the flesh-and-blood author of the work in question. Rather, what he has in mind is, in a sense, the text itself understood as the product of an author. As he explains,

> rhetoric can escape the objection of falling back into the "intentional fallacy" . . . inasmuch as what it emphasizes is not the alleged creation process of the work but the techniques by means of which a work is made communicable. These techniques can be discerned in the work itself. The result is that the only type of author whose authority is in question here is not the real author, the object of biography, but the implied author.
>
> (1988, vol. 3, p. 160)

The author *is* the architect of the work in question, then, and the intention that interests us *did* govern the creation of the text, but that intention is to be discovered, not through psychological intuition, but through a painstaking stylistic examination of the text's structure.

Explanation appeals to the laws of grammar and the lexical values attached to the words of the text in establishing the prima facie legitimacy of some readings and simultaneously ruling out as illegitimate a great many others. But structural explanation cannot constitute the whole of interpretation, for, in restricting its focus to the self-enclosed system of differences and oppositions that is language, it fails to engage with the subject matter of the work. Understanding, in Ricoeur's estimation, as in Gadamer's, is a matter of entering into a dialogue with the text concerning its subject matter. What makes this dialogue possible, freeing the interpreter from the tyranny (the monologue) of a strictly univocal reading, is the surplus of meaning that attaches to all linguistic expressions word-length or longer.

Considered in isolation, individual words and expressions are sheer potential—mere sets of possible usages. Placed in juxtaposition within a sentence, however, individual words can no longer lay equal claim to all of their potential meanings; for, contextualized within the sentence, words screen out as inapplicable many of the potential meanings associated with their neighbors. Thus, the syntactic dimension of the sentence constricts for each and every word in the sentence the semantic dimension belonging to it, until eventually there emerges, out of an array of initially open-ended possibilities, a more or less determinate meaning. In addition to the denotations attaching to individual words, however, there are also connotations and emotional colorings. These too are subjected to the process of sifting caused by the juxtaposition of words in the sentence. But because these associations are often highly subjective, and also because of their comparative imprecision, connotations are not as susceptible as denotations to definitive screening. As a result, room for disagreement always arises with respect to the nuances and emotional coloring of a sentence or work, even if there is virtually no disagreement possible with respect to its explicit propositional content. This lack of closure with respect to the screening of connotations guarantees the perpetual openness of literary works to reinterpretation.

According to Ricoeur, it is the initial surplus of meaning that necessitates our speaking "of semantic regulation by the content and not simply of structural regulation" (1974, p. 48). In other words, given the capacity of a text to be taken in many different ways, the reader must turn to the subject matter of the text—which is to say, to his own experience of the subject matter of the text—in order to decide finally between the various readings that are possible. Thus, the text provides, for each new reader, an occasion for reflection on its subject matter.

An important parallel exists between the language-discourse relationship and the tradition-interpretation relationship. Our tradition constitutes what is given to us before we begin to formulate in discourse the interpretations we arrive at on the basis of our personal experience. Thus, tradition, like language, is a system or structure that embodies and makes available interpretations, just as language is the system that embodies and makes available discourse. In each case, moreover, the system in question is in essence nothing more than sedimented function—that is, the possibility of repeating what has already been done, already been intended. But if system (either language or tradition) is sedimented function (either discourse or interpretation), it follows that neither of these systems is static in any permanent sense, for sedimentation is itself an ongoing process. Thus, innovation in discourse and interpretation, grounded in the particularity of the individual's lived experience, holds open the possibility of change and renewal for both language and tradition.

Ricoeur's most important and original contributions to interpretation theory are the fruits of his penetrating investigations into the workings of the actual "points of exchange" where the givenness of language and tradition first shape, and then in turn are shaped by, discourse and interpretation. Three of these crucial "points of exchange"—the metaphor, the symbol, and the narrative—particularly attracted his attention, and each became the subject of a book-length study.

On the subject of metaphor, Ricoeur embraces the interaction theory of I. A. Richards, which stresses that a metaphor is always composed of two parts: tenor and vehicle. When these are brought together, there is an illuminating irruption of one context upon another. A metaphor has cognitive significance—it *shows* us something—because the interaction of contexts that it brings about will only make sense if we can find some point of resemblance that makes the vehicle *fit* against the background established by the tenor. The recognition of this resemblance, which guides the creation of metaphor, is the same recognition of resemblance that underlies concept formation (and that thus governs all language use). Whereas in concept formation the recognition of similarity is all-important, however, in metaphor a disturbing tension arises: the tenor and vehicle, by virtue of their similarity, draw together and seem inclined to lose themselves in a single identity; at the same time, by virtue of the "inappropriateness" of their conjunction, they want to fly apart. This tension at the very heart of metaphor is, Ricoeur contends, something that we must take care to respect; for it is only while this tension persists that metaphor is alive and able to challenge us to see further than we have.

The symbol, like the metaphor, "invites us to think." It "calls for an interpretation, precisely because it says more than it says and because it never ceases to speak to us" (ibid., p. 28). To say, as Ricoeur is inclined to, that symbol is *opaque* is to say that it never gives up its whole store of meaning. This is because, in the analogy that the symbol essentially is, only one term—the material symbol itself—is clearly defined. In other words, in contrast to the situation where we recognize that an analogy can be drawn between two terms that are already thoroughly known, in our dealings with symbol we always arrive on the scene *after* the analogy is ensconced and *before* the second or symbolized term is thoroughly grasped. Thus, "a meditation on symbols starts from the fullness of language and of meaning already there; it begins from within language which has already taken place and in which everything in a certain sense has already been said" (ibid. 287–288). The symbol itself is indicated, and so too is the fact that, as symbol, it stands in an analogical relationship to some aspect of our situation. Interpreting the symbol, then, consists in clarifying what that second, and only incompletely specified, term in the analogy must amount to, given that an analogical relationship is known to exist.

According to Ricoeur, this interpretive meditation involves an interplay of speculation and reflection: speculation that begins from our preunderstanding of the significance of the symbol in question, but that is then drawn in new directions by the material nature of the symbol itself, and reflection that takes what is uncovered by such speculation and reintegrates it into the coherent body of our beliefs. This process, however, is fraught with danger in both directions, because reflective and speculative thought conflict. Reflection, which is by nature demythologizing, would, if given free rein, transform symbolism into allegory; and "allegory implies that the true meaning, the philosophical meaning, preceded the [symbol], which was only a second guise, a veil deliberately thrown over the truth to mislead the simple" (ibid., p. 299). Reflection, then, seeks the domination of the symbol by whatever spiritual doctrine is already in place. Speculation, on the other hand, left to itself, is prone to "rationalizing symbols as such, and thereby fixing them on the imaginative plane where they are born and take shape" (ibid.). This is the temptation of "dogmatic mythology" or gnosis—the temptation to allow the material symbol to carry thought wherever it will, unchecked by any need to remain consistent with an initial core of spiritual belief. These two dangers are to be avoided only by firmly yoking reflection and speculation together. Properly constrained, speculation, guided by the nature of the material symbol, extends and fleshes out the initial spiritual insight underlying the symbol, while reflection guards that original insight against the danger of heresy. Thus, when speculation and reflection are properly yoked, we can pursue a line of thought that is "at once *bound* and *free*" in the process of arriving at "an interpretation that would respect the original enigma of symbols, let itself be taught by this enigma, but, with that as a start, bring out the meaning, give it form, in the full responsibility of an autonomous systematized thought" (ibid., p. 300).

The symbol's capacity to carry thought in new and valuable directions even as it recovers insights to which we have a long-standing precommitment illustrates

> the double dependence of the self on the unconscious and on the sacred, . . . [which] is manifested only in a symbolic mode. In order to elucidate this double dependence, reflection must reduce the status of consciousness and interpret it in terms of the symbolic meanings that approach it from behind and ahead, from above and below. In short, reflection must embrace both an archaeology and an eschatology.   (Ibid., p. 333)

The form of "archaeology" that Ricoeur has in mind here is the psychoanalytic interpretation of religious symbolism, in the light of which religion is seen as "a projection of an ancient destiny, both ancestral and infantile" (ibid.). It is not necessary, however, to tie this claim too tightly to a specifically psychoanalytic interpretation of our symbols. In a broader sense, what is being suggested is that, in our efforts to come to know ourselves, we must reflect on both the past that has determined what we now are and the possibilities of new meaning that lie perpetually open before us. According to Ricoeur, this is the very essence of the hermeneutic task: to understand what might be on the basis of what is already given.

Not all expressions lend themselves equally well to the pursuit of this task. The symbol, in its opacity, and living metaphor, with its clash of contexts, each open up for us valuable avenues of understanding. But worthwhile as metaphor and symbol are in this regard, narrative offers still richer possibilities of understanding and self-discovery.

In "The Model of the Text," Ricoeur remarks that an action, like a text, can be understood only if it is meaningful and if it is given "a kind of objectification which is equivalent to the fixation of a discourse by writing" (1981, p. 203). Moreover, the action, like the text, possesses locutionary, illocutionary, and perlocutionary dimensions. These features found in both the text and human action—the fixation of meaning in structural form, the dissociation of this meaning (as a result of its fixation) from the intention of the author, the openness of the text or action to interpretation by anyone who takes an interest in it, and finally, the fact that the meaning of the text or action is something about which we are qualified (as inhabitants of the shared world of experience) to shape an opinion—are precisely the features that guarantee the possibility of objectivity in interpretation. To say that textual and historical interpretation are thus guaranteed a kind of objectivity, however, is to say only that the objectified form of the text or action must be done justice by any serious interpretation, and thus that a restriction is placed on possible readings. But again, because the meaning of a text or action does not reside exclusively within the fixed form, because meaning in its broader sense encompasses the three dimensions of locution, illocution, and perlocution (or significance), there are inevitably grounds for disagreement in the interpretation of human actions as well as of texts.

As humans, we are fascinated with narratives because they illustrate the possibilities of our nature—possibilities that cannot be known a priori, but that can be discovered by attending to what others have done. (What human nature has already demonstrated itself capable of, it obviously remains capable of.) Important as this recognition of more or less abstract possibilities is, it constitutes only a necessary preliminary to self-understanding, which entails, over and above this, the appropriation of what are specifically *one's own* possibilities of being—that is, those that speak to one's nature and open up new avenues of self-definition. According to Ricoeur, because one does define oneself, choosing to embrace some of the modes of being that one has uncovered and rejecting others, "the positing of the self is not a given, it is a *task*" (1974, p. 329).

Although each of the various "expressions in which life objectifies itself" has something to show us about the possibilities that are open to us as human beings, literature tends to have a unique advantage in this respect—the advantage of having been created for no other purpose than the imaginative exploration of possible ways of being human. The task of the playwright and the novelist "is to render as perfectly as possible the vision of the world that inspires [him]" (1988, vol. 3, p. 177) through the persuasive handling of plot and characterization. The corresponding task of the reader is to explicate and appropriate the type of being-in-the-world that the author has unfolded. This proposed world, moreover, "is not *behind* the text, as a hidden intention would be, but *in front* of it, as that which the work unfolds, discovers, reveals. Henceforth, to understand is *to understand oneself in front of the text*" (1981, p. 143).

What does it mean to say that the text opens up a "world"? When we read a novel, play, or historical narrative, we find ourselves called on to flesh out the actual account of events given in the text with our own sense of what is implied about how these explicit details of the narrative might relate to other circumstances and events that could be considered. Because the whole point of a fictional account is to persuade us that the events described might actually have occurred, it is implied that the sort of further information that is always, at least in principle, available in an account of real events is also available here. This additional information, however, is provided not by the author, but by the reader, who, under the guidance of what is explicitly given in the text, "fleshes it out" in her imagination. This fleshing out constitutes the world of the text—a world whose existence the text implies, but that is realized only by virtue of the reader's interpretation of the text (and that therefore, considered in its particulars, will differ somewhat from reader to reader).

In opening up these new worlds, literature invites the reader to consider alternative modes of being. As Ricoeur observes, "to understand is . . . to expose oneself to [the text]; it is to receive a self enlarged by the appropriation of the proposed worlds which interpretation unfolds" (ibid., p. 94). The reader, through projective identification with the characters of a novel or play, steps into—temporarily and "hypothetically"—an alien viewpoint, and in so doing achieves a certain measure of freedom from the circumstances of her own situation. This in turn affords the reader the sort of distance from herself that makes it possible for her to criticize her own nature and her own illusions:

> In the idea of the "imaginative variation of the ego," I see the most fundamental possibility for a critique of the illusions of the subject. . . . [T]he appropriation of the proposed worlds offered by the text passes through the disappropriation of the self. The critique of *false consciousness* can thus become an integral part of hermeneutics. (Ibid., p. 94)

In Ricoeur's estimation, this constitutes an answer of sorts to those critics of hermeneutics—such as Jürgen Habermas—who contend that too great a concern for appropriating the insights of one's tradition can only reinforce current ideologies and power structures. If exposure to the literary masterpieces of one's tradition increases the flexibility of one's outlook, surely this implies that one's commitments to institutions and practices already in place must become more thoughtful and more carefully qualified. In other words, literature has ethical significance. It shapes our understanding of what is right and wrong, valuable and insignificant, and thus determines in no small measure how we choose to live our lives. As Ricoeur puts it, "literature is a vast laboratory in which we experiment with estimations, evaluations, and judgments of approval and condemnation through which narrativity serves as a propaedeutic to ethics" (1992, p. 115).

Yet another way in which the reading of narratives contributes to the shape of one's self-understanding is in enabling one to see one's life as possessing narrative unity. This matters because "if [one's] life cannot be grasped as a singular totality, [one] could never hope it to be successful [or] complete" (ibid., p. 160). The successful life, after all, is one in which various projects are brought to fruition. But the completion of projects can itself only be understood in terms of a narrative structure—in terms of the initiation of action, followed by a sequence of intermediary events in which particular means are brought to bear for the sake of desired ends, which lead, finally, to the arrival of a conclusion.

This sense of the narrative unity of one's life, moreover, helps one to assimilate and make sense of those arbitrary and contingent aspects of experience that tend to disrupt and frustrate one's intentions. All narrative exhibits a "dialectic of concordance and discordance" (ibid., p. 147), by which Ricoeur means that any *interesting* story tells us how some intention was fixed upon, how its achievement was frustrated in various ways, and how these impediments were eventually surmounted and the goal in question was reached. What this implies is that the unexpected hindrance and, for that matter, the unexpected deliverance or benefit are essential elements of the narrative in which they appear. Beyond these contingencies, in fact, the narrative is constituted of only one other element—the character of the hero, which finds *its* expression in the hero's choice of goals and in the ways in which he responds to the various impediments and strokes of good fortune that come his way. But, according to Ricoeur, "it is the identity of the story that makes the identity of the character" (ibid., p. 148). "The contingency of the event contributes to the necessity, retroactive so to speak, of the history of a life. . . . The person, understood as a character in a story, is not an entity distinct from his or her 'experiences'" (ibid., p. 147). We come to recognize this, in particular, through the reading of literature; and insofar as our familiarity with literature enables us to grasp the narrative unity in our own lives, to see *ourselves* as characters in a story, our reading of literature paves the way to a proper appreciation of the significance of those arbitrary and contingent events that help to define us.

[*See also* Gadamer; Hermeneutics; Narrative; *and* Phenomenology.]

BIBLIOGRAPHY

Works by Ricoeur

La symbolique du mal. In *Philosophie de la volonté: Finitude et culpabilité,* vol. 2. Paris, 1960. Translated by Emerson Buchanan as *The Symbolism of Evil* (Boston, 1967).
De l'interprétation. Paris, 1965. Translated by Denis Savage as *Freud and Philosophy: An Essay on Interpretation* (New Haven, 1970).
Le conflit des interprétations. Paris, 1969. Translated as *The Conflict of Interpretations,* edited by Don Ihde (Evanston, Ill., 1974).
La métaphore vive. Paris, 1975. Translated by Robert Czerny, Kathleen McLaughlin, and John Costello as *The Rule of Metaphor* (Toronto, 1977).
Hermeneutics and the Human Sciences. Translated and edited by John B. Thompson. Cambridge and New York, 1981.
Temps et récit. 3 vols. Paris, 1983–1985. Translated by Kathleen Blamey and David Pellauer as *Time and Narrative,* 3 vols. (Chicago, 1984–1988).
Du texte à l'action. Paris, 1986.
Soi-même comme un autre. Paris, 1990. Translated by Kathleen Blamey as *Oneself as Another* (Chicago, 1992).

Other Sources

Ihde, Don. *Hermeneutic Phenomenology: The Philosophy of Paul Ricoeur.* Evanston, Ill., 1971.
Wood, David, ed. *On Paul Ricoeur: Narrative and Interpretation.* London and New York, 1991.

RON BONTEKOE

RIEGL, ALOIS (1858–1905), professor of art history at the University of Vienna at the turn of the century, pioneer of modern formal analysis, and spokesperson for a relativistic theory of artistic value. Both the latter endeavors were crystallized in Riegl's theory of a formally analyzable "artistic volition" *(Kunstwollen),* which develops throughout history, informs all artistic manifestations of a given period, and relates artistic form to a wider cultural context. One can judge art faithfully, Riegl thought, only in relation to its own *Kunstwollen,* not according to universal standards, and only in terms of form, not content.

The development of his theory of formal analysis is an illuminating example of a conservative revolution. In his studies and early scholarly work, Riegl's academic pursuits were in accord with the then current enthusiasm for realist artistic styles inspired by positivist intellectual trends. He sought to trace an evolutionary development toward realism throughout the centuries. From his perspective, artistic realism had a scholarly cast, as though art were a quasi-scientific method of gathering and analyzing data. This view was modeled on the empiricist education he received from his teachers at the University of Vienna in the 1870s and 1880s. Thus, while his Habilitationsschrift on the illustration of medieval calendars established the persistence of the Hellenistic tradition into the Middle Ages, it did so only to pinpoint the moment in the Middle Ages when artists departed from conventional models in order to study nature. He sought to preserve his quasi-scholarly view of art as, in following years, it encountered successive challenges both by philosophical developments with which he came in contact and by the artistic material with which he found himself confronted. By the end of his career, his attempt to preserve a representational theory of art based on realism led him to back into a nonrepresentational stance inspiring to Expressionist artists who created revolutionary abstract art early in the twentieth century.

The first challenge to Riegl's interpretation of the development of art in terms of realism alone came from the subject matter of his studies. His first professional position was as curator of textiles at the Austrian Museum of Art and Industry. Through it, Riegl moved out of necessity into the field of ornament. With ammunition in part provided by theories of the contemporary Arts and Crafts movement, he developed, in *Altorientalische Teppiche* (1891) and *Stilfragen* (1893), a complex theory of surface ornamentation. He kept this theory compatible with his quasi-scientific theory of realism by arguing that whereas representational art sought to approach a naturalistic rendering of the external world, ornamental art represented its own material, symbolizing the structure of the surface it covered through the construction and articulation of ornamental motifs. Riegl traced an evolutionary development in this type of "structural symbolism." His primary example was the Egyptian lotus ornament, whose fortunes he traced through its inception in Egypt to its transformations in Assyrian, Greek, Roman, and finally medieval Islamic ornament. According to Riegl, decorative motifs began as relatively simple parts, linked straightforwardly in rows. Through creative adaptation of the laws of (primarily vegetal) nature, however, they gradually developed more sophisticated methods of linkage. Ultimately, decorative motifs became extremely sophisticated representational tools with multilevel means for making a surface cohere visually and demonstrate flatness while maintaining visual interest. The makers of ornament, like Realist painters, studied and applied the laws of nature.

As close as the formal application of Riegl's theory may seem to mid-twentieth-century formalism, it remained a two-tiered notion of representation that left the role of artistic realism unquestioned. During the mid-1890s, however, Riegl's optimistic view of the ever-advancing discovery of the laws of reality through empirical study and classification faced serious challenges by subjectivist philosophies and art movements. Riegl reacted to this epistemological crisis by struggling to reveal and substantiate the element of physical reality and ultimately standards of value that he thought ensured the validity of the visual arts and all cultural endeavors. In so doing, he tried to incorporate into his theories elements of current subjective theories that threatened to undermine his attempts to preserve objectivity. The result-

ing synthesis, some of which can be seen in process in his posthumously published manuscript *Historische Grammatik der bildenden Künste* (1966), produced the impressive and puzzling work on which depends his historical significance. It led him to seek to reconcile the scientific model of art as the pursuit of knowledge with which he started with a voluntaristic, subjective model; to transform structural symbolism into perceptual psychology; to shift the locus of his endeavor from the work of art to the beholder; and ultimately to leave the field of art proper, and dwell on the ethical development of the beholder's system of values.

The concept of the *Kunstwollen*, which suggests subjectivity, came out of this endeavor. Riegl had employed the term loosely in *Stilfragen* as a symbol of artistic freedom to enlist creative artists in the struggle against "materialistic" theories of art based on the primacy of technique. In *Spätrömische Kunstindustrie* (1901) he canonized the *Kunstwollen*, and the "will" to which it refers, as the sole determinant of artistic form, expressly linked to the historically determined desire for a particular configuration of the visible world. At the same time, Riegl abandoned the distinction between the tasks of the fine and applied arts as incompatible with the notion of a singular *Kunstwollen*. The all-embracing *Kunstwollen* developed historically, and made itself known in the formal signs of outline, color, spatial and planar configurations. Tracing the development of the *Kunstwollen* through stages, Riegl developed a vocabulary that showed how a representational figure and an ornamental pattern play identical roles against their backgrounds, and allowed the central nave of a church to be perceived as acting similarly as a pattern against the background of its apse and side aisles. Using this concept, he could analyze all art in purely formal terms.

Although the *Kunstwollen* manifested itself only in formal relationships, however, Riegl was not ready to abandon art's relation to reality altogether. He used a widespread perceptual theory that allied objective reality with palpability to defend art's ability to represent material reality. According to Riegl's interpretation of the theory, the sense of touch isolated objects in order to validate their separate material existence, whereas the more intellectual optical sense united objects in large abstractions. The viewer who feels capable of touching an object is convinced that it exists. Riegl sought to harness this verifiability for artistic representation. Without claiming that the work of art represented external objects directly, he nevertheless thought that art could represent the impressions they made on the senses. Art could validate its representation within perception itself, through reference to the most objectively valid sense.

Historically, Riegl thought art began with the tactile, and increasingly admitted optical elements. In order to show how art could represent touch, Riegl developed a formal iconography of palpability based on the theories of the Arts and Crafts movement, translating the theory of representation articulated in *Stilfragen* into perceptual terms. He identified as signs of touch the elements that in *Stilfragen* he had thought symbolized the solidity and flatness of surfaces, among them hard outlines, flat planes of color, repetition, and symmetry. What he had seen as representations of (external) material became representations of the (internal) tactile sense. Such representational devices characterize surfaces as flat whether they are or not. Similarly, the artistic signs of visibility, the well-known artistic devices of Impressionism, could be used to characterize any surface as optical and ephemeral. Riegl, along with other German critics, regarded Impressionism as a movement concerned primarily with ephemeral qualities of light.

Formal relationships represented only perceptions, not the external world. Nevertheless, they had an important volitional tie to the external world. Using perceptual theory that conceived the optical sense as connecting objects within a single visual field, whereas touch separates objects from one another, Riegl defined the *Kunstwollen* as a demand that art visually reflect the relationships desirable in all domains of life at a particular moment. Art had an intellectual and a political significance, therefore. Opticality came to stand for connectives that are emotional, political, and even causal, whereas touch stood for separation, individuality, and power. Thus, the ornamental designs of buckles and pins acted out relations of both causality and might. In this respect, the historical development that Riegl postulated toward greater opticality articulated a theory of political and intellectual historical development, because greater opticality meant greater power to make connections conceptually as well as greater social cohesion with a looser hierarchy.

Through the mediation of art critics and essayists such as Wilhelm Worringer, the concepts of opticality, palpability, their formal components, and their meanings found echoes in the writings of Expressionist artists as they groped their way toward abstract art. Although their concerns differ widely from those of Riegl, traces of Riegl's spatial and perceptual terminology can also be found in formalist art historians and even in modernist critics, such as Clement Greenberg, in the mid-twentieth century. Thus, for decades Riegl was known chiefly for his system of formal analysis, and *Spätrömische Kunstindustrie* remained his most well known work. But far more significant for the present day are the works of his last few years, when he expanded the implications for the representation of relationships that preoccupied him in his study of late-antique ornament. *Das holländische Gruppenporträt* (1902) concerns seventeenth-century Dutch group portraits whose subjects look at the beholder. In it, Riegl developed a theory of "attentiveness" that addressed the issue of the relationship between the beholder and the work of art in formal and ethical terms. The desired relationship to the world is not simply reflected in the relationship between parts of the work of art, but in the

relationship it performs with the beholder. Art that looks back, for example, depends on the viewer to give the work formal coherence, but it can also, as does a Dutch group portrait, claim a right to its own existence and demand respect for itself. Thus, mutual regard involves a relationship of respect between art and beholder. In works of art contemporary to Riegl (genre paintings, for example), figures do not acknowledge the viewer. They allow themselves to be subsumed into the viewer's imagination, feeding the viewer's own subjectivity. A developmental theory informs Riegl's work on Dutch art, just as it does *Spätrömische Kunstindustrie*, but Riegl has to struggle to identify as progressive the demise of the later period, because it means the loss of the mutual respect exemplified in the Dutch paintings.

Both *Spätrömische Kunstindustrie* and *Das holländische Gruppenporträt* deliberately chose works of art undervalued by Riegl's contemporaries. He hoped to make the alien *Kunstwollen* known through an exploration of its differences from that of his own culture. The knowledge of alien values depended on an understanding of one's own in a form of hermeneutics that might today be called dialogic. Thus, Riegl's work, though it relied on developmental theories, had a relativistic edge, and has had the effect of encouraging research in minor or undervalued media and historical periods. The acceptance of historical changes in values is central to his important late theoretical essays on the subject of monuments, which stemmed from his work, from 1902 on, as conservator general of the Austrian Commission on Historical Monuments. These essays carried his ruminations on the ethical basis of the relation between beholder and object beyond the world of art. In the essay "Der moderne Denkmalkultus, sein Wesen, seine Entstehung" (in *Gesammelte Aufsätze*), he traced a hierarchy of values themselves, conceived in terms of the relation between man and the environment, and projected into a developmental history. A tendency to merge with the environment is conceived in optical, subjective terms and connected with the appreciation of aged objects, whose outlines become less defined, while the objective, crisp outlines of palpability suggest newness. As humanity becomes more subjective and optical, it is increasingly able to accept the ravages of time. Again, however, Riegl finds it difficult to embrace subjectivity wholeheartedly. In this essay, he historicizes the writing of history itself, attributing to the historian the tactile respect for the individual of the past. Although historical studies prepare humanity for the spiritual revolution signaled by the cult of age, the historian's respect for detail also comes across as the necessary antidote to the unchecked submission to the cult of subjectivity.

Because so much of it attempted to rescue the highly valued notion of representation from the onslaught of modern challengers, Riegl's work occupies a precarious position between the values he upheld and the antirepresentational theories that it would later help others to support. His work both exemplifies and signals the demise of the representational theory of art. Its pivotal character explains the resistance to easy appropriation by any one point of view that has contributed to its continuing significance. It has been given a variety of different readings, within and outside of the field of art history, that keep it useful and challenging from a formal, structuralist, or poststructuralist point of view. Early on, controversies over Riegl's significance centered on his work's political potential. Hans Sedlmayr's enthusiastic 1929 reading of the *Kunstwollen* as a totalizing concept that united a people, an era, and a country helped lead others, such as E. H. Gombrich and Ernst Bloch, writing in the postwar era, to condemn the concept of the *Kunstwollen* as protofascist. Marxist thinkers, however, had already begun to appropriate Riegl's ideas for their own, very different, aims. The notion of the near and the distant, for example, appealed to Walter Benjamin, who used it as the basis of his own idea of the "aura," which he developed in his essay "The Work of Art in the Age of Mechanical Reproduction" in 1937. Mikhail Bakhtin, although he was unaware of Riegl's protodialogic investigations into the relation between the beholder and the work of art, which he might have found of interest, appreciated Riegl's work for the content that he inscribed into his formalism. Bakhtin alluded to Riegl as a foil against the sterility of the Russian Formalists.

Although Riegl has never been neglected by scholars, his works were not translated into English for decades. The notorious difficulty of Riegl's German is usually given as the reason. Thus, the translation of several of his works into English suggests a renewed interest in Riegl. This new interest seems to be the result of the possibility of regarding Riegl from new points of view, some of them shaped by postmodernism. Interest in the conceptual foundations of art history, for example, has led to examinations of his historiographical methods in the context of Hegelian and Kantian ideas as part of the enterprise of a "critical history of art." The notion of the gaze, articulated in *Das holländische Gruppenporträt*, has attracted renewed attention in relation to recent theories of beholding. The eclecticism of postmodern architecture has encouraged an interest in his concept of the historical career of monuments, which he saw as eclectic because they belonged not only to the historical period that created them, but also to those that preserved, renovated, and modified them. Several signs, including the publication of Riegl's collected writings on historical preservation, attest to this current interest. But more broadly, the upsurge in interest in Riegl attests to the significance for the present, poststructural climate of art-theoretical and -historical practice, of Riegl's protodialogic hermeneutic investigation into the relationship between the beholder and the work of art and, more broadly, between our own values and those of the past.

BIBLIOGRAPHY

Works by Riegl

"Die mittelalterliche Kalendarillustration." *Mitteilungen des Instituts für österreichische Geschichtsforschung* 10 (1889): 1–74.
Altorientalische Teppiche (1891). Reprint, Mittenwald, 1979.
Stilfragen: Grundlegungen zu einer Geschichte der Ornamentik (1893). 2d ed. Berlin, 1923.
Spätrömische Kunstindustrie (1901; 2d ed., 1927). Reprint, Darmstadt, 1973.
Das holländische Gruppenporträt (1902). 2d ed. 2 vols. Edited by Karl M. Swoboda. Vienna, 1931.
Gesammelte Aufsätze (1929). Edited by Karl M. Swoboda. Berlin, 1995.
Historische Grammatik der bildenden Künste. Edited by Karl M. Swoboda and Otto Pächt. Graz, 1966.
Kunstwerk oder Denkmal? Alois Riegls Schriften zur Denkmalpflege. Edited by Ernst Bacher. Vienna, 1995.

English Translations of Riegl

"The Modern Cult of Monuments: Its Character and Its Origin." Translated by Kurt W. Forster and Diane Ghirardo. *Oppositions* 25 (1982): 21–50. Translation of "Der moderne Denkmalkultus, sein Wesen, seine Entstehung," in *Gesammelte Aufsätze,* edited by Karl M. Swoboda (Berlin, 1995), pp. 144–194.
Problems of Style: Foundations for a History of Ornament. Translated by Evelyn Kain. Princeton, N.J., 1992.
"Excerpts from *The Dutch Group Portrait.*" Translated by Benjamin Binstock. *October* 74 (1995): 3–35.

Other Sources

Bacher, Ernst. Introduction to Alois Riegl, *Kunstwerk oder Denkmal?* pp. 11–48. Vienna, 1995.
Binstock, Benjamin. "Alois Riegl in the Presence of *The Nightwatch.*" *October* 74 (1995): 36–44.
Forster, Kurt. "Monument/Memory and the Mortality of Architecture." *Oppositions* 25 (1982): 2–19.
Iversen, Margaret. *Alois Riegl: Art History and Theory.* Cambridge, Mass., 1993.
Kemp, Wolfgang. "Alois Riegl (1858–1905)". In *Altmeister moderner Kunstgeschichte,* edited by Heinrich Dilly, pp. 37–62. Berlin, 1990.
Kemp, Wolfgang. "Nachwort." In Alois Riegl, *Gesammelte Aufsätze,* pp. 207–222. Berlin, 1995.
Olin, Margaret. *Forms of Representation in Alois Riegl's Theory of Art.* University Park, Pa., 1992.
Pächt, Otto. "Alois Riegl" (1963). In *Methodisches zur kunsthistorischen Praxis: Ausgewählte Schriften,* edited by Jörg Oberhaidacher, Artur Rosenauer, and Gertraut Schikola, pp. 141–152. Munich, 1977.
Panofsky, Erwin. "Der Begriff des Kunstwollens." In *Aufsätze zu Grundfragen der Kunstwissenschaft,* 2d rev. ed., edited by Hariolf Oberer and Egon Verheyen, pp. 29–43. Berlin, 1974. Translated by Kenneth J. Northcott and Joel Snyder as "The Concept of Artistic Volition," *Critical Inquiry* 8 (Autumn 1981): 7–34.
Podro, Michael. "Riegl." In *The Critical Historians of Art,* pp. 71–97. New Haven, 1982.
Sauerländer, Willibald. "Alois Riegl und die Entstehung der autonomen Kunstgeschichte am Fin de Siècle." In *Fin de Siècle: Zur Literatur und Kunst der Jahrhundertwende,* edited by Roger Bauer et al., pp. 125–139. Frankfurt am Main, 1978.
Scarrocchia, Sandro. "'Al tempo la sua arte, all'arte la sua libertà': il Denkmalkultus di Riegl." In Alois Riegl, *Il Culto Moderno dei monumenti: Il suo caràttere e I suoi inizi,* translated by Sandro Scarrocchia and Renate Trost, pp. 9–23. Bologna, 1985.

Scarrocchia, Sandro. *Studi su Alois Riegl.* Ricerche dell'Instituto per i beni artistici culturali naturali della Regione Emilia-Romagna, no. 12. Bologna, 1986.

Scarrocchia, Sandro, ed. *Alois Riegl: Teoria e Prassi Della Conservazione Dei Monumenti: Antologia di scritti, discorsi, rapporti, 1898–1905, con una scelta di saggi critici.* Bologna, 1995.

Sedlmayr, Hans. "Die Quintessenz des Lehren Riegl." In Alois Riegl, *Gesammelte Aufsätze,* edited by Karl M. Swoboda, pp. xii–xxxiv. Augsburg and Vienna, 1929.

Worringer, Wilhelm. *Abstraction and Empathy: A Contribution to the Psychology of Style* (1909). Translated by Michael Bullock. New York, 1953.

Zerner, Henri. "Alois Riegl: Art, Value, and Historicism." *Daedalus* 105 (Winter 1976): 177–189.

MARGARET OLIN

ROCK MUSIC. Rock music has its own standards of evaluation, which differ in significant ways from those of traditional musical aesthetics. Rock musicians and serious listeners to rock music know and understand these criteria, which derive from the history and practices of rock music and its antecedents. The traditions from which rock arose (folk, blues, and country) emphasize performance rather than composition, and value the communication of feeling and emotion much more highly than either the formal complexity of the composition or the technical accuracy of the performance. Consequently, rock music is judged more by its effects on the listener's body than by a "disinterested" appreciation of its formal properties. The three principal criteria by which rock is judged are authenticity of voice, rhythm, and loudness. These categories do not exhaust what is important in rock music, but they point to its most obviously significant aspects.

Authenticity of Voice. Rock music succeeds where there is a direct emotional connection with the listener. The most important vehicle for expressing emotion in rock was originally the human voice, and this voice was judged by the conviction and intensity of the singing, because this was a sign of the authenticity or "truth" of the singer, a sign that the singer is singing from experience, and not simply "faking" emotions the singer has never felt. As is also the case with the blues, which is the basis for much of rock music, what matters is the singer's involvement in the material, as revealed by the amount of emotion and feeling in how the tones are sung. Whether the "correct" tones are sung, or sung at the "correct" time, is very much a secondary consideration, especially because the melody, rhythm, and even structure of the "same" song can vary so much from performance to performance that the very notion of a single "correct" tone is nearly meaningless. In rock and blues music, the "right" note is the one that is right for that performance, and depends on what has preceded the singing of that tone, and on what the performers are moving toward later in the performance. This is true, of course, of any performance-based and improvisational form of music, including jazz. In such music, the "song" is merely the framework for a performance, and it is the performance or the singer that is paramount, not the composition. As for the performance, what counts is whether the singer "tells the truth," that is, whether the expression of feeling is judged to be genuine. The criteria for determining authenticity are not formalizable rules but the effect of the voice on the body of the listener: the voice "rings true" or sounds "fake" depending on the complicated visceral response it arouses. This response is hard to describe, and it is unlikely that anyone could determine a set of "objective" criteria that could determine whether the response indicated a good or bad vocal performance, but it is immediately recognizable to the experienced listener.

These criteria of vocal expressiveness gradually were taken up by other instruments, and by the guitar in particular. Again, rock followed the lead of the blues, where artists such as Muddy Waters and B. B. King had made the electric guitar into a second "voice," rather than the mere accompaniment to the human voice that the guitar had been. Not surprisingly, the rock musicians who made the guitar into a vehicle of emotional expression were themselves strongly influenced by the blues, and the legacy of such pioneers as Eric Clapton and Jimi Hendrix is that, for succeeding generations of rock musicians, it is how the tones are played, and not the tones themselves or whether they are the "right" ones, that makes a rock performance successful. Occasionally, this emphasis on performance can degenerate into virtuosity for its own sake or "showboating." Sheer speed and flashiness will always have their place as part of rock's brazenness and rebelliousness, but discerning listeners value these less than the ability to convey feeling, which at times requires constraint, in much the same way as good rock singing is not all shouting, because on occasion more meaning is conveyed in a whisper than by a holler or a yell.

Rock's concern with emotional expressiveness rather than technical accuracy or faithfulness to a score should not be confused with lack of technique. There is a world of difference between someone who is trying to master the growling and howling of blues singing and someone, such as Muddy Waters or Janis Joplin, who is able to focus on what is being expressed rather than on the technique used to express it. A good rock musician is also sufficiently immersed in the forms and traditions of rock music to understand what can and cannot be given adequate expression in that idiom. Sometimes, a simple combination of exposure to the idiom and raw, inborn talent is enough; Elvis Presley was at his best when his singing was unschooled by anything other than an appreciation for blues and country music. In cases like these, the acquisition of "proper" technique serves only to obscure and distort a technique that had been acquired "naturally," which is to say, by a combination of innate gifts and lucky circumstances. Such "natural" technique might be confused with no technique at all, but these techniques are not easy; if they were, everyone could be an Elvis.

On the other hand, there is a significant body of rock music that claims to disdain technique altogether. This was notably the case with "punk rock," which arose in the 1970s in part as a protest against notions of technique and virtuousity. Many punk rockers could barely play their instruments, but were intent rather on creating an effect through sheer loudness, rhythmic intensity, and shrieking vocals. Nevertheless, punk rock was highly expressive, although the predominant emotions expressed were anger and aggression. Punk aficionados distinguished between authentic expressions of anger, such as Johnny Rotten's performances with the Sex Pistols, and inferior versions that were less capable of communicating significant emotion, or that did so less persuasively, or were seen as having nothing to say (the same Johnny Rotten, now John Lydon, in P.I.L.). It would be a mistake, then, to think that punk rock lacks technique. Rather, its technique relies on aggressive guitar chording and rapid tempo drumming, combined with aggressive vocals. It is a technique entirely opposed to the "art rock" of the period, the latter consisting of a technical mastery of an instrument that is not dissimilar from the virtuousity of a classical musician, and highly involved musical compositions that sometimes took on Wagnerian dimensions (the album by Yes, *Tales from Topographic Oceans*, is representative). Punk uses its instruments as aids in a dramatic enactment of emotions, rather than for their musical capabilities alone. This element, always present in rock music, became explicit in performances by The Who in the 1960s, which involved the drummer and guitarist physically destroying their instruments as an expression of pure rage. Punk took this element of rock performance and made it into nearly the entire content.

Given that punk rock strips rock to its bare essentials, and produces an antitechnical technique, the question arises as to whether the value of rock music is in any way based on its expressive capabilities or "authenticity of voice." In numerous publications, Simon Frith argues for a more sociological analysis of musical value. Popular music, including rock music, has value for a particular group if its style of performance embodies or expresses values with which the group identifies or toward which it feels an allegiance, and not all of these values need be "musical." This determines whether a certain kind of music will be popular with a certain social group, and the value of the music consists simply in its thus being valued by a social group. Values such as "authenticity" are no more than disguised expressions of the subjective preferences of the critic.

It could be argued, however, that criteria of "authenticity" are not those of a critic but those of a social group. Criteria of "authenticity" arise from the practices of musicians and listeners. These will vary according to the subcategories of rock music involved, each of which has its own norms and its own following. There is an enormous spectrum in rock music, from punk, grunge, thrash, and heavy metal at one extreme, to more balladic and lyrical folk rock and "adult-oriented" rock forms that verge into country and pop music. Within any of those subcategories, there are knowledgeable listeners capable of distinguishing between music of high quality, judged according to fairly objective and practice-based criteria, and music that they happen to enjoy for other reasons, such as political—the association of a piece of music with personal memories or with nonmusical symbols and values—or some other "subjective" criteria.

Rhythm. Rhythm is perhaps the most obvious and frequently remarked upon aspect of rock music. Rock music, like blues and country, was originally for dancing, and in dance the connection between the music and the listener's body is felt and enacted, rather than merely contemplated. A good rock song is one that makes the listener's body want to move, and this cannot be done simply by observing the correct tempo and time signature: good rock musicians will sometimes deliberately vary the tempo in order to create a certain effect (speeding up the tempo to build excitement, or slowly building up and slowing down the tempo in order to build up tension in the body that is later released with explosive energy), and play behind, in front of, and around the beat, rather than right on it. Timing—knowing whether to play ahead of or behind or on the beat—is more important than tempo, and the "rightness" of the timing, tempo, and rhythm is judged by whether the music inspires the body to dance. Good rock musicians enter into a dialogue with the dancers, adjusting their performance according to the dancers' responses, which is something that requires a great deal of practice and training, but not the sort of thing that could be captured in a score or some other set of formalized instructions. For the musicians as well as the dancers, the body and its feelings reveal whether or not the performance is successful.

The importance of rhythm varies in the different genres of pop music. In rhythm and blues, soul, funk, and rap, rhythm is often the most important element. In some of the more intellectualized rock forms, such as psychedelia, "progressive rock," and some types of heavy metal, rhythm is sometimes of little consequence, because these are forms of rock that have departed from the constraints of dance-oriented music in order to give more free play to the voice of the instruments. But even when rock is not meant for dancing, the rhythmical element remains, in the tempo shifts, the repetitive figures (or "riffs"), and the impact of the drums and electric bass, both of which resonate in the body core and convey a feeling of movement, even if the movement is not expressed as dance.

Loudness. Rock music is notorious for being loud, but the sheer volume or loudness adds to its intensity and can be effectively used as a vehicle of expression. Loud music vibrates in the chest cavity and the body core, and this feature can be used to create feelings of being lifted up, let down, or driven backwards. Music that is uniformly loud can be simply exhausting, which sometimes is deliberate, as with some punk rock, but otherwise is a sign of ineptitude. Most of the better rock performances make extensive use of dynamics, utilizing the loudness made possible by electrical amplification as a means of expression, and not simply as a technological given. Amplification and loudness also enter into the authenticity of voice in rock music. Some passages of rock music do not sound right unless they are played loud, and amplification gives the musician a whole new register of possibilities, something rock discovered as early as the pioneering "Rocket 88" (sometimes called the first rock-and-roll record because of its use of the distorted electric guitar accompanying the boogie-woogie piano) and exploited to great effect in Hendrix's guitar playing. Distortion and feedback can give guitar either a very dense and "fat" sound (as in the Kinks' "You Really Got Me") or a high, wailing sound (for example, the guitar on the choruses of The Who's "I Can See for Miles"). Reverb, echo, and tape delays, developed in conjunction with amplification, have added to the sound of rock music since Elvis's recording of "Mystery Train" for Sun Records in the mid-1950s, and reverb in particular has been used to create a haunting, bluesy sound in the harmonica playing of blues artist Little Walter Jacobs and some of Clapton's early guitar playing (with John Mayall and Cream). Bad rock musicians take a mechanical, rule-based approach to dynamics (or eschew dynamic variation altogether), and tend to be dominated by the technology of amplification, treating the technology as an end rather than a means. But for good rock musicians, loudness creates further expressive possibilities.

Rock and Pop. Like other forms of popular music, rock can be characterized by its relative accessibility to listeners and musicians with little formal or academic training; and, like pop music, the basic form of rock music is the song, which results in an emphasis on qualities of vocal expressiveness. Much of popular music is meant for dancing, and hence has regular rhythms and meters. All of these elements in both popular and rock music speak directly to the bodily responses of the listener.

Rock diverges from other forms of popular music, however, in much the way its antecedents do, and in particular, blues and jazz. Early jazz is a form of blues, and, in its "hot" variety, remains close to the vocal expressiveness and rhythmic intensity of blues music. Like blues and some jazz, rock has a more intense and aggressive feel than other popular music. In some cases, this is because the rhythms are more aggressive, marked by strong downbeats and syncopation; it can also be a result of allowing more free play in the playing or singing of a tone, so that the sound rises and falls in microtones that would be controlled and smoothed into a more unified sound in pop music; and it is also the result of

a greater tolerance for dissonance (the use of overtones such as those in the blues harmonica or blues harp, seventh and ninth chords, feedback effects, and so on). The contrast between rock and the pop music of its period is similar to that between the Benny Goodman Orchestra's recording of "Sing Sing Sing" and the "sweet" dance music of the 1930s. Pop tends to be "easy listening," that is, more melodious, less dissonant, with more lilting rhythms and a gentler "swing." Although rhythm is always a component in rock, it can disdain "swing" altogether; Led Zeppelin's "Dazed and Confused" is exemplary in that regard. Although both pop rock and soft rock exist, rock is, in virtue of its origins, "hard."

For that reason, rock music has often been associated with aggression: with anger and rebellion (as in early rock and roll, and in punk rock) and with an aggressive form of sexuality (in the blues and its derivatives). Even in its gentlest moments, there is an undercurrent of tension and even violence in much rock music. The effect, then, is not of calm so much as of violent passions held in check. The violence of some forms of rock music, such as heavy metal, have tended to make them into exclusively male enclaves. On the other hand, there have been a number of female punk rock groups (Siouxie and the Banshees, the Slits), and the role of aggressive rocker has more recently been taken up by Courtney Love's grunge-rock group, Hole. In addition, in rock and soul music, a number of female vocalists, such as Aretha Franklin and Etta James, have used a very aggressive and "hard" vocal style with considerable success. The aggressiveness of rock has made it in many ways "a man's world," but it is also a world where assertive women have made themselves heard. Assertiveness or outright aggression, however, whether expressed through rhythm or through the intensity and unguardedness of vocal and instrumental expression, is the primary means of distinguishing rock from other forms of popular music. Even so, many of these characteristics of rock music can now be found elsewhere, particularly in the "new country" music that has developed since the 1980s.

Conclusion. Authenticity of voice, rhythm, and loudness are perhaps the principal characteristics of rock music. All three elements have a direct effect on the body, and their proper use is judged by how the body responds to them, rather than by any formal criteria. All three come from the performance-oriented tradition, in which listeners bodily participate in the music (whether through dance or more visceral responses), and there is a direct emotional connection between the musician and the listener that allows the listener to judge whether the musical expression of emotion is true to the listener's experience. Not that either the musician or the listener lives in a realm of pure immediacy; that is a fiction of antirock theorists, who would like to reduce rock music to the "animal" level. The listener's response and the musician's performance are both mediated by a history of practices, forms, and conventions. But when the music rings true, it is the body that tells us so. This is something that has to be experienced to be understood. As the song says, "I'd tell you 'bout the music that can free your soul, but it's like trying to tell a stranger about rock and roll."

[*See also* Music, *historical overview article; and* Popular Culture.]

BIBLIOGRAPHY

Eisen, Jonathan, ed. *The Age of Rock: Sounds of the American Cultural Revolution.* New York, 1969.

Escott, Colin, and Martin Hawkins. *Good Rockin' Tonight: Sun Records and the Birth of Rock 'n' Roll.* New York, 1991.

Frith, Simon. *The Sociology of Rock.* London, 1978.

Frith, Simon. *Sound Effects: Youth, Leisure and the Politics of Rock.* New York, 1981.

Frith, Simon. *Music for Pleasure: Essays in the Sociology of Pop.* Cambridge, 1988.

Frith, Simon. *Performing Rites: On the Value of Popular Music.* Oxford and New York, 1996.

Gaar, Gillian G. *She's a Rebel: The History of Women in Rock and Roll.* Seattle, 1992.

Gracyk, Theodore, *Rhythm and Noise: An Aesthetics of Rock.* Durham N.C., 1996.

Marcus, Greil. *Mystery Train: Images of America in Rock 'n' Roll Music* (1975). 3rd rev. ed., New York, 1990.

Marcus, Greil. *Lipstick Traces: A Secret History of the Twentieth Century.* Cambridge, Mass., 1989.

Miller, Jim. *The Rolling Stone Illustrated History of Rock and Roll.* Rev. upd. ed. New York, 1980.

O'Brien, Lucy. *She-Bop: The Definitive History of Women in Rock, Pop, and Soul.* Harmondsworth, England, 1995.

Palmer, Robert. *Deep Blues.* New York, 1981.

BRUCE BAUGH

ROMAN AESTHETICS. "And Rome was taken captive by its captives." Such was the opinion of the Romans themselves about their debt to Greek art and artists, and it has been the conventional view of Greek art—but not architecture—from Johann Joachim Winckelmann through generations of grecophilic German art historians and aestheticians until the present. But Roman art, the principles governing its generation and production, the objectives of its patrons, both public and private, and the nature of its reception are not so easily defined by this alleged self-determining dependency on the artistic culture of an "other." After all, works of Roman art were produced in unprecedented number for centuries—third century BCE to fourth century CE—over a very wide area, encompassing ethnically diverse populations and varied belief systems, all within a society that was sharply divided by class, by distinctions between "Romans" and "provincials," yet was also dominated by an urban culture that was remarkably consistent throughout the Roman Empire. Simplistic or reductive definitions of Roman aesthetics, aesthetic attitudes, or the

exercise of Roman taste, whether expressed in terms of relative servitude to Greek artistic norms or in response to and/or rejection of them, fail to do justice to the complexity of this first world art, the foundation of European art itself. To complicate matters further, not only is there no modern consensus about the essential character of Roman art, but the ancient Romans rarely exhibited self-conscious pursuit of "beauty," so essential to the conventional formulation of an aesthetic attitude.

To a considerable degree, Roman aesthetic attitudes were overtly impoverished by a studied indifference to the matter of "beauty" and to its embodiments and creators. Artists in Roman society were déclassé, deemed unworthy of specific mention among the members of the Roman cultural elite who left few verbal statements of their views but who repeatedly made informed, deliberate, if often eclectic choices among competing artistic traditions, or styles, and their masters. Roman attitudes must be extracted from the extensive evidence of the exercise of Roman taste in action and from the highly selective, programmatic patterns of patronage. Furthermore, there can be no question that the language and topics of critical, aesthetic discourse had been previously established by Greek philosophers and scholar-critics, from Plato and Aristotle to Xenokrates of Athens and Longinus—almost exclusively with reference to drama, epic, rhetoric, and poetics, and rarely applied to works of fine art and architecture. Some Greek artists and architects wrote treatises recounting the history of their art and its current practice, expressing inter alia their views about the relative merits of its practitioners, and many of these treatises were known to the Romans. Among the most important of them was a five-volume treatise, written by the neoclassical sculptor Pasiteles in the first century BCE as a guide to the arts and to good taste for the benefit of eager, unsophisticated, would-be Roman patrons and collectors.

These treatises, now unfortunately lost, entered Latin literature in epitomized form, most notably in the writings of Vitruvius, Cicero, Quintilian, and Pliny the Elder. In his *Ten Books on Architecture*, Vitruvius, a practicing architect in the early Augustan Age, composed a conservative treatise on contemporary architectural design and urban planning that included a canned history of Greek architecture and a highly schematic system of values, or proprieties, dependent on Greek precedents, especially on the late-Hellenistic architect-critic Hermogenes of Alabanda. About a century later, Pliny the Elder, a distinguished Roman politician and encyclopedist who died in the eruption of Vesuvius in 79 CE, prosaically inserted the most complete, if very condensed, history of Greek sculpture and painting that survived classical antiquity in books 34–37 of his compendium of practical knowledge, the *Natural History*.

Even Pliny's views about artworks and artists, if one can so dignify them, were shaped by Greek classicizing standards with little reference to past or present Roman artistic practice or taste beyond the most banal comments or annalistic remarks. He even repeated the received dogma that artistic creativity ended in the late second century BCE *(deinde cessavit ars),* although the creative energy of contemporary Roman art and architecture in the Flavian period would seem to belie such an assertion. Clearly, Pliny either had no eye for the present or was unable or unwilling to judge its qualities. Throughout its history, Roman aesthetic education would seem to have been blindly insensitive to Roman artistic achievement and stultified in its judgments, were one restricted to the passages of description, ekphrastic imagery, and the repetition of the stale criteria of value preserved, here and there, in Roman literature. But there are the monuments, and they tell a different story.

The principal Roman writers on aesthetic topics—Cicero, Horace, and Quintilian—clearly responded to their Greek sources but in their own terms, especially with regard to the importance of style as a value-laden construct, carrying familiar, associative meanings, deemed appropriate for particular situations. These authors emphasized the rhetorical power of art to elicit desired responses from an audience that has its place in the persistent Roman effort to use art instrumentally to further the psychological conditioning of well-prepared viewers. Rhetorical effectiveness can be rightly considered the objective of much Roman artistic activity; conversely, because it is so result-oriented, the degree to which that objective is reached, as measured by the receptivity of the viewing public, would qualify artistic achievement. Romans never quite articulate this cost-benefit relationship, perhaps because it would have been too crass, too undignified, but they were always interested in creating a favorable impression by whatever means.

This endeavor to reach the heart and mind of Romans through the eye impelled artists and architects toward splendid visual effects, increasingly evident in later Roman Imperial art. It is symptomatic of the desire of those in power to exert their control over the spectating audience, as if that audience could be made ever more visually sensitive to the theatrical potential of monuments. In the process, the audience's great thirst for spectacular presentations was further stimulated: thus, the extravagant public ceremonies—the triumph in the bedecked Forum, the bloody games and battles in the stadia, the vicious gladiatorial contests in the arena, the wild chariot races in the circus, the ornamented luxury of public bathing—all participate in creating the urban culture of spectacle. This intensely visual Roman culture responds to a manifest preference for optical effects in painting, mosaic, and sculpture and for dematerialized forms, even in architecture, that substitute the *simulacrum* and the *signum* for the physical presence of solid things. This visual approach to the aesthetic experience constitutes the Roman opposition to the characteristically Greek exploitation of the physical reality of plastic forms that appeals directly to the sense of touch, the appreciation

of mass. This distinction between so-called Greek haptic naturalism and Roman optical abstraction was never absolute, nor were the differences ever fully resolved in the course of Roman art, although a progressive move toward abstraction informs late-antique art.

In its formative phase from the Middle Republic to the Early Empire, Roman art exhibited two very distinct tendencies, both developing under the liberating mantle of Greek artistic culture. One, characterized by modesty *(modestia)* of means and gravity *(gravitas)* of manner, is consistent with the old Roman tradition that stressed self-restraint as a virtue and with the cool, clarified idealism associated with neoclassical art, principally derived from Attic fifth-century models. Cicero and Augustus, in their own ways, clearly preferred this classicizing manner, or style, as the proper vehicle for the noble expression of Roman thought and art. This classicizing style retained its elevated image-value well into late antiquity, most especially during the reign of the philhellene Hadrian, and as a statement of cultural politics in the opposition of the "old Romans" to the newly Christianized Empire in the fourth century. But the doctrine of artistic restraint with a Republican and Stoic gloss also underlies the Vitruvian concepts of *decor* (beauty) and *proprietas* (fitness, suitability); these aesthetic propositions contribute to a moral attitude about the arts, *austeritas,* as a means of avoiding the excesses typical of Hellenistic art/architecture and of the Roman nouveaux riches. Paradoxically, this notion of austerity also advanced the claim of indigenous *Italian* art—unadorned, matter-of-fact, "realistic" but often inorganic, in sum, plain—to be truly representative of native Roman culture and society, unaffected, it was asserted, by Greek pretensions. This nativist tendency, sometimes erroneously termed "plebian," has its own long history, its relative importance waxing and waning as urban and provincial subcultures challenged the hegemony of the Roman elite. The plain style is especially prominent under Trajan and from the Severan emperors to the Tetrarchs, when Roman absolutism was fully established.

The other tendency, loosely called "baroque," is no less a combination of Greek and indigenous elements, but it looked to the Hellenistic world for inspiration. This rich, sumptuous manner emphasized extravagant effects, lavish combinations of colorful materials, heightened expression, and a taste for ostentatious splendor and conspicuous consumption. Romans associated these qualities with *luxuria,* whose active, if costly, pursuit soon became one of the operative principles of Roman aesthetics. *Luxus* (splendor or magnificence) is deeply implicated in the Roman ideology of display. Perhaps because *luxus-luxuria* carried some residue of moral opprobrium or the taint of decadence—a view offered by Cato, that dour defender of Roman virtue—this lavish mode was categorized as "Asiatic" in the rhetorical tradition or "Pergamene" in art and architecture, after that major center of Hellenistic art and architecture inherited by Rome in 133 BCE. This negative terminology, laden with adverse political and moral significance in the Late Republic, if much less so in the empire, sharply differentiated ostentatious opulence from the allegedly purified Attic of neoclassicism, although both modes derived their effectiveness as tendentious bearers of meaning from the creative *interpretatio romana* of the Greek artistic legacy—Roman literature was similarly bifurcated. A certain luxurious ambition in design and affect informs a number of Late Republican architectural projects (e.g., Palestrina), comes into prominence again under the Flavians, especially Domitian, and bursts into exuberant complexities of light, color, and aggressive affect under the Antonine emperors and in the Eastern Provinces.

These polar categories, separating the "neoclassical" from the "baroque," tend to be as much modern historiographical fictions as ancient value judgments, especially when one considers the combination of neoclassical, idealized forms with visual splendor so characteristic of Augustus, who found Rome a city of brick and left it one of marble. Yet, behind these subsets of "style," or modalities of artistic performance, lurk the tensions of an incomplete hybridization of the indigenous Italian and the imported Greek tradition. From this difficult situation arises the historiographic problem of isolating "Roman art" as a discrete entity and of characterizing its distinctive features. Clearly, a self-conscious, even deliberate eclecticism pervades Roman art throughout its history, a history punctuated as well by the constant revival of past "styles," always slightly different from their previous instantiation yet charged with "pure" and "impure" connotations, depending on the perceived motives of their patrons. This oscillation between a re-created past and a nostalgic present seems deeply embedded in Roman culture; it constitutes a framework of social and political action that ever renews itself through calculated self-reference as an artistic metaphor for the historical continuity of the state. Thus, the styles that together comprise Roman art and define its aesthetic horizon bespeak an attitude that prizes tradition—or traditions—much as the *pax romana* relied on Roman law to bind together the disparate elements of a world state.

The Column of Trajan in Rome, that most classic if not classical of all Roman monuments, epitomizes the fundamental reliance on an externalized, highly visible field of signs—principally the helical relief—imposed on a simple, organizing structure (the column) that provides order, stability, and coherence to the ensemble. The column itself functions as a purified architectural symbol, recalling the Greek Orders from which it is derived as well as the Roman practice of using these Orders in a manner that robs them of their load-bearing, architectural role in favor of their ornamental prestige as noble elements of the classical tradition. Hadrian's Pantheon exemplifies this practice, juxtaposing the Greek temple front, dressed in marble, and the

ROMAN AESTHETICS. *Augustus of Prima Porta* (early first century), marble sculpture, h. 204 cm; Vatican Museums, Vatican State. (Photograph courtesy of Alinari/Art Resource, New York.)

great cylindrical volume of the vaulted interior, a triumph of space over mass, of surface over substance. Roman sculpture, too, may be considered a heavily freighted vehicle for the display of carefully confected sign systems; Roman togati, cuirassed emperors, modest matrons, mythological sarcophagi, triumphal arches, replicas of Greek "masterpieces," all instantiate the impulse to address the spectating audience with important messages for its consumption, messages displayed on the surfaces of the forms, often subsumed for this purpose. This is no less true with respect to large-scale Roman architecture—the Imperial Fora, the great baths—where perceptible axiality and bilateral symmetry provide the abstract armature that supports and frames space, the immaterial but basic constituent of this architecture.

If Roman art retains its rhetorical purpose over the centuries, there is a discernible movement from materialist values toward a greater dependence on the transcendent sign, the transparency of surfaces, and the immateriality of space—all characteristic of late-antique art. Perhaps one can extract from this phenomenological change a basic premise of Roman aesthetics: that the purpose of art is to convince the spectator of the truth of the proposition presented to his eye. In the third century, Plotinus might have asserted that the realities of prime forms lie behind the surface of things, only dimly perceptible through art, but the contemporary Roman artist would have argued, on the contrary, that such realities come into being before these surfaces in the mind's eye.

[*See also* Classicism.]

BIBLIOGRAPHY

Becatti, Giovanni. *Arte e Gusto negli Scrittori Latini.* Florence 1951.

Hölscher, Tonio. *Römische Bildsprache als semantisches System.* Heidelberg, 1987.

Jucker, Hans. *Vom Verhältnis der Römer zur bildenden Kunst der Griechen.* Frankfurt am Main, 1950.

Keyser, Eugénie De. *La signification de l'art dans les Ennéades de Plotin.* Louvain, 1955.

Pelikán, Oldrich. *Vom antiken Realismus zur spätantiken Expressivität.* Prague, 1965.

Pollitt, Jerome J. *The Ancient View of Greek Art: Criticism, History, and Terminology.* New Haven, 1974. See pp. 1–111.

Riegl, Alois. *Spätrömische Kunstindustrie.* 2d ed. Vienna, 1927.

RICHARD BRILLIANT

ROMANTICISM. [*To analyze the meaning and history of Romanticism both as a distinct period of art and as a general aesthetic category, this entry comprises three essays:*

> Philosophy and Literature
> Visual Arts
> Music

The first essay examines the philosophical roots of Romanticism and the development of Romantic literature. Because Romanticism has had different histories in the various arts, there are separate essays on the visual arts and music. For related discussion, see Aestheticism; Autonomy, *historical overview article;* Difficulty, Aesthetics of; Hegel; Kant; Novalis; Originality; Primitivism; Schiller; A. von Schlegel; *and* F. von Schlegel.]

Philosophy and Literature

Romanticism begins in an experience of anxiety at one's possible human unreality, an anxiety that is strongly voiced by Immanuel Kant in the *Critique of Judgment* and closely associated with him by his philosophical and literary successors. "How," Kant asks, "can I express my freedom and rationality, somehow lodged deep within me noumenally, in a phenomenal world ordered under physical causal laws?" "The concept of freedom is meant to actualize in the sensible world the end proposed by its laws" (*Critique of Judgment*). How? And if I can't thus actualize my freedom and rationality, what then am I? Perhaps I am capable of nothing more than the "almost savage torpor" that William Wordsworth saw in his urban countrymen ("Preface to *Lyrical Ballads,*" 1801). The achievement of expressive free-

dom, in writing and in life, is then seen as the task of humanity, as it seeks to raise itself out of mere naturalness.

As Philippe Lacoue-Labarthe and Jean-Luc Nancy cogently observe, Kant's "weakening of the subject" ontologically as a being no longer present to itself in inner intuition "is accompanied by an apparently compensatory 'promotion' of the *moral subject* which . . . launches a variety of philosophical 'careers'" (1988). In German Idealist philosophy, the effort is to overcome various forms of division—subject/object, value/fact, freedom/nature, consciousness/the unconscious, self/other—by systematically describing a developing metaphysical order that undergirds both nature and humanity, explains the present existence of those divisions, and secures the possibility of overcoming them to achieve expressive freedom.

Romanticism, in contrast, is more self-critical in pursuing this same ambition. Romantics are characteristically more aware that their efforts at expression arise out of and remain marked by the divisions that they wish to escape. They remain in anxiety about their receptions by their audiences. Their best works—in a generalization that holds true for Wordsworth, Samuel Taylor Coleridge, Percy Bysshe Shelley, John Keats, Lord Byron, Friedrich von Schiller, and Friedrich Schlegel—are characteristically either incomplete, or fragmentary, or self-critical, or finally ironic. This had led Lacoue-Labarthe and Nancy to speak of a "literary absolute" that is sought and imperfectly, infinitely, enacted in their works, and it has similarly led Jerome McGann (1983) to distinguish between a doctrinal "Romantic ideology" of the overcoming of dualisms and the more troubling, more self-critical work of "Romantic poetry" that never quite accomplishes its longed-for transformations.

The wish for achieving full humanity through expressiveness, coupled with an enduring anxiety about the possibility of success, while arguably simply part of human consciousness of temporality, also arises with special intensity around 1790 in part out of occasioning social-political and scientific circumstances. The development of a widespread commercial and early industrial economy, particularly in England, in the sixty or so years before 1790, led to increased division of labor and social mobility. Writers and other artists began to make their livings, when they could, through publication, performance, and sales, rather than through patronage. The necessities of doing this, and the uncertainties of reception in a divided economy, led to increased anxiety about both the specific offices of art and the possibility of expressing humanity generally. Rather than seeing humanity expressed collectively in the partial conformity of social structures to a divinely ordained archetype, individuals began to worry about how to win their particular places in the market. As the conditions for the expression and ratification of rationality, humanity, and freedom become more uncertain and tenuous, Schiller notes the "negative results of divided labor" ("On the Aesthetic Education of Man,"), and

Wordsworth alludes to "a multitude of causes, unknown to former times" ("Preface") that are acting to degrade the fitness of social life for humanity.

At the same time, human beings, as a result of the seventeenth-century revolution in mathematical physics and its associated achievements in engineering, are now beginning to possess greater powers to free themselves from natural misery, and hence more scope for the expression of individual personality. There is, in 1790, no going back to any ruder, premodern state without the benefits of technology. The effort is instead to blend modern achievements with more stable simplicities, to blend what Schiller called "the naive"—the pastoral, where mind and nature are one, often identified with the pre-Socratic Greeks—with "the sentimental," the modern realm of dividedness and self-consciousness. The movement of the imagination on the whole is forward toward synthesis, toward "something evermore about to be" (Wordsworth, *Prelude)*, not backward. The French Revolution, with its ideals of liberty, equality, and fraternity, is seen as an especially promising, but then desperately failed, response to these modern social conditions and plights of mind. After the September Massacres of 1792, the Terror of 1793–1794, and the growing domination of Napoleon from 1795 onward, writers increasingly turn inward in attempting to take up the Revolution's ambitions and to avoid its failures. The transfiguration of humanity comes to be posited or announced proleptically, in art or within the subject, not immediately in politics, though the difficulties of proclaiming a message that requires a new audience in order to be received lead such proclamations typically to be crossed by despair, self-doubt, or irony.

Romanticism's aims for humanity thus contrast powerfully with the ancient world's pursuit of naturalness and *eudaimonia,* with medieval Christianity's ideals of obedience, continence, and beatitude, and with the Enlightenment's commitment to scientific understanding, material improvement, and satisfaction. Instead of any of these, expressiveness, or what Wordsworth and Ralph Waldo Emerson call Power, is the aim, wherein subjective personality and social reciprocity support one another, rather than being locked in conflict. Social peace is to be won without sacrificing individuality and spontaneity.

A number of thematic and stylistic features distinguish the Romantic writing that pursues this aim from its predecessors.

1. There is a prominent retrospective stance that expresses a consciousness of fallenness or dividedness. "Was it for this . . .?" Wordsworth asks about his present impotent state in the *Prelude* in undertaking to review his life; "That time is past, / And all its aching joys are now no more, / And all its dizzy raptures," he laments in "Tintern Abbey." In his 1808 "Lectures on Dramatic Art and Literature"—the principal critical document on Jena Romanticism for both Madame de Staël and Coleridge, who transmitted its analyses to France and England, respectively—August Wilhelm

von Schlegel remarks that "The Grecian ideal of human nature was perfect unison and proportion between all the powers—a natural harmony. The moderns, on the contrary, have arrived at the consciousness of an internal discord which renders such an ideal impossible." This consciousness of discord and division traces back to Schiller's essay "On Naive and Sentimental Poetry," and before that to Kant's remarks in his historical and anthropological essays on humanity's fitful progress through alienation. In France, it is expressed in Jean-Jacques Rousseau's opposition to the idea that the arts and civilization have led to an improvement in manners; in England, in the mythologies of loss of William Blake, Keats, and Shelley, and in Wordsworth's complaints about modern urban life.

2. In opposition to the neoclassical ideal of decorum in style aiming at pleasure, Romanticism reconceives the work of art as flowing from imagination, *poesis,* or genius, in relative freedom from rules. Wordsworth condemns "false refinement" and "what is usually called poetic diction," and he urges the merits of "prosaisms" ("Preface"). Taste is stigmatized as "a passive faculty" unable to engage with "the profound and exquisite in feeling, the lofty and universal in thought and imagination" (Wordsworth, "Essay, Supplementary," 1815). Instead, "Imagination . . . / Like an unfathered vapour that enwraps, at once, some lonely traveller" (Wordsworth, *Prelude)*, is to move us, in art and in life. "Internal authority alone is decisive" in the arts, August Wilhelm von Schlegel observes, and we ought not to accord "an unlimited authority" to the ancients ("Lectures"). A marked emphasis on originality—according to Kant the "primary property" of genius *(Critique of Judgment)*—issues in a pervasive antimoralistic, antinomian stance that has led some twentieth-century critics to accuse Romantics of sentimentality, vapidity, and a cult of idle sincerity in homage to nothing. Yet, the Romantic animus against borrowing and imitativeness—"even what we borrow from others, to assume a true poetical shape, must as it were be born again within us" (August Wilhelm von Schlegel, "Lectures")—also powerfully undermines dogma and complacency, in politics, art, religion, and life. In opposition to formalisms, the decorous, and the hierarchical, Romanticism's direction of thought is generally democratic-individualist. Wordsworth's "Muse," William Hazlitt observes, "is a levelling one" ("The Spirit of the Age").

3. Seeking to avoid both materialistic-oriented naturalisms and abstract moral or religious formulas, Romanticism moves epistemologically between empiricism and rationalism. The mind is typically pictured as quickened or awakened to autonomy and self-productive power in and through its engagements with certain natural scenes, numinous places, or genius loci of sublimity or beauty. "The sentimental poet" of modernity, as Schiller puts it, "*reflects* upon the impression that objects make upon him, and only in that reflection is the emotion grounded which he himself experiences and which he excites in us" ("On Naive and Sentimental Poetry"). The mind is both receptive and active, in its engagements with nature. Ordinary experience, figured by Wordsworth as "humble and rustic life" ("Preface"), reveals itself as uncanny—both in need of and in admitting of the unleashing of as yet muted powers.

4. Where medieval Christianity sought to locate humanity cosmologically within an exterior order, Romanticism tends to find either our home or the route toward our transformation in a descent within the psyche, so much so that it is possible to speak, with Northrop Frye, of the "internalizing of reality in Romanticism proper" (1963) or the internalization of quest romance. As Geoffrey Hartman puts it, the effort is "to draw the antidote to self-consciousness," in its present alienation and dividedness, "from consciousness itself," through a movement of descent. ". . . in such strength / Of usurpation, when the light of sense / Goes out, but with a flash that has revealed / The invisible world, doth greatness made abode, / There harbours whether we be young or old. / Our destiny, our being's heart and home, / Is with infinitude, and only there" (Wordsworth, *Prelude*).

5. As a result of its political and religious antinomianism and its emphasis on the transfiguration of our condition, Romanticism reintroduces anticlassical, Augustinian themes of the existence of standing struggles within the person, between the person and society, and between opposed sectors within society. Charles Taylor notes the Romantics' "resistance to a one-dimensional picture of the human will and their recovery of the sense that good and evil are in conflict in the human breast" (1989). Instead of knowing what we want, individually or collectively, we find that our impulses are divided, polymorphous, in need of a kind of harmonization that is never wholly achieved.

6. The typical protagonist of a Romantic text is more or less a solitary—from Wordsworth's *Prelude* persona, to Shelley's Prometheus, Keats's Hyperion, and Friedrich Schlegel's Julius. Often this protagonist is locked in a struggle with chthonic forces, internal and external, in an effort to achieve free expressiveness. Often the implied author-protagonist stands somewhat outside the fragmentary work as the locus of a hazy power of assemblage and vision. Even when others are presented in Romantic narratives, they typically appear as potential members of a small band, a company apart or an intellectual-political-artistic coterie, that has lifted itself out of generalized humanity's more vulgar commercial self-stultifications. For example, some of Jane Austen's happily married pairs self-consciously stand apart in this way in her endings, at home in higher tastes and manners that are supported by economic privilege. The ordinary travails of finding a job and earning a wage are rarely presented as providing opportunities for the development of identity. The action of identity development tends to take place in mythic arenas, or in pastoral seclusion, or in conditions of economic privilege. This has led some readers to regard Romantic impulses toward rebirth in retreat as a politically escapist bourgeois indulgence. Whether this is so depends in large measure on what one makes of the presence of problems of expressiveness within many or most human lives, and on the resources for addressing those problems that one sees in the arts and in internal descent, in contrast with class- or group-based political organization.

7. In seeking to retreat from commercial, public life, and ultimately to transfigure it, Romantics often turn to various forms of the vernacular or the exotic, against the public high culture of the neoclassical period. Figures from the Arab world or the Orient appear in works of Wordsworth, Novalis, and Coleridge and are associated with archaic-visionary alternatives to Western public culture; or the Greek gods are treated as such figures of human possibility, as in Keats and Shelley. Medieval Christianity is sometimes seen as an alluring time of social harmony and meaningfulness, especially in Novalis's "Christianity or Europe." Older quest romance literary forms and figures are reconsidered and rewritten. Interest in the North and in the medieval competes with and jostles attraction to the ancients and to Latin. William Shakespeare, Aristo, and Ossian are seen as significant predecessors, Ovid much less so. As August Wilhelm von Schlegel notes,

> the word [*romantic*] is derived from *romance*—the name originally given to the languages which were formed from the mixture of the Latin and the old Teutonic dialects, in the same manner as modern civilization is the fruit of the heterogeneous union of the peculiarities of the northern nations and the fragments of antiquity; whereas the civilization of the ancients was much more of a piece.   ("Lectures")

A sense of the artistic attractiveness of mixtures and liminal figures, rather than smoothness of finish, predominates. "No one," Friedrich Schlegel remarks, "can be the direct mediator for even his own spirit" ("Ideas").

8. Crossed with self-consciousness and opposed to neoclassical ideals of formal completion, many of the most important Romantic works are either unfinished or continually self-revising, including Wordsworth's *Prelude* and *The Excursion,* Coleridge's *Kubla Khan,* Keats's Hyperion poems, Shelley's "The Triumph of Life," Blake's *The Four Zoas,* and Friedrich Schlegel's *Lucinde* and "Critical Fragments," "Athenaeum Fragments," and "Ideas," among many others. In their fragmentariness or their self-revisions, these works often seek indirectly to suggest the persistence of a poetic, self-formative power beyond or outside the work. As Friedrich Schlegel puts it:

> The romantic kind of poetry is still in a state of becoming; that, in fact, is its real essence: that it should forever be becoming and never be perfected. It can be exhausted by no theory and only a divinatory criticism would dare to try to characterize its ideal. It alone is infinite, just as it alone is free.
>
>   ("Athenaeum Fragments")

Likewise Novalis: "The great mind would make of every acquaintance, every incident, the first item in an infinite series—the beginning of a never ending romance" ("Miscellaneous Writings"). Movement is all. Romantic doctrinal conclusions, when they occur, are often forced and unconvincing, unless they arrive at either irony, as in Byron, or despair, as in Coleridge.

The extent to which Romanticism has been supplanted as a form of sensibility, aspiration, and artistic expression by realism or modernism or postmodernism remains in dispute. Each of these movements takes up some aspects of the Romantic style and often in one way or another continues its tropes of rebirth and its emphasis on the movement of becoming. The social conditions of commerce, industry, and public life that influenced Romanticism have intensified, not disappeared, and human consciousness of temporality and wishes for rebirth and recognition have not altered structurally, even while the continuing deferral of the satisfaction of Romantic aspirations—itself noted in Romantic writing—has furthered our sense of being trapped in complexities and divided against ourselves.

[*See also* Classicism; Coleridge; Emotions; Genius, *conceptual and historical overview article;* Goethe; Irony; *and* Wordsworth.]

BIBLIOGRAPHY

Abrams, M. H. *The Mirror and the Lamp: Romantic Theory and the Critical Tradition.* New York and Oxford, 1953.

Abrams, M. H. *Natural Supernaturalism: Tradition and Revolution in Romantic Literature.* New York, 1971.

Abrams, M. H. "Neoclassic and Romantic." In *A Glossary of Literary Terms,* 6th ed., pp. 125–129. Fort Worth, Tex., 1993.

Frye, Northrop, ed. *Romanticism Reconsidered.* New York, 1963.

Gaull, Marilyn. *English Romanticism: The Human Context.* New York, 1988.

Lacoue-Labarthe, Philippe, and Jean-Luc Nancy. *The Literary Absolute: The Theory of Literature in German Romanticism.* Translated by Philip Barnard and Cheryl Lester. Albany, N.Y., 1988.

Lockridge, Laurence S. *The Ethics of Romanticism.* Cambridge and New York, 1989.

Lovejoy, Arthur O. "The Meaning of 'Romantic' in Early German Romanticism" (1916) and "On the Discrimination of Romanticisms" (1934). In *Essays in the History of Ideas,* pp. 185–206 and 228–253. Baltimore, 1948.

McFarland, Thomas. *Romanticism and the Forms of Ruin: Wordsworth, Coleridge, and Modalities of Fragmentation.* Princeton, N.J., 1981.

McGann, Jerome J. *The Romantic Ideology.* Chicago, 1983.

Mellor, Anne K. *English Romantic Irony.* Cambridge, Mass., 1980.

Seyhan, Azade. *Representation and Its Discontents: The Critical Legacy of German Romanticism.* Berkeley, 1992.

Taylor, Charles. *Sources of the Self: The Making of the Modern Identity.* Cambridge, Mass., 1989.

Wellek, René. "The Concept of Romanticism in Literary History" (1949) and "Romanticism Re-examined." In *Concepts of Criticism,* edited by Stephen G. Nichols, Jr., pp. 128–198 and 199–221. New Haven, 1963.

RICHARD ELDRIDGE

Visual Arts

Books on Romanticism—even when the term's application is restricted, as here, to a European movement of around 1790 to 1850—begin by stressing its sprawling nature and the consequent difficulty even of approximate definition. When attention is focused on Romantic art, in all its variety, matters seem hardly more tractable, so that one can sympathize with Stendhal's verdict that Romantic art is what pleases people "in the present state of their customs," classical art what pleased their grandfathers. To take just the case of painting, Romantic works, unlike those of Dutch genre painting or French Impressionism, are not to be grouped by a distinctive subject matter, style, or technique. Gallery visitors ignorant of intellectual history would have no reason to gather, under a single "ism," the geometrical drawings of William Blake, the somber crucifixions of Caspar David Friedrich, the "misty" works of Joseph Mallord William Turner, and the "exotic" canvases of Eugène Delacroix.

It is tempting to conclude that the only common factor among such artists is the very individualism that also separates them, that the "essential distinguishing characteristic of Romantic art" is the artist's personal "authenticity" (Honour, 1991, p. 20). A better conclusion is that Romantic art is identifiable only in relation to Romantic aesthetics. Crudely, artworks are Romantic to the extent that they are informed by, or manifest tenets of, Romantic aesthetic thought—"crudely," because not all Romantic artists were self-consciously executing a particular aesthetic, and in the case of those who were, it is not always obvious how their works relate to their program. Philipp Otto Runge proclaimed the familiar Romantic idea that "art should be the expression of . . . religious mysticism," but specialized in static portrayals of fat children.

Efforts to articulate the aesthetic that informed Romantic art range from locating some overarching tenet (the supreme value of the creative imagination, the achievement of the unity of spirit and matter, or whatever) from which more particular artistic ambitions might flow, to drawing up a long list of Romantic predilections (for emotion, spontaneity, movement, expression, individuality, and so on), some sufficient set of which the Romantic artwork must reflect. The danger in the former attempt is that of Procrusteanism; in the latter, that of failure to lend any order and coherence to the ideas informing the artworks.

A way of bringing into relief the Romantic aesthetic in its bearing on the visual arts, which steers between those two dangers, is to attend to several hierarchical classifications typically subscribed to by Romantic thinkers:

1. the superiority of the artist over the scientist, even over the philosopher, and certainly over everyone else;
2. the superiority, among the arts, of music and literature over the visual arts;

3. the superiority, within the visual arts, of painting over sculpture and architecture.

These hierarchical orderings are themselves ordered. Not only do they become increasingly specific, but the reasons for a later ordering stem from an earlier one. The predilection for painting—and, within that art, for landscape—ultimately stems from reasons for elevating the artist's calling over any other.

Before addressing the three hierarchies, a word is needed on the famous distinction between Romantic and neoclassical attitudes. Modern scholarship is apt to soften the impression of agonistic dichotomy that once prevailed. It is true that August Wilhelm von Schlegel, the first seriously to elaborate the distinction, recognizes in both tendencies a similar ambition, the expression of a sense of harmony, albeit one that in the classicist is "natural," in the Romantic striven for in the teeth of an initial "awareness of inner dissension" between "the intellectual and the sensual" (quoted in Willson, 1982, p. 183f.). It is true as well that artworks of the period do not all fit unambiguously under one or other label. The "neoclassicist" Jacques-Louis David's *The Death of Marat* is as expressive and moving as anything by Delacroix, although the latter portrayed classical figures, such as Medea, as often as David. Still, it is grossly exaggerated to write that "neoclassicism . . . is no more than an aspect of Romanticism" on the grounds, apparently, that the Romantics, too, often looked back to and "revived" earlier styles, such as the Gothic (Janson, 1986, p. 575). Hence, it is a constraint on any framework for elucidating Romantic aesthetics that it bring out the contrasts between Romantic and neoclassical aspirations, even if these are more blurred than older histories of art suggest.

Artists, Scientists, Philosophers. A constant lament of Romantic thinkers is that Enlightenment science has disastrously misrepresented nature, ourselves, and the relation between the two. "The world must be romanticized" again, wrote Novalis, after its "disenchantment" at the hands of science. At least three charges were leveled against science. First, it is atomistic and hence divisive, portraying the world as so many discrete items instead of the organic whole we sense it to be. In particular, as Friedrich Hölderlin complained, it teaches people to feel separate from—at best as interacting with—what surrounds them, nature. Second, it offers a completely mechanistic account of the world, thereby dismissing the testimony both of those "dark feelings" that for Wilhelm Wackenroder, evoke an "invisible" realm (in Schmitt, 1980, pp. 84ff.), and of experiences of "sublime" nature, replete with processes not captured under discoverable laws of cause and effect. Third, it treats the world as something objective, awaiting discovery: but this is to ignore, as Blake put it, that "this world is all one . . . vision of . . . imagination," that imagination which, in Samuel Taylor Coleridge's famous phrase, is the "prime

agent" in forging the world as we can ever encounter it (in Wu, 1994, pp. 108 and 574).

Therefore, it cannot be science that is the epitome of human activity. For some idealist philosophers, notably George Wilhelm Friedrich Hegel, it was philosophical reason that would demonstrate the unity and character of reality that science is incapable of doing. But, for the Romantics among them, philosophy was too much in cahoots with science to achieve this, thus leaving art as the only possible vehicle. First, as Friedrich Schlegel explains, "the Highest" cannot be "reached . . . by reflection." It is "unrepresentable," for reflection and representation employ concepts that are at once limited in their scope and divisive of what they are applied to (Bowie, 1990, chap. 2). Art, of course, cannot *represent* "the Highest," the Absolute, but it can exhibit that "longing" for something unlimited that philosophy pretends to delimit. Moreover, in the "play-drive" that Friedrich von Schiller postulated, art can embody those unities—notably between the intellectual and the sensual—that reason cannot explain. It is for such reasons that Friedrich Wilhelm von Schelling pronounced art the "organ of philosophy" (1988, p. 695).

Second, if nature is a whole of which we are integral parts, then it is something that "courses through" each of us: hence, the most promising strategy for insight into nature is not that of disengaged spectating but "espousing the inner élan . . . or impulse" of nature within us, and by "expressing" this to "make what was hidden manifest both for myself and others" (Taylor, 1989, p. 375). The person supremely fitted to do that is the artist.

Finally, if in a sense the world is a creature of the imagination, then the best place to turn if one is to explore those passing "worlds" so created is, as Schelling and Johann Gottfried von Herder insisted, to those self-consciously imaginative myths, allegories, and artworks through which human beings have, over the ages, expressed their visions.

The Romantic elevation of artists over everyone else affords them a very different status and role from the (neo)classically envisaged ones. In particular, the artist's function is not the relatively modest one of mimesis or representation. For Nicolas Poussin and Sir Joshua Reynolds, admittedly, the artist should not represent what is superficially before him but, in the "grand manner," capture ideal forms, "representing in every one of his figures the character of its species." But this ambition reflects just that assumption of an objectively ordered nature, awaiting rational discovery, whose rejection entailed a new conception of art as imaginative expression of a vision whose full articulation we can only ever "long" for.

Music, Poetry, and Visual Art. It is a striking feature of Romantic aesthetics that, in quantity at least, the literature on visual art pales in comparison to that on poetry and music. We have Wackenroder's and Runge's ruminations on painting, Charles Baudelaire's essays on Delacroix, and

ROMANTICISM: Visual Arts. Joseph Mallord William Turner, *Moonlight, A Study at Millbank* (c. 1797), oil on canvas, 314 × 403 cm; Tate Gallery, London. (Copyright by Clore Collection, Tate Gallery, London; photograph courtesy of Art Resource, New York.)

John Ruskin's celebration of Turner in *Modern Painters*, but little else of note to compare with the voluminous theorizing on the nonvisual arts by the Schlegel brothers, Coleridge, E. T. A. Hoffmann, and many others. This discrepancy reflects the conviction that the visual arts come in third after music and literature. (Opinions differed as to which came in first.) Influenced, doubtless, by the prevalence of neoclassical or "academic" painting and sculpture, the common impression was that visual artworks were too static, mimetic, or limited to be the ideal media for giving full expression to the creative imagination, the inchoate sense of the unity of everything, and the "dark feelings" of an organic nature coursing through the veins.

Reversing Immanuel Kant's judgment, music gets praised precisely because it is nonconceptual. Unencumbered by representational, conceptual devices, music addresses us as "spirit speaking directly to spirit." It is because he "leaves behind" what is "determinable by concepts" that Ludwig van Beethoven, according to Hoffmann, can "devote himself to the unsayable," the Absolute (quoted in Bowie, 1990, p. 184). Music, moreover, as Hegel observed, is better placed than painting to express the "inward" life that was the special concern of the Romantics—and this because it, like the life of mind and will, moves in time. (Arthur Schopenhauer was to claim that music is an immediate "copy" of the Will, the ineffable principle of reality in itself.) If Hegel's point alludes to the melodic aspect of music, other writers, exploiting Kant's remark that music is suited to express the "idea of a connected whole," stressed the harmonic dimension. The rich chord is the perfect "sensuous," yet nonconventional, symbol of that unity-in-difference that, for Romantics, reality is. Finally, the composer is more free than the visual artist, able to give vent to his imagination by combining notes with a spontaneity and élan that, emulated by the painter, would result in a mere mess.

It is the freedom enjoyed that is also a reason for placing the poet above the painter. Language, Percy Bysshe Shelley argues, permits "more various and delicate combinations, than colour [and] form," and hence is more "obedient" to the "arbitrary" imagination than the materials of the visual artist, which "limit" and "interpose between conception and expression" (quoted in Wu, 1994, p. 958). Poetry, moreover, is the ideal vehicle for that "romantic irony," of which the Schlegels made so much, through which the artist draws attention to his own creative procedure, thereby driving home the Romantic message that we stand to things not as reflective mirrors but imaginative producers. (Here, of course, is a significant affinity with those latter-day critics of the "Enlightenment project," the postmodernists.)

The subordination of painting and sculpture, and the lessons that were drawn for the practice of these arts, would have been impossible for neoclassicists to accept. In their canon, still echoed in Kant's remarks on music, the merely "sensuous," nonconceptual character of music made it the Cinderella of the arts; and although the visual arts could claim no superiority over poetry, they were no less capable of portraying the ideal types and "noble and serious actions" that, for Poussin, were every artist's true calling.

Painting, Sculpture, and Architecture. Schelling's aphorism "architecture is frozen music" is only the best known of many statements attesting to the Romantics' idea that the visual arts should emulate music or poetry. Baudelaire, for example, was to demand that painters should use their colors as "epic poets" do their words (1992, p. 59). (Emulation was sometimes taken rather literally, as when the Hudson River school painter Thomas Cole tried to construct a "piano" that produced colors instead of sounds.) Artists were often judged according to their success in such emulation. Delacroix, for Baudelaire, was the "true painter" of the nineteenth century because he was "a poet in painting," whereas, for Ruskin, it was Turner who deserved that title, not least because, as in a "choral harmony," each element in his paintings "helps" every other element, with nothing "fortuitous" (Ruskin, 1987, pp. 492ff.). Other Romantic painters, such as Friedrich and Runge, saw themselves engaged in an essentially literary exercise, deploying symbols in original combinations, rather as the poet juxtaposes metaphors.

Unsurprisingly, the visual arts were typically ranked according to their assumed capacity to emulate music or literature—the usual order being painting, sculpture, and architecture. Painting, it was argued, was clearly better placed to achieve such characteristically Romantic ambitions as expressing a vision of nature and rendering visible aspects of the "inward" life. Sculpture, after all, was preeminently representation of the human form, and no one could sculpt the sky or sea. As Hegel observed, mere "shape as such" is not the medium for communicating the "grief, agony, . . . deep feeling, and emotion" that are the "proper content of the . . . romantic imagination" (Hegel, 1975, p. 788). One reason he gives is that such communication requires greater and more subtle contrasts between light and dark than sculpture affords. This illustrates the emphasis on the central role of color, as against line and form, that became familiar in Romantic criticism. It was mainly in his depiction of color that the "truth" of Turner resided, according to Ruskin, whereas, for Baudelaire, too keen an eye for line is a positive hindrance to the expression of "atmosphere," "spirituality, . . . [and] yearning for the infinite," in all their indefiniteness, to which Romantic art aspires (1992, pp. 53 and 58). Still less could sculpture vie with painting in expressing the "spontaneous," "arbitrary" feelings of the artist. A "spontaneously" carved statue, after all, is likely to fall down. It is no accident that the most striking Romantic sculptures were not free-standing works, but the almost flat reliefs of Auguste Préault. His critics might have endorsed August Wilhelm von Schlegel's remark that "modern sculptors are too much painters" (quoted in Willson, 1982, p. 180).

With painting favored as closest to music and literature, architecture suffered even more than sculpture in comparison, sometimes being denied the title of "art" at all. More typical was Schopenhauer's verdict that architecture is the lowest grade of art, because the solid matter and forces of gravity it explores are at a far remove from the processes of organic life and human behavior that are the "higher" embodiments of the Will (1969, pp. 214ff.). There were several reasons, doubtless, why it was Gothic architecture that most appealed to the Romantic imagination—a phenomenon paralleled to some degree by the German Nazarene and British Pre-Raphaelite enthusiasm for medieval painting. The great cathedrals, after all, belonged to an age when, supposedly, humans still experienced the world about them as the Book of God. But an important reason was the alleged affinities between Gothic architecture and music or literature. The sheer complexity and copious use of symbols in a medieval church made it more akin than a simple Greek temple to a literary work. And Walter Pater was echoing a familiar analogy of the time in contrasting the "mere *melody*" of a temple with the "harmony" and hence "richer music generated by opposition of sounds" of Notre-Dame d'Amiens (quoted in Honour, 1991, p. 148).

The elevation of painting, and the consequent demands made on the other visual arts, strikingly conflict with neoclassical convictions. Indeed, sculpture and architecture suffered in the Romantic period from their status as the paradigmatically classical arts, ideal conveyors of Johann Joachim Winckelmann's "noble simplicity and calm grandeur." For August Wilhelm von Schlegel, "the spirit of all the art . . . of antiquity is plastic, just as that of modernity is picturesque" (quoted in Willson, 1982, p. 180). For Hegel, classical sculpture necessarily belongs to the past, because it perfectly expressed just that "immediate" unity of spirit and body that is no longer recognized, as the Romantics' obsession with the "inward" all too clearly exhibits.

Romanticism was indeed a broad tendency and there are aspects—a taste for the "exotic," say, or the idea of a *Volksgeist* as a source of inspiration—that have not been touched on in this essay. In the case of the visual arts, at least, these aspects did not play a vital role in shaping the best work of the period—Delacroix's "Arab" paintings being an outstanding exception—although it is not too difficult perhaps to appreciate their appeal to some Romantics. For example, an interest in the different ways that different peoples have envisioned the world is a natural corollary to abandonment of the idea of a single, universally valid representation of reality. To the extent, however, that Romantic visual art reflected an aesthetic, the debt was to the *idées mères*—such as holism and the centrality of the imagination—of the response to radical Enlightenment.

[*See also* Hölderlin.]

BIBLIOGRAPHY

Baudelaire, Charles. *Selected Writings on Art and Artists* (1972). Translated and edited by P. E. Charvet. Harmondsworth, England, 1992.

Bowie, Andrew. *Aesthetics and Subjectivity: From Kant to Nietzsche.* Manchester, 1990.

Hegel, G. W. F. *Aesthetics: Lectures on Fine Art.* 2 vols. Translated and edited by T. M. Knox. Oxford, 1975.

Honour, Hugh. *Romanticism* (1979). Harmondsworth, England, 1991.

Janson, H. W. *History of Art.* 3d ed. Revised and expanded by Anthony F. Janson. New York, 1986.

Kant, Immanuel. *Critique of Judgement.* Translated by James Creed Meredith. Oxford, 1952.

Ruskin, John. *Modern Painters.* Abridged in one volume by David Barrie. London, 1987.

Schelling, Friedrich Wilhelm von. *System of Transcendental Idealism* (1800). Translated by Peter Heath. Charlottesville, Va., 1978.

Schmitt, Hans-Jürgen, ed. *Romantik,* vol. 1. Stuttgart, 1980.

Schopenhauer, Arthur. *The World as Will and Representation.* 2 vols. Translated by E. J. F. Payne (1958). New York, 1969.

Taylor, Charles. *Sources of the Self: The Making of the Modern Identity.* Cambridge, Mass., 1989.

Willson, A. Leslie, ed. *German Romantic Criticism.* New York, 1982.

Wu, Duncan, ed. *Romanticism: An Anthology,* Oxford and Cambridge, Mass., 1994.

DAVID E. COOPER

Music

A powerful mythology connects music and Romanticism, defining each in terms of the other. "Music is the most romantic of the arts," declared E. T. A. Hoffmann in 1814; and Friedrich Nietzsche wrote, in 1888: "I fear I am too much of a musician not to be a romantic." These pronouncements have little to do, on the surface, with Romantic music as an artistic category roughly bounded by their two dates. In the history of European music, Romanticism generally designates the period between the classical and the modern, or a set of compositional practices and attitudes relatively independent of chronology, or a canon of names (usually including Franz Schubert, Carl Maria von Weber, Frédéric Chopin, Hector Berlioz, Robert Schumann, Felix Mendelssohn, Franz Liszt, Richard Wagner, and Johannes Brahms) within the wider range of nineteenth-century music. None of these categories applies to Hoffmann's remark, which alludes to composers now regarded as classical: Josef Haydn, Wolfgang Amadeus Mozart, and Ludwig van Beethoven. (Nietzsche was thinking of Wagner.) A symphony by Mozart or Beethoven was Romantic, for Hoffmann, in that it seemed to represent a separate, ineffable domain—an "Orphic world," he called it—complete in itself, free from human contingency or social purpose, independent of language yet coherent as the most rigorous grammatical logic. It was music in its purest and highest sense, music in its very essence—music itself. Revolutionary when first propounded at the close of the eighteenth century by the early German Romantics, this idea of music as a pure, "absolute" art gained rapid and long-lived ascendancy. In the classical-music sphere, it determines to this day most people's idea of what music is, and as a result scarcely any Western musical practice, theory, custom, or institution can be fully understood apart from it.

One practice that the twentieth century inherited from the nineteenth is a sharp distinction between classical and popular music, for the aesthetics of pure music implies an opposition between high and low cultures, between the elite few and the philistine crowd. Class distinctions swept away by the French and industrial revolutions were reborn not only in a hierarchy of talents, according to the Napoleonic creed, but in a new aristocracy of artists and a cult of high art. Music had a leading role to play in that cult: it promised accession to a truth beyond reason and language, the now-discredited foundations of the old order, and it rested that promise in "great" works that could be prized as timeless "classics." Whereas literature and the fine arts possessed canons of great works reaching back to antiquity, music outside the church had tended to vanish with its time; a concert-hall canon, in the modern sense, emerged only with Hoffmann's trio of Viennese classics, and with the late eighteenth century's new historical consciousness, cult of individual genius, and helpful developments in music printing. What is often called the "Romantic rebellion" was highly selective in its rebelliousness: it rejected, from the past, neoclassical models of good taste and correctness, while reviving artists of power (William Shakespeare being the prime example) spurned by the neoclassics. The cult of Johann Sebastian Bach, the enthusiasm for early music in general, the primacy of German music, the establishment of a standard concert repertoire based on that primacy, the idea of the musical work as a unified whole intended for performance "as written," all date from the Romantic period.

Hoffmann's "romantic" epithet must consequently be understood, in part, as polemical: it claimed a new dignity for music against its detractors of long standing; and it set "great" music apart from the trivial and the mediocre. The existence of incontrovertible masterpieces in the art of music, such as Beethoven's Fifth Symphony (1807), made it possible to argue a demonstrable permanence about an art traditionally disparaged as ephemeral by the very nature of its medium. In his *Critique of Judgment* of 1790, Immanuel Kant concedes that music "moves the mind in a greater variety of ways and more intensely" than poetry, but objects that it does so only "transitorily." With Kant, as with the neoclassics, music's very intensity of effect remains cause for suspicion: as an art of performance in sound, music has the power to act directly on the senses and thus to undermine the faculty of reason essential to the social order. But if philosophers since Plato had feared music for its sensual power, they had attacked it chiefly for its lack of conceptual content. Music was the least amenable of the arts to the neoclassical principle, inherited from Aristotle, whereby art's chief task was the imitation of a moral, ideal nature: as "mere sensations without concepts," according to Kant, music was of "less worth than any other of the fine arts." From this lowly position, music could redeem itself only in conjunction with the voice, capable of articulating "concepts" that could explain and "motivate" the music. Instrumental music had little place in such an aesthetic, which summoned music to remember its place as handmaiden of the word, and instruments to remain servants of the voice. It was a veritable declaration of independence—and evidence of a sweeping reversal of values—when Hoffmann not only claimed for music supreme status among the arts, but did so on the basis of instrumental music, the most denigrated of its manifestations. For Hoffmann, as for Johann Gottfried von Herder who, in 1800, directly responded to Kant's aspersions, music's evanescence, its action on the imagination and the senses, its "vagueness" of content were the very secret of its power and the foundation of its supremacy among the arts.

In a general sense, Hoffmann's "romantic" epithet served to decree a separate province for art, symbolized by the self-contained world of the masterpiece, safe from the intrusions of the everyday. During the 1830s, Schumann, Berlioz, and Liszt used the word *poetic* for similar purposes in fighting engulfment by a bourgeois *prose*. The threat to the "poetic," as they perceived it, came from both without and within: from a callous society concerned only with business and profit; and from musicians (such as virtuosos) who turned their art into a business, or from their old-guard teachers at the Paris Conservatoire, who, in the name of rules, forms, and formulas—including the formulas of commercial success—opposed anything that smacked of innovation. In response, rebel adepts of the new creed become educators and campaigners, priests of the religion of Art, defenders of music as equal to the greatest literature or philosophy. They found a forum for their efforts in the first music journals, where they subjected the objects of their devotion to the new practices of musical analysis and interpretation. In these writings, Beethoven was the supreme model—first inspiring, later inhibiting—against whom all other composers were judged. Among those who did not quite measure up were Gioacchino Rossini and Giacomo Meyerbeer, the two most-adulated composers of the first half of the nineteenth century. Others were Daniel Auber, Adolphe Adam, Ferdinand Hérold, Jacques-François Halévy, Gaetano Donizetti, and Vincenzo Bellini, or virtuosos such as Liszt himself, whose conversion to "high art" in the 1830s ultimately led him to renounce his pianistic career, incompatible with his role as purveyor of the new cult. That cult has stood squarely in the way of appreciating an entire "other" nineteenth-century repertoire, which derives from an earlier, performance-based aesthetic vigorously opposed but never fully supplanted by the "Romantic" one.

Set against the background of French military and cultural hegemony, and the resistance to both by the German Romantics, Hoffmann's aspiration to transcendence through art suggests a conservative withdrawal and retreat, at best an inner liberation through art. As such, it prefigures the art-for-art's-sake philosophy formulated in the 1820s and 1830s, and, at the end of the century, the Symbolist movement, explicit in its reverence for music and its wish to make of poetry a kind of music. It was also in tune with the rise of German idealism, a succession of philosophies that gave music an importance (especially with Georg Wilhelm Friedrich Hegel and Arthur Schopenhauer) it had not had since Plato. Rather than Plato, to be sure, Hoffmann's idea of music recalls the esoteric Pythagorean tradition, gone underground with modern science but kept alive in Gottfried Wilhelm Leibniz's description of music as "an unconscious exercise in mathematics" and in Jean-Philippe Rameau's elegantly rationalist system of chordal harmony. In the last decades of the eighteenth century, a more precise link was forged through the teachings of Karl Philipp Moritz, professor of "the fine arts and the relevant science of mathematics" at the University of Berlin, whose lectures on artistic autonomy were followed by Ludwig Tieck and Wilhelm Heinrich Wackenroder, Hoffmann's fellow adepts of the musical sublime. In the second half of the nineteenth century, this early Romantic musical aesthetics brought forth both idealist and formalist offshoots in musical theory, the latter associated with the name of Eduard Hanslick. Twentieth-century formalism derives from this lineage, with the ironic result that Romantic musical aesthetics, divested of its metaphysics, is the precursor of a modernist aesthetic established in scornful opposition to Romanticism.

What modernism has scorned in Romanticism is in fact a very different set of qualities from those of Hoffmann's Orphic world: qualities—sometimes extreme—of individual and social expression. Far from offering a retreat, Romantic art most often exposes and engages in all levels of the real, summoning up the widest possible range of inward and outward experience. If classical art seeks the general, Romantic art explores the particular. As such, it requires a capacity for expressiveness that Hoffmann's conception of music, read in formalist terms, would seem to exclude. Indeed, the question whether music could express or evoke anything outside itself was the central issue of nineteenth-century musical aesthetics, a question aired especially in the polemics over program music. When Berlioz's *Symphonie fantastique,* subtitled "Episode in the Life of an Artist" and accompanied by a programmatic story, was first performed in 1830, the critic François-Joseph Fétis condemned the genre with the help of Hoffmann, whose essay on Beethoven had ridiculed program music as exhibiting a woefully trivial conception of the art. In the 1850s, Liszt defended his programmatic conception of the symphonic poem (and, subsequently, the aesthetic of Wagner's music dramas) in the face of similar attacks from Hanslick, whose influential tract *On the Beautiful in Music* appeared in 1854. Yet, Berlioz and Liszt had no quarrel with the rejection of narrowly imitative views of music. They claimed kinship with Beethoven, as a model neither of imitation nor abstraction but of expression—the expression of human energies and emotion. Hoffmann himself maintained that the symphony had become "the opera of the instruments." More specifically, later critics understood the instrumental "opera" or drama as lyrical in content, distinguished by the direct or indirect revelation of an author's inner self. Symphonic music after Beethoven was conceived in large measure as episodes in the lives of its composers, though with little need, after Berlioz, for explicit programs. Those programs could be found in abundance elsewhere, such as in Schumann's song cycles, to many the quintessential Romantic music.

Among the implications for musical aesthetics of this implicit or explicit narrative of the "self" was an unprecedented freedom of form and emphasis on individual style. While denouncing conventional genres and procedures, Romantic composers made free use of any and all of them, assimilating styles and techniques from earlier periods, other cultures, and various social settings with an appetite that prefigures the postmodern. In Chopin's preludes, études, mazurkas, and waltzes, genres divested of their earlier functions supply color and character in a style so original it is best labeled "Chopinesque." In Schubert's "Moments musicaux," Mendelssohn's "Songs without Words," or Schumann's *Phantasiestücke* or *Nachtstücke,* the imaginative titles (the last two borrowed from Hoffmann's tales of the fantastic) suggest both independence and rivalry with respect to words, and a notion of genre limited only by the composer's imagination. Liberated from the classical hierarchy, vocal and instrumental textures contribute as equals to melodrama, *Lieder* and *mélodies,* and venturesome forms of opera and oratorio: Berlioz's *Damnation of Faust* blends opera, oratorio, and symphony to produce a work illustrating no genre but its own. Liszt, with the symphonic poem, attempted to create a genre bearing the prestige of the symphony without the strictures of its form. Even works designated as "symphony" or "sonata" in the nineteenth century, make such independent use of harmony, timbre, and rhetorical gesture as to blur or erase the classical implications of the labels.

Musical expression after the French Revolution meant not only individual expression, with its potential for difficulty and alienation, but also a force for communal utterance and social purpose, as in the Revolution's mass festivals. In the political chanson, popular melodrama, choral societies and their music, French grand opera with its political themes and crowd scenes, religious music, and efforts toward mass musical education, the Romantic period displays strong convictions of music's power to affect society. Like Beethoven, the composer of the popular "Ode to Joy" as well as the late quartets, Berlioz the uncompromising innovator spoke also to the masses in broadly conceived works for national occasions. Giuseppe Verdi and Wagner drew from the same tradition, from French grand opera, and from Berlioz in works designed to guide and inspire a nationalist spirit. Influenced by Schopenhauer, Wagner strove to sublimate that purpose and transcend spectacle in a music drama incorporating the early Romantic ideal of "pure" music. Nietzsche understood that ideal but questioned its motives. Critics today face a similar need to question motive and assumption in the aesthetic debates of musical Romanticism, in the current debates that issue from them, and even in the books that best help understand them.

[*See also* Music, *overview article; and* Wagner.]

BIBLIOGRAPHY

Barzun, Jacques. *Berlioz and the Romantic Century* (1950). 3d ed. New York, 1969.

Blume, Friedrich. *Classic and Romantic Music* (1958). Translated by M. D. Herter Norton. New York, 1970.

Brown, Marshall. Review of John Daverio, *Nineteenth-Century Music and the German Romantic Ideology. Nineteenth-Century Music* 18.3 (Spring 1995): 290–303.

Dahlhaus, Carl. *The Idea of Absolute Music* (1978). Translated by Roger Lustig. Chicago, 1989.

Dahlhaus, Carl. *Nineteenth-Century Music* (1980). Translated by J. Bradford Robinson. Berkeley, 1989.

Daverio, John. *Nineteenth-Century Music and the German Romantic Ideology.* New York, 1993.

Kramer, Lawrence. *Music as Cultural Practice, 1800–1900.* Berkeley, 1990.

Le Huray, Peter, and James Day. *Music and Aesthetics in the Eighteenth and Early-Nineteenth Centuries.* 2 vols. Cambridge and New York, 1981.

Lippman, Edward, ed. *Musical Aesthetics: A Historical Reader,* vol. 2, *The Nineteenth Century.* New York, 1988.

Lippman, Edward. *A History of Western Musical Aesthetics.* Lincoln, Nebr., 1992.

Neubauer, John. *The Emancipation of Music from Language: Departure from Mimesis in Eighteenth-Century Aesthetics.* New Haven, 1986.

Rosen, Charles. *The Classical Style.* New York, 1972.

Subotnik, Rose Rosengard. *Developing Variations: Style and Ideology in Western Music.* Minneapolis, 1991.

KATHERINE KOLB

ROUSSEAU, JEAN-JACQUES (1712–1778), Swiss-French philosopher, political theorist, writer, and composer. Rousseau made his name among the philosophes of Paris as the musician and playwright who condemned the artistic and intellectual achievements of the Enlightenment for having destructive effects on social life. Rousseau's aesthetic theory, therefore, is both informed by his experience as an artist and serves to advance his broader philosophical analysis of society.

Music was the art to which Rousseau remained closest throughout his life. He became a musician as a young man, and his *Confessions* describe his misadventures as an aspiring music teacher in provincial France. He arrived in Paris with a proposal to reform musical notation, which he presented to the French Academy of Sciences in 1742. While in Paris he presented several works, including his great success, *The Village Soothsayer* (1752), which was presented at court and remained in the repertory of the Opera for half a century. During this time, and indeed until his death, he earned money as a music copyist. The success of *The Village Soothsayer* led to the staging of a one-act comedy, *Narcissus,* written many years before, which, however, received only a handful of performances. Rousseau worked on several other plays in the 1740s and 1750s—but none was presented publicly, and some remained unfinished. In 1760, he published *Julie, or the New Héloïse,* which became perhaps the best-selling novel of the eighteenth century.

At its core, Rousseau's aesthetic theory is quite traditional: he holds that the fundamental principle of the fine arts is imitation. This definition of art as essentially mimetic is directed against the view that it is a matter of creating pleasing sensations. Rousseau links these two opposing conceptions of art to two opposing conceptions of human nature. He associates the sensationalist view with the materialism espoused by Enlightenment thinkers, according to which human beings are nothing more than complex physical systems. Rousseau argues, however, that human freedom—that is, the ability to choose whether or not to obey natural impulses—reveals a "spiritual" dimension of human nature. This possibility of freedom is what gives human life its moral potential, and Rousseau uses the term *moral* to describe the features of experience that are distinctively human.

It follows for Rousseau that in the human being sensations have two aspects: they are physical events, but they also have meaning:

> Whoever wishes to philosophize about the power of sensations must therefore begin by distinguishing between exclusively sensory impressions and the intellectual and moral impressions which we receive by way of the senses but of which the senses are merely the occasional causes. . . . Colors and sounds can do much as representations and signs, and little as simple objects of sensation. (*Essay on the Origin of Languages* [1781], chap. 15)

As signs, sensations can have what Rousseau calls moral effects, that is, effects concerning our status as conscious, choosing beings. Rousseau's mimeticism rests on this understanding of sensation: artists exploit the full power of their media, and address their audiences as fully moral beings, when the sensations caused by their works function as more than sources of sensory pleasure, that is, serve to represent things other than themselves.

Rousseau illustrates his view of the centrality of imitation with a discussion of the art of painting. The lovely colors of a painting in and of themselves might offer a pleasurable visual stimulation, but that stimulus has no effect beyond the pleasure it yields; it cannot generate an emotional or cognitive response. Thus, Rousseau's view is hostile to abstraction: he would say that a painter who worked merely with swaths of color would be limited to eliciting merely physical responses from viewers, rather than responses that spring from the viewers' full mental lives. What truly involves us in a painting, Rousseau argues, is its figurative aspect, that is, its status as an imitation, for we are able to grasp what the painting is of by interpreting the outlines of the figures as signs representing the subject. Only then can we respond to that subject in human terms.

Rousseau's remarks on painting serve largely as an analogy, to explain his view that music is a mimetic art. He argues that while harmony plays the role of color, providing mere physical stimulation, melody plays the role of figuration, enabling sounds to become signs. Melody, he holds, is intrinsically related to speech, because music and language both emerge out of the primitive vocalizations by which early human beings expressed their various passions. Rousseau does not argue that music is mimetic in the same way as language, that is, in virtue of a conventionalized semantics. Rather, it imitates a subject indirectly, by expressing the passion one feels in the subject's presence. Thus, for example, a melody directly imitates the inflections of a voice expressing an emotional response to a majestic forest, and thereby indirectly serves as a sign for the forest itself. Because the essence of fine art is imitation, it follows that melody is the essential element of music.

Rousseau insisted on the preeminence of melody in music in the face of the leading musical theorist of the day, the noted composer Jean-Philippe Rameau. Rameau held that harmony was the fundamental feature of music, and indeed that he had discovered universally valid principles of musical expression, based in the nature of sound and of human perception, that specified the proper harmonic structure for any composition. Although Rousseau initially accepted Rameau's views, which he incorporated in articles on music he wrote for Denis Diderot's *Encyclopedia,* he later came to reject them.

This rejection was announced in Rousseau's contributions to the "Querelle des Bouffons," a dispute over the relative merits of French and Italian opera sparked by the performances of Italian comic opera (opera buffa) in Paris in the early 1750s. He restated his position in his *Dictionary of Music* (1768). The Italian style contrasted strongly with French opera: the latter was formal and aristocratic, emphasizing elaborate music; the former was simpler and more popular, emphasizing melodic arias. Rousseau defended the Italians, arguing that because their language is itself melodic, musical settings of Italian could preserve the musical power of melody. By contrast, because French is an unmelodious language, composers are forced to compensate by devising elaborate harmonies to produce any musical effect.

In his *Essay on the Origin of Languages* (1781), Rousseau generalizes this criticism of French into a conjectural account of the degeneration of music. He argues that, in the earliest times, the ease of life afforded by warm southern climates led to the creation of sonorous languages well suited to the poetic expression of passion. By contrast, the harshness of the North forced people to speak harshly: with greater clarity, but less expressiveness. The barbaric invasions at the close of the Roman Empire spread the rough languages of the North across Europe. Because Northerners' singing could not, in virtue of their language, be melodic, they learned to create pleasant effects with harmony. Gradually, musicians developed complex theories of harmony, which now dominate musical practice. The music that results is now the product of rules and conventions, rather than a direct expression of natural passions.

This conjectural "fall" of music parallels the accounts of the "fall" of humanity that Rousseau offers in his *Discourse on the Sciences and Arts,* or *First Discourse* (1750), and his *Discourse on the Origin of Inequality,* or *Second Discourse* (1755). In the former, Rousseau argued that Enlightenment culture in general has a corrupting effect on social life. Whereas in primitive society, people's behavior reveals their thoughts directly, in contemporary society the arts contribute to strict rules of decorum that enable people to conceal their true thoughts behind masks of politeness. In a corresponding fashion, Rousseau elevates melody, in which passion finds a direct expression, over harmony, in which feeling is lost in a web of artificial conventions. In the latter discourse, Rousseau describes the progression of humanity from an original state of nature, through a golden age of

primitive communities, to the unjust, inequitable bourgeois society of the present. Again, his views on music reflect his general valorization of the original, natural condition of human life over the artificial condition that human beings have constructed for themselves.

In addition to his extensive writings on music, Rousseau published an important work on theater. The *Letter to d'Alembert* (1758) is an extended argument against Jean Le Rond d'Alembert's suggestion, offered in his article on Geneva in the *Encyclopedia,* that the city drop its Calvinist prohibition of performances of plays. Rousseau's views owe much to book 10 of Plato's *Republic,* which he paraphrased in preparation for writing the *Letter.* Like Plato, Rousseau discusses theater less from a purely aesthetic standpoint than a moral—and ultimately political—one.

Rousseau frames his argument by asking about the usefulness of a theater to its city. Will the presence of a playhouse make the citizens' way of life better or worse? Rousseau examines this question from two perspectives. First, he considers theater's status as a mimetic art, noting that it represents the working out of human passions, allowing the audience to see itself on the stage. But he notes that the spectators must respond favorably to the characters in a play or the play will fail. Thus, in order to succeed, authors will depict the passions in a way that accords with the audience's preexisting values. It follows that plays tend to reinforce the audience's attitudes and way of life. Where these are good, theater will make them better; where these are bad, it will make them worse.

Rousseau's argument leads him to deny the neoclassical account of catharsis, whereby the dangerous passions of characters are countered by appropriate passions in the spectators. Following Plato, Rousseau worries that exposure to characters' passions in the theater—in particular erotic passions, identified with women—makes spectators more vulnerable to their own, which they will be unable to control at all. If anything is likely to be purged in the theater, it is the spectators' sense of responsibility, for they might feel satisfied with their own consciences because they have taken pleasure in the imaginary moral actions performed on stage, without meeting the challenge of acting morally in their actual lives.

The second perspective that Rousseau adopts toward theater is to consider it as an institutional presence in society. From this perspective, because time spent at the theater is time spent away from other pursuits, the value of theater is inversely related to the value of other activities available to the citizens. In the degraded culture of contemporary Europe, exemplified for Rousseau by Paris, theater serves a useful function, because it keeps its audience out of worse trouble. Here again, Rousseau pursues the attack on Enlightenment culture that he announced in his *First Discourse* and elaborated in the series of replies to various critiques of his views. Indeed, in the *Preface* to his play *Narcisse* (1753), the critic of theater declared: "I would count myself most happy to have a Play a day hissed, if at that price I could keep the evil intentions of but a single one of its Spectators in check for two hours."

But if the institution of theater has a salutary effect in Paris, it would be a disaster for Geneva. Geneva was Rousseau's native city, and in his writings he represents it as a preserve of cultural purity. He notes that its citizens entertain themselves by participating in small social clubs called circles, and argues that the circles inculcate values and habits that support the city's republican political regime. A theater would distract the Genevans from their circles, leading to the corruption of their way of life. Not least of the damaging consequences would be the mixing of the sexes—men and women had their own circles—which in turn would result in the feminization of men. Following the tradition of civic republicanism, Rousseau construes feminization as a danger to republican political institutions.

Rousseau concludes that the effects of theater as an institutional presence outweigh the effects resulting from its mimetic content. Thus, on balance, although theater is acceptable in Paris, it is to be kept out of Geneva. But Rousseau is quick to emphasize that cities such as Geneva ought to stage appropriate spectacles to serve as entertainments. He concludes the *Letter to d'Alembert* with a call for "republican festivals," in which "the spectators become an entertainment to themselves." His suggestions range from contests of skill that honor socially useful activities, to a series of balls for the marriageable young.

Rousseau clearly suggested these participatory spectacles as alternatives to the traditionally accepted fine arts. Indeed, they appear to invert his criterion for the fine arts: they appear to be nonmimetic, because the participants present themselves to each other as themselves, not as fictional characters. It should be noted, however, that, at a deeper level, the festivals are indeed mimetic; for, through their participation in the festivals, the participants experience a representation of the structure of their social relations.

From a purely aesthetic point of view, Rousseau's theory—with its insistence on the centrality of mimesis—may today seem outmoded, if not somewhat quaint. One must bear in mind, however, that this insistence stems from his subordination of purely aesthetic considerations to moral concerns. Rousseau is less interested in artworks in and of themselves than he is in their status as elements in the cultural life of society. Perhaps the central topic in his political theory is the role of culture in the maintenance of just political regimes. Rousseau firmly agrees with the ancients that it is the function of culture to mold citizens, and this moral responsibility outweighs any other value that artworks might have. The appalling totalitarian implications of Rousseau's conception of art are today abundantly clear. (Indeed, these implications emerged shortly after Rousseau's death, when the French revolutionaries made

use of his views on art in their spectacular popular festivals, designed by the painter Jacques-Louis David.) It is therefore quite possible to criticize Rousseau's aesthetic theory as a whole on the moral ground that he himself prefers.

Nonetheless, by raising the issues of the moral function of culture, Rousseau's theory of art certainly speaks to questions that continue to be relevant today. For example, the *Letter to d'Alembert* is in large part an inquiry into whether popular culture merely reflects or actively changes public opinion. The current debate over the role of mass media is often pursued in precisely these terms. Thus, in an obvious instance, it is suggested both that television eroded public support for the Vietnam War and that it only broadcast criticisms of U.S. policy after the mood of the public had already turned against the war effort. On another front, in the debate over advertising as an element of popular culture, Stuart Ewen has argued that advertising generates new consumer demand for previously unwanted products, whereas Michael Schudson has responded that advertisers merely detect and exploit already existing trends. These and other current discussions pick up threads of a long-standing debate, in which Rousseau took a strong and influential stand.

[*See also* Theater.]

BIBLIOGRAPHY

Works by Rousseau

The First and Second Discourses Together with the Replies to Critics and Essay on the Origin of Languages. Translated by Victor Gourevitch. New York, 1986.

Politics and the Arts: Letter to M. d'Alembert on the Theatre. Translated by Allan Bloom. Reprint, Ithaca, N.Y., 1968.

Œuvres complètes. 5 vols. Edited by Bernard Gagnebin and Marcel Raymond. Paris, 1964–1995.

Other Sources

Barber, Benjamin R. "Rousseau and Brecht: Political Virtue and the Tragic Imagination." In *The Artist and Political Vision,* edited by Benjamin R. Barber and Michael J. Gargas McGrath, pp. 1–30. New Brunswick, N.J., 1982.

Cranston, Maurice. *Jean-Jacques: The Early Life and Work of Jean-Jacques Rousseau, 1712–1754.* New York, 1983.

Dent, N. J. H. *A Rousseau Dictionary.* Oxford and Cambridge, Mass., 1992.

Hamilton, James F. *Rousseau's Theory of Literature: The Poetics of Nature.* York, S.C., 1979.

O'Dea, Michael. *Jean-Jacques Rousseau: Music, Illusion, and Desire.* London and New York, 1995.

Trachtenberg, Zev M. *Making Citizens: Rousseau's Political Theory of Culture.* London and New York, 1993.

Verba, Cynthia. "Jean-Jacques Rousseau: Radical and Traditional Views in his *Dictionnaire de musique.*" *Journal of Musicology* 7.3 (1989): 308–326.

Wokler, Robert. *Rousseau on Society, Politics, Music and Language: An Historical Interpretation of His Early Writings.* New York, 1987.

Woodward, Servanne. *Diderot and Rousseau's Contributions to Aesthetics.* New York, 1991.

ZEV TRACHTENBERG

RUSKIN, JOHN (1819–1900),   English art critic and social theorist known especially for his four-volume *Modern Painters*. Ruskin is significant historically as the first English writer on art with a national and international audience. His themes are so wide-ranging as to be a compendium of cultural and social ingredients of the nineteenth century. The ways in which Ruskin shook up and recombined these themes opened up new possibilities for thought and action across several arts. He inducted diverse audiences into existence as a new sort of public gathered around his persona. Over five decades, this public evoked from Ruskin streams of jumbled, yet somehow coherent, communications. Ruskin also targeted more particular audiences during his self-shaped career of fifty years: evangelical religionists and tourists during its first half, and the civic-minded throughout. Early on he listened to writers, later to architects, always to painters. Ruskin stimulated considerable interaction across such groups, often serving as a catalyst.

Learning to See. What had begun in Ruskin's *Modern Painters* as a way of comparing Joseph Mallord William Turner's presentation of nature in painting with the "truth" of nature as observed became a general way to help others learn to see. Initially, Ruskin described this as sheer attentiveness without previous schemata, without preconceptions. Rejecting classical idealist inventories for looking, he addressed not simply the artist or the aristocratic connoisseur, but all of an emerging public willing to read and to look for itself. In "Of the Truth of Skies" (*Modern Painters*, vol. 1, section 3), for example, Ruskin took to task those who fail to look up at the part of creation that is accessible to every creature, who thus get along with secondhand images of skies and clouds.

Ruskin directed readers to look for themselves like scientific observers, to explore their visual perceptions. He often interspersed directions for visual experiments. These prescriptions derive from and appeal to the interest in optics, carried on from the eighteenth century, and to a popular fondness for amateur scientific experiments in books and lecture demonstrations. Even if his readers did not actually carry out the experiments, the possibility of "doing" could draw them into the ideas he was presenting. To engage the reader or hearer, to bring them into the center of the action, were his continual strategies.

With *The Elements of Drawing* (1857), Ruskin invited his reader pupils to share his experience of drawing to see. Writing with clarity and directness, he rejected the notion of drawing as polite accomplishment, even though he was addressing amateurs:

> . . . if you wish to learn drawing that you may be able to set down more clearly . . . records of such things as cannot be described in words . . . to obtain quicker perceptions of the natural world . . .

This was a serious endeavor; but it required no previous training, education, or "taste."

Ruskin's style in his drawing manual was conversational; there were both benevolent dictates and supportive, empathetic comments. He addressed the reader as "you" throughout. This personal rhetoric of teaching is a mode that Ruskin used frequently and effectively, especially in his lectures. His drawing exercises were easy to follow, although they demanded meticulous, patient care—which was his own way of working in his lifelong, daily pursuit of drawing. He again provided experiments in optics and perception, bringing his students back to the truth of their own eyes and hands.

Ruskin's teaching methods were based on a knowledge of the visual process from his own experience and from his reading. That the eyes explore and scan across a visual field, fixating on many points in succession, was confirmed by the then current knowledge about the structure and function of the eye's focusing capacity. Addressing the question of depth of field, Ruskin was especially interested in the boundary points of distance from the viewer, at which recognition and processing of detail changes over to a more generalized sense of light and dark masses and textual quality and infinite complexity. In painting, this "truth" is represented by the artist's fine-tuning of these transitions and by faithful and ingenious presentation of the "mystery" inherent in our close-up or faraway view of nature, "never distinct and never vacant." Ruskin points out that the "mystery" is always there, hovering on the bounds of seeing, and it is part of literal, visual truth. Thus, the artist is charged with mimicking what the eyes would see clearly—and suggesting what they could not see—in looking at an actual landscape. But it is clear too that the artist (especially if he is Turner) is editing, manipulating, arranging the elements of that scene to lead and convince the spectator's eyes and perceptions.

Having placed the viewer before the painted landscape with plenty of visual incentives to form conceptions of what is there, the artist has fulfilled the first "great end." The beholder's work is to practice the kind of visual awareness, the curiosity, and the readiness to meet the artist's imagination that Ruskin has modeled in his own writing. The beholder must be "both watchful of [the work's] every hint, and capable of understanding and carrying it out." This "power of continuing or accepting the direction of feeling given" is, Ruskin thought, "less a peculiar gift . . . than a faculty dependent on attention and improvable by cultivation." The beholder's effort must be earnest and he must take time to know the work of art.

Ruskin's rhetoric called on the beholder much as a preacher might call on the believer: be vigilant, be alert, watch and pray! Clearly, from Ruskin's viewpoint, and from the beginning, this is spiritual work. The habit of approaching art with a worshipful attitude was to develop during

Ruskin's century and become an element in cultural and social class attitudes about cultural tourism and museum going.

Thus, Ruskin brought together the maker and the beholder of art:

> Between the painter and the beholder, each doing his proper part, the reality should be sustained; and after the beholding one should be able to say, I feel as if I were at the real place, or seeing the real incident.

This is a moral activity, not only in the messages and values expressed, but in the making and apprehension of the work of art. The artist produces the truest work he can, and it is the beholder's obligation to interact with it, to participate with his truth and integrity as well. Beauty happens in that process.

Moving to See. The other basic method that Ruskin offered for learning to see was more social and historical. It was to take his readers (or listeners) along on a guided visual tour. The invitation to participate in a journey of the eyes and perceptions came of Ruskin's own experiences as a sightseer. On such a tour, the audience is meant to see with Ruskin's eyes, as enhanced by his descriptive power. This is a crucial area on the Ruskinian map. Here are found connections and concordances with thought and practice of the Romantic tradition, with natural science, and with cultural, social, and economic developments.

Early on, illustrated books of travel narratives were a fixture in Ruskin's parlor. Many of the engraved pictures in these books were by topological artists and were "open composition" scenes in which, rather than a single, contrived focus, there were many areas of detail to be discovered. Ruskin used his experiential knowledge of visual perception in an authoritative and convincing way, scanning a natural landscape much like a painting.

Truly, the eyes can see only part of a rushing stream or a copse of trees at a time, but the observer can learn to chain together the sequence of discrete visual experiences, to go search out structure of movement, growth, and relation. This linking of perceptions to build a dramatic sequence was one of Ruskin's main stylistic tools: skillfully he manipulated phrase rhythms, making a narrative of visual images. It was at once a prose work of art and a model for viewing art and nature, and indeed it fits well into the modern ecological theory of viewing enunciated by perceptual psychologist James Jerome Gibson (1979).

Ruskin's way of presenting ideas is similarly sequential, narrative, and accumulative. Beginning in childhood journeys with his parents, Ruskin spent much of his lifetime traveling. Travel was for him a stimulus, an occasion for intense study and acquisition of material; at other times, it was a period of convalescence from physical or psychological illness (this latter use of travel was common with other Victorians of his class as well). Many of the key events of

Ruskin's life and art took place in travel, especially those that are, as Wolfgang Kemp notes, "conversion experiences."

For example, in Turin, before a painting by Paolo Veronese, Ruskin experienced a revelation signaling loss of his Protestant evangelical faith around 1858, an "unconversion" through which a positive belief in the glorious nature of man began to inform his thinking and writing. Documentary scholarship has concluded, however, that Ruskin created some of the "conversion scenes" in various versions and at later dates. Nonetheless, they are significant as "types" in his understanding and representation of his life's progress and, in turn, as factors in his developing aesthetic and social ideas. Tied to a sense of historical change and a cultural preoccupation with autobiography, these cognitive and aesthetic changes are associated with being away in a different space, where new self-definitions might occur.

Just as the Ruskin family extended its travel beyond Britain to Germany, the Alps, and Italy, so others like them ventured further afield. Their mode was very different from that of the aristocrat on the road. Destinations were often different, less well known, not conventional stations of the upper-class grand tour. Of the nouveaux travelers, Kemp says: "In a sense, they filled in the gaps between other people's destinations" (1990). Kemp sees this typical middle-class traveler as often alone, "free," looking at nature—or at a public art collection—as an individual experience.

These habits of travel may be seen as a kind of symbolic expansion for those who were in the process of defining themselves socially and culturally. They were staking out their own territory as cultured travelers. As the range of travel destinations widened, so did the range of what was considered aesthetically significant, or worth looking at. Old guidebooks registering a few "sublime" spots gave way to more detailed and practical handbooks that included geological information and natural history lists. The Ruskin family, and throughout his life John himself, returned again and again to "their" places. For him, it was a reconnection with the earlier experiences in which he had scanned and studied. In a sense, it was a returning home.

Ruskin's most widely known book, *The Stones of Venice*, asks the reader to participate in the narrative reconstruction of a city, to be led into the stone-yard with the author to find out, from the very cutting of the stones, how Venice was built in both architectural and human, historical terms.

The first volume includes descriptions of stonecutting and the laws of structural dynamics as he understands them. Throughout the work, he introduces consideration of structural necessities, as well as "laws" that fit a particular style or specific materials. As he states in an 1853 lecture, he believes that everyone can—and ought to—learn architecture, "because all are concerned with it."

At the close of the introductory volume, the reader is finally conveyed to a gondola, and, in a stirring word voyage,

Venice—decaying Venice of the 1850s—comes into view. Ruskin uses imaginative descriptions to introduce places, to highlight comparisons, to underscore ideas. Most often, these employ movement in space. His comparative scenarios of the approach to an English cathedral close and the approach to the Venetian Church of San Marco are alike classics. They are satisfying to the armchair traveler as well as the British tourist who goes to Venice, Ruskin's book in hand.

Reaching His Audiences. Ruskin reached out and seized his readers with passionate weavings of insights ever more diverse and yet each keyed to himself. One of the Ruskinian paradoxes is that although he had, increasingly, little trust that his audiences would heed or even understand what he was saying, his ideas continued to be formed in the heat and heart of his styles of communication. From having been the observer who once wished to lose himself in observation, to be unobserved, Ruskin went on to become the observer who as artist and critic moves outward seeking relations, whether joyful or painful. His message—that his audiences must read the signs well and endeavor to change their environment in order that art may survive and beauty flourish—became the impetus for his work as lecturer and for his most direct and interactive communication with his audiences, his serial "journal" *Fors Clavigera* (1871–1884).

Ruskin worked in many genres, however: the guidebook to landscapes or cities or art collections or exhibitions; the travel essay; the popular science handbook; the polemical pamphlet; the texts of lectures; serialized essays; books on art history and theory. Frequently, he even mixed styles within a single presentation, as George Landow (1971) described in his analysis of Ruskin as Victorian sage. Ruskin could move from relaxed and humorous commentary to a detailed analysis of art, to topical events, to a lashing satirical harangue, and, finally, to an inspiring biblical close, all in the course of one lecture.

When Ruskin began writing, critical discussions of artists' interpretations of nature had been largely in terms of literature. The "rules" for viewing pictures in a classical literary sense put the viewer at some remove from both the work of art and its creator. This was true socially: a sense of aristocratic patronage, connoisseur's taste, and socially separated knowledge clung about painting and sculpture long after it had ceased to be relevant to the art being produced. The visual artist was in an anomalous position: no longer a servant but not quite accepted as a professional, a learned man yet also an entrepreneur. (Turner is an example of just such a mixture.)

There had also been distancing visually that Ruskin was to override. His description of Turner's painting *Coventry* (*Modern Painters*, vol. 1) is a beautiful example of Ruskin's way of pulling the viewer into the picture, linking detailed observations into a visual narrative, increasing the pace of his language, building to a climax, and then providing, as

the painter has done, a quiet close. During this period, Romantic poetry and novels also beckoned the growing English reading public to new ways of regarding both nature and the writer, and Ruskin set out to communicate his correspondingly intense experiences in viewing paintings. Even though he used analysis of literary works to illuminate processes of perception and imagination in the visual arts, he was intent on "reading" pictures and poems differently, beyond the classical framework. He created not so much narratives about the work of art, but rather, stories of a visual and kinesthetic journey round about a landscape painting or into an Italian sixteenth-century work, or into a medieval city. Similarly, when Ruskin discussed a poem or a play, he was inside the text, moving about among images and characters, tasting and testing the validity of the work.

Ruskin believed that his audiences, whoever they might be, had the potential to learn how to see art and nature well. Ruskin was aware, as lecturer and preacher, of the character and possibilities of audiences. With his writing of the late volumes of *Modern Painters* and completion of the magnificent *Stones of Venice*, he brought the reader even more explicitly into the story, dramatizing this participation in visual and spatial, and finally, social, terms.

Ruskin's styles as a verbal artist always predicate interaction with his audiences, as they teach interaction with the visible world, the work of art, and the artist. He spoke to the consumers he assumed were "out there." Sometimes these are straw men—or women—delineated to prove a point. He spoke also to the ideal consumers whom he wanted to create. He challenged them continually—sometimes gently, as in his manual *The Elements of Drawing*, sometimes sharply, as in his huge public lectures to industrialists and townsfolk, of Midlands cities and of Edinburgh—to participate actively in the seeing and understanding of art, and to make that activity part of their own self-determination.

He made some assumptions about his audience. There are occasions when he addresses women directly, as in his preface to his published lectures, *Sesame and Lilies* (1871). In fact, many women corresponded with him, as amateurs using his drawing manual. Sometimes they are regular correspondents seeking information and guidance on collecting art. Often they are responders to his challenging and frequently outrageous comments in his serial journal *Fors Clavigera*.

In speaking to his "beholder," Ruskin was clearly looking for people who were ready to be active in their looking at art. Writing of "finish" in art, Ruskin advanced the argument that overdone finish deprives beholders of any share in completing the suggestions of the artist. He hoped for readers who have an interest in the natural world, ready to plunge into the study of water, clouds, or stones as "diligent amateurs."

An artist may be merely the viewer's "conveyance, not his companion." But then, says Ruskin, if the artist "talks to [the viewer], makes him a sharer in his own strong feelings and quick thoughts; hurries him away in his own enthusiasms, guides him to all that is beautiful; snatches him from all that is base" then the viewer experiences "the sense of having not only beheld a new scene, but of . . . having been endowed for a time with the keen perception and impetuous emotions of a nobler and more penetrating intelligence" (*Modern Painters*, vol. 1, chap. 1).

Ruskin's initial ideas on the collaborative nature of the artist and viewer relationship partake of this image of the artist as a sort of demigod "endowing" the viewer. Such a connection with the "highest art" can probably only be attained by those who are themselves of superior intellect and imagination, he said. As he moved on to look more closely, however, he began to form ideas of imagination as a creative process infusing many human activities. He began to describe and define imagination more carefully, moving away from a high-Romantic description and closer to his own experience as a draftsman and painter, and also, interestingly, toward scientific modes of analogies.

In what form did Ruskin's theories and high visions about art reach those consumers most active in the contemporary English art world, in particular those attending the increasingly crowded and mundane annual exhibition in London of the Royal Academy of Art? In 1855, Ruskin began writing an annual critique of the Royal Academy Exhibition, which he called "Academy Notes," an outgrowth, he says in his Preface, of the circular letter he had been writing in response to the requests of friends, "to mark for them the pictures in the exhibitions that appear to me the most interesting, either in their good qualities or in their failure." Ruskin's pamphlet proved to be hugely successful, going into many additional printings. The "Notes," expanded to include the Watercolour Societies' exhibitions and also the occasional exhibition of French paintings, were then published in book form in 1859, and once more in 1875.

Aesthetics. A good deal of the first two volumes of *Modern Painters* is devoted to attempts to articulate formal philosophical and theological frameworks for what was becoming a vastly expanded work. Ruskin continued to use some older specialized categories for aesthetic content and experience, in particular from the Romantics—"sublime" and "grotesque," for example—but he is in fact demonstrating a way of seeing that can be applied to anything under the sun, in nature or in art: cliffs, rocks, cathedral walls, clouds, tree branches, waterfalls, whether Turner's or Tintoretto's or a Pre-Raphaelite's painting. This initial structuring did provide a kind of order for Ruskin's flood of observations, images, and polemics, and parts of it remained as keynotes throughout all five volumes of *Modern Painters*. It served also as an offering of intellectual credentials from a still-young author.

Ruskin's most consistent purpose in aesthetics was to describe and analyze the creative process. He was writing amid an environment of ideas in which empiricist psychologies and philosophies of perception made the viewer the main focus, not the object, and much less the continuing interaction among viewer and object and creator. Ruskin was familiar with works on the physiology of vision and with writings of John Locke and many of his later interpreters, among them, Archibald Alison, author of a widely read work titled *Essays on the Nature of Principles of Taste* (1790, with many nineteenth-century editions). Alison's theory of "associationism" held that the key to perception and the literary aesthetic experience is the triggering, by a sensory event, of a sequence of emotion and associated ideas. Ruskin was uncomfortable with this theory on the grounds of its relativism and its implication of a sort of passivity in the aesthetic response. Nevertheless, he came to include associationism by modifying it to suit his purposes. [*See* Alison.]

What Ruskin really knew with authority was his own experience as an intense observer of nature, a collector and recorder of visual experience; and he wrote as an artist who had "been there," struggling with the process of making a painting or a poem. At the close of volume 1 of *Modern Painters*, he talks of the critic's role:

> to tell us whether we are making our best painter do his best . . . none are capable of doing this but those whose principles of judgment are based on thorough practical knowledge of art, and on broad general ideas of what is true and right, without reference to what has been done . . . in one school or another. . . . such references to former excellence are the . . . refuge and resource of persons endeavoring to be critics without being artists.

Clearly, Ruskin believed that he had the necessary artistic qualifications.

In a delightful passage that rings true to personal experience, Ruskin described the "unimaginative painter." He traced a series of missteps by the unfortunate artist, who begins with a carelessly routine form of a tree, proceeds to follow "rules" about drawing trees, gets into all sorts of trouble as each element he adds forces a change in the other elements, and ends in a shambles.

The "imaginative painter," in contrast, knows the laws of nature but follows no rules; he goes out on his own to discover, and he moves boldly. He begins with an overall, holistic vision: "He saw his tree, trunk, boughs, foliage and all, from the first moment; not only the tree, but the sky behind it." All the elements fit together and all are essential to the whole conception. Ruskin introduced the idea that within this unity of the imaginative conception each part is imperfect, but each is "corrected by the presence of the other." The result is "a whole, an organized body with dependent members." This process of creation is, "as far as I can see, absolutely inexplicable." But Ruskin went on to liken it to a chemical change in which the elements are not seen to react in sequence but rather to interact simultaneously. This kind of near-mystical leap—"the possession-taking power of the imagination," he called it, is what he saw in Turner's work.

The artist's sense of the whole conception, for Ruskin, should inform the compilation of truths that include associated ideas, a "garland of thoughts." Ruskin made it clear that this is not merely "composition," which he valued and described in some of his fine analyses of Turner's drawings; rather, it is an overall process in which all the artist's activities operate by means of the "law of help," Ruskin's image for a kind of coordination and life-enhancing energy that runs through the whole creation. Indeed, Ruskin's model of the maker's work seems to be a vision of the unity he longed for in his own life and in his society.

How, then, might the viewer participate in this seemingly separate and rather godlike process? The assumption that Ruskin made was that perception can be trained to an open-ended awareness toward a work of art. He always stressed the active nature of the aesthetic experience: not only did he think, with Locke, that we do not really see until that sensory input has been registered and stored in organized structure in the mind, but he also described the perceptual activity as having a "bodily sensibility" that is clearly physical and also emotional, "both loving and moral," as he put it.

The essentially moral relation between the artist and the beholder that Ruskin advocates differentiates him from theories and practices of the later movement called Aestheticism. Walter Pater, its purest exponent, was a follower of Ruskin; but his ideas and prose departed from those of the master. For Pater, the beholder's effort was an intense focus on an experience snatched from physical and mental flux, an isolated activity in which each individual might find his or her spiritual "abiding place" in the cosmos. Although Pater wrote with great sensitivity and eloquence about individual artists, the moment in time of seeing their art is separated from them and belongs to the viewer only. Ruskin was wary of loading that sort of expectation onto the viewers' perception and, as he called it, the "weariable imagination." [See Pater.]

Seeing well and plainly is, in the end, worth more to Ruskin than is ecstasy, because the viewer may thus participate more nearly in the artist's work and in the Creation. This religious sense is always a ground base for Ruskin, even though its variations are multiple in the course of his life. Marcel Proust, also profoundly influenced by Ruskin and a first translator of many of his works, pointed this out when he wrote to refute other French works that placed Ruskin as the founder of Aestheticism. [See Aestheticism.]

Of Architects and Painters. Ruskin's verbal and pictorial descriptions of Gothic buildings in Venice, together with his theories of architecture, as in *The Seven Lamps of Architecture* (1855), helped change the face of British cities. This happened in the way in which many of Ruskin's artistic practices and values were disseminated. He intensified the interest in and discussion of architecture that had already begun around issues of religious practice and urban development.

A Ruskin-inspired building would most likely have hallmarks of massiveness, a certain squareness and solidity of form that made it intelligible, with nothing hidden and no materials masquerading as something else. Above all, the building should be decorated, preferably in color, using the natural color inherent in the material. A building should reach the beholder emotionally, should engage the creative imagination just as surely as a painting might. Architects agreed and disagreed with Ruskin, picked and chose, sometimes being quite literally Ruskinian, and often negotiating compromises with the institutions for which they were building. Ruskin was often involved in this, he and the architect frequently playing off against one another with ideas, support, encouragement, and discouragement.

It was with architects that Ruskin came closest to collaborative work, despite massive limits to the practicality of Ruskin's themes for architects. He was against the use of iron and steel, against the very idea of progress, and yet, through his opposition to modular design, at the same time against much of the classical Roman tradition in architecture. But some of his social utopian themes that might seem merely naive today struck a strong note in the era, and architects learned to be selectively practical. Perhaps painting had too much of plumbing, of a practical trade unmixed with speculation, to respond as readily.

The Americans seemed particularly adept at picking and choosing among Ruskin's strictures, meant though they were to be taken as a whole. Andrew Jackson Downing, the best-known American landscape architect of mid-century, was an admirer of Ruskin and a proselytizer for his ideas, but did not blush to build his own mansion in stucco against Ruskin's strongest stricture to build only in materials true to their appearance and function. Downing and his associate, the architect Arthur J. Davis, seemed to have come rather independently to some of the same themes as Ruskin, in the same decade.

There remain questions about Ruskin's great impact on architecture. For all his focus on the creative process, Ruskin's central concern, speaking in political economy terms, was consumption, not production. Ruskin was against machines, against steam, indeed, against working professionals. Producer of superb drawings, he could not abide diagrams—like machines, they spoke of mechanistic reproduction rather than imaginative creation. Ruskin had little concern even with the "production" of daily living, urging that no decoration be bestowed on chimneys, which were merely utilitarian. Ruskin focused on the decorative pattern, the colors and masses of buildings seen as rocks, rocks with rich but solid interiors. He indeed was obsessed with the problematics of roof design, going so far as to say, in his lectures as the first Slade Professor of Art in Oxford, that building design was just roofs (roofs over the interiors that Ruskin wished to disdain as being mere building, not architecture).

One answer to the puzzle is just this texture and color that Ruskin treated together and gave first place in importance for buildings, just as for paintings and landscapes. One generation after another of young architects felt liberated by this positive emphasis and took up structural polychromy. Another answer is Ruskin's enunciation of themes that played into the emerging desire for more beautiful, planned cities and neighborhoods. After all, Ruskin saw buildings primarily as elements in a landscape to be judged in the overall design. These account for the greater reception given to *The Seven Lamps of Architecture* than to almost any book on architecture perhaps before or since.

Ruskin's influence on the actual practice of painting was much more muted. He began with the study of paintings, and he drew every day of his life, whereas he had no such direct connection with building. Ruskin saw considerably more of painters than of architects, even later after his turn toward issues of social welfare and justice.

Evidence for Ruskin's impact on actual practices of painters is sparse. The clearest example is William Holman Hunt's acting on Ruskin's encouragement to take up the evangelical themes that most interested Hunt. Ruskin certainly tried to direct and shape style as well as content in other painters, but to little effect except in commissioned portraits.

Ruskin was coming into his own as a public figure during the emergence of the Pre-Raphaelites. During the course of his annual "Notes" on Royal Academy shows, Ruskin had discussed not only the works of the three artists in the original core of the Pre-Raphaelite group, but also works of the many who clustered around the group stylistically. He was, if anything, more discriminating in praising this sort of painting than any other. He noted that, with each year, Pre-Raphaelitism was becoming more a norm than an aberration. "Animosity has become emulation," he commented, and in 1858 he announced that "Pre-Raphaelitism has entirely prevailed (as I stated five years ago that it would)."

Then he made another prediction: the many rather ordinary followers of Pre-Raphaelitism will come to be disappointed at no longer being noticed, because they are no longer considered sensational. But, he said, beyond the comfort of "being right," there is this:

> The kind of painting they now practice is capable of far more extended appeal to the popular mind. The old art of trick and tradition had no language but for the connoisseur; this natural art speaks to all men . . . pictures will become gradually as necessary to domestic life as books; they will be largely bought.

This observation was partly true, perhaps, but offered little specific guidance to painters and in no way affected the continuing current of banal and sentimental genre scenes in the established Academic patterns.

It was a publicist, as mentor, and as patron that Ruskin constructed his relationships with the various Pre-Raphaelite artists. The content and context were quite different from his connection to Turner. When he came to write about them, he often used their work as a jumping-off point for more generalized history and theory, as, for example, the decline of religious belief and the corresponding decline of art, post-Raphael. He praised much of their work for its observant study and rendering of natural form, but he made it clear that this was only to be considered a beginning.

It was other artists, such as William Dyce, who first had recognized merit in the Pre-Raphaelite Brotherhood and literally tugged at Ruskin's sleeve to make him pay real attention to Millais's famous and infamous work *Christ in the House of His Parents* at the 1850 Royal Academy exhibition. Then, in 1851, the poet Coventry Patmore, a recent acquaintance of Ruskin's and a friend of Millais, wrote to Ruskin (at Millais's request) asking the critic to write in defense of the Brotherhood's works. Ruskin's first letter was quite moderate in its praise but did include the key statement that the artists were at "a turning point in their career from which they may either sink into nothingness or rise to very real greatness." In a second letter, he recorded hopes for the "foundations of a new school of art nobler than the world has seen for three hundred years." Millais and Holman Hunt then wrote Ruskin directly, thanking him, and Ruskin's more personal relationship with the Pre-Raphaelites, and their followers, began. With the third member ot the original Pre-Raphaelite Brotherhood, Dante Gabriel Rossetti, Ruskin was more directly a patron. He bought Rossetti's work and helped finance his living expenses and art trips to the continent. He attempted to be the painter's mentor, a role in which he was largely ignored by Rossetti.

There was a close relationship between Ruskin's lessons in basic drawing at the Working Men's College in London and his understanding and support of the Pre-Raphaelite group (some of whom he recruited to teach there also). The kind of truthful observation and meticulous rendering that were characteristic of the Pre-Raphaelite Brotherhood and its followers coincided with the approach that Ruskin taught in *The Elements of Drawing*.

Conclusion. Ruskin's writing and scholarship, sometimes diffuse and overdone, often purposeful and powerful, transformed the discussion of art: he pointed his audiences toward empirical experience of art, emphasizing its accessibility; he linked the practice, the consumption, and the economics of art; he insisted on correlations between images and the societies in which they were born; and he continually crossed boundaries among art, architecture, natural history, religious practice, mythology, social behavior, labor, capital, and ethics. His painterly, descriptive style blurred the boundaries between artist and critic to provide a new literary form for writers on art and architecture.

[*See also* Landscape, *article on* Landscape from the Eighteenth Century to the Present.]

BIBLIOGRAPHY

Works by Ruskin

The Works of John Ruskin. 39 vols. Edited by E. T. Cook and Alexander Wedderburn. London, 1903–1912.
The Elements of Drawing. Edited by Bernard Dunstan. London, 1991.

Other Sources

Altholz, Joseph L., ed. *The Mind and Art of Victorian England.* Minneapolis, 1976.
Ball, Patricia M. *The Science of Aspects: The Changing Role of Fact in the Work of Coleridge, Ruskin, and Hopkins.* London, 1971.
Baxandall, Michael. *Patterns of Intention: On the Historical Explanation of Pictures.* New Haven, 1985.
Brooks, Michael W. *John Ruskin and Victorian Architecture.* New Brunswick, N.J., 1987.
Gibson, James Jerome *The Ecological Approach to Visual Perception.* Boston, 1979.
Gillet, Paula. *Worlds of Art: Painters in Victorian Society.* New Brunswick, N.J., 1990.
Helsinger, Elizabeth. *Ruskin and the Art of the Beholder.* Cambridge, Mass., 1982.
Hewison, Robert, ed. *New Approaches to Ruskin.* London and Boston, 1981.
Hilton, Timothy. *John Ruskin*, vol. 1, *The Early Years, 1819–1859.* New Haven, 1985.
Hunt, John Dixon. *The Wider Sea: A Life of John Ruskin.* London, 1982.
Kemp, Wolfgang. *The Desire of My Eyes: The Life and Work of John Ruskin.* Translated by Jan van Heurck. New York, 1990.
Landow, George P. *The Aesthetic and Critical Theories of John Ruskin.* Princeton, N.J., 1971.
Pater, Walter. *Selected Writings of Walter Pater.* Edited by Harold Bloom. New York, 1974.
Rosenberg, John D. *The Darkening Glass: A Portrait of Ruskin's Genius.* New York, 1986.
Schuyler, David. *Apostle of Taste: Andrew J. Downing, 1815–1852.* Baltimore, 1996.
Walton, Paul H. *The Drawings of John Ruskin.* Oxford, 1972.
White, Harrison C. *Careers and Creativity: Social Forces in the Arts.* Boulder, Colo., 1993.

HARRISON COLYAR WHITE and CYNTHIA WHITE

RUSSIAN AESTHETICS.

[*To examine the relationship between Russian art and aesthetics, this entry comprises three essays:*

Religious Aesthetics
Russian Formalism
Socialist Realism

The first essay pays particular attention to religious aesthetics because it played a dominant role in the history of Russian art and aesthetics. The other essays address two distinct and influential twentieth-century Russian aesthetic movements. See also Bakhtin; Constructivism; Eisenstein; Stravinsky; *and* Suprematism.]

Religious Aesthetics

Russian religious aesthetics is the oldest and most peculiar trend in Russian aesthetics that has continued to exist within Orthodox culture from the eleventh to the twentieth century. The history of Russian religious aesthetics can be divided into four periods: medieval (or Old Russian; c.1000–1650); transitional (c.1650–1700); conservative or preservative (c.1700–1900); and neo-Orthodox (c.1900–1950).

Medieval Period. The first period, Old Russian aesthetics, is marked by an implicit type of aesthetic consciousness that finds its most adequate expressive forms in art, liturgy, and religious (in particular, monastic) life, and not in theories and concepts that are set in writing. Even on the conceptual level, however, a variety of texts of diverse genres (chronicles, saints' lives, religious polemics, rulings of church councils) reveal a rather complete picture of aesthetic ideas of medieval Russians.

Old Russian aesthetics has two main sources: the artistic culture and mythological consciousness of pre-Christian Eastern Slavs, and Byzantine aesthetics, whose influence in Rus began at the end of the tenth century. The Eastern Slavic (inner, archetypal) element of Old Russian aesthetic consciousness is characterized by tendencies to perceive spiritual phenomena as concrete, material, and palpable; to view nature as sacred; to visualize the world beyond and perceive it as "documented" and determinate; and to experience a feeling of mutual magical connection of all things. The Orthodox Byzantine culture and aesthetics that arrived in Rus with the Christianization of the Slavs are superimposed on this substrate—already rich, wholesome, and self-sufficient in its own way—and both reshape it and receive strong influences from it. The written sources of about 1000–1350 well reflect the process of formation of Christianized aesthetic ideas. The *Slovo o polku Igoreve*, the "Story of the Bygone Years" *(Povest' vremennykh let)*, as well as the writings of Illarion, Kirill Turovsky, Hegumen Daniil, and other learned writers reflect the views of medieval Russians on beauty (natural, spiritual, artistic), art, the sublime, and the heroic, which combine the elements of both pagan and Christian Weltanschauungen. Books, as the main carriers of spiritual values, inspire particular reverence in medieval Rus. Together with them, all that belongs to the sphere of spirituality is apprehended primarily aesthetically—as leading man toward God and bringing spiritual pleasure and joy—and is designated as beautiful. The characteristic features of Old Russian aesthetics are paying particular attention to the sensibly apprehended realizations of spiritual beauty; endowing the beautiful with palpable thingness; thinking of beauty as an expression of the true and the essential; developing specific sensibility to the beauty of artistic activity; having an increased emotionality and positive mind-set; and thinking of light (primarily visible light) as an important modification of the beautiful. In arts (architecture, painting, applied arts), Old Russian aesthetics values artistic wroughtness, grandeur, colorfulness, luminosity, brightness, and the presence of precious materials. The church building is apprehended, first of all, as an immense luxurious work of jeweler's art. The sacred apprehension of nature by Eastern Slavs is replaced by the understanding of nature as a beautiful work of the supreme artist. They now see in it a beautiful order *(stroj)* that delights the human soul. The main characteristics of natural beauty are magnitude, height, roundness, "artistic wroughtness," a particular ability to stand out in space. Toward the middle of the sixteenth century, moral beauty gains a prominent position in the aesthetic consciousness of Russians.

The period from about 1400 to 1600 is the time of growth and consolidation of a united and mighty Russian state—the Muscovite Rus—which is headed by the Great Prince whose powers rival those of the Byzantine emperor. Russian political thought advances the idea of Great Russia as the direct successor of the Byzantine Empire in spiritual and political matters. Sixteenth-century Russia sees the rise of the popular theory of "Moscow as the third Rome." Orthodoxy forms the spiritual and ideological foundation of the new "empire." Hence, religious mentality during this period is actively developed, and church art, literature, and aesthetics thrive. The aesthetic consciousness of this period includes a number of principles that are most adequately realized in art but only partly acknowledged by the medieval Russians themselves. In Russian religious aesthetics, they do not become the subject of literary discussion until much later—in the nineteenth and twentieth centuries. These are such principles as the *sobornost'* of aesthetic consciousness, the *sophiynost'* of art and artistic activity in general, the systematic character (or certain synthetism) of church art, its increased artistic symbolism, its high spirituality, and its canonicity.

Sobornost' signifies the essentially extrapersonal (suprapersonal) and atemporal nature of aesthetic consciousness. This is the consciousness of a community *(sobor)* of people, akin in spirit, who, in the process of communal liturgical life, have reached a spiritual unity both with each other and with the higher spiritual levels, ideally with God, that is, a people who receive gracious help from above. For this reason, medieval Russian art and other products of the spirit are essentially anonymous. The medieval Russian learned writer, icon painter, or architect does not consider himself personally as the author or creator of his own work, but only as a voluntary executor of the supreme will that acts through him, a middleman in artistic activity, or an instrument guided by the communal *(sobornoe)* consciousness of the Orthodox church. The communal *(sobornoe)* consciousness not only inspires creative activity in medieval artists, but also preserves carefully the forms, schemes, and methods that have been worked out in the process of this activity,

and that are considered to be the most capacious and adequate carriers and expressions of the Orthodox spirit.

It is for this reason that canonicity becomes the main principle of medieval creative activity. The artistic canon reflects and embodies the spiritual and aesthetic ideals of the epoch and establishes the system of representational and expressive methods that is most adequate to those ideals. In particular, the iconographic canon of Old Russian art, which goes back to its Byzantine prototype, determines the ideal visual structures that contain the ultimate graphic expression, for the Orthodox Middle Ages, of the essence of the portrayed phenomenon (a personage or an event from sacred history).

Faith in the divine origin of artistic activity leads to the understanding of a work of art (icon, church building, literary text) as a carrier of a certain supreme union of wisdom, beauty, and art. It is not until the twentieth century that this trait of Old Russian art receives the name *sophiynost'* (Florensky, 1993; Bulgakov, 1917) and a rather detailed theoretical elaboration in the Orthodox culture, resulting in the high spirituality of this art, for nothing transient, material, or base can penetrate into the sphere of *sophiynost'*. The artistic aim to express supreme spiritual values of culture leads to the raising of the level of abstraction of the language of art, as well as to the deepening of the degree of conventionality of artistic expressive means, that is, to artistic symbolism.

The system of these principles achieves its highest perfection and expressive completeness in the art of Andrei Rublev (around 1400), the most prominent painter of medieval Rus. Epiphanij Premudry, the most gifted hagiographer of that epoch, together with his literary colleagues, devise and put into practice the principles of a highly aestheticized literary style, which they call "word weaving" *(pleteniye sloves)* and which consists in infinite multiplication of metaphors and exquisite and complicated epithets around one thought.

The period around 1500–1600 is marked by a more pronounced literary expression of aesthetic views in medieval Russia. The leader of the ascetically oriented monks, Nil Sorsky, works out a Russian variant of "asceticist aesthetics," and Iosif Volotsky, his opponent in regard to the organization of monastic life, is occupied with the rethinking of liturgical aesthetics. It is he who, for the first time in Rus, expounds, in a rather detailed way, the Orthodox theory of the icon and the iconographical program for icon painters.

In the sixteenth century, a contribution to the consolidation of medieval aesthetic views is made by such thinkers as Maxim Grek, Vassian Patrikeyev, Zinovij Otensky, the monk Artemij, Prince Andrei Kurbsky, and the church councils of 1551 (the so-called *Stoglav*) and 1554. During this period, the sphere of the aesthetic—primarily literature and church art—is closely intertwined with the political, ecclesiastical, and ideological struggle between various church and state factions. Canonicity and traditionalism are acknowledged as the most important principles of art, but at the same time artistic practice gradually departs from them—a fact that foreshadows the beginning of the crisis of the medieval type of artistic thinking that comes to completion around 1700. A sharp polemic is initiated concerning complex religious allegorical representations that appear in church icon painting, as a result of which the symbolic theology of Pseudo-Dionysius the Areopagite, and in particular his concept of "unlike likenesses," is being interpreted, for the first time in the Orthodox aesthetics, as the theoretical foundation of religious painting.

Transitional Period. The characteristic feature of the second period of Russian religious aesthetics—the transition from the Middle Ages to modern times—is the spirit of sharp polemic between traditionalists and innovators regarding the main aesthetic problems and the gradual departure from the medieval style in art under the influence of sixteenth- and seventeenth-century western European art. The seventeenth century sees the appearance of manuals of grammar, rhetoric, and arithmetic in Russian, the creation of special treatises on music and painting, regulative handbooks (chinovnik, from Russian chin, "order") on ceremonial aesthetics ("The Chinovnik of Archpriestly Service," "The Order [chin] of the Blessing of Water," "The Order of Anointing for Kingship," "The Wedding Order," "The Order [uryadnik] of Falconry," etc.), where the aesthetic problematic holds a prominent place. The characteristic tendency of the specific treatises on art that are written between about 1650 and 1700—as a rule, promoting new methods and styles in religious art that differ from the medieval—is an attempt to prove that their methods do not contradict the medieval (and even the patristic) tradition, but, on the contrary, realize it more profoundly than the earlier ones.

Thus, Simeon Polotsky, the most prominent court poet, playwright, and theoretician of art in this period, undertakes to replace the traditional prose Slavonic translation of the Book of Psalms with a free poetic interpretation. He justifies his efforts not so much by the fact that the Hebrew original was also in verse, as by an observation that poetic text allows for a more laconic expression of thoughts, while it also emphasizes and interprets their inner meaning. According to him, poetic form (meter and rhyme) brings spiritual delight to the reader and thus facilitates the process of penetrating the spiritual depths of the text.

Nikolai Diletsky and Ivan Korenev, the authors of *Musikijskaya grammatika,* the first treatise on music, published in 1679 in Moscow, defend the advantages of the new polyphonic ecclesiastical chant against the old unison one and believe that, far from denying the medieval tradition, the new chant continues it on a higher level. A similar tendency manifests itself in treatises on painting. The treatise of Iosif Vladimirov, a "new" icon painter *(ikono-pisets)* and *zhivo-*

RUSSIAN AESTHETICS: Religious Aesthetics. *Nicholas the Wonderworker* (third quarter of the sixteenth century), Russian (attributed to Tver'); Ikonen-Museum Recklinghausen, Germany. (Photograph courtesy of Ikonen-Museum Recklinghausen; used by permission.)

pisets (Russian for *painter,* literally, the *painter of life,* this term not being in use before the second half of the seventeenth century), is especially noteworthy for its fullness and depth. Consistently defending the advantages of the new "lifelike" (*zhivo-podobnaya,* i.e., tending first of all toward an illusionist and naturalistic representation of man) painting against the icons of the older style, he supports his claim by the arguments of Byzantine iconodules in defense of mimetic images (which only existed in Byzantium at an early stage)—in particular, the legend of the "made without hands" *(acheiropoietos)* image of Christ (i.e., the image-imprint of the ideal face of Christ on a piece of cloth that was imprinted by Christ himself). In the seventeenth century, such "made without hands" images were painted with great technical skill by Simon Ushakov, a friend of Vladimirov. The seventeenth- and eighteenth-century traditionalists (first of all the so-called *staroobryadtsy*—the "Old Believers"—but not only them) fight frantically against all those Westernizing (and, in their understanding, heretical) innovations in church art and its theory, but they find little support from their mainstream contemporaries. The artistic culture of Russia relentlessly departs from the medieval Weltanschauung and artistic language in all genres of art. Within Russian religious art itself, new tendencies take shape: toward the secularization of art, aesthetics, and culture, and a departure from medieval mentality. They become dominant in Russia in the eighteenth and nineteenth centuries.

Conservative or Preservative Period. In the eighteenth century, the cultural and political reforms of Peter I actively contribute to the process of secularization of culture. From Byzantium, Peter inherits the tendency toward the consolidation of monarchical empire, in which even the church is fully subject to the monarch. Thus, it is Peter who abolishes the highest ecclesiastical rank of "Patriarch of All Russia." In matters of culture, he abandons the course of national and religious isolation of Russia from the West and starts to develop actively a variety of Western trends in culture and art (often alien to the Russian mentality) on Russian soil. Beginning with Feofan Prokopovitch (1681–1736)—a priest of the new orientation and a devoted follower of Peter I, who writes *Poetics* and *Rhetoric* according to the spirit of similar ancient and western European treatises—Russian thinkers, writers, and art critics of the eighteenth and nineteenth centuries actively rework and introduce the ideas of ancient (Greco-Roman) and modern European aesthetics into Russian culture. The views and teachings of the Enlightenment, classicism, Romanticism, sentimentalism, and classical German aesthetics receive wide circulation during these centuries, especially as part of university courses on aesthetics.

The nineteenth century sees a rapid formation, under the influence of Western ideas, of democratic views and sentiments among the Russian intelligentsia in areas ranging from science to literature and art. These views also hold sway in the areas of artistic creation and aesthetic thought. A new democratic trend in aesthetics is formed, represented by such prominent figures as Alexander I. Herzen, Nikolai A. Dobrolyubov, Vissarion G. Belinsky, Nikolai G. Chernyshevsky, and Vladimir V. Stasov. In this situation, Russian religious aesthetics is pushed to the far background of culture and survives only in part among the Old Believers, in the monasteries, and in the minds of certain thinkers and writers.

Among the latter is one of the most prominent Russian writers Nicolai Gogol (1809–1852), who realizes, from his own experience as a writer, the absolute futility of the tendency—very popular at that time—of "aesthetic humanism," or an attempt to introduce morals into society by means of secularized art. He reserves the power to overcome the tragic dissonance between aesthetic and moral principles only for the sphere of religion, and points out the importance of the problem of a relationship between the church and culture, as well as of a Christian metamorphosis of secular culture. He is the first among Russian thinkers to introduce conscientiously the notion of "Orthodox culture." He sees the mission of the artist only as awakening souls for the encounter with God, in their moral purification, and in the theurgical experience of a realization of divine justice *(pravda)* on Earth.

The movement of "Slavophiles" *(slavyanofily),* and in particular the activities of Alexei S. Khomyakov (1804–1860) and Ivan V. Kireevsky (1806–1856), becomes another noteworthy phenomenon in Russian religious aesthetics. Their aesthetics is based on a peculiar mixture of ideas from German Romanticism and Orthodox aesthetics. It is Khomyakov who, for the first time in Orthodox culture, finally gives a definition of *sobornost':* according to him, it is a mystical "unity of God and man," or a certain ideal spirit of the people enlightened by the Christian faith. He understands art as an expression of this spirit on the basis of divine love, or as an artistic "self-consciousness of life" through the mediation of the artist.

Alexander M. Bukharev (monastic name Archimandrite Feodor; 1824–1871)—a prominent figure in nineteenth-century religious culture—attempts to overcome the narrow ecclesiastical rigorism and present all contemporary culture and art (including nonecclesiastical) as imbued with the "light of Christ" and cherished by the "secret warmth" of the church. By that, he tries to overthrow the (in his opinion) unnatural idea of secularism in culture. According to him, any creative activity is an act of divine grace, even if it has no clear external indications of its religious or ecclesiastical character. Bukharev's conception thus removes the tragic character of the situation that overwhelms Gogol in the late period of his life and forces him to destroy the second volume of *Dead Souls* as belonging, in his opinion, to secular rather than to Orthodox culture.

After Gogol, the relationship and interaction between the aesthetic element and Christian ethics in culture becomes one of the most important problems in Russian religious aesthetics. This problem becomes particularly acute for the great nineteenth-century Russian writers. Like Gogol, Konstantin N. Leontyev (1831–1891)—a prophet of pure aestheticism—toward the end of his life resolves this problem in favor of Christian ethics. Fyodor Dostoyevsky centers his literary activity on his attempts to resolve the tragic conflict between the ethical and the aesthetic. As a result, the Russian writer chooses the ideal of early Christian ethics—the highest beauty that will "save the world," or Jesus Christ himself in his eschatological aspect—over against the modernized (or diabolic, in Dostoyevsky's interpretation) Roman Catholic "rationalistic" ethics of the Great Inquisitor. The great Russian writer Leo Nicolaevich Tolstoy (1828–1910) is also among those trying to find a clue to the complex dialectic of the ethical and the aesthetic. Toward the end of his literary activity, he turns to the Christianity of the early church fathers and severs his ties with secular culture, which he served for decades in his writings, with the official church, and with aesthetics as such. He experiences a tragic inner discord between his personal mystical experience and western European rationalism that has been acquired from the outside. As a result, both his manifesto *What Is Art?* and his other works are subject to a strict dictate of panmoralism. Beauty has nothing in common with the good. It follows that art based on aesthetic principles is an empty amusement that leads humanity away from goodness: "aesthetic pleasure is a pleasure of a lower rank." In the late period of his life, Tolstoy rejects almost all famous names in art (Eurypides, Dante, William Shakespeare, Rafael, Michelangelo, Ludwig van Beethoven) and accepts only art that contains "truth" in a simplified religious form that is accessible to people.

Neo-Orthodox Period. The new stage in Russian religious aesthetics begins with the philosopher Vladimir S. Solovyov (1853–1900) and reaches its apogee in the writings of his followers: the philosopher Nikolai A. Berdyaev (1874–1948) and especially the theoreticians of neo-Orthodoxy Florensky (1882–1937) and Bulgakov (1871–1944). This period coincides with tempestous social and political commotions in Russia and world culture in general, the latter undergoing essential changes under the influence of a positivist and materialist world outlook and the rise of scientific and technological progress. Russia is not left behind in this process. The Russian monarchy is on the verge of a crisis, and many democratic and progressive-minded figures in early twentieth-century culture actively contribute to its downfall. The representatives of the avant-garde in contemporary art and aesthetics—especially the Futurists and the Constructivists—support all revolutionary movements in Russia, including the Communist revolution. The representatives of Russian religious aesthetics, however, maintain their traditional conservative attitude in politics, although the general atmosphere of a mighty shift in culture has some influence even on their views. The "Russian religious renaissance" of the beginning of the twentieth century is largely an attempt of the most educated and creatively minded Orthodox thinkers to bring Orthodoxy into some degree of correspondence with the contemporary zeitgeist.

The aesthetics of Soloviev—the founder of "neo-Orthodoxy"—whose thought is based on Neoplatonism, German classical philosophy (mainly Friedrich Wilhelm von Schelling), and many ideas of nineteenth-century Russian aesthetics, is much broader than religious, let alone Orthodox, aesthetics as such. His philosophical concept of universal unity *(vseyedinstvo)*, his understanding of art as mystical "free theourgy" that transforms the world on the way to its spiritual perfection, his concept of the symbol, and the mystical intuition of Sophia as a cosmic and artistic creative principle (his sophiology) have a strong influence on aesthetic theories at the beginning of the twentieth century, in particular on the theorists of Russian Symbolism and neo-Orthodox aesthetics.

The aesthetic views of Berdyaev, which follow from his personalist philosophy, are of a mystical and romantic orientation. One of the main themes in his philosophy is the concept of creative activity that brings to their logical completion the ideas of theourgy (in art, culture, life, and being as a whole) that are present in Russian aesthetics since the time of Gogol and are partly developed by Solovyov and Vyatcheslav I. Ivanov. Berdyaev sees the meaning of human life in creative activity, for it is only in it that man can truly assimilate himself to God the creator and the supreme artist, and achieve, with his help, a breakthrough from the "ugly" earthly life to the supreme cosmic "life in beauty." To this point in history, creative activity realizes itself most fully in art. Art is tragic, however, for it has not been able to fulfill its main—theourgical—goal and has remained stuck in earthly reality, instead of rising to the level of cosmic being. Berdyaev distinguishes between Christian and pagan art. Pagan (Greco-Roman) art reaches the classical completeness of its forms in this earthly immanent world. It knows of no other higher world and does not long for it. Christian art, on the contrary, is the art of "transcendental longing" for another world, of "transcendental breakthrough" into that world. This is why it is essentially incomplete, in its highest sense, for it does not reach the other world in reality, but only points at it in its symbols.

Berdyaev distinguishes between the two main types of artistic activity: realism and symbolism. He sees realism as the ultimate form of adaptation of art to "this world," which in its foundation is ugly. Therefore, realism is the "least creative form of art." True art—especially Christian art (in a broad sense, the art of Christian regions in general)—is always symbolic to a certain degree, for it creates the symbols of the other world. It follows that art attains its highest state in Symbolism as an artistic trend from about 1850 to 1900. It is also in Symbolism, however, that it reaches the limit of its own capacities, or its own crisis. Symbolism reveals the tragic character of artistic activity in a particularly acute manner. The symbol is a "bridge crossing over from the creative act to the hidden, ultimate reality" and hanging over empty space with its other end. In Symbolism, artistic activity outgrows itself and goes beyond the limits of art in its traditional understanding: it leaves the sphere of culture and flows into being itself. It is Berdyaev who gives, finally, a clear definition of theourgy, to which the aesthetic consciousness of Orthodoxy is constantly drawn throughout almost all of its history: "It is not culture that theourgy creates, but new being; theourgy is above culture. Theourgy is art that creates a different world, different being, different life, beauty as being. . . . Theourgy is man's acting together with God: acting in a divine way, joint creative activity of God and man" (Berdyaev, 1916). In addition to this, Berdyaev considers the problem of art as theourgy mainly as a Russian problem, and it is with theourgy that he connects the future "Slavo-Russian renaissance."

Florensky—one of the most prominent Orthodox theologians and a scholar of encyclopedic knowledge and universal orientation who draws on all previous experience and achievements of human culture—pays particularly close attention to aesthetics and art. For him, it is God who is the supreme beauty, through the participation in which all becomes beautiful. Hence, the aesthetic, according to his definition, is not some particular section of being or consciousness, but a force, or energy, that penetrates all layers of being. Beauty and (spiritual, divine) light are important ontological and epistemological factors in his system. It is in them and through their mediation that man "cognizes" the trihypostatical truth in the mystical acts of liturgy, contemplation of icons, and, above all, monastic feats, which fills him with ineffable spiritual joy. In Florensky's understanding, then, the main aesthetic subjects are monks who devote their whole life to the contemplation of spiritual light. On the other hand, asceticism is, in the full sense of these terms, aesthetics and art. Ascetics themselves, Florensky stresses, call their activity the "art of arts," and the goal of their activity—"contemplative knowledge"—the "love of beauty" (this is how Florensky translates *philokalia,* in opposition to the traditional ecclesiastical translation "love of goodness"), as distinct from the rational "love of wisdom" *(philosophia).* Moreover, this activity does not limit itself only to contemplation, but even—ideally—has a goal of real transformation of the flesh of an ascetic into a more spiritual and luminous substance already in his lifetime, that is, a real crossing of the border between the material and spiritual worlds. On the level of cosmogony, it is sophia the wisdom of God who dwells at this border: a certain unknowable person and the creative principle of God, his creating energy, the spiritual foundation of the world and man who makes them beautiful. Hence, the sphere of the aesthetic and beauty, in its most intricate forms, is the transitional sphere between the heavenly and earthly worlds. The supreme beauty, however, in its pure form, is revealed only to select monk-ascetics, and therefore its real carriers in the world are symbols in liturgy and art (in its purest form—the icon).

Florensky understands the symbol not only as a semiotic unit but also as an ontological entity. Not only does it signify something else, but it also manifests it in reality, possesses its energy, and appears as a "living mutual interpenetration of two entities." Florensky extends the ancient Jewish understanding of the symbol (or name) as a bearer of the essence, together with the Byzantine notion of the liturgical symbol, to the general concept of the symbol. Among such symbols he includes, first of all, the icon, which he considers to be the highest achievement of the art of painting of all times and nations. When he considers in detail the peculiarities of the artistic language of the icon—including its canonicity, "reversed perspective," particular ways of organizing space, symbolism of color, and conventional character of forms—and compares all this with the

language of modern European painting ("Renaissance-type," in his terminology), he comes to the conclusion that it is with the "great" masters of the Renaissance who had rejected the medieval Weltanschauung and artistic language that the decline of representational art begins. Florensky is convinced that the essence of art is not the conveyance of visible forms of the material world, or of psychological states of man, but symbolic expression and the ascent, with the help of conventional images of art, to the everlasting spiritual world, and ultimately to God. Florensky pays much attention to the question of the synthesis of arts in liturgy, as well as to the philosophy and aesthetics of the ritual, the problems of the canon, and the organization of the space-time continuum in art.

Bulgakov largely continues Florensky's tradition in aesthetics. The cornerstone of his teaching is sophiology: the essentially antinomical teaching about sophia, which appears to him as "impossible" for the intellect, as an alogical mediator between God and the world, as a "round square," as a "square root of minus one," and, at the same time, as the original aggregation of all ideas of the creation—a neo-Orthodox rethinking of the (Neo) platonic theory of preexistent ideas—and as a creative principle of being and art. In fact, his sophiology can rightly be called neo-Orthodox aesthetics in the full sense of the word. At the center of it, Bulgakov, like Florensky, places the teaching about the icon, which he sees as an essentially antinomical phenomenon (because of its ability to represent the nonrepresentable God) ideally embodying the *sophijnost'* of the creation because of its canonicity. Under *sophijnost',* Bulgakov understands the expression of the primordial ideality of the material world in this world itself. The main criterion and indicator of the level of *sophijnost'* of a thing or a work of art is beauty, which is at the same time understood as the "revelation of the Holy Spirit" in matter, as the "sacred, without sin, palpability and perceptibility of the idea," that is, as "spiritual, sacred corporeity." Bulgakov draws particular attention to the category of corporeity in its ideal understanding, or "spiritual corporeity," for it forms the foundation of art. The artist "intuits beauty as the realized sacred corporeity" and strives to express it in his own art. In Bulgakov's opinion, the ancient Greeks perfectly succeed in this task in their sculpture (especially in nude figures), as do the medieval Orthodox artists in their icons. Hence, he defines the work of art as an "erotic encounter of matter and form, their enamored confluence, the idea that has been felt and has become beauty: it is the shining of the ray of *sophijnost'* in our world" (1917). Bulgakov makes no essential distinction between beauty in art and nature. The latter he understands as a "great and wondrous artist," and art he understands very broadly, as is customary for the Orthodox tradition in general. It is man, in all his "spiritual corporeity" and ideal "life in beauty," who is the main work of art. This "life in beauty" for the human being is difficult and tempting, however, for here—Bulgakov recalls Dostoyevsky—is the field of battle between the devil and God. "Earthly beauty is enigmatic and ominous, like Gioconda's smile. . . . Longing for beauty, torments through beauty, is the scream of all the universe" (ibid.). It is possible to overcome this tragic character of beauty in the world (an idea common to the whole of neo-Orthodox aesthetics) with the help of the theurgical function of art, which would then cross the boundaries of its proper works and in reality transform the world and man on their way of eschatological *sophijno-aesthetic* transfiguration, or the uplifting of the created world to its preexistent beauty, or sophia.

One more significant theme in aesthetics—the relationship between culture and civilization—is taken up by Russian religious aesthetics in the twentieth century. Vladimir V. Weidle (1895–1979), a prominent religious art critic and thinker who left Russia after the October Revolution, perceives a well-pronounced crisis and even "dying" in contemporary art (cf. his principal work, *The Dying of Art*, 1937). The causes of the latter he sees in the domination of rationalism and mechanistic principles, in the rift between the humanity and nature (these principles he defines as the traits of civilization, which is taken in opposition to culture), and ultimately in the loss of religious faith and religious *Weltanschauung*. True sound art, he believes, is always closely connected to religion and is religious in its foundation (whether the artist recognizes himself as a believer or not), "for artistic experience is in its very depth religious, because no creative act can exclude an expression of faith, and because the world that harbors art is ultimately transparent only to religion" (Weidle, 1996). Even the basic notions lying at the foundation of the interpretation of art, according to Weidle, are rooted in religious thought. Among these notions are transfiguration, incarnation, sacrament, antinomical wholeness, and miracle. The phenomena described by these notions belong as much to art as they do to religion, although art and religion as a rule are not identical. Art and religion are "con-natural" in their essence, and the "logic of art is the logic of religion." They do not, however, substitute, but supplement and strengthen, each other in culture. Certainly, even in modern times not all artists of genius have been religious in a narrow ecclesiastical sense. Yet, they were creating in a world that was still penetrated with "secret religion," a world that was "truly human, guided by conscience." Contemporary art is dying not because the artist ceased to be a believer but because he stopped acknowledging his creative act as a sacrament.

From about 1900 to 1930, Russian religious aesthetics had a strong influence on Russian culture in general and affected the views of many artists, writers, and thinkers. It is this aesthetics, for example, that, together with other spiritual trends, serves as a foundation for the main theoretical treatise—*Concerning the Spiritual in Art*—and the deeply mystical artistic activity of Vassily V. Kandinsky, a founder of abstract art. The founder of Suprematism, Kazimir Malevich, who is otherwise removed from any particular religious tradition, sees his *Black Square* as the new icon of the twentieth century. One of the most prominent twentieth-century Russian poets, Aleksandr Aleksandrovich Blok, receives the Russian Revolution of the 1917 in a mystico-Christian light. The image of Christ plays a prominent role in the art of Mark Z. Shagall, a Russian Hasidic Jew. One also finds echoes of Russian religious aestheticism in the aesthetic system of Alexei F. Losev (1893–1988), a prominent Russian aesthetician, philologist, and philosopher, one of the followers of Soloviev, who was secretly consecrated as a monk in the Soviet era. In his book *The Dialectic of Artistic Form* (1927), he outlines a system of aesthetic categories—in a rigorous dialectical form that is characteristic for him—relying on Neoplatonism, phenomenology, and Orthodox aesthetics. This system includes successive categories that generate (express) each other, such as eidos, myth, symbol, person (art belongs to this level), the energy of the essence, and the name of the essence. A strong influence of neo-Orthodox aesthetics can be felt in the way Losev develops such categories as symbol, person, energy, and name, as well as in his consciously acknowledged principle of antinomies, although as a whole his aesthetic system transcends the boundaries of Russian religious aesthetics as such.

The destiny of the last representatives of Russian religious aesthetics, like that of most of the Russian intelligentsia of the beginning of this century, is tragic. After the establishment of Communist rule, many were deported or forced to emigrate. The ones who stayed in Russia fell victim to repression (e.g., Florensky, who was executed in a Stalinist concentration camp) or were forced to change their occupation (e.g., Losev who devoted himself mainly to the study of antiquity after serving his term in a labor camp).

[*See also* Byzantine Aesthetics; Icon; Religion and Aesthetics; *and* Tolstoy.]

BIBLIOGRAPHY

Berdyaev, Nikolaj A. *Smysl tvorchestva, Opyt opravdaniya cheloveka* (The Meaning of Creative Activity, the Experience of Justification of Man). Moscow, 1916.

Bulgakov, Sergij N. *Svet nevecherniy, Sozertsaniya i umozreniya* (Contemplations and Meditations). Moscow, 1917.

Bychkov, Victor V. "Schönheit verweist auf Transzendenz, Maxim Grek: Zur Entwicklung des philosophisch-aesthetischen Gedankens in der Alten Rus." *Zeitschrift für Ästhetik und allgemeine Kunstwissenschaft* 34.1 (1989): 73–81.

Bychkov, Victor V. "L'esthétique internationale en Russie au 17ᵉᵐᵉ siècle, Juraj Krizanic et Nicolai Milescu Spatarul." *Syntesis Philosophica* 9 (1990): 161–182.

Bychkov, Victor V. *Russkaya srednevekovaya estetika, XI–XVII veka* (Medieval Russian Aesthetics). Moscow, 1992.

Bychkov, Victor V. *The Aesthetic Face of Being: Art in the Theology of Pavel Florensky*. Translated by Richard Pevear and Larissa Volokhonsky. Crestwood, N.Y., 1993.

Bychkov, Victor V. "Künstlerische und ästhetische Aspekte in der Sophiologie Vater Sergi Bulgakows." *Stimme der Orthodoxie* 4 (1994): 26–30.

Florensky, Pavel A. "Statyi po iskusstvu." In *Sobraniye sochineniy,* vol. 1 (Essays on Art. in Complete Works), edited by N. A. Struve. Paris, 1985.

Florensky, Pavel A. *Analiz prostranstvennosti i vremeni v hudozhestvenno izobrazitelnykh proizvedeniyakh* (The Analysis of Spatiality and Time in the Works of Representational Arts). Moscow, 1993.

Likhachyov, Dmitrij S. *Poetika drevnerusskoj literatury* (Poetics of Old Russian Literature). Moscow, 1979.

Rozanov, Vasilij V. *Religiya i kul'tura* (Religion and Culture). Saint Petersburg, 1899.

Rupnik, Marko I. *L'arte memoria della comunione. Il significato teologico missionario dell'arte nella saggistica di Vjaceslav Ivanovic Ivanov.* Rome, 1994.

Spidlik, Tomas. *L'idée russe: Une autre vision de l'homme.* Troyes, France, 1994.

Weidle, Vladimir V. *Umiraniye iskusstva, Razmyshleniya o sud'be literaturnogo i hudozhestvennogo tvorchestva* (The Dying of Art, Meditations on the Destiny of Literary and Artistic Activity, 1937). 2d ed. Moscow, 1996.

Zernov, Nicolas. *The Russian Religious Renaissance of the Twentieth Century.* London, 1963.

VICTOR V. BYCHKOV and OLEG V. BYCHKOV
Translated from Russian by Oleg V. Bychkov

Russian Formalism

Russian Formalism comprises a group of literary and aesthetic doctrines held by a number of early twentieth-century Moscow and Saint Petersburg linguistic and literary scholars and theoreticians. They founded the Society for the Study of Poetic Language, known by the Russian acronym OPOYAZ, in 1916. OPOYAZ was dedicated to the premise that literary language was autonomous in its function (the "self-sufficient word"), and operated against the background of a nonrepresentational aesthetics. As a discrete movement, Formalism came to an end in 1930, after which time it was denounced as "Western" and "bourgeois" (the term *Formalist* itself was later destined to become one of the strongest pejorative terms in the Soviet critical vocabulary). The later characterization of "bourgeois" seems ironic in view of the fact that the Formalists were leftists in the context of Soviet politics of the 1920s.

Still, a certain amount of clandestine Formalism continued to survive in the Soviet Union after 1930, more in literary theory than in actual criticism of specific literary works; with the reappearance of greater freedom of expression in the 1970s, Formalism became the chief literary approach followed by Soviet theoreticians, now blended with more recent Western trends in literary theory such as semiotics (though this use in literary theory and criticism developed to a degree out of Formalism and was only indirectly "Western").

Formalism is vaguely Kantian in its philosophical foundations, especially in its epistemology and its faith in art

as displaying "purposiveness without purpose," but in the Russian context it sprang more directly from a number of positivist philosophers such as Alexander Potebnja (1835–1891), who was influenced in part by Alexander von Humboldt. But the most powerful intellectual influence on Formalism was its close contact with linguistic theory and the Formalists' insistence that literature was the "art of the word" and not the "art of images," as certain nineteenth-century German aestheticians and their Russian followers had insisted.

The Russian Formalists were particularly unhappy with the prevailing eclecticism in literary theory and criticism, tending to follow biographical (biography of the writer), psychological, sociological, philosophical, cultural-historical, and other approaches, and often intermingling them without any precise methodological plan. The Formalists sought to create a "science of literature" (they used the term *poetry* more often than *literature,* not in order to exclude prose, but to emphasize that kind of literature in which verbal play had its fullest effect). The Formalists rejected the traditional duality of form and content; this dualistic concept was much too crude: it implied that content was poured into a kind of mold called form, which gave it a literary "shaping." Indeed, they rejected all external use of devices in literature: rhyme and rhythm were not mere ornaments but an intrinsic part of the organic work of art.

Instead of form and content, the Formalists postulated a new duality, that of material and device. Words are the "material" of literature, to be given shape by the application of devices.

"Device" was probably the basic concept in the Formalist arsenal. It was introduced by Viktor Shklovsky (1893–1984), a philosophically grounded Formalist. In a seminal article published in 1917, Shklovskij introduced his famous slogan "Literature as Device." Device makes it possible to bring fresh perspectives to the word, which is thus freed of its banal ties to everyday life. Besides purely poetic devices such as rhyme and rhythm, the concept includes distortion, both of meaning and syntax, and the insertion of the word in new, previously unused contexts, both semantic and syntactic. Shklovskij likened the thus renewed perceptions of the word to viewing a landscape through a pair of colored spectacles, which serve to revive its freshness.

The central poetic device that Shklovskij postulates is "defamiliarization" or "making strange" (Russian *ostranenie*). Banal words are introduced into strange, often distorted contexts (e.g., the illicit use of the verb *overcome* as intransitive in the civil-rights hymn), a use that gives it greater effect than the correct transitive use would permit. Defamiliarization is intended to revive words and impart to them a new vividness and freshness, especially in a revivified literary context. But, though literary satire shows a great deal of defamiliarization (e.g., *Gulliver's Travels*) in the form of distortions of ordinary reality, it would be difficult to apply this device to the language of all literature (e.g., in the Russian tradition, to Leo Nicolaevich Tolstoy's realistic novels, though Shklovskij strove, partly in vain, to accomplish this).

A second major device for Shklovskij is that of "making difficult" *(zatrudnenie):* writers deliberately make their writings difficult, partly in order to stimulate readers to make a greater effort to enter into the literary work and to comprehend it. This seems acceptable, but radical simplicity may seem to be an equally effective and compelling device. Another weakness in Shklovskij's thought is his frequent failure to differentiate verbal devices from nonverbal ones, as the other Formalists usually did. The distortions that Shklovskij finds in *Gulliver's Travels* more often concern descriptions of people and their stature than they do the use of language as such.

The force and the partial validity of the notion of defamiliarization proceed chiefly from the Formalists' insistence that the work of art is an artifact, a construct. But because it also has semiotic significance in works of satire, where the revivified words and images take on satiric effect, there is a considerable confusion here, restricted principally to Shklovskij's brand of Formalism. In his confusion on this point, Shklovskij attempted to show that much of Tolstoy's realism was actually satire.

The most radical and extreme Formalist was no doubt Roman Jakobson (1896–1982), later prominent as a Prague structuralist (both literary and linguistic), and still later active in the United States. Rather than defining rhythm as a condition of the lexicon and syntax of the poet's language, Jakobson declared it to be "organized violence perpetrated by the poetic form on the language." He began with the dictum, "Poetry is indifferent to the object of expression." The first dictum happened to fit well into Shklovskij's views, but the second goes far beyond them. Jakobson insisted that a poet who writes a love poem is not necessarily in love, and a poet who writes a religious poem is not necessarily religious. Later, Jakobson partly recanted the latter view, because it might have been difficult to take literature seriously if it was viewed as having no relevant content whatsoever. None of the other Formalists went so far: while denying the importance, or even the relevance, of content, they would dismiss these by the door in order to admit them again through the window.

Jakobson introduced the concept of "laying bare the device" *(obnazhenie priema),* familiar in parody, burlesque, travesty, and commonly occurring in advertising. Laying bare the device means exposing the techniques of the author, stripped from their message or content, and so displacing or "defamiliarizing" that message or content. Laying bare the device was the favorite technique of the Formalists' beloved Laurence Sterne in *Tristram Shandy* (1760–1767).

Formalism supplied a useful critical method for analyzing short poems and short stories, giving rise to literary studies not unlike those of the later Anglo-American critics (who were not aware of the Formalists). But the Formalists rarely tackled larger literary forms, and no Formalist ever attempted a history of literature. Shklovskij did suggest a most important dialectic force motivating the historical progress of literature: parody. The Formalists broadened the notion of parody beyond the humorous: parody was the opposition, through distorted imitation, of the younger generation to the older one. What is often viewed as the peaceful inheritance of literary forms by a younger generation is in fact the dialectical thrust of parody, which liberates the young writer from the tyranny of the older one, and makes it possible for him to advance literarily. Thus, the young Fyodor Dostoevsky parodies Nikolai Gogol in his first novel, *Poor Folk* (1846), but later finds his own independent path. In Sterne's celebrated novel *Tristram Shandy,* Shklovskij found a perfect parody of the developing novel form and its devices, verbal and imagistic.

Another dialectical notion popularized by Shklovskij is his theory that higher prose forms often represent the canonization of inferior genres. Thus, Dostoevsky employs the devices of the French boulevard novel, as Giovanni Boccaccio had the bawdy jokes of his day. These theories are interesting, but it is easy to see why Shklovskij could not construct a coherent history of literature based on them. Another manifest difficulty in Formalist historical theory, one observed by Viktor Zhirmunskij (1881–1971), is the fact that periods in the development of world literature often correspond to periods in the other arts, such as music, painting, and architecture.

In their analysis of narrative, the Formalists made another fundamental dialectical distinction between "fable" *(fabula)* and "plot" *(suzhet).* "Fable" denoted the basic narrative stuff that the author employs as raw material, which for fiction may be a "true" story; "plot" designates that material as rearranged or restructured by the application of devices. Such devices include repetition of episodes, alterations in temporal sequence, including flashbacks, retardation and acceleration, parallelism of episodes, and so on. Both stages are creatively essential to the work, though "plot" of course achieves the status of artifact and is closer to the finished work of art.

Although the Formalists wrote relatively little about other arts, one, Vladimir Propp (1895–1970), did apply Formalist analysis to the structure of the fairy tale: his *Morphology of the Folktale* (1928) attempted to reduce the structure of fairy tales to a limited number of functions; other criteria of classification, such as the identity of the characters, were shown to be irrelevant: for example, the character who plays the role of villain may be a sorcerer, a dragon, or even a bear without affecting the basic nature of a tale; in other words, it is the villain's role or function in the tale that is important, not his superficial characterization.

Formalism had a powerful influence on creative writing in Russia, particularly on such writers as Evgenii Zamyatin

(1884–1937), Veniamin Kaverin (b.1902), and Jurii Olesha (1899–1960). This did not survive the school itself, but abroad, Formalism had an enormous shaping effect on all the branches of literary and linguistic structuralism that subsequently emerged: on Polish integralism and Czech structuralism of the prewar period; on French and Bulgarian structuralism of the postwar era and their international impact, as, for instance, in the United States, and on a kind of homegrown structuralism in the Soviet Union (the so-called Tartu School of Juri Lotman). Structuralism even finds earlier precursors in the Soviet Union, as in the work of the Formalists Jurii Tynjanov (1894–1943) and Mikhail Bakhtin (1896–1975) in the 1930s, though Bakhtin in particular worked under great constraints. In its insistence on the autonomy of artistic language, Formalism shows itself as a kind of literary criticism that has clearly risen to a higher *étape* of an accepted set of generalizations that scarcely can be rejected any longer from the literary critical arsenal, at least not in toto.

Formalism, in its stress on semiotics, provides a model for the French structuralist notion of "deconstruction," though some of the deconstructionists employed their new technique for political and social purposes, which the Russian Formalists always eschewed, in spite of their leftist political orientation.

[*See also* Formalism; Poetics; Semiotics; *and* Structuralism.]

BIBLIOGRAPHY

Erlich, Victor. *Russian Formalism: History, Doctrine.* 4th ed. The Hague, 1980.

Harkins, William. "Slavic Formalist Theories in Literary Scholarship." *Word* 7.2 (1951): 177–185.

Matejka, Ladislav, ed. *Readings in Russian Poetics.* 2 vols. Michigan Slavic Materials, nos. 2, 5. Ann Arbor, 1962–1964.

Medvedev, Pavel N., and Mikhail M. Bakhtin. *The Formal Method in Literary Scholarship: A Critical Introduction to Sociological Poetics.* Translated by Albert J. Wehrle. Baltimore, 1978; reprint, Cambridge, Mass., 1985.

Pomorska, Krystyna. *Russian Formalist Theory and Its Poetic Ambiance.* The Hague, 1968.

Steiner, Peter. *Russian Formalism: A Metapoetics.* Ithaca, N.Y. 1984.

Striedter, Jurij, ed. *Texte der russischen Formalisten.* 2 vols. Munich, 1969–1972.

Terras, Victor, ed. *Handbook of Russian Literature.* New Haven, 1985. See "Formalism," pp. 154–155.

Thompson, Ewa M. *Russian Formalism and Anglo-American New Criticism: A Comparative Study.* The Hague, 1971.

WILLIAM E. HARKINS

Socialist Realism

Socialist Realism is a twentieth-century prescriptive doctrine aimed at defining and delimiting the content and, to an extent, the form of works of literature and art in the Soviet Union and in other socialist countries. Socialist Realism is sometimes claimed by its advocates to be an aesthetic, but at best it is a *politically correct* aesthetic. The elaboration of the doctrine of Socialist Realism did not prevent Soviet philosophers from developing unrelated systems of aesthetic theory, generally imagistic and deriving from Plato, G. W. F. Hegel, and other philosophers.

The sources of Socialist Realism are not obvious. The concept clearly does not derive from the teachings of Karl Marx, Friedrich Engels, or Vladimir Ilich Lenin, none of whom had very much that was specific to say about literature or art. The Soviet writer Maxim Gorky has generally been credited with providing at least models for the doctrine, and he did play a leading role in providing models for its formulation. But, though the doctrine seems to be ideological in nature, it is increasingly clear that it was created as a method aimed at restricting and focusing works of literature and the other arts. Its introduction forms one of the changes introduced by Joseph Stalin and his followers in Soviet ideology during the early 1930s, which served to put an end to the "class struggle" and introduce (at least in principle), a more conservative, classless society.

The doctrine of Socialist Realism was ratified in 1932 by a decision of the Seventeenth Congress of the Soviet Communist Party. The decision was set into the context of a thoroughgoing reorganization of the Union of Soviet Writers, and this union was entrusted with the enforcement of the new doctrine. As promulgated, Socialist Realism had relatively little content, but it did point to a few works of literature, notably Gorky's early revolutionary novel *The Mother* (1906), as models for writers to follow. Stalin's dictum that "Writers are engineers of human souls" was also taken as a key leitmotif of the new doctrine, though its actual meaning is not entirely clear.

The effect of this paucity of sources was to leave very great power to officials of the Union of Soviet Writers and to Soviet critics, and in effect to overweigh the balance normally obtaining between authors and their critics. Critics became umpires enforcing the "rules" of Socialist Realism, though in effect such rules had hardly been laid down. Only with time and the interplay of creative writing, critical stricture, and theoretical writing could it become clear what Socialist Realism meant. Paradoxically, definitions were more readily reached outside the Soviet Union than inside it, for outside the Soviet Union it could often be given real meaning and real social pathos by Marxist writers and critics who wrote in greater freedom.

Socialist Realism had been preceded by the proletarian movement, vested with authority in literature in the Russian Association of Proletarian Writers (RAPP), which dominated the literary scene at the end of the 1920s. The RAPP and its literary controls were based on a theory of class adherence and class cultural values; this theory would no longer be relevant when the Soviet Union proclaimed itself a "classless society" in the early 1930s. The prevalent Communist Party cultural ideology in the 1920s had favored "proletarianism," a view according to which the Communist proletariat would create a new socialist culture based on its own class values and its role in the Marxist class struggle. But Stalin was seeking to construct a new society and a new state order, for which an effort to sharpen the dialectical division of Soviet people into proletarians and others would have been counterproductive. A monolithic, "classless" writers' union seemed to point to greater freedom, when in fact the system under Socialist Realism would become even tighter.

Socialist Realism is a compound term, and this is both an advantage and a disadvantage in seeking a definition. *Socialist* might seem obvious, except that its use might seem to imply the elimination of a great deal of literature dealing with individual human life and with "eternal themes" such as love, fulfillment, ambition, family, and freedom that evidently evade the category of "socialist." *Socialist* implies that all literature should deal with the building of socialism and socialist society. This is true even in the past, where Marxist historical categories, such as bourgeois versus feudal, can be used as part of a system of historical *étapes* leading up and pointing forward to socialism. Even love and individual existence can be subsumed in such a way under the great theme of the building of socialism, though clearly always as secondary themes.

Historical fiction was largely discouraged in this light, but not totally excluded: "progressive" forces working toward the eventual order of socialist society could carry the heroic burden in a historical novel. Similarly, novels or dramas (these were the preferred forms of Socialist Realism) could be set in foreign countries where members of the local Communist Party or other "progressives" could play the heroic role.

The term *realism* is equally vexed. In part, its use stems from a desire to legalize a style current, popular, and acceptable to the Soviet rulers. Additionally, its use derives, no doubt, from the apparent truth implications of the word. One controversy (subsequently lost by the rebels) sought to find greater freedom in "Socialist Romanticism," but this concept survived only as a minor and nonobligatory subtype of Socialist Realism.

Realism in part corroborates the term *socialist:* the building of socialism is the great "truth" of our times; but "realism" is also an artistic method—only "realism" can give us any truth. In its application to painting, this was even clearer and simpler: distortion and abstraction were condemned totally.

In historical perspective, this meant that literature must not advance beyond the stylistic means of portrayal used by writers such as Tolstoy, Ivan Sergeevich Turgenev, or Anton

RUSSIAN AESTHETICS: Socialist Realism. Vitaly Komar and Alexander Melamid, *The Origin of Socialist Realism* (1982–1983), oil on canvas, 72 × 48 in.; Private Collection, Chappaqua, New York. (Photograph by D. James Dee; courtesy of the artists and Ronald Feldman Fine Arts, New York; used by permission.)

Pavlovich Chekhov. Again, Gorky (though there is a certain amount of Expressionism in his work) could serve as a model. This view hardly follows a priori from the doctrine itself, but it does seem to follow from a need not to complicate aesthetic means beyond the intellectual capacities or tastes of uneducated or semieducated persons of Stalin's generation, who were cultural parvenus. Curiously, in music this implied a *romantic* taste (Pyotr Ilich Tchaikovsky rather than Sergei Prokofiev or Dmitri Shostakovich) instead of a "realist" one ("realism" scarcely exists in music).

A facile application to literature was the factory novel, in which the building of a factory or the accomplishment of its assigned task could be equated both metonymically and metaphorically with the building of socialism. Secondary themes, such as love affairs, could readily be integrated into the woof of the whole without great risk. Valentin Kataev's

Five-Year Plan novel, *Time Forward!* (1932), about the construction of the Magnitogorsk chemical combine, was appropriated to serve as a model for this type of socialist novel.

Although Socialist Realism provided a method for dealing with the past, it did not resolve the problems and contradictions raised by the literature of the past. The term "bourgeois realism" was created by the critics for "bourgeois" realists such as Turgenev and Tolstoy, whom they were loath to discard completely; such writers, it was claimed, had pointed out many of the social problems and contradictions inherent in past Russian society, though without showing the way to the socialism of the future. But still, "bourgeois realism" could not extend back very far into the past: what does one do with a writer such as Aleksandr Sergeevich Pushkin, for instance, a poet of aristocratic origins and tastes, but still a Soviet favorite? He too was salvaged as a "realist," though hardly a "bourgeois" one. There were even attempts to label medieval Russian literature as "realist."

Although Socialist Realism arose as a literary doctrine, one enforced by the Union of Soviet Writers, it soon spread to the other arts. In painting, it had perhaps its greatest success, and tended to reduce Soviet painting to the level of mere copying. Abstraction was ruled out totally. Curiously, because the doctrine had little implication for the technique of Soviet painting (unlike literature), technique did not always suffer, at least not directly. What did suffer was the thematic poverty and the tendency to sentimentality of the great bulk of new Soviet painting.

Soviet film was largely a reflection of literature; films were either directly based on works of literature or on scripts that could be analyzed according to the criteria of Socialist Realism. The Soviet film, which had been created by such greats as Sergei Eisenstein, Vsevolod Ilarionovich Pudovkin, and Aleksandr Dovzhenko, was impoverished as much as literature or painting.

In music, the concepts of Socialist Realism could be applied readily to opera, ballet, and program music, and were so employed; attempts to apply them to more abstract music were largely abortive, as might have been expected; sometimes such works were dealt with as music with implicit programs, drawn from the life of the composer or the circumstances or period of composition. The popularity of nineteenth-century Russian opera and ballet, as of Tchaikovsky, for instance, made it impossible to circumscribe the older repertoire (this had not always succeeded in literature either), so that many compromises and exceptions had to be made where the popularity of older works was concerned. But new operas and ballets, such as Aram Khatchaturian's *Spartacus*, were created according to the formulas of Socialist Realism.

Literature produced for children (as well as other art) partly escaped the constraints of Socialist Realism. Of course, Socialist Realist works were created for children, but there was also a large repertoire of fairy tales and other imaginative writing. Russian folklore, venerated by Soviet critics as "progressive," also escaped proscription, though new Soviet works in a "folklore spirit" were also created in the mold of Socialist Realism.

Three fundamental corollaries were subsequently added to the basic doctrine of Socialist Realism. *Partiinost* ("Party orientation") implied making clear the role of the Communist Party in leading socialist progress. Non-Party factory workers in a work of fiction had either to be converted to the Party or act under the Party's mentorship. *Ideinost* ("ideological attitude") was in fact an older romantic notion of the need for ideology in political and cultural thought; the term now implied Communist ideology. *Narodnost* is the most difficult of the three concepts; the term implies not only "nationality," but also "folk" or "popular quality." What it should mean in literature was unclear; some critics equated it with the use or influence of popular folk forms such as proverbs or folk songs, while others argued that it meant the achievement of a good Russian style, an idea that was largely redundant.

The excesses of the doctrine brought a parodying reaction in the plays of Nikolai Virta (b. 1906), who, in the late 1950s, wrote "conflictless" dramas. Virta argued, obviously tongue in cheek, that, because there were no more vestiges of bourgeois attitudes in the Soviet Union, there could no longer be any impedance to the building of socialism, at least not inside the Soviet Union, and hence dramas could no longer have conflicts, but only pseudoconflicts, based on faulty communication or temporary misunderstandings. Virta's ironic logic did not long deceive his critics, however, and they denounced him as someone who had strayed from the true path.

After Nikita Khrushchev (1960s to date), the doctrine of Socialist Realism fell largely into abeyance and writers no longer took the categories of the doctrine very seriously. Still, until about 1985, a good deal of lip service was paid by critics to the idea, probably because criticism lagged behind original creation.

In the Soviet satellite countries—especially Poland, Czechoslovakia, and Hungary—the doctrine was accepted as official and unilateral, less so perhaps in art and music. Even in literature, however, there was a certain tendency to pay lip service to Socialist Realism and then write as one wished—without, of course, attacking the idea of socialism itself.

Outside the Soviet Union, the doctrine had considerable influence on Marxist writers and critics, though lack of a firm definition coming from the Soviet homeland meant that it was taken more as an enthusiastic slogan than as a doctrine. Still, a number of writers, prominent among whom are the French Communist Louis Aragon (1897–1982) and the Hungarian Communist György Lukács (1885–1971), did employ both the term and the concept in their literary theory and criticism. Aragon had the difficult and probably thankless task of reconciling it with his Dadaism and Surrealism. Lukács had taken up residence in the Soviet Union for some fifteen years beginning in 1929, and was there during the early years of development of the doctrine. But he broadened the concept into that of "socialist humanism," and later was reproached by his fellow Hungarian Communists for his apparent preference for "bourgeois realism" to "Socialist Realism."

In linking literary (and artistic) quality to a political base, Socialist Realism may be viewed as one (though of course not the only) source for the present widespread notion of "politically correct."

[*See also* Ideology; Lukács; Marxism; *and* Realism.]

BIBLIOGRAPHY

Ermolaev, Herman. *Soviet Literary Theories, 1917–1934: The Genesis of Socialist Realism.* Berkeley, 1963.

Hayward, Max. "The Decline of Socialist Realism." *Survey* 18.1 (1972): 73–97.

James, Caradog Vaughan. *Soviet Socialist Realism: Origins and Theory.* London, 1973.

Mozejko, Edvard. *Der sozialistische Realismus.* Leipzig, 1977.

Ovcharenko, Aleksandr I. *Sotsialisticheskiĭ realizm i sovremenny i literaturnyi protsess.* Moscow, 1968.

Terras, Victor, ed. *Handbook of Russian Literature.* New Haven, 1985. See "Socialist Realism," pp. 429–431.

Tertz, Abram [Andrej Sinyavsky]. *On Socialist Realism* (with *The Trial Begins*). Translated by Max Hayward and George Demis. Berkeley, 1960.

WILLIAM E. HARKINS

S

SAID, EDWARD WILLIAM. *See* Orientalism; *and* Postcolonialism.

SANTAYANA, GEORGE (1863–1952), Spanish-born philosopher and poet who was educated and later taught in the United States, and who wrote in English. Santayana's life and writings are punctuated with irony, including his place in the study of aesthetics. Although considered a principal figure in the development of aesthetic inquiry, Santayana abandoned efforts to delineate or discuss the nature of aesthetics shortly after his first book, *The Sense of Beauty* (1896). Nevertheless, the impact of his first major work is significant, marking a turning point in the theory of art and discussions of the sense of beauty. Santayana's later comments on aesthetics foreshadow modern discussions.

Philip Blair Rice wrote in the foreword to the 1955 Modern Library edition:

> To say that aesthetic theory in America reached maturity with *The Sense of Beauty* is in no way an overstatement. Only John Dewey's *Art as Experience* has competed with it in the esteem of philosophical students of aesthetics and has approached its suggestiveness for artists, critics and the public which takes a thoughtful interest in the arts.
> (p. ix)

Santayana's clear influence on aesthetic inquiry results largely from his method of analysis, which differs sharply from the preceding intellectualist traditions of aesthetics. This radical approach is emphasized in Arthur C. Danto's "Introduction" to the 1988 critical edition in which he says that Santayana brings "beauty down to earth" by treating it as a subject for science and giving it a central role in human conduct (p. xxviii).

The argumentative force of *The Sense of Beauty* lies in its dramatic and epigrammatic thesis: beauty is pleasure objectified. Why is this a daring thesis? In the nineteenth century, aesthetics and morals were considered by many as distinctive characteristics setting human beings apart from other animals and from scientific investigation. The sense of beauty was considered central to human experience, informing action as well as reflection. Beauty was not an abstract point of discussion related to art in museums or music in concert halls, but was an integral part of quotidian life, which was both elevated and evaluated by the sense of beauty. In 1928, Santayana wrote to the aesthetician Thomas Munro:

> You must remember that we were not very much later than Ruskin, Pater, Swinburne, and Matthew Arnold: our atmosphere was that of poets and persons touched with religious enthusiasm or religious sadness. Beauty (which mustn't be mentioned now) was then a living presence, or an aching absence, day and night.
> (Letters, pp. 238–239)

Santayana assumes the centrality of the sense of beauty, but instead of being a distinctly human characteristic and beyond scientific investigation, Santayana squarely places the sense of beauty in the pleasurable, in the satisfaction of individual desires that occur in particular settings. The satisfaction of a desire indicates as much about the nature of the person or animal having the desire as it does about the desired object. Furthermore, desires are not uniquely distinctive of human beings; they are a part of all animal experience. If one says that a sunset or an opera is beautiful, one is objectifying one's own pleasure as if it were characteristic of the sunset or the opera. By assuming that one's pleasure characterizes an existing object, one is projecting beauty as an objectified quality, as if beauty were a physical property rather than an objectified pleasure. This projection is natural but, if taken literally, is false. Hence, Santayana concludes that the sense of beauty is a reflection of the individual, not of an existing property in the world; it is a projection of one's pleasures on objects in the world. If this is true, then careful analysis conducted by able scientists may discern the origin of the sense of beauty, although the qualities projected on the object, according to Santayana, cannot become the subject of empirical research because they are individual, both in their origin and in their being. In his mature outlook, Santayana refers to the objects of consciousness as essences, universals that have no existence in the physical world but are the terms of consciousness, and he sometimes refers to the consciousness of aesthetic qualities as supervening on the physical relations.

Although the basic naturalism of Santayana's later philosophy is incipient in *The Sense of Beauty,* this work relies too heavily on the subjective experience of beauty to be fully in line with his more mature naturalism. There are some obvious problems with characterizing beauty as objectified pleasure. Does not the beautiful sometimes come without pleasure? Hence, it would appear that any rigid identification of beauty with objectified pleasure will not hold in all cases. Is beauty the only form of objectified pleasure? If there are other forms, then what is their relationship to the sense of beauty? These questions, and others, may have caused Santayana to pause in reconsidering his epigrammatic analysis of beauty and pleasure, but his assessment was more fundamental. There was something basically wrong with the approach he had taken.

He later characterizes his early philosophical method as relying too heavily on literary psychology, being neither true philosophy nor reliable psychology. Literary psychology is the analysis of experience without a full appreciation of the role of imagination or of the physical and social circumstances of that analysis and of the experience itself. "My whole little book *The Sense of Beauty* was written from a subjective point of view" (Santayana, 1967, 421 n. 2). A focus on radical empiricism, on experience alone, may become art if raised by imagination to the level of poetry and literature, but it is neither good philosophy nor good science. Hence, the role of the imagination, of possible meanings, is taken to be fundamental in aesthetics and other value-laden aspects of human existence. In *Interpretations of Poetry and Religion* (1900), Santayana maintains that imagination makes religion and poetry celebrations of life, but, if either is taken for science and not as rich imaginative works, the art of life is lost along with the beauty of poetry and religion. At their best, poetry and religion are identical; then "poetry loses its frivolity and ceases to demoralise, while religion surrenders its illusions and ceases to deceive" (1990, p. 172). This conclusion is found in his early correspondence with his father and appears as late as 1946 in *The Idea of Christ in the Gospels*, where Santayana presents the idea of Christ as poetic and imaginative, contrasted with a reading of the Gospels as historical events.

For Santayana, aesthetic experience is infused throughout everyday life. It is not uncommon, and, as a result, it is difficult or impossible to discern a particular field of experiences that can be isolated as subject to aesthetic analysis or to designate a particular set of characteristics that are definitive of the sense of beauty. To understand beauty, one must look beyond the experience of beauty and of pleasure objectified. Although Santayana abandons his definition of the sense of beauty as pleasure objectified, the basic direction of Santayana's aesthetics is clear even in *The Sense of Beauty*: the experience of beauty is more important than understanding it, and an understanding of it cannot rest solely on the experience.

Santayana wrote *The Sense of Beauty* as counterpoint to Josiah Royce's idealism and William James's radical empiricism, believing both of these to be literary and psychological without acknowledging it. Plato, Aristotle, and Immanuel Kant influence Santayana's account of beauty, and other intellectual influences include Rudolf Hermann Lotze's aesthetic metaphysics, Hermann Ebbinghaus's physiological psychology, Georg Simmel's critical account of abstract concepts, Herbert Spencer's evolutionary theories, and Friedrich Paulsen's account of Greek ethics. Prominent among the historical influences is Arthur Schopenhauer's *The World as Will and Idea* with its focus on objectification. "The world is my idea" is Schopenhauer's central notion in his system of the world as will objectified. Although owing much to Schopenhauer, Santayana's objectification is not a metaphysical necessity. It is a natural, evolutionary accident that, if understood, leads to a better understanding of the nature of the sense of beauty and of its origins in the physiology and social settings of the individual. This perspective is reminiscent of Simmel's account of abstract conceptions originating in the physical base of impulse and habit.

Being a product of the late nineteenth century, Santayana's outlook was shaped in part by his account of evolution and tempered by his view of Greek rational ethics. For Santayana, evolution is directionless and without goals, but from the perspective of the individual organism the ideal goal is a vital equilibrium between individual and the environment. Conscious experience is an accidental occurrence in a world of material forces and is incidental to any explanatory account of events in the world. Aesthetic experience is not lessened by this discovery, however; rather, it is the lyric cry in the wilderness of unconscious physical forces. The experience of beauty gives life meaning and significance when there is no meaning or significance in the world apart from that projected on it by individuals, but this is true not only for the sense of beauty but for any value projected on material events or objects. Santayana's view of evolution, supported by his reading of Spencer and coupled with his respect for Greek rational ethics, enabled him to account for the sense of beauty as originating in an organism that is at momentary harmony with the environment, whose pleasure is in the moment, and who revels in that fleeting delight in a world of conflicting and unthinking forces. Such passing harmonies may result in a sense of beauty, but they may also result in emergence of other moral values that reflect animal interests in an uninterested world. As a result, Santayana found it difficult to designate aesthetics as a discrete discipline, let alone designate specific characteristics of the beautiful or of art in general.

As early as 1904, Santayana abandons the notion that aesthetics is a separable field of inquiry: "Now the word 'aesthetics' is nothing but a loose term lately applied in academic circles to everything that has to do with works of art or with the sense of beauty" (1936, p. 32). He goes on to say:

Aesthetic good is accordingly no separable value; it is not realizable by itself in a set of objects not otherwise interesting. Anything which is to entertain the imagination must first have exercised the senses; it must first have stimulated some animal reaction, engaged attention, and intertwined itself in the vital process; and later this aesthetic good, with animal and sensuous values imbedded in it and making its very substance, must be swallowed up in a rational life; for reason will immediately feel itself called upon to synthesize those imaginative activities with whatever else is valuable.   (Ibid.)

In a 1927 reappraisal of *The Sense of Beauty,* Santayana writes:

Nor was the phrase "objectified pleasure" a definition of beauty, a visionary essence utterly indefinable: it was an indication of the conditions and manner in which the momentary apparition of beauty arose and vanished. If I tried now to give such an indication I might perhaps say that beauty was a vital harmony felt and fused into an image under the form of eternity.

(Santayana, 1967, p. 422 n. 2)

In brief, Santayana's mature view of aesthetic experience is as an accidental feature of evolutionary nature, rooted in the unique physiological and environmental circumstances of the individual and enveloped in a complex system of interests and values that find their expression in momentary vital harmonies. His account of aesthetics, as with his account of morals, is remarkably individualistic and creates difficulties in understanding how artistic criticism and a sense of community among artists are possible. Moments of aesthetic consciousness, taken collectively, would appear to be an anarchy of values, each legitimate in its origin and being. Yet, Santayana is a major cultural and art critic of his day, and he clearly had a sense of community among artists. How is this possible? Primarily, the answer lies in his naturalism. The growth of aesthetic experience is based on the physiological development of the individual and the environment, and, once this is clear, appraisal and community can be understood as natural outgrowths of the material world, fleeting and momentary though they may be.

One of Santayana's best appraisals of twentieth-century art is found in "Penitent Art" (reprinted in *Obiter Scripta*), an essay representing his approach to art criticism. He sustains an evolutionary approach to painting (although he maintains the criticism applies to other arts as well), which he describes as developing in three stages: blooming, flowering, and desiccating. Penitent art is in the last stage when art, having had its initial stages of innocence and then self-consciousness and sophistication, employs elaborate contrivances to retain its former status. When these contrivances dissolve and more genuine forms appear, art is penitent, rightly giving up its previous glory and accepting its present state. Santayana goes on to give an account of pure color and caricature in modern art, which many critics viewed as primitive. But for Santayana such penitent art is highly refined, revealing and enveloping its previous history in simplicity and suggestion. It is the integrity of the art to its heritage and present culture that determines its role in human history. Holding to the past without the spontaneity requisite for the present is a characteristic of dying art. Penitent art delights in the present, responding to the world in an imaginative and spontaneous manner while respecting artistic heritage.

Santayana's sense of community is the subject of "An Aesthetic Soviet." Published in 1927 and reprinted in *Obiter Scripta,* his allusion to the Soviet Union is clear, but by *soviet* Santayana means a "caucus of comrades." A central question is how can there be a community of artists if aesthetic experience is radically individual and momentary. Fundamental to the aesthetic soviet is valuing an image for its pure immediacy. Setting aside personal gain, practical consequences, and patronage to industry or custom, the aesthetic soviet revels in the spontaneous acts and intuitions that are not subject to institutional control. The basis for the community is, as one might suspect, animal motivation and natural circumstances that generate intuition, or consciousness, and enable an individual, and those of a similar nature, to be a part of the aesthetic community. By analogy, Santayana argues that fish swim in schools even though the water has no paths, and just as naturally those with an artistic physical base will be a part of each other's company.

To say that Santayana abandons aesthetics in his later philosophy is not fully accurate. He expanded the notion of aesthetics and subsumed it under a more complete notion of consciousness. Based on delighting in a present image, Santayana develops the idea of a spiritual life—a life that generates consciousness or intuition of images and delights in their presence without projecting one's own interest on them or taking them for anything other than as they appear. Hence, the spiritual life, for Santayana, is not a religious life necessarily; rather, it is a life of aesthetic enjoyment of the present, an enjoyment that is spontaneous and not forced. Individuals who have and cultivate the constitution and environment for such a life are the fortunate ones, and their spiritual life is not bounded by religion, art, or museums. It is, rather, a spontaneous celebration found in everyday living.

[*See also* Beauty; *and* Poetics.]

BIBLIOGRAPHY

Works by Santayana

The Sense of Beauty: Being the Outlines of Aesthetic Theory (1896). In *The Works of George Santayana,* edited by William G. Holzberger and Herman J. Saatkamp, Jr., vol. 2. Cambridge, Mass., 1988.

Interpretations of Poetry and Religion (1900). In *The Works of George Santayana,* edited by William G. Holzberger and Herman J. Saatkamp, Jr., vol. 3. Cambridge, Mass., 1990.

Reason in Art. In *The Life of Reason; or, The Phases of Human Progress,* vol. 4. New York, 1905.

Obiter Scripta: Lectures, Essays and Reviews. Edited by Justus Buchler and Benjamin Schwartz. New York, 1936.

The Idea of Christ in the Gospels: or, God in Man. New York, 1946.

Animal Faith and Spiritual Life. Previously Unpublished and Uncollected Writings by George Santayana with Critical Essays on His Thought. Edited by John Lachs. New York, 1967.

Other Sources

Arnett, Willard E. *Santayana and the Sense of Beauty*. Bloomington, Ind., 1955.

Ashmore, Jerome. *Santayana, Art and Aesthetics*. Cleveland, Ohio, 1966.

Cory, Daniel, ed. *The Letters of George Santayana*. New York, 1955.

Jones, John, and Herman J. Saatkamp, Jr. *George Santayana: A Bibliographical Checklist, 1880–1980*. Bowling Green, Ohio, 1982.

Levinson, Henry Samuel. *Santayana, Pragmatism, and the Spiritual Life*. Chapel Hill, N.C., 1992.

McCormick, John. *George Santayana: A Biography*. New York, 1987.

Rice, Philip Blair. "Foreword." In *The Sense of Beauty* (Modern Library Edition), pp. ix–xii. New York, 1955.

Schilpp, Paul Arthur, ed. *The Philosophy of George Santayana*. Library of Living Philosophers, vol. 2. Evanston, Ill., 1940.

Sprigge, Timothy L. S. *Santayana: An Examination of His Philosophy*. Rev. enl. ed. London and New York, 1995.

HERMAN SAATKAMP, JR.

SARTRE, JEAN-PAUL (1905–1980), French philosopher, playwright, novelist, and political activist. Perhaps no philosopher in the twentieth century has so typified the union of philosophy, politics, and art as Sartre. The presence of these often mutually conflicting interests gives a richness as well as a tension to his aesthetics that surfaced in his famous theory of committed literature. But the speculative source of these concerns lies in his conviction that imaging consciousness is the paradigm of consciousness in general. This explains his ready adoption of Edmund Husserl's phenomenology, with its use of "eidetic reduction" or the free imaginative variation of examples to yield an insight into the essence or intelligible contour of any object in question. Sartre's seminal *The Psychology of Imagination* (1940) employs such a method to reveal the essence of the image. The image, in turn, is the key to his aesthetic theory and practice.

Elements of a Sartrean Aesthetic. Although Sartre never wrote a treatise on aesthetics, one can glean the basic principles of such a theory from his ontology and philosophical psychology with significant additions drawn from his numerous essays on individual artists and interviews regarding his own literary works. Ontologically, he defended a dualism of spontaneity/inertia throughout his career. The spontaneous is usually described as "being-for-itself," though later as "praxis," and the inert is denoted as "being-in-itself" and later as the "practico-inert." The human individual is an ambiguous mixture of both dimensions and so, in Sartre's famous phrase, "is what it is not and is not what it is." This lack of self-coincidence, this inner distance, that we bring to every situation is the source of our freedom and of our creativity. As Sartre summarizes: "Human Reality is free because it is not a self but a presence to self." This ontological freedom is best exhibited in our imaginative creations that invite others to exercise their recreative freedom as they accept the artist's gift and respond to her appeal.

Imaging consciousness. Sartre's phenomenological description warrants the following definition: "The image is an act that intends [literally, "aims at" *(vise)*] an absent or nonexistent object in its corporeality by means of a physical or psychical content which is given not for its own sake but only as an 'analogical representative' [*analogon*] of the intended object." The image is not a thing but a conscious act. As conscious, it "intends" an other-than-consciousness (Husserl's thesis that all consciousness is intentional or *of* an other). Both imaging consciousness and perceptual consciousness intend their objects in their concrete individuality, not as mere simulacra. The object imaginatively presented is one we would perceive, were it a matter of perceptual awareness. But unlike perception, which grasps its object simply as present, imaging attains its object as *present-absent* or, as Sartre will sometimes say, as "derealized."

The analogon. The pivotal term for Sartre's aesthetics is the "analogon" or "intellectual representative." Introduced in *The Psychology of Imagination*, Sartre continued to defend his theory of the analogon throughout his career, eventually applying it to historiography as well, where the historian's narrative it taken as the analogon of the past event. The term denotes the *function* of the medium (the physical or mental content) as rendering the object present-absent, that is, present in the imaginary mode. The written words are the physical medium that serves as the "analogical representative" of the novel, just as the organized pigment on canvas does for the painting, the spoken words and gestures for the theater, or the eye movements for hypnagogic images. Although external images have a sensible residue aside from their function as analogues, Sartre believes that mental images do not. In any case, the physical artifact is the material component of the aesthetic object that appears when and so long as one intends the artifact in the aesthetic manner. Unfortunately, Sartre never provides a theory of analogy to support this pivotal concept, nor does he clearly distinguish between aesthetic and other forms of imaging. His increasing criticism of art for art's sake, however, reflects both his opposition to aestheticism and the correlative presence of the political dimension in his aesthetic theory. The imaginary comes to pervade his entire work. It appears in the "image" of the kind of person one thinks we all should be when one makes a moral choice and it emerges in the ideal of the "city of ends" that directs one's political commitments. Late in life, Sartre would insist that "everything is aesthetic," which should not be taken to imply that nothing is real. Rather, the relation between the imaginary and the real was one of his lifelong concerns. His multivolume study of Gustave Flaubert turns on it, as do his other "biographies" of Charles Baudelaire, Jean Genet, and Stéphane Mallarmé.

Presence. If Sartre's aesthetics is "representational," it is not mimetic. His use of Husserlian intentionality precludes the latter. But the concept of *presence* emerges as a basic aesthetic value for Sartre. Several examples support this claim. In his description of a woman doing an impersonation of Maurice Chevalier, we are led by various signs, such as the announcement that an impersonation is about to occur and the straw hat (cognitive elements), and by the actions of the impersonator herself (the physical analogue), to overlook the incongruity of the situation—for example, a woman of small stature (adoption of the imaginative attitude)—as we make present-absent Chevalier. But what "brings the performance off" is her ability to elicit from us an effective reaction similar to what we would feel in the presence of Chevalier himself. Correlative to this affective consciousness is the affective meaning of Chevalier's face, "a certain indefinable quality which we could call its 'meaning' [*sens*]." This *sens* synthesizes the various signs and gestures, animating them, as it were, with Chevalier's *presence*. Similarly, he distinguishes Francesco Guardi's paintings of Venice from those of Canaletto (Giovanni Antonio Canal) in that the latter are simply reproductive views of the city, "mere identity cards," whereas "Venice is *present* in each of [Guardi's] canvases, as we have all *experienced* but as no one has seen." Again, it is the *sens* of Guardi's work that the other lacks. Suggesting the overlap of aesthetics and historiography in his thought, Sartre argues that the entire Renaissance is present in Michelangelo Buonarroti's *David* and in the *Mona Lisa*'s smile as the German Baroque age is present in a Brandenburg Concerto. *Sens* always denotes a totality achieved through the artist's style.

Sens and signification. Sartre draws a sharp distinction between meaning *(sens)* and signification precisely to account for "meaning" in the nonsignifying arts. *Sens* is correlative to imaging consciousness, signification to signs. Thus, he can claim that music has a *sens* but no signification, which is why he has trouble with the political commitment of "pure music." This is the root of his well-known distinction between "poetry" and prose. "The poetic attitude," he explains, "considers words as things and not as signs. . . . Rather than using it as a *sign* of an aspect of the world, [the poet] sees in the word the image of one of these aspects." And again: "One does not paint significations; one does not put them to music." He concludes that "the empire of signs is prose." But he warns that prose is primarily an attitude of mind, one that uses language for utilitarian purposes. Hence, it is more the *use* to which one places art than its essential character that grounds his distinction between poetry and prose. Sartre only gradually came to acknowledge that at least some "poetry" could be politically committed.

Freedom. Sartre insists that whatever aesthetic principles he may have developed stem from the idea of freedom and not from that of commitment, which is more the by-product of freedom. The evolution of his understanding of freedom was echoed in his aesthetic theory. Just as Sartrean freedom in the mid-1940s broadened to include that of all people (one cannot be free unless all are free) and thickened to include socioeconomic freedom (freedom in the concrete sense), so the political dimension of artistic creation grew accordingly. Although it is an exaggeration to claim that Sartre abandoned art for political action, it is true that later in life he moved from writing plays and art criticism to devoting himself to the massive study of Flaubert's life and times, *The Family Idiot*. But even this he described as "a novel that is true" and characterized it as a sequel to *The Psychology of Imagination*. What he hoped would be a model of "socialist biography," this complex and prolix work stands as the crowning synthesis of those philosophical, political, and aesthetic interests that marked Sartre's lifework.

The work of art is an invitation from one freedom (the artist's) to another (the viewer's) in a manner that neither forces nor alienates. As such, the artwork is the model of nonalienating communication. But what it communicates is neither information nor emotive values. It invites a free agent to realize itself and thereby "reveal" Being. Human reality is a "revealer," that is, "man is the means by which things are manifested." But if we are inessential to the things revealed (through perceptual consciousness), we are correspondingly essential to the revelation of being in imaging consciousness. Art both as created and as *re*-created by the audience is a revelation of our freedom as revealers of being. Thus, the atheistic Sartre joins more theistic aestheticians in claiming that aesthetic experience is an image of Creation itself. But its source, like that of our freedom, is our consciousness: "the same insufficiency enables man to form images and prevents him from creating being."

The aesthetic event. It follows that, for Sartre, the aesthetic object is more an event than a "thing." Even immobile and spatial objects such as sculpture, for which Sartre showed little appreciation (with the exception of Alberto Giacometti, David Hare, and Alexander Calder), can be seen as aesthetic "events" when the viewer "derealizes" them into analogues for aesthetic enjoyment. This phenomenological aspect of Sartre's theory is buttressed by an existentialist dimension of freedom and its corresponding moral responsibility. Art, when it succeeds, increases our freedom and responsibility. Not that Sartre would subscribe to moralizing or censorship of any kind. In fact, he warned: "Beauty is a value which is only applicable to the imaginary and which requires the negation of the world in its essential structure. That is why it is stupid to confuse the moral with the aesthetic." But his linking of imaging consciousness and freedom makes it impossible, in his words, to produce an authentic work of art that proposes to enslave people or undermine their freedom. Hence, his animus against anti-Semitic "literature" and propagandistic "art."

Sartre and the Genres. As a creative artist in his own right (he was awarded but refused the Nobel prize for literature in 1964), Sartre could claim both the studio and the gallery views of the artwork. Given his ontological commitments, it was natural that his theory should focus on the nature of the artwork and the contrast between representation and imitation.

Literature. Sartre's most influential contribution to literary theory is the set of essays published as *What Is Literature?* in which he draws the prose/poetry distinction and introduces the concept of committed literature. Despite attacks from proponents of the *nouveau roman* among others, he continued to defend this distinction, albeit in a somewhat nuanced form, for the rest of his career.

True to his theory of the imagination, he claims that reading, like the apprehension of any work of art, is a synthesis of perception and creation. But the literary work of art, "though realized *through* language [the *analogon*], is never given *in* language." In fact, the appearance of a work of art is "a new event which cannot *be explained* by anterior data." It is a "directed creation" that, as an absolute beginning, is brought about by the freedom of the reader. He concludes that the writer "appeals to the reader's freedom to collaborate in the production of his work." Sartre's ontology and politics converge in the constitution of the work of art when he writes:

> One cannot address oneself to freedom as such by means of constraint, fascination, or entreaties. There is only one way of attaining it; first by recognizing it, then having confidence in it, and finally, requiring of it an act, an act in its own name, that is, in the name of the confidence that one brings to it.   (1988)

This is what he calls, in his posthumously published *Notebooks for an Ethics* (1992), the "gift-appeal" relationship. He takes it as the paradigm of all nonalienating interpersonal relations. But he does not recognize this gift-appeal phenomenon in nature, so he insists that "our freedom is never called forth by natural beauty."

But *The Family Idiot* reminds us of the role of criticism in Sartre's work, for it constitutes, among other things, a major study of French literary history in the nineteenth century. Although his critical essays on William Faulkner, Albert Camus, Francis Ponge, and others continue to be of interest and his "existential psychoanalyses" of Charles Baudelaire, Jean Genet, and Stéphane Mallarmé remain both insightful and controversial, except for a few occasional pieces, Sartre seems to have abandoned explicit art and literary criticism for political writing in the late 1960s.

Theater. Although his first novel, *Nausea,* made his name in literary circles, he is best known as a playwright. In addition to having written such plays as *The Flies, No Exit, Dirty Hands, The Condemned of Altona,* and *The Devil and the Good Lord,* Sartre reflected at length on the theater as a literary genre in essays and interviews over the years. His ethical and political concerns conspired to produce what has been called "a theater of situations," where the emphasis is on action (intention) and character rather than on the "pessimistic naturalism" of bourgeois deterministic behavior.

Here too his themes reflect his evolving understanding of "freedom" and "responsibility." They echo the political theater of Bertolt Brecht and others. But he appeals to understanding (the *Verstehen* of German social theory) over Brechtian explanation when he recommends that we combine the strengths of dramatic and epic theater, the subjective and the objective, in a postbourgeois theater where the play is presented to the audience as an image in which the spectators sympathetically participate rather than as an object that they view.

Painting. Sartre wrote essays on Jacopo Tintoretto and Titian (Tiziano Vecellio), and on several twentieth-century artists. His phenomenological method is especially apt to describe the absence of imitation in favor of "presentation." Appealing to his basic distinction between signification and *sens,* he remarks that the painter does not wish to trace signs on his canvas, that he wishes to create a thing; and if he gathers together some red, yellow, and green, it is not to give the ensemble a definable signification, that is, so as to refer to another object. He notes that "Tintoretto did not choose that yellow rent in the sky above Golgotha in order to 'signify' anguish or to 'provoke' it; it 'is' anguish and yellow sky at the same time." The "directed creation" of our response takes its cue from the suggestive power of the *analogon.*

But what of abstract painting? How does the theory of the *analogon* fare in this approach? It fares in a manner similar to that of music and other nonrepresentational art. The physical object becomes an *analogon* of itself; in other words, it invites the "presence" of any successful aesthetic object. To claim that such art is "meaningless" is to confuse signification with *sens.* Abstract art has meaning without necessarily carrying any signification. In fact, most "poetic" art will be of this sort. Of course, the emotive and informational components of any *analogon* cannot be discounted. They help to "direct" the re-creative act of the viewer. But these do not point "beyond" themselves as signs of an external object. Rather, they are ingredients in the synthetic "derealizing" act that constitutes the aesthetic object itself.

Sculpture. Given Sartre's valuing of dynamic being-for-itself over inert being-in-itself, it is not surprising that he favored sculptors such as Calder and Giacometti who attempted to overcome the limitations of their medium by appeal to motion and to bidimensionality, respectively. Whereas "for three thousand years sculptors have been carving only cadavers," in Sartre's view, Calder's mobiles exist "halfway between matter and life," while Giacometti confers "absolute distance on his [sculptured] images just as a painter confers absolute distance on the inhabitants of his canvas." True to his concept of the *analogon,* Sartre insists that "a statue truly resembles neither what the model *is* nor what the sculptor *sees.*" As Sartre explains it, Giacometti, for example, has recourse to elongation "to give perceptible expression to pure presence." What gives sculpture aesthetic value in Sartre's eyes is its ability to be what it is not and to not be what it is—like the human subject for which it exists.

Music. Although an amateur pianist himself, Sartre wrote little about music or musicians. Appealing to his *sens*/signification distinction, he claims that the eighteenth century is "present" in the sounds of a Brandenburg Concerto "just as the Renaissance smiles on the lips of the *Mona Lisa.*" But music cannot be "committed" as can prose, for it is a nonsignifying art. Rather, its revolutionary power is a function of the freedom inherent in every work of art as constituting a gift-appeal relationship: "Bach furnished the image of a freedom which, though seeming to remain within a traditional framework, transcended tradition toward a new creation." What Sartre says of the composer expresses his view of any artist: "the artist reflects *by anticipation*" of possibilities not realized in the present state of art or in the society that sustains it. In a pair of interviews on modern music given two years before his death, Sartre reflected on the works of Arnold Schoenberg, Krzysztof Penderecki, Luigi Nono, Iannis Xenakis, and others. Admitting his preference for music as "the art of sounds," he questioned what place is left for beauty in much contemporary "art of noise *(bruit).*" His remarks on Duke Ellington and John Coltrane remind us that he was an aficionado of jazz since his early years.

Art and Life. As the foregoing indicates, Sartre's existentialist aesthetic is a valorization of freedom in its many dimensions. None of these is a flight from reality, which he conceives as the realm of purposive action and dialectical counterfinality. Although his first novel, *Nausea,* seemed to defend art as a kind of salvation, his subsequent theory of "committed" literature in the 1940s placed art at the service of social justice, and his much-publicized abandonment of imaginative literature for political action in the 1960s was more apparent than real. Sartre's continued work on his "true novel" of the life and times of Flaubert was both a labor of creative imagination and an act of political and social critique. He never abandoned his conviction formed in the immediate postwar years that the artist has a social responsibility inherent in the freedom of the human condition not to pander to those who would deny this freedom but to foster it by the risk of artistic creativity, which is an act of confidence in the other's freedom. For Sartre, the moral, the political, and the aesthetic coalesce in the authentic work of art.

[*See also* Imagination; Literature, *article on* Literary Aesthetics; Marxism; Phenomenology; *and* Theater.]

BIBLIOGRAPHY

Works by Sartre

Essays in Aesthetics. Edited and translated by Wade Baskin. New York, 1963.
Literary and Philosophical Essays. Translated by Annette Michelson. New York, 1955.
Œuvres romanesques. Edited by Michel Contat and Michel Rybalka. Paris, 1981.
Sartre on Theater. Edited by Michel Contat and Michel Rybalka, translated by Frank Jellinek. New York, 1976.
The Family Idiot: Gustave Flaubert, 1821–1857. 5 vols. Translated by Carol Cosman. Chicago, 1981–1993.
The Psychology of Imagination (1940). New York, 1948.
What Is Literature? and Other Essays. Cambridge, Mass., 1988.

Other Sources

Barnes, Hazel E. *Sartre and Flaubert.* Chicago, 1981.
Bauer, George H. *Sartre and the Artist.* Chicago, 1969.
Flynn, Thomas R. "The Role of the Image in Sartre's Aesthetic." *Journal of Aesthetics and Art Criticism* 33.4 (Summer 1975): 431–442.
Goldthorpe, Rhiannon. *Sartre: Literature and Theory.* Cambridge and New York, 1984.
Hollier, Denis. *The Politics of Prose: Essay on Sartre.* Translated by Jeffrey Mehlman. Minneapolis, 1986.
Howells, Christina. *Sartre's Theory of Literature.* London, 1979.
Jameson, Fredric. *Marxism and Form: Twentieth-Century Dialectical Theories of Literature.* Princeton, N.J., 1971.
Jameson, Fredric. *Sartre: The Origins of a Style.* 2d ed. New York, 1984.
Kaelin, Eugene F. *An Existentialist Aesthetic: The Theories of Sartre and Merleau-Ponty.* Madison, 1962.
Kaelin, Eugene F. "On *Meaning* in Sartre's Aesthetic Theory." In *Jean-Paul Sartre: Contemporary Approaches to His Philosophy,* edited by Hugh J. Silverman and Frederick A. Elliston, pp. 124–140. Pittsburgh, 1980.
Sicard, Michel. *Essais sur Sartre, Entretiens avec Sartre, 1975–1979.* Paris, 1989.
Tenney, Charles D. "Aesthetics in the Philosophy of Jean-Paul Sartre." In *The Philosophy of Jean-Paul Sartre,* edited by Paul Arthur Schilpp, pp. 112–138. LaSalle, Ill., 1981.

THOMAS R. FLYNN

SAUSSURE, FERDINAND DE. *See* Metonymy; Semiotics, *article on* Semiotics as a Theory of Art; *and* Structuralism.

SCHAPIRO, MEYER (1904–1996), Lithuanian-born American art historian. Raised in Brooklyn, he was first exposed to art in evening classes at the Hebrew Education Society Settlement House, Schapiro continued his studio training at the art school of the Brooklyn Museum. His membership in the Young Peoples Socialist League expanded the political and ideological dimensions of his early education. Schapiro entered Columbia College in 1920 at the age of sixteen; his course of studies was broad, including Latin, modern languages, ancient and modern literature, anthropology, philosophy, mathematics, and art history—a range that was to inform and characterize his work throughout his career. He continued his graduate studies at Columbia—where, he confessed, his classes with Franz Boas and John Dewey were more important than any in art history. In 1929, he submitted his dissertation for the Ph.D., the first in fine arts and archaeology awarded by Columbia. "The Romanesque Sculpture of Moissac," parts of which were published in the *Art Bulletin* of 1931, opened entirely new critical perspectives for the study of medieval art (*Selected Papers*, vol. 1).

Schapiro traveled widely in Europe and the Near East in 1926–1927, viewing a vast range of art, preparing the foundations for his subsequent work, and leaving behind a trail of anecdotal legends that continued to be recounted long afterward by those who met the brilliant young graduate student—including Bernard Berenson, who compared the perceptive eloquence of the "very handsome youth" to the sweetness of Solomon's discourse on the hyssop in the wall.

Schapiro began his teaching career at Columbia in 1928 and rose through the academic ranks, becoming full professor in 1952; he was named University Professor in 1965 and became University Professor Emeritus upon his retirement in 1973. Elected a member of the National Institute of Arts and Letters in 1976, he was awarded a five-year MacArthur Foundation Fellowship in 1987.

Throughout his career, Schapiro moved between the Columbia campus on Morningside Heights and his home neighborhood in Greenwich Village, between the university and the city at large. From the late 1930s and through the 1940s, he lectured as well at the New School for Social Research, thereby reaching the wider community of the New York art world, especially the artists, in the years when New York was becoming the dynamic center of contemporary art. An engaged intellectual and a painter himself, Schapiro was as comfortable in the studios of the artists as in the realms of ideas and politics. Such a complex reach of experience was an essential component of the dialectics of his critical achievement.

Between Past and Present: The Reclamation of the Artist. As an art historian, Schapiro moved between the medieval and the modern, in full awareness of the reciprocal dynamics of his dual focus. His experience of developments in modern art opened him to phenomena in older art that had hitherto been ignored or uncomprehended by a too generalized or limited art historiography. Qualities of "perfection, coherence, and unity of form and content"—the subject of a later essay (1966; *Selected Papers*, vol. 4)—he recognized in the Romanesque sculpture of Moissac as well as in the paintings of the modern era. To each he brought a searching precision of analysis. He was attentive to the nuanced decisions, conscious and unconscious, of the sculptors of Moissac, Souillac (1939; *Selected Papers*, vol. 1), and Silos (1939; *Selected Papers*, vol. 1); that same close critical attention allowed him to articulate the creating brush strokes and constructive color choices of the Impressionists and Henri Matisse (1932).

The larger aim of Schapiro's project might be termed the reclamation of the artist in and from history. From the beginning his method involved effectively reconstructing the creative process; through close and sympathetic stylistic de-

scription he discovered unsuspected sources of vital expression in art. From the expressive physiognomy of the work of art, discerned in accordance with what he termed "general psychological laws," there emerged a persona of its creator. Behind the style, Schapiro sought and found the artist. To support his search for the explicitly "artistic character" of works of medieval art, he enlisted as unlikely allies from the medieval past harsh but sensitive critics such as Saint Bernard of Clairvaux. Reading Bernard's diatribe against the Cluniac art of his time in positive terms, Schapiro discovered a powerful voice on behalf of his own radical thesis "On the Aesthetic Attitude in Romanesque Art" (1947; *Selected Papers*, vol. 1): namely, that within church art there had emerged "a new sphere of artistic creation . . . imbued with values of spontaneity, individual fantasy, delight in color and movement, and the expression of feeling that anticipate modern art." This creativity was to be found, significantly, on the margins of the religious work, and it inspired a new appreciation for the beauty of the materials and craft of art distinct from its religious meaning. Invoking the "aestheticism" of troubadour poetry, Schapiro set out, in effect, to secularize the achievements of the medieval artist, to isolate his professional ambition and skill.

The marginal figures of jongleurs at Silos, he argued, affirmed "the self-consciousness of an independent artistic virtuosity." In contrast to the traditional, exclusively religious interpretation of this art, he emphasized the significance of these

lay artists, free, uninstitutionalized entertainers whose performance is valued directly for its sensuous and artisan qualities; just as in modern art, which is wholly secular, painters so often represent figures from the studio or from an analogous world of entertainment—acrobats, musicians, and harlequins—consciously or unconsciously affirming their own autonomy as performers and their conception of art as a spectacle for the senses."
(Ibid.)

The Dialectics of Marginality: The Social Bases of Art. Even as he sought the individual personality of the artist in the anonymous creations of the Middle Ages, Schapiro knew well that "individuality is a social fact." The artists he discovered in history were embedded in and conditioned by larger realities, material and ideological; their prospects were hardly unlimited. It was precisely the tense dialectic between the individual and the social that attracted him. That tension reflected the complexities of his own personal conflicts and commitments, including his Jewish background and his socialist beliefs. If, in his personal life, he deliberately rejected religion as a barrier to intellectual freedom, he remained committed to the ideals of socialism; he assumed a leading position for his moral principles in the political debates of the radical left in the late 1930s.

At the first American Artists' Congress against War and Fascism in 1936, Schapiro delivered a paper titled "The Social Bases of Art." Possibly against expectation, he opened by denying that his intention was "to reduce art to economics or sociology or politics." Art, he insisted, "has its own conditions which distinguish it from other activities. It operates with its own special materials and according to general psychological laws." He went on to define the marginal situation of the artist in modern society, his professional isolation: "Yet helpless as he is to act on the world, he shows in his art an astonishing ingenuity and joy in transforming the shapes of familiar things." Not unlike his medieval predecessors, then, the modern artist liberates himself from oppressive social constraint through the aesthetic, the free operations of his art. Schapiro's was a dialectics of marginality.

In the *Marxist Quarterly* of January–March 1937, he published a paper titled "The Nature of Abstract Art" (*Selected Papers*, vol. 2). Responding to the pioneering exhibition Cubism and Abstract Art organized by Alfred H. Barr, Jr., at the Museum of Modern Art, Schapiro countered the essentially formalist schema of Barr's art history and its assumption of the autonomy of art, its presumption of the independence of modern abstract art from modern historical realities. Schapiro insisted instead on the moral dimensions of that art, its intimate, if complex, rapport with the values of modern bourgeois life.

The shifting, unconventional, unregulated vision of early Impressionism offered "an implicit criticism of symbolic social and domestic formalities." Schapiro isolated the "informal and spontaneous sociability" of Impressionist imagery, the urban idylls of bourgeois recreation. Where others had celebrated the presumed insignificance of subject matter in this art *pour l'art,* he saw the very choice of subjects as integral to the new aesthetic devices of the art. Impressionist touch and broken color found their social base in Schapiro's criticism:

> In enjoying realistic pictures of his surroundings as a spectacle of traffic and changing atmospheres, the cultivated rentier was experiencing in its phenomenal aspect that mobility of the environment, the market and of industry to which he owed his income and his freedom. And in the new Impressionist techniques which broke things up into finely discriminated points of color, as well as in the "accidental" momentary vision, he found, in a degree hitherto unknown in art, conditions of sensibility closely related to those of the urban promenader and the refined consumer of luxury goods.

With a critical sensibility that joined the aesthetic perception of the studio—as a student he had been inspired by the writings of Roger Fry, and he himself continued to draw and paint—with a Marxist vision grounded in social and material reality, Schapiro's essay established an entirely new basis for the understanding of modern art, one that acknowledged it as part of a larger social life. He made the visual delights of the bourgeois art of Impressionism more intelligible and much more interesting, and he demonstrated

the complexity of values, "the burden of contemporary experience," inherent in more recent abstract art, which "bears within itself at almost every point the mark of the changing material and psychological conditions surrounding modern culture." Yet, these were the conditions, ultimately, of personal expression: "there is a burden of feeling underlying this 'geometrical' art," he declared of the *White on White* of Kazimir Malevich.

The Correlation of Form and Meaning. In the essay "On Perfection, Coherence, and Unity of Form and Content" (1966; *Selected Papers,* vol. 4), Schapiro addressed the "ascription of certain qualities to the work of art as a whole . . . , which are regarded as conditions of beauty." It was the last of the three that most engaged his attention, for the dynamic relationship between content and form and the distinction between content and subject constituted core issues for him. "Content and form," he wrote, "are plural concepts that comprise many regions and many orders within the same work." The essay epitomizes many aspects of Schapiro's larger effort. Early in his career he had argued the perfection and coherence of the Romanesque monuments, and his critical focus had always remained on the relation of part to whole. Now, considering Michelangelo's Sistine Chapel ceiling, he again felt compelled to acknowledge the content of form, the "pictorial meaning of each figure as a form" in its "unmistakable physiognomy." Like the anonymous Romanesque carver, the celebrated Renaissance master was to be reclaimed for art:

> Here the forms have become for us the main content of the work in a literal sense; they speak to us powerfully and we feel that we have perceived through them the force of the artist's creative powers, his imagination and conception of man, his style as a living person.

Seeking to explain stylistic change in "From Mozarabic to Romanesque in Silos" (1939; *Selected Papers,* vol. 1), Schapiro defined his method as the "critical correlation of the forms and meanings in the images with historical conditions of the same period and region." That method, with its essentially Marxist assumptions, proved more tractable and fruitful in confronting problems in nineteenth-century art, as demonstrated in "Courbet and Popular Imagery: An Essay on Realism and Naïveté" (1940–1941; *Selected Papers,* vol. 2). Woven into this study of the origins of realism in a "consciousness of the community," awakened by the Revolution of 1848, were themes that Schapiro found central to the values of modern art: a direct engagement of reality, a rejection of authority, an appreciation of the primitive and the naive—especially in the drawings of children.

The assumed correlation of form and meaning is what allowed Schapiro to move so easily between the large and small dimensions of style, between the work of art as a manifestation of shared social values and as the most personal expression; it is what permitted him to identify the work so intimately with its maker. In "The Still Life as a Personal Object" (1968; *Selected Papers*, vol. 4), Schapiro rejected Heidegger's reading of a pair of shoes painted by Vincent van Gogh as those of a peasant woman, and therefore redolent of the earth and symbolic of the world of the peasant. Instead, he identified them as the artist's own and argued the meaning of such identity, as "a memorable piece of his own life, a sacred relic." In "Further Notes on Heidegger and van Gogh" (1994; *Selected Papers*, vol. 4), he wrote of the painting as a "picture of objects seen and felt by the artist as a significant part of himself—he faces himself like a mirrored image—chosen, isolated, carefully arranged, and addressed to himself."

Precisely that identity, of image and maker, charged Schapiro's most sustained essay on the subject, "The Apples of Cézanne: An Essay on the Meaning of Still-Life" (1968; *Selected Papers*, vol. 2). Establishing the special place of apples in Cézanne's biography—in his study of literature and his own poetic efforts and in his early friendship with Émile Zola—Schapiro proceeded to demonstrate the significance of choice of subject matter to meaning in the genre itself and of the very act of depicting such objects. Acknowledging that in Cézanne's "habitual representation of the apples as a theme by itself there is a latent erotic sense, an unconscious symbolizing of repressed desire," Schapiro nonetheless admitted that such a formulation leaves much unexplained. Although responsive to the possibilities of psychoanalytic theory, he had severely criticized Sigmund Freud's interpretive essay on Leonardo da Vinci for the a priori limitations of its focus, its failure to recognize the contributing conditions of a larger social world, and its cultural conventions ("Leonardo and Freud: An Art-Historical Study" [1956; *Selected Papers*, vol. 4]). In considering Cézanne's apples, he expanded the discussion to engage that larger world and to explore the more general implications of the painter's activity and choice of subject, the synaesthesia of its appeal, especially to touch and taste. The apples are the "themes par excellence of an empirical standpoint wherein our knowledge of proximate objects, and especially of the instrumental, is the model or ground of all knowledge." He goes on to quote George Herbert Mead: "The reality of what we see is what we can handle."

The personal world of the tabletop, with its idiosyncratic selection of assembled objects, became for modern artists, the Cubists especially, the "plane of our active traversal of the world, into an intimate vertical surface and field of random manipulation," Schapiro wrote in "The Social Bases of Art" (1936). Schapiro's phenomenology was built from the full range of his own experience, as a viewer, a reader, and a painter. But it was particularly on his deep understanding of the creative choices of the artist, the formal decisions and marking gestures, that his vision was based.

The Operations of Art: Frame and Field. Schapiro's criticism was essentially empirical, a direct encounter with the work. On a larger scale, he was involved in a search for the operational principles that distinguished art, and his main concern as a scholar was with those periods in the history of art when the basic elements of image making were subject to the most fundamental pressures and reevaluation. In the dialectical conflict between frame and field, he located the tension between the artist and the determining social order; this was the arena of creative challenge, latent with possibilities. In Impressionism, as in Hiberno-Saxon and Romanesque art, the picture plane itself is viewed as a dynamic field of conflicting energies and ambiguous relationships, the resolution of which resides in the inventive act of design—and in the responsive act of interpretation.

Those elements and principles of pictorial representation that concerned Schapiro throughout his studies he most succinctly and systematically enumerated in a paper titled "On Some Problems in the Semiotics of Visual Art: Field and Vehicle in Image-Signs" (1969; *Selected Papers*, vol. 4). The issues themselves go directly to the heart of image making in its several dimensions—historical, cultural, psychological. Schapiro begins his discussion with the invention of the smooth prepared surface, reminding the reader that "such a field corresponds to nothing in nature or mental imagery." Related to this prepared ground is the concept of its boundaries: "we tend to take for granted the regular margin and frame as essential features of the image," but we are then reminded that the frame itself is a relatively late invention. Taking nothing for granted in the mechanics of picture making, Schapiro continues by isolating still further "non-mimetic elements of the image-sign and their role in constituting the sign." He isolates position and direction within the context of the field, the relative values of high and low, right and left, and the format of the field itself.

Finally, he turns to the sign-bearing matter of the picture, the "image-substance of inked or painted lines and spots." These are nonmimetic elements that have properties different from the objects they represent. The line that bounds a depicted face may be thick or thin, continuous or broken, and, whereas those qualities may lend a particular character to the face rendered, the line itself remains "an artificial mark with properties of its own." The ambivalence of the alternating function of the mark, mimetically referring to the face it denotes or graphically declaring its own independent existence, epitomizes the situation of the surface as a basic locus of tension and conflict. These contradictions constitute a crucial part of the aesthetic experience. "The artist and the sensitive viewer of the work of art are characterized by their ability to shift attention freely from one aspect to the other, but above all, to discriminate and judge the qualities of the picture substance itself." (Schapiro developed this theme in the essay "Eugène Fromentin as Critic" [1949; *Selected Papers*, vol. 4], which may be read as a highly personal credo.)

Schapiro quite naturally adduced as his example Impressionist painting, "in which the parts have been freed from the rule of detailed correspondence to the parts of an object." Throughout, in his lectures and in his writing, he consistently presented this art as central to any view of the art of the twentieth century, for in it the terms of the debate between the mimetic and the nonmimetic, between image-sign and image-substance, were fully articulated. If abstract art has capitalized on the liberation of the mark in representational art, the independent stroke nonetheless retains an indelibly physiognomic character, determined by "many of the qualities and formal relationships of the preceding mimetic art."

The Physiognomics of Expression. "The picture-sign seems to be through and through mimetic." This declaration may stand as key to Schapiro's own aesthetic values. In a different art-historical context, criticizing the polarities of another scholar who had posited in Romanesque monumental art a "contradiction" between architecture and sculpture, a contrast of order and disorder, Schapiro suggested instead a distinction between "constructive and physiognomic forms" ("On Geometrical Schematism in Romanesque Art" [1932; *Selected Papers*, vol. 1]). His selection of terms here implicates a system of values that extends beyond merely formal distinctions, for in Schapiro's usage, whether in regard to medieval or modern art, "physiognomic" properties suggest the deliberately expressive, the willfully inventive, the projection of human feeling and freedom. He himself responded to the "exuberant fantasy which delights us in Romanesque art," in the variety of capitals in an arcade, the individualization of the parts regardless of their functional identity, in the "wild involvement of monstrous aggressive beasts and human figures" in a Cistercian manuscript, and which he found "astoundingly modern in their freedom of conception" ("On the Aesthetic Attitude in Romanesque Art" [1947; *Selected Papers*, vol. 1]).

It is in the perception and analysis of such freedom and inventiveness that Schapiro consistently made reference to the concept and function of the frame, the "constructive" context within which he gauged the operations of the "physiognomic" element. In his vision, the two elements interact, creating that dynamic interplay that will define the field itself and its special properties, an arena projected by, even as it hosts, the forces of creative freedom.

What might be termed the humanism of Schapiro's critical attitude can be further gauged in his discussions of another set of basic options in pictorial representation: the alternative between frontal and profile. In *Words and Pictures: On the Literal and the Symbolic in the Illustration of a Text* (1973), this distinction informs a discussion of aspects of narration. Schapiro builds on a linguistic model: The profile is like the grammatical form of the third person, "the impersonal 'he' or 'she' with its concordantly inflected verb," whereas the frontal view of the face "corresponds to the role of the 'I' in speech with its complementary 'you'." Such grammatical analogies, however, retain their full social phenomenology: The profile face "is detached from the viewer and belongs with the body in action (or in an intransitive state) in a space shared with other profiles on the surface of the image" (ibid.). The frontal face enters into a dialogic relationship with the viewer, seeming to "exist both for us and for itself in a space virtually continuous with our own" (ibid.). Schapiro is ultimately less concerned with the generalized rule than with the individual case, and he carries this concern directly to the level of affect and response.

Too keenly aware of the variety, the alternatives and inflections, available within any determining context—and especially to the vigorously inventive artist—Schapiro stops short of the definition of laws:

> The plurality of meaning in each of these two appearances of the head would seem to exclude a consistent explanation based on inherent qualities of the profile and the frontal or full-face view. It is like the difficulty of finding in colors a universal, culturally unconditioned ground for their symbolic use, though we experience colors as strongly charged with feeling.   (Ibid.)

Schapiro's critical language is characterized by a special candor, a clarity of thought and directness—even simplicity—of expression. The markers of his argument are references to the essentials of the art: frame and field, figure and ground, mimetic and nonmimetic. Such basic terms, however, are never presented as abstractions or as absolute values. He refused to subordinate the artist's freedom to the laws of art; he insisted on that freedom, even if it be latent rather than actual.

Questions of Style. It was this attitude that made it difficult for Schapiro to accept the great descriptive and explanatory models of the earlier generation of theorists he so admired for their intellectual ambition. His earliest published paper (1925) was a discussion of Emanuel Löwy's *Rendering of Nature in Early Greek Art*, which analyzed the development from archaism to realism in seven stages. Here Schapiro first confronted the concept of the archaic, including its analogies to other primitive arts and to the drawings of children; it is a concept that was to prove central to his own investigations of Romanesque art. As important, the young Schapiro, uncomfortable with the traditional valorization of realism, began his own search for fundamental principles, asking the questions that were to challenge him throughout his career, the search for "a comprehensive study of the 'forms' of art." In the magisterial article "Style" (1953; *Selected Papers*, vol. 4), he reviewed the efforts of the earlier theorists: the stylistic polarities postulated by Heinrich Wölfflin, the cyclical pattern conceived by Paul Frankl, the phenomenological duality of Alois Riegl, as well as Löwy's progressive stages. Each is found wanting, as is the crude application of Marx to the explanation of style by the forms of social life.

"A theory of style adequate to the psychological and historical problems has still to be created," Schapiro concludes, somewhat wistfully. "It waits for a deeper knowledge of the principles of form construction and expression and for a unified theory of the processes of social life in which the practical means of life as well as emotional behavior are comprised."

Through his teaching, public lectures, and publications, as well his direct impact on several generations of practicing artists, Schapiro offered a model of engaged criticism. By the example of his own involvement and the nature of his inquiry, he affirmed the value of art as an essential unifying quality of humanity.

[*See also* Marxism; *and* Style.]

BIBLIOGRAPHY

Works by Schapiro

Words and Pictures: On the Literal and the Symbolic in the Illustration of a Text. The Hague, 1973.
Selected Works, vol. 1, *Romanesque Art.* New York, 1977.
Selected Works, vol. 2, *Modern Art, 19th and 20th Centuries.* New York, 1978.
Selected Works, vol. 3, *Late Antique, Early Christian and Mediaeval Art.* New York, 1979.
Selected Works, vol. 4, *Theory and Philosophy of Art: Style, Artist, and Society.* New York, 1994.

Essays Cited

"On Emanuel Löwy's *Rendering of Nature in Early Greek Art.*" *The Arts* 8 (September 1925): 170–172.
"The Romanesque Sculpture of Moissac." *Art Bulletin* 13.3 (September 1931): 249–352; 13.4 (December 1931): 464–531. Reprinted in *Selected Papers,* vol. 1, pp. 131–264.
"Matisse and Impressionism." *Androcles* 1.1 (February 1932): 21–36.
"Über den Schematismus in der Romanischen Kunst." *Kritische Berichte zu kunstgeschichtlichen Literatur* 1 (1932–1933): 1–21. Reprinted as "On Geometrical Schematism in Romanesque Art," in *Selected Papers,* vol. 1, pp. 265–284.
"The Social Bases of Art." In *First American Artists' Congress,* pp. 31–37. New York, 1936.
"The Nature of Abstract Art." *Marxist Quarterly* 1.1 (January–March 1937): 77–98. Reprinted in *Selected Papers,* vol. 2, pp. 185–211.
"From Mozarabic to Romanesque in Silos." *Art Bulletin* 21.4 (December 1939): 313–374. Reprinted in *Selected Papers,* vol. 1, pp. 28–101.
"The Sculptures of Souillac." In *Medieval Studies in Memory of A. Kingsley Porter,* edited by Wilhelm R. W. Koehler, pp. 359–387. Cambridge, Mass., 1939. Reprinted in *Selected Papers,* vol. 1, pp. 102–130.
"Courbet and Popular Imagery: An Essay on Realism and Naïveté." *Journal of the Warburg and Courtauld Institutes* 4.3–4 (1940–1941): 164–191. Reprinted in *Selected Papers,* vol. 2, pp. 47–85.
"On the Aesthetic Attitude in Romanesque Art." In *Art and Thought: Issued in Honour of Dr. Ananda K. Coomaraswamy,* pp. 130–150. London, 1947. Reprinted in *Selected Papers,* vol. 1, pp. 1–27.
"Fromentin as a Critic." *Partisan Review* 16.1 (January 1949): 25–51. Reprinted in *Selected Papers,* vol. 4, pp. 103–134.
"Style." In *Anthropology Today,* edited by Alfred Kroeber, pp. 287–312. Chicago, 1953. Reprinted in *Selected Papers,* vol. 4, pp. 51–102.
"Leonardo and Freud: An Art-Historical Study." *Journal of the History of Ideas* 17.2 (April 1956): 147–178. Reprinted in *Selected Papers,* vol. 4, pp. 153–300.

"On Perfection, Coherence, and Unity of Form and Content." In *Art and Philosophy: A Symposium,* edited by Sidney Hook, pp. 3–15. New York, 1966. Reprinted in *Selected Papers,* vol. 4, pp. 33–50.
"The Apples of Cézanne: An Essay on the Meaning of Still-Life." *Art News Annual* 34 (1968): 35–53. Reprinted in *Selected Papers,* vol. 2, pp. 1–38.
"The Still Life as a Personal Object: A Note on Heidegger and van Gogh." In *The Reach of Mind: Essays in Memory of Kurt Goldstein,* edited by Marianne L. Simmel, pp. 203–209. New York, 1968. Reprinted in *Selected Papers,* vol. 4, pp. 135–142.
"On Some Problems in the Semiotics of Visual Art: Field and Vehicle in Image-Signs." *Semiotica* 1.3 (1969): 223–242. Reprinted in *Selected Papers,* vol. 4, pp. 1–32.

Other Sources

Epstein, Helen. "Meyer Schapiro: A Passion to Know and Make Known." *Artnews* 82.5 (May 1983): 60–85; 82.6 (Summer 1983): 84–95.
Special issue "On the Work of Meyer Schapiro." *Social Research* 45.1 (Spring 1978).
Oxford Art Journal 17.1 (1994). Special issue devoted to Meyer Schapiro.
Schapiro, Lillian Milgram. *Meyer Schapiro: The Bibliography.* New York, 1995.

DAVID ROSAND

SCHELLING, FRIEDRICH WILHELM JOSEPH VON

(1775–1854), German idealist philosopher. Schelling contributed to aesthetics early in his career, especially in 1798–1803, years spent in Jena with the Romantic critics Karl Wilhelm Friedrich von Schlegel, and August Wilhelm von Schlegel, but close to the classicist Weimar of Friedrich von Schiller and Johann Wolfgang von Goethe. His work in aesthetics was theoretical rather than critical, exploring the interfaces between epistemology, psychology, and hermeneutics or philosophy of language. On the formal side, he followed Immanuel Kant in treating aesthetics as a quasi-cognitive domain, but deepened the theory of "aesthetic genius" by adding an account, inspired by Baruch Spinoza and Goethe, of unconscious knowing and producing in the artist. By focusing on the dialectic of conscious and unconscious intention in the artist's psyche, Schelling shifted the inquiry from the cognitive processes of the artist to the work of art itself, to its multiply determined (or "symbolic") meaning inside the public world of cultural objects. Implicit in his treatment of aesthetic production as the function of imagination *(Einbildungskraft)* was a general theory of semiotics (or "schematism"). Schelling found symbolism or schematism at work in all artistic domains: formative, plastic, and literary arts; in this he differed from August Schlegel, who thought the medium of language necessary for the highest arts.

On the side of content, Schelling's originality lay in his identification of the content of fine art with that of religion, with Greek mythology serving as the world-historical center of gravity for both art and religion. Rather than preferring classical to Romantic art, or the reverse, Schelling argued for a necessary unity of objective and subjective modes of symbolic communication. Modern art—Romantic, Christian, optimistic, embodying the poetics (and politics) of freedom—is meaningful only in contrast to the structured form and necessity embodied in classic art and pre-Christian religions. In his critical remarks on specific works, Schelling generally followed Schiller's in the formative and plastic arts and August Schlegel's in the literary arts, but he defined himself as a systematic philosopher, not a practicing critic. Whatever the thematic thread that shaped his total systematic view—identity philosophy (1800–1806), or philosophy of history (1809–1815), or philosophy of God (1821–1846)—he always viewed philosophy of art as one specialized but culturally accessible form of philosophical metatheory.

In his early years (1794–1800), Schelling worked alongside Johann Gottlieb Fichte to develop a self-standing philosophical system based on Kant's critical writings. Fichte brought Kant's three forms of reason—intellect, will, and judgment—under the umbrella of practical reason. The I is in essence act or self-deed. Affected by a vanishing but irremovable not-I, the I's act is intelligence. Expressed within the natural and social worlds, it becomes the various forms of will: biological drive, emotive striving, arbitrary choice, submission to social and moral laws. The watchword of Fichte's Kantianism was the "primacy of praxis." It left a deep imprint on Goethe's *Faust*, on Friedrich Hölderlin's poetry, and on the critical theories of the Schlegel brothers.

While Schelling supported the program of Fichte's *Wissenschaftslehre* as the logical ground for any transcendental philosophy, his early essays of 1794–1800 search for an alternate real ground for systematic philosophy. The 1797 *Ideas for a Philosophy of Nature* supplements Fichte's account of consciousness with a philosophy of nature inspired by Kant's *Metaphysical Foundations for Natural Philosophy*. Schelling argued that the same opposed activities that transcendental philosophy postulates to explain the "I think" of consciousness also explain the ladder of natural phenomena, from matter up to the animated body that is the platform of consciousness. Just as the I is "constructed" (i.e., explained) as a dynamic interplay of two activities, one unbounded, another limiting, so matter's basic property of filling space is explained as a dynamic balance between expansive and contractive forces.

A second attempt to systematize Kant's philosophy is found in the 1800 *System of Transcendental Idealism*. Following the clue of Schiller's *Letters on the Aesthetic Education of Humanity*, Schelling makes aesthetics the region that unites theoretical and practical philosophy, not the passive experience of viewer, auditor, or reader, but the peculiar productive activity of the artist: "aesthetic intuition." In Kant's language, an intuition of *x* is both my representation of *x* and the production of the *x* represented. In producing the work of art, the "intuitive" creator performs a knowing-as-doing that is more fundamental than the nonproductive knowing

and the noncognitive production that differentiate "knowing" and "doing" in other phenomenal contexts. Also, conscious and unconscious productivity, the forces constructive of the natural and social worlds, merge here in the artist's psyche as the interplay of conscious and unconscious intention. In the very independence of the finished work of art from the material and psychological sources of its production is proof that the artist produces more than she literally knows.

How can artistic production ground a philosophical system or serve as the capstone for a series of other philosophical inquiries? Schelling argued that because the artist's activity—aesthetic intuition—taps into the primary divided energy that first produces an objective world for the I and then ceaselessly conquers its objectivity by the I's knowledge and action, it is not a case of ordinary activity but a laying bare of foundations. What kinship can there be between the ground of being and the artist's activity?

In the 1800 *System*, Schelling utilized a vocabulary given currency by Kant and Fichte for naming the ultimate active ground of being. Kant had defined sensible intuition in opposition to a hypothetical intellectual intuition where, for example, God knowing *y* would also mean God realizes *y* or causes it to exist; Kant first noted in 1770 that artists seem to have some faculty analogous to this conceptually defined divine creativity. Fichte had used the term to designate the immediate certainty of agency involved in self-consciousness, the *doing* involved in the thinking of "I think." Schelling now uses *intellectual intuition* to indicate at the start of the system a pure (thus empirically unavailable) act of spontaneity that transcendental philosophy must postulate to explain self-consciousness: the analytical $I = I$ that mutates into the synthetic $I = \sim I$. The philosopher imitates this primal act by a freely undertaken conscious exercise—mediated by language, hence by imagination and by time, the primary schematism. The philosophical narrative that results is a "construction of consciousness"; in it the original synthesis of the I, which would be both conceptually clear and empirically there if the philosopher *had* the (merely) postulated intellectual intuition, is unpacked into epochs of the "history" of understanding and will. Schelling is clear that this "history of consciousness" is just an explanatory device; his work as a philosopher is primarily imaginative in Kant's sense: it translates the all-at-once of the I's self-constituting act (the fundamental synthesis that cannot be understood) into a series of acts that are at once objective and subjective (and that explain each other, at least minimally, in their succession). These acts form a "pragmatic history" of consciousness—not an empirical history, but a heuristic construction that shows how the features of self-consciousness and of objective nature nest inside the original synthetic act like Chinese boxes.

Despite the brilliance of these initial moves, Schelling was unable to close the story of the unfolding consciousness with a return to original identity. The inability rested on a logical prohibition. Because transcendental philosophy aimed at establishing the conditions for the possibility of experience, what explains and what is to be explained must be of different orders, one hypothetical, the other empirical. If the transcendental philosopher posits spontaneous self-realizing activity as the nonempirical explanatory element, and meanwhile uses analysis of that activity to explain the structure of both natural and social phenomenal worlds, he must in the end bring forward some empirical *explanandum* that is obviously *a case* of spontaneous self-realizing activity. If the tie-down to experience is lacking, there is no explanation, and a metaphysical fantasy has been perpetrated. Schelling was able to argue to the case of spontaneously self-realizing activity ("aesthetic intuition") only from the ambiguous status of the work of art once it is detached from the process of its production. Because a work—say, Goethe's *Faust*—has different meanings to various actors, directors, and critics, Schelling maintained that the work carried an unanalyzable multitude of meanings, and that the artist, consciously and unconsciously, endowed the play with all these meanings. He thus thought that the work displayed the existence of the infinite (at least the indefinitely multiple) in the finite and that, therefore, the artist's aesthetic intuition was an empirical case of the postulated intellectual intuition, everywhere informing but factually missing in the philosopher's activity. Schelling thus surmised that aesthetic intuition was the phenomenal analogue of the (empirically absent) intellectual intuition claimed by the philosopher.

Although the transcendental stance of Schelling's early philosophy and the prominence he accorded aesthetic intuition in the 1800 *System* were not permanent features of his philosophy, they captured the political, moral, and religious yearning of the Romantic poets and literary critics who were first Fichte's, then Schelling's, fellows at the University of Jena. These features of Schelling's thought found their way into Samuel Taylor Coleridge's *Biographia Literaria*, and from there into English Romantic literature and American Transcendental philosophy. That Coleridge assembled its twelfth chapter on productive imagination from various early texts of Schelling occasioned the charges and countercharges about plagiarism that have followed that author and his editors.

Schelling's preference for aesthetic intuition over discursive reasoning as the philosopher's tool in the 1800 *System* threatened to dissolve philosophy itself into literary theory (or *Poesie* as it was then called). In 1801, Schelling pulled back from this radical aestheticism and, in a third phase of philosophical innovation, announced an absolute system, which he casually called "Identity Philosophy." In *Presentation of My System of Philosophy*, (*Darstellung meines System der Philosophie*, 1927) Schelling claimed that the philosopher not merely presupposes but possesses intellectual intuition, the synoptic faculty that Kant called "pure reason." If

the philosopher distances himself from what is arbitrary and subjective in his thought the way the artist distances himself from his personality, he can move in and with reason and so with purely logical means construct a theory of the absolute. The philosopher posits a logical domain of pure identity on the basis of concrete identities seen within the items of experience. Because these identities are combinatory, fashioned from differences, their mode of being is identity-in-difference; their conceptualization demands not a logic of bare identity but one that integrates universals and particulars, concepts and intuitions. These integrative structures motivate the philosopher's postulation of a ground of explanation whose logic is not that of abstract identity as opposed to difference, but of *in*difference or the identity of opposites. This absolute is a transcendental (or heuristic) posit, a noumenal unity of everything that phenomenally manifests itself as connected by difference.

Because this move is made with the necessity and universality of thought, Schelling felt that philosophy had become methodologically self-sufficient and no longer needed to appeal to the artist's aesthetic intuition as an empirical correlate of intellectual intuition. The 1802 dialogue *Bruno* demoted the artist to an unconscious collaborator of the philosopher. The artist, it is now said, produces an infinite fund of meaning in the work of art not by conscious agency, but by an unconscious outworking of a reality contained in the absolute as an "idea." This idea is the "soul" of the artist, but it comes to expression only partially and in distorted form in the artist's psyche and in the bodily movements that produce the separate artifact. This explains why there is so much bad art that is "personal," and so little grand art that is universal: most artists have small "souls" or limited empirical personalities. *Bruno* thus demoted artistic creativity from a transcendent to a robotic activity. What Schelling viewed as the conscious *and* unconscious character of aesthetic intuition in the 1800 *System* is viewed as merely unconscious production in 1802.

In 1802–1803 and 1804–1805, Schelling lectured on *the philosophy of art*. He did not publish these lectures in his lifetime, perhaps because of his dependence on August Wilhelm von Schlegel's Berlin lectures *On Dramatic Art and Literature* (1801–1803) for critical evaluation of particular literary artists and their achievements, for example, of Dante Alighieri's poetry and the plays of Pedro Calderón de la Barca and William Shakespeare. The lectures stand, nonetheless, as Schelling's most important contribution to aesthetic theory. In the general parts of the lectures, the topics of imagination, language, and symbolism are used to present the metaphysics of identity. The treatment of symbolism as a general function of expression stands on its own outside the metaphysical theory and is of interest to contemporary readers because Schelling used language itself as his primary example of a "symbol" or materially expressed meaning.

Once he had subjugated the arts to philosophy as inferior domains of cognition, as he had in 1802, Schelling could approach *philosophy* of art as a suitable vehicle for presenting metaphysics. If one can mix—as the later Schelling frequently did—abstract talk of "the absolute" with talk of the object of religion, the fine arts are the place where "God-talk" and metaphysics overlap. Not only are the contents of the highest visual and literary forms of fine art religious, but all the arts come to be in activities of expression or *informing—Einbildung,* as in *Einbildungskraft,* imagination. The absolute, or "God" in the language of these lectures, has an autopoetic or imaginative form of being; its essence is to express or affirm itself, to translate its reality from unarticulated identity into a differentiated world of form. As the essential identity of universality and particularity, or ideality and reality, God is the source of the various projections of one factor upon the other that make the phenomenal world a series of images *(Einbildungen)* of the absolute. God's perfect self-affirmation is the identification *(Ineinsbildung)* or equal informing of universality and particularity into perfect particulars or "ideas."

With these general metaphysical structures in place—God as expressive, informing universality and particularity into ideas in the absolute, and occasioning "reflected" imagings of ideas in the two phenomenal domains of nature and human culture—Schelling is able to generate a philosophical model of the cultural world as detailed and compelling as the model of nature he constructed in the two editions of *Ideas for a Philosophy of Nature.* The ideal phenomenal universe—which Georg Wilhelm Friedrich Hegel calls "spirit"—is structurally the reflection of reality (or particularity) into ideality (or universality). The root identity (of real and ideal) is expressed in three stages or under three *powers:* on the objective level as knowledge, on the subjective as action, and on the highest level as art, where the two factors are posited as equal. The realm of art is thus the place where ideality is realized in perfect, crystalline form as ideas or perfect particulars and where subjectivity is perfectly manifested in objective shape, as in the bodies the Greeks gave to their gods and goddesses in ancient sculpture. Schelling did not think it was accidental that the most penetrating naive art portrayed ideas as individual gods. Although he was aware of the mythologies of other cultures and keenly interested in the phenomena of comparative religion, Schelling asserted that the world of the Greek Olympians was the paradigmatic content of all art. The love of all things Greek fostered by German classicism and the unconscious Eurocentrism fostered by Christianity conspired in Schelling to shape the narrow view that art can have only two sorts of contents: the realistic mythology of Greece with its poetics of eternity and the idealistic mythology of Christianity's attempts to display the workings of providence in history.

Schelling's remarks on the formal side of art expanded on the idea of "expression" that ties God to the universe or phenomenal worlds; they also build on August Schlegel's discussions of original language as part of *Naturpoesie.* All art is symbolic in a general sense, because it is at once the purest expression of the absolute's ideality, but in an objectified form, under the guise of pure sensuous objectivity. Language is the basic symbol because it is idea materialized, its first conceptual expression. There are three specialized sorts of symbolism: schematism, where the particular is intended by the universal (as in painting or generally in language); allegory, where the universal is intended by the particular (as in music); and symbolism proper, where universal and particular are one (as in the plastic arts). The subjugation of all fine arts to language and of the metaphysics of art to symbolic expression makes it clear that Schelling assimilated art to cognition, and that his theory could comprehend art only insofar as it served a cognitive or informational function. There is little discussion of the sensuous in his lectures on the *Philosophy of Art* and no hint of the possibilities that later art forms explore of manipulating the sensuous media themselves to produce nonrepresentative content.

Schelling made a final contribution to aesthetic theory in an 1807 essay, "Concerning the Relationship of the Plastic Arts to Nature." This essay repeats themes familiar from the Identity Philosophy, for example, the way good art strikes a balance between naturalism and formalism, exhibited perfectly in the concreteness whereby the "ideas" of mythology and religion are shown in painting and sculpture. New to Schelling's theory as he advanced toward the Philosophy of Freedom of 1809 and thereafter are the ideas that art redeems a nature intrinsically frustrated and sorrowful and that, in artistic creator and spectator alike, the agent that unifies form and matter and that perceives their essence is "spirit" *(Geist).* After 1807, Schelling's interests in the arts and in philosophy of language fade as he gravitates toward philosophy of history and philosophy of religion. The aesthetic vehicle is discarded as the philosopher becomes confident of a historical-anthropological access to God.

BIBLIOGRAPHY

Works by Schelling

Bruno; or, On the Natural and Divine Principle of Things (1802). Edited and translated by Michael G. Vater. Albany, N.Y., 1984.

Concerning the Relationship of the Plastic Arts to Nature. Translated by Michael Bullock. In *The True Voice of Feeling: Studies in English Romantic Poetry,* edited by Herbert Read. London, 1953.

Darstellung meines Systems der Philosophie. In *Sämtliche Werke,* Jubilee Edition, vol. 3. Munich, 1927. Reprint of original edition in 14 vols. by K. F. A. Schelling (Stuttgart, 1856–1861).

Ideas for a Philosophy of Nature (1797). Translated by Errol E. Harris and Peter Heath. Cambridge and New York, 1988.

On the History of Modern Philosophy. Edited and translated by Andrew Bowie. Cambridge and New York, 1994.

On University Studies. Translated by E. S. Morgan, edited by Norbert Guterman. Athens, Ohio, 1966.

System of Transcendental Idealism (1800). Translated by Peter Heath. Charlottesville, Va., 1978.

Other Sources

Burwick, Frederick. "Perception and 'the Heaven-Descended Know-Thyself'." In *Coleridge's Biographia Literaria*, edited by Frederick Burwick. Columbus, Ohio, 1989.

Coleridge, Samuel Taylor. *Biographia Literaria; or, Biographical Sketches of My Literary Life and Opinions*. In *The Collected Works of Samuel Taylor Coleridge*, edited by James Engell and W. Jackson Bate, vol. 7. Princeton, N.J., 1983.

Fackenheim, Emil L. "Schelling's Philosophy of the Literary Arts." *Philosophical Quarterly* (St. Andrews) 4 (1954): 310–326.

Jähnig, Dieter. *Schelling: Die Kunst in der Philosophie*. 2 vols. Pfüllingen, 1966–1969.

Lawrence, Joseph. "Art and Philosophy in Schelling." *Owl of Minerva* 20 (1988): 5–19.

Marx, Werner. *The Philosophy of F. W. J. Schelling: History, System, and Freedom*. Translated by Thomas Nenon. Bloomington, Ind., 1984.

Seidel, George J. "Creativity in the Aesthetics of Schelling." *Idealistic Studies* 4 (1974): 170–180.

Snow, Dale. "The Role of the Unconscious in Schelling's System of Transcendental Idealism." *Idealistic Studies* 19 (1989): 231–250.

MICHAEL G. VATER

SCHILLER, JOHANN CHRISTOPH FRIEDRICH VON

(1759–1805), a poet, playwright, and aesthetician of the classical age of German literature, the so-called age of Goethe *(Goethezeit)*, which began toward the close of the eighteenth century. Schiller was born in Marback on the Neckar, Germany. He attended the Duke of Württemberg's military academy, and in 1780 he qualified as a surgeon. Although Schiller seemed to adapt well to military life, he began reading, and eventually writing, Sturm und Drang (verse and plays). In 1783, Schiller worked as a dramatist for the Mannheim theater, and the next year, he began publishing a theatrical journal, *Die rheinische Thalia*. In 1785, he moved first to Leipzig, then to Dresden, where he joined Karl Theodor Körner's literary circle. In 1787, he moved to Weimar; the next year he was appointed honorary professor of history at Jena. Schiller was ennobled in 1802.

Schiller's aesthetic writings consist in four major treatises and many smaller essays, most of them written between 1791 and 1795. Each of the treatises has been influential in the history of aesthetics, and so they deserve separate analysis here.

Much admired by Friedrich Schlegel, Friedrich Wilhelm von Schelling, Friedrich Hölderlin, and Georg Wilhelm Friedrich Hegel, Schiller's aesthetic writings played a formative role in the development of German Idealism and Romanticism. Schiller was indeed the central spokesman for the aestheticism of the age of Goethe, the founder of its faith in the redemptive value of art. Schiller's aestheticism consisted in his belief that the perfect person, society, and state is a work of art, and that one should strive to make them aesthetic wholes. The main theme of his aesthetic

writings is that a person, society, or state achieves excellence only through beauty. It is the task of the arts, Schiller also believed, to make people aware of their highest moral aspiration: the longing to recover their lost harmony with themselves, nature, and society.

The central influence behind the formation of Schiller's aesthetics was Immanuel Kant, whom Schiller began to study in 1791. His aesthetics is scarcely comprehensible without some understanding of Kant's doctrines, because Schiller began from the same problems, adopted the same vocabulary, and applied the same ideas to new fields. Nevertheless, it is a mistake to consider Schiller a Kantian or to measure his work only in Kantian terms, for Schiller criticized Kant as much as he borrowed from him. Precisely how and why Schiller differs from Kant is a complex and controversial issue, which this essay will attempt to unravel.

Although Kant was the central figure in the development of Schiller's aesthetics, Schiller was also influenced by other writers. He was steeped in most classical and eighteenth-century sources. In the winter of 1792–1793 alone, the formative period for the development of his mature aesthetic view, he read Johann Georg Sulzer, Henry Home, Moses Mendelssohn, Edmund Burke, Raphael Mengs, Johann Joachim Winckelmann, and Charles de Batteux. Schiller's early *Philosophische Briefe* (Philosophical Letters; 1786) reveals the influence of Anthony Ashley Cooper, earl of Shaftesbury, whose doctrine of the unity of beauty, truth, and goodness continues to color his mature views.

It is also important to recognize that Schiller's philosophy antedates his acquaintance with Kant. In the early 1780s, Schiller became preoccupied with the question of the role of the artist in society, and his early essays on the German theater, *Über das gegenwärtige deutsche Theater* (On the Present German Theater; 1782) and *Die Schaubühne als eine moralische Anstalt betrachtet* (The Stage as a Moral Institution; 1784), laid the foundation for much of his later work. Schiller also sketched the rudiments of his metaphysics and ethics in the *Philosophie der Physiologie* (Philosophy of Physiology; 1779), the doctoral dissertation "Versuch über den Zusammenhang der tierischen Natur des Menschen mit seiner geistigen" (Essay on the Connection between Our Animal and Spiritual Nature; 1780), and the *Philosophical Letters* (1786). All these early writings are important for the problematic of Schiller's later aesthetics. In them, Schiller poses the questions that his later works will attempt to answer: "How is it possible to explain the unity of human nature?" "How is it possible to reconcile enlightened criticism with religious belief?" and "What is the role of the artist in the modern world?"

The Analysis of Beauty. Schiller laid the foundation for his mature aesthetic views in a series of letters to Gottfried Körner, which he wrote from the end of January to the end of February 1793. He intended to publish these letters under the title *Kallias oder über die Schönheit* (Kallias, or on Beauty), but the planned work never appeared. Although they are virtually complete and polished in substance and style, they are usually available only in collected editions of Schiller's correspondence.

In the first letter, Schiller outlines his own position vis-à-vis the prevailing views of his day, specifically those of Burke, the Wolffians (Alexander Gottlieb Baumgarten, Sulzer, and Mendelssohn), and, above all, Kant. There are, Schiller explains, four possible ways to explain the beautiful: the objective or the subjective, according to whether beauty exists in things or only in our perception of them; and the sensible or the rational, according to whether it is an empirical or an intellectual property, one determined by the senses or reason. Burke's theory is subjective and sensible; the Wolffians' is objective and rational; Kant's is subjective and rational. The fourth possibility is Schiller's own: that beauty is objective and sensible. In other words, Schiller thinks that beauty is an empirical and objective characteristic inhering in objects themselves.

The main problem with the Burkean theory, in Schiller's view, is that it regards beauty as simply a kind of sensation, so that aesthetic judgment must forfeit all claim to universality. The Wolffians rightly see that beauty must be a quality of objects themselves; but they go astray in placing it entirely in its purely rational or formal properties, especially perfection or unity in multiplicity. Schiller gives two reasons why beauty cannot consist in such properties alone. First, they are characteristic of mathematical regularity, which is not beautiful; and, second, they can be imposed on the object, so that they distort its real nature.

What, then, is wrong with Kant's position? According to Schiller, Kant had demoted beauty to a subjective quality, to the feeling of pleasure involved in the free play of our cognitive faculties, which has no reference to objects themselves (even as appearances). Schiller maintained, however, that beauty must be based on at least one characteristic inherent in the object itself: namely, whether the object is *self-determining*, that is, whether it is free from external influences and acts according to its own inherent nature alone. We cannot have an experience of beauty, Schiller argues, if what we perceive does not express its inner nature, if it is somehow subject to constraint, whether moral or physical. Here Schiller was developing a point made by Kant himself, who stressed that a work of fine art is beautiful only if it appears like nature and does not seem to conform to the rules of art (*Critique of Judgment*, section 45).

The *Kallias Letters* are essentially a defense and elaboration of Schiller's definition of beauty: freedom in appearance *(Freiheit in der Erscheinung)*. This definition recurs as a leitmotif throughout Schiller's aesthetic writings. Some analysis of each of its terms—*freedom* and *appearance*—is therefore necessary.

The "freedom" of beauty means that an object is autonomous, not subject to foreign ends or influences. Follow-

ing Kant, Schiller insists that an aesthetic object must be an end in itself and not a means to physical or moral ends. To be subject to such ends would be a form of constraint, and so they would distort the inner nature of an object. This autonomy or self-determination does not mean, Schiller is quick to add, that an aesthetic object is completely free from necessity and acts in a totally arbitrary manner. On the contrary, it is subject to rules or laws. Nevertheless, these are compatible with, and indeed necessary to, freedom, because they are *self-imposed* or follow from its inner and characteristic nature. Like Kant, Schiller thinks that freedom consists not in the absence of law, but in autonomy, the self-imposition or consent to law.

Schiller gives several reasons why beauty is freedom *in appearance*. First, the aesthetic object, though it is subject to rules and thus necessity, must *seem* or *appear* to be free. Second, the freedom of an aesthetic object, which must appear to the senses, is not the same as moral freedom itself, which is purely intelligible or transcendental, and so not given in the realm of appearances. The aesthetic object must therefore simply appear to be free, because it cannot really be free in the moral sense. In other words, aesthetic freedom is only an analogue to or symbol of moral freedom.

Ultimately, for all its sophistication, the *Kallias Letters* is a flawed work, suffering from inner tensions, mainly because of Schiller's ambivalent relationship to Kant. Although Schiller wants to establish an objective concept of beauty in opposition to Kant, his other Kantian premises undermine him. According to Kant, freedom cannot be a property of objects themselves in the natural world. Although we sometimes read the ideas of practical reason into objects in the sensible world, we have no right to assume that they really do act for ends; we can at most think of nature *as if* it were free (*Critique of Judgment*, sections 15, 58). Schiller himself adopts this Kantian point when he insists that we can regard appearances as only analogues of freedom. Yet, it is a doctrine that is scarcely compatible with his attempt to provide an objective concept of beauty.

This hardly means, however, that Schiller's theory, when consistent, collapses into Kant's. One of its more striking and novel characteristics is Schiller's subsumption of aesthetic judgment under the domain of practical reason, his placing of beauty within the domain of morality. Schiller maintains that aesthetic judgment is a form of moral judgment, because, when we see an object as beautiful, we subsume it under the concept of freedom, the fundamental concept of morality. Kant held that aesthetic judgments are distinct from moral judgments because each kind of judgment has a distinct subject matter or object: whereas aesthetic judgments appraise appearances in the sensible world, moral judgments assess moral intentions in the rational world. Yet, Kant failed to see, Schiller thinks, that there is an aesthetic use of moral judgment, because, in determining beauty, we have to apply moral concepts. Ironically, toward the close of the first part of the *Critique of Judgment* (section 59), Kant himself had prepared the ground for this doctrine. Here he argued that beauty is a symbol of the ideas of morality, and he even suggested that the demand for universal agreement in aesthetic judgments depends on it. Nevertheless, the main thrust of his teaching was that art belongs to a sui generis domain apart from science and morality, so that the beautiful is distinct from both truth and the good. It was the aim of Schiller to reunite the realms of the good and the beautiful that had been so sharply separated by Kant.

Grace and Dignity. Schiller's treatise *Über Anmut und Würde* (On Grace and Dignity), written in spring 1793, is not a work in aesthetics in the narrow sense. Although it attempts to provide precise definitions of the concepts of grace and dignity, which were common fare of eighteenth-century aesthetics, its central aim is to explain the fundamental role of these concepts in moral philosophy. Schiller's argument is primarily directed against Kant's ethics of duty, which he criticized for its narrow conception of human perfection.

Schiller's analysis of grace and dignity must be placed firmly in its eighteenth-century context. His work was influenced by Home, Christoph Martin Wieland, Sulzer, Lord Shaftesbury, and Mendelssohn, who all analyzed these concepts. Like most of his contemporaries, Schiller maintains that grace is a specific form of beauty: the beauty of human action and movement. He also agrees with his contemporaries about some of the defining characteristics of a graceful action: that it is performed naturally and spontaneously, without effort or compulsion, and that it complies with rules without acting because of them or for their sake alone. These characteristics also follow, of course, from the definition of beauty in the *Kallias Letters*.

Schiller's analysis of grace stresses, however, its moral rather than its aesthetic characteristics. In other words, grace involves less the beauty of an action—whether it is pleasing to the senses—and more the motives and personality behind it. Thus, Schiller stresses that graceful actions must be voluntary, having their source in personality or character rather than any physical or inherited characteristics. He therefore distinguishes the *architechtonic* beauty of human action and form, which is simply a gift of nature, from its *rational* beauty, which depends on the will alone. The architechtonic beauty comprises anatomy, posture, and complexion, whereas rational beauty consists in the motives or spirit behind an action. A person possesses grace, Schiller further explains, when his moral education has become "second nature" to him. According to this account, then, the aesthetic dimension of grace virtually disappears, because a person could possess grace even if his actions appeared awkward and ungainly to the senses.

The most controversial feature of Schiller's treatise is his application of the concept of grace to Kant's moral philosophy. To many of his contemporaries, Kant's moral philosophy seemed unduly rigoristic because it gave a too strict analysis of moral worth. Kant had maintained that the only actions having moral value are those done for the sake of duty or because of moral principle. Apparently paradoxically, he excluded actions done from benevolent as well as selfish inclinations; but Kant's reasoning was plausible enough: generous impulses stem from nature no less than selfish ones, so they too do not depend on the will, the ultimate source of all moral value.

The source of Schiller's quarrel with Kant has often been misunderstood. Schiller did not wish to defend the moral worth of benevolent impulses or a good heart, which have their source in nature alone. Furthermore, he expressed his agreement with Kant's analysis of moral action: to have a moral worth, an action must be done for the sake of duty, and its value must stem from the will. Wishing to minimize his differences with Schiller, Kant himself stressed these common points in a footnote to his *Religion innerhalb der Grenzen der blossen Vernunft* (Religion within the Limits of Reason Alone, 1793). Schiller was delighted with Kant's remarks.

Nevertheless, such apparent agreement should not obscure the deeper differences between Schiller and Kant. The main point of friction between them concerns not the analysis of moral action but human excellence or perfection; in other words, they differ over the conditions for becoming a good person, not the conditions for performing a morally good action. Schiller argued that Kant had given a much too narrow account of human perfection. The sole excellence of a human being could not be simply the execution of moral duty, for this failed to cultivate a person's sensibility, to develop his feelings and desires, which are as distinctively human as reason. If doing duty for its own sake is made into the sole or chief human virtue, Schiller contended, then Kant's ethic degenerates into a moral tyranny where reason dominates and eventually represses human sensibility. An excellent or perfect human being is, for Schiller, someone who acts as a whole, someone whose reason and sensibility are in perfect harmony, so that the demands of duty and inclination never conflict.

It is in this context that Schiller applies his concept of grace. A graceful action is one that stems from a person's whole character, from his reason and sensibility acting in harmony. It is not done simply from natural desire or inclination, and still less from a sense of duty alone. Rather, the person does his duty from desire and with feeling. These desires and feelings are not, however, simply those given by nature, which are still raw and selfish, but those created by moral education. In a graceful action, then, desires and feelings are neither repressed nor indulged. Rather, they are refined and ennobled, or, to use a more modern term, "sublimated."

For Schiller, dignity is the complement of grace. Although the graceful or "beautiful" soul acts in harmony with his feelings and desires, the dignified soul has full mastery over them in those extreme cases where duty demands sacrifice. Dignity is more self-possession than self-renunciation, however. Like grace, it shows no signs of external compulsion or effort, and no trace of righteousness or zealotry.

In stressing the value of dignity, Schiller recognized that there are some cases where duty and desire, moral principle and inclination, conflict. In an ideal world, people would need only grace; but in the real world they must also sometimes act with dignity. Schiller stressed that the ideal person has both grace and dignity. These virtues are, indeed, necessary to each other: a person acts with grace rather than simply a good heart if he can act according to dignity; and he acts according to dignity if his actions show grace rather than severity and punctiliousness.

Aesthetic Education. Schiller's most influential work on aesthetics was his *Über die ästhetische Erziehung des Menschen, in einer Reihe von Briefen* (On the Aesthetic Education of Mankind, in a Series of Letters), which he wrote in the summer and autumn of 1794. This work can be seen as a reply to Plato's and Jean-Jacques Rousseau's strictures against the arts. Schiller does not banish the arts but celebrates them. They are the chief instrument of political education and enlightenment in his republic. The arts, he contends, do not corrupt us with pleasant illusions but inspire us to live according to the laws.

The context of the *Aesthetic Letters* was the reception of the French Revolution in Germany. Like many of his contemporaries, Schiller admired the goals of the Revolution—liberty, equality, fraternity, and the rights of man—but disapproved of its violent methods. The bloodshed, strife, and anarchy in France seemed to show that the people were not ready for the high ideals of a republic. The key to political reform and stability, Schiller believed, was the enlightenment and education of the people. This task, however, demanded more than moral preaching, simply propagating the principles of reason. Most people already knew these principles; the problem was to make them act according to them. The most effective means of encouraging the people to do so was to educate their sensibility, to transform their hearts and feelings. The chief impulses for human action, Schiller explained, lay not in the cold reasoning of the intellect but in the desires and feelings of the human heart.

Schiller therefore saw art as the key to the education of the people. It was art, and art alone, that could address desire and sentiment. It alone could appeal to a person's feelings and imagination, and so inspire him to act according to the principles of reason. Hence, art had none of the limitations of philosophy or religion. Whereas philosophy could at best address a person's intellect, religion had lost its credibility in the Age of Reason.

In stressing the value of art in addressing the passions, Schiller was, in effect, attacking one of the weakest points in Plato's criticism of the arts: his failure to understand *akra-*

sia, that we can know the good but have no desire to live according to it. If Plato only fully admitted this point, Schiller seemed to be saying, then he would have seen the important role of the arts in his republic; for, if philosophy is necessary to know the good, art alone inspires and motivates to act according to it.

Schiller's faith in the redemptive powers of art in the *Aesthetic Letters* reflects, in part, the argument of his earlier work *The Stage as a Moral Institution*. Here Schiller argued that the theater is "a school of practical wisdom, a guide through civil life, an infallible key to the most secret passages of the human soul." Although the theater does not preach a new morals or religion, it holds up a mirror to human life and action, making us more aware of moral issues and so creating a greater civic consciousness. By directly appealing to our imagination and feelings, it provides a more effective sanction for the laws than religion or philosophy.

It would be a mistake, however, to see the argument of the *Aesthetic Letters* from the perspective of this earlier work alone. Schiller does not rest his case against Plato and Rousseau on his belief in the moral effects of the arts, and he even concedes that history shows the arts to flourish only when morals and the state decline. In the tenth letter, he explains that his main argument lies elsewhere: that he wants to prove the value of the arts a priori, by showing how beauty is "a necessary condition of humanity."

The heart of Schiller's tract is his argument from the eleventh to the fifteenth letters that beauty alone unifies the two fundamental drives of human nature, the intellectual and the sensible, the formal and the material. Whereas the formal drive attempts to give form to matter, to universalize the particular, or to internalize the external, the material drive tries to give content to form, to particularize the universal, or to externalize the internal. Each drive, Schiller explains, has its characteristic limit or constraint: the formal drive stands under the constraint of moral laws, whereas the material drive is subject to physical needs. What unites these two drives is beauty, the unity of form and content, of the universal and the particular, or of structure and life. This unity comes into existence through a third drive, what Schiller calls the "play drive." He chooses this term because the creation of beauty is like a form of play, in that we are no longer subject to the contraints of moral duty or physical need.

The dense and difficult argument in behalf of beauty in the *Aesthetic Letters* becomes clearer when we recall some of Schiller's early works. Schiller presupposes the definition of beauty in the *Kallias Letters*. If beauty is the appearance of freedom, then the play drive must create beauty, because it is only in play, Schiller argues, that we become free, liberated from the constraints of physical need and moral duty. Schiller also assumes the analysis of grace and dignity in *On Grace and Dignity*. The unity of the formal and material drives will be a form of beauty also because it consists in grace, those actions where we act from our whole nature.

Although Schiller's *Aesthetic Letters* have been ridiculed for their idealism and naïveté, these criticisms do not come to terms with its main argument. Schiller's case does not rest on the good effects of the arts—watching plays, reading poems, or listening to music—but on his anthropology, his belief that human beings are complete and fulfilled only as aesthetic wholes. The argument is, then, that if we were self-realized as human beings, we would become like works of art ourselves. This point alone, Schiller believes, and not any case for the good effects of the fine arts, means that we should recognize the significance of the aesthetic dimension in our lives.

The Naive and Sentimental. The last of Schiller's major works on aesthetics is his *Über naive und sentimentalische Dichtung* (On Naive and Sentimental Poetry), which appeared in Schiller's journal *Die Horen* from November 1795 to January 1796. This work is important in the history of aesthetics because of its influence on the development of Romanticism. The young Friedrich Schlegel's ideal of Romantic poetry was inspired by Schiller's concept of the sentimental.

Schiller's tract begins with an observation of Kant's: that sometimes we are pleased with objects simply because they are natural (*Critique of Judgment*, section 42). If something apparently natural turns out to be artificial (for example, a flower), then we lose our pleasure in it. This shows, Schiller thinks, that our pleasure is not really aesthetic. Both the artificial and the natural flower are beautiful, possessing the same formal characteristics; yet we still prefer the natural one. Therefore, the question arises: Why do we prefer the natural over the artificial? In what does our pleasure in natural objects consist?

Schiller's answer is that our pleasure in nature has more a moral than an aesthetic source. What we enjoy is not so much the objects themselves as the moral ideas we read into them. We project into natural objects the ideas of "quiet creative life, of acting from within oneself, of existence according to one's own laws, of inner necessity, and of eternal unity with oneself." In short, nature represents a state of complete independence, of total self-sufficiency, the absence of need and constraint.

When we observe natural objects, Schiller explains, we are moved because they represent something we have lost and to which we long to return. We once lived in a state of complete independence because we were in harmony with ourselves, with others, and with the external world. This is the state enjoyed by children and primitive man. But it has been lost with the development of civilization. The growth of bureaucratic government, of the division of labor, and of the arts and sciences has divided man from himself, from nature, and from others. Still, we hope to restore what we have lost, to re-create what was once given to us. The civi-

lization that has destroyed nature for us should also become the means for our return to it. Through the development of the arts and sciences, we will once again achieve that harmony with others, ourselves, and the external world.

Schiller's distinction between naive and sentimental poetry derives from this utopian philosophy of history. According to it, we stand in two possible relations with nature: either we are part of nature and it is given to us; or we have lost nature and desire to return to it. Naive poetry is the imitation of a nature that is given to us; sentimental poetry is the idealization of a nature that we have lost and to which we long to return. Schiller maintains that naive poetry is characteristic of the poetry of classical antiquity, when people lived more in harmony with nature, whereas sentimental poetry is characteristic of the modern age, which has fallen from its unity with nature.

Against the hidebound classicists, Schiller argues that each kind of poetry is valid in its own right, and that we should not attempt to measure modern poetry by classical standards. To be sure, classical poetry attained a high degree of perfection, but that was only because its aim was simply to describe its object; having such a limited goal, it had little trouble in achieving it. Modern poetry does not achieve such perfection, yet it has the great merit of aspiring to an infinite ideal—the expression of complete independence, of our harmony with nature, ourselves, and others. This means that modern poetry enjoys more freedom and flexibility: whereas ancient poetry stuck to a definite genre, one manner of seeing and feeling things, modern poetry reflects on its object in all kinds of ways, approaching it from many different angles.

Schiller's defense of modern or sentimental poetry stimulated the young Friedrich Schlegel, who had been a convinced classicist before reading Schiller's tract. Schiller's concept of sentimental poetry indeed anticipates Schlegel's own ideal of Romantic poetry in some striking respects: like Romantic poetry, sentimental poetry mixes genres, idealizes its object, and expresses the longing for an infinite ideal. In these respects, Schlegel's Romantic aesthetic simply canonized the virtues of Schiller's sentimental poetry.

Aesthetic Autonomy and Morality. How can Schiller insist on both the autonomy of art and its beneficial moral effects? It would seem that the arts benefit society and the state only by serving moral or political ends, and thus by forfeiting their autonomy.

This was a problem that Schiller himself addressed on several occasions, and to which he had various solutions. He discussed it most explicitly in his 1792 essay "Über den Grund des Vergnügens an tragischen Gegenstände" (On the Basis of Our Pleasure in Tragic Objects). Here, under the influence of Kant, Schiller seems to distance himself from his earlier views on the mission of German theater. Now he states that the purpose of art is to give pleasure, and that it should not submit to moral ends. He criticizes the old aesthetics of the Gottschedian school, which made art the servant of morality. The attempt to make art conform to moral ends, he insists, had led all too often to bad art. Nevertheless, Schiller immediately adds that this does not imply that the aim of art is merely entertainment, and that it cannot serve higher ends. The enjoyment of art, he explains, is a "free pleasure," and as such is opposed to the physical pleasures of our sensibility, which are subject to natural laws. The free pleasure of art rests on moral conditions, because it consists in the self-awareness of our freedom, the recognition that we are moral beings who stand above the causality of the natural world. According to Schiller, then, morality is only a means to the end of art—free pleasure—and we should never confuse means with ends by making art the servant of morality.

Schiller addressed the paradox from another angle in letters twenty-two and twenty-three of the *Aesthetic Letters*. He explains that a good work of art acts on a person as a whole and not on any faculty in particular. Art imparts energy and power to all of our capacities, but it does not determine how any one of them is applied. It does not, then, attempt to make us more moral because it does not prescribe any specific principles or action. Still, by acting on our whole nature, it stimulates all of our faculties, and so allows each of them to perform its specific function more effectively.

In the end, Schiller's belief in the moral value of art rests on an apparent paradox. The great value of art, he argues in most of his work, is that it helps us to achieve freedom. If art only does this, then it has promoted the highest moral value of all, namely, freedom. Yet, the paradox is that this great moral value can be attained only if art helps us to transcend the constraints of morality, which demand the suppression of our desires and so limit the expression of our whole nature. Hence, ironically, art achieves its greatest moral end only in virtue of its autonomy, its freedom from all moral constraint.

[*See also* Beauty; Education, Aesthetic; Kant; *and* Romanticism, *article on* Philosophy and Literature.]

BIBLIOGRAPHY

Works by Schiller

Schillers Werke: Nationalausgabe. 44 vols. Edited by L. Blumenthal and B. von Wiese. Weimar, 1943. This is now the standard edition of Schiller. For the aesthetics, see volumes 20 and 21. For Schiller's correspondence with Gottfried Körner, see volume 26, pp. 174–229.

Translations of Works by Schiller

The Aesthetic Letters, Essays and the *Philosophical Letters of Schiller.* Translated by J. Weiss. Boston, 1845.
Naive and Sentimental Poetry, and *On the Sublime: Two Essays by Friedrich von Schiller.* Translated by Julius A. Elias. New York, 1966.
On the Aesthetic Education of Man in a Series of Letters. Edited and translated by Elizabeth M. Wilkinson and L. A. Willoughby. Oxford, 1967.
On the Naive and Sentimental in Literature. Translated by Helen Watanabe-O'Kelly. Manchester, 1981.

Aesthetic Reconstructions: The Seminal Writings of Lessing, Kant and Schiller. Translation by Anthony Savile. Aristotelian Society Series, vol. 8. Oxford and New York, 1987.

Other Sources

Berger, Karl. *Die Entwicklung von Schillers Ästhetik.* Weimar, 1894.
Borcherdt, Hans Heinrich, ed. *Schiller und die Romantiker: Briefe und Dokumente.* Stuttgart, 1948.
Cassirer, Ernst. "Die Methodik des Idealismus in Schillers philosophischen Schriften." In *Idee und Gestalt: Goethe, Schiller, Hölderlin, Kleist,* pp. 79–108. Berlin, 1921.
Ellis, J. M. *Schiller's Kalliasbriefe and the Study of His Aesthetic Theory.* The Hague, 1969.
Hell, Victor. *Schiller: Théories esthétiques et structures dramatiques* Paris, 1974. On the aesthetics, see part 2, chap. 2, pp. 146–251.
Heuer, Fritz. *Darstellung der Freiheit: Schillers transzendentale Frage nach der Kunst.* Cologne, 1970.
Janz, Rolf-Peter. *Autonomie und soziale Funktion der Kunst: Studien zur Ästhetik von Schiller und Novalis.* Stuttgart, 1973.
Kerry, S. S. *Schiller's Writings on Aesthetics.* Manchester, 1961.
Kühnemann, Eugen. *Kants und Schillers Begründung der Ästhetik.* Munich, 1895.
Miller, R. D. *Schiller and the Ideal of Freedom.* Oxford, 1970.
Norton, Robert E. *The Beautiful Soul: Aesthetic Morality in the Eighteenth Century.* Ithaca, N.Y., 1995.
Reed, T. J. *Schiller.* Oxford and New York, 1991.
Sychrava, Juliet. *Schiller to Derrida: Idealism in Aesthetics.* Cambridge and New York, 1989.

FREDERICK BEISER

SCHLEGEL, AUGUST WILHELM VON (1767–1845), German literary critic. Along with his brother Karl Wilhelm Friedrich von Schlegel (1772–1829), he inaugurated the project of early German Romanticism (known as the *Frühromantik*), a project that established the foundation of modern literary history and criticism. The emergence of this new movement at the end of the eighteenth century in the German university town of Jena proved to be a turning point in the history of criticism. Influenced by the critical insights and writings of their literary forebears Gotthold Ephraim Lessing and Johann Gottfried von Herder, and drawing on the intellectual fruits of the philosophical revolution in Germany, the early Romantics relieved modern poetry from its burden of allegiance to an exemplary classical past and recognized it as the decisive and enduring aesthetic expression of modern consciousness. The Romantic paradigm of literary criticism was formulated in the pages of the journal *Athenäum*, founded by the Schlegel brothers and published during the years 1798–1800 in Jena. The journal represented one of the most fruitful literary and editorial collaborations of the age and counted among its contributors the greatest critical talents of the time, including Ludwig Tieck, the poet-philosopher Novalis (Friedrich von Hardenberg), the theologian Friedrich Schleiermacher, Caroline Schlegel-Schelling, and Dorothea Schlegel.

Schlegel was born in Hannover into a family known for its scholarly accomplishments. His father, Johann Adolf

Schlegel, and his uncle, Elias Schlegel, were prominent critics. He studied classical philology at the University of Göttingen with the renowned Hellenist Christian Gottlob Heyne and matriculated on 3 May 1786. Between 1787 and 1792, Schlegel wrote extensively for several literary journals, among them the *Göttinger Musenalmanach,* and contributed many articles to Friedrich von Schiller's *Horen* and *Musenalmanach* from 1795 until the poet and the Schlegel brothers had a final falling out in 1799. In 1798, Schlegel was offered a teaching position *(Extraordinariat)* at the University of Jena. Thus, the Romantic literary movement, whose critical gaze was trained on an unprecedented universality of literary representation, gained legitimate entry into the university. In 1818, Schlegel was invited to teach at the University of Berlin. He chose to go to the University of Bonn, however, where he was professor of Indology from 1819 to his death in 1845. During his tenure at Bonn, he served as the rector of the university from 1824 to 1825.

Schlegel was a prodigious man of letters, linguist, classicist, Orientalist, and one of the most accomplished translators of all times. In addition to the members of the Romantic school and Schiller, he was acquainted with the leading literary figures of Germany, including Johann Wolfgang von Goethe and Tieck, author of the quintessential German Romantic novel, *Franz Sternbald's Wanderungen* (Franz Sternbald's Travels). He was a devoted friend of the French writer Mme Germaine de Staël, who, under his tutorship, became an ardent student of modern German letters and published the widely reviewed and popularly received book *De l'Allemagne,* which introduced the modern German literary scene to French readers. Between 1797 and 1810, Schlegel translated most of William Shakespeare's plays into German, and to this day his translations are considered the best rendering of the bard's work in German. He also translated numerous works from French, Spanish, and Portuguese. During the latter part of his literary career, Schlegel became a highly regarded scholar of Sanskrit. Between the years 1820 and 1830, he published the journal *Indische Bibliothek* (Indian Library) and made available critical editions of the *Bhagavadgītā* in 1823 and the *Rāmāyaṇa* during the years 1829–1831.

Friedrich Schlegel and Novalis, the two major theorists of the Romantic school, are credited with translating the Kantian notions of critique and the autonomy of the work of art and Johann Gottlieb Fichte's philosophy of reflection, respectively, into usable terms of Romantic criticism. Although the theoretical strength of Schlegel's aesthetics was questioned by later critics, it is generally acknowledged that his comprehensive treatment of literature through history, language theory, and criticism is the most impressive trait of his oeuvre. Schlegel undertook the steady and laborious task of recovering and contextualizing, in the frameworks of modern poesy, a long history of forgotten, lost, and occulted literary traditions and histories. The desire to make accessible a significant but often misunderstood past, the past as a foreign territory, informed all of Schlegel's work. This work saw the light of day in a comprehensive array of formal vehicles, including translations, letters, essays, reviews, critical editions, fragments, and perhaps most significant, lectures. In their printed form, these lectures were widely read. Schlegel's vast knowledge of the history of world literatures and his reading of individual works of antiquity, the Middle Ages, and ancient India in a hermeneutically informed context reevoked a fast-receding and fading literary history in the imaginary universal library of German Romanticism.

Romantic poetry is defined as "progressive universal poesy" in the oft-cited *Athenäum* fragment 116. In the early Romantic lexicon, the word *Poesie* (poesy) referred to both literary arts and poetics. This fragment, considered an early manifest of the Romantic project, equates modern poetry with the Romantic. The aim of Romantic poesy is to reintegrate separated domains of human knowledge, combining philosophy with rhetoric, poetry with prose, inspiration with criticism, and poeticizing life as well as infusing poetry with life. Romantic poesy strives to embrace all forms of poetic expression, from the greatest systems of art to the artless song of a child. Although other forms of poetry have come full circle and are complete, Romantic poesy is in a state of becoming, which is its essential characteristic. It reflects on itself and sees this reflection in an infinite series of mirrors. Thus, in the Romantic idiom, modern poetry expresses a progressive striving.

In Schlegel's university lectures, the critical agenda of German Romanticism, which was partially articulated in the *Athenäum* fragments, finds its comprehensive and elaborate format of expression. The lecture series, starting with the Berlin *Vorlesungen über schöne Literatur und Kunst* (Lectures on Beautiful Literature and Art; 1801–1804) after the dissolution of the *Athenäum* group and including the 1808 Vienna *Vorlesungen über dramatische Kunst und Literatur* (Lectures on Dramatic Art and Literature), delineate against a vast panorama of literary historical detail the particular artistic destiny of modern Romantic poesy. To a certain extent, Romanticism's poetic paradigm owes its inception to an earlier controversy of literary history known as the Quarrel of the Ancients and the Moderns, the confrontation between the proponents of classical antiquity and those of aesthetic modernity. In the seventeenth and eighteenth centuries, French and English critics began to advocate the freedom of modern art from its subordination to classical models. Toward the end of the eighteenth century, the debate had penetrated German literary territory and became a formative impetus in the historical self-understanding of early Romanticism. Romanticism moderated this debate by acknowledging the mutability of genres, the emergence of novel forms, and the role of creative imagination in ordering these in new configurations. Romantic literary criticism gained its formative critical position from the famous distinction between Romanticism and classicism articulated by the Schlegels and developed to precision in Schlegel's *Lectures on Dramatic Art and Literature*. Unlike the Quarrel of the Ancients and the Moderns, the Romantic versus the classical distinction is not a strictly oppositional one. Rather, as Schlegel demonstrates in his many formulations, it is complementary, for the Romantic incorporates the memory of past forms and myths into the present moment of poetic self-reflexivity and reevaluation. Thus, Romantic criticism becomes a completion and complementation of its subject, the work of art, both ancient and modern.

In the *Lectures on Dramatic Art and Literature*, Schlegel sees the function of the history of art forms as recording what has happened and that of theory as teaching what ought to be accomplished by art. Without an intermediate link, however, history and theory alone cannot elucidate their respective concerns and remain inadequate forms of inquiry. Criticism is the mediating term between the history of art forms and the theory that furnishes their cognitive map. It illuminates the conditions for the production of the work of art. Like Romantic poetry, Romantic criticism is a generative field duplicating the gestures of its object of study and cannot operate as a closed system. Nations and individuals who are fettered by educational conventions, dictates of taste, and habits of mind lack the capacity for genuine criticism. Schlegel concludes that no person can be a true critic or connoisseur without a universality of mind and an understanding of other times, places, and systems of art and thought. He applies this notion of universality to the history of fine arts and observes that the reverent reception of antiquity had been fatally misguided and undermined the true appreciation of modern art by judging it only in terms of its imitation of ancient models. Finally, in the recent past, several critical minds, mostly Germans—here Schlegel is implicitly referring to the *Frühromantik* circle—attempted to redress this poverty of judgment by giving the moderns their due without detracting from the value of the ancients. They named the modern spirit of art *romantic* as opposed to the ancient and classical. Schlegel finds this a fitting description, because the word derives from *romance*, a name given to languages derived from a mixture of Latin and Teutonic dialects. As a reconfiguration of the characteristics of northern peoples and fragments of classical cultures, the modern age represents a heterogeneity in contrast to antiquity, whose culture was much more homogeneous and unified. Furthermore, drawing on Dutch philosopher and aesthetician Frans Hemsterhuis's critical observation that the ancient painters were too much sculptors and the modern sculptors too much painters, Schlegel sees the formal character of classical art and poetry as plastic and that of the modern or romantic as picturesque.

Schlegel's lectures set the terms of difference between the historical impulse of Greek antiquity and that of Romantic modernity. Classical art represents a finished product, a closed cycle. Romantic art, on the other hand, is always a state of becoming and characterized by the ethos of infinite perfectibility. The poetry of the Greeks, Schlegel argues in his Vienna lectures, marked a final settlement. It was housed in tropes of rest, arrest, and closure, whereas modern poetry needs continually to negotiate between remembrance and anticipation. There was a clear dichotomy between dissimilars in antiquity. In Romantic modernity, however, there is an intimate link between opposites such as nature and culture, poetry and prose, remembrance and anticipation, and the mortal and the divine. The classical and the modern represent different modes of the world of human experience. The Grecian ideal of human nature assumes perfect accord and harmony between all faculties. No gap separates fantasy and understanding, and the world exists as a coherent mythos. The modern age, however, is marked by a consciousness of internal discord where impression and reflection are divided. Thus, modern poetry strives to heal this breach in its construction of a "new mythology" that can recreate the internal coherence of the mythical condition in the contemporary world.

Every chapter of Schlegel's scholarly writing is marked by a vast comparative understanding of literary histories and the contingencies of historical modes of evaluation, and a universal acuity of aesthetic appreciation. This expanded historical consciousness of literary pasts led the Romantic critics to the retrieval of neglected and erased cultural forms that did not necessarily conform to the perceived superiority of classical standards. The Romantic recovery of fairy tales, the literature of the troubadours, the culture of the European Middle Ages and of ancient India, and the enthusiastic reappraisal of Dante Alighieri, Giovanni Boccaccio, Miguel de Cervantes, Pedro Calderón de la Barca, and Shakespeare, all more or less eclipsed by the sun of antiquity, marked a new appreciation of the diversity of literary forms, histories, and mythologies.

Whereas Schlegel's Vienna lectures historicized the ideas of early Romanticism and summarized in retrospect its broad range of literary activity, his earlier lectures in Berlin are characterized by highly original formulations. They register the critical impulse of early Romanticism in a nuanced fashion. *Poesie*, Schlegel argues, is neither bound to things and concepts nor generated by them. Rather, it is a self-creation, an "aesthetic invention," that transforms the nature it touches. Schlegel maintains that ultimately all poetry *(Poesie)* is indisputably poetry of poetry *(Poesie der Poesie)*. This felicitous phrase coined by Friedrich Schlegel refers in the first instance to the Romantic notion that poetry is always a reflection or commentary on poetry, on the coming into being of poetry, in other words, metapoetry. Borrowing from Immanuel Kant's philosophical lexicon, Friedrich Schlegel also called this metapoetic character of modern poetry *Transzendentalpoesie*. August Wilhelm von Schlegel appropriates the phrase to further elucidate the intimate chain of signification between language and poetry and to underscore the self-generative and autonomous nature of poetry.

Poetry presupposes language, which in turn is an invention of poetic sensibility, and the latter is the constantly self-transforming and never-ending poem of humanity. The transcendental view of poesy allows Schlegel to maintain that language itself is poetry and the literary work is poetry raised to a higher power, poetry of poetry. Schlegel sees a reciprocal and unbroken chain of signification between all things. This signification process is grounded in the symbolizing capacity of language, which, in the process of self-recreation, produces poetry. Poetry is born of language and builds on mythology, which itself is a "potentiated" language of the representation of nature. Poetry uses the material of mythology to carry it to a higher level of aesthetic expression. In this way, poetry constantly regenerates itself and never leaves humanity, accompanying it through the first words of childhood to the highest peaks of speculative thought and back to the ocean of its birth. Here, Schlegel makes the radical claim that poetry reproduces itself out of its own resources. Poetry constitutes a world with its own internal laws, measures, and relations.

The Berlin lectures also redefine mythology in a Viconian sense. Very much in the spirit of Giambattista Vico's understanding of myths as a cognitive approach to the world of experience, Schlegel sees in the human need to mythologize not merely an allegorical expression of complicated ideas or the replacement of an abstract concept with an image. Rather, mythology takes into its purview the complete field of intuitions that transcend the limits of understanding and lends them a sensible form. Like language, myth forms a structural system of human cognition. Certain mythologies, such as those of ancient Greeks, go through different stages of development and may become obsolete as belief systems of a particular people. Even after the demise of myth as religion, however, the poetic essence of myth remains. Artists and poets of later ages have continued to re-create ancient myths, albeit in selective, fragmentary, or reconfigured fashion. But quite apart from this conscious and deliberate reproduction of myths, our experience of the world is informed by a tendency to mythologize that manifests itself in the metaphorical transformation of everything we come in contact with. In his critique of Enlightenment ideals, Schlegel reimagines the relation between understanding and imagination as the dialectic of light and darkness. In the sunshine of reason we see the conditions of reality, but these are suspended at night, gently concealed, in order to highlight a new realm of possibilities. Reason and imagination are the common forces of our lives, and whereas reason insists on unequivocality, imagination validates the free play of ideas in unbound diversity. It is in the dark recesses of imagination, so to speak, that the magic of life and the spirit of poetry reside.

The understanding of the dialectical relation of language, poetry, and mythology requires a genuinely critical vision.

After a historically informed presentation of Romantic poetry, Schlegel formulates a hermeneutic approach to the reading of texts, which he names a "synthetic" procedure. Friedrich Schlegel's and Novalis's critique of Kantian and Fichtean idealistic philosophies took issue with the highly analytic nature of their systems. Novalis argued that true criticism had to take "both the analytic and the synthetic road" to understanding and knowledge. In a lesser philosophical vein, August Wilhelm von Schlegel argues that mere explanations of words or accidental characteristics of a work of art do not contribute to our understanding of language and art. In order to analyze poetry, we need to look at the poetic whole. Here, the true method of criticism is synthetic and hermeneutic, whereby individual poetic forms need to be understood in the larger context of *Poesie* and the theory of *Poesie* is derived or synthesized from the particularities of poetic forms. Ultimately, Schlegel's work on Romantic aesthetics enacts this synthesizing process that he advocates in the practice of criticism.

[*See also* Novalis; Poetics; *and* Romanticism, *article on* Philosophy and Literature.]

BIBLIOGRAPHY

Works by Schlegel

A. W. Schlegel's Lectures on German Literature from Gottsched to Goethe, Given at the University of Bonn and Taken Down by George Toynbee in 1933. Edited by H. G. Fidler. Oxford, 1944.

Course of Lectures on Dramatic Art and Literature. Translated by John Black. Revised by A. J. W. Morrison. London, 1846; reprint, New York, 1973.

Kritische Schriften und Briefe. 7 vols. Edited by Edgar Lohner. Stuttgart, 1962–1974.

Other Sources

Behler, Ernst. *Die Zeitschriften der Brüder Schlegel.* Darmstadt, 1983.

Behler, Ernst. *Frühromantik.* Berlin and New York, 1992.

Ewton, Ralph W. *The Literary Theories of August Wilhelm Schlegel.* The Hague, 1971.

Haym, Rudolf. *Die romantische Schule.* 3d ed. 2 vols. Berlin, 1914.

Lohner, Edgar. "August Wilhelm Schlegel." In *Deutsche Dichter der Romantik: Ihr Leben und Werk,* edited by Benno von Wiese, pp. 135–162. Berlin, 1971.

Sauer, Thomas G. *A. W. Schlegel's Shakespearean Criticism in England, 1811–1846.* Bonn, 1982.

Schenk-Lenzen, Ulrike. *Das ungleiche Verhältnis von Kunst und Kritik: Zur Literaturkritik August Wilhelm Schlegels.* Würzburg, 1991.

Schirmer, Ruth. *August Wilhelm Schlegel und seine Zeit: Ein Bonner Leben.* Bonn, 1986.

Schirmer, Walter F. *Kleine Schriften.* Tübingen, 1950.

Schlegel, Friedrich. "Athenäums Fragmente." In *Kritische Ausgabe,* edited by Ernst Behler et al., vol. 2, pp. 165–255. 35 vols. to date. Paderborn, 1959–.

Thalman, Marianne. *August Wilhelm Schlegel: Gedenkschrift zum 200. Geburtstag.* Bad Godesberg, 1967.

Wellek, René. *A History of Modern Criticism, 1750–1950,* vol. 2, *The Romantic Age.* New Haven, 1955.

AZADE SEYHAN

SCHLEGEL, KARL WILHELM FRIEDRICH VON (1772–1829), German aesthetician during the early formative phase of Romanticism, the period known as *Frühromantik*, which flourished from 1797 to 1802. Born in Hannover, he was educated at Göttingen and Leipzig. He later moved to Jena, where he developed his influential concept of Romantic poetry, formulated his famous idea of literary irony, and, together with his brother August Wilhelm, edited the journal of the early Romantic circle, *Athenäum*.

What did Schlegel mean by "romantic poetry" *(romantische Poesie)*? Obviously, that is the crucial question regarding the aesthetics of German Romanticism. But it is not easy to answer, partly because Schlegel's explanations are obscure and fragmentary, and partly because his meaning heavily depends on his intellectual context. "I cannot send you my explanation of the word 'romantic,'" he wrote his brother in December 1797, "because it would be two thousand pages long." With that in mind, this essay will only sketch an explanation here, beginning with a few basic points about Schlegel's use of the term *romantische Poesie*.

First, Schlegel began by using the term not only in a normative or stylistic sense, but also in a descriptive or historical one to refer to a specific period of literature. Romantic poetry denoted early modern in contrast to classical literature. More specifically, it signified the literature of the late Middle Ages and the Renaissance written in the Romance languages and in the countries of the former Roman Empire. This historical use of the term was common in the eighteenth century. Schlegel probably acquired it from Johann Gottfried von Herder, who, in his *Briefe zur Beförderung der Humanität* (1793–1794; Letters toward the Promotion of Humanity), used it to distinguish early modern from classical literature. The great authors of early modern literature were, in Herder's view, Miguel de Cervantes, Petrarch, Dante Alighieri, and William Shakespeare. What was characteristic of their work, he explained, is that it mixes all kinds of genres, portrays the spirit of its age, and expresses a spirit of love and adventure. Schlegel first used the term virtually in the same sense as Herder.

Second, Schlegel gradually stopped using the term in a historical sense and eventually defined it only in a normative one. As early as 1798, he stated that Romantic poetry is the ideal of *all* poetry, so that even forms of classical poetry were romantic. Schlegel combined and confused the historical and normative senses for many years, and only started using the term in a fully normative sense in his 1812 lectures *Geschichte der alten und neuen Literatur* (History of Old and New Literature).

Third, Schlegel never used the term *romantische Poesie* to refer to a specific kind or genre of poetry. It is not necessarily poetry in the sense of verse—speech with rhyme or meter—because it can also be prose. But it is not even a kind or genre of literature—poetry, drama, or novel—because one of its essential characteristics is that it is a *mixture* of genres.

In his *Brief über den Roman* (Letter on the Novel), Schlegel insisted that Romantic poetry was not a genre but an element or quality that could be applied to any genre. What was characteristic of the Romantic was "a spirit of love," "a sentimental material in a fantastic form," qualities that could be attributed to novels, plays, or poems.

Fourth, the term *romantic poetry* is indeed connected with *der Roman*, but more in the older sense of a romance than in the modern sense of a novel. This connection has been the subject of some dispute. In 1870, Rudolf Haym, in his monumental *Die romantische Schule* (The Romantic School), maintained that Schlegel's *romantische Poesie* essentially meant *romanartig* (like a novel). This point was strongly denied in 1916 by Arthur Lovejoy, who argued that the connection was accidental and negligible. In the 1950s, Haym's point was rehabilitated by Hans Eichner (1956), who argued that the terms *romantische Poesie, Romanpoesie,* and *Roman* were virtual synonyms. Eichner demonstrated that Schlegel used *der Roman* in the eighteenth-century sense to refer to the romances of early modern literature, the works that were the precursors of the modern novel (namely, Shakespeare and Cervantes). It is important to recognize, however, that Schlegel himself wanted to disassociate Romantic poetry from the verse stories of Samuel Richardson or Henry Fielding, which are closer to the novel in the modern sense.

Obviously, these basic points do not take us very far. We still do not know the specific characteristics of Schlegel's Romantic poetry, and still less why he advocated them. The most straightforward answer to these questions is to turn to Schlegel's intellectual development. Schlegel's ideal of Romantic poetry was essentially, but not entirely, a reaction against his own earlier classicism. One can understand what Schlegel meant by *Romanticism,* and why he championed it, only if one examines his classicism and why he rejected it.

Schlegel began his career as a classical philologist. His main aim was to do for the history of Greek poetry what Johann Joachim Winckelmann had done for Greek sculpture. The motives for Schlegel's classicism were, of course, more aesthetic than antiquarian. Like Winckelmann, Schlegel believed that German culture could revive only on a classical foundation through the imitation of Greek models. He regarded the Greeks as the very model of civilization, contrasting their purity, simplicity, and harmony with the corruption, complexity, and discord of modern life.

The main work of Schlegel's neoclassical period, *Ueber das Studium der griechischen Poesie* (1795; On the Study of Greek Poetry), is a sustained argument in behalf of the virtues of ancient poetry. Schlegel makes a sharp distinction between ancient and modern poetry that is heavily slanted in favor of the classical form. According to his distinction, the fundamental value of ancient poetry is beauty. Beauty means (1) that a work is complete in itself, not depending on moral and political ends; (2) that it conforms to the laws of a definite genre, so that it is an ode, an epic, or a satire but nothing more; and (3) that it is objective, imitating nature, and not subjective, expressing the sentiment of the artist. Modern poetry is the antithesis of ancient. Its aim is not to attain beauty but to be "interesting," to catch the reader's attention with novel and striking effects. It violates the basic law of aesthetic autonomy by pandering to public taste and attempting to express the spirit of the age; and, rather than conforming to the rules of a definite genre, it mixes all genres. Modern poetry is indeed so corrupt, Schlegel thinks, that its only law is to be lawless. Schlegel maintained that modern poetry is bankrupt because its quest for effects would eventually exhaust itself. Only the perception of beauty, provided by classical art, gives complete satisfaction.

Schlegel soon began to have serious doubts about his neoclassicism, however. He already had the idea of Romantic poetry in the *Studium,* and in his 1797 notebooks he began to elaborate it. In his 1797 *Lyceum Fragments* he formally repudiated his earlier classicism, dismissing the whole idea of imitation and ridiculing the belief that the ancients had a monopoly on good art. Then, in his famous 1798 *Athenäum* fragment 116, Schlegel finally revealed his new ideal of Romantic poetry.

In some respects, Schlegel's ideal is a synthesis of his earlier concepts of classical and modern poetry. Romantic poetry, he says, should be both subjective and objective, expressing sentiment (like modern poetry) and portraying its object (like classical). But, in other respects, Romantic poetry simply absorbs the characteristics of the earlier modern poetry, and so is still conceived in opposition to classical poetry. To an important extent, then, Schlegel reverses his old position, celebrating and embracing the modern poetry he once condemned. Although recent research has tended to emphasize the continuities in Schlegel's development—that he already had the idea of Romantic poetry and doubts about classical literature in the *Studium*—there is still an indisputable rupture, an indubitable volte-face, which is apparent from the many contradictions between the *Lyceum Fragments* and the *Studium*. The problem of Schlegel scholarship is to explain this reversal, not to smooth it over or deny it.

In the *Athenäum Fragments,* Schlegel attributes at least four characteristics to Romantic poetry that are at odds with classical poetry. First, whereas classical poetry strives for completion, Romantic poetry is *progressive,* constantly in a process of becoming. Second, if classical poetry sticks to a genre, Romantic poetry is a *mélange des genres,* mixing and fusing together all kinds of literary styles. Third, Romantic poetry, unlike classical, aspires to be the portrait of an age, not to create ageless beauty. Fourth, whereas classical poetry adheres to rules, Romantic poetry knows none except the caprice of the author.

To reconstruct the reasons behind Schlegel's romantic conversion, at least three factors should be emphasized:

First, Schlegel admitted even in the *Studium* that the classical aesthetic is no longer attainable in, or appropriate to, the modern age. The poetry of the Greeks arose from their immediate relationship to nature, which allowed them to imitate its objects. This relationship had disappeared in modern life, however, with the growth of individual freedom and self-consciousness. The more modern man grew in his powers of self-reflection, the more he separated himself from the natural world. Second, Schlegel had always recognized that modern culture has its own unique values, and that they are equal to those of ancient culture. If the chief principle behind ancient culture is the law of nature or instinct, that of modern culture is the law of freedom or understanding. Like Friedrich von Schiller and Johann Gottlieb Fichte, Schlegel admired modern culture for its striving for freedom, its progressive tendency. The distinction between these cultures raised the question, however, why each should not have its own distinctive art form. Why should the moderns imitate the ancients if their culture is governed by different principles? Third, under Schiller's influence, Schlegel recognized that modern poetry has its own distinctive worth. Just as classical poetry expressed the ethos of ancient culture, so modern poetry did the same for its culture.

Schlegel was converted to Romantic poetry, then, because he eventually recognized that it is more appropriate for modern culture, that it alone expresses its free, progressive, and intellectual spirit. The concept of Romantic poetry had acquired an ethical quality that modern poetry did not have in the *Studium* essay. Romantic poetry no longer stemmed from the quest for interesting effects, as modern poetry, but from a deeper moral purpose, the need to express the characteristic strivings of modern man.

Ultimately, the foundation for Schlegel's belief in Romantic poetry was his philosophy of history, which he inherited from Immanuel Kant, Fichte, and Schiller. This philosophy is essentially a secularized version of the biblical drama of paradise–Fall–redemption. There are three main stages to history, as in the biblical fable. In the first stage, man lives in harmony with nature and society. This period is best represented by the classical scholar's equivalent of the Garden of Eden: Greek civilization in the Periclean Age. In the second stage, this primitive harmony is destroyed with the growth of individuality, freedom, and self-consciousness. This period is best represented by the decline in the classical polis and the growth of the Middle Ages. The rise of Christianity expresses a longing to return to mankind's original unity and harmony; but because this is impossible on Earth, it is projected onto an imaginary heaven. In the third or final stage, the modern era, mankind strives to regain its lost unity with nature and the community. What had been given to the Greeks, and what the Christians had held on faith, it is now the task of modern man to create through his own efforts. The kingdom of God will be realized on Earth through endless struggle and striving. Of course, it is not possible to attain this ideal; but we have a duty at least to approach it.

The task of Schlegel's Romantic poetry was to express, and ultimately to promote, the striving of modern man to achieve his lost ideal. The starting point of modern culture, Schlegel wrote in his *Athenäum Fragments,* is the revolutionary wish to realize the kingdom of God on earth; but the end of every romantic work, he said in his *Lyceum Fragments,* is the *Vaterunser,* the wish that God's kingdom would come. But just as this ideal could be approached but never achieved, so Romantic art would be progressive but incomplete, the expression of a struggle to attain the unattainable.

It is in this context that Schlegel's famous concept of irony should be placed. Irony was the artist's recognition that his ultimate goal is unattainable, that he can approach it but never achieve it. If the artist fully understood this point, Schlegel believed, then he would be able to distance himself from any one of his productions, for each would be only finite and imperfect, and therefore inadequate to express his infinite and perfect ideal. In number 108 of his *Lyceum Fragments,* Schlegel wrote of irony: "It contains and excites the feeling of the irresolvable conflict between the unconditioned and condition, the impossibility and necessity of complete communication." Complete communication is impossible because any creation is finite and imperfect; but it is also necessary because it is only through striving and creating anew that we approach our ideal. Irony was thus, as Schlegel also put it in *Athenäum* fragment 51, the "constant change from self-creation to self-negation."

It should be clear from this general analysis of Schlegel's Romantic aesthetic that it does not conform to the common stereotype of Romanticism as escapism, a flight from a grim reality into an imaginary heaven. Rather, the aim of Romantic art was to *transform* reality, to bring humans closer to heaven on Earth. Its aim was to re-create the lost magic, beauty, and mystery of the world, so that humans could once again feel at home in it. If they could only achieve the final goal, then all of nature, society, and the state would become works of art. Romanticism was thus the aesthetics of modern utopianism.

[*See also* Irony; Poetics; *and* Romanticism, *article on* Philosophy and Literature.]

BIBLIOGRAPHY

Works by Schlegel

Dialogue on Poetry and Literary Aphorisms. Edited and translated by Ernst Behler and Roman Struc. University Park, Pa., 1968.
Friedrich Schlegel's Lucinde and the Fragments. Edited and translated by Peter Firchow. Minneapolis, 1971.
Kritische Friedrich-Schlegel-Ausgabe. 35 vols. Edited by Ernst Behler et al. Paderborn, 1958. The standard edition.
Literary Notebooks, 1791–1801. Edited by Hans Eichner. Toronto, 1957.

Other Sources

Ayrault, Roger. *La genèse du romantisme allemand.* 4 vols. Paris, 1961–1976.
Behler, Ernst. *Frühromantik.* Berlin and New York, 1992.
Belgardt, Raimund. "Romantische Poesie in Friedrich Schlegels Aufsatz über das Studium der griechischen Poesie." *German Quarterly* 40 (1967): 165–185.
Brinkmann, Richard. "Romantische Dichtungstheorie in Friedrich Schlegels Frühschriften und Schillers Begriffe des Naiven und Sentimentalischen." *Deutsche Vierteljahrschrift für Literaturwissenschaft und Geistesgeschichte* 32 (1958): 344–371.
Eichner, Hans. "Friedrich Schlegel's Theory of Romantic Poetry." *Publications of the Modern Language Association* 71 (1956): 1018–1041.
Haym, Rudolf. *Die romantische Schule.* Berlin, 1870.
Kluckhohn, Paul. *Das Ideengut der deutschen Romantik.* Tübingen, 1941.
Lovejoy, Arthur. "On the Meaning of 'Romantic' in Early German Romanticism." *Modern Language Notes* 31 (1916): 385–396; 32 (1917): 65–77.
Pikulik, Lothar. *Frühromantik: Epoche, Werke, Wirkung.* Munich, 1992.

FREDERICK BEISER

SCHLEIERMACHER, FRIEDRICH DANIEL ERNST (1768–1834), a systematic theologian of nineteenth-century Protestantism. He achieved sudden public reknown with the appearance of his first book, *Reden über die Religion* (On Religion: Speeches to Its Cultured Despisers), in 1799. This was followed in short order by two works on ethics, *Monologen* and *Grundlinien einer Kritik der bisherigen Sittenlehre.* His major theological work, *Der christliche Glaube* (The Christian Faith), was published in 1821–1822. Among his other accomplishments was a three-volume translation of Plato's dialogues into German.

Schleiermacher's relevance for contemporary aesthetics stems primarily from his position as the first major theorist of the modern hermeneutical tradition. During his lifetime he published nothing on hermeneutics, but among his posthumous papers were three sets of lecture notes on the subject. The importance of these (published as *Hermeneutics: The Handwritten Manuscript* [1977]) was first made clear by Wilhelm Dilthey, who saw himself as continuing and extending into the sphere of historical interpretation Schleiermacher's methodology of textual interpretation.

Before Schleiermacher, inquiry into the problems of interpretation tended to take the form of discipline-specific rules of thumb. Historians, philologists, and scriptural exegetes would leave their colleagues advice on how to discern the meanings of texts within their own fields without paying any significant attention to how scholars in other fields dealt with their parallel problems. What was lacking was any systematic approach to the problem of interpreting written texts in general. Schleiermacher changed this situation, establishing textual interpretation as a single clearly defined subject of inquiry, by drawing out the implications of the principle of the hermeneutic circle—a principle "of such consequence for hermeneutics . . . that one cannot even begin to interpret without using it" (Schleiermacher, 1977, p. 196). The basic idea is that a whole can be understood only in terms of its parts, which in their turn can be understood only in terms of the whole to which they belong. This deceptively simple principle operates on a multiplicity of levels. Thus, words are the parts of which sentences are the wholes, sentences are the parts of which texts are the wholes, texts are the parts of which an author's total literary output is the whole, and the lifework of a given author is itself, considered as a unit, merely one part of the whole of a culture's literary tradition. Similarly, a word or expression is a part of language, a text belongs to, and is thus a part of, a particular literary genre, and a genre in turn is a part of the whole of literature. In each case, the parts and the whole in question must be understood reciprocally.

The idea that the applicability of hermeneutical rules of thumb would vary substantially from discipline to discipline was based, in Schleiermacher's opinion, on the mistaken conviction that "understanding occurs as a matter of course," and thus that the methods of hermeneutics need only be applied to difficult cases of interpretation. Schleiermacher's contention, in contrast, is that the "more rigorous practice of the art of interpretation . . . is based on the assumption that misunderstanding occurs as a matter of course, and so understanding must be . . . sought at every point" (ibid., p. 110). "This more rigourous practice," he explains, "presupposes that the speaker and hearer differ in their use of language and in their ways of formulating thoughts, although to be sure there is an underlying unity between them" (ibid.).

Without the "underlying unity" of a shared language, there would be no possibility of a hearer's coming to understand a speaker. But the degree to which speaker and hearer possess a *genuinely* shared language is easily exaggerated. Because a given word acquires its meanings only by virtue of the various contexts within which it is encountered, and these contextual encounters with a given word are always encounters on the part of some particular speaker, whose track through the social forum of linguistic communication will not be exactly the same as anyone else's, it follows that the connotations attached to a word will necessarily vary from speaker to speaker. What this means, Schleiermacher contends, is that interpreters must be aware that the seemingly unproblematic utterance, expressed in familiar terms, may in fact have a meaning quite other than that which they attribute to it. Because even contemporaries "differ in their use of language and in their ways of formulating thoughts," the task of interpretation "is not limited to what is fixed in writing, but arises whenever we have to understand a . . . series of thoughts expressed in words" (ibid., p. 182). Thus, rather than a science dedicated to the deciphering of texts distantly removed from the reader by period or culture,

hermeneutics is, for Schleiermacher, simply the art of understanding language. In every case of interpretation, moreover, the task confronting one is the same, although it consists of two clearly distinguishable parts: on the one hand, to determine the manner in which the speaker is inclined to formulate his thoughts and, on the other, to discover the speaker's personal style in his use of language.

The two-sidedness of interpretation—the fact that it consists of what Schleiermacher calls a "grammatical" and a "technical" (or "psychological") side—is grounded in the fact that speech is intimately related both to the language in which it is presented and to the thoughts of the speaker. Thus, grammatical interpretation is based on a mastery of such things as vocabulary, punctuation, sentence structure, and genre—including an understanding of how these features of language have changed historically—as well as a sensitivity to the nuances of style. Technical or psychological interpretation, by contrast, is concerned with establishing how the text in question fits into the context of its author's intellectual life. This requires an investigation of the author's biography, an examination of the social conditions of the time and place in which she lived, and a consideration of how one text should be read in the light of the author's other texts.

Schleiermacher describes the aim of technical interpretation as the complete understanding of an author's personal style. This way of putting the matter alerts us to the interdependence of the two sides of interpretation, for "we are accustomed to restrict the term 'style' to the way language is handled" (ibid., p. 148), and yet, because thoughts and language are intertwined, the way in which an author reveals her character in the organization and development of her ideas is also a matter of style. Thus, the technical and grammatical sides of interpretation involve two different ways of trying to bring the same object into view. Given this common target of the two sides of interpretation, the task of understanding "is finally resolved when either side could be replaced by the other, though both must be treated, that is to say, when each side is treated in such a way that the treatment of the other side produces no change in the result" (ibid., p. 100). The task is finished, in other words, when what we have learned about the meaning of a text by reconstructing the author's character and way of thinking (through an investigation of her life and times) serves only to confirm, and no longer to augment, what we have learned about the meaning of the text by examining the way in which it is presented in language, and vice versa.

The task of interpretation *would* be resolved if that point were reached, but according to Schleiermacher, it is in principle unreachable. "The goal of technical interpretation," he writes, "can only be approximated. . . . Not only do we never understand an individual view exhaustively, but what we do understand is always subject to correction" (ibid., p. 149). Indeed, it is precisely because neither side of interpretation can ever be brought to genuine completion that the two sides of interpretation have to be pursued in tandem. It is necessary to move back and forth between the grammatical and technical sides of interpretation because, when we are confronted, on the grammatical side, with two possible readings of a passage and there is nothing that we can discern in the author's use of language that enables us to choose between them, it is often the case that insights concerning the author's character and way of thinking—insights gathered, in other words, on the technical side of interpretation—will help us decide which of the possible readings is probably correct. On the other hand, what is learned about an author on the technical side invariably leaves open a number of directions in which her thinking might have turned at a given point, and an examination of the way in which she actually chose to express herself is of course the best way to determine what the author had in mind.

Each of the two sides of interpretation is an art, Schleiermacher contends, because it "constructs something finite and definite from something infinite and indefinite" (the clues to be found in the language of the text and in the life of the author) without the benefit of "rules which may be applied with self-evident certainty" (ibid., p. 100). The language of a text is "infinite" in that the meaning of an expression is a function of the countless relations in which its individual components stand to all the other elements of language. So, too, the nuances of individual thought processes, the ways in which they come to be affected by prior events, the ways in which ideas are interrelated within those processes, and the ways in which those processes in turn influence the thinking of others and events in the world generally, are also infinitely variable.

The art of interpretation depends, then, on the reader's possession of two separate talents: a command of language and a knowledge of human nature. According to Schleiermacher, "to the extent that a person is deficient in one of these talents, he is hampered [in his capacity to grasp the text], and the other gift can do no more than help him choose wisely from the suggestions made by others" (ibid., p. 101). Again, because both sides of interpretation have to be pursued simultaneously, so that each can be used as a check on the other, an interpreter who, for example, has a fine ear for language but little insight into human nature is not, on that basis, excused from pursuing the technical side of interpretation. On the contrary, given his handicap, he will have to be especially circumspect in his approach to the psychological side.

Schleiermacher speaks, with respect to each of the two different sides of interpretation, of two methods—divination and comparison—that are to be employed by turns. In technical interpretation, divination involves a projection of oneself into the position of the author and an attempt to anticipate on this basis what the author intended in her work.

One cannot, of course, project oneself into the position of the author without first having ascertained, at least in general terms, what the author's position actually was, and that requires a certain amount of research. On the other hand, one can never expect to re-create completely the circumstances of a person's life merely by means of research. Indeed, if one *could* perfectly re-create the author's position in this way, divination would be unnecessary, for divination is employed to compensate for the fact that what we can learn through research alone is inevitably limited with respect to detail and lacking in discriminations of significance. In the process of divination, we appeal to our shared humanity in order to get a sense of what must have seemed trivial and what important to the author, given her interests and circumstances. Thus, divination is based "on the assumption that each person is not only a unique individual in his own right, but that he has a receptivity to the uniqueness of every other person" (ibid., p. 150). Because the interpreter's act of projection is always grounded in (potentially inadequate) prior research, however, the conclusions arrived at by means of divination are always at first merely hypothetical, and become certain only when they are corroborated through the process of comparison.

According to Schleiermacher, each conclusion arrived at through divination can be thought of as "subsuming the author under a general type" (ibid.); that is to say, anything we might feel inclined to suggest on the basis of our immediate intuition of the author's intent—that the text is ironic, tragic, lyrical, and so on—can be represented as a claim about what *sort* of author she is. Whenever such a claim is advanced, moreover, it needs to be confirmed through a comparison of this author and her work (*as* an ironist, a tragedian, or a lyricist, etc.) with the work of others of the same type, the same period, and the same culture. This process of comparison establishes the range of literary possibilities available to the author in her own day. Establishing these boundaries is significant because, although it is always conceivable that the author in question has creatively extended the range of literary possibilities, if *as* an ironist, a tragedian, a lyricist, and so on she seems to have written in entirely unprecedented ways, there is good reason to believe that one's first intuitions about the text are mistaken.

The point of research carried out on the technical side of interpretation is to enable the reader to put himself in the position of the author. This is not an end in itself, but rather a mere preliminary to the reader's interpretive re-creation of the text. The relationship that is assumed here, between occupying the position of the author and understanding the text, gives rise to the best-known and most contentious of Schleiermacher's remarks on hermeneutics: that the task of interpretation is "to understand the text at first as well as and then even better than its author" (ibid., p. 112). The idea that the reader of a text should be in a position to understand it *better* than the person who actually selected each word that it contains and whose intention was realized in the writing of it has been criticized by many theorists of interpretation on the obvious grounds that the interpreter comes to the text, after all, as a stranger who cannot possibly recover, through any amount of research, the privileged relationship to the work that authorship confers. Most of these same theorists argue, however, that as interpreters we should take no special notice of the privileged position the author enjoys. What *we* make of the text is presumed to be what counts. Today, then, the tendency is to follow Hans-Georg Gadamer in celebrating the fact that each of us "understands in a different way, if we understand at all."

But, given what Schleiermacher actually means by suggesting that the aim of interpretation is to understand the text better than the author did, the objection of those who follow Gadamer rather misses the mark; for it is not especially controversial to suggest that an author might have been unaware on a conscious level of some of the reasons for her constructing a text as she did, and that nonetheless an interpreter might manage to bring those reasons to light. The author, after all, need not be aware of her own psychological predispositions, motivations, and personal prejudices in order for these things to have an effect on her work. In the process of interpretation, however, the reader must first recognize *that* these determining factors have played a role in the production of the text and then must establish *what* that role is.

To understand a text better than its author did is thus neither a meaningless nor an altogether unachievable goal. Schleiermacher, however, sees the attainment of this goal as nothing more than a by-product of the interpreter's pursuit of the proper—and genuinely unattainable—goal of interpretation; for the stronger, more accurate formulation of the task of hermeneutics is the "historical and divinatory, objective and subjective reconstruction of a given statement" (ibid., p. 111). This task has four parts to it:

1. "objective-historical" reconstruction, which involves "consider[ing] the statement in [its] relation to the language as a whole, and consider[ing] the knowledge it contains as a product of language";
2. "objective-prophetic" reconstruction, which involves "sens[ing] how the statement itself will stimulate further developments in the language";
3. "subjective-historical" reconstruction, which involves determining "how the statement, as a fact in the person's mind, has emerged"; and
4. "subjective-prophetic" reconstruction, which involves "sens[ing] how the thoughts contained in the statement will exercise further influence on and in the author." (Ibid., p. 112)

According to this more stringent formulation of the task of hermeneutics, the interpreter is to concern himself not only with establishing (in its entirety) the history of the text's creation as the product of a particular language and the product of a particular person embedded within the social fabric of her time, but also with anticipating the impact that the text will have, first, on the author's own future work, and second, on the future of the language in which it was written. "So formulated," Schleiermacher writes, "the task is infinite, because in a statement we want to trace a past and a future which stretch into infinity" (ibid.).

In his pursuit of this ideal interpretation of a text—one that correctly situates it in the web of historical and linguistic influences acting on and emanating from the text—the interpreter is necessarily drawn into a number of different fields of inquiry. He becomes, of necessity, a biographer, a psychologist, a historian, and a linguist, as well as a literary critic. Each of these fields, however, is another interpretive discipline, dominated in its turn by the open-endedness of the hermeneutic circle relating (discipline-specific) parts to their correspondent wholes. Thus, in each of the various disciplines that the interpreter finds himself having to traverse in pursuit of a correct and thorough reading of a text, the interpreter is confronted with yet another in principle incompletable task. The nature of the author's character, the nature of the social world in which she lived, the nature of the language in which she wrote, the nature of the text's genre—the comprehension of each of these things is an adjunct to the interpretation of the text itself, and yet none of these can ever be fully comprehended. The task of textual interpretation, then, is in principle incompletable for any number of reasons. The one finally correct and true interpretation of a text *is* approachable, through the application of the divinatory-comparative method on both the grammatical and technical sides of interpretation, but approachable only asymptotically. In the real world of time constraints, limited resources, and personal motives, Schleiermacher observes, "the question of how far and in which directions interpretation will be pressed must be decided . . . on practical grounds" (ibid.).

[*See also* Hermeneutics.]

BIBLIOGRAPHY

Works by Schleiermacher

Der christliche Glaube. 2 vols. Edited by Martin Redeker. Berlin, 1960. Translated as *The Christian Faith* by H. R. Mackintosh and J. S. Stewart (Edinburgh, 1928).

Hermeneutics: The Handwritten Manuscripts. Translated by James Duke and Jack Forstman, edited by Heinz Kimmerle. Missoula, Mont., 1977.

Monologen. Edited by Friedrich Michael Schiele and Hermann Mulert. Leipzig, 1914. Translated as *Soliloquies* by Horace Leland Friess (Chicago, 1926).

Reden über die Religion. Edited by G. C. B. Pünjer. Braunschweig, 1879. Translated as *On Religion: Speeches to Its Cultured Despisers* by Richard Crouter (Cambridge and New York, 1988).

Sämtliche Werke, 1835–1864. Published in three divisions: I, theological; II, sermons; III, philosophical and related subjects.

Schleiermacher's Introductions to the Dialogues of Plato. Translated by William Dobson. New York, 1973.

Vorlesungen über die Ästhetik aus Schleiermacher's handschriftlichem Nachlasse und aus nachgeschriebenen Heften. Edited by Carl Lommatzsch. Berlin, 1974.

Other Sources

Brandt, Richard B. *The Philosophy of Friedrich Schleiermacher.* New York, 1941.

Dilthey, Wilhelm. *Leben Schleiermachers.* Berlin, 1870.

Scholtz, Gunter. *Die Philosophie Schleiermachers.* Darmstadt, 1984.

RON BONTEKOE

SCHMARSOW, AUGUST (1853–1936), German educator and art theoretician. Schmarsow was born in Mecklenburg and died in Baden-Baden. As a student, after abandoning his original plan to study cultural history with Jacob Burckhardt in Basel, Schmarsow attended courses in art history with Rudolf Jahn (Zurich) and Carl Justi (Bonn); classical archaeology with Adolf Michaelis (Strasbourg); history with Julius Weizsäcker and Hermann Baumgarten (Strasbourg); German literature and philosophy with Wilhelm Scherer (Strasbourg), Karl Simrock, and Alexander Reifferscheid (Bonn); and philosophy with Ernst Laas (Strasbourg). His doctoral dissertation was in German philology on the grammarian Georg Schottelius, published in part in 1877 under the title "Leibniz und Schottelius." Schmarsow started his professional career as an assistant at the Berlin *Kupferstichkabinett* (Copper Engraving Department), moved to the directorship of the Göttingen museum in 1881, and then on to an academic career that took him from Göttingen to Breslau and Leipzig (1893), where he taught for twenty-six years. This brief summary indicates that, in his studies as well as his subsequent teaching and writing, Schmarsow had founded his theories on a broad basis, with an emphasis on cultural sciences *(Kulturwissenschaft)* rather than on any specific discipline. Although Schmarsow's academic work is today almost totally neglected, he was without doubt one of the most influential figures of his time, both as a teacher and as a theoretician. His theory of architecture had the most far-reaching effects.

Schmarsow's published work shows that his interest followed two directions. The first phase of his academic career was marked by in-depth research that resulted in monographs on a number of artists as well as detailed analysis of individual works of art. Upon taking up the chair in Leipzig, a second tendency gained prominence. His interest was now primarily in establishing general principles *(Grundbegriffe)* for the newly emerging *Kunstwissenschaft* (science of art). His intention to combine aesthetics and historic analysis of art resulted in the establishment of the foundation of a systematic science of art based on psychological and philosophical principles.

Schmarsow's inaugural lecture at Leipzig, titled *Das Wesen der architektonischen Schöpfung* (The Essence of Architectural Creation), was to prove programmatic for most of his major writings over the next quarter of a century. Schmarsow diagnosed the position of architecture within the context of a science of art as one between two extreme positions, neither of which can do it justice. For aestheticians, architecture cannot be regarded as an art per se, but as an "unfree art" indistinguishable from tectonics and handicrafts. On the other hand, "thinking architects" regard architecture as *Bekleidungskunst* (art of cladding) and therefore view their activity as scarcely anything other than an external composition of a purely technical and decorative nature, a pasting of inherited styles onto the frame of a functional structure. For Schmarsow, Gottfried Semper's notion of architecture as the "art of cladding" lent itself only too readily to an interpretation that gave undue prominence to the outside appearance of a building, that is, the way in which the building "presents" itself, externally, its facade. This (mis)interpretation, however, was all the more convincing because it seemed to reflect the actual state of architecture throughout much of the nineteenth century, which was marked by an unprecedented historical eclecticism and by a growing preoccupation with new, industrially produced materials and techniques of construction (e.g., Karl Friedrich Schinkel, Henri Labrouste). An architect might then, indeed, choose from among a number of readily available "styles" while placing increasing emphasis on the functional aspects of building.

To overcome the deplorable "aesthetics from without," Schmarsow demanded an "aesthetic from within." In doing this, he alluded to Gustav Theodor Fechner's contrasting pair of "aesthetics from above" and "aesthetics from below." Fechner, in his psychophysics, had sought to replace the speculative, idealist "aesthetics from above," whose main aim was to define the principles of beauty. In its place he advocated an "aesthetics from below," a purely experimental science of beauty, based on direct observation. With his "aesthetics from within," however, Schmarsow evoked an internal psychological point as opposed to an "external" one that concentrated on form and formal changes. Yet, as it emerged in his lecture of 1893, it was also meant in the very concrete sense of "interior space" as opposed to the prevalent formal preoccupation with the exterior of architectural creation. Schmarsow's double claim to an "aesthetics from within" set his theory apart from a number of contemporary theories that concentrated almost exclusively on the effect of the exterior of architectural constructs. Thus, he avoided viewing the essence of architecture as a purely physical response to the relation of load and force or as an art of corporeal masses. Rejecting Semper's categorical distinction between the "Caribbean hut" and architecture as an "unhistorical and unphilosophical" art, Schmarsow argued that notwithstanding the differences in material and technics of construction, both the Caribbean hut and the most sophisticated building shared a common denominator that determined their status as architecture, namely, that every human-made structure is a spatial construct.

Schmarsow was one of the first scholars to develop and employ simultaneously methods of the recently established science of art. Greatly influenced by both the physiological and psychological theories of Hermann Lotze and Wilhelm Wundt, but also by the scientific genetic methodology of the historian Karl Lamprecht, Schmarsow was a firm advocate of a genetic approach, which placed him in marked contrast to Semper's establishment of a classificatory-taxonomical system. Because the creating and/or appreciating individual is at the center of all artistic manifestations, Schmarsow concluded logically that the enclosing of a subject is the crucial criterion in the human understanding of space and consequently in the creation of space, that is, architecture.

Schmarsow's premise, based mainly on Wundt's and Lotze's theories that human perception of space is a psychological synthesis between sensory experience and spatial intuitions *(Vorstellungen)* originating in the human body, was shared by many of his contemporaries. These intuitions were rooted in a similar part of the psyche where mathematical thinking, the psychological basis of the science of space, is to be found. The only difference between the *Raumwissenschaft* (science of space) and the *Raumkunst* (art of space) lies in the fact that architecture as an art of space strives to transform inner intuition into external appearance and concrete representation, whereas science on the contrary operates only in the abstract without a concrete product. History shows the two to be inseparable in the evolution of human culture. The ideal is always pure intentional form, the laws of which are investigated by the science of space, whereas the *Baukunst,* which executes its creation in the physical world, has to come to terms with circumstances of setting and physical laws. Both are ruled by basic intellectual laws, however, which constitute the basis of the order that humans perceive in the external world. This ideal form was, for Schmarsow, evident in the tendency inherent in human nature toward regularity, repeatability of parts, and purity of forms exhibited by all human interventions in the environment. The organization of the human body affects unconsciously all products of human creation, tools as well as the decoration of the environment and the body (tattooing). In the next step, and as a continuation of his argument, Schmarsow analyzed human experience of three-dimensional space by relating each dimension to the human subject, who—as postulated—is at the center of this space, whose directional axes intersect in us.

Schmarsow developed his theory of architecture by focusing on interior space (domestic space and the basilica). It was, indeed, the crucial postulate of his theory. The experience of the exterior of an architectural construct is fundamentally and conceptually different as we experience the architectural construct as another object or body *(Körper)* external to and opposite to our own body in space. In viewing the exterior, humans arrange their own meridians as middle axes, thereby enforcing their inherent law of symmetry and proportion.

Schmarsow further elaborated his theory of architecture into a full-fledged theory of the arts that connects all of them in a coherent system of basic principles. In 1896, at a public meeting of the Royal Saxonian Society of Sciences, Schmarsow delivered a lecture titled "Über den Werth der Dimensionen im menschlichen Raumgebilde" (On the Importance of Dimensions in Human Spatial Creation) that contained most of the ideas that were further established in his *Grundbegriffe der Kunstwissenschaft am Übergang vom Altertum zum Mittelalter* (Basic Principles of the Science of Art at the Transition from Antiquity to the Middle Ages) of 1905. Schmarsow's definition of art as our creative coming to terms with the world into which we have been placed presupposed two poles: the human being and the external world. Our creative coming to terms with the world is determined by our physical and psychic organization and constitution. Elaborating on his theory as presented in the 1893 lecture, Schmarsow distinguished three essential constituents of the human anatomy that are of crucial importance in our experiencing of the world and consequently make their mark in any aesthetic creation: our erect position, which distinguishes us from animals; our physical organization in pairs, such as two eyes, arms, ears, hands, breasts, legs, feet; and our pronounced frontal orientation (face, directional axis of the arms, legs, and feet).

Our coming to terms with the world follows the three-dimensionality of the intuited category that we call space. In a psychophysiological interpretation, Schmarsow identified the three peculiarities of the human anatomy as decisive in the experience of the three dimensions. Thus, height, as the dominant first dimension, is deduced from a human's vertical axis; width, the second dimension, is primordially experienced as a correlate of the extension of our shoulders, emphasized by our outstretched arms; the third dimension, depth, is correlated to our pronounced frontality, which determines our forward looking and moving. The location of the different organs, the peculiarity of their positioning, the degree of their mobility, their dependence on the torso, their degree of cooperation—all these determine not only our orientation in space but even our understanding of it and our rendering of space in the arts.

Schmarsow then established each of the three dimensions or axes as the generating force for one of the fine arts. It is with perfect inner logic that Schmarsow spoke in his 1896 lecture of *Raumgebilde* (creation in and of space), referring to all three fine arts. According to his elaborate system, the first dimension or vertical axis predominates in sculpture, the *Körperbilderin* (shaper of bodies); the second dimension or axis of width in painting, the *Flächengestalterin* (creatress of surfaces); and the third dimension or axis of depth in architecture, the actual *Raumgestalterin* (creatress of space). Following Semper's tripartite classification, Schmarsow arrives at the three principles of proportionality, symmetry, and rhythm, the latter replacing Semper's term *direction*. The principle of proportionality follows the different segmentations along our own vertical axis and is the determining principle for sculpture. Our own "symmetrical" organization (eyes, ears, breasts, arms, legs) requires a demand for symmetry that is established as a decisive principle for painting. The principle of rhythm, according to Schmarsow, is the natural outcome of our own breathing and heartbeat as well as our rhythmical moving forward. Consequently, rhythm is the decisive principle for architecture.

Schmarsow's complex construct can be represented in the following schema:

Human body	Dimensions	Fine art	Creative principle
Vertical axis	1st dimension	Sculpture	Proportion
Horizontal axis	2d dimension	Painting	Symmetry
Direction (depth)	3d dimension	Architecture	Rhythm

In establishing his system of basic principles of art, Schmarsow placed overriding emphasis on the human body and its particular organization in the experience of space. Yet, in doing so, he did not rely on an exclusively physiological or psychological position, nor did his theory conform to Robert Vischer's *Einfühlung* (empathy). Already in his *Grundbegriffe* he explicitly distanced himself from the "scientific or more specifically physiological basis" that he, like many others—including Alois Riegl and Adolf von Hildebrand—had thought essential, "from which we originally expected the highest triumph of exact science." Schmarsow now called it an *Abweg* (the wrong track) that "has to be renounced if we want to proceed."

Comparing the different stages in the development of Schmarsow's theories, an evident, increasing tendency toward phenomenological thinking emerged. Throughout his work there are increasing indications of implicit affinities between his theories and those of the early phenomenologists. It is, however, only in his 1919 essay "Kunstwissenschaft und Kulturphilosophie mit gemeinsamen Grundbegriffen" (The Basic Concepts Underlying a Science of Art and Cultural Philosophy) that he referred openly to phenomenology and especially to Max Scheler's *Der Formalismus in der Ethik und die materielle Weltethik* (Formalism in Ethics and Material World Ethics). In this essay, Schmarsow took up Scheler's distinction of the human body as *Körper* and *Leib*. For Scheler, the term *Leib* refers to the consciousness of our having a body that transcends our experience of our body as a *Körper*, that is, the sum of internal and external sensations.

Schmarsow used this distinction already in his *Grundbegriffe*, without, however, providing a reference for it. There he stated that the human subject's coming to terms with the external world begins with his own *Leib*, and, a few lines later, that the condition of the organic creature that finds itself *Körper* determines its relation to the world. Schmarsow's insistence on the determining factor of movement regarding the third dimension, of space, shows affinities to Edmund Husserl's theory of kinesthesia as being constitutive for the notion of space. Furthermore, the relevance of the "ground," the *Grund und Boden*, for man's experience of the world is emphasized on several occasions in the *Grundbegriffe*. Out of this relation to the common "ground" that we share with all other bodies arises also the basic condition for all artistic creation.

Thus, although it would be exaggerated to classify Schmarsow as a phenomenologist, numerous references throughout his theories clearly indicate a development away from positivistic psychology into a phenomenology of the visual arts.

[*See also* Architecture.]

BIBLIOGRAPHY

Works by Schmarsow

"Leibniz und Schottelius: Die 'unvorgreiflichen Gedanken'." Strasbourg, 1877. Reprinted in *Quellen und Forschungen zur Sprach- und Culturgeschichte der Germanischen Völker* 23 (1877): 1–43 (doctoral dissertation).

Das Wesen der architektonischen Schöpfung. Leipzig, 1994. Inaugural lecture given at the University of Leipzig on 8 November, 1893.

"Über den Werth der Dimensionen im menschlichen Raumgebilde." *Berichte über die Verhandlungen der königlich Sächsischen Gesellschaft der Wissenschaften zu Leipzig, Philologisch-historische Klasse* 48 (1896): 44–61. Address delivered to the society on 23 April 1896.

Beiträge zur Ästhetik der bildenden Künste. 3 vols. Leipzig, 1896–1899.

Barock und Rokoko: Eine kritische Auseinandersetzung über das Malerische in der Architektur. Leipzig, 1897.

Plastik, Malerei und Reliefkunst in ihrem gegenseitigen Verhältnis. Leipzig, 1899.

Grundbegriffe der Kunstwissenschaft am Übergang vom Altertum zum Mittelalter, kritisch erörtert und in systematischen Zusammenhänge dargestellt. Leipzig, 1905.

"Kunstwissenschaft und Völkerpsychologie: Ein Versuch zur Verständigung." *Zeitschrift für Ästhetik und allgemeine Kunstwissenschaft* 2 (1907), part 1: 305–339; part 2: 469–500.

"Raumgestaltung als Wesen der architektonischen Schöpfung." In *Kongress für Ästhetik und allgemeine Kunstwissenschaft, Berlin 9–10 Oktober 1913*, pp. 246–250. Stuttgart, 1914.

"Kunstwissenschaft und Kulturphilosophie mit gemeinsamen Grundbegriffen." *Zeitschrift für Ästhetik und allgemeine Kunstwissenschaft* 13 (1919), part 1: 165–190; part 2: 225–258.

"Rhythmus in menschlichen Raumgebilden." *Zeitschrift für Ästhetik und allgemeine Kunstwissenschaft* 14 (1920): 171–187.

"Zur Lehre vom Rhythmus." *Zeitschrift für Ästhetik und allgemeine Kunstwissenschaft* 16 (1922): 109–118.

"August Schmarsow: Rückschau beim Eintritt ins siebzigste Lebensjahr." In *Die Kunstwissenschaft der Gegenwart in Selbstdarstellungen*, edited by Johannes Jahn, pp. 135–156. Leipzig, 1924.

Other Sources

Mallgrave, Harry Francis, and Eleftherios Ikonomou, eds. *Empathy, Form and Space: Problems in German Aesthetics, 1873–1893.* Santa Monica, Calif., 1994.

Schwarzer, Mitchell. "The Emergence of Architectural Space: August Schmarsow's Theory of Raumgestaltung." *Assemblance* 15 (1991): 48–61.

ELEFTHERIOS IKONOMOU

SCHOENBERG, ARNOLD FRANZ WALTER

(1874–1951), composer and music theorist. Born in Vienna, Schoenberg (or Schönberg) came of age within the cultural and artistic traditions of the late nineteenth century, and he remained deeply committed to preserving and extending these. But he was also caught up in the revolutionary transformations that took place in his native city during the early years of the twentieth century; and balancing traditional and innovative elements, he forged from these circumstances a new compositional language with profound consequences for twentieth-century music and musical thought.

Most of Schoenberg's first fifty years were spent in Vienna, punctuated by two periods in Berlin (1901–1903 and 1911–1915). Dominated by conservative musical institutions, the city took little note of his work; often beset by extreme financial hardships, Schoenberg departed willingly and permanently in 1925 when offered the prestigious chair in composition at the Prussian Academy of Arts, Berlin, recently vacated by Ferruccio Busoni. With Adolf Hitler's rise to power in 1933, however, Schoenberg lost his position and, recognizing the implications for himself and his music, soon emigrated. After a brief period in Paris, he came to the United States, settling in California in 1934, where he spent the remainder of his life.

Schoenberg's musical aesthetic is inseparable from his compositional development. Largely self-taught, in the first years of the twentieth century he produced a remarkable series of compositions in a late-Romantic manner, motivated by both Wagnerian and Brahmsian influences and thereby synthesizing the "programmatic" and "absolute-music" lines of the Germanic tradition. In these works, Schoenberg pushed the boundaries of traditional tonal language to their breaking point. What distinguished him from others (Gustav Mahler, Claude Debussy, and Richard Strauss, for example), was his taking the final step toward "atonality" in fully abandoning the two primary attributes of traditional musical grammar: triadically constructed harmony and the privileging of a single, hierarchically elevated tone to which all others were subordinated. Tied to this was what Schoenberg called the "emancipation of dissonance": the treatment of dissonance not as the opposite of consonances, but as different only in degree. This move completely redefined the boundaries of what might be considered musically possible; and thereafter, no younger composer could approach musical material in quite the same way as before.

The final rupture with tonality occurred in 1907, initiating a period of intense creative activity for Schoenberg. Within a short period he composed a stream of new works, written as if improvised without conscious controls, and including several seminal works of musical modernism (most famously *Pierrot Lunaire,* a 1912 song cycle for soprano—employing *Sprechstimme,* a manner midway between speech and song—and five instrumentalists). To some extent, the atonal works can be viewed as extending developments initiated in the preceding ones. If there tonal definition was pushed to the breaking point, here it was annihilated; and if there traditional phrase structures and formal balances achieved ever more complex realizations, here they were abandoned entirely. The "last straw" effect produced by these developments was shattering, giving birth to a music of unprecedented formal fragmentation and expressive schism.

Following this initial explosive release, Schoenberg's work quickly approached a crisis point. Already between 1909 and 1916 fewer compositions appeared, and complete silence set in from 1916 until 1923. Far from being inactive in these years, Schoenberg experimented ceaselessly, attempting to develop a new compositional grammar to replace the traditional one that he had discarded. A move toward more conscious formulation is already evident in the works of 1909 to 1916 and can be traced in the gestation of a single composition, the one-act opera *Die glückliche Hand,* composed intermittently between 1909 and 1913, acquiring a significantly more rigorous complexion as it neared completion. During the period of silence, Schoenberg continued to work on numerous unfinished pieces, exploring new constructive principles designed to order and contain the highly chromatic musical material he felt to be the inevitable outcome of the dissolution of tonality.

In 1923, having completed his search, Schoenberg published the first works written according to a procedure he called the "method of composing with twelve tones which are related only with one another," subsequently known as the "twelve-tone system." (The tonal system, by contrast, uses seven primary tones, the remaining five being treated as departures.) Taking a particular ordering of all twelve pitches as a norm, uniquely chosen for each particular work, this "row," or "series," is placed within a larger configuration of symmetrical reflections: inversion, retrograde, and retrograde-inversion forms of the same row. This configuration then forms the basis for the pitch material used in the work, providing a basis for determining pitch choices within a fully chromatic, twelve-tone context while allowing for complete freedom in the determination of rhythm, texture, form, and other matters. (In this latter respect, Schoenberg's system differs fundamentally from the so-called integral serialism of the 1950s, where not only pitches are serialized but other compositional parameters as well, most notably rhythm.) Schoenberg stated that his system was based on the "principle of the absolute and unitary perception of musical space," putting it in marked contrast to the asymmetrical, unidirectional musical space of traditional tonality.

After 1923, Schoenberg again composed with relative ease, working primarily with his new method and exploring and extending its possibilities until his death in 1951. Once again he adopted traditional formal types, such as sonata and variation, discarded when he first abandoned tonality, bringing him back full circle to his initial formal presuppositions. Due to his persisting posttonal orientation, however, Schoenberg at this time was frequently paired and contrasted with Igor Stravinsky, who remained resolutely committed to tonality during these years (rethought by him as a more generalized play of "polar attractions"), the two becoming the leading representatives of what were considered the two principal compositional directions of the first half of the twentieth century. Theodor W. Adorno's *Philosophie der neuen Musik* (1948), for example, one of the most important early studies of musical modernism, is framed exclusively in terms of their divergent developments:

It is . . . not in the illusion of grand personality that only these two composers—Schoenberg and Stravinsky—are to be discussed. For if the total product of new music—as defined by its inner qualities rather than by chronology—were to be scrutinized in its entirety, including all transitions and compromises, these same extremes would again be encountered.

(Adorno, 1973, pp. 3–4)

Although Schoenberg thought of himself primarily as a composer, he was one of the major music theorists of his time, and an important teacher of composition. Always intensely self-aware, he expressed himself publicly on all aspects of his art. Unlike such nineteenth-century writer-composers as Robert Schumann, Hector Berlioz, and Richard Wagner, he did not limit himself to general critical and philosophical matters but addressed the mechanics of his craft. (In the preface to his *Theory of Harmony,* published in 1911, the first of several technical monographs, he states that his intent is to provide "a good practical theory," not "a bad aesthetic.") Among a number of major younger composers taught by Schoenberg (including such unlikely figures as Hanns Eisler and John Cage), the most closely—and famously—associated with him were his fellow Austrians Alban Berg and Anton Webern, the three eventually coming to be designated as the "second Viennese school."

Schoenberg was also a profoundly original amateur painter, the librettist for his three operas, and an inventor and designer of great skill. His intensely expressionistic, idiosyncratic paintings date almost entirely from one brief period, not coincidentally the years immediately following his liberation from traditional tonality, when his amateur

status as artist accorded well with his then commitment to unmediated personal expression. The painter Wassily Kandinsky, with whom Schoenberg was in close contact at the time, thought highly enough of his work to include two of his paintings in his almanac *Der blaue Reiter.* In an article he contributed for a 1912 *Festschrift,* Kandinsky commented:

We see *at once* that Schoenberg paints, not in order to produce "beautiful," "nice," etc. pictures; rather, while painting he does not even think about the picture itself. Ignoring the objective result, he seeks only to pin down his subjective "sensation," and in doing so, employs only those resources that appear to him at that moment indispensable. Not even all professional painters can boast of this manner of painting!

(Quoted in Hahl-Koch, 1984, p. 126)

Schoenberg's multiple talents were most fully united in *Die glückliche Hand,* for which he supplied the music and libretto, choreographed gestures and movements, painted the sets, and designed the lighting—a totality that he characterized as "making music with the media of the stage."

Despite his stress on technical matters, Schoenberg wrote eloquently on the aesthetic foundations of his art. His early creative evolution was shaped by Romantic—primarily Schopenhauerian—ideals of transcendental expression, which in his hands took on a distinctly expressionistic cast, encouraging rejection of inherited conventions in search of a unique inner vision and private compositional language. The idea that each work should define its own standards, independent of acquired rules or other restrictions, colors all of Schoenberg's early output. He articulated the position most emphatically in a series of letters written to Busoni in 1909: "My only intention is to have *no* intentions! . . . to place nothing inhibiting in the stream of my unconscious sensations. But to allow anything to infiltrate which may be invoked either by intelligence or consciousness." Two years later he wrote to Kandinsky:

Every formal procedure which aspires to traditional effects is not completely free from conscious motivation. But art belongs to the *unconscious!* One must express *oneself!* Express oneself *directly!* Not one's taste, or one's upbringing, or one's intelligence, knowledge or skill. Not all these *acquired* characteristics, but that which is *inborn, instinctive.* (Quoted in Hahl-Koch, 1984, p. 23)

Although this intuitive aesthetic was essential to Schoenberg's renunciation of tonality, it eventually raised issues in his own mind concerning the comprehensibility of his music. After the initial two years of intense activity, as his output declined, he began to question the advisability of composing in such a seemingly improvisatory manner. Whereas the final compositions of 1909, such as the violently eruptive psychological monodrama *Erwartung* (twenty minutes in length, and composed in a mere seventeen days), were not only "atonal" but also "athematic," without fixed, recurring melodic substance (Adorno writes of *Erwartung*'s "seismographic registration of traumatic shock"), subsequent pieces began to reveal more explicit melodic correspondences and even such traditional structural devices as canonic imitation. Having reached the extremes of unfettered expressivity, Schoenberg evidently questioned the possibility of sustaining such a high-wire act of creative intensity and began to introduce more conscious constraints. Looking back from 1941, he observed:

> From the very beginning such [atonal] compositions differed from all preceding music, not only harmonically but also melodically, thematically, and motivicly. But the foremost characteristics of these pieces *in statu nascendi* were their extreme expressiveness and their extraordinary brevity. At that time, neither I nor my pupils were conscious of the reasons for these features. Later I discovered that our sense of form was right when it forced us to counterbalance extreme emotionality with extraordinary shortness. Thus, subconsciously, consequences were drawn from an innovation which, like every innovation, destroys while it produces. New colourful harmony was offered, but much was lost. . . . Whether one calls oneself conservative or revolutionary, . . . one must be convinced of the infallibility of one's own fantasy and one must believe in one's own inspiration. Nevertheless, the desire for a conscious control of the new means and forms will arise in every artist's mind; and he will wish to know *consciously* the laws and rules which govern the forms which he has conceived "as in a dream." Strongly convincing as this dream may have been, the conviction that these new sounds obey the laws of nature and of our manner of thinking—the conviction that order, logic, comprehensibility and form cannot be present without obedience to such laws—forces the composer along the road of exploration. He must find, if not laws or rules, at least ways to justify the dissonant character of these harmonies and their successions. After many unsuccessful attempts during a period of approximately twelve years I laid the foundations for a new procedure in musical construction which seemed fitted to replace those structural differentiations provided formerly by tonal harmonies.
>
> (Schoenberg, 1975, pp. 217–218)

This "new procedure" was the twelve-tone system. Although its formalist orientation, as well as its coupling with traditional formal types, was consistent with the general anti-Romantic retrenchment and turn toward "sobriety" evident throughout European art in the years following World War I, the overtly systematic Constructivism of the new system assured that it attained considerable notoriety. Schoenberg was widely attacked for having turned music into a sort of mathematical game, and for the rest of his life he was considered by many to be little more than a modernist musical engineer. Yet, as his own words make clear, Schoenberg considered his path not in opposition to the Western musical tradition but as leading logically out of it. It is in this context that he remarked to one of his students in 1921 that the twelve-tone system would "insure the supremacy of German music for the next one hundred years."

With regard to historical process, Schoenberg was fundamentally traditionalist: he viewed his own work from the perspective of nineteenth-century notions of historical evolution and progress, as a logical and indeed necessary continuation of lines deeply anchored in the past. It was his belief that these lines traced a development toward ever greater concision and comprehensibility, the ornamental and unnecessary being progressively discarded so as to allow composers to say the "most important things in the most concentrated manner in every fraction of time." (In his earlier years, Schoenberg had confessed to Karl Kraus, inveterate opponent of all linguistic cant and imprecision: "I have learned more from you, perhaps, than a man should learn, if he wants to remain independent.") "This is why," Schoenberg noted, "when composers have acquired the technique of filling one direction with content to the utmost capacity, they must do the same in the next direction, and finally in all the directions in which music expands" (Schoenberg, 1975, p. 116). Through this process, music moved ever closer to its true nature. Schoenberg always emphasized, therefore, the close links between his own work and that of his forerunners, and stressed that any valid compositional technique had to be rooted in the past. He denied that he was a "revolutionary," convinced that everything he did "grew out of a necessity," servicing "progress in the direction toward an unrestricted musical language."

Schoenberg thus increasingly saw himself as an artistic prophet whose mission it was to chart music's path out of the modern wasteland—an idea powerfully brought to symbolic realization in the opera *Moses und Aron* (which remained, significantly, unfinished). Composing took on the aura of a responsibility, undertaken in response to an order from God (characterized as the "Supreme Commander"): "I knew I had to fulfill a task: I had to express what was necessary to be expressed and I knew I had the duty of developing my ideas for the sake of progress in music, whether I liked it or not" (ibid., p. 53)

This sense of duty made Schoenberg's journey both burdensome and lonely. In a 1910 aphorism, published in the periodical *Die Musik*, he stated: "Art is the cry of despair of those who experience within themselves the fate of all mankind." Indeed, pain and isolation are evident both in the difficulty of Schoenberg's music and in his belief that great art can only be for the few ("If it is art, it is not for all, and if it is for all, it is not art"). This acquired concrete expression in Schoenberg's formation of the Society for Private Musical Performances in Vienna in 1918, conceived so that performances of new works could be heard under carefully controlled conditions, divorced from normal concert life. Schoenberg's sense of alienation was also closely linked to his experience as an Austrian Jew, increasingly forced to see himself as an artistic, cultural, and racial outsider. Whether compelled or by choice, Schoenberg was always "in opposition."

The idea of "destiny," of taking "decisive steps" in response to historical necessity, cuts across the lines separating Schoenberg's tonal, free atonal, and twelve-tone compositions. It even informs his unexpected return to traditional tonality in several works written intermittently during the final two decades of his life. Typically, Schoenberg explained this move as an effort to close a lacuna in his own historical evolution: the Organ Variations, op. 48 of 1941, for example, were written to "fill out the gap" between the still-tonal Chamber Symphony (1907) and the immediately following atonal works. Similarly, a concerto by Georg Matthias Monn (1717–1750) was reworked in 1933 to lend it "true substance" by removing the "principal deficiencies of the Handel style" (Monn thereby being elevated to the "true" tradition).

Today, when such ideas have come to epitomize the hubris and masculine aggressiveness said to characterize the modernist endeavor in general, Schoenberg's aesthetic may appear hopelessly dated. Yet the composer's quasi-theological belief in artistic necessity must be measured against his overall artistic persona, with its profound contradictions in compositional output and aesthetic attitude. There is an almost schizophrenic split between Schoenberg's early position of unmediated expression and his later formalism and Constructivism; or between his deep distrust of all calculation, exact sequential repetition, and balanced proportioning in tonal music and his enthusiastic acceptance of the mirror symmetries underlying the twelve-tone system. There is also, though rarely acknowledged, the fact that Schoenberg's artistic self-consciousness and eclectic pluralism anticipate qualities now associated with musical postmodernism. The fundamental uncertainty reflected in Schoenberg's aesthetic and compositional shifts, along with the very extremity with which he espoused historical determinism, bespeak a tradition already in the throes of dissolution. Perhaps this helps explain one of the more perplexing features of music scholarship today: that this much-disputed composer, whose music remains almost as rarely performed today as during his own lifetime, retains such a defiant hold on contemporary musical consciousness.

[*See also* Modernism, *article on* Modern Music; *and* Music, *historical overview article*.]

BIBLIOGRAPHY

Works by Schoenberg

Letters. Edited by Erwin Stein, translated by Eithne Wilkins and Ernst Kaiser. London, 1964; reprint, Berkeley, 1987.
Style and Idea: Selected Writings of Arnold Schoenberg. Edited by Leonard Stein, translated by Leo Black. London, 1975; reprint, Berkeley, 1985.
Theory of Harmony (1911). Translated by Roy E. Carter. Berkeley, 1978.

Other Sources

Adorno, Theodor W. *Philosophy of Modern Music* (1948). Translated by Anne G. Mitchell and Wesley V. Blomster. New York, 1973.
Auner, Joseph H. "Schoenberg's Handel Concerto and the Ruins of Tradition." *Journal of the American Musicological Society* 49.2 (Summer 1996): 264–313.
Dahlhaus, Carl. *Schoenberg and the New Music.* Translated by Derrick Puffett and Alfred Clayton. Cambridge and New York, 1987.
Hahl-Koch, Jelena, ed. *Arnold Schoenberg/Wassily Kandinsky: Letters, Pictures and Documents.* Translated by John C. Crawford. London and Boston, 1984.
Kallir, Jane. *Arnold Schoenberg's Vienna.* New York, 1984. See on Schoenberg's paintings.
Morgan, Robert P. "Secret Languages: The Roots of Musical Modernism." *Critical Inquiry* 10.3 (March 1984): 442–461.
Ringer, Alexander L. *Arnold Schoenberg: The Composer as Jew.* Oxford, 1990.
Rosen, Charles. *Arnold Schoenberg.* 2d ed. Chicago, 1996.
Rufer, Joseph. *The Works of Arnold Schoenberg: A Catalogue of His Compositions, Writings, and Paintings.* Translated by Dika Newlin. London, 1962.
Schorske, Carl E. *Fin-de-Siècle Vienna: Politics and Culture.* New York, 1980. See chap. 7: "Explosion in the Garden: Kokoschka and Schoenberg."
Smith, Joan Allen. *Schoenberg and His Circle: A Viennese Portrait.* New York, 1986.
Stuckenschmidt, H. H. *Arnold Schoenberg: His Life, World and Work.* Translated by Edith Temple Roberts and Humphrey Searle. Reprint, New York, 1977.

ROBERT P. MORGAN

SCHOPENHAUER, ARTHUR (1788–1860), German philosopher who was an archrival of G. W. F. Hegel and who considered himself Immanuel Kant's only true heir in philosophy. Schopenhauer's aesthetics has arguably been more widely influential than that of any other philosopher of the past two centuries. Not only have subsequent philosophers, notably Friedrich Nietzsche, Henri Bergson, Ludwig Wittgenstein, and Susanne Knauth Langer, been much affected by his vision of the place and power of art, but a wide array of writers, composers, and intellectuals have testified, either explicitly or in their own works, to the power of that vision and of the metaphysics in which it is embedded: Richard Wagner, Gustav Mahler, Stendhal, Leo Tolstoy, Rainer Maria Rilke, Thomas Mann, Sigmund Freud, Marcel Proust, Thomas Hardy, Joseph Conrad. It would be fair to say that Schopenhauer's aesthetics has been, in the twentieth century, the artist's favored philosophy of art.

One cannot understand Schopenhauer's aesthetics without some understanding of Schopenhauer's metaphysics, and it is impossible to understand Schopenhauer's metaphysics without at least a passing grasp of the metaphysics of Kant, Schopenhauer's great predecessor and chief mentor among philosophers. Fortunately, however, it is possible to understand Schopenhauer's aesthetics without understanding Kant's aesthetics—though here too, naturally, influences and similarities can be noted. Thus, for the purposes of this essay, we can make do with thumbnail sketches of Kant's and Schopenhauer's metaphysics, and then proceed to the main topic, Schopenhauer's aesthetics.

The Metaphysical Background. The central notion in Kant's philosophy, the philosophy of transcendental idealism, is that the empirical world, the world known in perception, is in significant part a product of the mind's active structuring of the raw data of experience. This structuring is in terms of the forms of sensory intuition, namely, space and time, and the categories of the understanding, such as substance, causality, and relation. This structuring, furthermore, has a necessary or a priori status; without it, coherent experience of an objective world would not be possible, nor would knowledge of the sort represented by arithmetic, geometry, and pure physics. Hence, the world as it is known to us cannot, in virtue of such extensive and ineluctable structuring by the knowing mind, be identified with the world as it is in itself. The former has features that, because they are contributed by our very mode of knowing, cannot be features of the latter. The world as it is in itself must thus be granted—at least negatively, as a limiting condition of the world of experience—while evidently remaining beyond the possibility of being known as such. The known, or phenomenal, world is not all there is to reality: there is an unknowable, noumenal world, in some way underlying the appearances constituting the phenomenal one, and in unfathomable correspondence with it.

Schopenhauer takes over Kant's transcendental idealism wholesale, but with certain simplifications. Although he accepts space and time as primary modes of perceptual structuring, Schopenhauer reduces Kant's twelve categories of the understanding to one, causality, and regards space, time, and causality as in fact all forms of the Principle of Sufficient Reason, that everything must have a reason or ground for existing in just the way it does, which applies to all appearances or representations. The Principle of Sufficient Reason is valid only for the world of phenomena, including human action, and has no application beyond it. As we shall see, Schopenhauer ultimately entertains a notion of knowing "outside of" the Principle of Sufficient Reason, a knowing that finds its clearest exemplification in art, but this remains confined to the phenomenal realm, because still participating in and thus affected by the fundamental condition of knowledge in general, namely, the distinction of subject and object, or knower and known. For Schopenhauer, "subject" and "object" are correlative terms: all objects are inherently objects for a subject, and all subjects are inherently subjects cognizing objects; moreover, the characters of subjects and objects so correlated are always themselves importantly parallel.

Schopenhauer refers to space, time, and causality collectively as the *principium individuationis*. The existence of a plurality of distinct individuals and the existence of a framework of spatial, temporal, and causal relations are, for Schopenhauer, inseparable. But because space, time, and causality are aspects of the human way of knowing, individuality and plurality are themselves artifacts of that way of knowing, and cannot bear on the world as it is in itself. Noumenal reality must be nonplural, or nondivided, in nature. But can anything more be said, in a more positive vein, about that reality?

This is where the most distinctive part of Schopenhauer's metaphysics emerges. Although Schopenhauer, as a Kantian, holds throughout that the in-itself can, in the nature of things, never be known as such, there are still experiences available at the phenomenal level that give some insight into the nature of noumenal reality, and that ground a certain kind of extrapolation to its character. The key to this knowledge, albeit relative, of the thing-in-itself, of the inner nature of the world, is one's own person, and more particularly, one's own body. As Schopenhauer puts it, "we ourselves are the thing-in-itself" (1958, vol. 2, p. 195).

All other objects one knows only from the outside, as items in space and time enmeshed in a web of causes and effects. One's own body, on the other hand, is known also from within, introspectively and noninferentially. The purposeful movements of this body, observable to all externally, are known at the same time by the agent, internally, as acts of will. My body and my will are one: what manifests itself outwardly as matter moving through space manifests itself inwardly as agency or volition. What is more—and this is the crucial step in Schopenhauer's metaphysical argument—in knowing my body from the inside, I am knowing it in a way that gives some indication (the most it is possible for me to have, from this side of the phenomenal fence) of what it is like in and of itself, because certain of the forms of structuring that operate to generate phenomenal appearances are absent. In particular, the appearance of bodily action from within is freed of the filter of space, and, to some extent, causality, even though such an appearance is still in time, that is, apprehensible only successively, and still reflects, as an appearance, the essential division of knower and known.

Thus, Schopenhauer proclaims, my entire inner nature is willing—desiring, striving, urging—and all varieties of affect and emotion, pleasure and pain, that conduce to or inhibit action. Furthermore, one must take this as the best indication one has been vouchsafed as to the noumenal character of one's self: since when the distorting forms of phenomenal appearance are partially removed, the in-itself reveals itself as essentially conative, we can only assume that were they to be all removed, the in-itself would display a character somehow further along in that direction. (Schopenhauer is careful to caution, though, that we can have no assurance that this would be so; what the world is in itself absolutely, apart from all knowing, remains for him, as for Kant, unknowable.) Finally, by a second extrapolation, relying in part on the previously established nonplurality of noumenal reality, Schopenhauer draws the conclusion that the inner nature or noumenal character of everything is, again, to our best approximation, on the order of will as well. "If all other phenomena could be known by us just as immediately and intimately [as our own actions], we should be obliged to regard them precisely as that which the will is in us" (ibid., p. 197). All natural phenomena, including physical forces, are to be understood as forms of the sort of willing or agency with which we are familiar in our own cases, and the phenomenal world as a whole as the manifestation of a single, undifferentiated, so to speak cosmic, Will. In fact, and serving as a kind of empirical confirmation of this metaphysical deduction, the whole of nature, organic and inorganic, according to Schopenhauer, shows itself when suitably viewed as nothing other than a theater in which the universal will manifests itself in innumerable ways, and in the playing out of which conflict, frustration, and suffering are ubiquitous and inevitable.

This brings us, naturally, to Schopenhauer's famous pessimism. Human nature is at its core essentially striving or desire. But desire is a state of lack—of not having—and is thus an inherently unpleasant and disagreeable condition. Furthermore, the needs and wants of a given individual are generally both internally in conflict and externally in conflict with those of others; thus, as might be expected, the unclouded satisfaction of desire only infrequently occurs. Finally, such satisfaction as occurs is a very minor good, for three reasons. First, it has an entirely negative character, being just the pleasure of momentary cessation of desiring. Second, any desire actually fulfilled, and so extinguished, is as a rule quickly replaced by a multitude of others, whose noisy demands soon drown out the sensation of relief just noted. Third, in the odd event that new desires do not immediately surge up to take the place of those that have been quelled, what one has is nothing more than a state of perfect boredom or ennui, no more pleasant than the more usual state of constant unfulfilledness. It should be borne in mind that the foregoing diagnosis, which might seem to be based simply on a somewhat jaundiced observation of human psychology, together with some conceptual analysis, is, for Schopenhauer, undergirded by the metaphysical conviction that persons, and indeed the whole of existence, have willing as their essential and thus inescapable nature. Thus, insofar as one remains anchored in willing as a spatiotemporally bound individual—a bundle of strivings and cravings—suffering is virtually guaranteed.

Schopenhauer's Aesthetics. There is, however, a means of temporary escape from this sorry condition. It is afforded by aesthetic experience. Aesthetic experience, unlike ordinary perception, is focused not on material particulars in space and time, but on the perceivable essences or universals that such particulars embody, and that Schopenhauer, following Plato, calls Ideas. In the course of focusing on such objects, the perceiver is in effect transmuted: spatiotemporally rooted, practically oriented individuality gives

way, and what Schopenhauer calls the "pure subject of knowing," the same in everyone, takes its place. In aesthetic experience, one knows the world independently of the Principle of Sufficient Reason, grasping not the "why" or "how" of things, but only the "what": the knowledge faculty, ordinarily the servant of the will, becomes merely the mirrorer of Ideas, which are not "interesting" to the individual in which this faculty resides.

There are thus two sides to aesthetic experience, an objective and a subjective. On the objective side, there are the Ideas embodied in concrete particulars, on which attention now rests, and whose natures are grasped in contemplation; the aesthetic experience is thus centrally a cognitive one. On the subjective side, there is the transformation of the perceiver from an interested bundle of willing, concerned with objects only insofar as they are related, spatiotemporally and causally, to the satisfaction of needs and desires, into a disinterested beholder of Ideas, with which individual willing can have nothing to do. The disengagement of the subject's will and the shift in focus from one sort of object to another are two sides of the same coin; as noted earlier, subject and object for Schopenhauer are always correlated.

Schopenhauer thinks of the Ideas as grades of objectification of will, or thing-in-itself, on the phenomenal level. Ideas are intermediary between the nonplural will and the plurality of spatiotemporal individuals, but an Idea is still a representation for a subject, and thus not a thing-in-itself. Ideas are the most direct of the will's objectifications, or manifestations for a knowing mind, logically prior to the plurality of individuals that Schopenhauer conceived as in effect arising from the refraction of the Ideas through the lenses of space, time, and causality. The Ideas are something like the fundamental kinds of the phenomenal world, or the essences of them. There are Ideas corresponding to the species of living things, the varieties of natural forces, and the innumerable individual human characters, conceived of by Schopenhauer as virtually each a species unto itself. Unlike abstract concepts, however, Ideas are intuitively apprehensible; they are grasped in perception, and not through reason or language. (But how the Ideas of living things, say, can be both perceptually graspable, and yet entirely nonspatial, is not something for which Schopenhauer ever gives a satisfying explanation.)

The artist or man of genius, according to Schopenhauer, is one who is particularly gifted in two respects. First, through an excess of intellect beyond what is required for the practical purposes of daily living, the artist is enabled to perceive the Ideas in things more readily, more widely, and more sustainedly than the ordinary man, who as a rule has just enough understanding to grasp things in their spatiotemporal-causal, and thus will-relevant, relationship to him. "Whereas to the ordinary man his faculty of knowledge is a lamp that lights his path, to the man of genius it is the sun that reveals the world" (1958, vol. 1, p. 188). Second, the artist has the ability to embody this apprehension of Ideas in an artwork, a perceivable object in which the Idea has been made more vivid, more striking, more easily discerned than it was in nature, and so capable of triggering in the ordinary perceiver the sort of will-less contemplation that the artist had before nature unassisted. Yet, Schopenhauer stresses that the "power of recognizing in things their Ideas, of divesting themselves for a moment of their personality . . . must be present in all men in a lesser and different degree, as otherwise they would be just as incapable of enjoying works of art as of producing them" (ibid., p. 194). Schopenhauer can be viewed as taking up Plotinus's response to Plato's notorious charge against art of merely copying the ontologically already inferior, by stressing that the artist embodies in his work not the mundane, imperfect, and atypical object—even when this serves as model or ostensible subject—but rather its Idea or essence, and in such fashion that others are enabled to experience the sort of transcendence of self in viewing it that the artist achieved unaided in his interaction with the world.

So far, this essay has highlighted the cognitive dimension of aesthetic awareness more than the hedonic, but Schopenhauer's conception certainly includes the latter. The pleasure of aesthetic experience on his account would seem to be twofold. One part, that most stressed by him, is purely negative: temporary relief from the pain of constant striving, through transcendence of the standpoint of the individual willer. But a second part, less stressed though no less important, is of more positive character, and connects the hedonic aspect with the cognitive: satisfaction in contemplation of the given Idea and in the insight thus afforded into the timeless manifestations of Will. In effect, this is a delight in knowing, such as Aristotle and Kant, in different ways, posit as well. The negative pleasure of relief from the cycle of want and desire is provided equally, it seems, by any object offering an Idea for will-less contemplation; the positive pleasure from knowledge of an Idea, though, rather varies with the significance of the Idea involved.

Appreciation of beauty in nature and appreciation of beauty in art are both founded in contemplation of Ideas. In the one case, Ideas, or visible essences of willing, are simply strikingly evident in the world itself, in its unmodified state; in the other case, Ideas grasped in the world through the extraordinary perceptions of genius are embodied in a created object—the distilled experience of the genius—so as to be available to those of only modest powers of perception. At one point, Schopenhauer remarks that "everything is beautiful." What he means is that because everything embodies Ideas, if only those of the simplest sort, everything can in principle be made the object of disinterested contemplation. But, on the other hand, as he also remarks, "some things are more beautiful than others." This is because, in virtue of their forms, whether natural or human-made, or in virtue of the value of the Ideas they offer to contemplation,

objects will differ in the readiness with which they prompt such contemplation and in the worth of the contemplation they so prompt. Schopenhauer, with Kant, is thus one of the important sources of the idea of the aesthetic attitude as disinterested attention that can theoretically be brought to bear on anything, whatever its nature or degree of fashioning, thus potentially "aestheticizing" the world. Schopenhauer's emphasis on the nonspatiotemporal Idea rather than the concrete particular as the object of aesthetic attention might also be seen as cousin to Kant's notion of the disinterestedness of aesthetic judgment as rooted in the disconnectedness from "real existence" of the object so judged.

Schopenhauer, like Kant, distinguishes the sublime from the beautiful, and the account he offers is more convincing than Kant's. The difference between beauty and sublimity for Schopenhauer resides in the differing relation of the Ideas embodied to the human will, and a concomitant difference in the mode of engagement with the object that embodies them. "What distinguishes the feeling of the sublime from that of the beautiful is that, with the beautiful, pure knowledge has gained the upper hand without a struggle" (ibid., p. 202). In the case of the beautiful, the Ideas presented by an object are either agreeable or else neutral with respect to human nature, thus enabling the shift from interested perception to pure contemplation to occur passively, with a purely pleasurable upshot. In the case of the sublime, the Ideas presented by an object are inimical or threatening to the human mode of being, and so a shift to contemplation of them occurs only with the active participation of the subject, in a partly willful manner, resulting in pleasure with a painful undercurrent. Contemplation in the case of the sublime requires a forcible disengagement of the will, consciously and effortfully maintained, a free exaltation beyond the relations of the object recognized as unfavorable to human existence. The subject experiencing the sublime focuses on the fearful aspect of the object, while at the same time inhibiting the practical responses that the will would ordinarily have toward such hostile forces. Such a subject is aware of the antagonistic relationship of the object—for example, a maelstrom or thunderstorm—to human existence generally, but suspends, through an effort of will, the sense of threat to his personal well-being. The reward is the peculiarly mixed exhilaration known as the sublime.

Schopenhauer provides a categorization of the different arts, according to the grade of Ideas embodied and the quality of cognition thus afforded. On this scheme, the arts run from the lowest, architecture (whose objects manifest primarily the simple Ideas of gravity and rigidity), through landscape painting, animal painting, sculpture, historical painting (whose objects manifest, respectively, Ideas of vegetal nature, animal life, human body, and human character), to the highest, tragedy, for Schopenhauer a species of dramatic poetry. Tragedy deals with the conflict of human wills at the highest level, epitomizing the inevitability of suffering, the futility of aspiration, and the inexorability of fate, and thus ultimately teaching—what Schopenhauer endorses in his ethics—resignation and denial of the will.

The only art with no place in this scheme is music, and yet, for Schopenhauer, it is perhaps the greatest art of all. It lacks a place in that scheme because, as Schopenhauer was well aware, being nonrepresentational, it presents for contemplation no Ideas, no perceivable objectifications of willing, and thus seemingly provides no occasion for the transformation of the individual into a momentarily will-less pure subject of knowledge.

Two signs, for Schopenhauer, that music has an especially intimate relation with the deep nature of things are, first, that its effect on us is so profound, and second, that it is immediately understood by all. Thus, music does not copy or present Ideas, concludes Schopenhauer, but rather Will itself. Music, in all its forms, is willing made audible, in all its inner variety. Music and the phenomenal world are in fact parallel—complete, though different, expressions of the nature of Will. Confirmation of this is the fact that structural similarities between the two abound, and Schopenhauer is quite resourceful in suggesting analogies between aspects of the natural world and such musical features as melody, bass, fixed-scale positions, major and minor modes, cadences, modulations, and the impossibility of equal temperament.

There may appear to be a difficulty in the thesis that music is a complete alternate expression of Will, namely, that of music's itself being phenomenal, that is, bunches of sounds or sound waves. What this suggests is that it is music as repeatable pattern or succession, rather than as concrete event, that is meant here, or alternatively, sticking with music as concrete sonic phenomenon, that such a phenomenon is to be regarded as a microcosm of Will, in contrast with the phenomenal world as a whole, inclusive of music, taken as a macrocosm of Will.

Whether or not Schopenhauer's grounds for postulating this parallelism between music and world are fully adequate, there is a more pressing problem for his philosophy of music, one that might be labeled the "paradox of music's appeal." Music confronts a listener most directly with the awful inner nature of the world, being in effect a direct copy of the cosmic Will, the source of universal suffering, while at the same time offering no Ideas with which to engage objective contemplation and thus afford the subject momentary relief from willing. How, then, can music be even tolerable to us, much less immensely appealing? How can music gratify us, if what it centrally offers is the unfiltered spectacle of the root of all evil?

Schopenhauer provides a number of hints as to how this paradox might be resolved, and others can be offered on his behalf. First, although music by hypothesis confronts one directly with willing, the bane of existence, in a pure form, it is will-in-general, rather than some particular manifestation

of willing, that thus serves to divert attention from one's own situation and its incessant demands; contemplation of the universal will thus puts one's individual will in abeyance. Even though, in auditing music, the subject is not presented with any Ideas, disengaging practical concern in virtue of their utter unrelatedness to the subject in spatiotemporal terms, there supervenes a similar attitude of effectively selfless absorption in an image—that of Will itself—that has nothing to do with the phenomenally situated self and its materially tethered needs and desires. Second, music is still a representation of willing—even of the most immediate sort—rather than willing itself, and is furthermore divested of the particulars, spatial and causal, that characterize any real instance of willing; thus, emotions, even violent ones, may be reflected in musical flow, but being stripped of their concrete motivations and targets, they are not found personally distressing. Third, there is cognitive satisfaction in knowing will more completely by confronting it in its most transparent manifestation, that of music. Fourth, there is in contemplating music a kind of elation in grasping one's ultimate identity with and nonseparateness from the world, if in fact everything is at bottom the same blind will or life energy. Finally, it can be suggested that music models the vicissitudes of willing in ways that, however misleadingly, give impressions from time to time of purposefulness, rightness, or closure, which thus provide real if transient satisfactions, offsetting the distress that the naked image of Will might induce.

Schopenhauer's general view of the arts other than music as vehicles for contemplation of Ideas, affording temporary release from willful strife, is certainly not above criticism. First, much art seems very much concerned with unique particulars, with getting us to relish distinctive features of the concretely real, rather than allowing us to break free of such particularity. Second, much art appears designed to engage, rather than detach, our passionate or willing natures, even if still preserving some distance between art and life. Third, much art appears aimed at an active consumer, rather than one in whom the will is to be passively neutralized, through the presentation of objects supremely uninteresting to it, that is, ones that can only be contemplated. Finally, much art seems capable of providing a portion of positive, outgoing, and unadulterated pleasure much greater than that which Schopenhauer's view is able to accommodate, with its emphasis on the negative, crabbed pleasure of relief, however seconded by satisfactions of a cognitive sort. Underlying this, of course, is Schopenhauer's metaphysically driven overestimation of the degree to which people are indeed the suffering slaves of their willing natures, awash in a sea of dissatisfactions broken up only by islands of boredom.

Some of the ideas in Schopenhauer's aesthetics that are of lasting importance, ideas largely detachable from their metaphysical moorings, are the following: aesthetic attention as in principle capable of being brought to anything; art as a means of transcending the self and overcoming the narrow bounds of individuality; art's reward as lying partly in the cognitive insight it affords into the nature of things; the artist's essential power, that of heightened perception, as continuous with that of appreciators of art; an art form's value as bearing a strong relation to its range of concerns or subject matter; and music as fundamentally different from, and more immediately affecting than, the other arts.

[*See also* Disinterestedness; Kant; Music, *historical overview article; and* Nietzsche, *article on* Nietzsche, Schopenhauer, and Disinterestedness.]

BIBLIOGRAPHY

Works by Schopenhauer

Parerga and Paralipomena. 2 vols. Translated by E. F. J. Payne. Oxford, 1974.
The Fourfold Root of the Principle of Sufficient Reason. Translated by E. F. J. Payne. La Salle, Ill., 1974.
The World as Will and Representation. 2 vols. Translated by E. F. J. Payne. Indian Hills, Colo., 1958; reprint, New York, 1969.

Other Sources

Alperson, Philip. "Schopenhauer and Musical Revelation." *Journal of Aesthetics and Art Criticism* 40.2 (Winter 1981): 155–166.
Budd, Malcolm. *Music and the Emotions.* London and Boston, 1986. See chap. 5.
Diffey, T. J. "Schopenhauer's Account of Aesthetic Experience." *British Journal of Aesthetics* 30.2 (April 1990): 132–142.
Hamlyn, D. W. *Schopenhauer.* London and Boston, 1980.
Jacquette, Dale, ed. *Schopenhauer, Philosophy, and the Arts.* Cambridge and New York, 1995.
Janaway, Christopher. *Self and World in Schopenhauer's Philosophy.* Oxford, 1989.
Janaway, Christopher, ed. *The Cambridge Companion to Schopenhauer.* Cambridge and New York, forthcoming.
Knox, Israel. "Schopenhauer's Aesthetic Theory." In *Schopenhauer: His Philosophical Achievement,* edited by Michael Fox, pp. 132–146. Brighton, 1980.
Krukowski, Lucian. *Aesthetic Legacies.* Philadelphia, 1992. See chap. 3.
Magee, Bryan. *The Philosophy of Schopenhauer.* Oxford, 1983.
Young, Julian. *Willing and Unwilling: A Study in the Philosophy of Arthur Schopenhauer.* Dordrecht and Boston, 1987.

JERROLD LEVINSON

SCIENCE AND AESTHETICS. [*To treat the relationship between science and aesthetics, this entry comprises two essays:*

Conceptual and Historical Overview
Contemporary Thought

The first essay is an overview of the aesthetics in and of science, especially during two major transformations of science in the seventeenth and twentieth centuries. The second essay is a critique of common misconceptions about science and art that have, it is argued, unduly influenced aesthetics in ways that this critique may help to reverse. For related discussion, see Bachelard; Color; Mathematics and Aesthetics; Sensibilité; *and* Synaesthesia.]

Conceptual and Historical Overview

From Johannes Kepler to Albert Einstein and beyond, the aesthetics of science was governed by mathematical aesthetics. "A physical law must possess mathematical beauty," Paul Dirac famously said in 1956. The statement itself defines his views and practice of physics from the 1930s onward. By that time, both the question of the relationships between mathematical objects, beautiful or not, and physical law (or among mathematics, physics, and nature in general) and the question of the ontological and epistemological status of mathematical objects themselves acquired extraordinary complexity. Several radical developments in mathematics and science (in particular quantum physics, to which Dirac made an extraordinary contribution), philosophy, and the arts were responsible for transforming thinking concerning all these issues. By so doing, they also introduced new dimensions and complexities into the mathematical aesthetics of science, or into the aesthetics of mathematics itself, although one can trace some of these complexities (aesthetic or epistemological) to much earlier events and, in a certain sense, to the known origins of mathematics and science, or philosophy. As a result, the very concept of mathematical beauty has become increasingly ambiguous and problematic. The role of aesthetic considerations, however, especially those of a mathematical nature, both in the practice of science itself and in our understanding of this practice, has been extraordinary throughout Western intellectual history.

It is true, of course, that in mathematics and science, consistency and rigor, agreement with experimental data, and other (as they might be called) logico-epistemological factors are ultimately more significant than and take priority over aesthetic considerations, to the point (it has been argued) of making the latter irrelevant. This last claim requires much qualification, even if one leaves aside the complexity of the constitution of such nonaesthetic factors (including whether, or to what degree, they are independent from aesthetics), which have been the subject of powerful critical scrutiny. At the very least, aesthetic considerations have always played a major role in establishing directions for the development of mathematics and science—local (selecting one venue or another in approaching a given problem) or global (that of a given field or even discipline as a whole). One of the main reasons for this role is their prominence in the work of key scientists, who have given a primary or, sometimes (as in the case of Dirac), even *the* primary significance to the aesthetic dimensions of their work or their view of mathematics and science, or of nature itself. It may be that this aesthetic ideology—that is, the significance and implications (scientific, philosophical, or political) of certain aesthetic principles and ideas—defines the work of a small minority of major practitioners, such as Kepler, Einstein, and Dirac. Their aesthetic choices, however, and their aesthetic ideology as a whole often shaped the direction of modern mathematics and science at key points and crossroads of their development, and limited (sometimes severely) other venues of mathematical and scientific pursuit.

As a—or even *the*—paradigmatic example of this ideology of mathematical aesthetics, one might consider Kepler's famous "longing for harmonies" and "noble proportions," and his grand vision of the "harmony of the world." Following the Pythagoreans, Kepler's theory of planetary motion connects arithmetic and geometric harmonies—the harmony of numbers and of figures. The connections established by Kepler are elegant and beautiful by most classical criteria but complex in structure, especially in view of the elliptical (rather than circular) character and, one might say, the elliptical harmony of planetary motion around the sun, discovered by Kepler. Kepler "saved" the principle of harmony by introducing a more complex harmony into nature, or claiming this harmony for nature, which may well have been his greatest achievement. Ever since Kepler, this strategy has defined much of the history of mathematics and science, and of their aesthetics, as part of the aesthetic ideology of modern science. More generally, in all of their aspects, Kepler's aesthetics and aesthetic ideology have been decisive for developing modern mathematics, physics, and astronomy, no less—and sometimes more—than the scientific or explanatory aspects of his discoveries. As (along with astronomy) the earliest scientific discipline in the modern sense, mathematics was a natural prototype for Kepler's, and then post-Keplerian, science. This science, as Martin Heidegger argues, is not only mathematical, but is also experimental because it is mathematical, in view of the connections it establishes between measurement and its representation of natural objects by means of mathematical objects, a kind of reduction of natural objects to mathematical objects. Galileo Galilei's work is, arguably, most crucial in this respect, although his aesthetics and his understanding of the project of science were, ideologically, quite different from both Kepler's and Isaac Newton's. In spite of such differences between different projects and views of science (or indeed aesthetics), however, the aesthetics of science has been powerfully shaped by this mathematico-experimental determination of modern science and by reflecting and interconnecting the aesthetics of mathematics and the aesthetics of experimentation.

Kepler both mathematized and mathematically aestheticized Tycho Brahe's experimental data, and by so doing he established a paradigmatic model of modern mathematical science. Both his science and its aesthetics are Pythagorean in the sense that a mathematical "harmony" also "shapes" the data, unless one believes that reality (material or spiritual) already possesses this harmony. From the modern perspective, there may not be any data that would be "unshaped"—that is, not conditioned by theoretical, cultural, political, and other forces acting within situations where these data are generated. In any given situation, this shaping may also be aesthetic to one degree or another. Brahe's data, too, possessed a complex organization, some of which may be seen as aesthetic, and Kepler's own reorganization and re-aestheticization of these data is a complex issue. A full mathematization of planetary motion in the sense of modern physics—that of mathematical equations defining physical laws—came essentially with Newton (and took its modern form even later, with Joseph-Louis Lagrange and Sir William Rowan Hamilton), although in terms of aesthetics Kepler's contribution has been the greatest since Pythagoras. Newtonian and post-Newtonian physics also extended the mathematical aesthetics of science by complementing Kepler's geometric harmonies with those of algebra and the emerging calculus, following the mathematics of René Descartes (whose analytic geometry connected algebra and geometry) and Pierre de Fermat. Copernican and Ptolemaic systems had their own harmonies, mathematical and other. The choice between them in Kepler's (or Galileo's) case had complex aesthetic (or, of course, scientific, theological, philosophical, and political) determinations. As indicated earlier, however, Kepler's theory both enabled a better fit and introduced the aesthetics of complex harmonies into science, which finds its contemporary manifestations in the Riemannian geometry of Einstein's relativity or in the broken symmetries of quantum physics.

In general, although it entails a certain—beautiful—"simplicity," mathematical beauty should not be identified with mathematical simplicity. As Dirac argued, Einstein's theory of gravity (general relativity), while more complex than Newton's, is also more beautiful. First, the relationship to the experimental evidence, which classical physics can no longer account for, affects aesthetic considerations. Second, from Pythagoras and Plato onward, the mathematical harmony reflects the relationships—or a kind of harmony—of complexity (for example, the complexity of the parts) and simplicity (for example, that of connecting the parts into the whole). The same would refer to most economy principles, such as Occam's razor, which reflect a similar complexity—or, again, economy—of the relationships between parsimony and excess. These considerations apply at both levels—that of specific configurations and that of broader theoretical matrices or fields. Most grand programs in mathematics, physics, and other sciences are based on this double economy relating simplicity and complexity. The programs of unification of fundamental forces in modern physics offer arguably the best-known example in this respect. The search for mathematically and otherwise harmonious theories, and in particular unifying and unified theories, has shaped much of modern science. The concept of the One that would unify the diversity of immense and perhaps infinite richness (as in Gottfried Wilhelm Leibniz and Georg Wilhelm Friedrich Hegel), or an undifferentiated One lurking behind the diversities (as in Plotinus), has long governed much of the aesthetics of mathematics and science. Obviously, the significance of these concepts is much broader. They have also exerted immense philosophical, ideological, and political force throughout their history in mathematics and science. These nonaesthetic dimensions of their functioning in mathematics and science have powerfully affected and, reciprocally, have been affected by the aesthetic ones. This reciprocity is a manifestation of a more general fact that, whatever form it might take, the aesthetics of mathematics and science inevitably acquires a complex constitution that requires and has received, especially in recent years, an equally complex critical analysis—scientific, philosophical, historical, political, and, of course, aesthetic.

Much of the preceding discussion would apply to the aesthetics of nonmathematical science. Without considering the latter separately, several key examples of scientific discoveries and their aesthetics may be offered here in order, first, to illustrate key points and, second, to show the complexity of the relationships between mathematical and nonmathematical science and their respective aesthetics.

Dmitri Ivanovich Mendeleev's periodical table of the elements—a sort of Kepler's system of chemistry—is one of the greatest examples of scientific classification. The harmonies of Mendeleev's arrangement may or may not be seen as mathematical, although it would be hard to deny their mathematical dimensions. Obviously, chemistry in general has its own aesthetics, mathematical and other—the aesthetics of molecular arrangements, chemical equations, experiments, and so forth. As it happens, Mendeleev's table reflects the underlying mathematical harmony of atomic structures, which, once discovered (by Niels Bohr), added to both its scientific and its aesthetic significance.

Spectrography offers an analogous example. It never quite found its Mendeleyev's table, although the so-called Balmer's formulas and Rydberg's constant for the hydrogen spectrum played a somewhat similar role on a limited scale. It is only with Bohr's 1913 theory of atomic structure, in the wake of Max Planck's and Einstein's discoveries concerning the quantum nature of radiation, that spectra received their Mendeleev's system. It was, of course, the same system that explained the order that Mendeleev discovered. Jointly, these discoveries produced an extraordinary example of a complex harmony in nature and implied a still more complex one, which was eventually discovered by the (new) quantum mechanics of Werner Heisenberg and Erwin Schrödinger and subsequent developments in quantum physics, and which enabled a full theoretical understanding of atomic spectra. Bohr's explanation of Balmer's formulas and Rydberg's constant have been compared to Kepler's laws and the harmony of the world they represented, or,

again, to Pythagoras. The key elements of spectrographic analysis, based on the so-called Fourier analysis, are, fundamentally, the same, or rather offer a rigorous mathematical rendition of the numerical principles of musical harmony discovered by Pythagoras. Analogous harmonies and harmonics describe both musical chords and the music of the world, cosmic or atomic—the mathematical-aesthetic unity or, again, harmony of the world, which Bohr both enriched and undermined by his discoveries and his philosophy of science. By so doing, Bohr made major contributions to both old and new quantum theory, and he may be seen as the central figure who moved from Keplerian to more radical epistemology and aesthetics, combining old and new harmonies and dissonances.

In crystallography, overtly the most aesthetic of scientific disciplines, the geometric structure and symmetry of crystals is mathematically described by means of group theory, the most general mathematical embodiment of the principle of symmetry. Here, too, the underlying (micro)physics responsible for the (macro)harmony of crystals proved to be atomic and, ultimately, quantum (micro)physics, defined by its own complex symmetries. Louis Pasteur's work on the polarization of crystals would be another example of the discovery of the broken symmetry in nature. "L'univers est dissymétrique," Pasteur proclaimed. The handedness of the so-called weak interactions and other broken symmetries of quantum physics tell us that Pasteur might have been more right than he thought, although a better maxim might be: the universe is both symmetrical and asymmetrical.

Finally, in biology, Charles Darwin's theory of evolution offers an example of what might be called the dynamic (temporal or historical) organization of the data it considers. The complex aesthetic planes of Darwin's theory and of subsequent biology and genetics emerge at many levels—in their classification, structures, experiments, and so forth. Preceding (and subsequent) investigations in botany, zoology, and other fields that were concerned with morphology and gestalt have shaped the history of aesthetics in biology and elsewhere. The nature of the processes responsible for the phenomena at issue in Darwin's theory have not yet emerged. The discovery of the genetic mechanisms responsible for evolutionary processes was a crucial step, which may be compared to Newton's more systematic rethinking of Kepler's laws. The explosion of biology and genetics in the twentieth century has established complex networks of connections between physics, chemistry, and biology, and various levels of mathematization of biological processes. The aesthetics in/of biology has been extended accordingly. At this point, however, only God knows how this mechanism really works, and, as in quantum physics, this God, contrary to Einstein's belief, appears to be playing dice. As a result, modern biology has significantly affected developments in the epistemology and aesthetics of science. It is quite clear already that its mathematization involved some among the most complex—structurally and aesthetically—areas of mathematics. Many key aspects of the systems involved conform to mathematics and the mathematical aesthetics of such theories as probability and statistics, the so-called dynamic system, and more recently chaos theory and complexity theory, and hence to the theories and aesthetics of the interaction of chaos and order. It may well be that modern biology will reveal as yet unheard-of harmonies and dissonances—scientific, philosophical, and aesthetic.

[*See also* Helmholtz.]

BIBLIOGRAPHY

Cartier, Pierre. "Kepler et la musique du monde." *La Recherche* 278.26 (1995).

Chandrasekhar, S. *Truth and Beauty: Aesthetics and Motivations in Science.* Chicago, 1987.

Curtin, Deane W., ed. *The Aesthetic Dimension of Science.* New York, 1982.

Dirac, Paul. "The Relation between Mathematics and Physics." *Proceedings of the Royal Society* (Edinburgh) 59 (1938–1939): 122–129.

Feynman, Richard. *The Character of Physical Law.* Cambridge, Mass., 1967.

Heisenberg, Werner. *Across the Frontiers.* Translated by Peter Heath. Reprint, Woodbridge, Conn., 1990.

Kragh, Helge. "The Principle of Mathematical Beauty." In *Dirac: A Scientific Biography.* Cambridge and New York, 1990.

Lyotard, Jean-François. *The Postmodern Condition: A Report on Knowledge.* Translated by Geoff Bennington and Brian Massumi. Minneapolis, 1984.

Poincaré, Henri. *Science and Method.* Translated by Francis Maitland. Reprint, New York, 1952.

Weyl, Hermann. *Symmetry.* Princeton, N.J., 1952.

Wigner, Eugene P. *Symmetries and Reflections: Scientific Essays.* Bloomington, Ind., 1967.

ARKADY PLOTNITSKY

Contemporary Thought

Pernicious stereotypes underwrite the opposition of art and science. Art, it is said, seeks beauty, science seeks truth; art induces pleasure, science discloses facts; unfettered inspiration makes for art, slavish adherence to methodological canons, for science; art is subjective, science objective. Such stereotypes consign art and science to hostile camps. In so doing, they misrepresent both. By dispelling such stereotypes, we gain a better understanding of the relations between the two disciplines.

Counterexamples are legion. Michelangelo Buonarroti's *Last Judgment,* Joseph Conrad's *Heart of Darkness,* and Gustav Mahler's Ninth Symphony are dark, disconcerting, even horrific works. They are not beautiful. But we do not and should not consider them defective on that account.

To preserve the stereotype, we could revise our assessments, exiling such works from the aesthetic realm for their lack of beauty. But as the list of exclusions lengthens, the plausibility of such a strategy wanes. Alternatively, we might contend that the beauty relevant to aesthetics is distinct from being pretty, attractive, pleasing to the senses or the sensibilities. Aesthetic beauty, so construed, would be compatible with ugliness, hideousness, and so on. We retain the term *beauty,* then, by leaching out its content. What remains is just a label for whatever makes for artistic excellence. That art seeks whatever makes for artistic excellence may be true, but it is hardly informative. It seems best, then, to retain our familiar notion of beauty and admit that beauty is not always art's objective.

Equally vulnerable is the contention that science single-mindedly seeks truth. Science is riddled with approximations, idealizations, and simplifying assumptions that make no pretense of being true. The ideal gas law, for example, is a fundamental principle of thermodynamics. It is not true. Nothing in the world displays the features the law ascribes to the ideal gas. To construe such an express untruth as true would, of course, be an error. We would misunderstand both the phenomenon and the science if we took the ideal gas law to state a truth. But untruths, *acknowledged as such,* are often vehicles of scientific understanding.

So is beauty. Concern for beauty explains the appeal of symmetry principles, and the aversion to ad hoc excrescences. Concern for truth does not. Theories incorporating symmetry principles are no more likely to be true than theories that exclude them, nor are theories that make ad hoc assumptions more likely to be false than theories that eschew them.

Sometimes art induces pleasure. Sometimes it does not. Its effect depends on the audience as well as the art. The orchestra continued to play while the *Titanic* went down. But regardless of its merits, the listeners probably did not enjoy the performance. That a besotted swain delights in his beloved's braying monotone is no evidence that she is a talented singer. Kitsch that pleases philistines displeases connoisseurs. Atonal music that pleases sophisticated audiences displeases the hoi polloi. Evidently not all pleasure or displeasure occasioned by works of art is a measure of aesthetic merit.

Perhaps a distinctive sort of pleasure—aesthetic pleasure—is a measure of aesthetic merit. Because only people with refined sensibilities have the capacity for such pleasure, the reactions of the masses are aesthetically irrelevant. The difficulty is that connoisseurs do not always agree. Nor do they always enjoy the works whose merits they acknowledge. Only a sadist would take pleasure in Francisco de Goya's *Disasters of War,* or Sophocles' *Oedipus Rex.* Even if the responses of suitably sensitive, suitably receptive audiences afford evidence of aesthetic merit, no single response functions as a merit monitor.

Science often discloses facts. But it need not do so. A cosmology that acceptably accounted for currently known facts would be counted a success, whether or not it disclosed any new ones. A science strives to produce a systematic, integrated understanding of diverse phenomena. Disclosure of particular facts is far from its central concern.

A science does not, in any case, accept an antecedent demarcation of what constitutes the facts it studies. It contrives a conceptual framework that fixes its facts. Chemistry organizes its domain in terms of discrete chemical elements. Until it has done so, there is no fact of the matter as to whether copper is lighter than zinc; for until the two are recognized as distinct sorts of substances, the issue of their respective weights does not arise.

Science, moreover, devises methods—not just for disclosing facts, but also for making approximations, calculations, models, and so on. A powerful method may constitute a greater scientific advance than any particular finding of fact it facilitates.

Art also discloses facts. In seventeenth-century Dutch still lifes, for example, the juxtaposition of opulent materials with decaying fruit and dying flowers reveals the Calvinist burghers' ambivalence about worldly success. Toni Morrison's *Beloved* spells out the enormity of the psychological price slaves had to pay in order to survive. Science has no monopoly on facts, then, nor has art a monopoly on pleasure.

The widespread conviction that scientific inquiry consists in mechanical application of prescribed methods cannot do justice to the conceptual and methodological innovation crucial to scientific progress. It cannot, for example, explain the development of the theory of relativity, which involved reconceptions of space, time, mass, and other physical magnitudes. Nor can it account for the ingenuity needed to apply even well-established methods and concepts in recalcitrant cases. Science, like art, is a creative enterprise.

And art, like science, is conditioned by constraints. Some are formal—the requirements on linear perspective or counterpoint or iambic pentameter, for example. Others derive from medium, method, motif, or style. A poem need not, of course, be seventeen syllables long. But unless it is, it is not haiku. Nor need a sample respect the requirement of variety of evidence. But unless it does, it is not statistically significant. Of course, science and art have resources for challenging, revising, even repudiating accepted constraints. Both are open to innovation. But to recognize this is not to deny that constraints—sometimes quite severe ones—frame the activities of artists and scientists alike.

Art and science deploy symbols of many kinds. One mode of symbolization operative in both is exemplification, whereby a symbol exhibits and refers to some of its own features. A Piet Mondrian painting, for example, exemplifies squareness. It not only contains squares, it refers to and focuses attention on the squares it contains. A positive litmus test exemplifies the presence of acid. Because litmus paper turns pink only when acid is present, its turning pink serves as a symbol that points up the presence of acid. By

highlighting particular features, an exemplar affords epistemic access to them. The features in question may be elusive. Elaborate contrivance is sometimes necessary to bring them to light. Thus, a complex experiment is mounted to exemplify subtle differences between closely related viruses; and intricate stage setting is devised to exemplify the differences between very similar moods—nostalgia and melancholy, for example. Exemplification, moreover, need not be literal. Constantin Brancusi's *Bird in Flight* metaphorically exemplifies soaring, and a computer simulation of the behavior of electrons at absolute zero metaphorically exemplifies the disappearance of resistance.

Fiction is a staple of art. That their protagonists do not exist is no criticism of *Faust,* or *Madame Bovary,* or *The Birth of Venus.* Perhaps surprisingly, fictions are common in science too. Thought experiments are among the most obvious examples. Even though no one ever rode on a light wave, Albert Einstein was able to elaborate implications of the theory of relativity by considering what someone riding on a light wave would see. Nor is the role of scientific thought experiments merely heuristic. Erwin Schrödinger's cat and the two-slit experiment are integral to quantum mechanics. The conviction that fiction is antithetical to serious science is false.

We have seen that science, like art, can be beautiful, creative, pleasurable, and that art, like science, can disclose facts, respect rigorous constraints, engage reason. Both make use of fictions, exemplars, and metaphors. Both advance understanding. Is there, then, no difference between science and art?

Such differences as there are derive from the sorts of symbols the disciplines favor; and their rationales for favoring the sorts of symbols they do stem from their cognitive values and priorities.

Science values repeatable results and intersubjective accord, for it is a collaborative enterprise in which independent investigators build on one another's findings. Science thus places a premium on being able to tell just what results it reaches. If every difference in a magnitude constituted a distinct finding, one could never tell that two samples were the same, for identical readings might obscure differences beyond the threshold of measurement. Science, then, has reason to partition its domain into discrete, disjoint alternatives, and set a lower bound on the precision of its computations. It restricts its parameters, regiments its units of measure, and counts its measurements accurate only up to a specifiable number of significant figures. Finer-grained differences are ignored. Far from being more precise than art, science sacrifices precision to achieve accord.

As far as possible, it eschews vagueness, ambiguity, and other forms of semantic indeterminacy on the same ground, for such symbols invite divergent interpretations. If disagreements in interpretation are irresolvable, science cannot safely build on its results.

Art's priorities are different. It values delicacy of discrimination more highly than accord and aspires to irreproducible results. It thus favors dense, replete symbols, where the finest differences in certain respects matter and where a symbol may symbolize along indefinitely many dimensions at once. In a scientific graph, for example, only the shape of the line and its distance from the axes are significant. In a drawing, not just the line's shape and position, but also its precise shade, thickness, and texture at every point may be significant, as may the color, texture, and weave of the paper, the contrast between figure and ground, and so on. What the graph symbolizes is readily determined. What the drawing symbolizes may be permanently in dispute.

There are, of course, differences within the arts. Symbols in the visual arts are syntactically dense. The finest differences in shape, color, position, and the like affect their identity. But *Middlemarch* is *Middlemarch* regardless of the typeface, ink, or paper on which it is printed. All that matters is spelling. Literary works, then, are syntactically differentiated, their symbols being constructed from the finite list of alternatives that an alphabet supplies. Such works are, however, semantically dense. A natural language has the resources for drawing the finest distinctions among items in its field of reference. Literature makes use of these resources. In a scientific study of, say, the responses of commuters to traffic delays, the choice between *grumble* and *grouse* would probably make no difference. In a literary work, it can carry enormous weight.

Literary symbols are, moreover, relatively replete. That Ernest Hemingway avoided polysyllabic prose is no accident. The austerity of his language reflects the austerity of the world his characters confront. Sentence structure, cadence, juxtapositions, omissions, literal and metaphoric resonances, both within and beyond a work, may be aesthetically significant. One paraphrases at one's peril. Although substituting *one-half gallon* for *two quarts* would be unobjectionable in a scientific context, in a literary context such a substitution is impermissible, for some significance may attach to the fact that the volume is characterized as twice another, or that the expression *two quarts* contains exactly two, equally stressed syllables, or that the letter *q* appears. Debate about which, and how many, of these features are significant and about what they signify may be endless.

Ambiguity, vagueness, and indeterminacy are aesthetic virtues. They foster multiple, often incompatible, interpretations of a single work. There is no hope of deciding once and for all whether Hamlet was genuinely mad. Nor should we want to. Much of the power of the work derives from the interplay of divergent interpretations.

Art's susceptibility to multiple interpretations is perhaps the source of the final stereotype—that art is subjective, science objective. But such susceptibility does not ordinarily make for subjectivity. An ambiguous term such as *bank* admits of different readings. But we cannot ordinarily choose to take it to refer to whatever we like—a flock of geese, for example. Nor can we simply opt for the accepted interpretation we prefer, regardless of context and operative presuppositions. In the context of an agreement to repay an auto loan, for example, we cannot elect to construe it as pertaining to the river's edge.

Interpretation of works of art is, of course, more difficult than interpretation of ordinary language. But in neither sort of interpretation is it the case that just anything goes. Under no acceptable interpretation is *Medea* a comedy of manners or Rembrandt van Rijn's *Sacrifice of Isaac* a joke.

Interpretation in the arts is subject to constraints. Because several sets of constraints may apply, and a given set of constraints may be multiply satisfiable, a given work can admit of several acceptable interpretations. Still, reasons can be adduced to support or undermine a proposed interpretation and consensus on its acceptability often is reached. Availability of constraints, support by reasons, and the prospect of consensus are hallmarks of objectivity. Granted, the constraints are debatable, the reasons less than conclusive, and the consensus far from assured. But these weaknesses are not peculiar to art. Science holds out the promise that physics will eventually settle on a unique interpretation of quantum mechanics, but cannot guarantee that the promise will be kept. Art is objective if science is.

[*See also* Goodman.]

BIBLIOGRAPHY

Einstein, Albert. *Relativity: The Special and the General Theory: A Popular Exposition.* Translated by Robert W. Lawson. Reprint, New York, 1961.

Elgin, Catherine Z. "Understanding: Art and Science." In *Philosophy and the Arts,* edited by Peter A. French, Theodore E. Uehling, Jr., and Howard Wettstein, pp. 196–208. Midwest Studies in Philosophy, vol. 16. Notre Dame, Ind., 1991.

Elgin, Catherine Z. "Relocating Aesthetics." *Revue Internationale de Philosophie* 46 (1993): 171–186.

Elgin, Catherine Z. *Considered Judgment.* Princeton, N.J., 1997.

Elgin, Catherine Z., ed. *The Philosophy of Nelson Goodman.* 4 vols. New York, 1997.

Goodman, Nelson. *Languages of Art: An Approach to a Theory of Symbols.* 2d ed. Indianapolis, 1976.

Goodman, Nelson. *Ways of Worldmaking.* Indianapolis, 1978.

Goodman, Nelson, and Catherine Z. Elgin. *Reconceptions in Philosophy and Other Arts and Sciences.* Indianapolis, 1988.

Gombrich, E. H. *Art and Illusion: A Study in the Psychology of Pictorial Representation* (1960). 2d rev. ed. Reprint, Princeton, N.J., 1969.

McAllister, James W. *Beauty and Revolution in Science.* Ithaca, N.Y., 1996.

Wollheim, Richard. *Painting as an Art.* Princeton, N.J., 1987.

van Fraassen, Bas, and Jill Sigman. "Interpretation in Science and in the Arts." In *Realism and Representation,* edited by George Levine, pp. 73–99. Madison, Wis., 1993.

CATHERINE Z. ELGIN

SCULPTURE. Attempts to establish a specific sculptural aesthetics have rarely been undertaken in the history of philosophical reflection on the visual arts. Fundamental issues such as the essence of visual arts, the ontological status of the work of art, aesthetic experience, or art as expression have mainly been explored with regard to the painted image, which was taken as *pars pro toto* for the visual arts. In fact, it has been widely held that there are no essential differences between the visual problems and values of painting and sculpture. From the late Renaissance until after the middle of the twentieth century, painting was regarded as the superior art practice on the assumption that art represents (that is, imitates, simulates, or even re-creates) reality, and that the painted image is most suited to fulfill this task and to carry transcendental meaning. The bias toward painting is also rooted in a dominant anthropocentric view of the world that is inextricably linked to the preference of a single viewpoint, and thus to the picture plane and a central perspective as respective modes of representation. The sculptural object, being a three-dimensional body with potentially an indefinite number of aspects, does not fit comfortably into this conception of the world.

Although numerous philosophical works deal with the specific forms, developments, and functions of sculpture and its technical peculiarities from antiquity to the present day, consistent theories of sculptural aesthetics are mostly of fairly recent origin. Historically, the generic debates from the eighteenth to the twentieth century played a crucial part in establishing modern sculpture as an aesthetic form and practice distinct from painting.

From Antiquity to the Nineteenth Century. Plato and Aristotle regarded mimetic representation of nature as the goal of art. According to Aristotle, beauty is an inherent law of nature and determined by order, symmetry, and definiteness (*Poetics*, 1078b). He distinguishes between an internal morphology (order and symmetry) and an external structure (definiteness) of beauty through which a work of art stands out from the accidental, arbitrary, incoherent, and conflicting features of the world. For him, size matters as an important aspect of definiteness:

> Beauty is a matter of size and order, and therefore impossible either . . . in a very minute creature, since our perception becomes indistinct as it approaches instantaneity; or . . . in a creature of vast size . . . as in that case, instead of the object being seen at once, the unity and wholeness of it is lost to the beholder.
> (Ibid., 1450b)

Rooted in Aristotle's definition of beauty as symmetry, order, and definiteness is an Occidental tradition that restricted the ideal of beauty to these categories, particularly in the Middle Ages. Yet, the understanding of beauty changed from an integrated "organic" unity to a "unity in variety" as manifest in Galen's summary of the canon of beauty: "Beauty does not consist in the elements, but in the harmonious proportion of the parts, the proportion of one finger to the other, of all fingers to the rest of the hand . . . of all parts to all others, as it is written in the canon of Poli-

clitus" (quoted in Eco, 1986, p. 29). Before Galen, Vitruvius, who in his treatise *De architectura* focused on the aesthetic structures of the plastic arts, defines harmony as "arising out of the details of the work itself; the correspondence of each given detail among the separate details to the form of the design as a whole" (ibid.). The relational, quantitative conception of beauty as either inherent in all things, or only in the human body, yet not as a specific quality of human artifice, explains why, on the whole, medieval thinkers were above all concerned with the internal conditions of beautiful things rather than their "edifice." Wholeness being achieved by "coherence" (that is, mathematical proportions) potentially pointed toward infiniteness rather than definiteness.

Concepts of physical beauty in the Renaissance, which dealt with an ideal canon of measured proportions, also took up an Aristotelian stance by generally emphasizing that beauty lies not only in the shape of an object but also in its intended function. Based on an analogy between nature and art, the work of art became equated with an organism in which every part plays its part within a whole, as put forward by Leon Battista Alberti, who defines perfect beauty as "a Harmony of all the Parts, in whatever Subject it appears, fitted together with such Proportion and Connection, that nothing could be added, diminished or altered, but for the Worse" (quoted in Beardsley, 1966, p. 125). Until the late Renaissance, considerations of sculptural form and practice had their place mainly in technology, and found articulation as rules in treatises, because sculpture was treated as a mechanical art, that is, a craft that relied on skill and manual labor, and fulfilled, above all, material and practical needs rather than intellectual and spiritual ones. The amount of physical labor involved in sculpture provides Leonardo da Vinci with a crucial argument for the "Paragone" at the beginning of his *Treatise on Painting,* which stimulated a dispute over the precedence of art among many Renaissance artists and thinkers. Sculpture, because it involves a great amount of physical effort, remains essentially a craft inferior to the liberal art of painting. In contrast, Benvenuto Cellini, along with Michelangelo Buonarotti and others, argues that this very aspect redounds to the privilege of sculpture, and that the skill and craftsmanship involved elevate the sculptor over the painter. To prove the latter point, Cellini brings up the multifaceted nature of sculpture whereby only a truly dedicated artist can achieve eight views of equal quality (Wittkower, 1991, p. 144).

When, during the Renaissance, sculpture became gradually emancipated from its existence as visual design bound to architecture as its matrix, interest began to shift toward aspects and modes of representation in the arts that were interrelated with changing ideals of beauty but still firmly grounded in a normative approach. Influenced by René Descartes's rationalism, thoughts on the arts in the seventeenth and early eighteenth centuries concentrated on establishing rules and systems, hierarchical canons of styles, and genres governed by the principle of art as imitation of beautiful nature.

Generic definitions of sculpture, which arose mainly in the second half of the eighteenth century and the early nineteenth century, took the classical Greek tradition as a paradigm. In the neoclassical spirit of his time, Johann Joachim Winckelmann revived the concept of the *beau ideal* based on an early sixteenth-century Italian scheme of *divinia proporzione*. In his *Geschichte der Kunst des Altertums,* published in 1764, Winckelmann demands for sculpture "noble simplicity and quiet grandeur." He justifies a strong predilection for immaculate white marble with the argument that "a body is all the more beautiful the whiter it is." A high degree of unity, firm contours, and simple proportions within the human figure are emphasized through the whiteness of the stone, thus sublimating beauty (Winckelmann, 1966, p. 148). This notion, based on the assumption that Greek sculpture originally existed in "pure" substance, remained unchallenged until well into the nineteenth century, despite mounting evidence undermining its very foundation, and a sculptural practice of the past (from antiquity to the Renaissance) that had indulged in color without hesitation. [*See* Winckelmann.] Saint Augustine, for instance, claims that the beauty of the body lies in a "harmony of its parts with a certain pleasing colour" (Eco, 1986, p. 28).

The controversial debate about whether color is an intrinsic property of sculpture sheds light on complex aesthetic inquiries into the question of the nature of truth in the work of art. Reservations against the use of color in sculpture reach back to antiquity. Although Plato, for instance, acknowledged the use of color in the sculptural practice of his time, he did not think of it as an essential criterion of beauty. His argument—that color above all serves an imitation of reality, that is, that color is potentially deceptive or mendacious—returns in the debate of the eighteenth and nineteenth centuries—in the writings of Denis Diderot and Johann Gottfried von Herder, for instance, who share a concern for the rules of art insofar as they are not mere external application but inscribed in the structure of the work. Their writing is symptomatic insofar as it signaled a general shift from an interest in a normative canon of forms to the effect the work of art has on the viewer. Both equate sculpture with truth on the basis of its materiality. Hegel, in positing that the aim of sculpture lies in the representation of "an abstract side of the human body," emphasizes: "The spirit which sculpture presents is spirit compact in itself, not variously splintered into the play of accidents and passions" (1985, p. 85). Color in sculpture could only mean detraction from the "real existence of the spirit" by bringing the object too close to the "singularity" and "particularity" of real phenomena—the equation of color with naturalism is not far removed from Georg Wilhelm Friedrich Hegel's argument (Drost, 1996,

p. 64). A growing minority of Hegel's contemporaries, on the other hand, thought of color as perfection of the plastic work; but polychromatic concepts only began to gain currency in the second half of the nineteenth century, particularly in Symbolist and Art Nouveau sculpture. Throughout these debates about color there were two crucial issues: Is there a single truth in the visual arts and, if so, where does it emanate from? Is it possible to operate with two seemingly incompatible sets of truths: truth to color (i.e., illusion) and truth to material (i.e., real substance)?

Because of its specific material qualities, such as solidity, stability, and durability, sculpture was held to preserve and hand down images with "ideal significance," that is, the stone or the bronze as the embodiment of seemingly permanent and universal values. Its authoritative status was not least generated from the costs, effort, and time involved in the making of the object. For centuries, from Polykleitos to Michelangelo, from Gianlorenzo Bernini to Henry Moore, this aspect had helped to determine both its public character, scale, and format (as statue and monument) and the range of its respective functions (commemorative, celebrative, votive, etc.).

In his influential essay "Laokoön" published in 1766, Gotthold Ephraim Lessing, writing in the rationalist tradition, compares painting as *pars pro toto* (and ideal) for the visual arts with poetry. According to Lessing, the visual arts are concerned with bodies in space, and imitate physical beauty. This separates them from poetry as an art that represents action—that is, exists in time. The visual work of art as an interplay between formal elements is perceived all at once. The simultaneous nature of perception stands at the core of the instantaneous presence of a statue or painting. Although, Lessing adds, bodies exist in time, too, he points out that a visual objet d'art can suggest action—that is, time—only as a fixed moment in time through the specific relationship between coexisting bodies (Lessing, 1910, p. 102). Simultaneity of vision takes the picture plane as ideal for the visual arts. Thus, Lessing's comparison is oriented toward a recurrent notion of sculpture in proximity to the relief, a sculpture that champions a principal view rather than a sculpture in the round. [*See* Lessing.]

Attempts to develop a systematic approach to the arts reached their zenith in Hegel's lectures on the philosophy of art written between 1820 and 1829. His thoughts proved instrumental in shifting the emphasis from a concern for beauty toward the "cognitive significance" of art. Hegel's systematic description of the arts is based on the exploration of the specific character of the relationship between the "Idea" and formal properties in individual art forms. Summing up a notion of the essence and function of sculpture that had prevailed in Western art since the Renaissance, he assigned sculpture to the classical art form, to which an equilibrium between the meaningful content of the object and its material form is fundamental. "For through sculpture the spirit should stand before us in blissful tranquility in its bodily form in an immediate unity therewith, and the form should be brought to life by a content of spiritual individuality" (Hegel, 1975, p. 85). Sculpture as a self-contained, bodily object generates its potential meaning in and through the image of the human body as the "real existence of the spirit." This individuality of the human figure is to be represented in "abstract spatiality and the totality of its dimensions" (ibid.).

Sculpture as a three-dimensional body in space exists as part of the object-reality and, therefore, its external and internal structure has been regarded as important, in order for it to maintain a reality and significance of its own; hence the centrality of the categories of unity and wholeness in aesthetic debates. "The compact unity in itself which the god has in sculpture disperses into the plurality of the inner lives of individuals whose unity is not sensuous but purely ideal" (ibid., p. 86). The firm attachment of aesthetic values such as beauty and truth to formal unity and structured wholeness based on the representation of the human (and animal) body can be traced backward to antiquity and forward into the nineteenth century and beyond. [See Hegel.]

Hegel, among others, acknowledges the multifaceted aspect of sculpture and draws attention to the nature of its perception as a process of successive vision, that is, of taking in, comparing, and synthesizing the different aspects of a sculptural object to acquire an overall view while circumnavigating it. In practice, a type of sculpture had been cultivated that enabled the viewer to gain a "synoptic grasp" at once, as in the work of Antonio Canova. Thus, frontality—as the principal view that contained all information vital for the recognition, reading, and appreciation of the sculptural object—went along with a preference for formal principles, such as clear contours, and conventionalized narrative subjects through which a high degree of unity and wholeness could be achieved. The focus on perception as an integral part of an aesthetic experience provided arguments for a restrictive use of materials, against (or for) the application of color, and for championing the single figure in moderate movement, as they facilitate a clear identification of the object as art and its contemplation. A fixed subject-object relationship is implied a priori, however, when contemplation is taken as the appropriate mode of aesthetic reception.

Adolf von Hildebrand's influential work *Das Problem der Form in der bildenden Kunst* (The Problem of Form in Painting and Sculpture), published in 1893, rekindled a controversial debate on the formal properties of sculpture in relation to the process of perception that they induce in the viewer. On similar grounds as some of his predecessors, he suggested that a three-dimensional object ought to fit into a two-dimensional picture plane of "perceptual space," that is, a space exclusively created for the eye. Therefore, he took the relief as the ideal form of sculpture. His approach tried to overcome the prevailing disdain for the sculpted work by bringing it into proximity with the picture plane and the central perspective at a time when "plastic art" had already degenerated into an empty and pompous phrase.

Sculptural Aesthetics in the Twentieth Century. Innovative generic forms and aesthetic practices indicated a growing crisis of representation toward the end of the nineteenth century. Two intertwined developments in sculpture, most apparent in the work of Auguste Rodin, seem of particular significance. First, the body fragment (i.e., the torso) as a genre in its own right—distinguished from the archaeological fragment, the Michelangelesque *non finito*, and conventionalized entities such as the portrait bust—threw into question the traditional concepts of completeness and wholeness based on the human form. Second, the appearance of the body fragment as a genre cannot be conceived of without a process in which the common concept of a linear translation of a figure's anatomical facts into meaning was already abandoned, and with it the traditional notion of narrative structures as being literally embodied. The surface, constituted by interior and exterior forces, by the object's internal "life" and the external process of its making, has become the "locus of meaning" (Krauss, 1981, p. 28). Phenomenological ideas, expressed particularly in Edmund Husserl's thoughts on "intersubjectivity and the intersubjective world," that is, on the relationship between the self, consciousness, and experience of the life-world, may provide a rationale for early modernist sculpture and its rupture between surface, volume, and representational content. Taking the "paradox of the alter ego" as a point of departure, Husserl argues that the self is not a hermetic entity, sealed from direct access from the outside, but formed at the juncture of consciousness and the surface of the body. From there derives the ability to think of a synchronous interrelation of the "surface configuration" of the sculpture and its unpremeditated experience (ibid.). Experience is understood as unpremeditated and immediate through a sensuous grasp of formal relations.

In the visual arts, the relationship between extrinsic and intrinsic values became an issue of discussion with the emergence of abstract painting. Roger Fry and Clive Bell, among others, divorced formal qualities from any representational aspect and claimed that the essence of aesthetic values lay in "purely formal relations"—that is, form is the only intrinsic quality of a work of art and thus the "one constant quality of art" (Fry, 1926, p. 197). A representational content of the object awakes an aesthetic interest only as form, because only form produces "aesthetic" emotions. Representation is regarded as either "irrelevant" or merely "descriptive," that is, as an extrinsic element, for it potentially detracts from both the creation of a work of art and its appreciation. In this way, formalist theories helped to free the debate on sculpture from its tight focus on the depiction of the human and animal body, and subsequently raised awareness of its specific formal condition and expressive potential. Through the sculptural work of artists such as

Constantin Brancusi, Henry Laurens, and Pablo Picasso, the relationship between expressive values of volume and space became reappraised in practice and in theory.

Until the early twentieth century, aesthetic analyses concentrated on the body, while the space in which it existed was considered as merely necessary, passive surrounding. Herbert Read, among others, elaborates on the concept of "touch-space" and emphasizes the essentially palpable character of the plastic object. In *The Art of Sculpture* (1941), he argues that the established convention of making sculpture accessible only for the visual sense is a violation of its true haptic nature (that is, vision mediated through touch), which demonstrates the hegemony of vision in Western culture. Taking up Alois Riegl's notion of "space-shyness," Read reinvestigates the historical development of sculpture and comes to the conclusion that the truly free-standing sculpture with a multiplicity of viewpoints is a recent achievement and heavily indebted to *Kleinplastik* (small statues). Only the small-scale entity can warrant an analysis by the sense of touch as well as by sight, in a processual character of perception in which the multiple aspects are synthesized into an overall sensation.

Susanne Knauth Langer, whose work is founded on developments in logic and linguistics, describes the nature of sculpture as haptic; yet she argues that "the business of sculpture is to translate its data into entirely visual terms, i.e. to make tactual space visible" (1953, p. 89). She considers form in sculpture to be the abstract presentation of a virtual object that is apparent only to sensory perception. Volume and space are engaged in a synthetic relationship, in which space actively participates in the constitution of form, as the void that possesses expressive qualities. In *Feeling and Form,* published in 1953, she writes:

> The volume, however, is not a cubic measure, like the space in a box. . . . it is space made visible, and it is more than the area which the figure virtually occupies. The tangible form has a complement of empty space that it absolutely commands, that is given with it and only with it, and is, in fact, part of the sculptural volume. The figure itself seems to have a sort of continuum with the emptiness around it, however much its solid masses may assert themselves as such. The void enfolds it, and the enfolding space has vital forms as a continuation of the figure.
> (Ibid., p. 88)

Langer's concept of sculpture projects a fixed object-subject positioning [*see* Langer]:

> Sculpture is literally the image of kinetic volume in sensory space. . . . Though a statue is, actually, an object, we do not treat it as such; we see it as a center of a space all of its own; but its kinetic volume and the environment it creates are illusory—they exist for our vision alone, a semblance of the self and its world.
> (Ibid., p. 91)

Maurice Merleau-Ponty's phenomenological investigations abandon the dichotomy between subject and object by ren-

SCULPTURE. Eva Hesse, *Untitled (3 Nets)* (1966), three net bags with painted papier mache weights, 42 1/2 × 11 1/2 × 6 in. (Copyright by the Estate of Eva Hesse; photograph courtesy of Robert Miller Gallery, New York; used by permission.)

dering fixed centers such as self and world nonexistent. The human body is subject and object in one. For Merleau-Ponty, it is the perceiving body that forms the intersection between the world and consciousness, because consciousness is necessarily embodied. From there emanates art—that is, sculpture transcends the human experience of existing as body in the world.

> I see things, each one in its place, precisely because they eclipse one another, and . . . they are rivals before my sight precisely because each one is in its own place. Their exteriority is known in their envelopment and their mutual dependence in their autonomy. Once depth is understood in this way, we no longer call it a third dimension. . . . Depth thus understood is, rather, the experience of the reversibility of dimensions, of a global "locality"—everything in the same place at the same time, a locality from which height, width, and depth are abstracted, of a voluminosity we express in a word when we say that a thing is there.
> (Merleau-Ponty, 1994, p. 290)

SCULPTURE. Sol LeWitt, *Tower* (1990), painted cinder block, 24 × 10.8 × 10.8 ft.; Commissioned by the Wexner Center for the Arts, Ohio State University; collection of the artist. (Photograph by Kevin Fitzsimons; copyright 1998 by Sol LeWitt/Artists Rights Society, New York; courtesy of Wexner Center for the Arts; used by permission.)

Merleau-Ponty, extrapolating his position in respect to painting, turns against the notion of spatiality as a third dimension altogether and puts into place a synchronous, relational time-space concept; he thus provides a tool to disentangle the internal principles of sculpture from an anthropocentric bias. [*See* Merleau-Ponty.]

Merleau-Ponty's idea of voluminosity as an expression for a certain quality of presence is echoed in Adrian Stokes's and Kurt Badt's Platonistic reference to "plasticity" as the metaphysical presence of a tangible idea, a surge of energy from the center of a work of art, notwithstanding the medium in which the idea is embodied. Initially, the distinction between sculpture and plastic art is rooted in the difference between two basic generic practices: carving and modeling. Sculpture is derived from the Latin verb *sculpere* and implies a process that works from the outside to the inside of resistant material. The other term, *plastic,* derived from the Greek *plastikos,* is associated with modeling and malleable materials, that is, a process in which material is added from the inside to the outside. Through a historically extended use of the term *sculpture,* it came to be accepted to cover both practices.

Addressing the inherent contradiction of surface and spatial morphology, of flatness and volume as inherent to sculptural practice, Stokes and Badt establish the fundamental structure of sculpture as an interrelation between the organic (i.e., plastic) form and geometry as the ordering and regulative principle. Their position implies the equation of a work of art with an organism and the view that "life" is the telos of art, a position that also motivates Langer's "virtual kinetic volume that is created by—and with—the semblance of living form" (Langer, 1953, p. 89). Stokes's and Badt's concepts, however, embrace a notion of unity and wholeness that potentially allows for open structures and constructed form based on geometry as the unifying principle through which a sense of definiteness is achieved in the object. Their theory provides a rationale for constructive sculpture, as a new generic practice and the apparent "descent" of modeling in the twentieth century. Artists such as Vladimir Tatlin, Aleksandr Rodchenko, and Naum Gabo, and later David Smith and Anthony Caro, employed the "tools and techniques" of the engineer as well as the natural properties of new materials and thus freed the sculptural volume from its mass, weight, and self-contained character. Their objects—often resonant of architectural engineering or machine design—explore the conditions of the physical world in a concrete mode.

Unlike Gabo's and Antoine Pevsner's expansion of sculpture into the fourth dimension of time (as proclaimed in their "Realist Manifesto" of 1920), neither Stokes's and Badt's elaboration on "plasticity" nor Langer's "kinetic volume" implies that time might constitute an inherent property of sculptural structure and provide a necessary and sufficient criterion for its definition. In a traditional way, they consider time to be an external element of perception rather than an internal structural component of the object. In contrast, artists such as Umberto Boccioni, Alexander Calder, László Moholy-Nagy, and Jean Tinguely used "real" movement as an integral part of their sculpture.

Artists' and art critics' concerns were central to the recurrence of generic debates from the 1950s to the 1970s. They grew out of an increasing diversity of creative strategies and pluralistic styles, which went hand in hand with a collapse of traditional generic practices. Approaches from that direction concentrate on a reconsideration of sculpture's goal, explore the relationship between sculpture as object and as representation of reality, or focus on the genesis of specific morphologies in an evaluative way. Jack Burnham's *Beyond Modern Sculpture* (1968) or William Tucker's *The Language of Sculpture* (1974) might serve as examples for the rich literature of this kind. Burnham draws a link between kinetic sculpture, technological progress, and the human craving to re-create life in order to extrapolate sculpture's ability ultimately to bridge the gap between art and life by replacing the human organism. Tucker, on the other hand, reconsiders the sculptural tradition through a focus on the object's earthbound character, its existence in the round, and its close relation to a perception that is mediated through bodily experience.

In his influential essay "Art and Objecthood," Michael Fried links purity of form with value. He writes: "The concept of quality and value—and to the extent that these are central to art, the concept of art itself—are meaningful, or wholly meaningful, only within the individual arts. What lies within is theatre" (1969, p. 142). Sculpture that enfolds not only in space but in time, sculpture as a performative act, poses a threat to its representational function by "theatricalizing" the space, and, ultimately, blurring clear-cut object-subject positionings. Its essence also comes under attack for an overbearing scale and repetitive pattern. Fried turns against the increasing anonymity of Minimalist sculpture because of its impersonal composition and the fact that, with the use of industrial materials and the aestheticization of technology, traces of the creative process were completely eliminated by artists such as Robert Morris and Donald Judd during the 1960s. With reference to Constructivism and in opposition to the highly emotionally and psychologically charged subjective gesture in art, artists such as Dan Flavin, Carl Andre, and Frank Stella imposed the clarity of mathematical formulas onto their works. By operating with series of similar objects, they accentuated both the arrangement of the parts into a simple rational order and the whole of the composition, rather than its individual elements, in order to achieve a high degree of immediacy.

This attitude is intertwined with a break between the "language" of sculpture and an "extraneous" content. According to Fried, these artists put in jeopardy sculpture's essential qualities such as "presentness and instantaneousness." Insisting on a tight-knit unity and wholeness as essential qualities of the sculptural object based on the instantaneous nature of its perception, he writes:

> It is this continuous and entire presentness, amounting, as it were, to the perpetual creation of itself, that one experiences as a kind of instantaneousness; as though if only one were infinitely more acute, a single infinitely brief instance would be long enough to see everything, to experience the work in all its depth and fullness, to be forever convinced by it. (Ibid., p. 146)

Fried's conception of sculpture as constancy that grows out of its perception comes close to Hildebrand's demand of sculpture having to submit to a "perceptual space." In addition, Fried's derogatory use of the term *theater* excludes those visual forms from the concerns of sculpture that reach out for the dimension of time, such as the kinetic object, installation, and performance.

Different strategies employed from different perspectives have oscillated between a dissolution or an expansion of generic boundaries. Of great influence were structuralist and semiotic theories that regarded art in general as text with a vocabulary of symbolic forms, and a system of syntactic and semantic codes that provided unifying principles. As early as the beginning of the twentieth century, Benedetto Croce developed the view that aesthetic expression necessarily entails embodiment in a material form but is founded in the artist's intuition. The notion of wholeness and unity is replaced as a criterion by intuition as a coherent, self-contained idea formulated in the mind of the artist that completes the work of art. In order to grasp the work, the artist's intuition has to be re-created in the viewer's own imagination. This concept has been of utmost importance for the many strands of conceptual art in which the process of conceiving an idea takes precedence over the realization and existence of the actual (material) object.

Umberto Eco's (1989) theory of the *opera aperta*, the open work of art, comes as a response to the problem of an ever-greater diversity of complex and contradicting aesthetic practices, from, on the one hand, Marcel Duchamp's conceptual approach to Sol LeWitt's Minimalist concept, from Alberto Giacometti's figurations to the Fluxus movement, and, on the other hand, the exclusive nature of necessarily confining generic boundaries. Eco draws on information theory and phenomenology in his linkage between "formal innovation," "ambiguity," and "information." The modern work of art is defined as an ambiguous one that breaks with the codes of practice, whereas the traditional work is based on conventions through which it remains potentially unambiguous, and therefore closed. Ambiguity evolves from formal innovation and generates information. Eco sees information in contrast to meaning. The former points toward unpredictability, toward infiniteness and incompleteness, and thus potentially opens up the work of art in terms of its material structure and its readings, whereas the latter ultimately means fixture and closure. The work of art operates at the center of a complex and multidirectional field of possibilities. This field interacts with the viewer and revokes the traditional notion of a polarization between subject and object on the basis of stable identities. [*See* Eco.]

Whereas Eco's approach potentially dissolves generic terms in an open field of innovative cultural practice, other approaches, such as Rosalind E. Krauss's analysis in "Sculpture in the Expanded Field," aim at keeping generic terms that are traditionally marked by a specific aesthetic practice. Krauss expands the field in which this practice is suspended, in order to turn away from a situation in which modernist sculpture only exists as "ontological absence," as *negativum*, neither constructed nor natural. The binary opposition of nonarchitecture and nonsculpture is opened up into a "quaternary field" by adding their positive terms through inversion: "Sculpture is no longer the privileged middle term between two things that it isn't. Sculpture is rather only one term on the periphery of a field in which

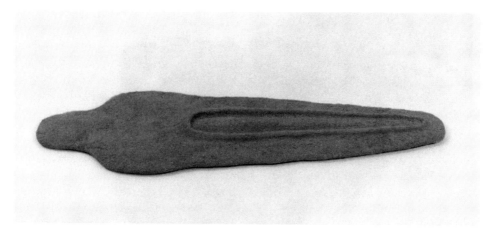

SCULPTURE. Ana Mendieta, *Nile Born (Nacido del Nilo)* (1984), sand and binder on wood, 2 3/4 × 19 1/4 × 16 1/2 in. (7 × 48.9 × 156.2 cm); Museum of Modern Art, New York (Gift of Agnes Gund). (Photograph copyright 1998 by the Museum of Modern Art; used by permission.)

there are other, differently structured possibilities" (Krauss, 1985, p. 284).

The flood of new labels for an increasing pluralism of innovative aesthetic practices in the twentieth century has highlighted the problems involved in defining an objet d'art in terms of classified groups of artifacts. Addressing the changed nature of the objet d'art and Duchamp's readymades in particular, Arthur C. Danto (1992) and George Dickie (1992) argue that neither intrinsic formal properties nor aesthetic values constitute the essence of art according to which it could be independently classified and appreciated. Rather, art's "not exhibited properties"—that is, the institutional framework in which art is presented, the "artworld"—define what is aesthetically appreciated. An artifact aquires the status of "candidate for appreciation" when it is put forward as such by a "person acting on behalf of the artworld." "The only difference between the appreciation of art and the appreciation of non-art is that they have different objects" (Dickie, 1992, p. 439). Therefore, a work of art achieves its meaning through the context of the institutions and its potentially indefinite number of "subsystems," such as sculpture. The subsystem's rules impose the terms and conditions of the reception of the object. This approach ultimately regards the question of inherent aesthetic qualities and their link to generic considerations as irrelevant for philosophical investigations into the nature of contemporary art.

[*See also* Bourgeois; Constructivism; Judd; Minimalism; *and* Monuments.]

BIBLIOGRAPHY

Aristotle. *The Poetics of Aristotle*. Translation and commentary by Stephen Halliwell. London, 1987.
Badt, Kurt. *Raumphantasien and Raumillusionen: Wesen der Plastischen.* Cologne, 1963.
Beardsley, Monroe C. *Aesthetics from Classical Greece to the Present: A Short History.* New York, 1966.
Bell, Clive. *Art.* London, 1914.
Burnham, Jack. *Beyond Modern Sculpture: The Effects of Science and Technology on the Sculpture of This Century.* New York, 1968.
Croce, Benedetto. *Aesthetic as Science of Expression and General Linguistic.* Translated by Douglas Ainslie. 2d ed. London, 1922.
Danto, Arthur C. "The Artworld." In *The Philosophy of the Visual Arts*, edited by Philip Alperson, pp. 426–433. New York and Oxford, 1992.
Dickie, George. "What Is Art? An Institutional Analysis." In *The Philosophy of the Visual Arts,* edited by Philip Alperson, pp. 434–444. New York and Oxford, 1992.
Drost, Wolfgang. "Colour, Sculpture, Mimesis: A 19th Century Debate." In *The Colour of Sculpture, 1840–1910,* pp. 61–73. Amsterdam, 1996.
Eco, Umberto. *Art and Beauty in the Middle Ages.* Translated by Hugh Bredin. New Haven, 1986.
Eco, Umberto. *The Open Work.* Translated by Anna Cancogni. Cambridge, Mass., 1989.
Fried, Michael. "Art and Objecthood." In *Minimal Art: A Critical Anthology,* edited by Gregory Battock, pp. 116–147. London, 1969.
Fry, Roger. *Art and Design.* London, 1926.
Hegel, Georg Wilhelm Friedrich. *Aesthetics: Lectures on Fine Art.* 2 vols. Translated by T. M. Knox. Oxford, 1975.
Herder, Johann von Gottfried. *Plastik: Einige Wahrnehmungen über Form und Gestalt aus Pygmalions bildendem Traume.* Berlin, 1964.
Hildebrand, Adolf von. *The Problem of Form in Painting and Sculpture* (1893). Translated by Max Meyer and Robert Morris Ogden. Reprint, New York, 1945.
Husserl, Edmund. *Formal and Transcendental Logic.* Translated by Dorion Cairns. The Hague, 1969.
Krauss, Rosalind E. *Passages in Modern Sculpture.* New York, 1977; reprint, Cambridge, Mass., 1981.
Krauss, Rosalind E. "Sculpture in the Expanded Field." In *The Originality of the Avant-Garde and Other Modernist Myths,* pp. 276–290. Cambridge, Mass., 1985.
Langer, Susanne K. *Feeling and Form.* London, 1953.
Lessing, Gotthold Ephraim. "Laokoön." In *Laokoön: Lessing, Herder, Goethe* (1766), edited by William Guild Howard, pp. 19–154. New York, 1910.

Merleau-Ponty, Maurice. "Eye and Mind." In *Art and Its Significance: An Anthology of Aesthetic Theory*, 3d ed., edited by Stephen David Ross, pp. 282–298. Albany, N.Y., 1994.

Plato. *The Dialogues of Plato.* 3d rev. corr. ed. 5 vols. Translated by Benjamin Jowett. Oxford, 1892.

Read, Herbert. *The Art of Sculpture* (1941). New York, 1956; reprint, Princeton, N.J., 1977.

Stokes, Adrian. "The Stones of Rimini." In *The Critical Writings of Adrian Stokes*, vol. 1, pp. 181–302. London, 1978.

Tucker, William. *The Language of Sculpture.* London, 1974.

Winckelmann, Johann Joachim. *Geschichte der Kunst des Altertums* (1764). Facs. ed. Baden-Baden, 1966.

Wittkower, Rudolf. *Sculpture: Processes and Principles* (1977). Reprint, London, 1991.

KERSTIN MEY

SEMIOTICS.

[*To clarify the meaning of semiotics, a theory of signs, this entry comprises three essays:*

Semiotics as a Theory of Art
Semiology of Music
Semiotics and Architecture

The first explains the development of semiotics in general and in contemporary art history. The other two essays treat semiotics as it has been practiced in connection with music and architecture, two other arts wherein a semiotic or linguistic turn has taken place. For related discussion, see Barthes; Eco; Kristeva; Peirce; Structuralism; Theater; *and* Theories of Art.]

Semiotics as a Theory of Art

The basic tenet of semiotics, the theory of signs and sign use, is an antirealist one. Human culture is made up of signs, each of which stands for something other than itself, and the people inhabiting culture busy themselves making sense of those signs. The core of semiotic theory is the definition of the factors involved in this permanent process of sign making and interpreting, and the development of conceptual tools that help to grasp that process as it goes on in various arenas of cultural activity. Art is one such arena.

Semiotic debates focus on such issues as the polysemy of meaning; the problematics of authorship, context and reception; the implications of the study of narrative for the study of images; the issue of sexual difference in relation to verbal and visual signs; and the truth claims of interpretation. This essay is limited to the first two, and focuses on the critique of disciplinary tenets. In all these areas, semiotics challenges the positivist view of knowledge.

Context. The problem here lies in the term *context* itself. Precisely because it has the root *text* while its prefix distinguishes it from the latter, *context* seems comfortably out of reach of the pervasive need for interpretation that affects all texts. Yet, this is an illusion. As Jonathan Culler (1988) has argued, the opposition between an act and its context seems to presume that the context is given and determines the meaning of the act. Context, however, is not given but pro-

duced; what belongs to a context is determined by interpretive strategies; contexts are just as much in need of elucidation as events; and the meaning of a context is determined by events.

Context, in other words, is a text itself, and thus consists of signs that require interpretation. What we take to be positive knowledge is the product of interpretive choices. The art historian or critic is always present in the construction she or he produces. In order to endorse the consequences of this insight, Culler proposes to speak not of context but of "framing": "Since the phenomena criticism deal with are signs, forms with socially constituted meanings, one might try to think not of context but of the framing of signs: how are signs constituted (framed) by various discursive practices, institutional arrangements, systems of value, semiotic mechanisms?" (1988, p. xiv).

This proposal does not mean to abandon the examination of "context" altogether, but to do justice to the interpretive status of the insights thus gained. Not only is this more truthful, but it also advances the search for social history itself; for, by examining the social factors that frame the signs, it is possible to analyze simultaneously the practices of the past and our own interaction with them, an interaction that is otherwise in danger of passing unnoticed. What art historians are bound to examine, whether they like it or not, is the work as effect and affect, not only as a neatly remote product of an age long gone.

Semiotics, following the structuralist phase of its evolution, has had to examine the conceptual relations between *text* and *context* in detail, in order to ascertain the fundamental dynamics of socially operated signs. When a particular work of art is placed "in context," it is usually the case that a body of material is assembled and juxtaposed against the work in question in the hope that such contextual material will reveal the determinants that make the work of art what it is. But, from a semiotic point of view, it cannot be taken for granted that the evidence that makes up *context* is any simpler or more legible than the text or image upon which such evidence is to operate. The observation is directed against any assumption of opposition, or asymmetry, between *context* and *text*, such that here lies the work of art, waiting for context to order its uncertainties, and over there is the context, as that which will act upon the work of art and transfer to the latter its own certainties and determination. The idea of "context" invites us to step back from the uncertainties of text to context, posited as platform or foundation. But once this step is taken, it is by no means clear why it may not be taken again; that is, *context* implies from its first moment a *mise-en-abîme*, a potential regression "without brakes."

Semiotics has been obliged to confront this problem head-on, and how it did so has shaped the history of its own development. In its "structuralist" era semiotics (Ferdinand de Saussure) frequently operated on the assumption that the meanings of signs were determined by sets of internal oppositions and differences mapped out within a static system. In order to discover the meanings of the words in a particular language, for example, the interpreter turned to the global set of rules (the *langue*) simultaneously governing the language as whole, outside and away from actual utterances *(parole)*. The crucial move was to invoke and isolate the synchronic system, putting its diachronic aspects to one side; what was sought, in a word, was structure. The critique launched against this theoretical immobility of sign systems pointed out that a fundamental component of sign systems is their aspects of ongoing semiosis, of dynamism. The changeover from theorizing semiosis as the product of static and immobile systems to thinking of semiosis as unfolding in time is indeed one of the points at which structuralist semiotics gave way to poststructuralism.

From this perspective, *context* appears to have strong resemblances to the Saussurean signified. Against such a notion, poststructuralist semiotics argues that *context* is in fact unable to arrest the fundamental mobility of semiosis for the reason that it harbors exactly the same principle of interminability within itself. J. L. Austin's remark concerning speech act theory is a case in point: "the total speech act in the total speech situation is the *only actual* phenomenon which, in the last resort, we are engaged in elucidating" (1975). Semiotics' objection to such an enterprise focuses primarily on the idea of mastering a totality, together with the notion that such a totality is "actual," that is, that it can be known as a present experience.

The problem concerns the stroke or bar (/) between the terms *text* and *context*. That mark of separation presupposes that one can, in fact, separate the two, that they are truly *independent* terms. Yet, the relation between *context* and *text* (or *artwork*) that these terms often take for granted implies that history stands prior to artifact; that context generates, produces, gives rise to text, in the same way that a cause gives rise to an effect. But often the sequence (from context to text) is actually inferred from its end point, leading to the kind of metalepsis that Friedrich Nietzsche called "chronological reversal."

Elements of (visual) texts migrate from text to context and back, but recognition of such circulation is prevented by the primary cut of text-stroke-context. The operation of the stroke consists in the creation of what, for semiotics, is a phantasmic cleavage between text and context, followed by an equally uncanny drawing together of the two sides that had been separated. The stroke dividing *text* from *context* is a move that semiotic analysis would criticize as a rhetorical operation.

Semiotics is averse neither to the idea of history nor even to the idea of historical determination. But meanings are always determined in specific sites in a historical and material world. Semiotics does not work to avoid the concept of historicity; rather, its reservations concern forms of historiography that would present themselves in an exclusively aoristic or constative mode, eliding the determinations of historiography as a performative discourse active in the present. The same historiographic scruple that requires us to draw a distinguishing line between "us" and the historical "them"—in order to see how they are different from us—should, in the semiotic view, by the same token urge us to see how "we" are different from "them," and to use *context* not as a legislative idea but as a means that helps "us" to locate ourselves instead of bracketing out our own positionalities from the accounts we make.

Senders. No less problematic is the status of the concept of "artist" (painter, photographer, sculptor, here "author"). It might seem at first that the idea of the author is, again, a natural term in the order of explanation, and one that is now much more substantial and tangible than "context." The author of a work of art is surely someone we can indeed point to, a living (or once living), flesh-and-blood personage with a palpable presence in the world. Yet, as Michel Foucault points out, the relation between an individual and his or her proper name is quite different from the relation that obtains between a proper name and the function of authorship. The name of an author or artist oscillates between designation and description: when we speak of Homer, we do not designate a particular individual, we refer to the author of the *Iliad* or the *Odyssey*, of the body of texts performed by the rhapsodists at the Panathenaic Festivals, or we intend a whole range of qualities, "Homeric" qualities that can be applied to any number of cases (epics, epithets, heroes, types of diction, of poetic rhythm—the list is open-ended). A "J. Bloggs" is in the world, but an "author" is in the works, in a body of artifacts and in the complex operations performed on them. Like "context," "authorship" is a work of framing, something we elaborately produce rather than something we simply find.

Some of the processes of this enframement can be seen at work in the strategies of attribution. Perhaps the first procedure in attribution is to secure clear evidence of the material traces of the author in the work, metonymic contiguities that move in a series from the author in the world, the flesh-and-blood J. Bloggs, into the artifact in question. The traces may be directly autographic—evidence of a particular hand at work in the artifact's shaping; they may be more indirect—perhaps documents pertaining to the work, or the physical traces of a milieu (as when an artifact is assigned to the category "Athenian, c.700 BCE"). Attribution in art history involves further operations that lead away from science and technology into subtler, and more ideologically motivated, considerations concerning quality and stylistic standardization. Before, the "author" referred to a physical agent in the world, but now it refers to the putative creative subject. In the drastic changeover from scientific procedures built on measurement and experimental knowledge, to the highly subjective and volatile appraisals of quality and stylistic uniformity, one already sees how multifarious are the principles that "authorship" bring into play.

A further and quite different range of the arbitrary is found in the procedures for "setting limits" to what counts within authorship. The author, under the forensic principle, is the origin of all the physical traces that point to her presence in the world. But "authorship" is an exclusionary concept. On one side, it works to circumscribe the artistic corpus, and on the other it works to circumscribe the archive. As a concept, "authorship" turns out after all to entail the same regressions and *mise-en-abîme* involved in "context"; and, as it operates in practice, "authorship" manages these receding vistas through many variations on the theme of nonadmission.

The forces of authorship must also include the protocols of writing and the rules governing what is to count as a correct mode of narration. For instance, a catalogue raisonné would be breaking those rules if it wandered into the realm of an author's doodles and napkin sketches, just as a biography of the author would be breaking them if it widened the aperture of relevance to the proportions of a *Tristram Shandy*. That such deviant narratives are rarely encountered is proof of the efficiency of the "authorship" operation. By a rule of correct narration or "emplotment," only those aspects of an author's innumerable wanderings through the world that may be harmonized with the corpus of works will count as relevant, whereas, on the other side, only a certain number of an author's traces will count as elements of the authorized corpus. The exclusionary moves are mutually supportive, and "correct" narration will set up further conventions concerning exactly how much latitude may be permitted in describing the perimeters.

Authorship, then, is no more a natural ground of explanation than is context. The moment of narrative closure, when all the metonymic chains draw to a convergent close, can also be read as a denial of the actual continuation of the contiguities in which the narrator stands. The movement of contiguities in fact passes on from the artwork into the (art) historian's own situation; the work of art is also contiguous with her or him. But the modernist discourses, which foreclose metonymic movement by getting the chain to end with the artwork, can work to deny this, making "contiguity then" eclipse and elide "contiguity now." The draining of hagiographic qualities from the "author" in the past can also be said to justify a corresponding emptying out of the qualities of positionality, motivation, and investment present in the author of the historical narrative.

Semiotics assumes that not only artworks, but the accounts we fashion for them, are works of the sign. From the viewpoint of semiotics, the modernist no less than the humanist discourses are constructed in such a way as to prevent realization that when we confront works of art we enter the field of the sign and of semiosis, of potentially infinite regressions and expansions, and that we deal with this situation by delimiting it from the place where we stand "now." In this process of concealing where we stand, the concept of "author" plays a crucial role, if as a result of its operation "author then" comes to mask—and to mask the masking of—"author now."

Receivers. Semiotics is centrally concerned with reception. It will describe the logic according to which meanings are engendered. Semiotic analysis of visual art does not set out in the first place to produce interpretations of works of art, but rather to investigate how works of art are intelligible to those who view them, the processes by which viewers make sense of what they see. Standing somewhat to one side of the work of interpretation, its object is to describe the conventions and conceptual operations that shape what viewers or readers do.

Reception semiotics usually draws a distinction between "ideal" and "empirical" spectators. "Ideal" refers to the various roles ascribed to viewers by the paintings they see, the set of positions or functions proposed and assumed by each of the images on display. Within modern art history, for example, the ideal spectator has been a continuing focus of interest, from Alois Riegl's *Dutch Group Portraiture* through the reception studies of Wolfgang Kemp to Michael Fried's *Absorption and Theatricality*. Bringing empirical spectatorship into sharper focus has been the goal of a far more materialist analysis which begins by investigating the actual traces left by actual encounters between viewers and works of art. This project and its approach accord closely with semiotics' own understanding of the concreteness, materiality, and sociality of sign-events.

But if analysis of reception discloses particular social groups, whose visual responses to particular works of art vary in semiotic terms; if different groups possess different codes for viewing even the same work, the idea of *possession* of codes of viewing cannot be taken for granted. If one is really going to address reception, it must be recognized that possession of codes of viewing is a process, not a given, and that members of groups acquire their familiarity with codes of viewing, and their ability to operate those codes, to varying degrees. Access to the codes is a matter of unevenness: codes have to be learned and their distribution varies (and changes) within a group. The danger here is that the term *group* may function as an unacknowledged, and undetectable, synecdoche: in fact, members of the group have different levels of access to the group's codes, varying degrees of competence and expertise; but the condition of expertise is generalized to all of them.

What semiotic analysis draws attention to is the plurality and unpredictability at work in contexts of reception. Surrounding those forms of looking that have given rise to discursive configurations that actually figure in the archive are other, submerged series of procedures that addressed other needs, procedures whose traces can still be derived from the forcefulness of the attempts to repress them. Such series will include codes of viewing that represent residual practices edged out by the rise of those later codes that come to replace them, and, conversely, codes that are hardly yet formed, emergent ways of seeing whose coherence has not yet been established and whose energies have not yet taken root, still tentative and faltering configurations that still have to find each other and lock together to form a configuration that may be seen emerging into the historical record. In a separate category are complete idiolects of viewing, private languages of memory and habit that reorder the dominant codes into secret configurations of desire and identity, codes that may or may not be revealed to another human being, whose nature may or may not be consciously recognized.

A semiotic analysis of reception seeks to add a question and to shift the claim. The better question to ask would be: from where, from what position, is the reconstruction being made? Discussions of reception seem to move between two poles: the plural, dispersed, often submerged "polytheism" of actual, empirical reception; and the delimitations of a discourse on viewing that produces out of this plurality a cast of viewers whose responses are said to follow the most determinable contours. Out of the welter of concrete reception is distilled a character, "the viewer" whose attributes vary from one narration to another. But however this figure is defined, the viewer is essentially a character, a personification, in stories of viewing written in the first place according to the disciplinary norms of the narratives they work within.

History and the Status of Meaning. But what about history? Three issues complicate the historical search: intertextuality, polysemy, and the location of meaning. The term *intertextuality* was introduced by the Soviet philosopher of language Mikhail Bakhtin. It refers to the ready-made quality of linguistic—and, one can add, visual—signs, that a writer or image maker finds available in the earlier texts that a culture has produced. This concept does not quite overlap with iconographic precedent. Iconographic analysis tends to take the historical precedent as the source that virtually dictated to the later artist what forms can be used. But one may consider the work of the later artist as an active intervention into the material handed down to her. This reversal, which also amounts to a deconstruction of the relation between cause and effect, already challenges the idea of precedent as origin, and thereby makes the claim of historical reconstruction problematic.

A second difference is the place of meaning. Iconographic analysis frequently avoids statements about the meaning of the borrowed motifs. To borrow a motif is not a priori also to borrow a meaning. The concept of intertextuality, in contrast, implies precisely that: the sign taken over, because it is a sign, comes with a meaning. This is not to say that the later artist necessarily endorses that meaning; but she will inevitably have to deal with it: reject or reverse it,

ironize it, or simply, often unawares, insert it in the new text. Thus, referring to Albrecht Dürer's *Melencolia I* in the pose of the aggressive elder in his *Susanna* in Berlin, Rembrandt van Rijn cannot help bringing in the quite unsettling meaning of that precedent, suggesting that illegitimate and abusive looking paralyses the transgressor.

A third difference resides in the *textual* character of intertextual allusion. By reusing forms taken from earlier works, an artist also takes along the text out of which the borrowed element is broken away, while constructing a new text with the debris. Reusing a pose used earlier in a self-portrait, Rembrandt inserts the discourse of self-portraiture into his *Bellona* of 1633 (New York, Metropolitan Museum). The new text, say, a mythography, is contaminated by the discourse of the precedent, and thereby fractured, so to speak, ready at any time to fall apart again. The fragility of the objectifying, distancing device of mythography is displayed by this taint of "first person" subjectivity. The historical narrative is infected by subjective discourse. Such a view obviously has consequences for the interpretation of this painting in terms of gender.

One can push this reflection of the implications of intertextuality further, in the direction of the kind of self-reflection advocated by Jürgen Habermas; for the reader cannot help but bring to the pictures her own legacy of discursive precedents, and reading texts or images entails the inevitable mixture of these signs with those perceived in the work. The allusion to *Melencolia,* for example, occurred to us for reasons that Habermas would wish us to explore further, and of which it is obvious that they have to do with contemporary gender issues. This input from the present is emphatically not to be taken as a flaw in our historical awareness, or a failure to distance ourselves from our own time, but as an absolutely inevitable proof of the presence of the cultural position of the analyst within the analysis. To take that presence into account makes the analysis, in fact, more rather than less historically responsible.

This leads to the second issue, that of *polysemy.* Because readers and viewers bring to the images their own cultural baggage, there can be no such thing as a fixed, predetermined, or unified meaning. Attempts to fix meaning provide the most convincing evidence for this view. The field in which struggles over meanings are fought is a social arena where power is at stake. A good example of this mechanism is allegory, the interpretation of, say, a mythical story and all its representations as referring to something outside itself. On the one hand, allegory demonstrates the fundamental polysemous nature of signs. If stories can mean something entirely outside of themselves, then there is no constraint. But take the allegorical interpretations of mythical stories of rape as "really" dealing with tyranny and the establishment of democracy. Intertextual analysis will bluntly refuse such abdication of the meaning imported by the sign: if rape means political tyranny, then the bodily, subjective experience of the woman raped cannot be divorced from the politics at stake. The myth of Lucretia, then, is allegorical, but with a vengeance. The *allos* of allegory is, after all, not only "other," but also "within."

This problem with allegory is, in turn, allegorical for a larger problem implied by polysemy; for the dynamism of signs implied in this view might be mistaken as an abdication of the scholarly position altogether. In spite of the attraction of this idea, especially as a corrective to the remants of positivism still pervasive in the humanities, it needs emphasis that the play of interpretation is surely not entirely free, or else there would be no cause for chagrin about power relations and exclusions in academic practice. In agreement with Ludwig Wittgenstein's concept of the language game, semiotics proposes to see signs as active, and requires them to be both deployed according to rules and public. A sign, then, is not a thing but an event. Sign-events take place in specific circumstances and according to a finite number of culturally valid, conventional, yet not unalterable rules that semiotics calls codes. The selection of those rules and their combination leads to specific interpretive behavior. That behavior is socially framed, and any semiotic view that is to be socially relevant will have to deal with this framing, precisely on the basis of the fundamental polysemy of signs and the subsequent possibility of dissemination.

[*See also* Art History.]

BIBLIOGRAPHY

Austin, J. L. *How to Do Things with Words.* 2d ed. Edited by J. O. Urmson and Marina Sbisa. Cambridge, Mass., 1975.

Bal, Mieke. *Reading Rembrandt: Beyond the Word-Image Opposition.* Cambridge and New York, 1991.

Bal, Mieke, and Norman Bryson. "Semiotics and Art History." *Art Bulletin* 73.2 (June 1991): 174–208.

Bryson, Norman. "Art in Context." In *The Point of Theory: Practices of Cultural Analysis,* edited by Mieke Bal and Inge E. Boer, pp. 66–78. New York, 1994.

Culler, Jonathan. *Framing the Sign: Criticism and Its Institutions.* Norman, Okla., 1988.

Derrida, Jacques. "Living On: Border Lines." In *Deconstruction and Criticism,* by Harold Bloom et al., pp. 75–176. New York, 1979.

Derrida, Jacques. *Dissemination.* Translated by Barbara Johnson. Chicago, 1981.

Derrida, Jacques. *The Truth in Painting.* Translated by Geoff Bennington and Ian McLeod. Chicago, 1987.

Eco, Umberto. *The Role of the Reader: Explorations in the Semiotics of Texts.* Bloomington, Ind., 1979.

Eco, Umberto. *Semiotics and the Philosophy of Language.* Bloomington, Ind., 1984.

Fried, Michael. *Absorption and Theatricality: Painting and Beholder in the Age of Diderot.* Berkeley, 1980.

Goodman, Nelson. *Languages of Art: An Approach to a Theory of Symbols.* 2d ed. Indianapolis, 1976.

Holly, Michael Ann. "Past Looking." *Critical Inquiry* 16 (Winter 1990): 371–396.

Shapiro, Meyer. "On Some Problems in the Semiotics of Visual Art: Field and Vehicle in Image-Signs." *Semiotica* 1.3 (1969): 223–242.

MIEKE BAL and NORMAN BRYSON

Semiology of Music

If one accepts the minimal idea that the sign is, as Saint Augustine said, something that *refers* to something else for someone, then music is a semiological phenomenon in two ways: (1) The musical sign refers to other musical signs. This is the intrinsic or formalist conception of musical meaning: music is a language that signifies itself. (2) The musical sign refers to the experienced, affective, imaging, cultural, ideological world.

If this is so, then one can see in the semiology of music, if not a discipline, in any case an activity or a point of view (1) according to which one can question the symbolic possibilities of music: in this sense, a project of musical semiology has an ontological dimension (which makes a philosophical and aesthetic investigation of interest); and (2) according to which one analyzes music: musical semiology is thus one of the possible forms of musical analysis, and as such, it already has its place, as is evidenced in the *New Grove Dictionary of Music and Musicians,* in the history of analysis and musicology (Bent, 1980).

Even if it has rarely been formulated in these terms, the question of the semiological status of music is at the heart of the millennial aesthetic reflection on music (Fubini, 1983). When Plato assigned distinct ethical values to different modes in the *Republic,* considering some of them dangerous for society, he recognized in music a power of influence *exterior* to sonorous structures themselves. When Eduard Hanslick opened the way to the modern aesthetic of music in 1854 by making the claim that one must not look for musical *thought* anywhere but in the sounds themselves—and in this, he was to be followed by Igor Stravinsky, Anton Webern, and Pierre Boulez—he acknowledged that music possessed a semiological dimension, but on an intrinsic level. In truth, one could compile a history of the musical aesthetic that would show how the semiological pendulum has oscillated between the extrinsic pole and the formalist pole. In the seventeenth century, when instrumental music got the upper hand over the vocal music of the Renaissance, Bernard Le Bovier de Fontenelle exclaimed, "Sonata, what do you want from me?" ("Sonate, que me veux-tu?"). Once instrumental music had acquired its autonomy, Richard Wagner swung the pendulum back in the other direction by making music the servant of drama, whereas Franz Liszt invented the symphonic poem. Johannes Brahms never wrote one, leaning on classical forms in his symphonies and chamber music. When an innovator such as Claude Debussy wrote *La Mer,* some conductors made it their objective to render present the play of the waves and the ringing of the Tritons (Ernest Ansermet), while others stressed above all the modernity of the construction and sonority (Boulez). It soon becomes clear that the semiological status of music (does it refer to itself or to the lived world?) not only runs through aesthetic reflection but implicates the composers and performers as well.

It seems unnecessary to choose between the two options and among the intermediary positions that Leonard B. Meyer (1956) has brilliantly distinguished—the pure formalists, the absolutist expressionists, the referentialist expressionists, and the pure referentalists. One can certainly adopt a normative semiologico-aesthetic position, but the day will come when it will be necessary to violate it. Because the most intransigent formalist will never be able to prevent descriptive music from existing (without mentioning opera music), the most expressionist of musicians will never be able to deny that a work exists first as an ensemble of sonorous configurations. Therefore, one can hear more expressions and indeed more sentiments in a Webern piece than he wanted to put in it; one can be more interested in the rhythmic structures of *Le Sacre du Printemps* than in seeing a pagan ritual in it. This is because another, more fundamental distinction characterizes the semiological functioning of music beyond the opposition between referentialism and formalism. The perceptive strategies, relative as much to forms as to sentiments expressed, do not necessarily correspond to compositional strategies, even if there exists something between the two that is at once the point of departure and the end point: a constellation of sonorous combinations.

SEMIOTICS: Semiology of Music. *Microstructure and macrostructure in the first fifteen bars of "Le Cathédrale Engloutie, Préludes" by Claude Debussy.* (Courtesy of Jean-Jacques Nattiez.)

Following the model proposed by J. Molino (1990), and which, in fact, can be applied to every form of work or human practice, one can call the "semiology of music" every area of reflection or every kind of musical analysis that, as much from the standpoint of form as from that of expression, endeavors to distinguish what Molino denotes as the *poietic* (compositional strategies), the *neutral level* (immanent structures), and the *aesthesic* (perceptive strategies) and to study the modalities of their articulation (Nattiez, 1976, 1987, 1990).

Before presenting a few instances of this semiological conception of musical aesthetics, its relevance may be illustrated with the example of a tripartite musical analysis. To this end, particular aspects of the first fifteen bars of Debussy's *La Cathédrale Engloutie* will be examined (see Figure 1).

An analysis of neutral level (an immanent one) may, among many other characteristics of this piece, note in the opening of the text the following phenomenon of repetition and variation. The motif D-E-B in bar one is taken up again an octave higher in the same bar, but without the B. This group is found again in bars 3 and 5. In bars 14 and 15, the motif D-E-B reappears, again repeated an octave higher, but this time with a high B. The whole forms a descending mirror form at bar 15. One finds a transformation of this motif of a second plus a fifth in the theme, in bars 7 and 8: C#-D#-G# also presents the intervallic succession of second and fifth. The same motif is transformed in bars 9 and 10 and 11–12 (G#-A#-D#). The motif D-E-B is also present in these first fifteen bars on a macroscopic level: the first chord of bars 1, 3, and 5 displays a high D; the E of the motif is present, in the form of an ostinato, from bar 5 to bar 13; and the B intervenes as the top note of the first chord in bar 14.

One speaks here of a neutral type of analysis, for it has been content with noting the recurrence of a motif with its variations without asking questions of poetic and aesthetic relevance.

The poetic question occurs when one asks if these repetitions and transformations form part of Debussy's compositional strategies. The answer is unhesitatingly yes. The specificity of the intervallic configuration of second and fifth and the identity of the motif D-E-B in bar 1 with the larger macroscopically stretched motif can hardly be the product of mere chance.

On the other hand, it is not evident that, when one hears this piece in real time, the ear should be able to establish all these connections that musicology may find in its laboratory analysis. Is the high B of bar 15 perceived as the complement to that which was left in suspense at the end of bars 1, 3, and 5? Can the listener establish a link between the motif D-E-B and its stretching out over fifteen bars? Research following the lines of experimental psychology (which will be dealt with elsewhere in detail) shows that the repetition of the motif in bars 1, 3, and 5 is noticed by the majority of listeners. The motif's transformation in the theme, however, is perceived by a much smaller group. The two other phenomena (completion at bars 14–15 of the expectation created at the beginning, and correspondence between the micro- and macrostructure) are not perceived by anyone.

This example well illustrates the necessity of distinguishing, in musical analysis, between immanent, poetic, and aesthetic points of view. How do things lie in the aesthetic domain?

A good number of musicians and musicologists have difficulty accepting the pertinence of this tripartite distinction, and here, many different configurations are possible. There are those for whom music is nothing other than a formal game (described by Molino as the analysis of the neutral level). What is the point, then, in worrying about the poietic and the aesthesic? For others, music would not exist without the gesture of the composer. For others still, it is made above all to be heard. Few theories have attempted to embrace the relationship between these three levels, either because theorists do not recognize the necessity of a level of immanent description of music or because they do not acknowledge the "discrepancy" between the poietic and the aesthesic.

Why is this so? First of all because of the bias, conveyed by certain semiologists (Roman Jakobson, Umberto Eco), but shared by many, according to which a musical work (or a film, a poem, a sentence) is supposed to be a phenomenon of communication: a *common code* to the sender and the receiver is supposed to make communication possible, and the task of the semiologist is to make an inventory of these codes. Unfortunately, one quickly discovers that there are an infinite number of "codes" implied in "communication." It appears theoretically and empirically more appropriate, if not easier, to examine which *interpretants* (in Charles Sanders Peirce's sense) intervene in musical production and musical perception, that is, which traits or aspects of lived, musical, semantic, expressive, and ideological experience are connected to sonorous structures, and this, for the composer, performer, or listener.

Second, a large majority of musicians consider harmony to be equally constitutive of the foundation of the tonal system. For them, the other parameters are subordinated to it, and the principles of harmonic functioning have remained unvaried from Johann Sebastian Bach to Wagner. How could one acknowledge the slightest gap between the poietic and the aesthesic before such stability? Even if the cycle of fifths seems quite constant during the entire period of so-called common practice, and even though the cycle of thirds are strongly present in the nineteenth century, it is necessary all the same to wonder why a treatise of melody (Anton Reicha) considered independently of harmony appears at the beginning of the nineteenth century; why Hec-

tor Berlioz, in composing one of the first treatises of orchestration, sanctions a new autonomy of timbre that will lead to electro-acoustic music; why modern theorists such as Fred Lerdahl and Ray Jackendoff (1983), all the while acknowledging the fundamental ideas of harmony according to Heinrich Schenker, base their analytic approach on a metrico-rhythmic cadre.

Confining our discussion to the West, tonal music is far from constituting a harmonious hierarchized group. The diverse parameters that constitute it—melody, rhythm, meter, harmony, timbre—have, to use the terminology of Étienne Gilson, a specific physical mode of existence. To put it roughly, the melodic line extends over the duration; harmony is constituted by vertical entities; and rhythm is what remains when the pitches, and so on, have been removed. In short, it is possible to distinguish them, and thus, the parameters and their components have experienced different rhythms of historical evolution for more than three centuries. Consequently, it is difficult to decide if Ludwig van Beethoven is a classicist or a Romantic in the *Periodisierung* of German musicology. Harmony and phraseology are still considered classical in it, but in Beethoven there is already a thematic construction based on the cell that will become fundamental for Brahms and that will appear again at the root of the Schoenbergian series.

The relative equilibrium between the poietic and the aesthesic seems only to characterize the brief classical period. The works of experimental psychology have confirmed that the series was not made to be perceived, having opportunely recalled that, during an audition, a talented conservatory student could not differentiate the subject, the countersubject, and the answer of a fugue of Bach (Francès, 1958). This is because of the fact that one finds in the musical phenomenon what could be called purely poietic instruments that are far from having authority over communication. Conversely, the act of musical perception is not a phenomenon of reception, but of construction. It suffices to read the diverse descriptions of Debussy's style, for example, to realize that although characteristic traits such as parallel fifths or the tonal scale (which was already picked up because of its novelty by Marcel Proust, who was not a musician) are cited by everybody, as soon as one enters into details, the corpus of more detailed traits that are specific to Debussy vary according to the perception of the individual. Is this to say that the description of style is eminently subjective? No. This means simply that style, like every other aspect of the musical phenomenon, is a symbolic reality with three dimensions: it is not only a phenomenon of perception, but a poietic phenomenon (from which musical tradition—Frédéric Chopin, the Russians, Emmanuel Chabrier, André Messager—did Debussy develop his own style?) and a phenomenon of structure: there are harmonies and melodic phrases that are found nowhere else except in Debussy.

It soon becomes clear that, starting from an aesthetic and ontological reflection on the semiological nature of music, we have imperceptibly moved toward musical *analysis*. Do specifically semiological analytic approaches exist?

At first, as we have just seen concerning the example of style, the semiological tripartition makes it possible to classify the diverse types of musical analysis—an undertaking that is pedagogically of cardinal importance, because each inventor of an analytic paradigm is evidently convinced of having proposed the best and the last one. When Boulez analyzes rhythm in *Le Sacre du Printemps,* he deliberately proposes an *immanent analysis*. When Rudolph Réti draws the hypothesis, based on text of *La Cathédrale Engloutie,* that Debussy used the third and the fourth as "generative intervals," he proceeds from what can be called an *inductive poietic*. If, on the contrary, one projects onto the text a piece of information exterior to the work such as the preliminary studies of Beethoven or Wagner, one undertakes an *external poietic*. The situation is symmetrical on the side of perception: Meyer and Lerdahl and Jackendoff practice an *inductive aesthesic* in drawing the hypothesis of perceptive behavior from the musical text on the basis of general rules of perception. Conversely, experimental psychologists (Robert Francès, Michel Imberty) and cognitivists today construct an *external aesthesic* in interrogating subjects about what they have effectively perceived and then projecting their responses onto the text subject to inquiry. Finally, there are theorists such as Schenker for whom the analysis of harmonic structures is poietically pertinent and normatively determines how the work should be perceived. If it were systematically put into practice, this classification of analyses would facilitate discussion between specialists, because there is no point in accusing an author of neglecting an aspect of a work if it is clear that he or she tackled a single side of its symbolic dimension that is incompatible with the others.

Can one say that there are musical analyses that are specifically semiological? This is the qualifier that has often been given to the technique of paradigmatic decomposition of the musical syntagma proposed by Nicolas Ruwet (1972, 1987) and inspired by the structuralism of Jakobson and Claude Lévi-Strauss. Paradigmatic analysis is an effective instrument in the analysis of immanent structures because of two aspects: the systematic rewriting of open units and the rendering explicit of procedures utilized. The paradigmatic technique lends itself to a large number of uses: the hierarchization of the formal unities of a piece; the analysis of processes of variation throughout a work; the reconstruction of protomelodies; the establishment of scales; and the assessment of recurrent harmonic schemata. This method is specifically semiological if one considers music an "introversive" semiological system, as Jakobson (1973) indicated when he specifically cited the paradigmatic technique as a means to describe the play of signs between musical units.

But even from the immanent point of view, the paradigmatic model is not the only appropriate one. The intramusical semiological sign does not only exist between taxonomic units. One must also take into account the prolongational phenomena so well demonstrated by Schenker on the harmonic level and of which Meyer seems to have shown the specific semiological dimension in analyzing melodic phenomena in detail. Finally, these two forms of immanent description—taxonomic and prolongational—only constitute a first step toward bringing together poietic strategies at the origin of the sonorous with aesthesic strategies that reconstruct it with semantic associations that link it to the lived universe of the composer or listener.

The musical semantic without a doubt provides the most concrete example of the difficulty that one encounters in establishing links between musical structures and that to which they refer. Insofar as it is prudent to understand musical significance as referring to every kind of intra- and extramusical sign, if one does not want to fall into the frequent trap of taking language as a model of all symbolic functioning, the term *semantic* must be reserved for the part of musical semiology that treats verbal associations that are conceptualized by means of music. On the poietic side, it has been the object of a certain tradition in the history of music, notably in the theories described in the eighteenth century as *Affektenlehre,* which were essentially elaborated in the Baroque era. On the aesthesic side, experimental psychology has constructed many often statistically sophisticated tools to obtain and classify the data obtained from subjects listening to music. Contrary to the widespread idea that these experiments have discovered what was already known, they have made it apparent that beyond the central tendencies, networks of associations existed that were not less real for being a minority. They have equally allowed "semantic maps" of style to come to light: for example, the works of Imberty (1979, 1981) reveal the interweaving of diverse types of water in Debussy: waters that are clear and demonstrated; waters that are cascading, transparent, torrential, flowing, undulating, heavy, despairing, majestic, weighty, or imposing; waters that allow listeners to link the musical phenomenon to the most profound in their imaginary.

One will be able to speak about musical semiology, strictly speaking, when one has succeeded in putting one's finger on the intermediary symbolic behaviors between verbal associations and sonorous structures and in clarifying the nature of the connection between the two. Despite the fact that the enormous cultural interferences probably constitute one of the deepest mysteries of musicology—indeed, of the human sciences—Imberty managed to establish a patent connection between the type of response obtained and the degree of heterogeneity in the musical form calculated according to the frequency of melodic intervals and the duration of metrical intervals. C. Boilès, for his part, demonstrated (1967, 1969) that, in the civilizations he studied (the Otomi and the Tepehua in Mexico), one could make precise meanings correspond to stable musical figures in a ritual context. Undoubtedly, more civilizations than is generally realized possess a system of semantic association: the evidence of Geneviève Calame-Grialue (1965) drawn from the Dogan people, and the work of Nicole Beaudry (1983) on the music of Haitian vodun and of Monique Desroches (1980) on that of the Hindus of Martinique would seem to confirm this.

Semiological research on music must allow music to be situated among the other symbolic forms, while avoiding the pitfall of taking human language as the standard. Music and language certainly have two common traits: linearity and organization in discrete units. It has been said often enough that music is *lacking* a first articulation, without, however, examining if it does not have something "more" as well. In any case, it could well be that, on the basis of the information furnished by the history of music and ethnomusicology, without having the status of a substitute for spoken language, the immersion of music in limiting contexts, notably religious ones, has given it a power of semantic expression that is stronger than what one is often ready to recognize in it today.

[*See also* Music, *historical overview article*.]

BIBLIOGRAPHY

Beaudry, Nicole. "Le langage des tambours dans la cérémonie vaudou haïtienne." *Revue de musique des universités canadiennes* 4 (1983): 125–140.

Bent, Ian. "Analysis." In *New Grove Dictionary of Music and Musicians,* edited by Stanley Sadie, vol. 1. London, 1980.

Boilès, C. "Tepehua Thought-Song: A Case of Semantic Signaling." *Ethnomusicology* 11.3 (1967): 267–292.

Boilès, C. "Otomi Cult Music." Ph.D. diss., Tulane University, 1969.

Calame-Griaule, Geneviève. *Ethnologie et langage: la parole chez les Dogon.* Paris, 1965.

Desroches, Monique. "Validation empirique de la méthode sémiologique en musique: le cas des indicatifs de tambour dans les cérémonies indiennes en Martinique." *Yearbook of the International Folk Music Council* 12 (1980): 67–76.

Francès, Robert. *La perception de la musique.* Paris, 1958.

Fubini, Enrico. *Les philosophes et la musique.* Translated by Daniele Pistone. Paris, 1983.

Hanslick, Edvard. *On the Musically Beautiful: A Contribution towards the Revision of the Aesthetics of Music.* Translated and edited by Geoffrey Payzant. Indianapolis, 1986.

Imberty, Michel. *Entendre la musique.* Paris, 1979.

Imberty, Michel. *Les écritures du temps.* Paris, 1981.

Jakobson, Roman. "Le langage en relation avec les autres systèmes de communication." In *Essais de linguistique générale,* translated by Nicolas Ruwet, vol. 2, pp. 91–103. Paris, 1973.

Lerdahl, Fred, and Ray Jackendoff. *A Generative Theory of Tonal Music.* Cambridge, Mass., 1983.

Meyer, Leonard B. *Emotion and Meaning in Music.* Chicago, 1956.

Meyer, Leonard B. *Explaining Music.* Berkeley, 1973.

Molino, J. "Fait musical et sémiologie de la musique." *Musique en Jeu* 17 (1975): 37–62. Translated into English as "Musical Fact and the Semiology of Music," *Music Analysis* 9.2 (1990): 105–156.

Musique en Jeu 1–33 (November 1970–November 1978). See nos. 5, 10, 12, and 17.

Nattiez, Jean-Jacques. *Fondements d'une sémiologie de la musique.* Paris, 1976.

Nattiez, Jean-Jacques. *Musicologie générale et sémiologie.* Paris, 1987. English translation by Carolyn Abbate published as *Music and Discourse: Toward a Semiology of Music* (Princeton, N.J., 1990).

Ruwet, Nicolas. *Langage, musique, poésie.* Paris, 1972. English translation of chap. 4 published as "Methods of Analysis in Musicology," *Music Analysis* 6.1–2 (1987): 3–36.

Stefani, Gino. *Introduzione alla semiotica della musica.* Palermo, 1976.

JEAN-JACQUES NATTIEZ
Translated from French by Terri Gordon
and Larsen Powell

Semiotics and Architecture

By the mid-1950s, confidence in the principles of modernism in architecture had reached a point of crisis—if not for architectural practitioners at large, then certainly for its most thoughtful historians and critics. Mainstream modernism's "functionalist" design methods had come to seem prosaic, and its long-accepted aesthetics of abstraction increasingly vacuous. In historical retrospect, it is evident that there were two particular bodies of theory outside architecture to which revisionist thinkers predominantly turned at that time, to seek intellectual reinvigoration for their discipline. These were "operations research," on the one hand, and theories of "perception" and of "reception," on the other. By means of a retheorization of "functionalism" in architecture, "operations research" led eventually to what came to be known as "systematic design methodology." The various theories of "perception" and "reception," on the other hand, through an intensified consideration of architecture's audience, led to an effort to apply semiotics to architecture.

One key venue at which both of these lines of inquiry were explored early on was the Hochschule für Gestaltung in Ulm, founded as a sort of "new Bauhaus" in 1955. Not a school of architecture in the usual sense, the Ulm Hochschule combined industrial and building design with visual communication and information—encompassing press, films, broadcasting, television, and advertising. At Ulm, all these design disciplines were intended to be explored from the perspective of what one of the school's notable early pedagogues, Gui Bonsiepe, named "technological rationalism." Tomás Maldonado—another of the leading figures at Ulm—eventually concluded that "operations research" alone could not adequately address the significance of form in architecture; as a result, like many of his colleagues, he found himself exploring theories of perception and reception as well. One important source was Max Bense, whose approach to communications was first outlined in his *Aesthetica* of 1954, and another one was the early American semiotician, Charles Morris, whose works had first appeared in the 1930s. Kenneth Frampton observed, in an essay on the Ulm school, that "operation" and "communication" were the two poles that were to "play major roles in the evolution of *Hochschule* theory" (1973). The school's commitment to technological rationalism meant that both these poles were being explored from a predominantly positivist philosophical vantage point.

The fact that this was so was not lost on an early visitor to Ulm, who was later to become one of the most committed critics of its "scientistic" intellectual orientation. This was Joseph Rykwert, whose 1958 lectures at the school eventually took the form of an essay (to be discussed later) titled "The Sitting Position: A Question of Method." Rykwert had already published the previous year an essay; "Meaning in Building," in which he lamented what he saw as the vulgar and banal consequences of a "preoccupation with rational criteria" for the design process, and called instead for architects to "acknowledge the emotional power of their work," insisting further that such an acknowledgment would depend on "investigations of a content, even of a referential content in architecture" (1982). In choosing to employ a term such as "referential content," Rykwert challenged the supposedly transparent abstract aesthetics of mainstream modernism head-on, and opened the way to the explicit consideration of the semiological "signifier" and "signified" in architecture, which was to commence some years later. "The Sitting Position," moreover, emphasized the anthropological—as opposed to the functional—aspects even of such an "operational" discipline as ergonomics. (Both of Rykwert's prescient essays of the late 1950s were later compiled in a collection titled *The Necessity of Artifice* [1982].)

As it happens, the first publication of Rykwert's "Meaning" essay was in the Italian magazine *Zodiac*, no. 6, and Italy became the home of the next notable series of efforts to apply semiotics to architecture. For example, in 1964, Giovanni Klaus Koenig published his *Analisi del linguaggio architettonico*, the first extended text devoted explicitly to the study of the possible application of the models of semiotics to architecture along parallel lines to those that had been explored at Ulm. (Appropriately enough, Koenig's text was preceded by an introduction by Maldonado.) In 1967, Koenig's book was followed by Renato de Fusco's *Architettura come mass medium* of 1967—this being a text whose very title foregrounded what was coming to be known as "reception theory"—in particular, the influence of the celebrated Canadian media theorist Marshall McLuhan. Then, in 1968, the rapidly evolving Italian perspective on semiotics was put into a definitively sharp focus with the publication of Umberto Eco's *La struttura assente*. Eco's comprehensive text not only summarized the whole earlier history of the various intellectual strands that made up the theory of semiotics up to that date; it put into context the contributions of Koenig and de Fusco to a possible semiotics of ar-

chitecture, and went on to set out the clearest, most detailed, and most broadly based application of the such principles to architecture that had appeared up to that time. (Eco made a number of efforts to translate this text into English, but eventually abandoned the effort, instead folding its arguments into a later book, which he wrote in English, *A Theory of Semiotics* (1976), and incorporating its architectural contents, translated into English, in a 1980 anthology discussed later in this essay.)

In a stream of thinking parallel in many ways to that of the Ulm thinkers and the Italians, a group of French scholars had begun to make their own significant contribution to the emerging field. From 1954 to 1957 had appeared the now-famous series of feuilletons of Roland Barthes that were compiled in French under the title *Mythologies* (1957). The following year, Barthes's text was joined by the French edition of Claude Lévi-Strauss's equally influential *Structural Anthropology*. Like most of the "structuralist" French texts of that period, both of these were more heavily dependent on their respective authors' debts to the linguistic theory of the Swiss pioneer Ferdinand de Saussure than on the work of either Charles Morris or Charles Sanders Pierce, even though the French scholars, like Eco, acknowledged the significant role played in the early development of semiotic theory by such figures. As a result of the rapid rise to prominence of Barthes's and Lévi-Strauss's typical methods of cultural interpretation, their works rapidly achieved considerable intellectual influence in an increasing number of nonliterary cultural fields—painting, photography, and cinema no less than architecture itself. With the French publication of Barthes's *Elements of Semiology* in 1964, this growing influence reached a definitive first culmination.

Among the revisionist theoreticians of architecture who eagerly read Lévi-Strauss's and Barthes's arguments of the early 1960s was the present author, who was engaged during the mid-1960s in the preparation of a doctoral dissertation in architecture at University College London. The professor of architecture there at that time was Richard Llewellyn-Davies, and he had made his school a British center of a revisionist architectural tendency known in those years in the English-speaking world as "systematic design methodology." Like their intellectual fellow travelers at the Ulm school, the British methodologists were engaged in an intellectual project intended to devise a new mode of designing that would possess the authority of science, and that would eschew any preoccupation with subjectivity, intuition, or myth.

It is difficult from the vantage point of three decades later to recall just how powerful this tendency appeared to be in the mid-1960s—especially in Britain, given how little influence it has managed to sustain in the years since. At the time, the advocates of this tendency bid fair to succeed in their project, at least insofar as they did manage to supplant the rapidly fading pieties of "orthodox" modernism, in numerous schools of architecture throughout the world, especially those of the former British Empire. Probably the first culmination of their project of revisionism was the publication in 1964 of *Notes on the Synthesis of Form* by Christopher Alexander. In this first of his many influential books, Alexander employed the concept of "fit" within the design process to devise a sort of utterly frictionless end point by which the ultimate appropriateness of any finally designed "form" could, as he saw it, be dispassionately assessed.

Revisionist theoreticians, who wished to see architecture regain a securer social role than mainstream modernism had been able to achieve for it, but who also believed that such a role needed to be one that was not limited to "functionality"—even to the sophisticated new versions of functionality that the design methodologists were claiming to find in applications of architecture of "operations research"—found highly promising the potential alternative applications of semiotics, particularly in the structuralist semiotics associated which the French intellectual lineage stretching back to de Saussure.

Among the intellectual efforts to realize that promise was a 1967 issue of *ARENA*, the journal of the Architectural Association School of Architecture in London, England, edited by the present author and devoted to the theme "Meaning in Architecture." Among the texts included in this issue that have proved to have some historical influence were "Typology and Design Method" by Alan Colquhoun, "The Sitting Position: A Question of Method" by Rykwert (the first English-language publication of the essay that had been first published in Italian in 1965 in *Edilizia Moderna*), and "*La Dimension Amoureuse* in Architecture" by George Baird. Colquhoun's essay was one of the first attempts to challenge the methodologies that had been developed at Ulm and at University College London, and was even framed as an explicit reply to Maldonado, whom Colquhoun had met when they were simultaneously visiting faculty at Princeton University. Baird's "*La Dimension Amoureuse* in Architecture" was one of the first published in English to set out a systematic exposition of the Saussurean concepts of *langue* and *parole,* of the "signifier" and the "signified," and of "system" and "syntax," as they might be employed to interpret architecture as a social field of meaning. In 1968, the journal publication was followed by a book of the same title, edited by Charles Jencks and Baird, and substantially expanded to include a number of additional texts on related topics by authors such as Françoise Choay, Gillo Dorfles, Kenneth Frampton, and Charles Jencks. In subsequent years, the book *Meaning in Architecture* went on to play a role in the dissemination of Saussurean semiotics as applied to architecture, first in the English-speaking world, and then also in Spain and in France, where foreign-language editions appeared.

In 1972, it became possible for the first time to discern the impact of the project of semiotics in architecture on an already established generation of thinkers, for in that year a still-controversial text was published that was much more directly oriented to the design of actual buildings than *Meaning in Architecture* had been, and was thereby more influential—at least in the English-speaking world. This was *Learning from Las Vegas,* by Robert Venturi, Denise Scott Brown, and Steven Izenour. Of this trio of authors, Venturi had already made himself famous as the author of the seminal revisionist text of 1966 *Complexity and Contradiction in Architecture*—probably the single most important of the critiques of the principles of "orthodox modern architecture," to use Venturi's sardonic term, that had preceded the historic application to architecture of the methods of semiotics. But the *Las Vegas* text went much farther down a revisionist road than Venturi's earlier text had done. Where *Complexity* had mounted a formalist critique of the compositional principles of modernism, *Las Vegas* went on to make a much more "sociological" and "populist" disparagement of modernism, and the precepts of semiotics formed a supportive methodological backdrop to it. For that matter, the choice by Venturi and his coauthors of Las Vegas itself as the putative exemplar of an identifiably distinctive—and popular—American urbanism was deliberately polemical.

It is interesting to note that the authors of this inflammatory book cited arguments from *Meaning in Architecture*, in particular Colquhoun's increasingly influential essay "Typology and Design Method." Indeed, during the early 1970s, the concept of "type" that had been so compellingly employed by Colquhoun in his 1967 essay merged with a body of ideas that had been being developed in Europe during those same years, and that revolved around the paired concepts of building "typology" and urban "morphology." Associated in the first instance with an Italian architectural lineage from Ernesto Rogers to Saverio Muratori and Aldo Rossi, the body of ideas comprising "typology/morphology" established a conceptual relationship of architecture to urban form that, like semiotics, was deeply embedded in the "social."

Five years after Venturi's *Las Vegas* came what is still probably the most influential English-language text on semiotics in architecture, Jencks's *The Language of Post-Modern Architecture* (1977). Where *Meaning in Architecture* set out a theoretical apparatus for consideration, and *Las Vegas* oriented this apparatus to "popular culture," Jencks's book not only recapitulated and extended both of these intellectual trajectories, but it also went on to illustrate a number of actual built examples, and explicitly linked the analogy of "language" in architecture, based on semiotics, with the specific architectural tendency then coming to be known as "postmodernism." For the next decade, the postmodernist tendency rapidly took over the practice of architecture throughout the English-speaking world, now intellectually sanctioned by the apparatus of "semiotics." In the United States, architects who became very prominent celebrities—

such as Michael Graves, Charles Moore, and Robert A. M. Stern—all did so as perceived practitioners of the new "postmodernist" style, and they in turn were followed in the world of more commercial architecture by practitioners in large corporate firms.

In 1980, a shift from popularizing texts back to more scholarly ones occurred in the English-speaking world with the publication of a follow-up volume to *Meaning in Architecture,* edited by one of that book's coeditors, Jencks, this time joined by Geoffrey Broadbent and Richard Bunt. *Signs, Symbols and Architecture* brought together a revised version (and English translation) of the portion of Eco's *La struttura assente* that had been devoted to architecture, with various texts by other authors. These included specific, detailed applications of semiological analysis to specific building elements (by Eco and Jencks, as well as by Mario Gandelsonas and David Morton), texts of a more sociological character (by Judith Blau and Maria Luisa Scalvini), and even certain expressions of skepticism in respect to the whole project of semiotics in architecture (by Xavier Rubert de Ventos and Bunt).

Historically speaking, the contribution to this book by Gandelsonas and Morton (a reprint of an essay that was first published in 1972) is particularly interesting, because it was devoted to semiological interpretations of the work of a number of American architects, including Peter Eisenman. Eisenman was soon to become part of a polemical backlash against the influence of semiotics in architecture. As of 1980, it was still politically possible for his work to be discussed in a volume of essays largely oriented to it affirmatively. It is true, of course, that at an earlier point in his career, Eisenman had been interested in a loose linguistic analogy with architecture, based on the concept of "deep structure" that had been framed by the American linguist Noam Chomsky. By 1980, Eisenman had abandoned the influence of Chomsky, but this did not prevent Gandelsonas and Morton from reprinting in that year an earlier text that discussed his work in terms primarily in terms of its "syntactics."

As the 1980s proceeded, and as the populist and popular phenomenon of "postmodernism" in architecture grew ever more ubiquitous throughout the world, it became increasingly uncommon to emphasize the "syntactic" aspects of the application of semiotics to architecture. Instead, the overwhelming bias of postmodern architecture toward the "semantic" utterly overwhelmed mainstream architectural practice. At the same time, the parallel urban ideas that had been framed in Europe in relation to the concepts of "typology" and "morphology" similarly lost their former sharp focus. Worst of all, other related aspects of this bias became strikingly evident as well. Instances were, on the one hand, the increasingly reactionary polemics in favor of a historicist, populist urbanism propounded by Britain's Prince of Wales and, on the other, the newly systematic appropriation of the tech-

niques of "postmodern" architecture then being undertaken by the Disney Corporation for its proliferating theme parks.

An undercurrent of dissent also became increasingly visible among leading theorists and critics in those years. The increasingly "scenographic" character of postmodernist architecture—in both its historicist and its more commercial theme-park modes—precipitated stronger and stronger objections among its critics, who pointed to its increasingly evident loss of cultural authenticity. What is more, some of these identified the application of semiotics to architecture as a cause of the perceived undesirable direction of architecture that had become so widespread. Polemical counterattacks on postmodernism—and at least implicitly on semiotics—grew increasingly vociferous in the late 1980s and early 1990s, and most of them derived from two distinct, but related, cultural/intellectual positions. The first was a resurgent architectural neo-avant-gardism, and Eisenman was a prominent representative of it. He had, of course, from the very beginning of his career had avant-gardist leanings, and the accommodationist political success of postmodern architecture offended him. Its historicist iconography, its mainstream popularity, and its corporate acceptability—all these eventually made postmodernism anathema for such American neo-avant-gardists as himself. His turning away from the ideas of Chomsky, and toward those of Jacques Derrida, only speeded up his neo-avant-gardist antipathy to "pomo," as he famously labeled it.

But perhaps equally as important in the backlash against postmodernism—as well as against typology/morphology studies—in intellectual circles was a distinct new commitment by a younger generation of critics to a phenomenological philosophical stance that was hostile not only to postmodern architecture, but to structuralist theory itself. Appropriately representing this position is Alberto Perez-Gomez, whose Gadamerian, hermeneutical *Architecture and the Crisis of Modern Science* had appeared in 1983. For the phenomenological position as represented by Perez-Gomez, the entire intellectual project of structuralism, including semiotics and typology, had to be rejected as "preconstituted" and thereby as inauthentic knowledge. Occupying an intermediate position between Eisenman and Perez-Gomez was Daniel Libeskind, who rose to fame during the period of the loss of credibility of postmodernism, effectively combining the charisma of the neo-avant-gardist designer with the moral indignation of the phenomenological critic of inauthenticity. By the mid-1990s, the impact of the combination of neo-avant-gardist and phenomenological attacks on postmodernism—and by implication on semiotics and structuralism as well—was effective enough to largely destroy the intellectual legitimacy that architecture and urban design had inherited from those bodies of theory two decades previously.

As a result, during the decade of the 1990s, a bifurcation of orientations to architecture split the intelligentsia of the profession off from its mainstream practitioners more severely than at any time since the early part of the twentieth century. On the one side, the popular project of postmodernism, launched in the 1970s, in large part in the name of semiotics, continues to dominate commercial architectural practice and popular taste. On the other, architectural education in leading schools, following on from the avant-gardist, phenomenological attack, has completely rejected postmodernism, committing itself instead to an architecture of critique and to an at least hypothetical tectonic integrity, which defines itself precisely in opposition to current mainstream practices.

If it can be said at the present time that the project of semiotics in architecture is to have any chance of intellectual rediscovery, it may well be as follows. It has become apparent that the architecture of critique is now a largely exhausted trope and cannot any longer sustain substantial new design creativity—even in predominantly academic architectural circles. At the same time, the inability of the neo-avant-gardism promulgated by figures such as Peter Eisenman and Libeskind to come compellingly to terms with the "social" and with the urban is evidently troubling to an increasing number of contemporary observers. The revisionist theory of the 1960s and 1970s—now so long in disrepute as to have been forgotten—appears to be becoming a topic of increasing interest to a younger generation of architectural historians and theorists. Perhaps the combination of the inadequacies of the once-ascendant avant-gardist project, combined with the aura of historical rediscovery, will yet reinvigorate the historic project of semiotics and architecture.

[*See also* Architecture; *and* Postmodernism.]

BIBLIOGRAPHY

Alexander, Christopher. *Notes on the Synthesis of Form.* Cambridge, Mass., 1964.

Barthes, Roland. *Mythologies.* Paris, 1957.

Barthes, Roland. *Elements of Semiology.* Translated by Annette Lavers and Colin Smith. London, 1967.

Broadbent, Geoffrey, Richard Bunt, and Charles Jencks, eds. *Signs, Symbols and Architecture.* Chichester and New York, 1980.

Eco, Umberto. *La struttura assente: Introduzione alla ricerca semiologica.* Milan, 1968.

Eco, Umberto. *A Theory of Semiotics.* Bloomington, Ind. 1976.

Frampton, Kenneth. "Apropos Ulm." *Oppositions* (New York) 3 (1973): 17–36.

de Fusco, Renato. *Architettura come mass medium.* Bari, 1967.

Jencks, Charles A. *The Language of Post-Modern Architecture.* 6th ed. New York, 1991.

Jencks, Charles, and George Baird, eds. *Meaning in Architecture.* London, 1969.

Koenig, Giovanni Klaus. *Analisi del linguaggio architettonico.* Florence, 1964.

Lévi-Strauss, Claude. *Structural Anthropology.* Translated by Claire Jacobson and Brooke Grundfest Schoepf. New York, 1963.

Perez-Gomez, Alberto. *Architecture and the Crisis of Modern Science.* Cambridge, Mass., 1983.

Rossi, Aldo. *The Architecture of the City.* Translated by Diane Ghirardo and Joan Ockman, revised by Aldo Rossi and Peter Eisenman. Cambridge, Mass., 1982.

Rykwert, Joseph. *The Necessity of Artifice: Ideas in Architecture.* New York, 1982.

Venturi, Robert. *Complexity and Contradiction in Architecture.* 2d ed. New York, 1977.

Venturi, Robert, Denise Scott Brown, and Steven Izenour. *Learning from Las Vegas: The Forgotten Symbolism of Architectural Form.* Rev. ed. Cambridge, Mass., 1977.

GEORGE BAIRD

SEMPER, GOTTFRIED

SEMPER, GOTTFRIED (1803–1879), German architect and theorist. Born in Hamburg, Semper first studied mathematics at Göttingen University before attending briefly the Munich Academy of Fine Arts. He next traveled to Paris, where he learned architecture at a private school. From Paris he embarked on a three-year tour of Italy, Sicily, and Greece, during which time he developed an interest in classical polychromy. In 1834, Semper received a chair at the Dresden Academy of Fine Arts. In that city he built a major architectural practice with notable designs for the Hoftheater and Art Gallery. This promising career as a monumental builder was rudely halted by the political uprising of 1849, in which Semper and Richard Wagner participated; their involvement led to their political exile. Semper lived first in Paris but then crossed the English Channel to London, where he eventually taught at Henry Cole's Department of Practical Art (later Victoria and Albert Museum). In 1855, Semper moved to Zurich to head the architecture department of the newly created federal Polytechnikum (now ETH). Eventually, he returned to practice; counted among his late works are the Winterthur town hall (1864–1870), the second Dresden Hoftheater (1869–1878), the Vienna Art History and Natural History Museums (1869–1891), and the Hofburg Theater (1871–1888).

The formative impulse to Semper's architectural and aesthetic theories was his trip to Greece in 1833. He had left Paris in 1830 on the heels of Jacques-Ignaz Hittorff's address to the Académie des Beaux-Arts, at which the noted architect displayed his brilliantly colored reconstruction of a Sicilian monument. In Athens, Semper recorded patches of paint on the Hephaesteum and Parthenon on both the interior and exterior walls. In the preliminary publication of his findings in 1834, he responded to the inadequacy of Johann Joachim Winckelmann's "white" vision of the past and insisted that color was not only essential to Greek plastic works but also held the key to their conception of art. Temples were painted for artistic and environmental reasons (the sunny climate, the variegated landscape) as well as for symbolic ones. The hanging of flowers, branches, implements, shields, and other emblems on early temples initiated a process whereby these motifs were later incorporated into monuments plastically. What gave these elements a higher artistic calling, however, was the addition of paint, gilding, draperies, baldachins, spectators, priests, choruses, and processions—all of which elevated the temple to the center point of elaborate communal rituals. These dramatic *Gesamtkunstwerken,* as it were, functioned more theatrically than religiously in their sentiments; their development paralleled the perfection of the classical Greek stage.

Semper's busy Dresden practice prevented the completion of his planned folio on polychromy, but his beliefs remained firm and were enriched in the 1840s by new archaeological and ethnological findings. Another force affecting his intellectual development was the arrival in Dresden in 1842 of the young Richard Wagner. The latter's first operas were performed in the theater that Semper had designed and the two men became close friends. Their spirited artistic debates, during which Wagner also came to form his view of a classical synthesis of the arts, became a focal point of Dresden's lively artistic culture.

The Dresden uprising of May 1849 ended this happy period and Semper suffered greatly as a result of his exile. With his career in ruins, he turned his attention to writing. His plans for a major work of theory faltered, but in 1851 he published a short work titled *The Four Elements of Architecture.* The first few chapters were a defense of his earlier views on polychromy; in the second half of the study, however, he developed the theme of architecture's conceptual origins.

Drawing on Gustav Klemm's cultural history and the Assyrian findings of Sir Austin Henry Layard and Paul Émile Botta, Semper proposed that architectural forms were generated by four primal motives or ideas: walling, roofing, mounding, and hearth gathering. The last was the social motive for civilization; tribes gathered around the fire after the chase. The other three motives appeared to protect the hearth against inclement weather: the mound raised the fire off the damp earth; the roof shielded it overhead; the wall protected it from wind. Each motive developed formally in different ways in different cultures. Each motive also spawned its own art industries. The hearth gave rise to the ceramic and metal arts. From the roof came the idea of carpentry or the concept of a fixed framework. The notion of mounding was developed in earthworks and waterworks, later evolving into terracing and masonry.

The fourth element, the vertical enclosure or wall, was the most significant in Semper's theory. He was struck by ethnological descriptions of aboriginal abodes in which crude mats were hung vertically from timber frames, the mats serving as walls. These hangings, Semper reasoned, gave rise to the art of textiles, but just as importantly to the spatial motive of architecture: the separation of an inner world distinct from the outer. Later, as more durable walls were erected, textile fabrics continued to be hung inside solid walls as symbolic reminders of their primordial past.

Still later, these dressings give rise to other types of sheathing or paneling, whose decorative motifs and stylistic details often alluded to their textile forerunners. This was a stage exemplified for Semper by the Assyrian bas-reliefs in alabaster. The Greeks inherited this "dressing principle" *(Bekleidungprinzip)* from the East, which they exploited in their polychrome temples.

In 1851, Semper became involved in laying out some of the national exhibits for the Great London Exhibition. The commissions in themselves were insignificant, but they allowed him access to the one million square feet of wares on display. He was able to examine artifacts from the so-called primitive nations as well as the latest implements of industrialized technology. At the close of the event, he wrote a lengthy review of its significance, *Wissenschaft, Industrie, und Kunst* (Science, Industry, and Art).

This book, presaging ideas of Walter Benjamin, is a masterful analysis of industrialization and its effect on traditional conceptions of art. If the art of the past was based on handicraft methods of fabrication, new industrial forces and the division of labor were quickly rendering this approach obsolete. Machines now sew, knit, embroider, paint, carve, encroach deeply on the field of human art, and put to shame every human skill. This devaluation of labor results in a devaluation of meaning, as art made in the traditional way comes to be seen as eccentric. This abundance of means, moreover, is aided by the speculative forces of capitalism, which has insinuated itself into the marketplace with its values of fashion and consumption. If artistic forms produced for the masses worked well with some items such as carriages or musical instruments, this process was having a stultifying effect on the traditional arts. High art, in particular, was being mortally hit.

After Semper moved to Zurich in 1855, he began in earnest his major work of theory: *Style in the Technical and Tectonic Arts, or Practical Aesthetics.* It appeared in two lengthy volumes between 1860 and 1863. A planned third volume devoted to architecture was never started.

Semper's masterwork carried forward many of his earlier ideas, but it also expanded greatly the scope and depth of interests. In essence, he conceived the book as a general theory of artistic forms—a study of the ornamental and formal development of motifs from their origin in the four industrial motives of textiles, ceramics, tectonics, and stereotomy. Semper now placed more emphasis on the symbolic values of forms and their evolution, for instance, how a simple wreath might signify the notion of eurythmic binding or how an ornamental pattern might derive from the art of tattooing. In parts of his study, he undertook psychological analyses of the formal significance of certain artistic paradigms, such as his cultural interpretation Egyptian *situla* and Greek *hydria.* In other parts, he showed how a basket weave in textiles or the specific curvature of a ceramic vase might be transposed to a column capital or entablature molding. Even linguistic analysis played a prominent role in his method. The German word for "hem" or "border" *(Saum),* for instance, shares a linguistic similarity with the German word for "hedge" *(Zaum).* Both also have the additional meanings of "fillet" and "fence." Again, the word for "clothing" *(Gewand)* is related to the word for "partition wall" *(Wand).*

The heart of his aesthetic theory, however, lay in those passages dealing with the "masking of reality" in the arts. Drawing on Romantic themes going back to Friedrich von Schiller, Semper cited the improvised and brilliantly endowed festival stage of antiquity as the motive for the permanent monument—an event that makes its Dionysian entry in Attic times. Now the polychrome "dressing" that was inherited from the East becomes a dissimulating fabric, a conscious masking of the material reality and thematic content of artistic forms. If Greek drama with its chorus and masked actors sought to represent life's tragic and comic underpinnings, he argued, so monumental Greek art strove to become a symbolic masking of life's ennobling cultural forms. He identifies the "haze of carnival candles" as the "true atmosphere" for all high art—from the "stone dramas" of Phidias to the "carnival sentiment" of William Shakespeare.

Semper joined with Wagner in Munich in the 1860s to put these ideas into practice in the design of a colossal opera house, a building intended to stage the nearly completed *Ring* cycle. The glorious design, the forerunner to the less-ambitious theater at Bayreuth, was never realized—in part a result of Ludwig II's tenuous grasp of reality, in part of Wagner's scandalous behavior. But it was significant in other respects.

Friedrich Nietzsche began reading Semper in the summer of 1869 and took notes of those passages dealing with the Greek stage and its connection with monumental architecture. The following winter, Nietzsche delivered two lectures that dealt with Greek drama. Their leading theme was that the known works of Aeschylus and Sophocles are only stripped-down librettos of far more complex choral works. If modern man were somehow transposed back into Attic times, he would find these more satiric performances both foreign and barbaric in their emotional display. Nietzsche expanded this theme in his first book, *The Birth of Tragedy* (1872), in which he argued that Greek tragedy was born out of the union of Apollonian and Dionysian elements—a union in which, however, the Dionysian tendency dominated. This union effectively ended at the height of classical Greek culture when the rational tendencies of Euripides and Socrates purged the Dionysian component.

This theme gains additional relevance because, during these same months, Semper was preparing the iconographic scheme for his second Hoftheater in Dresden, in which he too paid homage to the "return of Dionysus" at the expense of more traditional Apollonian motifs. He saw his theater in emotional terms as a frenzied realm of a Dionysian dithyramb, as a dramatic *Gesamtkunstwerk* in which reality should be masked.

By the time of his death in 1879 Semper dominated the German architectural world and his ideas continued to assert themselves across Europe and North America for the next two decades. But his thought was equally influential in such areas as archaeology, anthropology, art history, and aesthetics.

Semper's impact on aesthetics was long-standing. In Zurich he was close to Friedrich Theodor Vischer, and the latter's "Kritik meiner Aesthetik" (Critique of My Aesthetics, 1866) almost certainly owes much to Semper's criticisms of Hegelian notions. Conrad Fiedler's essay "Observations on the Nature and History of Architecture" (1878) was written as a commentary to Semper's book on style, and in it Fiedler lauded the idealism of Semper for its many revelations. Heinrich Wölfflin's dissertation, "Prolegomena to a Psychology of Architecture" (1886), also owes a large debt to Semper's thought. August Schmarsow's inaugural address at the University of Leipzig, "The Essence of Architectural Creation" (1893), is entirely Semperian in its conception. One can measure Semper's importance at this time by Wilhelm Dilthey's contemporaneous characterization of him as the "real successor to Goethe."

Perhaps the most devout Semperian was the Viennese art historian Alois Riegl. As curator of textiles at the Austrian Museum for Art and Industry in the late 1880s, Riegl was intellectually raised on Semper's body of thought. In his early writings, he followed Semper's lead closely and his book *Stilfragen* (Questions of Style, 1893) is driven by his spirited defense of Semper's idealism against the materialist excesses of latter-day Semperians. Ironically, it was Riegl's subsequent and inexplicable reversal of this argument in 1901 that confused critics and art historians for more than three-quarters of a century.

[*See also* Architecture; *and* Riegl.]

BIBLIOGRAPHY

Works by Semper

Gottfried Semper: Ein Bild seines Lebens und Wirkens. Berlin, 1880.
The Four Elements of Architecture and Other Writings. Translated by Harry Francis Mallgrave and Wolfgang Herrmann. Cambridge and New York, 1989.

Other Sources

Bayer, Josef. "Gottfried Semper." *Zeitschrift für Bildende Kunst,* vol. 14. Leipzig, 1879. Also in *Baustudien und Baubilder: Schriften zur Kunst,* edited by Robert Stiassny (Jena, 1919).
Berry, J. Duncan. "The Legacy of Gottfried Semper: Studies in Späthistorismus." Ph.D. diss., Brown University, 1991.
Bletter, Rosmarie Haag. "Gottfried Semper." In *Macmillan Encyclopedia of Architects,* edited by Adolf K. Placzek, vol. 4 pp. 25–33. London, 1982.
Ettlinger, Leopold. *Gottfried Semper und die Antike: Beiträge zur Kunstanschauung des deutschen Klassizismus.* Halle, Germany, 1937.

Fröhlich, Martin. *Gottfried Semper: Zeichnerischer Nachlass an der ETH Zürich.* Basel, 1974.

Herrmann, Wolfgang. *Gottfried Semper: Theoretischer Nachlass an der ETH Zürich: Katalog und Kommentare.* Basel, 1981.

Herrmann, Wolfgang. *Gottfried Semper: In Search of Architecture.* Cambridge, Mass., 1984.

Laudel, Heidrun. *Gottfried Semper: Architektur und Stil.* Dresden, 1991.

Lipsius, Constantin. *Gottfried Semper in seiner Bedeutung als Architekt.* Berlin, 1880.

Magirius, Heinrich. *Gottfried Sempers zweites dresdner Hoftheater: Entstehung, künstlerische Ausstattung, Ikonographie.* Vienna, 1985.

Magirius, Heinrich. "Die Gemäldegalerie in Dresden: Ein Bau von Gottfried Semper." In *Gemäldegalerie Dresden.* Leipzig, 1992.

Mallgrave, Harry Francis. *Gottfried Semper: Architect of the Nineteenth Century.* New Haven, 1996.

Quitzsch, Heinz. *Die ästhetischen Anschauungen Gottfried Sempers.* Berlin, 1962.

Staatliche Kunstsammlungen Dresden. *Gottfried Semper, 1803–1879: Baumeister zwischen Revolution und Historismus.* Dresden, 1979; 2d ed., Munich, 1980.

Stockmeyer, Ernst. *Gottfried Sempers Kunsttheorie.* Zurich, 1939.

Technische Universität Dresden. *Gottfried Semper, 1803–1879: Sein Wirken als Architekt, Theoretiker und revolutionärer Demokrat und die schöpferische Aneignung seines progressiven Erbes.* Dresden, 1979.

HARRY F. MALLGRAVE

SENSIBILITÉ. Of all the major concepts of the French Enlightenment, none is quite so difficult to pinpoint as *sensibilité*. Etymologically, this term belonged to the same family of words as *sens, sensation, sentiment, sentimental,* and *sensiblerie.* Also associated with the term's moral and social vocabulary were notions such as sympathy, virtue, pity, benevolence, and various expressions for tender feeling and compassion. Yet, *sensibilité* was also central to physiological terminology beginning in the 1740s, when it edged out *irritabilité* as the word most commonly used to describe the innate capacity to react to stimuli that was held to underlie all the phenomena of life in the human body. The concept of *sensibilité* was thus invested with enormous connotative power in mid- to late eighteenth-century France, and figured prominently in fields as diverse as the philosophy of the mind, ethics and social theory, biomedical science, aesthetics, and literature—all of which belonged to the loose confederation of naturalistic discourses then known as the "sciences of man."

In fact, the various meanings attached to sensibility at this time tended to be mutually permeable, because the philosophes used the word as a bridging concept, a means of establishing causal connections between the physical and moral realms. From sensationalist philosophers of the intellect such as Étienne Bonnot de Condillac, Charles Bonnet, and Georges-Louis Leclerc de Buffon, to aestheticians such as Abbé Jean-Baptiste Dubos and Denis Diderot, to moralists such as Charles Duclos and Jean-Jacques Rousseau, to the vitalist theorists of the Montpellier medical school, French Enlightenment thinkers subscribed to the idea that

sensibility was the essential link between the human body and the psychological, intellectual, and ethical faculties of humankind. Sensibility was thus fundamental to this period's understanding of human nature: it was seen as the root of all human perceptions and reflections (G. S. Rousseau, 1976; Figlio, 1975); as the innate and active principle of sociability that gave rise to human society (Baasner, 1986); as a kind of sixth sense whose special affective energy was essential both to virtue and to art (Spink, 1977); and finally, as the paradigmatic vital force, whose actions could be detected in every bodily function, be it healthful or morbid (Williams, 1994). Sensibility was consequently far more than a fashionable cult of high-minded feeling or histrionic emotionalism, as some literary critics and historians have characterized it (Wilson, 1931). It was also the object of a unique culture: a "constellation of ideas, feelings, and events" that developed around the concept of sensibility throughout eighteenth-century Europe, albeit with often striking national differences (Barker-Benfield, 1992).

Three major traits distinguished the eighteenth-century French culture of sensibility from the ideas that surrounded the term elsewhere in Europe. First, sensibility and sentimentalism were closely associated in France with the process of secularization that the philosophes were intent on advancing (Denby, 1994). Second, French writers did not polarize sensibility in relation to sex and gender nearly as much as did their British counterparts (Barker-Benfield, 1992; Jones, 1993), at least not until the last few decades of the century; rather, even the most hard-boiled philosophes prided themselves on their sensibility, and saw nothing unmanly about cultivating this quality (Ridgeway, 1973). Third, sensibility was often imbued by French writers with a pronounced physicalist or materialist undertone, without provoking any major outcry from the defenders of morality and religion. One factor underlying the greater French tolerance for such approaches to sensibility was the unusual appeal that medicine held for this nation's intellectual and social elite (Coleman, 1974). To see just how physicalized the concept of sensibility became during the French Enlightenment, one need only consult the *Encyclopédie*, whose fifteenth volume contained two entries on the property: first, a lengthy medical article that affirmed sensibility's primacy in human physiology and pathology and described how it varied according to age, sex, temperament, the passions, and external factors such as climate; and second, a one-paragraph article on sensibility's extraordinary capacity to inspire virtue, to reinforce the intellectual faculties, and to persuade by appealing to the heart. The juxtaposition of these two articles is revealing, because it shows both the proximity of sensibility's physical and moral meanings and the prestige that was accorded to the physicians who rallied to the cause of sensibility during the second half of the century.

Chief among the theoretical inventions of eighteenth-century France was this working assumption: before one could assess an individual's moral disposition, one first had to determine how he or she reacted and interacted with the world as an organically sensitive being. Inspired by this assumption, a particular group of medical theorists set out at mid-century to develop a comprehensive and authoritative explanation of sensibility. These vitalistic-leaning theorists, based in Montpellier, called themselves *médecins philosophes;* their leader was Théophile de Bordeu, who was later cast in a somewhat caricatural form as an interlocutor in the *Rêve de d'Alembert,* Diderot's fictional dialogue on the origins of life. Bordeu and his followers seized on the landmark experimental studies of sensibility and irritability that the Swiss physiologist Albrecht von Haller had recently published and used them to refute the iatromechanistic doctrines that had dominated seventeenth- and early eighteenth-century European medicine (Moravia, 1978). Like Haller and contemporary English physicians such as Robert Whytt, the French medical vitalists believed that sensibility was conveyed via a system of natural, interorganic "sympathetic" coordination; they did not, however, perceive that system as limited exclusively to the nervous apparatus. Rather, using a metaphor that would soon reappear in other discursive contexts (such as Diderot's writings), they compared the sensible body to a beehive—a federation of semiautonomous parts, each of which followed rhythms determined by its particular dose of local sensibility. What held this "beehive" together, as Bordeu described it, was not the soul but rather a triumvirate of major vital centers (the brain, chest, and lower abdomen) whose influence over the local parts maintained the harmony of the general animal economy. The *médecins philosophes* then extrapolated this model of the animal economy onto the social economy, and concluded that it, too, was driven by sensibility and thus subject to medical intervention. In short, they saw the principle of sensibility as the key to forging not only new ways of diagnosing and treating the human body, but also a new, global understanding of the human race.

The *médecins philosophes* thus sought to catapult their field to the forefront of the Enlightenment movement by making physical sensibility the primary factor in the crusade to illuminate and improve humanity. They were, however, hardly alone in their efforts to use the notion of vital sensibility as a means of explaining the nonphysical phenomena of human life. A similar idea also resounded through the literature of the period—most particularly, the novel of sensibility. To be sure, sensibility was also central to eighteenth-century theater, especially to the hybrid dramatic genre known as the *drame bourgeois.* Yet, the literary genre in which sensibility's expanded meanings were most provocatively deployed was, without question, the novel. Prior to 1750, sensibility in the French novel was largely a worldly affair: upper-class sociability, as represented in fiction, was a mode of social intercourse that revolved around the acts of manifesting and deciphering such phenomena as

"delicacy" and "tender emotion" in oneself and in others (Marivaux, 1731–1741). After 1750, by contrast, the novel of sensibility became a fertile testing ground for exploring the medico-philosophical idea that all manifestations of sensibility were ultimately rooted in its organic foundations. Diderot, for example, created fictional works that both echoed and exploited Bordeu's conception of the body as a dynamically resonating sensible network. Rousseau, in turn, used his novel *La nouvelle Héloïse* to carry out the hygienically based *morale sensitive* that he, along with the Swiss physician Samuel-Auguste-André-David Tissot, envisioned as a means of containing sensibility within wholesome, moderate bounds. Later in the century, Choderlos de Laclos and Donatien-Alphonse-François de Sade produced libertine novels that ironically mimicked both the conventions of literary sentimentalism and the sexually bimorphic model of sensible constitution that emerged in the 1770s.

With its heavy emphasis on visualizing the invisible interior of the body—most particularly that of woman—the physiophilosophy of sensibility was not without a certain aesthetic dimension in its own right (Jordanova, 1989; Stafford, 1991). Equally intriguing, however, were the theories of fiction put forth in order to account for the ambiguous effects of sensibility, sentiment, and sympathy on aesthetic response (Marshall, 1988). Diderot, for example, argued vehemently in favor of creating literary works that would engage the reader-spectator intensely and involuntarily in touching scenes from the drama of everyday experience. His reflections on the aesthetic and ethical dimensions of fiction making are contained in a series of texts composed during the 1750s and 1760s: the *Entretiens sur le fils naturel* and *De la poésie dramatique,* where he set forth the principles underlying the new genre of *drame* with which he wanted to reform and update French theater; the *Éloge de Richardson,* where he described the epiphanic experience of reading Samuel Richardson's intimately absorbing novels; and *La religieuse,* where he explored the connections between the sympathy to which the novel of sensibility explicitly appealed and its implicit capacity to seduce its readers. As in his art criticism, Diderot called for the development of "detheatricalized modes of beholding" in theater and in the novel (Fried, 1988): he urged playwrights and novelists to forgo the contrived coups de théâtre typical of traditional French comedy, tragedy, and novels, and instead to present moving visual tableaux of sympathetic characters caught up in a moral crisis or a moment of strong emotion. Only then, Diderot maintained, would fiction truly stir the sensibility of its audience and give it the profound vision of moral and physical nature that great art should provide. To appreciate the austere pleasures of serious fiction, one had, in Diderot's view, to possess a pure and refined taste, a tender and honest soul, a good deal of experience in life, a noble mind, a slightly melancholic temperament, and "delicate organs" (Diderot, 1757). One had, in other words, to be a philosophe as he defined the figure: Diderot's ideal be-holder was a venerable, paternal bourgeois who, by being moved to tears before a dramatic tableau, would not only demonstrate his own sensitivity to the moral turmoil being represented, but also prompt his fellow reader-spectators to respond in kind (Caplan, 1985).

Although their literary works often revolved around the spectacle of a virtuous heroine in distress, Diderot and the numerous writers he inspired (these included Pierre-Augustin Caron de Beaumarchais, Louis-Sébastien Mercier, and the Marquis de Sade) promoted an aesthetic of sensibility that was not so much "feminized" or even sentimental as philosophical: by infusing their fictions with maximum intensity of dramatic effect, they hoped to put their audiences into direct, visceral contact with the great but often terrible energies of nature and the passions. One finds a similar effort to promote a more serious and emotional kind of fiction in the writings of Rousseau, but with an important difference: Rousseau was so deeply suspicious of the seductive powers of conventional French novels and theater that he deemed both to be beyond redemption. He thus took a dim view of contemporary efforts to transform these literary genres into forums for activating sensibility in the name of moral edification and sympathetic sociability, because he maintained that those virtues could only flourish beyond the boundaries of the existing social world. At the same time, Rousseau's phenomenally successful *La nouvelle Héloïse* was instrumental in popularizing the sentimentalist conception of fiction as an intensely affecting and potentially life-changing experience (Brooks, 1969).

In his emphasis on the problematic relationship between sensibility and society, Rousseau was closer to the other theorists of sensibility than he might have admitted. Although sensibility was largely seen as a gloriously harmonious and life-expanding force when held in the proper degree, it also seemed to lead people into physical disorder and moral decay when misdirected. Many medical theorists of the day perceived excessive sensibility to be a rising problem in the contemporary population, most particularly among their wealthy, idle, urban patients; hence, the peculiar mid-eighteenth-century fear that an epidemic of nervous maladies or "vapors" was overtaking France's cities—the very places where sympathy seemed most important, because of the complexity of the social interactions that took place there. The specter of vapors thus introduced an unsettling note into the theory of sensibility, a property that had once seemed to be the unequivocally positive mark of an ungendered moral elite, but was now increasingly associated with the debilitated, effeminate members of the leisure class (Foucault, 1961).

One response to this dilemma was semantic: new terms such as *sensiblerie* were coined during the 1770s and 1780s to differentiate positive from negative kinds of sensibility (Trahard, 1931–1933; Brissenden, 1974). Yet, there were also some interesting theoretical responses, as, for example, in Pierre Roussel's *Système physique et moral de la femme* (1775). Roussel's method of differentiating between types of sensibility was overtly anthropological: he divided the attributes of sensibility into complementary but incommensurate sets—feminine versus masculine, yielding versus resistant, womb-based versus cerebral. In other words, Roussel masculinized the noblest qualities of sensibility while feminizing those that he deemed primitive or less evolved, thus transforming the contemporary view of human nature into two perspectives: a progressive, meliorist perspective on man's nature, and a biologically deterministic perspective on woman's nature (Vila, 1995).

Roussel's bimorphic model of sensibility not only took so-called philosophical medicine in a new and troubling direction, but also demonstrated a growing tendency, both in medicine and beyond, to split sensibility into modes of expression that were often radically different. This conceptual movement, which became increasingly pronounced during the aftermath of the Enlightenment movement (the 1790s to 1830s), ran directly counter to the philosophes' efforts to devise a unified vision of humankind in which everything human could be seen as linked together in a seamless natural continuum. Sensibility and the jointly sentimentalist and vitalist ideas related to it remained popular even at the violent heights of the French Revolution (Trahard, 1936), and continued to be endowed with great explicative power in the biomedical sciences, philosophy, aesthetics, and literature. Yet, as nineteenth-century thinkers refined the meaning of sensibility for their particular fields, the old "enlightened" consensus over the property's integrated physico-moral-intellectual nature not only weakened, but was, in some cases, rejected outright.

In early nineteenth-century physiology, Xavier Bichat developed a new, more empirically grounded system for conceptualizing vitality in which sensibility was subdivided into two distinct modes: the inferior, involuntary mode characteristic of the organic or passional life, versus the highly developed, voluntary kind associated with the animal or intellectual life. Thanks in part to the greater precision that Bichat brought to vitalism, the monistic vision of sensibility persisted in medical theory well into the 1830s (Cabanis, 1802; Broussais, 1828). This concept of sensibility, however, encountered stiff opposition from rival biomedical theories of a dualist and politically conservative bent, which emerged after 1800 (Williams, 1994). A similar spiritualist, antimaterialist reinterpretation of sensibility was undertaken by philosophers such as Marie François Pierre Maine de Biran, who demoted it to an essentially passive role in the operations of cognitive perception and moral consciousness. And in literature, the antirevolutionary and generally antiphilosophe authors who launched the fledgling Romantic movement took pains to redefine the notions of sensibility and artistic genius in terms that were more restrictive, moralizing, and private, such that sensibility became endowed with religious and antisocial overtones that it had not had in the previous century outside of Rousseau's writings (Baasner, 1988).

The old unitary conception of sensibility thus fell victim after the end of the ancien régime to social upheaval, politics, new theoretical developments, and a pervasive urge to resacralize many of the aspects of human experience that had been desacralized during the Enlightenment: consciousness, personality, ethical imperatives, and the living process itself. *Sensibilité* did not disappear in the nineteenth century, but it did take a distinctly different form, most particularly in literature, philosophy, and aesthetics, where it became associated not with the rational and sociable qualities of humankind, but rather with imagination, mysticism, and the idiosyncracies of artistic temperament; hence, the emergence of a new dichotomy between sensibility and reason—a dichotomy that has since been misapplied to eighteenth-century France. That dichotomy does not, however, suffice to explain sensibility's complexity during the French Enlightenment, the era when *sensibilité* truly flourished and enjoyed a conceptual dynamism and breadth of meaning that have since been lost.

[*See also* French Aesthetics, *article on* Eighteenth-Century French Aesthetics; Science and Aesthetics; *and* Taste.]

BIBLIOGRAPHY

Primary Sources

Beaumarchais, Pierre-Augustin Caron de. "Essai sur le genre dramatique sérieux" (1757). In *Œuvres,* edited by Pierre Larthomas. Paris, 1988.

Bichat, Xavier. *Recherches physiologiques sur la vie et la mort* (1800). Paris, 1955.

Bonnet, Charles. *Essai analytique sur les facultés de l'âme* (1759). Reprint, Geneva, 1970.

Bordeu, Théophile de. *Recherches anatomiques sur la position des glandes, et sur leur action* (1752). In *Œuvres complètes,* vol. 2. Paris, 1818.

Broussais, François-Joseph-Victor. *De l'irritation et de la folie, ouvrage dans lequel les rapports du physique et du moral sont établis sur les bases de la médecine physiologique* (1828). Paris, 1986.

Cabanis, Pierre-Jean-Georges. *Rapports du physique et du moral de l'homme* (1802). Reprint, Geneva, 1980.

Diderot, Denis. *Entretiens sur le fils naturel* (1757). In *Le paradoxe sur le comédien, précédé des Entretiens sur le fils naturel.* Paris, 1981.

Diderot, Denis. *Discours sur la poésie dramatique* (1758). In *Œuvres complètes,* vol. 10. Paris, 1975.

Diderot, Denis. *La religieuse* (1760/1780–1782). Translated by Francis Birrell as *Memoirs of a Nun.* London, 1959.

Diderot, Denis. *Éloge de Richardson* (1761). Translated by Beatrix L. Tollemache as "An Eulogy of Richardson." In *Diderot's Thoughts on Art and Style.* London, 1896.

Diderot, Denis. *Le rêve de d'Alembert* (1769). In *Œuvres complètes,* vol. 17. Paris, 1975.

Fouquet, Henri. "Sensibilité, Sentiment (Médecine)" (1765). In *Encyclopédie, ou Dictionnaire raisonné des sciences, des arts et des métiers,* vol. XV. Reprint, New York, 1969.

Haller, Albrecht von. *Dissertation on the Sensible and Irritable Parts of Animals* (1755). Reprint, Baltimore, 1936.

Jaucourt, Louis de. "Sensibilité" (1765). In *Encyclopédie, ou Dictionnaire raisonné des sciences, des arts et des métiers,* vol. 3. 15. Reprint, New York, 1969.

Laclos, Choderlos de. *Les liaisons dangereuses* (1782). Translated and edited by Douglas Parmée. Oxford and New York, 1995.

Maine de Biran, Marie François Pierre. *Mémoire sur la décomposition de la pensée* (1805). In *Œuvres,* edited by François Azouvi, vol. 3. Paris, 1984.

Marivaux, Pierre Carlet de Chamblain de. *La vie de Marianne* (1731–1741). Translated Mary Mitchell Collyer as *The Virtuous Orphan.* Edited by William Harlin McBurney and Michael Francis Shugrve. Carbondale, Ill., 1965.

Mercier, Louis-Sébastien. *Du théâtre, ou Nouvel essai sur l'art dramatique* (1773). Reprint, Geneva, 1970.

Rousseau, Jean-Jacques. *Lettre à d'Alembert sur les spectacles* (1758). Paris, 1987.

Rousseau, Jean-Jacques. *La Nouvelle Héloïse* (1758). Translated by Judith H. McDowell as *Julie, or The New Eloise.* University Park, Pa., 1968.

Roussel, Pierre. *Système physique et moral de la femme, ou tableau philosophique de la constitution, de l'état organique, du tempérament, des mœurs et des fonctions propres au sexe* (1775). 7th ed. Paris, 1820.

Sade, Donatien-Alphonse-François de. *Justine, ou Les malheurs de la vertu* (1791). Translated and edited by Richard Seaver and Austryn Wainhouse as "Justine, or Good Conduct Well Chastised." In *The Complete Justine, Philosophy in the Bedroom, and Other Writings.* New York, 1965.

Sade, Donatien-Alphonse-François de. "Idée sur les romans" (1800). Translated by Austryn Wainhouse and Richard Seaver as "Reflections on the Novel." In *The 120 Days of Sodom and Other Writings.* New York, 1966.

Tissot, Samuel-André-Auguste-David. *Essai sur les maladies des gens du monde* (1770). In *Œuvres de M. Tissot,* vol. 4. Lausanne, 1788.

Other Sources

Baasner, Frank. "The Changing Meaning of 'Sensibilité': 1654 till 1704." *Studies in Eighteenth-Century Culture* 15 (1986): 77–96.

Baasner, Frank. *Der Begriff "sensibilité" im 18. Jahrhundert. Aufstieg und Niedergang eines Ideals.* Heidelberg, 1988.

Barker-Benfield, G. J. *The Culture of Sensibility: Sex and Society in Eighteenth-Century Britain.* Chicago, 1992.

Brissenden, R. F. *Virtue in Distress: Studies in the Novel of Sentiment from Richardson to Sade.* London, 1974.

Brooks, Peter. *The Novel of Worldliness.* Princeton, N.J., 1969.

Caplan, Jay. *Framed Narratives: Diderot's Genealogy of the Beholder.* Minneapolis, 1985.

Coleman, William. "Health and Hygiene in the Encyclopédie: A Medical Doctrine for the Bourgeoisie." *Journal of the History of Medicine* 29 (1974): 399–421.

Denby, David J. *Sentimental Narrative and the Social Order in France, 1760–1820.* Cambridge and New York, 1994.

Figlio, Karl M. "Theories of Perception and the Physiology of Mind in the Late Eighteenth Century." *History of Science* 12 (1975): 177–212.

Foucault, Michel. *Histoire de la folie à l'âge classique.* Paris, 1961. Translated by Richard Howard as *Madness and Civilization: A History of Insanity in the Age of Reason* (New York, 1965).

Fried, Michael. *Absorption and Theatricality: Painting and Beholder in the Age of Diderot.* Reprint, Chicago, 1988.

Jones, Chris. *Radical Sensibility: Literature and Ideas in the 1790s.* London and New York, 1993.

Jordanova, Ludmilla. "Natural Facts: An Historical Perspective on Science and Sexuality." In *Sexual Visions: Images of Gender in Science and Medicine between the Eighteenth and Twentieth Centuries.* Madison, Wis., 1989.

Marshall, David. *The Surprising Effects of Sympathy.* Chicago, 1988.

Moravia, Sergio. "From *homme machine* to *homme sensible:* Changing Eighteenth-Century Models of Man's Image." *Journal of the History of Ideas* 39.1 (1978): 45–60.

Ridgeway, R. S. *Voltaire and Sensibility.* Montreal, 1973.

Rousseau, G. S. "Nerves, Spirits, and Fibres: Towards Defining the Origins of Sensibility." In *Studies in the Eighteenth Century*, vol. 3, edited by R. F. Brissenden and J. Eade. Toronto, 1976.

Spink, John S. "'Sentiment', 'sensible', 'sensibilité': Les mots, les idées, d'après les 'moralistes' français et britanniques du début du dix-huitième siècle." *Zagadnienia Rodzajów Literackich* 20 (1977): 33–47.

Stafford, Barbara Maria. *Body Criticism: Imaging the Unseen in Enlightenment Art and Medicine.* Cambridge, Mass., 1991.

Trahard, Pierre. *Les maîtres de la sensibilité française au XVIIIe siècle, 1715–1789.* 4 vols. Paris, 1931–1933.

Trahard, Pierre. *La sensibilité révolutionnaire, 1789–1794.* Paris, 1936.

Vila, Anne C. "Sex and Sensibility: Pierre Roussel's *Système physique et moral de la femme*." *Representations* 51 (1995): 54–71.

Vila, Anne C. *Between Enlightenment and Pathology: Sensibility in the Literature and Medicine of Eighteenth-Century France.* Baltimore, 1997.

Williams, Elizabeth A. *The Physical and the Moral: Anthropology, Physiology, and Philosophical Medicine in France, 1750–1850.* Cambridge and New York, 1994.

Wilson, Arthur M., Jr. "Sensibility in France in the Eighteenth Century: A Study in Word History." *French Quarterly* 13 (1931): 35–46.

ANNE VILA

SEXUALITY. In present-day theoretical and critical usage in philosophy and the humanities, the term *sexuality* refers to an individual's historically determined and psychologically meaningful selection of erotic objects—not necessarily limited to partners of the opposite sex in genital intercourse—with the aim of satisfying sexual desire, understood to be an irreducible drive for pleasure in erotic activity. It is possible to classify social groups in terms of such selections, often described as an "orientation" or a "preference" when they seem endogenous and persistent; hence, different sociologically real sexualities can be defined. In the early part of the nineteenth century, however, "sexuality" referred to the teleological organization of human generation. In common usage as well as in modern biology, it generally denotes the possession and exercise of the reproductive functions as such. In aesthetics, sexuality can be broadly defined as the eroticism—even the pleasurableness—of art in its personal and intersubjective origins and significance. But it would also be possible to conceive it as the reproductive rationale of art (if any), for example, in its evolutionary emergence as a mode of human adaptation.

Eighteenth- and early nineteenth-century thinkers recognized different modes of personal eroticism and different institutions of sex and sexual feeling in society (for example, the "pederasty" of the ancient Greeks). But a systematic theory of erotic variability, including a typology of sexual "perversion," did not emerge until the second half of the nineteenth century. Psychiatric nosology, clinical observations of "contrary sexual feeling," suggestion therapy, and

sexual and criminal anthropology were coordinated in the many editions of Richard von Krafft-Ebing's *Psychopathia sexualis* (1st ed., 1886; 9th ed., 1894), a major reference until well into the twentieth century. Krafft-Ebing's work reflected its wider juridical-legal and social context. It investigated the relations between—and the balance of—the reflexive (or "irresponsible") and the volitional or ("ethical") dimensions of human sexual behavior and erotic feeling, an interest also expressed in the prepsychoanalytic work of Sigmund Freud (for example, in an 1888 essay, "The Brain"). *Psychopathia sexualis* was still implicitly taken up with the definition, punishment, or absolution of sodomy—nonprocreative and/or adulterous practices—as it had been treated in established canon law. It was also strongly influenced by contemporary and earlier antimasturbation movements (represented, for instance, in Heinrich Kaan's *Psychopathia sexualis* of 1844, an exclusively antionanism tract).

The modern theory of "sexuality" attempted to detach Krafft-Ebing's and similar "clinical forensics" of *psychopathia sexualis* from their traditional moralizing foundations and confusing typologies based on superficial patterns of behavior. Several thinkers sought to develop an empirically grounded or at least conceptually coherent concept of the sexual reflex in its long-term organization, beginning with its earliest observable manifestations in the human organism well before puberty. Ultimately, some "perversions" recognized by Krafft-Ebing, such as kleptomania, became less interesting to the newer approach, which saw them as offshoots of more fundamental structures; by the same token, the new approach recognized structures not distinguished in the earlier clinical forensics. The most influential version of the updated approach was the psychoanalytic sexology of Freud, stated in his *Three Essays on the Theory of Sexuality* (1st ed., 1905; 3d ed., 1915). Other thinkers, such as Magnus Hirschfeld, believed that sexual variation resulted from embryonic differentiation or mutation. These theories often appealed to reformers concerned to assert the criminal irresponsibility of alleged sexual perverts. But they lacked convincing empirical foundation until the endocrinological studies of the latter half of the twentieth century. Thus, it is with psychoanalysis that much of the literature on sexuality and the arts has been most closely connected.

Freud tracked the vicissitudes of the sexual drives from infancy through adulthood in relation to the habits of thought, speech, and behavior, psychosomatic symptoms, and imaginative constructions (whether private fantasy or conventionalized works of creative art), which serve, he believed, as relays in the transmission of the drive-energy ("libido") in its long-term arc from original stimulation to final discharge. Freud stressed both the archaic endogeny of sexual reflex—so-called infantile sexuality—and its "polymorphous" quality, the apparent fact that sexual stimulation can be obtained or desire directed at almost all parts or zones of the human body and in relation to almost any conceivable object of interest, including people of the same sex or inanimate objects. Such observations had been made before, but they had not been well integrated with a psychology as general as Freud's theories of the unconscious, of psychic defense ("repression"), and of dreams and parapraxes. Freud's approach was compatible with many forms of the biographical and historical analysis of persons and their imaginative productions; indeed, Freud's sexological theories were in part a response to certain traditions of art and literary production not only as they had been studied by Freud himself but also as they had been inherited by patients in Freud's client pool. Freud himself and a number of early followers produced pathographies of artists and writers, studies of works of art, and speculative anthropologies. Often criticized by art and literary historians, these endeavors nonetheless had an enormous impact on twentieth-century scholarship. They addressed aspects of aesthetic experience and of the history of the arts that other methods have barely broached. Not surprisingly, many twentieth-century artists became involved with Freudianism. Hence, twentieth-century art itself has made sexuality both one of its materials and one of its subjects. For this reason alone, sexuality is (or should be) a crucial analytic concern of aesthetics or of the history and criticism of the arts.

Psychoanalysis treats sexuality as a temporal process: it is both a cognitive history and a development, even a normative maturation, from an initial stimulation of the organism, whether innocuous or traumatic, to a satisfaction of the feelings created, sometimes retrospectively, by the stimulation and its analogues. Freud developed a complex account of the typical situations and thresholds of stimulation, trauma, and defense that organize a person—in or as his or her "sexuality"—from earliest childhood into adulthood. Each phase both retains and replaces elements of the earlier ones. In general, Freud saw much of emergent sexuality as a *Reizschutz*, a "shield against stimuli," in which a person protects and attempts to reproduce and augment what provides or has provided pleasure. In theory, then, one can work backward from a particular work of art—conceived as a relay of sexual reflex—toward earlier and possibly more defining conditions of the maker's "sexuality." By the same token, one can work forward from a work toward possible conditions of its reception—considering the ways, for example, in which it will or might stimulate an audience. Finally, one can work outward from a work to analogous or associated objects, persons, or situations in the artist's or the audience's life history. The work of art can be said to have—to express or to reflect—a "sexuality" in all of these directions just to the extent that it really is a node in the personal and social networks that transmit and organize eroticism.

But this is precisely the problem. Although the theories of sexuality have been widely embraced, methodology remains unclear. To what extent can a work of art relay sexuality when it must be conventionalized—responding to technical limits, stylistic norms, and social functions? Moreover, if completing the work requires active "repression" of motivating sexuality, as might be the case, to what extent can one rediscover sexuality *in* the work? Freud regarded the psychoanalysis itself as a manifestation of the patient's sexuality (brought into relation with the sexuality of the analyst). For this reason, the analysis is a platform from which a reconstructive archaeology can be launched. But in the case of art produced outside psychoanalysis, other means must be found to locate it in the historical web of a sexuality, presuming that sexuality itself is taken to be an intrapsychic and intersubjective reality. (An alternative—that sexuality is essentially a "textual" or aesthetic reality—will be considered momentarily, but it has less empirical and theoretical support.) For example, what an artist might offer as meaningful associations to an image within a psychoanalysis could be inferred by a historian from a pattern of stylistic or iconographic similarities among works of art. To take a similar example, what the analyst might interpret as a significant repeated symptom within a psychoanalysis could be inferred by the critic from a pattern of conventions—or seeming violations of convention—characteristic of a particular artistic canon.

In general, an archaeology of sexuality in the history and criticism of the arts requires properly clarified data in two domains. First, the temporal sequence of the production and reception of works of art must be charted comprehensively. This history supports analysis of sexual desire continuously represented and relayed in cognition and maturation. (In particular, long-term patterns of revision, erasure, and preservation should be studied; these might index a history of "repression.") Second, the relation of works of art to other constructions and activities of life must be mapped. This anthropology supports analysis of sexual desire continuously stimulated by and attached to situations, people, or objects. A substantial criticism of art can be conducted in the absence of this research, but it is unlikely to reveal much about sexuality (unless it is the sexuality of the critic). Of course, these topographies have little theoretical interest in themselves; they might conform to ordinary presentations of stylistic development or social history. The key will be provided by historically identifying or critically interpreting some aspect of style or history to be the satisfactory analogue of a symptom, parapraxis, or association—thus connected with stimulation, trauma, and defense—in the psychoanalytic sense. At this point, a stylistic or social history can be rewritten as a history of sexuality.

Influenced by linguistic and structuralist models in psychoanalysis, associated largely with the work of Jacques Lacan, many writers have urged that patterns of critical response to or social discourse about the arts can reveal the relay and pressure points of sexuality. For example, if popular response systematically avoided the homoerotic dimension of iconography, one could suspect that the images in question evoked forbidden or unspoken feelings of homosexual desire and anxiety. Although self-fulfilling to some extent, such accounts make sense if artistic languages and response systems as a whole—their points of articulation and slippage—are comprehensively understood: we need to know that a gap is, in fact, not *just* a gap but a silence or suppression. But although it is theoretically required, such a structural(ist) overview is rarely available.

More convincing have been a series of more strictly Freudian and Lacanian studies of the "letter" of artistic significance—that is, of the actual material structures of linguistic or imagistic usage in creative production, requiring painstaking attention to the temporality and rhythms of sexual desire charted by Freudian theories of defense, maturation (chiefly organized in the Oedipal complexes), and object relations, processes often called "subjectivity." Because Lacan considered subjectivity to be a basic "gap" in the person's relationship to language and other forms of representation (although this is not the place to review his several formulas), his students and followers could readily transform his psychoanalysis into a textual—or pictorial or cinematic—codicology and criticism, related to established philological as well as to phenomenological and deconstructive aesthetics. Like traditional Freudian pathographies, however, these inquiries risk implausible interpretations—for example, finding intricately coded but hidden features of a linguistic or visual structure. More troubling, they can readily lose sight of the human person and of the erotic status of aesthetic production for him or her; Lacanian criticism is highly formalistic.

Paradoxically, many recent students of sexuality in the arts oppose psychoanalysis, at least in part; they wish to reject the primacy it allegedly accords heterosexual male erotic experience and history. Feminists approach sexuality in relation to—sometimes even as a function of—the differences (biological, social, or experiential) between historically variable gender identities, histories, or positions. Gay and lesbian studies takes homosexuality as its central topic. In the 1990s, a broad "antihomophobia" movement arose out of contemporary feminism and gay and lesbian studies and an associated body of "queer theory." Like Krafft-Ebing, queer theory considers *all* nonstandard or "queer" sociosexual formations, such as transvestism or fetishism; like psychoanalysis, it treats normative sexuality (i.e., genital heterosexuality) as peculiar—that is, as a specific formation of the sexual reflex requiring cognitive and developmental analysis like any other. But, like feminism and gay studies, queer theory is substantially different in its intellectual foundation and direction from established sexological and psychoanalytic approaches. Three areas of divergence between established and newer approaches can be noted.

First, in feminism, gay and lesbian studies, and queer theory, Michel Foucault's historicist theories of discourse and subjectivity have provided attractive substitutes for the psychophysical and neurological platforms that Krafft-Ebing and Freud assumed. The *Introduction* to Foucault's *History of Sexuality* (1976) stressed that whatever its biopsychological matrix, homosexuality was and is the product of a social process of cultivation—namely, the formation of subjects in relation to classifications of sexual behavior, the chief effect, if not the sole cause, of which is to secure the purity, intelligibility, and reproducibility of the social order. Foucault's proposals about the actual history of this process in Western society were incomplete. But, as he intended, his deft blend of Freudian, Marxist, and structuralist insights offered a model for—if not quite a method for—a sociocultural history of sexuality. It is not clear what a Foucauldian art-critical perspective, or an aesthetics, strictly speaking, would look like. On the one hand, Foucault's historicism (his doctrine of the subject as slave) suggests that works of art might be vehicles for the social classification and management of sexual desire—as it were, creating or "calling into being" the sexuality of their makers and users. On the other hand, Foucault's strongly ethicist and libertarian views (his doctrine of the subject as ascetic), prominent in his later writing, might imply that art sustains a person's essential freedom to constitute himself or herself in a domain reserved from the surveillance and management of others. (Here Foucault's account of the human ego differs sharply from Lacan's account of the human subject.) Probably both of these aesthetic and art-critical perspectives could legitimately claim Foucault as godfather.

Second, the Freudian legacy has been reassessed. The research of social and cultural historians, many of them influenced by Foucault, tends to conceive Freud's sexology as a powerful interpretation—but also as a generalization—of specific erotic practices, social relations, and cultural traditions in the client pool Freud surveyed. This finding does not vitiate Freudian concepts of the unconscious, repression, identification, or anxiety; these remain central to all views of sexuality, including Foucault's. But Freud's model of infantile eroticism—what he called "bisexuality," a supposed lack of gender and other differentiation in sexual object choice—has come under strong pressure. Some scholars see it as Freud's ideological, albeit innovative, effort metaphysically to describe sexual variation in terms of latent or immanent potentials in order to satisfy the needs of his own commercial therapy of personal postnatal development. At the moment, quasi-psychoanalytic theories of primary undifferentiated sexuality and of a developmental history of erotic identifications and anxieties remain a touchstone for much feminism, gay and lesbian studies, and queer theory in aesthetics, histories of the arts, and cultural criticism. But some philosophers and critics of the arts have begun to explore (or, more exactly, to re-explore) the possibilities that sexuality, though it is surely constructed socially as a mosaic of intersubjectives and object relations, cannot be mapped as the history of the vicissitudes of a single sexual drive. This view—it ignores or opposes the founding doctrine of the sexual reflex with which psychoanalysis attempted to clarify sexological forensics—has remained popular in belles-lettres and nonacademic aesthetics and criticism since the end of the nineteenth century. There it tended to be connected with cultural conservatisms. Today, however, the deconstruction of the sexual reflex—and emerging ethical and aesthetic models of sexuality—tends to be connected with more radical, or at least libertarian, social and cultural philosophies.

Third, the history and anthropology of sexuality, on a worldwide and transhistorical scale, have been greatly enlarged. For the first time, evidence drawn from the arts has come to play a major role in the very theory of sexuality itself. Aesthetics has stressed the construction of fluid eroticisms in the specifically imagistic (i.e., visual, acoustic, tactile, kinesthetic) dimensions of sensation and thought and in the fields of gestural, sartorial, and interpersonal activity. Some theorists propose that, irrespective of the biopsychological nature of sexuality, it must always be presented or performed in a social arena using the cultural forms and aesthetic strategies available to or devised by the performers. This concept, trading on the close philosophical connection between erotics and aesthetics, probably generalizes from the social histories of specifically performative sexualities, such as transvestism. It certainly embodies familiar Wildean and Dadaist conceptions of the supposedly transgressive roles of art, theater, dress, and so on in private and public life. But, for this reason, it has helped aesthetics to grasp influential artistic movements of recent decades—from Duchamp to performance art—and to interpret historical practices of body ornamentation, cross-dressing, masquerading, interior design, and the like. Moreover, there are substantial overlaps, if not identities, between judgments of desire and desirability rendered in sexual and in aesthetic categories.

In the hands of some historians and critics of the arts, the performative theory of gender and sexuality often ascribes a high degree of self-conscious agency and creativity not only to the technical process of aesthetic construction itself, but also to the management of erotic identity—the supposed basis and aim of much artistic production. But the orthodox Freudian theory of sexuality and offshoots such as the Lacanian theory of subjectivity consider the infantile and longer-term aspects of eroticism, personal and intersubjective, to be largely outside the reach of such individual technical creation and recreation. Art might be repetition, revision, or symptom, and it could be therapy, but it is not sexuality as such. Moreover, some feminist and gay/lesbian critics have objected on ethical and political grounds to the idea that sexualities might be constructed and recon-

structed like works of art, even though it might be true that works of art are constructed and reconstructed in sexualities. Finally, the real theoretical difference, if any, between a "performative"-aesthetic theory of gender and sexuality and a standard philosophical model of intentionality in its complex—layered, nested, and reflexive—structures remains to be clarified.

At the present time, the theory, history, and criticism of sexuality in the arts find themselves at a complex crossroads; intellectually, they are positioned midway between Krafft-Ebing's *Psychopathia sexualis* and Oscar Wilde's "Decay of Lying." Freud's *Three Essays on the Theory of Sexuality* and Foucault's *History of Sexuality* remain indispensable points of reference, but neither offered an explicit perspective on the relation between sexuality and aesthetics. Many writers work from expectations based on a formal theory of sexuality, such as Freud's or Foucault's, to particular studies of individual works of art or aesthetic problems. But a formal aesthetic theory should also generate expectations guiding research into the most elementary data of sexual behavior and feeling. Some of the most compelling treatments of sexuality in the arts assume both of these analytic possibilities; they make about equal contributions, for instance, to psychoanalysis and to narratology, or to the history of painting and to the history of homosexuality. Any forced or limited choice between the options is likely to be unproductive.

[*See also* Foucault; Freud; Gay Aesthetics; Lacan; *and* Lesbian Aesthetics.]

BIBLIOGRAPHY

Bersani, Leo. *The Freudian Body: Psychoanalysis and Art.* New York, 1986.

Davis, Whitney. *Replications: Archaeology, Art History, Psychoanalysis.* University Park, Pa., 1996.

Foucault, Michel. *The History of Sexuality,* vol. 1, *An Introduction* (1976). Translated by Robert Hurley. New York, 1978.

Freud, Sigmund. *Drei Abhandlungen zur Sexualtheorie.* Vienna, 1905. Translated as *Three Essays on the Theory of Sexuality,* in *The Standard Edition of the Complete Psychological Works of Sigmund Freud,* edited James Strachey, vol. 7 (London, 1953), pp. 125–245.

Freud, Sigmund. *Eine Kindheitserinnerung des Leonardo da Vinci.* Vienna, 1910. Translated as *Leonardo da Vinci and a Memory of His Childhood,* in *The Standard Edition of the Complete Psychological Works of Sigmund Freud,* edited by James Strachey, vol. 11 (London, 1957), pp. 59–137.

Krafft-Ebing, Richard von. *Psychopathia Sexualis: Mit besonderer Berücksichtigung der conträren Sexualempfindung: Eine klinisch-forensische Studie.* 9th ed. Stuttgart, 1894.

Lacan, Jacques. *Écrits: A Selection* (1966). Translated by Alan Sheridan. New York, 1977.

Potts, Alex. *Flesh and the Ideal: Winckelmann and the Origins of Art History.* New Haven, 1994.

Rose, Jacqueline. *Sexuality in the Field of Vision.* London, 1986.

Sedgwick, Eve Kosofsky. *Epistemology of the Closet.* Berkeley, 1990.

Weeks, Jeffrey. *Sexuality and Its Discontents: Meanings, Myths, and Modern Sexualities.* London and Boston, 1985.

Wilde, Oscar. "The Decay of Lying." In *The Complete Works of Oscar Wilde*, edited by Robert Ross, vol. 4, pp. 3–57. New York, 1905.
Wollheim, Richard. *Painting as an Art*. Princeton, N.J., 1987.

WHITNEY DAVIS

SHAFTESBURY, EARL OF. *See* Cooper.

SIDNEY, PHILIP (1554–1586), a poet of the English Renaissance, who suffered an early death, from a battle wound. Sidney's *A Defence of Poetry,* published posthumously in 1595, is widely regarded as the most significant work of aesthetics in the Elizabethan era. Yet, Sidney did not live to witness the apex of Elizabethan drama and poetry—William Shakespeare was only twenty-two when Sidney died, and John Donne was fourteen. This may explain Sidney's disrespect for the contemporary theater, which he criticized for violating the Aristotelian unities and for the vulgarity of the public playhouses (though Shakespeare himself would soon be reproved on similar grounds). Indeed, Sidney is curiously ambivalent in his defense of both his own métiers, drama and the love poem. Although Sidney's production of courtly spectacles won him fame as an upscale "Master of the Revels," his enduring reputation as a poet rests on his amorous verse. Because Sidney's influence on aesthetics is owing almost solely to the *Defence*, however, this essay will focus exclusively on that work, which is a rich source of eloquently expressed ideas, both new and received.

Sidney's characterization of poetry as an art of imitation appeals explicitly to Aristotle, but the influence of Horace and Julius Caesar Scaliger can be seen in his gloss of poetic imitation as "a speaking picture—with this end, to teach and delight" (Sidney, 1966, p. 25). Similarly, although the *Defence* is clearly meant to answer the Platonic indictment of poetry, Sidney's Plato is always seen through the eyes of contemporary Puritanism. Sidney was particularly influenced by Stephen Gosson, whose *The School of Abuse* is the most famous tract in the Puritan sermon and pamphlet campaign against the theater, which culminated in the suppression of stage plays in 1642 by an edict of the Long Parliament. Sidney sought wherever possible to appease his opponents, even granting their complaint that poetry can be morally corrupting. Yet, because it can also serve as a powerful force for virtue, Sidney insists that the admitted "abuses" of poetry do not infect its proper use. He thus embraced a form of humanist aesthetics, which claims an ethical function for art. Yet, Sidney's humanism was less a moralistic constraint on poetry than an expression of his faith in the Horatian ideal, that the poet mingle the useful and the sweet, which elides any tension between moral and aesthetic demands.

Sidney expressly defends poetry against four charges: that poetry is a waste of time, that poets are liars, that poems indulge "sinful fancies," and that Plato banished the poet from his ideal republic. This last charge is dismissed with the dubious claim that Plato too disparaged only bad poetry. More authentically Platonic is Sidney's quick rejection of the triviality charge, on the grounds of poetry's ability to move us in morally significant ways, by giving us attractive pictures of virtue (although, of course, Sidney was far more sanguine about the effects of poetry than was Plato). But the bulk of Sidney's argument is directed against the charges of deception and sin. Although antecedents of both accusations can be found in Plato, their metaphysical and religious baggage was lost in the translation from antiquity. It has been questioned whether Plato actually held that poetry is inevitably misleading, but this reading was long standard. Cast in the Puritan idiom, it was expressed as the idea that poets are liars by nature. Plato's most serious charge, that poetry encourages emotional incontinence, was sexualized in the Puritan imagination. Thus, whereas Plato was primarily concerned with tragedy's power to induce such unmanly emotions as sorrow and fear, Sidney focuses on the idea that poetry encourages "wanton sinfulness and lustful love" (ibid., p. 54).

But there is a more profound difference between the burden of Sidney's defense of poetry and Aristotle's. Because Plato took pleasure to be intrinsically good, it follows that any argument against a form of pleasure must rest on the adverse consequences of its indulgence. In contrast, Sidney's Puritan opponents were innately suspicious of pleasure. Therefore, in defending poetry, Sidney had both a positive and a negative task: he needed to locate a suitably nonhedonic value of poetry, and to acquit the poet of the charges of deception and incitement. He found the positive value of poetry in its ability to teach virtue. Although Sidney develops this idea in a rather scattershot manner, his most distinctive humanist thesis is that "the poets' persons and doings are but pictures what should be, and not stories what have been" (ibid., p. 53). The two significant negative charges against poetry are handled quite differently. Sidney grants that the abuse of poetry can be an incitement to sin, but he denies that poets are even capable of lying. Thus, the *Defence* responds to both the positive and the negative challenge; but there is a tension at the center of Sidney's thought, which foreshadows his deeply conflicted legacy to aesthetics.

Sidney is perhaps best remembered for his uncompromising response to the deception charge. Although poets traffic in the depiction of imaginary scenarios, we are not asked to believe in them, nor do we. Rather, Sidney famously insists that "the poet, he nothing affirms, and therefore never lieth" (ibid., p. 52). This slogan was taken up by a variety of twentieth-century literary critics and philosophers, who wanted to claim that fiction can involve only the pretense of assertion, never the genuine article. Their motives for denying poetic assertion are diverse. It is a central tenet of modernism that aesthetic value is radically autonomous from the values of truth and goodness; and the New Critics in particular feared that to consider poetry as a vehicle for assertion inevitably leads to its being judged on adventitious criteria. Some postmodern successors of the New Critics, while rejecting their conception of aesthetic value, have embraced the related idea that literature can speak only of itself, and not of the world. One major philosophical theory attempts to ground fictionality on the speech act of pretended assertion.

It is much easier, however, to hold that we are not expected to believe in the poet's scenarios, or that some flimsy stage prop is the gate of Thebes, than it is to claim that a fable does not actually assert its moral. There is good reason to think that Sidney never meant to make this stronger claim, or to hold that poets literally assert nothing. The poet can be acquitted of being a liar by nature once we see that we are not being asked to believe in the fictitious persons and doings he depicts. Any more thoroughgoing denial of poetic assertion is deeply problematic, and typically rests on a faulty theory of assertion or a tendentious view of fiction. Moreover, it would belie the distinctive aspect of Sidney's humanism: his idea that the poet shows us what should, or should not, be. If the poet makes moral claims, then he does assert something rather than nothing; and he is therefore capable of error and deceit, after all. There are several ways one might seek to reconcile Sidney's humanism with his claim that poets never lie; but the route most in keeping with the gist of Sidney's view retreats somewhat from his most famous dictum. Although poets are capable of moral deception, by putting forward pernicious views of what should be, we are not in danger of being taken in, because though moral motivation is lamentably scarce, moral knowledge is easily had.

However Sidney might have resolved this tension, had he recognized it, two aspects of his view cannot be doubted: first, he pays poetry the Platonic compliment of thinking it powerful enough to be dangerous; and, second, his commitment to humanist aesthetics is undaunted by poetry's acknowledged dangers. Although Sidney allows that "by the reason of his sweet charming force, [poetry] can do more hurt than any other army of words" (ibid., p. 55), he nevertheless insists that, when properly used, it can also do the most good. Even so, unless we can be convinced that the "proper use" of poetry accommodates both moral and aesthetic demands, Sidney's position seems vulnerable to charges of moralism. Perhaps Plato was right, and it is just when poetry is most charming that it is also most treacherous.

[*See also* Literature, *article on* Literary Aesthetics; *and* Poetics.]

BIBLIOGRAPHY

Work by Sidney

A Defence of Poetry (1595). Edited by Jan A. Van Dorsten. New York and Oxford, 1966.

Antecedents of Sidney's *Defence*

Aristotle. *Poetics.* Edited by D. W. Lucas. Oxford, 1968.
Gosson, Stephen. *The School of Abuse.* London, 1841.
Horace. *The Art of Poetry.* In *Horace on the Art of Poetry,* edited by Edward Henry Blakeney. London, 1928.
Plato. *Republic.* Translated by G. M. A. Grube. Indianapolis, 1974.
Scaliger, Julius Caesar. *Poetics.* In *Select Translations from Scaliger's Poetics,* edited by Frederick Morgan Padelford. New York, 1905.

Other Sources

Abrams, M. H. *The Mirror and the Lamp: Romantic Theory and the Critical Tradition.* New York and Oxford, 1953.
Buxton, John. *Sir Philip Sidney and the English Renaissance.* 2d ed. London, 1964.
Frye, Northrop. *The Anatomy of Criticism: Four Essays.* Princeton, N.J., 1957.
Graff, Gerald. *Poetic Statement and Critical Dogma.* Evanston, Ill., 1970.
Heninger, S. K., Jr. "Sidney's Speaking Pictures and the Theater." *Style* 23.3 (Fall 1989).
Jacobson, Daniel. "Sir Philip Sidney's Dilemma: On the Ethical Function of Narrative Art." *Journal of Aesthetics and Art Criticism* 54 (Fall 1996): 327–336.
Wimsatt, W. K., and Cleanth Brooks. *Literary Criticism: A Short History.* New York, 1957.

DANIEL JACOBSON

SIGN. *See* Prague School; Semiotics; *and* Structuralism.

SIMMEL, GEORG (1858–1918), German sociologist who explored the different facets of culture. Besides history, religion, ethics, and economics, Simmel also examined the arts and the lives of various artists as illustrations of his cultural theory. He did not, however, develop a systematic philosophy or sociology of art. Writings on art include articles about artists such as Michelangelo, Stefan George, Auguste Rodin, and Rembrandt van Rijn, to whom he also devoted an entire book in 1917, *Rembrandt: A Philosophical Essay on Art,* after already publishing a book on *Goethe* (1913). In other essays, he analyzed aesthetic phenomena such as the picture frame, the handle, the face, the portrait, and the caricature. Simmel also drew attention to the aesthetic dimensions of cities, ruins, and landscapes. In his book *The Philosophy of Money* (1900), he applied an aesthetic perspective to the analysis of money and its symbolic function in society. In his late articles on realism, style, naturalism, and art ("L'art pour l'art," 1914), Simmel introduced criteria concerning the ontological status of artworks and their specific properties. Overall, his widespread deliberations about the arts stand in a systematic relationship with his other studies on history and on the development and effects of culture.

Background. Simmel was born in Berlin, the youngest child of a converted Jewish merchant family. He studied history, ethnopsychology, philosophy, Italian, and the history of art at the University of Berlin, where he encountered the historicist and the neo-Kantian movement. His dissertation on ethnomusicology was rejected in 1881. It was considered too aphoristic and unscientific, a criticism that Simmel would be confronted with throughout his life. He finally earned his doctorate with a treatise on Immanuel Kant. Although the department accepted his Habilitationsschrift, he initially failed the oral defense, where he openly criticized the views of his mentor Eduard Zeller. Simmel subsequently taught in Berlin as Privatdozent without attaining a full professorship until 1914, when he finally received a call to Strasbourg.

Artists such as Rodin and Max Liebermann and the poets Rainer Maria Rilke and George were among Simmel's acquaintances. He also held weekly private meetings in his house where issues of art were discussed. Like Wilhelm Dilthey and Max Weber, Simmel was among those turn-of-the-century intellectuals who responded to the challenge posed by modernity: the need for the humanities *(Geisteswissenschaften)* to rethink their theoretical foundation given the success of modern industrialization and rationalization. Simmel's scope from early on was to understand the origin of culture, and how its change could be explained. The analysis of different artists lies at the core of his theory of understanding culture and his concept of modern history as the development of individualization. The arts are seen as a resort from the process of alienation, harmonizing the tension between subjective creativity and objective culture. In response to Henri Bergson's work Simmel turned to a philosophy of life *(Lebensphilosophie),* which manifested itself in his essay collection *Philosophical Culture* (1911), his studies on Goethe (1913) and Rembrandt (1916), and his last book, *Views of Life* (1918). During the last part of his life, he increasingly devoted himself to aesthetic questions and deliberations on a philosophy of art.

The Theory of Culture. Simmel's theory of culture is crucial to his philosophy of art, because he analyzes art in light of its reflection of a cultural form. In his essay "Personal and Objective Culture" (1900), he stipulates that in modern times the cleavage between subjective culture—that is, the intellectual work of an individual—and the objective culture as the totality of cultural products of a society has increased as a result of the division of labor. We are alienated from the objective culture, because we feel surrounded by an increasing number of anonymous objects and thus retreat into individual isolation, Simmel maintains in "The Future of Our Culture" (1909). Only the artist is able to combine objective culture with his own subjective culture by achieving a harmony between the reception of the objective culture and his own creative production.

At the same time, the objective culture, Simmel states in "On the Essence of Culture" (1908), is also the result of the individual's attributing value to it. In "On the Concept and Tragedy of Culture" (1911), he calls it the tragedy of culture that subjective life—being a continuous flow—cannot achieve its own end from within itself, but only via the objectified and flowless form of culture. Only for the genius is the development of his subjective spirit the same as selfless devotion to the objective task; he succeeds in harmonizing the subjective life and the objective culture by giving objective form to his own life. Particularly in his later work, Simmel refers to the dualism between cultural subject and object as a dualism between life and form ("Change of Cultural Forms" [1916]). In "The Conflict in Modern Culture" (1918), he applies his philosophy of history to a theory of conflict between life and form. History is examined as the change of cultural forms whereby life—constantly changing—opposes the objective validity of its own forms and products. The conflict of modern culture is that life can only realize itself in forms that limit its liberty. Simmel's analysis of various artists serves to show that they can overcome that conflict.

As one of the first gender theorists, Simmel also analyzes culture in the light of gender difference. In "Female Culture" (1902), he claims that culture is not gender-neutral but male, because it is defined by male forms of productivity. The lack of female cultural products is the result of the fact that female creativity does not match the existing male cultural forms. In most of women's cultural products Simmel sees friction between the content derived from female experience and the form pertinent to a male world. In cases where women found their authentic means of expression, such as Käthe Kollwitz, they appear to communicate a holistic understanding of the world alien to a man's cultural production.

Sociological Aesthetics—Aesthetic Sociology. Simmel not only analyzed the arts as illustrations of his cultural analysis, he also applied aesthetics as a method to examine sociological phenomena, which brought him the reputation of being an aestheticist. He aestheticizes in the following ways: (1) he chooses and examines his objects of analysis (e.g., sociological phenomena) with respect to their aesthetic qualities, such as purposiveness, symmetry, formal relations between parts and whole, and/or symbolic features; and (2) he relates attitudes that individuals take toward society and/or the objective culture to aesthetic categories such as distance and self-sufficiency.

In his article "Sociological Aesthetics" (1896), Simmel had already introduced his aesthetic perspective to sociology. He focuses on the sense behind the appearance, on the examination of rules and symmetries behind the outer senselessness. Society as a whole can become a work of art when one can attribute sense and meaning to each of its parts by virtue of their contribution to the whole. The social organization itself is aesthetic to the extent that it develops a purposiveness to the functioning of its parts and their interrelationship.

In his *The Philosophy of Money* (1900), Simmel claims that any object can be examined aesthetically. This aesthetic quality of perception should be used for an analysis of society. Money is only a symbol for the interrelationship of objects, exemplifying the aesthetic category of analogy by making objects analogous with regard to their monetary value. As a symbol of exchange, money represents the interrelation between culture and its form, just like a work of art. Money thus becomes objectified culture similar to the arts, religion, or law. At the same time, Simmel values the autonomy of means from any purpose as a condition for aesthetic pleasure. In money, as a means without content, this aesthetic pleasure must reach its peak.

According to Simmel, our attitude toward society is also aesthetic in that we try to distance ourselves from our surroundings as a reaction to the obtrusiveness of the modern world.

In "Fragments from a Psychology of Women" (1904), as well as in "On Psychology of Women" (1890), Simmel compares the female psyche to the character of artworks with respect to their self-sufficiency and autonomy. The close relation between world and individual experience is inherent to the inner self of women so that—similar to artworks—their inner life gains universality only by the expression of its very personal form.

Artists Expressing Their Age. Simmel analyzed different artists and their work as an illustration of the history of cultural forms developing to an increased individualization. Each age, however, evolves a specific idea about the interrelation between the subjective expression and the objective form, the analysis of which is the task of a philosophical sociology.

The central idea of the Renaissance is embodied in "Michelangelo" (1911). Michelangelo's figures do not show the individual but the classical ideal, that is, the unity of life above all individual forms. The tragedy of his work is that, at the same time, it also represents melancholy deriving from the actual dualism of life and form that Michelangelo only forced into a synthesis. Similarly, Leonardo da Vinci—as Simmel pointed out in "Leonardo da Vinci's Last Supper" (1905)—created an ideal space that allows the simultaneity of temporally different events, thereby condemning us to recognize our own powerlessness with respect to our finiteness.

Rembrandt—as Simmel tried to show in his *Rembrandt Studies* (1914), as well as in his 1917 book on the artist—finally overcame the dualism between life and form inherent to the Renaissance. In his portraits, he captured the individual's development as rooted in a life history, thus depicting the stream of life in one form, and expressing what Simmel called the individual law. Form in Rembrandt's baroque art appears to be a part of life, whereas Michelangelo's work uses life to lend content to a given form. Michelangelo's figures, therefore, seem unfree, despite their formal perfectionism.

Rodin, as Simmel pointed out in articles on the artist in 1902 and 1911, succeeded in expressing modernity. The unity of life and form is realized in such a way that its elements are explicitly shown as separate. By deliberately leaving his sculptures unfinished, Rodin satisfies the modern desire to have as much autonomy as possible in interpreting the work. His statues express movement, which makes the liveliness of the whole human being visible, and which is able to combine form and content. Similarly, George's poems express movement through their musicality, thus giving an adequate form to the subjective experience. The entire fate of life becomes apparent, not as a general idea as in Michelangelo, but in its immediacy. In three essays on George from 1898, 1901, and 1909 ("The Seventh Ring"), Simmel describes George's poetry as going beyond the individual feeling by making feelings art. George's interest does not lie in the content but in the artistic form. The content has become the means for sheer aesthetic values expressing the inner life.

Cities and Landscapes. Simmel also analyzed the aesthetic role of cities and landscapes with regard to his sociology of forms and his philosophy of life. As Simmel pointed out in an article on his contemporary Arnold Böcklin in 1895, landscapes, like works of art, are self-sufficient, enabling us to look beyond our momentary fate. In "Philosophy of the Landscape" (1913), Simmel claims that the concept of landscape also implies the idea of individualization as opposed to nature. Thus, the objectivity of landscapes is actually forged as unity, that is, subjective form by the artist. In this way, landscapes are a human construction. In his article "The Alps" (1911), Simmel maintains that the Alps in their monumentality serve as a symbol of the transcendent, which compels us to realize that there is something higher and purer than our life. Thus, Simmel illustrates his idea of cultural development as a process of increasing individualization that involves the acknowledgment of a higher force. His essays on three cities—"Rome, an Aesthetic Analysis" (1898), "Florence" (1906), and "Venice" (1907), serve similar purposes. Whereas Rome expresses the simultaneity of different time periods, Florence unites nature and spirit by forming its surrounding nature—Tuscany—through culture. Whereas the Roman unity is still a tension between ancient and modern culture, the synthesis of Florence is from within life and culture itself. Venice, on the other hand, shows a unity that is just a mask, disguising life so that the appearance of the city can only offer artificiality.

Aesthetic Phenomena. In "Picture Frame" (1902), "Handle" (1911), and "Ruin" (1911), Simmel discovers phenomena that are aesthetically pertinent because of their status at the border between art and reality, art and usefulness, and art and nature. The picture frame keeps art at a distance from the outer world, thus enhancing aesthetic pleasure. It emphasizes the unity of art against the observer and the world, and, at the same time, mediates between the two. Similarly, the handle of a vase represents the interrelation between art and the world of purposes. The handle presents art and usefulness as unity, thus pointing to a higher beauty where idea and life find their synthesis. Simmel sees this function of the handle reflected in the fate of the human soul, which, on the one hand, is self-sufficient and part of our being, and, on the other, has to reach out to the world and its purposes. The ruin, finally represents nature regaining power over a cultural form, which results in a new unity between nature and art, deriving its new purpose from the secret harmony of the unintended. The tension between purpose and chance, nature and culture, past and present reaches an outer unity in the form of the ruin.

In "The Aesthetic Significance of the Face" (1901), Simmel finally examines the face as a synthesis of body and soul, of symmetry and individuality. It is the bodily and geometric space where the inner personality can express itself. This is the reason why Simmel, in his 1918 essay on the portrait, regards it as the most important object of painting. The challenge for the painter is to attribute an inner necessity to the outer visibility. The artistic form of the portrait proves anew the unity of body and soul. By showing this unity in a portrait, the work of art is guided by the soul, which functions as a law of singular traits.

Toward a Philosophy of Art. In his late work, Simmel introduces criteria to determine what art is as opposed to nonart. In his essay "On the Third Dimension of Art" (1906), he maintains that the artwork has to legitimize its quality by offering meaning beyond what can be seen. The meaning has to be experienced in the perception of the artwork, however: it is the "third dimension" that adds to the actual sensual properties of the artwork a quality that spells itself out as enrichment and reinforcement of the two-dimensional content. It derives its force from the artist's ability to organize imagination, thus adding a specific nuance to the perceptual properties. The third dimension is the form that the artist gives to the relationship between himself and the world. In his "Fragments from a Philosophy of Art" (1916), Simmel elaborates his concept of the third dimension as the sensibility immanent in a work of art. In his posthumously published piece "Lawfulness in the Work of Art," he describes art as an objective form whose reality is idea and law: the artistic criterion is an individual law that arises from the creation of art itself, and whose own ideal necessity serves as its guideline. The work of art at the same time creates the problem it wants to address. This is the reason why style receives a rather negative connotation in Simmel's concept of art. He claims that style is a general principle that limits the individuality of an artwork. A great artwork derives its power from the individual law, unlike crafts, which follow a general principle of style ("The Problem of Style" [1908]).

Finally, the realism of an artwork has nothing to do with the imitation of reality. First, without imitating reality, the artwork can provoke the same psychological reactions with different means. Second, the artist sees in reality only what he intends to create. Receptivity and activity are the same in the artist. Third, art does not even gain its specific aesthetic quality from its outer appearance as it compares to reality. It derives its force from the third dimension, where things are independent of appearance ("On Realism in Art" [1908]). Simmel rejects naturalism precisely for its claim that one should find the given in art. Art is not supposed to reach out to the world, but to lead the world into art. Truth in art does not refer to a correspondent relationship between art and reality, but to the truthful expression of the artist ("The Problem of Naturalism" [posthumous]). In "On the Philosophy of an Actor" (1908), Simmel points out that the actor as much as the painter creates a new world that shares some of its properties with the "real" world because their contents both stem from all being. It is only art, however, if this content is artistically experienced, thus not realizing a certain content, but making it sensual. A work of art has a double character in that it excludes the world and our lives, but at the same time is part of our life. Art is self-sufficient only because behind its self-sufficiency there lies the deeper dimension of its relationship with life ("L'art pour l'art" [1914]).

[See also Sociology of Art.]

BIBLIOGRAPHY

Works by Simmel

Philosophische Kultur: Über das Abenteuer, die Geschlechter und die Krise der Moderne (1911). 3d ed. Berlin, 1983. Contains "The Alps," "Handle," "Ruin," "On the Concept and Tragedy of Culture," "Michelangelo," and "Auguste Rodin."

Goethe. Leipzig, 1913.

Rembrandtstudien (1914). Basel, 1954.

Rembrandt: Ein kunstphilosophischer Versuch (1917). Edited by Beat Wyss. Munich, 1985.

Zur Philosophie der Kunst: Philosophische und kunstphilosophische Aufsätze von Georg Simmel. Edited by Gertrud Simmel. Potsdam, 1922. Contains "Rome, an Aesthetic Analysis," "Florence," "Venice," "Picture Frame," "The Portrait," "L'art pour l'art," "Leonardo da Vinci's Last Supper," "Stefan George," "The Seventh Ring," and "Arnold Böcklin."

Fragmente und Aufsätze aus dem Nachlass und Veröffentlichungen der letzten Jahre. Edited by Gertrud Kantorowicz. Munich, 1923. Contains "Lawfulness in the Work of Art," "On the Philosophy of an Actor," and "The Problem of Naturalism."

Das Individuum und die Freiheit (1957). Berlin, 1984. Contains "Philosophy of the Landscape," "The Aesthetic Significance of the Face," "The Future of Our Culture," "On the Essence of Culture," "Change of Cultural Forms," and "Sociological Aesthetics."

George Simmel, 1858–1918: A Collection of Essays. Edited and translated by Kurt H. Wolff et al. Columbus, Ohio, 1959. Contains "The Handle," "Ruin," and "The Aesthetic Significance of the Face."

The Conflict in Modern Culture and Other Essays. Translated by K. Peter Etzkorn. New York, 1967. Contains "The Conflict in Modern Culture," "Sociological Aesthetics," "On the Concept and Tragedy of Culture," and "On the Third Dimension of Art."

Das individuelle Gesetz: Philosophische Exkurse (1968). Edited by Michael Landmann. Frankfurt am Main, 1989. Contains "Handle," "Fragments from a Philosophy of Art," "On the Concept and

Tragedy of Culture," "The Conflict in Modern Culture," and "Sociological Aesthetics."

On Individuality and Social Forms. Edited by Donald N. Levine, translated by Donald N. Levine and Kurt H. Wolff. Chicago, 1971. Contains "The Conflict in Modern Culture."

The Philosophy of Money. Translated by Tom Bottomore and David Frisby. London and Boston, 1978.

Essays on Interpretation in Social Science. Edited and translated by Guy Oakes. Totowa, N.J., 1980.

Gesamtausgabe. 20 vols. Edited by Otthein Rammstedt. Frankfurt am Main, 1989–.

Vom Wesen der Moderne: Essays zur Philosophie und Ästhetik. Edited by Werner Jung. Hamburg, 1990. Contains "The Problem of Style," "On Realism in Art," "Rome, an Aesthetic Analysis," "Florence," "Venice," "Picture Frame," "The Portrait," "L'art pour l'art," "Stefan George," "The Seventh Ring," and "Auguste Rodin."

Other Sources

Böhringer, Hannes, and Karlfried Gründer, eds. *Ästhetik und Soziologie um die Jahrhundertwende: Georg Simmel.* Frankfurt am Main, 1976.

Dahme, Heinz-Jürgen, and Otthein Rammstedt, editors. *Georg Simmel und die Moderne.* Frankfurt am Main, 1984.

Dörr, Felicitas. *Die Kunst als Gegenstand der Kulturanalyse im Werk Georg Simmels.* Berlin, 1993.

Frisby, David. *Sociological Impressionism: A Reassessment of Georg Simmel's Social Theory.* London, 1981.

Frisby, David. *Simmel and Since: Essays on Georg Simmel's Social Theory.* London and New York, 1992.

Jung, Werner. *Georg Simmel zur Einführung.* Hamburg, 1990.

Levine, Donald N. *The Flight from Ambiguity: Essays in Social and Cultural Theory.* Chicago, 1985.

Liebersohn, Harry. *Fate and Utopia in German Sociology, 1870–1923.* Cambridge, Mass., 1988.

Utitz, Emil. "Georg Simmel und die Philosophie der Kunst." *Zeitschrift für Ästhetik und allgemeine Kunstwissenschaft* 14 (1920): 1–41.

Weingartner, Rudolph H. *Experience and Culture: The Philosophy of Georg Simmel.* Middletown, Conn., 1962.

MONIKA BETZLER

SIMULACRUM. *See* Baudrillard; *and* Deleuze.

SITUATIONIST AESTHETICS. There is no such thing as Situationism, there are only Situationists—those who construct situations. This makes it difficult to ascribe a general aesthetic to Situationists as a whole, because the principal characters involved were too individually creative to be generalized. The problem is exacerbated by deep fractures within the movement—if movement it is—and made worse still because the notion of a Situationist aesthetic would be anathema to Situationist philosophy: by definition, situations are conceived as the opposite of works of art.

At their origin, the different strains of Situationist agreed only that the political and technical progress that marked the twentieth century had invaded individual creativity, colonizing and enclosing a territory in which the imagination was supposed to run free. United against passive submis-

sion to the "society of the spectacle"—as articulated by Guy Debord, their foremost philosopher, Situationists formed a caucus of opposition to the mediated experience of life under capitalism. They issued a call for the simultaneous dissolution and transcendence of art, for a return to pleasure, to spontaneity, to instinct and prelogical creativity. As Raoul Vaneigem—a leading theorist of situations—argued: "men live in a state of creativity twenty-four hours a day. Once that's clear, power's scheming use of freedom forces to birth the idea of lived freedom, inseparable from individual creativity" (1972). The situation to which they collectively aspired was one in which the imagination was freed, in and by an environment that allowed and encouraged liberated expression. Clearly, such a move would reduce the validity of, and necessity for, a discrete concept of "Art," and, indeed, various Situationist tendencies relegated Art to an inspirational historical entity at best, and at worst to a reactionary impediment to freedom. In general, Situationists understood that even the radical cultural alternatives offered by Dada and Surrealism had been "emasculated" by bourgeois culture. Combining a Surrealist admiration for the marvelous and the subconscious with Dada's anarchic adventure, they sought, in very varied ways, to recapture the anti-art fervor of their predecessors, and to continue the revolutionary program.

The immediate progenitors of the Situationist International included Lettrisme, an obscure and extremist group dedicated to the reinvention and reempowerment of languages, led by Isidore Isou; and the philosophy of Henri Lefebvre, a Marxist academic whose *Critique de la vie quotidienne* was published in 1947. Lefebvre introduced the notion of everyday life into political science, and his definitions are, if not the source of Situationist theory, clearly allied to it.

> Let us simply say about daily life that it has always existed, but permeated with values, with myths. The word "everyday" designates the entry of this daily life into modernity: the everyday as an object of programming, whose unfolding is imposed by the market, by the system of equivalences, by marketing and advertisements. (1991)

Lefebvre contemporaneously taught Jean Baudrillard, whose concept of the hyperreal reveals a shared influence, and he was at one time close to Debord and other leading members of the Paris-based Situationist International.

Other European Situationists were made up of members of the Movement for an Imaginist Bauhaus (IMIB), and CoBrA, this latter being a well-known group of expressive, abstract, and gestural painters founded in 1948 by Asger Jorn, Christian Dotremont, and Constant (Niewenhuis). Articulating the frustrations that these disparate groups shared, Constant wrote in a 1948 manifesto: "this culture, unable to make artistic expression possible, can only make it impossible." A multifaceted artist, architect, and theorist,

Constant was—paradoxically—later excluded from the Situationist International, in part because of ideological failures discerned in his designs for a utopian city, "New Babylon."

Both Constant and Jorn were involved with IMIB, a small international coterie whose members also included painter/collagist Enrico Baj and Debord. Apparently in agreement with the early aims of the Weimar Bauhaus, they saw its descent into Formalism as a clear sign of the degenerate effects of technology on cultural thought and action. They proposed a fresh attempt to integrate art and society, this time avoiding the commercially driven rationalism of the German original.

Situationist groups operated as a network rather than a movement—a shifting association of artists and activists who agreed simply on the derelict state of culture, on the imprisoned condition of the collective imagination, and on the harmful alienation that scientific progress and capitalism had combined to induce in the nuclear world. Their history can only be dimly discerned in an almost parodic succession of schisms and factions, coalescing and dividing around a number of conferences spread across Europe through the 1950s and early 1960s. Their fundamentally anarchic ambition provided fuel for many disparate versions of Situationist argument and activity, including publication of at least two periodicals: the *International Situationist* and the *Situationist Times*. There were also numerous exhibitions, conferences, articles, brochures, films, books, and tracts; and, of course, innumerable situations were constructed.

The First Conference of International Situationists took place in 1957, in Alba, Italy, a site that had in other years seen the formation of similarly polysyllabic organizations such as the First World Congress of Liberated Artists (1956) and the International Movement for an Imaginist Bauhaus (1953). Many of these groups were composed of the same people, presumably summering at the artists' colony known from 1956 onward as the Experimental Laboratory, under the directorship of Dr. Giuseppe Pinot-Gallizio, a sometime Situationist who produced an astonishing hybrid between painting and architecture: pseudoindustrially produced rolls of paint-splattered canvas that could be used as wall and furniture covers.

Jorn appears to have been a constant presence at these gatherings. An artist who, by the early 1950s, had garnered an international reputation as a painter of wild, weird, and colorful nightmares, often produced automatically or through chance processes, Jorn's works exemplify the Situationist concept of *détournement*—an adaptation of collage as developed by Dada—particularly his 1959 exhibit of junk-store paintings, crudely overpainted to pervert their original status and deliberately confuse their message. An avid discussant and theorist, Jorn believed that color was capable of provoking immediate and indescribable meaning.

He initiated, participated in, and financially or morally supported a number of artist groups, each sharing internationalist, revolutionary, and essentially playful characteristics, and once proposed, for example, a "Scandinavian Institute for Comparative Vandalism." One Situationist authority has detected among Jorn's personal influences such disparate concepts as "happy Christianity," Johan Huizinga's concept of *homo ludens,* and, of course, Dada. Jorn's expansive and restless nature caused him to consider founding another Nordic Situationist Bauhaus in 1960 and led him to closer connections with Gruppe SPUR, a Munich-based group of expressive painters whom he first encountered in 1953. Grafted onto the Situationist International after 1959, the Gruppe SPUR was "officially" excluded from the group in 1961, shortly after the Fifth Congress in Gothenburg.

Constant had conceived of "an architecture of situation" in 1953, and architecture—or at least, human reaction to the built environment—was a common concern, particularly the insidious but accelerating effects of industrial culture. According to Debord, their original desire had been for a city that would incite and deploy unbounded new passions. In the rapidly expanding cities of postwar Europe, however, where bomb-blasted historic centers were being overrun and overshadowed by massive and depersonalized development, life was, in Situationist terms, becoming a visual and virtual embodiment of aggressive capitalism. New conceptual tools were required to identify, experiment with, or oppose these phenomena, and these devices included, most famously, the spectacle and the *dérive*.

Debord, whose career had begun with Lettrisme, and whose activities included filmmaking in addition to cultural criticism, did most to develop the concept of the spectacle. He argued that the perceptible world was being transformed into a very effective illusion, in the way that media stars become mere representations of living human beings, surrendering their "real" life to the collective fantasy of their alienated audiences. Life had become pseudolife, lived in spectacular time, by virtue of having been turned into an endless succession of commodities through the inevitable machinations of capitalism. More than an imposition of values, and more abstract even than money, the spectacle is "not just the servant of pseudo-use—it is already in itself the pseudo-use of life" (Debord, 1994). Debord's provocative condemnation, increasingly persuasive with the passage of time, is perhaps one reason for the continued pertinence of Situationist thought.

The *dérive*, although translated as a "drift," was originally an active urban exploration of environmental effects—showing its roots in Surrealist automatism. Drifting across Amsterdam, London, or Rome in small select groups, directed only by the psychic topography, and occasionally aided by walkie-talkie, the *dérive* fulfilled useful research functions for the architectural, theoretical, and political arguments being developed by Debord and others, particularly the notion of unitary urbanism. A form of "living criticism" that linked areas of the city psychogeographically, unitary urbanism operated on the level of a subversive activity. As an International Situationist editorial made clear; 'all space is occupied by the enemy. We are living under a permanent curfew. Not just the cops—the geometry. True urbanism will start by causing the occupying forces to disappear."

Ultimately, Situationists were appealing for liberty, believing that this both entailed and would bring about complete and creative human expression. Such a state is generally antithetical to classification and categories, and in turn makes a coherent Situationist style unlikely. "Nothing could have been wider off the mark," wrote Gordon Fazakerly, sometime editor of the *Situationist Times*, "had some cretin stood forth with a pictorial belief" (1992). It is not surprising, therefore, that Situationist production varies enormously in style, medium, and quality, from hermetic drifting in groups, to Hardy Strid's biting Pop collages, to publicity-grabbing guerrilla pranks. Although pavement graffiti might seem to be at odds with, for instance, Debord's disruptively challenging films, both clearly aim at a joint societal target, and both offer, in the words of Bjørn Rosendahl, "playful revelations of society's absurdity" based on the premise that life could be viewed as one gigantic "happening" (Rosendahl, 1992). Similarly, although there are considerable formal differences between complex architectural theory and the *co-ritus*—free-form multimedia community actions instigated by Jorgen Nash—both looked toward a defined moment of life concretely and deliberately constructed by the collective organization of a unitary ambiance and a game of events.

All Situationist works attempted to tamper with the conventional relationship between individual and society, and to render explicit the implied assumptions therein. Without regard to normal aesthetic considerations, their intent was effected in any way that seemed appropriate—by deflecting and subverting intended meaning through *détournement,* by an insistence on artistic collaboration, or in the form of direct intervention.

Cultural terrorism was widely practiced by Situationists, sometimes in an arena directly connected to the visual arts, as in an outrageous anti-Documenta assemblage-cum-happening inflicted on the fifth Documenta (an international art show in Kassel, Germany held about every five years); and at other times connected to ideological targets, such as the Lettriste's famous proto-Situationist assault on the Cathedral of Notre-Dame, in which a fake Dominican priest read Serge Berna's antitheist, anti-Catholic tract to a horrified and hostile congregation. Probably the most notorious scandal surrounded the 1964 decapitation of Copenhagen's well-known bronze symbol, the Little Mermaid, and the subsequent disappearance of her head. The police were led to suspect members of the Movement for a Scan-dinavian Bauhaus Situationniste (MSBS), after Nash hinted to journalists that he knew the identity of the culprit. As a prank at the expense of the spectacle-hungry mass media, it leads a field that includes a Lettriste attack on Charlie Chaplin, Nash's dissonant disruption of the Copenhagen Opera, and, in a slightly different vein, the diversion of student funds to publish an excoriating critique of student life. Having gained control of the University's Student Union in 1966, Strasbourg Situationists used their newly acquired budget to print and distribute Mustapha Khayati's pamphlet *De la misère en milieu étudiant;* conventional authority was suitably scandalized, and the widely disseminated text became—ironically, perhaps—an instant classic.

Since the early 1960s, Situationists had been divided both by geography and, increasingly, by ideology. The conventional distinction between "artistic" northerners and "political" Parisians only foregrounds two rather conventional artist groupings at the expense of more obscure cells—particularly as, in an unofficial census published in 1974, Christopher Grey lists seventy individual Situationists from more than a dozen countries, collected into eight sections. There is evidence, however, of a predilection for theory from France contrasting with action and exhibition centered on Sweden. Calling themselves the Movement for a Scandinavian Bauhaus Situationniste, and based around a rambling farmhouse known as "Drakkabygget," which was also the title of their publication, three or four members of the "original" Situationist International, including some from Gruppe SPUR, were joined by various self-styled Situationists, who continued to produce paintings, collages, films, actions, and scandals until their 1972 attempts to overthrow the official Documenta. After a short lull, a continuously changing group including Yoshio Nakajima continued the anarchist, activist heritage of the Situationists through a proliferation of correspondence art, outrageous performance, and Jean Sellem's heroically unpopular exhibitions in the university town of Lund.

The Paris-based "Central Council," including Michélé Bernstein, Attila Kotányi, and Guy Debord, had always operated on the perimeters of the far left, and had, during the 1960s, been involved with the producers of the radical journal *Socialisme ou Barbarie.* They created an impressive legacy, largely based on their critical social theories and increasingly political philosophy, which eventually provided the inspiration for some involved in the 1968 uprisings in Paris. There is dispute about the exact nature of their connections with the worker-student riots, but there is no doubt that some aspects of the failed revolution were influenced and encouraged by their ideas, if only as upholders of an imaginative contrarian tradition. Certainly, a number of the famous Situationist slogans seen on the streets of Paris are as much distillations of William Godwin or Pierre-Joseph Proudhon as they are Surrealist imprecation: "The passion for destruction is a creative passion," wrote Mikhail

Bakunin; "Beneath the cobblestones, the beach!" answered the mob.

Along with Debord's *The Society of the Spectacle*, the most well known text from the Parisian Situationists is Vaneigem's *The Revolution of Everyday Life*. Each text acts as a critique of bourgeois consciousness, and each essays a wide variety of subject areas; from the proletariat as subject and representation, through time and history, to the decline and fall of work. Both were published in 1967, and both had been translated and freely republished in English by the early 1970s, although Debord's text is better known, and his concept of the spectacle has been subsequently popularized almost to the point of parody.

This text-based Situationism has been widely dispersed and has spawned a number of progeny on the radical fringes of cultural theory and architectural or artistic practice. It is argued that Malcolm McLaren's manipulation of the Sex Pistols, and the early moments of Punk, are natural heirs to this activism: the inherent aggression and nihilist leanings, combined with a slash-and-paste approach to production, give credence to this idea and thus place Punk in the widening wake of anti-art.

The legacy of the Situationists is as anti-aesthetic as the original, and even more diffracted. In the 1970s and 1980s, their ideas were spread largely through the blossoming of live art forms; through small press publications—often without copyright; and through international correspondence art circuits, which operated as a kind of World Wide Web using kitchen-table technology. Situationist activities continue to diversify into—among other things—direct political activism, legally questionable performance, postmodern projects to attack conventional culture, poetic terrorism, fiction, and, increasingly, academies, where the "crime" of categorizing the revolution is undertaken with sardonic humor.

Situationists might be seen as among the last heroes of modernity, cast into the paradoxical role of the antihero. Disrupting and distorting the comfortable hierarchy of the spectacle, and unmasking the "natural" order of culture, they have, despite—or because of—their apparent authenticity, assumed the mantle of the romantic rebel, a symbol whose value as entertainment is in inverse proportion to its revolutionary significance. On the other hand, when viewed as standard-bearers of the ancient impulse to refuse authority, to disobey, to turn, turn, and turn again, Situationists should not be dismissed. Despite naive, 1960s assumptions, despite turgid nit-picking tracts and petty personality contests magnified into ideological tirades, the construction of situations remains as a valuable step toward individuality, spontaneity, and finally, freedom.

[*See also* Anti-Art; *and* Installation Art.]

BIBLIOGRAPHY

Bernstein, Michéle. "In Praise of Pinot Gallizio" (1958). Translated by John Shepley. In *Guy Debord and the Internationale Situationniste*, special issue edited by Thomas F. McDonough. *October* 79 (Winter 1997): 93–94.

Debord, Guy. *La société du spectacle*. Paris, 1967. Translated by Donald Nicholson-Smith as *The Society of the Spectacle* (New York, 1994).

Fazakerly, Gordon. "The Ferry Boat." In *Bauhaus Situationist*, special issue edited by Jean Sellem. *Lund Art Press* 2.3 (1992): 131–133.

Gray, John. *Action Art: A Bibliography of Artists' Performance from Futurism to Fluxus and Beyond*. Westport, Conn., 1993.

Home, Stewart. *The Assault on Culture: Utopian Currents from Lettrisme to Class War*. London, 1988.

Knabb, Ken, ed. *Situationist International Anthology*. Berkeley, 1981.

Kotányi, Attila, and Raoul Vaneigem. "Unitary Urbanism." Translated by Christopher Grey in *Leaving the Twentieth Century: The Incomplete Work of the Situationist International*. London, 1974.

Lefebvre, Henri. *Critique de la vie quotidienne*. 3 vols. Paris, 1947–1981. Volume 1 translated by John Moore as *Critique of Everyday Life* (London and New York, 1991).

Marcus, Greil. *Lipstick Traces: A Secret History of the Twentieth Century*. Cambridge, Mass., 1989.

Rosendahl, Bjorn. "Bauhaus Situationist in Sweden: A Retrospective." In *Bauhaus Situationist*, special issue edited by Jean Sellem. *Lund Art Press* 2.3 (1992): 23–27.

Sellem, Jean. *Hardy Strid's Work and Swedish Modernism in Art from 1935 to 1980*. Munich, 1981.

Stokvis, Willemijn. *Cobra: An International Movement in Art after the Second World War*. Translated by J. C. T. Voorthuis. New York, 1988.

Vaneigem, Raoul. *Traité de savoir-vivre à l'usage des jeunes générations*. Paris 1967. Translated by John Fullerton and Paul Sieverking as *The Revolution of Everyday Life* (London, 1972). Also translated by Donald Nicholson-Smith (2d ed., Seattle, 1994).

SIMON ANDERSON

SMITH, ADAM (1723–1790), Scottish economist. Smith was born in Kirkcaldy, Scotland, and educated at the Universities of Glasgow and Oxford. In 1751, he became professor, first of logic and then of moral philosophy, at Glasgow. He resigned in 1764 to travel abroad as a private tutor to the young Duke of Buccleuch, and he returned to Scotland in 1767. Between 1773 and 1776, he advised the government in London on economic matters, and returned to Edinburgh in 1778 as a commissioner for customers. The two major books he published during his lifetime were *The Theory of Moral Sentiments* (1759), and *An Inquiry into the Nature and Causes of the Wealth of Nations* (1776). His collected works and correspondence were published only in 1976, and include lectures on rhetoric and jurisprudence, and various essays on philosophical subjects.

Smith wrote no comprehensive theory of aesthetics, or "criticism," as it was typically called, and most of his remarks are incidental to some other discussion, such as those on morality or effective communication. But Smith himself read widely, even by the standards of the day, took part in a number of literary and artistic activities, and wrote one, probably late, essay on imitation. It has to be conceded that Smith's remarks on the arts had almost no influence on later writers.

Like his close friend David Hume, he was much influenced by the writings of the abbé Jean-Baptiste Du Bos, whose *Réflexions critiques sur la poésie et sur la peinture* first appeared in 1719. Smith agreed with the view that poetry is the first form of human discourse, although both dancing and primitive music may predate it as pleasurable social activities. The "fine arts" develop later, on the basis of the leisure, wealth, and political stability of self-sufficient communities.

Smith said little about the three aesthetic issues that most occupied his contemporaries: the nature of beauty, taste, and critical judgment. But, in his lectures on rhetoric, he wrote at length on kinds of effective communication, and elsewhere on ways in which works of art represent their "subjects" and convey their meaning to audiences. Smith developed Hume's emphasis on the need to identify the proper contexts for critical judgment, by arguing that the overriding concern is with the meaning of works; hence, the very high intellectual pleasure that accompanies sensual pleasure in the arts. Like Hume, Smith derives his views mainly from reflection on literature, and his observations on painting and the "decorative arts" ignore the special character of the medium. He does, however, recognize the unique expressive and nonrepresentational character of music.

For Smith, if the main purpose of history is instruction, that of epic or romance is entertainment; but the fundamental difference between them lies in the fictionality of the latter's stories. Moral instruction requires that narrated facts be real, because the moral worth of actions depends on the worth of the agent's motives; the worth of art depends crucially on its effects. Poetic license is allowed to poets only because their task is to amuse. Smith agrees with Hume that utility is one of the main sources of beauty, but it is usually a derivative rather than a fundamental source. In the field of morality, as elsewhere, the aesthetic dimension can be accorded illicit priority.

In the 1750s, the nature of taste was extensively discussed in Edinburgh by philosophers such as Smith, Hume, Alexander Gerard, Lord Kames, and the painter Allan Ramsay. In *The Theory of Moral Sentiments* (part 5), Smith argued that two related principles, fashion and custom, influence all judgments concerning beauty. Poetry, music, and architecture are just as subject to their influence as dress and furniture. Smith implicitly links such views with the notions of style and tradition, emphasized by later theorists. He holds that however dominant a fashion becomes, it is entirely contingent which styles become accepted as fitting and appropriate.

Smith's most sustained thinking about problems in aesthetics occurs in an incomplete essay on "imitation," much of which was probably written in the 1780s (in Smith, *Essays on Philosophical Subjects*, 1980). He is mainly interested in how both expressive and cognitive meaning are conveyed and recognized in the different mediums of the various arts. Like most of his contemporaries, he used the term *imitation* to cover any kind of what might be called "representation,"

whether natural or symbolic; and he explicitly linked the notions of imitation, representation, resemblance, correspondence, and expression, sometimes using them interchangeably.

Some of the viewer's pleasure in the imitative arts may derive from the skills exercised in the medium, but admiration for difficulties overcome ought not to be carried over into admiration of a work's content; meaning should always be clear, however recalcitrant the medium in which it is expressed. The primary burden is on the artist to be perspicuous, and spectators, for Smith, carry less responsibility for effort and attention than they do for Hume. In urging that even inexpert spectators derive pleasure from, and achieve modest understanding of, at least the best works, Smith forgets to mention his earlier insight that everyone has to learn a repertoire of responses in a familiar tradition and culture. He also reflects on the mutual advantages of juxtaposing arts in different media, such as painting and sculpture. He here conflates two issues, however, namely, the overall harmony of different works in a setting, where judgment focuses on the whole effect, and the influence of one work on another when each is considered singly.

Music and dancing are the most natural pleasures, Smith holds, but, in its power to express a meaning with clarity and distinctness, dancing is superior to music, and poetry to dancing. He moves toward a distinction between the transitive and intransitive sense of expression; that is, between a view that music elicits response because it both expresses emotion and implants it, possibly in a reduced and transformed state, in a listener, and the view that the expressive character of unaccompanied instrumental music is in the music itself. Such music implants its moods by virtue of one's mental capacity to attend to, and remember, the sequence and character of its sounds.

BIBLIOGRAPHY

Works by Smith

The Glasgow Edition of the Works and Correspondence of Adam Smith. 6 vols. Oxford, 1976–1983. Consists of vol. 1, *The Theory of Moral Sentiments;* vol. 2, *An Inquiry into the Nature and Causes of the Wealth of Nations;* vol. 3, *Essays on Philosophical Subjects;* vol. 4, *Lectures on Rhetoric and Belles Lettres;* vol. 5, *Lectures on Jurisprudence;* vol. 6, *Correspondence.*

Other Sources

Avison, Charles. *An Essay on Musical Expression.* London, 1752.
Bonar, James. *A Catalogue of the Library of Adam Smith.* 2d ed. London, 1932.
Dubos, Jean-Baptiste. *Réflexions critiques sur la poésie et sur la peinture.* Paris, 1719.
Gerard, Alexander. *An Essay on Taste.* Edinburgh, 1759.
Hume, David. "Of the Standard of Taste." In *Four Dissertations,* pp. 203–240. London, 1757.
Jones, Peter. *Hume's Sentiments: Their Ciceronian and French Context.* Edinburgh, 1982.

Jones, Peter. "The Aesthetics of Adam Smith." In *Adam Smith Reviewed,* edited by Peter Jones and Andrew Skinner, pp. 56–78. Edinburgh, 1992.

Jones, Peter. "Hume's Literary and Aesthetic Theory." In *The Cambridge Companion to Hume,* edited by David Fate Norton. Cambridge and New York, 1993.

Ramsay, Allan, Jr. "A Dialogue on Taste." In *The Investigator,* 2d ed., pp. 1–77. London, 1762.

Richardson, Jonathan. *An Essay on the Theory of Painting.* London, 1715.

Ross, Ian Simpson. *The Life of Adam Smith.* Oxford, 1995.

PETER JONES

SOCIOLOGY OF ART. Only a few decades ago, a survey of the sociology of art would have begun and ended with contentiously worded assertions about the relations of the arts and society. A number of scholars would have affirmed that art mirrors society, but there consensus would end. Whereas some have insisted that art reflects societal production relationships, serving as an ideological tool to support dominant groups, others, equally positively, would have maintained that art—at least great art, the rest not being worthy of attention—is an autonomous sphere, capable of surmounting material constraints, that reaches for higher values, or presages cultural and societal trends. Deriving from the materialist orientation of Karl Marx, who actually wrote little about art, it provides the foundation of Arnold Hauser's massive analysis of artistic creativity through the ages, *The Social History of Art.* Of the many anti-Marxist variants on the idea that art mirrors society, the one elaborated by Pitirim Sorokin in an equally massive work viewed art as representative of the spirit of its age.

Other social theorists, such as Émile Durkheim, have thought of art as a substitute religion, a secularized spirituality of emotional support or constraint for individuals, which helps to hold society together. For Max Weber, on the contrary, in an increasingly rationalized modern world the aesthetic sphere may, under certain conditions, foster a discourse that competes with the ethical sphere of society (Weber, 1946, pp. 340–342).

As different as they are, these interpretations of the relations of the arts and society aim to unearth hidden postulates of art in relation to broad social structural processes. Whether from the standpoint of Marxist macrostructural analysis, anti-Marxist idealist perspectives, or those that look on art as a quasi religion, these universalizing conceptions of art represent a western European, hierarchicizing scheme of cultural classification. In particular, its presumption of an aesthetic domain analytically divorced from society is questionable and, in any case, idiosyncratic. Work by anthropologists, who see art as a cultural system that needs to be understood according to its cultural context, shows the inadequacy of such assumptions (Geertz, 1983).

Even though these perspectives continue to underlie some of the current analyses of the arts, in practice they have given way to different concerns and questions. Regardless of the political or intellectual stance of individual scholars today, their ambitions are far more modest. Sorokin embraced twenty-five hundred years of civilization, and Hauser's study starts from the even earlier point of prehistoric cave painting, and both extended their discussion to include contemporary artists. Today's social analysts rarely undertake to encompass such magisterial breadth. This does not necessarily entail a narrowing of vision, however, because the types of art that contemporary researchers consider worthy of analysis are far more varied than what their predecessors documented. Neither Hauser nor Sorokin paid much attention to non-Western civilizations, and barely any at all to primitive and folk forms and, except disparagingly, commercial art and entertainment (Hauser, 1982). Neither considered the absence of women artists as a question to be examined. Even within the domain of fine art, both shared a largely unexamined, but generally unfavorable, opinion of avant-garde art. Finally, like most of their more aesthetically oriented peers, although they dealt with changing genres and stylistic modes, they accepted extant categories of art as unproblematic givens, without considering that other forms of expression might be contenders for inclusion in the aesthetic field. Yet, beyond their ambitious reach, what is remarkable about the Hauser and Sorokin studies is that they were exceptional: on the whole, social scientists gave short shrift to the subject of art.

More recently, however, culture and the arts have become increasingly visible in sociological publications (Peterson, 1976; Becker, 1982; Crane, 1987; Balfe, 1993), disciplinary recognition, and professional organizations, both in the United States and elsewhere (Zolberg, 1990). This essay begins by considering the place that this field has occupied in sociology, and suggesting why it has changed. It examines developments within sociology itself, and trends exogenous to it that impinge on its composition. Work in the sociology of art today is characterized by four trends. First, sociologists elaborate the roles of the institutions and processes that give rise to or constrain the emergence of artworks. Second, they analyze the artistic practice of creators, and patterns of appreciation and acquisition of patrons and collectors. Third, they investigate degrees of access of new and different publics to the arts, and the role of the arts in status reproduction. Fourth, most radically, some scholars call into question the very nature of the arts, arguing that their definition as art needs to be understood not as self-evident, but as a social construction that requires analysis.

Art: In the Periphery of Sociology. Aside from literary and aesthetic scholars who touched lightly on the social contexts or cultural history surrounding the arts, in the first half of the twentieth century the sociology of art was largely the concern of a few European, and even fewer American, scholars. Among Europeans, a single major work by Weber (1958) dealt directly with a specific art form—music—as a case of his theory concerning the cultural rationalization in the West. Durkheim placed what he termed aesthetic sociology into the matrix of the sociology that he was trying to establish, but only under the residual rubric *divers,* and did no study of it himself (Zolberg, 1990, p. 38). Only Georg Simmel wrote frequently about the arts, though less as a social scientist than as a literary and art critic, philosopher, or fashionable essayist (Coser, 1965).

Even though American sociology had its origins in, and continued to look toward, European theoretical formulations, by the end of World War II, with the destruction or undermining of much European scholarship by totalitarian regimes, or under their military occupation, American sociology, along with American science more generally, had become the most dynamic and expansive in the world. This growth was a counterpart to the prominence of the United States on the international scene as the champion of Western humanist values during the war and defender of freedom during the cold war.

American social-scientific scholarship, however, had hardly acknowledged the arts as a legitimate object of study. This stance had its nearly symmetrical correlative in the opposing and equally intransigent stance on the part of humanist scholarship, including literature, aesthetics, art theory, musicology, cultural history, toward what seemed the threat of the social sciences. The foundations for this antagonism are situated at least as much in scholarly, institutionally strategic, and political domains as in intellectual considerations. The increasing preeminence of the exact sciences during and after the war had drawn many social scientists to adopt the presuppositions, techniques, and methodologies of these disciplines, an orientation that cast a shadow over humanist subjects and qualitative interpretive methods. Still, as higher education was expanded, despite official emphasis on the exact sciences, the social sciences and the humanities were expanded as well. Far from being only an American phenomenon, universities swelled in most European countries as well, providing structural conditions in which both scientific and humanist fields might flourish. Although the legacy of earlier misgiving persists, it has become considerably muted because of changes in both sets of disciplines that have produced convergences in their orientations (Zolberg, 1990).

In the United States, that the arts were studied at all had been largely the result of émigré scholars, especially members of the Frankfurt School such as Theodor Adorno (1976). Straddling the intersection of the humanities and social science, these exiles remained marginal to the mainstream, were treated as outsiders, and saw themselves in that light (Wilson, 1964, p. v). This marginality was enhanced by the Marxist orientation to which some adhered, combined more generally with their critical views on American sociology's scientist empiricism and, in many cases, contempt for what they took to be its intellectual shallowness (Zolberg, 1990, p. 72). They deplored the development of mass society and culture and its impact on individuals and intellectual life. Their insistence on a value-laden stance and rejection of what they regarded as a fictive scientific objectivity reinforced their exclusion from the academic mainstream of sociology. Nevertheless, some of them attracted a following of American scholars, intrigued by their inquiry, in the spheres of both high culture and commercial culture.

Foundations for a New Social Study of the Arts. Although in many countries a considerable body of scholarship was devoted to aesthetics, it was only in the post–World War II period that an autonomous field of sociology of art distinct from philosophy, history, or criticism materialized. This was the case in France, as Raymonde Moulin (1986, p. xiv) has observed, where, through the efforts of Pierre Bourdieu and his associates (1990; 1984) and of Moulin herself (1986; 1992), intellectual leadership and institutional support led to the development of new perspectives. German philosophical, musicological, and art-historical scholarship continued to straddle the social domain, as successors to the Frankfurt School tradition for whom the arts, both fine and commercial, were foci of study. English literary and historical scholarship infused Raymond Williams's (1981) social analysis of what he saw as the hegemonic role of the arts, and underpinned the development of British culture studies. In the United States, the multifaceted challenge to the university as an agent of government policy, especially the Vietnam War, and "normal" sociology in particular, challenged what was seen as scientist biases of the social sciences.

Simultaneously, the art world itself was undergoing transformations that included an enormous increase of the numbers of aspiring artists, a shift to New York as the center of the international art market, initiation by the national government of public subsidies for the arts, and growth of private foundation support (Crane, 1987). The arts themselves exploded their boundaries, as artists introduced new media, broke the barriers separating genres, and reversed conventional hierarchical arrangements. The process, begun earlier in the century when Marcel Duchamp gathered (or invented) "found objects"—ceramic urinals, snow shovels, bicycle wheels—"assisted" them to the status of art by supplying them with titles and an (alleged) artist's signature, had shaken standard conceptions. With renewed interest in his (and other Dadaists') innovations, artists and composers began routinely to wreak havoc with artistic tradition.

John Cage serves as archetype of this revival in the post–World War II period. Cage composed music on the basis of throwing *Yi jing* sticks, thus creating aleatory music—music by chance. He organized open-air concerts to which the audience was invited to bring transistor radios and turn them on as loudly as possible to any station they wished, thus producing the "music." In this way, he extended to new media the innovations of the literary Dadaist Tristan Tzara, who wrote poetry by tossing about printed words that he had clipped from newspapers, and which he then pasted together in whatever way they fell (Zolberg, 1990).

It may be argued that this mayhem developed in response to the magnified consumerism of late-capitalist society. This is not a trivial idea—economics rarely is trivial—but it does not explain everything, either in sociology or in the arts. The entry of large numbers of aspiring artists into the avant-garde art world, and the growth of foundation, corporate, and government support for the arts, must be included in the economic expansion (Crane, 1987). The United States during this period offered an unprecedented hospitable environment for social scientists interested in culture and the arts—in relation to consumerism, as a right of citizenship, and in creative innovation. Aside from a few articles, no major sociological works had increased the small pre-1950 bookshelf. On the basis of what had become "normal sociology" of the 1950s and 1960s, it would have been difficult to predict that an efflorescence in the sociology of art was in the offing.

An indication of this trend appeared in the exploratory work *The Arts in Society* (1964) by Robert Wilson, who wrote and compiled a number of essays on aspects of the arts in society. Justifying his choices by taking as his point of departure the fairly orthodox idea that artists could "often see what is going on in the society or the psyche a good bit earlier than other men do" (1964, p. vi), and unabashedly "concerned with the products and producers of high culture," Wilson's own selections analyze the role of the artist, poet, composer, and dancer. Essays by others included in the book focus on artworks, writers, and literary personages as exemplars of their social milieus (Lowenthal; Speier). Still others analyze the effects of institutional arrangements on artistic practice (White and White; Graña). Opting for high culture, the essayists pay little attention to popular or mass culture. In what must be seen as a paean to democratic pluralism, and a riposte to the Frankfurt School (and other) attacks on mass society, Edward Shils's essay "The High Culture of the Age" argues that far from deteriorating (ibid., p. 321), high culture is enriched by expanding education to make increasingly sophisticated publics, that enlarging the markets for art liberates the artist from the trammels of private patronage.

Only a few years later, another collection of essays heralded an "institutional" approach that examines the functions of the arts in meeting human needs, and maintaining social stability (Albrecht, Barnett, and Griff, 1970). The editors included studies on the relationship of forms and styles to various social institutions; artists' careers and their interactions in a variety of artistic milieus; distribution and reward systems; the roles of critics, dealers, and the public in recognizing artists and works. Despite its structural-functionalist orientation, dominated by the idea of art as an integrative force to maintain the social system and meet emotional needs, the editors were generously open to divergent views that encompassed even Marxian analysts such as Lucien Goldmann (pp. 582–609). Yet, these essays also demonstrated the infancy of the field: of the authors represented, only one fourth were actually sociologists, whereas the rest were in anthropology, comparative literature, history, and art history, or were practicing artists, painters, dancers, and writers. The happy result of this *omnium gatherum* was that Albrecht and his coauthors created an American field that integrated European contributions and was strongly cross-disciplinary, ranging over the fine arts, classical and contemporary, as well as folk art, music, dance, and literature, and their corresponding institutional grounding.

A Sociological Space for Art—Current Trends. Ever-greater diversity has become the hallmark of the sociological study of culture and the arts today. Methodological approaches range from empiricism that relies on quantitative tools to analyze masses of available data, such as the degree of access to cultural resources (Blau, 1988), to survey data of art-world practices and audience studies (Gans, 1975). Equally empirical, but based on microscopic observation and qualitative analysis of cultural practices, is the ethnography of Howard S. Becker's *Art Worlds* (1982). Historical and semiotic perspectives have been imported from literary analysis into the social studies. Even more striking is that the range of works and art forms investigated has burgeoned and includes the commercial domain. But, rather than seconding Shils's triumphalism, sociologists have recognized that the arts may be a means to exclude certain classes of aspiring artists, such as women and racial minorities, from what were defined as the most distinguishing and distinguished art forms (Bourdieu, 1984).

The most distinctive American school of sociology has been a synthesis of scattered approaches to the social study of science, religion, and work, brought together under the rubric of the "production of culture" (Peterson, 1976). Defining culture in a broad sense that allied it to anthropology—comprising art, popular culture, science, religion, and symbols, Richard Peterson urges that the questions broached should themselves determine the use of synchronic or diachronic modes according to their appropriateness. Proponents of this approach considered how cultural products were constituted, accentuating the effects of institutional and structural arrangements, both as facilitators of or impediments to creation. Characteristically, they reject macrosociological ambitions in favor of granting priority to middle-range and microscopic levels of analysis that, they believe, more effectively reveal the impact of laws, culture industry practices, and gatekeepers on the form and content of artworks.

Peterson also championed a "genetic" perspective, which treats culture as the "code by which social structures reproduce themselves" as the foundation for understanding how culture is "received" by individuals bearing different social characteristics. This involves a focus on the role of family, education, media, and other enculturating institutions and agencies that, at the time, was not being actively pursued by most American sociologists in relation to the arts. Their approach was considerably expanded through their intermingling with European and non-Western scholarship.

Institutions and processes. The role of certain institutions, such as official academies and government agencies or ministries, in providing support for artistic creation or, conversely, foiling it has been decried by critics and artists since their establishment. However, the pioneering sociological study by Harrison White and Cynthia White of the French painting world in the nineteenth century (1965) was one of the first to analyze systematically the changing structure of opportunity that the French Academy provided for artists. The Whites reconstructed quantitative data to show how the Academy's recruitment, educational, and marketing functions succeeded in drawing an increasing number of applicants to what was an honorable and lucrative profession. But the Academy's very success caused it to be overwhelmed by aspirants, to the point that both would-be artists and even already successful academicians had to turn to art dealers who had been cultivating a new middle-class clientele in order to sell their works. As this market expanded, new art styles, such as Impressionism, came to a prominence that the Academy's conservatism had begrudged them.

A more recent study of how academies selected among those allowed entry, and the implications for artists, was carried out by Gladys Engel Lang and Kurt Lang (1990). Focusing on the revival of etching as an art form in the nineteenth century, they show how the exclusion, or severe limitation, of women as students and members by most European academies impeded their entry into the highly regarded world of oil painting. Diverted to other, lesser media, such as etching and watercolor, whose professional organizations were newer and less restrictive, aspiring women artists were able to gain entry, and a measure of status and recognition.

Research on French art institutions has continued to thrive with the work of Moulin (1992) on the interplay among art museums, the art market, and government policy in providing official recognition for innovative art. In the United States, a system in which the national government's support for the arts is far more limited, and declining, the study of the effect of institutions on the arts has advanced under the leadership of Paul DiMaggio (1986). In fact, with the postwar growth of government subsidies in many countries, the effects of governmental policies are being investigated in other countries as well. Following the lead of Bour-

dieu and his associates (Bourdieu et al., 1990), English researchers have examined changing cultural institutions, especially museums, in representing the arts to new publics (Lumley, 1988), as have Dutch sociologists (Gubbels and Van Hemel, 1993).

Artistic practices and worlds of art. Inside the creative processes themselves, a major contribution to understanding how the arts are constituted was Becker's *Art Worlds* (1982). By adapting a "sociology of work" approach to study what is customarily viewed as unique creations of individual geniuses, Becker starts from the premise that making art is not qualitatively different from other social activities. Controversially, he sets out the convincing argument that, far from being an individual act, the making of art needs to be understood as a collective process, in which interactions among participants, of whom the named artist is only one, result in in the production of "artworks." The other participants—support personnel—may range from assistants to servants, to managers or agents, critics, buyers, and organizations.

Taking into account the size and complexity of modern societies, Becker does not reduce the arts to a single art world. Instead, he argues that art making is constituted in four principal art worlds, each characterized by a particular style of working, as based on its own conventions. Thus, the Integrated Professional artist is trained according to the conventions of an art form such as music, painting, and dance, within the domain of either high culture or commercial culture. The Maverick is also trained according to those conventions, but refuses to abide by them, preferring risk of isolation and failure in order to innovate and go his own way. The Folk Artist works within conventions traditional in his community's lore. Finally, outside of actual constituted art worlds, the least integrated is the Naive artist, untrained in art and following an internal urging, whose works represent idiosyncratic experiences that may include religious symbolism, representations of personal remembrances, or even aberrations and madness. Whereas the other art worlds have ties to regular art-world institutions or practitioners, or make it their goal to develop ties to them, Naive artists must be "discovered" by others, or else remain unknown.

Internal structures among informal groups of creative artists (or scientists) and their ties to their societal context have been analyzed by Charles Kadushin (in Peterson, 1976, pp. 107–122). His framework highlights circles within, and networks of, communications to external supporters. In his inquiry into the rise of the New York school of Abstract Expressionism, he shows how the circles of adherents promoted creativity *against* conventional forms, providing mutual support in the face of rejection by established art-world gatekeepers. Lacking channels for entrée to galleries or prestigious institutions, these mavericks and their supporters initiated networks of relationships to important external agents, media, and organizations, through which they eventually achieved recognition. In their turn, however, they became increasingly reserved about accepting newcomers into their midst, thus provoking the creation of competing circles.

Art and its publics: Status reproduction and taste. One of the most misleading adages of all time must be "de gustibus non disputandum est." In fact, taste is always being disputed. Thorstein Veblen was one of the first social scientists to interpret the symbolic meanings of expressed taste in his analysis of leisure class behavior during the Gilded Age (Veblen, 1899). Approximately a half century later, Russell Lynes published his classification of high-, middle-, and lowbrow taste preferences, in which artworks and fashion are taken as status markers (Lynes, 1954). On the basis of writings by these and other astute spectators, a number of sociologists have noted that taste, in art, design, and fashion, may be revealing of one's social standing. Far from viewing taste as trivial, purely personal, and difficult to fathom because it is nonrational, sociologists such as Bourdieu contend that taste is social in its formation, symbolic in its expression, and has social consequences for individuals and social institutions.

In his pioneering work on the taste cultures of American consumers, Herbert Gans (1974) treated the arts as a right of democratic choice. Contrary to the derision heaped on those of low educational level, living in rural areas or in relative poverty, for preferring popular, commercial art forms (pop music, country and western, gospel), Gans challenged both the government and commercial media to educate people to appreciate high cultural forms, and make them accessible, either directly or through radio or other media. If these institutions, agencies, and firms do not provide these cultural forms, he argued, they should abandon the judgmental manner that turns the "wrong" taste into a weapon of scorn against the culturally deprived.

Going beyond the idea of taste as a "right" of consumerism, Bourdieu (1984) takes observations of social differences in artistic taste to a more complex level of analysis. He shows the linkages among taste, symbolic status, and the mechanisms by which they tend to reproduce existing status hierarchies in society at large, from generation to generation. Treating taste as an aspect of the individual's cultural baggage, a durably structured behavioral orientation whose origin stems from early childhood and schooling, Bourdieu employs a variety of methods, quantitative and ethnographic, to show how taste functions as a form of capital to crystallize inequalities based on economic and social advantages or disadvantages. In this way, taste becomes a badge of social honor or scorn, signaling to influential groups that some are more acceptable than others.

English sociologists of culture have been pursuing cultural reproduction from a comparable standpoint. Although not as a rule using large surveys of taste, many have analyzed the content and uses of aesthetic culture, both high and popular. Williams (1981), beginning from a Marxian perspective, and moving between literary or film criticism and academic life, was a major influence on what became the field of Culture Studies. Beyond the simple base-superstructure correspondence of Marxism, in which culture is conceived as merely epiphenomenal to existing production relationships, Williams and his followers, including Stuart Hall (1980) and Janet Wolff (1993), among many others, conceived of culture as a constitutive practice in the construction of social meanings. They have tried to overcome the prevailing, decontextualized, literary-critical mode of analysis by elucidating the relations between, on the one hand, cultural images, objects, and practices, and, on the other, social institutions and processes. Scholars associated with the Birmingham Centre for Contemporary Cultural Studies analyzed many aspects of British youth subcultures and their relationship to new artistic styles.

Is taste a simple offshoot of socioeconomic status, a device of social reproduction? Or is the connection more complex? It would be misleading to suggest that there is complete agreement among sociologists about how taste and status are related, and with what consequences. Many find it essential to take into account observable changes in social stratification patterns, and the conditions of their expression. Whereas Bourdieu attributes expertise in manipulating symbolic capital through complex codes available in the lore of dominant class fractions, David Halle (1994), who has studied the collection and display of art *inside* of people's homes, argues differently. His interviews with elite collectors of abstract art reveal that they have little understanding of the works in their own homes, which are nearly as esoteric for them as for nonelites. In fact, Halle finds widespread sharing of taste across status lines, especially noting a nearly universal and, it appears, similar mode of appreciation of the landscape genre. Moreover, although educational level is an important enabler of high-culture taste, ethnicity and race play important roles in how people select works for the home, in contrast to their responses to questionnaires administered in public spaces.

Beyond the linkage established by Bourdieu, Gans, Lynes, and other investigators between social status and social class, or educational attainment, others find that our conception of social status needs to incorporate gender, race, and ethnicity in order to take into account both the volume and the variety of preferences that appear to vary among social classes. In studies of how musical tastes are related to occupational status, Peterson and Simkus (1992) suggest that although classical music continues to be a status marker for high-status occupational groups, more striking is the great breadth of their preference for a variety of musics. Thus, whereas fewer than a third of holders of prestigious occupations say that they like classical music best, surprisingly, a somewhat larger proportion of such respondents prefer country-and-western music to grand opera. What is more distinguishing is that high-status individuals participate in more cultural activities and enjoy a wider range of music than do those of lesser status. As Peterson and Simkus put it, they are "omnivores," as opposed to less elite groups, whose limited range of taste in music makes them "univores" (1992, pp. 152–186).

But what is art? In the past, scholars investigating the place of the arts in society have taken for granted the categories of art conventionally agreed to by art-world participants, but in recent times certain sociologists have turned their attention to how art classifications are constructed. Like the sociologist of science, Bruno Latour (1987), who questions the processes by which certain frameworks of analysis, categories, and findings come to be incorporated into the scientific canon, some see even more plausible reasons for interrogating how artistic canons are established. Art is a stake in the arena of competition that pervades much of social life, as Bourdieu contends, not only for artists themselves, but for their supporters, patrons, collectors, and dealers, and for the writers and scholars who compose the art worlds in which they exist.

Under pressure from potential publics, market forces, including collectors, and political action, and in light of the openness of the fine arts to new media, existing cultural institutions, such as art museums, are exhibiting works previously excluded from consideration as art. Whereas previously, for example, African carvings were largely consigned to ethnological collections, their entry into art museums has taken the form of an upward spiral; art of the insane has attained high market value (Anne E. Bowler, in Zolberg and Cherbo, 1997); and women artists are gaining a level of recognition that had routinely been denied them (Zolberg and Cherbo, 1997). In the worlds of culture industry as well, new musical forms such as rock-and-roll and rap have emerged from the interplay of business developments, technological innovations, and enacted statutes in such fields as copyright law, which set the parameters for works to come to public attention (Ennis, 1992, pp. 5–7).

Prospects. By now the study of culture and the arts has become a lively sociological arena in the United States, as it had already been in much of Europe. No longer a stepchild of the *serious* business of sociologists, the arts are, if not central, then at least a legitimate, as opposed to a frivolous, subject. This flowering has come about despite a traditional anti-aesthetic orientation in American social science, and, until recently, relative retarded development of much contemporary European social science. Despite this change, the position of the arts in the social-science disciplines is likely to remain tenuous, and requires renewed justification as an intellectual enterprise. The reasons for this have to do with both the intellectual outlooks that have become embedded in understandings of the arts and the social structures of their creation—or "production."

First, the crux of the arts since the Renaissance has been the artist as an individual, a tradition of several centuries that emphasizes the uniqueness of the actor and the work he (rarely, she) created. Although the notion of such an individual agent is relatively compatible with the discipline of psychology, it is less easily reconciled with the collectivist understanding of behavior by sociology. This perception underlies the view of art as a collective process (Becker, 1982) and sociologists' emphasis on the production, rather than creation of culture. Retaining or reinserting the individual artist as agent has both ethical importance, because it implies respect for the autonomy of the individual, and intellectual validity in a discipline that would easily reduce art to an outcome of overly general structures and processes.

A second reason, and one related to this disciplinary tradition, surrounds that of aesthetic judgment. This presents even more arduous barriers for sociologists, for whom scientific objectivity pervades their disciplinary orientation. But aesthetic judgment is problematic for literary and humanist scholars, many of whom avoid it. In part, this is because of the objective and scientific turn that humanist studies have taken, one of whose consequences is that categories of value are too deeply embedded in society to be disaggregated from it. Sociologists are only too aware of how contaminated our judgments of most things are, and the expanded notion of art today does not render evaluation any easier.

Finally, the extraordinary transformation of the international arena in recent years requires that scholarship move more explicitly outside of the scholarly world and into the domain of artists and policymakers. Knowledge of their functioning is essential if we are to grasp the future relationships of the arts and society in a world that brings together what had been largely national concerns. The arts are no longer understandable in terms of one society alone (if that was ever the case), because few societies are either homogeneous or sealed off from other geographic, national, or societal units. Thus, whereas it may still be possible to study such issues as arts censorship in the context of a single society, it is more likely that political transformations open the door to new conflicts, as a global phenomenon.

Related to globalization, a second set of factors that militates against retaining the single society as the primary unit of analysis stems from the opportunities offered by technological innovations such as developments in cyberspace and computer technology. Not only do they permit new forms of artistic expression, but they also enhance attempts to evade control over art content. Providing new avenues for artistic dissemination, they also substitute for direct contact with the storehouses of art, museums. These developments suggest that this contextual metamorphosis will set the parameters of the next phase of studies in the sociology of the arts.

[*See also* Art Market; Art World; Artist; Bourdieu; Cultural Studies; Institutional Theory of Art; Mannheim; Marxism; Museums; Politics and Aesthetics; Popular Culture; Simmel; *and* Taste.]

BIBLIOGRAPHY

Adorno, Theodor W. *Introduction to the Sociology of Music* (1962). Translated by E. B. Ashton. New York, 1976.

Albrecht, Milton C., James H. Barnett, and Mason Griff, eds. *The Sociology of Art and Literature: A Reader.* New York, 1970.

Balfe, Judith Huggins, ed. *Paying the Piper: Causes and Consequences of Art Patronage.* Urbana, 1993.

Becker, Howard S. *Art Worlds.* Berkeley, 1982.

Blau, Judith R. *The Shape of Culture.* Cambridge and New York, 1988.

Bourdieu, Pierre. *Distinction: A Social Critique of the Judgement of Taste* (1979). Translated by Richard Nice. Cambridge, Mass., 1984.

Bourdieu, Pierre, Alain Darbel, and Dominique Schnapper. *The Love of Art: European Art Museums and Their Public* (1969). Translated by Caroline Beattie and Nick Merriman. Stanford, Calif., 1990.

Coser, Lewis, ed. *Georg Simmel.* Englewood Cliffs, N.J., 1965.

Crane, Diana. *The Transformation of the Avant-Garde: The New York Art World, 1940–1985.* Chicago, 1987.

DiMaggio, Paul J. *Nonprofit Enterprise in the Arts: Studies in Mission and Constraint.* New York and Oxford, 1986.

Durkheim, Émile. *The Elementary Forms of the Religious Life* (1912). Translated by Joseph Ward Swain. New York, 1965.

Ennis, Philip H. *The Seventh Stream: The Emergence of Rocknroll in American Popular Music.* Hanover, N.H., 1992.

Gans, Herbert J. *Popular Culture and High Culture: An Analysis and Evaluation of Taste.* New York, 1975.

Geertz, Clifford. *Local Knowledge: Further Essays in Interpretive Anthropology.* New York, 1983.

Gubbels, Truus, and Annemoon Van Hemel, eds. *Art Museums and the Price of Success.* Amsterdam, 1993.

Hall, Stuart. "Cultural Studies and the Centre: Some Problematics and Problems." In *Culture, Media, Language: Working Papers in Cultural Studies, 1972–1979,* edited by Stuart Hall et al., pp. 15–47. London, 1980.

Halle, David. *Inside Culture: Art and Class in the American Home.* Chicago, 1994.

Hauser, Arnold. *The Social History of Art.* 4 vols. Translated in collaboration with the author by Stanley Godman. New York, 1951; reprint, New York, 1957–1958.

Hauser, Arnold. *The Sociology of Art* (1974). Translated by Kenneth J. Northcott. Chicago, 1982.

Lang, Gladys Engel, and Kurt Lang. *Etched in Memory: The Building and Survival of Artistic Reputations.* Chapel Hill, N.C., 1990.

Latour, Bruno. *Science in Action: How to Follow Scientists and Engineers through Society.* Cambridge, Mass., 1987.

Lumley, Robert, ed. *The Museum Time Machine: Putting Cultures on Display.* London and New York, 1988.

Lynes, Russell. *The Tastemakers: The Shaping of American Popular Taste* (1954). New York, 1980.

Moulin, Raymonde, ed. *Sociologie de l'art.* Paris, 1986.

Moulin, Raymonde, with Pascaline Costa. *L'artiste, l'institution et le marché.* Paris, 1992.

Peterson, Richard A. ed. *The Production of Culture.* Beverly Hills, Calif., 1976.

Peterson, Richard A., and Albert Simkus. "How Musical Tastes Mark Occupational Status Groups." In *Cultivating Differences: Symbolic Boundaries and the Making of Inequality,* edited by Michele Lamont and Marcel Fournier, pp. 152–186. Chicago, 1992.

Sorokin, Pitirim. *Social and Cultural Dynamics,* vol. 1, *Fluctuations of Forms of Art.* New York, 1937.

Veblen, Thorstein. *The Theory of the Leisure Class* (1899). New York, 1934.

Weber, Max. *From Max Weber: Essays in Sociology.* Translated and edited by Hans H. Gerth and C. Wright Mills. New York and Oxford, 1946.

Weber, Max. *The Rational and Social Foundations of Music.* Translated and edited by Don Martindale et al. Carbondale, Ill., 1958.

White, Harrison C., and Cynthia A. White. *Canvases and Careers: Institutional Change in the French Painting World.* New York, 1965; reprint, Chicago, 1993.

Williams, Raymond. *The Sociology of Culture.* (1981). Reprint, Chicago, 1995.

Wilson, Robert N., ed. *The Arts in Society.* Englewood Cliffs, N.J., 1964.

Wolff, Janet. *The Social Production of Art.* 2d ed. New York, 1993.

Zolberg, Vera L. *Constructing a Sociology of the Arts.* Cambridge and New York, 1990.

Zolberg, Vera L., and Joni M. Cherbo, eds. *Outsider Art: Contesting Boundaries in Contemporary Culture.* Cambridge and New York, 1997.

VERA ZOLBERG

SONTAG, SUSAN. *See* Camp; *and* Photography.

SOREL, CHARLES (c. 1600–1674), prolific author who engaged in fields as varied as science, historiography, moral theory, philosophy, fiction, and literary history. Although Sorel himself expressed a keen preference for his encyclopedic work *La science universelle* at the end of his career, he would be recognized by posterity for his novelistic creations above all. For example, in his masterly study *Le roman jusqu'à la Révolution*, Henri Coulet calls Sorel "the greatest comic novelist of the Baroque age" (1967). Sorel's importance in the evolution of fiction, and the definition of his aesthetics, are most evident in the conception of a genre in which he both experimented and served as main critic: the *histoire comique* (comic novel). In 1623 appeared the first part of the work with which his name is still associated by many readers: *Histoire comique de Francion*. The huge success of this text is attested by the numerous editions and translations it underwent over the course of the seventeenth century. *Francion* established a tradition that would include the *histoires comiques* of Scarron and Furetière, whose works also testify to the crisis in the aesthetics of fiction that occurred in France during the *grand siècle*.

Throughout his career as a writer, and particularly in his works of literary criticism (*La bibliothèque française* [1664] and *De la connaissance des bons livres* [1671]), Sorel tirelessly invoked "verisimilitude" as a criterion for judgment and a principle of evolution in fiction. Having elaborated, in *Francion*, the model of a novel designed to present "as realistically as possible the temperaments, actions, and ordinary conversations" of men, Sorel undertook in *Le berger extravagant* (1627) a systematic attack on the "absurdities" of the kind of fiction that was then in fashion (most particularly pastoral novels such as *L'astrée*). While imitating the formula of novelistic madness that was initiated by *Don Quixote*, Sorel went further: the parodical target of his text was explained in lengthy *remarques* in which he commented on the ineptitude of the existing models. *Le berger extravagant* (retitled *L'anti-roman* in the edition of 1633) was thus conceived essentially as the "tomb of fiction." With *Polyandre* (1648), Sorel attempted once again to bring the novel closer to everyday life, by breaking with the picaresque framework that he had in part followed in *Francion*, and embracing *bienséance* (decorum) that had become essential with the advent of classicism. Through the social milieu it presented, this third *histoire comique* (which inspired Molière) directly paved the way for Furetière's *Roman bourgeois* (1666).

The *histoire comique* as Sorel conceived of it was, therefore, above all a reaction against traditional fiction (the tale of chivalry, the pastoral, or the heroic novel). "Farcical heroes" and "chimerical adventures," which "incite all sorts of vices," should, according to Sorel, be abandoned in favor of "natural tableaux of human life" in which moral lessons could be artfully insinuated. "Verisimilitude" implied, moreover, "mixing conditions" and "temperaments." A novel's plot should, therefore, no longer focus on the idealized representation of love, or depict the torments of two young heroes of noble birth and spirit who often lived in a time and place that distanced them even further from the reader. It is even questionable whether one should use the term *hero* to refer to the protagonists of *histoires comiques*, who were generally bourgeois and more preoccupied with their social position than with the quest for pure love. Through its depiction of persons of "mediocre" social standing and its satiric intent, the *histoire comique* can be compared to comedy. Just like the tableaux of social mores created by Molière and other comic playwrights of the period, these novels resort to grotesque deformation as a means of presenting the vices of human nature via the portrayal of types or *caractères*—a term that Sorel used (well before Jean de La Bruyère) in *Polyandre*.

The critical works of Sorel and the preface to *Polyandre* underscore the importance of assuming a "natural" style that strikes a *juste milieu* (happy medium) between coarseness and affectation, in order to reinforce the effect of verisimilitude. From the very beginning of his career, Sorel decried exaggerated style and metaphorical abuses that undermine truthfulness. The most revealing emblem of his aesthetic principles is undoubtedly the "metaphoric" portrait of Charite in *Le berger extravagant*, which was illustrated by the famous engraver Crispin de Passe and thoroughly critiqued in the text. In this work, the painter entrusted with representing Charite transposes quite literally the "extravagant descriptions of poets" that the shepherd Lysis uses to describe his beloved. When he composed this "monstrous" portrait, Sorel sought to denounce the

disparity between figurative language and what it is supposed to translate, and allowed the reader to appreciate visually the absurdity that resulted from that gap.

The aesthetic principles that Sorel brought into play in his conception of the *histoire comique* cannot be separated from his freethinking philosophy, which he voiced most openly in *Francion*. Indeed, this text both contested traditional literary forms and questioned the social and moral conventions of the day. By virtue of its lack of fixed conventions, the *histoire comique* seemed to be the ideal format for expressing audacious ideas; libertine authors such as Théophile de Viau *(Première journée)* or Cyrano de Bergerac *(L'autre monde)* would exploit the genre's potential in this regard by also expounding "things that no one has ever been bold enough to say" *(Francion)*.

In the last analysis, beyond his contribution to the development of a genre that has been considered the "avant-garde of novelistic creation" (Serroy, 1981) and that contributed significantly to the expansion of this field, Sorel's entire body of works—including fiction, science, and history—came down to a single, essential principle: the defense of and quest for truth. When, in the novel bearing his name, Francion declares that his goal is to rid his mind of "vulgar opinions" so that he might seek to understand the "natural reason for all things," he expresses the objective that would guide *La science universelle*, where Sorel also refuted the "old authorities" and touched on the project of demystification that informed *Le berger extravagant*. Because it championed the improvement of reason over the course of time, along with the need for innovation in the field of literature, Sorel's thought was closely akin to the proclamations of those who belonged to the "moderns"; and, thanks to the longevity of the author, it presented an important reflection on—and of—the progression of seventeenth-century aesthetics toward classicism.

BIBLIOGRAPHY

Works by Sorel

Histoire comique de Francion. Paris, 1623; 3d ed., Paris, 1933. Reprinted in *Romanciers du XVIIe siècle,* edited by Antoine Adam. Paris, 1958.
Le berger extravagant. Paris, 1627; 2d ed., Paris, 1928; reprint, Geneva, 1972.
Polyandre, histoire comique. Paris, 1648; reprint, Geneva, 1972–1974.
La bibliothèque françoise. Paris, 1664; 2d ed., Paris, 1667; reprint, Geneva, 1970.
La science universelle: dernière édition revue et augmentée. Paris, 1668.
De la connaissance des bons livres, ou examen de plusieurs autheurs. Paris, 1671. Critical edition, edited by Luoia Moretti Cenerini (Rome, 1974).

Other Sources

Coulet, Henri. *Le roman jusqu'à la Révolution.* 2 vols. Paris, 1967–1968.
Debaisieux, Martine. *Le procès du roman: écriture et contrefaçon chez Charles Sorel.* Saratoga, 1989.
DeJean, Joan. *Libertine Strategies: Freedom and the Novel in Seventeenth-Century France.* Columbus, Ohio, 1981.

DiPiero, Thomas. *Dangerous Truths and Criminal Passions: The Evolution of the French Novel, 1569–1791*. Stanford, Calif., 1992.

Howells, Robin. *Carnival to Classicism: The Comic Novels of Charles Sorel*. Biblio 17. Paris and Seattle, 1989.

Showalter, English. *The Evolution of the French Novel, 1641–1782*. Princeton, N.J., 1972.

Suozzo, Andrew G., Jr. *The Comic Novels of Charles Sorel: A Study of Structure, Characterization, and Disguise*. Lexington, Ky., 1982.

Sutcliffe, F. E. *Le réalisme de Charles Sorel: problèmes humains du XVIIe siècle*. Paris, 1965.

Verdier, Gabrielle. *Charles Sorel*. Boston, 1984.

MARTINE DEBAISIEUX

SPORTS are an obvious topic for philosophical reflection. There are connections between a conceptual interest in sports and moral philosophy, the theory of mind, and the theory of action, to name but a few relevant areas of philosophy. This essay, however, is confined to mentioning a few respects in which sports are of interest in the philosophy of art.

One salient characteristic shared by sport and art is that they are among the most conspicuous of those human undertakings done for no obvious external reason. That human beings do such things ought to be of interest in many areas of philosophy, and it is of special interest in aesthetics. Sport and art are things we do that we do not have to do, at least not in the way in which we have to build shelters (in order to survive the elements and other degradations) and have to cultivate food (in order to eat). When it is possible for us to live indoors without building, then we do not build, and when we can get food without growing it, we do not grow it. Even if one thinks that there is some end for the sake of which art and sport are engaged, it is not "detachable" in the sense that we can suppose that if that end were otherwise available, we would forgo the actual art and sport. This is not to say that art and sports satisfy no need, but it is to say that whatever satisfaction they provide, that satisfaction is not available without the sport and the art themselves, and this seems to be true both of those who engage in these activities as participants and of those who observe. Nor, of course, is it to deny that some artists and athletes may well do what they do only because they are paid to do it, and if they could secure income otherwise, they would leave off making art and playing sports. It is to say only that, at their cores, both activities are carried on—and sustained in human history—because engagement in them seems to satisfy some human need that knows no other satisfaction. Finally, moreover, it is not to say that art and sport satisfy the same human need, nor that they are the only human enterprises thus irreplaceable ("social" conversation, experiencing nature, and engaging in religious ritual may be some among many other examples). But perhaps they both satisfy the same generic need. Is it, perhaps, that those things we do that are not things we have to do are precisely the things we do to "express ourselves"? These are things we are free not to do, and so when we do them, we do them freely, therein showing what we truly are as we do what we truly want.

There are several topics of interest in aesthetics when one looks to sports. The first is simply the interest in sporting activities as objects of what might be called "aesthetic appreciation," and the others take sports as a kind of parallel to art and inquire into just how appreciation of sports differs (or does not) from the appreciation of art.

Athletic performances are obvious occasions for the display of grace, elegance, beauty, and so on, and as such they are occasions for the appreciation of these features, just as works of art and their performances are. In some cases, there seems to be a kind of means/end distinction to be made in the case of sports but not in the case of art, whereas in other cases the distinction virtually is absent in the appreciation of sports. In the first case, the gracefulness of, say, a basketball player shooting a ball, or a third baseman fielding a hard ground ball in baseball, or a cricket batsman executing a perfectly stroked swing at a downward diving ball might be compared with the gracefulness of a ballet dancer executing a particular sequence—with this difference: the admirability of the athlete is understood at least in large part in terms of his scoring a basket, cleanly picking up the baseball, or knocking for six; that is, the gracefulness is exhibited in the service of something, of some end, whereas the gracefulness of the dancer seems to be just that, and it seems to be an object of appreciation, so to speak, in itself. In other cases—for instance, those of a gymnast or a figure skater—although there may be certain specific requirements built into the routine done by the athlete, the judgment of the athlete's exhibition seems very like that of the dancer, a judgment simply of the performance itself without reference to any specific end.

Sports players are, typically, appreciated for doing things that are *difficult*. So are artists. Why is this? Why is it admirable to do something difficult, and just what does it mean for something to be difficult to do? Does the difficulty consist simply in the fact that most other people could not do this thing? Is that why a performance by Sviatoslav Richter and a century struck (in cricket) by Hobbs are admirable, because almost no one else can play the piano like that or bat so successfully as that?

If both sports and art are of interest, at least in part and at least sometimes, because difficult things are done, why do some difficult things support extensive interest and appreciation whereas other equally difficult things do not? Why are tumbling (in gymnastics) and tennis playing substantially successful "spectator sports," whereas walking on one's hands and speed-typing are not? Why does figure painting have the status of high art and command substantial attention from the art-minded public, whereas dress designing does not?

When the difficulty being overcome is significant, and its apprehension is a matter of intense and deep appreciation, so that the performer (sports player or artist) may even be considered a virtuoso, how is it that the audience is aware of this difficulty? Is the difficulty of a task, so to speak, exhibited in the doing of the task itself, or does a competent appreciator need some independent experience in order to be able to gauge the level of difficulty? Must one have tried playing the piano or the violin to appreciate the virtuosity of an Alfred Brendel or a Itzhak Perlman? Must one have tried playing basketball to appreciate the stunning performance of Michael Jordan? It might be enough to have seen and heard enough people attempting to play the piano or the violin or basketball to begin to have an idea of just how difficult it is to do those things. Perhaps it varies, and some human endeavors are near enough to things we all do for us to infer just how difficult they are, and others are sufficiently arcane to contain a difficulty that novice observers will be unaware of. The matter is complicated by the fact that a mark of certain exhibitions of virtuosity is that the difficulty being overcome is concealed. Thus, some genuine virtuosos are complimented, as it is said, for making the difficult look easy. In such a case, genuine appreciation requires that we know the task is not easy despite the fact that it "looks" as if it were. If it does indeed look easy, then we will take it to *be* easy unless we have something to go on besides how it looks.

These matters seem well worth looking into, if only because they illustrate that "appreciation" is not only not confined to engagements with works of art, but that it might not even have its primary exhibition there. The matters are all related to the topic of spectator or audience "identification," and it is here, perhaps, that one can see most clearly that the phenomenon of aesthetic appreciation is linked closely to the phenomenon of the appreciation of sports. It is a commonplace that the appreciation of many works of art requires that an appreciator "identify himself with" someone else. Often the identification is to be with a fictional character, as in the appreciation of novels, stories, operas, plays, and movies. Sometimes the identification is to be with the artist. A common way of explaining both the emotional and the intellectual content of certain paintings and pieces of music is to say that the appreciator must come to understand that he himself would execute these brush strokes or write these harmonies if he were possessed of certain convictions or feelings, and were able to create these things. This requires somehow imagining oneself to be the painter of this painting, or the composer of this music. It is very difficult to give such an explanation clearly, and one of the immediate complexities is that what seems to be required is not identification with the painter or composer as such, but with the painter or composer insofar as this painting or this musical work is concerned; that is, for instance, it is not required that Igor Stravinsky have felt playful when he composed this section in one of his works, but that Stravinsky himself had to understand what a person feeling playful composing music of this kind might have done in this section; and the audience is required to achieve the same understanding.

There is an astonishing similarity to be found in the full appreciation of sports. To appreciate fully the achievement of some sportsman, it is necessary, frequently, to be able to do something that might be called imagining oneself to be doing what the sportsman does. How is this done if in fact one knows absolutely that one could not do that? Can one still imagine oneself doing it? Can one identify with the athlete? It seems that one can do something like this, however difficult it is to describe the achievement. That is why when one is pleased by a sporting achievement in which, say, the sportsman wins his game or scores his point, besides being pleased that the person or team the fan wanted to succeed has indeed succeeded, there is an additional, perhaps different, satisfaction that comes with feeling, virtually, that one has done the winning oneself. Many art theorists and artists have claimed something similar for the appreciation of art. Both R. G. Collingwood and Paul Hindemith, for instance, argue that the full appreciation of a work is achieved only by those who can feel themselves, and think of themselves, as creating the work.

If we think of sportsmen in this way, as people whose activities we appreciate in much the way that we appreciate the work of artists, then we must ask what kind of artists they resemble. Are they like authors, painters, and composers, or are they more like performers, typically those who perform works initially created by others? Perhaps the nearest analogy is with performers, but performers engaged in improvisation, such as certain kinds of jazz musicians and improvisatory actors. There is a background score or script to be performed *from* in nonimprovisatory cases, but in cases of genuine improvisation there is only something like a given melody or a topic or a situation. The sports player has the background of whatever sport or game he is engaged in, with its rules and their specification of what is allowable to him, but after that the sportsman, like the improvising artist, is to find his own way within whatever confines have been established. There remains the difference that, in typical sporting endeavors, there is in place an overall, controlling requirement that whatever one does be aimed at *winning*. In art, success is gauged in some other way. It is worth considerable thought to try to explain this artistic success, and in particular how it is, in some respects, rather like winning, but in other respects it is not like winning just because it does not require in any clear sense that anyone lose.

The philosophy of art has two main insights waiting to be gained in time spent considering sports. The first is the discovery that what is customarily thought of as "aesthetic appreciation," in all its complexity and subtlety, is to be found in the rich appreciation of sports, and therefore that aesthetic appreciation may not be linked essentially to art, but may have only a special provenance there. The second insight is a realization that the characteristic of art that it is pursued "for its own sake" does not by itself set art apart from other human endeavors. Both insights hold the promise of underwriting a deeper understanding of art by way of a precise formulation of just how art differs from sports, its surprisingly close cousin.

[*See also* Appreciation.]

BIBLIOGRAPHY

Andre, Judith, and David N. James, eds. *Rethinking College Athletics.* Philadelphia, 1991.
Journal of the Philosophy of Sport 1– (1974–). See especially no. 14 (1987), which contains an extensive bibliography.
Morgan, William, and Klaus Meier, eds. *Philosophic Inquiry in Sport.* Champaign, Ill., 1988.
Vanderwerken, David L., and Spencer K. Wertz, eds. *Sport Inside Out: Readings in Literature and Philosophy.* Fort Worth, Tex., 1985.

TED COHEN

STEIN, GERTRUDE (1874–1946), American poet and writer. For most of the twentieth century, Stein was considered the great eccentric of modern letters, a fascinating "character," more read about than read, the subject of memoir, biography, portraiture (from Pablo Picasso to Man Ray), and seemingly endless gossip. As someone who wrote no formal criticism, Stein the theorist is only now beginning to be recognized as one of the foundational modernist thinkers.

Stein's career is full of paradoxes. She lived most of her life in France; French was the language spoken in her salon but she boasted of never reading or writing in it. A writer of German-Jewish origins, she had as little taste for German culture as for the Jewish religion, always insisting that she belonged to the Anglo-American tradition, as it came down to her from William Shakespeare to George Eliot and Henry James. A writer who was lesbian, she expressed no interest in or enthusiasm for the work of other lesbian writers—or of women writers in general, unless, as in the case of Edith Sitwell, they played the role of disciple. Indeed, to the company of literary women or literary men she preferred the company of male artists, especially the artist who was in many ways her opposite, being a Catholic-born Spaniard, violent and volatile, with an enormous (heterosexual) libido and, at least later in life, a marked taste for radical left politics. The only critical monograph Stein ever wrote was an homage to this artist: her *Picasso* (1938), written, in violation of her own principles, in French.

There is the further difficulty of distinguishing between the official and the unofficial Stein discourse on literature. Her first invited public lecture, "Composition as Explana-

tion," given at Cambridge in June 1926 and published the following year by the Hogarth Press, was written to impress an audience that was quite unfamiliar with her major works, few of which had been published. Consequently, Stein exhibits a certain coy defensiveness that becomes even more pervasive in *Lectures in America* (written in 1935), written by the now best-selling author of *The Autobiography of Alice B. Toklas* (written in 1933), a sixty-year-old smiling public woman who has finally been invited to lecture in her native land in what turned out to be a grand coast-to-coast tour. *Lectures in America* creates the Stein persona most people still mistake for the actual Stein: a kind of female Douanier Rousseau, charmingly naive and "primitive," who is given to locutions such as the following in the lecture "Pictures":

> Having thus become familiar with oil paintings I looked at any and all of them and I looked at thousands and thousands of them. Any year in Paris if you want to look at any and all paintings you can look at thousands and thousands of them, you can look at them any day and everywhere. There are a great great many oil paintings in Paris.

This is by way of leading up to the recognition that "there is a relation between anything that is painted and the painting of it." Stein makes similar statements elsewhere, but in her more "unofficial" writings these are repeatedly revised, qualified, complicated, and recharged. Indeed, we do not have, in Stein's case, a corpus of critical writings detachable from a corpus of "primary" works, as is the case with T. S. Eliot or Virginia Woolf. Some of Stein's most profound theoretical speculation is found in her poems, her "portraits," her autobiographies, and in the various unclassifiable prose texts of the 1920s, beginning with "An Elucidation" (written in 1923) and culminating in the pieces collected in *How to Write* (written in 1931). For Stein, in short, writing, whatever the genre, is theory.

Consider, for starters, the opening piece of *Tender Buttons* (written in 1914), which is called "A Carafe, That is a Blind Glass":

> A kind in glass and a cousin, a spectacle and nothing strange a single hurt color and an arrangement in a system to pointing. All this and not ordinary, not unordered in not resembling. The difference is spreading.

Stein herself insisted that *Tender Buttons* was entirely "realistic" in the tradition of Gustave Flaubert. "I used to take objects on a table, like a tumbler or any kind of object and try to get the picture of it clear and separate in my mind and create a *word relationship between the word and the things seen*," she recalls in "A Transatlantic Interview—1946)" with Robert Bartlett Haas. What she no doubt means is that *reference* remains central to her project even if *representation* does not. Unlike Eliot or Ezra Pound, unlike, for that matter, the Cubist Picasso, she does not give us an *image,* however fractured, of a carafe on a table; rather, she forces us to reconsider what the objects in question are and how they function.

A carafe is, of course, "A kind in glass"—a kind of object belonging to the glass family, which includes its "cousins": bottles, pitchers, jugs, tumblers, wineglasses, and so on. A carafe is a "blind glass" because it is filled with wine, presumably red wine, and so one cannot see through it. It is also a blind glass in that it does not mirror the spectator. Nor can it be used, like a pair of glasses, to look at anything. One looks at it and through it ("a spectacle") but it does not improve our vision in any way. "Nothing strange" about this: one does not expect a carafe to be otherwise.

"A single hurt color": This carafe is evidently filled with red wine and one associate red with hurt. But "hurt" may also refer to some sort of contamination; something has bled into that single color (perhaps soda water) and changed it. At the same time, the carafe participates in what Stein calls "an arrangement in a system to pointing." Here "realism" meets Cubism: like the distorted, fragmented carafes of Picasso or Juan Gris, Stein's is part of a larger compositional arrangement, a grammar in which every verbal unit points to all the others. The carafe is "not ordinary" (i.e., not just a pitcher), "not unordered in not resembling" (it is distinct from all its "cousins," but they are all part of the compositional system). Stein concludes with the seemingly Derridean assertion "The difference is spreading." The more one studies such an "arrangement in a system to pointing," in other words, the more one becomes aware of the subtle differences between seemingly similar things. In this sense, Stein no doubt felt that she had established, as closely or "realistically" as possible, the relation between the word and the thing seen.

"A Carafe, That Is a Blind Glass" thus asks the reader to rethink the function of language in literature. There is no use, Stein implies, in giving minute verbal renditions of visual objects; words can never fully reproduce the thing seen anyway, and besides, a photograph can do the job much better. In the age of mechanical reproduction, she suggests, ostensive definition has become quite pointless. Accordingly, the aesthetic of *Tender Buttons* stands opposed to Pound's Imagist demand for "direct treatment of the thing, whether subject or object," and to William Carlos Williams's "No ideas but in things!" On the contrary, the conviction is that there are no "things" outside language to be "treated," whether directly or indirectly; there are only words. Poetic language, Stein implies, though she makes no overt statement on the subject, is not the verbal transcription of a preexistent content, nor does it provide us with what Eliot termed the "objective correlative"—"a set of objects, a situation, a chain of events which shall be the formula of [a] *particular* emotion"—for nothing can be the "formula" for anything else. But—and this is the paradox—the primacy of language does not mean that the literary text is autonomous, that it is a verbal artifact isolated from the real world. On the contrary—and here Stein's "fine new kind of realism," as her mentor William James called it, again comes into play—literature is always directly related to life.

We can see the same process at work in the "tender button" called "Custard":

Custard is this. It has aches, aches when. Not to be. Not to be narrowly. This makes a whole little hill.
It is better than a little thing that has mellow real mellow. It is better than lakes whole lakes, it is better than seeding.

Again, Stein avoids actual description. She gives us neither the recipe for making custard nor a visual image of a custard cup. Yet, consider the generative force of her words. Custard does not "ache" but it does shake or quiver. When we see something or someone shake, the inference that the movement is produced by the rhyming "ache" is reasonable. Custard quivers (aches) in a delicate way: overcook it and it turns solid—a hard lump. Conversely, beat the eggs insufficiently and it becomes runny, liquid—a lake. Thus, success depends on precision: "Not to be narrowly" and you get a "whole little hill"—"better than a little thing that has mellow real mellow." "Mellow" rhymes with "yellow"—custard color, a whole little hill of it.

But the last line is puzzling: what does "seeding" have to do with this custard? It is at this point that the sexual allusions, latent throughout the poem in the references to "custard," "aches when," "not to be narrowly," and "better than a little thing" come together. The "ache" of "custard" is "better than seeding": lesbian loving is more enjoyable than heterosexual sex. Like most of the poems in "Tender Buttons," "Custard" celebrates Stein's newfound erotic happiness with Alice B. Toklas, and feminist critics have been quick to read this and related texts as veiled sexual allegories in which each word or phrase really means something else. But such translation has a way of flattening out the work. The wit of "Custard" is that nothing is ever just one thing: for all we know, custard is, well, just custard, even as Marcel Duchamp's erotically charged readymade *Why Not Sneeze, Rrose Sélavy?* is, after all, a birdcage containing sugar cubes, a cuttle bone, and a thermometer. The main thing to note is that Stein's little poem is deeply ambiguous, but that its ambiguity is the function less of its figurative language, as would be the case in its Symbolist counterparts, than of its morphology and syntax.

"A Grammar," we read in "Arthur a Grammar," relates to "not liking to see again those you used to know" *(How to Write)*. "Those you used to know" are, in Stein's lexicon, nouns and adjectives. In "Poetry and Grammar," Stein declares:

A noun is a name of anything, why after a thing is named write about it. A name is adequate or it is not. If it is adequate then why go on calling it, if it is not then calling it by its name does no good. . . . just naming names is alright when you want to call a roll but is it any good for anything else.

And on the next page:

> . . . nouns as I say even by definition are completely not interesting, the same is true for adjectives. In a way anybody can know always has known that, because after all adjectives affect nouns and as nouns are not really interesting the thing that affects a not too interesting thing is of necessity not interesting.
>
> *(Lectures in America)*

Here Stein's rejection of the naming function recalls Ludwig Wittgenstein's critique in the *Philosophical Investigations* (1953; a work Stein could not possibly have known although it was drafted, like *Lectures in America*, in the mid-1930s) of the Augustinian theory of language, the notion that, in Wittgenstein's summary, "Every word has a meaning. This meaning is correlated with the word. It is the object for which the word stands." But what about words such as *is* or *but* or *five* that have no such object equivalent? What about nouns such as *game* or verbs such as *read*, whose specific meaning is determined only by its *use* in a specific context?

Stein was thus something of a Wittgensteinian *avant la lettre*. She was fascinated by the little words—articles, pronouns, prepositions—whose meanings necessarily depend on context. Pronouns, for example, "in not being his or its or her name . . . already have a greater possibility of being something" ("Poetry and Grammar"). "Arthur A Grammar" contains the following passage:

> What is it. Who was it. . . .
> He merely feels.
> Does he.
> Does it.
> He merely feels does it.
> He merely feels does he.
> Makes.
> In prints it.
> Prints prints it
> Forgotten.
> He has forgotten to count.
> He has forgotten how to count.

Here the slightest adjustment of preposition or pronoun *(in/on; does it/does he)* alters the meaning, reminding us of the strangeness of ordinary language. "He has forgotten to count": it is clear what that means. But when "how" is inserted before *to, count* can be construed as an intransitive verb and the sentence may thus mean "He has forgotten how to make his presence felt."

"When a sentence is called senseless," we read in the *Philosophical Investigations*, "it is not as it were its sense that is senseless. But a combination of words is being excluded from the language, withdrawn from circulation" (no. 500). The real question is then: why is this particular combination withdrawn? In her writings, Stein makes a similar case for a radical deconstruction of language and its function in culture. Why can we not say "Grammar will" or "Grammar an

angel"? Why can one not be "worried hours aloud" or refer to "our last hourglass"? How is it that we communicate as adequately as we do in daily life, when we must discriminate between phrases such as

> Two next
> To be next to it
> To be annexed
> To be annexed to it.   ("An Elucidation")

Think of the possibilities for writing varied and vivid sentences. "A sentence is an interval in which there is a finally forward and back." It follows that a real writer is someone who puts before us not intricate narrative, or the complex psychological interaction between characters, or subtly charged images, or even elegant sound structures, but rather someone who reinvents the language itself so as to make manifest the possibilities that have been there all along. "I am a grammarian," Stein declares in *How to Write*, and again, "Grammar. Fills me with delight. / I am having it as a habit"—which again recalls a Wittgenstein phrase, this time from his Cambridge *Lectures 1930–1932:* "In philosophy all that is not gas is grammar." Or, in what sounds like a Steinian aphorism, "There are no gaps in grammar; grammar is always complete."

If, then, as Stein insists, the writer's unit is not the image or the symbolic construct but the smallest grammatical unit that is the sentence, it follows that composition in the larger sense will depend on what Stein calls "using everything." In "Composition as Explanation" (1926), "using everything" is related to "beginning again and again" and the "continuous present"; these three compositional principles, Stein explains, first make their appearance in the early fictions generated by repetition and permutation: *Melanctha, The Making of Americans,* and *A Long Gay Book.* In his introduction to the paperback reprint of *The Geographical History of America* (written in 1935), William Gass has an excellent discussion of this aspect of Stein's work:

> Life is repetition, and in a dozen different ways Gertrude Stein set out to render it. We have only to think how we pass our days: the doorbell rings, the telephone, sirens in the street, steps on the stairs, the recurrent sounds of buzzers, birds, and vacuum cleaners. . . . Life is rearrangement, and in a dozen different ways Gertrude Stein set out to render it. We are not clocks, designed to repeat without remainder, to mean nothing by a tick, not even the coming tock, and so we must distinguish between merely mechanical repetition, in which there is no progress of idea, no advance or piling up of wealth, and that which seriously defines our nature, describes the central rhythms of our lives.
>
> Almost at once [Stein] realized that language itself is a complete analogue of experience because it, too, is made of a large but finite number of relatively fixed terms which are then allowed to occur in a limited number of clearly specified relations, so that it is not the appearance of a word that matters but *the manner of its reappearance.*
>
> (1973)

Not appearance but reappearance: this is what Stein has in mind when she speaks of "beginning again and again" and the "continuous present"; for repetition only becomes meaningful when the word or phrase or even whole sentence is repeated often enough—and repeated, of course, with the most delicate variations—to make a difference. But the third principle in the triad, "using everything," has implications for writers and artists whose mode and style may otherwise have little to do with Stein's. In the "Transatlantic Interview," she makes her meaning clearer:

> Everything I have done has been influenced by Flaubert and Cézanne, and this gave me a new feeling about composition. Up to that time composition had consisted of a central idea, to which everything else was an accompaniment and separate but was not an end in itself, and Cézanne conceived the idea that in composition one thing was as important as another thing. Each part is as important as the whole, and that impressed me enormously.

Here Stein is referring, however elliptically, to one of the cornerstones of modernist aesthetics. From the Renaissance to the late nineteenth century, painting distinguished between figure and ground, foreground and background, and Stein rightly (if somewhat schematically) attributes the breakdown of that basic distinction to Paul Cézanne—or, so far as literature is concerned, to Flaubert, especially the Flaubert of the *Éducation sentimentale,* whose canvas depends precisely on the conviction that "each thing is as important as every other thing." James, Stein goes on to say, still discriminates between figure and ground: he bathes his characters in an "atmosphere" that assumes great importance, but it is still atmosphere, against which a Maggie Verver or Lambert Strether is silhouetted. But in Stein's world, as in Picasso's or, for that matter, in Dada, "using everything" means that no part of the canvas (or, in her case, the poem or narrative) is more important than any other part. What this means in practice is that the writer does not begin with a central image or ruling myth or dominant symbol and then gather his or her materials around it, as, for example, William Butler Yeats does in his Byzantium poems. Rather, the process of writing is itself the "hero" of the work.

In art discourse, the notion of "using everything," of getting rid of the figure/ground distinction, has been taken as a given from Cubism and Futurism on down, but in literary theory, it remains a radical concept. It is interesting to compare Stein to Pound in this regard. Such well-known Pound theorems as "Use no word that does not contribute to the presentation," or his definition of the Vortex as a "radiant node or cluster . . . from which, and through which, and into which, ideas are constantly rushing," are based on precisely the premise that there is a focal point, a "radiant node" or "figure" to which everything else in the composition is subordinated. "Use no word that does not contribute to the presentation" makes no sense from a Steinian perspective because it implies that there are more and less important words—images that are central and "filler" words that connect those images. For Stein, by contrast, there are no filler words, no phrases such as "Petals on a wet black bough" that subordinate the preposition and the article to nouns and adjectives. Each thing is as important as every other thing.

The theory of "using everything," eccentric as it was taken to be in the poetics of the early twentieth century, has, ironically enough, become one of the important precepts of postmodern poetics. From the Objectivists and French Oulipo writers to such younger poet-theorists as Lyn Hejinian, Susan Howe, Steve McCaffery, Joan Retallack, Tom Raworth, and Charles Bernstein, the Stein injunction to "Act so there is no use in a centre" has become an article of faith. Accordingly, Stein is now hailed as the precursor of contemporary avant-garde movements.

Yet, one must be careful not to overdo such analogies. Despite Stein's radical critique of conventional theories of signification, she did not hold, as did Jacques Derrida, that language is no more than trace structure, the infinite regress whereby "words and concepts receive meaning only in sequences of differences" (Derrida, 1976). The notion that the signified (say, the mental image of a sugar bowl on the table, to which one points when one says, "Please pass the sugar") is "originarily and essentially . . . trace, that it is *always already in the position of the signifier,*" and that accordingly no word can have "full presence," would have been quite alien to Stein's pragmatist way of thinking. She would have scoffed that of course a sugar bowl is a sugar bowl (no more, no less), the question being, as in "Marry Nettie," how it functions in the text.

Here, as already suggested, the apposite figure is not Derrida (or any other poststructuralist theorist) but Stein's contemporary, Wittgenstein, for whom the meaning of a word is its use in the language. If you and I function within the same language community and I say to you, as we sit at the breakfast table, "Pass the sugar, please," you know exactly what I mean. The signifier *sugar* does not participate in the play of *significance,* the oscillation of presence and absence. But difficulties arise when you are not sure what language game I am playing:

> When I say that the orders "Bring me sugar" and "Bring me milk" make sense, but not the combination "Milk me sugar", that does not mean that the utterance of this combination of words has no effect. And if its effect is that the other person stares at me and gapes, I don't on that account call it the order to stare and gape, even if that was precisely the effect that I wanted to produce.
> To say that "This combination of words makes no sense" excludes it from the sphere of language and thereby bounds the domain of language. But when one draws a boundary it may be for various kinds of reason. . . . So if I draw a boundary line that is not yet to say what I am drawing it for.
>
> (Wittgenstein, 1968, nos. 498–499)

There may, in short, be a good reason to say "Milk me sugar." Stein, for that matter, wrote a poem called "Milk" that begins: "A white egg and a colored pan and a cabbage showing settlement, a constant increase." At first this sentence seems perverse: what is the resemblance between milk and egg or milk and cabbage? But if one consider what the "boundary lines" here might be, one soon notices that the poem describes quite accurately the process of boiling milk. Poured into one of those colored enamel pans, milk does look like an oval egg and, as it rises to the boil ("a constant increase") it settles into the hilly form of a cauliflower (a member of the cabbage family). If one takes the language game in question to be a cooking lesson, it all makes perfectly good sense.

Such defamiliarization—what Pound called "Make It New!"—was, of course, a central tenet of modernism. Where Stein's form of defamiliarization differs from that of most of her contemporaries (though not from such avant-gardists as Duchamp) is in her rejection of poetry (or fiction) as the representation of a particular subjectivity, as revelation of self. Or rather: she understood, long before it was fashionable to do so, that the self is at least partially a cultural construction, that context makes all the difference. "Arthur," in her scheme of things, is only "a grammar," and even in her more conventional works, such as *The Autobiography of Alice B. Toklas,* the principals—Picasso, his mistress Fernande, Guillaume Apollinaire, Marie Laurencin, Constance Fletcher—are seen as functions in a "system of pointing" rather than as individual characters. "'I,'" she might have said with Wittgenstein, "is a word like any other." It is in this respect that Stein seems very much our contemporary.

[*See also* Aleatoric Processes; Feminism; Modernism, *article on* Modern Literature; *and* Poetics.]

BIBLIOGRAPHY

Note: There is to date no collected or definitive edition of Gertrude Stein's works, and the published texts are by no means reliable, as Ulla E. Dydo points out in her excellent *A Stein Reader* (see below). In the Stein items listed, I therefore supply the original date of publication (often much later than the year of composition cited in the text), where relevant.

Works by Stein

Tender Buttons (1914). In *Selected Writings of Gertrude Stein,* edited by Carl Van Vechten, pp. 460–509. New York, 1990.
How To Write (1931). Los Angeles, 1995.
The Autobiography of Alice B. Toklas (1933). New York, 1990.
"An Elucidation" (1934). In *A Stein Reader,* edited by Ulla E. Dydo, pp. 429–442. Evanston, Ill., 1993.
The Geographical History of America (1935). New York, 1973.
Lectures in America (1935). Boston, 1985.
Selected Writings of Gertrude Stein (1946). Edited by Carl Van Vechten. New York, 1990.
"A Transatlantic Interview—1946." In *A Primer for the Gradual Understanding of Gertrude Stein,* edited by Robert Bartlett Haas, pp. 15–35. Los Angeles, 1971.
A Stein Reader. Edited by Ulla E. Dydo. Evanston, Ill., 1993.

Other Sources

Bridgman, Richard. *Gertrude Stein in Pieces.* New York and Oxford, 1970.
Derrida, Jacques. *Of Grammatology.* Translated by Gayatri Chakravorty Spivak. Baltimore, 1976.
Perloff, Marjorie. *The Poetics of Indeterminacy: Rimbaud to Cage.* Princeton, N.J., 1981.
Perloff, Marjorie. *Wittgenstein's Ladder: Poetic Language and the Strangeness of the Ordinary.* Chicago, 1996.
Pound, Ezra. *Literary Essays.* Edited by T. S. Eliot. New York, 1954.
Wittgenstein, Ludwig. *Philosophical Investigations* (1953). 3d ed. Translated by G. E. M. Anscombe. New York, 1968.
Wittgenstein, Ludwig. *Wittgenstein's Lectures, Cambridge, 1930–1932* (1980). From the Notes of John King and Desmond Lee, edited by Desmond Lee. Chicago, 1989.
White, Ray Lewis. *Gertrude Stein and Alice B. Toklas: A Reference Guide.* Boston, 1984.

MARJORIE PERLOFF

STOICISM. See Hellenistic Aesthetics.

STOKES, ADRIAN DURHAM (1902–1972), critic, heir to the nineteenth-century tradition of Walter Pater and John Ruskin. Stokes wrote about old master art as if it were part of a living cultural tradition. His greatest books, *Quattro Cento* (1932) and *Stones of Venice* (1935)—both reprinted in Stokes, 1978—presented a theoretical conception, modified but never abandoned in his later writing. What he calls "Quattro Cento" art—he turns the Italian *quattrocento* (fourteenth century) into a descriptive phrase—appears essentially atemporal. To these Quattro Cento carved works, the most visual kind of visual art, he contrasts that lesser painting and sculpture which, in its musical-like play with temporality, uses modeling. The familiar contrast between the carver's cutting into his medium and the modeler's building up a form thus is reinterpreted.

Stokes's early books, which aided the revival of interest in quattrocento sculpture, employ ways of thought that are alien to the modern art historian. Charles Seymour's scholarly account (1966, pp. 129–134) identifies the ideas that may have influenced Agostino di Duccio, the sculptor of the Tempio Malatestiano, Rimini. Stokes's deeply felt belief was that these relief sculptures express fantasies about the history of their materials. "Agostino's root preoccupation was with water forms and water movement" (Stokes, 1978, vol. 1, p. 229). Within modern art history, there is a broad division between iconographers' study of the literary sources of artworks and connoisseurs' concern with qualities that are immediately knowable visually. Like a connoisseur, Stokes is interested in what is directly knowable; but, unlike most connoisseurs, he is not concerned with attributions. Stokes believes that, in carving the stone, the artist entertained fantasies that can be intuited by an attentive observer.

Some art historians admire the "poetic" qualities of Stokes's writing, but even his admirers are unlikely to adopt his way of thinking, which today seems highly speculative. His ways of thinking about visual art deserve attention from aestheticians, both because of the intrinsically valuable literary qualities of his writing and for the challenge it poses to "normal" art history. It provides a highly original model of what can be done with that much-discussed topic psychoanalytic aesthetics. Stokes was primarily concerned with the materials of art, not with art as a vehicle for personal fantasy. Because his way of thought differs so radically from that of both traditional art historians and those revisionist historians concerned with poststructuralism, his work provides a valuable critical perspective.

The most important philosopher of art influenced by Stokes is Richard Wollheim, whose "Adrian Stokes" (1972) remains the best introduction to the thought of his friend.

BIBLIOGRAPHY

Works by Stokes

The Critical Writings of Adrian Stokes. Edited by Lawrence Gowling. London, 1978.

Other Sources

Carrier, David. *Artwriting.* Amherst, Mass., 1987. See chap. 3.
Seymour, Charles, Jr. *Sculpture in Italy, 1400–1500.* Baltimore, 1966.
Wollheim, Richard. "Adrian Stokes" (1972). In *On Art and the Mind: Essays and Lectures,* pp. 315–335. London, 1973; reprint, Cambridge, Mass., 1974.

DAVID CARRIER

STRAVINSKY, IGOR FEDOROVICH (1882–1971), Russian composer. As a prominent representative of musical modernism and advocate of an aesthetic of musical objectivity, Stravinsky had enormous influence on musical developments in Europe in the first half of the twentieth century. His artistic development, like that of many of his contemporaries, was shaped by political circumstances, which forced him onto a cosmopolitan compositional trajectory: born in Russia in 1982, he went to Paris in 1911, moved to Switzerland in 1914, to Paris again in 1920, to California in 1940, and lived in New York after 1969 until his death in 1971. His compositional oeuvre divides logically into three stylistic periods, which coincide with major geographic dislocations: the works of his early years (1903–1917) reflect Russian cultural traditions and evince the composer's attraction to primitivist aesthetics, which are most evident in the three ballets that Sergei Diaghilev commissioned for the Parisian programs of the Ballets Russes: *The Firebird, Petrouchka,* and *Le Sacre du Printemps.* His second stylistic period (1914 or 1922, depending on interpretation, to 1951) corresponds with his emigration to western Europe and gradual rejection of his Russian musical her-

itage in favor of a French-influenced "objective" style that his critics subsequently labeled neoclassical. This new approach to composition characterizes works ranging from the *Three Pieces for String Quartet* through the Concerto for Piano and Winds to *The Rake's Progress.* In his third, "late" stylistic period (1952–1963), Stravinsky surprised some of his followers by adopting and transforming the twelve-tone method of a composer whom critics since the 1920s had considered his nemesis: Arnold Schoenberg.

Stravinsky outlines his aesthetics most comprehensively in "Some Ideas about My Octuor" (1924), his autobiographical *Chronique de ma vie* (1935), and his *Poétique musicale* (1942), a publication resulting from the six Charles Eliot Norton lectures he gave in French at Harvard University from October 1939 to May 1940. It would be erroneous to consider these texts either as a comprehensive aesthetic or as a systematic explanation of the composer's thoughts on art throughout his life. They do, however, provide the most explicit account of Stravinsky's highly influential aesthetic of musical objectivity. Ideas presented here also reappeared later, with variations, in the numerous published conversations with Robert Craft.

Perhaps Stravinsky's most significant yet most misunderstood statement on musical aesthetics is contained in his *Chronique de ma vie:*

> I consider music, by its very essence, incapable of expressing anything at all, whether it be a feeling, an attitude, a psychological state, or a phenomenon of nature, and so on. Expression has never been the immanent property of music and in no way defines its essence. If, as is usually always the case, music seems to express something, it is only an illusion and not a reality. Expression is simply an additional element that we, because of some tacit or inflexible convention, have lent to or imposed on music like a name tag, a report, or, in sum, a posture, and that we have come to confuse with music's essence whether unconsciously or by habit. (1935)

In denying music the ability to express anything whatsoever, Stravinsky explicitly rejects nineteenth-century aesthetics of feeling, musical Expressionism, and the psychology of the individual subject. In their place, he envisions music as "a type of speculation formed in terms of sound and time" or conscious organization of tones. The musical work becomes an "artifice" or abstract order that is neither mimetic (i.e., representative of an outside reality) nor a vehicle for expressing human feeling. Rather, it reveals and justifies itself in the "free play of its functions" and is most analogous to an architectural structure.

Stravinsky solves the problem of how listeners can still perceive emotions in music even when the composer has not invested it with any by attributing to form the ability to present emotions independently of human agency. Form is defined as the "only emotive subject of composition"; and the means of composition become "emotive in themselves."

His description of emotions in music as the "heterogeneous play of movements and volumes" reveals that he understands emotion as universal and impersonal, and has so accepted the meanings music had acquired in Western culture that he had come to understand them as natural, or intrinsic to the notes. Largely uninterested in the sociocultural construction of musical meaning, Stravinsky was willing to deny that human subjects had originally invested such emotional content in music.

In Stravinsky's nonexpressive universe, the human subject and musical object are linked primarily through their existence in time: "the phenomenon of music is given to us with the sole aim of establishing order among things, especially between *man* and *time.*" Following Pierre Souvtchinsky, Stravinsky distinguishes between two kinds of music: one parallel to the course of psychological time, the other following ontological time. In the first type, music is subject to the composer's emotive impulses. Such music emphasizes contrast and variation, is most likely tonal, and is best exemplified by Richard Wagner's works. Stravinsky rejects this music in favor of the second type, or what Souvtchinsky calls "chronometric music," in which the musical process is in equilibrium with real time, or the beat becomes the identity of the subject. Stravinsky favors this type of music because he believes that "music is the only domain where man realizes the present. Because of the imperfection of his nature, man is forced to succumb to the passing of time—of the categories of past and future—without ever rendering real, in other words stable, the category of the present" (ibid.). In his *Poétique musicale,* Stravinsky encourages composers to link their music to ontological time by emphasizing the evident or hidden similarities between musical materials. In his music, he evokes the metaphor of ontological time by returning to the steady beat of Baroque music, echoing the effects of mechanical performance media, and encouraging a *perpetuum mobile*-style continuity that caused critics to compare his music to a "sewing machine." Wary of the hierarchy of tonal functions that characterize psychological time, Stravinsky advocates a harmony based on poles of attraction.

Stravinsky's aesthetic of an objective music based on ontological time is best revealed in practice in the so-called neoclassical works of his second period. First applied to Stravinsky's music by Boris de Schloezer in 1923, the term *neoclassical* originally served the function of distinguishing Stravinsky's work from that of Schoenberg, and of accentuating its affinity to classical as opposed to Romantic musical aesthetics. "Neoclassicism" is most useful as a means of defining the new relationship to musical materials that Stravinsky developed around the time he emigrated to western Europe and was exposed to the music and thought of Erik Satie and Jean Cocteau. Influenced also by the nonexpressive, kinetic choreography of Diaghilev's Ballets Russes and Vsevolod Meyerhold's revival of commedia dell'arte,

Stravinsky developed a compositional approach in his second period in which sounds involved the listener directly in an aural ritual, rather than acting as symbols or signs denoting emotional or expressive psychological content. By transferring the practice of juxtaposing and superimposing motivic cells that he had established in Russian ballets such as *Le Sacre du Printemps* to instrumental works such as *Three Pieces for String Quartet* and *Symphonies des Instruments à Vent,* Stravinsky objectified a practice of simultaneity originally associated with the violent rhythms of primitivist dance. These pieces evince ontological time as a metaphor for a musical practice in which the beat becomes the unit of measurement over metric accent. Surface discontinuities confuse the listener's sense of the beat, forcing him or her to concentrate on the passage of time, or the present. Using register, timbre, nonexpressive, experimental instrumental techniques, tempo, harmony, and silence to alienate highly differentiated cellular materials, Stravinsky focuses the listener's attention on isolated musical events and their formal development. Drawing on his experiences as a student of Nikolai Rimsky-Korsakov and on his knowledge of Aleksandr Scriabin's music, from which he developed an understanding of the octatonic system, and building on the polarized harmonic organization that he had established in *Petrouchka,* he developed a harmonic technique based on the interaction between diatonic and octatonic systems. Devoid of tonal hierarchies and marked by severe temporal discontinuity, this music could no longer communicate expressive and emotional content in the manner of Western art music.

Stravinsky broke most dramatically with nineteenth-century aesthetics of expression by alienating the musical material of his compositions in multiple ways. In *L'histoire du soldat,* for example, he used the visual scenario of a marionette theater, the instrumental colors and combinations of the fairground, and non-Western phrase structure and repetition in order to create a distanced, seemingly mechanical music. Inspired by the notion of abstract types as opposed to the more personally expressive individual, Stravinsky evoked the universal in this work by parodying characteristic genres such as the march and incorporating general, stylized allusions to other genres such as the tango and ragtime. Parody became for Stravinsky a vehicle for distancing listeners from musical materials in a nonjudgmental—that is, objective—way. In the commedia dell'arte ballet *Pulcinella,* he made listeners conscious of their emotional response to the original music by Giambattista Pergolesi and Domenico Gallo by recomposing the accompaniment of melodies, destabilizing the meter, distorting harmonies, shortening phrases, reorchestrating passages, and confusing the focus of the music by introducing unusual timbres and accents. In contrast to other classicists such as Ferruccio Busoni, Stravinsky did not manipulate these materials in order to comment on them, but rather, in the spirit of Aleksandr Benois's ballet scenario, to free them by liberating them from their conventional meanings. In the opera *Mavra,* begun a year later, he expanded his manipulation of musical artifacts by exploring within a modernist framework materials as diverse as the tonality of Western music, Mikhail Glinka's and Pyotr Ilich Tchaikovsky's styles, rudimentary jazz rhythms, and elements of Russian variety shows.

After the fiasco of *Mavra,* Stravinsky turned to instrumental works based on textbook, stereotypical classical forms such as the sonata, variations, and rondo. He did not intend to reconstruct these historical forms with all their compositional implications, but rather only to allude to them as a means of signaling to his audience that they should enter the formalist mode of listening. Even when tonality reappears, it is often drained of its goal-directed force and forced into a quasi inertia. In works such as the *Octet,* he evoked the style and classical sonata form of Franz Joseph Haydn and Ludwig van Beethoven, for example, only in order to undermine them with contradicting formal and stylistic strategies, like those of Johann Sebastian Bach. Styles, genres, and forms serve less as a compositional foundation than as neutral material that the composer mixed and matched at will. This practice is most clear in *Oedipus Rex,* in which Stravinsky fused a wide range of styles, among them those of George Frideric Handel, Giuseppe Verdi, Bach, and even the Folies Bergères, in order to destabilize the denotative meaning of the music and thereby achieve an extreme objectivity accentuated by the unidiomatic use of Latin and inclusion of a speaker satirizing the action. *Oedipus Rex* realizes objectivity by referencing past artistic achievements in an impersonal way. "Resolutely negating all individualism," Stravinsky's colleague Arthur Lourié wrote in 1927, Stravinsky, "revives impersonal yet solidly constructed forms of the culture of past centuries, making them serve new needs and aims" (1927).

Lourié's statement demonstrates that the emotional objectivity commonly associated with Stravinsky's neoclassical works results only partially from their inherent compositional features. To a large extent, the composer and his supporters created an aura of objectivity around these works through the words they used to describe them and the polemics surrounding their composition. In his writings, Stravinsky emphasizes his lack of emotional involvement in these works, for example, by referring to himself not as their composer but as their craftsman; he does not express himself, but rather *makes* this music in a productive process that follows controlled, rational principles to impose on the materials a form that he has consciously conceived. Avoiding the spiritual and psychological implications of the notion of inspiration by delegating it to the insignificant role of an "emotive disturbance," Stravinsky solidifies his theory of the artist as craftsman by seeking the source of his creative work in a less mystical "appetite for discovery" that, for the

composer, was a "natural need." The composer does not make ethical or aesthetic choices, but rather "ensures the rightness of [his/her] operation" by acquiring certain methods through experience, inventiveness, and apprenticeship. This experience is not personal, but rather "objective" and linked to "concrete values." Composers can make such proper aesthetic judgments because they have culture and inner taste—the necessary basis for being able to observe and thus compose. They have to deny their personalities, however, in order to recognize true principles of organization and realize them objectively in music.

Stravinsky is able to minimize the role of the composer and subjective expression in composition because he has reinstated a classical belief in transcendental rules of art and metaphysical values in his aesthetic system. He has accepted the metaphysical theory of the substantially unified human subject, for example: music "emanates from the integral man. I mean from a man armed with all the resources of his senses, his psychological faculties, and his intellectual capacities." He has also accepted without questioning the unity of the autonomous artwork, which is suprapersonal and suprareal, coherent and sufficient in itself. Finally, his entire poetic is based on the existence of a set of rules or dogmas that are "demanded by the very organization of the spiritual being" and resemble spiritual truths or religious laws. This dichotomy between a materialist or formalist approach to composition and a belief in metaphysical values led Enrico Fubini to label Stravinsky's aesthetic a "metaphysical formalism."

By evoking the authority of transcendental truths, Stravinsky absolves himself from the task of addressing the thorny issue of the moral obligation of the artist. From a liberal perspective, Stravinsky appears to be blindly accepting authority and refusing ethical responsibility for his work. His approach to ethics becomes clearer, however, in light of Jacques Maritain's Neo-Thomist philosophy of art, which Stravinsky came to know through Lourié in the 1920s and which strongly influenced his thought. In *Art et scolastique,* Maritain had proposed that art was not self-expression, but rather a virtue of the "practical intellect" whose goal was the goodness of the thing made. Art was distinct from moral virtue because it was "outside the human sphere; it had an end, rules, values, which were not those of man, but those of the work to be produced. The work was everything for Art; there was for Art but one law—the exigencies and the good of the work" (Maritain, 1965). Thus, the capacity of the artist to produce good artifacts was independent of his moral condition. Maritain could distinguish the artist's morality from his art because he believed in transcendent truth, as did Stravinsky. This faith in metaphysical values has been the subject of the most skeptical critical attacks on Stravinsky by postmodern critics.

Stravinsky's aesthetics had a wide influence throughout the twentieth century, creating disciples and provoking vivid critical response. Perhaps the most influential and incriminating critique came from Theodor W. Adorno, who rejected Stravinsky's goal of objectivity as the attempt to evoke a nonexistent "objective" society and to deny the reality of sociopolitical relations in his time. Adorno equated objectivity with an absence of meaning and the commercialization of art, and defined it as representative of the alienated state of consciousness of the modern subject. Dedicated to the project of ideology critique and sociological analysis of the Frankfurt School, Adorno necessarily rejected Stravinsky's attempts to create a nonmimetic art, which he interpreted as an escape into an "illusory realism." In his highly influential *Philosophie der neuen Musik* (1975), Adorno attacked the very backbone of Stravinsky's aesthetic approach: his interpretation of musical time. For Adorno, Stravinsky's ontological time was equivalent to a rejection of subjectivity and a reduction of humanity to a thing. Because he interpreted art as the encounter between the conscious compositional subject and socially established material, Adorno could hardly have had less sympathy for Stravinsky's Neo-Thomist notions of craftsmanship. He likewise rejected Stravinsky's neoclassicism as the impossible attempt to reconstitute styles of the past that reflected the society of their time and could thus only appear false in the present.

Adorno's writings had an overwhelming influence on how Stravinsky's aesthetics were received in Europe, particularly in Germany. The German musicologist Rudolf Stephan has reinterpreted Stravinsky's aesthetics within the context of Russian Formalism. Although Stravinsky and Russian Formalists pursued radically different objectives, Stephan and others have noted their affinity in terms of the alienation of musical material through parody. This technique enables the composer to objectify material and enter into a dialogue with the musical past, and offers a new means of understanding a nonexpressive form of composition.

More recently, Stravinsky's aesthetics have come under attack from the American musicologist Richard Taruskin. In the tradition of Adorno, Taruskin condemns the reactionary ideology that allowed Stravinsky to submit to rules and deny human subjectivity. Taruskin pinpoints the fundamental problem of Stravinsky's aesthetics: namely, how do we assure the moral responsibility of the artist if we accept rules and orders uncritically as eternal and given? Taruskin's writings are representative of the postmodern trend toward rejecting the aesthetic postulates of modernism.

[*See also* Modernism, *article on* Modern Music; Music, *historical overview article; and* Russian Aesthetics.]

BIBLIOGRAPHY

Works by Stravinsky

"Some Ideas about My Octuor." *The Arts* (January 1924). Reprinted in Eric W. White, *Stravinsky: The Composer and his Works* (London, 1966), pp. 528–531.

Chronique de ma vie. Paris, 1935.
Poetics of Music in the Form of Six Lessons. Bilingual Edition. Translated by Arthur Knodel and Ingolf Dahl. Cambridge, Mass., 1947.
Conversations with Igor Stravinsky. With Robert Craft. London, 1958.
Memories and Commentaries. With Robert Craft. London, 1959.
Expositions and Developments. With Robert Craft. Garden City, N.Y., 1962.
Dialogues and a Diary. With Robert Craft. London, 1968.
Retrospectives and Conclusion. With Robert Craft. New York, 1969.
Themes and Conclusions. With Robert Craft. London, 1972.
Selected Correspondence. 3 vols. New York, 1985.

Other Sources

Adorno, Theodor W. *Philosophie der neuen Musik.* Edited by Rolf Tiedemann. Frankfurt am Main, 1975.
Druskin, Mikhail. *Igor Stravinsky: His Life, Works, and Views.* Translated by Martin Cooper. Cambridge and New York, 1983.
Fubini, Enrico. "L'estetica di Stravinskij." In *Stravinskij Oggi: Convegno internazionale, Milano, 28–30 Maggio 1982,* edited by Anna Maria Morazzoni, Quaderni di Musica/Realta 10, pp. 32–45. Milan, 1986.
Griffiths, Paul. *Stravinsky.* New York, 1992.
Lourié, Arthur. "Oedipus-Rex." *La revue musicale* 8.8 (April–October 1927): 240–253.
Maritain, Jacques. *Art et scolastique.* 4th ed. Paris, 1965.
Messing, Scott. *Neoclassicism in Music: From the Genesis of the Concept through the Schoenberg/Stravinsky Polemic.* Ann Arbor, 1988.
Pusler, Jann, ed. *Confronting Stravinsky: Man, Musician, and Modernist.* Berkeley, 1986.
Schloezer, Boris de. *Igor Stravinsky.* Paris, 1929.
Souvtchinsky, Pierre. "La notion du temps et la musique." *La revue musicale* (1939): 310–320.
Stephan, Rudolf. "Zur Deutung von Strawinskys Neoklassizismus." In *Igor Stravinsky,* Musikkonzepte 34/35, pp. 80–88. Stuttgart, 1984.
Stravinsky, Vera, and Robert Craft. *Stravinsky in Pictures and Documents.* New York, 1978.
Taruskin, Richard. "The Pastness of the Present and the Presence of the Past." In *Authenticity and Early Music,* edited by Nicholas Kenyon, pp. 137–210. Oxford and New York, 1988.
Taruskin, Richard. "Back to Whom? Neoclassicism as Ideology." *19th-Century Music* 16.3 (Spring 1993): 286–302.
Taruskin, Richard. *Stravinsky and the Russian Traditions: A Biography of the Works through Mavra.* 2 vols. Berkeley, 1996.
Walsh, Stephen. *The Music of Stravinsky.* Reprint, Oxford, 1993.
Walsh, Stephen. *Stravinsky: Oedipus Rex.* Cambridge and New York, 1993.
Watkins, Glenn. *Pyramids at the Louvre: Music, Culture and Collage from Stravinsky to the Postmodernists.* Cambridge, Mass., 1994.
White, Eric Walter. *Stravinsky: The Composer and His Works.* 2d ed. London, 1979.

TAMARA LEVITZ

STRUCTURALISM. One might sum up structuralism by saying that it is a theory that conceives of all cultural phenomena, including artistic artifacts, as sign systems, and those systems as operating according to the dictates of a deep structure (one might think of the latter as being analogous to a genetic program). Its roots lie mainly in the linguistic theories of the Swiss linguist Ferdinand de Saussure, although the work of the early Soviet school of literary theorists, the Russian Formalists (plus those connected with them in their brief heyday following the Russian Revolution), also played a part in structuralism's development. Structuralism has had an impact on many areas of intellectual endeavor in the twentieth century—aesthetic theory and criticism, anthropology, and psychoanalysis, to name some of the most prominent.

Saussure's linguistic theories, as expounded in his *Course in General Linguistics* (put together, after his death in 1913, by his students from their notes of his lecture program at the University of Geneva), are based in the first instance on the principle that language (that is, the whole family of human languages) is a self-contained system with its own rules and regulations governing its internal operations—in other words, that there is an underlying grammar to all human language. The "linguistic model" that resulted from Saussure's research was put forward as a model for how all systems operated, and structuralism as it has developed since Saussure's death relies heavily on this original model as the basis for its analyses of cultural phenomena. Language, for Saussure, was to be divided into two main parts: *langue* and *parole*. The former referred to language as a system, the latter to the body of individual utterances made by human beings within that system. *Langue* was where Saussure's interest was almost exclusively concentrated, that is, with language as a system, its grammar, and its methods (*parole* being more a matter of behavior than of rules). In his favorite analogy, language was like a game of chess, in that it was self-contained, self-regulating, and bound by rules as to how the pieces could be used. The grammar of chess dictated that pawns could make certain moves only, knights others again, and so on with castles, bishops, queens, and kings. The consequence of this conception of systems was that the elements of the system (the chess pieces, for example) were to be defined by their function: to ask the meaning of a pawn was to be told its function within a game of chess, and equally, of a linguistic unit (such as a verb) its role within the grammar of the linguistic system. Individual elements were, in fact, to be defined by their difference from other elements within the given system; thus, to be a pawn was to have a function different from a bishop (etc.), and to stand in a clearly defined relationship to that figure within the confines of the game.

Language was taken to be a system of signs to which we respond in a more or less predictable way (as, to use an example of a rudimentary sign system with a very restricted grammar, we would to traffic lights). Signs were made up of a signifier and a signified (basically, a word and its mental concept), which combined together in the mind, in an act of understanding, to form the sign: the union of the word *cat* and the mental concept "cat," for example, signaled the object being referred to. The bond between signifier and signified was described as arbitrary, meaning that any word at all, in theory, could be used to signify a given object; all that was needed was a consensus among a linguistic community

at any given time as to the particular word being used to refer to a particular object. Proof of the arbitrariness of the bond could be found in the fact that different words were used to describe the same object across the family of human languages: *cat* in English, *chat* in French, *gatto* in Italian, and so on. There was nothing intrinsic to the word *cat* itself that required that it be associated with that particular animal. For Saussure, language was dominated by this principle of arbitrariness, although in practice the need for consensus meant that any changes in the meanings of words tended to happen gradually. He argued, therefore, that the arbitrariness was relative only, and that systems displayed order rather than disorder. Finding order within systems has remained a primary preoccupation of structuralist analysis.

Saussure saw language as operating according to a series of binary oppositions (such as the *langue/parole* distinction). The relations between words could be either syntagmatic or associative. In a sentence constructed according to the rules of, say, English grammar (subject-verb-object, "The book is on the desk"), the words were joined together in a linear sequence (or "syntagma"). Associative (later also called "paradigmatic") relations depended on looser connections, in effect, something more like association of ideas: teaching/education/apprenticeship being one example of such a sequence given by Saussure. Language was also to be seen in either synchronic or diachronic perspective, the former being a case of observing the system as a whole, the latter in one of its dynamic phases (the difference between the game of chess as a totality, with a set of rules governing its operation, and a particular move in a game initiating a change in the state of play). The diachronic perspective enables structuralist analysts to scrutinize selected aspects of the whole against the background of the total system, thus communicating a sense of historical change.

Saussure is also famous for predicting the development of a "science of signs," or "semiology," as he called it (now more generally referred to as "semiotics"). This discipline is effectively coterminous with structuralism, and language is only one of many systems that it studies, although arguably the most important, in that it provides the basic model for semiotic inquiry (for the psychoanalyst Jacques Lacan, for example, even the unconscious is a sign system structured like a language). The promise that semiology held out was that ultimately we could come to understand the workings of all cultural phenomena. Structuralism appeared to offer a key to unlock the secrets of the myriad sign systems in human experience, a way of coming to terms with the complexity of the world. When applied to aesthetic matters, structuralism enabled us to see how works of art could be read as sign systems designed to elicit certain responses from their audiences, and to grasp how those responses were generated. Not the least of the virtues of structuralism is that it is a relatively easy method to assimilate, and it very quickly enables the practitioner to amass large amounts of data about works of art—the details of the internal grammar, the relations between its various elements, and how these compare to the grammar and elements of other works. Comparative analysis, and the wider understanding that is engendered by it, are a logical outcome of the structuralist approach. Structuralism also aspires to universal applicability, and, by ranging over so many fields, it has helped to foster interdisciplinary inquiry, which in itself has helped to give a broader picture of the world by cutting across intellectual specialization.

Russian Formalism prefigured structuralism's systematic approach to the study of narratives. In *The Morphology of the Folktale,* for example, Vladimir Propp broke down folktales into a series of narrative functions (or conventions), which appeared each time around but in subtly different forms across a range of tales (the concept later known as "transformation," and in that guise a key element in Claude Lévi-Strauss's methodology). Roman Jakobson, another theorist from the Formalist milieu, emphasized the role of linguistics in literary analysis and helped to influence the direction of Lévi-Strauss's thinking when they were colleagues together in New York during World War II.

Of the many practitioners working in what can be called the "high structuralist" tradition (the 1950s and 1960s, when the theory was at the height of its popularity, particularly in France), arguably the two most important are Lévi-Strauss and Roland Barthes—although the latter eventually moved away from structuralism to a certain extent, and is even considered poststructuralist in his later career by many commentators. The emphasis in the work of each thinker is on the notion of unity. All narratives are considered to contain common features, or codes, and to share a common sense of structure. In Lévi-Strauss's case, this led him to conclude that groups of myths were all variants of a central myth ("variations on a theme," to use his musical analogy), and that it was the task of the analyst to chart the variety of ways (the transformations) in which the same set of narrative conventions were deployed over a range of narratives. These transformations signaled that, although the surface details might be different, the underlying structure remained in force. If a myth demanded the intervention of the gods as one of its structural elements (or "functions"), then that intervention might be accomplished by various means: the gods might take human form, or animal form, even insect form, or work through natural phenomena such as the weather (storms, for example, having a long tradition of being read as evidence of the gods' wrath being expressed against humankind). Barthes similarly insisted, in his high structuralist phase, on the unity of narratives, treating them as linked by their deep structural elements, and arguing against the possibility of there being any chance elements involved: everything had to be accounted for in terms of the overall pattern. In each and every case, there was a deep

structural grammar to be identified, and it was the analyst's role to reveal this. Barthes applied this principle over a wide-ranging series of analyses of cultural phenomena (all of which he treated in the manner of a narrative), such as advertising, the fashion industry, and cultural politics, in each instance being concerned to notate the underlying grammar (that is, sense of order) involved.

Structuralism even reached into Marxism, with the "structural Marxism" of Louis Althusser and his followers having a considerable vogue from the 1950s to the 1970s. Althusser posited the existence of large-scale institutional structures within an ideology that worked to control the thought and behavior of individual human beings (thus functioning like the deep structure of ideology). These structures were Ideological State Apparatuses (ISAs for short) and the Repressive State Apparatus (RSA). The former category included such phenomena as the legal and educational systems and the media, the latter the government, police, and army. Collectively, these entities worked to prevent questioning of the dominant ideology of a society, as well as to hide the contradictions that were encoded within that ideology (it being part of Althusser's definition of ideology that it contained contradictions that it was in the interest of the ruling class to conceal). Althusser's theories were adapted to the field of literary theory by his disciple Pierre Macherey, in the highly influential study *A Theory of Literary Production,* which advocated "reading against the grain" of texts in order to uncover the ideological contradictions hidden within narratives. The point of this technique was to reveal the ways in which ISAs and the RSA were controlling the thought processes of a society, even down to the level of artistic activity. Literary texts, to Macherey, were first and foremost productions of ideology, and, by an act of critical "interrogation," they could be made to yield up the secrets of that ideology.

Barthes's *S/Z* represents a desire to escape from what many were beginning to regard by the 1970s as the rigidity of structuralist methodology, with its demand that all cultural phenomena conform to the workings of the linguistic model and display an underlying sense of order. *S/Z* approached texts as inexhaustible sources of meaning and interpretation (a text being a "galaxy of signifiers"), and demonstrated, by a reading of Honoré de Balzac's novella *Sarrasine,* how the narrative was a complex sequence of overlapping codes (five in number in this case). Barthes's interest had now switched to narratives that invited multiple interpretations ("writerly," as he called them), such as the open-ended texts of the modernist tradition, which, he maintained, encouraged active participation on the part of the reader. These "writerly" texts were to be compared to "readerly" texts, which required a passive response only from the reader. In later Barthes, the reader becomes an increasingly important figure in the literary process, with Barthes announcing the "death of the author" as an authority figure controlling the reception of a text's meaning, and upgrading the reader's role accordingly.

Similar moves to Barthes can be seen in the work of the semiotic theorists Umberto Eco and Julia Kristeva, who provide some of the most important developments in later structuralism. Kristeva put together a hybrid of semiotic, Marxist, and Freudian theory that she called "semanalysis," and that was designed to break away from the linguistic model inherited from Saussure. By the time Kristeva entered onto the French intellectual scene, structuralism was under attack from a new wave of poststructuralist thinkers such as Jacques Derrida, and semanalysis was an attempt to reconstitute semiotics on a more scientific basis than hitherto (mathematics and logic were where Kristeva drew her inspiration from at this stage). An important contribution of Kristeva's to semiotic discourse was the notion of intertextuality. For Kristeva, every text was intertextual, that is, a signifying system made up of a "mosaic of quotations" drawn from other signifying systems. Texts were, therefore, plural, and incapable of being reduced to a single meaning or interpretation. Eco's answer to the apparent restrictiveness of the interpretive model of high structuralism was the notion of the "labyrinth," which also allowed for multiple interpretations of a given text. The labyrinth was to be considered as a form of net, such that any one point on its surface could be joined to any other point. In Eco's words, the net was "an unlimited territory." This meant that there was an infinite number of routes through the territory in question, with a different collection of connected points being possible on each and every occasion. Eco gives as an example the fact that one is not compelled to pass through Saint Louis on a trip from New York to Dallas, and that one could never exhaust the possible routes between the two points. There is no prescribed interpretation of a text using semiotic theory, therefore, although there is an overall framework within which the analysis has to take place. Like Kristeva, Eco takes issue with the primacy accorded the Saussurean linguistic model in semiotic analysis, complaining that it is arguable that all sign systems are comparable in nature, as the high structuralists, taking their lead from Saussure, had assumed.

The notion of a deep structure, or underlying program, determining how systems operate, and ultimately how human beings behave, has come in for considerable criticism. Critics of humanist bent have objected that it leaves little scope for the exercise of individual free will and reduces individuals to the status of mere puppets for the working out of amorphous forces. Ideas such as the "death of man" (announced by Michel Foucault in *The Order of Things*), and the "dissolution" of man (Lévi-Strauss, *The Savage Mind*) are also at odds with the humanist ideals of modern Western culture, which emphasize the improvability of humankind and the importance of the individual in the cultural scheme of things. Structuralism's emphasis on the system at the expense of the individual (and that individual's assumed freedom of action) has led to it being described on occasion as antihumanist in orientation.

Even more trenchant criticisms of the structuralist project have come from within the poststructuralist movement, with Derrida in particular being very harsh on what for him is structuralism's teleological bias and interpretive rigidity. For Derrida, it is a case of structuralists knowing beforehand what they will find in their analysis, because it is in the nature of their theory to impose a sense of structure on any work or discourse. Derrida considers this method to be authoritarian in that it closes off the creation of new meanings and new interpretations of texts. It is also argued to be essentialist because it assumes that the deep structure is the essence of each text, and can only envisage texts as expressions of that deep structure.

Another criticism of the structuralist enterprise has been that it has turned Saussure into something like an idealist philosopher, when in real terms he was a linguist pure and simple. This is the criticism voiced by Leonard Jackson (1991), who has also remarked scathingly of the system-building side of structuralism that it amounts to little more than "cultural meccano." Certainly, there is a sense in which structuralist analysis can become highly predictable (identify the grammar, specify how it works in the particular instance in question, and your analytic inquiry is all but complete), and it is also open to the charge that it does not actually say a great deal about the meaning, or value, of texts, or of cultural phenomena in general. What it *does* say a great deal about is function, but ultimately, it could be argued, this provides a somewhat impoverished view of texts, no less than of cultural phenomena. To be told how the various parts of a text relate to each other reveals very little about the nature of its emotional impact on its audience, or why some texts have a greater resonance over time than others.

Despite such criticisms, structuralism has made enormous contributions to twentieth-century thought. It remains a superb basis for comparative analysis (between cultures or literary genres, for example), and it has had many notable successes in this regard, with the work of Barthes in particular still finding an audience and informing current critical practice and debate. Few methods of cultural or aesthetic inquiry have not adopted something from structuralism, and many of its techniques have now become absorbed to the point where they are simply taken for granted by critics and teachers alike.

[*See also* Barthes; Formalism; Kristeva; Poststructuralism; Prague School; Russian Aesthetics, *article on* Russian Formalism; *and* Semiotics.]

BIBLIOGRAPHY

Althusser, Louis. *Lenin and Philosophy and Other Essays.* Translated by Ben Brewster. New York, 1971.

Barthes, Roland. *S/Z*. Translated by Richard Miller. New York, 1974.

Barthes, Roland. *Image-Music-Text*. Translated and edited by Stephen Heath. New York, 1977.

Culler, Jonathan. *Structuralist Poetics: Structuralism, Linguistics, and the Study of Literature*. Ithaca, N.Y., 1975.

Culler, Jonathan. *Saussure*. London, 1976.

Derrida, Jacques. *Writing and Difference*. Translated by Alan Bass. Chicago, 1978.

Eco, Umberto. *Semiotics and the Philosophy of Language*. Bloomington, Ind., 1984.

Foucault, Michel. *The Order of Things: An Archaeology of the Human Sciences*. New York, 1970.

Jackson, Leonard. *The Poverty of Structuralism: Literature and Structuralist Theory*. London and New York, 1991.

Kristeva, Julia. *The Kristeva Reader*. Edited by Toril Moi. New York, 1986.

Lévi-Strauss, Claude. *The Savage Mind*. Chicago, 1966.

Lévi-Strauss, Claude. *Mythologies I: The Raw and the Cooked*. Translated by John Weightman and Doreen Weightman. New York, 1970.

Macherey, Pierre. *A Theory of Literary Production*. Translated by Geoffrey Wall. London and Boston, 1978.

Propp, Vladimir. *The Morphology of the Folktale*. Translated by Laurence Scott. Austin, Tex., 1958.

Saussure, Ferdinand de. *Course in General Linguistics*. Edited by Charles Bally, Albert Sechehaye, and Albert Reidlinger. Translated by Wade Baskin. New York, 1959.

STUART SIM

STYLE. The word style has produced more than its share of definitions and descriptions; the *Oxford English Dictionary* finds twenty-eight variants for the term, with even the common elements among them inviting as many questions as they resolve. Because of the central place of artistic style in this broader history, the analysis of its structure has been equally complex. Closely tied to the concept of art as such, discussions of artistic style have, furthermore, constantly faced the question of whether and how art and style are to be distinguished. The common view of style as a "way" or manner implies the existence of an act that the manner qualifies; the difficulty of determining where these two elements of art diverge is at once a clue to their relationship and an important factor in the analysis of style.

The etymology of *style* reverts to the Latin, appearing there as a metonymy in which the *stilus,* used for inscribing wax tablets, represented the manner or quality of writing in contrast to its content. The claim has been made as well of an earlier source in the Greek *stylos* ("column") based on the several orders of entablature, but the evidence for this reference is less clear. In any event, the Greek commentators (e.g., Theophrastus, *On Style*) also associated style almost exclusively with rhetoric, relating it to the latter's persuasive function and using its categories to distinguish among various rhetorical means and effects in contrast to the substantive assertions communicated.

This instrumental origin influenced subsequent discussions of style, which, continuing to the present, have emphasized the "how" of stylistic expression as distinguished from its presumably non- or extrastylistic "what"—for example, the threefold distinction in Latin rhetoric among the grand, the mixed or middle, and the plain styles, a distinction based on the "levels" of language used, as these took account of the audience addressed and the specific purpose intended, with the combined effect of these then judged to be the "decorum" of the speech made. Quintilian summarized the art of rhetoric as "speaking well," and again in this phrase, it is the adverbial "how" that makes style an issue.

These early accounts, however, also recognized the importance of the relation between the rhetorical means and the subject articulated by it—beginning with the contingent character of that relation (as in Aristotle's criticism of those who speak "casually about weighty matters or solemnly about trivial ones"), but then moving on to suggest a stronger, intrinsic connection, the "form" of a work then reciprocally affecting and affected by its "content." The latter conceptualization of style has come increasingly to the fore since the shift of stylistic analysis to a focus on the arts that gains strength in the Renaissance; it has been the source at once of the most important advances and of the most troublesome issues in the analysis of style.

Almost without exception, modern accounts of style have ascribed to it a characteristic regularity or reiteration—in Meyer Schapiro's (1961) phrase, a "constant form"—which must also, however, be expressive (or, in related terms that are sometimes used, exemplary or symbolic). *Natural* regularities—the shape of an oak leaf or the pattern of an EKG—are not ordinarily held to be pertinent to style, although Nelson Goodman (1975) cites a "sunrise in Mandalay style" as one of what would then be many exceptions. On most accounts, even "human-made" regularities are not features or instances of style unless they are also integral to the works in which they appear: the sequential page numbers of a novel are not relevant to its style, although their total number may well be (i.e., in contrast to the characteristic length of the short story). For the purpose of making attributions, "connoisseurship" in the visual arts has at times relied on physical elements so limited as to be nonexpressive—ranging from characteristics of the parts of figures represented (ears, eyes) to the texture of brush strokes; but such elements seem in themselves no more relevant to style than the artist's fingerprints would be as identified on a canvas.

Viewed historically, both the categories of style and individual stylistic features appear not as "natural kinds" but as conventions varying among cultures, developmentally *within* cultures, and in and sometimes across specific arts. This contingent status argues against the possibility of determining universal categories of style or even of specifying stylistic properties in contrast to those that count aesthetically but nonstylistically in the individual artwork. There seems no part of a work (even its "grammar," insofar as violations of syntactic norms may reflect stylistic intention) that cannot in principle function as an element of style—an openness so broad that commentators such as Monroe Beardsley have regarded it as diminishing the usefulness of style in critical or aesthetic discourse. But the continued referral to categories of style in interpretation and evaluation suggests their relevance notwithstanding this disadvantage; the histories of art criticism and critical theory would be unrecognizable without reference to stylistic elements such as patterns of figurative discourse, distinctions among genres, or the classification of artworks by school or group.

A leading example of the conceptual tension affecting the analysis of style has been the issue of synonymy—the claim that two expressions can be identical in meaning yet differ in form. Theorists such as E. D. Hirsch (1975) have held synonymy to be a necessary condition of style; others, such as Goodman, have denied the possibility of synonymy (in style or elsewhere) and advanced a conception of style without it. The pertinence to style of synonymy (if it *were* possible) is unmistakable, because it would provide a systematic basis for the distinction between the way something is formulated and its "what" or substance. Even if synonymy is ruled out strictly speaking, the fact that certain locutions come closer than others to realizing that condition may be all that is necessary for grounding stylistic categories in the form-content distinction. In any event, the claim that the content and the expressive form of a work's style are intrinsically connected, with their relationship then varying contextually, does not mean that differences asserted between the two must be arbitrary; the shifting line would reflect the functional status of style—resembling in this respect the work's nonstylistic features (some aesthetic, some not) from which its own are distinguished.

The stakes in applying categories of style in interpretation and evaluation become progressively higher as those applications have shifted from their early focus on rhetorical distinctions to the more diverse and less immediately utilitarian arts. The modern typology of the arts coincided with the increasing recognition accorded individual artists in the Renaissance. The new emphasis on "self" in and outside art, together with the growing professionalization of the arts and artists, led the analysis of style to consider more closely the individual character (and identity) of its creator—that is, the artist's "signature." This use of the categories of style as a means of reaching back to the artist continues to have a place (on some accounts, a central one) among the definitions of style, but it seems even here subordinate systematically to the conception of style as generally expressive; that is, as going beyond the person or history of the individual artist. The emphasis on style as signature, furthermore, is problematic in its own terms, insofar as some identifying markers (such as a painter's *literal* signature) have nothing to do with style, and some typical features of style are only marginal indicators of the individual artist's or even group identity (as in the use of broadly accepted artistic conventions such as those governing perspective or tonality).

It has been claimed of style (e.g., by Richard Wollheim [1993]) that its attribution to groups or schools—the "Post-Impressionist" painters, the "metaphysical" poets—is no more than an ad hoc shorthand that, for external reasons, brings together independent instances of individual style. This view of group style as essentially derivative has been contested, however; not only is the emphasis on style as expressing the artist's individual "physiognomy" (in Arthur Schopenhauer's term) relatively recent in art's own history, but even a recognizably personal style does not preclude indebtedness to other styles (of individuals *or* groups). One need not, moreover, posit a collective mind to acknowledge the social origins of much, or aspects of all, individual expression. Features of a group style are sometimes more notable than those of individual styles, and there is sufficient historical evidence of reciprocity between the two to speak noninvidiously of style in both connections. The question of priority between individual and group style seems as much open to dispute—and similarly, more than only a historical or an empirical question—as the question of priority, in theories of human nature, between a socially constituted self and a private, autonomous one. It has often been noted that the most radical stylistic innovations are typically *not* found in artists who are the most celebrated individually.

To attribute to style an expressive or representational role underscores the question of what it is that style expresses or represents. This question impinges on the general issue of artistic representation, and although the analysis of style is not alone accountable for resolving that issue, one element of style in particular—the factor of choice—bears directly on it. No more for style than for art in general can accident or nature by themselves explain its development or varieties; deliberation or choice are thus in some sense implicated (leaving Goodman's reference to "natural style" as metaphoric at best). The intentional character of style is pertinent to the practical and historical analysis of art as well as to its ontology; Leonard Meyer (1989), for example, traces specific changes and genre distinctions in the history of musical style to the contrast between options rejected by various composers and those that they selected and then elaborated. Ascribing a role to choice in style supports the view of artistic representation and meaning that has been charged with the "intentional fallacy"—although even agreement on a role for intentions in the formation of style leaves open the question of what the specific relation is between intentions and artistic meaning.

It is evident in any case that stylistic "choice" is not only a matter of deciding among determinate options, like choosing among different dishes on a restaurant menu. Some stylistic choices may be of this sort, but others involve the creation of the options among which choice is then made. This does not imply that style is even here free of historical constraint (thus, Heinrich Wölfflin's statement that, stylistically, "Not everything is possible at any [particular] time" [1951]); it leaves room for originality in individual or group style while insisting that it occurs always within a historical context. (The objection against linking style to choice because the artist's "character" to which style is related will then also have been "chosen" seems to argue for rather than against the connection.)

The problem of synonymy also bears on the contingency of the categories of style insofar as attempts to determine common or universal categories have failed; there is, and arguably can be, no fixed list of stylistic predicates or categories either within the individual arts or across them. Franz Kafka's use of the preposition *aber* ("but") two or three times more frequently than the norm among German writers may or may not be stylistically significant; a connection would have to be shown between it and the characteristic expression of his works (the relevance to style of the general property of word-use frequency would also have to be tested by such particular instances). Similarly, the curve of a painted or sculpted or dancer's arm may or may not be stylistically significant—as would be the case for the gracefulness (or grace*lessness*) of the same curve. Stylistic categories or their instantiations, like the connection between style and expression on which they depend, can thus be validated (or rejected) only contextually, that is, by the other aesthetic categories or properties with which they stand in contrast in the artwork. This circularity in identifying what is stylistically significant has been a central factor historically in the instability of stylistic categories—as these have evolved in relation to changes and decisions within or among the arts as well as in relation to history external to art. It is not only that individual styles develop in these ways, but that accounts and appreciation of the "same" style or the "same" stage of a style also change; the history of the reception of painting in the twentieth century provides numerous examples of such alteration—as does the varied reception over time of many of the now-canonical figures in all the arts. Whatever style is style *of*, furthermore, discloses a similarly labile character, evoking Roland Barthes's metaphoric description of style as an onion: peeling away its layers in the hope of reaching a "core," the viewer of style has to settle in the end for the layers themselves. For these same reasons, the identification of stylistic features in art requires imagination in the critic comparable if not identical to the artist's in constituting them.

The categories of style, moreover, are typically conceived after the fact: Pyotr Ilich Tchaikovsky did not set out to be a "Romantic" composer or Pierre Corneille a "neoclassical" dramatist. This retrospective feature of style strengthens the resemblance between style and art; neither is prescriptive or rule-governed. Certainly, the development of particular styles does not seem to be dictated by formula or entailed by the stylistic past—although, as for other questions related to style, the opposing view on this question of origins has had its advocates. Thus, stylistic "explanation" has at times claimed to enumerate the sufficient conditions for particular styles, basing this on an internal logic and full-scale determinism. The best-known instance of the latter is Georg Wilhelm Friedrich Hegel's view of the history of art as moving necessarily from the "symbolic" to the "classical" to the "romantic" stages. Beyond this progression, Hegel conceived the phenomenon of art itself as a stylistic "moment"—one that he claims has ended and been superseded in the life of "Spirit" first by religion and (that) then by philosophy.

Numerous more limited efforts than Hegel's have been made to identify a developmental logic in the history of particular styles (as in Early, High, and Late Renaissance art). Such attempts have often identified useful categories (as in Wölfflin's five-paired distinction between Renaissance and Baroque art), although these categories do not justify the claim sometimes made for them as reflecting a *necessary* progression. Common or analogous stylistic patterns may appear in different media (as in the related features of Baroque music and Baroque architecture), and such likenesses may extend beyond the arts as well. But the assertion of a *Weltgeist* that, on the Hegelian concept, imparts a common style to all contemporary modes of expression seems more than the evidence supports, if it is verifiable at all.

Style is sometimes invoked as itself a positive attribute, as when a person "has style" or acts "with style" (or *is* "stylish")—although, on the other hand, something designedly "in" a style may by that fact be presented as less than the real thing (as a "Georgian-style" building would not be *quite* Georgian). Furthermore, individual categories may have positive connotations; it would be as unlikely to find a "unified" theme cited in evidence of a work's failure as it would be for "incoherence" to be a positive feature. Often, however, stylistic terms are neutral in evaluative connotation, as they mark differences between one work and others of a kind, or between the one kind and others, or call attention to particular aspects of the work that subsequently affect its evaluation. Whether stylistic features are executed well or badly in a given work is a separate question from that of their presence or identity; even an unusually distinctive style provides no more assurance of aesthetic quality—kitsch is an example of this—than would less distinctive ones, although to find that a work is *without* style would ordinarily be a negative and probably decisive judgment.

Many standard stylistic categories now applied descriptively and neutrally originally had evaluative connotations (as *Baroque* denoted the bizarre or absurd and *Mannerist* an affected or exaggerated quality). The claim that all stylistic categories were initially evaluative, as E. H. Gombrich (1968) asserts for those of art history, is debatable; it seems clear, in any event, that not all terms evaluative of art are style terms, beginning with "beauty" itself. Insofar as an expressive function is intrinsic to style, the categories of style *would* be closely associated with the intensity of an audience's reaction to corresponding features of the artwork itself.

Categories employed in descriptive stylistics may affect critical evaluation internal to the category (as in distinguishing between a good and a bad instance of Gothic) or by external comparison (the Gothic as judged superior or inferior to the Romanesque). An individual work may be judged a failure or a success in its style, but such judgment implies an independent stylistic baseline. Even if the distinction is at some points indeterminate, the difference between a work of "bad" style and one with no style seems worth preserving (even for an evaluative relativism that refuses to judge among styles, the absence of all style would be noteworthy). To the extent that stylistic features are distinguished from other aesthetic features, it follows that a "bad" style may be outweighed by other features, and that a "good" style (necessarily more than only *being* a style) would not be sufficient for similarly judging the whole. Not all aesthetically relevant or even all "good-making" features of a work are features of style; the "thought" ingredient in literature, for example—as noted in Aristotle's *Poetics* among the six elements of tragedy—extends beyond style (as in respect to judgment of its truth or importance) even though it also may also appear as an aspect of individual or group style.

Style can be imitated or forged, with the latter's most successful examples no doubt hanging undetected in museums or wrongly attributed in library catalogs. The claim that forgeries too are stylistically identifiable in relation to their creator has been made for many that have been discovered, but this is no more compelling a basis for assuming that all forgeries are in principle detectable than for inferring that all forgeries *will* be detected. This constraint suggests that a forger's style might succeed in *being* that of the original artist, although an objection to that possibility registers in Cardinal John Newman's contention that somebody could "as well say that one man's shadow is another's as that the style of a really gifted mind can belong to any but himself." Such emphasis on the uniqueness of individual style— a still-recurrent theme inherited from Romanticism— narrows what style does in art to the function of representing the artist's persona or emotional state; Jonathan Swift's brief tribute to style that places expression in a broader, more impersonal framework—"Proper words in proper places"—offers an instructive contrast.

In recent aesthetic theory and art criticism, the role of style and its categories has been attacked from various directions; at an extreme, style, whether as phenomenon or concept, is denied all warrant. Some objections to this effect come from antiformalist theories that, committed to psychological, cultural, or material bases of interpretation, dispute the usefulness or even the possibility of translating

those grounds into stylistic categories. A different source of opposition appears in the objections of postmodernist or poststructuralist theory to the reification it finds in interpretations of style where the artist appears as its source or embodiment, or to what it claims is the imposition of an "essentialist" unity of style on disparate aesthetic features. The latter assumptions are attacked as tendentious: if style is an epiphenomenon, aesthetic analysis should see through it; and if the self is not unified, styles that are described as unified expressions of the artist's self would have had that unity imposed by the "stylist" (for reasons that may have little to do with art). Such objections have not, however, prevented the use of *postmodernist* itself as a stylistic category, applied first to architecture but then to other arts as well, as traditional norms of style in them are subverted—replaced, however, by what turn out to be almost "constant forms" like the pastiche or (in Fredric Jameson's [1994] categorization) "dirty realism."

Coincident with attacks on style from this direction has been an extension of the concept to forms of expression not previously associated with it, as in "styles" of historical, philosophical, or scientific discourse, and in the still more inclusive "lifestyles." The proposed extension to these areas conflicts with the more traditional ideal of truth or cognitive content as unaffected by its means (or styles) of presentation. This conflict calls attention to an often unnoticed condition of style as a pluralistic and, to that extent, skeptical concept that presupposes alternate possibilities—no one style, in other words, without (at least) two. The denial of this condition implies a view of the content of art or of other discourses as supralinguistic and, still more clearly, suprastylistic—a recurrent theme of rationalism that is epitomized in Baruch Spinoza's statement that "God has no particular style in speaking." Situated in this way between denials of the existence of style, on the one hand, and proposals to find it everywhere, on the other, the present status of style promises a future hardly less unsettled than its past.

[*See also* Baroque Aesthetics; Benjamin, *article on* Benjamin's Writing Style; Japanese Aesthetics, *article on* Kire and Iki; Literature, *article on* Literary Aesthetics; Narrative; Nietzsche, *article on* Nietzsche's Literary Style; Schapiro; *and* Wölfflin.]

BIBLIOGRAPHY

Ackerman, James. "A Theory of Style." *Journal of Aesthetics and Art Criticism* 20 (1962): 227–237.

Chatman, Seymour, ed. *Literary Style: A Symposium.* New York and Oxford, 1971.

Clifford, James, and George E. Marcus, eds. *Writing Culture: The Poetics and Politics of Ethnography.* Berkeley, 1986.

Danto, Arthur C. *The Transfiguration of the Commonplace.* Cambridge, Mass., 1981.

Foucault, Michel. "What Is an Author?" In *Language, Counter-Memory, Practice: Selected Essays and Interviews,* translated by Donald F. Bouchard and Sherry Simon, pp. 113–138. Ithaca, N.Y., 1977.

Gombrich, E. H. "Style." In *International Encyclopedia of the Social Sciences,* vol. 15, edited by David L. Sills, pp. 353–361. New York, 1968.

Gombrich, E. H. *Norm and Form* (1966). 4th ed. London, 1985.

Goodman, Nelson. *Problems and Projects.* Indianapolis, 1972.

Goodman, Nelson. "The Status of Style." *Critical Inquiry* 1.4 (June 1975): 799–811.

Gross, Alan G. *The Rhetoric of Science.* Cambridge, Mass., 1990.

Hegel, Georg Wilhelm Friedrich. *Aesthetics: Lectures on Fine Art.* 2 vols. Translated by T. M. Knox. Oxford, 1975.

Hirsch, E. D. "Stylistics and Synonymy." *Critical Inquiry* 1.3 (March 1975): 559–579.

Hough, Graham. *Style and Stylistics.* London, 1969.

Jameson, Fredric. *The Seeds of Time.* New York, 1994.

Kennedy, George. *The Art of Rhetoric in the Roman World.* Princeton, N.J., 1972.

Kristeller, Paul Oskar. "The Modern System of the Arts." *Journal of the History of Ideas* 12.4 (October 1951): 496–527; 13.1 (January 1952): 17–46.

Lang, Berel, ed. *The Concept of Style.* Rev. exp. ed. Ithaca, N.Y., 1987.

Lang, Berel. *The Anatomy of Philosophical Style: Literary Philosophy and the Philosophy of Literature.* Oxford and Cambridge, Mass., 1990.

Meyer, Leonard B. *Style and Music: Theory, History, and Ideology.* Philadelphia, 1989.

Schapiro, Meyer. "Style." In *Aesthetics Today,* edited by Morris Philipson, pp. 91–113. Cleveland, Ohio, 1961.

van Eck, Caroline, James McAllister, and Renee van de Vall, eds. *The Question of Style in Philosophy and the Arts.* Cambridge and New York, 1995.

White, Hayden. *Metahistory: The Historical Imagination in Nineteenth-Century Europe.* Baltimore, 1973.

Wölfflin, Heinrich. *Principles of Art History: The Problem of the Development of Style in Later Art.* Translated by M. D. Hottinger (1932). New York, 1951.

Wollheim, Richard. *The Mind and Its Depths.* Cambridge, Mass., 1993.

BEREL LANG

SUBLIME. [*To analyze the role of the concept of the sublime in aesthetics, this entry comprises three essays:*

> The Sublime from Longinus to Montesquieu
> The Sublime from Burke to the Present
> Feminine Sublime

The first essay traces the early history of the concept of the sublime before and up to the birth of aesthetics. The second essay continues this history from that period up through contemporary theories of the sublime. The final essay introduces the notion of the feminine sublime, which serves as a critical challenge to the traditional understanding of the sublime. For related discussion, see Beauty; *and* Nature.]

The Sublime from Longinus to Montesquieu

Belonging to an old Greek and Latin tradition, the concept of the sublime experienced two main "renaissances": the first began not in the Romantic age, but at the height of classicism; the second appeared in the late twentieth century along with the rise of postmodernism. In order to understand the grounds for such resurgences, one has to consider the first writings on the sublime, and the various points of view they represented.

Adjective or Noun? First of all, the absence of homogeneity between a long literary tradition and a philosophical one must be stressed. In the former, *sublime* is not infrequently an adjective, synonymous with *grave, elevated, strongly conceived,* or *impressive.* In the latter, on the contrary, *sublime* designates a category opposed to the beautiful, both aesthetic and trans-aesthetic, the theoretization of which in the mid-eighteenth century accompanies the birth of the aesthetic problematically: does it confirm the closure of aesthetics, or, to the contrary, demonstrate the impossibility of such closure?

In fact, a profound duality of origin is hidden under the current uniformity in the vocabulary of the sublime: whereas the same term, pronounced differently, is used in English, French, Italian, and Spanish, as a simple or substantivized adjective, reflection on the sublime has developed historically from Greek and Latin terms of dissimilar grammatical and etymological nature. The Greek *hypsous* is a noun, belonging to a rich and well-constructed family of terms all derived from the adverb *hypsi. Hypsous* commonly means "height," conceived as a spatial dimension and opposed to width and length, and takes on the figurative meaning of a climax. On the contrary, the Latin *sublimis* is an adjective, and indeed an unusual one, with a problematic meaning. It is derived from *sub,* which marks the displacement toward the high, and from *limis* or *limus* (oblique, askew), which characterize a certain direction of gaze, such as that of cross-eyed Athena, or a certain type of ascension nonorthogonal to the ground. Quintilian sanctions this use in the expression "sublime type of speech" *(genus sublime dicendi).* In fact, it is impossible to substantivize adjectives in Latin—a language lacking articles. As for the term *sublimity (sublimitas),* it is certainly not correctly rendered as *hypsous,* because it does not designate the full range of things that are sublime, but the simple fact of being sublime.

In theorizing about the sublime, this leads to considerable divergences of evaluation. On the one hand, it is the idea of the sublime that commands attention and one endeavors to elucidate its genesis and status. On the other hand, one is concerned more with styles or levels of discourse, in order to try to determine one or several sublime traits. Thus, two conceptions of invention come face-to-face: one defining its object according to the theory of stylistic genres and the other locating the force of the conception in its nascent state, in its creative virtue.

But between an adjective, conceived as a simple descriptive and evaluative tool, and a substantive, which refers to an essence, a gap appears that seems essential. Indeed, the real problem is to understand the sublime as simultaneously being (1) in its more or less contingent vehicles; (2) in its effects, which cannot be reduced to the strict combination of admiration and pleasure; and (3) in its principles, which appear bound to the constitution of the subject as self-transcending. On this single condition it would be possible to avoid not only the uncontrolled usage of the concept, which seems bound up with the generalization of adjectival employment, but also its dogmatic use, based on a specific theory. Having avoided the radical dispersal of the sublime in the sensible world, the difficulty lies in not hypostatizing the idea of the sublime. One must preserve absolutely the operational and critical sense of the concept historically attributed to it. The sublime remains a question that is always subdividing, for one can discriminate certain modes of "entry" or angles from which an artwork, a deed, or even a life might be considered sublime.

Accordingly, it is important to investigate by which type of variation—spontaneous, or more or less voluntary—one privileges certain values in a given field or space. Only a certain selection allows the sublime to emerge in its entirety. Now, is not the desire to encourage one type of redistribution and develop the appreciation of the sublime the basis for a truly educating education?

Longinus and the Founding of the Sublime. Such is the case in the sole treatise on the sublime that antiquity has bequeathed to us, under the name of *Peri Hypsous* (On the Sublime) and whose orientation is presented from the very start as practical. *On the Sublime* does not concern itself with defining the sublime theoretically for a public assumed to be unaware of it, but rather with finding "by what means" we might be able to lead "our natural gifts to a certain degree of elevation." This work, baptized the "golden book" by Isaac Casaubon (1605), nearly disappeared in antiquity and was revived in the Renaissance, broken off in seven places and attributed to a fictional author. It is reasonable to assume at present that this anonymous or pseudoauthor, who we still call Longinus, lived during the reigns of Claudius and Nero, perhaps in Alexandria. His culture was principally Hellenistic, he quotes Genesis once, and he presents his treatise as a missive to a Roman friend. Accordingly, *On the Sublime* is situated at the crossroads of three great traditions and it is quite significant that the category of the sublime was elaborated in a time of unprecedented change: one in which Christian monotheism asserted its authority, while the power of Rome grew greater out of the wreckage of the Republic. In a period of crisis affecting all values, does not the sublime correspond to a will to recapture what dazzles and deserves to dazzle?

Longinus essentially studies the sublime immanent in discourse. He excludes the idea of a sublime transcending all manifestation, but not that of a natural sublime. True to the anthropocentric tendency in Greek philosophy, he concentrates on humankind more than on the external world. Nevertheless, under his aegis, although only in an incidental clause of chapter 35, the sublime acquires a body, a hydrography, and a cosmography: on the one hand, the vast and indefinite, on the other, the unpredictable and terrible. No

mere rivers inspire astonishment, but great ones and, even more, the ocean; it is not the burst of a slight flame that sears, but the lights tearing through the celestial darkness and rivers of fire pouring down from Mount Etna.

Prevalent in the rhetorical and poetic spheres, the sublime is defined as "a certain distinction and excellence in discourse." It aims neither at persuading nor pleasing; it is neither useful nor agreeable. Rather, it causes rapture or ecstasy by storm. The violence is indeed accepted, but it is violence all the same—attesting to the properly "irresistible" character of the sublime. The dazzled witness then tends to identify with the source, acting as if the constraint emanated not from without, but from within himself, "for, as if instinctively, our soul is uplifted by the true sublime; it takes a proud flight, and is filled with joy and vaunting, as though it had itself produced what it has heard" (Longinus, 1899).

Analyzing the sources of the sublime, Longinus insists on the reversibility of art and nature. Art does nothing but reveal nature, whereas nature itself cannot act without art. As for nature, the power of conception and the vehement and inspired character of passion constitute the sources of the sublime. As for art, on the contrary, we distinguish the due formation of figures, nobility of expression, and, lastly, the dignity and elevation of the composition. But the redundancy of the expression clearly shows the circle in which we are caught: the sublime arises out of what is already sublime. Its character is to require itself. If we vacillate then in the interpretation, opting at times for a hierarchization of the sources that puts greatness of mind at the forefront, at other times for equal dignity for each source, this really results from an inability to think the unity. The sublime is not one among many other possible qualities. It radiates from all sides at once, like what is achieved in the singular melding of genius with its instruments. One must say of sublime discourse, then, not that it possesses sublimity, but that it *is* the sublime in nascent state.

The Sublime and Genus Dicendi. One Latin translation played a large role in the history of the resurrection of Longinus's treatise even before the principal edition of the Greek text. Gustavo Costa has attributed it to Fulvio Orsini and has demonstrated its influence, from the outset of the cinquecento, on the intellectual environment of the Farnese and, particularly, on Michelangelo. Apart from this exception and the first Italian version of 1639, all later editions use the expression *sublime genus dicendi* in their titles. We must try therefore to analyze on what basis the junction of sublime style and the Longinian *hypsous* can have been brought about.

The theory of types of speech *(genera dicendi)* begins with Theophrastus in the fourth century BCE. The meager *(ischnos)* and mean *(mesos)* styles, corresponding to the Latin terms *gracilis* and *mediocris,* respectively, were opposed by the Greeks to the muscular or robust *(adros)* style. The *Rhetorica ad Herennium* (c.86–83 BCE), which is the oldest

Latin source, distinguishes between three genres: grave or imposing *(gravis),* intermediate *(mediocris),* and diminished *(extenuatus* or *attentuatus).* Cicero picks up on this triad in one of his last works, *The Orator* (46 BCE), and coins the adjective *grandiloquent,* to which he gives a laudatory sense lost today. The grand style is characterized by the abundance of gravity, but Cicero adds three new criteria: vehemence, variety, and impressiveness. Choice of style is made according to the criterion of appropriateness: "to prove is proper to necessity, to charm proper to agreement, to yield proper to victory." Nevertheless, the grave style overshadows the other criteria because, concentrating on the greatest power, it arouses the wonder of peoples and dominates them. Thus, Quintilian awards the palm cleanly to the sublime style, acknowledging that it leaves the audience defenseless. "Delivered to the disorder of his senses, beyond himself, the judge gives himself entirely over to the orator without concerning himself with the matter of the case." In fact, the sublime of Quintilian has in common with the Longinian *hypsous* the "fascinating splendor" that plunges the discussion of facts into shadow and that, far from soberly persuading the audience, ravishes it in ecstasy, even against its will; and so the handling of it should be reserved to honest men.

Moreover, we have at our disposal Demetrius's treatise *On Style,* dating back to the first century BCE or perhaps earlier. Demetrius contrasts the elevated style *(megaloprepēs)* to the vehement style *(deinos),* in order to set both over against simple style. Elevated style, exemplified by Thucydides, is characterized by a solemn gravity and already eludes ordinary language, whose clarity makes emotive power disappear. Vehement style, illustrated by Demosthenes, evokes combatants dealing blows at close quarters and goes so far as to seek darkness, in the belief that what is suggested by allusion has more value than what is flatly exposed.

Although Demetrius treats a question of style, and not the sublime properly speaking, he has the merit of introducing a remarkable tension: should we seek the sublime more in terms of the force of conception, or more in terms of that of passion? Morpurgo Tagliabue (1980) believes it possible to show that Edmund Burke's sublime of the terrible is closer to the *deinos* of Demetrius than the *hypsous* of Longinus. But, if Longinus makes the sublime first and foremost "the echo of a great spirit," and if he affirms that *pathos* is not absolutely necessary to the sublime, he nevertheless recognizes that "there is no tone so lofty as that of genuine passion, in its right place."

Nicolas Boileau and the Revision of Rhetoric. Boileau was the first to uproot the sublime explicitly from the categories of rhetoric and to use the substantivized adjective in the title of his translation of Longinus, *A Treatise on the Sublime; or, on the Marvelous in Discourse* (1674): "We must therefore know that by 'sublime' Longinus does not

understand what orators call sublime style. . . . A thing can be in the sublime style yet fail to be sublime, that is, fail to have anything extraordinary or astonishing." The Longinian revolution consists in suppressing the opposition between the simple and sublime styles at the heart of the theory of the *genera dicendi*—put another way, it was to rehabilitate the simple and make it consubstantial with the sublime.

Boileau no doubt ends up making a caricature of Longinus's thought by projecting onto it his own rationalist and normative conception of art in which clarity of expression follows from excellence of conception, which, in turn, follows from a single, universal precept: "to please at length and never to make weary." Such is Boileau's aim, where Longinus found, above all else, ecstasy.

That Boileau bestowed a dignity on the English sublime is nevertheless implicitly acknowledged by Samuel Johnson when he declares that "'the sublime' is a Gallicism, but now naturalized." But the translation of *hypsous* as "sublime," which in itself seems suitable in Romance languages, continues to pose problems in English. According to W. Rhys Roberts, who nevertheless adopts the term in 1899, "a misconception has been the result, a misconception which the existence of Burke's homonymous treatise *On the Sublime and the Beautiful* has done much to increase" (Longinus, 1899).

The Invention of New Landscapes: From the Rhetorical to the Natural Sublime. However powerful the impulse of Boileau to reconsider the sublime, the decisive fact derives less from deliberated theoretical change than from a radical change in sensibility. Under the influence of new *practica* with nature and of new scientific and technical discoveries, attention was no longer directed just toward the inhabited earth, but to the mountain, the littoral, the sea, and the desert. On the one hand, the custom of the grand tour, mountaineering, medicinal sea baths; on the other, the challenge to geocentrism and geostatism, as well as the discovery of the richness of nature viewed with the new optical apparatuses (the microscope and telescope)—all contributed to shape a new way of looking at the phenomenal world that the "natural sublime" perfectly symbolizes. If Samuel Monk (1960) could maintain that, in the eighteenth century, the history of the sublime generally coincides with interpretations of Longinus, that is doubtless primarily because the new sensibility could think itself prefigured in chapter 35 of his work, mentioned earlier as involving the sublime of great rivers, oceans, and volcanoes.

It is striking that all the traits that Charles de Marguetel de Saint-Denis de Saint-Évremond, for example, negatively emphasizes in his *Dissertation on the Word "Vast"* (1685) might easily be called on to characterize the sublime. Stigmatizing inordinate and excessive grandeur, kindred to the ugly and horrible, and sign of the impermeability to culture or of a destruction just exerted, Saint-Évremond defines in a premonitory way what will become the natural sublime:

> vast things do not suit things that make an agreeable impression upon us. . . . Vast forests frighten us. The view dissipates and disappears in looking upon vast fields. . . . Rivers that are too large, overwhelming things, and floods displease us by their unrest and our eyes are unable to endure their vast extent. . . . *Vasius quasi vastatus,* vast. It is nearly the same as decayed and ruined.

The first writer who, far from disapproving of it, expresses a fascination with physical grandeur is Thomas Burnet, to whom we owe a "novel" about the earth compatible with biblical teaching and illustrated with engravings designed to excite the imagination: the *Telluris Theoria Sacra,* which appeared in 1681, with an English translation by 1684. Burnet praises, in an entirely new way, the magnificence of the ocean and of mountain ranges: "The greatest objects of Nature are, methinks, the most pleasing to behold; and next to the great Concave of the Heavens, and those boundless Regions where the stars inhabit, there is nothing that I look upon with more pleasure than the wide Sea and the Mountains of the Earth." Quite impressed by Burnet's theory, John Dennis in 1693 describes the "delightful horror" in which he is plunged by the contemplation of the Alps: "we may well say [of nature] what some affirm of great Wits, that her careless, irregular and boldest Strokes are most admirable. For the Alps are works which she seems to have design'd, and executed too in Fury" (1693).

Anthony Ashley Cooper, earl of Shaftesbury, will powerfully echo these themes in *The Moralists* of 1709, more precisely in part 3, which praises the beauty of wild places and deserts: "The wildness pleases," declares Theocles, "we seem to live alone with Nature. We view her in her inmost recesses, and contemplate her with more delight in these original wilds than in the artificial labyrinths and feigned wilderness of the palace." [*See* Cooper.] But the text that exercises the most influence is undoubtedly Joseph Addison's famous series "On the Pleasures of Imagination," which appeared in *The Spectator* in 1712. Addison, who had been Burnet's student, focuses his analysis on the great, an aesthetic category that he sets over against both the uncommon and the beautiful: "By greatness, I do not only mean the bulk of any single object, but the largeness of a whole view, considered as one entire piece. . . . Our imagination loves to be filled with an object, or grasp at anything that is too big for its capacity" (1712). Thus, Addison glorifies Longinus as being one of the few critics able to take into consideration "something more essential, to the art, something that elevates and astonishes the fancy, and gives a greatness of mind to the reader" (ibid.).

Of an Overwhelming Principle Grasped in Astonishment. What was the status accorded to the constitutive experiences of the new landscapes? How can one explain that the vacillation caused by the awareness of new phenomena and by the progression of our faculties beyond their accustomed bounds can be converted into delight? A peculiar form of reality arises along with the sublime, which questions us while it dazzles us. But the odd thing is that we would be able to draw from this experience a form of pleasure.

It is with Giambattisa Vico that we encounter, in the first half of the eighteenth century, the most extraordinary attempt to grasp in *uncivilized* humankind the wondering that permits the constitution of a properly human world. The metaphysics of the first humans—neither rational nor abstract, but felt and imagined—will allow us to understand how imagination and thought were set in motion and how a similar stimulation can be renewed in our own time in the experience of the sublime, conceived as a conversion in the poetic order of an originary impact. Recall the cardinal experience of a shock that it is the property of the sublime to restore in its values of actualization: one hundred years after the Flood, when the earth was finally dry, the sky hurled bolts of lightning and terrifying claps of thunder. "Thereupon a few giants, who must have been the most robust . . . were frightened and astonished by the great effect whose cause they did not know, and raised their eyes and became aware of the sky" (Vico, 1968). From this followed a belief in a god, search for shelter in caverns, and, by degrees, divination, marriage, and agriculture. Therefore, one would have to show how in Vico's work man becomes everything, not by understanding the world, but by *not* understanding it *(homo, non intelligendo, fit omnia)*. Man feels himself confronted by irreducible alterity, whose marvelous halo, paradoxically, it attains in the most trying of circumstances. The progress of civilization provides extraordinary testimony of this awareness.

In another register—no longer involved with converting an emotion, but rather with an emotion already converted by the agency of art—recall the eulogy of continual surprise that one finds in Montesquieu's *Essay on Taste,* translated by Burke in 1759: surprise is born of the contrast between what we know and what we see; above all, it springs out of the consideration of an almost unbearable spectacle. "In the Passion in the gallery in Florence, Michelangelo has painted the Virgin upright, looking upon her crucified son without sadness, pity, regret, or weeping. He assumes her aware of this great mystery and therefore makes her bear the sight of this death with grandeur" (1759). Does the horror of death yield to the sublime of consent? The witness remains placed before the door of the mystery, where what appears immediately slips away and where the imminence of the inaccessible is felt. View and review the object as we might, "our suspension and, I dare say, our ignorance, still remains" (ibid.). The essential is no doubt of a different order than positive knowledge; the experience of the sublime is fundamental in that it brings about a relativization of knowledge. Thus Montesquieu assigns the disappearance of the sublime to "that new philosophy which only talks of general laws and which removes from the mind all particular thoughts of divinity" (ibid.)—in short, to the philosophy that Vico principally opposed as built on a misunderstanding of the power of the imagination and the nature of language in its poetic mode of constitution.

Thus, everything seems now in place for Burke to systematically oppose the sublime to the beautiful: the beautiful settles us in the world, the sublime dazzles and bewilders by transgressing form and confusing reference. Burkean astonishment will upset the subject in his intimacy, thanks to the revelation of a radical principle of dispossession, which Burke's originality is to apprehend independently of any religious or moral consideration. Moreover, looking for the sources of the sublime in the phenomenal world, Burke tries to define the qualities belonging not only to single objects, but to atmospheres, as we would say today. "When danger or pain press too nearly, they are incapable of giving any delight, and are simply terrible; but at certain distances, and with certain modifications, they may be, and they are delightful, as we every day experience." Thus, the problem will be to understand the "distance" and the "modifications" that allow the terrifying principle to be converted into the sublime principle, and the effect of fright into that of astonishment.

But how to distinguish the true mystery from the seeming mystery and the deepest awe from superficial dread? One can see how easily the sublime could arouse suspicion and be changed into its contrary. If we want to avoid the misunderstandings caused by Demetrius's and Burke's theory, we must state that the sublime is not only an immediate overwhelming power, but also a lasting incitement to critical reflection.

[*See also* Longinus.]

BIBLIOGRAPHY

Addison, Joseph. "On the Pleasures of Imagination." *The Spectator* (June–July, 1712).
Boileau-Despréaux, Nicolas. Preface to translation of Longinus, *Traité du sublime*. Paris, 1674.
Burnet, Thomas. *Telluris Theoria Sacra*. Londini, 1681.
Cooper, Anthony Ashley, Earl of Shaftesbury. *Characteristics of Men, Manners, Opinions, Times*. London, 1711.
Demetrius. *Demetrius on Style: The Greek Text of Demetrius, "De Elocutione," Edited after the Paris Manuscript*. Edited and translated by W. Rhys Roberts. Cambridge, 1902.
Dennis, John. *Miscellanies in Verse and Prose*. London, 1693.
Longinus. *Longinus on the Sublime: The Greek Text Edited after the Paris Manuscript*. Edited and translated by W. Rhys Roberts. Cambridge, 1899.
Monk, Samuel H. *The Sublime: A Study of Critical Theories in Eighteenth-Century England*. New York, 1935; reprint, Ann Arbor, 1960.
Montesquieu, Charles de Secondat, Baron de. *Essai sur le goût*. Paris, 1757.
Saint Girons, Baldine. *Fiat lux: Une philosophie du sublime*. Paris, 1993.
Vico, Giambattista. *The New Science of Giambattista Vico* (1744). Rev. ed. Translated by Thomas Goddard Bergin and Max Harold Fisch from the 3d ed. of 1774. Ithaca, N.Y., 1968.

BALDINE SAINT GIRONS
Translated from French by Fred L. Rush, Jr.

The Sublime from Burke to the Present

The modern history of the notion of the sublime begins with the discovery of the fragments of the classical text *Peri Hypsous* (rendered as *On Elevation, On Greatness,* or *On the Sublime*). This text is now attributed to Longinus or Pseudo-Longinus who lived in the first century CE. Formerly it was attributed to Cassius Longinus, a rhetorician and teacher of rhetoric taken to have lived in the third century CE. This text had a profound impact on the world of modern European letters from the time of Nicolas Boileau's translation into French in 1672. The treatise's basic contribution was to reanalyze the stylistic hierarchy of speech—the high, middle, and low styles—to argue that rhetoric involved not merely the capacity for recognizing and deploying a style appropriate to one's subject matter but also included a judgment on a rhetorical performance or a literary work. For the moderns, it came to be seen as a central statement of the view that art involved the achievement of a previously unanticipated success, what would later be known as the "je ne sais quoi" or the "grace beyond the reach of art" that made successful works of art seem not just successful but surprisingly so. As a registration of the difficulties of resolving artistic accomplishment or greatness into prescriptive formulas that artists might simply follow, the classical text came to be the modern pretext for insisting on the aesthetic as an arena of the surprising, the unexpected—a position that seemed only to have been enhanced by the fact that the treatise's rediscovery made it look like an intriguing interruption of literary tradition, a kind of classical novelty.

Longinus's fragmentary treatise had posed a significant challenge to the very tradition that it participated in. If the rhetorician had most frequently seen himself as teaching others how to be rhetorically effective, Longinus, by contrast, stressed the limitations of conventions and formulas and instead appealed to the significance of audience reaction as evidence of those limitations. What would once have been described as correct came to be seen as "merely correct." Although Longinus's remarks, particularly because of their imperfect state of preservation, constituted something more like practical criticism than a full-blown theory of rhetoric, their general tendency became especially important for the examination of the sublime under the auspices of a formalist aesthetics, in which neither the original intention of the author nor the originary context of a work was seen as particularly important in justifying a claim about the aesthetic power of that object.

The clearest version of that argument would, however, only emerge with Immanuel Kant's *Critique of Judgment* (1790). Initially, the rediscovery of the sublime took the form of investigating the impact of both objects of experience and literary works on observers. The sublime was routinely coupled with the beautiful to produce a classificatory system for judgments about experience. In Edmund Burke's empiricist treatment, the analysis of the beautiful and the sublime was simply a way of noticing the physiological effects of objects on individuals. Thus, his *A Philosophical Enquiry into the Origin of Our Ideas of the Sublime and Beautiful* (1757) insisted first on the reliability and universality of the testimony of the senses, and tried to uncover large patterns in that testimony by organizing it under the categories of the beautiful and the sublime. The beautiful, which Burke continually related to the social emotions of companionability, encompassed a range of qualities that all shared familiarity and comprehensibility; the sublime, which Burke linked with the more strenuous purposes of heroism, he associated with the sense of exertion brought on by a confrontation with the surprising or unfamiliar, with objects of experience extending beyond an individual's reach. In keeping with this general division, things that were diminutive and smooth were conceived as beautiful because they seemed to conform especially well with the human sensory organs, and things that were novel, obscure, and terrible were conceived as sublime because they seemed to challenge those organs. Thus, Burke saw himself as demonstrating, for example, the aptness of sweetness for the tongue by describing how sugars, as versions of several "perfect globes," move on the taste buds in such a way as to confirm the taste in its own conformation. Analogously, he described the ways in which such things as darkness or excessive light would seem sublime on account of the difficulty that the senses had in working with them.

Especially in the most insistently physiological discussions, Burke's *Enquiry* suggested that beauty and sublimity were properties of objects, persistent attributes that could be discovered by experience. The judgment of taste, from this standpoint, appeared merely a way of categorizing experiences of that were unequivocal. Yet, even as he pursued that claim, he was also simultaneously advancing another somewhat different view, one in which the purpose of aesthetic experience was not so much to reveal the stable and intrinsic properties of objects as to draw attention to the various aspects under which they might be considered. Thus, he made it clear that the same object might be viewed in various "distinct lights": "The description of the wild ass, in Job, is worked up into no small sublimity, merely by insisting on his freedom, and his setting mankind at defiance; otherwise the description of such an animal could have had nothing noble in it" (II, v).

What Burke had accomplished in his *Enquiry*, then, was both to suggest that rhetoric had traditionally been credited

with power inasmuch as it dealt in obscure connections between understanding and affect and to argue that not only language provided instances of such difficulties. Although his introduction on taste had implied that he was merely cataloging the uniformity of reactions that all people would have to objects of experience, he had ended by discovering the extent to which representation itself produced a new set of elements to be responded to. Memory and anticipation began to complicate the testimony that he developed about the sensory experience of objects, and the specific words and images of a speech from Homer or a passage from Job came to appear less like testimony about physiological regularity than like an occasion for new sensations.

Yet, if Burke's attention could be said to shift in the *Enquiry* from the objects of experience to the various senses through which they were represented—and, indeed, to various representational systems such as poetry or language— Kant's *Critique of Judgment* (1790) reoriented the project of the sublime. Turning away from the more nearly Burkean perspective that he had adopted in his earlier *Observations on the Feeling of the Beautiful and Sublime* (1763), in which he had tried to scan the collections of objects that he identified as beautiful or sublime and to talk about their common properties, he foregrounded the differences between aesthetic judgments and both epistemological claims and moral judgments. This project involved him in dividing the beautiful and the sublime in a novel way. While most commentators on the sublime proceeded, as Burke had, by treating both natural objects and human artifacts as beautiful or sublime, Kant restricted the sublime—or what he termed the "sublime properly so-called" (section 23)—to judgments on *natural* objects alone. His purpose in making such a restriction was not to argue that one could not see stirring and thus sublime themes or effects in art or in other human productions. Rather, he isolated the sublime in cases that demonstrated natural might or infinitude because he wanted to call attention to the ways in which judgments on the sublime were no less important for not being objective, for not being readily resolved into claims about the nature of the object under scrutiny or about the conditions under which it was viewed. The natural sublime thus provided a clear instance of an individual judgment that could appeal to no evidence outside itself: one could neither solicit confirmation from other people nor appeal to the conventions and conditions under which the object had been produced. Sublime aesthetic experience was important because it involved treating what was not produced to be meaningful to us as if it were meaningful, or what he called, in one of the *Critique*'s most significant phrases, "purposiveness without purpose." What the experience of the sublime contributed, over and above the experience of the beautiful, was restlessness as opposed to satisfaction, a drive toward the as yet unapprehended, that would come to be associated with the claim that sublime aesthetic experience contained within it a commitment to avant-gardism.

Kant identified two different kinds of sublimity: (1) the mathematical, in which the reflective judgment is occupied not with measuring an object but with recognizing "in our imagination a striving toward infinite progress and in our reason a claim for absolute totality" that surpasses "every standard of sense"; and (2) the dynamical, in which one confronts the difference between human limitations as natural creatures and the nonsensuous standard of reason that enables us to find "in our mind . . . a superiority to nature even in its immensity." In the sublime, Kant sought to identify the curious pleasure that an individual might have in the experience of a negative; that is, he argued that we do not subscribe to the conventions that underwrite a mathematical series or acknowledge natural might out of a sense of necessity, or from the conviction that human society or nature require us to accept them. Rather, both human conventions and natural necessity become supportable, and indeed interesting, because sublime experience enables us to imagine them as reflection allows, so that reflection seems to allow for choice in relation to even the least elective aspects of experience. If the beautiful seemed to Kant to present particular difficulties and particular richness because it raised the question of how one might perceive new aspects of previously identified objects (the beauty of objects that had been made to be serviceable, for instance), the sublime, by contrast, involved a claim that the judgment needed to use an encounter with a *presentation* in the external world to discover the inadequacy of the presentation: "We must seek a ground external to ourselves for the beautiful in nature, but seek it for the sublime merely in ourselves and in our attitude of thought, which introduces sublimity into the representation of nature" (section 23).

The sublime in nature thus becomes a particularly pure instance of aesthetic judgment, because it is peculiarly unavailable to epistemological claims both about objects and about the nature of representational systems or the conditions of perception. Although judgments about beauty may well overlap with judgments about a particular concept (so that it becomes difficult to say how far one appreciates a flower, say, because it is beautiful, and how far one appreciates it because it is a good example of a flower), Kant attempted to describe the sublime independent of conceptual categories. Although he acknowledged the plausibility of describing a whole range of experiences and artifacts with the adjective *sublime,* he was not committed to identifying a general field of associations for the term or properties of objects that could be said to be sublime. Instead, he foregrounded the way in which nature might represent sublimity to humans, because he wanted to stress that nature harbored no views for or about persons. (It is a particularly important implicit theme of Kant's Third Critique that he is not describing nature as a book on which a divinity has en-

rolled a statement of its will.) Moreover, the ventriloquism that was involved in imagining that nature might speak to humans as they took it to be sublime made it possible to imagine what Kant meant in talking about the disinterestedness of the aesthetic judgment; an aesthetic judgment about sublime nature could not, by its nature, involve a claim about what a human agent had meant in making it a particular way. Because the significance of a sublime object existed in reception rather than in production, it would be especially difficult to describe sublime interest in any ordinary lexicon of motivation.

It may have been partially in reaction to Burke's affectivism, which Kant characterized as his capacity for penetrating observations from empirical psychology, that Kant introduced into the notion of the sublime a distinction between the mathematical and the dynamical sublime. His account of the dynamical sublime resembled Burke's account of the sublime generally; it involved a staged process of representing an object as exciting fear, recognizing that one "can regard an object as *fearful* without being afraid of it," and feeling pleasure that "in our rational faculty we find a different, nonsensuous standard" that reminds us of our own powers. The consciousness of nature's power over the sensuous aspect of human beings yields to the consciousness that "nature is here called sublime merely because it elevates the imagination to a presentation of those cases in which the mind can make felt the proper sublimity of its destination, in comparison with nature itself" (section 28). The mathematical sublime involved a less contestatory rhetoric. It enabled Kant to register the point that all standards (whether they have a tree, an English mile, or the human body as their unit) are themselves aesthetic, that "we can never have a first or fundamental measure" (section 26), and to suggest that this recognition could lead not simply to skepticism about the usefulness of measurement but to a pleasure in the mind's production of its own insatiable demand for a measure that could be enlarged to achieve a totality.

Friedrich von Schiller's brief essay *On the Sublime* (1801) extends an essentially Kantian position about the significance of the supersensible aspects of aesthetic experience. What Schiller draws from Kant's *Critique of Judgment* is the basic sense that the significance of aesthetic experience is its subjective character. Thus, whereas a figure like Burke had seen it as a limitation in aesthetic experience that it might be so subjective and variable as to be unavailable as knowledge, Schiller echoes Kant's distinction between cognitive statements and aesthetic judgments. Aesthetic objects therefore come to have less interest because of what they might teach us about the things they depict and greater interest because of what they lead us to recognize about human capacities. Opening his discussion by quoting from Gotthold Ephraim Lessing's *Nathan the Wise*, "No man must 'must,'" Schiller focuses his discussion on the support that he takes aesthetic judgments to lend to the will. For Schiller, human beings are, above all else, characterized by the capacity to will. This capacity manifests itself in what might, from Burke's perspective, look like a failure in aesthetic judgment. Whereas it might seem like a deficiency in the aesthetic judgment that one might not be able to communicate one's particular judgments to other people and that one might not be able to replicate one's particular judgments even for oneself, Schiller argued forcefully that this apparent weakness was not a failure in human understanding. It was, he thought, instead an indication that "the will is the genetic characteristic of man as species, and even reason is only its external rule" (Schiller, 1966).

If Burke had stressed the importance of natural might that reminded human beings of the comparative insignificance of their own powers and had argued that a consciousness of having escaped annihilation produced energizing emotions, Schiller proceeded from a diametrically opposed position. For him, the experience of the sublime involved the affirmation of human identity as the refusal to suffer violence from any of the "countless forces" that are superior to man's own and wield physical mastery over him. In an intensification of the Kantian view that what is termed "sublimity" can only be applied to external objects through a "subreption" of a descriptive language that ought, properly speaking, to be applied only to human consciousness, Schiller devotes his attention almost exclusively to that consciousness. He argues that "Man can no longer be the being that wills if there is even a *single* case in which he simply must do what he does not will" (ibid.), developing in the process a defense of "aesthetic education" as the process of enhancing the natural human powers with the kind of artificial enhancement that they can gain as they develop their consciousness of the importance of their wills in altering what might look like necessity. With the emphasis on aesthetic education as the development of character and the consolidation of a subjective technology, the sublime comes scarcely to seem attributable to external objects, which are significant largely as a series of obstacles that human consciousness seeks to overcome.

In Georg Wilhelm Friedrich Hegel's view, as he set it forth in his Berlin lectures on aesthetics of the 1820s, Schiller's opposition between natural necessity and the freedom of the human will only dramatized what he took to be a fatal weakness in Kantianism—that it tended to make the phenomenal world look merely conjectural. Hegel's criticism of Kant would operate on a number of different philosophical fronts; he would characteristically hold that Kant continually condemns experience to seeming possible rather than actual. With relation to aesthetic judgments, he criticized Kant's willingness to sacrifice objective knowledge to what he took to be the requirements of subjectivity, and to insist on the postulate that aesthetic experience might not be unified but that we had to treat it as if it were.

Thus, Hegel replies to Kant's statement that "the faculty of judgment must assume as a principle for its own use that what is contingent for us contains a unity, which for us indeed is not knowable, but yet thinkable, in the connection of the manifold with an implicitly possible experience" with the charge that this fixes "Being-in-itself" "once for all . . . outside of self-consciousness" and conceives the "Understanding . . . only in the form of the self-conscious, not in its becoming another."

The term *sublime* comes under considerable pressure in the substantial disagreement between Kant and Hegel. Kant had isolated the sublime from the beautiful along lines that were radically different from those of most commentators; that is, he had argued that the sublime was an interesting category precisely because it included no human artifacts, because its objects were identifiable as objects only through an individual subjective act of judgment. In so doing, he had made it seem merely metaphoric to speak of "sublime poetry" or "sublime painting," because those arts obviously had to have been made by someone and thus already had an objective existence that was independent of a particular viewer's experience of them. In Hegel's account, this Kantian notion of "purposiveness without purpose," with its emphasis on the *look* of intentional significance, comes under particular attack. Kant's account of the sublime had revolved around what Hegel singled out as objects with only "external adaption to end," and had thus pointed to the way in which Kant had defined the sublime not as an attribute of existing objects, but instead as a statement made on behalf of the human faculty of reason. From the perspective of Hegelian phenomenology, Kant's account of the sublime was thus unacceptable in its simultaneous suggestion and refusal of illusion. Hegel thus occupies himself exclusively with the fine arts insofar as they instantiate a unity of content and its presentation, and he tends to locate the sublime as one of the three basic relations of the Idea to its configuration. Arguing that "art begins" when "the Idea, still in its indeterminacy and obscurity, or in bad and untrue determinacy, is made the content of artistic shapes," he identifies sublimity as an an insufficiently individualized version of symbolic form, one in which "abstraction and one-sidedness leave its shapes externally defective and arbitrary." In the sublime mode, which he associates with the earliest stages of the historical unfolding of art, "the first form of art is . . . rather a *mere search* for portrayal than a capacity for true presentation; the Idea has not found the form even in itself and therefore remains struggling and striving after it" (ibid). Whereas Kant had spoken of the sublime as providing an understanding of the motives for art that always lies beyond the reach of actual art, Hegel's effort is to identify the sublime as an aspect of art with specific limitations that can be, and are, overcome. Thus, he instances the incompatibility of the relationship between the Idea and natural objects that are thoroughly determinate in their shape as an instance of the sublime, and describes the incompatibility as "a *negative* one," because "the Idea, as something inward, is itself unsatisfied by such externality, and, as the inner universal substance thereof, it persists *sublime* above all this multiplicity of shapes which do not correspond with it."

If Hegel had revived the notion of representational strain in his account of the symbolic mode of sublime art, Theodor W. Adorno, in his *Aesthetic Theory* (1997), identified Hegel's determination to viewing "spirit as a defining characteristic of works of art" as a significant weakness, one that hypostatized spirit's "objectivity as a kind of absolute identity," a simple epiphenomenon of the Hegelian system. In so doing, he revived interest in Kantian aesthetics for its principled ambiguity in "beginning with a sense of necessity and at the same time denying necessity's existence" (1997). He thus adapts Kant's account of the sublime, treating it as the prototype of contradictory experiences of the same object, and describing it as particularly well instanced in the "kind of art that vibrates and quakes by suspending itself for the sake of a non-illusory truth content, while simultaneously being unable to slough off its illusory quality as an art" (ibid.). For Adorno, then, the sublime does not remain outside of art (as it had in the Kantian account). Indeed, Kant's recognition of the sublime in a feeling for nature is simply a historical fact, evidence of the fact that Kant "had not yet experienced great subjective art." And if Adorno comes to aver that it "might be better to stop talking about the sublime completely," because "the term has been corrupted beyond recognition by the mumbo jumbo of the high priests of art religion" (ibid.), he retains a commitment to seeing the sublime as an essentially oppositional structure. Although the Kantian depiction of the sublime in terms of "the resistance that spirit marshals against the prepotence of nature" may have a limited purchase on an aesthetic practice that has thoroughly incorporated subjectivity into itself, Adorno's commitment to the critical function of art continually holds aesthetic experience up as staging just such a resistance. The targets of this resistance may shift from the prepotence of nature to the prepotence of authoritarian government and, indeed, to the prepotence of subjective art itself, and the resistance need not have any direct political consequence. Yet, Adorno is clearly interested in recuperating from Kantian aesthetics an image of the sublime that serves to provide an explanation of modernity's relentless search for novelty and, moreover, to depict it as a spiritual restlessness. In his view, Hegel's major contribution is to have acknowledged art in terms of the human consciousness of need, and his interest in sublimity is in interrogating that need in such a way as to distinguish the "objectively spiritual" aspect of works of art from their materials, to identify what separates works of art "in principle from food and drink."

Against just such a repudiation of the materiality of works of art, Jacques Derrida was interested in examining the sublime to locate the importance of the notion of the limit in philosophical thought and in language and to argue that the sublime only apparently involves a movement beyond its material presentation toward the supersensible. Thus, in *The Truth in Painting,* he takes up the question of the relationship between a beautiful painting and its frame to prepare the way for a discussion of the sublime. Arguing for the importance of the material features of the presentation of an aesthetic object, Derrida advances the view that the frame around a painting should not be thought of as merely an accessory, a parergon or hors d'oeuvre that comes in physical contact with the "work itself" but has no significant relationship to it. Rather, the parergon, "this supplement outside the work," establishes itself as what Derrida calls a "transcendent exteriority" that presses "against the limit itself" and intervenes "in the inside only to the extent that the inside is lacking" (1987). In other words, the encounter with beautiful paintings suggests that the constant distinction between frame and painting, what is an accessory and what is the real work, would not be necessary if works of art established their own boundaries in the terms that have seemed available in accounts of internal coherence, harmonious balance, and imitative adequacy. By contrast with the beautiful painting, the sublime cannot have a "parergon." As an infinite, the sublime has no obvious physical limit; it is not, Derrida says, "bordered" or bounded. For Derrida, the sublime epitomizes the process of establishing limits for the illimitable, a process that he sees as omnipresent in ordinary linguistic operations in which individuals delimit the significance of linguistic signs that are, by virtue of what he terms "iterability," always potentially repeatable with a difference and, he argues, infinite. In making this suggestion, Derrida obviously rejects the distinction between the understanding and the imagination on which the Kantian account had turned. Kant had affirmed, in his discussion of the mathematical sublime, that the understanding frequently rests content with something less than concrete comprehension of an absolute and infinite whole. Indeed, the interest of the sublime for him lay in its imposing a new demand—a demand that imagination comprehend all the elements of an infinite series in just such an absolute whole—that marked off aesthetic experience as distinctive. Derrida's account aims at suggesting that we might want to extend the claims made for aesthetic judgment in the Third Critique to our more general understanding of language, which Derrida wants to detach from the Kantian emphasis on intentionality in the process of arguing that written language does not so much produce evidence of the existence of a conscious author as militate toward a sense of the superfluousness of such an author (as a written message implies for him the disposability of its maker).

For Jean-François Lyotard, the sublime was a topic that opened on a variety of social and ethical problems. Although he published lectures exclusively devoted to Kant's Analytic of the Sublime (1991), Lyotard was less concerned with identifying an exclusively aesthetic domain than with examining the implications that aesthetic experience has for knowledge more generally. By contrast with Derrida, he was less concerned with identifying the material conditions of judgment and instead emphasized the importance of the Kantian notion of the sublime for directing attention to the tension between logical descriptions and individual intention. In such an account, the importance of the sublime lies less in the notion of challenging or transcending conventions than in designating the possibility of movement from one set of rules or conventions to another. The sublime thus becomes a way of designating a passage to a new perception. He shrewdly recognized that Kant may have departed from Burke in most respects but that he "ransacked" Burke's aesthetic for its "major gambit—to show that the sublime is kindled by the threat that nothing further might happen" (1991). Thus, in *The Postmodern Condition: A Report on Knowledge* (1984), Lyotard examines the sublime as an index to the importance of the avant-garde. What he calls "modern" in art is an art committed to the sublime, which he characterizes, following Kant, as taking place "when the imagination fails to present an object which might, if only in principle, come to match a concept." Insofar as sublime ideas—ideas of the infinitely great, the infinitely powerful, and the like—are "unpresentable," they "impart no knowledge about reality" and interfere with the free union of the faculties that occurs in the response to the beautiful. Instancing figures such as Kazimir Malevich, Paul Klee, and Barnett Newman as artists of "negative presentation," he argues for an art that dedicates its "'little technical expertise'" to "present the fact that the unpresentable exists" (ibid.). By contrast with what he characterizes as Jürgen Habermas's commitment to consensus as an appropriate goal, Lyotard attacks the "task which academicism had assigned to realism: to preserve various consciousnesses from doubt," and instead defends the project of a sublime avant-garde art that is "perpetually flushing out artifices of presentation which make it possible to subordinate thought to the gaze and to turn it away from the unpresentable" (ibid.).

With the work of Adorno and Lyotard, the sublime recovers the social function that Longinus had attributed to it: it becomes the arena for a recognition of the force of the unanticipated, the success that seemed not to have been predicted. If the notion of "negative presentation" does not entirely seem to convey the nature of the shock of recognition that the sublime produces, it registers the increasingly strong claim that commentators on the sublime have made for its significance in altering the usually tacit rules of the games of social interchange.

[*See also* Burke; Kant, *article on* Kant on the Sublime; *and* Lyotard.]

BIBLIOGRAPHY

Adorno, Theodor W. *Aesthetic Theory.* Edited by Gretel Adorno and Rolf Tiedemann, translated by Robert Hullot-Kentor. Minneapolis, 1997.
Bourdieu, Pierre. *Distinction: critique sociale du jugement.* Paris, 1979. Translated as *Distinction: A Social Critique of the Judgement of Taste* by Richard Nice (Cambridge, Mass., 1984).
Burke, Edmund. *A Philosophical Enquiry into the Origin of Our Ideas of the Sublime and Beautiful.* Edited by James T. Boulton. Oxford, 1987.
Crowther, Paul. *The Kantian Sublime: From Morality to Art.* Oxford, 1989.
de Man, Paul. "Phenomenality and Materiality in Kant." In *Hermeneutics: Questions and Prospects,* edited by Gary Shapiro and Alan Sica. Amherst, Mass., 1984.
Derrida, Jacques. "Economimesis." In *Mimesis: des articulations.* Paris, 1975.
Derrida, Jacques. *La vérité en peinture.* Paris, 1978. Translated as *The Truth in Painting* by Geoff Bennington and Ian MacLeod (Chicago, 1987).
Ferguson, Frances. *Solitude and the Sublime: Romanticism and the Aesthetics of Individuation.* New York and London, 1992.
Ginsborg, Hannah. *The Role of Taste in Kant's Theory of Cognition.* New York, 1990.
Guyer, Paul. *Kant and the Experience of Freedom: Essays on Aesthetics and Morality.* Cambridge and New York, 1993.
Hegel, Georg Wilhelm Friedrich. *Aesthetics: Lectures on Fine Art.* 2 vols. Translated by T. M. Knox. Oxford, 1975.
Hegel, Georg Wilhelm Friedrich. *Hegel's Introduction to Aesthetics: Being the Introduction to the Berlin Aesthetics Lectures of the 1820s.* Translated by T. M. Knox. Oxford, 1979.
Kant, Immanuel. *Critique of Judgment.* Translated by Werner S. Pluhar. Indianapolis, 1987.
Lyotard, Jean-François. *Le différend.* Paris, 1983. Translated as *The Differend: Phrases in Dispute.* by Georges Van Den Abbeele (Minneapolis, 1988).
Lyotard, Jean-François. *Leçons sur l'analytique du sublime.* Paris, 1991. Translated as *Lessons on the Analytic of the Sublime* by Elizabeth Rottenberg (Stanford, Calif., 1994).
Lyotard, Jean-François. *The Postmodern Condition: A Report on Knowledge.* Translated by Geoff Bennington and Brian Massumi. Minneapolis, 1984.
Nancy, Jean-Luc. "L'offrande sublime." *Poésie* 30 (1984): 76–116.
Schiller, Friedrich von. *Naive and Sentimental Poetry and On the Sublime.* Translated by Julius A. Elias. New York, 1966.
Weiskel, Thomas. *The Romantic Sublime: Studies in the Structure and Psychology of Transcendence.* Baltimore, 1976.
Žižek, Slavoj. *The Sublime Object of Ideology.* London and New York, 1989.
Žižek, Slavoj. *Tarrying with the Negative: Kant, Hegel, and the Critique of Ideology.* Durham, N.C., 1993.

FRANCES FERGUSON

Feminine Sublime

From Longinus's day until today, writers have viewed the sublime as a more or less explicit mode of domination. The vast majority of theorists conceptualize it as a struggle for mastery between opposing powers, as the self's attempt to appropriate and contain whatever would exceed, and thereby undermine, it. Within the tradition of Romantic aesthetics that sees the sublime as the elevation of the self over an object or experience that threatens it, the sublime becomes a strategy of appropriation. For Immanuel Kant, its most authoritative and influential theorist, the sublime moment entails the elevation of reason over an order of experience that cannot be represented. Typically, the sublime involves a moment of blockage followed by one of heightened lucidity in which reason resists the blocking source by representing its very inability to represent the sublime "object"; it thereby achieves supremacy over an excess that resists its powers. Thus, the central moment of the sublime marks the self's newly enhanced sense of identity; a will to power drives its style, a mode that establishes and maintains the self's domination over its objects of rapture. Without domesticating the sublime by defusing its profound and important connections to the realms of power, conflict, and agency, or suggesting that the feminine sublime is merely another, more intense version of the beautiful, it is important to emphasize that, rather than represent the object of rapture as a way of incorporating it, as does the traditional sublime, the feminine sublime does not attempt to master or dominate its objects of rapture.

The feminine sublime is neither a rhetorical mode nor an aesthetic category but a domain of experience that resists categorization, in which the subject enters into relation with an otherness—social, aesthetic, political, ethical, erotic—that is excessive and unrepresentable. The feminine sublime is not a discursive strategy, technique, or literary style that the female writer invents, but rather a crisis in relation to language and representation that a certain subject undergoes. As such it is the site both of women's affective experiences and of their encounters with the gendered mechanisms of power from the mid-eighteenth century (when the theory of the sublime first came to prominence) to the present, for it responds specifically to the diverse cultural configurations of women's oppression, passion, and resistance.

The sublime is a theoretical discourse, with its unique history, canon, and conventions, about the subject's diverse responses to that which occurs at the very limits of symbolization, and gender plays a crucial yet unexamined role in the history of this theory. The theory of the sublime not only describes the subject's encounters with excess but also defines the ways in which excess may or may not be conceptualized. Theories that seem merely to explain the sublime also evaluate, domesticate, and ultimately exclude an otherness that, almost without exception, is gendered as feminine. The texts that form the canon of the sublime— Longinus's *Peri Hypsous* (On the Sublime), Edmund Burke's *A Philosophical Enquiry into the Origin of Our Ideas of the Sublime and Beautiful* (1757), Kant's Third Critique— are able to represent the sublime only through recourse to metaphors of sexual difference; moreover, the structure of the sublime depends on (and results from) a preexisting construction of "the feminine." What appears to be a theory of how excess works actually functions to keep it at bay.

The notion of spectatorship as the site of sublime experience is one of the principal strategies through which such a neutralization occurs. Joseph Addison's "Essay on the Pleasures of the Imagination," from the *Spectator* papers of 21 June through 3 July 1712 (nos. 409, 411–421), emphasizes sublime experience as that of the spectator of an overwhelming event, landscape, or text, and thereby suggests a principal avenue of inquiry that Burke and Kant were to explore more thoroughly. Why, he asks, do we "take delight in being terrified or dejected by a Description, when we find so much Uneasiness in the Fear or Grief which we receive from any other Occasion?" Addison explains that such pleasures depend on a comparison between our own state of safety and the danger or terror we contemplate:

> When we look on such hideous Objects, we are not a little pleased to think we are in no Danger of them. We consider them at the same time, as Dreadful and Harmless; so that the more frightful Appearance they make the greater is the Pleasure we receive from the sense of our own Safety. . . . In the like manner, when we read of Torments, Wounds, Deaths, and like dismal Accidents, our Pleasure does not flow so properly from the Grief which such melancholy Descriptions give us, as from the secret Comparison which we make between ourselves and the Person who suffers.

The distinguishing features of the sublime, however, unsettle the very notion of spectatorship on which Addison and subsequent theorists rely. [*See* Addison.] Although Addison, Burke, and Kant regularly posit a subject who observes pain or terror without partaking of or being directly affected by it, the very hallmark of sublime experience is an identification between auditor and orator or between reader and text in which, as Longinus was the first to observe, "we come to believe that we have created what we have only heard" (7.2). Such a moment, in which the subject, whether in thought or in fact, merges with that which she perceives distinguishes sublime discourse from language that, in Longinus's words, is merely "persuasive and pleasant" (1.4). It is important to emphasize that the very nature of the sublime—its ability to blur distinctions between observer and observed, reader and text, or spectator and event—undercuts the claim on which its theorists rely to explain and defuse its peculiar force. The internal contradiction so central to the history of the sublime is that its theorists regularly claim for the spectator a state of detachment that, were it to exist, would nullify the very features of rapture, merger, and identification that characterize and define the sublime, for the sublime event is precisely one in which what happens to "the other" also happens to the subject who perceives it.

The sublime of William Wordsworth, Samuel Taylor Coleridge, John Keats, and Percy Bysshe Shelley finds its most typical expression in epic or narrative (rather than lyric) poetry, yet there is nothing inherent in the genre of poetry that makes it uniquely suited to or evocative of the sublime. The genre of sublime poetry was effectively closed to women. Dorothy Wordsworth, or any woman of her period, could not have written a poem such as "Tintern Abbey," with its celebration of "A presence that disturbs me with the joy / of elevated thoughts; a sense sublime / Of something far more deeply interfused" and abiding faith in the poet's infinite ability to "revive again." Wordsworth, the poet of the "egotistical sublime" that so provoked Keats, inherits as his birthright a self-assurance, entitlement, and confidence in his right to speak and be heard that no woman of his era could share. The moment of conversion that Wordsworth experiences in *The Prelude* when he encounters a blind beggar in the streets of London—"My mind did at this spectacle turn round / As with the might of waters" (VII, lines 643–644)—is a paradigm of Romantic transcendence and celebrates a kind of power that was forbidden to women. It also privileges a subject who subsumes all experience into an infinitely expanding "I," as if the goal of the Wordsworthian sublime were to consume the very otherness it appears to bespeak and demonstrate mastery over an experience that had seemed overwhelming.

Keats criticizes the "Wordsworthian or egotistical sublime" as "a thing per se" that "stands alone." Unlike Wordsworth, he views the sublime as residing in the extinction and not the enhancement of identity: "poetical Character," he observes, "is not itself—it has no self—it is every thing and nothing—it has no character": to be sublime is to have "no Identity . . . no self." As with Keats, Coleridge's sublime also depends on the self's awareness of its own absence. His comments on the sublimity of a Gothic cathedral provide a striking contrast to Wordsworth's response to the craggy peaks in the Mount Snowdon passage of *The Prelude* or Shelley's rhapsodic identification with Mont Blanc:

> But Gothic art is sublime. On entering a cathedral, I am filled with devotion and with awe; I am lost to the actualities that surround me, and my whole being expands into the infinite; earth and air, nature and art, all swell up into eternity, and the only sensible expression left is, "That I am nothing!"

Whereas Wordsworth's sublime culminates in what Thomas Weiskel describes as "an infinitely repeatable 'I am'" (1976), in the sublime of Keats and Coleridge individual consciousness is subsumed by the eternal. The grandeur of the Gothic church suspends Coleridge's self-awareness; all the self can know of itself is that is "nothing." [*See* Coleridge *and* Wordsworth.]

In contrast to Wordsworth's "I am every thing" and Coleridge's "I am nothing," the feminine sublime neither celebrates self-presence and the self's capacity to master the other nor consecrates the immediacy of its absence. If Coleridge's identity is diminished by the sublime, whereas Wordsworth's expands, the feminine sublime contests the logic of identity that conceives of the self in exclusive terms

of presence or absence. Here, one might envision a sublime in which the self neither possesses nor merges with the other but attests to a relation with it.

No innate femininity or unique style of women's writing accompanies the feminine sublime. Indeed, the very search for an essential difference that would function outside any specific context to fix, determine, guarantee, and control meaning is precisely what the sublime contests. At stake in the notion of the feminine sublime is the refusal to define the feminine as a specific set of qualities or attributes that might be called irreducible and unchanging. Here the term *feminine* functions as a synonym for textual and/or political practices that contest binaries, including a rigid notion of sexual difference that would insist on separate male and female selves. The appeal to a "feminine sublime" is not to a specifically feminine subjectivity or mode of expression, but rather to that which calls such categories into question. It is one name for what cannot be grasped in established systems of ideas or articulate within the current framework in which the term *woman* has meaning.

To investigate the feminine sublime is not to embark on a search for an autonomous female voice, realm of experience, or language, although these categories may be valuable as a dimension of the strategic interventions of feminist practice. What is specifically feminine about the feminine sublime is not an assertion of innate sexual difference, but a radical rearticulation of the role that gender plays in producing the history of discourse on the sublime and the formulation of an alternative position with respect to excess and the possibilities of its figuration. To assert the importance of the feminine in this context is not to reinscribe normative gender categories, but to offer a critique of a tradition that has functioned historically to reassert masculine privilege. In this sense, the notion of the feminine does not refer to a particular affinity group, gender, or class, but rather to a putting in question of the master discourse that perpetuates the material and psychological oppression of actual women.

The word *feminine* refers to the socially constructed category of woman that has endured universal and transhistorical oppression and thus underscores the reality of women's patriarchal order, whether it is perpetuated and sustained by biological women or by men. Here, the term does not so much refer to actual women as designate a position of critique with respect to the masculinist systems of thought that contribute to women's subjugation. Although such a conception of the feminine does not suspend reference to existing women, it does suspend the notion of an ultimate feminine identity that could function as the ground of sexual difference. Rather, it becomes one name for a residue that disrupts the oppositional structure male/female and thereby calls for a radical rearticulation of the symbolic order:

> If we had a keen vision and a feeling for all ordinary human life, it would be like hearing the grass grow and the squirrel's heart

beat, and we should die of that roar which lies on the other side of silence.   (George Eliot, *Middlemarch*)

The Borderlands are physically present wherever two or more cultures edge each other, where people of different races occupy the same territory, where under, lower, middle and upper classes touch, where space between two individuals shrinks with intimacy. . . . A border is a dividing line, a narrow strip along a steep edge. A borderland is a vague and undetermined place created by the emotional residue of an unnatural boundary. It is in a constant state of transition. The prohibited and forbidden are its inhabitants.   (Gloria Anzaldúa, *Borderlands/La Frontera*)

She listened, but it was all very still; cricket was over; the children were in their baths; there was only the sound of the sea. She stopped knitting; she held the long reddish-brown stocking dangling in her hands a moment. She saw the light again. With some irony in her interrogation, for when one woke at all, one's relations changed, she looked at the steady light, the pitiless, the remorseless, which was so much her, yet so little her, which had her at its beck and call (she woke in the night and saw it bent across their bed, stroking the floor), but for all that she thought, watching it with fascination, hypnotized, as if it were stroking with its silver fingers some sealed vessel in her brain whose bursting would flood her with delight, she had known happiness, exquisite happiness, intense happiness, and it silvered the rough waves a little more brightly, as daylight faded and the blue went out of the sea and it rolled in waves of pure lemon which curved and swelled and broke upon the beach and the ecstasy burst in her eyes and waves of pure delight traced over the floor of her mind and she felt, It is enough! It is enough!
                                          (Virginia Woolf, *To the Lighthouse*)

Woman is not to be related to any simple designatable being, subject, or entity. Nor is the whole group (called) women. One woman + one woman + one woman will never add up to some generic entity: woman. (The/a) woman refers to what cannot be defined, enumerated, formulated or formalized. Woman is a common noun for which no identity can be defined. (The/a) woman does not obey the principle of self-identity, however the variable x for self is defined. She is identified with every x variable, not in any specific way. Presupposed is an excess of all identification to/of self. But this excess is no-thing: it is vacancy of form, gap in form, the return to another edge where she retouches herself with the help of—nothing. Lips of the same form—but of a form that is never simply defined—ripple outwards as they touch and send one another on a course that is never fixed into a single configuration.
                                          (Luce Irigaray, *Speculum of the Other Woman*)

To hear the roar that lies within silence, and write it; inhabit a borderland (not a wasteland) in which boundaries overlap and differences of race, class, sexuality, and geography collide; to see waves of light breaking upon the beach as a movement in which otherness appears; or to define *woman* not as a shared fantasy of sexual identity, but in a way that contests any notion of essence, feminine or otherwise—across different trajectories Eliot, Anzaldúa, Woolf, and

Irigaray articulate crucial aspects of the feminine sublime, for each makes explicit the subject's encounter with and response to an alterity that exceeds, limits, and defines her.
   [*See also* Feminism.]

BIBLIOGRAPHY

de Bolla, Peter. *The Discourse of the Sublime: Readings in History, Aesthetics, and the Subject.* Oxford and New York, 1989.

Burke, Edmund. *A Philosophical Enquiry into the Origin of Our Ideas of the Sublime and Beautiful* (1757). Edited by Adam Phillips. Oxford and New York, 1990.

Ferguson, Frances. *Solitude and the Sublime: Romanticism and the Aesthetics of Individuation.* New York and London, 1992.

Freeman, Barbara Claire. *The Feminine Sublime: Gender and Excess in Women's Fiction.* Berkeley, 1995.

Guerlac, Suzanne. *The Impersonal Sublime: Hugo, Baudelaire, Lautréamont.* Stanford, Calif., 1990.

Hertz, Neil. *The End of the Line: Essays on Psychoanalysis and the Sublime.* New York, 1985.

Kant, Immanuel. *Critique of Judgment.* Translated by Werner S. Pluhar. Indianapolis, 1987.

Longinus. *"Longinus" on Sublimity.* Translated by D. A. Russell. Oxford, 1965.

Lyotard, Jean-François. *The Postmodern Condition: A Report on Knowledge.* Translated by Geoff Bennington and Brian Massumi. Minneapolis, 1984.

Lyotard, Jean-François. *The Differend: Phrases in Dispute.* Translated by Georges Van Den Abbeele. Minneapolis, 1988.

Monk, Samuel Holt. *The Sublime: A Study of Critical Theories in Eighteenth-Century England.* New York, 1935; reprint, Ann Arbor, 1960.

Weiskel, Thomas. *The Romantic Sublime: Studies in the Structure and Psychology of Transcendence.* Baltimore, 1976.

Yaeger, Patricia. "Toward a Female Sublime." In *Gender and Theory: Dialogues on Feminist Criticism,* edited by Linda Kauffman, pp. 191–212. Oxford and New York, 1989.

                                          BARBARA CLAIRE FREEMAN

SUGER (Abbé of Saint-Denis.) *See* Gothic Aesthetics.

SULZER, JOHANN GEORG (1720–1779), Swiss aesthetician and philosopher. Born in Winterthur, the son of a Protestant minister, Sulzer studied theology, philosophy, mathematics, and botany and was greatly influenced by the critic Johann Jakob Bodmer. In Germany, he became friends with the representatives of the Berlin Aufklärung. In 1750, he was elected to the Royal Academy of Arts and Sciences of Berlin, and from 1775 onward he presided over its speculative philosophy class. He contributed to keeping the influence of Christian Wolff's philosophy alive. In 1755, he translated David Hume's *Inquiry concerning Human Understanding.* Written within the framework of the physicotheological movement of the interpretation of nature, his first essays on aesthetics are devoted to natural beauty and to its moral use. His major work, the *Allgemeine Theorie der schö-*

nen Künste (General Theory of Fine Arts), is truly an encyclopedic synthesis of the aesthetics of the period.

The aesthetic thought of Sulzer, whose best work can be found in various essays written between 1750 and 1770 and in his *Allgemeine Theorie,* reflects both the theoretical eclecticism and the refusal to develop a philosophical system that characterized the "popular philosophy" of the German Aufklärung. Even if he remained largely within the intellectual scope of later rationalism and of the aesthetics of perfection elaborated by Wolff, Alexander Gottlieb Baumgarten, Georg Friedrich Meier and Moses Mendelssohn, Sulzer approached aesthetic and philosophical problems from a highly psychological perspective. Thus, he played an important mediating role by combining the new themes of the French and English aesthetics of sentiment (Anthony Ashley Cooper, earl of Shaftesbury, Joseph Addison, Abbé Jean-Baptiste and Dubos) with a subjectivist interpretation of Leibnizian monadology. Sulzer's psychology, in particular his analysis of pleasure, rests on a Leibnizian interpretation of the fundamental tendency of the soul to produce continuously new representations for itself. In opposition to Baumgarten, who accentuated the "logic of sensual knowledge" (*cognitio sensitiva*), Sulzer approached aesthetics from the point of view of the perceiving subject's feeling of pleasure. He insisted on the mediating dimension of the fine arts, whose main task is to awaken the moral feeling of the good, thus preparing the subject for moral action. Although the subordination of the beautiful to the good and the moral orientation of aesthetics remain a constant of later rationalist aesthetics, Sulzer's originality was to have limited both moral sense and the faculty of desire to the sphere of feeling. In all likelihood, this stemmed from the influence of English and Scottish aesthetics and moral thought. Thereafter, Sulzer assigned an almost instrumental function to aesthetic sensibility.

Sulzer's strict aesthetic moralism is accompanied by a real sense of aesthetic problems. Sulzer identified two primary faculties of the soul: the faculty of representation, or apperception, through which the soul is absorbed in the object; and the faculty of sentiment or feeling, through which the soul is absorbed in its own state of being. Between the state of distinct perception, where one feels nothing, and the state of strong sensation, where one sees nothing, Sulzer distinguished an intermediary state of "contemplation." This latter state, which acts as mediator between the two other states, and which also serves to mediate between speculative ideas (which are clear but inert) and practical ideas, is equated with taste. Taste is defined as the ability to perceive the beautiful, the latter being the result of the simple subjective perfection of the form of the object: this perfection is said to be subjective because it consists in the free and effortless representational activity of the imagination, the outcome of which is a pleasant sensation. Thus, the notion of "aesthetic form" developed by Sulzer may be placed in the overall process of

subjectivization of the "aesthetic of perfection" initiated by Baumgarten (article "Schön" of the *Allgemeine Theorie*). Although at times Sulzer seems to develop the theoretical tools that would enable him to give a more complex explanation of the specificity of the aesthetic sphere and its relation to both understanding and moral sensibility, the moral instrumentalism that governs his aesthetics tends to undermine the most original ideas contained in his theory of taste and art. Thus, beauty is simply formal and must be completed by a beauty of a superior order, "which is born from the union of the perfect, the beautiful, and the good" (article "Schön"); only "thinking sensations" render the soul "sensitive to moral goodness," and it is "in this that the highest end of the fine arts resides" (article "Sinnlich").

Regarding questions about the intermediary position of taste, the critique of the rationalist notion of "perfection," and the relationship between taste and morality, Sulzer paved the way for Immanuel Kant's aesthetics and foreshadowed the theory of the tripartite faculties of the soul (Johann Nikolaus Tetens, Mendelssohn, Kant). Although Sulzer was severely attacked by the representatives of the Sturm und Drang, who rejected both his morals and his encyclopedism, his aesthetics advanced certain themes later developed by them. For example, like the Sturm und Drang, his conception of genius conceives of art not as an imitation of nature, but rather as the imitation of the creative process of nature itself. Moreover, genius is a state of enthusiasm, an intensification of the representational activity of the entire soul that spreads itself throughout the work of art by a radically original representation.

BIBLIOGRAPHY

Works by Sulzer

Versuch einiger moralischer Betrachtungen über die Werke der Natur. Berlin, 1745.

Unterredungen über die Schönheit der Natur. Berlin, 1750; new ed., Berlin, 1770; reprint, Frankfurt am Main, 1971.

Allgemeine Theorie der schönen Künste. 5 vols. Leipzig, 1771–1774; reprint, Hildesheim and New York, 1967–1970.

Vermischte philosophische Schriften. 2 vols. Leipzig, 1773–1781.

Other Sources

Baker, Nancy Kovaleff, and Thomas Christensen, eds. *Aesthetics and the Art of Musical Composition in the German Enlightenment: Selected Writings of Johann Georg Sulzer and Heinrich Christoph Koch.* Cambridge and New York, 1995.

Dobai, Johannes. *Die bildenden Künste in J. G. Sulzers Ästhetik, seine Allgemeine Theorie der schönen Künste.* Winterthur, 1978.

Gross, Karl Josef. *Sulzers Allgemeine Theorie der schönen Künste.* Berlin, 1905.

Heym, L. M. *Darstellung und Kritik der ästhetischen Ansichten J. G. Sulzers.* Leipzig, 1894.

Leo, Johannes Hermann. *Zur Entstehungsgeschichte der "Allgemeinen Theorie der schönen Künste" J. G. Sulzers.* Heidelberg, 1906.

Nivelle, Armand. *Les théories esthétiques en Allemagne de Baumgarten à Kant.* Paris, 1955. German translation published as *Kunst- und Dichtungstheorien zwischen Aufklärung und Klassik.* 2d ed. (Berlin, 1971).

Palme, Anton. *J. G. Sulzer Psychologie und die Anfänge der Dreivermögenslehre.* Berlin, 1905.

Sommer, Robert. *Grundzüge einer Geschichte der deutschen Psychologie und Ästhetik Von Wolff-Baumgarten bis Kant-Schiller.* Würzburg, 1892.

Tumarkin, Anna. *Der Ästhetiker Johann Georg Sulzer.* Die Schweiz im deutschen Geistesleben, vols. 79–80. Leipzig, 1933.

DANIEL DUMOUCHEL

SUPREMATISM. Exemplified and defined by the iconic work *Black Square* (1915), Suprematism is a direction in early twentieth-century abstract painting that was launched in December 1915 by Kazimir Malevich (1878–1935). The movement was inaugurated in Petrograd as a cohesive artistic orientation with the display of thirty-nine paintings shown at "0.10: The Last Futurist Exhibition." The term *Suprematism* was coined by Malevich, a key figure of the Russian and Ukrainian artistic avant-gardes of the 1910s and 1920s, to define not only an artistic style, but also a philosophical stance propounding the revelatory and transformative power of art. Suprematism consummated this power by negating conventional form. Malevich's concept of "zero-form" brought to a close the disjunctive rendering of three-dimensional objects and ushered in new categories of interpreting reality.

As an aesthetic of nonfigurative art, Suprematism put an end to the formalist manipulation of the painted surface through the convention of static collage and countered the subversion of represented images by resorting to an overt and unadulterated pure nonobjectivity. By abandoning the heterogeneity of collage that separates form from subject, Suprematism reestablished form and its content on the same ontological level of meaning. It explored new concepts of relief and weight based on the deliberate and calculated arrangement of autonomous, monochromatic geometric shapes floating homogeneously on a white, seamless background in a vast, undetermined space. Leaving behind the materialist illusionism of observed reality, Suprematism was instead guided by a philosophical imperative that put forth a transcendent, rather than empirical, order for art. Suprematism, as implied by its name, was to be a new and prophetic kind of painting, representing a world to be, rather than one that is.

To the degree that Malevich abandoned the mimetic tradition of Western art, he also embraced ever more profoundly the canon of Orthodox iconographic practice. The Iconoclastic Controversy did not lead to an absolute refusal of the image but challenged the precepts by which the iconographer could express man's supernatural nature and his rise toward eternity. Under the influence of Hellenism, the iconographer overcame illusionistic figuration (and the risk of idolatry) through the use of abstract planimetric modules to relay key theological and spiritual meaning via a monumental, but flexible, format. In the Orthodox icon, various elements of the subject are organized along curved planes confined within rectangular areas. Archetypal paradigms for the various iconographic subjects were made available in guidebooks called *podlinnyky*. In them, the depiction of sacred figures overlay substructures of squares inscribed within circles, or along diagonals determined by arcs and single curved lines extending from the top to the bottom of the icon panel. Such prescriptions prevented the iconographer from transgressing canonic form and bespoiling the content, which was to remain whole and unchangeable within a fixed framework.

Malevich's *Black Square* is the iconic template of Suprematist painting. The square within a square format derives from the geometric structure of traditional icons, while the seriality of Suprematist paintings parallels the devolution of icons from a single archetype. That the *Black Square*, the seminal piece of "0.10: The Last Futurist Exhibition," hung strategically at the juncture of the walls and ceiling planes in the corner of the "Suprematist" room in the Dobychina Gallery, gives further evidence of its iconic function, for the installation appropriates the sacred or "beautiful" corner of a typical peasant home where the patron icon was ordinarily situated.

The tension between Suprematism as a painting style and its transcendental or spiritual dimensions is enacted in the production of the 1913 Futurist opera *Victory over the Sun*. Although the opera predates Suprematism's official and public birth, its production provided a laboratory where Malevich was able to formulate his theory of painting. The opera spawned Malevich's venture into a sphere that surpassed the material and rational world. The action outlined in a libretto written by the Futurist poet Alexei Kruchenikh, aspired to a "Tenth Land"—a utopian realm that bore no resemblance to a present physical world constrained by materiality. The key ideas of the opera were presented reductively in two acts, demonstrating at once opposition and progression, as well as opposition to (technological) progress. Act 1 marks the end of a present world, an experience of the "here and now" that is connected to a delusive and inert realm of appearances, filled with unease caused by the invasive influx of technology. Act 2 defines a new land, dimensionally removed by a passing from zero to ten, a measured and metaphoric distance from the chimeric field of illusion, and is characterized by the cataclysmic destruction of an old cultural order. Here, new technologies are neutralized (a plane crashes to the earth) and, in their place, a new conception of art (and life) is put forth. It is ensconced in a box of concrete, shielded against space, time, and history. Two years hence, when Suprematism would be introduced to the world for the first time, the black square on a white background would dare not be referred to as an empty flat space, void of meaning.

The genesis of Suprematist content can be traced to the absolute darkness brought about by the dramatic eclipse in

SUPREMATISM. *Last Futuristic Exhibition 0.10* (1915), Petrograd (Saint Petersburg), Russia. (Photograph courtesy of Avery Architectural and Fine Arts Library, Columbia University, New York; used by permission.)

Victory over the Sun. This was the point of transition between the acts (and two distinct realms of experience) in the opera, occurring at the instant that the sun is vanquished. The iconology of the play is connected to its place in the perspective of Russian culture of the time, a culture profoundly affected by the feeling of the death of a civilization explored by the Symbolists. Yet, the violent gesture of destroying the sun opens up possibilities of a new and unstifling reality experienced without the inhibitions of time and restrictions of space. This crossing over barriers from one realm into another creates a new sphere of understanding, a dimension of perception unhampered by the mimetic limits of representionalism. The physical and materialist world is thus liberated by an ethereal and transcendental reality—a New Realism. The sun, as a symbol of tired conventions (cf. the Apollonian myth, enlightenment, rationalism, materialism, and the use of chiaroscuro for the palpable rendering of form), can no longer obstruct or interfere with the transmigration of experience into unknown, numinous territories.

As part of the current dialogue concerning the expansion of consciousness about the world and new states of awareness, discussions regarding the "fourth dimension" surfaced in Russia by 1911, when *Tertium Organum* was published by the Russian philosopher on hyperspace Peter Demianovich Ouspensky. Ouspensky had a popular influence on the reception of the fourth dimension, largely because of the efforts of Mikhail Matiushin, composer of the opera *Victory over the Sun.* In 1911, Matiushin had begun to write on the subject and, during winter 1912–1913, he composed an essay with Ouspenskian overtones titled "The Sensation of the Fourth Dimension." When, in 1913, Matiushin translated excerpts from Albert Gleizes and Jean Metzinger's *Du cubisme* (1912) into Russian, he included among the passages quotations from Ouspensky's books *The Fourth Dimension* (1909) and *Tertium Organum.* Later,

Matiushin, through the concept of *zorved* (see-know), would develop ideas on broadened vision that related color to space and time. Under such influences, Malevich began to refer to his colors as "real colors"—making visible the pure sensation of color not of this world, but in another reality of a different dimension—a new, "painterly realism."

References such as "Color Masses in the Fourth Dimension" in the subtitles of Malevich's Suprematist paintings were mechanistic devices that disclosed his intuitive understanding of the concept. Indeed, the inauguration of Suprematism, coinciding with the end of Futurism, marked the institution of a new kind of reason in the visual arts. The annihilation of the sun in the Futurist opera meant the destruction of old and worn devices in art, but it also enfeebled a worn vocabulary no longer capable of defining a reality beyond this world. Kruchenikh's "transrational" language *(zaum)* obfuscated a lexicon of crude utterances that could not contain the emphatic iconographic "logos"—the coherent, complete, and compact message contained in icons. With the old notion of "style" presupposing a manipulation of discrete painterly elements suddenly obliterated, style and its vocabulary began to assume one and the same form where only the laws of pure form presided. Thus, Suprematism is not a subjectless art. It divines the conquest of chaos through the power and mystique of a vast and absolute nothingness—the ultimate reality.

The visionary interpretation of nature as it undergoes physical demise is a theme explored by the Symbolists and lies at the base of Suprematism. For Malevich, it stemmed, in part, from the mystical (and occult) inclinations of the Blue Rose painters, a small group of Moscow Symbolist artists who were engaged in an intense and persistent quest for eternal truth as espoused by the Russian philosopher Vladimir Soloviev. Malevich's early Symbolist paintings of around 1905–1907 focus Soloviev's apocalyptic metaphors as the artist seeks to reconcile inner subjective impulses with the contemplation of immutable cosmic energies. A series of frescoes from this period, exhibited by Malevich at the Golden Fleece exhibitions, explore Symbolist content by dwelling on themes of transfiguration of life by way of a Promethean regenerative wholesomeness. To the degree that Symbolism had outlined its own search for a new contemporary language through the metaphoric value of color, it opened up the possibility for a transition from the real world to one that was more meaningful. Blue Rose painting emphasized the immateriality of physical experience by submitting its workings to the expressive forces of music defined by such abstract features as rhythm, movement, texture, and *gama* (color). With it came a process of depiction that strove toward simplicity and restraint to preserve the tremulous feeling of nature. As in the ambiguous, twilight world of the Blue Rose, where the color blue transcends and fructifies the literal references to the sky and water, so Malevich, in his 1916 booklet *From Cubism and Futurism to Suprematism,* describes the forms of Suprematism as a "construction of forms out of nothing"—the fertile stimulus or starting point of an artistic image that permits one to soar above reality.

Part of this redirection was rooted in Malevich's concurrent interest in the chaste values of indigenous folk art traditions embodied in Russian Neo-Primitivism (c.1905–1913), which inspired the work of Natalia Goncharova, Mikhail Larionov, David Burliuk, and others and could be found in the harmonious rhythms and compositional unities unveiled by a fluid calligraphic handling of icons. It is at this point that Malevich turned to the simple graphite pencil as a way of releasing in a work of art direct but meaningful expression, free of all affectation. Fellow Neo-Primitivist Alexander Gritchenko, in his 1913 essay "On the Relationship between Russian Painting with Byzantium and the West from the Thirteenth to the Twentieth Century," traced the legitimate role of the icon as a formal inspiration for contemporary painting. He claimed that the foundations of the "new painting" (which included all the Picassos dutifully studied by the members of the Russian avant-garde in the collections of the Moscow magnates Ivan Morozov and Sergei Shchukin) go back to the Byzantine iconographic tradition. Thus, in response to philosopher Nikolai Berdyaev's warnings about the contemporary "crisis of art," Gritchenko countered that the crisis only exists in our not knowing how to approach contemporary painting, namely, through pure form and pure color.

Suprematism manifested an end to formalist experimentation. As an abstract style, it was given impetus by contemporary Cubist and Futurist positions about visual representation that found resonance in Malevich's works just prior to Suprematism's debut. Hence, the Futurist breaking up of kineticized elements into repetitive compositional units aggressively penetrating space and form alike, as in Malevich's *Knife Grinder* (c.1913), and the Cubist exploration of relativity, both in the process of observing objects and in recording them as temporal and visual shifts of overlapping planes, as translated by Malevich in a series of paintings from 1914 (e.g., *Lady at the Advertisement Pillar, Private of the First Division,* and *An Englishman in Moscow*), established what Malevich called an "alogical realism"—a play between illusionistic reality and its tactile materiality *(faktura)* that blurred over shifts of time and space. Displayed at exhibitions of the Union of Youth, a society that sponsored many events to publicize the aims of the avant-garde in Saint Petersburg and Moscow, these works of alogical (or transrational) realism, rendered in painting by visual cleavages and ruptures of logical syntax and meaning, served as Malevich's springboard to Suprematism.

It was only in the 1920s that Malevich began to incorporate references to "relativity" and the fourth dimension in his writings. By that time, the inability of Malevich's contemporaries to reconcile the style with his personal philosophy resulted in Suprematism's evolving into a one-man movement. Suprematism would have been a logical construct for Russian post-Revolution society seeking, through political ideology, to build a new world and a new humanity. Even Malevich entertained brief interludes for implementing Suprematism into potentially functional habitats *(arkhitektony)* and "space stations" *(planity)*, and, under the aegis of Unovis, the organization that sprang up after the Russian Revolution for the Advocacy of the New in Art, he designed proletarian tea services and published pamphlets with a Suprematist New Art logo, a square within a square, inscribed by a circle. But except for El Lissitzky's *Prouns*, which had their starting point in Suprematism, Malevich's conception of Suprematism's being an art for a new transformed reality had no true followers, even though his theories on art prevailed until the late 1920s. Two distinct generations benefited from Malevich's efforts. The first, known as the Supremus Circle, extolled Malevich's system by planning a journal in 1916 under the name *Supremus* (a plan that never materialized) and included artists such as Ivan Kliun, Liubov Popova, and Olga Rozanova who successfully employed Suprematist forms in their paintings and found equally (but differently) provocative resolutions to the objectives of the wartime avant-garde. A second generation of adherents included a group who, connected through Unovis, responded to post-Revolution demands and made of Suprematism an applied art form. These included design artists such as Nikolai Suetin and Ilya Chashnik, both of whom studied with Malevich in Vitebsk.

Ultimately, Suprematism's intuitive and subconscious premises were translated, and only temporarily at that, into cognitive functions of art that laid the way for Constructivists such as Aleksandr Rodchenko to address the immediate concerns of the artist's role as engineer in making art that was socially meaningful. Suprematism's universal system for the reshaping of life as a whole thus gave way to the reforming of the physical attributes of an earthly environment alone.

[*See also* Bauhaus; Constructivism; Malevich; Modernism, *overview article; and* Russian Aesthetics.]

BIBLIOGRAPHY

Andersen, Troels. *Malevich: Catalogue Raisonné of the Berlin Exhibition 1927, Including the Collection in the Stedelijk Museum.* Amsterdam, 1970.

Andersen, Troels, ed. *K. S. Malevich: The World as Non-Objectivity; Unpublished Writings, 1922–1925.* Translated by Xenia Glowacki-Prus and Edmund T. Little. Copenhagen, 1976.

Anderson, Troels, ed. *K. S. Malevich: The Artist, Infinity, Suprematism; Unpublished Writings, 1913–1933.* Translated by Xenia Hoffmann. Copenhagen, 1978.

Bowlt, John E., ed. and trans. *Russian Art of the Avant-Garde: Theory and Criticism, 1902–1934* (1976). Rev. enl. ed. London and New York, 1988.

Bowlt, John E., and Charlotte Douglas, eds. *Kazimir Malevich, 1878–1935–1978.* Special issue of *Soviet Union/Union Soviétique* 5.2 (1978).

Douglas, Charlotte. *Swans of Other Worlds: Kazimir Malevich and the Origins of Abstraction in Russia.* Ann Arbor, 1980.

Douglas, Charlotte. *Kazimir Malevich.* New York, 1994.

Gray, Camilla. *The Russian Experiment in Art, 1863–1922* (1962). Rev. ed. by Marian Burleigh-Motley. London and New York, 1986.

Groys, Boris. *The Total Art of Stalinism: Avant-Garde, Aesthetic Dictatorship, and Beyond.* Translated by Charles Rougle. Princeton, N.J., 1992.

Henderson, Linda Dalrymple. "Transcending the Present: The Fourth Dimension in the Philosophy of Ouspensky and in Russian Futurism and Suprematism." In *The Fourth Dimension and Non-Euclidean Geometry in Modern Art*, pp. 238–299. Princeton, N.J., 1983.

Kasimir Malewitsch zum 100. Geburtstag. Cologne, 1978. Exhibition catalog, Galerie Gmurzynska.

Kazimir Malevich, 1878–1935. Amsterdam, 1988. Exhibition catalog, Leningrad, Russian Museum; Moscow, Tretyakov Gallery; Amsterdam, Stedelijk Museum.

Kazimir Malevich 1878–1935. Los Angeles, 1990. Exhibition catalog, Armand Hammer Museum of Art and Cultural Center.

Marcadé, Valentine. *Le renouveau de l'art pictural russe, 1863–1914.* Lausanne, 1971.

Nakov, Andrei B. *Kasimir Malevich.* London, 1976. Exhibition catalog, Tate Gallery.

Simmons, W. Sherwin. *Kasimir Malevich's Black Square and the Genesis of Suprematism, 1907–1915.* New York, 1981.

Zhadova, Larissa A. *Malevich: Suprematism and Revolution in Russian Art, 1910–1930.* Translated by Alexander Lieven. London, 1982.

MYROSLAVA M. MUDRAK

SURREALISM.

[*To explain the aesthetics of Surrealism, an early twentieth-century art movement, as well as the impact of Surrealism on aesthetics, this entry comprises two essays:*

Surrealism and the Visual Arts
Surrealism and Literature

Because Surrealism emerged and developed separately in the visual arts and literature, the first essay treats the visual arts and the second deals with literature. For related discussion, see Avant-Garde; Bataille; Breton; *and* Modernism, *overview article.*]

Surrealism and the Visual Arts

Surrealism proper—literary Surrealism, or a less genre-specific aesthetic project of fusing life and art, dream and reality, conscious and unconscious experience—was a highly theorized entity, full of self-conscious manifestos. Yet there was no mention in these earliest declarations of how the visual arts specifically could be Surrealist, partly because the movement's main theoreticians were not even convinced that a properly Surrealist art could exist. A challenge by Pierre Naville in the pages of *La révolution surréaliste* in 1924 and 1925 started the debate. Naville argued that painting would always fail to represent adequately the pure psychic automatism unfettered by the control of reason sought by Surrealists, because painting was quite simply too mediated a technique—it had neither the speed of execution nor the apparent immediacy and transparency of written or spoken language. Naville's stance clearly illustrates the hegemonic status enjoyed by automatic writing in Surrealism's early history; its privileged position put all other techniques—and all other artistic mediums—out of reach for orthodox Surrealists.

André Breton was thus forced to defend the possibility of Surrealist art: his response to Naville, *Surrealism and Painting,* was published as a series of articles between 1925 and 1927. Breton pointed out that the works already being produced by artists associated with the movement were valuable contributions to the investigation of the surreal, and he went on to discuss these artistic practices in terms of their formal strategies. In Breton's essays, Surrealist art is defined according only to its proficiency in serving the larger goals of revealing the unconscious in representation, dismantling the opposition between the real and the imaginary, and expressing pure thought. From Pablo Picasso's Cubism, which was interpreted as a demonstration of the "treacherous nature of tangible entities," to Max Ernst's collage with its poetic juxtapositions of outmoded banalities, from Man Ray's photography, which blurred the boundaries between real and unreal, animate and inanimate, to André Masson's automatic paintings with their speed of execution and lack of aesthetic concern, Breton identified the different and varied formal solutions employed by these artists as routes to the surreal without ever defining what *surreal* could be for the visual arts.

Breton expressed contempt for those who would reduce Surrealism to style or technique, although he would, in his later writings on Surrealism, divide Surrealist art practice into two categories, automatism and dream transcription. At the time of his earliest writings, however, Breton avoided a stylistic definition of Surrealism in the face of what would seem to be an unreconcilable variety in Surrealist aesthetic procedures. Later historians of the movements who treated *form* or *style* as the central term to their definitions of Surrealist aesthetics would face this problem as well: how to find the common stylistic terms in which to describe work that ranged from painting and sculpture to collage and photography, and in which activities that fell outside of traditional aesthetic categories (for example, the Surrealist object or wanderings through Paris), were difficult to separate from other, more traditionally bound, practices?

If Breton avoids providing a definition of Surrealist art or aesthetics in his essay on the subject, one can turn to other writings, notably the First Manifesto of Surrealism (1924), *Nadja* (1928), *Les vases communicants* (1932), and *L'amour fou* (1937), for concepts that prove more fruitful in the analysis of Surrealist visual art production: the marvelous, and its subcategories or cognates, convulsive beauty and objective chance. These three concepts can be understood as organizing principles of Surrealist production, in both the literary and the visual arts.

The marvelous provides the most complete manifestation of a Surrealist aesthetic philosophy, because, Breton states

in the First Manifesto, "the marvelous is always beautiful, anything marvelous is beautiful, and in fact only the marvelous is beautiful." Signifying an almost miraculous rupture in the natural order, the marvelous was essentially a challenge to rational causality. Louis Aragon, in his important text "La peinture au défi" (1930), is even more emphatic in his attitude toward the marvelous; he defines it as the "refusal of *one* reality, but also of the development of a new relationship, a new reality liberated by that refusal," and declares that "it is Surrealism's *duty* [which he characterizes in specifically ethical terms] to make the point of the marvelous" (1970). It is only in the miraculous negation of the real that a synthesis or conciliation of the real and the marvelous can—and must—occur.

According to Breton, the marvelous, in the form of convulsive beauty, was produced in the confusion of animate and inanimate (veiled-erotic), or in the sudden stop of something that ought to be in motion, something that has been taken out of its normal flow of existence, or the arrested motion of a body become image (fixed-explosive). Its effects were also produced by the found object or found verbal fragment that, though part of the external, material world, carries a message informing the recipient of his own desire, and thus acts as a sign of that desire—the marvelous, in other words, is also an effect of the Surrealist notion of objective chance.

These notions—the marvelous, objective chance, and convulsive beauty—held in common their capacity to provide access to the unconscious. It is, indeed, the unconscious and its mechanisms that most interested Surrealists: Breton alleged in *Surrealism and Painting* that art would refer to a "purely interior model" or would cease to exist. Defining Surrealist *visual* art according to an understanding of the poetic image, and thus as a hypnogogic vision or upwelling of the unconscious in the mind's eye, he insisted that the job of the Surrealist artist was to reproduce faithfully that image, whether by automatism or dream transcription, making all attempts to bypass the rationalizing structures of thought. To a certain degree, Breton was resuscitating the premises of an outmoded realism, in which painting was understood to be a window onto a parallel reality, and in which the image is thought to exist a priori. At the same time, however, he declared perception to be wholly subjective and recognized the role of the unconscious in molding an individual's perception of reality according to secret desires and buried memories, and by doing so effectively critiqued the premises of realism.

It must be made clear, however, that the Surrealists' interest in psychoanalysis, and especially Sigmund Freud's version of it, was not simply on the level of the motif; rather than a superficial metaphorization of Freudian thought, what the Surrealists sought—and, for the most part, achieved through its various techniques—was a way of structuring representation according to psychic operations of dreaming, a poetic understanding of the *operations* and not just the content of the unconscious. In order to explore the mechanisms at work in the unconscious, the Surrealists explored the language of dreams and the process of dream work; however, Surrealism's use of psychoanalysis was not diagnostic but poetic, focusing rather on the aesthetic and critical potential of this new psychology.

Of these psychic processes, the one that seems to explain much Surrealist practice—artistic and extra-artistic—is that of the uncanny. Freud's concept of the uncanny (translated from the German *unheimlich*) is all that is not "homely" or "familiar"; it is the return of a familiar phenomenon (image or object, person or event) made strange by repression. Its primary effects are threefold: first, an indistinction between the real and the imagined; second, a confusion between animate and inanimate; and third, a replacement of physical reality by psychic reality. All three effects are basic to the Surrealist project—the Freudian uncanny is simply another way of thinking or describing the Surrealist idea of the marvelous.

In this understanding of the psychoanalytic structure of Surrealist practice, explored most extensively by the art historian Hal Foster (1993), the marvelous as convulsive beauty is seen as the uncanny confusion between animate and inanimate states, and the marvelous as objective chance is seen as an uncanny reminder of the compulsion to repeat. Brassaï's untitled photograph of 1933, in which a woman's torso is seen from behind and cropped such that it could be mistaken for a phallus, or Man Ray's photograph *Explosante-fixe* (1934), in which a dancer in the throes of a rhythmic frenzy is stopped, crystallized, by the click of the photographer's shutter in an unnatural state of limbo between life and death, are both examples of the uncanny logic of convulsive beauty. In these cases, the animate approaches the inanimate, and, in Foster's words, "not only natural form and cultural sign but also life and death become blurred" (1993).

It would be a mistake, however, to concentrate solely on the structural conditions of the Surrealist work of art in one's analysis of Surrealism, for this interest in psychoanalysis and the operations of dreaming also played a role in determining the artist's approach to—or moral stance toward—the marvelous. In other words, there was an interest on the part of many Surrealists, including artists, in speaking from the place of the unconscious, and in inhabiting madness, rationalism's ultimate destabilizer. Even the notions of convulsive beauty and objective chance can be seen in this light, for the ultimate goal of both these phenomena was to produce shock, a route to the unconscious related to hysteria, and thus a simulation of madness itself.

Max Ernst's description of his discovery of collage ("One rainy day in 1919, . . . I was struck by the obsession which held under my gaze the pages of an illustrated catalogue" [1948]) makes clear that the operations of the uncanny not only structure the collages themselves, but played a part in Ernst's own obsessional fascination with the catalog of outmoded illustrations that provoked a succession of hallucinatory visions in him. In Ernst's description of his discovery of frottage, there is an uncanny sense of the compulsion to repeat, because this memory is almost identical to his memory of the birth of collage:

> On the tenth of August, 1925, an insupportable visual obsession caused me to discover the technical means which have brought a clear realization of this lesson of Leonardo. . . . I was struck by the obsession that showed to my excited gaze the floor-boards upon which a thousand scrubbings had deepened the grooves.
>
> (Ibid.)

In both descriptions, Ernst refers to a childhood memory of his father on the occasion of Ernst's own conception; one sees the eruption of the past in the present as Ernst returns (compulsively?) to an unresolved, disturbing, and clearly sexually charged experience of his childhood—a primal fantasy—which he has contained and repressed, and presents it as the starting point of his creative activities.

Perhaps no other artist better exemplifies this desire to speak from the place of not merely the unconscious but of madness itself than Salvador Dalí. Dalí's paranoiac-critical method of painting took Breton's and Paul Éluard's experiment in *The Immaculate Conception*, in which the poets attempted to simulate various states of madness in order to demonstrate the fluid boundaries between sanity (rationality) and insanity (irrationality), one step further. Paranoiac-criticism attempted to reproduce paranoiacs' ability to systematically interpret the world through the imposition of their own desires and to make other people believe in the reality of their impressions. The double image of Dalí's paranoiac-critical paintings was described by him as "a representation of an object that is also, without the slightest physical or anatomic change, the representation of another entirely different object, the second representation being equally devoid of any deformation or abnormality betraying arrangement" (1930). The number of images that could be projected onto a single form was limited only by the degree of paranoiac capacity. Using this method, Dalí actively sought "to systematize confusion and thus to help discredit completely the world of reality" (ibid.) because it allowed the artist continually to call into question the stability and intransitory nature of images in the external world.

Ernst's canvas *Surrealism and Painting* (1942) introduces a final problematic into this discussion of Surrealist aesthetics. It represents a fantastic, many-headed bird of monstrous proportions and uncertain anatomy, working on a small automatist canvas, paintbrush in hand. What is striking about Ernst's canvas, which promises through its title to make clear the uneasy relation between painting and Surrealism, is that the canvas on which Ernst's bird works is the least interesting aspect of the image. Ernst's work points out

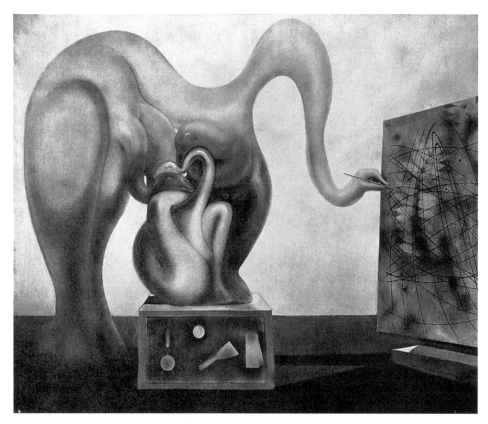

SURREALISM: Surrealism and the Visual Arts. Max Ernst, *Le Surrealisme et la Peinture* (1942), oil on canvas, 76 3/4 × 91 3/4 in.; private collection. (Copyright 1998 by the Artists Rights Society, New York/ADAGP, Paris; photograph courtesy of Avery Architectural and Fine Arts Library, Columbia University, New York; used by permission.)

the element of Surrealism that makes all traditional categories of formalism, connoisseurship, style, or perhaps even aesthetics, inappropriate for an effective understanding of the movement: in Surrealist art, the art object is not the end but the beginning of the Surrealist experience. The Surrealist work of art was not just the record or reproduction of the artist's contact with his or her unconscious; it was evidence of the artist's psychic state, which could be analyzed after the fact to reveal deep desires, and a tool by which the viewer could also experience that sublime state of pure thought, unfettered by rationalizing controls of perception.

Ultimately, however, one must return to Breton's Manifesto of 1924, in which he declares Surrealism outside any moral or aesthetic consideration, and to Naville's original objection to the idea of a Surrealist visual art, which claims the inadequacy of painting to capture "the street, kiosks, automobiles, screeching doors, lamps bursting the sky . . .": in both cases, the authors declare aesthetics to be obsolete—Breton because of his objection to Enlightenment thought, Naville because of his insistence on the synthesis of life and art in the face of twentieth-century spectacle culture. How, then, to map an aesthetic program for a movement whose most radical potential was found in its understanding of the

inseparability of life and art rather than in a removal of art into an aesthetic realm, and which was, despite its claims, highly aestheticized?

BIBLIOGRAPHY

Aragon, Louis. "Challenge to Painting." In *Surrealists on Art*, edited by Lucy R. Lippard, pp. 36–50. Englewood Cliffs, N.J., 1970. Originally published in March 1930 as "La peinture au défi."

Breton, André. *Surrealism and Painting.* Translated by Simon Watson Taylor. New York, 1972. Originally published in 1965 as *Le surréalisme et la peinture.*

Dalí, Salvador. "L'âne pourri." *Le surréalisme au service de la révolution* 1 (1930): 9–12.

Ernst, Max. *Max Ernst: Beyond Painting; and Other Writings by the Artist and His Friends.* New York, 1948.

Fer, Briony. "Surrealism, Myth and Psychoanalysis." In *Realism, Rationalism, Surrealism: Art between the Wars,* edited by Briony Fer et al., pp. 170–249. New Haven, 1993.

Foster, Hal. *Compulsive Beauty.* Cambridge, Mass., 1993.

Greenberg, Clement. "Surrealist Painting." In *Clement Greenberg: The Collected Essays and Criticism,* vol. 1, edited by John O'Brian, pp. 225–231. Chicago, 1986. Originally published in *The Nation,* nos. 12 and 19 (August 1944).

Krauss, Rosalind E. "The Photographic Conditions of Surrealism." In *The Originality of the Avant-Garde and Other Modernist Myths,* pp. 87–118. Cambridge, Mass., 1985.

Krauss, Rosalind E. *The Optical Unconscious.* Cambridge, Mass., 1993.

Krauss, Rosalind E. and June Livingston. *L'amour fou: Surrealism and Photography.* New York, 1985.

Kuspit, Donald. "Surrealism's Re-vision of Psychoanalysis." In *Psychoanalytic Perspectives on Art*, vol. 3, edited by Mary Mathews Gedo, pp. 197–209. Hillsdale, N.J., 1985.

Lippard, Lucy R., ed. *Surrealists on Art.* Englewood Cliffs, N.J., 1970.

Mundy, Jennifer. "Surrealism and Painting: Describing the Imaginary." *Art History* 10.4 (December 1987): 492–508.

Nadeau, Maurice. *The History of Surrealism.* Translated by Richard Howard. New York, 1965; reprint, Cambridge, Mass., 1989.

Rubin, William S. *Dada and Surrealist Art.* New York, 1968.

Rubin, William S. *Dada, Surrealism, and Their Heritage.* New York, 1968. Exhibition catalog, Museum of Modern Art.

Spitz, Ellen Handler. *Museums of the Mind: Magritte's Labyrinth and Other Essays in the Arts.* New Haven, 1994.

ARUNA D'SOUZA

Surrealism and Literature

The question is probably *not* whether Surrealism occupies, in the literature of the twentieth century, the central place held in the visual arts of the twentieth century, according to most critics, by Cubism; for that can be, and generally is, answered in the positive. The question is, rather, the more meaningful one about why this should be so.

The easy answer is that automatism, the freeing of the mind by the unthinking tracing of a text or a drawing, has itself to be examined. As it is, the history of automatism, even within Surrealism, is not untroubled. At one point, even Surrealism's leader, André Breton, will allege automatic writing to have been a catastrophe. (For those who have played the games associated with it, even the deservedly celebrated Exquisite Corpse, they can find themselves full of repetition, triviality, and—worst of all—fakery. Each human mind has its obsessions and its limited vocabulary: it is these drawbacks that tend to dominate, in the long run, the material that the "unguided" and unthinking mind is supposed so freely to pour forth.) It is not this technique or any other that in the long run accounts for the tremendous impact that Surrealism has had, and continues to have, on the contemporary mind and its productions. Rather, it is a basic and remarkably *serious* optimism.

It is often said that Dada, the movement that originated in 1917 in Zurich, was based in the Cabaret Voltaire, and spread to Berlin and Hannover before coming to Paris with some of its adherents, is generally negative and anarchic, and that Surrealism is its more organized and more positive side. It is certainly true that Tristan Tzara, Hugo Ball, and Richard Huelsenbeck, the papas of Dada, were ecstatically negative, reacting to the militaristic endeavors around them with mockery and to everything organized with scorn, all of them being presidents of Dada, for example. It is true that Tzara called on the Dadas and those who would join them in their poetics and politics to befoul all the embassies and places of authority, shitting in bright colors on everything

everywhere. He and his cohorts chose to race down the mountains of built-up sentimentality like a vivid poison, purging the veins of all the slow-moving emotions that would, like so much chocolate, block the clarity of the dynamic nay-saying Dada intellect. All his notes on art and on poetry confirm this rapidity and this joyous destruction. His notes on Negro art and his importation into his poetry and thought of the "primitive" impulse and of the particular sophistication of African art play the same role for Dada and, subsequently, for Surrealism as does African art for Cubism.

It is equally true that Tzara's image of the yes and the no meeting on street corners like grasshoppers is taken over in Breton's formulation of the contraries meeting and communicating—as in the famous image of and theorization of communicating vessels in the book by the same name. That particular meeting of contraries has a double origin, for it appears also in the contemporaneous writings of the "Cubist" Pierre Reverdy, in the article "The Image," appearing in both French and English in Reverdy's 1917 publication *Nord-Sud,* North-South like directions of the subway line. The two elements of the image, says Reverdy, must be taken from different and opposing realms in order for an illumination or shock to take place. Breton will develop this seed into a full-blown theory of the meeting of day and night, of life and death, of up and down, so that reality and dream combine in a kind of Hegelian synthesis of thesis and antithesis.

Guillaume Apollinaire, a great poet and terminologist, who himself wanted to be called a Futurist, but who, when he was discouraged by Filippo Tommaso Marinetti in this endeavor, called his movement Orphism, coined the term *Surrealism* in his make-more-babies satire *The Breasts of Tiresias.* It stuck to what was originally to be called superrealism, but ended up as Surrealism, because the former term grazed too closely on the land of the spiritual. Surrealism, as it finally develops, is authentically antireligious: at one point, the "truest" gesture of a Surrealist was not to go down into the street and shoot the first passerby—a sentiment briefly flirted with—but to spit at passing priests. There was even a hero of this heroic gesture, and Benjamin Péret, Breton's most loyal and long-enduring sidekick, is photographed in such a heroic stance. In any case, superrealism turns into Surrealism, and Surrealism, influenced by German Romanticism and by French poets such as Charles Baudelaire and Arthur Rimbaud, and the odd Uruguayan Lautréamont—author of the image of the sewing machine and the umbrella meeting on the dissection table and a proponent of collective writing—defined at the start as having to do with this automatism of writing and drawing and speaking, gradually deepens.

In the beginning, a sentence was heard tapping on the window of Breton's brain. With Philippe Soupault, he wrote out a series of these automatic givens and called them *Les champs magnétiques* (1919; Magnetic Fields), and he imagined, superbly, how humans are soluble in their own thought: an odd version of idealism, touching also on the material world, which undergoes a "crisis of the object." The *Surrealist Manifesto* of 1924 formulates the idea of automatism and the freeing of the spirit. The initial enthusiasm was great, in all the endeavors: automatic writing, hypnotic sleep and texts, dream transcriptions, public performances. The major Surrealists, along with Breton, their leader with the mane of hair, the serious stance, and the charismatic personality, abounded in dramatic gestures and undertakings, desirous of changing the mental world the way Marxism was to change the political world and the world of the mind in the way Rimbaud wanted to—in a sense, especially the latter sense, it did so.

Under the political impulse, the journal of the Surrealists, *La révolution surréaliste,* changes its name to *Le surréalisme au service de la révolution,* and there is a period of association with the Communist Party. Then Surrealism as such separates from the party as such, and affiliates with Leon Trotsky in Mexico, where Breton and his wife Jacqueline Lamba the painter, visit and where Breton and Trotsky write a *Manifesto for an Independent Art* (although, for political reasons, the manifesto is signed by Breton and Diego Rivera). As the years go on, there are dissociations (Louis Aragon and Paul Éluard remain with the Communist Party), banishments (Robert Desnos for having a job), disillusions and uncertainties, as with all movements. The *Second Surrealist Manifesto* of 1930 speaks of all this, and has a sermonizing air about it. By the time Breton writes *Prolegomena to a Third Surrealist Manifesto,* the movement has hardened and become both less flexible and less interesting. When Breton and others go to Marseille for shelter during the war, with the aid of Varian Fry, and then to New York, where they start the journal VVV, after a brief association with the journal *View,* the movement changes character. Breton was never to learn English, and so his relation to the non-French world has a flavor of otherness to it; when he returns to France after the war, Tzara lectures against him in the Sorbonne; the group has a coterie of younger members, and gradually becomes more aesthetic, even mystical, than revolutionary.

But always, and more than most groups, during the early or heroic period of the 1920s, and even later, to its end, Surrealism really grouped. In the various cafés the group patronized, they would assemble every day in the late afternoon, Breton with his Mandarin curaçao, most of the others following in his wake, and undertake organized discussions. The *ordering* Breton favored is what springs to the eye: the games played were played to a purpose. From the Game of Truth, aimed at releasing all prudery about sexual matters by questions of the most intimate sort (when, how often, what position, etc.), to the game of the Exquisite Corpse, play was aimed at release, but also at serious construction

by the collective of something that would reveal what social and intellectual habit could not. Thus, in the Exquisite Corpse, the first player writes a noun on a piece of paper and folds the paper so that the subsequent entries will be only attached by a hidden and not an obvious logic. The second player places an adjective on the folded paper, folds it again, the third puts down a verb, the fourth another noun, and the fifth an adjective again, so that a French sentence emerges fresh and of a kind unlikely to be available to the waking deliberate mind: the name comes from the first game played—"The Exquisite Corpse Will Drink the New Wine." The results in the visual realm were oddly delightful: three, four, or five players would construct a whole by folding the paper over, leaving just a connecting line for the next part, defined in advance: a head, a neck, a middle, legs, and feet, depending on the number of players, or then an umbrella, a trunk, and various other elements, with ribbons stringing it all out: variations are endless. The point, of course, is the illogical and marvelous connection made without the working mind. This is the ludic equivalent of the marvelous in everyday life, in which an object in the outside world responds to a question one did not know one had.

Part of the particular fascination of Surrealism for present readers has to do with moral and political issues related to aesthetics. For example: in a restaurant, a waiter drops his purse. Should the Surrealist group return it, or is that a bourgeois gesture? How does a group react to a chance event? Another example: with Claude Lévi-Strauss and Roger Caillois, Breton examines a Mexican jumping bean. What makes it jump? Do they open it, do they leave it closed and simply speculate about it, or do they, as Breton later says he suggested, use their wits at speculating about it and then open it at the end? What should be, in short, the attitude of the artist or the writer toward the chance event and the marvelous? What is certain is that the high points of emotion and imagination are to be cherished above deadening daily happenings and customs.

What survives from Surrealism, apart from the visual art (generally agreed to be less powerful than the written), is a kind of group spirit and group vibrancy, as well as some remarkable writings. Heavily influenced by Sigmund Freud, whom Breton disappointingly visited, with neither quite understanding the other (see the texts at the end of *Communicating Vessels*), the various endeavors of the Surrealist imagination—from the short-lived Office of Surrealist Dream Research, staffed by Antonin Artaud among others, to the novels of Aragon and Desnos, to the lyric essays of Breton and the great poems of Éluard, and the aesthetic writings of Aragon, Georges Limbour, and others—are often masterpieces. One of the most mind-blowing is the attempt by Aragon and Éluard to simulate the writing of various mental derangements: *The Immaculate Conception,* these texts are called. Another is the collective three-person poetry of Breton, René Char, and Éluard, called *Slow Down*, or *Ralentir travaux*. Among the more remarkable speculative texts by Breton, *Communicating Vessels* stands out, together with his lyric meditations on love (*Nadja* and *L'amour fou* [Mad Love]). In *Nadja*, the fact that the author of so many invocations to madness should have been, as he avows himself, "unable to love Nadja," the madwoman, remains as valuable and disturbing evidence of how the mind and reality do not always fit. In *L'amour fou*, Breton's madly loved wife leaves him after the glorious early days, so that the final pages, a letter to his small daughter, express both the hope that she will be "madly loved" and the sad certainty that sublime love and the "sublime point" in which, so famously, all the contraries were to meet could be pointed out but not lived in, any more than the "crystal house" of complete transparent truth that Breton had believed for a moment he could inhabit. *Arcane 17*, the written account of the finding of a new love and a new kind of peaceful accord between desire and actuality, is a lyric evocation of the Gaspé Peninsula in Canada, and of what Surrealism in its late period can do, more calmly, in the mind. It is here that Breton invokes Mélusine the mermaid, the power of the woman-child singing forever in the imagination of man, the power of the irrational and the unmilitary that could, were it given a chance, undo the warring instinct in the heart of man.

Aragon's early novels are nothing short of brilliant: *Anicet ou le Panorama;* (1936; Anicet or the Panorama), a spoof on the art world, leads to the famous invocation of the architectural and mental glassed-in wandering place or *passage* dwelled on by Baudelaire and Walter Benjamin, in Aragon's unforgettable *Paysan de Paris;* (1926; The Peasant of Paris). The strange and compelling prose of Desnos in *Deuil pour deuil* (Grief for Grief) and *La liberté ou l'amour!;* (1993; Freedom or Love!) remains as testimony to a moment, lasting, and promising still.

[*See also* Benjamin, *article on* Benjamin and Surrealism; Dadaism; *and* Play.]

BIBLIOGRAPHY

Primary Sources

Aragon, Louis. *The Peasant of Paris.* Translated by Simon Watson Taylor. London, 1971; reprint, Boston, 1994.

Breton, André. *Nadja* (1928). Translated by Richard Howard. New York, 1960.

Breton, André. *Communicating Vessels* (1932). Translated by Mary Ann Caws and Geoffrey Harris. Lincoln, Nebr., 1990.

Breton, André. *Mad Love* (1937). Translated by Mary Ann Caws. Lincoln, Nebr., 1987.

Breton, André. *Conversations: The Autobiography of Surrealism* (1952). Translated by Mark Polizzotti. New York, 1993.

Breton, André. *Manifestoes of Surrealism* (1962). Translated by Richard Seaver and Helen R. Lane. Ann Arbor, 1969.

Breton, André. *Poems of André Breton: A Bilingual Anthology.* Translated and edited by Jean-Pierre Cauvin and Mary Ann Caws. Austin, 1982.

Breton, André. *Œuvres complètes.* 2 vols. Edited by Marguerite Bonnet, Étienne-Alain Hubert, José Pierre, Marie-Claire Dumas, and Philippe Bernier. Paris, 1988–1992.

Works on Breton

Balakian, Anna. *André Breton: Magus of Surrealism.* New York and Oxford, 1971.

Balakian, Anna, and Rudolf Kuenzli, eds. *André Breton Today.* Iowa City, 1989.

Caws, Mary Ann. *André Breton.* Rev. ed. New York, 1996.

Polizzotti, Mark. *Revolution of the Mind: The Life of André Breton.* New York, 1995.

Other Sources

Balakian, Anna. *Surrealism: The Road to the Absolute.* Rev. enl. ed. New York, 1970.

Caws, Mary Ann. *A Metapoetics of the Passage: Architextures in Surrealism and After.* Hanover, N.H., 1981.

Caws, Mary Ann. *The Surrealist Look: An Erotics of Encounter.* Cambridge, Mass., 1997.

Caws, Mary Ann. *The Surrealist Painters and Poets.* Cambridge, Mass., 1997.

Chénieux-Gendron, Jacqueline. *Surrealism.* Translated by Vivian Folkenflik. New York, 1990.

Gershman, Herbert S. *The Surrealist Revolution in France.* Ann Arbor, 1969.

Matthews, J. H. *Surrealism and the Novel.* Ann Arbor, 1966.

Nadeau, Maurice. *The History of Surrealism.* Translated by Richard Howard. New York, 1965; reprint, Cambridge, Mass., 1989.

Philbrick, Jane, ed. *Return of the Cadavre Exquis.* New York, 1993.

MARY ANN CAWS

SYMBOL. *See* Cassirer; Goodman; Langer; Metaphor; Semiotics; *and* Symbolism.

SYMBOLISM. By evoking a forest of symbols in a sonnet, "Les Correspondances," Charles Baudelaire launched a poetic terminology of which he never suspected the consequences. It was a simple sonnet on relationships between mental states and the world of nature; but in the last six lines, a shift occurs. Baudelaire initiated a language that integrated the spiritual and the material into single images that appealed to several of the senses in a synaesthetic manner. Although principally a Romantic poet, in his major work, *Les fleurs du mal*, Baudelaire left a number of poems that create the conjunction of the mind and the senses that, without recourse to the supernatural, expand the enjoyment and range of sensual realities ad infinitum. Some of his symbols were to become a springboard for the poets of the later decades of the nineteenth century.

Literary historians and critics recognize Symbolism as a literary movement that creates a cenacle in France around 1885–1886. Its theories are illustrated in a flurry of poems appearing in special journals such as *La revue wagnerienne, La plume, La vogue, Vers et prose,* and *Décadance.* Paul Verlaine and Stéphane Mallarmé form the axis of Symbolist direction. A decade earlier, Verlaine had written a manifesto-poem, "L'art poétique," in praise of ambiguity and musicality. But Mallarmé's theories had more precise aesthetic principles: a poem must not narrate or describe but evoke little by little an unnamed object or mood. He proposed two ways of arriving at relationships between the poet's inner world and the objective exterior world. One sprang from an inner mood, undefined, which was projected onto an object, figure, or landscape; the other direction emanated from a concrete object whose effect on the poet gradually penetrated him and aroused an inner state of being. Synaesthesia was no longer a promise of supernal experience but a strictly human possibility dependent on verbal achievement. Mallarmé became the mentor of the group, which gathered at his home every Tuesday between 1885 and 1895. Mallarmé's disciples were a generation younger than he and have become less prominent with the passage of time than in their own era. Those poets and novelists in the group who did not reach beyond the decadent ambience of the "Belle Époque" remained representative of a limited cultural moment rather than emerging as avant-garde innovators. But they elaborated on Verlaine's and Mallarmé's precepts and gave the movement aesthetic dimensions. In the coterie were Gustave Kahn, who liberated French poetry from the alexandrine, which had dominated it for four centuries; René Ghil, who tried to establish a correlation between instrumental sounds and associable combinations in poetic language; the Greek Jean Moréas, who proliferated classical settings for Symbolist poetry; and two Americans, Francis Vielé-Griffin and Stuart Merrill, both brought up in France, who became strong proponents of free verse in French poetry. Rubén Darío passed through the experimental climate of Parisian Symbolism and took it back to Latin America to incorporate its concepts into Hispanic modernism. The first generation of Symbolists explored synaesthetic effects, tried to strengthen the bonds between literature and music, and used the language of ambiguity to suggest the indeterminism of meaning that music has. The Symbolists adopted Richard Wagner as their patron saint because he had promoted the alliance of music and art, and subsequently the coordination of all the arts into closer unity. In the waning years of the nineteenth century, Symbolism spread to international proportions in both its philosophical and its literary dimensions. It crystallized the post-Darwinian existential shake-up relating to questions of origin and destiny, human necessity and objective chance. As the uncertainties of the human condition were compounded and human values ceased to be *givens,* the poet searched through the use of certain tropes for a language to express the uncertainties and concern over the evanescence of human life and over the survival of its imprint through the permanence of the arm forms; Symbolist writing became recognizable globally and outlived its emblematic messages. It also found structures that spread from poetry to the other genres. Proceeding from a nonnational grouping in Paris, the movement spread all over Europe and into the Western Hemisphere. It had its apogee in the first three decades of the twentieth century. Symbolist literature became a body of writings integral to a profound philosophical crisis in which poesis became a conduit to a substitute universe.

Although French literary historians mark the end of the Symbolist movement in the 1890s, in the long view Mallarmé's theories had their aesthetic and philosophical impact on the major poets and dramatists of the early part of the twentieth century both in Europe and in other parts of the world.

Beyond these specific historical boundaries, there occurs an aesthetic evolution that has wider scope. Symbolism's more permanent permeation contradicts the general notion that it is the tail end of Romanticism. The basic problem for Mallarmé was how to suppress the overt "I" from poetry, so dominant in Romanticism, and yet to filter the subjectivity of the poet into the poem. Symbolism also reflects an entirely different ontology and its ontology creates a new function for poetic discourse. Although through Baudelaire, the Symbolists made use of Swedenborgian language, their perspective was totally different. Emanuel Swedenborg said: "Everything that springs from the spiritual world is called 'correspondences.'" Romanticism, which espoused this Christian sense of duality, made of poetry the reflector both of the subjectivity of the writer, expressed through the personal "I," and the image of a supernal world. It developed the Swedenborgian forest of symbols, such as flowers, soaring birds, meaningful gardens, boats, veils, fountains, and Promethean figures in search of the divine. The symbols on earth had direct meanings (correspondences) in heaven. The Symbolists often used the same symbols in totally opposite contexts. Their correspondences eliminated the sacred and emphasized relationships between human states and nature.

In the distortion of the Romantic image, the Symbolists developed an internationally recognizable series of key images of their own. The obvious similarities that arose from the interchange among poets created a linguistic code intended to suggest the ephemeral quality of being, the purity toward which humans aspire, and the putrefaction that awaits them. The swan, beautiful in its solitude and state of exile, had been previously evoked by Baudelaire in a famous poem by that name, a figure identified as an inhabitant of land, sea, and sky, but a stranger on all three planes, representative of the poet's uncomfortable position on all the common spaces of existence. Mallarmé's swan poem describes the swan metonymically and does not name it until the end of his poem, "Le vierge, le vivace et le bel aujourd'hui"; the image of the creature's wings trapped in an ice-cold lake is not overtly associated with classical references of alienation, and refers more implicitly to the poet without direct self-identification.

Other flying creatures, from seagulls to fireflies, images of solitary parks, vacant mansions, a wide range of musical instruments, pale virgins fearful of life, all contribute to suggest the "daily tragic," the precarious human condition in the process of losing confidence in divine assistance. Poets searched not for the blue flower of Romanticism but for Mallarmé's "absent" one "from all bouquets," boats run into dry dock, lakes become stagnant pools, green valleys become glaciers, the wasteland that T. S. Eliot was eventually to use as the title of his major poem.

The cult of imagery had a direct effect on a coterie of American poets who called themselves "imagists," but it left a much more important mark in aesthetics in its evolution among the major poets of the twentieth century, such as William Butler Yeats, Paul Valéry, Rainer Maria Rilke, Federico García Lorca, Jorge Gillen, Hugo von Hofmannsthal, Endre Ady, Aleksandr Blok, Andrei Bely, Eliot, and Wallace Stevens. Symbolism in its broader sense developed its ontological dimension, derived principally from Mallarmé, and reflecting, as Stevens said, the "age of inconstancy." It faced the philosophically renewed problem of the artist in society, his position between the subjective and objective worlds, a reexamination of long-fatigued concepts such as reality, representation, and communication. Indeed, it probed the nature of nature itself. Those who saw beyond the mere technical innovations of Symbolism confronted an ever-widening sense of reality that linked the inner dream with outer phenomena; they experimented with alternatives to representation that introduced interference into mimetic reflection so that Narcissus saw not his own image in the water but another, and communication no longer aimed to convey information or even a mood from the writer to the reader or respondent in direct discourse but to instigate in indirect discourse a bond from the writer's perception to the reader's capability to connect the poem with his own mental or moral state or associations. As Eliot remarked, "The ambiguities may be due to the fact that the poem means more, not less, than ordinary speech can communicate."

The symbol became a mediator between the writer and his readers. Symbolist poetry developed a selective system of communication that identifies, without any intention of clarifying, the domains of human perplexity in respect to time and place; it extended its domain beyond the "interpreted universe," in Rilke's words, and it suggested the discontinuity of events and the perceived reality of an indifferent universe. Poets who followed in the path of Mallarmé expressed the disjunction between the cosmos and the human world, by demolishing the relationship in normal linguistic expression between the signifier and the signified. Words absolved of previous relationships to one another were stripped of congealed codes. Mystery was moved from what was "behind the veil" into language itself. The poet generated his symbols but left the responsibility of interpre-

tation to his readers. This kind of occultism differs from traditional gnosticism and hermeticism; it is not a palimpsest, eventually decipherable, but a communication containing multiple, simultaneous connotations.

The hermetic character of Symbolism was intended to create a breach between literature and journalism. Verlaine had ended his "Art poétique" with the line "Et tout le reste est littérature," using *literature* in a derogatory sense to mean *reportage* and to create a cleavage between Symbolist writing and popular literature.

Verlaine's other theories that were adopted by "Symbolist" poetry—ambiguity and musicality—were to be modified in meaning as time went by. When he gave instances of the ambiguous, he used images of vagueness and veiled objects. The words themselves were vague. Later practitioners of Symbolist *écriture* followed Mallarmé's rather than Verlaine's perception of aesthetics and use of language: the words were no longer veiled but very clear and concrete. Ambiguity consisted of a conscious search for an idiom of polyvalences. The enigma was created by the freeing of signifiers from their usual significations, the destruction of clichés, the return from heavy and congealed connotations to original denotation, to etymological meanings, the play between several meanings contained in a single word; their range of substitution of words, principally by projecting the subjectivity of the "poet" into images of other artists and performers such as painters, acrobats, dancers, clowns, weavers. The aesthetic course taken in poetics leading to the most sophisticated forms of Symbolist *écriture* went from analogy to metaphor, from metaphor to metonymy, which opened up the meaning of closed symbols, and finally to the use of single words that could assume the prismatic character of multiple and simultaneous evocations. Valéry remarked that the power of the single word is "limitless." The association of words with one another was not necessarily through meaning but through semantic contagion and phonemic contamination.

The references to the divine and the sacred changed in signification. They passed from a dualistic vision of existence to a monistic one bringing exterior physical nature into complicity with a fictitious cyberspace of the artist's own creation. Language tried to convey archaeological or discontinuous time, which Mallarmé had illustrated in his enigmatic poem *Hérodiade*, the suspension of time or static time best illustrated in the plays of Maurice-Polydore-Marie-Bernard Maeterlinck and coming all the way down to the writings of Samuel Beckett.

Musicality, explicit in Verlaine's "Music above all things", turned from its function as imitation of the sound of music, *la chanson grise,* to that of the process of musical composition. Mallarmé's understanding of the parallel was not confined to the creation of a mood but in making poetry that is "architectural and premeditated," the result not of vague inspiration but conscious strategy, composed of specific, calculated annotation like musical composition, which avoids explicit meaning but challenges the receiver's imagination and elicits various interpretations of the uncertainty of meaning that it carries.

Mallarmé's major poetry was not simply musical, it contained an episteme. Between more and more awareness of the perishable character of human existence and the unreliability of the material world of uncontrollable phenomena, the work of the artist looms as the only immutable refuge. The artist withdraws into his own shell and into the product of his own mind, which carries him into total introspection. Edmund Wilson grouped the generation after that of the coterie of Symbolists under the title *Axel's Castle*. Axel was a character in a play written by a contemporary of the Symbolists, Auguste, comte de Villiers de l'Isle-Adam, who preferred annihilation to the life of ordinary man. "Live?" asked Axel. "Let my servants do that for me."

Eventually, the linguistic devices created new associations that in their turn became congealed into codes that could be decoded because of the frequency of imitative referents, robbing Symbolism of its mystery. Eliot's "objective correlative," evolving from Symbolist correspondences, returned poetry to the demon of allegory. Poetic language became stylized, produced new conventions, the range of interpretations waned, narration returned to poetry, the philosophical elements were no longer self-contained but reverted from verbal alchemy to versified philosophy expressed in direct discourse. Symbolist writing became a signature. It also got confused with *decadent* literature, which identifies with the Symbolists' philosophy but is a direct and overt expression of it.

It took another movement, Surrealism, to make an even more invasive attack on language and establish a deeper association between the inside world of the subconscious and an ever-expanding external universe. Surrealist poets also confronted chance and chaos, but they attempted to show how man could transform his own existence and the work of his imagination if, instead of avoiding the natural hazards, he capitalized on them, making of chance a necessity, replacing a nihilistic philosophy with a more positive view of the challenges of human life. Elsewhere, the subjective "I" returned even more vigorous and overtly collective and universal, particularly in American poetry under the increasing impact of Walt Whitman. By the end of the twentieth century, most poets preferred the descriptive style of ecological expression and the direct confessional discourse of psychiatry.

[*See also* Baudelaire; Mallarmé; *and* Poetics.]

BIBLIOGRAPHY

Abastado, Claude. *Expérience et théorie de la création poétique chez Mallarmé.* Paris, 1970.
Balakian, Anna. *The Symbolist Movement: A Critical Appraisal* (1967). New York, 1977.
Balakian, Anna. ed. *The Symbolist Movement in the Literature of European Languages.* Budapest, 1982.
Balakian, Anna. *The Fiction of the Poet: From Mallarmé to the Post-Symbolist Mode.* Princeton, N.J., 1992.
Bertocci, Angelo Philip. *From Symbolism to Baudelaire.* Carbondale, Ill., 1964.
Boon, James A. *From Symbolism to Structuralism: Lévi-Strauss in a Literary Tradition.* New York, 1972.
Bowie, Malcolm. *Mallarmé and the Art of Being Difficult.* Cambridge and New York, 1978.
Bowra, C. M. *The Heritage of Symbolism.* 3 vols. London, 1943.
Cornell, Kenneth. *The Symbolist Movement.* New Haven, 1951.
Cornell, Kenneth. *The Post-Symbolist Period: French Poetic Currents, 1400–1920.* New Haven, 1958.
Decaudin, Michel. *La crise des valeurs symbolistes.* Toulouse, 1960.
Hertz, David Michael. *The Tuning of the Word: The Musico-Literary Poetics of the Symbolist Movement.* Carbondale, Ill., 1987.
Houston, John Porter. *French Symbolism and the Modernist Movement.* Baton Rouge, La., 1980.
Lawler, James R. *The Language of French Symbolism.* Princeton, N.J., 1969.
Michaud, Guy. *Message poétique du symbolisme.* 3 vols. Paris, 1947.
Porter, Lawrence M. *The Crisis of French Symbolism.* Ithaca, N.Y., 1990.
Symons, Arthur. *The Symbolist Movement in Literature.* London, 1899; reprint, New York, 1958.
Weinberg, Bernard. *The Limits of Symbolism.* Chicago, 1966.
Wilson, Edmund. *Axel's Castle: A Study in the Imaginative Literature of 1870–1930.* New York, 1931.

ANNA BALAKIAN

SYNAESTHESIA. The classic view that each of the five senses—touch, sight, hearing, taste, and smell—has its proper and distinct sphere of activity was first formulated by Aristotle (*De anima* II, 6 [418a]; III, 1 [425a–b]), and was reinforced in the early nineteenth century by Johannes Müller's influential physiological law of the "specific nerve energies." But during Müller's own lifetime (1801–1858), several cases of individuals who had the capacity to experience involuntarily two sensations simultaneously as the result of a single stimulus were reported. The phenomenon, which was identified by the adjective *synesthétique* for the first time in a French dictionary in 1872, attracted the attention of many psychologists, especially at first in Germany, Switzerland, and England (Fechner, 1876–1877; Bleuler and Lehmann, 1881; Galton, 1883); the number of identified cases had increased so much by 1890 that the Congrès International de Psychologie Physiologique decided to sponsor a thorough investigation in that year. The heyday of the scientific study of synaesthesia was between about 1880 and 1930; it has only recently become accessible and interesting to neurologists and experimental psychologists again because of the development of more exact and sophisticated techniques of monitoring the activity of parts of the brain (Cytowic, 1993; Harrison and Baron-Cohen, 1994).

It can be no accident that the earliest phase of intense scientific interest in synaesthesia coincides with the European

Symbolist movement for, although there have been reported instances of the synaesthetic operation of taste, smell, and touch, by far the majority of recorded cases have involved sight and hearing, and have therefore been especially accessible to visual and aural art. The most commonly experienced variety of synaesthesia has been colored hearing—originally, it seems, an English term, but more often referred to in its French form, *audition colorée,* in which a particular musical or spoken sound evokes a particular color. Two artists closely associated with Symbolism, the French poet Arthur Rimbaud and the Russian composer Aleksandr Scriabin, provided some of the best-known cases of synaesthetic perception; the Russian nonrepresentational painter Wassily Kandinsky also appears to have possessed the faculty of synaesthesia, and to have been notably sympathetic toward its aesthetic potential. From the point of view of aesthetics, synaesthesia may be seen as having provided a positivist inflection for the ancient and still-persistent concern to engage several senses simultaneously, usually in the context of theater or religious ritual (Schrader, 1969), a concern that, again in the period of Symbolism, involved the demands of coherence implicit in the *Gesamtkunstwerk.* In practice, even the nineteenth-century total artwork was scarcely able to give equality to each of the senses, and its founding father, Richard Wagner, was insistent that his music dramas could best be appreciated with closed eyes. Scriabin's *Prometheus Symphony* (op. 60, 1910/11) was performed in its earliest years without the light accompaniment *(tastiera per luce)* that the composer had written into it, but that, for technical reasons, proved very difficult to supply (Peacock, 1985). Yet, the investigation of the phenomenon of synaesthesia offered the possibility of basing aesthetic coherence on physiology.

Although Aristotle had supposed that it was the function of the various senses to keep the perceptions of the sensible properties of natural objects distinct, he also posited some "common sensibles" that might be perceived simultaneously by more than one sense. The examples he gave were movement, magnitude, and number; but, in the event, he was only able to instance movement, as perceptible to sight and to touch. Conversely, he only gave a single example, yellow bile, of objects whose multiple characteristics were more or less simultaneously apprehended by more than one sense, in this case sight and taste. He was above all anxious to preserve a clear demarcation between subject and object, and this was equally so in his influential suggestion (*De sensu et sensili,* 439b) that the unknown principles of color harmony might be inferred from the known mathematical principles of musical harmony, by assuming that the intermediate colors were all composed of exact numerical proportions of white and black. The many theories of the relationship of colors to musical sounds (for example Immanuel Kant's in the *Critique of Judgment,* sections 14, 51), and the many instruments devised to exemplify this relationship before the late nineteenth century, all started

from this "objective" proportional analogy. The best-known of these instruments, the *clavecin oculaire* of the French Jesuit Louis-Bertrand Castel, which he developed between about 1725 and 1755, but perhaps never made fully operable, became the focus of interest for the debate on the relationship between visual and aural harmonies for more than a century (Franssen, 1991).

The ancient tradition (Vitruvius, *Ten Books on Architecture,* I,i,3) that music was an essential study for the architect because of the geometric proportionality common to both arts had a particularly vital revival in the Italian Renaissance (Wittkower, 1962, Onians, 1984); and it was still capable of elaboration in the Romantic period in England, when Francis Webb extended the fragmentary ideas of the painter Giles Hussey (1710–1788) into a comprehensive theory of the universal relationship of geometric proportion in form and color, in his *Panharmonikon* of 1814 (Gage, 1993). As late as 1888, Georges Seurat's polymathic friend Charles Henry, drawing on the unpublished notes of Leonardo da Vinci, issued his *rapporteur esthétique* (aesthetic protractor), in which all measurable proportions were interiorized as psychological perceptions. It is striking that Seurat's late compositions, painted under the influence of Henry's ideas—*La Parade, Le Chahut,* and *Le Cirque*—unite carefully calibrated line and color with the imagery of music. Another symptom of the period of Symbolism, indeed, in which synaesthetic research was seen to flourish, was that the color-music analogy moved from common proportions to the subjective ground of instrumental color: musical sound was now seen as akin to color not by virtue of their similar harmonic structure but because of its perceived quality, its *timbre,* in German, its *Klangfarbe.* This related the old color-sound analogy far more closely to the newer *audition colorée.*

Rather more common than the evocation of color sensations by pitched (i.e., musical) sounds has been the synaesthetic experience of colored speech. Although whole words, such as numbers and days of the week or months of the year, and even historical periods, have been seen to evoke colors, most reported cases have involved single discrete sounds: consonants or, more frequently, vowels. Rimbaud's sonnet "Voyelles" (1871), with its opening line "A noir, E blanc, I rouge, U vert, O bleu: voyelles" (which should be spoken in the original French, because it is the sound rather than the visual form of the letter that is in question), was introduced into the scientific literature very shortly after its first publication, by Verlaine, in 1883 (Rochas, 1885). But in a note to the poem in "Une saison en enfer" (1873), Rimbaud claimed that he had invented these correspondences in order to open the poetic word to all the senses; and, in "Voyelles," he did indeed introduce metaphors of touch and smell as well as of color.

The early literature on colored hearing tended to treat it as neurologically based and even as pathological, but the most recent investigations, including those by neurologists themselves (Cuddy, 1985, Cytowic, 1993), have emphasized the structural links with the processes of language formation, to which metaphor is intrinsic. This has helped to modify the apparently irreducible lack of agreement about color-sound equivalents among various synaesthetes, which has seemed to some investigators to place it beyond the scope of scientific investigation. As Francis Galton wrote as early as 1883:

> Persons who have colour associations are unsparingly critical. To ordinary individuals one of these accounts seems just as wild and lunatic as another, but when the account of one seer is submitted to another seer, who is sure to see the colours in a different way, the latter is scandalized and almost angry at the heresy of the former.

This understanding of synaesthesia as a particularly vivid and compelling kind of metaphoric structure has brought it closer to the more expansive rhetorical activity of symbolizing, an activity that has similarly—for example, in Jungian psychology—been seen to function at a profound and quasi-biological level.

One of the obstacles to treating color-hearing synaesthesia as a function of rhetoric is that it is commonly found more frequently in children than in adults (Vernon, 1930; Reichard, Jakobson, and Werth, 1949; Marks, 1978). This may be related to the earliest formation of phonemes in infancy, and the perception of letters in early reading (Harrison and Baron-Cohen, 1994); and it is true that a good deal of interest has been shown in the phenomenon of colored hearing by structural phonologists such as Roman Jakobson (Jakobson, 1968). One of the most fascinating cases to be investigated to date has been that of a young multilingual female subject studied by Jakobson in the 1940s (Reichard, Jakobson, and Werth, 1949), who gave one of the most extended accounts of the acquisition of sound-colors:

> As time went on words became simply sounds differently colored, and the more outstanding one color was the better it remained in my memory. That is why, on the other hand, I have great difficulty with short English words like *jut, jug, lie, lag* etc.: their colors simply run together and are obscured by the longer words that stand near them.
>
> I like to play with words. I like to listen to new sound combinations and to arrange them in color patterns. For example, Russian has a lot of long, black and brown words, like Serbian words; in both these languages the combinations of *ya* or *yu* are little sparkling stars. The German scientific expressions are accompanied by a strange, dull yellowish glimmer, the word *English* and many English words are steel blue to my mind. Hungarian with its frequent *cs, zs, cz, sz* twinkles in violet and dark green, while French, the language I love most, is richest in colors, colors that at the same time carry a tone: hence a vivid mental picture when I listen to French.

The investigation of a phonetic basis for colored hearing goes back to Jakobson's association with the Moscow Lin-

guistic Circle in the 1910s, and especially to the writing of Velimir Khlebnikov who, unusually, regarded the correspondence of verbal sounds and colors as a universally understandable language. It can thus be closely related to that search for a universal language of visual form and color by such early nonrepresentational artists as Kandinsky and another associate of Jakobson and Khlebnikov, Kazimir Malevich.

If children have been more prone to synaesthetic experiences than adults, there also seems to be a perceptual asymmetry between the sexes. Although the first substantial collection of case histories of colored hearing, published in 1890, recorded only thirty-nine female subjects among the 134 investigated (Suarez de Mendoza, 1890), modern research has reversed that proportion, finding that in some tests females were two or three times more susceptible to synaesthetic perception than males (Shanon, 1982). It has been suggested that this unbalance may reflect an underlying sex-linked genetic factor (Baron-Cohen et al., 1993), just as color-deficient vision is identifiable in about 2 percent of the male white population, but in less than .03 percent of females.

Rimbaud's Symbolist "derangement of all the senses" had been understood by the previous generation of writers in France as the creation of "correspondences," where, in Baudelaire's sonnet of that title, "Les parfums, les couleurs et les sons se répondent" (Perfumes, colors, and sounds (cor)respond to one another). These sublime and apparently involuntary metaphors had often, in Théophile Gautier, in Baudelaire, and perhaps in Rimbaud himself, been a by-product of experiments with drugs. Depressants such as alcohol and hashish *(cannabis indica)* are well-known stimulants to synaesthetic experiences, just as stimulants such as caffeine inhibit them. These antithetical and characteristic effects of drugs have been interpreted as the result of shifting the emphasis of brain activity from the cortex (the rational brain) to the limbic system (the emotional brain) (Cytowic, 1993). Yet, just as Baudelaire maintained that hashish could only enhance what is already present in the mind, so the increased activity of the limbic brain does not seem to create synaesthetic perception, but simply to facilitate it.

It remains that, although synaesthesia, in its looser sense of metaphor and association (sometimes called "pseudo-synaesthesia"), is very widely experienced in Western societies, in its stricter sense of a wholly involuntary multisensual response to a single stimulus, it seems to be rather rare. One estimate suggests that there may be only a single synaesthete in a hundred thousand of the population (as already noted, synaesthesia is far more common among children than among adults, and among females than among males). This, together with the almost wholly individual character of synaesthetic perceptions—as opposed to a possibly common neurological process lying behind them—makes it at present unlikely to be available to aesthetics conceived as a potentially universal system, even though this seemed to be a distinct possibility when the topic was first introduced into Gustav Theodor Fechner's experimental aesthetics in the mid-nineteenth century, and it remained so until at least the early years of the twentieth.

[*See also* Perception; Psychology of Art; Science and Aesthetics; *and* Symbolism.]

BIBLIOGRAPHY

Baron-Cohen, Simon, John Harrison, Laura H. Goldstein, and Maria Wyke. "Coloured Speech Perception: Is Synaesthesia What Happens When Modularity Breaks Down?" *Perception* 22.4 (1993): 419–426.

Bleuler, Eugen, and K. Lehmann. *Zwangsmässige Lichtempfindungen durch Schall und verwandte Erscheinungen auf dem Gebiete der andern Sinnesempfindungen.* Leipzig, 1881.

Cuddy, L. L. "The Color of Melody." *Music Perception* 2 (1985): 345–360.

Cytowic, Richard E. *The Man Who Tasted Shapes: A Bizarre Medical Mystery Offers Revolutionary Insights into Emotions, Reasoning, and Consciousness.* New York, 1993.

Fechner, Gustav Theodor. *Vorschule der Ästhetik.* 2 vols. Leipzig, 1876–1877.

Franssen, M. "The Ocular Harpsichord of Louis-Bertrand Castel: The Science and Aesthetics of an Eighteenth-Century *Cause Célèbre.*" *Tractrix: Yearbook for the History of Science, Medicine, Technology, and Mathematics* 3 (1991): 15–77.

Gage, John. *Color and Culture: Practice and Meaning from Antiquity to Abstraction.* Boston, 1993.

Galton, Francis. *Inquiries into Human Faculty and Its Development.* London, 1883.

Harrison, John, and Simon Baron-Cohen. "Synaesthesia: An Account of Coloured Hearing." *Leonardo* 27.4 (1994): 343–346.

Jakobson, Roman. *Child Language, Aphasia, and Phonological Universals.* The Hague, 1968.

Marks, Lawrence E. *The Unity of the Senses: Interrelations among the Modalities.* New York, 1978.

Onians, John. "On How to Listen to High Renaissance Art." *Art History* 7.4 (December 1984): 411–437.

Peacock, K. "Synaesthetic Perception: Alexander Scriabin's Color Hearing." *Music Perception* 2 (1985): 483–506.

Reichard, G. A., R. Jakobson, and E. Werth. "Language and Synesthesia." *Word* 5 (1949): 224–233.

Rochas, A. de. "L'audition colorée." *La Nature* 1 (1885); 2 (1885).

Schrader, Ludwig. *Sinne und Sinnesverknüpfungen: Studien und Materialien zur Vorgeschichte der Synästhesie und zur Bewertung der Sinne in der italienischen, spanischen und französischen Literatur.* Heidelberg, 1969.

Shanon, Benny. "Color Associates to Semantic Linear Orders." *Psychological Research* 44.1 (May 1982): 75–83.

Suarez de Mendoza, F. *L'audition colorée: étude sur les fausses sensations secondaires physiologiques et particulièrement sur les pseudo-sensations de couleurs associées aux perceptions objectives des sons.* Paris, 1890.

Tornitore, Tonino. *Scambi di Sensi: Preistorie delle Sinestesie.* Turin, 1988.

Vernon, P. E. "Synaesthesia in Music." *Psyche* 10 (1930): 22–40.

Wittkower, Rudolf. *Architectural Principles in the Age of Humanism.* 3d rev. ed. London, 1962.

JOHN GAGE

T

TAINE, HIPPOLYTE ADOLPHE (1828–1893), French philosopher, historian, and critic. Taine is known as the historian who, immediately after the Paris Commune (1871), started to write the *Origines de la France contemporaine* (1876–1896). He wrote in the most important journals of the time, such as *Le journal de l'instruction publique* and *La revue des deux mondes,* and he published extensively in both philosophy and literary criticism. *Les philosophes classiques du XIXe siècle en France* (1857), and especially *Essais de critique et d'histoire* (1858) and *Histoire de la littérature anglaise* (1863–1864), made him one of the most visible critics in France, and situated him in the camp of the Positivists, as a follower of Auguste Comte. In addition, Taine had an important role in aesthetics, as the author of *Philosophie de l'art* (1865). His position within aesthetics was both the logical extension of his general interest in philosophical systems and history and the result of his first academic position, as professor of aesthetics and art history at the École des Beaux-Arts. What is probably most interesting about Taine today is the contradiction between the classical aim of his whole philosophy of art and the influence of his style on the Symbolist generation of art critics at the end of the century.

Taine was new to the field of art when, in 1864, he was appointed as professor at the École des Beaux-Arts, a position previously held by the architect Eugène-Emmanuel Viollet-le-Duc. It is impossible to separate his aesthetic vision from his whole system in philosophy, literature, and history, where he was perceived as a controversial figure, and a dangerously modern one: his theoretical motto was *race, milieu, moment* (race, social milieu, historical moment), the phrase that gave its deterministic impulse to his monumental *Histoire de la littérature anglaise,* published just before he was appointed to the Beaux-Arts, where he would lecture for twenty years in front of large crowds. Some contemporaries—such as the literary critic Charles-Augustin Sainte-Beuve and the art critic Ludovic Vitet—commented on the paradox that somebody so modern in criticism would embody the classical trend. Vitet was not wrong in considering him as a scholar who could be "a real friend of the Parthenon." In fact, since his opening lecture, the critic, who was, together with Ernest Renan and Émile Littré, the initiator of the new scientific approach to research, insisted on the perfection of Greek sculpture and of Italian Renaissance painting. Taine was obsessed by ques-

tions of Positivist method, and hardly commented on the most discussed artistic topics of the time: his appreciation of Eugène Delacroix comes up once in May 1854 in his correspondence, and once in 1867 in his article "Les beaux-arts en France." This essay is a short fiction envisioning a conversation between Taine himself and an elegant Italian tourist sensitive to the beauty of Renaissance art, and Delacroix is considered as an example of how the moderns are inferior to the ancients for their style; but Taine acknowledged that the Romantic painter powerfully expressed the anguish of the present.

Taine's aesthetics was the result of translating his philosophical and historical framework into the field of art. It placed the ideal of classical beauty within the modern scientific ambition suggested by nineteenth-century physiology, founded on factual and experimental truth, and capable of classifying events according to their "degree of importance." Taine was influenced by Georg Wilhelm Friedrich Hegel's vision of Greek sculpture, but his method was mainly informed by Comte's *Cours de philosophie positive.* Already in 1856, Taine expressed his enthusiasm for Théodore Jouffroys's *Cours d'esthétique,* which he defined in *Les philosophes français du XIXe siècle* as the only book that one could read after Hegel's *Aesthetics.* His vision of Italian Renaissance art and history was indebted to Stendhal's *Histoire de la peinture en Italie.*

Taine's whole aesthetic enterprise, as expressed in his lectures at the Beaux-Arts, first published in his *Philosophie de l'art* in 1865, aimed to "understand the precise conditions and the fixed laws" of the making of art, to define its nature and object, its role and character. Here Taine declared his ambition to consider nothing but *facts* and their causes, to constitute a truly "modern" aesthetics that would be "historical and not dogmatic, capable of reporting laws rather than imposing precepts." That historical approach encompassed a division in chronological periods and national characteristics that structured also his *Voyage en Italie* (1866). Taine adopted the historicist idea that flourishing periods are followed by decay, and therefore that there are periods of great art and of decline. Sculpture in ancient Greece and the art of the Italian Renaissance were the highest artistic productions in human history (two large sections of the *Philosophie de l'art* explore those periods): they both represented the beauty of the human body. The Middle

Ages, on the contrary, is presented as a dark Christian and feudal epoch, when plague, hunger, "universal misery and filth" reigned together with the terror of God. No wonder, for Taine, that its art was sad and gloomy.

Taine was not interested in the philological study of a work's attribution, and his formula was quite simple: history of art depends on history itself, and on the identification of historical periods with economic, political, and cultural characteristics. His conception simplified the Hegelian identity between aesthetics and art history, while his Positivist explanatory system lacked the dynamics of Hegelian dialectics (as has been pointed out by his detractors, such as Péladan in 1906). Taine's aesthetics is the example of a critical model that is rooted outside the medium itself: structural phenomena are considered as the sources of art, which seems, among human activities, the most erratic. The evidence on which he built his sociological system in the fine arts was the same on which, following Comte and Sainte-Beuve, he established his literary history and criticism, centered on the author's biography. A simple chain of causal relations ties an element to another, which Taine called "the larger whole": one work of art is linked to the other works of the same artist; one artist is linked to the school or group of artists in the same country and historical period to which he belongs; and, finally, the group of artists depends on the world surrounding them, which is the same as for the audience.

Works of art and artists are not isolated phenomena. It would be a mistake, for example, to consider Peter Paul Rubens as a unique case, because it would suffice to go to Belgium, and visit the churches of Ghent, Brussels, Bruges, or Antwerp in order to realize that there was a whole group of painters whose talents were similar to his. Dealing with painting in Holland, Taine showed that artists such as Albrecht Dürer, Jan van Eyck, and Hans Holbein existed because of the spirit and the habits of the German race, and because of the national character of Flemish and Dutch art. Taine founded his idea of race on a whole theory of climate, completely in tune with the conceptions of the time, which are also present in aesthetic conceptions very different from Taine's, such as those of Delacroix and Charles Baudelaire. Taine argued that the northern people did not tend toward the ideal but tried to reproduce what existed in nature; they did not concentrate on the sole nude, but, without fear of being trivial, looked for the real in all its aspects, and liked all its elements, such as buildings, landscapes, animals, and costumes.

The idea of nation and national character was shaped from within the historical vision: Taine's history represents fully and exactly what today's conceptions are departing from. In typical nineteenth-century overtones, similar to the narratives of historians such as Augustin Thierry and Jules Michelet, Taine describes the genealogy of races and geographic settlements, together with the physical and mental effects of climate, as preceding any artistic production, which then becomes the visible expression of those elements. Taine's aesthetics is not important today as a set of rules that could inform contemporary research, but as evidence of the historicist-national vision prevailing at the moment it asserted itself and claimed its own modernity within the institution of the École des Beaux-Arts and of the publishing market (namely, Hachette), totally open to the new generation.

Taine's aesthetics is especially interesting to see within the network of contradictions within a supposedly coherent ideology. The "real friend of the Parthenon," who, in a period of intense artistic debates, appreciated the realistic paintings of Constant Troyon, and, as a traveler in London, was suspicious of the enthusiasm for Joseph Mallord William Turner, was unsuspectedly tending to a vision of classicism that had little to do with historical truth. The second chapter of his *Philosophie de l'art*, whose title is "De la production de l'œuvre d'art" (On the Production of the Work of Art), contains this law: "The work of art is determined by the general state of mind and surrounding habits." One of the cases illustrating this theory is Greek art. But the deterministic perspective did not have the dryness of a statistical study: Taine ended up constructing a wonderful fantasy, close to Hegel's judgment on Greek sculpture, and already sketching the classical myth typical of decadent painters and Symbolist art critics. The fable started more or less three thousand years ago, in the unique milieu that was the Greek city-state, in the unique harmony between mind and body that characterized everyday life as well as gods, who had a human physical presence: sculptors could produce such perfect human forms because in the world in which they lived, they could constantly admire beautiful bodies. Page after page, description after description, Taine seems to forget his Positivist distance, and almost sounds like the fin de siècle critic Walter Pater writing on Johann Joachim Winckelmann's vision of ancient Greece: the whole ideal of the nude in art seemed to derive from the beauty of naked young and healthy people freely showing their bodies in athletic exercise and everyday life.

Paradoxically, Taine's aesthetics influenced the Symbolist generation. His teaching, more than confirming his sociology of art, touched those who looked for a type of art criticism completely separated from art history and any historical concern. This astonishing reversal was possible because of Taine's accuracy as a historian who was dutifully presenting periods of decadence as well as periods of splendor, and also because of an inner contradiction within his work where the project of a "philosophy of art" was doubled by another literary genre devoted to the pleasure of describing works of art: voyage literature. Taine's contradiction can be seen as a continuous temptation of blending in his colorful descriptions what his scientific criticism wanted to keep separate: facts of knowledge and facts of feeling. Having identified the Middle Ages as one of the four epochs of European civilization from Greek and Roman antiquity to contemporary industrial democracy, he extensively described art in that period, as well as the beginning of the Renaissance. He therefore emphasized those periods that were not valuable for the classicists, but would matter highly for the decadents and the Symbolists. In *L'art moderne* (1883), Joris-Karl Huysmans attacked Taine's systematic approach, and reversed it in order to establish his own passion for modern painters, the Primitifs, and Gothic cathedrals. Beyond the question of art and history, Taine's taste for descriptions favored the *écriture artiste*, the descriptive talents of such writers and art critics as the brothers Edmond and Jules Huot de Goncourt, Huysmans himself, or Jules Laforgue, who audited Taine's lectures at the Beaux-Arts and was enthusiastic about his presentation of Beato Angelico. Thanks to his descriptions, Taine the art historian produced the rich and ornate prose that would characterize art criticism in favor of Impressionist art. Taine himself, coherent with his abstract historical and philosophical stand, never commented on an Impressionist painter. Nevertheless, in 1889, discussing the Realist painter Édouard Bertin, he contrasted at length the differences between the optical performances of the painters aiming at the precision of design, and those sensitive to the infinite vibrations of color. If the masters of design are judged as achieving the most splendid artistic results, the most intense descriptions are displayed for the Impressionist technique and its nervous sensitivity. The Positivist thinker, who endlessly described the perception of light and color in his psychology masterpiece *De l'intelligence,* offered the model of the physiological explanation of Impressionism that became fashionable among its critics and historians.

[*See also* Symbolism.]

BIBLIOGRAPHY

Works by Taine

Les philosophes français du XIXe siècle. Paris, 1857.
Histoire de la littérature anglaise. 4 vols. Paris, 1863–1864.
Philosophie de l'art. Paris, 1865. After 2d ed. of 1872, 2 vols.
Voyage en Italie. 2 vols. Paris, 1866.
De l'idéal dans l'art. Paris, 1867. After 1882, included in *Philosophie de l'art.*
De l'intelligence. Paris, 1870.
Notes sur l'Angleterre. Paris, 1872.
"Les beaux-arts en France" and "Édouard Bertin." In *Les derniers essais de critique et d'histoire.* Paris, 1894.
H. Taine: sa vie et sa correspondance. 4 vols. Edited by Victor Giraud. Paris, 1902–1907.

Other Sources

Delacroix, Eugène. "Des variations du beau." *La revue des deux mondes* 9 (March 1857): 908–914.
Huysmans, Joris-Karl. *L'art moderne.* Paris, 1883.
Laforgue, Jules. *Œuvres complètes,* vol. 3, *Mélanges posthumes.* Paris, 1903.
Péladan. *Réfutation esthétique de Taine.* Paris, 1906.
Sainte-Beuve, Charles-Augustin. "Entretiens sur l'architecture par Viollet-le-Duc." In *Nouveaux Lundis,* vol. 7. Paris, 1867.
Vitet, Ludovic. "Les arts du dessin en France." *La revue des deux mondes* 54 (November 1864): 92–99.

PATRIZIA LOMBARDO

TAOIST AESTHETICS. *See* Daoist Aesthetics.

TASTE. [*In tracing the history of the concept of taste and its development in aesthetics since the concept first emerged (even before aesthetics itself), this entry comprises two essays:*
     Early History
     Modern and Recent History
The first essay explains the origins of taste and its history up to the eighteenth century, when it becomes a main aesthetic concept, especially in the British tradition. The second essay offers a critique of the concept of taste and at the same time explains the rise and fall of taste in aesthetic theory up through the twentieth century. See also Beauty; Disinterestedness; Food; Perception; Pleasure; Rasa; *and* Sensibilité.]

Early History

The centrality of "taste" as a theoretical concept is part of the rise of modern aesthetics in the eighteenth century. "Taste" extended the empiricist paradigm based on sense to critical practice and aesthetic appreciation. It provided a way to account for the subjective immediacy of aesthetic response in the context of judgment and discrimination. The prominence of the concept in the eighteenth century makes its origins of special interest. Conventional histories of aesthetics trace the concept to seventeenth-century Mannerism. It has classical roots, however, and Renaissance writers on art and art theory anticipate and develop the concept in its modern form.

Aristotle assigned to sense an important position as a starting point for judgment and wisdom. Sense is the immediate element, which in turn leads to memory. Memory makes possible experience, and experience leads to judgment. In the *Metaphysics*, sight is the primary sense, but in *De Anima*, a different priority is given to touch, which is a necessary condition for sentient beings. Aristotle also considers touch as the basis for taste because one can only taste what the tongue can touch. It is possible on these Aristotelian grounds, therefore, for taste to become the most immediate and discriminating sense.

Taste can only become a fully theoretical aesthetic term when the universals of Plato and Aristotle are replaced by the empiricism of the seventeenth and eighteenth centuries. Prior to that point, however, many of the elements were in place. Umberto Eco (1986, p. 110) points out the increasing empiricism of the later Middle Ages, citing Thomas Aquinas (*Summa theologiae*, I,78,4; Comm. *De anima*, III,4,633). Medieval art continued to subordinate sense to transcendent forms represented in traditional iconography, however. One must look to the Renaissance for the expressive emergence of the artist, and with that expression, the increasing dependence on personal factors that ultimately led to a theory of taste.

Among the first to use the metaphor of taste in connection with judgment was Leon Battista Alberti (1404–1472). Alberti regarded taste as a negative concept that undermined rules, however. Leonardo da Vinci (1452–1519) is similarly ambivalent on how the senses are related to judgment. Sense and experiment are important, but they are a means to imitation, not an independent source of knowledge. Much of the High Renaissance reference to sense is still within the Aristotelian mode in that it subordinates the senses to a judgment that operates at a higher level.

Taste comes to be linked directly to judgment and wit in later sixteenth-century Italian writers on art and painting. As the individuality and expressiveness of the artist became central, taste took its place as an indicator of the makeup of the artist and the means of transforming the artist's sense into a form of expression. This appeal to sense moves beyond the reliance of Alberti and Leonardo on sense as a means for artistic imitation. One place that this can be seen is in the shifting importance of illusion. In classical art, illusion had something of the quality of a forbidden fruit. It fascinates, but it also shows the fundamental unreliability of the senses. In the sixteenth century, a fascination with illusion and skill takes a different direction. The classical appeal is to the ability to fool the audience. One has anecdotes such as Zeuxis birds that are deceived and peck the painted fruit. The Renaissance appeal is to sense itself. One is not fooled; the pleasure depends on recognizing the illusion. For example, Sabba di Castiglione (1485–1554) connects decorative illusion with judgment. Theory is moving in the direction of a connoisseurship that connects taste and desire. Desire is a physical appetite, a lack that seeks to be satisfied. What is desired is a product of taste. Individual desire finds its expression in one of the marks of Mannerism, design, which is understood as satisfying an appetite. All of the elements of a theory of taste except the explicit application of the metaphor are present at this point.

The Venetian Paolo Pino's *Dialogue on Painting* (1548) offers an interesting distinction in the way that sense is being promoted by linking color and style as individual expression. Pino's idea was that color should reflect the skill of the artist, bringing honor to those who master its use. This judgment provides the basis for comparing individual painters. Pino's definition of charm as relish made this a matter of taste. The medieval *claritas* as it is found in Aquinas's threefold definition of beauty (integrity, harmony, clarity) is transformed into individual expression.

The emphasis on style as a reflection of individuality is a necessary step in the construction of taste as a critical term. Lodovico Dolce, in the *Dialogo della pittura intitolato l'Aretino* (Venice, 1557) provides an interesting example of how this individuality of expression is incorporated into critical judgments. In defending Raphael's superiority to Michelangelo, Dolce assigned it to a "je ne sais quoi" that fills the mind of the spectator with delight. This "je ne sais quoi" requires an immediacy of sense because it cannot be given a principled formulation. It gives pleasure without depending on anything other than direct contact. Critically, that poses a problem for a classical theory that looked to rules and rational forms. The only principle at work is pleasure, and the "je ne sais quoi" is accessible only to sense. Both source and critical means are sensibles. One is once again led back to contact, touch, and the analogy of taste.

Dolce also provides a link to *maniera*—"manner"—which is important. Dolce regards "manner" as negative—a stylization that subordinates the subject to the artist's manner. But the root of *maniera* is *some* individuality. If it is not the artist's, it is the subject's. The alternative, positive sense stresses the free play that the artist indulges in by his manner, thus developing his own style that exhibits his good taste. The positive sense of "manner" can be illustrated from Giorgio Vasari's *Lives of the Painters* (Florence, 1550). Vasari lists five achievements that advance painting beyond its earlier stage: rule, order, proportion, design, and manner *(regola, ordine, misura, designo, maniera)*. He goes on to define manner as a choice of parts. Although this definition represents manner as a stylized idealization, it also identifies it with a style that cedes the authority for the process to the artist. Without the ability to select, there is no manner, no beautiful figure. Thus, artists compete to develop a style that exhibits more and more detail, more and more of the ideal in concrete form. More is better. Elaboration is a positive move. Above all, the artificial is a product of the judgment of advanced artists. Vasari specifically sees this new style as a move beyond the simplicity of Giotto.

Taste corresponds to the essentially personal nature of a new form of judgment. A striking example is provided by Vasari's description of Jacopo Pontormo. Pontormo painted what he pleased for whom he pleased. Behavior that nowadays seems merely stereotypical of artists struck Vasari as exceptional, and in fact it could only occur in an eccentric such as Pontormo, who shut himself up with a work for years only to produce something so singular that it baffled his contemporaries (the fresco in the Temple of San Lorenzo). Vasari's estimation of that work (which was covered over in the eighteenth century) is thrown back on individual judgment. Something so singular can only be judged directly by the response of each person who sees it. To lose oneself in this way still appears to a Renaissance critic as madness (as it may well have been in Pontormo's case).

Mannerism retained the classical ordering of sense but shifted the emphasis. One of the tenets of Mannerism was that the combination of forms that presented beauty must go beyond mere imitation of nature and even beyond the earlier reliance on idealization. What now appears as elaboration and even distortion was central to the Mannerist desire to exhibit a beauty that could not be found naturally. In his *Dei veri precetti della pittura* (1586 or 1587), Giovanni Battista Armenini added one additional factor to the traditional theories of imitation and illusion: "If Zeuxis had not possessed a unique personal style [*singolar maniera*] in addition to his great diligence, he would never have been able to harmonize the beautiful individual parts he copied from so many virgins" (1977, p. 160). Armenini effectively connects Mannerist theory and taste by linking style and person. One who has a singular manner—a manner that is unique, individualistic, and not imitative—can unite elements and go beyond imitation, just as one who has a common sense can unite the five senses into a single sensory impression. Armenini's singular manner makes manner into a kind of sense. Style plays the same structural role as a common sense. Because taste is the analogy that worked best for the classical writers, it is a natural move to identify having taste with having the Mannerist style. If such a style, or a response to it, is instinctive, then not only are manner and taste linked, but taste can operate immediately and take on even more of the sense characteristics of its empirical origin.

The primary function of such judgment was productive. The final move to an explicitly metaphoric use of taste as a critical and aesthetic term can be located in the Mannerist writers who make explicit the connection between judgment and taste. Federico Zuccaro writes in his *L'idea de' pittori, scultori et architetti* (1607), "Grace is . . . a soft and sweet accompaniment which attracts the eye and contents the taste . . . ; it depends entirely on good judgment and good taste [*gusto*]" (quoted in Blunt, 1940, p. 146). The essentially aesthetic property "grace" is linked to the eye, and good judgment is explicitly identified with a second sense, taste. Zuccaro effectively unites the Aristotelian sense theories in a new way.

Renaissance and seventeenth-century writers evidently found grounds for the metaphoric extension of "taste" not directly in Aristotle but in the classical rhetorical tradition. Both Ernest Robert Curtius and Benedetto Croce cite Cicero and Quintilian as sources for seventeenth-century authors who use *taste* as a critical term (Curtius, 1953, p. 296; Croce, 1922 p. 193). Quintilian says, for example, that "It is no more possible to teach it [judgment/*iudicium*] than it is to instruct the powers of taste and smell" (VI, v, 1–2). But in context, although the analogy is suggested, taste and smell remain just what they were for Aristotle—senses that are lower on the scale of mental operations than the imagination, memory, and reason. It is not clear that either Cicero or Quintilian would be able to import a direct sensible ele-

ment in the way that it came to be applied later. Only when *taste* became critically reflective did it become the dominant critical term that is at once normative and individual.

The final critical assimilation of taste and *maniera* came in the seventeenth century. Balthasar Gracian (1601–1658) is widely acknowledged as the principal source of this critical transformation, but clearly taste was already being used in the necessary sense by earlier Mannerist writers such as Zuccaro and Armenini. Gracian treated taste as something that could be acquired and imitated independently of intellect. In this regard, its character as sense is taken for granted. Metaphorically, taste is a form of judgment and discrimination. It relates directly to Gracian's concept of *agudeza*, "acuteness," which is an essentially prudential principle. Prudentially, the variability of taste leaves the critic or the would-be connoisseur exposed. Knowledge in this case is not Aristotle's higher form but simply knowing what is going to be accepted. Gracian does not mean that vulgar taste will win, but clearly one does not want to be the one who is different. Bad taste is just eccentric taste.

Thomas Hobbes (1588–1679) is roughly contemporary with Gracian and uses *taste* in the same way, though he is much less happy with the moral consequences of such use. Speaking of those who ignore science and retain the philosophy of the schools, Hobbes accuses them of being dependent only on their own taste:

> They make the rules of good and bad, by their own liking and disliking: by which means, in so great diversity of taste, there is nothing generally agreed on; but every one doth (as far as he dares) whatsoever seemeth good in his own eyes, to the subversion of commonwealth.   (Hobbes, 1994, part 4, chap. 46)

Both Hobbes and Gracian take for granted the importance of taste as a sense. In becoming a critical term, sense was transformed into a normative judgment. Good and bad taste are ways of praising and blaming.

Taste was rapidly assimilated into the critical vocabulary of Europe in the later seventeenth century, particularly in France and England. It retains a substantial element of the prudential, personal quality that it had in the Mannerists. For example, Dominique Bouhours, in "The Conversations of Aristo and Eugene" (1671), uses taste with regard to men, who have a certain "je ne sais quoi." The concept of taste finds a particular use in empiricist philosophy after John Locke (1632–1704). Both Anthony Ashley Cooper, earl of Shaftesbury (1671–1713) and Francis Hutcheson (1694–1746) draw on Locke's limitation of knowledge to ideas to locate aesthetic and moral judgment within the individual. If knowledge is conceived of as wholly dependent on ideas and ideas are the product of individual experience, then, they reason, the source of aesthetic ideas must be an aesthetic sense on the model of physical taste. Beauty may remain the nominal object of those ideas, but taste is the sense that alone can make aesthetic judgments.

Taste is also a feeling. Lord Shaftesbury, Hutcheson, and David Hume (1711–1776), most prominently, develop the sentiment of taste into a dominant aesthetic. A taste for something just is the subjective pleasure that one takes in it. Lord Shaftesbury's *Characteristics of Men, Manners, Opinions, Times* (1711) and the *Critical Reflections on Poetry and Painting* of Abbé Jean-Baptiste Du Bos (1719) begin with the indisputable nature of that pleasure and seek to cultivate and explain it. The primary datum is the pleasure itself. Its source is something that operates like an empirical sense to the extent that its operation is natural and automatic. "Internal sense" in the sentimental line is never simply a sixth or seventh sense without qualification, but the pressure of the empiricist model makes it much closer to the external senses than the Aristotelian common sense or the Augustinian and medieval internal sense that acted as a unifying and judging faculty. The sentimentalist line thus takes taste as a hedonistic principle of human nature.

For the sentimentalists, taste alone cannot be trusted. For Lord Shaftesbury, aesthetics becomes the problem of educating and restricting taste. This is a genuine dilemma, because the analogy of taste suggests that although one's taste may change, it is, in its immediate occurrence, beyond dispute. The solutions offered turn on increasing delicacy and discrimination. A more discriminating palate and a finer and more subtle perception are the goals of taste, but in the last analysis, a preference for such refined pleasures is difficult to justify. Lord Shaftesbury clings to classical values and justifies refined taste because it ultimately leads back to and coincides with virtue. Hutcheson is more empirically rigorous and finds the justification in taste's perception of order and purpose. Both also believe that taste is allied to benevolence and offers quantitatively more pleasure when the social and communal virtues are perceived. Lower tastes and selfish tastes are neither as perceptive nor as naturally satisfying according to these forms of sentimentalism as those attested to by classical virtues and benevolence.

Du Bos and Hume are more willing than Lord Shaftesbury and Hutcheson to grant a complete independence to taste. For Du Bos, the audience cannot be wrong. The problems for Du Bos are how to explain and predict taste so that one can be both prudentially with the majority and constructively productive. His explanations include elaborate comparisons on national and even climatic causes. Hume goes much deeper than Du Bos in granting to emotion, passion, and sentiment an epistemological authority. Taste is one element in a thoroughgoing empirical reliance on impressions and ideas. As such, taste is evidential. It discloses regularities in aesthetic and moral responses. Hume looked back to Lord Shaftesbury to link taste with character, but, for Hume, character has no existence apart from its expression in stable forms of moral and aesthetic behavior. When we judge taste, as we inevitably do, we are judging the stable identity that virtue and aesthetic preferences exhibit. Hume

thus founds an aesthetic and moral personhood on sentiment and taste.

The sentimentalist line appeared much too subjective and hedonistic for other empiricists as well as for most neoclassical critics and theologically influenced philosophers. Lord Shaftesbury and Hume tended to be grouped with Bernard Mandeville, whose *Fable of the Bees* (1714–1729) was seen as defending the hedonistic utility of vice. Nevertheless, taste became the dominant term for the more conservative aesthetic philosophers as well. Experience, on its new scientific and empiricist models, displaced Neoplatonic forms of beauty. Taste was either good taste or bad taste, depending on whether it conformed to or differed from the naturally founded artistic rules. Thus, Joshua Reynolds (1723–1792) expects painting to conform to rules that are discovered by painters through experimentation and learned through time and history by study of the masters. Beauty may be what is felt, but the whole aesthetic apparatus has become a quasi-scientific empirical exploration of the applicable rules of art to which taste conforms. Taste becomes a sign of an educated patron, a connoisseur. As Hume's cousin, Henry Home, Lord Kames, explained in *Elements of Criticism* (1762), "Do we not talk of a good and bad taste? . . . What is universal, must have a foundation in nature. If we can reach that foundation, the standard of taste will no longer be a secret" (vol. 2, p. 383).

Both main lines of development of the concept of taste in the eighteenth century are empiricist in their origins, therefore. Rationalist aesthetics in the tradition of Alexander Baumgarten (1714–1762) had little use for the concept of taste. Voltaire (1694–1778) summed up both lines in his *Philosophical Dictionary*. On the one hand, he defined taste as a sense. On the other hand, it is only an analogy. Good taste perceives actual beauties. In the last analysis, taste is a kind of national or cultural trait to be developed over time by nature. "Is there not a good and a bad taste? Without doubt; although men differ in opinions, manners, and customs. The best taste in every species of cultivation is to imitate nature with the highest fidelity, energy, and grace" (Voltaire, 1901, pp. 48–49). Denis Diderot (1713–1784) concurred: "What, then, is taste?" he asks. "A facility, acquired by repeated experiences, for grasping the true or the good, as well as those circumstances that render either of them beautiful, and for being promptly and keenly affected by them" (1966, p. 167). The empiricism of Hume is far more radical than this language, but its spirit is similar.

Two problems dominate discussions of taste in the later eighteenth century. The first is how to move beyond the "je ne sais quoi" of early taste theories. In order to give taste coherence and order, it needs to be traced to some more fundamental psychological principles. The dominant psychology is associationist. Taste is understood as a response to associations provided by the external senses. Alexander Gerard, in his *Essay on Taste* (1759), attributes the operations of taste to the imagination. This is a significant move because it leads in the direction of treating taste as a form of expression rather than a passive sensory response. Ultimately, taste takes its place in the *Critique of Judgment* (1790) of Immanuel Kant (1724–1804) as a response to pure intuition based on the free play of the imagination.

The second persistent problem concerning taste is how to establish a standard of taste. Hume, famously, juxtaposed two equally obvious alternatives: there is no disputing about taste, but it is absurd to say that someone who prefers Ogilby to John Milton is right. Kant turned this paradox into the antinomy of taste: taste is subjective, but it judges universally. Hume sought the standard in the character of the judges rather than in taste itself. Others, such as Lord Kames and Gerard, maintained, somewhat inconsistently, that taste was subject to rules if they could just be discovered. Kant ultimately moved the dispute onto new ground by arguing that a disinterested intuition was at once both universal and subjective. This displaced taste as it had been understood and replaced it in the course of the nineteenth century with a form of attention. Then, instead of a standard of taste, what one needed was a different way of experiencing that was uniquely aesthetic and beyond (rather than the subject of) critical disputes.

A number of factors tended to reduce the importance of taste toward the end of the eighteenth century. Aesthetic senses tended to multiply. By the time that Archibald Alison wrote his *Essays on the Nature and Principles of Taste* (1790), every aesthetic predicate could be regarded as requiring a separate sense: the sense of grace, of elegance, and so on. The passive, immediate receptivity of Lockean sense has been replaced by the actively associationist and imaginative operations of a mind that is expressing its own powers in its aesthetic activities and takes pleasure in those activities primarily because that is the way that it comes to know itself.

Kant, whose *Critique of Judgment* sums up theories of taste, also displaces them by shifting aesthetic perception to a form of intuition that underlies not just beauty but all theoretical and practical judgment as well. Taste achieved its centrality in aesthetics by uniting judgment and perception. Kant separates judgment into interested and disinterested forms. Disinterested judgment is independent of practical and theoretical considerations that belong to science and morality. Practical criticism is effectively moved out of aesthetics. In its place, disinterestedness, which had gradually assumed aesthetic importance in the eighteenth century, takes its place. Taste is the means of responding aesthetically and disinterestedly, but genius is the ability to produce aesthetically. Gerard and others had already begun to use *genius* in this sense. In effect, imagination and genius explain the two functions of taste. The imagination creates and recreates. Genius exercises a primary form of imagination, as Samuel Taylor Coleridge argued, and then what genius has

created can be re-created by imaginative reproduction in audiences and other, lesser artists.

After Kant, idealist aesthetics had other ways of explaining what is aesthetic. The unification of taste with judgment is pulled apart again. In *Modern Painters* (1843), John Ruskin distinguishes taste from judgment. Taste is the ability to take pleasure in true works of art; judgment is a separate activity. The determination of what is a true work no longer depends on taste, which is reduced to the role of refined sensibility. In the mid-twentieth century, taste reappears briefly as a matter of concern just because it is understood not to be rule-governed and plays no theoretical role. It is contrasted to attempts to define art that are under attack by philosophers influenced by Ludwig Wittgenstein. Their notions of taste are far more limited, however, than the central sense of taste that shaped seventeenth- and eighteenth-century empiricist aesthetics.

[*See also* Alberti; Cooper; Du Bos; Hume; Hutcheson; Kant; *and* Vasari.]

BIBLIOGRAPHY

Aristotle. *The Basic Works of Aristotle.* Edited by Richard McKeon. New York, 1941.
Armenini, Giovanni Battista. *On the True Precepts of the Art of Painting.* Edited and translated by Edward J. Olszewski. New York, 1977.
Blunt, Anthony. *Artistic Theory in Italy, 1450–1600.* Oxford, 1940.
Cooper, Anthony Ashley, Earl of Shaftesbury. *Characteristics of Men, Manners, Opinions, Times.* Edited by John M. Robertson. Indianapolis, 1964.
Croce, Benedetto. *Aesthetic.* Translated by Douglas Ainslie. 2d ed. New York, 1922.
Curtius, Ernest Robert. *European Literature and the Latin Middle Ages.* Translated by Willard R. Trask. New York, 1953.
Diderot, Denis. "Essay on Painting" (1765). In *Diderot's Selected Writings,* edited by Lester G. Crocker, translated by Derek Coltman, pp. 161–168. New York, 1966.
Du Bos, Jean-Baptiste. *Réflexions critiques sur la poésie et sur la peinture* (1719). Paris, 1993.
Eco, Umberto. *Art and Beauty in the Middle Ages.* Translated by Hugh Bredin. New Haven, 1986.
Gerard, Alexander. *An Essay on Taste* (1759). Facsimilie of 3d ed (1780). Gainesville, Fla., 1963.
Gracian, Balthasar. *The Art of Worldly Wisdom.* Translated by Joseph Jacobs. New York, 1945.
Hobbes, Thomas. *Leviathan.* Edited by Edwin Curley. Indianapolis, 1994.
Home, Henry, Lord Kames. *Elements of Criticism* (1762). 2 vols. in 1. Boston, 1796. First American from the seventh London edition reprinted from the edition of 1763.
Hume, David. "Of the Standard of Taste." In *Essays, Moral, Political, and Literary,* rev. ed., edited by Eugene F. Miller, pp. 226–249. Indianapolis, 1987.
Hutcheson, Francis. *An Inquiry into the Original of Our Ideas of Beauty and Virtue.* London, 1725.
Kant, Immanuel. *The Critique of Judgment.* Translated by Werner S. Pluhar. Indianapolis, 1987.
Klein, Robert. "Judgment and Taste in Cinquecento Art Theory." In *Form and Meaning: Essays on the Renaissance and Modern Art,* translated by Madeline Jay and Leon Wieseltier, pp. 161–169. New York, 1979.

Klein, Robert, and Henri Zerner, eds. *Italian Art, 1500–1600: Sources and Documents.* Englewood Cliffs, N.J., 1966.

Quintilian. *Institutio Oratoria.* 4 vols. Translated by H. E. Butler. Loeb Classical Library. Cambridge, Mass., 1958–1960.

Voltaire. *A Philosophical Dictionary. In The Works of Voltaire.* vol. 7, part 2, translated by William F. Fleming. New York, 1901.

DABNEY TOWNSEND

Modern and Recent History

Philosophies of taste were developed in the eighteenth century in response to two questions: What is the nature of beauty and other aesthetic qualities? What kind of perception enables one to find an object beautiful? Aesthetic evaluations were termed "judgments of taste," and a "man of taste" was viewed as someone sensitive to beauties of both nature and art.

Issues of taste became urgent in the philosophical climate of the Enlightenment, because under the influence of empiricism it was widely agreed that "beauty" names no objective quality but signals the pleasure of the perceiver. To identify beauty with pleasure, however, runs the risk of dismissing it as merely a matter of idiosyncratic enjoyment, but judgments of beauty are at the center of important disputes and thus are not merely matters of personal preference. Therefore, eighteenth-century theorists searched for a standard of taste that would reconcile subjective aesthetic pleasure and a shared way to evaluate objects of that pleasure.

Taste has been employed since about the sixteenth century as the metaphor of choice for aesthetic evaluation, because it captures the sense of immediacy of aesthetic pleasures and of the phenomenon of savoring and enjoying experienced qualities. But although the pleasures of eating are comparable to aesthetic pleasures in that both demand intimate, firsthand experience to assess, they are importantly different. Disagreement about tasty foods is seen as a matter of individual preference with no pressing need to adjust to a standard; pleasures of beauty and art are as important as ethical evaluations and require mutual agreement. Indeed, many Enlightenment thinkers regarded moral and aesthetic sensibilities as close kin and beauty as the countenance of goodness.

Philosophers such as Francis Hutcheson, David Hume, and Immanuel Kant developed theories of taste that rely on a concept of common human nature, such that judgments of aesthetic value signal a special sort of pleasure that is in principle sharable with all human perceivers. Although their philosophies are very different, they agree that it is important to recognize a pleasure that is free from desire, a condition that has become known as "disinterestedness." Interest, or, more precisely, self-interest, hinders agreement on aesthetic matters because it is concerned with personal desires and advantages. The absence of personal interest in a judgment of taste is thus philosophically important because it

permits evaluations that tap into a source of pleasure common to all human beings. For similar reasons, it is important to stipulate that aesthetic approval is distinct from other sorts of evaluations, including practical or instrumental assessments, because these vary with cultural and individual contexts. A "pure" judgment of taste is pleasure in an object presented to the senses or to the imagination, freed from special individual desire. Taste so understood is a particularly developed ability to discern the fine qualities of art and nature. Thus, good taste both describes individuals of particular refinement and is based on a disposition common to all people. Eighteenth-century philosophies of taste laid the foundation for the development of the modern discipline of aesthetics. Assumptions about the need to refer to a special sensitivity to explain the perception of aesthetic qualities persist well into the twentieth century, as is evident in the influential essay by Frank Sibley, "A Contemporary Theory of Aesthetic Qualities: Aesthetic Concepts" (1959).

The latter part of the twentieth century saw a mounting criticism of the concept of taste and skepticism about the notion of a common human nature that underlies these philosophies. Several probing questions have served as avenues for the deconstruction of the concept of taste: What sort of "perceiver" is envisioned in theories of human nature presumed by philosophies of taste? What social context prompts the development of taste? What is the relationship between the perceiving subject and the aesthetic object? Critics of Enlightenment theories call attention to what they see as a conservatism built into the concept of taste: A person with good taste all too frequently comes to appreciate the very artifacts that have been appreciated for centuries. He thus enters an elite company of people with good taste, who are suspiciously coincident with people of wealth and social standing within a select group of European nations. Thus, it is argued, the notion of a standard of taste universal to all is covertly an imposition of national and class-based preferences.

Sociologically minded scholars have analyzed philosophies of taste by calling attention to the historical context of their development. The eighteenth century saw the rise of bourgeois social influence in Europe and the spread of democratic ideals. In this climate, the newly powerful middle classes conceived of themselves as active subjects who could regulate themselves politically and morally without the imposition of governing authorities. Philosophies of taste were appealing to many because they claim a universal ability to appreciate art that expands the privileges of good taste beyond a small elite; yet, at the same time, the exercise of taste is effectively limited to a class of people who have the leisure to develop the refinement of their perceptions. The universality of taste by this account is a fiction; taste really describes appreciation for the accepted canon of art that perpetuates the cultural hegemony of an elite. This phenomenon is disguised by the fact that so many people willingly subscribe to the aesthetic ideas of their times. Michel Foucault demonstrated that power is not only exercised by some central social authority but is most effective when values are absorbed by a population and enacted in daily social practice. So it is with taste: what appears to be an exercise of common dispositions is the acceptance of values as one's own that mimic and thereby confirm social privilege. The concept of the aesthetic, with taste preferences supposedly reflecting the proclivities of common human nature, crystallizes the self-regulation of this class of citizens. Scholars such as Terry Eagleton (1990) and Janet Wolff (1993) have offered analyses of theories of taste that translate philosophical concerns into the social exigencies of modern Europe. Approaching the subject by emphasizing the historical context within which aesthetics developed, taste appears to concern common human nature less than the power of certain classes and nations to select cultural artifacts for special attention, and to denigrate as base or savage the artifacts both of popular, nonelite provenance and of alien cultures.

Sociologist Pierre Bourdieu offers another trenchant criticism of taste in *Distinction: A Social Critique of the Judgement of Taste* (1984). Bourdieu also assails early modern defenses of a uniform standard of taste as disguised class hegemony that regulates values of domination and submission in European societies. He particularly takes issue with Kant, who most stringently purified aesthetic pleasures from practical contexts. Rather than providing the grounds for universal aesthetic pleasures that transcend the differences of individuals, Bourdieu argues, Kant's disinterested pleasure is a product of history that prescribes a contemplative, detached attitude only possible among people wealthy enough for leisure.

Bourdieu amassed data from different strata of French society, and concluded that "good taste" in art, fashion, or food is only that which is preferred by the bourgeois classes; it rarely matches the actual preferences of the working classes. Although eighteenth-century theory insisted on the distinction between aesthetic taste, about which it is important to have common judgments, and gustatory taste, about which individual preferences reign, Bourdieu argues that the two kinds of taste are comparable. A diet full of meat and heavy food is considered healthy and tasty for one who labors with his body, yet this food does not achieve the ranks of "gourmet" taste. Similarly, enjoyment of classical music describes the taste of a cultural elite that is socially powerful enough to determine what is "good" taste. Values are intrinsic to the habitus within which one lives, the subtle material and cultural influences that operate more or less below the level of awareness and shape one's pleasures. The concept of a standard of taste is an illusion rooted in the attempt to make class distinctions irrelevant to contemplative ideals of aesthetics; far from being irrelevant, they were only rendered invisible.

Collapsing the distinction between gustatory tastes and the aesthetic sense of taste is philosophically provocative, for it redirects attention to the traditional assumption that although taste for food is not of great importance beyond the nourishment of an individual, taste for cultural artifacts such as artworks is important enough to be a matter for public debate and resolution. Food has not figured importantly in aesthetic theories or philosophies of art in part because the sense of taste is a "bodily" sense rather than a "distance" sense such as sight or hearing. According to long philosophical tradition, only the distance senses detach the observer sufficiently from the state of his own body to yield "objective" knowledge. Bodily senses such as taste, smell, and to some degree touch are understood to be merely more subjective and to direct attention inward to one's own body; they also yield pleasures that are "merely animal" and run the risk of overindulgence, a point emphasized by the Aristotelian ethical tradition. The late twentieth-century philosophical turn to the body and interest in its role in cognition and evaluation opens up opportunities to consider food and the sense of taste more seriously as philosophical subjects.

Not only class but also gender enters into the construction of an ideal consumer of art. The "man of taste" is a person positioned with a degree of social power manifest in his confident survey of the world for his aesthetic enjoyment. Theoretically, a woman of taste is also in this position. Yet, at the same time, women's social position differs from that of men. The bodies and faces of women are regularly conceived as representative objects of beauty, and, when this is the case, women occupy the positions of both perceiver and perceived. Feminist writers have reexamined the "disinterested attitude" of the person of taste and argued that the aesthetic distance prescribed for the exercise of taste is an objectifying, controlling distance that is apt to pinion women as aesthetic objects. This is especially evident if one considers certain works of visual art. What position of viewing is presumed to appreciate aesthetically a painting such as the Rokeby Venus (one of many European paintings of nude females in erotic poses)? Certainly, sexual desire needs to be distanced to permit aesthetic assessment, traditionally understood. But the appreciative position, however disinterested, is still a masculine one from which a heterosexual male views and savors the form of a beautiful female body. "Disinterestedness" thus does not free the perceiver from gender, for any viewer is positioned by such art traditions in the masculine role of surveyor. Similar analyses have been articulated to probe the appreciation of foreign, primitive, or exotic subjects of art.

There is much at stake philosophically in the dispute between traditional philosophies of taste and social deconstructions of the concept of taste; and feminist critics have raised deep issues about the psychology of perception and the social construction of aesthetic points of view. Even if one is persuaded that traditional concepts of taste fall prey to gender, class, or national biases disguised as universalism, the questions that originally prompted philosophies of taste are not answered by cultural analysis alone. In assessing all these matters, several questions need to be kept distinct. What historical conditions fostered the development of theories of taste, and how important are these conditions for the formulation of philosophical problems and standards of taste? To what degree is appreciation of art constructed by gender, class, and national determinants, and do such influences exhaust the freedom of the imagination to appreciate disinterestedly? Finally, what philosophical problems do theories of taste continue to address? One may grant the salience of historical context and the near impossibility of true disinterested appreciation, and yet acknowledge that there are questions about aesthetic qualities and standards for judgments still to be answered.

[*See also* Bourdieu; *and* Food.]

BIBLIOGRAPHY

Bourdieu, Pierre. *Distinction: A Social Critique of the Judgement of Taste.* Translated by Richard Nice. Cambridge, Mass., 1984.

Dickie, George. *The Century of Taste: The Philosophical Odyssey of Taste in the Eighteenth Century.* New York and Oxford, 1996.

Eagleton, Terry. *The Ideology of the Aesthetic.* Oxford and Cambridge, Mass., 1990.

Kivy, Peter, "Recent Scholarship and the British Tradition: A Logic of Taste—the First Fifty Years." In *Aesthetics: A Critical Introduction,* edited by George Dickie, Richard Sclafani, and Ronald Roblin, pp. 254–268. 2d ed. New York, 1989.

Mattick, Paul, Jr., ed. *Eighteenth-Century Aesthetics and the Reconstruction of Art.* Cambridge and New York, 1993.

Pollock, Griselda. *Avant-Garde Gambits, 1888–1893: Gender and the Color of Art History.* London and New York, 1993.

Sibley, Frank. "A Contemporary Theory of Aesthetic Qualities: Aesthetic Concepts." *Philosophical Review* 68.4 (1959): 421–450.

Wolff, Janet. *The Social Production of Art.* 2d ed. New York, 1993.

Woodmansee, Martha. *The Author, Art, and the Market: Rereading the History of Aesthetics.* New York, 1994.

CAROLYN KORSMEYER

TEA CEREMONY. *See* Japanese Aesthetics.

TELEVISION. [*To treat the modern, global social-aesthetic phenomenon of television, this entry comprises two essays:*

An Overview

Contemporary Thought

The first essay explains the history of television and explores the various ways it has been studied culturally. The second essay examines the relevance of television (and, specifically, television series) to the philosophy of art. For related discussion, see Cultural Studies; Popular Culture; *and* Video.]

An Overview

As an object of study, television is a confounding concept. It calls for attention from the sciences, social sciences, and humanities, but requires each to acknowledge ways in which the others might alter or challenge basic and originating assumptions. It is experienced in the most common and offhand fashion, yet it synthesizes complex technological, economic, regulatory, aesthetic, psychological, and cultural categories. It is, in many respects, a global phenomenon, while remaining in most instances the strongest indigenous example of a "cultural industry," far more powerful and direct than cinema in addressing national audiences, preserving linguistic distinction, and developing or maintaining local and regional identities.

In spite of these multiple connections and relations, however, television is still most often approached from single perspectives. Those perspectives, and attendant methods of analysis or argument, generally reflect deep interests directed toward specific agendas. Thus, for the social psychologist concerned with the welfare of children, any study of television must gather data of a certain sort, capable of securing a voice in the arena of public policy, or at least in the attendant bodies of academic literature that might be cited in public debate. For the political economist focused on international flows of media, however, children's programming might be examined as a relatively inexpensive commodity best understood with "public good" economic theory. Programming thus cited might be considered an example of why certain producing entities or nations have come to have particular influence in world markets. Yet, for the critic interested in the history of fictional forms, the same body of programs might be "read" as versions of expressive culture, works that rely on familiar forms of narration, stories that can be placed within a very long tradition of "representation."

But by far the most interesting questions begin to emerge when the critic suggests to the social psychologist that it is impossible to study children's responses without some sophisticated notion of narrative theory, or when the political economist argues that the relatively limited number of story forms is the result of powerful interests in control of "storytelling" in all cultural and social contexts. What these interactions suggest is that television can best be understood not as an entity—economic, technological, social, psychological, or cultural—but as a site, the point at which numerous questions and approaches intersect and inflect one another. For this reason, television should also be thought of as "television," somehow "marked" to remind that no single definition or set of terms can gather or control the power and significance of this most ubiquitous entity. Indeed, in this tendency to complicate singly focused approaches, television has also become the site at which various theories and methods—not to say larger systemic constructions such as "the social sciences" or "the humanities" or "critical theory"—have been forced to recognize shortcomings and attempt conversation, if not always conjunction, with others.

Moreover, the difficulties posed by television's complexities are further greatly perplexed by variations among national contexts. Any discussion of critical approaches to television must acknowledge these distinctions, even as it recognizes the enormous international influence of U.S. television. An analysis of the crime genre in British television, for example, must establish connections with British literary and cinematic traditions, but must also deal with the ways in which imported U.S. programming, growing from its own traditions, influenced British program development. Yet, to make such a comparison fully applicable, the analysis must also deal with the intersecting problems facing the study of television as outlined earlier, and deal with them in terms of the basic facts of two very different television systems:

- Britain's public service system versus the U.S. system of advertiser-supported, commercially oriented television;
- Resulting from this basic distinction, Britain's much more highly regulated programming procedures versus a virtually unregulated U.S. system;
- Resulting from these regulatory differences, one possible explanation for generic distinctions regarding the representation of violence, power, and authority;
- Finally, the recognition that these distinctions bear direct relation to concerns for the monitoring and regulating of social behavior in the two societies, concerns often addressed and processed in crime fiction in many media.

Such an example could be easily multiplied—and greatly entangled by comparing cultural and social contexts even more distinct from one another than the Anglo-American case. Yet, even within a single national-cultural context, this recognition of multiple interrelated questions and issues must inform a growing body of work grounded in critical, theoretical, and historical approaches best defined as "television studies." The development of these complex approaches grew, in a relatively short period, from more narrowly focused projects, often tentative, but perhaps necessary as foundational efforts to understand the medium. This growth of "television studies," however, hardly occurred in a vacuum. Much to the contrary, these approaches had to make their way into or adjacent to a massive existing discourse guided by the notion of "television as a social problem."

Following World War II, the shattered infrastructures of broadcasting throughout Europe began to rebuild at varying speeds, most often in accordance with other elements of economic and material redevelopment. From that period until the present, television growth in postcolonial, nonaligned, developing nations has also continued as part of technological and economic development. In the postwar United States, however, the widespread implementation of television at national and local levels exploded, so rapidly in fact that the Federal Communications Commission imposed a "freeze" on the allocation of new television frequencies in 1948. Originally planned as a brief interlude, the freeze lasted until 1952, and during this period competing interests struggled for control of various aspects of the medium. When the freeze was lifted, "television" in the United States was configured in a pattern that remained in place until the mid-1980s, when new technologies and newly organized older technologies brought an end to what might be called television's "network era."

From the late 1940s through the mid-1970s, almost all serious attention to television was filtered through a model of American social science designed to explore and determine the "effects" of the medium. Serious attention was focused on the effects of television on children, on political processes, and on general problems related to the representation of violence on television. Much of this work is cited or referenced in a series of summary studies published in the mid- to late 1970s (e.g., George Comstock and Marilyn Fisher, *Television and Human Behavior: A Guide to Pertinent Scientific Literature*, Santa Monica, Calif. 1975). Often conducted with substantial funding from government sources, the studies conducted from this general epistemological model were instrumental in establishing certain forms of American social science that, when applied in the construction of a growing number of departments of communications studies, educated generations of faculty, forged curricula, and filled academic journals.

Humanistic approaches to television were fugitive in nature, often appearing in general readership magazines such as the *Nation* or *Saturday Review*. Critical, analytic work focused on textual analysis, aesthetic evaluation, or interpretive studies did not appear in academic journals, even in the increasingly available venues devoted to the study of film. Film studies had begun to find a place in academic settings during this same period, largely because "film as art" focused on European and other national cinemas rather than "Hollywood film." This term, with its connotations of "commercial," "superficial," "popular," or "mass," was synonymous with "inferior" or "unworthy," and prohibited "serious" study of these forms of expression. (Early in the history of television in the United States, live broadcasts of original single plays had been conceived by journalists as a new art form, honored with serious attention. When the economic configuration of the medium pushed production to Hollywood and filmed series, this early period was immediately identified as the "golden age" of American television and discussed with reverence and awe. In some circles, this remains a dominant perspective.)

In the mid-1970s, a number of influences led to the development of new approaches to the study of television. In the United States, the study of popular culture grew out of departments of English, history, and sociology. Scholars paid serious attention to popular genres such as the western, mysteries, and science fiction in literature and film, and to the "auteurs" who created these works. Often ridiculed in the popular press itself, and battled in academic settings, interest in such endeavors nevertheless continued to spread. Recognition of the pleasures and complexities of popular music (the Beatles' influence) and some forms of visual representation (Pop art) suggested that lines between "popular culture" and "high culture" could be blurred—despite ongoing and often rancorous debates in scholarly journals. Television, however, remained the latest and most despised of debased forms.

But other perspectives, other voices, were at work. A major influence in the growth of attention to television came from serious journalists who recognized the deep cultural roots of the medium's forms of expression. Gilbert Seldes had dealt seriously with television in *The Public Arts* (1956), and in 1962 Robert Lewis Shayon, columnist for the *Saturday Review,* introduced *The Eighth Art,* a collection of essays, largely written by journalists. More significantly, Shayon again addressed a larger public with his 1971 book *Open to Criticism,* in which he reprinted a number of his columns and discussed them in a style of metacriticism. His book was a study of the critical process—that its subject was television made the analysis all the more remarkable.

Other cultural institutions were also "discovering" the significance of other discursive formations developing around the newer medium. As early as 1966, Patrick Hazard's *TV as Art: Some Essays in Criticism* had suggested a role for serious academic study of the medium. Published, significantly, for the National Council of Teachers of English, this collection went largely unnoticed. In the mid-1970s, the Aspen Institute for Humanistic Studies sponsored conferences that resulted in two influential anthologies, edited by Richard Adler and Douglass Cater, *Television as a Social Force* (1975) and *Television as a Cultural Force* (1976). These collections called for and provided examples of television analysis and criticism that resembled the best work in literary and film studies, as well as other essays that explored the reasons for a lack of serious cultural discussion of television.

Horace Newcomb's 1974 monograph *TV: The Most Popular Art* offered genre-by-genre analysis of American television's most popular program types, the first full-length study of this material from a perspective more directly grounded in the humanities than in the social sciences. In 1976, Newcomb's anthology of television criticism drawn from journalistic and academic writing, *Television: The Critical View,* became a widely used text-reader for the growing number of courses devoted to the study of television. (Four subsequent editions, each containing new essays, have traced the expansion of television studies.) From the mid-

1970s to the present, the field has grown rapidly and influences from the United Kingdom and from European critical theory have been central to this development.

Early U.S. approaches to television were focused largely on defining formal qualities of the medium, relating those forms to a heritage of generic influence from literature and film, and engaging in interpretive analyses of the relations of those forms to American culture. Although British and Continental approaches to mass culture generally, and television in particular, dealt with similar topics, they were also informed from the very beginning stages by concern for issues of politics, ideology, and all forms of social power. Clearly, much study of popular culture forms of all sorts was influenced by the work of Raymond Williams, long a television commentator for *The Listener.* But his *Television: Technology and Cultural Form* (1975) most clearly related study of this medium to economic and technological formations.

During this same period, significant work on television and other popular cultural formations was being conducted at the Centre for Contemporary Cultural Studies at the University of Birmingham, England. Working Papers in Cultural Studies, a mimeographed series describing ongoing studies and projects, was circulated with great influence in various academic circles. One of these papers, Stuart Hall's "Encoding/Decoding" (published in 1980 as "Encoding/Decoding in Television Discourse") was extremely significant in its articulation of relations among ideological formations, industrial structures, textual practices, and audience responses. In some ways, Hall's essay prefigured later, more fully developed studies exploring these fundamental elements of television.

An equally influential book, *Reading Television* by John Fiske and John Hartley (1978), was a powerful demonstration of the ways in which television required an approach that exceeded narrow formalism, methodologically driven social-scientific approaches, or subjective interpretation. Here again, ideology formations were central topics, but complex formal questions informed the ideological analysis. Recognizing the range of possible meanings within individual television programs and genres, Fiske and Hartley presented television content as a site of struggle for cultural and social meanings. Television was presented as a "bardic" voice, at once the presenter of the pressures within social formations and a centralizing force that tends to "claw back" alternative ideological notions to an acceptable manner of representation.

By this point in the development of television studies, several issues were constantly in play. Concern for the ideological power of television led to a strong influence from Continental sources. Significant among these was the recognition, following Louis Althusser, of television's role as an ideological state apparatus. Other forms of structuralism and psychoanalysis were central to film studies during this

period, and attempts to apply approaches from film theory had brought an increasing number of film scholars to the study of the related medium. "Screen Theory" (from the journal *Screen*) sought to relate television viewing to processes of "subject positioning" prominent in the study of film. Here again, the final concern was with the reinforcement of dominant ideology. But Screen Theory argued that the process not only occurred through narrative techniques, story, and plot, but was located as well within the very cinematic apparatus. Ways of filming, modes of exhibition, and the resulting forced forms of spectatorship led (almost) inevitably to certain ideological "effects" or "effectivities." The apparatus forced a replication of psychological states and stages of development, and these deeper structures, it was argued, reestablished unequal gender relations and other forms and expressions of power. When applied to television, the range of genres and modes of address led the argument toward the conclusion that these psychological functions were structured, especially in U.S. television, within an ideology of consumer capitalism. All desire was directed, in some cases toward products, but more generally toward the acceptance of consumerism as both "natural" and appropriate.

But various forms of structuralism, ideology studies, and audience analysis soon seemed to falter on the recognition of actual differences between film and television. In 1980, Hall and others published an edited collection, *Culture, Media, Language: Working Papers in Cultural Studies, 1972–79*. Here, Hall's "Encoding/Decoding" essay received much wider dissemination. Following Antonio Gramsci's use of the concept of hegemony as a noncoercive means of ideological persuasion and enforcement, Hall suggested that the producers of television (encoders) worked within unstated, professionally defined, dominant ideological boundaries. The resulting messages/meanings/representations were thus "structured in dominance." But his attention was also focused on the "decoding" process in which audiences variably interpreted and responded to these messages. Although there is relatively little detailed analysis in the essay, Hall points to possible differences in interpreting ideological central messages. Substantial portions of an audience would, he argued, "read" the content within the accepted, dominant framework. Others, however, because of particular social formations, would perform an "oppositional" reading. His example here is of trade unionists rejecting a news report explaining causes of and responses to a labor dispute. He also holds out the possibility of a middle ground, a "negotiated" reading, that would draw on a range of possible meanings. With this outline of the social processes surrounding television, Hall effectively established a taxonomy of foci for television studies. That arrangement of conceptual issues can be presented as follows:

- The encoding process, which is sometimes also termed "production studies." This work focuses on

the modes of production, organization of labor, technological apparatus and influence, policy and regulatory contexts (including specific national variations), and fundamentally, the economic system in which television is produced, transmitted, and received (ever more frequently focusing on the roles of transnational corporations).

- The programs/texts of television. Work here includes studies of narrative structures, the analysis of particular genres and individual programs, the roles of individual performers, writers, producers, and directors. Additional attention is paid to the arrangement of television programs into a "schedule," a far more complex notion of "text." Much of this work is descriptive and interpretive in nature, often focusing on the representation of specific groups (racial, ethnic, class, gender-defined) and on ideological constructs. Examining and explaining the hegemonic processes that appear in the content of television are central goals of much textual analysis, and general issues of ideology are often at the forefront of this work.

- The television audience. Work related to understanding the behavior and interpretive processes of television audiences has become increasingly central to television studies since the mid-1980s. Often arguing against narrowly defined "effects studies," audience analysis has oscillated between two radical poles, one seeing the audience as effectively positioned by the apparatus of television (industry, text, modes of transmission and exhibition), the other positing an audience radically free to create individual or group judgments and interpretations. Actually, few studies would be found at either extreme. Most focus on specific cases and operate cautiously in some more moderate space.

In practice, many specific instances of television studies combine some aspects of all these categories, and placement of any particular project in one or the other suggests a central focus or tendency rather than purity of accomplishment.

In the earlier stages of television studies, relatively few works concentrated on production studies, and those that did often placed significant emphasis on the texts that emerged from the production process. One major approach in this body of work involves case studies or particular productions. Philip Elliot's *The Making of a Television Series* (1972), and Manuel Alvarado and Ed Buscombe's *Hazel: The Making of a Television Series* (1978), follow an entire production process in order to explain how a particular text emerges. These studies depend on participation or close observation, and both require intimate access to the production arena for primary sources. Another approach focuses on the role of individuals within this production process, often attempting to identify degrees of control and the use of this industrial medium as a means of personal expression (e.g., David Marc and Robert J. Thompson's *Prime Time, Prime Movers: From I Love Lucy to L.A. Law,* Boston, 1992). A related concern finds this logic of control and expression not in individuals, but in organizations such as production companies. *MTM: Quality Television* (Feuer et al., 1984) is the most thorough exploration of the "company signature" approach to understanding commonalities in a body of work for television. Todd Gitlin's *Inside Prime Time* (1983) provides case studies in an overview that combines several of these approaches; but his focus, again, is thrust toward understanding the large ideological significance of the medium as a whole. The study is the strongest recent example of the legacy of the Frankfurt School attitudes toward mass culture, and, in Gitlin's view, television is the fullest expression of "recombinant culture," a culture of exhaustion.

Gitlin draws his conclusion from his combined study of production (encoding) and interpretive (textual) practices. But specific textual studies of television are far more extensive and varied than studies of production, and offer a wider range of conclusions. They can be indicated here only by representative instances such as David Marc's highly personalized accounts of television programs, particularly television comedy (1989, 1996), or Robert Thompson's study of quality programming in the 1990s (1996). Numerous studies of individual genres exist, but perhaps the soap opera has been studied more thoroughly than any other. In some ways, this emphasis is exemplary of the rise of television studies, for in a suspect medium, soap opera is perhaps the most suspect instance. It is also one of the most complicated; for here, fundamental issues and problems of television's textuality come to prominence. The central questions may be put this way: What is it that one studies when one studies "television"? What is a television text? Do we study individual episodes of programs, the entire run of a program's episodes (impossible until the advent of videocassette recording devices), the genre in which the program exists, or the schedule in which the program, and the episode, are embedded?

In the United States, the soap opera, specifically designed for industrial purposes, not only raises all these questions, but also requires consideration of fundamental notions of textuality developed for literary, dramatic, and film study. Programmed daily and constructed around an intertwined set of never-ending narratives, the form explodes the Aristotelian dictum that stories have beginnings, middles, and ends. The American soap opera is designed as a perpetual middle, a perpetual second act. The very fact that the form is created for such continuous attendance and potential pleasure contributes, in some views, to its debased status. Much of this discrimination is related to the designation of soap opera as not merely a "women's genre," but as a genre for "woman domesticated."

Yet, feminist scholars have examined the form frequently, often recouping a substantial range of value and significance, and in so doing, claiming a power for both creators and viewers. Studies by Muriel Cantor and Suzanne Pingree (*The Soap Opera,* Beverly Hills, Calif., 1983), Suzanne Frentz (*Staying Tuned,* Bowling Green, Ohio, 1992), and Carol Traynor Williams (*"It's Time for My Story,"* Westport, Conn., 1992) explore a range of production practices, social experience, and textual strategies. Martha Nochimson (*No End to Her,* Berkeley, 1994) examines soaps in light of feminist social and psychological theory. Mary Ellen Brown (*Soap Opera and Women's Talk,* Thousand Oaks, Calif., 1994), Christine Geraghty (*Women and Soap Opera,* Cambridge, 1991), C. Lee Harrington and Denise D. Bielby (*Soap Fans,* Philadelphia, 1995), and Laura Stempel Mumford (*Love and Ideology in the Afternoon,* Bloomington, Ind., 1995) all study the form with a view of social relations, seeking to identify and analyze the particular pleasures and uses of soap opera by viewers. Like Robert C. Allen in *Speaking of Soap Operas* (1985), many of these studies also present crucial elements of the production and industrial processes underlying soap opera. This has particularly been the case as the influence of soap opera has spread to prime-time television. The massive international response to programs such as *Dallas* and *Dynasty,* as well as the generic experimentation in such crime programs as *Hill Street Blues,* are directly related to the adoption of serial narration in these programs; and because soap operas are increasingly international in their production, distribution, and popularity (as the Latin American *telenovela* and the Quebecois *téléroman* attest), they raise questions focused on international economics and policy as well as cultural influence.

If the soap opera is a concentrated version of the problem of television textuality and the locus of fundamental questions related to the place of television in both social and cultural formations, it is also the site on which textual studies blur into the study of television audiences. No area has received so much attention in the recent past as the study of the television audience. The central issue of this discussion has focused on possible degrees of audience freedom, the freedom to variously interpret and apply discourse presented in television constructed within dominant industrial, economic, regulatory, and expressive contexts. These issues were being presented and refined as early as the publication of Hall et al.'s *Culture, Media, Language.* There, Dave Morley, in the essay "Texts, Readers, Subjects," expanded on Hall's notion of variable decoding, and, in later work on the television program *Nationwide,* offered grounded analyses of how these variations might rise from the social contexts of viewers. His findings—that social class might not always be a defining predictor of interpretive strategies and that gender and domestic arrangements, as well as technology (the remote control device), are major factors in the decoding process—have been supported in a range of other studies with reference to other programs and genres. Ien Ang (1991, 1996) has provided the most thorough theoretical surveys of this issue, as well as close analysis of specific cases (1985). In almost every case, the issue of interpretation continues to be framed in terms of viewer relations to ideological formations. As such, these projects have continued an emphasis on the ideological role of the medium, and questions of form and history have been subordinated to that fundamental concern.

This brief survey of some core issues and texts in television studies (which has not cited a burgeoning periodical literature) suggests a progressive identification of issues, topics, themes, and approaches to the medium. These studies also reflect a continuing application of critical theory common to other expressive forms such as literature and film. Structuralism, semiotics, genre study, cultural studies, feminist theories and other approaches have been honed and focused in terms of their specific subjects, and television has often proved exceptionally difficult to "capture" with any single method. Among the most useful texts for television studies have been Robert C. Allen's *Channels of Discourse: Television and Contemporary Criticism* (1987) and *Channels of Discourse: Reassembled* (1992). These collections demonstrate specific connections between television and a wide range of theoretical perspectives. But they also illustrate the difficulty of explaining the medium with any single theory, any unified approach.

As suggested earlier, television demands, and television studies now acknowledges, the application of intersecting theoretical and methodological examinations. Early examples of this sort of work already cited include Gitlin (1983) and Feuer et al. (1984), both of which explored interactions of industrial practice and textual strategy, but offered less specific analysis of audiences. The most recent contributions to this field have maintained an interest in specific topics, but have more and more often sought to explore that topic as the locus of interacting forces. Jostein Gripsrud's study of the television series *Dynasty* (*The Dynasty Years: Hollywood Television and Critical Media Studies,* London and New York, 1995), for example, explores the international circulation of that program and others, the cultural responses in differing national contexts, and consequent problems for the entire field of "critical media studies." He demonstrates the necessity for framing much of television in terms of international cultural and policy issues, while pointing to the role of multinational flows of capital as another central means by which to understand television. At the same time, however, Herman Gray's (*Watching Race: Television and the Struggle for Blackness,* Minneapolis, 1995) examination of the representation of "blackness" on U.S. television focuses on specific *national* issues. He forges a context comprising economic conditions, Reaganism, the growing power of certain black performers, and changes in the television industry. The acknowledgment of both spe-

cific local sites of production and cultural significance, as well as the international implications of artifacts and their economic and cultural roles, is now a necessary part of television studies. The oscillation between local and global contexts—so common a theme in much culturally based work—is increasingly acknowledged and practiced in the study of this medium.

Still, for all its familiarity, all its massive cultural influence on a global scale, few of the details of the development of television are known. Fortunately, therefore, many of the more recent studies demonstrating complex webs of explanation have been cast as histories. As such, they acknowledge the fact that there are now sufficient supplementary studies of specific programs, genres, individuals, archival institutions, events, and policies to support such explorations, as well as minimal technical devices such as the videocassette recorder to make detailed study possible. Additionally, they demonstrate strong forays into relatively unsupported primary sources—the television industry is notorious for randomly disposing of its own product as well as for its close proprietary control of records and details, but new archival endeavors have uncovered important resources, and oral histories and case studies of events have added vastly to the store of knowledge regarding the medium.

William Boddy's *Fifties Television: The Industry and Its Critics* (1990) is a model for the analysis of complex interactivity that must be untangled in any definition of "television." Examining industrial strategies, critical response in both journalistic and public interest arenas, and governmental actions, he outlines television's shift from the context of "live" production in New York to the culture industry in Hollywood. By providing detailed industrial and policy contexts for the development of the medium at a crucial time, he presents a new perspective on the nation's adoption of this medium as a central aspect of social and cultural life. Moreover, he presents these events in the history of television as a struggle to control "television," and shows how the outcome of these contests related to and reinforced other interests and power relations. From a very different perspective, Lynn Spigel's *Make Room for TV: Television and the Family Ideal in Postwar America* (1992) provides a social history to detail the more personal, home-centered responses to television as a domestic device and a general entertainment medium. Relying on sources such as print advertisements for television sets, Spigel shows how the very spaces in which American families lived were transformed by this technology. But she also shows how the redefinitions generally reinforced existing gender relations, child-rearing practices, and personal interactions. On yet another front, Christopher Anderson's *Hollywood TV: The Studio System in the Fifties* (1994) offers a series of detailed case studies providing specific information about the transformation of the film industry and the invention of television's narrative structures. He also explains how television was deeply implicated in large-scale leisure industries, such as Disneyland, which were on the verge of transforming leisure and entertainment experiences.

These three studies all employ a variety of interpretive strategies, sources, and analytic approaches, and in so doing demonstrate the now-recognized necessity for examining television as an intersection of social and cultural forces. More important, however, they can be seen as interlocking pieces of the "map" of television as it developed from the late 1940s through the 1950s. Only by shifting from the national, policy, and industrial arenas limned by Boddy, to the specific studios and individuals making television as presented by Anderson, and finally to the domestic and personal experiences analyzed by Spigel can we capture anything approaching the more complete sense of what the coming of television meant in a particular place at a particular time. Television exists in the making of policy and the exchange of huge capital outlays, in the industrial processes that produce programs and schedules, and in the experience of families and individuals who live with it in quotidian experience. Perhaps no single study can capture the overlapping layers of influence and participation. But, as the new television histories provide more and more detail, the map is drawn more precisely.

One of the most recent additions to television studies comes close to providing such a detailed map for a particular period. John Thornton Caldwell's *Televisuality: Style, Crisis, and Authority in American Television* (1995) seeks to define closure for the "network era." His argument holds that by the 1980s "television" as it had been commonly produced, recognized, and received no longer existed. In its place was something quite familiar, but now defined by constant efforts for stylistic distinction that might draw attention, stop the ceaseless "channel surfing," and afford economic success. The situation he describes is dependent on a rigorously detailed delineation of changes in technology, government policy, and industrial composition. His explanations of how economic and technological shifts altered the fundamental structure of the television industry, and consequently, the fundamental structures of television programs, are powerful examples of such interactions; and his interpretations of specific texts, fully cognizant of their multiple meaning structures, provide extraordinarily subtle connections to the shifting ideological and cultural formations of this crucial period. Although he does not depend on specific ethnographic or observational studies of audiences, he makes clear the options open for varieties of interpretation. He also offers a thorough analysis of industry attempts to manufacture new audiences and interpretive communities, often defined demographically in the interests of sponsors and advertising agencies. Thus, Caldwell, as much as any scholar to date, has managed to present the complex interactions of the three broad categories of television studies: encoding/text/decoding.

Claims such as Caldwell's—attempts to define truly transitional moments of huge import—are always fragile in some respects, but there is little question that "television" as it has been known for a brief period of half a century is in a stage of momentous alteration. New technologies have outstripped existing policies. Fundamental terms such as *broadcasting* are now obsolete. Once a central and centralizing medium comparable in power to the church of the Middle Ages, "television" has become fragmented and personalized, and the linkage of "television" with the personal computer suggests even more individualization to come. In some ways, cultures and societies intimately familiar with television are moving from a relationship defined by that earlier ecclesiastical model to that of the newsstand or the massive lending library. The probability of hundreds of available channels is inevitably, perhaps ironically, linked to the probability of control by fewer and fewer massive media conglomerates. The relation of these institutions, these channels of distribution, to these audiences lacks clear focus and perspective. Barely two decades of television studies have only begun to offer an understanding of the period just ending, yet the field already faces an imperative to make sense of a fluid future.

BIBLIOGRAPHY

Adler, Richard, and Douglass Cater, eds. *Television as a Social Force.* New York, 1975.

Adler, Richard, and Douglass Cater, eds. *Television as a Cultural Force.* New York, 1976.

Allen, Robert C., ed. *Channels of Discourse: Television and Contemporary Criticism.* Chapel Hill, N.C., 1987. Second edition published as *Channels of Discourse: Reassembled: Television and Contemporary Criticism* (Chapel Hill, N.C., 1992).

Ang, Ien. *Watching Dallas: Soap Opera and the Melodramatic Imagination.* Translated by Della Couling. London and New York, 1985.

Ang, Ien. *Desperately Seeking the Audience.* London and New York, 1991.

Ang, Ien. *Living Room Wars: Rethinking Media Audiences for a Postmodern World.* London and New York, 1996.

Boddy, William. *Fifties Television: The Industry and Its Critics.* Urbana, Ill., 1990.

Brown, Mary Ellen. *Soap Opera and Women's Talk: The Pleasure of Resistance.* Thousand Oaks, Calif., 1994.

Caldwell, John Thornton. *Televisuality: Style, Crisis, and Authority in American Television.* New Brunswick, N.J., 1995.

Feuer, Jane. *Seeing through the Eighties: Television and Reaganism.* Durham, N.C., 1995.

Feuer, Jane, et al., eds. *MTM: Quality Television.* London, 1984.

Fiske, John. *Media Matters: Everyday Culture and Political Change.* Minneapolis, 1994.

Fiske, John, and John Hartley. *Reading Television.* London, 1978.

Gitlin, Todd. *Inside Prime Time.* New York, 1983.

Hall, Stuart, et al., eds. *Culture, Media, Language: Working Papers in Cultural Studies, 1972–1979.* London, 1980.

Hartley, John. *Tele-ology: Studies in Television.* London and New York, 1992.

Hilmes, Michelle. *Hollywood and Broadcasting: From Radio to Cable.* Urbana, Ill., 1990.

Marc, David. *Comic Visions: Television Comedy and American Culture.* Boston, 1989.

Marc, David. *Demographic Vistas: Television in American Culture.* Rev. ed. Philadelphia, 1996.

Morley, Dave. *The Nationwide Audience: Structure and Decoding.* London, 1980.

Morley, Dave. *Family Television: Cultural Power and Domestic Leisure.* London, 1986.

Newcomb, Horace. *TV: The Most Popular Art.* Garden City, N.Y., 1974.

Newcomb, Horace, ed. *Television: The Critical View.* 5th ed. New York and Oxford, 1994.

Newcomb, Horace, and Robert S. Alley. *The Producer's Medium: Conversations with Creators of American TV.* New York, 1983.

Pribram, E. Diedre, ed. *Female Spectators* [*sic*]: *Looking at Film and Television.* London and New York, 1988.

Spigel, Lynn. *Make Room for TV: Television and the Family Ideal in Postwar America.* Chicago, 1992.

Thompson, Robert J. *Adventures on Prime Time: The Television Programs of Stephen J. Cannell.* New York, 1990.

Thompson, Robert J. *Television's Second Golden Age: From Hill Street Blues to ER.* New York, 1996.

Thompson, Robert J., and Gary Burns, eds. *Making Television: Authorship and the Production Process.* New York, 1990.

Williams, Raymond. *Television: Technology and Cultural Form.* New York, 1975.

HORACE NEWCOMB

Contemporary Thought

The technical possibilities of television, and with them the aesthetics of television, have been changing and will continue to change with great rapidity. For some time, however, a staple of television has been standard commercial broadcasting, and much of it remains in place despite recent alterations. It remains a good, difficult topic for the philosophy of art. This essay considers only those thirty-minute, sixty-minute, and occasionally longer programs that constitute what are called "series." These include so-called dramatic series, often involving police, detectives, hospitals, lawyers, and the like, and also comedy series. Other staples of television programming are certainly of interest, but it is with these that the philosophy of art might first begin to make its way.

Two main topics are the objects themselves and the audience for these objects. In both cases, theorists are confronted with virtually unprecedented phenomena, and it is of the first importance to describe these phenomena accurately. Television is often held in low esteem, especially by American academic intellectuals, and, whether or not that opinion is justified, it often seems to arise from a failure to apprehend the phenomena accurately.

The Objects. Just what is a television series, metaphysically, so to speak? An example likely to be chosen from the "narrative" arts—say, a movie, a short story, a novel, or a play—is a self-contained entity, however its temporal and spatial dimensions are to be described. So is a television program. But a television series is different. It is discontinuous: its elements are spread out in time, separated from one another, typically, by a week. Thus, it is a very peculiar object of aesthetic appreciation. In some cases—for instance,

those of some "situation comedies"—each episode is largely self-contained, with plots that are resolved entirely during one program, but even with them the sustaining characters appear week after week, and a sense of the characters—especially of those that develop throughout the series—requires attention to more than a single program. In other cases, in which plots are not begun, developed, and concluded in the same program in which they begin, there is a profound difference from other kinds of narrations. The tempo and rhythm of such a continuing series is manifest not in a single program, but in a succession of them, sometimes occupying many weeks or even more than a year. When such a series is done with appreciable skill, use is made of the temporal separation of programs; that is, the series is constructed to exploit the fact that anyone watching one of the programs has not seen the series for the last seven days. The simplest exploitation of this fact is the use of a presumption that a week has elapsed since the characters in the program were last seen: the viewer is made to feel that the characters he sees have been active during the week in which they have not been seen; that is, it is not as if one put aside a novel for a week and then resumed reading at the point at which one broke off, but it is as if one were periodically witnessing an hour's worth of the time in the lives of the program's characters, having missed all the time since seeing them for an hour a week ago.

A failure to credit television series with their ample dimensions, with the fact that the actual object of appreciation is spread out over a very long time, often leads to the idea that television is a rather simple medium, producing objects that, if they are artistic at all, are of very little complexity or subtlety. It is difficult to sustain this idea once one attempts to account for the structural features of a genuine series. Correlatively, the idea that television programs are "easy" to appreciate, perhaps too easy to be genuine works of art, may have to give way in the face of the fact that those members of the audience who do engage in easy viewing (often called "passive") are simply viewers not responding to all that is there. Standard commercial television series may just be examples of a kind of art familiar elsewhere, namely, that kind of art that somehow supports both sophisticated, intense audience responses and less arduous, easier, more superficial responses. Operas by Giuseppe Verdi, novels by Charles Dickens, poems by Robert Frost, much jazz music, and even some plays by William Shakespeare are all like that. It scarcely shows the inferiority or slightness of these works that they have long sustained audiences deriving simple pleasures and enjoyment, because they also support very complicated and intricate considerations from audiences with a taste for that. Neither should that fact about television, by itself, underwrite a low estimation of television programs, should it be possible—as it almost certainly is—to subject television series to complex aesthetic analyses.

The Audience. It is arguable that the appreciation of movies, certainly in the early history of movies and in some quarters even today, suffers from a persistent tendency to view movies as if one were seeing a play. Whatever we make of that misapprehension and how damaging it may be to an adequate appreciation of movies, it seems true that the appreciation of television often derives from a tendency to view television as if one were seeing a movie. Even if it does not increase one's estimate of at least some television to correct this misapprehension, it is useful to approach the description of television programs in terms of their difference from movies. To begin, one might note that for almost all the history of commercial television, television pictures have had less vivid and interesting colors than movie pictures, they have been less sharply and accurately focused than movie pictures, and because of their much smaller size they have not had the capacity for the same spatial dynamism available to movie pictures.

The development of a sensibility adequate to television, or to the movies, or perhaps to any art, is different for different people, especially when the people are of different ages and the art in question has developed during their lives. For a certain group of people, now among the oldest part of the population, in the development of movies they witnessed the addition of sound (to silent pictures), whereas in the development of television they witnessed the addition of pictures (to radio). Thus in "talking pictures" they heard the people they had been seeing, whereas in television they saw the people they had been hearing. In both cases, it took some time for the newly added element to seem more than a novel, contingent addition, that is, for the new element to begin to seem essential and to be "exploited" artistically. But for those born later, and especially those born, say, since 1950, both the movies and television were sight and sound from the beginning. These younger viewers are far less likely to have assimilated movies to theater, or television to movies. Indeed, for many of them, their earliest experience of movies was on television sets, and these people have had to separate movies from television, not television from movies, and there has been no background sense of theater in play at all.

No art has had an audience like the audience for television. Television's audience has a size and structure unique in the history of art. This is changing with alterations in television programming and especially with the increasingly wide use of recording devices, but for a time the situation of the television audience was this: At a certain time—say, 10 P.M. United States Eastern Standard Time—a certain program, say, an episode of *Hill Street Blues,* came on, and several million people spent the following hour watching. Movies have had audiences of millions, no doubt, and so have musical works and literary works, but these audience members are spread out in time. The television audience is spread out in space, but not in time. This means that when

one is watching that particular program, even though one might be watching alone in one's own room, one is part of an enormous audience, none of which is present to oneself. The members of this audience know that one another are watching, and a concomitant feature of the appreciation of television is the ongoing conversation supported by the communal experience. Thus, the mornings after *Hill Street Blues* was shown, millions of viewers engaged one another in conversation about the preceding night's episode. Some people, no doubt, experience art in isolation, and it is no part of their appreciation to share this experience, but for many people it is a vital dimension of their aesthetic experience that others participate in it. It is one thing, and a very important one, that a person be enraptured by a Wolfgang Amadeus Mozart divertimento. It is another thing, and a very common and vital one, that the person so enraptured be aware that his rapture is available to all those to whom the divertimento is accessible. Thus, one recommends the piece or a particular performance of it to another. But with the mass television audience, the experience is not only shared, but it is participated in cotemporally. So it is with the audience at a movie or a musical performance. But, paradoxically, the television audience is immensely larger while, at the same time, a much smaller part of it is present to any other part. Whether the experience of television is an "aesthetic experience" or not, it is still of interest that it is a common shared human experience in which the aspect of sharing is unique. If art does indeed have the power to create communities of those who respond to it, television does this in a particularly direct and dramatic way.

BIBLIOGRAPHY

Adler, Richard, and Douglass Cater, eds. *Television as a Cultural Force.* New York, 1976.
Cavell, Stanley. "The Fact of Television." *Daedalus* (Fall 1982).
Cohen, Ted. "Objects of Appreciation: Early Reflections on Television with Further Remarks on Baseball." In *Philosophy and Art,* Studies in Philosophy and the History of Philosophy, vol. 23, edited by Daniel O. Dahlstrom. Washington, D.C., 1991.
Nehamas, Alexander. "Plato and the Mass Media." *Monist* 71 (April 1988).
Newcomb, Horace, ed. *Television: The Critical View.* 5th ed. New York and Oxford, 1994.

TED COHEN

TEXT. Despite being one of the more frequently used terms in contemporary aesthetics, cultural studies, literary theory, and critical theory, *text* is one of the more difficult to define. It is used in a number of radically different and even conflicting senses for varying sets of purposes. The history of the concept of text is long and somewhat convoluted, and is complicated even more by the exponential growth of varying theories of the text during the twentieth century. Nevertheless, one might divide conceptions of text into two distinct groups: the classical concept of text and the contemporary concept of text. Making a fundamental distinction between two conceptions of text will help to avoid the unfortunate trend in aesthetics toward conflating these widely differing conceptions.

Textus. Variations of the concept of text have been in circulation since Greek antiquity, but whereas contemporary usage of the concept tends to make distinctions among related concepts such as work, artifact, and artistic production, the classical usage of the term does not. One frequently finds the term *text* used interchangeably with, say, *work,* to denote the concept of text. What is more, there is a long history of arguments by philosophers in support of the impossibility of even defining the concept of text, from Aristotle's *Physics* (192b20) through Ludwig Wittgenstein's *Philosophical Investigations* (sections 65–67).

The first use, though, of *textus,* the Latin root of *text,* is in Quintilian's major contribution to rhetoric and literary theory, the *Institutio oratoria* (IX, 4, 13). Here, *textus* is used by Quintilian as a metaphor that regards an instance of language use as a woven tissue or texture. This metaphor has been employed in many of the classical and contemporary codifications of the meaning of *text.* The idea of woven texture appears, for example, in the Romance language regard for the term as representing the connection of the different parts of a literary work. It also plays a central role in the contemporary notion of intertextuality—an idea developed by the semiotician Roland Barthes that involves the notion that all texts have other texts present within them to some degree. As such, most of the usage of the term *text* up to the twentieth century (that is to say, what we shall call the classical usage of the term) has treated the domain of *text* to be exclusively a linguistic or written domain. Even Barthes, in his entry on *text* for the *Encyclopaedia universalis,* limits the concept of text only to written entities, and not spoken ones. *Text* has thus become widely regarded as the linguistic texture of the written discourse that constitutes it. As we shall see, one of the hallmarks of the contemporary concept of text is that its domain is not limited to written entities.

Since the Middle Ages, the denotation of *text* has ranged from (1) an abstract, immaterial, verbal entity that may be instantiated in different concrete, material entities to (2) a specific, concrete verbal inscription existing as a particular material object or event. One important difference between the former entity and the latter is that the abstract, verbal text is repeatable, whereas the specific, concrete text is not. Contemporary aesthetics, following a distinction made by Charles Peirce, has called these transcribable texts "tokens," and the original or archetype of the transcription a "type." The type-token distinction compels us to see in every written realization a more or less veiled reflection of a text whose nature has been taken by many philosophers to be purely mental. To a great extent, the ways in which texts are produced and reproduced determine our position as to

what a text is. It has also led to the widespread belief that the text is not part of the "furniture of the world," so to speak—that it is something toward which particular transcriptions or tokens approach but never replicate.

The Classical Concept of Text. Although there are many variations of the classical concept of text, each regards *text* as an autonomous, stable, and coherent object with a determinate identity. From the Stoics through the middle of the twentieth century, this classical concept of text maintained that a text is a written message involving two major components: a signifier and a signified. The former, the signifier, manifests itself in the materiality of the text, that is to say, its letters, words, sentences, and so on. The latter, the signified, is a univocal and definitive meaning—a meaning that is positively closed to multiple meanings. This notion of text, while firmly established by Geoffrey Chaucer's time, gained particular prominence through the work of the American literary critical movement known as the New Criticism.

During its heyday in the 1930s through the 1960s, the New Criticism had a monumental effect on the focus of literary studies. Although the members of this movement differed on many of the specifics of criticism, they were united in the view that literature should be treated objectively, and that works of literature are self-contained, autonomous, and exist for their own sake. Extrinsic factors such as authorial intention are not important for a determination of the identity and meaning as they serve only to divert the reader from the text. W. K. Wimsatt and Monroe Beardsley (1946) dubbed such diversions the "intentional fallacy." Oddly enough, with regard to authorship, there is some similarity of view between the New Critical and the seemingly antithetical poststructuralist position on authorship, which was presented most famously in Barthes's "The Death of the Author" (1968).

The New Critics sought to replace biographical and philological approaches to literary works with a text-centered approach. In this regard, they stood squarely in opposition to philological views of the text that not only emphasized the material boundaries of the text, but also insisted that understanding texts involved determining the intentions of the writer. The New Critics insisted that emphasis be placed on close reading of the text with an eye toward the complex interrelations of form and content—a distinction that would later be dismantled by the contemporary, semiological concept of text. By championing the beauty, complexity, and speciality of literary language, the New Criticism foregrounded the text as an object of aesthetic appreciation. Both the aesthetic qualities and the meaning of the literature come from its text and not its author, and form and content are inexorably linked. [*See* New Criticism.]

One of the major debates in twentieth-century aesthetics, especially in the United States and Britain, was over the source of the identity of the autonomous, stable, and coherent classical notion of text. For some, from Roman Ingarden in *The Literary Work of Art* (1931) to Wolfgang Iser in *The Implied Reader* (1974), the text is a set of schemata with indeterminacies awaiting concretization. For Stanley Fish (1980), a reception theorist like Ingarden and Iser, the identity of the artistic text is bestowed on it by its interpreter, and is not an inherent property of the object. Fish's position that textual identity is a social construction implies, for example, that authorial intention plays little role in the identity of the text. It also implies that different interpretations entail different texts. For Fish, there is no difference between explaining a text and changing it. His view might be said to conflate questions of interpretation with those of identity.

Other theorists of the classical text associate textual identity with inherent properties of the text. Nelson Goodman (1976), for example, argues that the identity of a text is defined by the identity of its syntax and its language—the former involves all of the characters and marks that constitute the text, and the latter implies that translation, for example, will yield a text with a different identity.

A number of attempts have been made in Anglo-American aesthetics to define a text that stands somewhere between the flexibility of Fish's classical concept of text and the rigidity of Goodman's. However disparate the definitions may seem, at the center remains a text with some type of an essence and identity—a notion of text that is squarely opposed to notions of the text developing on the Continent. Some theorists, such as Richard Rorty (1991), have tried to find a type of middle ground for texts between essentialist Anglo-American positions and antiessentialist Continental views. One particularly rich source in this area is the work on text by Umberto Eco (1976, 1979).

A text, for Eco, is a "lazy machinery" that asks someone to do part of its job, and is meant to be an experience of transformation for its reader. Aesthetic or open texts serve as the "structured model for an unstructured process of communicative interplay" (Eco, 1979). Labyrinthine structures can be located at the foundation of every aesthetic text, as well as every sign function. These mazelike structures of the aesthetic text stimulate reactions, rather than communicate contents. Open texts are organized such that their interpretation by a reader forms a significant part of the compositional and narrative strategy of the author. The completion of the open text is possible only through the participation of the reader, yet even so, the completion of a truly open work is only temporary and provisional. The opposite of the open text—the closed text—elicits almost a predetermined response from its reader. A good example of a closed text would be Ian Fleming's James Bond novels, and an exemplary open text would be James Joyce's *Finnegans Wake*. Open texts lack the specific, privileged point of view of closed texts from which the message may be interpreted. Nevertheless, for Eco, closed texts, like open texts, are always texts, and as such can elicit infinite readings. [*See* Eco.]

Classical conceptions of text, then, are closely associated with criticism's demand for a fixed textual meaning; and, if meaning necessarily involves some degree of identity, then classical notions of text must determine the amount and source of textual identity. Although each of the positions defended necessarily involves maintaining some degree of stability and determinate identity between signifier and signified, there is no consensus as to the source of that identity. It is located to varying degrees and combinations, in the text, the author and the critic.

The Contemporary Concept of Text. By the 1960s, the domain of text had extended from its traditionally delimited space of written discourse to that of any object whatsoever—written or spoken, aesthetic or otherwise. Some theorists, including Juri Lotman and Jacques Derrida, went so far as to view the world itself as text. Why did this shift take place? What compelled theorists to broaden the scope of text to such a degree?

The key to understanding this shift is to recognize that it involves nothing less than a rejection of the classical notion of text, and a reconceptualization of the linguistic and philosophical foundations of language. The contemporary concept of text departs from the classical concept by following through on some of the implications of the structural linguistics of Ferdinand de Saussure. He held that the material and nonmaterial differences among signs determine language, and that language is not representational. The sign system is a convention, and signs have neither an existential nor an analogical relation to what is represented. Saussure began nothing less than a revolution in the way in which we view the structure of the elements of language—a revolution that in turn compelled many to explore a new conception of text. [*See* Structuralism.]

Saussure and the structuralists proposed that it is only through functional structures that we are in any sense aware of reality, and maintained that language, including art, abstracts utterances or cultural products from their existential and historical context. Language, in effect, imposes form on nature and makes it manifest as the given of a certain structure. For some structuralists, such as Michel Foucault, codes are the sum total of a discourse, whereas for others, such as Barthes, the forms of the already given order themselves into the cultural codes of the language. For Barthes, then, codes are the forms imposed by language on reality that determine our perception of it, and the text of art amounts to nothing more than a set of codes that control its production. All told, the structuralist text can be said to be motivated by three elements: the sign; the codes that order the signs into the already said of a culture; and the discourses to which sets of codes belong.

In the twentieth century, the multifarious semiological movements and their successors became the major forces shaping the contemporary concept of text. From the philological tradition, the semiologists inherited a reverence for the materiality of the text. They also removed it, however, from an idealism which philologists contended stabilized and fixed textual meaning. One of the major figures in the semiological reshaping of the concept of text was Louis Hjelmslev. In the early 1960s, Hjelmslev proposed the innovative view of text as process. By replacing Saussure's opposition of *langue* to *parole* with an opposition of *system* to *process*—that is to say, *language itself* to the *text*—Hjelmslev was able to argue that language cannot be individuated and defined except by starting from processes. Texts come into existence *against* the background of systems that govern and determine their development. The tradition established by Hjelmslev regarded texts as related to linguistic systems, but not coextensive with them. [*See* Semiotics.]

Clearly, though, the most influential group of writers on the contemporary concept of text in the twentieth century was the *Tel Quel* group. Founded in 1960, the avant-garde journal *Tel Quel* included among its associates three seminal theorists of the text: Barthes, Julia Kristeva, and Jacques Derrida. The *Tel Quel* group's concept of text as *écriture* displaced the idea that the meaning of a text is singular and upheld the notion that textual meaning is polysemic. Derrida's (1976) view of *écriture* is based on the idea that the meaning of texts is not stable or fixed, but is rather a series of supplements, deferrals, and substitutions. Derrida contests long-standing philosophical tradition when he argues that speech is not to be privileged over writing. For Derrida, speech is *always already* writing, and both speech and writing lack presence and are indeterminate. [*See* Barthes; Kristeva; *and* Derrida.]

According to Barthes (1975), texts are structures of language in which authorial intention has no role in the meaning of the text. Meaning not only is produced independently of the author, but also resists closure. The reader interacts with the text to produce meaning that is many times a source of *jouissance*. Barthes makes a sharp distinction between this type of entity, which he calls a text, and something he calls a work. The latter is laden with authorial intent, finitely meaningful, and ultimately interpretable. Whereas a text is an unstable entity that is produced by the reader, a work is a stable entity consumed by the reader. The predominant view among Anglo-American aestheticians is that the objects of aesthetic inquiry are works, whereas among Continental theorists, the view is quite the opposite: the objects of aesthetics are more like Barthes's texts. Generally speaking, the differences between works and texts mirror the differences between classical and contemporary concepts of text.

It should be noted that even though Barthes restricts the domain of *text* to written entities only, and treats spoken entities as the domain of *discourse,* many of the poststructuralists who succeeded him do not follow this practice. Rather, they use the term *text* to refer to any entity—written, spoken, or otherwise—that produces meaning through the infi-nite play of signs. Others, such as Émile Benveniste, extend the range of *discourse* to include both spoken and written entities, thus using *text* synonymously with *discourse.*

Kristeva (1969) treats the text not as a communicative process of social exchange based on the sender-receiver model of communication, but rather as a generative activity that she calls "productivity." As productivity, texts—aesthetic and otherwise—have a redistributive relationship to the language in which they are situated, and because of this are regarded by her as translinguistic entities. For Kristeva, texts are regarded as revolutionary transformations of the language because of the dialectical relationship that she establishes between language and text. Of primary concern is the dynamics of the production of texts, rather than the actual product. One of the factors determining the polyphonous character of texts, intertextuality, is not simply a matter of literary influence. The text is an intersection, absorption, and transformation of other texts and codes, and comprises in some sense the entirety of contemporary and historical language. The analytic process, comprised of the *phenotext* and *genotext* stages, is one of dissolution that inevitably leads to the hidden meanings of the text. The phenotext is the textual surface structure that can be described empirically by the methods of structural linguistics. The genotext is the level of textual deep structure wherein the production of signification takes place. Characteristics of the genotext include exteriority to the subject, timelessness, and a lack of structure. The genotext contains the possibilities of all languages and signifying practices as its predisposition before it is masked or censured by the phenotext. Textual analysis, for Kristeva, shows that, whenever a text signifies, it participates in the transformation of reality by capturing it at the moment of its nonclosure.

The World as Text. As mentioned earlier, since the 1960s, there has been not only a reshaping, but also a broadening, of our sense of text. Although Hjelmslev, Barthes, and Kristeva capture some of the broadening, the domain of text for them is narrow when compared with the text theories of Mikhail Bakhtin, Juri Lotman, and Derrida. Perhaps the broadest sense that text can take is reference to entities of *any* code. It is this sense of text that many theorists employ when they regard all cultural phenomena—from film and dance to music and carnival—as text. According to this broad definition, all of the objects of aesthetics should be treated as texts.

As a proponent of this position, Bakhtin (1986) regarded the text, both written and oral, as the primary given of all of the disciplines making up the human sciences, including literary studies, aesthetics, and philosophy in general. For Bakhtin, the text is the unmediated reality of thought and experience, and the only reality from which the disciplines of the human sciences can emerge. Where there is no text, claims Bakhtin, there is no object of study, or even an object of thought. A text is any coherent complex of signs. The structure of the sign complex is such that in itself it reflects all texts with the bounds of a given area—texts are a type of monad. According to Bakhtin, the study of the arts is the study of texts whose structures are a mosaic. Through his close readings of writers such as Fyodor Dostoyevsky and François Rabelais, Bakhtin has shown how literary texts, in particular, have a *dialogic* or *polyphonous* structure because they are a layered mosaic of other texts. [*See* Bakhtin.]

Other theorists have worked to refine this broad sense by narrowing the notion of text to mean the basic unit of culture, and claim that texts are the product of cultural codes. Texts occur within a situational context that involves textual and extratextual elements. In *The Structure of the Artistic Text* (1977), Lotman differentiates the textual and extratextual by the criteria of expression and demarcation. Because the text *is* its expression, it is materially fixed in the signs of a system. According to Lotman, the textual is opposed to the extratextual structures of *langue,* which are not expressed within the text. By its demarcation, the text is opposed to all material signs of the context not contained in the text. In general, any kind of sign activity within a given sign system may be called a text. "From this point of view," Lotman explains, "we may speak of a ballet, of a play, of a military parade, and of all of the other sign systems for behavior of texts, in the same measure in which we apply this term to a text written in a natural language, to a poem or to a picture" (1977).

Lotman also observes that in widely different cultures a tendency arises to see the world as text, and, as a consequence, to treat our knowledge of the world as tantamount to a reading, understanding, and interpretation of this text. This view of the world as text is related to long-standing religious views of the text—a position that is nicely summarized in Francis Bacon's quip from *The Advancement of Learning* that there are two texts laid before us by God: Scripture and the creatures that express God's power (I. vi. 16). A similar position can be seen in the Russian Symbolists' view that the world presents itself as a hierarchy of texts dominated by one universal text.

The vision of the "world as text" outlined by Derrida argues that there is nothing outside of the text ("il n'y a pas de hors-texte"). Aesthetic texts, as well as all others, are, for Derrida, a place of the effaced trace—the play of presence and absence. The breadth of Derrida's notion of textuality is evident when one considers that not only is textuality the object of study, it is also the subject that studies. As such, the subject-object distinction does not hold for Derrida—he is said to have *deconstructed* it. Whereas structuralists such as Barthes contended that reconstruction of the object in a way that manifests the rules of its functioning is the goal of critical activity, Derrida challenged a position predicated on the ability to objectively describe objects in the world. His textualism asserts that we cannot provide answers to questions such as "What is X?"—whether X is art in general or a particular painting or musical composition. Although Derrida's grammatological structure is discernible, it denies us the possibility of objective description in aesthetics.

The Limits of Expansion. One of the reasons for the expansion of *text* as a key term in philosophy in general, and aesthetics in particular, is the impact of the "linguistic turn" on twentieth-century philosophers. Interest in language among philosophers has achieved a status unprecedented in the history of philosophy. Philosophers from differing philosophical trends have together agreed that not only are philosophical questions closely related to questions of language, but also that truth is linked in some ultimate sense to language. Some philosophers have even gone so far as to say that outside of language there are no facts, and that reality is only available to us through language—that the dream of "seeing through" language or making it more precise is not the way to knowledge and truth. As such, the contemporary concept of text has appealed to many philosophers, as has viewing the world as text. One of the problems with this approach, though, is that it can easily give way to forms of relativism or linguistic idealism.

The main tension that has arisen in the expansion of text is not whether the concept should be central to philosophy, but whether it should be the classical or the contemporary concept of text that is fundamental. On the one hand, the classical concept of text allows us to conceive of text as an autonomous object capable of being evaluated in terms of its formal unity, and as integrating various historical, literary, and sociological influences and sources into a new unity. On the other hand, the contemporary concept of text pushes us to reveal the codes that integrate the text into a whole of signification, and suggests that we view text as a function of linguistic and ideological discourse. The latter concept of text is also theoretically more fruitful in a technological world that reinscribes texts into an economy of production and consumption, and does not value uniqueness. Despite attempts by some, such Rorty and Eco, to bridge the two conceptions, however, there has yet to be an entirely satisfactory compromise between the two conceptions. The differences between them seem almost insurmountable.

[*See also* Discourse; Ecphrasis; Hypertext; Imagery; *and* Ut Pictura Poesis.]

BIBLIOGRAPHY

Bakhtin, Mikhail M. "The Problem of the Text in Linguistics, Philology, and the Human Sciences: An Experiment in Philosophical Analysis." In *Speech Genres and Other Late Essays,* translated by Vern W. McGee, edited by Caryl Emerson and Michael Holquist, pp. 103–131. Austin, 1986. English translation of "Problema teksta v lingvistike, filologii i drugikh gumanitarnykh naukakh: Opyt filosofskogo analiza" (1959–1961).

Barthes, Roland. "The Death of the Author" (1968). In *The Rustle of Language,* translated by Richard Howard, pp. 49–55. New York, 1986.

Barthes, Roland. "From Work to Text" (1971). In *The Rustle of Language,* translated by Richard Howard, pp. 56–64. New York, 1986.

Barthes, Roland. "Texte (théorie du)" (1973). In *Encyclopaedia universalis,* vol. 7, pp. 996–1000. Paris, 1985.

Barthes, Roland. *The Pleasure of the Text.* Translated by Richard Miller. New York, 1975. English translation of *Le plaisir du text* (Paris, 1973).

Benveniste, Émile. "The Semiology of Language" (1969). In *Semiotics: An Introductory Anthology,* edited by Robert E. Innis, pp. 226–246. Bloomington, Ind., 1985.

Derrida, Jacques. *Of Grammatology.* Translated by Gayatri Chakravorty Spivak. Baltimore, 1976. English translation of *De la grammatologie* (Paris, 1967).

Ducrot, Oswald, and Tzvetan Todorov. *Encyclopedic Dictionary of the Sciences of Language.* Translated by Catherine Porter. Baltimore, 1979. English translation of *Dictionnaire encyclopédique des sciences du langage* (Paris, 1972).

Eagleton, Terry. *Criticism and Ideology: A Study in Marxist Literary Theory.* London, 1976.

Eagleton, Terry. *Literary Theory: An Introduction.* Minneapolis, 1983.

Eco, Umberto. *A Theory of Semiotics.* Bloomington, Ind., 1976.

Eco, Umberto. *The Role of the Reader: Explorations in the Semiotics of Texts.* Bloomington, Ind., 1979.

Fish, Stanley. *Is There a Text in This Class? The Authority of Interpretive Communities.* Cambridge, Mass., 1980.

Goodman, Nelson. *Languages of Art: An Approach to a Theory of Symbols.* 2d ed. Indianapolis, 1976.

Hjelmslev, Louis. *Prolegomena to a Theory of Language.* Rev. ed. Translated by Francis J. Whitfield. Madison, Wis., 1961.

Jameson, Frederic. "The Ideology of the Text." In *The Ideologies of Theory: Essays, 1971–1986,* vol. 1, pp. 17–71. Minneapolis, 1988.

Kristeva, Julia. *Séméiotiké: recherches pour une sémanalyse.* Paris, 1969.

Kristeva, Julia. *The Kristeva Reader.* Edited by Toril Moi. New York, 1986.

Lotman, Jurij. *The Structure of the Artistic Text.* Translated by Ronald Vroon and Gail Lenhoff. Ann Arbor, 1977. English translation of *Struktura khudozhestvennogo teksta* (Moscow, 1970).

Mowitt, John. *Text: The Genealogy of an Antidisciplinary Object.* Durham, N.C., 1992.

Ricoeur, Paul. "What Is a Text? Explanation and Understanding." In *Hermeneutics and the Human Sciences: Essays on Language, Action, and Interpretation,* edited and translated by John B. Thompson, pp. 145–164. Cambridge and New York, 1981.

Rorty, Richard. "Texts and Lumps." In *Objectivity, Relativism and Truth: Philosophical Papers,* vol. 1, pp. 78–92. Cambridge and New York, 1991.

Wimsatt, W. K., Jr., and Monroe Beardsley. "The Intentional Fallacy" (1946). In *The Verbal Icon: Studies in the Meaning of Poetry* by W. K. Wimsatt, Jr., pp. 3–20. Lexington, Ky., 1954.

JEFFREY R. DI LEO

THEATER. Until recently, there have been remarkably few sustained investigations into the nature of theater, by either philosophers, theater scholars, or practitioners. For a comprehensive overview of important theoretical positions, one must ferret through a disparate assortment of texts in disciplines that have had little discourse with one another. With a few notable exceptions—such as Georg Wilhelm Friedrich Hegel, for whom theater occupied the "highest phase" of all the arts—philosophers have examined theater only fleetingly in the context of aesthetic theories developed through detailed analyses of the visual arts or music. Theater scholars have produced mostly critical studies of particular dramatic texts or performances and historical studies of particular periods or movements, and theater practitioners typically advance manifestos declaring what theater *should* be. Such descriptive and prescriptive analyses inevitably rest on assumptions about the general features of theater, but rarely do they explicitly articulate, and even more rarely do they defend, these assumptions.

The most basic assumption concerns what sort of thing theater is. The issue is not how to *define* theater in the sense of identifying necessary and sufficient conditions (an issue considered later in this essay), but how to *categorize* it, situating theater among related phenomena. The perspective one assumes toward theater helps to determine both the way one answers many basic questions and the questions that one sees fit to ask in the first place, much as a scientific paradigm determines the terms of scientific research.

Paradigms. Various approaches have been taken to categorizing theater. This section examines several paradigms.

Theater as enacted literature. In the *Poetics,* Aristotle defines tragedy as a species of mimesis or imitation, and specifically as a genre of poetry. The four most important elements in his ranking of the six elements of tragedy—plot *(mythos),* character *(ethos),* thought *(dianoia),* and diction *(lexis)*—pertain exclusively to the dramatic text; only the last two elements—song *(melos)* and spectacle *(opsis)*—pertain to theatrical performance. Aristotle describes these two performance-related elements as "embellishments" and ascribes the power of tragedy chiefly to dramatic structure. Aristotle's *Poetics* dictated the terms of dramatic theory from the time that text was rediscovered in the Renaissance through the Enlightenment, with the primary goal of most theorists, from Julius Caesar Scaliger in the sixteenth century to Voltaire in the eighteenth century, being to establish rules for the proper construction of tragedies and, by extension, plays in other genres. Even after the authority of Aristotle's *Poetics* waned after the Enlightenment, many serious thinkers who concerned themselves with drama continued to follow Aristotle in devaluing performance. In the nineteenth century, the British critic Charles Lamb argued that William Shakespeare's plays exist fully only on the page, and that performances corrupt the texts' purity. For a generation of scholars following World War II, the dominant paradigm for analyzing plays was New Criticism, which treated plays as extended metaphors to be subjected to "close readings," minimizing the significance of even such quasi-theatrical features as the sequence of the dialogue and its attribution to specific characters.

Theater as sign system. In the twentieth century, the most extensive body of theory analyzing the general nature of theater employed an approach that combines, in varying proportions, the structuralist semiology of the Swiss linguist

Ferdinand de Saussure and the pragmatic semiotics of the American philosopher Charles Sanders Peirce. The underlying assumptions of semiotic theories of theater are that the primary function of theater is communicative and that theater constitutes a distinctive system of signs with its own syntax and semantics. Theater semiotics has come in two waves. The first occurred in Prague during the 1930s and 1940s, when members of the Prague Linguistic Circle emphasized the conventional and dynamic nature of theatrical signs: a single signifier, such as an actor or a prop, can convey virtually any type of meaning, including information about a character or place. This early semiotic program paid particular attention to those theatrical practices that highlighted the conventionality of the theater event, such as puppetry, and folk and experimental theater. It came to an abrupt halt when the Soviet authorities—who had declared Socialist Realism the only valid style for drama and theater—disbanded the Prague Linguistic Circle in 1948. The second wave of theater semiotics, beginning in the late 1960s, was international in scope. Theater semioticians such as Tadeusz Kowsan, Patrice Pavis, Marco De Marinis, Keir Elam, and Erika Fischer-Lichte worked to provide a systematic account of the theatrical sign system. This project involved, among other things, breaking theater down into component sign systems such as language, gesture, and costume, determining the way these component systems operate both separately and together, and, most problematically, trying to identify a minimal syntactical and semantic unit equivalent to words in verbal language. By the early 1990s, the semiotic paradigm seemed to have fallen out of favor, and many self-described theater semioticians had abandoned the effort to identify universal features of the supposed "language" of the stage, turning instead to issues concerning the ideology and historical contingency of theater practices. [See Prague School; and Semiotics.]

Theater as phenomenon. One objection to the semiotic paradigm is that it fails to account for the vitality of human presence on the stage. In response to this limitation, a number of theater theorists, such as Bert States and Stanton Garner, have adopted an approach they call "phenomenological," loosely inspired by the work of such Continental philosophers as Maurice Merleau-Ponty, Gaston Bachelard, and to a lesser extent Roman Ingarden and Mikel Dufrenne. From a semiotic perspective, a live actor is just another kind of signifier, and theater is little different than film; indeed, according to some semioticians, the former is a subset of the latter, which incorporates virtually all of the sign systems of theater and adds additional systems such as montage. From a phenomenological perspective, however, live performance and film are radically different. Phenomenology shifts the focus away from theater as a medium for communication and examines the way different dramatic and performance strategies manipulate spectators' perceptions of the performance event, and in partic-

ular their subjective experience of time and space, their sensitivity to the elements of risk and spontaneity implicit in live performance, and their awareness of the corporeality of the actor's body. This emphasis on the body dovetails with issues in feminist theory such as "gender construction" and "the gaze," and theorists including Judith Butler and Peggy Phelan have employed variations of the phenomenological approach to analyze the way performance manipulates people's perception of gender and sexuality. [See Phenomenology.]

Theater as art form. Philosophers of art such as Susanne Knauth Langer, Richard Wollheim, Nicholas Wolterstorff, and Kendall Walton have carved out a place for theater within their aesthetic theories, albeit usually as an afterthought. Analyzing theater as an art form tends to deemphasize the relationship between theater and literature that, until recently, has preoccupied most academic theater specialists, and highlights theater's kinship with other art forms. As a medium of representation, theater has much in common with both painting and sculpture; scenery often incorporates elements of both these media, and one might view an actor as a sculpture made of flesh. At the same time, many of theater's nonrepresentational features relate theater more closely to music: both music and theater involve a temporal dimension and the concept of "performing a work." Because theater shares key features with other art forms, philosophers often find it easy to apply to theater their solutions to problems presented by other forms. Theater, however, also presents some distinctive philosophical challenges of its own, and these have received less attention. By using flesh-and-blood human beings to represent human beings, and real actions to represent fictional actions, theater blurs the lines between reality and representation in a way that no other art form does. Actors function at once as artists and media, analogous to both the musician and the music, simultaneously giving voice to dramatic language and becoming aesthetic objects in their own right.

Theater as performance. Since the mid-1970s, an increasing number of theorists have situated theater within a larger field called performance studies, whose earliest champions were the experimental theater director Richard Schechner and the anthropologist Victor Turner. Performance studies encompasses not only Western and non-Western theater traditions, but also dance, performance art, circus, shamanistic rituals, sporting events, political rallies, parades, wedding ceremonies, and medieval tournaments. Performance studies inherits its populist, antiliterary impulses from 1960s avant-garde theater and performance art, and at the same time responds to the growing emphasis on multiculturalism in all disciplines in the arts and humanities. A number of writers have followed Schechner in defining performance as "restored behavior," that is, any behavior that can be rehearsed and repeated, but there is little emphasis on establishing a rigid definition; the focus is rather on identifying multiple points of similarity and variation within an open-ended range of phenomena. A precedent for the performance studies paradigm occurred early in the twentieth century when the "Cambridge school anthropologists" Gilbert Murray and F. M. Cornford argued that Greek tragedy and comedy, respectively, evolved from pagan rituals enacting the myth of the Year-Daemon. Although most classical scholars rejected this proposal, the underlying idea of analyzing theater from an anthropological perspective rather than a literary or aesthetic one has had enormous influence. Another key influence on performance studies was sociologist Erving Goffman's use of theater as a governing metaphor to analyze a wide range of social behavior, demonstrating the usefulness of an extended concept of "performance."

Theater as play. A number of theorists—among the most prominent being the cultural historian Johan Huizinga and the hermeneutic philosopher Hans-Georg Gadamer—have analyzed theater as a species of play, classing theater with children's games of make-believe and other games that involve an element of role playing. The performance studies approach sometimes subsumes this paradigm, for it includes any game performed for spectators within its province. [*See* Play.]

Theater as mode of cultural production. Starting in the 1980s, a great deal of theory set out to de-aestheticize theater, analyzing it as a mode of cultural production alongside such practices as advertising, news reporting, popular music, and television. This approach is grounded in Marxist theory, and in particular the work of twentieth-century cultural materialists such as Antonio Gramsci, Louis Althusser, and the Frankfurt School, as well as Michel Foucault's analyses of history and power. Its objective is to explore the way theater—both as an institution and through particular works—participates in the propagation or subversion of the "dominant ideology." Advocates of this approach emphasize the need to "historicize" theory, that is, to base it in an understanding of a particular cultural context, and so tend to be skeptical of "essentializing" claims about the nature of theater.

Problems. Regardless of which paradigm is adopted in the analysis of theater, certain problems arise. They will be discussed in this section.

Definition of theater. Most theorists, whatever their preferred paradigm, agree that theater as conventionally practiced within the Western tradition consists of one or more actors performing a play for an audience, which in turn entails conveying a narrative by means of role playing. Not all theorists would accept every element of this loose definition of theater as a necessary condition. In particular, some regard the existence of a "play" as optional, thereby allowing for improvised forms of theater—though certain definitions of "play" do accommodate certain kinds of improvisation. Others regard "narrative" as optional, thereby

allowing for Happenings and other types of avant-garde performance—though even many avant-garde performance artists consider some hint of narrative content, however fragmented or ambiguous, to be integral to theater. For example, Alan Kaprow, who coined the term *Happening* in the late 1950s, insists that Happenings *not* be regarded as theater. Some even question the necessity of "audience," thereby making room for fully participatory events that do not distinguish between performer and spectator. Most philosophical controversies concerning theater, however, arise from the way theorists characterize the constituent elements of this definition and, even more, the precise relationship between these elements. The most salient controversies have concerned the relationships between play and performance, performance and narrative, and actor and role.

Play and performance. Semiotic theories distinguish between the "dramatic text" that a reader encounters on the page and the "performance text" that an audience encounters in the theater. This "two-text" model is consistent with at least six ways of characterizing the relationship of performance text to dramatic text, each of which has had prominent proponents. Proponents of an *incorporation* theory (e.g., Jiří Veltruský) regard the dramatic text merely as the "verbal component" of the performance. The relationship between play and performance, on this view, is one of part to whole: a performance, in addition to containing other kinds of signs, contains the dialogue of the play. According to a *translation* theory (such as Pavis's view), dramatic text and performance are related by virtue of what they represent, with the performance attempting to say in the language of the stage what the text says in words. A *realization* theory (such as Jean Alter's) is similar to a translation theory, but instead of regarding the dramatic text as the representation of a fictional narrative, it regards it as the representation of an idealized performance. An *interpretation* theory (such as Fischer-Lichte's) responds to the fact that performances do not strive merely to replicate content already present in the text or that once existed in the mind of the playwright, as the translation and realization theories imply, but inevitably add a tremendous amount of information, including, but not limited to, the specific appearance of the props and scenery and the actors' inflections and movements. These creative contributions convey the director's, designer's, and actors' interpretation of the play. Advocates of *adaptation* theories (e.g., Benedetto Croce, Ingarden) are similarly impressed by the extent of a production's creative contribution, but draw the conclusion that the resulting production should therefore be regarded as a new work altogether, analogous to a film based on a novel. Finally, proponents of *execution* theories (e.g., John Searle, De Marinis, Anne Ubersfeld) regard the dramatic text as a series of instructions, commands, or suggestions to actors and designers, though they offer contrasting proposals regarding the specific illocutionary force of the stage directions and dialogue.

Many contemporary analytic philosophers conceive of plays as logical *types* whose *instances* are performances. This proposal, first advanced by Wollheim in *Art and Its Objects* (1968; 1992), implicitly rejects the two-text model, which conflates the concept of the "play" with that of the dramatic text. The relationship between a play and its performances, on this view, is less like that of a novel to its translations than a novel to its copies or a silk screen to the prints made from it. One strength of this view is that the concept of a "play" need not presuppose the existence of written dialogue, as long as it is capable of providing a set of principles that allow performers and audience members to determine what counts as a performance of the work. Among the areas of contention surrounding the type-token theory are when a performance ceases to be an instance of the play and becomes a new work, and whether the primary object of aesthetic interest for the audience is the type (the play) or the token (the performance). Wollheim, for example, regards the play as the aesthetic object and the performance as a means of access to it; Paul Thom, by contrast, concedes that theatrical performances are not artistic "works," as plays are, but maintains nonetheless that they are primary objects of aesthetic interest. The theory also raises many issues that have as yet received little attention, such as the status of the production. A play such as *Hamlet*, for example, receives a great many productions by different directors and casts of actors, and each of these productions usually has many performances. Hence, a theatrical performance is typically the token of two types: a play and a production, and productions themselves are simultaneously tokens with respect to plays and types with respect to performances.

Performance and narrative. Precisely how theatrical performances convey narrative information is one of the key issues in theater theory. [*See* Narrative.] A major concern has been the relative role of what Peirce called "symbols" (convention), "icons" (which can be characterized in terms of either resemblance or exemplification, concepts that some theories conflate), and "indexes" (physical cause or contiguity). Prague school semioticians emphasized the role of convention, as did the American playwright Thornton Wilder in his reflections on theater theory; many more recent semioticians, such as Umberto Eco, have emphasized iconicity, and some, such as Elam, have argued that indexical signs play an extensive role. Other theorists, such as Jean-Paul Sartre and Walton, have offered nonsemiotic theories of theatrical representation emphasizing the role of the spectators' imagination. According to Walton, for example, representational art functions in general by serving as "props" in the spectators' "games of make-believe" (1990). What distinguishes theater from other art forms is its extensive use of *reflexive* props: when spectators watch an actor playing Hamlet, they not only imagine that they are seeing Hamlet, as they would if confronted with a painting of Hamlet, but they imagine *of the actor* that *he* is Hamlet.

In addition to analyzing how theater works as a medium of representation, some theorists have questioned the possibility of a nonrepresentational theater. Some theorists, such as Michael Kirby, Josette Feral, and Jean-François Lyotard, argue that "de-semiotic" strategies of performance can arrest signification and produce a theatre of pure "surfaces" or "libidinal energy." Others, such as States, Marvin Carlson, and Herbert Blau, argue that all such strategies are doomed to failure, and nothing can ever simply be "itself" on the stage; the theatrical frame inevitably initiates a process of signification or illusion.

Actor and role. A hotly contested issue, especially since the posthumous publication of Denis Diderot's *Paradox of Acting* in 1830, has been the degree to which actors should identify with their roles. Diderot took the position that actors should remain psychologically detached from their characters and acutely aware of their audiences. At the same time, they should produce the illusion of identification with the character and immersion in the fictional scene, creating the impression that an invisible "fourth wall" separates the world of the stage from that of the audience. Diderot's advocacy of fourth-wall realism in the theater correlates with his illusionistic theory of painting, which Michael Fried aptly describes as "dramatic," and anticipates the realistic aesthetic that was to dominate the Western stage by the end of the nineteenth century. At the same time, Joseph Roach (1985) has traced an intimate connection between Diderot's theory of acting and the arguments about emotion, sensibility, and spontaneity set forth in his writings about physiology and biology.

During the first three decades of the twentieth century, the Russian director and actor Konstantin Stanislavsky (1948) developed a systematic approach to actor training known simply as the "System." Stanislavsky's objective was to help actors consistently achieve a state of inspired creativity and intense emotional involvement with their parts. His quasi-scientific attempt to uncover timeless laws of acting drew inspiration from the nascent science of psychology, and in particular the work of the French psychologist Théodule Ribot. Stanislavsky insists that the *illusion* of identification is not sufficient; actors must act "truthfully" and "become the character." According to Stanislavsky, a commitment to "inner truth" does not entail a realistic aesthetic; on the contrary, he began work on the System precisely as his interests as a director shifted from Naturalism to Symbolism. Consequently, Stanislavsky's position inverts Diderot's: whereas the former insists on the identification between actor and character but not the illusion of external realism, the latter insists on the illusion of reality but rejects actor-character identification. Nevertheless, the System has become closely associated with realism, and in particular American domestic realism, through its appropriation and modification by members of New York's Group Theatre in the 1930s. The various American incarnations of the System became known collectively as the "Method," and achieved worldwide fame through the spectacular film success of Method-trained actors such as Marlon Brando. Method performances have proved especially well suited to film, because they are not only capable of withstanding the close scrutiny of the camera, but they thrive on the camera's ability to convey subtleties of expression and subtext. In turn, film's emphasis on the visual elements of the performance has no doubt contributed to the diminution of language's role in much modern and postmodern theater.

Bertolt Brecht devised his widely influential theory of "epic acting" in the late 1920s when he embraced Marxism, and abandoned it toward the end of his career in favor of a more nuanced approach. This theory shares Diderot's position regarding the means, but disagrees with both Diderot and Stanislavsky about the desired ends. Actors should not even *appear* to identify with their characters or be immersed in the fictional scene. They should adopt a third person perspective on their characters, cultivating a "gestus of showing" to keep the audience conscious at all times that it is watching a play, and conveying a clear attitude toward the character for the audience to assess critically. Humanist approaches to acting that cultivate empathy between character, actor, and spectator, Brecht argues, universalize the play's meaning by encouraging the spectator to focus on individual psychology rather than the larger sociopolitical context.

Diderot, Stanislavsky, and Brecht differ in their empirical assumptions (for example, about what approach to acting most effectively elicits the audience's empathy) and artistic objectives (for example, whether audience empathy is to be encouraged or avoided), but not in the range of possibilities for which their theories allow. Brecht, for example, presupposes the possibility of identifying with one's character, just as Stanislavsky presupposes the possibility of adopting an objectified attitude toward one's character. Underlying all these theories, however, are unresolved philosophical issues concerning the concepts of both character and identification. What is a dramatic role? Is that concept the same as literary character? Is it the same in all forms of theater? Little philosophical work has been done to address these questions explicitly, though philosophers often, with little reflection, construe their general theories about fictional character to extend to the case of theater. Both Diderot and Brecht describe dramatic characters as social types; Stanislavsky, by contrast, advocates a humanist view of characters, explicitly warning actors to avoid playing general types and instructing them to invent details about the character's biography. This view of character links Stanislavsky to nineteenth-century literary critics such as A. C. Bradley, who scoured through Shakespeare's plays for hints about the characters' lives; but whereas Bradley analyzes literary characters as if they were autonomous human beings, Stanislavsky does not ultimately grant characters an autonomous existence. Stanislavsky maintains that, in the end, actors should play themselves, acting truthfully *as if they* were in the character's given circumstances.

The influential director and theorist Jerzy Grotowski (1968), inspired by Antonin Artaud's vision of a "Theater of Cruelty," similarly regards character on stage as a role that the actor must truthfully assume, but he "depsychologizes" the concept. Rather than defining the role in terms of a character's fictional situation, he defines it as a "score" of precise physical actions, and conceives of the actor's disciplined performance as a ritualistic process, an act of self-sacrifice with symbolic overtones. Although Grotowski's approach has been described as apolitical, Grotowski has retrospectively described his productions in the Soviet-controlled Poland of the 1960s as subversive rituals of freedom and self-expression within an oppressive society. Grotowski's work assumed a different significance in the United States during the 1960s, where its raw, uncompromising emotional expressiveness and physicality, coupled with its rejection of realistic conventions, constituted a rebellion against the values and restrictions of the bourgeois "establishment," and a utopian attempt to achieve a more authentic mode of being.

A second philosophical issue underlying the debates about whether the actor should identify with the character concerns the notion of "identification." Many writers have defined the idea of "becoming the character" in terms of emotional empathy. The philosophical problem then becomes explaining what an actor's emotional empathy with a character entails. Although philosophers have devoted little attention to this problem, the many conflicting theories about the nature of an audience's emotional involvement with music and fiction clearly have a bearing here.

In his later work, Stanislavsky de-emphasized the significance of emotional identification and argued that the key challenge for the actor is to truthfully perform a character's actions. This goal raises one of the few sharply defined philosophical controversies about acting's logical limitations. A number of philosophers have asserted that actors do not perform *real* actions on stage, but only *pretend* to perform actions. Although some philosophers have argued that *all* action on stage is pretense, the most influential position has been Searle's, which applies specifically to the status of speech acts. Searle argues that the fictional frame of a theatrical performance suspends the illocutionary force of any utterance made during a play. Theater semioticians regularly cite this argument with approval, because it supports the semiotic view that everything placed on stage becomes a sign. If this argument is correct, then Stanislavsky's insistence that actors "really" perform actions is quixotic, and boils down to an injunction for actors to create a particularly effective illusion of real action. The argument that the theatrical frame eliminates illocutionary force, however, fails to account for the function of speech acts in improvisations, where, for example, one actor's command that a partner sit down often does cause the partner to sit down. If speech acts performed during improvisations retain some degree of illocutionary force, so, at least under certain circumstances, might speech acts performed during scripted performances.

[*See also* Alembert; Brecht; Diderot; Dryden; Goethe; Performance; Performance Art; Rousseau; Sartre; Tragedy; *and* Wilde.]

BIBLIOGRAPHY

Artaud, Antonin. *The Theater and Its Double*. Translated by Mary Caroline Richards. New York, 1958.

Blau, Herbert. *To All Appearances: Ideology and Performance*. New York and London, 1992.

Brecht, Bertolt. *Brecht on Theatre: The Development of an Aesthetic*. Translated and edited by John Willett. New York, 1964.

Carlson, Marvin. *Theories of the Theatre: A Historical and Critical Survey, from the Greeks to the Present*. Exp. ed. Ithaca, N.Y., 1993.

Cole, Toby, and Helen Krich Chinoy, eds. *Actors on Acting*. New rev. ed. New York, 1970.

Dukore, Bernard F., ed. *Dramatic Theory and Criticism: Greeks to Grotowski*. New York, 1974.

Elam, Keir. *The Semiotics of Theatre and Drama*. London and New York, 1980.

Fischer-Lichte, Erika. *The Semiotics of Theater*. Translated by Jeremy Gaines and Doris L. Jones. Bloomington, Ind., 1992.

Grotowski, Jerzy. *Towards a Poor Theatre*. New York, 1968.

Pavis, Patrice. *Languages of the Stage: Essays in the Semiology of the Theatre*. New York, 1982.

Phelan, Peggy. *Unmarked: The Politics of Performance*. London and New York, 1993.

Reinelt, Janelle G., and Joseph R. Roach, eds. *Critical Theory and Performance*. Ann Arbor, 1992.

Roach, Joseph. *The Player's Passion: Studies in the Science of Acting*. Newark, Del., 1985.

Saltz, David Z. "How to Do Things on Stage." *Journal of Aesthetics and Art Criticism* 49.1 (Winter 1991): 32–45.

Schechner, Richard. *Performance Theory*. Rev. exp. ed. New York and London, 1988.

Searle, John R. "The Logical Status of Fictional Discourse." In *Expression and Meaning: Studies in the Theory of Speech Acts*, pp. 58–75. Cambridge and New York, 1979.

Stanislavsky, Konstantin. *An Actor Prepares*. Translated by Elizabeth Reynolds Hapgood. New York, 1948.

States, Bert O. *Great Reckonings in Little Rooms: On the Phenomenology of Theater*. Berkeley, 1985.

Thom, Paul. *For an Audience: A Philosophy of the Performing Arts*. Philadelphia, 1993.

Walton, Kendall L. *Mimesis as Make-Believe: On the Foundations of the Representational Arts*. Cambridge, Mass. 1990.

Zarrilli, Phillip B., ed. *Acting (Re)Considered: Theories and Practices*. London and New York, 1995.

DAVID Z. SALTZ

THEORIES OF ART. There is no limit to the number of theories that might be applied to art. Almost any account of social life or of human concerns might be extended to it.

There are also many possibilities for theories focusing specifically on art's various aspects, such as artistic creativity, performance, reception, criticism, and the histories and sociologies of these. Another area involves comparison of the arts of different cultures. One rather special theoretical enterprise, that of definition, attempts to outline what it is in virtue of which a thing is what it is. Definitions of art take different theoretical approaches—the functional, the procedural, and the historical. Moreover, individual philosophers (Plato, Plotinus, Thomas Aquinas, Francis Hutcheson, Alexander Baumgarten, Immanuel Kant, David Hume, Georg Wilhelm Friedrich Hegel, Arthur Schopenhauer, Friedrich von Schiller, Søren Kierkegaard, Friedrich Nietzsche, Martin Heidegger, John Dewey, and Roman Ingarden) developed philosophical systems in which the analysis of the aesthetic and of art was accorded an important place. Theories of art also have been developed by artists (such as Samuel Taylor Coleridge, John Ruskin, Oscar Wilde, T. S. Eliot, Wassily Kandinsky, Richard Wagner, and Igor Stravinsky) and by critics and historians (such as F. R. Leavis, Clement Greenberg, Susan Sontag, E. H. Gombrich, and Heinrich Wölfflin).

This essay begins by sketching some views that have been historically important in the aesthetics of Western art. These variously identify mimesis, expression, form, or historical process as central to art's distinctive character or purpose. Two broad trends in the approach to art—autonomism and contextualism—are then contrasted. The suppositions of autonomism have dominated the discussion of art over much of the past two hundred years; contextualism represents a recent reaction to autonomism. Next, the suppositions of modernism and their rejection by postmodernists are outlined. A final section considers Marxism, psychoanalysis, and feminism in their application to art. These accounts of psychological and social life have widely influenced the way in which art is discussed, analyzed, and made, just as they have affected the wider intellectual climate of the times.

Art as Mimesis. Plato (c.427–347 BCE) characterizes art as mimetic—a notion covering imitation, representation, and embodiment. Because he regards the appearance of reality as but a shadow of the world of the Forms, wherein truth and stability reside, and art merely as a copy of that shadow, he sees art as doubly removed from the eternal verities. Accordingly, his conclusions are negative: art is an unreliable source of truth and is faulty as a pedagogical tool. Moreover, its power to work on the emotions, thereby subverting reason, makes it liable to mislead. In arriving at this assessment, Plato seems to assume that art would be valuable only if it could convey reliable information about the world of the Forms. One could challenge this assumption in two ways: by rejecting the Platonic doctrine of the Forms while arguing that art reveals truths about reality; or by suggesting that art's value does not depend solely on its capacity to inform us about the way the world is. In developing this last idea, it could be suggested that many artworks represent or generate fictional worlds the exploration and comprehension of which are interesting and worthwhile independently of the extent to which these fictions correspond to the real world. The point was made by Aristotle (384–322 BCE), who argued that the mimetic arts present the idea of a *possible* world. [*See* Aristotle.]

Provided one includes narration within the scope of mimesis, the mimetic theory applies to many of the arts—to drama, song, dance, poetry, and literature, as well as to painted or sculpted depictions—but it does not cover all the forms of art and it does not capture all that is important about some of the arts to which it does pertain. Instrumental music and some paintings, sculptures, and dances appear to be abstract in nature. Meanwhile, the expressive power of many pieces, not their depictive character, is the more distinctive of them as art.

There are several ways by which one could try to save the mimetic theory by extending it to these alleged counterexamples. It might be argued that, as well as description and depiction, mimesis includes any form of symbolization or expression. Contra Plato, all art, including the abstract varieties, could be said to represent aspects of human experience that are not immediately apparent in appearances presented directly to the senses. If we cannot always describe what art represents, this might be because the aspects of human experience depicted in artworks are not readily describable. One might maintain, alternatively, that abstract works represent themselves, the materials from which they are constructed, or the techniques used in their construction.

None of these strategies is attractive, however. Given the differences between them, the assimilation of description, depiction, symbolization, and expression, rather than discovering an underlying commonality, imposes an artificial unity. Also, it is difficult to support the claim that art communicates the ineffable when there is so little agreement about the profundities allegedly conveyed by artworks, especially abstract ones. Moreover, there is no reason to think that abstract works refer to their properties or materials, as opposed merely to possessing or using these. To follow the suggestions mooted would drain the notion of mimesis of explanatory power and resilience.

It might be thought that no theory describing art as serving a referential function via mimesis can do justice to the fact that artworks interest us for themselves, not as instruments for conveying ideas lying beyond their boundaries. This objection is not so compelling as might first appear, though. Where it is fictional, or offered as such, a work's contents draw one in, rather than directing one elsewhere. It is a distinctive feature of art that the "message" is not easily to be separated from the "medium," that the significance of a work and the means by which this is imparted to it are re-

lated so intimately that a pursuit of the former usually leads to an awareness of the latter. If art serves a referential function in being mimetic, it does so in a fashion drawing attention to its own nature and to the techniques employed in it. It is opaque, not transparent, with respect to its import. Thus, an interest in representational artworks for themselves is consistent with a concern with their mimetic character. Even if it is not the prime purpose of artistic depictions to convey information about the world, it does not follow that an aesthetic interest in them could or should be indifferent to their depictive character or to the subjects they represent.

Art as Expression. Leo Tolstoy (1828–1910) maintains that the function of art is the communication of feeling from the artist to the audience. The relevant feelings should encompass or be consistent with the highest religious and moral perceptions. Art derives its value and purpose from its expressing those feelings (such as ones of human fellowship) that give meaning to life in general. Works whose sole aim is to be beautiful are dismissed as mere entertainment, whereas those that promote cultural elitism and social division are rejected for opposing art's true function.

Tolstoy's is a revisionist theory; on his view, works that do not conform to his analysis are not art. He explicitly rejects the art credentials of many works, including some of William Shakespeare's plays, that are generally recognized as artistic paradigms. But if we think of artworks as generating and exploring fictional worlds that remain distinct from, even if they take inspiration from, the actual world, and if we are inclined to value them not solely for the moral lessons they might teach but also for the pleasure we gain from contemplating them on their own terms, we might prefer to stand by the notion of art with which we are already familiar. It should be noted, moreover, that a theory such as Tolstoy's does not apply readily to abstract works, such as Johann Sebastian Bach's fugues. [*See* Tolstoy.]

A different version of the expression theory, one that highlights the expression of emotion as against expression of the more general feelings that concern Tolstoy, is propounded by Benedetto Croce (1866–1952) and R. G. Collingwood (1889–1943). They regard artistic creation as a process through which the artist's inchoate feelings and impulses are brought to a definite form. The emotion present in, and communicated by, the artwork is constituted through the act of expression, having no prior identity; that is, the unique character of the emotion expressed is a product of the manner of the emotion's artistic expression. Collingwood regards art as expression at the level of imagination, whereas Croce characterizes art as intuitive expression. Like Tolstoy, both tend to dismiss as not genuine artworks that do not accord with their theories.

These authors regard the work as existing in the artist's mind and as inseparable from the act of expression. A work can be created without being "externalized," but the creation of a public object in a physical medium is necessary if the artist wishes to communicate his work to others. This public object is not strictly the work, but is, rather, a vehicle by which awareness of the work is transmitted to the audience. The audience comes to know the work if contemplation of the public object leads it to recognize or share the mental condition that is the work's existence. Collingwood denies, however, that it is the function of art to arouse emotion. This is because an artist could aim to arouse a particular emotion only if he could identify in advance the emotion he intended to provoke, which he cannot do because the emotion expressed in his work cannot be identified prior to its successful expression. Collingwood holds that art is primarily concerned with the self-awareness accomplished by the artist through his act of expression. [*See* Collingwood; *and* Croce.]

This version of the expression theory invites some obvious objections: It overemphasizes the private, mental dimension of both artworks and emotions, and thereby relegates their public forms and embodiments to the role of dispensable concomitants. In consequence, it renders mysterious the process by which the audience becomes acquainted with, and confirms its knowledge of, the artwork. Moreover, it must treat the work's content as largely independent of the physical medium in which the artist works, whereas many artistic properties seem to rely on, or otherwise derive from, the manner in which the work's material is treated.

Another philosopher who regards art as primarily concerned with the expression of emotion is Susanne Knauth Langer (1895–1985). She argues that artworks are symbols of the emotions. Unlike discursive symbols, of which ordinary language is the main example, artworks are presentational symbols that represent feelings by echoing their forms. The various art forms differ in the manner in which they generate structures iconic with those of feelings. Neither the rules governing the projection of feeling into narrative, paint, sound, and the like, nor the individual character of the emotions thereby expressed, can be described in language. But the similarity between the forms of artworks and the forms of feeling, as well as reference from the former to the latter, is intuitively recognized by those who appreciate art.

There is a tension in Langer's theory produced by her attempt to account in language for that which she characterizes as ineffable and indescribable. Moreover, it is doubtful that the phenomenological forms of emotional experiences serve to distinguish adequately between their various types and instances, or between emotions and other kinds of dynamic processes, including nonmental ones. Finally, it might be thought that art expresses the content or feeling of emotions, not merely their structures. [*See* Langer.]

Art as Form. Aesthetic formalism often is associated with the theory of beauty offered by Kant (1724–1804),

who, in his *Critique of Judgment,* is concerned to characterize judgments of taste as objective, even though they do not provide knowledge. He regards judgments of aesthetic value (as distinct from moral and practical ones) as "disinterested." The objects of such judgments are viewed apart from their conceptual categorizations, functions, moral relevance, and existence, as well as the subjective interests, goals, desires, and appetites of the judger. Normally, the faculty of "imagination" collects and presents sensory "intuitions" that are synthesized and brought under concepts by the faculty of understanding. The knowledge that results, when harnessed to desire or duty, might then issue in action. In the case of aesthetic judgments, by contrast, the exercise of these faculties leads to their combination in a kind of contemplative "play" that is free in being both disinterested and nonconceptual. Where their interaction is harmonious, the free play of the imagination and understanding is pleasurable. We judge to be beautiful those objects of sensory intuition that produce delight when contemplated disinterestedly, and we regard beauty as autonomously valuable because its apprehension affords us a kind of pleasure unobtainable in other ways. Although aesthetic judgments are grounded only in feeling, and are not subsumable under rules, therefore, they have the character of universal, rather than subjective, judgments because they are made disinterestedly and, hence, ought to be arrived at by every person.

The formalism apparent in Kant's theory is a function of the nonconceptual, noncognitive character of aesthetic experience as he describes it. The raw data for aesthetic experience are delivered by the imagination and consist of that which is perceived without being brought under definite concepts by the understanding. In Kant's view, these data, as explored by the faculty of understanding, are the *form* of the object of intuition. The understanding seeks "purposiveness without purpose"; that is, it looks for, or considers the possibility of, design, while approaching its object as divorced from the ideas, concepts, or functions that would give moral or practical point to that design. The outcome, as previously noted, is "free play" of the imagination and the understanding, a pleasurable process coming to no natural conclusion or completion. [*See* Kant.]

In the early twentieth century, Clive Bell (1881–1964) argued that the feature distinctive of paintings is "significant form." Because all works have some kind of form, the qualifying adjective must carry the explanatory burden. Bell's account of significant form seems to render the notion both empty and circular. Works are said to possess significant form if they are artistically meritorious, and artistic merit then is analyzed as the possession of significant form. A more perspicuous account of formal significance, however, will likely lead one either to an unacceptably narrow formalism, one that treats representation and expression as artistically irrelevant, or to a notion of "form" that, in acknowledging the contribution of representational and expressive elements to the artistic whole, does not treat structural factors as the sole source of aesthetic interest and value. [*See* Bell.*]

For the reasons just indicated, formalism is at its most appealing when applied to art forms that are essentially abstract, with "pure" instrumental music being the prime candidate. The music critic Eduard Hanslick (1825–1904) developed such a view. He claimed that beauty in music resides solely in the attractiveness of "tonally moving forms." Music is not capable of expressing or embodying emotions, he holds, though it might be described metaphorically in terms of emotions or processes (such as the weather) that are analogous in their dynamic structure. Peter Kivy has advocated an "enhanced formalism" for instrumental music. He differs from Hanslick in holding that musical features can be intrinsically expressive of emotions and also in maintaining that limited representation is possible in instrumental music. If Kivy's is the more plausible account, it is so to the extent that it rejects narrow formalism by conceding that the appreciation of music frequently depends on an awareness of much more than purely sonic structures. [*See* Hanslick.]

Art as Historical Process. Hegel (1770–1831) regards art as a source of metaphysical knowledge; art has the aim of presenting truth, or insight into the divine, through a sensuous medium. When this goal is achieved, art is superseded by religion and then by philosophy, which offer progressively higher, conceptually based acquaintances with the nature of metaphysical and cultural truth. Human history is a progress toward self-consciousness and self-revelation. Art provides an essential step in this process, but progress in the history of art comes to an end when art's purpose is fulfilled. At that time, art no longer advances the dialectic of human history; doing so becomes the task of religion and philosophy.

According to Hegel, Greek art attained a harmony and consistency between its subject matter and its sensuous mode of expression. Accordingly, he maintains that art fulfilled its historical destiny some two thousand years ago; it had conveyed about the nature of spirit all of which it was capable. Subsequent historical developments left art behind, as it were. By the Christian era, art could only present truths already known through religion. There was no longer a perfectly balanced connection between form and content in art, between Beauty and Truth. From that time to the late eighteenth century, art increasingly concerned itself with its own techniques and forms; that is, with the mechanics of style.

The interpretation of Hegel's thesis is difficult and controversial. Some commentators have pointed out that Hegel draws attention to changes in the attitude to art, from a devotional to a critical one that evaluates art against other sources of knowledge and questions its authority. By contrast, other commentators have recommended the view that art returns to importance as the epochs of a civilization replace each other cyclically. The philosophical consciousness attained at the end of one epoch might give way to art that represents a higher level of self-awareness at the beginning of the next, and so the spiral continues. In that case, it is not obvious how Hegel would regard the art of the present day. Whatever interpretation is appropriate, it is plain that Hegel's theory of the end of art presupposes his more general philosophies of culture and history. The obscure metaphysics and teleological assumptions that underpin these might always be questioned. [*See* Hegel.]

Arthur C. Danto (b.1924) has taken inspiration from Hegel's views in offering a different theory that stresses the self-referential, inward-looking character of recent art: the purpose of art's historical progress has been the revelation of its own essence. The past tense is appropriate here because art completed its historical destiny in the twentieth century, according to Danto. Marcel Duchamp's readymades and Andy Warhol's appropriations of the images of popular culture raise within art the question of its own nature and intimate the answer to that question. The query could not have been posed within art at an earlier time because it was only with the twentieth century that it became acceptable to create as art items that, to the untutored eye, are perceptually indistinguishable from "mere real things." These revealed that what makes something art is not, as traditionally thought, its appearance, nor is it a matter of mimetic or expressive function. Something is art if it is surrounded by an "atmosphere" generated by the traditions, practices, and institutions of artists, performers, critics, and audiences. A piece so located cannot collapse the differences between itself and blank reality, or between itself and items with a different cultural or historical location. The history of art, as a progress toward that moment of self-discovery and awareness, then came to an end. Art continues to be made in its posthistorical phase, but it can have nothing new to say.

One wonders how readily Danto's apocalyptic vision can be generalized from the visual, plastic arts to others. There may be different ways of explaining the presently confused condition of art, and the alienation from it of the wider public, without committing oneself to a view according to which artistic change is irreversible and seemingly inevitable. Even if this were a plausible account of the development of artistic traditions, one might doubt that their development involves progress, as opposed merely to change, or that current artistic practice better reveals the nature of art than did historically prior ones. [*See* Danto.]

Accounts that focus on art's self-referential character might miss a crucial consideration that the theories characterized earlier aimed to capture. Art possesses interest and value only because it engages human concerns, aspirations, and sympathies. It might make this connection through narration, depiction, expression, or in other, less direct, ways.

Even outwardly abstract artworks are experienced as infused with the effort, intellect, and feeling that go into their creation and elaboration. Not every artwork establishes a direct link to the world of human experience, but we approach and appreciate art as such against a background that supposes the regularity and vitality of that bond. Without acknowledgment of this, it is difficult to explain the importance of art and the role it occupies in any culture's attempt to define itself.

Autonomism versus Contextualism. From the eighteenth to the early twentieth century, the philosophy of art was dominated by views such as the following: The fine arts are to be distinguished from crafts and decorative practices. Works are to be approached "for their own sakes"—for the enjoyment of their aesthetic properties, which are given directly to the senses. Beauty and sublimity are the primary aesthetic qualities and these are displayed more often in form than in content. The beautiful and the sublime are present in nature, just as they are in art. Access to a piece's aesthetic properties is provided by the faculty of taste, the exercise of which might require the adoption of a special perceptual mode or frame of mind, the aesthetic attitude. In adopting this attitude, the audience is to separate the work from its historical and social context and to divorce it from all practical concerns. This is deemed necessary for the perception and appreciation of its aesthetic character. Great artworks are produced by geniuses and artistic creation cannot be formulaic but must be unconstrained by rules. Works are valued for their individuality and originality.

Much of the philosophical aesthetics of the second half of the twentieth century might be seen as a reaction against the aesthetic autonomism just caricatured. This response was ignited by developments in the world of art, such as the revolutionary character of Duchamp's readymades and the rise of mass art, as well as by changes within the discipline of philosophy, which witnessed a move toward relativism, antirealism, and nihilism. The recent trend is toward a contextualized, historicized account of art's place and purpose.

Central planks of the autonomist platform have been challenged. For example, George Dickie (b.1926) argues against the idea that there is a distinctively aesthetic mode of perception or psychological attitude. Also, a wider range of aesthetic properties are considered relevant and attention is devoted more to artistic properties—nonsensuous features depending for their significance on semantic or referential relations—than to aesthetic qualities. [See Dickie.] As Danto has argued, if an artwork has properties different from "mere real things" from which it would be perceptually indistinguishable were it mistaken for another of their kind, then the artistic significance of artworks cannot reside in the appearances they present to the uninformed observer. The character of an artwork will be apparent only to the person who can locate it within or against an appropriate context, which is generated by the institutions, practices, writings, and actions of artists, critics, and audiences. As Joseph Margolis (b.1924) puts it, artworks are culturally emergent artifacts. Art has a history of making and of appreciation; it takes place within a tradition. This means not only that artists are inspired or revolted by the art of others and by the writings of commentators and historians, with this reaction showing in their own works, but also that what it is possible for artists to achieve depends on their place within the tradition. What might be a plausible continuation of the "narrative" that is art's history will depend both on who offers it (on what that person has done and said so far) and on the tradition as it then stands (on its works, its prevailing ideas, and its values). As a result, no artist can achieve by the same means what some other artist has done, which explains, as the autonomist view cannot readily do, the differences between an original and a forgery. It follows, then, that we can appreciate and understand art only if we bring to it a knowledge of its provenance and background, of the practical problems posed by its medium, of its intended and likely function, and so forth. The work takes its identity and its character from its relation to the art world and, more generally, to its social and historical surroundings; so, contrary to autonomism, it cannot be appreciated "for itself" if these relations are disregarded.

Modernism versus Postmodernism. *Modernism* is an umbrella term for the assumptions, values, and methods derived from the autonomism of writers such as Kant and Schopenhauer (1788–1860) by their followers in the twentieth century, such as Bell and the Bauhaus. Modernists stress the autonomy, unity, integrity, and high purpose of the fine arts, regard art as distinct from the other products of culture, and see art as a providing knowledge of absolute, transcendental truths that could not be communicated by other means. They assign to art a central place in systematic, overarching, totalizing theories that dealt more generally with metaphysical reality, morality, and historical inevitability.

As used within philosophy, *postmodernism* is a term applying to a range of theories that find their roots in contextualism and are united in their rejection of modernist doctrines. Postmodernism is suspicious of "metanarratives," of grand theories and systems. It rejects claims to absolute value or truth, along with the possibility of total consensus, of authority, and of neutral, objective, exterior perspectives on the nature of culture or history. Such notions are replaced by a commitment to indeterminacy, instability, openness, and multiplicity. More particularly, principled distinctions between fine art and mass art, and between art and the other products of social life, are discarded. Postmodernism favors eclecticism, individuality, pastiche, incongruity, and difference in art, and celebrates the polyglot impurity of popular art, while treating all explicit pretension to aesthetic value with irony. All this is accompanied not with the angst that so often attends the rebellious overthrow of one set of ideals by another but, rather, with a deflationary "who cares?"

Some philosophers whose accounts are regarded as postmodern include Derrida, Foucault, Lyotard, and Baudrillard. Jacques Derrida (b.1930) considers texts not as repositories of given, fixed meanings determined by their authors, but as intrinsically dynamic, linguistic arrays to be treated creatively by the playful reader who, in exploring their multidimensional resonances, thereby contributes to their significance. Michel Foucault (1926–1984) stresses the extent to which social "realities" are fabricated as discourses; that is, are culturally and linguistically relative. Jean-François Lyotard (b.1925) argues that social groups and the roles of authority within them are constituted by self-legitimating narratives. The values invoked in such narratives are internal to them and different narratives appeal to incommensurable values, so none can justify its superiority to another. Jean Baudrillard (b.1929) suggests that the signs and social images of mass culture now function as "hyperreal" commodities. They have become reified simulcra, replacing, rather than referring to, reality. The works of these authors are not solely (nor even primarily) concerned with art, but nevertheless are frequently taken to entail the aestheticization of life and culture. Where meaning and culture are arbitrarily constructed and there is no fundamental difference between the actual and the fictional, life cannot be distinguished from art.

The Continental philosophers with whom postmodernist aesthetics is associated often seem to make these equations: the collapse of the ideals and values of modernism with the end of artistic value as such; the historicity of art with the inaccessibility of the past (so that past art must be entirely remade by its current audience in light of their own values and desires); multivalency, ambiguity, and multiple interpretability with radical insecurity of meaning; the recognition that fundamental perspectives are relative to changeable, socially grounded conventions and practices with the demise of most standards for truth and objectivity. By contrast, some Anglo-American philosophers draw a different moral and philosophical goal from the demise of modernism. Their project appears to be that of demonstrating that a naturalized, historicized, socialized contextualism is compatible with objectivity in the description, interpretation, and evaluation of both present and past art. To this end, they argue that the multiple interpretability of artworks does not entail the legitimacy of all interpretations of a given work; that a knowledge of the history and conventions of art can make it possible to understand and appreciate the art of the past for what it was created to be, as well as permit the benefits of hindsight; and, more generally, that appropriate relativizations are not inconsistent with widely applicable standards for meaning, acceptability, merit, or truth.

Psychological or Social Theories External to Art.
This section discusses the place of some general accounts of human psychology and social structure as these have been applied to the discussion of art: Marxism, psychoanalysis, and feminism (treated as if they were unitary theories).

Karl Marx (1818–1883), in his attempt to explain the material (economic) relations that determine social relations, and the implications of these for the unfolding of history, regarded art, and "culture" in general, as belonging to sets of ideas (the "superstructure") in a society that are determined by economic relations (the "infrastructure") and the patterns of power generated by these relations. [See Marxism.] Sigmund Freud (1856–1939) presented an account of human psychosexual development and of the mental structures and forces that govern transactions between the public and private aspects of the individual. Although he viewed artworks much as he did dreams and fantasies—as symptomatic of unconscious desires from which they are derived by a process of symbolization—he took inspiration from art and myth and named thematic patterns of human development after Oedipus (and Elektra). [See Freud.] Feminism, as a political and intellectual movement, has been concerned to uncover and alter the masculinist attitudes that have led to the suppression, deprivation, and exclusion of women with respect not only to their proper social, political, and economic place, but also to their spirit, moral ethos, and character. Art, as a prime manifestation of culture, has been viewed by feminists both as an instrument employed for women's oppression and as providing an opportunity for renewal and change. [See Feminism.]

These theories are relevant to art in three ways. First, they provide theoretical frameworks in terms of which to view artistic practice as a whole, either to illustrate the theories or to expose the forces shaping that practice. The theories can be applied in producing broad-based accounts of the creative process, of performance, of audience reception, of the social dynamics of the art world, and of themes persistently presented within artworks. For instance, the Marxist György Lukács (1885–1971) considers many literary works for their modernist (bourgeois) or realist (socialist) tendencies and John Berger (b.1926) notes how the contents of paintings serve to illustrate or imply the social status of the owner or commissioner, thereby revealing the role of art as an economic commodity. The Freudian Otto Rank (1884–1939) offers a detailed account of artistic creativity. Feminists such as Kate Millett (b. 1934) have exposed masculinist attitudes expressed toward women in literature in *Sexual Politics* (New York, 1970). Feminists also have drawn attention to the fact that skilled women's work, such as needlepoint, has been denied the status of art by being dismissed as a decorative, domestic craft. Germaine Greer (b.1939), among others, has—in *The Obstacle Race: The Fortunes of Women Painters and their Work* (New York, 1979) pointed—to the past exclusion of women from the leagues of creative artists and she documents the frequent dismissal and trivialization of the works of the comparatively few women artists who produced artworks under their own names.

When it comes to discussing the contents of artworks, such theories do not always confine themselves to the straightforwardly narrative or depictive types. Theodor W. Adorno (1903–1969), a Marxist and a progressivist, looks for social meaning in instrumental music. When the composer takes control of the material of music, as Arnold Schoenberg did with his method of composing with twelve tones, greater creative freedom results. Regressive artworks, such as Stravinsky's neoclassical pieces, do not look forward to social transformation, Adorno claims. The feminist Susan McClary suggests in *Feminine Endings: Music, Gender, and Sexuality,* (Minneapolis, 1991) that the confrontational and combative ethos of the sonata form—the structure most commonly used in classical music between about 1760 and 1910—is essentially phallocentric. She concludes that truly feminist music requires the evolution of different structural patterns. Freud himself made intriguing observations about a striking feature of the symphonies of Gustav Mahler—the prevalence at moments of high emotional intensity of banal themes, such as those played by brass bands—as a result of questioning the composer about his childhood.

Second, the theories can be applied to the interpretation of particular pieces, providing new insights into the artist or the work. Ernest Jones's (1879–1958) explanation of Hamlet's (alleged) procrastination and Freud's accounts of Leonardo da Vinci's painting of Saint Anne, Mary, and the Christ child, as well as of Michelangelo's *Moses,* are examples of the psychoanalytic approach. McClary's feminist analysis of Georges Bizet's *Carmen* points to an association between Carmen's sensuality and chromaticism in the music associated with her. Chromaticism, which is connected in music's history with instability and deviation, calls for resolution and a return to order. Carmen also is expected to conform (for the sake of the patriarchal social order) and is sacrificed for failing to do so.

Third, such theories may inspire or provoke artists in their creative efforts. Under Joseph Stalin, Marxism was interpreted as suggesting that art should serve the proletariat. It could do so by pursuing realism while idealizing the goals and values of socialism and condemning those of capitalism. This political agenda was forced upon artists, many of whom did not find it congenial. Alternatively, it is argued by Adorno and Bertolt Brecht (1898–1956) that Marxism is compatible with antirealist styles of art that audiences will find challenging and sophisticated. In his plays, Brecht sets out to reveal both the social forces lying behind the events considered and the mechanisms employed in bringing all this to the stage. Meanwhile, the painters of the Surrealist movement, among many others, self-consciously employed a mode of symbolism with a Freudian character; and the artworks of many contemporary women artists express a distinctive female consciousness and celebrate the place, lives, interests, and values of women.

Three kinds of objections, none of which is entirely convincing, are often raised against the analysis and interpretation of art in terms of theories such as these. The first objection is to the theories' generality: because they focus on broad patterns and trends, and in doing so must overlook the welter of detail, such theories are ill suited to characterizing that in which the interest and importance of art resides, which is the individuality of works. If people's choices in clothes, or cars, or friends can illustrate the themes of Marxism, or psychoanalysis, or feminism as readily as do their arts, then these theories fail to reveal what is distinctive to, and valuable in, art.

In response, one can note that, although art might be used (as the objection recognizes) with the purpose of illustrating the theory, this is by no means the only way the two can be brought into relation. These theories can provide revealing perspectives on the wider social settings within which art is created, presented, and received. That background is of interest in its own right, but it also connects intimately with the work's character, because artistically significant properties of the work can be affected by its relation to these contexts. Moreover, the individual work and its interpretation can become the focus of concern. Just as a general theory of gravity and force can be applied to the specific case, say, of explaining how a plane becomes airborne, so Marxist, psychoanalytic, or feminist theories can be applied to the detail of a particular artwork. The generality of these theories is a function of the range over which they might be applied, not of the manner of their operation on the particular.

The second complaint is raised against the anachronistic use of such theories in interpreting works created prior to their espousal. How could it be that Hamlet is paralyzed by an inner Oedipal conflict when Shakespeare could not have conceived of such a possibility? Is it not arrogant of us to judge art depicting the treatment of women in other times by standards grounded in, and shaped by, our own sociotemporal location?

A reply might take this form. The theories under discussion claim to be true—if not of all cultures at all times, then of patriarchal or capitalist/feudal ones, and of those in which children are raised by their parents against a background of sexual taboos. Thus, they deal with most societies, if not all. If they are true, for example, of the societies in which John Bunyan penned *The Pilgrim's Progress,* Sophocles scripted *Oedipus Rex,* and Samuel Richardson wrote *Clarissa,* and if these authors are astute observers of custom and human nature, then the theories can be employed to discuss their works. Artists of any time might see and record the effects of the psychological processes and social forces analyzed by Marxism, psychoanalysis, and feminism, because these processes and forces predated their systematic description and categorization.

This is not to say that artists always think about the psychological or social significance of their ideas as they work. They might remain unaware of the underlying causes of the outcomes they describe, depict, or convey. Indeed, psychoanalysis predicts that the processes it discusses are often cloaked from consciousness. It is likely that the social dynamics discussed by Marxists and feminists often operate like Adam Smith's famous "hidden hand"—as producing overall patterns that are not aimed at directly, but that occur as a consequence of many individual decisions, each of which is made with a view only to immediate, local goals.

The third objection takes up a point mentioned in the previous reply by questioning the truth or credibility of the theories under discussion. Marxism and psychoanalytic theory now are, if not entirely discredited, treated with reserve and skepticism, and feminism is not without its critics. If the appropriateness of using such theories in art criticism depends on their claim to truth, then there is room for doubting their applicability.

A first line of response remarks that the theories in question might contain many insightful parts even if the whole is flawed. (More than a hundred years' persistent attractiveness speaks for the likely truth of elements in Marxism and psychoanalysis, and the depth of recognition and engagement awakened in many women by feminist theory suggests that, at worst, it contains an important kernel of truth.) Because Marxist, psychoanalytic, and feminist theories usually are applied to art in piecemeal fashion, their use in analyzing the art of the past is sufficiently justified by the insights they encompass. The second response was foreshadowed above: contemporary artists constantly draw on these theories, false or not, so interpretation of the resulting pieces requires reference to them. To take some obvious examples, George Orwell's novels are overtly political; the protagonists of J. D. Salinger's *The Catcher in the Rye* and Philip Roth's *Portnoy's Complaint* address their stories to their psychoanalysts; Doris Lessing's *The Golden Notebook*, Marge Piercy's *Woman on the Edge of Time*, and Marilyn French's *The Women's Room* are all about women's personal liberation. The theories of Marxism, psychoanalysis, and feminism are embedded so pervasively and deeply in the intellectual life of our times that it is legitimate to extend their use even to works that seem not to invite this regard.

[*See also* Autonomy; Discourse; Expression Theory of Art; Formalism; Historicism; Mimesis; Modernism; Ontology of Art; Postmodernism; Semiotics; Sociology of Art; Text; *and* Theory.]

BIBLIOGRAPHY

Adorno, Theodor W. *The Philosophy of Modern Music*. Translated by Anne G. Mitchell and Wesley V. Blomster. London, 1973.
Adorno, Theodor W. *Aesthetic Theory*. Edited by Gretel Adorno and Rolf Tiedemann, translated by Robert Hullot-Kentor. Minneapolis, 1997.
Aristotle. *The Poetics of Aristotle: Translation and Commentary*. Translated by Stephen Halliwell. London, 1987.
Baudrillard, Jean. *Jean Baudrillard: Selected Writings*. Edited by Mark Poster. Stanford, Calif., 1988.
Bell, Clive. *Art*. Reprint, New York, 1958.
Berger, John. *Ways of Seeing*. London, 1972.
Brecht, Bertolt. *On Theatre: The Development of an Aesthetic*. Edited and translated by John Willett. London, 1964.
Collingwood, R. G. *Principles of Art*. Oxford, 1938.
Croce, Benedetto. *Aesthetic as Science of Expression and General Linguistics*. Translated by Douglas Ainslie. Reprint, London, 1953.
Danto, Arthur C. *The Transfiguration of the Commonplace: A Philosophy of Art*. Cambridge Mass., 1981.
Danto, Arthur C. *The Philosophical Disenfranchisement of Art*. New York, 1986.
Derrida, Jacques. *Writing and Difference*. Translated by Alan Bass. Chicago, 1978.
Dickie, George. *Art and the Aesthetic: An Institutional Analysis*. Ithaca, N.Y., 1974.
Eagleton, Terry. *The Ideology of the Aesthetic*. Oxford and Cambridge, Mass., 1990.
Freud, Sigmund. "The Moses of Michelangelo." In *Collected Papers*, vol. 4, translated by Joan Riviere, pp. 257–287. London, 1957.
Freud, Sigmund. *Leonardo da Vinci and a Memory of Childhood*. Translated by Alan Tyson. Harmondsworth, England, 1963.
Hanslick, Eduard. *On the Musically Beautiful: A Contribution Towards the Revision of the Aesthetics of Music* (8th edition of 1891). Translated and edited by Geoffrey Payzant. Indianapolis, 1986.
Hegel, Georg Wilhelm Friedrich. *Aesthetics: Lectures on Fine Art*. 2 vols. Translated by T. M. Knox. Oxford, 1975.
Kant, Immanuel. *The Critique of Judgement*. 2d rev. ed. Translated by J. H. Bernard. London, 1914.
Kivy, Peter. *Sound Sentiment: An Essay on the Musical Emotions*. Philadelphia, 1989.
Kristeller, Paul Oskar. "The Modern System of the Arts: A Study in the History of Aesthetics." *Journal of the History of Ideas* 12.4 (October 1951): 496–527; 13.1 (January 1952): 17–46.
Langer, Susanne Knauth. *Philosophy in a New Key*. Cambridge, Mass., 1942.
Langer, Susanne Knauth. *Feeling and Form*. New York, 1953.
Lukács, György. *The Meaning of Contemporary Realism*. Translated by John Mander and Necke Mander. London, 1962.
Lyotard, Jean-François. *The Postmodern Condition: A Report on Knowledge*. Translated by Geoffrey Bennington and Brian Massumi. Minneapolis, 1984.
Margolis, Joseph. *Art and Philosophy*. Atlantic Highlands, N.J., 1980.
Plato. *The Republic*. Translated by H. D. P. Lee. Harmondsworth, England, 1955.
Rank, Otto. *Art and Artist: Creative Urge and Personality Development*. Translated by Charles Francis Atkinson. New York, 1932.
Sparshott, Francis. *The Theory of the Arts*. Princeton, N.J., 1982.
Tolstoy, Leo. *What Is Art? and Essays on Art*. Translated by Aylmer Maude. Oxford, 1930.

STEPHEN DAVIES

THEORY, HISTORY OF. [*The role of theory has become an important, if controversial, topic in contemporary aesthetics, art history, literary studies, cultural studies, and many other disciplines related to art and culture. This entry provides the conceptual background for such debates by tracing the history and practice of the concept of theory in general (not just in connection* *with art) from the Greeks up to the end of the nineteenth century, when theory seems to get displaced (for reasons analyzed here), only to reemerge late in the twentieth century.*]

A theory is a consistent, coherent, complete, critical body of ideas believed to provide a clearer, more comprehensive, or more adequate understanding of some object or objects than less systematic, pretheoretical perspectives. In aesthetics, theory is a body of ideas about the aesthetic, including within its scope topics such as the phenomenology of processes through which natural or cultural objects come to be perceived or designated as aesthetic, the ontology of such objects, and the analysis of ways in which art is created, experienced, and/or critically understood and evaluated.

In ancient Greek philosophy, Aristotle established the philosophical contrast between theory and other forms of activity with a tripartite distinction between *theoria* (an activity whose end is knowledge of the universal and eternal), *poiēsis* (an activity whose end is things made rather than knowledge), and *praxis* (an activity that produces change in the agent; good or worthwhile action in the sense of *praxis* is its own end). This triple division was subsequently simplified to a distinction between theory and practice, and in its contemporary usage theory is usually contrasted with practice (or praxis) in a modern philosophical tradition extending from Immanuel Kant through Georg Wilhelm Friedrich Hegel to Karl Marx and beyond. Contemporary discussion of relationships between theory and practice also occurs in other areas of philosophy besides aesthetics, such as ethics and political philosophy, and in the social-scientific disciplines of cultural anthropology, sociology, clinical psychology, and political science. This expanding discussion across and within academic disciplines and fields has produced an impact on aesthetic discussions of the topic. Although current discussion of theory inside and outside of aesthetics differs in significant ways from the views expressed in ancient philosophical texts, it is necessary to grasp the understanding of theory present in Plato and Aristotle in order to appreciate contemporary discussion. The following summary of views about theory thus begins with ancient Greece, then turns to a brief survey of contributions to the topic by Kant, Hegel, and Marx, and concludes with suggestions about the relationship between contemporary understandings of theory and aesthetics.

Etymology. Greek understanding of theory as a topic in philosophy presupposes a complex etymology. The origins of the English word *theory* are found in three Greek words associated with vision—*theorein, theoros, theoria*—and word for the divine, *theos*. Together, these words imply root ideas that informed the work of Plato and Aristotle and that continue to play a role in modern and contemporary discussions. These ideas include the priority of sight over other senses, the truthfulness or reliability of a privileged way of seeing, and a possible link between this reliable way of see-

ing and transcendence of the merely visible. *Theorein* means to look at attentively, to behold, to contemplate, or to survey. The centrality of sight over other senses in Greek culture is captured by Hans Blumenberg: "The light in which the landscape and things that surround the life of Greeks stood gave to everything a clarity and (in terms of optics alone) unquestionable presence that left room for doubt regarding the accessibility of nature to man only late, and only as a result of thought" (1983). Hans Jonas, in his essay "The Nobility of Sight," notes several consequences of the Greek visual bias, including the atemporal quality of sight and a resulting Greek preoccupation with unchanging and eternal presence; the distance between subject and object established by sight accompanied by a predisposition to believe in the neutral observation of the latter by the former; and the great reach of sight as an influence on the idea of infinity.

A *theoros* was originally a spectator at festival theater performances, athletic contests, and other public events. In later usage, the term assumed a more restricted, technical sense of one who has a faculty for seeing farther, for discriminating, judging, comparing, criticizing, or savoring what he sees. According to Terence Ball, "A spectator in this sense is not one who seeks immediate sensual or perceptual gratification but rather one who seeks understanding and wisdom" (1979). Hans-Georg Gadamer emphasizes the sacral character attributed to the vision of a *theoros:*

> We can recall the concept of sacral communion that lies behind the original Greek concept of *theoria. Theoros* means someone who takes part in a delegation to a festival. Such a person has no other distinction or function than to be there. Thus the *theoros* is a spectator in the proper sense of the word since he participates in the solemn act through his presence at it. Thus sacred law accords him a distinction: for example, inviolability.   (1989)

Finally, according to Hartmut Böhme (1984), this communion-oriented emphasis on vision was especially evident in pre-Socratic thought. Böhme implies cultural movement from an earlier, communion-oriented understanding of vision to a subsequent understanding of vision emphasizing separation between the viewer and the object of vision. This suggestion is further supported by F. M. Cornford's (1991) observation that the Orphic version of *theoria* included a sense of emotional involvement, whereas its later Pythagorean replacement did not.

The question as to whether theory represents a way of seeing separating the theoretician from the theorized, or rather indicates a unique form of insight leading to communion between theoretician and object, is further complicated by the change from Greek to Latin. As Martin Jay notes, "The Latin *speculatio*—along with *contemplatio*, the translation of *theoria*—contained within it the same root as *speculum* and *specular* which designate mirroring. Rather than implying the distance between subject and object, the specular tradition . . . tended to collapse them" (1993). The question of theory as communion or separation from its objects returns in Kant and Hegel.

Theory also has links to *theoria*. A *theoria* was an official delegation from one Greek polis to another. It served an important function in Greek civic life by attesting to the occurrence of an important event, first witnessing the event as it occurred, and later certifying that it had actually taken place. Wlad Godzich, in his "Forward: The Tiger on the Mat" (in Paul de Man, *The Resistance to Theory*), emphasizes the contrast between the collective, official work of the *theoria* and individual acts of perception or *aesthēsis*.

> Their [the *theorias'*] function was one of see-and-tell. . . . while other individuals in the city could see and tell . . . the city needed a more official and ascertainable form of knowledge if it was not to lose itself in endless claims and counterclaims. The *theoria* provided such a bedrock of certainty: what it certified as having seen could become the object of public discourse.
>
> (1986)

There are, finally, associations between *theorein, theoros, theoria,* and *theos* or god. The gods of Greece were believed to have been visibly manifest to humans, and were frequently depicted in sculpture, mosaics, and painting, suggesting links between the visualization associated with theory and the sacred. Plutarch and early Christian authors such as Gregory of Nyssa, Basil the Great, and Pseudo-Dionysius all note the link between *theorein* and *theos*, suggesting that true *theoria* involves more than mere seeing; it may involve observation of nature from a divine perspective. At the same time, the dangers of vision misdirected—to the one who sees or to the object of seeing—are the subject of Greek myths, notably those of Narcissus, Orpheus, and Medusa. The possibility implied by these myths—that sight/insight improperly used may lead to death—does not diminish the importance of vision, but serves rather as a balance to the otherwise positive understanding of vision in Greek iconography.

The etymology of *theory/theoria* demonstrates that prior to Plato's discussion of theory as a unique kind of seeing done by a philosopher, or Aristotle's praise of a life dedicated to theory over one given to practice, there was already a complex background in Greek culture and language that emphasized the precedence of vision over other senses in the search for truth, recognized the sight of some persons as privileged, and implied the possibility of such sight performing a positive or a negative revelatory role.

Plato and Aristotle. For Plato, theory is a superior form of seeing not wholly communicable in language. In the *Republic* (474B–478), Glaucon mentions a resemblance between the sightseers at festivals and philosophers. Socrates, while conceding a resemblance between the two forms of activity, emphasizes the philosopher's task as more than mere seeing. Philosophy is the pursuit and love of knowl-

edge *(epistēmē)*, defined by Plato as an understanding of an eternal, immutable, and unchanging *eidos* or idea, "which is like a visible form blanched of color" (Jay, 1993). Such knowledge is direct, unmediated, in some ways similar to a religious vision, as well as being incommunicable in speech according to the image of the dazed philosophical visionary returning to the cave from his encounter with the central *eidos*—the good—in the *Republic*. While there is no sharp separation in Plato between theory in the transformative sense of contemplation of the divine, and theory in the reductive sense of scientific analysis through dialectic, in later dialogues such as the *Statesman,* the *Laws,* and the *Sophist,* the theorist is cast as a "stranger" and given no name, thus emphasizing the strangeness of philosophy. At times, Plato even suggests that theorizing means taking leave of life, a kind of separation or type of death. Plato's final understanding of theory in effect replaces the collective citizen *theoria* with an individual philosopher, who is to perform that office by virtue of unique qualities of soul. Plato also assumes that a philosopher cannot fully achieve the final goal of *theoria*—knowledge of the good—until a polis is governed by philosophers.

In later, Neoplatonic thinking, this Platonic inheritance of the strangeness of philosophy and longing for an ideal city is developed in the light of a different ideal: union with the divine One. This otherworldly ideal leads to a further distinction between theory as science and theory as contemplation. "With Gregory of Nyssa Christian theology . . . takes over this distinction. In his homily on the Song of Songs Gregory distinguishes between two sorts of *theoria*: one which corresponds to the Platonic dialogues and thus to science . . . and another which is a 'seeing of God in darkness,' that is, contemplation" (Lobkowicz, 1977). For Aristotle, as noted earlier, theory is one of three distinctive ways or forms of life. *Theoria* is the highest or best way of life consisting of noninstrumental, continuous activity aiming at self-sufficiency *(autarkēs)*. This activity is dedicated to a wisdom (nous) capable of grasping undemonstrable first principles, the permanent, unchanging characteristics of being as such (*Nicomachean Ethics*, 6.2, 1140b31–41a8). It is in such theoretical activity that human minds most closely approximate the pure, unmediated activity of God as pure thought, a form of life in which there is perfect coincidence between subject and object of knowledge. A life devoted to *theoria* is in marked contrast to the leisured life of desire pursued by the wealthy. This way of life is sharply criticized by Aristotle (in the *Rhetoric* 2.15–16. 1390b14–91a19) as "worthless" *(euteles)* or "foolish" *(aonoētos)*. Finally, there is the life of an engaged citizen of a polis, dedicated to praxis. Praxis is a form of activity whose goal is the perfection of the doer, requiring practical wisdom *(phronēsis)*: the ability to deliberate about "living well as a whole" (*Nicomachean Ethics*, 6, 1141a20–25). Such practical wisdom can only be acquired through repeated experience in the exercise of the various moral and intellectual excellences *(aretē)* of character, for it is in this way that an individual actor comes to recognize and embody a mean of excellence relative to himself. This form of practical rationality, about one's life and the lives of people one knows, enables one to resolve the problems of a city, while simultaneously developing one's character. All of these ways of life presume a degree of leisured independence, unlike the life of an artisan or daily wage earner focused on poeisis, the form of intentional activity through which various objects are made according to a plan.

Aristotle assumes, in his account of *theoria,* that human beings have a natural desire to know, ultimately to comprehend reality in the fullest sense possible, and further, that when the mind is fully engaged in such activity, it achieves a type of unity with its object in ways that echo the notion of communion between seer and seen present in the vision of a *theoros.* [*See* Plato; *and* Aristotle.]

Kant and Modernity. To understand Kant's contribution to the idea of theory, it is important to recall the ways in which the philosophical context of his work differs from the work of Plato and Aristotle. Medieval Christianity's understanding of the distinction between theory and practice had moved between the alternatives of Plato and Aristotle as these were developed by Augustine and Thomas Aquinas and their followers, with the obvious difference that, for Christians, the world, however understood, was to be seen as the good product of an all-powerful, benevolent Creator as only the penultimate locus of human life. Whether theory was understood in a Neoplatonic sense as a form of inner, mystical union with the One or in a neo-Aristotelian sense as the work of the active intellect in grasping the forms of sensible things, the common theological and ecclesial background of thought about theory precluded development of the idea of theory as critical in the modern sense.

In the period of scientific discovery and creativity in western European society that immediately preceded Kant, this commonly accepted theological and ecclesial background either disappeared altogether or was relegated to a minor place in the progress of scientific discovery. With both traditional practices and beliefs of Christianity under increasing attack within and outside churches, theory was no longer commonly understood as necessarily linked to a religious tradition or as serving religious purposes. To the contrary, true theory now came to be seen by many secular intellectuals as the result of independent, empirical, scientific investigation in explicit contrast to the received understandings and practices of religious tradition. Such scientific discoveries, though requiring no justification in practice, were nevertheless believed by many modern thinkers, such as Thomas Hobbes, to offer an independent, material basis for human conduct thanks to an accurate, empirical understanding of the fundamental characteristics of reality. At the same time, progress in mathematical discovery in thinkers

as diverse as René Descartes and Gottfried Wilhelm Leibniz suggested an alternative to this empirical tradition: that theory as an understanding of the fundamental structures of reality was closer to the deductive work of mathematicians than to the inductive work of scientific experimentation. The philosophical work of Descartes, Leibniz, and Baruch Spinoza follows this model of theory.

Kant rejects the claims of both "speculative metaphysics" (his term for the mathematically based form of theory) and empiricism to have achieved reliable, truthful knowledge about the nature of reality as it might exist independent of the human mind. For Kant, theory is to be understood in three different and somewhat contradictory ways. First, Kant sharply rejects and criticizes theory as useless and illusory the claims of "speculative metaphysics," the rationalists' attempt to achieve knowledge of reality independent of the empirical work of science. There is no knowledge of an independent reality "as it is," prior to experience. Second, Kant challenges the claims of modern scientific theory to have achieved the truth about reality in his logical criticism of the limits of scientific understanding (what he calls a "metaphysics of nature"). The task of theoretical reason as presented in the *Critique of Pure Reason* is largely negative: to demonstrate that the methods of science can achieve nothing more than an interpretation of sense-data. Theoretical reason in its strictest sense denies the knowableness of "things in themselves." Third, there is a positive understanding of theory in Kant such as can be found in his definition in a 1793 essay, "On the Proverb: That May Be True in Theory, but Is of No Practical Use." There theory is "a collection of rules, even of practical rules . . . envisaged as principles of a fairly general nature . . . which, nonetheless, necessarily influence their practical application" (Kant, 1983). In this essay, as well as in the *Critique of Practical Reason* and other writings on morality, Kant understands theory as providing an account of the rational basis for moral action, a basis that includes both the general rules governing moral action (the categorical imperative) and a grasp of necessary "postulates" (God, freedom, and immortality) that allow men to believe their pursuit of virtue to be in accord with reality. Theory in this final sense is the basis of normative judgment capable of shaping and directing an autonomous moral will.

Kant also introduces the idea of judgment as a middle term between theory and practice in this essay: "For to the concept of the understanding that contains the rule must be added an act of judgment by means of which the practitioner decides whether or not something is an instance of that rule" (1983). Further development of this "middle term" occurs in the later *Critique of Judgment,* whose import is especially evident for aesthetics in Kant's discussion of the "antinomy of taste." Kant proposes a "dialectical" tension between a thesis—that "A judgement of taste is not based on concepts; for otherwise one could dispute about it (decide by means of proof)" (ibid.)—and an antithesis: "A judgement of taste is based on concepts; for otherwise . . . one could not lay claim to other people's necessary assent to one's judgment" (ibid.). He resolves the antinomy by claiming that whereas judgments of taste are indeed based on a concept, the concept is "of a general basis of nature's subjective purposiveness for our power of judgement" (ibid.). Although this concept is indeterminate, telling us nothing about the perceived object that has inspired it, it is still the basis for a universal claim about the kind of being who makes the judgment—what Kant calls the "supersensible substrate of humanity."

Kant's often-quoted remark, in his preface to the second edition of the *Critique of Pure Reason,* that he had intended to "abolish [speculative] knowledge [in order] to make room for [moral] belief" suggests both the radical character of his work and his intent to maintain a determinative role for theory. Kant's work is radical to the extent that he denies the possibility, implied in the Greek notion of *theoros,* of a form of human activity that unites the theorist with the object of his knowledge, if by "object" one means anything other than the content of one's mind. Yet, for Kant, a properly chastened theory still has a (negative) role to play in guiding the work of science, and, in its normative applications, theory as a form of practical rationality can provide a positive, principled basis for understanding the universal character of moral and aesthetic judgments in marked contrast to the empirical, psychological basis for claiming that such judgments are subjective, as found in Scottish Enlightenment figures such as David Hume, Francis Hutcheson, and Adam Smith. Where the latter must appeal to "common sentiments" or cultural convention to secure a possible basis for shared normative judgments about particulars, Kant claimed to provide a link between the particular objects of sensation and universal ideas in his notion of judgment as an aspect of (practical) reason itself. Hegel and Marx attempt to provide a stronger theoretical basis for the link between theory and practice in their different understandings of reason as a historical process and a social product. [*See* Kant.]

Hegel and Marx. Although Hegel and Marx are often seen as polar opposites on questions of theory and practice, they share a strong appreciation for the cultural, social, and political power of theory. Hegel shares Aristotle's understanding of theory as the highest form of activity and Kant's appreciation for the limits of classical speculative metaphysics. Unlike Aristotle, who saw God as independent of the world, Hegel understands Spirit *(Geist)* to be immanent and evident in the processes of natural and historical change. These processes always involve a dialectical movement between three basic terms—thought, action, and object (thing)—each of which is able to play its distinctive role only in interplay with the other two; one of these three terms must always mediate between the others. Hegel's account of the evolution of human consciousness in *The Phenomenology of Spirit* equates the historical and social processes by which persons have become able to grant recognition to each other as fully autonomous beings with the gradual growth in God's recognition of God in that which is truly "Other"—natural and human conscious processes. Unlike Kant, for whom theory had a primarily limiting function, theoretical reason was expansive and radically inclusive for Hegel. Although powered by the "negative" (i.e., by consciousness's ability to reject a partial truth about an initial object of awareness and move dialectically to a higher perspective), reason is not separate from historical process; it always reflects the determinate stage of development reached by that process. Ultimately, all of the contradictions experienced in historical life, such as those between nature and culture, self and other, God and world, or being and nonbeing, are to be understood as overcome in a form of knowing that combines permanence and process in a cohesive vision of the whole. Partial truths, such as those implicit in art or religion as contrasts or contradictions, are finally understood as aspects of an overarching unity in philosophical discourse, the truest medium of Spirit. Hegel writes:

> The essential category is that of unity, the inner connection of all these diverse forms. We must firmly grasp this, that there is only *one* Spirit, *one* principle, which leaves its impress on the political situation as well as manifesting itself in religion, art, ethics, sociability, commerce and industry, so that these different forms are only branches of one trunk.   *(History of Philosophy)*

Marx decisively rejects Hegel's idealism in the name of dialectical materialism and insists on the supremacy of praxis over theory, claiming that all social life is practical and, in his famous eleventh thesis on Ludwig Feuerbach, that "The philosophers have only *interpreted* the world in various ways; the point is, to *change* it" *(Theses on Feuerbach).* Yet, Marx was no less confident than Hegel in the power of theory. Where, for Hegel, theory in the form of philosophical wisdom fully expresses the sense of a culture or age, making further development possible, for Marx, theory, in uncovering the material forces and processes that have produced cultural institutions, objects, and relations, is a critical tool, one that can enable revolutionary change led by those most profoundly alienated by modern culture, the urban workers whom he designated a "proletariat." The first task of such a critical theory in Marx's sense is to expose the oppressive ideology embedded in cultural institutions and the role played by that ideology in producing resistance to change when internalized by members of an oppressed class. Genuine change in the direction of an egalitarian community can only come about through a combination of theoretical understanding and action. The former prevents action's ineffectiveness or dissipation, while the latter, altering the material conditions under which men live, provides the necessary basis for a humane social order. Criticizing Hegel for collapsing theory and practice into one, Marx claimed that only a revolutionary yet genuinely self-critical practice could mediate between thought and things, that only such a practice was already thoughtful enough to be "objective" in a nonpositivistic sense. Objectivity, for Marx, means constant awareness of real, human individuals as the basic units of thought rather than of statistical patterns. Marx writes: "The chief defect of all hitherto existing materialism . . . is that the thing, reality, sensuousness is conceived only in the form of *object* or *contemplation,* but not as *human sensuous activity, practice*" (ibid.). Where Hegel defined the activity of a theorist as an attempt to render a phenomenon comprehensible, Marx saw theoretical activity as the attempt to master the phenomenon. Reason is an instrument or weapon of living, sensuous men who suffer, and true thinking is a form of practice, not contemplation at a distance. These extraordinary, albeit different, claims for the power of theory in Hegel and Marx failed to be realized in the twentieth century. Hegel's vision of theory achieving a comprehensive grasp of the "objective spirit" of an age manifest in a unified, common culture has been rendered problematic, in part by the development of a global, multicultural society, fragmented into distinctive cultural identities based on nation, language, race, religion, and ethnicity. In spite of this apparent fragmentation of culture into cultures, some cultural theorists continue to argue for a more expansive role for theory, as James Clifford does in his essay "On Collecting Art and Culture" (1988). For Clifford, it is possible for a theorist to gasp universal, dynamic processes at work in contemporary culture, such as the movement of cultural artifacts between points on a semiotic grid. These "points" are represented by terms such as "fine art objects," "representative artifacts of material culture," "examples of technology," and "curios or commodities," and it is claimed that artifacts are routinely displaced from point to point on the grid by a system of cultural institutions and meanings that classifies them and assigns them relative value. Although a Marxist or neo-Marxist version of critical theory is capable of seeing through the machinery such as Clifford's "art-culture system," belief in the power of critical practice to bring about any final, progressive, revolutionary change has also been rendered suspect by the betrayal of Marx's humanism in Soviet and Chinese state Communism, and by the collapse of self-identified "Marxist" or socialist regimes throughout eastern Europe. Yet, in spite of these theoretical and empirical difficulties, combinations of Hegel's and Marx's understanding of theory continue to provide a necessary starting point for the ideas of theory found in the work of such diverse contemporary French thinkers as Jean Baudrillard, Maurice Blanchot, Gilles Deleuze, Jacques Derrida, Michel Foucault, Jacques Lacan, Emmanuel Lévinas, and Jean-François Lyotard, taken in combination with the work of Friedrich Nietzsche,

Edmund Husserl, Martin Heidegger, and other existential phenomenologists, such as Jean-Paul Sartre, Maurice Merleau-Ponty, and Paul Ricoeur. Another, parallel discussion of theory in the Frankfurt School among authors such as Theodor W. Adorno, Walter Benjamin, Max Horkheimer, Herbert Marcuse, and Jürgen Habermas also presupposes the work of Hegel and Marx. The discussion of such work, however, belongs more properly to survey essays on postmodernism and on individual French and German authors than to this general survey of ideas about theory. [*See* Hegel; *and* Marx.]

Theory and Contemporary Aesthetics. This brief summary of perspectives on theory ends with the nineteenth century, well before the phenomena of modernism and postmodernism. Although it would be possible to expand discussion of work on theory into the twentieth century in a similar survey fashion, covering some or all the individual Continental authors just mentioned, apart from limitations of space, the greater problem is that much of what has been traditionally understood as "theory" has been displaced today into cultural locations other than philosophy. Part of this displacement is the result of the influence of a growing number of interdisciplinary or cross-disciplinary texts such as those of Foucault. It is increasingly difficult, in the work of contemporary academic authors on aesthetics influenced by such texts, to draw sharp lines separating the humanities and the social sciences or dividing discrete disciplines such as philosophy, literary criticism, religious studies, anthropology, or psychology. Combinations of elements of all of these and other disciplinary conversations, not always clearly designated or noted as such by authors, often shape texts "occasioned" by an artwork or a traditional aesthetic problem. When reading a contemporary work of theory dealing with a familiar topics in aesthetics such as Pierre Bourdieu's *Distinction: A Social Critique of the Judgement of Taste,* it may be possible to discern an educational background focused on the literatures of specific fields (cultural anthropology and modern works on aesthetics in Bourdieu's case), but the primary evidence for such a background is often to be found less in the substance or style of the argument than in the texts referenced in footnotes or the bibliography.

The displacement of theory also involves the blurring of lines between text and context, work and commentary, or artist and audience, typically associated with postmodernism. Where modernism in art and art writing often rejected self-conscious efforts to be "theoretical," it is a commonplace of contemporary writing about art and the aesthetic that the work of many postmodern artists embodies explicit theoretical beliefs or positions, and that such work is directed at an audience presumed to be theoretically informed, if not always theoretically sophisticated. Sherrie Levine's, Barbara Kruger's, and Cindy Sherman's photographs all involve a theoretical stance on the defining characteristics of photography, on "originals" versus "copies," and on the role of the artist in the artwork, without which the visual experience of their work remains opaque. It is often the case in such works, and in writing about them by art critics and aestheticians, that a form of "praxis" response by an intended audience (i.e., action of some kind in a political, social, or communal sense rather than appreciation or contemplation of a work) is part of the primary aim of individual or collective artists. Whether "theory" is understood by such artists or in such works as a form of ideology, or as a constantly expanding metadiscourse about paradigms or epistemes of ideologies and their instantiations, or as itself a form of practice, it is increasingly difficult to draw precise lines distinguishing artworks from theory. Given the proliferation of a wide diversity of theories of art claiming an explicit basis in practice and/or in sui generis forms of experience of varied groups identified by sex, gender, ethnicity, or race, it is also difficult to find a common point of reference by which diverse theories could be compared, if not critically evaluated. The evaluation of a theoretical discourse in such instances is often found in its ability to provoke action or to consolidate the unique experience of members of a group sharing a common identity.

Finally, in the case of some contemporary site-specific works such as Robert Smithson's environmental works, John Ahern's South Bronx bronzes, or projects of new genre public artists such as Suzanne Lacy or the Chicago "Culture in Action" group, it is often difficult to determine at what point artists and/or a critical/appreciative audience is/are experiencing, analyzing, or acting. Many of these works, like much of the theoretical writing about them, have deliberately indeterminate, anticlosural qualities that invite supplementation, and resist framing by any one, unitary discourse. In such a cultural context, it is impossible to offer any definitive concluding generalization about theory in relation to aesthetics other than to remark that parallel work by philosophers in ethics and political theory faces a similar set of cultural challenges.

It is possible, however, to note how postmodern cultural contexts problematize the central ideas implied in the Greek etymology of theory. To the extent that one accepts an image-laden cultural background characterized by constant vacillation between signified and signifier as the defining attribute to postmodern culture, it is possible to imagine that the work of a *theoria* or the words of a *theoros* can no longer be confined to designated individuals recognized for their special abilities. The postmodern world is not one in which difference has been simply absorbed into identity. It is, rather, a world in which determinate identities, of either cultural objects or cultural fields—once said to be established by theory—can no longer be produced because the cultural conditions for such production are absent. It is not yet evident what forms of thought or genres of expression

will come to be regarded as theory in the twenty-first century.

[*See also* Theories of Art.]

BIBLIOGRAPHY

Ball, Terence. "Plato and Aristotle: The Unity versus the Autonomy of Theory and Practice." In *Political Theory and Praxis: New Perspectives*, pp. 57–69. Minneapolis, 1977a.

Ball, Terence, ed. *Political Theory and Praxis: New Perspectives*. Minneapolis, 1977b.

Bernstein, Richard J. *Praxis and Action: Contemporary Philosophies of Human Activity*. Philadelphia, 1971.

Blumenberg, Hans. *The Legitimacy of the Modern Age*. Translated by Robert M. Wallace. Cambridge, Mass., 1983.

Böhme, Hartmut. "Sinne und Blick: Variationen zur mythopoetischen Geschichte des Subjekts." In *Konkursbuch*, 13 (1984).

Bourdieu, Pierre. *Outline of a Theory of Practice*. Translated by Richard Nice. Cambridge and New York, 1977.

Clifford, James. *The Predicament of Culture: Twentieth-Century Ethnography, Literature, and Art*. Cambridge, Mass., 1988.

Cornford, F. M. *From Religion to Philosophy: A Study in the Origins of Western Speculation*. New York, 1957; reprint, Princeton, N.J., 1991.

de Man, Paul. *The Resistance to Theory*. Minneapolis, 1986.

Foster, Hal, ed. *The Anti-Aesthetic: Essays on Postmodern Culture*. Port Townsend, Wash., 1983.

Gadamer, Hans-Georg. *Truth and Method*. 2d rev. ed. Translation revised by Joel Weinsheimer and Donald G. Marshall. New York, 1989.

Godzich, Wlad. "Foreword: The Tiger on the Paper Mat." In Paul de Man, *The Resistance to Theory*, pp. ix–xviii. Minneapolis, 1986.

Harrison, Charles and Paul Wood. *Art in Theory, 1900–1990: An Anthology of Changing Ideas*. Oxford and Cambridge, Mass., 1992.

Jay, Martin. *Downcast Eyes: The Denigration of Vision in Twentieth-Century French Thought*. Berkeley, 1993.

Lobkowicz, Nicholas. "On the History of Theory and Practice." In *Political Theory and Praxis: New Perspectives*, edited by Terence Ball, pp. 13–27. Minneapolis, 1977.

Kant, Immanuel. "On the Proverb: That May Be True in Theory, but Is of No Practical Use." In *Perpetual Peace and Other Essays*, translated by Ted Humphrey. Indianapolis, 1983.

Salkever, Stephen G. *Finding the Mean: Theory and Practice in Aristotelian Political Philosophy*. Princeton, N.J., 1990.

Stepelevich, Lawrence S., and David Lamb, eds. *Hegel's Philosophy of Action*. Atlantic Highlands, N.J., 1983.

Taylor, Charles. *Hegel*. Cambridge and New York, 1975.

Tessitore, Aristide. *Reading Aristotle's Ethics: Virtue, Rhetoric, and Political Philosophy*. Albany, N.Y., 1996.

Wallis, Brian, ed. *Art after Modernism: Rethinking Representation*. New York, 1984.

DAVID H. FISHER

TOLSTOY, LEO NIKOLAEVICH (1828–1910), Russian novelist and theorist. Tolstoy was born on his family's estate, Yasnaya Polyana, in central Russia. He attended the University of Kazan for three years, from 1844 to 1847, but did not take a degree. He lived the dissolute life of many young Russian aristocrats during this period. He saw military service in the Caucasus, and in the Crimean War, during the 1850s. During this period, he also found his vocation as a fiction writer. Most of the rest of Tolstoy's life was spent at Yasnaya Polyana.

Tolstoy's writing life divides quite sharply between two periods, which are separated by a time of spiritual and psychic crisis. In the earlier period, he wrote his greatest works of fiction. In the later, although he continued to write fiction, he concentrated on the ethical, political, and aesthetic implications of the religious views he had developed during that crisis (which he describes in *A Confession*).

Tolstoy has special relevance for aesthetics in three ways. First, he was, by common critical assessment, one of the supreme fiction writers who has ever lived. Moreover, he was a writer who attempted self-consciously to engage philosophical issues in his fiction. In *War and Peace*, he not only wrote a great historical novel about the conflict between Napoleonic France and Russia filled with memorable characters (and much of his own family's history), but he also reflected on the nature of human history. Second, Tolstoy was concerned with the nature of fiction and participated in some of the lively critical debates in nineteenth-century Russia about the possibilities of fiction. Third, late in his life, he wrote a book titled *What Is Art?* in which he presented a critique of previous theories of art, and in which he proposed his own definition and analysis of art. This work, though not the product of a trained philosopher, has been one of the most provocative in the history of aesthetic theory. Interestingly, Tolstoy denounces his own earlier writings (including *War and Peace* and *Anna Karenina*) in this book from the perspective of his late religious views. After a brief overview of Tolstoy's view of fiction and *What Is Art?* this essay will discuss Tolstoy's own definition of art and some of the more common objections to it.

Tolstoy's View of Fiction. Although Tolstoy was not a philosopher, he began his career as a writer of fiction at a time when philosophical issues permeated the atmosphere of Russia. He both attempted to deal with philosophical—even metaphysical—issues in his fiction and engaged in the lively critical debates about the nature of fiction that were so prominent among writers in the 1850s and 1860s. A terminology derived from Georg Wilhelm Friedrich Hegel helped frame these debates. Much of the tradition of critical discussion about Tolstoy stresses what is seen as his divided nature. For Isaiah Berlin, for example, in *The Hedgehog and the Fox*, Tolstoy was best understood as a fox (someone who knows many different things) who wanted to be a hedgehog (someone who knows one big thing—who has achieved a systematic understanding of reality). It was, however, a commonplace of the time to think of analysis as the detailed understanding of individual elements and events, and synthesis as the capacity to integrate these particulars in a single unifying vision. Moreover, the relationship of these two capacities was thought of as dialectical—a Hegelian term often used of Tolstoy by his contemporaries. To a writer such as Henry James, the novels of Tolstoy with their natu-

ralistic and metaphysical ambitions must appear to be "large loose baggy monsters," but, for Tolstoy, the naturalistic representation of life would be incomplete without a reflective attempt to understand the meaning of life.

Tolstoy was obsessed by basic philosophical issues throughout his life—such issues as the true nature of a human being, the relationship of the individual to history, the nature of goodness, the possibility of human happiness—and he sought to embody, and to investigate, these issues, first in his fiction, later in his essays and in his life. Perhaps the most important philosophical influence on him was Jean-Jacques Rousseau; even late in life he identified Rousseau and the Gospels as the principal influences on his thought and art. Tolstoy's understanding of Rousseau's view of human nature underlies much of his fiction in the earlier period of his writing career. By the time he came to write *What Is Art?* Tolstoy had repudiated what most people judge to be his greatest artistic achievements. This was not because his fundamental concerns had changed, however, but because he had reached new religious conclusions about those concerns. Well before his religious conversion, he regarded his fiction as philosophical and didactic. He never held the view of "art for art's sake," and although he was committed to a broadly naturalistic view of fiction, he always felt that it was his task to go beyond the representation of possible realities in order to attempt to achieve an integrated understanding of those fictional realities.

What Is Art? The context of the title's question already shows the direction of Tolstoy's thought. He asks this question by considering the money that is spent on art, the effort and expense of training performing artists such as opera singers and ballet dancers, and the effort involved in a rehearsal of an opera. (In the famous passage describing the opera rehearsal, he achieves an alienated distance from what he describes by pretending that he has no acquaintance with the cultural practice of opera.) The question of the justification for all this activity requires an answer to the more basic question of what art is: what does it do for human beings?

Tolstoy gives a brief history of aesthetic theorizing (derived mainly from Max Schasler's history of aesthetics) in order to show that this history consists of a chaos of conflicting opinions. He writes that "Art in all its forms is bounded on one side by the practically useful, and on the other by unsuccessful attempts at art. How is art to be marked off from each of these?" (1959). This is the task of definition, and he goes on to give his own definition of art, which he then uses to judge what has been offered as art in his own time. Of that, he writes that he has come to the "conviction that almost all that our society considers to be art, good art, and the whole of art, far from being real and good art, and the whole of art, is not even art at all but only a counterfeit of it" (ibid.). It is his sense of the endemic threat of fraudulence in art that motivates much of what

Tolstoy writes. He gives special attention to the refutation of aesthetic theories that depend on notions of beauty or pleasure, though he also attempts to explain the historical origin of such theories. Tolstoy also devotes considerable attention to the evaluation of art.

Tolstoy's Theory of Art. At the outset, a number of different questions asked about art by Tolstoy should be distinguished:

1. What is art as opposed to nonart?
2. How is art, as art, to be evaluated? (Tolstoy makes a not always successful effort to separate this from the first question.)
3. How is the content of art to be evaluated? (It is here that Tolstoy introduces his own religious views.)
4. Which works are examples of good art, bad art, and nonart? (Tolstoy's critical judgments, presented as answers to this question, have occasioned outrage among most readers of his book.)

Tolstoy claims that the first question can only be answered by considering the purpose that art may serve "in the life of man and humanity. . . . [Art is] one of the conditions of human life. Viewing it in this way we cannot fail to observe that art is one of the means of intercourse between man and man" (1959). Tolstoy then draws a fairly crude distinction between thought and feeling, and suggests that whereas speech is the medium for the communication of thought, the essence of the intercourse of art is the transmission of feeling. Of course, not all transmission of feeling from one human being to another is art, though art is based on the human capacity to share the feelings of fellow humans. Here is Tolstoy's definition of art from *What Is Art?*:

> To evoke in oneself a feeling one has once experienced and having evoked it in oneself then by means of movements, lines, colours, sounds, or forms expressed in words, so to transmit that feeling that others experience the same feeling—this is the activity of art.
>
> Art is a human activity consisting in this, that one man consciously by means of certain external signs, hands on to others feelings he has lived through, and that others are infected by these feelings and also experience them.   (Ibid.)

Several aspects of this definition require comment. First, Tolstoy emphasizes both the expression of feeling by the artist and the reception of feeling by the audience. Because his theory is often broadly categorized as an "expression" theory, it is worth noting that, for Tolstoy, expression, to be achieved, requires reception by an *other*. Moreover, he requires that the audience experience the *same* feeling as that experienced by the artist, rather than that they understand what the feeling was that the artist experienced. (Unfortunately, Tolstoy has no philosophical account of feeling or emotion to offer here, so the implications of this definition are difficult to assess.) It is immediately obvious from this

definition that sincerity of the artist is required for something to be art (a requirement that Tolstoy shortly makes explicit.)

Second, one should note that his definition does include a reference to the media of the various arts ("movements, lines, colours, sounds, or forms expressed in words") and that he requires a conscious manipulation of the medium by the artist. Tolstoy has been criticized for his lack of attention to the formal elements of the arts, and it is true that he pays very little specific attention to these elements throughout *What Is Art?* Nonetheless, there is a place for them in his theory. The artist must have a command of these elements adequate to fashion an object capable of evoking in an audience the feeling experienced by the artist. Art is not produced by the simple spontaneous expression of emotion.

Third, however, it should be noted that this definition covers more than had come to be classified as part of the "fine arts" by the time Tolstoy wrote. His own example of artistic activity is of a boy telling of his frightening encounter with a wolf, producing in his audience the feelings he has experienced. This feature of Tolstoy's theory was welcome to its author who, as we shall see, was opposed to almost everything considered to be a part of the "fine arts" not only of his own time but throughout history.

The second question—"How is art, as art, to be evaluated?"—is the point at which Tolstoy's view of the relationship between art and morality/religion should be discussed. Tolstoy has commonly been interpreted as holding a moral view of art, which he specifically opposes to the "art-for-art's-sake" aestheticism of the nineteenth century. This interpretation may ultimately be compelling, but his presentation of his view is complex. He holds that it is a necessary condition of a work of art that it produce an "infection" of its audience of its author's "condition of soul" or feeling. When he gives a criterion for what he calls the "quality of art (which depends on its form) considered apart from its subject-matter," he writes that "not only is infection a sure sign of art, but the degree of infectiousness is also the sole measure of excellence in art. . . . *The stronger the infection the better is the art*, as art" (ibid.). Here we seem to have a criterion of evaluation that is decidedly nonmoral. That Tolstoy intends this seems to be confirmed by his statement, "If a work is a good work of art, then the feeling expressed by the artist—be it moral or immoral—transmits itself to other people" (ibid.). This seems to imply that there can be a good work of art whose content is immoral, which would be precluded by any simple equation of the artistically good with the morally good. Of course, this would still leave open the possibility that works of art can be subject to moral judgment—it would just refuse the claim that nothing can be a good work of art unless it is morally good.

Matters become complicated, however, with Tolstoy's answer to the third question: "How is the content of art to be evaluated?" Tolstoy carefully distinguishes the quality of art considered apart from its subject matter from the quality of the feelings that form the subject matter of works of art, and deals with these issues in separate chapters. For judgments about the former, the degree of infectiousness is the criterion, and that degree is determined by the individuality of the feeling, the clarity of its transmission, and the sincerity of the artist (and Tolstoy claims that sincerity entails individuality and clarity). For judgments about the latter, one must employ moral/religious truth. Tolstoy claims that the value of the feelings transmitted by works of art must be judged in terms of the highest religious perception of the age, and that the religious perception of *his* age is

> the consciousness that our well-being, both material and spiritual, individual and collective, temporal and eternal, lies in the growth of brotherhood among men—in their loving harmony with one another. . . . And it is on the basis of this perception that we should appraise all the phenomena of our life and among the rest our art also.　　　　　(Ibid.)

It might seem that we now have two standards of evaluation that might not be in agreement: one standard evaluates the quality of the work of art in terms of infectiousness; the other evaluates the quality of the content of the work in terms of religious truth. This picture is complicated by the fact that Tolstoy has a normative view of sincerity, however. He holds that the religious perception articulated above is true; therefore, feelings not in accord with it are what he calls "perverted." Because an artist who expresses such feelings is necessarily alienated from the truth of his or her nature, such expression can never be deeply "sincere." Hence, despite that fact that he attempts to separate the evaluation of art as art, and the evaluation of its content, Tolstoy may have a moral criterion for true art after all.

Finally, the fourth question: which works are examples of good art, bad art, and nonart? The most famous feature of *What Is Art?* is Tolstoy's almost complete rejection of the traditional "canon" of fine arts. Here is a list of some of the artists whose work Tolstoy condemns as pseudoart or bad art: Aeschylus, Sophocles, Euripides, Aristophanes, Dante Alighieri, Torquato Tasso, William Shakespeare, John Milton, Johann Wolfgang von Goethe, Charles Baudelaire, Stéphane Mallarmé, Maurice-Polydone-Marie-Bernard Maeterlinck, Henrik Ibsen, Gerhart Hauptmann, Michelangelo, Raphael, Édouard Manet, Claude Monet, Auguste Renoir, Camille Pissarro, Alfred Sisley, most of Johann Sebastian Bach, late Ludwig van Beethoven (especially the Ninth Symphony), Franz Liszt, Hector Berlioz, Richard Wagner, Johannes Brahms, Émile Zola, Rudyard Kipling, and almost all of the literary works of Tolstoy (including *War and Peace* and *Anna Karenina*). Tolstoy does give some examples of works that satisfy his criteria of arthood and value; these include primarily folk art and religious literature of great antiquity, but also a few modern literary works. Among the latter are *Les Misérables,* some works of Charles

Dickens, the works of Fyodor Dostoyevsky, George Eliot's *Adam Bede,* and some stories by Aleksandr Sergeevich Pushkin, Nikolai Gogol, and Guy de Maupassant. One might note that Tolstoy's particular critical judgments result from his application of his theory, and that one might agree with the theory and still dispute those particular judgments. Some have attributed Tolstoy's late repudiation of the tradition of high art that he had loved to his deeply divided personal nature. He was also a deeply sensual man, who railed against human sensuality. Ultimately, for Tolstoy, his aesthetic theory was one more weapon to be used against the social institutions of his culture. Nonetheless, his insistence that art is one of the conditions of human life, and must be understood in relationship to human nature and human communication, has provided inspiration to later theorists.

[*See also* Expression Theory of Art; Literature, *article on* Literary Aesthetics; *and* Russian Aesthetics.]

BIBLIOGRAPHY

Work by Leo Tolstoy

What is Art? and Essays on Art. Translated by Aylmer Maude. Reprint, New York and Oxford, 1959.

Other Sources

Bayley, John. *Tolstoy and the Novel.* New York, 1967; reprint, Chicago 1988.
Matlaw, Ralph, ed. *Tolstoy: A Collection of Critical Essays.* Englewood Cliffs, N.J., 1967.
Orwin, Donna Tussing. *Tolstoy's Art and Thought, 1847–1880.* Princeton, N.J., 1993.
Silbajoris, Rimvydas. *Tolstoy's Aesthetics and His Art.* Columbus, Ohio, 1990.
Steiner, George. *Tolstoy or Dostoevsky.* New York, 1959; 2d ed., New Haven, 1996.
Wasiolek, Edward. *Tolstoy's Major Fiction.* Chicago, 1978.
Wilson, A. N. *Tolstoy.* New York, 1988.

　　　　　　　　　　　　　　　　STANLEY BATES

TRAGEDY. [*To examine several of the key stages in the history and genre of tragedy within the history of aesthetics, this entry comprises three essays:*

　　　　　　　　Greek Tragedy
　　　　　　　　Hume on Tragedy
　　　　　　　　Freud on Tragedy

The first essay explains the origins of tragedy in Greek drama and philosophy. The second essay explains David Hume's contribution to the aesthetics of tragedy. The last essay examines Sigmund Freud's ideas on tragedy and their place in his psychoanalytic aesthetics. For his central analysis of tragedy, see Nietzsche. *See also* Music; *and* Theater.]

Greek Tragedy

Greek tragedy developed in the late sixth century BCE, in a society whose dominant form of communal organization was the "citizen state" (polis). As the modern traveler knows, impressive remains of ancient theaters can still be visited at sites in many areas where Hellenic civilization flourished; even in the fifth century BCE, a hundred years before the huge expansion of Greek culture in the wake of the conquests of Alexander the Great, tragedies were put on in a range of locations, from Sicily to Macedonia. Yet, the source of the tragic phenomenon lies within just one polis: democratic Athens. An understanding of the Athenian context of tragedy is a prerequisite for the interpretation of the genre.

Context. Tragedies were performed at the City Dionysia, a spring festival in honor of the god Dionysus. Three playwrights each put on four plays. First came three tragedies, in which stories from the mythical past were retold through the actions, speech, and song of masked actors and chorus. Each set of three tragedies was followed by a "satyr play," a mythological burlesque that raucously disrupted the tone of what went before. A panel of citizens, chosen by lot, awarded the prize to whichever dramatist they adjudged the best.

Several points about the Dionysia need to be emphasized. First, it involved citizen participation on a large scale. In addition to tragedies, there were also competitions for comic drama and choral singing, so around fifteen hundred people must have been actively involved in mounting each festival, quite apart from the audience of perhaps fifteen thousand. Second, the festival represented the polis on display, not just before its own members but, in symbolic terms, before the rest of Greece: tribute from states belonging to the city's empire was ostentatiously brought into the theater, and distinguished visitors from outside Athens had privileged seats. Third, the competitive element enabled the community to keep artistic innovation within the bounds of what was felt appropriate to tradition. It is clear, then, that Athenian tragedy was the very opposite of a coterie art form appealing exclusively to the taste of an elite. Although it is unlikely that many slaves ever attended performances, and although the presence of women in the audience is a matter of heated debate—some scholars rule it out altogether—it nevertheless remains undeniable that tragedy was aimed at a mass public to which it was directly accountable, for the point of selecting judges at random was surely to ensure a representative verdict.

Were performances "religious"? Were they "rituals"? Like the festival, the theater belonged to Dionysus: his priest sat in the middle of the front row. But the relationship between the god and the tragedies staged within his precinct is intricate and indirect. Although most plots explore the relations between humans and gods, few concern Dionysus himself. Because Dionysus was a god of reversals and "ecstasy" ("standing outside oneself"), however, tragedy may be thought of as "Dionysiac," at least insofar as it constituted an arena for temporary, licensed role reversal, in which masked, male citizens stood outside their own identities to portray slaves, women, heroes, and gods.

As for "ritual," the situation is equally complex. With rare exceptions, each play put on was new—not an exact repetition of a sacred drama, but a fresh reinterpretation of the past in the light of present concerns. Like other aspects of Athenian life, rituals (marriage songs, hymns, funeral dirges) were reworked for theatrical purposes. In spite of repeated attempts by modern scholars to find the key to tragedy's structure in a ritual pattern, however, the genre's fluidity resists the imposition of such a restrictive framework.

Tragic Myths. Tragedies explore experience by means of exaggeration. The dramatized myths portray some of the most extreme types of transgression imaginable: incest between son and mother (*Oedipus the King*), matricide (Aeschylus's *Oresteia*, and the *Electra* plays of Sophocles and Euripides), infanticide (Euripides' *Medea* and *Heracles Mad*), fratricide (Aeschylus's *Seven against Thebes*), cannibalism (the story of Thyestes' unwitting consumption of his own children, again recounted in the *Oresteia*). Yet, such stories simply take to their ultimate, catastrophic conclusion tensions potentially felt by any person living within a family. Similarly, the dilemma experienced by Sophocles' Antigone—whether to leave one's traitor-brother unburied or to defy the city's ruler—shows in extreme form some of the conflicts generated in ordinary life by that other framework for social life, the polis. Borrowing a phrase from engineering, one might describe tragedy as "testing to destruction" the norms of the society within which it grew. The Athenian polis was in precisely the kind of historical situation to foster such a self-examination: a democracy coming to terms with the aristocratic world out of which it had developed.

Action and Character. Aristotle famously observed that tragedy was "an imitation, not of human beings, but of action and life." The profound truth highlighted by this observation, sometimes obscured by critics interested in peeping behind the mask of tragic characters to examine the supposed person beneath, is nowadays widely recognized. Greek tragedy depicts *the unfolding of an action*. Thus, *Antigone* represents the consequences of Creon's edict forbidding the burial of a traitor, who happens to be the brother of Antigone. The work begins by focusing on the "heroine," yet ends by virtually ignoring her and concentrating on the shattered ruler, who enters bearing his son's dead body in his arms. Similarly, in another Sophoclean play, *Women of Trachis*, which explores the doomed attempt of Deianira to recover the love of her husband Heracles, the two central figures never meet onstage: as the action develops, it is first the wife who takes center stage, and only later the monster-slayer. The corollary of this emphasis on the unfolding of an action as opposed to the in-depth exploration of character is that the minutiae of an individualized, idiosyncratic personality play no part in this genre. To come to Greek tragedy with expectations derived from George

Eliot or Henry James is to forget the crucial importance of the mask.

Space. From their seats in the half-bowl-shaped auditorium beneath the Acropolis, the Athenian audience looked down on a multifaceted space. Immediately below lay the *orchestra,* the circular "dancing place" where the chorus (twelve, later fifteen in number) danced and sang to provide a context for and link between the "episodes" involving actors. Beyond the orchestra was the *skene,* a low, flat-roofed stage building with at least one door, allowing entrances and exits. Beyond, again, was the territory of the city outside the theater. No hermetically sealed theatrical world, this: the other public spaces of the polis, notably its arena for political debate, were a short walk away.

Greek theater did not aim at illusionistic realism. Instead, "reality" was created through language. In the manner celebrated by the chorus at the start of William Shakespeare's *Henry V,* the audience's imagination was called on to breathe life into the prospect before them. The imaginary space of tragedy was, indeed, varied and elaborate. The scene of the *Oresteia* shifts from Argos to Delphi to Athens, with the city of Troy looming repeatedly as a significant offstage presence; Euripides' *Helen* is set in Egypt, *Prometheus Bound* (ascribed to Aeschylus) in the Caucasus; numerous other stage sets occur, within and outside Greece. Recently, scholars have drawn attention to the way in which "other" places are used to explore contrasts and comparisons with the home city of Athens. Ideologically speaking, tragedy was both "here" and "not here," as well as being both "now" (thanks to its exploration of contemporary moral and political issues) and "not now" (being set in the mythical past). This combination of proximity ("here"/"now") and distance ("not here"/"not now") offers an intriguing analogy with the famous Aristotelian identification of pity and fear as the combination of emotions aroused by tragedy, because, for Aristotle at least, pity was aroused by contemplating the suffering of others, fear by the sense that "it might happen to *me.*"

Speech and Song. Tragedy incorporates many types of poetic meter and linguistic register. Choruses sang, to the accompaniment of a double-pipe player, in a variety of "lyric" rhythms, and in language whose tinge of Doric dialect set it, for an Athenian audience, apart from the everyday. Closer to the conversational was the iambic verse in which most dialogue between the actors was spoken. But actor speeches had their own stylizations, such as the extended passages of alternate-line dialogue known as "stichomythia," and the narratives of news bringers ("messengers"), who typically use a form of the past tense that approximates it linguistically to the narratives of Homeric epic.

Due attention to tragic language enables us to dispel the trivial observation that "nothing happens in Greek tragedy." For example, the violence that many theatrical traditions exhibit on stage was, in Greece, enacted in words. Oedipus's self-blinding, Hippolytus's gruesome downfall, and Pentheus's rending by his mother lose nothing by owing their theatrical realization to an audience's imagination rather than its eyesight. Again, a recurring aspect of tragic "action" is persuasion. The psychic invasion of Pentheus by Dionysus in Euripides' *Bacchae* is as clear a case as there could be of "something happening"; the same goes for Clytemnestra's mastering of Agamemnon's will in the *Oresteia,* as a result of which he leaves the stage, trampling over fabric the color of darkened blood, on his way to meet death within the house.

Stagecraft. Greek tragedy may be, supremely, a drama of the spoken word, but it also derives much of its power from apparently simple gestures and stage movements. Toward the end of *Heracles Mad,* the returning hero lies onstage a shattered wreck, surrounded by the corpses of his family, whom he had just slaughtered in a fit of madness sent by the goddess Hera. Heracles has shrouded his head, through fear of bringing religious pollution upon those around him; but his friend Theseus uncovers him, so restoring him to the world of human intercourse. A comparably momentous act occurs in Sophocles' *Philoctetes,* when the exiled, naively trusting hero places his one, priceless possession—his magic bow—into the hands of Neoptolemus, the young man who, as the audience knows, is part of a conspiracy to steal the bow. Many significant exits and entrances in tragedy tell the same story, as a powerful emotional charge is concentrated into a simple movement—nowhere more impressively than in the case of the deathward exit of Agamemnon just mentioned.

The Uses of Convention. The commonest difficulty faced by anyone attempting to introduce Greek tragedy to a contemporary public is that the plays' conventions may be felt to constitute a barrier to appreciation. Two such conventions are the chorus and the *ekkuklema.* Brief consideration of these should demonstrate that the barrier need not exist.

The chorus's contribution to dramatic meaning is often underestimated by modern audiences/readers because the frequent cross-references to other stories from the corpus of mythology can seem obscure or tedious. Yet, in fact, choruses have a pivotal role within the overall dramatic structure. Typically, they occupy a position of "ritual centrality." They may sometimes be wrong; their lack of perception may set them at an ironical disadvantage compared with characters or audience; but their proverbial, communal voice remains a vital counterpoint to the transgressions and exaggerations implicit in the conduct of those who decide and act. "Why should I dance?" sings the chorus of old men in *Oedipus the King,* faced with the prospect that the direction in which the action is vertiginously heading may threaten everything—including ritual dancing—which they have hitherto regarded as securely rooted in experience and tradition.

The *ekkuklema* was, it seems, a platform that could be rolled out from the *skene*, bearing a tableau of characters from within. Like any sharply defined theatrical convention, it lent itself to parody—as Aristophanes gleefully showed. But, within its tragic context, it had a perfectly valid function. Thanks to this piece of machinery, a moment of past action could be frozen onstage, for the contemplation of the audience. In the first two plays of the *Oresteia*, the corpses of Agamemnon and Cassandra, and later those of Clytemnestra and Aegisthus, are brought from the house, their postures fixed as at the moment of death, to be gazed at and meditated upon by dramatic characters and audience alike. One central theme of the trilogy is the dragging of the dark past into the glare of the present; another is the revealing of the generations of horrors concealed within the household. The *ekkuklema* is not a *restrictive* convention, but one that allows a particular kind of dramatic statement to be made.

Evaluation. How, finally, do ancient and modern evaluations of Greek tragedy differ? Many modern critics relish the presence in the genre of paradox, ambiguity, and irony, and stress what they see as the questioning and even subversiveness to be found there. There is, however, no evidence that the *admiration* for tragic paradox/ambiguity/subversion was so widely shared in antiquity. (Intriguingly, the tetralogy of which *Oedipus the King* formed part came no higher than second in the dramatic competition; this *might* imply that the qualities that modern critics find in that play were not so highly valued by the ancient jury.) Where the issue of evaluation is addressed, the angle of approach usually concerns either a play's effectiveness in "teaching" its audience, or its success in arousing emotion. Neither of these is unproblematic. The sense in which tragedy could be said to "teach" is far from certain—"by providing moral paradigms" is one answer implicit in our sources, but this obviously leaves out much of the genre's complexity. Again, privileging emotional arousal (as some modern critics would wish to do, following Aristotle and the Sophist Gorgias) risks belittling the undeniable presence of intellectual, speculative elements in these works.

Surely, the most sensible strategy is to accept that Greek tragedy can accommodate all of these approaches: the plays are unsettling *and* paradigmatic *and* moving. Such multivalence is one of the reasons why this remarkable art form—both popular and profound—has continued to fascinate for two and a half millennia.

[*See also* Aristotle, *survey article; and* Katharsis.]

BIBLIOGRAPHY

Goldhill, Simon. *Reading Greek Tragedy.* Cambridge and New York, 1986.

Heath, Malcolm. *The Poetics of Greek Tragedy.* London, 1987.

Jones, John. *On Aristotle and Greek Tragedy.* London, 1962; reprint, Stanford, Calif., 1980.

Pickard-Cambridge, Arthur. *The Dramatic Festivals of Athens.* 2d ed. Revised by John Gould and D. M. Lewis. Oxford, 1968.

Silk, Michael S., ed. *Tragedy and the Tragic: Greek Theatre and Beyond.* Oxford, 1996.

Taplin, Oliver. *Greek Tragedy in Action.* London, 1978.

Vernant, Jean-Pierre, and Pierre Vidal-Naquet. *Tragedy and Myth in Ancient Greece.* Translated by Janet Lloyd. Atlantic Highlands, N.J., 1981. Reprinted as *Myth and Tragedy in Ancient Greece* (New York, 1988).

Winkler, John J., and Froma I. Zeitlin, eds. *Nothing to Do with Dionysos? Athenian Drama in Its Social Context.* Princeton, N.J., 1990.

RICHARD BUXTON

Hume on Tragedy

Although "Of the Standard of Taste" is undoubtedly David Hume's most significant contribution to philosophical aesthetics, his essay "Of Tragedy" is of considerable interest, both as a contribution to the philosophical discussion of the "paradox of tragedy" and as an application of the theory of the passions worked out in book 2 of his *A Treatise of Human Nature*. The topic of the essay has been the subject of debate by philosophers and literary theorists at least since Aristotle's statement that "The tragic pleasure is that of pity and fear" (*Poetics,* chap. 14): how is it that we can take pleasure in tragedy, given that the sorts of response that it characteristically elicits from us (indeed, which on Aristotle's view are partly definitive of the genre) are on the face of it far from pleasant? What sort of pleasure is it, Hume asks, that stems "from the bosom of uneasiness" and "which still retains all the features and outward symptoms of distress and sorrow" (1987)?

Hume begins by considering two attempts to explain the appeal of tragedy, both of which he finds inadequate. The first claims that human beings naturally prefer emotional excitement, even if the emotions involved are negative, to the "languid, listless state of indolence, into which [the mind] falls upon the removal of all passion" (ibid.). Hume accepts that there is something in this, but argues that it fails to explain the pleasure that we take in tragedy: after all, "real-life" tragedies are hardly a source of pleasure, despite their invigorating powers. The second explanation suggests that we can take pleasure in literary or dramatic tragedy because we know that it is fictional; this knowledge, in Bernard Le Bovier de Fontenelle's words (quoted by Hume), "serves to diminish the pain which we suffer . . . and to reduce that affliction to such a pitch as converts it into a pleasure" (ibid.). Hume has more sympathy with this suggestion, but again finds it inadequate. He notes, first, that the distress we experience in response to fictional tragedy may be acute, and second, that in some cases we take pleasure in the tragic representation of events that we do not take to be fictional. How can this be?

Hume's suggestion is that the key to understanding the peculiarly ambiguous nature of our experience of tragedy lies in recognizing that the pleasure and the distress that we may experience in responding to tragic works have different causes and objects. The negative emotional responses that are aroused in us are directed at *what is depicted*—at the suffering of the characters, the horror of the events, and so on. In contrast, the pleasure that tragedy affords us is directed at *the manner of depiction*—at what he describes as "that very eloquence with which the melancholy scene is represented" (ibid.). This pleasure "predominates" over the feelings of distress that we also experience, and "converts" them into pleasurable feelings. As Hume says, "The uneasiness of the melancholy passions is not only overpowered and effaced by something stronger of an opposite kind; but the whole impulse of those passions is converted into pleasure, and swells the delight which the eloquence raises in us" (ibid.). Thus, for example, in responding to *King Lear,* we attend not only to the plight of Lear and Cordelia and Gloucester, but also to William Shakespeare's eloquence and to the art of the actors, director, stage designer, and so on; and the pleasure that we take in the latter "overpowers" and "effaces" and "transforms" the distress that we feel at the former.

Understanding Hume's account of tragic pleasure clearly depends on understanding this rather obscure talk of the "conversion" and "transformation" of passions. What does this process amount to? Hume cannot mean that, in our experience of tragedy, sorrow or terror (say) are somehow rendered pleasant, for, in book 2 of his *A Treatise of Human Nature,* the passions are identified with "simple and uniform" reflective impressions; a change in the feeling of a passion from pain to pleasure would on this account be impossible, because it would necessitate a change in the impression and hence a change in the passion itself. As he says in "Of Tragedy," "You may by degrees weaken a real sorrow, till it totally disappears; yet in none of its gradations will it ever give pleasure" (ibid.).

But if Hume is not suggesting that painful passions are themselves rendered pleasant in our experience of tragedy, it is far from clear precisely what he *is* suggesting. At some points in the essay, he talks explicitly of the transformation of one passion into another: for example, "the subordinate passion is here readily transformed into the predominant one" (ibid.). At other points, he writes as though the conversion he has in mind is not strictly of the passions themselves, but of the "impulse" or "vehemence" or "motions" that accompany or "arise from" the passions: for example, "The impulse or vehemence, arising from sorrow, compassion, indignation, receives a new direction from the sentiments of beauty" (ibid.).

These remarks are reminiscent of parts of his discussion of the passions in the *Treatise* where, for example, Hume speaks of the "principle, that every emotion, which precedes or attends a passion, is easily converted into it" (1978, book 2, part 3, section 5). Unfortunately, however, the discussion of this principle in the *Treatise* is hardly less opaque than it is in "Of Tragedy." In both works, the best

that Hume offers by way of illumination is a series of examples of the phenomenon with which he is concerned. For instance, "parents commonly love that child most, whose sickly infirm frame of body has occasioned them the greatest pains, trouble, and anxiety in rearing him. The agreeable sentiment here acquires force from the sentiments of uneasiness." Again, "jealousy is a painful passion; yet without some share of it, the agreeable affection of love has difficulty to subsist in its full force and violence." These and the other examples that Hume gives in both the *Treatise* and "Of Tragedy" constitute virtually the only support he offers for the principle that underlies his view of tragic pleasure, and commentators have differed over just how much support they do actually provide.

The central difficulty facing Hume's account of tragic pleasure, then, lies in the obscurity of his talk of the conversion and transformation of passion. Doubtless not least as a result of that obscurity, Hume's account has found few supporters in subsequent philosophical discussion of tragedy. Attenuated versions of his account, however, which abandon his notion of conversion but retain his suggestion that the pleasure and the distress involved in our experience of tragedy have different causes and objects, have not been uncommon. It is questionable whether this sort of position represents any advance on Hume's account, however. As Hume recognized, we value tragedy in large part because of, and not despite, the fact that it arouses in us the sort of "uneasy" or distressing emotional experience that it does. To construe the pleasure afforded us by tragedy as essentially separate from the distress that it also evokes, then, is to pull apart one of the crucial respects in which we value tragedy from the pleasure that it affords us. For Hume, who held a hedonic theory of value, that would be unacceptable; hence, his insistence that tragic pleasure has its source at least partly *in* the distress. In his words, the seemingly "unaccountable pleasure" is pleasure "which the spectators of a well-written tragedy *receive from* sorrow, terror, anxiety and other passions that are in themselves disagreeable and uneasy" (ibid.; emphasis added): not a pleasure that accompanies or runs alongside the "uneasiness" of "passions that are in themselves disagreeable," but—paradoxical though it seems—the pleasure *of* those passions. The tragic experience has a unitary character, albeit a difficult and ambiguous one; and it is just this that Hume's thesis about the conversion and transformation of passion in our experience of tragedy is meant to account for. Without that thesis, we are left with an account that misses a crucial aspect of the nature of the "singular phenomenon" with which he was concerned. With the thesis, however, we have an account that is at best highly obscure, based on associative principles that Hume himself never fully explains.

[*See also* Hume, *survey article.*]

BIBLIOGRAPHY

Works by Hume

A Treatise of Human Nature. 2d ed. Edited by P. H. Nidditch. Oxford, 1978.
"Of Tragedy." In *Essays Moral, Political and Literary,* rev. ed., edited by Eugene F. Miller. Indianapolis, 1987.

Other Sources

Budd, Malcolm. "Hume's Tragic Emotions." *Hume Studies* 17 (1991).
Eaton, Marcia. "A Strange Kind of Sadness." *Journal of Aesthetics and Art Criticism* 41 (1982): 51–63.
Feagin, Susan. "The Pleasures of Tragedy." *American Philosophical Quarterly* 20 (1983): 95–104.
Hill, Eric. "Hume and the Delightful Tragedy Problem." *Philosophy* 57 (1982): 319–326.
Hipple, Walter. "The Logic of Hume's Essay 'Of Tragedy'." *Philosophical Quarterly* 6 (1956): 43–52.
Neill, Alex. "Yanal and Others on Hume and Tragedy." *Journal of Aesthetics and Art Criticism* 50 (1992): 151–154.
Packer, Mark. "Dissolving the Paradox of Tragedy." *Journal of Aesthetics and Art Criticism* 47 (1989): 212–219.
Paton, Margaret. "Hume on Tragedy." *British Journal of Aesthetics* 13 (1973): 121–132.
Quinton, Anthony. "Tragedy." *Proceedings of the Aristotelian Society* Suppl. vol. 34 (1960): 245–264.
Schier, Flint. "Tragedy and the Community of Sentiment." In *Philosophy and Fiction,* edited by Peter Lamarque. Aberdeen, 1983.
Schier, Flint. "The Claims of Tragedy: An Essay in Moral Psychology and Aesthetic Theory." *Philosophical Papers* 18 (1989): 7–26.
Yanal, Robert J. "Hume and Others on the Paradox of Tragedy." *Journal of Aesthetics and Art Criticism* 49 (1991): 75–76.

ALEX NEILL

Freud on Tragedy

Sigmund Freud's contribution to the study and interpretation of tragedy begins with his letters to Wilhelm Fliess, for it is there that he announces that he has discovered a thematic continuity between the tragic drama *Oedipus the King* by Sophocles and William Shakespeare's *Hamlet.* That reading of the two plays established a lifelong involvement and fascination with Greek classical and Shakespearean tragedy. It also set the interpretive pattern for Freud's commitment to a biographical element in literary psychology, for he believed that the authors of tragedies gained their deep psychological insights through personal experience, though usually unconscious, of inner conflict. Two programs are initiated in the letter of 15 October 1897: the first, to examine great literary writings for psychoanalytic insights; the second, to connect those insights to the private life of the author.

> The Greek legend [of Oedipus] seizes upon a compulsion which everyone recognizes because he senses its existence within himself. Everyone in the audience was once a budding Oedipus in fantasy and each recoils in horror from the dream fulfillment here transplanted into reality. . . . the same thing might be at the bottom of *Hamlet* as well. I am not thinking of Shakespeare's conscious intention, but believe, rather, that a real event stimu-

lated the poet to his representation, in that his unconscious understood the unconscious of his hero.   (Freud, 1985)

Freud's wide reading in European literature, especially drama, led him to discoveries that he believed supported his own understanding of psychic development, and lent support to his theoretical observations. This support encouraged him to extend the literary interpretations even further in the light of the clinical, and thus psychoanalytic inquiry and the literary analysis of character came to reinforce one another. Psychoanalytic essays, in which long-debated literary problems are given psychological solutions, and neglected passages brought into the center of interpretation, and thus are seen in a new light, appear throughout Freud's writings.

In his many books and essays, Freud frequently returned to tragic drama because, of all the arts, it offered the most compelling and insightful representations of the kinds of family constellations and conflicts that psychoanalysis discovered in the consulting room. When *The Interpretation of Dreams* (1900) was published, Freud elaborated on the insight communicated to Fliess, making it clear that one may postulate a historical development in tragedy that shapes the tragic conflict in its various representations, though the psychological roots remain constant. The psychoanalytic theory of tragedy distinguishes two components, historical and psychological: "Shakespeare's *Hamlet* has roots in the same soil as [Sophocles'] *Oedipus Rex,*" Freud wrote.

> But the changed treatment of the same material reveals the whole difference of the mental life of these two widely separated epochs of civilization: the secular advance of repression in the emotional life of mankind. In the *Oedipus* the child's wishful phantasy that underlies it is brought into the open and realized as it would be in a dream. In *Hamlet* it remains repressed; and—just as in the case of neurosis—we only learn of its existence from its inhibiting consequences.   (1953, vol. 4, p. 264)

Modern audiences remain unknowing about Hamlet's psychological problem, that is, his inability to act, because of the psychological repression characteristic of our time. Freud argued that while literary critics advance a variety of interpretations to explain Hamlet as a person, they all miss the essential, unconscious conflict that immobilizes him:

> Hamlet is able to do anything—except take vengeance on the man who did away with his father and took that father's place with his mother, the man, who shows him the repressed wishes of his own childhood realized. . . . I have translated into conscious terms what was bound to remain unconscious in Hamlet's mind.   (Ibid., p. 265)

Beyond the historical and psychological forces that shape tragedy, Freud insisted, a biographical cause can be postulated in the case of Shakespeare because there is sufficient evidence to tie the plot of Hamlet to the playwright's life:

> It can only be the poet's own mind that confronts us in Hamlet. . . . *Hamlet* was written immediately after the death of

Shakespeare's father (1601), that is, under the immediate impact of his bereavement and, as we may well assume, while his childhood feelings about his father had been freshly revived.   (Ibid.)

Freud, like his predecessor in the interpretation of tragedy, the philosopher Georg Wilhelm Friedrich Hegel, used the method he had evolved for solving problems outside the aesthetic to read and interpret a number of tragic dramas. Whereas in Hegel's case the method was his general philosophy, then relied on as an interpretive tool to analyze a variety of problems, in Freud's case it was his psychoanalytic theory and its method of interpretation that opened up a number of cultural problems, especially in the arts. The two thinkers are alike in that both postulate a manifest content and a latent content in tragedy, to be connected through the method of inquiry that each has worked out. For the psychoanalytic, that means a double connectedness: first from the manifest content of the drama, as in Hamlet's inability to act, with its unconscious underpinnings in infantile psychic conflict, Hamlet's "Oedipus complex," and then to search in the biography of the author for evidences of the conflict, expressed in conduct, letters, and contemporary historical facts. Freud's method thus led him to explore a wide variety of conditions, internal and external to the particular drama in question. He was able to observe, in a sensitive application of his theory, common themes that tied together plots from various sources. Freud discovered in both linguistic and material art a universal preoccupation with conflicts that necessarily emerged in the sexual development of men and women. Tragedy derives its emotional force in part from its establishment of the irresolvability of these conflicts. Tragic pessimism mirrors the psychoanalytic view of human nature.

In contrast, it might be pointed out, that Hegel's readings of tragedy, for all his recognition of tragic conflict, emphasized a progressive movement toward resolution and enlightenment in the historical process. Freud, although firmly committed to the power of his method in the clinic to better the human condition, saw no optimism in the tragic dramas he analyzed. Their clear-sighted representations of the ever-present political and sexual conflicts stood as evidence that human nature has not changed and does not change through the ages.

Two major essays develop the psychoanalytic interpretation of tragedy, and exemplify the broad scope of the theory: "The Theme of the Three Caskets" (1913) and "Some Character-Types Met with in Psychoanalytic Work" (1916). In the first, Freud analyzes scenes from *The Merchant of Venice* and *King Lear;* in the second, themes in *Richard III, Macbeth,* and Henrik Ibsen's *Rosmersholm.*

Tying together dramas that at first seem as disparate as the *Merchant of Venice* and *King Lear* is the subject, Freud observes, of a man making a choice of one among three women. The women, symbolized in the *Merchant of Venice*

by the three caskets from which the suitors must choose, and directly represented in *King Lear* by the three daughters, are a manifest dramatic presence symbolizing a latent meaning. The essay "The Theme of the Three Caskets" searches for the hidden inner meaning of such a dramatic presentation. Freud suggests that underlying the choice in both cases of the most beautiful yet silent woman lies the human necessity to deny life's finitude, to turn that which is most repellent, death, into that which is most alluring, beautiful, and sexually desirable. Both dramas perpetuate a mythic theme, choosing one of three women, a theme that is seen in other stories: the choice by Paris of Aphrodite, who promises him the most beautiful woman in the world, Helen, and the choice in fairy tales of the most beautiful, though apparently least worthy, Cinderella. Another example of the choice is to be found in Apuleius's tale of Psyche.

In the *Merchant of Venice*, Bassanio chooses the lead casket, characterized as silent and unworthy, but within is hidden the painting of Portia, so beautiful it stuns the beholder. Silence and lead symbolize death, as does Cordelia's silence before Lear. Freud made this identification with the help of his own clinical work, for, he observed, in dreams reported by patients, dumbness symbolized death, and therefore he was led to ask if the same symbolization appeared outside of dreams. Setting as a hypothesis that the symbolization does indeed extend beyond dreams, he examined the way tragic drama intensifies the dream thoughts in dramatic scenes of great power. He also observed audience response, for these dramas make clear to the audience the high worth and sexual attractiveness of the woman. One may then postulate that the woman, so attractive and so desirable is at the same time a symbol of death and death's loss of dominion, a deep and universal wish of all human beings: let death be transformed into that which is most to be sought.

Freud goes on to argue that in every life there are three women, the woman who is mother, the woman who is lover, and finally, the woman who, as in Nordic myth, carries away the dying person, death itself. Underlying all of these narrative representations in which there is affirmation of choice, yet recognition of finality, is the Greek trio of the Fates, women who preside over every life. The terror of death they inspire becomes transformed in dramas such as the *Merchant of Venice* and *King Lear* into the one beautiful woman, freely, joyfully chosen from among her two companions.

Latent and manifest content are woven into a denial and an affirmation that penetrate into the audience's unconscious, for, Freud argued, works of tragic art are able to show us that through an aesthetic structure we are enabled to look upon that which, outside of art, would simply force us to turn away. Freud concludes his remarks on *King Lear:* "Let us now recall the moving final scene, one of the culminating points of tragedy in modern drama. Lear carries Cordelia's dead body on to the stage. Cordelia is death" (1958 vol. 12, p. 301). With this bold *is* of psychoanalytic interpretation, Freud demonstrates the identification on which his whole theory rests: a manifest representation is translatable into a latent meaning. Once that is discovered, the force and power, the hidden inner meaning, of the dramatic scene is disclosed, and we gain an understanding of why and how tragedy moves us so deeply.

Discussing *Macbeth*, in the essay "Some Character-Types Met with in Psychoanalytic Work," Freud discovers a theme at once obvious, yet implying hidden meanings. Central to the tragedy is the childlessness of Macbeth and Lady Macbeth. Moving beyond the tragic plot, Freud saw its political implications, for tragedy always hides, even in its psychological shrewdness, a political reality with which all societies must cope. Psychoanalytic theory of tragedy is sensitive to the close affinity between tragic conflict and the real political conflicts in everyday life. In the case of *Macbeth*, the political reality is a covert mirroring of the childlessness of Queen Elizabeth: "The accession of James I," Freud points out, "was like a demonstration of the curse of unfruitfulness and the blessings of continuous generation. And the action of Shakespeare's *Macbeth* is based on this same contrast" (1957, vol. 14). Childlessness has many ramifications, and in following them out, Freud gives a psychoanalytic reading of the play that pulls together several seemingly disparate scenes.

Scenes that appear remote from one another gain consistency and coherence. The words of the Weird Sisters, the fate of Banquo, the advancing "trees" of the forest, the terrifying night noises, all contribute to a cosmic ruin politically expressed by Macbeth in his cruel violence, and psychologically by Lady Macbeth in her madness. The protagonists are driven to tear apart the public social fabric and to pervert the private psychic balance as a consequence of the despair induced by lack of descendants. Freud writes:

> I believe Lady Macbeth's illness, the transformation of her callousness into penitence, could be explained directly as a reaction to her childlessness, by which she is convinced of her impotence against the decrees of nature. . . . The dramatist can indeed, during the representation, overwhelm us by his art and paralyse our powers of reflection; but he cannot prevent us from attempting subsequently to grasp its effect by studying its psychological mechanism.   (Ibid. Vol. 14, pp. 321–323)

Freud's studies of tragedy led him to conclude that these "mechanisms" are represented in the same terms in literature as they are in clinical experience.

In order to apply the psychoanalytic method to its fullest extent, the interpreter of works of art ought to be conversant with psychoanalytic naratives produced as "case histories," for they themselves are stories with tragic elements embedded in them. A study of Freud's cases highlights two recurring elements that appear frequently in tragic drama. One is the riddle, the other a psychological process to which Freud applied the term *splitting*.

Riddles appear over and over again in tragic drama, the most obvious in *Oedipus the King*. They are central also in *Hamlet, King Lear, Macbeth,* and many of the Greek tragedies. The person setting forth into psychoanalytic treatment pursues the deepest riddle that all human beings confront, their own innermost nature. So too the tragic heroes are engaged in a like searching, and in the search come upon the contradictions human being sees in itself. Watching a tragic drama unfold is very like a quest into the self. This observation led Freud to propose tentatively a hypothesis about how audience response to tragedy can be at once frightening and pleasurable. Splitting is the psychoanalytic answer to Aristotle's inquiry into the pleasure appropriate to tragedy, even while the audience suffers the emotions of pity and fear. Splitting allows the audience to gain pleasure from witnessing even the terrifying scenes in tragedy. Freud describes the psychological process of splitting in his late essay "An Outline of Psychoanalysis": "Two psychical attitudes [coexist], one which takes account of reality, and another which under the influence of the drives detaches the ego from reality. The two exist alongside of each other." Even though they are "contrary and independent of each other" they can be maintained at the same time. This doubleness allows the audience to identify both with the action on the stage, its aesthetic wholeness as narrative representation, beautifully composed, and the reality of private conflict within the self, which though it may remain unconscious, is brought into congruity with the dramatic unfolding (1964, vol. 23, pp. 202–204, 275–277).

Although Freud created a method of interpretation that stands beside those of Aristotle, Hegel, and Friedrich Nietzsche, from all of whom the psychoanalytic draws some of its powers, the psychoanalytic emphasizes interpretations of tragedy that complement those sources by discovering the deep unconscious conflicts that all cultural traditions must confront, and that in the West were best represented and aesthetically tamed in tragic drama.

[*See also* Freud, *article on* Survey of Thought.]

BIBLIOGRAPHY

Euben, J. Peter. *The Tragedy of Political Theory.* Princeton, N.J., 1990.

Freud, Sigmund. *The Interpretation of Dreams* (1900). In *The Standard Edition of the Complete Psychological Works of Sigmund Freud,* vols. 4 and 5, edited by James Strachey. London, 1953.

Freud, Sigmund. "Some Character-Types Met with in Psychoanalytic Work." In *The Standard Edition of the Complete Psychological Works of Sigmund Freud,* vol. 14, edited by James Strachey, pp. 309–333, London, 1957.

Freud, Sigmund. "The Theme of the Three Caskets." In *The Standard Edition of the Complete Psychological Works of Sigmund Freud,* vol. 12, edited by James Strachey, pp. 289–301. London, 1958.

Freud, Sigmund. "An Outline of Psychoanalysis." In *The Standard Edition of the Complete Psychological Works of Sigmund Freud,* vol. 23, edited by James Strachey, pp. 141–207. London, 1964.

Freud, Sigmund. "Splitting of the Ego in the Process of Defense." In *The Standard Edition of the Complete Psychological Works of Sigmund*

Freud, vol. 23, edited by James Strachey, pp. 271–278. London, 1964.

Freud, Sigmund. *The Complete Letters of Sigmund Freud to Wilhelm Fliess, 1887–1904.* Edited and translated by Jeffrey Moussaieff Masson. Cambridge, Mass., 1985.

Garber, Marjorie. *Shakespeare's Ghost Writers: Literature as Uncanny Causality.* New York and London, 1987.

Girard, René. *Violence and the Sacred.* Translated by Patrick Gregory. Baltimore, 1977.

Green, André. *The Tragic Effect: The Oedipus Complex in Tragedy.* Translated by Alan Sheridan. Cambridge, 1979.

Jones, Ernest. *Hamlet and Oedipus.* New York, 1949.

Kuhns, Richard. *Tragedy: Contradiction and Repression.* Chicago, 1991.

Rorty, Amélie Oksenberg, ed. *Essays on Aristotle's Poetics.* Princeton, N.J., 1992.

Rudnytsky, Peter L., and Ellen Handler Spitz, eds. *Freud and Forbidden Knowledge.* New York, 1994.

Steiner, George. *Antigones.* New York and Oxford, 1984.

Vernant, Jean-Pierre, and Pierre Vidal-Naquet. *Tragedy and Myth in Ancient Greece.* Translated by Janet Lloyd. Atlantic Highlands, N.J., 1981. Reprinted as *Myth and Tragedy in Ancient Greece* (New York, 1988).

RICHARD KUHNS

TRIBAL ART. Also termed "ethnographic art" or, in an expression seldom used today, "primitive art," tribal art is the art of small-scale nonliterate societies. Some of the traditional artifacts to which the term refers may not be art in any obvious European sense, and many of the cultures where they occur may not, strictly speaking, be tribal in social structure. The rubric nevertheless persists because the arts produced by small-scale cultures share significant elements in common. The tribal arts that have gained the greatest attention in the West come from the Americas (such as the Inuit, Southwest and Plains Indians, and isolated areas of Central and South America), Oceania (including Melanesia and Australia, Polynesia and New Zealand), and sub-Saharan Africa. The characteristics that define a small-scale, traditional society are (1) isolation, politically and economically, from civilizations of Europe, North Africa, or Asia; (2) oral traditions in the absence of literacy; (3) small, independent population groupings, usually in villages of no more than a few hundred souls who live a life of face-to-face social interaction and informal social control; (4) a low level of labor/craft specialization; (5) subsistence by hunting, fishing, and gathering and/or small-scale agriculture; (6) little technology beyond hand tools, and that often of stone rather than metal; and (7) slow rates of cultural change prior to European contact. Of this list, small size, lack of written language, and isolation from large civilizations are the essential features of societies whose art is discussed here.

As the European interest in "primitive" art grew in the second half of the nineteenth century, attention was first captured by carvings and masks, as these were the easiest to transport back to the capitals of colonial empire. The arts of small-scale societies include, however, far more than transportable artifacts: musical and dance performance, oral literatures, textiles and jewelry, and relatively perishable or ephemeral arts, such as sandpainting and body painting. Cultures tend to specialize in some arts at the apparent expense of others; the Sepik peoples of northern New Guinea, for example, are renowned for their wood carving, whereas their countrymen in the interior highlands hardly carve at all, but focus extraordinary care and attention on stunning body decorations. The acute aesthetic sensibilities of peoples of small-scale societies extend beyond crafted arts. Nilotic cattle herders of east Africa, such as the Dinka, have a refined sense for the natural colors and forms of cattle markings, around which they have built a subtle aesthetic vocabulary for critical discourse.

Whether such activities and artifacts amount to art at all in the European meaning of the term is a question persistently raised in anthropological and aesthetic literature. Rudolf Arnheim has claimed that tribal art "is not made to produce pleasurable illusions," but is "a practical instrument for the important business of daily living" (1974). More recently, anthropologist Alfred Gell has argued that the importance of tribal art lies in its utility as a magical technology, rather than in its aesthetic appeal (1993). Thus, the colorful appearance of a canoe may dazzle a trading partner, the decorations on a spear may help it find its target, or a carving's importance may derive from the fact that it is occasionally inhabited by a god or by the ghost of an ancestor; it follows that the Europeans' valuing of such objects merely because of their beauty would be ethnocentric. Gell's emphasis on the remoteness of tribal arts from familiar European aesthetic interests can be bolstered by considering some of the remarkable practices in the local contexts of tribal arts: for instance, *malangan* figures of New Ireland are sometimes unceremoniously burned following the ritual for which they were a centerpiece.

Yet, it is arguable that too much stress has been placed on the differences between Western and tribal arts. For instance, there are folk traditions in European Christianity in which an icon of the Virgin may temporarily be inhabited by her spirit, and it develops that New Ireland artists may have very good reason for wanting to burn a laboriously produced *malangan*, if, in the course of a rite, the carving has acquired potent magical powers that could be put to malevolent use were it not destroyed. Generally, it is difficult to find a practice involving tribal art in its original magical, religious, political, or entertainment context for which there cannot be discovered a plausible analogue involving acknowledged "art" products and practices in the civilizations of Asia and Europe.

Moreover, even when Westerners are ignorant of the original context of use of tribal arts, the immediately perceptible visible organization of a putative work of tribal art—color, imaginative representation, order, and balance—seems often to mark its aesthetic status. In this respect, what Robert Goldwater (1938) has termed the "directly visual" impact of tribal arts is no more mysterious (and no less powerful) than the encounters, however decontextualized, with fragments of ancient artworks of the West. Furthermore, even the most culturally remote or naive audience will recognize a human face or human body in a work of art, and this can provide a point from which appreciation can begin (this fact may explain, incidentally, why the most desirable tribal carvings in the Western market for such art continue to be renderings of the human form).

The characteristics of the art of tribal societies have been cataloged by H. Gene Blocker (1994). According to Blocker, the tribal art object normally (1) is of aesthetic (sensual or imaginative) interest, (2) is made by a specialist producer of art, (3) is subject to critical appraisal, (4) is set apart from ordinary life, (5) represents the real or a mythological world or events either literally or symbolically, (6) is intended to be understood as a symbolic or as mimetic representation, (7) involves the possibility of novelty within a tradition, and (8) is made by a person often seen as "eccentric" or socially alienated within the indigenous context. Although one might dispute the applicability of any of these criteria to every small-scale society (e.g., carving is a special activity of an elite few in some Polynesian cultures, whereas in most of Melanesia virtually any man can try his hand at it), the list is nevertheless a useful reminder that tribal arts are very far from being crude or primitive in any aesthetic sense, but are the mature, fully developed arts of technologically less developed societies.

An imaginative challenge to the claim that the artistic status of tribal artifacts is necessarily perceptible in visible form has been mounted by Arthur C. Danto (1988), who suggests a thought experiment: imagine two tribes, the Pot People and the Basket Folk, both of whom produce what are, to European eyes, indistinguishable pots and baskets. In the minds of these tribal peoples, however, there is an enormous difference between Pot People pots and Basket Folk pots (and conversely with baskets), for the pots are works of art, embodying deep symbolism for the Pot People, whereas they are mere utilitarian artifacts for the Basket Folk. Because this is, for Danto, a conceivable situation, it follows that for these imagined tribes, and possibly generally as well, the status of an artifact as work of art results from the ideas a culture applies to it, rather than from its inherent physical or perceptible qualities. Cultural interpretation (an art theory of some kind) is therefore constitutive of an object's arthood.

If supportable, Danto's thought experiment would have important implications for the Western encounter with tribal arts, for it would follow from it that knowledge of the cultural context of, say, an Oceanic ancestor figure was not merely an enriching support to the immediate aesthetic impact of the object. Rather, its original culture would exhaustively determine whether the object was art at all; apprecia-

TRIBAL ART. *Canoe Prow* (nineteenth to twentieth century), Solomon Islands; private collection. (Photograph courtesy of Denis Dutton.)

tion of formal aesthetic qualities in the absence of considerable cultural knowledge therefore risks being completely delusive. Nevertheless, it is difficult to imagine circumstances where something like Danto's example could actually exist. Those works of tribal art that embody dense cultural meaning are in small-scale societies normally ones into which are invested the greatest care, craftsmanship, and critical discernment. In Danto's example, even though one can well imagine that Europeans might find it difficult or even impossible to distinguish between Basket Folk baskets (works of art) and Pot People baskets (utilitarian craft objects), it is hard to envision the situation where the basket weavers of the Basket Folk would not be able to tell the difference (one might mistake a Terborch for a Hals, but it is unlikely Terborch or Hals ever did so).

Nevertheless, Danto's approach to the problem of cross-cultural aesthetic understanding, even if overdrawn, is a useful reminder of the importance of cultural knowledge in grasping works of tribal art. As they are deeply embedded in their cultural contexts, tribal arts are governed by systems of rules as complex as those that govern Western art forms. Moreover, it seems probable that societies that lack writing as a means of recording information and tradition invest artworks with a greater density of meaning than do literate societies. It may also be the case that an isolated society that has no access to alternative visual representations outside of its own art develops highly sophisticated and aesthetically powerful stylizations. It is perhaps for this reason that many judges both from within and outside of small-scale societies have remarked on the degradation of tribal arts once they come in close contact with industrial societies.

Whether such a view is fair to indigenous artists or instead represents ethnocentric prejudice is a topic of fierce debate. Many knowledgeable collectors and curators of tribal arts wish mainly to acquire and display works made in a traditional style for a traditional religious or social use that are thus designated "authentic." The market in tribal art therefore places a premium on African masks that have been used in a dance, Philippine carvings encrusted with years of oil and blood offerings, or decorated New Guinean fighting shields peppered with arrowheads from combat. At the same time, contemporary tourist or "airport" art made explicitly for sale to foreigners is passed over as inferior, because it does not reflect the indigenous values of the society, but only the demands of an alien market. This Western valorization of authenticity has been sternly criticized by Larry Shiner, who argues that it "is not merely an ethnocentric reflection of the modern discourse of Fine Art; it is also a piece of ideology, an unintended justification of a continuing exploitative power relation" (1994). Westerners fantasize that old, authentic works were produced by tribal artists in the unspoiled, Edenic state of such societies prior to colonial contact. Yet, as Shiner points out, there was a healthy circulation of ideas with much artistic and cultural borrowing in tribal societies before European contact; the fact that tribal artists now borrow from the West itself is a continuation of an authentic tradition of cultural exchange. Such a value system works against contemporary indigenous artists, unless they become adept at producing the countless faked "old" masks and carvings that have flooded the tribal art market in recent years.

Yet, although it may be unjust that the airport art of developing societies should be disparaged by those more wealthy cultures that brought the airports in the first place, it is not unreasonable that historians and collectors should retain an abiding interest in the art of small-scale societies as they existed before the onslaught of the consumer economies of colonizing powers. The passionate, imaginative visions of tribal arts, expressing as they often do modes of life and thought that have been abandoned since contact

with Western culture, have significantly expanded the West's notion of how art can have meaning. For those in the West willing to open their eyes and minds, they offer a wondrous gift.

[*See also* African Aesthetics; *and* Folk Art.]

BIBLIOGRAPHY

Abusabib, Mohamed A. *African Art: An Aesthetic Inquiry.* Uppsala, 1995.

Arnheim, Rudolf. *Art and Visual Perception: A Psychology of the Creative Eye.* New rev. exp. ed. Berkeley, 1974.

Blocker, H. Gene. *The Aesthetics of Primitive Art.* Lanham, Md., 1994.

Coote, Jeremy, and Anthony Shelton, eds. *Anthropology, Art, and Aesthetics.* Oxford, 1992. Includes articles by Ruth Barnes, Ross Bowden, Raymond Firth, Alfred Gell, Susanne Küchler, Robert Layton, Howard Morphy, Jarich Oosten, Anthony Shelton, and Jeremy Coote.

Danto, Arthur C. "Artifact and Art." In *Art/Artifact: African Art in Anthropology Collections,* edited by Susan Vogel. New York, 1988.

Dissanayake, Ellen. *Homo Aestheticus: Where Art Comes from and Why.* Reprint, Seattle, 1996.

Dutton, Denis. "Tribal Art and Artifact." *Journal of Aesthetics and Art Criticism* 51.1 (Winter 1993): 13–21.

Dutton, Denis, "Mythologies of Tribal Art." *African Arts* 28.3 (Summer 1995): 32–43.

Gell, Alfred. *Wrapping in Images: Tatooing in Polynesia.* Oxford and New York, 1993.

Goldwater, Robert J. *Primitivism in Modern Painting* (1938). Enl. ed. Cambridge, Mass., 1986.

Shiner, Larry. " 'Primitive Fakes,' 'Tourist Art,' and the Ideology of Authenticity." *Journal of Aesthetics and Art Criticism* 52.2 (Spring 1994): 225–234.

DENIS DUTTON

TRUTH. Underlying the ancient debate about truth and art—a debate at the very core of aesthetics—are profound philosophical issues concerning the acquisition of knowledge (epistemology), the ultimate nature of reality (metaphysics), and the sources of goodness (ethics). Beginning with some scattered observations in Homer about representation and the different functions of the poet and seer, the debate (in the Western philosophical tradition) has evolved considerably over two-and-a-half thousand years, reflecting not just changing views about art but radically different conceptions of truth, reality, and knowledge. In the broadest terms, the truth issue in aesthetics boils down to two fundamental questions: What features of art, in particular involving relations between works of art and reality, support the claim of art to truth? Is the conveying of truth to be counted among the primary functions and thus values of art?

It is a mark of the complexity of the topic that specialist terms have been developed to characterize the truth-bearing relations between art and reality: *mimesis,* representation, "mirror" (of nature), realism, verisimilitude, didacticism, and naturalism, among others. These conceptions are by no means interchangeable and confusion often results from running them together. Nor is their connection with truth by any means straightforward. The question, for example, whether art aims at lifelikeness or verisimilitude should be distinguished from the question whether art aims at truth in some more direct cognitive sense (in parallel to philosophy or science). Also, the imaginative truths that the Romantics (William Wordsworth, Samuel Taylor Coleridge, John Keats) claimed for lyric poetry are not the same—nor based on the same conception—as the truths that the eighteenth-century neoclassical theorists (Alexander Pope, John Dryden, Samuel Johnson) identified with poetry, nor indeed those sought by nineteenth-century Realist novelists (Honoré de Balzac, Émile Zola) or painters (Gustave Courbet, Edgar Degas), even though these views developed within a span of little more than one hundred years. Furthermore, not all arts lend themselves to the truth idiom, which is most commonly applied to the literary arts (drama, poetry, the novel) and the visual arts (painting, sculpture, film), but less to architecture, music, and dance, except where these are deemed to have representational content.

It is possible to discern different kinds of theories relating art and truth, which might be crudely sketched as follows:

1. *Mimetic theories.* The term *mimetic* covers a range of views, some of which will be discussed below, according to which works of art are seen as "imitating" or "mirroring" reality (be it a transcendent reality of Platonic Forms or a social reality or the mental reality of philosophical idealism or yet other kinds). The "imitating" might occur through verisimilitude (likeness), the transmission of universal truths, or the realization of an ideal type. [*See* Mimesis.]

2. *Didactic theories.* Characteristic of such theories is the notion that art is (can be, should be) a vehicle for instruction, be it religious doctrine, moral truth, or political ideology. The potential of art for teaching, imparting belief, even propaganda, has long been recognized, though as often deplored as applauded. [*See* Politics and Art; *and* Religion and Aesthetics, *article on* Religion and Art.]

3. *Moral theories.* Those theories that emphasize the moral nature and responsibilities of art, the idea that great art in some essential way is connected to moral truth, can often be viewed as a subclass of didactic theories; but they deserve a category of their own because they do not necessarily imply a teaching function for art and have at their core a criterion for art's fundamental value. [*See* Morality and Art.]

4. *Authenticity theories.* Sometimes the concept of truth in art is associated with truthfulness, sincerity, or authenticity. According to such theories, works of art are to be valued for their honesty, lack of sentimentality, clarity, or directness, whereby an artistic vision is presented without self-indulgence or distracting artifice; such works are praised for their "truth," though this need not be either moral truth or in any straightforward sense an "imitation" of nature.

The first three categories, in their varied manifestations, have found expression throughout the history of aesthetics. In contrast, authenticity theories, the fourth category, are essentially modern (post-eighteenth century), arising only when Romantic or expressive conceptions of art began to develop, although those who hold authenticity views often (however anachronistically) project them back onto earlier periods. Already the distinction between mimetic, didactic, moral, and personal or expressive truth shows just how diverse are the concerns in the debate about truth and art. Tracking the history of the debate is fraught with difficulty not only because of the profound changes in epistemological and metaphysical presuppositions, but also given the very elusiveness of the key terms *truth* and *art.* It would be deeply misleading to suppose that all the contributors to the debate shared any common, clearly defined set of premises or even any universal conception of the subject matter.

The Classical Foundations of the Historical Debate. In the classical debate, two fundamental positions on the question of how art might stake a claim to truth are defined by Plato (428–348 BCE) and Aristotle (384–322 BCE). Plato's views on knowledge and on the nature of reality played a determining role in his attitude to art. In the allegory of the Line (*Republic,* 1941, book 6), he divided cognition into four levels from the highest *(noesis),* a form of reason giving access to the basic principles of reality, to the lowest *(eikasia),* the perception of "shadows" and appearances. He assigns the products of art to the lowest level. The true reality of the world of ideas can only be grasped through a disciplined exercise of philosophical reasoning. Pictorial, sculptural, and literary art are all a form of mimesis or "imitation." But what the artist imitates is simply the imperfect and deceptive appearances found in this world. Plato illustrates the point in his famous example of the bed (ibid., book 10, pp. 597–599), according to which the craftsman (carpenter) imitates the Form of a bed while the painter merely imitates that imitation, thus locating his work at two removes from reality. In this same passage, Plato introduces the analogy of art and a mirror, a metaphor that was to become so influential among neoclassical theorists, by way of showing how easy it is to be a "maker" of (images of) all things on Earth (i.e., by holding up a mirror to them).

Of all Plato's strictures against art, none is stronger than his discrediting of art as a source of truth. For one thing, artists purport to a knowledge that they do not in fact possess and base their productions on unreliable opinion; a poet might successfully mimic the speech of a doctor without having any of the doctor's skills. Worse still, poets can beguile their readers, through the charm of their verse, into ascribing to them an authority that they have not earned. Plato recognized the seductive power of art and had much to say in its favor but on balance tended to stress its dangers over its benefits. In depicting the poets as irrational (even mildly insane), as lacking true knowledge of their subject matter, as mere "imitators" (in a largely negative sense), as pursuing pleasure before truth, as producers of potentially harmful effects, and therefore in need of censorship (ibid., book II; *Laws,* 801), he laid the foundations for a line of thought about art that has proved remarkably resilient. [*See* Plato.]

Aristotle's response to Plato comes in his *Poetics,* where he deals specifically with the genre of tragedy. He agrees with Plato that art must be defined as a type of mimesis, but he extends the possible objects of mimesis: the poet, like the painter, can imitate "one of three things, that is, what was or is, what is commonly said and thought to be the case, and what ought to be the case" (*Poetics,* 1972, 1460b). Aristotle emphasized the natural propensity of humans to take pleasure in imitations. In rejecting Plato's metaphysics of Forms and locating universals (the proper objects of knowledge) in particulars *(in re)* rather than in some ultimate reality of their own *(ante res),* he was not committed to the idea of art as an "imitation of an imitation" and was able to accord to poetry an epistemically respectable place between philosophy and history: "poetry is at once more like philosophy and more worthwhile than history, since poetry tends to make general statements, while those of history are particular" (ibid., 1451b). Far from denigrating poetry as a source of truth, he even identified, at least in the case of tragedy, the nature of the truths it can impart: "the poet's function is to describe, not the thing that has happened, but a kind of thing that might happen" (ibid.). In tragedy, the principal object of imitation is human action (not character), and the way the plot is structured, with its own internal necessity, is of paramount importance in yielding both the cognitive and the emotional (cathartic) payoff that gives tragedy its unique artistic value.

In his response to Plato, then, Aristotle does not question the basic premise that it is a function of art to tell the truth or to "imitate" reality and that failure to do so makes art morally objectionable. But he meets Plato's worries about the poet's merely simulated knowledge by locating the dramatist's distinctive contribution not in the recounting of particulars but in the revelation of deeper universal principles. As for the poet's use of artifice, this is no longer seen as serving mere trickery or beguiling illusion but as part of the craft of constructing a convincing plot from which the universal truths can emerge. [*See* Aristotle.]

The notion, broadly conceived, of a mimetic function (and value) of art came to provide a basis for the discussion of truth in art for nearly two millennia, even though conceptions of the appropriate objects of imitation and the realities against which art was matched shifted radically. It is only with the Romantic period in Europe in the mid- and late eighteenth century that truth in the ordinary, cognitive sense came to be challenged as irrelevant to the nature and function of art.

Both Plato and Aristotle are concerned with the philosophical (or moral) rather than the historical (or factual) truth of art. It is indeed arguable that classical comments on art put a higher premium on verisimilitude or lifelikeness than on historical accuracy. In summarizing debates about the Arts in classical Greece, Plutarch (c.46–after 119 CE) says about Simonides (c.556–c.468? BCE) that he held that though painting and poetry (and in poetry he includes history) "differ in material and manner of imitation," they both have the same goal: the best historian "is he who brings his narrative to life like a picture with emotions and personalities"; and, continues Plutarch, the Greeks also held that "poetry owed its charm and honour to its power to express things in a lifelike way: as Homer says [*Odyssey,* 19.203], 'she spoke many lies, resembling truth'" (*Moralia,* 1972, 346^f ff.). The concern for verisimilitude also emerges in Aristotle's much-quoted dictum that "one ought to prefer likely impossibilities to unconvincing possibilities" (1972, 1460a). These remarks illustrate not only that the question of the verisimilitude of a work of art is different from that of its (literal) truth, but that it was commonly accepted through the classical period that historical truth and accuracy had lower priority than verisimilitude. The function of poetry, the art in which the question of truth has always arisen in its most acute form, was, in Horace's (65–8 BCE) words, held to be "to do good or to give pleasure—or, thirdly, to say things which are both pleasing and serviceable for life" (*Ars poetica,* 1972, pp. 333–334). Both poetry and history had the rhetorical function to edify or amuse, and it did not then matter whether the tale was literally true or not.

The Late-Classical and Medieval Period. Throughout the classical period, there was a continuous concern with verisimilitude in sculpture and painting. A great deal of virtuosity is displayed in rendering sculpturally the peculiar individuality and specific look of a subject, something commented on by Pliny (23–79 CE) in his *Natural History* (xxxv, 88). Pliny also gives an account of the development of the technique of painting from a simple beginning to something like full realism (ibid., xxxv, 56–62). There is, however, little sustained discussion of the issue of truth in aesthetics between the seminal writings of Plato and Aristotle and that of the Neoplatonist Plotinus (204–270 CE). In *Ars poetica,* Horace offered some fleeting contributions, but although his views are often quoted, out of context, they remain undeveloped. Sextus Empiricus (second century CE) used his general skepticism to question whether poetry contains truth *(Against the Grammarians).*

What is notable about Plotinus is that although he adopted many of the metaphysical precepts of Plato, he more or less reversed the position that Plato assigns to art in the levels of cognition. Although the beauty of art (actual art objects) falls well short of the eternal Beauty (the essential Form, for Plotinus, identical with the Good), recognition of this worldly beauty is nevertheless a path to knowledge of the higher form. In a clear reference to, and repudiation of, Plato, he writes in *The Enneads:*

> Still the arts are not to be slighted on the ground that they create by imitation of natural objects; for, to begin with, these natural objects are themselves imitations; then we must recognize that they give no bare reproduction of the thing seen but go back to the Ideas from which Nature derives, and, furthermore, that much of their work is all their own; they are holders of beauty and add where nature is lacking. Thus Pheidias wrought the Zeus upon no model among things of sense but by apprehending what form Zeus must take if he chose to become manifest to sight. (1956, v.8.1, "On Intellectual Beauty")

Far from being restricted to imitating objects in the natural world, the artist, like the philosopher, can justly aspire to revealing truths at a higher plane.

In the early development of Christianity, the influence of Plato was strong, including his own ambivalence toward art and poetry. Classical literature was tolerated only to the extent that it could be useful in education, but drama was viewed—for example, by Saint Augustine (354–430 CE)—as morally suspect. Augustine observes that although poetry is often "full of lies," it nevertheless has "the aim . . . to delight rather than to deceive" (*Soliloquies,* II, ix, 16). By addressing the question of fiction and (in the case of stories and poems) replacing imitation with invention, he takes a significant step on from classical mimetic theories.

Perhaps a bigger step still comes in the theory of scriptural interpretation. Augustine (in *De doctrina christiana*) had discussed how to penetrate the obscure passages in Scripture to reveal their spiritual truth, but it was John Cassian (360–435) who postulated four levels of scriptural meaning—the literal, allegorical, tropological, and analogical—a distinction that was to become standard throughout the Middle Ages. The distinction allowed for the uncovering of otherwise unnoticed symbolic meanings (and thus truths) in the Bible, but it soon became connected to a wider metaphysical doctrine that the world itself was replete with symbolic meaning, natural objects doubling as things *(res)* and signs *(signa),* which could be "read" like a book. The development of allegorical literature, such as the *Divine Comedy, The Faerie Queen,* and *Pilgrim's Progress,* springs from the same intellectual sources. Truth was present in art, as in nature, but had to be elicited through interpretation. A parallel movement in pictorial representation led to increasingly arcane uses of Christian iconography to the point where the blending of Christian and pagan mythological figures in Baroque art makes the meanings virtually irrecoverable except to the cognoscenti. Nevertheless, medieval didactic art—morality plays, the frescoes of Giotto—whose function was to convey the revealed truths of Christian doctrine is often perfectly accessible.

The Renaissance. For all the flourishing of creative activity that occurred in the fifteenth and sixteenth centuries, especially in Italy, there is not a great deal of advance in the debate about art and truth. Leon Battista Alberti (1409–1472) conceived of a painting as a "window through which we look out into a section of the visible world" and insists, in a typically empiricist and nominalist manner, that "the painter has nothing to do with things that are not visible" (1956). The representational nature of painting and the need for verisimilitude are taken for granted. There is also an emphasis on painting as a species of natural philosophy, however, embodying general knowledge about the human form, the laws of nature, and mathematics. In his *Treatise on Painting,* Leonardo da Vinci (1452–1519) explicitly sought to incorporate painting into natural science, a view that led him to elevate painting above poetry, insisting that the former "represents the forms of nature's works with more truth than does the poet" (1956).

The spirit of Plato lived on in Puritan attacks on poetry and drama (e.g., Stephen Gosson's *School of Abuse,* 1571). The most notable, though by no means unique, "defense of poetry" is that of Sir Philip Sidney (1554–1586), whose *A Defence of Poetry* (1579/80) encapsulates the characteristic anti-Platonic (neo-Aristotelian) line in the Renaissance. The poet reveals the universal by combining the philosophical (teaching by precept) and the particular (teaching by example), but even where dealing with historical fact rather than "invention," the poet "nothing affirms, and therefore never lieth." Poetry in its productions "bodies forth" "in effect another nature," but the principles that govern this production are the same rational principles of probability and necessity that govern nature itself. Sidney thus retains the mimetic view of poetry, allied to the Horatian formula that its aim is to "teach and delight." The truths that poetry tells are not historical truths but truths about how things ideally should be: "[nature's] world is brazen, the poets only deliver a golden."

The Neoclassical Period. The seventeenth century saw a rapid growth in the prestige and spread of science as well as a new emphasis on reason as the source and guarantee of the validity of all human knowledge. Science was concerned with the exploration of nature, whereas reason guaranteed the validity of the mind's outlook on nature. Conceptions of art were developed that emphasized the importance of reason. "Love reason then," Nicolas Boileau (1636–1711) insists, "and let whate'er you Write / Borrow from her its Beauty, Force, and Light" (*Ars poetica* [1674], canto 1, lines 37–38). The goal of art was to imitate nature correctly, as Pope (1688–1744) wrote in *An Essay on Criticism* (1711):

> First follow NATURE, and your Judgement frame
> By her just Standard, which is still the same:
> *Unerring Nature,* still divinely bright,
> One *clear, unchang'd,* and *Universal* Light,

Life, Force, and Beauty, must to all impart,
At once the *Source,* and *End,* and *Test of Art.*

(1961, lines 68–73)

The view that nature, properly understood, is the standard against which art is measured is found equally in theories about painting. "Have recourse to nature herself," says Joshua Reynolds (1723–1792), "who is always at hand, and in comparison of whose true splendour, the best coloured pictures are but faint and feeble" (1852, vol. 1, p. 320). Art is not merely an imitation of nature as casually perceived, however, but of universal nature:

> There is an absolute necessity for the painter to generalize his notion; to paint particulars is not to paint nature, it is only to paint circumstances. When the artist has conceived in his imagination the image of perfect beauty, or the abstract idea of forms, he may be said to be admitted to the great council of Nature.
>
> (Ibid., vol. 2, p. 257)

Similar remarks abound in the writings of the literary critics of the period, perhaps the most famous being Johnson's (1709–1784) remark in *Rasselas* (1759) that "The business of the poet is to examine, not the individual, but the species; to remark general properties and large appearances; he does not number the streaks of the tulip, or describe the different shades of verdure of the forest" (1990); or his remark in his "Preface to Shakespeare" (1765) that "Nothing can please many, and please long, but just representations of general nature" (1968). For the neoclassical theorist, then, the highest aim of art is to exhibit those eternally valid truths that the rational mind discloses, and to do so with the clarity, simplicity, and moral seriousness that was thought to be the mark of a classical golden age.

The development of science, however, also pointed in another direction, which in philosophy manifested itself in empiricism, in particular in Britain. In scientific reports, it was important to get the facts right and empiricist philosophy insisted on the importance of particular sense impressions as the building blocks of knowledge. In the arts, this empirical emphasis showed itself in an insistence on close observation and lifelike detail. In literature, it provided part of the background that made possible the development of the novel, with what Ian Watt (1957) has called its formal realism. In early novelists such as Henry Fielding (1707–1754) and Samuel Richardson (1689–1761), there is a marked concern with verisimilitude grounded in accuracy of observation and knowledge of the world. "First then," says Fielding in chapter 1, book 8 of *Tom Jones,* "I think it may be very reasonably required of every writer, that he keeps within the bounds of possibility. . . . Nor is possibility alone sufficient to justify us, we must keep likewise within the rules of probability." Richardson, too, in the "Preface" and "Postscript" to *Clarissa* (1747–1748), defends his portrayal of the character of Clarissa as well as his technique (the epistolary form and the amount of minute, circumstantial detail) in terms of the probable and the lifelike.

The Romantic Period. Until the last quarter of the eighteenth century, the notion of artistic truth was nearly always closely bound up with prevailing notions of philosophical or scientific truth. In the most general terms, artistic truth was taken to consist in some sort of "imitation" or reproduction of an external reality (however conceived), and the debate about truth in art was a debate about how far, if at all, art could successfully present important truths about such a reality. With the change in the intellectual climate toward the end of the century, however, which saw the breakdown of the Enlightenment confidence in reason and the increased emphasis on the irrational and passionate side of man's nature, views on the aspirations of art, and consequently on artistic truth itself, underwent a radical change. What became paramount was not, as for the neoclassicists, the studied delineation of a rationally ordered world but the artist's own sensibility, an inner world of intense, sometimes disorderly, feelings.

Art came to be seen as the expression of these feelings; as the poet Charles Baudelaire (1821–1867) remarked later, "Romanticism is precisely located neither in choice of subject nor in exact truth, but in a way of feeling." Art was both caused by emotion and affected its audience emotionally, and the value of art was seen as in a large part bound up with its emotive origins and impact. The emotions that were essentially linked to art, however, were also a source of knowledge. Poets and painters were thought to possess a special gift, a sort of emotional intuition, which enabled them to participate feelingly not only in the inner life of other human beings, but in the inner life of the world itself. As Wordsworth (1770–1850) says in the "Preface" to the 1802 edition of *Lyrical Ballads:*

> It will be the wish of the Poet to bring his feelings near to those of the persons whose feelings he describes, nay, for short spaces of time perhaps, to identify his own feelings with theirs; [the] object [of poetry] is truth, not individual and local, but general, and operative; not standing upon external testimony, but carried alive into the heart by passion; truth which is its own testimony.

Reason being discredited, the key faculty for the artist became imagination, which came to be seen as a mode of thought seizing directly on deep, mysterious truths involving man's sentience, which reason could not reach: artistic truth became imaginative truth.

This new role for the imagination required a new conception of imagination itself. Coleridge (1772–1834) distinguished between imagination and fancy, the *primary* imagination being "the living Power and Prime Agent of all human Perception," the *secondary* imagination being "an echo of the former" but a faculty that can be exercised at will in artistic creation: "It dissolves, diffuses, dissipates, in order to recreate; or where this process is rendered impossible, yet still at all events it struggles to idealize and to unify." The fancy, on the other hand, was what had heretofore been called imagination, having "no counters to play with, but fixities and definites," and being "no other than a mode of Memory emancipated from the order of time and space" (1983, chap. 13). Imagination affects, in the words of William Hazlitt (1778–1830), "the intuitive perception of the hidden analogies of things" and is "what stamps the character of genius on the productions of art more than any other circumstance: for it works unconsciously, like nature" ("On the English Novelists" [1819], in *Works*, 1967, vol. 6, p. 109). Similar views of the role of the imagination were developed on the Continent by theorists such as Joseph Joubert (1754–1824) ("Imagination is the faculty of making sensuous what is intellectual, of making corporeal what is spirit: in a word, of bringing to light, without depriving it of its nature, that which in itself is invisible" [*Les Carnets* (1938 ed.), vol. 2, p. 493]) and poets and artists such as Baudelaire: "Imagination is, as it were, a divine faculty, which perceives directly, without the use of philosophical methods, the secret and intimate relationships of things, their correspondences and analogies" (Introduction to his translation of Edgar Allan Poe, *Nouvelles histoires extraordinaires* [1857], *Œuvres complètes*, vol. 7 [1933], p. xv).

For all the grand claims made on its behalf, the Romantic conception of imaginative truth is deeply problematic. Because imaginative truth is essentially subjective—literally the product of one subject's felt response to the world—the line between truth and falsehood must itself rest on subjective criteria, for example, that which "rings true" or is "true to" another individual's own response. This means that only like-minded people will recognize each other's truths. Yet, if imaginative truth contrasts so strongly with more familiar notions of truth, in science and common sense, which at least aspire to objectivity (so important for Enlightenment thought), then it is not clear that "truth" is being used univocally; nor is it clear in what sense imaginative truth could be "deeper" or more important than scientific truth. These have been recurring problems for all attempts to shore up the otherwise attractive conception of imaginative truth that has been an enduring legacy of Romanticism. [*See* Romanticism.]

It is significant that the two towering figures of philosophical aesthetics in this period, Immanuel Kant (1724–1804) and Georg Wilhelm Friedrich Hegel (1770–1831), took quite different views on the truth debate. For Kant, who stressed the beauty of nature over art, who played down the cognitive elements in aesthetic appreciation, and was a key architect of Romantic conceptions of genius and the sublime, the question of truth in art held little interest. For Hegel, on the other hand, the truth issue was central, but his approach to it was eccentric. Art occupied a key role in Hegel's elaborate Idealist philosophy, being, along with religion and philosophy, one of the three modes of apprehension of the Absolute Idea. The basic aim or "vocation" of art is "to unveil the *truth* in the form of sensuous artistic configuration" (1975, vol. 1, p. 55). Hegel emphasized the historical development of art and the changing relations between the spiritual and the material: in Symbolic art, the spiritual Idea is overwhelmed by the material medium; in classical art, the two are perfectly in harmony; in Romantic art, the Idea dominates the sensuous. This in turn allows Hegel to propose a hierarchy of the arts: architecture is supreme in Symbolic art, sculpture in classical art, and poetry (ahead of painting and music) represents, in Romantic art, the final stage of freedom from the material. Nowhere is it plainer than in Hegel's philosophy how the truth debate in aesthetics hinges on a wider metaphysical context. [*See* Kant *and* Hegel.]

Later Nineteenth-Century Developments. Another leading conception in the nineteenth-century truth-in-art debate after the Romantic period was that of Realism, although the idea was developed more by artists themselves than by philosophers, who remained mostly under the spell of Idealism and Romanticism. The term *réalisme* first appeared in print in 1826 (*Le Mercure français du XIXᵉ siècle*) and was immediately associated with truth ("la littérature du vrai"). At a superficial level, the guiding notion once again was that of verisimilitude, but there were more interesting currents at a deeper level. One was the continuing influence of experimental science. For Zola (1840–1902), a leading exponent of the doctrine (though he preferred the term *naturalism*), "the novelist is equally an observer and an experimentalist . . . the naturalistic novel . . . [being] . . . a real experiment that a novelist makes on man by the help of observation" (1894). Gustave Flaubert had spoken of "the precision of the physical sciences" and the "pitiless method" of his novels (1857; *Correspondance IV*), and earlier still, Balzac identified the need to "study the causes or central cause of . . . social facts, and discover the meaning hidden in [them]" ("Preface" to *La comédie humaine*, 1846). In painting too the same language was being deployed; John Constable (1776–1837), in his fourth lecture to the Royal Institution (1836), described painting as "a branch of natural philosophy, of which pictures are but the experiments."

In contrast to the Romantic view, the pursuit of truth for the Realists was conceived in terms of scientific objectivity and fidelity to fact. The means adopted in this pursuit took various forms. There was a preference (not universally adhered to) for a subject matter representing lowlier aspects of life, the gritty struggles of ordinary people, rather than the idealized (and exotic) lives of romantic heroes. In novels, characters were drawn in highly particularized detail set in a real-life background; conventional plots were replaced by individualized stories displaying a finely meshed causal and temporal nexus; and the narrative language lacked undue ornament or embellishment. The overall (desired) effect—

in the service of truth—was to make the narrative more like reportage, concealing the art (or artifice) in the name of "scientific" neutrality. What is evident in the development of Realism as an aesthetic conception is the markedly different emphases given to these various aspects: Realism being associated sometimes with a strong scientific view of truth, sometimes with mere verisimilitude; as primarily a feature of subject matter or just as a mode of writing; as a mirror held up to society or as a tool for deeper explanation.

It is interesting to note that, as an aesthetic doctrine, Realism declined in France just as the new social sciences were being established. It is arguable that this decline was partly the result of the recognition that the social sciences performed much better at the task the Realists had set themselves. What is notable is that although the strong cognitive claim for Realism—that realistic art afforded a special neoscientific access to (social) truth—was abandoned or modified, the Realist mode of writing (and, indeed, painting) survived into the twentieth century, even if for a time it was overshadowed by modernism. Realism did not need the strong claim to truth, nor, as we shall see, did the claim to truth need realism.

In the twentieth century, the debate about realism (and truth) took different forms. Within Marxist aesthetics, for example, the idea of "Socialist Realism" was used both as a theoretical weapon against modernism and as a renewed attempt to identify a truth role for art. György Lukács (1885–1971), a Marxist theoretician who helped refine the notion of realism, admired the literary form of the nineteenth-century Realist novel but rejected what he called the "pseudo-objectivity" of the "mechanical imitation of life" ("Art and Objective Truth," 1965), preferring the "partisanship of objectivity," which drew on, and revealed, deeper processes of historical change. Another Marxist, Bertolt Brecht (1898–1956), in "The Popular and the Realistic" (1958), sought a conception of realism "broad and political, free from aesthetic restrictions and independent of convention," but nevertheless one with a cognitive function, "laying bare society's causal network / showing up the dominant viewpoint as the viewpoint of the dominators" (1964). He rejected the constraint of verisimilitude (in effect disagreeing with Lukács) and famously advocated in the theater the "alienation effect" *(Verfremdung)*, thereby breaking down the illusion of reality and the tendency of audiences to empathize with the characters. Theodor W. Adorno (1903–1969) took a similar view, yet had no hesitation in speaking, in an unqualified way, of "truth" in art; he championed (e.g., in *Aesthetic Theory*) the most austere modernist art against all forms of popular culture on the grounds that the latter colluded with prevailing ideologies, whereas the former could give a truthful, if "negative," image of the fragmented and alienated condition of bourgeois society. For these latter theorists, the notions of realism, truth, and verisimilitude are pulled apart altogether. [*See* Realism.]

There are tendencies in this direction from other quarters as well. Nelson Goodman (b.1906) has argued (1976) that realism need not imply verisimilitude, claiming that realistic depiction is fundamentally a matter of convention; what seems realistic is a function only of how familiar is the system of representation used. Roland Barthes (1915–1980), who (unlike Goodman) denied any representational function in narrative ("Introduction to the Structural Analysis of Narrative," 1966), described realism as simply "a reality effect" ("The Reality Effect," 1967). It should be emphasized, though, that the relation between realism and verisimilitude, like that of representation and resemblance, is still a matter of contention among aestheticians, even if the strong claims of the early French theorists probably have few remaining supporters.

Another later nineteenth-century development was the art-for-art's-sake movement, which grew up alongside, although in opposition to, that of French Realism. Like Romanticism, it involved a sharp repudiation of the classical mimetic theory. The phrase *l'art pour l'art* was first popularized by Théophile Gautier (1811–1872) in the preface to *Mademoiselle de Maupin* (1834). Oscar Wilde's (1854–1900) often-quoted paradox that "Life imitates art far more than Art imitates Life" nicely pokes fun at centuries of orthodoxy about mimesis, as does his view that "the more we study Art, the less we care for Nature" (both in "The Decay of Lying," 1891). In fact, the ideas can be traced back to the Kantian aesthetics of disinterestedness and Friedrich von Schiller's conception of art as "play"; they also anticipate formalist developments in the twentieth century. The aestheticist movement emphasized the autonomy of art, conceived sometimes in terms of the social isolation of the artist, sometimes, more philosophically, in terms of the intrinsic value of aesthetic experience and the subjection of art to its own law-governed sphere. A. C. Bradley (1851–1935) wrote of poetry that it is "not a part, nor yet a copy, of the real world . . . but . . . a world by itself, independent, complete, autonomous," though he qualifies this by speaking of a "connection underground" between "life and poetry" ("Poetry for Poetry's Sake," 1909). Aestheticism broke not only with mimetic theories, but also with moralistic theories. Clive Bell's (1881–1964) assertion that "Once we have judged a thing a work of art, we have judged it ethically of the first importance and put it beyond the reach of the moralist" (1914) is not far removed from Wilde's aestheticist's epigram that "There is no such thing as a moral or an immoral book. Books are well written, or badly written. That is all" (*The Picture of Dorian Gray*, 1891). [*See* Aestheticism.]

Twentieth-Century Developments. Descendants of the Romantics, the art-for-art's-sake movement, and the cognitive Realists have manifested themselves in diverse strands of the twentieth-century truth-in-art debate. Formalists, autonomists, and structuralists, on the one hand, as well as those who adopt wider skeptical attitudes to truth itself, take a broadly "antitruth" stance, while realists, Marxists, and certain metaphysicians and moral philosophers, on the other, form the "pro-truth" camp.

The truth idiom is prominent, for example, in Martin Heidegger's (1889–1976) aesthetics in accord with his sense of truth as "unconcealment." Art can uncover the "hiddenness" of being. In Heidegger's famous discussion of Vincent van Gogh's painting of what Heidegger takes to be peasant shoes, he argues that the painting, through revealing facets of the peasant's work, "has shown us what shoes are in truth" (1964). Jean-Paul Sartre's (1905–1980) existentialist philosophy stressed the freedom of artistic creation and the use of imagination to disclose the world, but in a more political vein he encouraged the idea of "la littérature engagée" (*What Is Literature?* 1948) whereby writers could not shirk political commitment in the name of artistic autonomy. [*See* Heidegger *and* Sartre.]

The dominant and most vocal form of antitruth theories in the twentieth century have been structuralism and its descendants, poststructuralism and postmodernism. Four antecedents (at least) helped shape this complex of ideas. First, there is Friedrich Nietzsche's (1844–1900) view that there are "no facts only interpretations" a view he dubbed "Perspectivism" (*The Will to Power*, 1901); the rejection of absolute or universal truth is a central tenet of poststructuralism. Second, there is the general Marxist doctrine that the significance of art lies as much in what it conceals—its ideology, the conditions of its production—as in what it overtly displays. Third, there is the antihumanist attack on the autonomous self or subject, drawing on (but going far beyond) the work of Sigmund Freud (1856–1939). Fourth, there is the crucial influence of Ferdinand de Saussure (1857–1913), whose *Cours de linguistique générale* (1916) was interpreted as claiming that language (into which human beings are born) does not mirror reality but helps constitute reality.

For structuralists, all cultural phenomena, including works of art, are products of "systems of signification" whose signs acquire sense through their internal relationships rather than their relations with an external reality. Such phenomena are viewed essentially as "texts" constituted in much the same way as linguistic texts. The sentence analogy is imposed on all sign systems, including painting, architecture, sculpture, or film, whose general meaning properties are taken to be conventional and "arbitrary" on the pattern of the linguistic sign in Saussure's theory. This view is often thought to be encapsulated in the slogan, lifted from Jacques Derrida's (b.1930) *De la grammatologie* (1969), "Il n'y a pas de hors-texte" (p. 227) (deliberately ambiguous between "There is nothing outside the text" and "There is no outside text," that is, no ultimate urtext or master text that can be used as a point of reference for truth). On the issue of art and truth, this can only imply a

strong "antitruth" stance. What is rejected are not only all forms of mimesis (there is nothing for art to imitate, and even verisimilitude is a mere "reality effect"), but also the Romantic notion of an expressive (authorial) self, which is seen as one more social construct. At best, works of art are deemed to be self-referential, tracking their own history of production and the sign systems in which they are embedded. Poststructuralism goes further, emphasizing the inherent instability of all sign systems, suggesting that determinate meaning (not to speak of truth) is permanently undermined in every text. The traditional ascendancy of philosophy over literature is reversed, as the latter, through foregrounding its rhetorical tropes and fictionality, is judged to be less "deluded" than the former, which still strives vainly for universal truth and rational argument. Poststructuralists also have little use for the concept of "art" itself; the concept embodies too many humanist assumptions that they reject, as well as a value system that they see as ungrounded. [*See* Structuralism *and* Poststructuralism.]

Postmodernism, both as a body of theory and as an art practice, owes much to certain strands of poststructuralism. Characteristically, postmodernist theory rejects, as based on spurious "metanarratives" (Lyotard, 1984), any intellectual enterprise—that of aesthetics par excellence—that aspires to universal application; the very concepts of truth, meaning, value, reality, and reason, which have been thought to provide foundations for theorizing, are radically relativized or dismissed as repressive and authoritarian. Postmodernist artists also self-consciously turn against the aesthetic; their principal mode is ironic self-reflection, delighting in the ephemeral and the fragmented, denouncing the false reverence of the art gallery or the museum, rejecting the distinction between "high art" and "popular art," and, above all, mocking the higher aspirations of art in terms of truth, self-expression, or morality. Curiously, one of the more outlandish postmodernists, Jean Baudrillard, has come to see reality itself as a kind of simulacrum or simulation ("the cinema and TV are America's reality" [Baudrillard, 1988, p. 104]), suggesting the ultimate collapse of the distinction between art and the world. [*See* Postmodernism.]

Within analytic aesthetics, the truth debate has largely been focused on the logical peculiarities of fiction, but opinions remain divided for and against artistic truth. Early in this strand of the debate, I. A. Richards (1893–1979) had proposed a sharp distinction between two "functions of language," the "referential" and the "emotive," identifying science broadly with the former and poetry with the latter (1923, chap. 7). In his *Principles of Literary Criticism* (1924), he insists that the "scientific sense" of "truth" is "little involved by any of the arts" and that within criticism "truth" is most commonly used to mean "acceptability" and "sincerity" (1926, pp. 212–213). He speaks of the "pseudo-statements" of poetry. Although the notion of "emotive" meaning largely ran out of steam with the demise of logical positivism, the idea that the language of fiction fulfills a special, nonreferential, function has had wide support. The idea, as a logical thesis, probably originated with Gottlob Frege (1848–1925), who had written in his essay "On Sense and Reference" (1892) that, in the case of poetry (i.e., fiction), "the question of truth would cause us to abandon aesthetic delight for the attitude of scientific investigation. Hence it is a matter of no concern to us whether the name 'Odysseus', for instance, has reference, so long as we accept the poem as a work of art" (1980). Many logicians, and in turn logically minded aestheticians, came to think of poetic or fictional language as lacking truth-value (a view anticipated perhaps by Sidney, as quoted earlier); a stronger view still, though less influential, deriving from Bertrand Russell's theory of names, sees fictional sentences as simply false.

For many, though, it is far from clear that such logical theses imply the cognitive inertness of all fictional literature (and, by analogy, other representational arts). On this issue, a vigorous debate has been pursued. The proponents of truth have moved in two directions, either relocating the truths of fiction or seeking different conceptions of truth. On the former, it is pointed out that although works of fiction do contain sentences describing fictional states of affairs that cannot literally be true, they also contain, explicitly and implicitly, propositions that make a legitimate claim to truth: these are generalizations found in fictional texts (King Lear's "As flies to wanton boys, are we to th'Gods; / They kill us for their sport") or implied truth claims elicited by readers ("Even Kings are mere mortals," identified as a theme of Shakespeare's history plays). The crucial step in the pro-truth argument is not that these propositions are genuine truth-bearers, which can be readily conceded, but that their truth is relevant to the aesthetic value and interest of the works. The latter is hotly disputed: Morris Weitz (1955), John Hospers (1946, 1960–1961), Francis Sparshott (1967), R. K. Elliott (1966–1967), D. H. Mellor (1968), and Richard Miller (1979) have argued in favor, while Arnold Isenberg (1954–1955), Joseph Margolis (1965), Mary Sirridge (1974–1975), Peter Lamarque and Stein Haugom Olsen (1994) have argued against. The case against often rests on emphasizing the distinctive ("institutional" or aesthetic) nature of literary works (including the generalized propositions in or derived from them) and the dangers of assimilating them to other (truth-centered) modes of discourse.

A different strategy on the pro-truth side involves loosening the connection between truth and propositions. The notions of "truth to" (Hospers, 1946) or of truth as "authenticity" (Dorothy Walsh, 1969) or of "knowing how" (David Novitz, 1987) or "knowing what it is like" (Walsh, 1969) in contrast to "knowing that" are sometimes proposed. Iris Murdoch has sought to explain the "truth" of great works of art in terms of their "vision" as against the propositions they express (Murdoch, 1970, 1992, 1997). Other philoso-

phers (e.g., Martha Nussbaum, 1990) have tried to assimilate literary works into moral philosophy. The objection to such moves is that they either deploy a weakened and unexplained notion of truth or that they lose sight of the unique contribution of literature.

One thing is clear, namely, that merely investigating the logic of fictional sentences is not sufficient to resolve the deeper, more long-standing issues about literary truth. It should be noted that there is a conception of "truth in fiction" that is not to be confused with this wider issue: the idea of truth "within a fictional world," whereby a distinction is drawn between, say, the truth of "Sherlock Holmes is a detective" and the falsity of "Sherlock Holmes took up ballet dancing." This distinction between truth and falsity is drawn within the parameters of the fictional context. There is extensive debate as to how best to explicate this notion: in terms of "possible worlds" (David Lewis, 1978) or speech act theory (John Searle, 1979) or even to play down the significance altogether (Richard Rorty, 1982).

The deeper questions about literature and art in relation to truth are not amenable to any simple categorizations in logic. Among other things, they go to the heart of what counts as, and might be the benefits of, a liberal humanist education. As intellectual and philosophical fashions come and go, it is unlikely that this debate will find any determinate and uncontested resolution.

[*See also* Alienation, Aesthetic; Epistemology and Aesthetics; *and* Fiction.]

BIBLIOGRAPHY

Alberti, Leon Battista. *On Painting.* Translated by John R. Spencer. New Haven, 1956.

Aristotle. *Poetics.* Translated by M. E. Hubbard. In *Ancient Literary Criticism: The Principal Texts in New Translations,* edited by D. A. Russell and M. Winterbottom. Oxford, 1972.

Auerbach, Erich. *Mimesis: The Representation of Reality in Western Literature.* Translated by Willard R. Trask. Princeton, N.J., 1953.

Augustine. *De doctrina christiana.* Translated by Thérèse Sullivan. Washington, D.C., 1930.

Barthes, Roland. "From Work to Text." In *Textual Strategies: Perspectives in Post-Structural Criticism,* edited by Josué V. Harari. Ithaca, N.Y., 1979.

Barthes, Roland. "The Reality Effect" (1967). In *The Rustle of Language,* translated by Richard Howard New York. 1986.

Baudrillard, Jean. *America.* Translated by Chris Turner. London and New York, 1988.

Beardsley, Monroe C. *Aesthetics from Classical Greece to the Present: A Short History.* New York, 1966.

Beardsley, Monroe C. *Aesthetics: Problems in the Philosophy of Criticism.* 2d ed. Indianapolis, 1981.

Bell, Clive. *Art.* London, 1914.

Bradley, A. C. "Poetry for Poetry's Sake" (1909). In *Oxford Lectures on Poetry* (1909). Reprint, London, 1965.

Brecht, Bertolt. "The Popular and the Realistic" (1958). In *Brecht on Theatre: The Development of an Aesthetic,* edited and translated by John Willet. New York, 1964.

Coleridge, Samuel Taylor. *The Collected Works of Samuel Taylor Coleridge,* vol. 7. 1–2. *Biographia Literaria; or, Biographical Sketches of*

My Literary Life and Opinions, edited by James Engell and W. Jackson Bate. Princeton, N.J., 1983.

Culler, Jonathan. *Structuralist Poetics: Structuralism, Linguistics, and the Study of Literature.* Ithaca, N.Y., 1975.

Culler, Jonathan. *On Deconstruction: Theory and Criticism after Structuralism.* Ithaca, N.Y., 1982.

Derrida, Jacques. *Of Grammatology* (1969). Translated by Gayatri Chakravarty Spivak. Baltimore, 1976.

Elliott, R. K. "Poetry and Truth." *Analysis* 27 (1966–1967): 77–85.

Falck, Colin. *Myth, Truth, and Literature: Towards a True Post-Modernism.* Cambridge and New York, 1989.

Frege, Gottlob. "On Sense and Reference." In *Translations from the Philosophical Writings of Gottlob Frege,* 3d ed., edited by Peter Geach and Max Black. Oxford, 1978.

Goodman, Nelson. *The Languages of Art: An Approach to a Theory of Symbols.* 2d ed. Indianapolis, 1976.

Hart, H. L. A. "A Logician's Fairy Tale." *Philosophical Review* 60 (1951): 198–212.

Hegel, G. W. F. *Aesthetics: Lectures on Fine Art.* 2 vols. Translated by T. M. Knox. Oxford, 1975.

Heidegger, Martin. "The Origin of the Work of Art." In *Philosophies of Art and Beauty,* edited by Albert Hofstadter and Richard Kuhns. New York, 1964.

Horace. *Ars poetica.* Translated by D. A. Russell. In *Ancient Literary Criticism: The Principal Texts in New Translations,* edited by D. A. Russell and M. Winterbottom. Oxford, 1972.

Hospers, John. *Meaning and Truth in the Arts.* Chapel Hill, N.C., 1946.

Hospers, John. "Literature and Human Nature." *Journal of Aesthetics and Art Criticism* 17 (1958–1959): 45–57.

Hospers, John. "Implied Truths in Literature." *Journal of Aesthetics and Art Criticism* 19 (1960–1961): 37–46.

Isenberg, Arnold. "The Problem of Belief." *Journal of Aesthetics and Art Criticism* 13 (1954–1955): 395–407.

Johnson, Samuel. *The Yale Edition of the Works of Samuel Johnson,* vols. 7–8, *Johnson on Shakespeare,* edited by Arthur Sherbo. New Haven, 1968.

Johnson, Samuel. *The Yale Edition of the Works of Samuel Johnson,* vol. 16, *Rasselas and Other Tales,* edited by Gwin J. Kolb. New Haven, 1990.

Lamarque, Peter. *Fictional Points of View.* Ithaca, N.Y., 1996.

Lamarque, Peter, and Stein Haugom Olsen. *Truth, Fiction, and Literature: A Philosophical Perspective.* Oxford and New York, 1994.

Leonardo da Vinci. *Treatise on Painting.* 2 vols. Translated by A. Philip McMahon. Princeton, N.J., 1956.

Lerner, Laurence. *The Truest Poetry: An Essay on the Question: What Is Literature?* London, 1960.

Lewis, David. "Truth in Fiction." *American Philosophical Quarterly* 15 (1978): 37–46.

Lukács, György. "Art and Objective Truth" (1965). In *Writer and Critic and Other Essays,* edited and translated by Arthur D. Kahn. London, 1970.

Lyotard, Jean-François. *The Postmodern Condition: A Report on Knowledge.* Translated by Geoff Bennington and Brian Massumi. Minneapolis, 1984.

Martin, Graham Dunstan. *Language, Truth, and Poetry: Notes towards a Philosophy of Literature.* Edinburgh, 1975.

McCormick, Peter J. *Fictions, Philosophies, and the Problems of Poetics.* Ithaca, N.Y., 1988.

Mellor, D. H. "On Literary Truth." *Ratio* 10.1 (1968): 150–168.

Miller, Richard W. "Truth in Beauty." *American Philosophical Quarterly* 16 (1979): 317–326.

Murdoch, Iris. *The Sovereignty of Good.* London, 1970.

Murdoch, Iris. *Metaphysics as a Guide to Morals.* London, 1992.

Murdoch, Iris. *Existentialists and Mystics: Writings on Philosophy and Literature.* Edited by Peter Conradi. London, 1997.

Nelson, William. *Fact or Fiction: The Dilemma of the Renaissance Storyteller.* Cambridge, Mass., 1973.

Newsom, Robert. *A Likely Story: Probability and Play in Fiction.* New Brunswick, N.J., 1988.

Nietzsche, Friedrich. *The Will to Power* (1901). Translated by Walter Kaufmann and R. J. Hollingdale, edited by Walter Kaufmann. New York, 1967.

Nussbaum, Martha C. *The Fragility of Goodness: Luck and Ethics in Greek Tragedy and Philosophy.* Cambridge and New York, 1986.

Nussbaum, Martha C. *Love's Knowledge: Essays on Philosophy and Literature.* New York and Oxford, 1990.

Nuttall, A. D. *A New Mimesis: Shakespeare and the Representation of Reality.* London and New York, 1983.

Plato. *Republic.* Translated by Francis MacDonald Cornford. Oxford, 1941.

Pliny. *The Elder Pliny's Chapters on the History of Art.* Translated by K. Jex-Blake, commentary by E. Sellers. London, 1896; reprint, Chicago, 1968.

Plotinus. *The Enneads.* 2d ed. Translated by Stephen McKenna, revised by B. S. Page. New York, 1956.

Plutarch. *Moralia.* Translated by D. A. Russell. In *Ancient Literary Criticism: The Principal Texts in New Translations,* edited by D. A. Russell and M. Winterbottom. Oxford, 1972.

Pope, Alexander. *The Poems of Alexander Pope: The Twickenham Edition,* vol. 1; *Pastoral Poetry and An Essay on Criticism,* edited by E. Audra and A. Williams. New Haven, 1961.

Reynolds, Joshua. *The Literary Works of Sir Joshua Reynolds.* 2 vols. London, 1852.

Richards, I. A. *Principles of Literary Criticism* (1924). 2d ed. London, 1926.

Richards, I. A., and C. K. Ogden. *The Meaning of Meaning.* London, 1923.

Rorty, Richard. "Is There a Problem about Fictional Discourse?" In *Consequences of Pragmatism: Essays, 1972–1980.* Minneapolis, 1982.

Sartre, Jean-Paul. *What Is Literature?* Translated by Bernard Frechtman. New York, 1965.

Saussure, Ferdinand de. *Course in General Linguistics* (1916). Edited by Charles Bally, Albert Sechehaye, with Albert Riedlinger, translated by Roy Harris. London, 1983; reprint, La Salle, Ill., 1986.

Searle, John R. "The Logical Status of Fictional Discourse." In *Expression and Meaning: Studies in the Theory of Speech Acts.* Cambridge and New York, 1979.

Sirridge, Mary J. "Truth from Fiction?" *Philosophy and Phenomenological Research* 35 (1974–1975): 453–471.

Sparshott, Francis E. "Truth in Fiction." *Journal of Aesthetics and Art Criticism* 26 (1967): 3–7.

Stern, J. P. *On Realism.* London and Boston, 1973.

Walsh, Dorothy. "The Cognitive Content of Art." *Philosophical Review* 52 (1943): 433–451.

Walsh, Dorothy. *Literature and Knowledge.* Middletown, Conn., 1969.

Walton, Kendall L. *Mimesis as Make-Believe: On the Foundations of the Representational Arts.* Cambridge, Mass, 1990.

Watt, Ian. *The Rise of the Novel: Studies in Defoe, Richardson, and Fielding.* Berkeley, 1957.

Weitz, Morris. *Philosophy of the Arts.* Cambridge, Mass., 1950.

Weitz, Morris. "Truth in Literature." *Revue Internationale de Philosophie* 9 (1955): 116–129.

Wilde, Oscar. "The Decay of Lying" (1891). In *The Works of Oscar Wilde,* new coll. ed., edited by G. F. Maine. London, 1948.

Zola, Émile. "The Experimental Novel." In *The Experimental Novel and Other Essays,* translated by Belle M. Sherman. New York, 1894.

PETER LAMARQUE and STEIN HAUGOM OLSEN

U

UGLINESS. The common conception that ugliness is simply the antonym of beauty, its polar opposite on the spectrum of aesthetic value, can easily obscure the subject's inherent subtlety and complexity—features that have made it both fascinating and perplexing to aesthetic theorists throughout the ages. Although there is no doubt an opposition between beauty and ugliness, it is an opposition that can be understood in a good many ways; and although beauty marks an extreme of aesthetic positivity, ugliness sometimes present itself in manifestations whose effects are not altogether negative. Philosophical reflection on the nature of aesthetic ugliness has centered on three issues: (1) the conceptual problem of providing a correct analysis of ugliness, particularly in its relation to beauty; (2) the ontological problem of determining whether ugliness exists (i.e., whether there are any things that truly *are* ugly) and, if it does, how it becomes engaged in aesthetic judgment; and (3) the critical problem of accounting for ugliness's salubrious effects both within and without the world of art.

The Analysis of Ugliness. It seems apparent that ugliness cannot be abstractly identified with some set of characteristics common and peculiar to all ugly objects. For one thing, the kinds of ugly objects and the ways in which they can be ugly are remarkably diverse; for another, ugliness is often supposed to consist less in features of things than in a form of reaction they call up. It might be thought that this reaction, an expression of serious aesthetic disfavor or disapproval, could itself serve as a defining characteristic of ugliness, except that there are arguably many instances of ugly objects—grotesques appearing in certain artworks, for instance—that, far from evoking disfavor or disapproval, seem to evoke something approaching their opposite. It is hardly surprising, therefore, that the consensus view throughout the history of debate on the concept has been that attempts to analyze ugliness in terms of this or that feature in things or in our reactions to things are destined to miss the mark unless they frame the analysis as an expression of the complementarity of these features or reactions to those of beauty. This is because, as nearly everyone agrees, the chief point of the standard deployment of this concept is to mark a pronounced contrast or distance between objects we call ugly and those we call beautiful. In ascribing ugliness to this thing or that, we are at the very least declaring it to be unbeautiful, or at odds with beauty (or perhaps very unbeautiful, very much at odds with it). But in what way is this opposition to be understood? Quite different accounts of ugliness follow from different accounts of its way of contrasting with beauty, and controversies over these differences have proved especially heated and long-lived.

Four main camps have emerged from the debate. The first takes the view that ugliness is related to beauty as its absence, or privation, much as cold is simply the absence of heat. This view is rooted in Plato's treatment of the ugly as this or that detraction from the power of beauty—as what is less than fitting, inappropriate, or limited in practical value. Plato's point is extrapolated and given a moral-theological cast by Plotinus:

> All shapelessness whose kind admits of pattern and of form, as long as it remains outside of Reason and Idea, has not been entirely mastered by Reason, the matter not yielding at all points and in all respects to Ideal Form, is ugly by that very isolation from the Divine Thought. . . . We may even say that Beauty *is* the Authentic-Existents and Ugliness is the Principle contrary to Existence: and the Ugly is also the primal evil; therefore its contrary is at once good and beautiful, or is Good and Beauty: and hence the one method will discover to us the Beauty-Good and the Ugliness-Evil.

Similarly, Saint Augustine speaks of ugliness as simply the inverse of beauty, a "privation of form," and most medieval philosophers down through Saint Thomas Aquinas follow his lead. As they saw it, one principle governs both beauty and ugliness, so that the presence or absence, increase or decrease, of the one is ipso facto the absence or presence, decrease or increase, of the other. A fundamental problem facing this view is that of accounting for callilogical neutrality. Not everything that fails to be beautiful is generally taken to be to that degree ugly. In fact, some things (the number seventeen, for example) seem to be altogether unbeautiful without thereby being in the least bit ugly.

A second view responds to this problem. It is the position that ugliness is not just the inverse of the scale of beauty; instead, it and beauty occupy polar extremes on a single scale of aesthetic value whose gradations descend from each pole toward a middle state of neutrality. On this account, beauty and ugliness are related more as pleasure to pain than as heat to cold. Just as some experiences are neither pleasurable nor painful, so some objects are neither beautiful nor ugly. Early modern philosophers seem generally to have gravitated to such a position. Thomas Hobbes, David Hume, and Edmund Burke apparently held such a view. More recent thinkers often complicate the position with moral or practical judgments flavoring the way in which both "beautiful" and "ugly" are to be understood. John Dewey, for example, attributed beauty to whatever serves the purpose for which an artifact was designed and ugliness to whatever thwarts that purpose. In *Art as Experience,* he illustrates the distinction with the example of a common chair:

> A chair may serve the purpose of affording a comfortable and hygienically efficient seat, without serving at the same time the needs of the eye. If, on the contrary, it blocks rather than promotes the role of vision in an experience, it will be ugly no matter how well adapted to use as a seat.

But it is clear that Dewey accepted the view that some artifacts are neither so successful in their design to be counted beautiful nor so unsuccessful as to be deemed ugly. In this second version of opposition, whatever is credited to the account of beauty is not thereby deducted from that of ugliness; still, anything that is found beautiful cannot be to any degree ugly, and vice versa, because ascriptions of each are made on opposite sides of neutrality. This view is, therefore, no more capable than its predecessor of making sense of the claim that things may be both ugly and beautiful at once.

The third view accepts the plausibility of this conflation by placing beauty and ugliness on the same scale and allowing either or both to permeate the neutral meridian. Here, ugliness is conceived of as related to beauty much as humility is to pride; while some actions may be purely proud or purely humble, some display what seems aptly described as humble pride or, conversely, proud humility. Two prominent versions of this view have emerged. In the first, ugliness is seen as a negative species of beauty distinguished from the more familiar, positive species by the challenge its negative aspects pose to appreciation. George Santayana, Bernard Bosanquet, and W. T. Stace, among others, subscribed to variations of this view; but it was Samuel Alexander who embraced it most explicitly as a pivotal point in his aesthetic theory: "Ugliness . . . is an ingredient in aesthetic beauty, as the discords in music or the horrors of the tragedy. When it becomes ugly as a kind of beauty it has been transmuted. Such ugliness is difficult beauty" (Alexander, 1968). Thus understood, ugliness contributes to the effect of (positive) beauty by challenging the attentive intellect to respond in unorthodox ways to phenomena in which appealing elements are combined with repelling ones. No doubt such a view owes some of its credibility to the emergence of modern psychology, a study that points up the constructive contribution made by elements of experience hitherto regarded as altogether untoward. (It is worth noting that some theorists—for example, Burke—retain the idea that beauty and ugliness are mutually exclusive opposites while allowing that ugliness partially overlaps with the sublime. Others (e.g., August Schlegel) propose that, while the two are opposites, certain forms of ugliness may contain elements of the beautiful). The second version derives from Hegelian idealism rather than empirical science; it characterizes the ugly as one stage in a dialectical process whereby the beautiful is more perfectly realized. In this view, most ambitiously expressed in the work of Benedetto Croce, ugliness abets beauty's role in the development of spirit's progress toward its ultimate destiny by serving as its aesthetic counterpoint. Just as the individual consciousness cannot discover what it is without considering what it is not, beauty requires an antithetical value to evolve through synthesis into something that goes beyond both on the path of intellectual liberation. Far from relegating ugliness to the role of beauty's foil or sparring partner, the dialectical accounts often speak quite admiringly of its constructive partnership with beauty, especially as the two are linked together in art. As Karl Rosenkranz puts it, "If art is not to represent the idea in a merely one-sided way it cannot dispense with the ugly. . . . If mind and nature are to be admitted to presentation in their full dramatic depth, then the ugly of nature, and the evil and diabolic, must not be omitted" (*The Aesthetic of Ugliness,* 1853).

The chief complaint against both versions of the third view is that they equivocate on the question of whether ugliness is really negative. In trying to establish the claim that aesthetic awareness of the ugly can be valuable, proponents of this view are driven to say that ugliness is both appealing and unappealing, both pleasant and unpleasant, both positive and negative. But it can be argued that this is not so much a concession to aesthetic complexity as it is to muddle a thing's ugly aspects with others coexisting in close proximity to them. Just as a bad man may do a good deed because he sometimes is motivated otherwise than by his badness, so an ugly thing may have its appealing, even beautiful aspects without thereby becoming "negatively beautiful," or beautifully ugly.

The fourth view avoids the conflation problem by denying that ugliness and beauty occupy the same scale of aesthetic value. The contrast between the two might be thought of as similar to that between the risible and the pathetic. While these characteristics occupy independent scales, so that any degree of risibility is consistent with any degree of pathos in a subject, an attenuated form of opposition between them persists in that, in civil society, the recognition of the truly pathetic rightly inhibits laughter, rendering it boorish and contemptible. Likewise, ugliness and beauty might be conceptually independent yet exercise a shaping or braking influence on each other as they operate in certain contexts. The seeds of such a view were planted by Schlegel and Bosanquet, who insisted that while ugliness and beauty both express positive value, they do so in altogether different ways. More recently, Stephen C. Pepper distinguished ugliness from the lack of beauty (in artworks) by turning the former, but not the latter, into an ascription of moral disapproval. Artworks might be ugly, he supposed, if they exhibit "aesthetic dishonesty" through actions by artists that sacrifice the integrity of their work by deliberately distorting or perverting the audience's attention. A particularly strident defense of the view has been mounted by Mark Cousins, who insists that because aesthetics cannot deal with ugliness save as a negation of beauty, its proper analysis must be left to other disciplines. His own deconstructive, psychoanalytic account presents ugliness as the experience of dislocation or mislocation; "The ugly object is an object which is experienced both as being there and as something that should not be there. That is, the ugly object is an object which is in the wrong place" (Cousins, 1996). Although on this account ugliness has admittedly little to do with beauty, an opposing relation between the two may still be detected at a certain level of experience. For, while the dislocating force of ugliness makes our relations to the experienced world seem "precarious," the countervailing force of beauty makes them seem less so.

The obvious charge to be leveled against theories that put beauty and ugliness on different scales is that in so doing they abandon the very notion of complementary opposition without which ugliness is freed from beauty only to be bound in confusion with a host of other values. If ugliness has nothing to do with beauty it becomes the expression of any aesthetic antipathy one pleases, dissipating its force in the vagaries of taste, intuition, and ideology. Efforts by proponents of the different-scales view to retain some portion of the polarity they reject, as in admitting the "natural" conflict between the lessons of beauty and ugliness in certain contexts, are bound to seem desperate expedients, or unwitting betrayals of an incapacity to abandon what has been disavowed.

The Ontology of Ugliness. A common indictment of theories equating ugliness with the privation of beauty is that they tend to deny reality to ugliness altogether. If all things are beautiful in varying degrees—say, in proportion to the excellence of their form—then ugliness is simply a hypothetical limit on quotients of beauty, an absence beyond its smallest presence. But this absence, like formlessness itself, simply does not exist, so nothing can truly be ugly. Such a conclusion is, of course, impossible to square with the general acknowledgment that many real things are ugly; and this consequence is widely regarded as a reductio ad absurdum of ugliness-as-privation theories.

Not everyone, however, regards the unreality of ugliness as an unwelcome, let alone absurd, belief. To Augustine, for example, it is simply a reflection of the recognition that God's handiwork in this world is permeated with aesthetic as well as moral goodness. If something should seem ugly, that fact is taken as symptomatic of a deficiency in perceptual capacities

or in responsiveness to the formal order and harmony pervading all things. One need not share Augustine's sanguine theological outlook to discount the reality of ugliness as a failure of appreciation. Bosanquet, for instance, regards apparent ugliness simply as a matter of incomplete expressiveness, a condition growing out of humanity's as-yet-unsuccessful attempt to relate freely and fully to the objects of our awareness. Since, in his view, every object of awareness is already to some extent expressive, and since what is expressive is beautiful, what at first seems ugly is properly understood as a stimulus to aesthetic effort on the part of the observer—an effort whose success consists in the conversion of initial ugliness to eventual beauty. Nor need one subscribe to idealist metaphysics to take such a view. Pepper rejects all negative aesthetic value on the ground that value runs through all of life. Francis J. Kovach argues along Deweyan lines that the ugly is simply a limitation on the beauty of beautiful things—a condition of impediment or shortcoming—and, while this condition may add piquancy or depth of meaning to experience as a whole, it is only a deficit in real things, and no real thing itself.

Philosophers are not the only ones to deny the reality of ugliness. It is a point of pride among some artists to insist that a special, heightened aesthetic awareness permits them to see beauty in all things, nullifying whatever ugliness others see. Thus, for example, John Constable is said to have boasted: "No, madam, there is nothing ugly; *I never saw an ugly thing in my life:* for let the form of an object be what it may, —light, shade, and perspective will always make it beautiful." Frequently, it is difficult to determine from what they say whether artists are claiming that nothing is ugly and they have a facility for seeing that this is so or that whatever things are ugly can be transformed and presented as beautiful under the spell of their talents. It is, in fact, apparent that among both theorists and practitioners rejecting the reality of ugliness rarely has the effect of denying its real consequences, and for this reason it is usually more instructive to take note in these expressions of what existences are affirmed than of what are denied. In general, the lines between affirming a thing's existence and commending it and between denying its existence and condemning it are extremely thin.

It would be natural to suppose that theorists who defend the reality of ugliness break into the two familiar camps of objectivism (locating the existence of ugliness in things and their qualities) and subjectivism (locating it in the reactions of consciousness to things perceived) along the Kantian divide, paralleling the historical development of corresponding positions in the theory of beauty. But this would be a mistake. After Immanuel Kant, ugliness theorists are overwhelmingly subjectivists, and before him most theorists denied independent existence to ugliness altogether. Consequently, there are virtually no objectivist ugliness theories. All the interesting debates among the reality affirmers have been between rival conceptions of the experiential process involved in making judgments about ugliness rather than between claims about its location.

One strand of theory takes judgments of ugliness to mark a distinctive species of painful experience—usually involving a kind of pain that rises above the merely unpleasant by virtue of its perceived contrast to the pleasures supplied by beauty. Stace is a prominent defender of such a view, strands of which he derives from Aristotle's earlier reflections on the value of aesthetic pain. Another strand emphasizes disapproval rather than displeasure. It identifies the ugly with the inappropriate, the ignoble, the unseemly, and so forth, even when the experience of these does not occasion a painful response. Theorists as various as Schlegel, Croce, and Cousins have defended such views. Sometimes the disapproval takes on a moral tone, and the judgment involved mingles with ethical judgments, as when in Hobbes, for instance, the ugly is associated with the base, or when in G. E. Moore, it is identified as whatever it is evil to contemplate admiringly. Yet another strand regards the experience of ugliness as consisting mainly of pleasure, albeit of a peculiar kind—a contorted form of allure, fascination, or amusement. Santayana sometimes seems inclined to such a view (on the ground that "everything is capable in some degree of interesting and charming our attention"), and several of his followers have embraced it explicitly. Of course, we have already mentioned the Hegelian position that ugliness is not a feature of any one human faculty, response, or taste verdict but rather a reiterated component in a complex, dialectical action incorporating many elements of evolving consciousness. There are other views as well—perhaps as many as there are aesthetic epistemologies. While the diversity of these views exposes the depth of historical controversy over the conceptual mechanism of aesthetic judgment, it also reveals the breadth of effort that has been expended on extracting value from ugliness in the exercise of that mechanism. For, in almost all instances, the theorists have built their theories with one eye fixed on the objective of showing how our experience of ugliness can be edifying, no matter how negative its inherent character.

The Value of Ugliness. If our contact with ugly things is usually or always distasteful or disagreeable, it would seem we should wish to avoid or minimize our exposure to them. The displeasure we feel is more than just a feeling of dislike or a bad taste; it involves a cognitive aversion to what is wrongly formed and therefore debilitating or debilitated. Yet, curiously enough, the experience we derive from that contact is frequently pleasant, engaging, and even ennobling. We may call this the "paradox of ugliness." It is easily recognized to be the generic parent of the better-known "paradox of tragedy." The latter concerns our special reactions to representations of ugly, untoward, and hideous objects and conduct on stage, whereas the former concerns the way we react to ugly objects and events wherever we find them. Explanatory accounts of our admiration of ugliness in art often founder on the issue of what object is being admired, diverting attention to the skill or ingenuity of the artist and away from the ugly thing portrayed. Questions about how an artist manages to convert what was once ugly into beauty and why we are pleasantly moved by the ugly so converted are neither as fundamental nor as challenging as the question of how ugliness can be so powerfully and positively affecting, whether or not it is touched by art. At least four kinds of answers have been given to this question.

Descending from Aristotle's treatment of the therapeutic effects of unpleasant elements in tragedy, the dominant early strand of answers took the negativity of ugliness seriously and conceived of its salubrious effects as strictly antidotal. Some exposure to ugly things and actions can, according to this account, defend and improve us by providing what amounts to inoculation against later, more dangerous uglinesses. The pleasure we experience in relation to ugly objects is taken to be a symptom of the rightful satisfaction we feel at being well warned and armed against hazards that might confront us from without or erupt from our own unwary souls.

A second pattern of answers began to appear in the heady turbulence of post-Renaissance individualism, when introspective curiosity demanded a full accounting of our mental powers and their interplay. Ugliness was deemed particularly instructive in acquainting us with internal tensions between these powers. A strong antipathetic reaction to something might awaken an awareness not only of the grounds of aversion but of the distinctive way we consider and manage such a response. Kant's analysis of sublimity set the tone for advocacy of this position in the modern period. In the experience of sublimity, horror of the overwhelming is a vital element in revealing the grounds of human dignity. Similarly, ugliness could be seen to show us hidden corners of our powers that are activated in facing and overcoming the untoward. Later, Hegelian strands of the self-awareness answer insisted that ugliness could not properly be understood except in its partnership relations with other elements (the comic, the sublime, the beautiful, etc.) in the wider scheme of intellectual and spiritual fulfillment.

A third kind of answer emerged from postindustrial realism, a strident reaction to what was seen as the excesses of theory in preceding ages. If philosophers held that ugliness was unreal, that it was an odd kind of beauty, or that it was only part of a grand process of human improvement, then, the realists responded, they had to be wrong. For the world, as people normally experience it, is gritty, messy, and indelibly ugly here and there. We should, they insisted, see it for what it is, not what it is imagined or hoped to be; and in doing so we will reap the benefits of honest vision, ontological tolerance, and respect for the natural order of things. Inspired by the ascendancy of anti-Panglossian scientism (especially in the field of psychology), they insisted that ugliness, like death, malevolence, and disease, should be faced up to and not denied.

In recent times the role of ugliness as a concept expressing aesthetic disapproval has fallen into disuse. The negative force it once had has largely been transferred to ethics. Beginning with the *fin de siècle* decadence movement, literature and the arts undertook to challenge old divisions between bad and good on the broadest front. They called on us to look again at ugly things with eyes prepared to find beauty. Or perhaps it would be more accurate to say that they asked us to look at things through neither concept so that we might see them beyond the distortion of both. What had been realist respect for ugliness as part of common experience now became avant-garde fascination with ugliness as an exciting frontier of unusual experience. That positive effects might be experienced in relation to objects commonly regarded as ugly is not hard to understand; they are simply the undiscovered aspects of things that could be revealed only after the old, dichotomous borders were broken down. Postmodernism has, of course, led this assault on old lines of theory, but it has not been alone. Analytic aestheticians like Guy Sircello have not hesitated to join in this response, urging that what we gain from experiencing ugliness is surprisingly similar to what we gain from experiencing beauty; it is an intensification of our awareness of the qualities in our world most deserving of attention.

Each of these approaches throws light on facets of the contribution that appreciative awareness of ugliness makes to aesthetic intelligence. No doubt any fully satisfactory rejoinder to the paradox of ugliness will need to take stock of all of them. That there is considerable value to be gained from contemplation of the ugly things in life is beyond dispute; the debate has shifted to consider what part of this contemplation should involve rejection of ugliness in defense of beauty and other positive aesthetic values and what part can be given over to enjoying its dark, exotic pleasures.

[*See also* Beauty; Ontology of Art; *and* Value.]

BIBLIOGRAPHY

Alexander, Samuel. *Beauty and Other Forms of Value*. Reprint, New York, 1968.
Beardsley, Monroe C. *Aesthetics from Classical Greece to the Present*. New York, 1966.
Bosanquet, Bernard. *Three Lectures on Aesthetic*. London, 1915.
Cousins, Mark. "The Ugly." *AA Files* 28 (1996): 61–64; 29 (1996): 3–6.
Garvin, Lucius. "The Problem of Ugliness in Art." *Philosophical Review* 17 (1948): 404–409.
Kovach, Francis J. *Philosophy of Beauty*. Norman, Okla., 1974.
Pepper, Stephen C. *The Basis of Criticism in the Arts*. Cambridge, Mass., 1945.
Stace, W. T. *The Meaning of Beauty*. London, 1929.
Stolnitz, Jerome. "On Ugliness in Art." *Philosophy and Phenomenological Research* 11 (September 1950): 1–24.
Stolnitz, Jerome. "Ugliness." In *Encyclopedia of Philosophy*, edited by Paul Edwards, vol. 8, pp. 174–177. New York, 1967.

RONALD MOORE

UNIVERSALS. What impresses any observer of art, and our human interactions with art, is how much these differ from place to place, even from person to person, and how much they change over time. Nonetheless there have been persistent attempts by theorists of the arts to identify, beneath all the diversity and change, certain universals. One can usefully distinguish four different dimensions of art and interactions with art in which theorists have claimed to spy universality—of one sort or another.

Begin with evaluations. It is here especially that the observer is struck by diversity and variation: what one person judges admirable, another judges despicable or boring. Relativism seems unavoidable. Now no one denies that judgments of quality in works of art are in fact extremely diverse and variable. But there is a powerful body of thought about art that invites the observer to look deeper.

From within this whole mass of evaluations, one must, first, single out those that are aesthetic evaluations. It has proved extremely difficult to state, with rigor and precision, which evaluations those are. The general idea that guides the attempt to do so is clear enough, however. Aesthetic evaluations are those based on what one finds good in the object itself when contemplating it—as opposed to those based on what one finds good in how the object fits into the fabric of human purposes and desires. Aesthetic evaluations are those made when one contemplates the object disinterestedly.

A question that inevitably comes to mind is this: When contemplating objects disinterestedly, which features of those objects are in fact found good? Which features of objects make such contemplation of them rewarding? Which features give satisfaction in such contemplation? Which features ground, account for, aesthetic delight? To this question it would, of course, be possible to answer, "It varies"— and let it go at that. But few of those who have struggled to isolate the aesthetic dimension have in fact been content with that answer. The strategy for answering the question that Monroe Beardsley adopts in his now-classic book *Aesthetics* is paradigmatic. Beardsley concedes that human beings find aesthetic delight in a wide variety of different features of objects. But he does not regard these features as an unstructured smattering. To the contrary: he argues that everything humans find aesthetically good in objects is a specific case of either unity, complexity (richness), or expressiveness. Beneath all the variety, there are these universals.

A modern aestheticist like Beardsley is continuing the line of thought found in the medieval reflections on beauty. The medievals thought of beauty as that which pleases upon contemplation. They did not explicitly add the qualifier *disinterested*. But that they implicitly assumed this qualifier is clear from the answers they offered to the question, What is it in objects that accounts for pleasure upon contemplation? In their terminology that question is the same as, What is it about objects that makes them beautiful? Among the answers standardly offered were *unity, due proportion, clarity, brightness,* and *perfection.* The relevant point is that these were understood as features of objects that always and everywhere make for beauty.

Immanuel Kant, in his *Critique of Judgment,* pressed the quest for universality, in grounds for evaluation, one decisive step further. Suppose that what gives one person delight in contemplating some object is its melancholy character, whereas that very same character makes another person dislike contemplating it. For Beardsley, the fact that the latter person differs from the former in this way does not imply that the former person's satisfaction is not aesthetic. Our tastes for particular species of expressiveness may differ, as may our tastes for particular species of unity and of complexity; but if it is the unity, the complexity, or the expressiveness of an object that grounds one's satisfaction in contemplation, it is certain that the satisfaction in question is aesthetic. The medievals would happily make the parallel point for beauty. Although the due proportion of an object makes it beautiful, it may well be that human beings differ from each other in their tastes for specific versions of due proportion. Kant, however, laid down as a condition of aesthetic satisfaction not only that it be disinterested, but that it be universal, in the sense that it be grounded in shared human nature rather than in any particularity of makeup or training. If the melancholy character of the work gives a person no delight in the contemplation thereof, that establishes that the delight experienced in its melancholy character is not aesthetic. Indeed, if it is so much as possible that someone have no taste for melancholy expressiveness, that is sufficient to establish that such expressiveness is irrelevant to judgments of beauty. It is not possible in this discussion to explain which features of objects Kant regarded as grounding judgments of beauty, given his double requirement of disinterestedness and universality.

From evaluation consider what might be called artistic impulse. Nobody would deny that what motivates the composition and creation of works of art is multiple and diverse. But on this point, too, a rather large number of theorists have contended that if one digs through the variety and diversity one comes to a universal—to the universal artistic impulse. Although in every specific case other impulses may be operative as well, one always finds this universal. For example, Johan Huizinga, in his well-known *Homo Ludens,* suggests that it is the play-impulse that generates art.

Most of these attempts to discover some universal artistic impulse come and go with considerable rapidity. Various attempts to define "art," or "work of art," presuppose some such universal, however; and some of these definitions have proved of more abiding interest. Two examples will suffice to make the point. In *What Is Art?* Leo Tolstoy argues that art comes about when someone evokes in others an emotion that he or she has had by composing or creating an artifact expressive of that emotion. Such an artifact, and only such an artifact, is a work of art, said Tolstoy. From this it can be inferred that Tolstoy was of the view that the impulse to communicate or transmit emotions in the way indicated is the universal artistic impulse. R. G. Collingwood's view, expounded in his *Principles of Art,* is similar to Tolstoy's in its emphasis on emotions, but is nonetheless significantly different. Human beings often try to form constructs of the imagination with expressive qualities that match (fit, correspond with) some emotion that is felt. Such a construct of the imagination, says Collingwood, is a work of art. The artist may try to "objectify" this construct of the imagination in some medium, with the intent of producing in other persons knowledge of the emotion of which that construct was expressive—perhaps even with the intent of evoking that emotion in others. But this is not essential to art, and whatever impulse there may be to produce such objectifications, that is not the artistic impulse. The universal artistic impulse is just that impulse to "express" one's emotions by forming imaginative constructs that are expressive of one's emotions.

This reference to expressiveness leads naturally into a third dimension of art and commerce therewith in which theorists have claimed to spy universality beneath diversity and variability. It was suggested above that human beings differ from each other with respect to the kinds of artistic expressiveness that they like and dislike: some like works of melancholy character, others do not. In that way they differ in their tastes. It is equally obvious that they disagree in their identification of the expressiveness of objects: where one person spies melancholy, nothing of the sort. More generally, people differ in how they respond to works of art. People differ in construals of what the works represent or symbolize, in interpretations of what is said, in emotional reactions—and, as mentioned, in apprehensions of their expressiveness. Yet here, too, in this vast realm of actuality of response, theorists have claimed to spy universals.

Among the most interesting and provocative of such claims are those that emerge from the experiments of the psychologist Charles E. Osgood and associates, in which universals in the apprehension of the expressiveness of objects were uncovered. Osgood freely admitted that if one took complex objects and simply asked people to state what they perceived them as expressive of, highly diverse answers would be forthcoming. Nonetheless, he uncovered two fascinating phenomena beneath the diversity. He invited people to judge the expressive character of objects by locating the object on a qualitative continuum, with the two ends of the continuum picked out by antonyms. Is the object more fast than slow or more slow than fast? Is it more joyful than sad or more sad than joyful? And so on. What Osgood discovered is that, for all subjects, if sufficient continua for evaluation are offered, and those offered are selected randomly, these continua fall into three groups, of the following sort: If I know how a subject would evaluate an object on one of the continua belonging to a certain group, I can predict, with considerable reliability, how that subject will evaluate that object on other continua belonging to that same group. If a subject, for example, evaluates the expressive character of a painting as more fast than slow, then it is likely that she will also evaluate it as more sharp than dull. Second, Osgood and his associates discovered that if the entities given for evaluation are qualities rather than highly complex objects, then there is often astonishing agreement across cultures on their expressive character. There is massive agreement across cultures, for example, that heavy is more thick than thin, and that sharp is more red than green. (The Osgood results are summarized and scrutinized in Nicholas Wolterstorff, 1980a pp. 96–110.)

The fourth dimension of art concerns the claim by a good many theorists that universals are discovered when considering the ontological status of works of art. One hears two musical performances. But fully to describe the situation, one is compelled to say something more; namely, that the two performances are of the same sonata. One scrutinizes two graphic-art impressions—two etchings. But fully to describe the situation one is compelled to say something more; namely, that they are both impressions of the same print. One reads a poem in two different books. But fully to describe the situation, one is compelled to say something more; namely, that it was the same poem read in two different books. And so forth. What then is the sonata, as distinct from performances thereof, the print, as distinct from impressions thereof, and the poem, as distinct from copies thereof? A considerable number of theorists (including the author of this article) have contended that there genuinely are these entities—sonatas, prints, poems, and that given that they are capable of multiple instantiation in performances, impressions, and copies, these entities are universals. As one would expect, this claim has been controversial. Some, while conceding that there are ontological universals in art, would contend that they are of a somewhat different nature than that suggested above. More radically, "conceptualists" have argued that in addition to such spatiotemporal particulars as performances, impressions, and copies, there are only such mental entities as images, memories, concepts, and so forth; and "nominalists" have argued that in addition to the spatiotemporal particulars, there's nothing at all. Talk about sonatas, prints, and poems is nothing but a dispensable—albeit useful—fashion of speech.

These, then, are four dimensions of art and of interactions therewith in which theorists have claimed to discover universals. Within each dimension, many more examples could be given. And in every case, the claims made have proved controversial. Indeed, some of the most fascinating and perennial debates concerning art are clustered around these claims of universality. On this occasion we have only been able to indicate the focus of these debates, not to enter them.

[*See also* Definition of Art; Essentialism; Evaluation; Ontology of Art; Qualities, Aesthetic; *and* Relativism.]

BIBLIOGRAPHY

Beardsley, Monroe. *Aesthetics: Problems in the Philosophy of Criticism.* New York, 1958.
Collingwood, R. G. *The Principles of Art.* Oxford, 1938.
Currie, George. *An Ontology of Art.* New York, 1989.
Kant, Immanuel *Critique of Judgment.* Translated by Werner S. Pluhar. Indianapolis, 1987.
Huizinga, Johan. *Homo Ludens: A Study of the Play-Element in Culture.* Translated by R. F. C. Hull. London, 1949.
Goodman, Nelson. *The Languages of Art: An Approach to a Theory of Symbols* (1968). 2d ed. Indianapolis, 1976.
Kivy, Peter. *The Corded Shell: Reflections on Musical Expression.* Princeton, N.J., 1980.
Tatarkiewicz, Wladyslaw. *A History of Six Ideas.* Translated by Christopher Kaspareh. The Hague, 1980.
Tolstoy, Leo. *What Is Art?* Translated by Almyer Maude. New York, 1930.
Wolterstorff, Nicholas. *Art in Action: Toward a Christian Aesthetic.* Grand Rapids, Mich. 1980a.
Wolterstorff, Nicholas. *Works and Worlds of Art.* Oxford, 1980b.

NICHOLAS WOLTERSTORFF

UT PICTURA POESIS. The phrase *ut pictura poesis* first appears in the *Ars poetica* of Horace. Translated literally it means "as a painting, so a poem," and it occurs in a passage urging greater flexibility in critical judgments of poetry when Horace implies that a poem, like a painting, can please both in its detail and in its overall conception. The passage, in Latin, reads:

> Ut pictura poesis: erit quae, si propius stes,
> te capiat magis, et quaedam, si longius abstes.
> haec amat obscurum, volet haec sub luce videri,
> iudicis argutum quae non formidat acumen;
> haec placuit semel, haec deciens repetita placebit.

Ben Jonson's translation is as follows:

> As Painting, so is Poësie: some man's hand
> Will take you more, the nearer that you stand;
> As some the farther off: this loves the dark.
> This, fearing not the subtlest Judge's mark
> Will in the light be viewed: this, once, the sight
> Doth please, this ten times over will delight.

Thus, in a casual, incidental way appears the simile that becomes one of the great commonplaces in the history of aesthetics, initiating the tradition of comparisons between the sister arts of painting and poetry. Its basic assumption, that painting and poetry shared a common objective—namely, the vivid representation of nature—was not argued but simply implied. Nonetheless, it provided the departure point for countless discussions of the similarity and differences between these two liberal arts, discussions that reached their greatest application and refinement between the fifteenth and eighteenth centuries. After the eighteenth century, as theories of poetic inspiration shifted to a Romantic doctrine of original genius, references to *ut pictura poesis* diminish, although it can be argued that many of its preoccupations are reformulated to reappear in other guises in modern aesthetic thought.

In antiquity, the phrase did not possess the full theoretical meaning it was later to accrue. It appears, for example, in Plutarch's *De gloria Atheniensium* in another phrasing that would reappear in more extended discussions. When quoting Simonides of Ceos, Plutarch refers to painting as "mute poetry" and to poetry as a "speaking picture," a version of the comparison that would shift the balance from visual to verbal art in later formulations. Plutarch also invokes the analogy between painting and poetry when, in his *Moralia* (17f–18a), he suggests that a young man studying poetry be given "a general description of the poetic art as an imitative art and faculty analogous to painting."

The assumption that poetry and painting are mimetic arts, unstated by Horace and unargued by Plutarch, is more directly addressed by Plato in book 10 of *The Republic*. As is well known, Plato found the efforts of both poets and painters to imitate ideal beauty to be defective. His conception of Beauty as an ideal form, both ontologically real and having a metaphysical status prior to the existence of material nature, inevitably relegated both verbal and visual art to a secondary role relative to the work of the philosopher, but his emphasis on the mimetic nature of the sister arts would become a fundamental aspect of subsequent discussions of *ut pictura poesis*. Moreover, in his discussion he gave to this developing aesthetic theory one of its most persistent metaphors relative to the concept of *ut pictura poesis*, the idea of the painting or poem functioning as a mirror held up to nature.

Aristotle, in his *Poetics* (2, 1), also emphasized the mimetic function of painting and poetry as the essential meeting place of these two sister arts, but he redirected that mirroring function toward the material world. In doing so, he added yet another element to the accrual of associations around the phrase *ut pictura poesis*, the notion that the proper object of imitation for both painters and poets was human nature in action. Moreover, Aristotle also stressed that, as mimetic arts, poetry and painting are nonetheless distinguished from each other: painting by imitating through color and form and poetry by imitating through language, rhythm, and harmony. Thus, he opened the discussion of the likeness between the sister arts to a consideration not only of their distinguishing features but also of their respective strengths and weaknesses. Painting, limited to form and color, could portray many but not all things. Poetry, conversely, would excel in depicting those topics whose sequential nature made them best presented through language. Aristotle thus introduced an important refinement to the aesthetic theories originating in *ut pictura poesis*: he made clear that when the arts were classified by the means of imitation, they would differ from each other; when classified by the objects of imitation, they would be more closely associated.

Finally, Aristotle introduced one more variable to the discussions premised on the assumptions of *ut pictura poesis*. In section 5 of the *Poetics*, he noted that the tragic dramatist should follow the example of the painter who produces a portrait that, without losing the likeness, yet idealizes the sitter. Thus, to his assertion that the proper object of imitation is human nature, Aristotle added the notion that the poet should seek not simply to imitate but to improve nature, and in this endeavor his best role model was the painter. [*See* Aristotle.]

One other figure from antiquity should also be mentioned in the history of the evolution of *ut pictura poesis*. Chrysostom (Dion of Prusa), in his *XII Olympic Speech*, anticipates some of the differences between painting and poetry that Gotthold Ephraim Lessing would detail at greater length in the eighteenth century, when he observes that a poem develops in time whereas a painting remains the same. Additionally, he asserts, a poem can "evoke images of anything that comes to mind," including things that cannot be visually depicted, like abstract thought. A painting, according to him, can only represent the human image. Finally, other classical writers (e.g., Cicero, in his *Tusculans*, 5) also made reference to analogies between painting and poetry, but these too, like the other mentions from antiquity, were only in passing and remained undeveloped.

In the Middle Ages, the formula *ut pictura poesis* was known and commented on, usually in periods of classical renaissance like the Carolingian and Ottonian revivals. Many *arts poétiques*, influenced by Horace, were produced (and have been collected and summarized by Edmond Faral). At the same time, most medieval discussions of the association of poetry with painting also emphasized the greater difficulty in understanding and processing poetry but identified this difficulty as both source and sign of the greater value of the written text. They concurred with Augustine (*In Ioannis Evangelium*, 24.2) that writing was capable of addressing spiritual matters and in stimulating spiritual responses in ways that painting could not. Thus, the Middle Ages gave to the *ut pictura poesis* discussion the argument that writing had the greater moral and religious value. It offered more lasting satisfaction than paintings could produce.

Whereas the classical world saw painting as the model for poetry insofar as its use of color and form made it superior in representing material nature, the early Christian world not only privileged the superior spiritual efficacy of words but, in its more iconoclastic moments actively distrusted painting. Isidore of Seville is typical in his definition of painting:

Pictura is a representation expressing the appearance of anything, which when it is beheld makes the mind remember. *Pic-*

tura is, moreover, pronounced almost *fictura*. For it is a feigned representation, not the truth. Hence it is also counterfeited, that is, it is smeared over with a fabricated color and possesses nothing of credibility or truth.   (*Etymologarium,* 19)

While the medieval world, deeply divided in its attitudes toward its classical past, thus added little to the aesthetic theories that were being shaped by the evolution of the phrase *ut pictura poesis,* Renaissance theorists welcomed, revived, and extended it. In fact, the period from the fifteenth century in Italy to the eighteenth century throughout Europe made the greatest identification of painting and poetry, sometimes collapsing altogether any distinction between them.

Fifteenth- and sixteenth-century Italian theorists, responding to both Horace and Aristotle, extended the growing complex of ideas surrounding *ut pictura poesis* in two directions. On the one hand, following Aristotle, they gave greatest attention to that aspect of "nature" that emphasized the nobility of human nature in action. On the other, they developed two, partially antithetical, extensions of the mimetic function of art, one toward greater naturalism, or the trompe l'oeil effect, the other toward greater idealism through a doctrine of imitation that argued for the imitation of human beings not as they are but, in Aristotle's phrasing, "as they ought to be." Over time the arguments shifted from an emphasis on the exact imitation of nature to an emphasis on an ideal imitation of nature, but the two could coexist, and the same theoretician who argued for art as imitating the ideal within the natural might also be found describing the painter's ability to be the "ape of nature" as his most important accomplishment.

Leon Battista Alberti, in his *De pictura* (c.1435), represents the first category of theorist, those who stressed that reality should be imitated closely and exactly. In his technical discussions of perspective and composition, he relies heavily on the sister-arts comparison, arguing that the painter should be like the poet in compiling the different levels of a painting. Just as the poet first joins letters into syllables, then syllables into words, and words into sentences, so the painter must compose a painting by first outlining surfaces, then joining surfaces, and finally combining these surfaces into forms. When Alberti moves his discussion from technical matters to choices of subject, he again touches on the poet/painter comparison, but here he moves more in the direction of suggesting that what poet and painter imitate is not simply human experience but an enhanced version of that experience. The "historia" that is the painter's subject will move the spectator more if it is inspiring, and, in a later section, Alberti recommends that the painter turn for inspiration to the poet. In reminding his readers that Phidias was said to have learned how best to depict Jupiter by reading Homer and that it is Lucian's verbal description of Apelles' lost painting of Calumnia that

"excites our imagination when we read it," Alberti inverts *ut pictura poesis* to serve the painter's needs. [*See* Alberti.]

As one scholar, Jean H. Hagstrum, has observed, "The chief, if not sole, reason for the importance of *ut pictura poesis* in Renaissance criticism was that it somehow served the purposes of artistic naturalism" (Hagstrum, 1958). The shift from the exact to the ideal imitation of nature suggests that the complex of theoretical approaches subsumed under *ut pictura poesis* also served a concept of both arts that saw them as mirroring not only human experience but also the hidden order of the universe. Boccaccio, for example, although he uses the reference "ape of nature," which is more frequently associated with exact imitation, seems to be gesturing toward something hidden in nature as equally the poet's objective:

The epithet [ape of nature] might be less irritating [than ape of philosopher] since the poet tries with all his powers to set forth in noble verse the effects, either of Nature herself, or of her eternal and unalterable operation . . . the forms, habits, discourse, and actions of all animate things, the course of heaven and the stars, the shattering force of the winds, the roar and crackling of flames, the thunder of the waves, high mountains and shady groves, and rivers in their course . . . so vividly set forth that the very objects will seem actually present.

(*Geneaologiae Deorum* 14.7)

Here the "forms, habits, discourse, and actions of all animate things" imply that the poet's objective is moving beyond literal representation.

Thus, although the concept of literal representation was, in Rensselaer W. Lee's words, "a realistic point of view and practice among those artists who were striving strenuously to capture the perfect illusion of visible nature," it can be seen that even for those who, like Alberti, were deeply engaged in the technical aspects of producing realistic effects, the sister arts' mirror could be held up to an idealized nature.

This latter point is most important for the author of the major humanist treatise on painting in the late Italian Renaissance, Lodovico Dolce (*Dialogo della pittura,* 1558). Dolce invokes the usual comparison of painters and poets, saying not only that "writers are painters" but also that "poetry is painting, history is painting, any composition by a learned man is painting," and he retells the familiar stories about Zeuxis and Parrhasius in which painted objects deceive the viewer. In his more precise discussion of imitation, however, Dolce demonstrates how that fundamental empiricism becomes qualified by the idealism that marked many Renaissance departures from strict mimeticism. Discussing the perennial question of whether the painter should imitate nature directly or rather be guided by imitating his classical predecessors (who had the advantage of living closer to nature in the golden age), Dolce makes it clear that imitation is not an end in itself but a means to an end, the representation not of empirical nature but of the ideal hidden within or behind it.

Exactly how the ideal was associated with the empirical remained an open question, not just for Dolce but for others as well. Theorists varied in their emphases (occasionally within the same discussion), sliding between Aristotle's theory of the selective imitation of nature and the Neoplatonic emphasis on ideal beauty, the image of which might be reflected in the artist's mind but whose source was in God rather than in nature.

Dolce is also important in respect to *ut pictura poesis,* moreover, for his discussion of the response of the spectator to painting. According to him—relying on the Renaissance understanding of faculty psychology whereby the imagination was seen as that capacity of the soul that created and refined images out of materials collected by the senses—a profoundly religious painting could stimulate and even improve the viewer's soul. Thus the painter, at least in a few instances, could generate as empathetic a response as could the poet, historian, or orator. Images, Dolce concluded, were thus not only books for the ignorant, they could also arouse devotion in those who had understanding by directing them toward the contemplation of what was being represented. Dolce thus offered a corrective to the medieval emphasis on the word as the more spiritually efficacious medium.

A more ardent and passionate champion of this point of view—although unfortunately without influence, since his observations remained hidden in his notebooks—was Leonardo da Vinci. Leonardo argued aggressively for the superiority of painting to poetry, contending that painting appealed to the eye, the highest of the senses, that painting engaged directly with nature, the creation of God, and that painting in its immediacy could effectively represent the harmonious nature of beauty, whereas poetry's successive depiction of it could only result in the tedium of boring description. In language, he asserted, the parts of beauty are divided in time and thus forgetfulness intervenes and the effects, which painting could present simultaneously, are separated from each other in language and lose their focus. Parodying Simonides, he observed sarcastically that "if you call painting mute poetry, poetry can itself be called blind painting" (1956, p. 18).

Leonardo's position was extreme, however, and most Renaissance critics engaging with *ut pictura poesis* held the dominant view of poetry that stressed its image-making capacity and superior ethical and spiritual value. English theorists were no exception here. As Sir Philip Sidney, the best known among them, observed in his *Defense of Poesy,*

> Only the poet, disdaining to be tied to any . . . subjection, lifted up with the vigor of his own invention, doth grow in effect another nature, in making things better than nature bringeth forth, or, quite anew, forms such as never were in nature . . . so as he

goeth hand in hand with nature, not enclosed with in the narrow warrant of her gifts, but freely ranging only within the zodiac of his own wit. Nature never set forth the earth in so rich tapestry as divers poets have done . . . Her world is brazen, the poets only deliver a golden.

Sidney's words thus sum up the dominant view of *ut pictura poesis* in the Renaissance: while the splendors of painting—especially naturalistic painting profiting from the technical developments achieved through the use of perspective and oil-based paints—were impressive, poetry was still privileged for its greater epistemological and spiritual efficacy. Nevertheless, Sidney's use of the vocabulary of painting to describe the effects of poetic inspiration and accomplishment demonstrates just how closely each of the sister arts had affected the other. [*See* Sidney.]

Although theorists of the Enlightenment still used the vocabulary and assumptions associated with *ut pictura poesis,* there are several indications that that influence was fading and had run its course. Late seventeenth- and eighteenth-century theorists, for example, accepted as axiomatic the sister-arts analogy so fundamental to *ut pictura poesis,* and, at least initially, they seem to differ little from their Renaissance predecessors. Charles Dufresnoy's Latin poem, *De arte graphica* (c. 1644–1653), translated into French by Roger de Piles (1668) and into English by John Dryden (1695), summarized the doctrine of *ut pictura poesis* and reinvested it with some of the vigor of its initial formulations. Nevertheless, opposition to the unity of the sister arts had begun to surface. That opposition was most clearly and fully expressed by Lessing in *Laocoön; or, The Limits of Painting and Poetry* (1776).

Lessing's argument was similar to Leonardo's, although presented in more unified and accessible fashion. Essentially, he argued that painting should concern itself with bodies in space and that the proper domain of poetry lay in action through time. Additionally, the signs that comprised language were largely arbitrary, their significance established by convention, while the signs composing a painting were natural. The highest genre, however, was that which came closest to converting arbitrary signs into natural, and that was drama. [*See* Lessing.]

Moreover, the image-making capacity of poetry also began to be questioned. Edmund Burke in *A Philosophical Enquiry into the Origin of Our Ideas on the Sublime* (1757) pointed out that words do not necessarily generate images and indeed that the visual imagery produced by poetic images can sometimes be absurd, even chaotic. Poetry, he concluded, affects by "sympathy" rather than by imitation. It is not truly an imitative art. [*See* Burke.]

The similarities that had linked the sister arts were thus increasingly downplayed or denied while their differences were accentuated. Most critically, the element that had originally united them, the assumption that they were each mimetic arts with the common goal of representing the natural world, came increasingly into question. Poetry came to be seen as less and less like a picture, and the phrase *ut pictura poesis* disappeared almost entirely from aesthetic discussions. In the Romantic era, interest in the topic was limited. In fact, poetry was more frequently compared to music than to painting, and when its image-making potential was discussed, it was in the context of a new phrase, the picturesque. By the end of the nineteenth century, although there was much discussion on the nature of poetic imagery and although in the twentieth considerable attention has been given (in the Symbolist movement, for example) to the image-making potential of language, little of this discussion has been in the context of *ut pictura poesis*, largely because painting itself had begun to turn toward abstraction and thus away from the mimetic function on which its analogy with poetry had been predicated. Moreover, it has been generally agreed that the mental images evoked by a literary text are selectively constructed, varying enormously among individual viewers and thus not fundamentally susceptible to visual analysis.

One might argue, however, that some of the attention to the representational aspects of painting and poetry that concerned the theorists of *ut pictura poesis* has returned in part through semiotic poetics. The work of C. S. Peirce, for example, can be seen to reformulate *ut pictura poesis* as the thesis that the iconicity of a literary work is attributable to systems of signs in which there exists a resemblance between the signifier and the signified. Since, however, certain elements of iconicity must also be in the form of symbols, which semioticians term conventional signs, they thereby lack any natural resemblance to their signified objects. More fundamentally, since the dominant thrust of such systems is to turn everything to text, the sister-arts analogy no longer works in both directions, and thus *ut pictura poesis* has really been erased rather than reinstated.

Thus, while the final word on *ut pictura poesis* has doubtless not yet been written, its epitaph has been prepared. In the words of John Ashbery from his poem "And *Ut Pictura Poesis* Is Her Name," "You can't say it that way any more."

[*See also* Discourse; Ecphrasis; Imagery; Literature, *article on* Literary Aesthetics; Poetics; Renaissance Italian Aesthetics; *and* Text.]

BIBLIOGRAPHY

Dundas, Judith. *Pencils Rhetorique: Renaissance Poets and the Art of Painting.* Newark, Del., 1993.

Faral, Edmond. *Les arts poétiques du XIIe et du XIIIe siècle.* Paris, 1924.

Farmer, Norman K., Jr. *Poets and the Visual Arts in Renaissance England.* Austin, Tex., 1984.

Gent, Lucy. *Picture and Poetry, 1560–1620.* Leamington Spa, England, 1981.

Hagstrum, Jean H. *The Sister Arts: The Tradition of Literary Pictorialism and English Poetry from Dryden to Gray.* Chicago, 1958.

Land, Norman E. *The Viewer as Poet: The Renaissance Response to Art.* University Park, Pa., 1994.

Lee, Rensselaer W. *Ut Pictura Poesis: The Humanistic Theory of Painting.* New York, 1967.

Leonardo da Vinci. *Treatise on Painting.* Translated by A. Philip McMahon. Princeton, N.J., 1956.

Markiewicz, Henryk. "Ut Pictura Poesis: A History of the Topos and the Problem." *New Literary History* 18 (1987): 535–559.

Mitchell, W. J. T. "*Ut Pictura Theoria:* Abstract Painting and Language." In *Picture Theory: Essays on Verbal and Visual Representation,* pp. 213–239. Chicago, 1994.

Park, Roy. "*Ut Pictura Poesis:* The Nineteenth Century Aftermath." *Journal of Aesthetics and Art Criticism* 28 (Winter 1969): 155–169.

Steiner, Wendy. *The Colors of Rhetoric: Problems in the Relation between Modern Literature and Painting.* Chicago, 1982.

"Ut Pictura Poesis: A Selective, Annotated Bibliography of Books and Articles, Published between 1900 and 1980, on the Interrelations of Literature and Painting from 1400 to 1800." *Yearbook of Comparative and General Literature* 32 (1983): 65–124.

Word and Image: A Journal of Verbal and Visual Inquiry 4.1 (1988).

ANN HURLEY

V

VALUE. Value is one of the weightiest, most indispensable, and perhaps most mystified concepts in aesthetics and, beyond that, in formal thought. Like a number of other terms, such as *meaning* and *reality*, that have strong currency in informal speech and long histories as the focus of theoretical analysis, the term seems to name an aspect of the world so fundamental to our thinking—so elementary and at the same time so general—as to be both irreducible and irreplaceable. Like any other term, however, *value* has a history of variable and complex usage.

From the time of its earliest recorded occurrences through to the present, the English word *value* (like *worth* and the corresponding French and German terms *valeur* and *Wert*) has maintained two parallel—related but distinct—senses. In the first sense, value is understood as the equivalence-in-exchange of a thing: its price in some cash market, its equivalent when compared to or traded for something else in some more general domain of reciprocal transactions. In the second broad sense, the value of a thing is a more abstract matter of its utility in relation to some purpose, its measure with respect to some dimension, or its position on some scale (e.g., courage in battle, temporal duration of a musical tone, or abstract numerosity of a variable in a mathematical equation). Value in this second sense, then, is something like relative plusness or amount or degree of positivity. Because both senses of the term involve two key ideas (namely, comparison and positivity) that relate to an extensive range of human practices, it is not surprising that the concept of value appears so important and, so to speak, invaluable.

As this last somewhat paradoxical possibility reminds us, however, the more or less pragmatic, quotidian senses of the term may be negated or reversed in the specification of one or another highly privileged (i.e., valued) type of value. Thus, it may be asserted that the essential, spiritual, moral, sentimental, symbolic, or aesthetic value of a thing has nothing to do with comparison, measure, utility, money, materiality, or exchange, but is, on the contrary, unique, noninstrumental, ineffable, immeasurable, and unexchangeable. It appears that when the experienced positive operations or effects of a thing are especially intense, extensive, or significant but also especially heterogeneous and subtle, those operations and effects are likely to be indicated and theorized by way of contradistinction from other rela-

tively more specific, palpable, or readily describable values. There also seems to be a strong general tendency to project the experienced effects of any complex set of conditions back into the most salient (i.e., visible, concrete, palpable) of those conditions—with the resulting idea of value as an autonomous and inherently objective property of objects themselves that is independent of the actual, possible, posited, or even imagined experience of those objects by particular situated subjects.

Although the general idea of essential or intrinsic value is more closely associated with the humanistic disciplines and ethics or aesthetics than with social theory, various social theorists—including anthropologists, sociologists, and economists—have entertained or been affected by the idea of an essentially inherent and fixed value that is distinct both from fluctuating market price and from subject-variable experienced or attributed value (Appadurai, 1986). The conception of value as embodied labor could be explored in this connection (Steedman et al., 1981), as could Karl Marx's somewhat ambiguous allusions to use-value as a historically, subjectively, and otherwise variable attribute of objects and as a product or shadowy twin of their physical, material, and presumably objective properties.

Complicating current conceptualizations of value are the classically perplexed relations between objects and subjects in the realm of human experience. It seems clear that experiences and judgments of the value of particular objects—in the sense of subjective registerings and overt verbal assessments of their adequacy in satisfying certain needs, serving certain purposes, or eliciting certain desired or desirable effects—are, like all other experiences and judgments, more or less subject variable and shaped by numerous other more or less variable conditions (contextual, cultural, historical). It could be said, then, that (the experience or judgment of) the value of any object is irreducibly contingent, meaning not arbitrary but, rather, dependent on conditions that are always to some extent variable and unpredictable. It may still be asked, of course, whether the value of an object (or at least some aspect of its value) could not be (or is not properly conceived of as) independent of the experiences and judgments of particular subjects, and thus as essentially intrinsic and objective. Given these classic perplexities, however, there seems no way to approach that question without also engaging a number of other chronic and currently significant philosophical issues—or, of course, presupposing particular but currently contested positions on them (essentialist or nominalist, realist or constructivist, phenomenological or naturalistic, and so forth).

An important consequence of the history of usage and conceptualization of value is the emergence, in the West, of a double discourse of value, that is, the stabilization of two strenuously antithetical discursive domains, both centered on articulations of value but defined largely through mutual contradistinction. In the first (profane, naturalistic) discourse, value is understood as instrumental, economic, material, often monetary, and essentially mutable and contingent: this is the domain of trade and industry, accumulation and profit, production and consumption, and individual self-interest. Value in the second (sacred, humanistic) domain is understood as nonutilitarian, noneconomic, immaterial, inherent, and essentially transcendent: this is the domain of ethics and religion, gifts and sacrifice, creation and appreciation, and, traditionally, art—at least high art. Differences among types and degrees of value are, of course, both individually and communally significant, but these polarized oppositions are evidently discursively constituted and only institutionally stabilized; that is, they are not otherwise given in the nature of things. Accordingly, the boundaries of the double domain of value require careful patrol and continuous (re)establishment, tasks characteristically undertaken by religious institutions and also, in relation especially to cultural productions, by the humanistic disciplines. Thus, the familiar implicit admonitions to discriminate between intrinsic value and mere utility, aesthetic value and mere hedonic enjoyment, artistic value and mere technical display, literary value and mere sociological interest, and so on. For the reasons already suggested, the differences thus set in polarized, hierarchized opposition can usually be recast as matters of relative or gradient difference in relation to some configuration of dimensions: for example, range of uses and effects, degree of subtlety, intensity, or heterogeneity, or extent of individual or contextual variability. It could also be argued, however, that there are important communal, long-range values served by the strenuous maintenance of at least some such absolute distinctions and hierarchies: notably, the protection of certain goods (in all senses) from commodification, debasement, and the risk of ultimate destruction.

Aesthetic value, often equated with the concept of beauty and associated with a particular type of pleasurable and otherwise (e.g., morally or politically) valuable sensory/perceptual experience, is widely understood as a distinctively noninstrumental positivity elicited by certain purely or at least primarily formal properties of certain natural or artifactual phenomena. So understood, it is also seen as especially characteristic or defining of (genuine) works of (fine) art, and as the product, expression, or manifestation of exceptional creative gifts on the part of artists and performers.

The proper or full experience of aesthetic value, so understood, is sometimes seen as limited to persons with special training or appropriate innate sensibilities but is also—and sometimes simultaneously—posited as ideally or potentially universal.

These interrelated characterizations and understandings of aesthetic value have operated quite well over the past two centuries for purposes of critical discourse (description, classification, explanation, interpretation, assessment, and so forth), at least among those (artists, audiences, patrons, critics, curators, academic scholars, and so forth) educated in the classical high culture of Europe. Certain conceptual incoherences and otherwise problematic features of that set of ideas have become more evident, however, as relevant research and analysis in empirical fields such as anthropology, cultural history, psychology, and sociology have been disseminated more broadly (see, e.g., Becker, 1982; Bourdieu, 1984; Braudel, 1982; and Douglas, 1979) and also as more conceptually exacting formulations have been attempted in formal aesthetics and elsewhere in philosophy (Danto, 1981; Derrida, 1981, 1987; Goodman, 1976, and Mothersill, 1984). At the same time and to some extent relatedly, the cultural provincialism and sometimes narrowly self-privileging normative assumptions of much traditional critical theory have become more notable as alternative formulations—many of them with significant political and institutional implications—have been developed and promoted by the members of a now more culturally diverse and heterogeneous academic, artistic, and critical community. Accordingly, contemporary discussions of aesthetic value are likely to stress the subjectively individuated, historically and culturally variable, and contextually specific nature of the experience and effects of artworks (Stewart, 1991); the historically and institutionally variable constitution of categories such as works of (fine) art, works of literature, and aesthetic experiences (Williams, 1977); and the social and political operations of aesthetic theory itself (Bennett, 1979; Eagleton, 1990; and Connor, 1992). More or less sophisticated efforts to redeem the idea of an essential aesthetic value and, with it, of a potentially or ideally universal aesthetic experience, do, however, continue to be pursued (Eagleton, 1990; and Guillory, 1993).

Most current conceptions of aesthetic value derive more or less directly from Immanuel Kant's *Critique of Judgment*, in which such value, under the term *beauty*, is associated with certain configurations of pure form. Although the details of Kant's elaborations of this idea have been a rich resource for phenomenological aesthetics and critical theory more generally, some of his relevant assumptions concerning the operations of human perception and cognition now appear dubious—and with them the related idea of an objectively (or universally subjectively) valid aesthetic judgment. Most significantly, it appears that our perceptual experiences of even such ostensibly pure stimuli as single musical tones, basic geometric figures, and simple visual or auditory patterns will be shaped by our experiential history of similar and related forms and by the particular contextual conditions in which we encounter them—which is to say, the experience and judgment of beauty will inevitably be both impure (in Kant's terms) and, contrary to the idea of universal subjective validity, more or less personally individuated.

The term *aesthetic value* operates in many informal critical discourses with more or less specific and stable senses (though not the same ones in all those discourses), and the idea of aesthetic value as a distinctive, determinate attribute has been important and perhaps indispensable in the development of Romantic and modernist critical theory. One reason for the increasing questioning of such theory, however, is that, in spite of the many painstaking attempts to do so, there does not appear to be any way to define clearly, consistently, substantively, and without circularity a particular type of value that is characteristic of just those phenomena or features of phenomena that are generally spoken of as aesthetically valuable or just the set of objects generally referred to as art at any particular time. Rather, it appears that the phenomena indicated as aesthetically valuable are irreducibly heterogeneous and that those highly specific, intensely focused, uniquely exciting or pleasing, richly evocative, analysis-defying, category-dissolving effects that we (sometimes) experience in our engagements with (what some of us now call) artworks are more or less continuous with our experiences of numerous other putatively nonartistic, nonaesthetic artifacts, activities, and states, including mass-produced commodities, popular entertainment, sex, sports, work, dreaming, drunkenness, and madness.

[*See also* Evaluation; Historicism; Qualities, Aesthetic; Relativism; *and* Universals.]

BIBLIOGRAPHY

Appadurai, Arjun, ed. *The Social Life of Things: Commodities in Cultural Perspective.* Cambridge and New York, 1986.
Bataille, Georges. "The Notion of Expenditure" (1933). In *Visions of Excess: Selected Writings, 1927–1939,* edited and translated by Allan Stoekl. Minneapolis, 1985.
Becker, Howard S. *Art Worlds.* Berkeley, 1982.
Bennett, Tony. *Formalism and Marxism.* London, 1979.
Bourdieu, Pierre. *Distinction: A Social Critique of the Judgement of Taste.* Translated by Richard Nice. Cambridge, Mass., 1984.
Braudel, Fernand. *Civilization and Capitalism,* vol. 2, *The Wheels of Commerce* (1979). Translated by Sian Reynolds. New York, 1982.
Connor, Steven. *Theory and Cultural Value.* Oxford and Cambridge, Mass., 1992.
Danto, Arthur C. *The Transfiguration of the Commonplace: A Philosophy of Art.* Cambridge, Mass., 1981.
Derrida, Jacques. "Economimesis" (1975). Translated by Richard Klein. *Diacritics* 11 (1981) 2: 3–25.
Derrida, Jacques. "Parergon" (1978). In *The Truth in Painting,* translated by Geoff Bennington and Ian McLeod, pp. 15–148. Chicago, 1987.
Douglas, Mary, and Baron Isherwood. *The World of Goods.* New York, 1979.
Eagleton, Terry. *The Ideology of the Aesthetic.* Oxford and Cambridge, Mass., 1990.
Fekete, John, ed. *Life after Post-Modernism: Essays on Value and Culture.* New York, 1987.
Goodman, Nelson. *Languages of Art: An Approach to a Theory of Symbols.* 2d ed. Indianapolis, 1976.
Guillory, John. *Cultural Capital: The Problem of Literary Canon Formation.* Chicago, 1993.
Kant, Immanuel. *Critique of Judgment* (1790). Translated by J. H. Bernard. New York, 1951.
Mothersill, Mary. *Beauty Restored.* Oxford, 1984.
Mukarovsky, Jan. *Aesthetic Function, Norm and Value as Social Facts* (1936). Translated by Mark E. Suino. Ann Arbor, 1970.
Smith, Barbara Herrnstein. *Contingencies of Value: Alternative Perspectives for Critical Theory.* Cambridge, Mass., 1988.
Steedman, Ian, et al. *The Value Controversy.* London, 1981.
Stewart, Stewart. *Crimes of Writing: Problems in the Containment of Representation.* New York and Oxford, 1991.
Williams, Raymond. *Marxism and Literature.* Oxford, 1977.

BARBARA HERRNSTEIN SMITH

VASARI, GIORGIO

VASARI, GIORGIO (1511–1574), Italian painter, architect, and art historian. Giorgio Vasari was born in Arezzo to a family of artisans, and his education in the Medici household in Florence prepared him well to become a highly successful courtier-artist. After some initial setbacks linked to political turmoil, he enjoyed the favor of many of the leading patrons of his day; from 1555 he worked for Cosimo I, duke of Florence, whom he served as painter, architect, and designer of elaborate court spectacles. Although his painting is now generally held in low regard (his architecture, on the other hand, still commands admiration), his achievement in bringing a new degree of rationalization to the productive process, especially to the management of large, complex collaborative projects involving literary advisers, on the one hand, and teams of artist-assistants, on the other, deserves recognition. The Accadémia del Diségno, the first formally incorporated academy of art, which he helped to establish in Florence in 1563 with the aim of imposing a similar kind of rationalization on artistic education, also set an example imitated throughout early modern Europe.

Vasari's enduring fame, and his interest in this context, depend on his book, *The Lives of the Most Eminent Painters, Sculptors and Architects,* first published in 1550, then again, in a greatly expanded edition, in 1568. The *Lives* is the first sustained account of the history of the visual arts in modern times, and it is as important for the interpretive structure it imposes on that history as for the information it provides about individual artists and their works. Written for cultivated amateurs as well as artists, it helped to establish and disseminate a system of aesthetic standards and a critical vocabulary for the discussion of art, the fundamental elements of which continued to enjoy currency all over Europe until the nineteenth century. Written in a lively style, with colorful descriptions, anecdotes, and character sketches, it is also a classic of Italian literature.

The biographies that make up the *Lives* are grouped into three sections corresponding to three phases that Vasari discerned in the development of Italian art from the late-thirteenth to the mid-sixteenth century, the period we have come to call the Renaissance. Vasari understood this development as one of progress, and likened the phases to stages in the growth of an individual: the first, extending roughly to the end of the fourteenth century, is represented as the "infancy" of art; the second, which covers the fifteenth century, as its "youth." The third phase, from the last years of the fifteenth century to Vasari's own time, is the period when art reaches "maturity" and perfection. The notion of the progress of art was available from ancient sources such as Pliny; the metaphor of organic development is found among ancient historians, and three-phase patterns are commonplace, but Vasari's combination of these ingredients deserves to be recognized as an original achievement: it creates an interpretive structure that has survived even the many revisions modern scholarship has offered to the substance of his account.

The progress of art involves the gradual improvement of the ability to "imitate nature": in the case of painting, the perfection of the ability to suggest the illusion of three-dimensionality and, in figures, of living presence. The leading artist of the first period, Giotto, is able to suggest the volume of forms by virtue of accurate drawing, consistent modeling in light and shade, and attentiveness to spatial relationships; Masaccio, an innovator of the second phase, refines on his predecessors by using the technique of linear perspective to create an altogether more consistent and convincing illusion of space; by making a careful study of anatomy he is also able to improve on earlier representations of the figure. Leonardo da Vinci, the artist who inaugurates the third phase, develops a style distinctive for its extremely delicate modeling, capable of capturing the subtlest and most fleeting effects: he brings to the mastery of linear perspective a sensitivity to the way in which forms are perceived through atmosphere—so-called atmospheric perspective—and his comprehensive study of nature enables him to represent all things, not just human anatomy, with extraordinary depth of understanding.

Besides naturalism there are other aspects to the progress of art. One is storytelling: an early painter like Giotto gives plausibility to his narrative scenes by appropriate costumes and effective characterization. Two hundred years later, Raphael possesses such a comprehensive sense of decorum that his pictures seem like the perfect equivalents of the texts they illustrate; beyond that, they seem to reflect a systematic, "philosophical" understanding of human nature, so that they become occasions for the contemplation of larger and deeper truths. Another aspect of the progress of

art is the capacity of pictures to convey abstract ideas through symbolism and allegory. Giotto pioneers allegorical representation in frescoes at Assisi; Vasari and his contemporaries are able, with the help of scholar-advisers, to concoct elaborate decorative schemes deploying all the resources of theology and humanist learning.

If art becomes more naturalistic, it also becomes more beautiful: at its best, it no longer imitates but surpasses nature. On the one hand, the path toward beauty is indicated by ancient art: the progress of sculpture, for instance, has as much to do with approaching the look of ancient statuary as with fidelity to nature, and Vasari believed that the study of ancient models had enabled the artists of his own time—Michelangelo above all—to surpass nature. On the other hand, the authority of ancient sculpture rests on the belief that the ancient masters selected only the best natural forms to imitate, often combining the most beautiful features of several specimens in order to produce an ideal form, a principle illustrated in the famous story of the painter Zeuxis and the maidens of Croton. The modern artist might also proceed in this manner, without having recourse to ancient models (some theorists, like Leonardo da Vinci, argued that the artist should only rely directly on nature), and thus even the standard of ancient art might be subject to critical revision, as it were, and surpassed. Vasari believed that, like nature, antiquity too had been surpassed in his own time, and again, by Michelangelo, whose figures must therefore be understood to possess a beauty unprecedented in the world.

Another feature of the progress of art, often neglected in accounts of the *Lives,* is the integration of the three arts of painting, sculpture, and architecture. The idea that painting and sculpture are kindred arts, dependent on the practice of drawing, and thus on the principle of design (the Italian word *diségno* can mean both an individual drawing and the concept of design in the abstract), was already a commonplace in the mid-fourteenth century; the notion that design *(lineaménta)* is an essential principle of architecture is found in Vitruvius. Ambitious art theorists—Leonardo among them—had suggested that design actually serves as the basis of many other disciplines as well: writing, mathematics, geometry, optics, astronomy, and mechanics. Vasari combined these ideas, and again made use of a biological metaphor, when he claimed that the three arts are daughters of the one father, *diségno*—thereby establishing the unity of the visual arts as well as the basis of their distinctness from other arts. This unity exists a priori, in principle, but the historical development that he traces brings it to realization or fulfillment: increasingly, artists are able to work in all three art forms and to integrate them into single works. This process, too, reaches its climax in Michelangelo, who brings each of the arts to perfection individually, but in so doing also demonstrates their unity in the principle of design.

Wishing to emphasize its importance, Vasari elaborated and clarified his treatment of design in the second edition of the *Lives:* he added discussions of individual artists' drawing styles to many of the biographies, and included at the beginning of the book, in an introductory section on the materials and techniques of art, a definition of design as a principle. This definition is the most explicitly philosophical passage in the *Lives:*

> Because design, the father of our three arts of architecture, sculpture and painting, proceeding from the intellect, derives from many things a universal judgment, like a form or idea of all things in nature—which [nature] is most consistent in its measures—it happens that not only in human bodies and those of animals, but in plants as well and buildings and sculptures and paintings, it [design] understands the proportion that the whole has to the parts and the parts to one another and to the whole. And because from this there arises a certain notion and judgment which forms in the mind that which, when expressed with the hands, is called design, one may conclude that this design is nothing other than a visible expression and declaration of that notion of the mind, or of that which others have conceived in their minds or given shape to in their imaginations.

The concept of "universal judgment" comes from the beginning of Aristotle's *Metaphysics;* the phrase "like a form or idea" invokes Platonic tradition. Vasari's point is simply that design is something that requires philosophical definition, a faculty of mind that qualifies the visual arts as modes of rational operation. Although scholars have criticized the rather superficial juxtaposition of the two philosophical vocabularies, Vasari's intention is obviously to suggest that no serious incompatibility exists between them as far as the definition of design is concerned.

The idea that design is the principle of the visual arts was given an institutional form in the Accadémia del Diségno. The first edition of the *Lives* ended with the biography of Michelangelo; the second edition carries the account forward in time to include discussion of the work of many of the young academicians and the projects in which they collaborated: the emphasis is less on the culmination of the history of art in Michelangelo and more on the perfection of the rules of art and their propagation through the teaching of the academy. In this way, too, the position of design as the fundamental rule or essence of art is confirmed by historical demonstration.

Another important dimension of Vasari's concept of artistic progress is the way in which it is linked to the progress of other disciplines during the same period and to the progress of art in antiquity:

> Having carefully considered these things, I conclude that it is a property and natural quality of these arts that they improve themselves little by little from a humble beginning, finally attaining the height of perfection; and I am further convinced, seeing that virtually the same thing happened in other disciplines, which, because there is a certain kinship among all the liberal arts, is no small argument in favor of its truth. Something so

similar must have occurred in ancient times that if the names were exchanged, the account would be exactly the same.

The correspondence between the progress of art and the simultaneous progress in other areas of learning serves to support Vasari's claim for the status of the visual arts as liberal disciplines; the correspondence between the progress of art in his own time and in antiquity suggests that even the pattern of its development in time is governed by rule, a formal consistency that further testifies to its rational nature. Both correspondences, synchronic and diachronic, serve to confirm for Vasari the real perfection of the art of his own time and the universal validity of the principles on which it is based; at the same time they confirm the correctness of his account of its history.

Belief in the relation between the liberal disciplines and their revival in modern times was central to the cultural ideology of humanism, and insisting on the kinship between, say, painting and poetry was a common way of allowing the visual arts a share in the prestige of the humanist project. This idea, often denoted by the phrase *ut pictura poesis,* would be rejected by modern aesthetics—along with the assumption that art is fundamentally rational—but Vasari's suggestion that a single pattern underlies the historical development of art in all times seems to have been the starting point for modern formalist notions of an internal necessity governing the evolution of style.

Although the progress of art might be defined as the discovery and application of the rules for making good art, Vasari also acknowledges that the highest perfection sometimes involves a willful disregard of rules. In contrast to the artists of Vasari's own time, those of the second phase are deficient because they lack "a certain license, which, while not of the rule, is yet governed by the rule." Neither did these artists possess "that correctness of judgment by means of which their figures, without having been measured, might have, in proper relation to their dimensions, a grace surpassing measure." The idea that perfection can involve something beyond rational calculation could have come from any one of a number of sources: the literature of manners, for instance, extolled the studied negligence of demeanor that produces the aura of effortless grace; essays on female beauty often praised the stray curl that enhances rather than detracts from the overall effect; ancient rhetorical theory always reserved a place for the bold and effective breaking of rules. The tension between freedom and rule need not pose much of a problem if one remembers what Vasari himself says: that successful departures from rule give the impression of pointing toward another, higher rule.

A similar sort of apparent tension is found in Vasari's sensitivity to the diversity of individual styles, on the one hand, and his sense, on the other, of there being a single all comprehending standard. Some contemporaries had claimed that Raphael was a better painter than Michelangelo: although admitting Michelangelo's preeminence in sculpture and architecture, they felt that his painting, concerned almost entirely with the ideal male nude, lacked the pleasant color harmonies, facile grace, and richness of narrative interest found in Raphael. Others argued that Titian possessed similar virtues in even greater measure. Vasari acknowledged the merits of these painters; still, he took care, in the second edition of the *Lives,* to insist that Michelangelo's mastery of the principle of design gives his paintings a profundity that compensates for their lack of incidental charm. Raphael's style, marvelous as it is, owes much of its strength to the example of Michelangelo; Titian's voluptuous color masks a deficiency in design.

Appreciative as he was of different styles, then, there were limits to Vasari's tolerance; indeed, his conception of the progress of art presupposes rather narrow and rigid standards. His exclusivity is sometimes shocking to the modern reader: because good architecture is classicizing in style, for instance, what we call Gothic is simply barbaric—not an alternative style but a nonstyle. His attitude toward older art in general is condescending: although Giotto deserves credit for having made brave efforts in a benighted age, his work merits only qualified admiration. Such confidence in current standards was characteristic of the time: cultivated people could believe that the art of Giotto and his contemporaries was simply outmoded—quaint at best, clumsy and downright ugly at worst; one writer even criticized Vasari for giving Giotto more attention than he deserved. Seen against this background, Vasari's commitment to a historical understanding of the way art had come to achieve perfection stands out as markedly enlightened; one might even say that his historical perspective points beyond the limitations of his art theory. An appreciation for medieval art, a sense of its representing an alternative as valid as that of classical antiquity, on the one hand, or the High Renaissance, on the other, did not begin to emerge until the mid-eighteenth century and was not generally accepted until the mid-nineteenth: it was only with John Ruskin that Vasari's account of history, grounded in a particular set of values, was effectively supplanted.

Vasari is often faulted for his regional loyalties and prejudices. His taste is that of an artist trained in Florence and Rome, and his view of history gives overwhelming preponderance to central Italian developments. In the second edition he tried to present more information about other centers, both in Italy and northern Europe, but he still treats them as provincial, and sometimes uses the occasion to insist on the superiority of Florentine and Roman practice. His reservations about Venetian painters such as Titian, for instance, are partly explicable in terms of regional preference.

In addition to the exclusivity, there is another feature of Vasari's conception of progress that surprises and disturbs modern readers:

This art is nowadays reduced to such perfection, and is so easy for someone who possesses skill in design, in invention and in the handling of colors, that where it once took a master painter six years to make one picture, we can now make six pictures in one year; I can swear to this for I have seen it done and done it myself; and [what is more] our works are more finished and perfect than those of even the leading masters of the past.

Such a passage reveals not only Vasari's smug attitude toward earlier art, but also that, on a deeper level, his notion of progress is rooted in a narrow, pragmatic—and frankly prosaic—conception of art as technique. His delight in the new facility of productive method seems to us almost embarrassingly simpleminded: disillusioned as we are by industrialization and nourished on the assumption that any such approach is alien to art virtually by definition, we must make an effort to imagine how he could regard it as something to be proud of. He could do so because the susceptibility of the creative process to this kind of rationalization was for him yet another sign of the rationality, hence the intellectual dignity, of art.

Much of Vasari's aesthetics is derivative, and much does not stand up to close philosophical scrutiny; one often hears it said that he was not an original or rigorous thinker. In his own way, however, he was both original and rigorous: he used a historical approach to gather and integrate, to superimpose, as it were, the various sources of art's interest; in so doing, he made history a means of demonstrating its intellectual depth and richness. The humanist historiography that he adopted as a model was regarded as a mode of philosophical inquiry: its aim was not simply to describe events, but to extract from them the enduring principles of human conduct. The *Lives* works in the same way: preserving the sources of art's human interest—in biography, in the drama of gradual development over time, for instance—it also tries to show how the universally and eternally true are revealed in time, and even how that process conforms to a pattern that transcends history. One might say that Vasari's philosophical achievement was to insist that art has a history, and that its historicity is essential to its philosophical interest.

[*See also* Art History; Narrative; *and* Renaissance Italian Aesthetics.]

BIBLIOGRAPHY

Works by Vasari

Le opere di Giorgio Vasari. 8 vols. Edited by Gaetano Milanesi. Florence, 1878–1885.
Le vite de' più eccellènti pittóri, scultóri e architéttori, nélle redazióni del 1550 e 1568. Edited by Rosanna Bettarini and Paola Barocchi. Florence, 1966–.

The Lives of the Most Eminent Painters, Sculptors, and Architects. 3 vols. Translated by Gaston du C. de Vere (1910). New York, 1979.

Other Sources

Belting, Hans. "Vasari and His Legacy: The History of Art as a Process?" In *The End of the History of Art?,* translated by Christopher S. Wood, pp. 65–120. Chicago, 1987.
Cast, David. "Reading Vasari Again: History, Philosophy." *Word and Image* 9 (1993): 29–38.
Kliemann, Julian. "Giorgio Vasari." In *The Dictionary of Art,* edited by Jane Turner, vol. 32, pp. 10–25. London, 1996.
Rubin, Patricia Lee. *Giorgio Vasari: Art and History.* New Haven, 1995.
Schlosser-Magnino, Julius von. *La letteratura artistica* (1924). 3d ed. Edited by Otto Kurz, translated by F. Rossi. Florence, 1977. See pp. 289–346.

ROBERT WILLIAMS

VENTURI, ROBERT. *See* Architecture; *article on* Modernism to Postmodernism.

VICO, GIOVANNI BATTISTA (1668–1744), Italian philosopher. Giambattista Vico was born in Naples and lived the whole of his life there, except for nine years (1686–1695) spent at Vatolla in the region of the Cilento south of Naples, where he served as tutor to the Rocca family at their castle, occasionally visiting Naples. He was professor of Latin eloquence at the University of Naples from 1699 to 1741. In 1735, under the rule of Charles of Bourbon, he was appointed royal historiographer.

Vico's major work is *Principles of New Science concerning the Common Nature of Nations,* which he published in two versions, the first in 1725 and the second in 1730 (the second was printed in a new edition in the year of his death). Vico is commonly considered to be the founder of the modern philosophy of history, but his *New Science* is also important for the origins of the philosophy of mythology and the philosophy of culture. Among his other works are a series of university orations presented in the first decade of his teaching career (1699–1707); these develop a conception of human education advocating the early study of poetry, metaphor, and rhetoric. Another book, *On the Most Ancient Wisdom of the Italians* (1710) is a refutation of Cartesian metaphysics. Vico opposes to René Descartes's method of certainty through doubt the principle he derived from Latin, that "the true is the made" ("verum esse ipsum factum"). He published a three-volume work on jurisprudence in the 1720s, under the general title *Il diritto universale* (Universal Law), in which he grounds natural law in the development of culture. Important to the understanding of Vico's philosophy is his autobiography, published in 1728 and continued in 1731. It is a first example of an original thinker providing a genetic account of his own intellectual development and discoveries. Vico wrote a large number of poems reflecting his knowledge of classical forms of composition, but these are occasional or commissioned pieces and are not regarded as having intrinsic artistic merit.

Although his career falls within the eighteenth century, Vico is not a figure of the Enlightenment. He does not hold doctrines of *illuminismo* or of specific progress either in history or in the development of the arts and sciences. Some commentators regard Vico as an enemy of the Enlightenment; others present him as accepting but transforming certain themes of modern science, and others consider him to be the final, summary figure of the tradition of Italian Renaissance humanism.

For aesthetics, the most important part of Vico's philosophy is his conception of "poetic wisdom" *(la sapìenza poètica),* which is the subject of the longest book in the *New Science.* Poetic wisdom is the form of thought and social life common to all nations at their origin. Poetic wisdom is the primordial state in which humans comprehend the world in terms of myths and create a world of civil institutions through rituals, customs, and common feelings. Vico claims that the first humans were poets who thought in terms of "imaginative universals" *(universali fantastici).* Vico uses the term *poetic* for what more modern thinkers such as Ernst Cassirer or Claude Lévi-Strauss would designate as "mythic." Vico's "poetic wisdom" is closer to the ancient notion of the poet as mythmaker, closer to *poiein* ("to make" and "to compose poetry"), on which concept Plato plays in book 10 of *The Republic,* and closer to the Latin *poeta* (maker, poet) than it is to the modern conception of poetry as a specific art form distinct from other forms of thought and consciousness. Vico claims that the first science to be studied should be mythology or the interpretation of fables because it is through the power of myths and fables that humans first organized their world and developed social institutions.

Vico's conception of poetic wisdom is based on his conception of *fantasìa.* Although normally translated as "imagination," *fantasìa* is not precisely equivalent to "imagination." Vico's notion of *fantasìa* has none of the sense of "fantasy," that is, nothing of the experience of a mental image of the "unreal," an illusion or phantasm. *Imagination,* when used not as a synonym for fantasy but in its sense of a deeply creative faculty that can perceive basic resemblances between things, is close to what Vico means by *fantasìa.* In the first stages of culture, according to Vico, human beings are unable to form abstract universals *(universali intelligibili)* such as are found in Aristotelian class logic, in which a given property can be univocally predicated of a number of things that compose a class. Humans are originally capable only of forming "imaginative universals"; through their power of *fantasìa* they are able to turn a particular experience into an image that carries universal meaning. A particular image formed by *fantasìa* can be univocally "predicated" of a multiplicity of particular entities. Thus, a hero or a totem is not one individual or thing among others but contains the total reality of the group. They all share in and fully embody its identity.

Vico's conception of imaginative universals is tied to his conception of history. Vico claims that history is cyclic. The life of any nation occurs in terms of *córso* and *ricórso*. Any given *córso* or *ricórso* moves through three ages, which Vico calls "ideal eternal history" *(stòria ideale etèrna):* an age of gods, of heroes, and of humans. In the age of gods, all natural phenomena, as well as all basic social institutions (religion, marriage, burial, etc.), are formed as gods. Thunder is formed by the imaginative universal of Jove; the thunderous sky, with lightning, is literally Jove. Juno is literally the institution of marriage. In the age of heroes, virtues that guide conduct and character cannot be formed as concepts but are formed in the poetic character of the hero. Thus, Vico says, valor is formed as Achilles, wisdom as Ulysses. In the age of humans, the primordial power of *fantasìa* fades, as a dominant force guiding human thought and society, giving way to written laws and conceptual structures. *Fantasìa* remains within the third age as the power that underlies poetry and art. Within the sphere of aesthetic experience the imaginative universal holds sway, but it is no longer what guides thought and the cultural world at large.

Vico's imaginative universal—that is, the basis of fables and myths in the ages of gods and heroes—remains a way to form "ideal truths" about the human world in popular consciousness. Because of this, Vico says there "springs this important consideration in poetic theory: the true war chief, for example, is the Godfrey that Torquato Tasso imagines; and all the chiefs who do not conform throughout to Godfrey are not true chiefs of war" (1984, axiom 47). Vico suggests that there is a poetry of everyday life in which "ideal truths" or characters that embody virtues or various features of the human condition are first imagined, and these continue to be basic to our organization and interpretation of the world. The imagination continuously supplies us with the *archai* from which to know and act in the world. There is an interplay between the poet, who often formulates master images such as Tasso's Godfrey, and the common or vulgar imagination through which we approach the world on an everyday basis.

Based on his conception of the three ages of ideal eternal history, Vico has a conception of the "true Homer" and the "true Dante" that is relevant to literary history. Vico considers Homer to be the summary poet of the first two ages of the *córso* of Western history, the age of gods and the age of heroes. The "true Homer" is the Greek people themselves. Homer represents the transition from poetic wisdom to the conceptual wisdom of the philosophers, who appear in the third age, the age of humans. With the fall of the ancient world, the *ricórso* of the West is marked both by a return to religion and by the later development of the heroes of medieval society. The summary poet of the *ricórso* is Dante, whom Vico calls the "Tuscan Homer." Dante's *Divina commèdia* marks the transition from the poetic wisdom of the *ricórso* to the philosophical wisdom of the Renaissance philosophers. For Vico, any work of literature can be read within the context of its place in the order of the ideal eternal history. What a work of literature means, for Vico, must include an understanding of its relationship to human culture.

Vico says that "imagination is the same as memory" ("la memòria è la stessa che la fantasìa). Thus the poet, in the modern age of humans, performs an act of memory; the poet is always attempting to recover that primordial power of *fantasìa* in an age in which such power is nearly lost. Behind the poet is always the ancient power of the myth and the fact that all words are centers of memory. Each word carries its own "truth" in its history of meanings, its etymology. James Joyce, who consciously used Vico's *New Science* as a "trellis" on which to base *Finnegans Wake* (as he had used Homer's poem for his novel *Ulysses*), adopted Vico's equation of imagination and memory as an aesthetic maxim. Joyce, as well as Ezra Pound and also William Butler Yeats, would be excellent examples of the view of the modern poet that emerges from Vico's approach to literature.

In aesthetic theory, the two thinkers who are most associated with the name of Vico are Benedetto Croce and R. G. Collingwood. Croce, in *Aesthetic as Science of Expression and General Linguistic*, devoted a chapter to the views of Vico. Indeed, Croce is one of the great figures in Vico scholarship generally. His *Philosophy of Giambattista Vico* was translated into English by R. G. Collingwood in 1913. Croce saw Vico as a precursor of Hegelian idealism and thus as an important source of his own idealist conception of culture. Croce credits Vico with the discovery of the true nature of poetry, in his conception of poetic wisdom, and calls Vico the inventor of the "science of aesthetic." Croce claims that in Vico's view, poetry and language are substantially the same, meaning that in its original form language is poetic and the instrument of the imagination. [*See* Croce.] Collingwood mentions Vico only twice in his *Principles of Art,* but Collingwood's general interest in developing a theory of imagination for understanding the principles of art, and his claim that art is knowledge, knowledge of the individual, are Vichian in spirit. [*See* Collingwood.] A third thinker who has given attention to Vico as important for a conception of myth and art is Cassirer. In his chapter on art in *An Essay on Man,* Cassirer presents Vico as the creator of a "logic of imagination," and he recounts Vico's conception of three ages as a basis for his own claim, that the mythmaker and the poet seem to live in the same world, that the symbolic form of myth always underlies and in one way or another is recalled in the productive activity of the poet.

Vico's *New Science* has historically had its greatest impact on the views of art and aesthetic experience in the idealist tradition. Vico has not become a source for work in contemporary aesthetics, although in literary studies such a writer as Herbert Read has praised Vico and been influenced by him. Vico does not have an aesthetic doctrine that is separate from his philosophy of history and philosophy of culture. Besides what Vico says specifically about the nature of the imagination and of poetic wisdom, the point that Vico's work holds out, to contemporary aesthetic theory, is the importance of grounding questions about art and aesthetics in the larger context of a philosophy of human culture.

Much work in the history of aesthetics has gone into the search for a definition of the artwork and for the determination of the essence of the artwork—the expression of emotion, pleasure, feeling, and so forth. In contemporary aesthetics a great deal of attention has been given to the cognitive status of the artwork and to the language of art. Most of such work in aesthetic theory is conducted as though art could be understood as something purely in itself, apart from the grounding of what art is in terms of a general theory of knowledge, philosophy of culture, or conception of society. When attention is given to art in these respects, a reductionist theory of art is often advanced in which art is reduced to politics, for example, in materialist or Marxist or other ideological terms.

Vico's view is instructive in that it implies that any proper conception of art, the arts, or aesthetic experience must begin where culture itself begins: with an understanding of myth or poetic wisdom, in the primordial use of *fantasia*. Although Vico does not formulate a theory of aesthetics per se, his *New Science* suggests that any aesthetics must be developed from an understanding of the origin of aesthetic experience in the origin of culture itself and that it must be understood against the particular stage of culture in which art occurs. This is not simply to advocate a historicist conception of art, because in Vico's view all development follows an ideal eternal pattern; thus, ultimately for Vico, any aesthetic view would require a grounding in a metaphysics of the nature of the human or civil world, one Vico claims to have given in his *New Science*.

[*See also* Poetics; *and* Renaissance Italian Aesthetics.]

BIBLIOGRAPHY

Works by Vico

The Autobiography of Giambattista Vico. Corr. rev. ed. Translated by Max Harold Fisch and Thomas Goddard Bergin (1944). Ithaca, N.Y., 1975.
The New Science of Giambattista Vico. Unabr. rev. ed. Translated from the 1744 edition by Thomas Goddard Bergin and Max Harold Fisch (1948). Ithaca, N.Y., 1984. Includes Vico's "Practic of the New Science."
On Humanistic Education: Six Inaugural Orations, 1699–1707. Translated by Giorgio A. Pinton and Arthur W. Shippee. Ithaca, N.Y., 1993. From the definitive Latin text, introduction, and notes of Gian Galeazzo Visconti.
On the Most Ancient Wisdom of the Italians, Unearthed from the Origins of the Latin Language. Translated by Lucia M. Palmer. Ithaca, N.Y., 1988. Includes Vico's *Disputations with the Giornale de' Letterati d'Italia.*
On the Study Methods of Our Time. Translated by Elio Gianturco (1965). Ithaca, N.Y., 1990. Includes Vico's "The Academies and the Relation between Philosophy and Eloquence," translated by Donald Phillip Verene.
Opere di G. B. Vico. 8 vols. in 11. Edited by Fausto Nicolini. Bari, 1911–1941.

Other Sources

Berlin, Isaiah. *Vico and Herder: Two Studies in the History of Ideas.* New York, 1976.
Danesi, Marcel. *Vico, Metaphor, and the Origin of Language.* Bloomington, Ind., 1993.
Grassi, Ernesto. *Rhetoric as Philosophy: The Humanist Tradition.* University Park, Pa., 1980.
Mali, Joseph. *The Rehabilitation of Myth: Vico's New Science.* Cambridge and New York, 1992.
Schaeffer, John D. *Sensus communis: Vico, Rhetoric, and the Limits of Relativism.* Durham, N.C., 1990.
Verene, Donald Phillip. *Vico's Science of Imagination.* Ithaca, N.Y., 1981.
Verene, Donald Phillip. *The New Art of Autobiography: An Essay on the "Life of Giambattista Vico Written by Himself."* Oxford, 1991.

DONALD VERENE

VIDEO. Defining video as an aesthetic medium has historically been a perplexing project. Written primarily as the evolution of its technology, video's history has been one of rapid, and of late, accelerating change. Since the introduction of the Sony Portapak in 1965, technological transformations of the video apparatus, such as the addition of color, high-resolution monitors, and on-line digital editing, have been inextricably allied with transformations of aesthetic effects. At the same time, video's diversity of formats, flexibility as a means of recording, and multimedia configurations have increasingly escaped traditional and modernist ontological categories. This chameleon-like quality, video's ceaseless process of becoming, can in part be traced to the specificity of the historical moment of its advent and cultural diffusion. Developed to complement broadcast technologies, videotape and video recorders were designed initially as accessories to commercial network television, which inflected the formal and technical properties of the video medium itself. Thus, at its origin, video lacked a secure and distinctive identity. Moreover, as a medium coming of age in the postindustrial era of information, video increasingly served as the audiovisual interface for interactive computer technologies, resulting in hybrid rather than pure video forms. From this perspective, the evolution of a unique video aesthetic can be read as the dialectical story of video's simultaneous self-discovery and abnegation as a medium, which can be charted in three roughly chronological periods: video's struggle for independence from the specificities of television, video's establishment of autonomy as a medium with distinct inherent properties, and video's re-

VIDEO.   Nam June Paik, *Magnet T.V.* (1969), Television set and magnet, Television: 11 × 17 × 11 in., Magnet: 5 1/4 × 1 3/4 × 1 3/4 inches. (Photograph courtesy of the artist and the Holly Solomon Gallery, New York; used by permission.)

turn to indeterminacy as an adjunct technology of multimedia.

Video as Antitelevision. As an accident of history, video contested the tenets of technological determinism, a prescriptive discourse concerned with the belief that technology dictates aesthetics. Coinciding with the determinist theories of television popularized by Marshall McLuhan, video's first practitioners appropriated the medium precisely in opposition to television; thus, video by default signified antideterminism and the negation of institutional mandates, advocating cultural resistance to and formal experimentation with a broadcast medium previously theorized as monolithic and inert. Shattering David Sarnoff's model of broadcast from a single point of active production (the professional studio) to a constellation of passive receivers (domestic television sets), the invention of the Portapak and video recorder released the medium of videotape from the industrial and aesthetic confines of commercial networks into the hands of individual artists, activists, and home consumers. These constituencies, concerned respectively with art, politics, and entertainment, began to distinguish the term *video* from *television* as an inverse relation. Whereas television became regarded as a conservative

medium of transmission (of other media forms, of capitalist ideology, of conventional programming), video was championed as a revolutionary medium of transformation (of art institutions, of the establishment status quo, of the network schedule).

In general, video artists adopted two strategies of negation: the first, a minimalist aesthetic and an assertion of real time as an interrogation into and detoxification of passive television spectatorship; the second, the modification of the codes of commercial television through quotation, allusion, parody, and protest in order to cue recognition of and distantiation from the objectionable qualities believed to inhere in industrial forms. Perhaps the video installations of Nam June Paik are most representative of these strategies of deconstruction and demystification: his prepared televisions (*TV Chair*, 1968), minimalist video sculptures (*TV Garden*, 1974–1978), recontextualized monitors (*TV Bra*, 1969), and distortions of received broadcast signals (*Magnet TV*, 1965) stripped television from its institutional and domestic environments in order to restore video as an aesthetic object.

Social activists who were contemporaries of Paik's appropriated video in order to intervene in the politics of television by organizing alternative production practices (variously referred to as street video, community video, or grassroots video) as modes of communication, consciousness-raising, and social change. Groups such as Videofreex, People's Video Theater, Global Village, and Ant Farm produced, distributed, and exhibited innovative underground documentaries, posed audiovisual culture as a positive alternative to print, and attempted to sublate the art/life dichotomy reified by bourgeois capitalism by integrating video into everyday praxis. In 1971, Michael Shamberg, a leader of the Raindance cooperative, advocated the decentralization of television as an aesthetically bankrupt and commercially corrupt medium in a manifesto titled *Guerrilla Television*. The appellation has persisted as a generic term for alternative video practices sharing similar sociopolitical goals.

Like early video art, activist video developed its aesthetic in opposition to commercial television. Against the slick postproduction values of network journalism, street video promoted an aesthetic of immediacy, which in part was technologically based. The unobtrusive nature of lightweight video equipment, its synchronous recording of sound and image, and the instantaneous replay of information encouraged a naturalistic, "real time" approach, which was, in turn, translated in terms of style as "realism" and of epistemology as "truth." Also opposed to the commodification of news as a product to be sponsored by commercial advertisers, activist video celebrated a more autotelic process accented by intimacy (an informal relationship between producers and subjects constituted by mutual participation and feedback) and by democracy (video's portability as a means to greater access and engagement for typically disenfranchised constituencies).

As many of the practitioners and goals of guerrilla video were absorbed and neutralized by television in the 1980s, the advent of home video consumer technologies, while domesticated in design and function, have been defended in some quarters for their potential resistance to broadcast imperatives for passive consumption. A substantial body of scholarship has documented the methods by which the video home system (VHS) video recorder has reactivated television reception. Its capacity for "time shifting," a function that records and saves broadcast programming for viewing at the spectator's convenience, intervenes in television's imperious "flow" by upsetting the designs of the network schedule to suit the idiosyncratic temporal rhythms of the household. The VCR's interactive features, such as pause, slow motion, and fast-forward, not only foster a writerly response to television texts but also liberate the viewer from ubiquitous advertisements and objectionable content. Finally, the growing market of prerecorded videocassettes available for playback increases access to subject matter not procurable from broadcast or cable, as well as preserves a corpus of texts for archival retention.

If the video recorder has fostered interactive reception, the video camcorder has encouraged proactive production.

As opposed to the economic and material restrictions of Super-8 film stock, videotape's low cost, extended recording time, and instant playback, as well as its capacity to be recycled, dubbed, and edited cleanly and efficiently, have substantially increased the range and volume of home-mode production practices exploring the possibility of non-broadcast forms (e.g., electronic diary, amateur porn, video will). As improvements to consumer equipment narrow the gap in quality between amateur and professional images, broadcast institutions have reacted by both adopting and adapting conventions of home video to fit those of commercial television. For example, the stylistic idioms associated with home video (hand-held camera movement, zooming, low light levels) have been embraced by advertising as markers of authenticity. More significantly, the subgenre of reality programming that solicits and airs amateur videotapes has substantially altered both audience expectations and Federal Communications Commission regulations of what constitutes broadcast image standards. The journalistic variation, inspired by George Halliday's footage of the Rodney King beating (1991) and represented by series such as *I Witness Video*, employs home video documents of crime, accidents, and disasters as eyewitness evidence; the more successful domestic variation, most notably *America's Funniest Home Videos*, blends the privatized experience associated with ritual family photography with the public, mass-marketed conventions of prime-time television. Commissioning amateur imagery for professional exploitation, reality-based programming of this nature in effect resituates activist video's populist origins as a democratic practice within a commercial context where, paradoxically, home video's ideologies of self-determination and familialism conflict. If amateur video may contest institutional hegemony, its commercial broadcast resurrects television's historic domestic ideologies, which may neutralize home video's potential for resistance.

Video as Video. Once liberated from its dependence on television, in order to achieve autonomy as a medium on an equal footing with the traditional arts, video would have to be reintroduced on its own terms, develop its own practices, and argue for the validity of its own aesthetic value. Resituating video within the Greenbergian discourse of inherent properties, which defines a medium by its supposed essential, unique formal characteristics, video artists began to create individual works foregrounding the materiality of the video apparatus, experimenting with its technological capabilities and constraints, and exploring its relation to painting, sculpture, Happenings, and kinetic, conceptual, and performance art.

If video's aesthetic of negation rejects the institution of television, video's aesthetic of inherent properties challenges the institution of art, in particular, the museum's archival agenda, sites of delivery, and modes of reception. Impermanent, videotape's signal decay and incompatibility with ever-changing delivery formats represent a denial of art as a precious, eternal object. Reproducible, video deviates from any policy dedicated to the protection and display of unique artifacts. Whether linear or multichannel, video's temporality, usually requiring a period of extended or intense viewing, clashes with the self-guided time of the museum's more leisurely pace.

Video installations, for example, reinvigorate the pedantic atmosphere of the museum by synthesizing real and electronic spaces into a visual, aural, and kinesthetic environment in which spectators can freely interact, moving about and behind the apparatus, while often appearing framed within monitors as part of the installation's raw material. Seminal works such as *Wipe Cycle* (Schneider and Gillette, 1969), *Corridor* (Nauman, 1970), *Dachau* (Korot, 1974), and *Mem* (Campus, 1975) aspired to the aesthetic of sculpture, by bringing separate units of image production (monitor, camera, VCR) into complex recorded and live closed-circuit configurations, and by treating the video signal as a tactile source of light rather than as a conduit of story or information.

Single-channel videotapes, like installations, often display a similar lack of commitment to narrative temporality and causal relations. Artists dedicated to a technique of synaesthetic abstraction reject the conception of videotape as a neutral recording device or a medium of representation, and instead generate electronic landscapes enabled by color processing, video keying, superimpositions, and computer inserts. Many early experimental tapes of this type focus on and exhaust the possibilities of one particular aspect of video's specificity: for example, instant replay (*Noise*, Benglis, 1972), live feedback (*Locating #2*, Holt, 1972), and electronic dubbing (*Generations*, Bolling, 1972).

Another genre of single-channel videotapes adopts the avant-garde aesthetic of montage as a method of parodic appropriation. At times referred to as "scratch" or "pastiche" video, works such as *P. M. Magazine* (Birnbaum, 1982), *Perfect Leader* (Almy, 1983), *Scenes from the Microwar* (Millner, 1985), and *Joan Does Dynasty* (Braderman, 1986) refashion popular and commercial imagery through a variety of editing and image-processing strategies, including the repetition of sound bites to expose the nonsensical redundancy of anonymous, authoritarian voice-overs; and the paradigmatic stacking of audiovisual fragments to betray the predictability and ideology of conventional narrative. As video dé-collage, these works offer a Brechtian metacritical discourse about industrial media's overt and hidden agendas, while reinvesting the appropriated material with a new understanding from a novel perspective.

Perhaps the most influential genre of single-channel tapes, performance videos foreground the presence of the artist's body as raw material, emphasize the author as both subject and object of enunciation, and incorporate personal experience for public display. The medium of video first at-tracted performance artists who had been staging live exhibitions as a way to control, edit, and preserve each piece in its final, perfected form; to repeat performances without having to be physically present; and to seek refuge from the unpredictable responses of a live audience in real time and space.

In particular, the economy of video production, as opposed to film, recommended the medium to feminists, who discovered through performance video a mode of electronic consciousness-raising and an audiovisual means to illustrate the popular liberationist slogan "The Personal Is Political." Works such as *Semiotics of the Kitchen* (Rosler, 1975), *Kaleidoscope* (Barry, 1977), *Binge* (Hershman, 1987), and *It Wasn't Love* (Benning, 1992) typify feminist concerns with revising female stereotypes, expanding the self through projective role-playing, and exercising the right of women to assert themselves as creative, speaking subjects. Generally produced in the artist's home or alone in a production facility and structured rhetorically by direct address to the camera, feminist performance videos in particular have inflected art video with an aesthetic of intimacy.

Other performance videos have achieved a variety of aesthetic effects by imagining the video apparatus as a distinctive metaphor of self-identity. For example, seminal works such as *Centers* (Acconci, 1971), *Now* (Benglis, 1973), and *Boomerang* (Serra, 1974), exploit video's technological capacity to record and transmit the image of the artist simultaneously as both the object and subject of the gaze, constructing a solipsistic model of the apparatus as an electronic mirror, thereby achieving an aesthetic of narcissism. Not all performance videos are, however, essentially narcissistic. *Anger* (Cohen, 1986) and *The Love Tapes* (Clarke, 1978–1994), for instance, use video as a mode of confession and as a channel for dialogue with the self and an undisclosed other. In these works, wherein subjects disclose private thoughts and feelings alone to a camera as a method of therapy, the apparatus is constructed as both mirror and screen, a vehicle for self-confrontation and for intimate face-to-face encounters made safe by the buffer of a private and anonymous electronic space.

This is not to say that all performance videos are purely autobiographical. In videotapes as varied as *Weather Diary I* (Kuchar, 1986), *I Do Not Know What It Is I Am Like* (Viola, 1986), *My Puberty* (Segalove, 1987), and *Everyday Echo Street* (Mogul, 1993), the artist's subjectivity is split between inscribing personal history and documenting the external world. These works construct the monitor and camera lens as mirror and window, a dialectical apparatus calibrating the gap between introjective musings about self-identity and projective representations of an environment in which the artist maintains a libidinal, social, or cultural investment. Conceiving of the video apparatus variously as mirror, screen, or window, performance videos illustrate that the medium lacks a basal ontology. Video's so-called inherent properties are, rather, revealed as enabling fictions that reconfigure the differential aesthetic, cognitive, and cultural effects of individual works into metaphorical models of the apparatus that can claim for video a specific essence as justification of the artist's preferred mode of practice.

Video as Multimedia. The modernist pursuit of video's specificity in the 1970s and 1980s often conflated received conventions, established art idioms, and available technologies as intrinsic aspects of the medium rather than as the cultural elaborations of its material capacities at a specific historical moment. In the 1990s, video's manifold affiliations with multimedia, its assimilation by cinema, and its protean transformations by computer machinations have even further undermined the search for video's inherent properties as a propitious enterprise. Once the idea of a necessarily fixed site for the production and reception of images has been attenuated by issues of interface, hybridity, and digitization, the very designation of a unique video aesthetic loses signifying force. Increasingly, video serves as a medium of interface networking previously disparate media: for example, the computer (video games, CD-ROM, on-line editing), photography (photo-CD, video printer), telephone (teleconferencing, electronic mail), and architecture (video walls, closed-circuit surveillance). Neither an autonomous medium free of all links to other forms of art and communication, nor entirely dependent on any one of them, video can only be described by the plurality of its multimedia relationships rather than as pure in and of itself.

For example, video's supplemental relationship to film has generated hybrid forms and practices transforming modes of cinematic production and reception. Complementing celluloid as a production tool, video has been employed to record rehearsals, animate storyboards, scout locations, and check for continuity. Film-to-tape transfers of exposed footage have increased the speed and flexibility of editing, allowed for the rapid execution of special effects, and shortened the time lag between production and distribution.

Films on video have also radically transformed cinema reception in the form of the videocassette. Not only are motion pictures more frequently viewed at home than in movie theaters, privatizing a previously public viewing environment, but in order to accommodate for the different aspect ratios of the cinema screen and the television monitor, video must write its own technology over the original film text, introducing peculiar effects such as panning, scanning, letterboxing, and image reduction.

The employment of video images within film also modifies the phenomenology of classical Hollywood narration. Appearing in works such as *sex, lies, and videotape* (Steven Soderbergh, 1989) and *Speaking Parts* (Atom Egoyan, 1989), video scan lines, pixels, SLR-framing, LED messages, and shuttle effects comprise a new set of hybrid codes. This "video in the text" reframed by the cinema screen becomes a factor in the spectator's viewing strategy by calling attention to the source of its images, often implicating the viewer as a voyeur of private moments.

If film has increasingly incorporated video, computer digitization threatens to subsume it altogether. Digitized video replaces traditional image-making tools (VCR, camcorder, videotape) with a set of algorithmic models that code and decode the analog image as a series of binary symbols not mediated by physical processes, but rather stored in abstract structures independent of the dispositions and aesthetic qualities of the original video substrate. While digital icons are not subject to distortion or degradation when processed or reproduced, they do undermine the authority of the video image and distance the artist from the actual process of image creation: whereas analog video's aesthetic has been perceived as immediate, literal, actual, and naturalistic, digitized video is construed as contrived, distanced, synthetic, and analytic.

The indeterminacies of multimedia derail the notion that video's essence will inevitably unfold as it evolves progressively toward its self-identity. Such media teleology myths have been countered by postmodern arguments claiming that, because of its radical heterogeneity (capacity for interface and hybridity) and radical homogeneity (capacity for digital simulation), video simultaneously explodes and implodes modernist boundaries. From these apparently paradoxical qualities, according to this logic, the medium's essence can be extrapolated: that is, the specificity of video is precisely that it lacks one.

While multimedia may suggest that video's ontology will remain amorphous, the question of its aesthetic continues to be reframed and newly posed in works that stress content as well as form. Exploring issues of history (*The Art of Memory*, Vasulka, 1987), postmodernism (*Leaving the Twentieth Century*, Almy, 1982), creativity (*J. S. Bach*, Downey, 1986), ethnicity (*Meta Mayan II*, Veldez, 1981), feminism (*A Spy in the House That Ruth Built*, Green 1981), postcolonialism (*History and Memory*, Tajiri, 1991), and homophobia (*Tongues Untied*, Riggs, 1989), contemporary videos experiment with the medium's formal properties not merely in and for themselves, but as innovative material signifiers by which to express a unique social, cultural, or political vision. In these experimental works, the indeterminacies of video reflect the precarious conditions of contemporary life.

[*See also* Film; *and* Television.]

BIBLIOGRAPHY

Armes, Roy. *On Video.* London and New York, 1988.
Battcock, Gregory, ed. *New Artists Video: A Critical Anthology.* New York, 1978.
Berko, Lili. "Video: In Search of a Discourse." *Quarterly Review of Film Studies* 10.4 (1989): 289–307.
Cubitt, Sean. *Timeshift: On Video Culture.* London and New York, 1991.
Cubitt, Sean. *Videography: Video Media as Art and Culture.* New York, 1993.

d'Agostino, Peter, ed. *Transmission: Theory and Practice for a New Television Aesthetic.* New York, 1985.

Garnham, Nicholas. "The Myths of Video: A Disciplinary Reminder." *Capitalism and Communication: Global Culture and the Economics of Information,* pp. 64–69. London, 1990.

Hall, Doug, and Sally Jo Fifer, eds. *Illuminating Video: An Essential Guide to Video Art.* New York, 1990.

Hanhardt, John G., ed. *Video Culture: A Critical Investigation.* Rochester, N.Y., 1986.

James, David E. "inTerVention: The Contexts of Negation for Video and Video Criticism." *Millennium Film Journal* 20/21 (Fall/Winter 1988–1989): 46–55.

Jameson, Fredric. "Video: Surrealism without the Unconscious." In *Postmodernism: or, The Cultural Logic of Late Capitalism,* pp. 67–96. Durham, N.C., 1991.

Kurtz, Bruce. "Video Is Being Invented." *Arts Magazine* 47 (December/January 1973): 37–44.

Marshall, Stuart. "Video: Technology and Practice." *Screen* 20.1 (Spring 1979): 109–119.

Marshall, Stuart. "Television/Video: Technology/Forms." *Afterimage* 8/9 (Spring 1981): 70–85.

Nmungwun, Aaron Foisi. *Video Recording Technology: Its Impact on Media and Home Entertainment.* Hillsdale, N.J., 1989.

Podesta, Patti, ed. *Resolution: A Critique of Video Art.* Los Angeles, 1986.

Renov, Michael, and Erika Suderburg, eds. *Resolutions: Contemporary Video Practices.* Minneapolis, 1996.

Shamberg, Michael, and Raindance Corporation. *Guerrilla Television.* New York, 1971.

JAMES M. MORAN

VIOLLET-LE-DUC, EUGÈNE-EMMANUEL. *See* Gothic Aesthetics.

VIRTUAL REALITY.

Virtual Reality is a synthetic technology combining three-dimensional video, audio, and other sensory components to achieve a sense of immersion in an interactive, computer-generated environment. Virtual Reality also appears under the title Virtual Environments or Virtual Worlds. Popular culture now uses the terms *virtual* and *virtual reality* in a weak sense that refers loosely to any kind of computer-mediated experience or even to any kind of imaginative experience, but the stronger usage of the term implies the application of immersion techniques that remain under development and are not yet widely available in the mid-1990s. It is these immersion techniques that distinguish the aesthetic novelty introduced by Virtual Reality.

Whereas traditional sculpture and architecture involve the viewer in three-dimensional space, Virtual Reality insulates the human sensorium in a full-surround computerized sensory feedback loop. The technical configuration used to achieve immersion differs, ranging from head-mounted displays and datagloves to room-size projections for unencumbered full-body interaction with artificial entities and autonomous agents. High-speed computing allows Virtual Reality systems to track the user's sensory responses and to provide real-time feedback of appropriate images, sounds,

and tactile pressure to create the feeling of immersion or being in a world. Some see in Virtual Reality the evolution of human–computer symbiosis, progressing from multimedia to cyberspace to virtual reality. A designer must take into account the specific immersion techniques and the kind of presence needed for the specific virtual world. The Virtual Reality artist can draw on a wide range of realism, from photographic realism to the softer realism of archetypal imagination. Virtual Reality has numerous applications in education, science, and industrial prototyping, as well as in telepresence and robotics, where it is used in surgery and in the exploration of outer space. As a metamedium, Virtual Reality will unfold its full potential only as artists gradually release it from the constraints of commercial and entertainment applications.

Definition in Historical Context. Virtual Reality functions as an umbrella concept for related research and commercial developments. The term *virtual reality* first appeared in the late 1980s with Jaron Lanier and his Virtual Programming Languages Incorporated (VPL), which introduced the first commercial system for controlling computer simulations through a dataglove and a stereoscopic head-mounted display (HMD). An artist himself, Lanier introduced Virtual Reality as a medium for shared self-expression. The fiber-optic glove or "dataglove" measures hand and finger movements and the helmet tracks the user's point of view so that the computer can adjust the stereo images to fit the user's position and hand gestures. The basic research behind the HMD and dataglove had been going on for twenty years before VPL, stretching back to Ivan Sutherland at Harvard and to several NASA research projects. Over the past decades, two major streams of Virtual Reality emerged: the one stream based on the HMD and the other stream based on the room-size projection of graphics for unencumbered interaction.

The helmet-based stream of Virtual Reality emerged not from the art world but from military flight simulators. The "supercockpit" was begun in the 1970s by Thomas A. Furness at Wright-Patterson Air Force Base. Along similar lines was the groundbreaking work of Ivan Sutherland during the 1960s at Harvard and at the University of Utah. Sutherland's head-mounted displays could work with primitive graphic simulations, not just aircraft flight. Early computer art, stemming from Michael Noll's experiments at Bell Labs, provided the computer graphics. Sutherland influenced Frederick P. Brooks, who founded the virtual worlds laboratory at the University of North Carolina. Brooks began designing virtual worlds for solving problems in medicine, physics, and engineering. The HMD pilot trainer became a universal simulator.

The other stream of Virtual Reality development came from the art world. Some of the kinetic and electronic art of the 1960s used cameras to create a feedback loop between the art objects and the participants. Interactive art, such as

Myron Krueger's Videoplace, suggested an unencumbered way of participating in real-time, computer-generated, graphic worlds. Krueger's Videoplace put people in separate rooms who could then relate interactively by mutual body painting, free-fall gymnastics, and tickling. Krueger's Glowflow, a light-and-sound room, responds to people's movements by lighting phosphorescent tubes and issuing synthetic sounds. Another environment, Psychic Space, allows participants to explore an interactive maze where each footstep corresponds to a musical tone, all produced with live video images that can be moved, scaled, rotated, without regard to the usual laws of cause and effect.

Krueger's line of Virtual Reality inspired commercial products such as the Mandala System and scientific research such as the CAVE at the Electronic Visualization Lab (EVL) of the University of Illinois at Chicago. At EVL, the CAVE (CAVE Automatic Virtual Environment) uses surround-screen, projection-based techniques to create an entire room in which users can explore virtual worlds unencumbered by physical trackers. Applications in the CAVE have included virtual environments for astronomy and physics. Krueger's influence was also manifest in the 1993 ALIVE (Artificial Life Interactive Video Environment) at the Massachusetts Institute of Technology Media Lab where semi-intelligent artificial agents with animated graphic bodies join human users who can relate to them with natural gestures.

Both streams of HMD and projection Virtual Reality share the common goal of providing an immersive experience. The user feels surrounded or immersed in a world of artificial, computer-generated entities with which he or she can interact. The "virtual" in *virtual reality* comes from the experience of being immersed in a world of entities that feel present when in fact they are not actually present, "virtual" meaning "in effect but not in fact." It is this illusory quality of Virtual Reality that establishes its link with trompe l'oeil painting and the many variants of aesthetic realism.

Virtual Reality can shade into telepresence. Telepresent Virtual Reality is an interactive immersion in a simulation linked causally, usually through robotics, to real-world entities. Virtual Reality telepresence allows NASA operators in Houston to move a Moon Rover across the lunar landscape while feeling as if they were actually present in the vehicle on the Moon. When linked to robotic graphics, Virtual Reality becomes a technology for telepresence, which means presence at a remote location.

The complex notion of presence is tied to subtle shadings of human experience. Research in Virtual Reality continues to explore the issues of what constitutes presence and what gives humans the ontological confidence to declare something to be real.

A related meaning of virtual reality has arrived with the advances in computer graphics. As sound systems were once praised for their high fidelity, present-day imaging sys-

tems now deliver "virtual reality." The images have a shaded texture and light radiosity that pull the eye into the flat plane with the power of a detailed etching. Landscapes produced on the GE Aerospace "Visionics" equipment, for instance, are photorealistic real-time, texture-mapped worlds through which users can navigate. These graphic dataworlds spring from the context of mission rehearsal and training in military flight simulators. Researchers now seek to bring these techniques to medicine, entertainment, and education. The claim of Virtual Reality aestheticians often goes beyond the claims of photographic realism or representation as users may experience the virtual entities to have ontological properties indistinguishable from the ontological properties of actual entities. Aesthetics in the virtual realm then often involves questions of presence and of ontological identity.

Relation to Tradition. Early Western psychology distinguished five senses plus a sixth or common sense *(sensus communis)* that coordinates the five other senses. The sixth or common sense produces the feeling of being focused on a unified, substantial entity on the basis of which the perceptions of the other senses are synthesized. Later aestheticians conceived this common sense as "sensibility" (called "universal subjectivity" in Immanuel Kant's *Critique of Judgment*), which changes over time and differs according to cultural conditioning. Cultural historians trace the variations in this conventional sensibility as shifts in perceptions. A similar postulate underpins Virtual Reality research. The notion of presence is intimately connected with whatever the senses perceive as given. The right sensory input can activate the sixth sense or feeling of presence, and the user experiences being present (virtually) among real entities in a real world. In this way, Virtual Reality brings aesthetics closer to ontology. Much twentieth-century philosophy—especially existentialism—revolved around presence as the key to reality. Pragmatists like William James also stressed the power of the human senses to entrain belief: you see it, you believe it—unless you consciously choose not to believe it. Because Virtual Reality raises basic questions of ontology and epistemology, its vocabulary resonates with much of Western art and philosophy, from Plato to Maurice Merleau-Ponty and Martin Heidegger. The scholars who one day will detail these connections will very likely cause the maps we have of past philosophies to be redrawn. Art, philosophy, and religion have from time immemorial discussed ways of transcending the immediate world. Knowledge, art, and thinking have achieved a considerable self-reflection on how to transcend bodily life. To this tradition Virtual Reality adds the factor of technology. Involvement with Virtual Reality may bring art, philosophy, and religion closer to the world of information.

Special Problems. The reference in Virtual Reality to "reality" or realism suggests a fundamental problem running throughout art history. If we want to create realistic experience, what indeed is reality? Is it largely a function of psychology or of empirical sense impressions? The introduction of technology does not answer this question but only heightens it—unless, that is, virtual reality shrinks to entertainment trivia and commercial applications. To achieve its potential as an art form, Virtual Reality will necessarily explore degrees of realism and of verisimilitude. What complicates the issue is the broad spread of disciplines from which Virtual Reality draws its sustenance: Virtual Reality combines art with technology, psychology with computer science, and electrical engineering with metaphysics. Another related problem is how to bridge the gap between the great expectations raised by the Virtual Reality concept and the actual achievements of research. The most widely available Virtual Reality systems today serve the limited goals of arcade games and commercial applications.

As Virtual Reality becomes a metamedium—combining theater, film, sculpture, dance, and so forth—artists will break it loose from the constraints of entertainment and commercial applications. Only in this way will its full potential unfold and truly appropriate applications appear. The learning curve will be high as Virtual Reality deviates from the experiential norms of previous art. One current example of such experiments is the visual sculpture done at the Institute for Simulation and Training in Florida. An interactive painting and sculpture environment gives participants some fuzzy-ball primitives to work with in three-dimensional space. The balls float scattered either loosely or densely in space according to the speed at which the user's hand moves through the space. The tracker sensor determines x, y, and z coordinates of the ball placement, but the other three degrees of hand movement (pitch, yaw, and roll) give color mappings for the balls. Colors change with the pitch of the hand, yaw controls the color saturation, and the intensity is controlled by the roll of the hand. Such nonisomorphic mapping requires considerable practice before art can be created, but the experiment shows the rich potential of Virtual Reality as a metamedium.

Closely related to the question of realism is the notion of immersion or presence. Granted that immersion is part of Virtual Reality, the question remains: How are users best immersed in virtual environments? Should users feel totally immersed? That is, should they forget where they are (in a graphics environment) and see, hear, and touch the world much in the same way we experience the primary phenomenological world? (We cannot see our own heads in the phenomenological world.) Or should users be allowed to see themselves as a cyberbody? Should they be aware of their primary body as a separate entity outside the graphic environment? What makes full-body immersion? The two different answers to this question split the field into the two kinds of immersion: the one derived from Krueger's Videoplace and the other from the head-mounted displays of Vir-

tual Programming Languages, NASA, and Brooks's lab at the University of North Carolina. The choice of different Virtual Reality platforms (HMD or projection) points to a deeper issue of Virtual Reality and concerns its relationship to primary reality. The aesthetic questions then impinge on ethical issues. Our bodies remain in primary reality, and our cyberbodies (whether first person headless, full graphic, or telepresent surrogate) add a secondary level of self-awareness. The unity of the human mind and its primary body becomes more tenuous than ever in virtual worlds. Pilots in the Persian Gulf War experienced an extraordinary detachment from their bombing raids after having trained themselves virtually on the same missions for weeks. The skills required to wield computer precision and power are producing what the Pentagon calls "Nintendo soldiers." Avant-garde doctors also speak of the Nintendo surgeon who operates through telemedicine and whose patients evaporate into bodiless bits and bytes. Similar to jet lag and flight-simulator sickness, the Virtual Reality gap between mind and body leads to alternate world syndrome (AWS) or alternate world disorder (AWD) where fragments of the psyche get stuck in one world while working in another. Researchers find Virtual Reality users pointing their fingers in the real world and expecting to fly as they do in virtual environments. The positive side of such maladies is the possibility that Virtual Reality artworks in "augmented reality" will be able to connect virtual and real images in ways that enhance and transform the human connection to primary reality.

[*See also* Artificial Intelligence and Aesthetics; Computer Art; Cyberspace; Digital Media; Hypertext; *and* Multimedia.]

BIBLIOGRAPHY

Aukstakalnis, Steve, and David Blatner. *Silicon Mirage: The Art and Science of Virtual Reality.* Berkeley, 1992.
Biocca, Frank. "Will Simulation Sickness Slow Down the Diffusion of VE Technology?" *Presence: Teleoperators and Virtual Environments* 1.3 (Summer 1992): 334–343.
Burdea, Grigore, and Philippe Coiffet. *Virtual Reality Technology.* New York, 1994.
Heim, Michael. *The Metaphysics of Virtual Reality.* New York and Oxford, 1994.
Heim, Michael. *Virtual Realism: The Art of Emerging Technology.* New York and Oxford, 1998.
Krueger, Myron W. *Artificial Reality II.* Reading, Mass., 1991.
Pimental, Ken, and Kevin Teixeira. *Virtual Reality: Through the New Looking Glass.* 2d ed. New York, 1995.
Rheingold, Howard. *Virtual Reality.* New York, 1991.

MICHAEL HEIM

VOLTAIRE, FRANÇOIS-MARIE AROUET DE. *See* French Aesthetics, *article on* Eighteenth-Century French Aesthetics.

W–Z

WAGNER, RICHARD (1813–1883), German composer. From *Der Fliegende Holländer* (1841), his first fully characteristic work, through *Tannhäuser, Lohengrin,* the mighty *Ring* cycle *(Das Rheingold, Die Walküre, Siegfried,* and *Götterdämmerung),* through *Tristan und Isolde, Die Meistersinger von Nürnberg,* to his final work, *Parsifal* (1882), Wagner's musical and dramatic explorations opened up terrains of the imagination that were to haunt almost every significant composer since his time. As a strictly musical phenomenon, then, Wagner's place in history is as secure and as clear as that of any seismic event could be. But why does he matter for aesthetics?

The answer to this question is immensely complex. One might begin, somewhat artificially, by distinguishing four separate senses in which Wagner's relationship to aesthetics is significant. First, Wagner can be seen as the product, or at least the accomplice, of an aesthetic—Arthur Schopenhauer's. Second, he can be seen as the inspirer of an aesthetic—most notably Friedrich Nietzsche's. Third, he can be seen as the producer of an aesthetic—through his own copious writings. Fourth, and most diaphanous, he can be seen as a disrupter of aesthetics—his musical works, and the reception of them, disturb and continue to disturb any settled sense of what art can be and do.

The first two of these can be dealt with quite quickly. Wagner discovered Schopenhauer's *The World as Will and Representation* in 1854, and what he found there was exciting and congenial. The innermost nature of the world, according to Schopenhauer, is vile: a blind, endlessly, and meaninglessly striving Will whose refracted representations constitute the world of human experience. Music, and music alone, is capable of penetrating the veil of representation. Indeed, music enjoys a uniquely privileged mode of access: it is (or can be) a "copy" of the Will. The sheer grandeur of Schopenhauer's vision, if not perhaps the actual vileness of it, appealed to Wagner immensely, as it would to any musician of ambition. Finding in Schopenhauer a warrant for his own most extravagant estimation of music's capacities, for his conviction that music was *the* metaphysically significant activity, he became an ardent admirer—to the extent that his book about Beethoven, supposed to be ardently admiring of Beethoven, refers to Schopenhauer about ten times as often as to its ostensible subject. Then, in 1868, Wagner met Nietzsche, himself already an avid Schopenhauerian. Nietzsche was hungry for a hero and was swiftly convinced that in Wagner he had found one. The final ten sections of *The Birth of Tragedy,* Nietzsche's first book, hail Wagner as the modern incarnation of Aeschylus, as a doer of metaphysical deeds whose like had not been seen since antiquity. Specifically, Nietzsche hails Wagner as the first post-Socratic artist to have penetrated the ("Apollonian") veil of representation so as to touch ground again with the ("Dionysian") reality beneath—a reality so dreadful that it could be borne only in the kind of intoxicated state that Wagner's music was so capable of inducing. Nietzsche fell out with Wagner shortly afterward. He also repudiated Schopenhauer. But whereas the break with Schopenhauer marked the decisive move into Nietzsche's all-too-brief philosophical maturity, the break with Wagner was much less clean. Nietzsche's estimation of the significance of art, and of music in particular, was permanently conditioned by his experience of Wagner. He returned to him again and again, as if to a peculiarly seductive sore—picking, squeezing, probing, hating, fond—and remains Wagner's most intimate and devastating critic.

No artist has so directly fed off or into the major philosophers of art as has Wagner. But if he had merely done that he would have been a prodigy, not a phenomenon. To capture his phenomenal quality better, one must turn to the third and fourth of the considerations mentioned earlier. The third concerned Wagner's own writings. Verbose, grandiloquent, and often tiresomely obscure, Wagner's reflections on music and musical drama represent by far the most sustained attempt by a musician of genius to express his hopes for and understanding of his own art (only Arnold Schoenberg comes close to him in this regard). Two of his larger ideas should be enough to suggest the thrust, and indeed the thrustingness, of his thought. First, there is the conception of the *Gesamtkunstwerk* (the "total work of art"). Wagner longed for a synthesis of the arts in a single work—a work in which the various arts would come together to yield a power and a totality of vision unavailable to any of them individually; and he sought, with a degree of success that is still the subject of debate, to realize that ideal in his own music dramas (for which he wrote both texts and music and, when he could, designed the sets). The second large idea concerns the relation of thought to feeling: "Nothing should remain," he said, "for the synthesizing intellect to do in the face of a performance of a dramatic work of art. . . . In drama we must become *knowers* through *feeling.*" Here, in all likelihood, Wagner felt that a sufficiently openhearted response to his own works would be enough to bear him out. These two ideas are not unrelated. Historically, both kick against the most important trend in nineteenth-century musical aesthetics. Music, it was increasingly coming to be held, was autonomous: it bore no natural allegiance to the other arts, did not depend on them or anything else for its significance, and was, in that sense, *pure,* that is, meaningful in a purely musical way. The *Gesamtkunstwerk* ideal turns this on its head. Music, for Wagner, is to be seen as a mere ingredient, as just one force in a field of significance whose import exceeds, no doubt impurely, anything that music might achieve by itself. Add to this the claim that dramatic art operates on thought via feeling, so that music, in its dramatic capacity, is significant for reasons other than purely musical reasons, and the repudiation of musical autonomy is complete. At a historical level, then, Wagner's aesthetic is strikingly nonconformist.

It is at a level that one might describe as cultural that Wagner's aesthetic is most striking. Nietzsche was probably the first to put his finger on (and to be disturbed by) the wider character of Wagner's artistic ambitions. The aspiration to a totality of vision, to an all-encompassing interpretation whose authority was to be grounded on the primacy of feeling, seemed, on Nietzsche's diagnosis, to be symptomatic less of an artistic impulse than of a religious one. Founders and furtherers of religions, he insisted, set out to combat the dissatisfactions engendered by the immanent, contingent nature of human existence. They do this by inventing for existence *complete,* and therefore transcendental, interpretations—that is, interpretations that, because they offer to account for everything, to make sense of everything, remove that "illusion" of contingency that dissatisfaction is caused by and feeds off; and the founders of religions exploit the passions of the dissatisfied in order to force those interpretations on them or, at any rate, to render them irresistible. In this sense at least, Wagner's aesthetic turns out to be a kind of substitute theology, expressly designed to comfort the afflicted and to foreclose the possibility of living in that honest acknowledgment of immanence and contingency that Nietzsche calls "noble" and "tragic." Small wonder that, having made this diagnosis, Nietzsche withdrew his youthful identification of Wagner's art as the *rebirth of tragedy.* Of course, the situation is more complicated than this. For one thing, Wagner—under the influence of Schopenhauer—came to accord to music a far greater significance than was consistent with his original conception of the *Gesamtkunstwerk.* But this is offset by his acceptance of Schopenhauer's metaphysics, itself a totalizing interpretation of existence driven, if the later Nietzsche is right, by the acutest feelings of dissatisfaction (Schopenhauer's "Will" is an all-embracing explanatory principle

that, once grasped, is supposed to alleviate pain by fostering renunciation—renunciation being a response to which Wagner had always attached great significance). Thus, Wagner's aesthetic remains quasi-religious, in Nietzsche's sense, even if his conception of the precise character of the metaphysical task to be fulfilled by art, and by music in particular, changed. What is beyond doubt, though, is that in a century on which religion proper had started to lose its grip, art was increasingly seen as its natural successor (*something* must comfort the afflicted); and of this new cult (which counted Hector Berlioz and Franz Liszt among its early adepts), few, including Wagner, seriously doubted that Wagner was to be high priest. Where "religion becomes artificial," he wrote, "it is the duty of art to save religion's essential core"; and when he opened the Festspielhaus at Bayreuth in 1876, built by him and specifically designed for the performance of his own works, its character as a temple and a place of worship was widely appreciated.

Many have been tempted to see rather more in Wagner's efforts to "save religion's essential core." Specifically, many have been tempted to see in it a commitment to another major nineteenth-century trend—the trend toward romantic nationalism. Insofar as Wagner would have liked, in part and at times, to reinvent Germany in the images of Nordic mythology, it is said, so his aesthetic/religious ambitions must necessarily have had a political dimension. But this is surely questionable. Wagner was, after all, a Schopenhauerian—and Schopenhauer's separation of aesthetics from politics was uncompromising. Nor is the suggestion, regularly made, that Wagner instead drew encouragement for an aestheticized nationalism from Nietzsche at all compelling: the nearest to a political position of any kind to be found in Nietzsche is an extreme contempt for nationalism in general and for German nationalism in particular. If the link between Wagner's quasi-religious ambitions and a romantic politics is to be made good, then, the evidence for it will have to be drawn from his music dramas; and here it is doubtful that what is needed can be found. Even *Die Meistersinger,* which might at first sight appear to offer the richest pickings, turns out to wear its nationalism lightly; and, to the extent that its politics is an aestheticized politics, it implies nothing more romantic than the musical or dramatic equivalent of a republic of letters. It seems unlikely, then, that Wagner is best to be regarded as a political phenomenon, however much politics may have figured in the reception of him in some quarters. The political is not, in other words, integral to an understanding of Wagner's work in the way that the religious is.

No one who is at all serious about life can remain indifferent to religion. Its claims and demands are unconditional; it abolishes, by fiat, the possibility of remaining neutral. One must be for it or against it; and so, for closely analogous reasons, and to an extent unequaled by any other artist, with Wagner. No one who is at all serious about music can be (or has been) indifferent to him; for the astonishing thing—and this brings us to the fourth of the considerations mentioned at the outset—is that Wagner's art succeeds, to a remarkable degree, in realizing and giving form to the fundamental tenor of his aesthetic. The larger-than-life, mythic quality of the characters and actions of his dramas, the huge and yet somehow hermetically sealed worlds in which they unfold, offer, or appear to offer, totalizing interpretations as complete and unconditional as those of any religion. As for the music, when Wagner demanded that a dramatic work of art should leave "Nothing . . . for the synthesizing intellect to do"—that "we must become *knowers*" of his interpretations "through *feeling*"—he neither overestimated the expressive capacities of his own music nor underestimated the radical power that such capacities might have. For sheer extremism, his is the most expressive music ever written. In its effects—seductive and intoxicating to the admirer, cynical and manipulative to the detractor—its power to polarize is unprecedented. No other artist has inspired worshipful fervor as Wagner has, nor has any artist been so brutally vilified. *Tristan und Isolde* is Wagner at his most Wagnerian. It is, as Michael Tanner has shown, his one fully religious work—not in the sense of having overtly religious subject matter, in which case the religious work would have been *Parsifal* (in fact his least religious work), but in the sense that it pushes so uncompromisingly at the limits of immanence and contingency that the only possible resolution of its dramatic impetus is transcendental—a possibility, moreover, of whose reality Wagner's music more than half persuades one. "Every religion," as Tanner puts it, is "a doctrine of extremes"; and in *Tristan,* "so paralysingly absolute in its demands," that doctrine is "humanism pressed to its limits, then exploded into transcendent metaphysics"—a metaphysics set to and apparently embodied in "music which has a compelling beauty of a kind that none other possesses" (1996). It is this sort of thing that makes neutrality in the face of Wagner a nonoption. Either one is prepared to be seduced by him, to be converted, however briefly, into a (quasi-religious) "knower" through "feeling," or else, because one suspects that this is what Wagner can do, and one refuses him the authority to do it, one must recoil from him and denounce the means through which his effects are attempted.

Yet, neither of these options has proved easy to pursue with any grace. The first, as the young Nietzsche found, degenerates too readily into idolatry: Wagner becomes a shrine at which one offers up one's integrity. The second, on the other hand, tests one's integrity to the limit: it requires that one first acknowledge the power of Wagner's music to do *to oneself* what one refuses it the authority to do—which, as the mature Nietzsche repeatedly discovered, makes the moral high ground almost impossible to identify, let alone to occupy. This, in turn, explains why the rejection of Wagner's own extremism—a rejection that may be attempted in all se-

riousness and good faith—so often, in his less courageous critics, degenerates into those extreme and self-serving modes of denunciation with which we are all familiar, for instance, the perennially popular one of pretending to have discovered traces, or even swaths, of proto-Nazism in his music (something that, music being music, could not be there). It is no accident, in light of this, that Wagner's most penetrating critics—Nietzsche, Thomas Mann—have also been the most ambivalent, perpetually torn between gratitude and revulsion, never settling for long into either. Wagner, like Christianity, puts the critic—indeed, Western culture itself—on the spot, to an extent that no other artist even begins to equal; and it is in this huge and acute sense that he continues to matter for aesthetics. What, as Nietzsche asked, is the *meaning* of Wagner?

[*See also* Music, *historical overview article;* Nietzsche; Opera; *and* Schopenhauer.]

BIBLIOGRAPHY

Work by Wagner

Prose Works. 8 vols. Translated by William Ashton Ellis. London, 1892–1899.

Other Sources

Cooke, Deryck. *I Saw the World End: A Study of Wagner's Ring.* New York and Oxford, 1979.
Dahlhaus, Carl. *Richard Wagner's Music Dramas.* Translated by Mary Whittall. Cambridge and New York, 1979.
Deathridge, John, and Carl Dahlhaus. *The New Grove Wagner.* London, 1984.
Donington, Robert. *Wagner's "Ring" and Its Symbols: The Music and the Myth.* London, 1963.
Kerman, Joseph. "Opera as Symphonic Poem." *Opera as Drama,* new rev. ed., pp. 158–177. London, 1989.
Large, David C., and William Weber, eds. *Wagnerism in European Culture and Politics.* Ithaca, N.Y., 1984.
Mann, Thomas. *Pro and Contra Wagner.* Translated by Allan Blunden. London, 1985.
Muller, Ulrich, and Peter Wapnewski, eds. *Wagner Handbook.* Translation edited by John Deathridge. Cambridge, Mass., 1992.
Nietzsche, Friedrich. *Nietzsche contra Wagner.* In *The Portable Nietzsche,* edited and translated by Walter Kaufmann. New York, 1954.
Nietzsche, Friedrich. *The Case of Wagner.* In *The Birth of Tragedy and the Case of Wagner.* Translated by Walter Kaufmann. New York, 1967.
Schopenhauer, Arthur. *The World as Will and Representation.* 2 vols. Translated by E. F. J. Payne. Reprint, New York, 1966.
Tanner, Michael. "The Total Work of Art." In *The Wagner Companion,* edited by Peter Burbidge and Richard Sutton, pp. 140–224. London, 1979.
Tanner, Michael. *Wagner.* London, 1996.

AARON RIDLEY

WARHOL, ANDY. *See* Pop Art.

WILDE, OSCAR (1854–1900), Irish poet, playwright, and critic. Perhaps the most entertaining aesthetic theorist of all time, Wilde's contribution to the transition between Victorian and modern views of art in society has been consistently underrated—even, as Jorge Luis Borges once observed, by his most ardent defenders, who tend to celebrate his irreverence and wit over the lucidity and insight that bore them out. In the more than a century since his release from prison, Wilde has been championed as a martyr to Victorian morality, as a radical and boisterous minister of an otherwise rather effete aesthetic gospel, and, more recently, as a fountainhead of such postmodern phenomena as queer self-consciousness, identity politics, and commercial self-promotion. Although none of these views is false or useless, they all tend to de-emphasize the intellectual aspect of his achievement in favor of its social and political aspect, and thus do Wilde the same disservice—much as contemporary accounts of his outrageous affectation and brilliantly modulated conversation once tended to obscure his remarkable kindness and generosity. This essay considers Wilde's critical theory on its own terms—that is, those of the main currents of Victorian thinking about art's function in society—and, equally, in terms of his own personal development.

Life. Oscar Fingal O'Flahertie Wills Wilde was born in Dublin in 1854, second son of Sir William Wilde and Lady Jane Francesca. Reared in an atmosphere of high-minded, intellectual bohemianism, Wilde spent three years at Trinity College, Dublin, before going up to Magdalen College, Oxford, in 1874, where he studied with John Ruskin and Walter Pater and distinguished himself as a first-rate classical scholar and flamboyant personality. In 1878, he moved to London, where he published a volume of poems and a verse play, and acquired almost instant celebrity as a wit and apostle of art, often sharing weekly headlines with James McNeill Whistler. In 1882, his fame firmly linked to that of Reginald Bunthorne, the aesthetic caricature in W. S. Gilbert's *Patience* (1881), Wilde embarked on a yearlong lecture tour of the United States, delivering his largely Ruskinian gospel of beauty in everyday life. On his return to England, he married Constance Lloyd in 1884 and had two sons, Cyril and Vyvyan. In 1886, he gave up lecturing in order to pursue a career in letters, writing numerous reviews, occasional pieces, and the fairy tales collected in *The Happy Prince and Other Tales* (1888). Between 1887 and 1889, he edited *The Woman's World,* a popular ladies' magazine, which he revamped to include articles on politics and social issues as well as fashion. In the ensuing years, Wilde wrote his most important works of criticism: "The Portrait of Mr W. H. (1889), "The Soul of Man under Socialism" (1891), and the four essays later published as *Intentions* (1891): "The Decay of Lying," an attack on realism; "Pen, Pencil and Poison," which explores the affinities of art and crime; "The Critic as Artist," the most complete statement of Wilde's critical theory; and "The Truth of Masks," a meditation on Shakespearean stage costume. The year 1891 also

saw the publication of two volumes of Wilde's fiction: *A House of Pomegranates,* a collection of allegorical tales, and *The Picture of Dorian Gray,* the now classic fable of a beautiful young man whose portrait bears the marks of age and debauchery, while he himself retains the innocent beauty that it first depicted. Although its initial notoriety proceeded largely from its distinctly homosexual overtones, the novel is now most fruitfully viewed as a culmination of this critical phase.

It was in the wake of *Dorian Gray*'s controversial reception that Wilde met Lord Alfred Douglas, the love of his life, and the instrument of Wilde's spectacular fall from public grace. During the early 1890s, Wilde found a lucrative market as a popular dramatist. Although *Salomé* (1891), written in French, was banned from the English stage, his series of comedies, *Lady Windermere's Fan* (1891), *A Woman of No Importance* (1892), *An Ideal Husband* (1893), and his masterpiece, *The Importance of Being Earnest* (1894), were all critical and financial successes. The last two were running simultaneously in the West End when the marquess of Queensberry, Douglas's father, delivered the last of a string of public insults with which he had been harassing Wilde for some time. At Douglas's urging, Wilde sued for libel, lost, and was subsequently tried, convicted, and sentenced to two years at hard labor for homosexual practices. In prison he wrote the long, cathartic letter to Douglas published posthumously as *De Profundis* (1905). Shortly after his release, he wrote "The Ballad of Reading Gaol" (1898), his best poem and last completed work. A social and professional pariah, Wilde lived out the remaining years of his life on the Continent under the assumed name of Sebastian Melmoth. He died in Paris, from complications of an ear infection, in 1900.

The Aestheticism of Self. Ian Small (1993) and other critics have argued that Wilde's celebrity as a social figure and the tragic trajectory of his later life have obscured the nature of his work as a critic and theorist. But Wilde's theory of self-cultivation is far too closely bound up with his own career of self-promotion, spectacular rise, and fall to allow for any easy suppression of his biography. Wilde himself famously remarked to André Gide that he had put his genius into his life, and only his talent into his works, and taking this claim seriously does illuminate certain important elements of Wilde's very particular contribution to aesthetic theory. Wilde's genius in life was for producing extreme and quite often opposing effects while sustaining a remarkably unified and consistent persona. In society he combined self-serving dissimulation with a radically satirical honesty. Professionally he advocated an aristocracy of art while devoting his energies to popular and financial success. His intellectual tastes combined the exquisite languors of Charles Baudelaire with the energetic rigors of Ruskin; his morals were equally narcissistic and public-spirited; his ethics were as radically individualistic as Friedrich Nietzsche's or Ralph

Waldo Emerson's, yet more sensitive to the effective operation of conventional norms than either. In personal matters, he was known for his extraordinary kindness and generosity, yet his conduct toward his wife can only be called cruel.

Many original personalities can be said to contradict themselves this way, but Wilde was the only one to claim it as a mode, rather than merely a symptom, of creative genius. "To turn truth into a paradox is not difficult," he once wrote in praising a modern novelist, "but [he] makes all his paradoxes truths, and no Theseus can thread his labyrinth, no Oedipus solve his secret." It was crucial to Wilde's work that he had a secret of his own, which he was always both careful to preserve and eager to flaunt. Richard Ellmann has suggested that Wilde's critical period of productivity was linked to his seduction and initiation into homosexuality by Robert Ross in 1886, and that the illicit, duplicitous existence into which it propelled him provided not only the basis for his fiction but the grounding of his critical thought as well, although it can as easily be said that Wilde's preoccupations with duplicity influenced the conduct of his erotic life. Either way, the public revelation of Wilde's sexuality is clearly central to his importance as a figure of Victorian transition into modernity, not only socially, but intellectually as well. Wilde's eloquent defenses of male love as a cultural inheritance of classical Greece revealed the erotic aspect of a familiar mode of thought and discourse; his defeat and decline underscored the irreconcilability of human experience to simple classifications of moral value. Other figures of the period—Charles Stewart Parnell, for example—had challenged conventional morality, demanding that one aspect of a man's character guarantee forgiveness for another. But Wilde's homosexuality was far more acutely linked to his public persona than any public man's private adulteries could be: rather than demanding forgiveness, it was a revelation that gave everything he had said and done before a new meaning, producing precisely the kind of shift in consciousness that, according to Wilde, it is art's business to effect.

The course of Wilde's life is a remarkable illustration of just those tensions between self and society, conceptual and perceptual experience, that came to define modernist self-consciousness. Wilde was himself a great exponent of modern selfhood, which identifies the individual as existing in opposition to a communal standard, albeit not completely alienated from it. In "The Soul of Man under Socialism," Wilde propounds his view of the artist's perfect freedom to cultivate sensation and experiment with new forms as the ultimate type of personal autonomy. According to his libertarian socialism, the elimination of private property and industrial labor will free everyone, rich and poor, to realize themselves fully in this manner, resulting in an entirely uninhibited culture, in which it will be possible "to express everything," as the artist is able to do. Although Wilde's belief in socialism's commitment to the supreme rights of the individual was sincere, his utopia is more of a platform than a projection. The abolition of authority in a state of perfect socialism is a step toward the abolition of "public opinion," a philistine monstrosity that limits the exercise of artistic temperament. Yet, it is in setting the counterexample for this very public that the artistic temperament is meaningful and empowering, and it is in this essay that Wilde asserts the possibility of good art being able to affect and improve public taste, provided that the artist is free from the need to satisfy public expectation; and he praises a great theatrical producer for having "created in the public both taste and temperament." Art, then, is for Wilde the means by which individual efforts at self-realization can be shared without resorting to the universalizing effects that invariably proceed from the imposition of moral standards or social prejudices.

Art also provides a model for the synthetic, rather than organic, development of the self, which for Wilde was a crucial feature of modern existence. Dorian Gray's identity composes and decomposes itself around a picture and a book, each brought into his life by a different man; Willie Hughes, the notional boy actor on whom the central theory of "The Portrait of Mr. W. H." is based, is literally composed of lines from Shakespeare's sonnets and the frustrated passion of an actor turned critic; in *The Importance of Being Earnest*, Jack Worthing's false identity trades places with his real one when the latter turns out to be the result of a substitution of a person for a work of fiction. The point is not only that the self is grounded in artifice, but that it grows and changes as art does, in the consciousness of other people as well as one's self. Conflicting attitudes toward the public—indifference and confrontation, deception and disclosure—are at the heart of all the phases of Wilde's individualism. In the Preface to *Dorian Gray*, he says that the artist commits himself to "reveal art and conceal the artist," while the critic's work is always "a mode of autobiography"—a species of self-disclosure that emerges from serious engagement with nature of his aesthetic responses. Yet, this engagement is precisely what makes the critic *into* an artist. In *De Profundis*, the source of self-realization has mutated from aesthetic experience to suffering, and takes the despised, redemptive Christ as the figure for the Ultimate Artist. The idea still partakes of the same paradoxical relation between a perfectly universal individualism—toward which Wilde saw all good as tending—and the communal background of social and moral standards against which it must be exercised. That he insists on sustaining this contradictory attitude toward others, rather than attempting either to evade to resolve it, is finally what makes Wilde's individualism more of a personal and practical philosophy than a social or political one.

The Aestheticism of Form. In the figure of the artist/dandy/critic, Wilde found his own method of enacting critical ideas of self-development that might well be (and has been, by Philip Rieff [1970]) called therapeutic, especially considering that Wilde was almost an exact contemporary of Sigmund Freud. But whereas Freud's theory depends on working out a relationship to authority through transference, Wilde's model of self realization presupposes an indifference to any authority save beauty, that interplay between form and feeling by means of which Wilde saw art doing its therapeutic work: "mere expression is a mode of consolation," he says in "The Critic as Artist": "form, which is the birth of passion, is also the death of pain." The birth of passion is also the birth of external, not just internal, experience of self. For Wilde, as Leon Chai puts it, "form belongs to life rather than simply to our perception of it" (1990). The apprehension of form is a means of connecting interior experience to exterior reality.

Both in Wilde's theory and in the course of his own life, the development of the self begins in this attentiveness to form. During his Oxford years, Wilde traveled to Greece with a former Trinity tutor, and returned with a fully "Hellenized" view of civilization and a settled commitment to the creed of beauty that would later qualify him to be representative of the so-called Aesthetic movement. A school of self-presentation as much as of ideas, its doctrine of sensational experiment and artistic detachment—the French dictum "art for art's sake" was its catchphrase—was to be expounded in a languid demeanor and various affectations of "exquisiteness" (long hair, cigarettes, anachronistic dress) as well as in an artistic and critical disdain for realism and a commitment to technique and atmosphere, principles influenced by such French writers as Baudelaire, Théophile Gautier, and Stéphane Mallarmé as well as by the English Pre-Raphaelites, Ruskin, and Pater. As he matured, Wilde's commitment to beauty crystallized into a commitment to individualism, but it maintained its grounding in aesthetic effects. It is precisely this aesthetic conception of self—an identity derived from experience rather than from universal precepts—that Wilde rightly understood to be a crucial aspect of modernity.

One of paradoxical things about Wilde that has confused his critics is that his aesthetic judgments—especially of poetry—often seem to belie his ideology. Wilde had none of the taste for hard, intellectual unprettiness that came to be a hallmark of modernist aesthetics; nevertheless, he recognized the greatness of two of its most important poetic precursors, Walt Whitman and Robert Browning: even as he denigrated the sounds of their poetry, he correctly understood and valued the more general aspect of their respective enterprises as modern artists. Grasping this distinction between deeper and more superficial modes of aesthetic affinity is crucial to understanding Wilde's thinking. For Wilde, form meant style and treatment, rather than structure or genre. It also meant, very importantly, a sense of beauty as a substantial element of experience. A great advocate of what he called "vitality" in art (a word he retained from Ruskin), Wilde despised the naturalism that emphasized quotidian

verisimilitude over the kind of truth that only beauty could make compelling. But although Wilde's resistance to "the morbid and unhealthy faculty of truth-telling" affects a superficially Romantic posture, it derives from a relation between art and life that, quite contrary to the transcendent operation of the sublime, deliberately asserted the limits of both. In an aphoristic couplet from the Preface to *Dorian Gray,* he makes it clear that the relation between beauty and realism, though conflicted, is not a simple opposition:

> The nineteenth-century dislike of Realism is the rage of Caliban seeing his own face in a glass.
> The nineteenth-century dislike of Romanticism is the rage of Caliban not seeing his own face in a glass.

It is Caliban Wilde rebukes here—that is, expectations of art that limit its function *either* to decoration or to description—not the tendencies of Realism or Romanticism, which in this case represent what he called conditions of art.

Much confusion about Wilde's aesthetic doctrine has derived from his association with decadence, that belated mutation of Romantic aestheticism. Although decadence certainly appealed to Wilde's tastes (which were in many respects rather conservative), and indeed he came to represent its precepts to many people, it had far less to do with his aesthetic theory than is generally supposed. According to decadent theory, the artist's detachment from sordid reality was essentially an escape—or at any rate a refuge—from society. For Wilde, the artist's relation to society was, on the contrary, exemplary and dynamic, and most important, vulnerable. All his myths of individuality—with perhaps the exception of his socialist utopia—entail risk: the artist's freedom had nothing to do with privacy, or insulation from the public, but rather freedom from restriction and censorship, which implies public exposure.

The aspect of Wilde's thought most significantly influenced by decadence was the affinity of art with crime that he explores in "Pen, Pencil and Poison" and that, in *Dorian Gray,* was predicated not just on the transgressive nature of artistic experiment but more specifically on the radical disjunction of moral valuation from aesthetic experience. But although Wilde saw the artistic judgment as legitimately deriving only from the latter, he by no means considered the artist himself as unavailable to the former. Wilde was far too steeped in Ruskin to adhere to the outright rejection of middle-class morality espoused by his French colleagues. Rather, he adopted the posture of rejection to serve what was for him the important truth: that there is more to a good society than good morals, that indeed a modern society cannot rely only on ethical or sentimental principles to sustain coherence and growth. He denounced Victorian didacticism not because it accorded works of art too much responsibility for moral behavior, but because it mistook and underestimated the power of aesthetic effectiveness, reducing art's enormous capacity for conveying and modifying individual experience to the schematic representation of social and moral codes. "An ethical sympathy," he wrote, "is an unpardonable mannerism of style."

Wilde's idea of the nature of aesthetic effectiveness is best outlined in "The Decay of Lying," which attacks not didacticism but realism, on the ground that art develops its own forms, which life can only imitate:

> The highest art rejects the burden of the human spirit, and gains more from new medium or a fresh material than she does from any enthusiasm for art, or from any lofty passion, or for any great awakening of the human consciousness. She develops purely on her own lines. She is not symbolic of any age. It is the ages that are her symbols.

When Wilde's argument extends from life to nature, it takes a more clearly phenomenological turn, and gives rise to one of his most famous critical paradoxes: that the brown fogs hovering over London were the invention of Impressionist painters. In glossing this very pointed turn on Ruskin's formulation in "The Nature of Gothic" (i.e., that the vaulted ceilings and archways of Gothic architecture had gradually assimilated the organic forms of trees, rather than the other way around), Wilde then pays homage to the creative susceptibility of Ruskin's eye. "Nature is no great mother who has borne us. She is our creation. It is in our brain that she quickens to life. Things are because we see them, and what we see, and how we see it, depends on the Arts that have influenced us."

The Critic as Artist. At this point, Wilde's agenda begins to emerge: he had shown that the priority of individual method and style over social convention was the expressive basis of modern art, and that the displacement of nature by artifice had become the material basis of modern life. It remained for him to demonstrate the superiority of interpretation over representation or instruction as the intellectual basis of aesthetic response, and so to deliver his version of the function of criticism. The influence of Matthew Arnold becomes important here, not so much in terms of critical method—Wilde was far more indebted in this sense to Ruskin and Pater—but as a benchmark in the critical tradition against which it was necessary for Wilde to define himself. It was Arnold, even more than Ruskin, who had established the scope of critical activity, and set the goal of a society informed and directed by the critic's aesthetic attunement to art.

Although Wilde rejected Arnold's utilitarian model of aesthetic cultivation, as also he outgrew his early Ruskinian socialism, his belief in art's beneficent effects on society remained quite as sincere and urgent as theirs. It is art's capacity to inform general perceptions *through* individual experience that engages Wilde's moral attention, and it is at the crux of his relationship to, and departure from, his precursors. Where Arnold and Ruskin adopted social rationales

for criticism, and Pater avoided its public or social implications, Wilde recognized that criticism was both an aesthetic enterprise that, like works of art, should not be held accountable to moral standards of value, and a communicative medium, whose purpose was to convey a comprehensive experience of beauty.

The concept of "The Critic as Artist" is inspired by Pater, but it is clear that Wilde did not use Pater's own procedure but rather the effects of it as an example of what criticism could be made to do. The difference is subtle but important, for Wilde's thinking was far more attentive to the interplay of personalities—in both art and criticism—than Pater would ever allow his to be. In conflating the activities of producing art and interpreting it, Wilde's critic as artist argues for a dynamic relation between perceptual and conceptual experience that recasts the old Romantic link between reality and imagination. In taking artifice and gesture rather than spirit and motive to be the touchstones of aesthetic experience, Pater had done something like this, but Pater stops short of acknowledging any relationship whatever between individual experience and the realities of common life, whether social or material. For Pater, to contemplate a work of art was to absorb its existence into one's own—and so to be relieved of the Ruskinian responsibility for considering how it has come to be made. Wilde, on the other hand, saw criticism as a kind of recapitulation of the creative process, transferred to another personality. He argued that the critic is the ultimate artist, not because the primacy of his own impressions is unencumbered by the material considerations of technique, but rather because his detachment from the exigencies of technique allows him to comprehend a wider range of material considerations than can the artist himself.

In setting a premium on the dissemination of aesthetic perception, Wilde's theory of the critic as artist owes more to Ruskin than either to Arnold, whose claims to objectivity he entirely inverted, or to Pater, whose impressionism Wilde criticized for being too passive, too disengaged from the production and the consequences of aesthetic effects. Wilde came to see, albeit in different terms from Ruskin, that the disposition to address the process by which aesthetic properties and values are communicated did not derive solely from the capacity to appreciate beauty in existing forms, but also from the impulse—Ruskin would call it duty—to participate actively in the world of persons and things and institutions, and to address them on new terms. Interpretation as Wilde understood it was itself a gesture of imaginative community, both with the artist and with the audience. He saw that the fundamental link between art and activism that Ruskin insisted on could only be effected in a criticism devoted to the mechanisms by which experience of objects informs a subject, and by which subjects in turn create objects of their own. The impressionism that was for Pater a retreat from—or a resistance to—the artist's representative function was for Wilde a means for engaging in and vindicating the same role.

This ability to cope with both the sources and the consequences of aesthetic effects, in which Wilde recognized the key to a truly modern artistry, extended beyond the scope of an individual work of art; it was, indeed, the means by which art could comprehend and leave behind its history. "The development of the critical spirit" will allow us

> to realize not merely our own lives, but the collective lives of the race, and so make us absolutely modern. . . . For he to whom the present is the only thing that is present, knows nothing of the age in which he lives. To realize the nineteenth century, one must realize every century that has preceded it and that has contributed to its making.

Here Wilde's radical individualism finds its balancing force: the critical intellect as an instrument of communication with the past. Wilde's critic thus prefigures T. S. Eliot's individual talent, which inevitably contributes to and alters the totality of the tradition that precedes him.

Critical Fictions. For all his hymns to fantasy in "The Decay of Lying," imagination was for Wilde an essentially interpretive faculty, a matter of selection and emphasis rather than invention or vision. Personality, the force of temperament, was the true essence of artistic activity. It is not surprising, then, that the critical art form for Wilde, the representative medium for his theory, turned out to be not poetry or fiction but drama. Wilde's own plays may appear to be rather conventional, but the role of the drama in his critical work afforded him a very potent model for artistic experience and practice. Where Ruskin found in architecture a totalizing, concrete medium through which nature's genius could be realized, and translated, as it were, into a society, Wilde recognized the ideal conditions for modern artistry in the actor, an individual who realizes—interprets, enacts, and communicates—a supreme fiction. This affinity of criticism and acting is a manifestation of a dramaturgical element in Wilde's thinking that is discernible in his earliest work, and that Edouard Roditi (1947) has recognized in the dialectical grace of Wilde's criticism. Nowhere, however, is it more potent than in his fiction.

The most important example of what might be called Wilde's critical dramaturgy is "The Portrait of Mr. W. H.," a work of criticism in the form of a fiction, in which Wilde sets up a dizzying sequence of personal and rhetorical relationships among his protagonists to frame the critical theory at its center, which is that the dedicatee of Shakespeare's sonnets was a boy actor named Will Hughes, who portrayed the great heroines and inspired the playwright to create his greatest female roles. This theory, derived from purely internal evidence of the sonnets by Cyril Graham, a young man whose genius for acting has been thwarted by Victorian mores and so has turned to literary criticism, is an authentic work of critical art, while the eponymous portrait,

which Graham finally produces to corroborate his theory, is exposed as a forgery. Unable to realize his genius legitimately either on stage or in the world of letters, Graham martyrs himself to his own idea to convince his doubting disciple, the older critic Erskine; the latter in turn forges his own suicidal martyrdom to convince the disillusioned narrator, who has the last equivocal word. In its multiple layers of narration, the story makes explicit the complexity of the link between criticism and acting discussed in "The Critic as Artist." That the critic's coup is the revelation of the unsuspected existence of an actor, and that that revealed actor should be in turn the impetus behind the greatest works of English literature, suggests at once the interdependence of creation and interpretation, and the inevitable pressure of ordinary life that this contingency brings to bear on the life of art.

The mimetic aspect of this pressure is pursued in *The Picture of Dorian Gray*. Here Wilde acknowledges his own mentors in Dorian Gray's relationship to Basil Hallward, the painter whose repressed love for Dorian initially manifests itself in the portrait, and Lord Henry Wotton, the aesthetic-minded critic who persuades Dorian that youth is itself an art and better than anything life can offer. Alone together in the opening sequence, they argue about whether or not the unfinished portrait should be shown, and the substance of their debate forms a subtle counterpoint to the clear echoes of Ruskin and Pater in their rhetoric: Lord Henry, the Paterian voice of self-engrossed aestheticism, unexpectedly argues that art's place in society must preserve a balance between aesthetic and human reality, while Basil, the more righteous and sentimental Ruskinite, turns out to be morbidly obsessed with keeping both his picture and his friend out of sight. In this equivocal fashion, the two men's influence on Dorian culminates finally in Dorian's peculiar, and entirely secret, relation to the portrait itself. The ensuing struggle for moral identity that occurs between the man and the work of art is enlarged by the figure of an actress, whose perfect artistry Dorian worships, but whom he rejects when, having found love, she loses her talent. Sybil Vane's art, the perfect realization of a personality not her own, is a morally purified version of Dorian's own development. Both pay—she with her life, he with his conscience—for their different confusions of art and life, which Wilde cannily arranges to undermine each other.

In light of his essays, it becomes clear that both these fictions were integral to Wilde's critical project. *The Picture of Dorian Gray* is not simply a prurient tale about the dangers of aestheticism, but rather a profound and complex meditation on the relation between the processes by which a self is formed, and those by which a work of art is made. Similarly, "The Portrait of Mr. W. H." is not simply a fanciful theory about Shakespeare prophylactically encased in a fiction, but a very economical presentation of two ideas: one is the difficult concept of persuasiveness in art, which raises questions not only about the conflict between aesthetic and ethical modes of integrity, but about the very possibility of belief; the other is the relation between interpretation and creation, which Wilde rightly understands is based on love. In the displacement of mentors by disciples, each story offers a different version of Wilde's central critical drama, whereby Romantic sincerity is supplanted by a critical self-consciousness, an acknowledgment of the inevitable artifice of every gesture.

But in the autobiographical flavor of his characters' sins, in the allegorical cast of his subjects, and in the tragic structure of his plots, Wilde's fiction also extends his criticism in a direction that his critical essays and dialogues could not go: it allows him to pursue to its fullest implications the fundamental trope of his critical thought: the identification of person with a work of art. Predicated in one way or another on a deception, both works of art in these stories survive their makers and even, in the case of Dorian's portrait—which returns to its original perfection once painter and subject are both dead—the corrupt contingencies of mimetic representation. Each figure—the enduring portrait, the ever-plausible theory—embodies a cluster of relationships between artifact and personality that are not only problematic and interconnected but continuous and unending, and thus perpetually open to fresh response. The life of culture in general is thus implicated in the processes of personal mythmaking engaged in by Dorian Gray and Cyril Graham, and crucially by Wilde himself. What we learn from their tragedies is that the connections between the moral life of the individual and the effectiveness of art cannot be reduced to the formulas either of vulgar sentimentalism or of aestheticized formalism; yet, it may not entirely escape them either, for the vitality of both art and artists depends on their openness to misinterpretation. If art is to express everything, it must risk everything as well.

[*See also* Aestheticism; Gay Aesthetics; Pater; Ruskin; *and* Theater.]

BIBLIOGRAPHY

Works by Wilde

The Artist as Critic: Critical Writings of Oscar Wilde. Edited by Richard Ellmann. New York, 1969; reprint, Chicago, 1982.
Letters of Oscar Wilde. Edited by Rupert Hart-Davis. London, 1962.
The Picture of Dorian Gray (1890, 1891). Edited by Donald Lawler. New York, 1988. Includes both versions.

Other Sources

Chai, Leon. *Aestheticism: The Religion of Art in Post-Romantic Literature.* New York, 1990. Chapter 5, "Art and Life," is on Wilde.
Cohen, Ed. *Talk on the Wilde Side: Toward a Genealogy of a Discourse on Male Sexualities.* New York and London, 1993.
Ellmann, Richard, ed. *Oscar Wilde: A Collection of Critical Essays.* Englewood Cliffs, N.J., 1969. Includes assessments by W. H. Auden, Jorge Luis Borges, Hart Crane, André Gide, James Joyce, Thomas Mann, Walter Pater, G. B. Shaw, and W. B. Yeats.
Ellmann, Richard. *Oscar Wilde.* New York, 1988.
Gagnier, Regenia A. *Idylls of the Marketplace: Oscar Wilde and the Victorian Public.* Stanford, Calif., 1986.
Knox, Melissa. *Oscar Wilde: A Long and Lovely Suicide.* New Haven, 1994.
Powell, Kerry. *Oscar Wilde and the Theatre of the 1890s.* Cambridge and New York, 1990.
Rieff, Philip. "The Impossible Culture: Oscar Wilde and the Charisma of the Artist." *Encounter* 35 (September 1970): 33–44.
Roditi, Edouard. *Oscar Wilde.* (1947) Rev. ed. New York, 1986.
Shewan, Rodney. *Oscar Wilde: Art and Egotism.* London, 1977.
Small, Ian. *Oscar Wilde Revalued.* Greensboro, N.C., 1993.
Woodcock, George. *Oscar Wilde: The Double Image.* Montreal and New York, 1989. Reissue of *The Paradox of Oscar Wilde* (1949).

ELIZABETH HOLLANDER

WILLIAMS, RAYMOND (1921–1988), literary and cultural critic who was one of the founders in the early 1960s of the intellectual movement known as "cultural studies." Williams was born in a Black Mountain village on the Welsh border in 1921, and followed a well-trod path from provincial isolation to upward mobility as a "scholarship boy" at Cambridge during the late 1930s and early 1940s. Between 1946 and 1960, Williams worked as an adult education tutor at Oxford University. The experience of teaching English literature to working-class students, combined with his own Welsh, working-class background, gave Williams an acute awareness of the contingency of ostensibly universal forms of cultural expression. His first book, *Culture and Society, 1780–1950,* was published in 1958 and, along with Richard Hoggart's *The Uses of Literacy* (1957) and Edward Palmer Thompson's *The Making of the English Working Class* (1963), is considered one of the founding texts of the cultural studies movement, and of the British New Left. Williams was professor of drama at the University of Cambridge until his retirement in 1983. His books include *The Long Revolution* (1961), *The Country and the City* (1973), *Keywords* (1976), *Marxism and Literature* (1977), *Politics and Letters* (1979), and *Problems in Materialism and Culture* (1980), among others, as well as several novels.

Williams's work as a cultural critic was influenced by two intellectual traditions. The first was the strain of "practical criticism" associated with the writings of Frank Raymond Leavis and the journal *Scrutiny* during the 1920s and 1930s. Leavis, along with Ivor Armstrong Richards, sought to bring greater rigor to the study of English literature through close attention to the specific aesthetic operations of a given text. This process of "close reading" required, however, that the text be isolated from its social and historical context. Williams embraced Leavis's concern with the material performance of the text, but rejected the social abstraction of practical criticism, developing instead a kind of "left-Leavisite" approach epitomized by his treatment of literary works in *Culture and Society* (Eagleton, 1976, p. 38).

Williams was concerned to relate the mechanisms by which cultural texts such as novels, plays, and films produce meaning for the viewer or reader to historically specific forms of social, economic, and cultural power. In *Culture and Society*, this linkage was based on a relatively organic concept of "culture" as the domain in which underlying social tensions could potentially be resolved. The second important influence in Williams's intellectual development was his gradual rapprochement with Marxist cultural theory, culminating in the publication of *Marxism and Literature* in 1977. Here, concepts such as "feeling," "creativity," "imagination," and the "aesthetic" were related to Williams's analysis of a "hegemonic" culture, based in part on the work of Antonio Gramsci and Louis Althusser.

As a writer, Williams was not, by and large, concerned with philosophical issues, although he did acknowledge the influence of theorists such as Lucien Goldmann and Görgy Lukács, along with Althusser and Gramsci, on his own intellectual development (Williams, 1980). There is little or no direct engagement with the traditions of aesthetic philosophy in his work; no critical exegesis of the writings of Immanuel Kant, Friedrich von Schiller, Francis Hutcheson, or Anthony Ashley Cooper, earl of Shaftesbury; no detailed investigation of the structures of taste or *sensus communis*. Moreover, at no point does Williams offer anything like a systematic philosophical account of his own definition of the aesthetic. Instead, the aesthetic is positioned within a loosely defined collection of terms—*culture, art, structures of feeling, creativity,* and *imagination*—that are at the center of his analysis of modernity. Williams defines the aesthetic pragmatically, through what he perceives to be its cultural effects. In *Keywords*, the aesthetic is described as an "element in the divided modern consciousness of art and society: reference beyond social use and social valuation which . . . is intended to express a human dimension which the dominant version of society appears to exclude" (1976, p. 32). The concept of a "divided" conscious links Williams's discussion of the aesthetic to a process of historical change and contestation that he defines elsewhere in terms of "dominant," "residual," and "emergent" cultural practices (1977, pp. 121–127). Thus, the aesthetic resides either in the past, at some point prior to the "division" of art and society, or in contemporary practices that have been suppressed or marginalized by the dominant social order. Alternately, the aesthetic might be understood here as a primarily symbolic form, the function of which is simply to "refer" to the possibility of a cultural practice that is "beyond social use."

The strength of Williams's approach to cultural analysis lies in his ability to chart the process by which apparently fixed concepts have shifted in meaning over time, through interaction with changes in the structure of social, political, and economic power. The aesthetic is understood not as having some absolute or a priori meaning, but rather, as having undergone a series of semantic transitions since its

original emergence in eighteenth-century German philosophy. This contextual specificity, however, is purchased at the expense of a certain conceptual clarity. At some points in Williams's work, the aesthetic is defined as the expression of an original creative, human impulse. In *Marxism and Literature*, he writes of the "aesthetic response" as "an affirmation . . . of certain human meanings and values which a dominant social system reduced and even tried to exclude" (1977, p. 151). Here, the aesthetic merges into Williams's definitions of "creativity" and "imagination" (it is "directly comparable with . . . creative imagination"). In other cases, Williams defines the aesthetic precisely as the process by which this creative impulse was abstracted from the totality of the human subject. It was the "controlling and categorizing specialization of the aesthetic," he writes, that functioned to reduce the "multiplicity" of writing into reified categories such as "fiction," "history," and biography" (ibid., p. 150). Williams associates this function of the aesthetic, and the consequent shift of focus in the philosophy of art from the intention of the producer to the experience of the viewer or reader, to the emergence in the nineteenth century of a "bourgeois economics" that privileged a model of subjectivity based on consumption (ibid.). The aesthetic is simultaneously a part of the system by which bourgeois culture contains and subdivides the "multiplicity" of writing and of the expressive human subject, and the germinal form of a common human desire to create and transform.

Williams is concerned to point to a transition that is particular to modernity in which an initially whole or integral subject underwent a process of fragmentation. This dynamic is clear in *The Long Revolution* when he writes of the "division" of human activity between "work" and "art," and between "Aesthetic Man" and "Economic Man" (1961, p. 38). As Williams points out, the term *art* first referred to a general skill or craft, but was gradually transformed during the nineteenth century to refer to a privileged form of production, elevated above culture in general. The aesthetic was initially defined in terms of sense perception, but gradually came to signify only those sensations produced by works of art (1977, p. 50). This passage from the general or common to the specific is accompanied by the attribution of a heightened moral value as well (art and the aesthetic are understood as superior and more civilized modes of production and of sense-based knowledge). The confusion in Williams's analysis between the isolation of a preexisting "aesthetic" experience and the "aestheticizing" operations of modernity is thus joined by a slippage among analytic terms such as *art, culture,* and the *aesthetic*. If these terms are not always fully differentiated in Williams's writing, it is in part because of the conceptual force generated by his underlying definition of modernity. This definition rests on a dynamic in which a whole or integral "way of life" is subject to a hierarchical division and segmentation, and on an implicit teleology leading to the eventual reintegration of the divided halves of human culture (Hunter, 1992). Williams is caught between the humanism of his Leavisite origins and the protostructuralism of his later work. As a result, it is not always easy to understand precisely how he might define the "subject" implied by his cultural analysis. Questions that have come to preoccupy cultural theorists concerning the construction of subjectivity or the specific relationship between discursive formations and individual experience or agency are left unresolved.

Despite this conceptual slippage, Williams nevertheless insists on the need to defend the "specificity of the aesthetic" (1977, p. 151). In *Marxism and Literature,* he offers what is perhaps his most nuanced and detailed account of this specificity. He compares the bourgeois commodification of art with the Marxist reduction of the aesthetic to mere epiphenomenal "ideology." Williams cites Lukács's work, specifically his situation of the aesthetic between the "practical" (instrumental) and the "magical" (ideal and unrealizable; the domain of "myth"), as an example of a more sophisticated Marxist cultural analysis. Williams is concerned, however, with the way in which Lukács's analytic system might be applied to the "multiple world of social and cultural processes," a world in which "actual making and reception" cannot simply be reduced to categorical forms (ibid., p. 152). He turns to the work of Jan Mukařovsky for a nonidealist definition of the aesthetic as a "function" or "practice." In *Aesthetic Function, Norm and Value as Social Facts* (1970), Mukařovsky argues that aesthetic value is not inherent in given objects (it is "not a real property of the object"), but rather is a condition that only manifests itself in objects "under certain conditions" (cited in Williams, 1977, p. 153). This contextual and pragmatic reading of the aesthetic clearly complements Williams's own analysis of the arbitrary division between fine art and mass culture. As he writes, art must "by ever more absolute abstraction" suppress and deny the social processes "within which it is contained" (ibid., p. 154). The virtue of Mukařovsky's approach, according to Williams, is that it effectively dismantles the framework of bourgeois aesthetics, thereby exposing the structural "function" of aesthetic value, and clearing the philosophical ground for a more fully developed Marxist aesthetic.

But what remains of a conceptually discrete aesthetic experience in the aftermath of Mukařovsky's demolition? On the one hand, Williams locates the specificity of the aesthetic in its status as the repository of a vaguely defined human essence ("known and pressing elements of human intention and response" that have been "excluded or undervalued" by "dominant elements of human practice") (ibid.). He argues that a "genuine" aesthetic practice can express a "humane response" and "human meanings and values" (ibid., p. 151) by registering a protest against the general instrumentalization and commodification of cultural values in bourgeois society. The aesthetic, like the unconscious, is created by repression. At the same time, Williams wants to replace Mukařovsky's aesthetic "function" with the concept of an aesthetic "situation" that is even more clearly rooted in a specific temporal and spatial context. A given object does not generate a single, unvarying aesthetic meaning, but rather, a "range" of potential meanings that can be made available to specific viewers in specific social situations (ibid., p. 155). Williams's faith in "practice," "variability," "relativity," "materiality," and the ultimately uncategorizable "multiplicity" of "actual" social encounters emerges as the last redoubt of a resistant subjectivity against the rationalizing drive of bourgeois culture.

The semantic shift from "function" to "situation" does not necessarily resolve the problems of immanence or of specificity, however. Thus, Williams contends that "situations" still require "works which are . . . designed to occasion" an aesthetic response (ibid., p. 154). At the same time, he roots the specificity of the aesthetic in a bodily response: the "real experience" of the aesthetic, the "true effects" of writing, "are indeed quite physical," including "specific alterations of physical rhythms, physical organization: experiences of quickening and slowing, of expansion and of intensification" (ibid., p. 156). This mode of experience must be viewed in continuity with other, equally "aesthetic" experiences produced by a "deliberately dividing society," such as "dulling," "lulling," and "chiming" (ibid.). In this view, the aesthetic acts as a site within bourgeois culture at which the status of somatic knowledge can be staged and potentially contested. Williams's analysis thus presents two sets of aesthetic meanings, each of which expresses a particular form of conflict. The aesthetic as somatic experience (the "expansion and intensification" evoked by the work of art) is coupled with an anaesthetic "dulling" and "lulling" (Buck-Morss, 1992). The aesthetic as an expression of (noninstrumental) "human values" is coupled with the aesthetic as an expression of the "categorization and specialization" of bourgeois culture. The dynamic interaction between these two terms—the body and the specific social situation undetermined by a priori conceptual forms—gives Williams's account of the aesthetic a contemporary resonance. The fact that both of these models of aesthetic experience continue to inform current debates and criticism suggests the prescience of his scholarship.

[*See also* Cultural Studies; Gramsci; Lukács; *and* Marxism.]

BIBLIOGRAPHY

Works by Williams

Culture and Society, 1780–1950. London, 1958.

The Long Revolution. London, 1961.

Communications. Harmondsworth, England, 1962; 3d ed., Harmondsworth, England, and New York, 1976.

The Country and the City. London, 1973.

Keywords: A Vocabulary of Culture and Society. London, 1976; rev. exp. ed., London, 1983.

Marxism and Literature. Oxford and New York, 1977.

Problems in Materialism and Culture. London, 1980.

Writing in Society. London, 1983.

Resources of Hope: Culture, Democracy, Socialism. Edited by Robin Gable. London and New York, 1989.

Other Sources

Buck-Morss, Susan. "Aesthetics and Anaesthetics: Walter Benjamin's Artwork Essay Reconsidered." *October* 62 (Fall 1992): 3–41.

Dworkin, Dennis L., and Leslie G. Roman, eds. *Views beyond the Border Country: Raymond Williams and Cultural Politics.* London and New York, 1993.

Eagleton, Terry. *Criticism and Ideology.* London, 1976.

Eagleton, Terry, ed. *Raymond Williams: Critical Perspectives.* Boston, 1989.

Eldridge, John Eric Thomas, and Lizzie Eldridge. *Raymond Williams: Making Connections.* London and New York, 1994.

Frow, John. *Cultural Studies and Cultural Value.* Oxford, 1995.

Gorak, Jan. *The Alien Mind of Raymond Williams.* Columbia, Mo., 1988.

Hunter, Ian. "Aesthetics and Cultural Studies." In *Cultural Studies,* edited, by Lawrence Grossberg, Cary Nelson, and Paula A. Treichler, with Linda Baughman and John Macgregor Wise, pp. 347–367. London and New York, 1992.

Mukařovsky, Jan. *Aesthetic Function, Norm and Value as Social Facts.* Translated by Mark E. Suino. Ann Arbor, 1970.

O'Connor, Alan. *Raymond Williams: Writing, Culture, Politics.* Oxford and New York, 1989.

Pinkney, Tony. *Raymond Williams.* Bridgend, Wales, 1991.

Prendergast, Christopher, ed. *Cultural Materialism: On Raymond Williams.* Minneapolis, 1995.

GRANT KESTER

WINCKELMANN, JOHANN JOACHIM (1717–1768), German archaeologist and art historian. Winckelmann is best known for his *Reflections on the Imitation of Greek Works* (1755) and *History of Ancient Art* (published 1764, though written some years earlier and continually under revision). Celebrated in his own lifetime, he became still more so in cultural retrospect. His place in the development of aesthetics stems largely from that acquired cultural status, namely, as founder of neoclassicism and of systematic art history.

Johann Wolfgang von Goethe hailed Winckelmann as the Columbus of a forgotten land. His picture of an ideal antiquity transformed eighteenth-century taste in the visual arts; the clear outlines of "noble simplicity and quiet grandeur" (*edle Einfalt und stille Grösse*; Winckelmann, 1987, pp. 32–33) influenced John Flaxman in England, Jacques-Louis David in France, and many others. In Germany, Winckelmann had an even larger impact on the literary culture. His humanist norm of *Bildung*—self-cultivation, self-development—shaped an entire scholarly and pedagogical tradition effective well into the twentieth century.

Besides this general significance for cultural history, however, Winckelmann may be said more specifically to have founded art history as a scientific discipline. Although certain aspects of his archaeology were outmoded soon enough, the dominance of Winckelmann's formalist approach may be traced down through Heinrich Wölfflin and Erwin Panofsky. Winckelmann's originality lay not just in his analytic observations of individual works, but also in his shift away from biographical chronicle to conjectures on the system of stylistic forms. More broadly, he went beyond Enlightenment models of political, pragmatic, or "universal" histories to suggest a new, singular conception of history that foreshadowed *Historismus.*

Inspired by Montesquieu, Winckelmann sought to place the arts in geographic, climatic, and above all political perspective. Although later (for prudential reasons) he would play down any republican intent, Winckelmann held that Greek art stemmed from democratic freedom, an idea that found an ideological resonance at the time of the French Revolution. Yet, it is not merely a question of context: Winckelmann casts art in a still more central role, namely, in articulating a particular culture; he thus anticipates the model of "expressive" explanation found in Johann Gottfried von Herder. For Winckelmann, art gave an insight into the "essential" in human society, and supplied the "systematic" angle on history that he thought his special contribution. "I understand the word *history* [*Geschichte*] in the larger sense that it had in the Greek language," he writes, "and my aim is to make an attempt at a system [*eines Lehrgebäudes*]" (1968).

The expressive model displays also a changed attitude to the past: no longer an Enlightenment search for the origins of the present, it sees all cultures as subject to an intrinsic development of growth and decay. "The history of art should teach us its origin, growth, alteration, and fall, together with the various styles of people, periods, and artists, and demonstrate this as far as possible from the remaining works of antiquity" (ibid.). Winckelmann's aim was not to diagnose an overall progress or decline—universal history in Enlightenment fashion—but to show how art (preeminently Greek sculpture) develops of its own accord, passing from schematic rigidity through a "high" style still marked by the older abruptness of outline, then to a "beautiful" phase in which all is gracefully rounded off, before degenerating into imitation and pleasing effects. This fourfold pattern of stylistic development configured the history of art from then on. Ironically—and it is hardly the last of Winckelmann's ironies—the Greek Ideal itself is internally split into "high" (or sublime) and properly "beautiful" moments: a duality repeated in Friedrich von Schiller, Georg Wilhelm Friedrich Hegel, and many others.

Winckelmann was the first to historicize art in a thoroughgoing way. At the same time, that achievement remains ambiguous. As Herder noted, Winckelmann retains a normative primacy for the classical Ideal, for metaphysical Beauty in an almost Platonic sense at odds with any historicizing of art (which would judge each culture in its own terms, whether of context or internal development). Alex Potts suggests that to force such inconsistency on Winckelmann verges on anachronism, and that if he did indeed effect a "paradigm change," it was in the proper Kuhnian sense of shifting discussion to new terrain and a different agenda of problems to solve: how to square history with system, empirical observation with formal distinction, norms of taste (in which Winckelmann strongly believed) with variant circumstance (Potts, 1994, p. 24f.). Such aesthetic problems remain part of the "normal science" of history to this day; Winckelmann was merely their originator. It should be no surprise that divergent traditions such as Weimar classicism, Romantic historism, or Rankean positivism claimed Winckelmann as progenitor.

This procedural resort cannot decide a further ambivalence in Winckelmann, namely, the dialectical chiasmus between history and art; for if Winckelmann *historicized* art, in turn History becomes *aestheticized*—as if it were (in Herder's image) a collection of picture galleries illuminated by the flickering glance of the historian's consciousness. Not only does an aesthetic perspective unify the whole, but it also demands a certain originality in the historian's composing of his account. Hence, the famous set pieces evoking the effect of looking at Laocoön, the Belvedere Apollo, Niobe, and so on: memorably vivid ekphrases in their day as influential as the developmental account in which they were embedded. Further yet, Winckelmann could be regarded as a forerunner of the systematizing of art itself, whereby culture is made in the image of a newly conceptualized "Art": no longer the several "fine arts," but a self-defining normative field. Art no longer appeared under the aegis of the old classicist canon, nor was it merely the object of "cultivated taste." In that sense, Hegel was right to declare (in a passage cited by Walter Pater) that Winckelmann was one of those who had "opened up for the spirit a new organ . . . a new sense for considering art" (Hegel, 1975, p. 63). Hegel notes that this had less influence on the theory of art, though his own account of the "classical Ideal" imitates Winckelmann's *History* verbatim.

If Winckelmann set out to re-create the original, so to speak, a similar dialectic operates in the appeal to "imitation." He writes in the *Reflections:* "The only way for us to become great or, if this be possible, inimitable, is to imitate the ancients" (1987, p. 5). On the face of it, this is more than paradoxical. It figures the Ideal as necessarily absent, value as found only when lost. It is as if Christopher Columbus glimpses his new land of art only (to recall Winckelmann's image at the end of the *History*) in waving tearful farewell to his beloved Greece. Following Jacques Derrida, Michael Fried (1968) calls such doubling of origins "supplemental": it requires a third term—the Renaissance—to give it referential stability, for then retrospective invention is naturalized as cyclical process. That argument could be extended

to the very conception of the Ideal, of a divine yet human beauty: an impossible identity of Idea and corporeal shape that needs adjacent terms such as the high and the derivative style for its postulation. One can more readily speak about imperfection; the fusion of elements in the beautiful style can only be hinted at.

Even Winckelmann's method suggests ambivalence. Having published the *Reflections,* he went on to pen a biting critique under a pseudonym, then rushed to his own philosophical defense. It shows an ironic awareness of conditions of circulation and publicity framing high speculation. Equally, Winckelmann owns up to the conjectural nature of his activity, applying the metaphor of "scaffolding" *(Gerüst)* to his own building practices (1968). Truth and fiction go hand in hand. His appeal to a system linking art and history—akin to a Linnean *systema* (Dilly, 1979, p. 95)—is an empirical construction, testable against the natural world. (Nor, one might add, is this so far from Hegel's understanding of "philosophical" history, beyond pragmatic, particular, or critical modes, but merging epistemological self-awareness with narrative drive; neither thinker is served by charging their constructions with a priori dogmatism.)

A figure caught between eras, Winckelmann today appears more complex than his marmoreal image implies. He is of contemporary interest in at least two further respects, linked to current revision of eighteenth-century studies: gender, and the bourgeois public sphere *(bürgerliche Öffentlichkeit).* First, not only does Winckelmann split the classical Ideal into the sublime and the beautiful, but he genders them in surprising ways. Edmund Burke's association of sublime with male and beauty with female has provoked recent comment. One might compare Winckelmann's suggestion that the "high" Ideal resists and finally overwhelms sensuous embodiment: Potts sees here "an allegory of desire," as if the masculine Idea ravishes the helpless figure of woman. With the beautiful, by contrast—as in Laocoön's graceful disposition of limbs even in agony—Idea and human (now male) body melt into each other: in this centerpiece, Winckelmann's male gaze longs for a masculine form.

The second area of contemporary interest concerns Winckelmann's venture into the public sphere of civil society, with its journals, reviews, prize essays, and institutionalized conversation. Here, it is notable how he fought to escape not just his poor social origins, but also the usual resort to a functionary's life as secretary, librarian, or academic (he refused university offers) in a Prussia he detested. Opting instead to become a private scholar and intellectual, he concerned himself with the artistic composition and most effective circulation of his own work in a nascent public sphere. One might compare the situation of a predecessor, Anne Claude de Tubières, comte de Caylus, in 1740s France: an aristocrat who moved beyond patronage yet was unable finally to secure a public forum for discussion of values (Crow, 1985, pp. 116–17). Winckelmann was more successful, even if much of the "conversation" about his neoclassical Ideal was posthumous. Here, too, one should attend to his social ambitions to be part of and even help form a "cultivated" middle class. In this respect, his own homosexuality, hinted at in his charged descriptions of sculpture, reveals a tension between private and public never successfully resolved in Enlightenment, or indeed later, aesthetics.

[*See also* Art History; Classicism; Herder; *and* Historicism.]

BIBLIOGRAPHY

Works by Winckelmann

Gedanken über die Nachahmung der griechischen Werke in der Malerei und Bildhauerkunst. Dresden, 1755. Translated by Elfriede Heyer and Roger C. Norton as *Reflections on the Imitation of Greek Works in Painting and Sculpture* (La Salle, Ill., 1987).

Geschichte der Kunst des Alterthums. Dresden, 1764; Vienna, 1776. Translation of 1849–1873 edition, as *History of Ancient Art* in 4 vols. (New York, 1968).

Other Sources

Crow, Thomas E. *Painters and Public Life in Eighteenth-Century Paris.* New Haven, 1985.

Dilly, Heinrich. *Kunstgeschichte als Institution: Studien zur Geschichte einer Disziplin.* Frankfurt am Main, 1979.

Fried, Michael. "Antiquity Now: Reading Winckelmann on Imitation," *October* 37 (1986): 87–97.

Goethe, Johann Wolfgang von. "Winckelmann and His Age" (1805). In *Essays on Art and Literature,* edited by John Gearey, translated by Ellen von Nardroff and Ernest H. von Nardroff, pp. 99–121. Princeton, N.J., 1994.

Hegel, Georg Wilhelm Friedrich. *Aesthetics: Lectures on Fine Art.* 2 vols. Translated by T. M. Knox. Oxford, 1975.

Potts, Alex. *Flesh and the Ideal: Winckelmann and the Origins of Art History.* New Haven, 1994.

MARTIN DONOUGHO

WINNICOTT, DONALD WOODS (1896–1971), British pediatrician and psychoanalyst. Noted for his work with children, Winnicott's contribution to aesthetics centers on a developmental theory of culture and on his concept of the "transitional object." His theory of the work of art as cultural object rests on a triadic epistemology: external reality, inner psychic reality, and a "third area" of play and make-believe shared by child and adult (usually the mother). Within that area, the child is inducted into culture. Psychoanalytically considered, the third area is the space within which therapeutic inquiry with children is carried on. It is from observations made during therapy that Winnicott developed his wider theory of art and culture.

In the process of acculturation, the child meets the first "work of art" as a "transitional object"—a blanket, a doll, a teddy bear, or simply a bit of cloth that the child can carry into the space outside the third area. Winnicott observed children in their early forays away from the mother, carrying the transitional object, as if a bit of maternal protection that allows the child to explore beyond the third area and then return to it. Within the third area, aesthetic-artistic events have their initial creation, for there the child plays a role, engages in imitations, responds to maternal teaching as roles are assumed, exchanged, and analyzed, and narratives are made up. Play with objects is often accompanied by explanations and interpretations.

Winnicott develops his theory of the "potential space" or "third area" in several directions. First, he elaborates Jacques Lacan's description of the child's first mirror of self-recognition by moving back to the earliest experience of the child with the mother. What the baby sees when he or she looks at the mother's face ought not be construed as a mirror experience, but rather something like this: what the mother looks like is related to what the mother sees in the baby. The child's feeling that the child exists depends on how the mother sees the child. This interrelational exchange characterizes externalizations in the case of cultural objects. And thus painting, sculpture, and narrative all are "seen" as they themselves *see*.

Second, works of art express and project as they are perceived and interpreted. That which they come to mean is a function of an interchange in which the object sustains itself against the perceiver's unconscious acts of destruction ("The Mirror-Role of Mother and Family in Child Development," in Winnicott, 1989).

Third, learning to use an object—that is, play in the "third area"—thus exhibits a developmental trajectory that leads to adult creation and use of cultural objects. Stages in development are as follows: (1) subject (child) relates to object; (2) child discovers the object is an independent event, not placed by the subject in the world; (3) subject "destroys" the object (in fantasy); (4) object survives "destruction"; and (5) subject can now use object in a creative way, for example, endow it with character, place it in a narrative context, shape it as an expression of the self ("The Use of an Object and Relating through Identifications," in ibid.). This use of the object is the first use of a symbol, for the object becomes the child's "first not-me possession." This symbol "is at the place in space and time where and when the mother is in transition from being . . . merged with the infant and alternatively being experienced as an object to be perceived rather than conceived of" ("The Location of Cultural Experience," in ibid.). In so describing the idea of symbol, Winnicott suggests that there is a psychological precondition that enables human beings to become symbol-using beings. The child comes to realize, through an unconscious process of assimilation, that separation in space and time from the mother can be as well union with the mother, now on a level that needs no actual physicality. Winnicott implies that a psychological-cultural development of this kind leads from this realization to adult aesthetic experience in all its complexity. Winnicott has grounded symbolism on a stage in the process of play.

Fourth, Winnicott now relates the early stages of cultural development to the adult whose objects are works of art, religion, and philosophy:

> The task of reality-acceptance is never completed; no human being is free from the strain of relating inner and outer reality, and relief from this strain is provided by an intermediate area of experience [art, religion, philosophy], . . . which is in direct continuity with the play area of the small child who is "lost" in play.
> ("Transitional Objects and Transitional Phenomena," in ibid.)

Winnicott's developmental theory has wide application to both the content of works of art and the process of perceiving-interpreting works of art. Aesthetic theory calls for a psychology of cultural objects that explains how humans become cultural beings that use and respond to material, tonal, and linguistic objects endowed with historical powers. Artists themselves often represent this process to which Winnicott has given a psychoanalytic explanation. The work of art as "transitional object" relating perceiver to tradition is the subject of paintings by Nicolas Poussin, Dominique Ingres, and Gustave Courbet; literary works by Virgil, Dante, and Giovanni Boccaccio in classical and Renaissance tradition, and T. S. Eliot, Wallace Stevens, and W. H. Auden in modern poetry; and the music of Maurice Ravel, Gustav Mahler, George Crumb. For examples, see bibliography.

[*See also* Freud; *and* Psychology of Art.]

BIBLIOGRAPHY

Work by Winnicott

Playing and Reality. London, 1971; reprint, London and New York, 1989.

Other Sources

Carrier, David. *Poussin's Paintings: A Study in Art-Historical Methodology.* University Park, Pa., 1993.
Kuhns, Richard. *Psychoanalytic Theory of Art: A Philosophy of Art on Developmental Principles.* New York, 1983.
Spitz, Ellen Handler. *Image and Insight: Essays in Psychoanalysis and the Arts.* New York, 1991.
Wollheim, Richard. *Painting as an Art.* Princeton, N.J., 1987.

RICHARD KUHNS

WITTGENSTEIN, LUDWIG JOSEF JOHANN.

[*To explore the importance of Wittgenstein's thought for aesthetics, this entry comprises three essays:*

> Survey of Thought
> Reception of Wittgenstein
> Wittgenstein and Literary Theory

The first essay is a survey of Wittgenstein's thought as a background for his views on aesthetics. The second essay explains how he influenced aesthetic theory in the second half of the twentieth century. The third essay discusses recent literary theory that has been inspired by Wittgensteinian philosophy. For related discussion, see Cavell; Conceptual Art; and Essentialism.]

Survey of Thought

The Austrian philosopher Ludwig Wittgenstein (1889–1951) was born in Vienna, the youngest of eight children. His father was one of the wealthiest men in the Austro-Hungarian Empire, and his mother was highly cultured and made the house a center of musical culture—Joseph Joachim, Johannes Brahms, and Gustav Mahler were frequent visitors. His brother Paul was a well-known concert pianist, while Wittgenstein himself had considerable musical talent. Engineering studies brought him to Manchester in 1908 and led to an interest in mathematics and then, through reading Bertrand Russell's *The Principles of Mathematics,* to the philosophy of mathematics. In 1911, he went to Cambridge to study with Russell and there began work on what was to be the *Tractatus Logico-Philosophicus.*

Despite physical disabilities and family connections, he enlisted as a common soldier when World War I began. He eventually became an officer and sought the most dangerous assignments. He had the manuscript of the *Tractatus* in his knapsack when taken prisoner by the Italians in 1918.

The conclusion of the *Tractatus* was that everything that philosophy tried to say was senseless and could not be said. Wittgenstein's intellectual honesty led him to abandon philosophy and he became a schoolteacher in rural areas of Austria. This experience ended unfortunately and for a while he worked as a gardener in a monastery and even considered becoming a monk. During this period, he designed and supervised the construction of a house for his sister in Vienna. Conversations with friends and other philosophers, however, led him to realize that the *Tractatus* had not disposed of all philosophical problems and in 1929 he returned to Cambridge and took his doctoral degree, submitting the *Tractatus* as his dissertation. He then began to lecture at Cambridge and to develop the thought that would eventuate in the *Philosophical Investigations,* published posthumously in 1953. In 1939, he was appointed to the chair of philosophy that George Edward Moore had resigned, but during the war he took leave to do volunteer war work. Although he lectured again after the war, he resigned his chair in 1947. He died of cancer in 1951.

Wittgenstein never produced systematic or extended writings in aesthetics, but it is clear that, along with ethics, aesthetics was a lifelong concern. In 1949, he remarked that although he found scientific questions interesting, it was only conceptual and aesthetic questions that really gripped him; he said he could be indifferent to the solution of a scientific problem, but not the other sort. Wittgenstein regarded art, especially music, with passionate intensity and said that it was impossible for him to say how much music had meant to him throughout his life. This concern is part of the background against which his philosophical work must be understood.

The *Tractatus* makes a distinction between the world as the totality of facts, those things that can be said (i.e., described and talked about), and those things that cannot be said, but can only be shown. The latter include ethics, aesthetics, and religion as well as the relation between language and the world it describes. Wittgenstein called all this, perhaps misleadingly, "the mystical." Any attempt to talk about these topics results only in nonsense. The significance of this was misunderstood by the logical positivists, who were much taken with Wittgenstein's work in logic and language. If it is nonsense and "mystical," they thought, then it must be dismissed as of no importance. Wittgenstein's mysticism, however, is not the usual one, but signals a view of the world as a "limited whole" in which ethics and aesthetics are seen as standing outside the world of facts and marking the only things that are of vital human importance.

In the *Notebooks, 1914–1916*, from which much of the *Tractatus* material was drawn, he described art as a kind of expression and said that ethics is the world seen under the aspect of eternity, whereas a work of art is an object seen under the aspect of eternity. The only reference to aesthetics in the *Tractatus* is the statement that ethics and aesthetics are one. These remarks are enigmatic, but are probably best glossed as follows: value is not a fact in the world, but is the result of the way in which one sees the world. One's moral stance to the world is shown in the character seen in the world and that character may be one's own for, he says, the world of the happy man is different from that of the unhappy man. Aesthetics, on the other hand, presents us with a view of a particular object. In 1930, he said that a work of art forces us to see an object in the right perspective, that is, as the artist saw it.

Wittgenstein never abandoned the saying/showing distinction that was the central thesis of the *Tractatus*, although it underwent important changes. In the *Tractatus*, the distinction is puzzling and, for many, obfuscating, which is not surprising because that work is a thoroughgoing piece of metaphysics. The philosophical practice of his later work in the *Philosophical Investigations* is intended to clear away the confusions of metaphysics, with the result that one can find there the wherewithal to make clear sense of the distinction.

In 1936, Wittgenstein spoke of the odd resemblance between a philosophical investigation and an aesthetic one. One clue to understanding the resemblance is found in Moore's report of the 1930–1933 lectures, in which Wittgenstein said that what aesthetics does is to give reasons why, for example, this word rather than some other is used in the poem or this musical phrase in the composition. This is done by drawing attention to the work and placing works side by side. To understand a particular work of art,

to understand what the artist is doing, the work must be seen alongside other of the artist's works, and even perhaps alongside that of other artists. In this way, attention is directed to the larger context of artistic endeavor with all its history, conventions, and practices that alone make the work intelligible. This is consistent with the remark in the *Lectures and Conversations on Aesthetics, Psychology and Religious Belief* that expressions of aesthetic judgments play a complicated role in the culture of a period, and to describe them the culture must be described. A description of the culture shows the role of these expressions.

A philosophical investigation also puts things side by side. Philosophical problems arise, Wittgenstein says, when language goes on holiday, that is, when words are taken out of any context in which they have a role to play. Wittgenstein's practice is to bring words back from their metaphysical to their everyday use by reminding us of their actual uses and by describing particular cases and situations in which words have a function and engage with life. These cases can then be put alongside the claims of philosophical theories so that we can see when work is being done and sense is being made and when it is not. Traditional philosophical arguments play little role in Wittgenstein's work; his procedure is to show language at work.

The aim of an aesthetic investigation is to realize the meaning and the value of a work of art for oneself and to change the way a painting is seen, a piece of music is heard, or a poem is read. Similarly, the aim of a philosophical investigation is to realize for oneself when language has gone on holiday and thus to bring us back to engagement with the world and with human affairs so that things are seen properly. In neither case is it of any avail simply to be told what is or what is not important, valuable, or intelligible. Both kinds of investigations aim at changing one's perspective.

In the *Lectures and Conversations*, Wittgenstein insists that the kind of reason and explanation that we seek in aesthetics is not causal and has nothing to do with psychology. He talks about aesthetic taste and appreciation with respect to such activities as selecting clothing, but says that we do not appreciate the tremendous things in art, that is, our reactions to great art are very different from our reactions to a well-cut suit.

In the *Philosophical Investigations*, Wittgenstein stressed the importance of language as an activity grounded in human life by constructing an analogy between language and games and spoke of the different uses of language as language games. He claimed that there was no essence of language, no factor common to all its multiple uses. To illustrate this, he pointed out that there is no essence of games, that is, no feature common to all games by virtue of which they are games. There are, however, characteristic and overlapping features that he described as family resemblances. He insisted that we "look and see" whether there are common features instead of assuming that there must be if the word *game* is to have a clear meaning. In the 1950s, philosophers such as Morris Weitz and William Kennick saw implications in this for attempts to construct theoretical definitions of "art" and argued that such attempts are fruitless because there is no factor common to all works of art and that, instead, "art" should be considered a "family-resemblance" concept.

Thus, it came to be thought that a Wittgensteinian aesthetics must be "antiessentialist." Although Wittgenstein did not discuss the notion of art in this way, his methods should suggest that there is no intelligible formulation of what could constitute the essence of art, of what could count as a common factor, and therefore he is neither an essentialist nor an antiessentialist. The question of whether there is an essence of art should be dismissed. The concentration on definition and theory makes it appear that the major concern is with identifying something as a work of art when the concern should be with the point of calling something art and with the way one engages with the work and reacts to it. The matter of engagement has important implications for our dealings with the avant-garde.

There are other issues relevant for aesthetics in the *Philosophical Investigations* of equal or greater importance than the matter of definition. Aesthetic appreciation and understanding are in large part a matter of how things are seen or heard. In part 2, section 11 of the *Philosophical Investigations,* there is an extended discussion of seeing that makes clear that there are a number of interrelated conceptions of perception and that many different kinds of things can count as objects of sight. Although much attention has been directed to the ambiguous duck-rabbit figure that can be seen either as a duck or as a rabbit, that curious creature serves only to introduce a whole series of different concepts of perception. The section begins with the notion of seeing likenesses and moves to seeing aspects and patterns of organization and investigates the relations between seeing, thinking, and interpreting and then modulates to the phenomenon of experiencing the meaning of a word. This, in turn, leads to the introduction of the idea of words having secondary senses.

This material has very important implications for understanding a number of issues that have puzzled philosophers—for example, the perception of design and composition in a work of art, the aesthetic character of language, and the use of expressions borrowed from other areas of human experience to describe works of art when those expressions do not appear to have any "literal" application to art (e.g., the ascription of emotional character to works of art).

Wittgenstein understands these questions to be conceptual or "grammatical" in nature. They are not psychological or in any way empirical. The problems arise because there is something about language that is misunderstood. The prob-

lem is to be dissolved by getting a better view of the actual workings of the relevant language. The implication for aesthetics is that these questions about aesthetic experience and aesthetic perception can be resolved without recourse to theories, whether of psychological processes or the ontology of "aesthetic objects."

Wittgenstein shared with twentieth-century analytic philosophy the view that philosophical problems are at bottom a matter of language, but he was not concerned, as analytic aesthetics has been, to construct theories of art or to map the logic of aesthetic concepts. His concern was always with the human importance of art and with those intellectual tendencies to misunderstand what is before our eyes that lead us to darken counsel by philosophical theory.

Although the *Philosophical Investigations* contains a number of insightful remarks and asides concerning aesthetics, aesthetics is not directly a major concern. The book's greatest importance is the view that it gives of the nature of philosophical problems and the techniques it teaches for resolving those problems. It is left to us to apply all that to aesthetics and the philosophy of art.

BIBLIOGRAPHY

Works by Wittgenstein

Tractatus Logico-Philosophicus. Translated by C. K. Ogden. London, 1922. Also translated by D. F. Pears and B. F. McGuinness (London, 1961).
Philosophical Investigations (1953). 3d ed. Translated by G. E. M. Anscombe. New York, 1968.
Notebooks, 1914–1916. Edited by G. H. von Wright and G. E. M. Anscombe. New York, 1961; 2d ed., Chicago, 1979.
Lectures and Conversations on Aesthetics, Psychology, and Religious Belief. Edited by Cyril Barrett. Berkeley, 1967. The material on aesthetics is from 1938.
Culture and Value. Edited by G. H. von Wright and translated by Peter Winch. Chicago, 1980. Material from 1914–1951.

Other Sources

Cavell, Stanley. *Must We Mean What We Say?* (1969). Cambridge and New York, 1976.
Elton, William, ed. *Aesthetics and Language.* Oxford, 1954.
Evans, Martyn. *Listening to Music.* Houndmills, 1990.
Haller, Rudolf, ed. *Aesthetics: Proceedings of the 8th International Wittgenstein Symposium.* Vienna, 1984.
Janik, Allan, and Stephen Toulmin. *Wittgenstein's Vienna.* New York, 1973.
Johannessen, Kjell S., and Tore Nordenstam, eds. *Wittgenstein: Ästhetik und transzendentale philosophie.* Vienna, 1981.
Kennick, William E. "Does Traditional Aesthetics Rest on a Mistake?" *Mind* 67.3 (July 1958): 317–334.
Mandelbaum, Maurice. "Family Resemblances and Generalization concerning the Arts." *American Philosophical Quarterly* (1965).
McGuinness, Brian. *Wittgenstein: A Life: Young Ludwig, 1889–1921.* Berkeley, 1988.
Monk, Ray. *Ludwig Wittgenstein: The Duty of Genius.* New York, 1990.
Moore, George Edward. "Wittgenstein's Lectures, 1930–1933." In *Philosophical Papers,* pp. 252–324. London, 1959.
Tilghman, B. R. *But Is It Art? The Value of Art and the Temptation of Theory.* Oxford and New York, 1984.

Tilghman, B. R. *Wittgenstein, Ethics and Aesthetics: The View from Eternity.* Houndmills, 1992.

Weitz, Morris. "The Role of Theory in Aesthetics." *Journal of Aesthetics and Art Criticism* 15.1 (September 1956): 27–35.

Wijdeveld, Paul. *Ludwig Wittgenstein, Architect.* Cambridge, Mass., 1994.

BENJAMIN R. TILGHMAN

Reception of Wittgenstein

It is remarkable that the writings of Ludwig Wittgenstein have exerted a great influence on aesthetics and the philosophy of art, because Wittgenstein actually wrote very little directly on the philosophical issues that arise in connection with the arts. But since the publication of the *Philosophical Investigations* in 1953, philosophers of art have found many of Wittgenstein's fundamental contributions to the philosophy of language and the philosophy of mind to hold significance for aesthetic questions, and like the impact his work made on the areas of language and mind, the aesthetic significance was regarded as revolutionary. Rather than accepting without question the problems that aestheticians traditionally faced and then proceeding to the development and elucidation of theories designed to answer those questions, Wittgenstein provided an avenue of escape from, or a new method for treating, those classic questions. Central among them were the essentialist questions of definition: "What essential properties must an object possess to qualify as a work of art?" and "What quality or property do all works of art have in common?" Wittgenstein's famous contribution to the problem of universals, the question asking why all members of a class are placed in that class (e.g., objects of knowledge, truth, beauty, justice, and art), was revolutionary in that it undercut rather than answered the question of universals. Wittgenstein's new proposal proceeded in terms of "family resemblance," but the great impact of this proposal led to the consensus that the significance that Wittgenstein's philosophical writings held for aesthetics could be summed up in antiessentialist terms. This is in fact untrue. Further topics include the often-hidden influences of language on our conceptions of artistic meaning; the complex interrelations among words, music, pictures, and gestures; the analogy between the arts and what Wittgenstein antireductively refers to as a "form of life"; the clarification of the ways in which art can embody thought; relations between philosophical conceptions of the self and conceptions of artworks; the role of the imagination in aesthetic perception; many complex interrelations between texts and contexts; nuances of self-revelation and autobiographical disclosure in literature; the relations between literary-interpretive and philosophical undertakings; the "logic" of criticism and the nature of critical reasoning and justification; and the separation of empirical and conceptual methods in aesthetics. There are also authors now reading

Wittgenstein as a philosopher of culture, extracting from his writings new understanding of how a tradition is transmitted, how to evaluate and diagnose the ailments of a culture, how to better see the relation between Wittgenstein's work and his own time, and how to see in the *Philosophical Investigations* a subtle—and unsettling—depiction of our own times. There is much greater aesthetic and cultural illumination to be had from Wittgenstein's philosophy than the antiessentialist consensus would begin to suggest.

The writings discussed here divide into five broadly defined areas. The first concerns the relations between the arts and the philosophy of language; issues and strategies from Wittgenstein's multifaceted investigations into language are transplanted into aesthetic contexts. Under this heading, Rush Rhees (1969) has inquired into the very possibility of an artwork's *character;* this naturally led him into an investigation of the relations between judgments of persons and works of art. Following Wittgenstein's observation that "we learn logic as we learn to speak," he suggests that we learn the concept of art and—broadly speaking—art criticism as we learn to speak, and that such concepts are embedded in our linguistic practices. Rhees also opened the discussion of Wittgenstein's remarks on the meaning of ritual in his comments on James Frazer's *The Golden Bough,* a topic that resurfaces throughout the multifarious writings on Wittgenstein, aesthetics, and cultural understanding.

Beginning with Wittgenstein's replacement of problem-solution with problem-dissolution, Carolyn Korsmeyer moved beyond the definitional question in aesthetics to the ontological question, asking "What do aesthetic adjectives modify?"—particularly, how do critical descriptions such as "mysterious," "eerie," "corrosive," "pompous," "stately," and similar aesthetic predicates reside in (if they do) the physical objects we regard as artworks? Korsmeyer brings into play the concept of gesture as an illuminating way of understanding the relation between aesthetic predicates and physical objects. Yet, to speak of relations here is dangerously misleading because "a major part of understanding a poem or other work of art is 'seeing' the expression it embodies, although the expression is nothing different from the work itself, just as an expression of sadness is not a face plus sadness, but a sad face" (Korsmeyer, 1978). Aesthetic predicates are "verbal equivalences" to the "gesture" made by the expressive work, and thus artistic meaning is not—consistent with Wittgenstein's groundbreaking work within the philosophy of language—to be understood as a mental shadow or hidden intention only contingently attached to its outward expression.

Furthering the use of the concept of gesture in its connection with linguistic meaning, Karlheinz Lüdeking observed that whenever Wittgenstein "considers art, he shows a remarkable tendency to compare it to the gestures of the human body" (1990), and he uncovered the aesthetic significance of a claim that is central to Wittgenstein's mature thought, namely, that language is invariably viewed as having roots in concrete practices rather than as an abstract calculus. Indeed, gestures, like works of art, are understood only "when one is familiar with their role in a form of life," and it is by looking into some human gestures as depicted in painting that Lüdeking uncovers valuable connections between Wittgenstein's gestural conception of linguistic meaning and the perception of expressive properties in art.

Showing that references to musical experience appear throughout Wittgenstein's writings and that these are primarily used to explore logical and linguistic matters, P. B. Lewis (1977) examined the parallel that Wittgenstein draws between understanding a sentence and understanding music. But whereas Wittgenstein usually employs this parallel to cast light on linguistic understanding, Lewis reverses the direction and investigates how Wittgenstein conceives of the understanding of a musical theme. Not surprisingly, relations to understanding persons, and particularly to understanding facial expressions, enter into the discussion; these topics too have become major themes in Wittgensteinian aesthetics.

The phrase "a form of life" appears throughout Wittgensteinian aesthetics, referring to the "complex of habits, experiences, skills, with which language interlocks in that it could not be operated without them and, equally, they cannot be identified without reference to it," as Richard Wollheim captures the meaning of Wittgenstein's phrase (1980). Wollheim shows why it would be wrong to attempt—as many aesthetic theorists have done and continue to do—to locate the artistic impulse or intention apart from and prior to the institutions and practices of art. He offers a diagnostic analysis of the erroneous presumption that the expressive content of a work of art can always be propositionally expressed apart from the expressive artwork itself. Wollheim uncovers some of the subtleties, and the often-veiled power to direct subsequent thinking, of the larger or more general analogy between language and art. Answers to questions concerning art-language analogies, as Wollheim's writing shows, are anything but simple and unitary.

Yet, it may still be the case that the language we use in aesthetic or critical contexts can be characterized generally, and B. R. Tilghman has offered such a characterization in terms of the secondary senses of words, a conception of linguistic meaning found in the latter sections of the *Philosophical Investigations*. Tilghman finds much significance for aesthetics in some of Wittgenstein's remarks on experiencing the meaning of a word, on the "soul" of a word, and on "understanding a sentence in the sense in which it can be replaced by another which says the same, but also in the sense in which it cannot be replaced by any other." Tilghman also investigates the autonomy of language games, a topic discussed at length by others mentioned later in this essay.

The second broad area into which Wittgenstein's writings relevant to aesthetics can be divided concerns the relations between aesthetics and the philosophy of mind, and the work here undertaken has particularly cast light on the significance that Wittgenstein's work holds for our understanding of artistic creation and perception. Roger Shiner (1982) has shown the philosophically pernicious effects of holding a Cartesian or dualistic (i.e., mind and body) conception of the self for our understanding of meaning, and he too turns to the significance of gesture in sorting out the relations between expressive content in art and in human behavior. He also shows why, once dualism is seen to lead us into conceptual confusion when contemplating artistic expression, we should avoid reaching for the polemical alternative to dualism, a monistic or reductive behaviorism. To insist on the distinction between a person and that person's expressive behavior is to lay the groundwork for the analogous distinction between a tangible art object and its intangible expressive properties, and that is to remain locked inside the dualistic categories from which Wittgenstein's work, as Shiner shows, releases us.

Wittgenstein's philosophy of mind has much to say about the nature of the self. But it also has much to say about perception, and Malcolm Budd (1989) has focused on the central topic of aspect perception. We do on occasion see an object (or a much-discussed ambiguous line drawing that can be seen as a duck or as a rabbit) and, while seeing it, know that although it has not changed, the way we see it does change. In what does this change consist, and what does it tell (or show) us about the role the imagination plays in perception? As Budd says, Wittgenstein returned to this kind of perceptual-imaginative phenomenon (actually, phenomena—he shows that they are not all alike) time and again in his writings on the philosophy of psychology, and these writings have exerted considerable influence in philosophical aesthetics. Budd's work, extending into aspect shifts, aspects of organization, the relations between sensational and representational properties in visual experience, and—most fundamentally—the role of imagination in visual interpretation, is primarily about the philosophy of mind, but his close examination of Wittgenstein's remarks hold great significance for aesthetics.

Some, notably T. E. Wilkerson, have argued that "interpreting pictures is a special case of seeing aspects" (1991), and Wilkerson has identified five features of aspect perception: it is typically detached from belief; it is subject to the will; noticing a change of aspect is akin to the experience of a sudden dawning of understanding; in seeing a Y-aspect in S, we focus attention on a resemblance between X and Y (e.g., in seeing a landscape in cracked plaster we focus on the resemblance between the contour of the plaster lines and the contour of landscape depiction); and, most important, aspect seeing is an exercise of the imagination. One can see how these features are immediately relevant to fundamental aesthetic questions, and Wilkerson goes on to show how the explanation of pictorial representation in terms of aspect perception does not rely too heavily on resemblances between picture and object, yet it preserves a place for it.

R. K. Elliott (1973) has also explored imagination, but he has taken the discussion in a somewhat different direction. Noting the density of significance in Wittgenstein's remark that when a printed triangle is seen as a mountain "it is as if an image came into contact, and for a time remained in contact, with the visual impression," Elliott focuses his concern on "types of imaginal experience in which the image which seems to come into contact with what is perceived is an image of something which is *not* depicted or described in the work, but which nevertheless achieves a certain strength of presence" (1973), and conducts a Wittgensteinian investigation into the roles imagination plays in aesthetic perception. Just as Wilkerson secures a carefully described place for resemblance (through the use of Wittgenstein's analysis of aspect perception) in an account of pictorial representation, so Elliott secures a carefully nuanced place for imaginal experience in aesthetic perception, showing how a misbegotten aesthetic objectivism—a position holding that a true and verifiable perception of an artwork would derive only from a direct perception of its intrinsic properties—would severely mischaracterize and impoverish genuine aesthetic experience.

A third major area of research in Wittgensteinian aesthetics is devoted to the relations between philosophy and literature, but because the subject is addressed in the following essay, the reader is referred here to works listed in the bibliography.

G. E. Moore's record of Wittgenstein's lectures in 1930–1933 has proven a valuable resource for those working in a fourth area, the philosophy of criticism. Moore writes: "He introduced his whole discussion of aesthetics by dealing with one problem about the meaning of words" (1972), and then follows this with a discussion of Wittgenstein's remarks on the word *game* and its application to the word *beautiful*. Richard Shusterman opens an essay on the Wittgensteinian sense of critical reasoning by referring to these lectures, and identifies three central themes of Wittgensteinian aesthetics: (1) the "radical indeterminacy of aesthetic concepts" (illustrated by the concept "game") but applied to genre concepts (tragedy, comedy, epic, etc.), to period concepts (Gothic, Baroque, Cubist, etc.), to the very concept of art itself, and to specific critical concepts (vivid, delicate, unified, elegant, etc.); (2) "the logical plurality of critical discourse," involving both the logical variety of critical statements and the critical plurality of critical frameworks; and (3) the "cultural historicity of art and art appreciation" (1986). But by returning to those lectures, and by proceeding to an examination of the rhetorically persuasive rather than strictly inductive or deductive nature of critical argumentation, Shusterman cautions that a *theory* of criticism built on these foundations "seems inconsistent with the very doctrines that engendered

it" (ibid.), and that if we are insufficiently mindful of the plurality of critical "language games"—indeed, a *family* of critical games—we may well ironically fall victim to the very conceptual dangers of which Wittgenstein's philosophy is designed to warn us.

Theory construction, or building, is anything but Wittgenstein's motivation, and Kjell S. Johannessen (1990) opens his study with an epigraph from Wittgenstein: "I am not interested in constructing a building so much as in having a perspicuous view of the foundations of possible buildings." And he employs a particularly resonant passage from Wittgenstein, that there is a "queer resemblance between a philosophical investigation . . . and an aesthetic one." Johannessen turns our attention to various critical activities and to how we actually get rid of aesthetic puzzlement; these show the kinds of things Wittgenstein had in mind by "aesthetic investigation."

Beginning with a discussion of some of Wittgenstein's observations on inexpressibility in aesthetics and the analogy between aesthetics and ethics, Joachim Schulte (1989) considers nuances of the expressibility and inexpressibility of the content communicated by works of art, thus implicitly furthering the discussion of intransitivity and explicitly furthering the discussion of the nature of criticism. Like other authors, Schulte integrates remarks from Moore's record of Wittgenstein's lectures, and he further advances the investigation into the delicate role of subjective judgment and personal taste within Wittgensteinian aesthetics. A central theme of Wittgenstein's philosophy of language and his philosophy of mathematics enters in here, specifically that of rule following in connection with the perception of aesthetic correctness. But Schulte shows that, indeed, rule following in artistic contexts does not reduce to one single mental phenomenon, nor do the experiences of noticing unusual aspects or particular features of works where those experiences play roles in our critical language specifically as they pertain to aesthetic rightness. Frank Cioffi (1984) has pursued these topics in detail, asking particularly when and why empirical methods bypass questions of aesthetic meaning and significance. Cioffi reminds us that Wittgenstein criticized Frazer for having launched an investigation into the origins of ritual, and Sigmund Freud for having responded to dreams by searching for causal relations between dreams and other aspects of our experience. These doubts concerning empirical explanation, extending, as Cioffi observes, well beyond Wittgensteinian exegesis, give rise to this problem:

> There are questions which present themselves as empirical, i.e. such that they require further information for their resolution, but with respect to which we are told, or come to feel obscurely for ourselves, that this is an illusion, that the consummation we are seeking is not to be found in more empirical knowledge, or via scientific explanation, but elsewhere and otherwise. What is the character of this "elsewhere and otherwise"?   (Cioffi, 1984)

In answering, Cioffi identifies errors (e.g., the conceptual model of dualism, taking causal explanation for all explanation, the mimicking of science) that Wittgenstein was opposing in his remarks on aesthetics. In sorting out these errors and in elucidating their significance for aesthetics, Cioffi relies on a quotation from an author who exerted a profound influence on Wittgenstein's thought, Heinrich Herz in *Principles of Mechanics:* "When these painful contradictions are removed, the question as to the nature of the force will not have been answered; but our minds, no longer vexed, will cease to ask illegitimate questions." This brings to the fore the replacement of problem-solution by problem-dissolution in Wittgenstein's philosophy, an idea also central to Wittgensteinian aesthetics.

The dissipation of perplexity is thus a fundamental aim of Wittgenstein's philosophical methods, and Richard Eldridge (1987) has provided an overview of these methods as they have influenced aesthetics since the publication of the *Philosophical Investigations;* he particularly sets the rooting of aesthetic and artistic concepts in human practices against the misleading influences of Cartesian dualism and definitional essentialism, and considers the possibility of a Wittgensteinian phenomenology of art. For this, he refers to the ideas of Immanuel Kant, particularly concerning the capacity of the arts to exhibit the mind's freedom.

A fifth major area of work in Wittgensteinian aesthetics is the philosophy of culture. This naturally involves further investigation into aesthetic practices, as well as into central areas of Wittgenstein's philosophy of language, including private language and rule following. Anthony O'Hear (1991) has shown the significance that these linguistic themes hold for our understanding of the cohesion and style of a culture and the transmission of that culture generationally. O'Hear views Wittgenstein's work not only from the more familiar point of view of Gottlob Frege, Bertrand Russell, and British empiricism, but also from that of Austro-Hungarian conservative thought and the "philosophical anthropology" one can extrapolate from it. Indeed, the very idea of tradition is illuminated, as O'Hear shows, by Wittgenstein's analysis of rule following, of the ineradicably social nature of language, and more specifically of linguistic meaning, and of the nature of the relations between self and society. O'Hear asks where the grounds of our practices are and are not intelligibly called into question, and he shows that Wittgenstein had a good deal of immediate relevance to the understanding of cultural activity on this score. But Wittgenstein's emphasis on the rootedness of the concepts of our community and, more widely, our culture, does not imply that these practices are immune to criticism. Wittgenstein was hardly complacent or satisfied with the state of his own culture.

J. Bouveresse (1991) quotes a phrase from a passage in the Preface to the *Philosophical Investigations* written in 1945: "It is not impossible that it should fall to the lot of this work in its poverty and in the darkness of this time, to bring light into one brain or another—but, of course, it is not likely." Wittgenstein's perception of cultural darkness was such that he wrote in the remarks published as *Culture and Value,* "My own thinking about art and values is far more disillusioned than would have been *possible* for someone one hundred years ago." But Wittgenstein adds that, rather than showing that his view is more correct than someone's a century ago, this "only means that I have examples of degeneration in the forefront of my mind which were not in the *forefront* of men's minds then." Also looking into the Austro-Hungarian and European contexts for Wittgenstein's cultural thinking, Bouveresse reconsiders his cultural pessimism and in particular his sense of *decline* and the relations of his view to those of Oswald Spengler, Robert Musil, Friedrich Nietzsche, and others. Appropriate to a Wittgensteinian study, Bouveresse assembles a large picture of the cultural context within which Wittgenstein developed these views and the set of cultural practices in which these concepts were rooted, particularly emphasizing Wittgenstein's doubts concerning the concept of progress. Indeed, Wittgenstein's preference for clarity and perspicuity, "values in themselves," over progress and the building of ever more complicated theories or explanations, is given a fuller context here, as is his remark, "I am not interested in constructing a building so much as having a perspicuous view of the foundations of possible buildings" (ibid.).

Wittgenstein had personal doubts about his philosophical work being properly understood in his cultural context, and such doubts may have been common, as George H. von Wright has pointed out, to many great philosophers. Did not many believe that they "could not be properly understood until an entirely new climate of opinion had come to prevail?" (von Wright, 1981). Perhaps not, for von Wright writes: "I still think that Wittgenstein's attitude to his time makes him unique among the great philosophers" (ibid.). In a line that resonates with some work surveyed earlier in this essay, von Wright shows how in Wittgenstein's thoughts on these and related matters (e.g., the belief that in a future culture with different patterns, the questions that tormented him will not arise), the "philosophic conviction that the life of the human individual and therefore also all individual manifestations of culture are deeply entrenched in basic structures of a *social* nature" (ibid.) is absolutely central. These structures are, as discussed throughout the larger field of Wittgensteinian aesthetics, *Lebensformen,* or forms of life, and language games. Von Wright also shows how the emphasis on the social (in language and in the psychology of the individual) is intertwined with Wittgenstein's conception of the nature of philosophy itself. If problems of philosophy have their origins in the malfunctions or conflations of language games, similar problems can manifest as "unhealthy habits of thought, permeating the intellectual culture of a time" (ibid.). Wittgenstein's philosophical methods are designed to do battle with such problems and pernicious habits, but a profound change in our practices (following a thorough investigation of them), which of course are inseparable from our concepts, can prove therapeutic and problem-dissolving. Von Wright quotes Wittgenstein from the *Remarks on the Foundations of Mathematics:* "The sickness of a time is cured by an alteration in the mode of life of human beings . . ."; von Wright goes on to consider the deep connections between language and ways of life, and he too pursues the comparison between Spengler and Wittgenstein on these issues. Von Wright reveals that Wittgenstein's "conception of philosophy is intimately allied to a way of viewing contemporary civilization" (1981), a view constituted in large part by the artistic and aesthetic dimensions of his culture.

Von Wright's essay is Stanley Cavell's (1989) point of departure in pursuing further questions in Wittgensteinian philosophy of culture. Is Wittgenstein's attitude to his times essential not only to understanding his intellectual personality, but also to understanding his philosophy? Cavell reconsiders the similarities, but primarily the contrasts, between Wittgenstein's position on culture and Spenglerian pessimism, and this naturally leads to a reconsideration of the idea of a form of life and the question whether Wittgenstein found disorders in language itself. In casting light on Wittgenstein's conception of philosophy and of philosophical problems (not by any means a straightforward task, as Cavell shows), he observes that although "Wittgenstein speaks of pictures holding us captive, of unsatisfiable cravings, of disabling sublimizings," he does not "say very much about why we are the victims of these fortunes, as if his mission is not to explain why we sin but to show us that we do, and its places" (1989). For Cavell, the multifarious philosophical undertakings of the *Philosophical Investigations* constitute an interminable war with skepticism; and we can link to this perspective the related observation that within some contexts, some language games, the question of giving grounds cannot arise, as argued by O'Hear. But, more specifically, Cavell is claiming that "there is a perspective from which the *Philosophical Investigations* may be seen as presenting a philosophy of culture," and can be seen as it stands, "as a portrait, or say as a sequence of sketches (Wittgenstein calls his text an album) of our civilization, of the details of what Spengler phrases as our 'spiritual history,' the image of '*our own* inner life'" (ibid.). In reading the *Philosophical Investigations* as an artistic representation, Cavell uncovers a good deal concerning the conception of philosophy that Wittgenstein's book slowly articulates.

Further works demonstrate various aspects of the influence of Wittgenstein's philosophy on aesthetics. For example, Roger Scruton's groundbreaking *Art and Imagination,* (1974), while extending its account of aesthetic experience far beyond the bounds of Wittgensteinian exegesis or commentary, incorporates a Wittgensteinian account of the imagination; more recently, Martyn Evans's *Listening to Music* (1990) incorporates Wittgensteinian conceptions of expressivity, judgment, and gesture into its subject; Frank Palmer's *Literature and Moral Understanding* (1992) incorporates the concept of the language game in its account of literary experience; G. L. Hagberg's *Meaning and Interpretation* (1994) explores literary interpretation as Wittgensteinian investigation and his *Art as Language* (1995) examines analogies between language and art as these have shaped much aesthetic theory.

Exclusive focus on the question of artistic definition would greatly impoverish our understanding of the significance of Wittgenstein's philosophy for aesthetics: work in this field, although perhaps generally unified in its broadly antitheoretical stance, in fact ranges throughout, and in many cases crosses over, the five major areas of Wittgensteinian aesthetics mentioned here. It uncovers and elucidates complex interrelations among visual art, language, gesture, imagination, music, architecture, literature, criticism, self-understanding, culture, aesthetic theory, methodology, and philosophy itself.

BIBLIOGRAPHY

Work by Wittgenstein

Lectures and Conversations on Aesthetics, Psychology, and Religious Belief. Edited by Cyril Barrett. Berkeley, 1967.

Other Sources

Bouveresse, J. "'The Darkness of This Time': Wittgenstein and the Modern World." In *Wittgenstein Centenary Essays,* edited by A. Phillips Griffiths, Royal Institute of Philosophy Lecture Series 28, pp. 11–38. Cambridge and New York, 1991.

Budd, Malcolm. "Seeing Aspects." In *Wittgenstein's Philosophy of Psychology.* London and New York, 1989.

Cavell, Stanley. "The *Investigations* as a Depiction of Our Times." In *This New Yet Unapproachable America: Lectures after Emerson after Wittgenstein.* Albuquerque, N.Mex., 1989.

Cioffi, Frank. "When Do Empirical Methods Bypass 'The Problems Which Trouble Us'?" *Philosophy and Literature,* edited by A. Phillips Griffiths, Royal Institute of Philosophy Lecture Series 16 (1983), pp. 155–172. Cambridge and New York, 1984.

Eldridge, Richard. "Problems and Prospects of Wittgensteinian Aesthetics." *Journal of Aesthetics and Art Criticism* 45.3 (1987): 251–261.

Elliott, R. K. "Imagination in the Experience of Art." In *Philosophy and the Arts,* edited by Godfrey Vesey, Royal Institute of Philosophy Lectures 1971–1972, vol. 6, pp. 88–105. London, 1973.

Evans, Martyn. *Listening to Music.* Houndmills, 1990.

Hagberg, Garry L. *Meaning and Interpretation: Wittgenstein, Henry James, and Literary Knowledge.* Ithaca, N.Y., 1994.

Hagberg, Garry L. *Art as Language: Wittgenstein, Meaning, and Aesthetic Theory.* Ithaca, N.Y., 1995.

Johannessen, Kjell S. "Art, Philosophy, and Intransitive Understanding." In *Wittgenstein: Towards a Re-evaluation,* edited by Rudolf Haller and Johannes Brandl, Proceedings of the 14th International Wittgenstein Symposium, pp. 323–333. Vienna, 1990.

Korsmeyer, Carolyn. "Wittgenstein and the Ontological Problem of Art." *Personalist* 59.2 (April 1978): 152–161.

Lewis, P. B. "Wittgenstein on Words and Music." *British Journal of Aesthetics* 17.2 (Spring 1977): 111–121.

Lüdeking, Karlheinz. "Pictures and Gestures." *British Journal of Aesthetics* 30.3 (July 1990): 218–232.

Moore, George Edward. "Wittgenstein's Lectures, 1930–1933." In *Aesthetics,* edited by Harold Osborne, pp. 86–88. Oxford and New York, 1972.

O'Hear, Anthony. "Wittgenstein and the Transmission of Traditions." In *Wittgenstein Centenary Essays,* edited by A. Phillips Griffiths, Royal Institute of Philosophy Lecture Series 28. Cambridge and New York, 1991.

Palmer, Frank. *Literature and Moral Understanding.* Oxford, 1992.

Rhees, Rush. "Art and Philosophy." In *Without Answers,* edited by D. Z. Phillips. London, 1969.

Schulte, Joachim. "Aesthetic Correctness." *Revue Internationale de Philosophie* 43.169 (1989): 298–310.

Scruton, Roger. *Art and Imagination: A Study in the Philosophy of Mind.* London, 1974.

Shiner, Roger. "The Mental Life of a Work of Art." *Journal of Aesthetics and Art Criticism* 40.3 (Spring 1982): 253–268.

Shusterman, Richard. "Wittgenstein and Critical Reasoning." *Philosophy and Phenomenological Research* 47.1 (September 1986): 91–110.

Tilghman, B. R. *Wittgenstein, Ethics, and Aesthetics: The View from Eternity.* Houndmills, 1991.

von Wright, George H. "Wittgenstein in Relation to His Times." In *Wittgenstein and His Times,* edited by Brian McGuinness, pp. 108–120. Oxford, 1981.

Wilkerson, T. E. "Pictorial Representation: A Defense of the Aspect Theory." *Midwest Studies in Philosophy* 16 (1991): 152–166.

Wollheim, Richard. *Arts and Its Objects.* 2d ed. with six supplementary essays. Cambridge and New York, 1980. See especially pp. 104–132.

—GARRY HAGBERG

Wittgenstein and Literary Theory

Ludwig Wittgenstein has had considerable impact on contemporary literary theory and criticism in spite of the fact that he wrote very little about literature and did not regard himself as producing a "theory" of language, literary or otherwise. Wittgenstein's thinking has nonetheless been important for contemporary literary theorists because it offers nuanced perspectives on the antifoundationalist assumptions that govern the most prominent work in criticism today. Moreover, the antifoundationalism of Wittgenstein's *Philosophical Investigations* may also offer a way beyond the impasses with which both deconstruction and neo-pragmatism have found themselves confronted. Wittgenstein's work can help move critics away from debates over what can or cannot be known with certainty about the (literary) text toward a deeper understanding of the responsibilities placed on readers when faced with the facts of the text's "undecidability."

Wittgenstein's importance for contemporary literary theory first became apparent in the context of the American appropriation of ordinary-language philosophy and speech act theory, especially in the work of Stanley Cavell, who drew extensively on Wittgenstein's later writings in the course of his engagement with the work of J. L. Austin. In the essays gathered in *Must We Mean What We Say?* and even more so in the chapters that comprise *The Claim of*

Reason, Cavell's understanding of what is at stake in the claims of "ordinary language" centers on a drama in which philosophy encounters the limits of what it can reasonably claim to know in the form of skepticism's irrepressible doubts. In Cavell's reading of Wittgenstein, skepticism is not so much opposed to philosophy as it is the condition and limit of philosophical discourse: as long as philosophy is to attempt to validate its claims to knowledge, it must acknowledge the threat of skepticism. Skepticism represents something that philosophy cannot overcome, but only avoid.

In this reading of Wittgenstein, skepticism and epistemology represent twin distortions of our relationship to the world and to others. When faced with the fact of these distortions, the task of philosophy must be to overcome itself. This process of therapeutic overcoming yields a return to the world of the ordinary, or to the "everyday." Its intent is to bring words back "home," or to a region in which their sense is obvious. Although the hope expressed in the *Philosophical Investigations* is for a "complete clarity," in which philosophical problems would finally disappear, later readers of Wittgenstein such as Cavell stress the fact that any return to the ordinary must take place in full view of the fact that skepticism cannot be defeated. In contrast to the Wittgenstein of the *Philosophical Investigations,* for whom our response to doubt must be to return words to their "home," the world of the ordinary in many of the recent literary-theoretical uses of Wittgenstein is seen as a space of contingent relationships in which rational coherence is available only within the framework of some provisional "language game" and in which there is no justification for, or theory of, what constitutes a language game in general. The "language game" has been taken as Wittgenstein's way of formulating what other antifoundationalist philosophers, from Martin Heidegger to Michel Foucault, have described in terms of the background "practices" against which all forms of human action establish their meaning.

The many dimensions of our contingent relationship to the world become especially visible in a Wittgensteinian reading of the literary forms of tragedy, romance, and novel. In tragedy (Cavell deals principally with *King Lear* and *Othello,* but others, including Anthony J. Cascardi and Richard Eldridge, have dealt with the novel), we find revealed the limits of what we can claim to know with certainty about the world. In disclosing the limits of knowledge, tragedy discovers that the demand for responsible action with respect to other human beings is without end. It leads to a demand for acknowledgment rather than knowledge as the basis for our dealings with others. In romance (Cavell looks at William Shakespeare's romances, especially *The Winter's Tale,* and at a genre of Hollywood film called the "comedy of remarriage"), Wittgenstein's understanding of the provisionality of language games helps disclose the fact that we stand in a contingent relationship to the world. For example, "marriage" is not the description of an original or natural set of facts; in these plays and films, "marriage" involves acceptance and consent; moreover, every "marriage" seems also to be a form of remarriage. In the case of the novel, a Wittgensteinian approach reveals the ways in which the coherence and continuity of narrative are at best internally generated; similarly, the forms of life that novelistic narrative supports are the products of deeply rooted conventions. In all these instances, the antifoundationalism of Wittgenstein's *Philosophical Investigations* informs and supports a nonnaturalist vision of the social self.

Wittgenstein's insights into the nature of "language games" has helped provide many other theorists with a richer understanding of what is at stake in the development of a nonfoundationalist philosophy. This work overlaps with, and in some respects surpasses, the assumptions that contemporary literary theory has adopted from deconstruction and neopragmatism. For the philosopher Richard Rorty, who approaches Wittgenstein via the work of John Dewey rather than Austin, Wittgenstein's thought represents a valuable lesson in "overcoming" philosophy that is every bit as powerful as the lessons that Friedrich Nietzsche and Heidegger taught in this regard. For Rorty, the problem facing philosophy that a Wittgensteinian approach can help resolve is how to "circumvent" the tradition of metaphysics. Especially during the Enlightenment, when philosophy staked its identity on the ability to locate a truly impartial critical position, the practice of critique amounted to an attempt to "unmask" every prior critical stance, to show that each is marked by some form of blindness, of which it is unaware. But at the end of the Enlightenment tradition it has become apparent that none of these so-called critical stances was powerful enough to put an end to the motives of suspicion that drive the demand for further unmasking, and indeed that no stance could ever have such power. Wittgenstein's philosophical therapy is particularly instructive in showing what philosophy might look like if it could overcome the desire for a final unmasking and set aside its desire to pronounce the final word on any given subject.

In Wittgenstein's work, the problem with traditional philosophy (metaphysics) lies in that it has been held captive by ideals of systematic completion and closure that it has never been able to achieve. The task of philosophy as Wittgenstein sees it is rather "to shew [*sic*] the fly the way out of the fly-bottle" (1958, p. 309). This does not mean finding the right solutions to all the "problems," but rather working to bring words back home, so that the "problems" of philosophy disappear. Thus, Wittgenstein can insist that the clarity he is seeking in his work is "complete clarity" (ibid., p. 133). Rather than find a better answer to a Kantian question such as "How is synthetic a priori knowledge possible?" Wittgenstein might propose to diagnose and resolve the strangeness of the desires that motivate such a question in the first place. By focusing on the problems of philosophy and the linguistic distortions that produce them,

Wittgenstein's work is nonetheless congruent with the irony that Rorty identifies as characteristic of literary discourse as opposed to philosophy. In Rorty's work, however, a much greater emphasis falls on the contingency of our relationship to language (and, for that matter, to social practices). For Rorty, the "ironic" writer recognizes the fact that his or her pronouncements can never aspire to be the final words, the summation of a discourse. The "ironic" writer foregrounds the facts that permeate all literary discourse: contingency, provisionality, and openness to revision by redescription. Rather than aim to be an accurate representation of the world, Rorty has proposed that philosophy should strive to be an edifying form of discourse; and, rather than aim to be complete, philosophy should strive to approximate the irony of literature by revoking its claims to necessity and to closure, recognizing instead the contingency of its own ambitions and goals. Rorty's neopragmatist desire to circumvent the tradition of metaphysics thus shares central assumptions with Wittgensteinian "therapy" even while it diverges from Wittgenstein's desire for "complete clarity."

The neopragmatist use of Wittgenstein is complemented by the deconstructive interest in Wittgenstein. Stressing the affinities between the Heidegger of the "end of metaphysics" tradition, the work of Jacques Derrida, and Wittgenstein's later writings, numerous poststructuralist theorists and practitioners of deconstruction have drawn on Wittgenstein in order to press a series of assumptions about the indeterminacy of the text. (Some, such as Henry Staten, have also emphasized the irreconcilability of Wittgenstein and Derrida.) Deconstructive uses of Wittgenstein often begin from the commonplace position that Wittgenstein's notion of the "language game" can support claims about the indeterminacy of meaning (and, by implication, of all structures); in so doing, they may betray Wittgenstein's desire for "complete clarity." But deconstructive and other poststructuralist uses of Wittgenstein can also yield insightful treatments of the notion of the "language game" as the expression of the contingency of human relations. Jean-François Lyotard's appropriation of Wittgenstein in the discussion of justice in *The Differend* (1988) is a prominent example of the latter. For Lyotard, Wittgenstein's philosophy fits squarely within the domain of poststructuralism. He argues that this is so because the Wittgensteinian notion of "language game" makes sense only where we accept the fact that there can be no a priori hierarchy of language games, no transcendental position from which all such games can be surveyed, coordinated, or ranked. Lyotard's use of Wittgenstein is placed in the service of a stance that he describes as "pagan." This postmodern "paganism" describes a world founded on a belief in the irreducible heterogeneity of language games. Lyotard remains sensitive to the demands for justice that arise from claims that fall between the language games that rule a given world; and although his use of Wittgenstein's notion of language games allows us to hear the claims of those who have been denied a voice and thus victimized by the reigning language games, it comes at the price of a blindness to other, equally attractive, conceptions of justice. Specifically, Lyotard advances a notion of justice that does not acknowledge the validity of principles such as "fairness" or "desert." By stressing instead the affinity between justice and notions of taste and tact *(justesse)*, Lyotard uses Wittgenstein in order to revoke the notion of "principle" itself. Many would argue that although a revocation of the notion of principle suits Wittgenstein quite well, Lyotard's world simply does not aspire to the "complete clarity" of the *Philosophical Investigations.* [*See* Lyotard.]

Wittgenstein's affinities with aesthetic modernism can offer literary theory something that both neopragmatism and deconstruction are bound to miss insofar as they remain preoccupied with the incommensurability of language games and the indeterminacy of meaning. This lies in Wittgenstein's insights into the qualities of action or modes of relation of the subject, which tend to be omitted from critical practices that stress strategic rather than purposive modes of action. Rather than simply provide the ground for an ironic questioning of identities, and rather than provide us with instruction in the incommensurabilities of language games, Wittgenstein's work in the *Philosophical Investigations* can be seen as calling for further reflection on the qualities we display and the attitudes we adopt in relation to the language games we accept as contingent. This further reflection, which does not follow any strict methodological path, is represented by Wittgenstein's emphasis in the *Philosophical Investigations* on the particular modes in which a subject speaks or acts. It involves an emphasis on articulation that requires us to turn our attention to the "rough ground" of experience rather than to the transcendental or quasi-transcendental issues that philosophical advocates of discourse theory, such as Jürgen Habermas, have continued to pursue. Among contemporary literary scholars who have detected such possibilities in Wittgenstein's work, Charles Altieri (1976, 1981) has argued cogently that this attention to quality has affinities with modernist literary and artistic practice. First, modernist art stands in an ironic relationship to the aesthetic tradition, which it cannot conclusively surpass. Instead, modernism takes its problematic relationship to the past as the basis for foregrounding the particular qualities of action that the subject is empowered to put into play. Second, where modernist art approaches the ideal of a subjectless work, it relieves us of the desire to approach the work of art as an accurate representation of the world and asks us instead to focus on the modes of being or qualities of action that are displayed in and through it. Ideally, the modernist work of art is not "about" the world; it is itself a field in which the qualities of subjects can be demonstrated, put in play.

Wittgenstein thus enables literary theorists to confront a set of questions that remain to be addressed even after deconstruction and neopragmatism have succeeded in gaining universal agreement about the undecidability of the text and the contingency of discourse. These further questions are remarkably close to the ones Cavell was asking in the course of his interlacings of Wittgenstein, ordinary-language philosophy, tragedy, and romance. Rather than concentrate on what we can know, can Wittgenstein prompt us to ask how we should act in light of the contingency that surrounds anything we might claim to know? Wittgenstein's work thus opens a further avenue of research into the links between ethics and aesthetics for contemporary theorists working at the intersection of literature and philosophy. Wittgenstein's critique of the philosophical tradition and its modes of discourse provides convincing evidence that there remain viable models of subjective agency to be recovered from literary discourse even after we have accepted its ironic and contingent nature.

[*See also* Literature, *article on* Literary Aesthetics.]

BIBLIOGRAPHY

Work by Wittgenstein

Philosophical Investigations (1953). 3d ed. Translated by G. E. M. Anscombe. New York, 1968.

Other Sources

Altieri, Charles. "Wittgenstein on Consciousness and Language: A Challenge to Derridean Theory." *MLN* 91 (1976): 1397–1423.

Altieri, Charles. *Act and Quality: A Theory of Literary Meaning and Humanistic Understanding.* Amherst, Mass., 1981.

Cascardi, Anthony J. *The Bounds of Reason: Cervantes, Dostoevsky, Flaubert.* New York, 1986.

Cascardi, Anthony J. "The Grammar of Telling." *New Literary History* 19 (1988): 403–417.

Cavell, Stanley. *Must We Mean What We Say?* (1969). Cambridge and New York, 1976.

Cavell, Stanley. *The Claim of Reason: Wittgenstein, Skepticism, Morality and Tragedy.* New York and Oxford, 1979.

Cavell, Stanley. *Pursuits of Happiness: The Hollywood Comedy of Remarriage.* Cambridge, Mass., 1981.

Eldridge, Richard. *On Moral Personhood: Philosophy, Literature, Criticism, and Self-Understanding.* Chicago, 1989.

Fischer, Michael. "Stanley Cavell's Wittgenstein." In *Redrawing the Lines: Analytic Philosophy, Deconstruction, and Literary Theory,* edited by Reed Way Dasenbrock, pp. 49–60. Minneapolis, 1989.

Law, Jules David. "Reading with Wittgenstein and Derrida." In *Redrawing the Lines: Analytic Philosophy, Deconstruction, and Literary Theory,* edited by Reed Way Dasenbrock, pp. 169–188. Minneapolis, 1989.

Lyotard, Jean-François. *The Differend: Phrases in Dispute.* Translated by Georges Van Den Abbeele. Minneapolis, 1988.

Rorty, Richard. *Philosophy and the Mirror of Nature.* Princeton, N.J., 1979.

Rorty, Richard. *Contingency, Irony, and Solidarity.* Cambridge and New York, 1989.

Staten, Henry. *Wittgenstein and Derrida.* Lincoln, Nebr., 1984.

ANTHONY CASCARDI

WITTKOWER, RUDOLF (1901–1971), German-American art historian. Wittkower studied at Munich and Berlin and taught at Cologne, London (Warburg Institute and University College), and Columbia. He was long considered one of the principal theoretical art historians writing in English, thanks to his *Architectural Principles in the Age of Humanism* (1949; 3d ed. 1962) for decoding the metaphysical (Pythagorean-Neoplatonic) aspect of Italian Renaissance church architecture as a manifestation of a humanist spirituality, thus revising the nineteenth-century secularist understanding of the Renaissance. In its diversity, however, Wittkower's larger project has become more legendary than familiar.

Like his mentor Adolf Goldschmidt, Wittkower did not believe that art-historical scholarship existed to advance grand Hegelian theory: he was interested in theory, notably Renaissance and Baroque architectural theory and eighteenth-century British aesthetics, for the sake of culture-historical understanding. One of several general papers on art history, a 1959 address to the Winterthur (Delaware) Seminar on Museum Operation and Connoisseurship titled "Art History as a Discipline" (1961) not only relates to Erwin Panofsky's "The History of Art as a Humanistic Discipline" (1940) but stands against the extreme of connoisseurship declared in Roger Fry's "Art-History as an Academic Study" (in *Last Lectures*, 1939), where German scholarship is criticized for taking artworks "almost entirely from a chronological point of view, as coefficients of a time sequence, without reference to their aesthetic significance": not that sensibility is unworthy, but Wittkower could not have acknowledged as a historical discipline a subject aiming (symbolistically) to "compare the state of mind which results from contemplating one work of art with that which results from contemplating another."

In one theoretical matter of his generation, Wittkower took a firm position: he was ethnologically a *diffusionist,* a believer that similar forms imply historical contact and transmission. Of course, the opposite term to diffusionism is not always clear: "functionalism," "independent invention" (which, not unlike spontaneous generation as false start to germ theory, may hide diffusion), psychologizing universalism, uncritical nominalism. In "East and West: The Problem of Cultural Exchange" (1966, p. iii), Wittkower cites Adolf Bastian as posing the question in the late nineteenth century with an evolutionary view of parallel cultural manifestations at equivalent developmental stages, "independent convergence." In the more synoptic than syncretic lectures *The Impact of Non-European Civilizations on the Art of the West* (1989), Bastian leads "antidiffusionists" as Wittkower warns that both sides may "forget that for the high civilizations with literary traditions diffusionism has been developed into a universally accepted technique of research; in art-historical controversies the degree and character of diffusion may be disputed but not the principle of

diffusion"—provided that lines of contact are verifiable and that "alert, critical judgment . . . be exercised at all times," for not all things that look similar are related.

Despite a strong skepticism toward the reification of period style, Wittkower participated in the modern (even modernist) establishment of Mannerism as a style occurring between "Renaissance" and "Baroque" and entailing a dialectic of classical and anticlassical tendencies. His joining the cause of Mannerism, however, not only shows Wittkower's implicit theoretical bent, but it also testifies to his opposition to Wölfflinian formal systematics even as he exercised subtly penetrating formal analysis. As for the Baroque itself, when he took up Gianlorenzo Bernini's case (first with H. Brauer, in *Die Zeichnungen des Gianlorenzo Bernini,* 1931), the emotive Counter-Reformation sculptor cannot have been any more respected in Berlin than in England, where he would still be distained by Wittkower's friend, that "Yorkshire Protestant" Herbert Read. As a writer, Wittkower can show stunning concision—famously in his Pelican handbook of Italian Baroque painting, sculpture, and architecture (1958). A few careful strokes, in his Bernini monograph (1955), and one knows exactly what is meant by saying (against much literary commentary confused by the concretization of metaphor) that *The Ecstasy of St. Theresa* (1645–1652) makes that mystic's text "real and visionary at the same time"; he also dilates eloquently, as on a certain drapery fold in *The Blessed Ludovica Albertoni* (1671–1674) as the "pang of death" (1955).

Wittkower was intellectually at home in the Enlightenment even with his passion for the Italian Baroque, Jesuits, and all (1972), the honor in which he (be)held the High Renaissance and its "Divine Michelangelo" (1964), his own humanist re-cognition of the earlier Renaissance, and even his fascination with the ancient East as point of origination: these were all features of a singular encyclopedic enthusiasm. If it were possible to build a system, like one building, to house such supposedly incompatible enthusiasms, its classical lintel might be inscribed "Burke," for his having rendered up to understanding the subjective aspect of art (also for being Roman-oratorical and writing handsome *prose*); first, however, at the entrance to the surrounding *jardin anglais,* one would have to pass the name of Anthony Ashley Cooper, earl of Shaftesbury, or the word *Design* from his title "Letter concerning Design" (1712)—the ideo-historical key not only to Wittkower's happy Anglo-Palladianism, but also to the ideal of his English king peacefully pronouncing directives of even a Labour government as hardly utopian. Like his hero Bernini, he did not bother much with France (leaving it to Anthony Blunt, with whom he collaborated on Nicolas Poussin's drawings in the 1930s under Walter Friedländer): when he said "Enlightenment," he might as likely have been thinking of Potsdam as of Paris. He always insisted that Lord Shaftesbury's influence on the French Enlightenment was underestimated.

Although in his early collaborations he might well be mistaken for a connoisseur, Wittkower became a prime member of the "iconological" avant-garde. When Aby Warburg introduced the concept of "iconology"—more culturally hermeneutical than simple iconography—in a lecture in Rome in 1912, Panofsky, present as a student, soon joined in Warburg's project. Wittkower (nine years younger) met Warburg in 1927 and was invited to work in the Warburg Library in 1928; he joined the staff after it left Hamburg to become the Warburg Institute in London in the 1930s. Recent theoreticians have tended to install Panofsky as unique heir to the Warburg iconological tradition at the expense of others now less read—Gertrud Bing, Fritz Saxl (Frances Yates is read, but more remotely from art), as well as Wittkower—who were long active in the inner orbit. Panofsky and Wittkower were friendly colleagues, and there are significant points of thematic convergence in their work (e.g., implications of the dichotomy "Gothic" versus "classic" [Wittkower, 1974]) as well as a shared anti-Wölfflinian pedagogical influence in America (on the latter, see C. Eisler, "Kunstgeschichte American Style: A Study in Migration," in D. Fleming and B. Bailyn, eds., *The Intellectual Migration: Europe and America 1930–1960* [1969]). But their work was different. To put the matter crudely, Panofsky mainly pursued a history of illustrated concepts (such as Francis Bacon's "notions"), mythic or rational, that have fortunately taken roost from time to time in written texts and datable objects; it is no wonder that his position seems close to the neo-Kantian thinking of Ernst Cassirer, who was at home in the Warburg Library early on. Wittkower was as fascinated by the way a motif could travel independently of meaning as by the ways meaning could take different forms. Where current "critical theory" tends to install Panofsky as the Warburgian hero of (synchronic) "contextualism" versus (diachronic) "formalism," whereas both scholars were more dialectical in praxis, there may be repressed idealism in an automatic preference for Panofsky as the more "theoretical."

Wittkower was ultra-Warburgian. Even his popular *Born under Saturn* (1963)—praised by Stefan Morawski for "a keen insight into the precapitalist situation of the artist" ("Major and Minor Functions of Art in a Context of Alienation," 1964)—is in the direct Warburgian line of Ernst Kris and Otto Kurtz's catalog of topoi, *Legend, Myth and Magic in the Image of the Artist: An Historical Experiment* (1929). As with Panofsky, the classical tradition was his C major key (the "classical tradition" being what the Warburg Institute is "for the study of"), though in Wittkower's Warburgianism it was the very basis of cosmopolitanism: compare the postwar London exhibition and catalog by him and Saxl, *British Art and the Mediterranean* (1948), with his Germano-British contemporary Sir Nikolaus Pevsner's *The Englishness of English Art* (Reith Lectures, 1955).

As a humanist, Panofsky tended to take art as a more or less crafty illustration of *literae humaniores;* in his different but equally humanist practice, Wittkower, who taught artists at the Slade School (University College London), was a proponent of painting, sculpture, and architecture as *artes liberales.* Panofsky might seem closer to having been a philosopher, not only as associated with Cassirer, but also in his philological bent; but it deserves to be asked if Wittkower's pragmatic directness toward all made things, including ideas, was not also philosophical. If expanded historical understanding expands the range of aesthetic awareness, for Wittkower that was itself a historical consequence of the framing in eighteenth-century British aesthetics of new categories, the picturesque and the sublime. Methodologically, this teacher conveyed a sense that the field of examples of any motif (formal or iconographic) potentially includes every instance ever, everywhere, as if in Random Access Memory: Warburg might have liked to cross-index the whole world, but Wittkowerian synthesis wanted selectivity and hierarchy (subject to change). The canonical work served as a nexus facilitating operational extension of typology and discourse into the unknown.

Unlike Panofsky's "The History of the Theory of Human Proportions as a Reflection of the History of Styles" (1921; in *Meaning in the Visual Arts,* 1955), concerned with representation of the human body from Egyptian antiquity to Albrecht Dürer, Wittkower's "The Changing Concept of Proportion" pertains to architecture and was first aimed at architects. Panofsky sets out from the Cassireresque idea that normative bodily proportions change as a function of artistic style; Wittkower begins, à la Edmund Husserl's "Origin of Geometry" (not cited), with Galileo Galilei's first treating proportion in the abstract, and the detachment of mathematics from priestly mystique in ancient Greece. Pythagoras (not mentioned by Panofsky) establishes "theoretical geometry," including "musical consonances," as canonized in the *Timaeus* (Plato is barely mentioned in Panofsky's longer essay); and the Pythagorean-Platonic understanding persists in medieval "geometric" proportion, with "irrational dimensions" and incommensurable ratios, followed by a Renaissance "arithmetic" proportion of commensurable ratios. Why, then, a Renaissance cult of the square? Its appeal was not only geometric but as a figure of "the ratio 1:1 (unison in music)." When, beginning in the seventeenth century, art had to escape "a universe of mechanical laws, of iron necessity," Edmund Burke's *Philosophical Enquiry into the Origin of Our Ideas of the Sublime and Beautiful* (1757) was crucial for its emphasis on the perceiver. From René Descartes down to Jay Hambridge in the twentieth century, the quasi-superstitious "golden section" has nothing serious to offer; but Le Corbusier's resort to modular elements cannily combines construction efficiency and Renaissance-classical arithmetic proportion in the abstract. Alfred North Whitehead testifies that physics has "vindicated" some Platonic sense of harmony in nature.

Wittkower could be as imaginative as he was rigorous. In "Interpretation of Visual Symbols" (1955, p. iii), contributed to A. J. Ayer et al., *Studies in Communication* (1955), he denotatively equates "A Child's Drawing" of a figure with a nude by Leonardo da Vinci. When the present writer once noticed a curious detail and asked Wittkower if he had drawn the figure, he smiled; years later, the image turned up in an early child psychology book, James Sully's *Children's Ways* (1897), given as a "reproduction" of a little girl's drawing (from an American source). Wittkower's illustration is a further redrawing, identical for purpose of argument but mimetically distinct in its halting line, details of feet, and, particularly, one hand. Now the source left hand is a zigzagged letter "W," the right, another "W" but haphazardly drawn; however, Wittkower's figure's right hand is like a good "R," so that the hands thus read from the viewer's left as the initials "R" and W'": even in hypothesis, he did not tell a documentary lie.

The burgeoning of art history in postwar America and its unfortunate overspecialization diminished the potential influence of Wittkower's orthodox but creative art history in the modern field. In the opening "Non-European" lecture, he maintains that the art of the whole nomadic Eurasian North "was to a large extent . . . abstract and non-representational" (followed up in the present writer's notes by the sentence, lacking in the *Selected Lectures of Rudolf Wittkower*, "Only after contact with the Southern civilizations did they incorporate animals into their style"). The last page of "'Sacri Monti' in the Italian Alps" (1959, p. iv) better accounts for the modern split between "high" and "popular" art, as a consequence of "idealistic classical art theory," than most studies of that question. Wittkower himself was contemporary with the first Bauhaus *student* generation, and he published contemporary exhibition reviews in the mid-1920s and an article on the politics of museums in the Soviet Union in 1931; in later life, he was prepared to analogize the young Raphael's stylistic pluralism to the young Pablo Picasso's (ibid.), and he spoke of Henry Moore, his contemporary, as "our Bernini"; as for architects, Le Corbusier had obviously inherited the mantle. Wittkower must have had other latter-day influences that would be more difficult to track (to his diffusionist satisfaction) than that in which this writer, while still his student, had occasion to explain his dialectical theory of the "English garden" to the artist Robert Smithson. Wittkower was an actively generalist-humanist art historian who said never to forget that to most people the "history of art" per se seems like a very specialized subject.

[*See also* Architecture; Classicism; Iconography and Iconology; Panofsky; *and* Renaissance Italian Aesthetics.]

BIBLIOGRAPHY

Works by Wittkower

Architectural Principles in the Age of Humanism (1949). 3d rev. ed. London, 1962.

Gian Lorenzo Bernini: The Sculptor of the Roman Baroque (1955). 3d rev. ed. Ithaca, N.Y., 1981.

Art and Architecture in Italy, 1600–1750 (1958). 3d ed. New York, 1980.

Born under Saturn: The Character and Conduct of Artists: A Documented History from Antiquity to the French Revolution. Collaboration with Margot Wittkower. New York, 1963.

The Divine Michelangelo: The Florentine Academy's Homage on His Death in 1564. Edited and translated by Rudolf Wittkower and Margot Wittkower. London, 1964.

Baroque Art: The Jesuit Contribution. Edited by Rudolf Wittkower and Irma Jaffe. New York, 1972.

Gothic versus Classic: Architectural Projects in Seventeenth-Century Italy. New York, 1974.

Collected Essays of Rudolf Wittkower. Edited by Margot Wittkower. London, 1974–1978. Consists of vol. 1, *Palladio and Palladianism;* vol. 2, *Studies in the Italian Baroque;* vol. 3, *Allegory and the Migration of Symbols;* vol. 4, *Idea and Image: Studies in the Italian Renaissance.*

Selected Lectures of Rudolf Wittkower: The Impact of Non-European Civilizations on the Art of the West (1964). Edited by Donald Martin Reynolds. Cambridge and New York, 1989.

Other Sources

Reynolds, Donald Martin, ed. *The Writings of Rudolf Wittkower: A Bibliography.* Rome and New York, 1989. Contains a reprint of Howard Hibbard, "Rudolf Wittkower (1901–1971): An Obituary," originally published in *Burlington Magazine* 114 (1972): 173–177.

JOSEPH MASHECK

WÖLFFLIN, HEINRICH (1864–1945), Swiss art historian. Born in Winterthur, Switzerland, Wölfflin grew to maturity in the fin de siècle world. His new art history became an influential part of this revolutionary world.

Wölfflin's continued influence lies in the two methods he devised for studying the history of art: the formal analysis of works of art and the comparison of formal characteristics of art from different periods and nations to determine the prevailing style. The power of Wölfflin's approach has always been in the ability to replicate these two methods. Through empirical means, Wölfflin discovered that a small number of forms were consistently used in the Renaissance and Baroque periods, and from this morphology of forms he created a lawful concept of style for both periods. From the outset, Wölfflin's scholarly work challenged the status quo by posing a radical reordering of the components of art history and aesthetics.

His books were short and spare compared to those of his contemporaries. They signified a turn away from philosophizing about art and its development to psychologizing about it. Wölfflin's psychological hypotheses mediated between art and its creators, viewers, critics, and historians. Early on, in his dissertation of 1886, his preferred psychological mediation was a one-to-one empathetic correspondence between man and his objects. The psychological mediations changed from book to book: from an organic analogy between man and architecture in his dissertation, to mood in his first book *Renaissance and Baroque* (1888), to attitude and vision in *Classic Art* (1899), to just vision in *The Art of Albrecht Dürer* (1905) and *Principles of Art History* (1915), and back to mood and feeling in *The Sense of Form in Art* (1931).

His theory of art has been considered purist and modern, or Hegelian and teleological, and even positivist in the Anglo-American tradition. There is some truth to all these claims, but when Wölfflin's work is considered as a whole, the consistency, complexity, and independence of his construct from all these interpretations becomes clear.

The cumulative image of Wölfflin is of a scholar who, at an early stage in his career, knew what kind of contribution he wanted to make and what he wanted to avoid. He refused to write the already popular biographies and monographs concerning artists, and concentrated on the material record of the works of art. He was inclined toward systematic and inductive research, and rarely diverged from it into anecdotal material. He balanced theoretical concerns against empirical research; he did not often exceed the bounds of what could be demonstrated. He was a circumspect humanist.

He was educated in a remarkable, intellectual milieu and was trained by some of the great minds of his time, such as historian Jacob Burckhardt, philosopher Wilhelm Dilthey, psychologist Hermann Ebbinghaus, philosopher and educator Friedrich Paulsen, historian Wilhelm Riehl, philosopher Johannes Volkelt, and classical archaeologist Heinrich Brunn. They all left a significant imprint on Wölfflin's work, which is evident in his thesis for Munich University, *Prolegomena zu einer Psychologie der Architektur* (1886). This "prolegomena for a psychology of architecture" summarized his university education. Philosophers Volkelt and Dilthey were both attempting to find the basis of artistic production and other cultural endeavors in psychology, although each proposed a different psychology. To investigate the idea of an "organic analogy" between man and architecture, Wölfflin found various common features, a similar organization, and function in man and architecture.

In finding these correspondences, he set the stage for his life's work: to discover a psychology of art. The new discipline of psychology, however, offered two discrepant models: an abstract and universal one in the work of philosophers Rudolf Hermann Lotze, Friedrich Theodor Vischer, and Volkelt, and a psychology based on low-level sensory functioning in the work of experimental psychologists Hermann von Helmholtz, Wilhelm Max Wundt, Gustav Theodor Fechner, and Ebbinghaus. Wölfflin used both models in his thesis, which explains the absence of the artist or other actors in his theory—they were missing in late nineteenth-century psychology also. [See Psychology of Art.]

The thesis on architecture for his degree in philosophy at Munich University was interdisciplinary, joining ideas from philosophy, art history, psychology, and aesthetics. Wölfflin was still uncertain about which of these paths would form

his life's work until he lived in Rome in 1886. In Rome, his interest in architecture flourished. With his first book, *Renaissance and Baroque* (1888), Wölfflin introduced the comparative analysis of the two styles, Renaissance and Baroque, with opposite characteristics—the method that became the hallmark of his work. He now favored a different psychological mediation—the "mood" *(Stimmung)* of a period.

Wölfflin became Burckhardt's successor as professor of art history at Basel University in 1893. In the intervening years up to the publication of *Classic Art* in 1899, Wölfflin was deeply influenced by the sculptor Adolf von Hildebrand, the writer Conrad Fiedler, and the connoisseur Giovanni Morelli.

Hildebrand and Fiedler believed that perception was the single most important element in artistic creation. Hildebrand developed a theory of perception to reinforce the superiority of his favorite art form, the classical relief, against Impressionism. He devised a modern form of the *paragone*, or comparison of media to determine which is superior, using new scientific theories of perception. Hildebrand defended his view in *The Problem of Form in the Fine Arts* (1893), which was extremely influential, primarily because he used new ideas from perceptual psychology.

Wölfflin reconciled historical practice with a "history of vision" in *Classic Art* (1899), which relied on Hildebrand's account of the effect of perceptual functioning on art forms. In *Classic Art*, Wölfflin compared fifteenth- and sixteenth-century Italian art. Again he chose to resurrect an unpopular style, this time sixteenth-century Italian art—notably of Leonardo da Vinci, Raphael, and Michelangelo—to demonstrate its beauty. Quattrocento art was much more highly valued at the end of the nineteenth century, as the works of Bernard Berenson, Aby Warburg, and Morelli attest and Wölfflin noted. The first part of *Classic Art* resembled *Renaissance and Baroque* with a characterization of classic art in terms of its opposite, fifteenth-century art. Differences in art as markers for cultural change were of the greatest importance to Wölfflin.

The second part of the book presented three different ways of analyzing the classic style and explaining its development: he described the subject matter in terms of patronage, society, and the artist; then he derived the nature of the style from the then current attitude toward beauty; and, finally, he determined the formal composition of images from the artist's vision. By 1899, Wölfflin had determined that art was clearly the result of both internal artistic and external social influences, which were interrelated.

Perception became the leading new explanatory variable for change in style. The autonomy of art and vision, however, jeopardized the claim that other, external factors played a part in creation. It was not until his classic book *Principles of Art History* (1915) that Wölfflin clarified this issue.

In 1901, Wölfflin became professor of art history at Berlin University, the most prestigious university in central Europe. He was cast into a foreign milieu, from small republican Basel to large and imperial Berlin. Kaiser William II virulently and emphatically opposed modern art and placed Wölfflin in the position of having to defend his friends, as well as his Swiss nationality. It is in this context that Wölfflin's next book, *The Art of Albrecht Dürer* (1905), must be understood, for it is exceptional among his publications. Despite concentrating on a single artist, Wölfflin did not relinquish his comparative method, for Dürer sought to integrate classic elements into his style.

The underlying theme of this book was national differences in art. By focusing on the premier northern artist, he described what was characteristic in northern art and its opposite southern style. Wölfflin claimed that Dürer was unique among northern artists in that he sought to become a classic artist. Perception, broadly defined, was the force that altered Dürer's course: he gradually abandoned his northern vision for that of the south. The irony is that Dürer was cherished as the great German artist, with all the nationalistic connotations of that faith. Wölfflin abandoned this myth by accentuating Dürer's Italian ambitions.

At the time Wölfflin was working on the Dürer book, he was living a life that emulated Dürer's and that of all the other great northerners who had lived in Italy. He took sabbaticals in Italy to paint and to associate with artists. Wölfflin was so enthralled with Italy that he planned to write a novel about a modern German artist who seeks salvation in Italy. Instead, he wrote about Dürer.

Wölfflin integrated the artist's life into the historian's. He identified with Dürer's creative path, as he followed it work by work, re-creating his aesthetic world using historical methods. Dürer's eye was initially naive and northern, recording nature in a realistic style. But, as Dürer matured, Wölfflin felt he was able to move from realism to idealism. Dürer transcended his native vision and attained an individual vision that he used to create at will. In a sense, Wölfflin was intent on enacting a realist epistemology, while he continued to theorize, to idealize, to find patterns that explained the experience of both artist and historian. The northern artist began with a realist epistemology, while the southern artist simplified, idealized, and monumentalized. The antinomies of Wölfflin's intellectual activity were allegorized and symbolized in the art he studied.

For the next ten years, up to World War I, Wölfflin worked on a synthesis of the many ideas he had considered since the beginning of his academic career. (He moved home to Munich University in 1912, where his father had ended his career.) The result was his classic book *Principles of Art History* (1915), which summarized the results of his comparative approach as applied to the two leading European styles—the Renaissance and the Baroque. In it, he compared northern and southern examples of Renaissance and Baroque painting, sculpture, and architecture. He concluded that there are two primary ways of perceiving and transcribing the world into art, corresponding to the Renaissance and Baroque styles. These two visions recurred over time, in the same order, with a classical, linear style the precursor to a baroque and painterly style. Like his method in *Renaissance and Baroque,* Wölfflin distinguished five essential characteristics of each style or schema: linear, planar, closed, clear, and multiplicity of focii for the Renaissance style versus painterly, recessional, open, unclear, and unity of focus for the Baroque style. Each characteristic mode of representation derived from vision, again the single most important factor for changes in style. [*See* Style.]

In *Principles of Art History,* Wölfflin asserted that perception has a history, which was revealed and reified in art: "not everything is possible at all times"; only at certain times could some perceptions occur. He attempted to harmonize the real historical flow of art with a theoretical construct to interpret it. Crucial to his notion of perception was his statement: "Determining and determined, it always overlaps into different spiritual spheres" (1932). In other words, perception was always simultaneously an independent agent and yet determined by other agents of culture and life. The visual schemas of the two styles were the end product of an ongoing exploration of a large amount of visual material.

Wölfflin combined an empirical, scientific method of analyzing art with a circular hermeneutical interpretation of artistic development. [*See* Hermeneutics.] Perception, defined as rational and psychological, mediated between them, because it preceded and grounded both. [*See* Perception.]

There are affinities between Wölfflin's theory and the sociologist Max Weber's theory of ideal types. One could compare an internally logical ideal type or style with the actual art. In comparing the hypothetical and the concrete, one could speculate about the differences. In making the comparison, an interpretive strategy was begun that might add new objects of analysis, change the initial ideal type or schema, and end in the construction of laws. Empirical and interpretive acts were intertwined. Weber and Wölfflin intended such a union. Wölfflin continually demonstrated that each publication was a work in progress, modified and elaborated in succeeding works. Unlike most scientists at work, humanists can revise, reinterpret, reengage; conclusion is not necessary, although readers generally expect it. Early on, Wölfflin reached closure on his overall strategy of interpretation of art's history, but not on the causes for historical change.

Wölfflin described his task as speculative. Perception was determining, but was itself driven by external forces; it incorporated a number of cognitive states: imagination, interpretation, representation. Perception was malleable, but conformed to a rather rigid framework of the visual schemas of five pairs of concepts that recurred, periodically, in a regular sequence. But Wölfflin never fully explicated how the whole system operated, for he claimed that more empirical work was necessary before the whole theory could be perfected. The ideal schemas of style and real works of art remained in permanent tension in Wölfflin's theory.

The last thirty years of Wölfflin's life reveal both continuity and discontinuity in his theorizing. He wrote four rebuttals to the critics of *Principles of Art History* between 1920 and 1940, in which he defended his earlier work by restating the arguments while slightly shifting ground. At the same time, he revised his theory quite substantially in his only major publication after 1915, *The Sense of Form in Art* (1931), as it is known in English, or *Italien und das deutsche Formgefühl*.

In this last unified book, Wölfflin examined national differences, comparing art in Italy and the Germanic world between 1490 and 1530, the late Renaissance and early Mannerist periods. Contradicting his claim in *Principles of Art History* that Renaissance art possessed the same features in the north and the south, he now attempted to demonstrate that there were significant national variations in the Renaissance style. He refashioned the five pairs of concepts from *Principles,* concentrating on classic stylistic traits.

One fundamental change was the status of the "eye," which now retreated into the background of the theory and was replaced by "form-psychological hypotheses," meaning primarily feeling and sensation. The "organic analogy" reappeared, along with the "mood of a nation." Now Wölfflin proposed a sociological approach: he suggested that one could examine national food preferences and sleeping habits and still discover the same types of differences found in a nation's art. The core of his theory was no longer perception, but the patterns of imagination and thought that nations possess and that inform their art. The intellectual climate had moved away from the dominance of rational, scientific perceptual theories to *Lebensphilosophie,* the irrational, spiritual, antipositivist. Wölfflin adapted to and participated in new general philosophical trends.

Fascism was ascendant in 1931 when *The Sense of Form in Art* was published. In his book, however, Wölfflin favored the Italians over the Germans. Wölfflin had been repelled by what was happening in Germany during the 1920s and fled back to Zurich in 1924 to live out his days in the safety of his neutral, republican homeland. Nonetheless, one cannot ignore that he claimed that each nation possessed a "racially different bodily organization." This kind of notion relates to the then popular belief in eugenics that became integrated into Nazi medical and social practice. Determining factors in the creation of art became more confused and contradictory in Wölfflin's book. National traits seemed to negate psychological forces and yet he still argued that psychological causes were responsible for the supremacy of certain forms. He subverted his previous argument that the development of European art was uniform.

Wölfflin dismantled the entire framework of *Principles of Art History* in *The Sense of Form in Art,* and also the harmony of hermeneutical, inductive, and perceptual psychological approaches. He returned to his earlier psychological theories without uniting them into a coherent whole. It appears that, in this last systematic book, he was attempting to humanize his abstract and logical theory. The artist became the "seer" and "feeler" who expressed through forms. Wölfflin, however, seemed to be moving the old variables around like pieces on a chessboard and the outcome was a stalemate.

Wölfflin struggled to create a systematic history of art. He was most successful in *Principles of Art History.* The basic framework of interpretation, with an empirical, hermeneutical, and psychological union was impressive. Like Weber, he created a heuristic model of art-historical styles against which he could compare individual works of art. Wölfflin laid an impressive foundation for even more ambitious models—particularly that of Erwin Panofsky, who understood the need to proceed from a formal analysis to a larger interpretive framework and who also used a hermeneutic method of interpretation. Wölfflin concentrated on formal design, much as the artists of the Bauhaus and other modern artists did. Current interpretations in the history of art propose a greater emphasis on the language of art—a project that Wölfflin initiated. Art for him was a language of form, to which signs either conformed through contour, color, and shading and were Renaissance, or did not conform in those ways and were Baroque. The hegemonic constructs today are the ones Wölfflin engaged: empiricism, hermeneutics, psychology.

[*See also* Art History; Baroque Aesthetics; Iconography and Iconology; *and* Renaissance Italian Aesthetics.]

BIBLIOGRAPHY

Works by Wölfflin

Renaissance and Baroque (1888). Translated by Kathrin Simon. Ithaca, N.Y., 1966.
Classic Art: An Introduction to the Italian Renaissance (1899). London and New York, 1952.
The Art of Albrecht Dürer (1905). Translated by Alastair Grieve and Heide Grieve. London and New York, 1971.
Principles of Art History: The Problem of the Development of Style in Later Art (1915). Translated by M. D. Hottinger from the 7th ed. New York, 1932.
The Sense of Form in Art: A Comparative Psychological Study (1931). Translated by Alice Muehsam and Norma A. Shatan. New York, 1958.

Other Sources

Gantner, Joseph, ed. *Jacob Burckhardt und Heinrich Wölfflin: Briefwechsel und andere Dokumente ihrer Begegnung, 1882–1897.* Basel, 1948.
Gantner, Joseph, ed. *Heinrich Wölfflin, 1864–1945.* Basel, 1982.
Hart, Joan. "Reinterpreting Wölfflin: Neo-Kantianism and Hermeneutics." *Art Journal* 42 (1982): 292–300.

Hart, Joan, Roland Recht, and Martin Warnke. *Relire Wölfflin.* Paris, 1995.

Hauser, Arnold. *The Philosophy of Art History* (1958). Cleveland, Ohio, 1965.

Mallgrave, Harry Francis, and Eleftherios Ikonomou, eds. *Empathy, Form, and Space: Problems in German Aesthetics, 1873–1893.* Santa Monica, Calif., 1994.

Minor, Vernon Hyde. *Art History's History.* Englewood Cliffs, N.J., 1994.

Podro, Michael. *The Critical Historians of Art.* New Haven, 1982.

JOAN HART

WOLLHEIM, RICHARD (b.1923), a British philosopher who has both contributed to aesthetics and written in a serious systematic way about art history. Analytic philosophers, it has often been observed, typically have little to say about art. Perhaps this reflects insensitivity to the properly poetic qualities of language; maybe it demonstrates that traditional philosophical aesthetics cannot survive modern critical scrutiny. Wollheim's work is a valiant attempt to develop a systematic aesthetic employing the standards of reasoning and the style of argumentation found in analytic philosophy.

The starting point of his *Art and Its Objects* is the ontological question: what is art? Posing this ontological question is a good way of comparing the various arts. In painting, the artwork is identified with a unique physical object; in literature, there are many copies of the artwork; and in music, the artwork might be identified with the score, or its performances. Therefore, really one should ask: What is painting? What is a novel? What is a musical work? and so on. When one then asks how artworks represent, or are expressive, discussion must take account of these distinctions. With painting, for example, the question to ask is how a physical object has expressive qualities. Until one thus understands how to define the arts, it is not possible to understand the nature of representation or expression; how interpretation works; or the strengths and limitations of psychoanalytic theorizing, Marxism, and other interpretive approaches.

As befits an analytic philosopher, Wollheim is cautious about making generalizations. He tends less to assert his own viewpoint directly than to back into it by identifying problems with less subtle approaches. For example, the view that art is a language, although it identifies the way that art communicates emotion, breaks down when we observe that artworks are not grammatical in the way that sentences are. The most illuminating statement of Wollheim's general position is provided by a preface, later suppressed, in one 1968 edition of *Art and Its Objects:* "As the audience of art or as the makers of it, we seem to be engaged simultaneously with artefacts and with a concept. Art, and its objects, come indissolubly linked. . . . Aesthetics . . . may be thought of as the attempt to understand this envelope in which works of art invariably arrive." Wollheim provides a piecemeal reconstruction of this envelope. His inability to give sweeping generalizations is compensated for by his capacity to provide numerous details about the relationships between the various arts and their corresponding objects.

The starting point of *Painting as an Art,* as one would expect in a book on painting, is narrower. The theory of representation is discussed, first from the artist's viewpoint, then from the spectator's. A significant artist has an individual style, which is to say that there is an internal relationship between his works. What we spectators see has been described by aestheticians in terms of illusion, make-believe, "seeing as," information conveyed; and using semiotic theories. What is important for Wollheim is less the details of his disagreements with other theorists than his deployment of a very far-reaching account of projection. Often in everyday life, one finds a scene in the external world that matches an emotion. Then "expressed emotion and perception fuse" (Wollheim, 1987, p. 82). In art, projection is guided by the artist. What one sees depicted is what the artist intended to show. Seeing the picture properly, one observes the artist's attitude toward his pictorial content. In his account of Adrian Stokes, Wollheim notes how "it becomes for the reader the most natural thing in the world . . . to assimilate a shape to a feeling" (Wollheim, 1973, p. 334). That is what happens also for the reader of his writing.

Once this theory is presented, Wollheim is prepared to look at the procedures of individual artists: Édouard Manet's appeal to a spectator within the picture; Pablo Picasso's play with the power of the gaze; Titian's metaphoric association of the painting with the body; and so forth. What links this account to traditional psychoanalytic approaches to art is the concern with art as a form of personal expression. We best understand Manet, Picasso, and some (not all) other painters, Wollheim suggests, by knowing something of their lives. (Such approaches, it has been often argued, are essentially reductive; they reduce art to mere autobiography. This is correct, Wollheim implies, only if we hold an impoverished view of the psychic processes that generate art.) The interesting complications arise in fitting Wollheim's practice of art-historical interpretation into his broader vision of mental activity. In the Preface to *Painting as an Art,* he argues that connoisseurship is the "best hope for the objective study of painting" (1987, p. 10). Connoisseurship usually is understood as the skill needed to separate the genuine works of a master from the school pieces, copies, and forgeries; and then to identify the sequence in which those genuine works were made. Connoisseurship is thus characteristically opposed to iconography, whose concern is with the meaning of the visual image, with its sources and its possible symbolic sense.

Connoisseurs' preoccupation with identifying quality closely associates them with collectors, who need reliable attributions to guarantee the value of the art they purchase.

Wollheim does not accept this characterization of connoisseurship, nor this conservative view of its political implications. Wollheim calls himself a socialist, but he is not interested in the radical protest art so influential during the 1980s. (It really is not clear, from his published writings, how exactly he would understand the link between politics, philosophy of mind, and aesthetics.) Politically leftist, Wollheim is, within the context of the American art world, aesthetically conservative; his is the prose of an aesthete, but he has the morality of a socialist. (His novel *A Family Romance* gives a vivid sense of his ways of dealing with what, to an outsider, would seem the obvious conflicts here.) Wollheim is not especially concerned with attributions. What for him defines connoisseurship is close, attentive looking, which reveals what the artist intended to depict. The essential qualities of the artwork can be identified visually. Study of the historical context can support, but never supplant, this evidence of the eye.

How, then, can Wollheim's accounts of what close looking reveals be tested? Not by any abstract philosophical argument; nor by appeal to historical evidence. We must see—literally, *see*—if his accounts of Manet, Picasso, Titian, and Nicolas Poussin are consistent with our experience. What is to be done when, inevitably, disagreements arise? Wollheim implies that the only ultimate source of disagreements is the inability of some viewers to see the artwork as it really is. Here, he rejects decisively the claims of cultural historians. Wollheim's version of connoisseurship depends on a bold faith in the universality of human nature. He does not have any way to explain different responses, except to assert that they arise because some people do not see the artwork accurately.

Is this a weakness of his position? Perhaps not, because for Wollheim, as with more traditional connoisseurs, focusing on disagreements may be misleading. Some attributions remain controversial, but on the whole connoisseurs achieve remarkable agreement. The easiest way to explain that agreement is to suppose that most people interested in visual art learn to see it correctly. Analogously, in interpreting art, interpersonal agreement very often is achieved. *Painting as an Art* in effect asks that the readers test Wollheim's claims to see if they match their experience. What is merely personal in his analyses thus can be corrected.

Wollheim attributes highly complex internal structures to the mind, giving special emphasis to our capacity to fantasize; rejecting historicism, positivism, and relativism, he is very optimistic about our capacity to retrieve these inner feelings revealed in our experience of art. Psychoanalysis, he argues, in extending commonsense ways of thinking, builds on the classical tradition of philosophy of mind. Connecting his view of visual art with the view of persons and morality presented in his *The Thread of Life* is no easy task. Nor is it easy to directly relate the reading of psychoanalysis in his *Freud* to the kinds of fantasy play discussed in *Paint-*

ing as an Art. In *Art and Its Objects,* Wollheim appeals to Ludwig Wittgenstein's much-discussed phrase, "form of life": "Art is, in Wittgenstein's sense, a form of life" (1980, p. 104). The significance of this enigmatic claim takes us back, again, to the title of the book. To understand art, we cannot merely appeal to the psychic processes characteristic of the artist; nor, as social historians would suggest, to the institutions that constitute the art world. Such understanding requires, rather, that we grasp the finely entangled relationship between the traditions of art, and the modification (or dismantlement) of those traditions such as occur in the practice of any interestingly original artist. To speak of art *and* its objects is to note, tersely, this unity of history and ongoing practice. When a great deal of traditional philosophy—especially philosophy in the analytic tradition—marginalizes art, as if art making were merely a rather subsidiary human activity, what is really revealed, Wollheim is suggesting, is an impoverished view of the mind and its activities. A politically sensitive aesthete, he implies, would understand the relation between art and social life.

The easiest way to unpack the interconnections here within Wollheim's aesthetic is through a comparison with the work of his near contemporary, Arthur C. Danto. Both are analytic philosophers; and both, seeking to define art, are centrally concerned with visual art. But they disagree entirely about the philosophical significance of contemporary art. Danto claims that Marcel Duchamp's readymade *Fountain* (1917) and Andy Warhol's *Brillo Box* (1964) show that visual art cannot be defined by its visual properties. What defines an artwork, he says, is not its visual qualities, but what he calls "a certain theory of art" (Danto, 1964, p. 581); what distinguishes *Brillo Box* from a Brillo box in the grocery store is the availability of some such theory. But Wollheim resists this claim. He argues that Duchamp's work has exercised more influence over contemporary aesthetics than it deserves.

What is at stake here is something more, and something other than disagreements about taste. Wollheim grants that readymades are artworks. (His 1965 essay "Minimal Art" [Wollheim, 1973, chap. 5], which discusses Duchamp, was probably the source for the name of that art movement, "Minimalism.") Danto, in turn, allows that the painterly art that Wollheim loves is the kind of art he also cares about most. But what Danto claims, and Wollheim certainly denies, is that such work is very significant for the philosophy of art. Why, then, do they disagree? Here, it is necessary to return to the ontological discussion in *Art and Its Objects.* If the goal is to define art, and the readymades are artworks, then what follows? "As our attention spreads over the object, more and more of its properties may become incorporated into its aesthetic nature" (Wollheim, 1980, p. 123). It seems impossible to view such banal objects as *Fountain* and *Brillo Box* in this way.

In "Minimal Art," Wollheim made a further helpful suggestion: "In the visual arts . . . we are called upon to concentrate our attention upon individual bits of the world" (1973, p. 110). Now, in one obvious way, this claim seems to be either false or circular. If *Fountain* and *Brillo Box* are artworks, then do they not show that in the visual arts one is not always called on to take this kind of aesthetic attitude toward individual bits of the world? They must be counterexamples to his general characterization of art. If, however, Wollheim is only saying that in *traditional* visual art individuals concentrate their attention thus, then his analysis is just circular. He simply rules out in advance any counterexamples such as Danto's.

But there is more going on here than this characterization of his claims indicates. Allowing that the readymades are artworks, Wollheim implies that they are an impoverished kind of art. It is revealing that in speaking of how art calls our attention to individuals, he speaks also of loving a particular individual, and not merely someone with certain qualities. At this point there are deep connections between his account of persons, his passionate interest in psychoanalysis, his socialism, and his aesthetics. His "Babylon, Babylone" (1962) dealt with Impressionism in a way that makes these connections. This remarkable essay, not much discussed in the art-historical literature, thus anticipated the concerns of recent social historians of Impressionism. These political themes are not taken up explicitly in Wollheim's recent work, but perhaps a similar approach is needed to do justice to this debate about Minimalism and defining art. Wollheim's aesthetic reveals its full significance only when linked with the broader concerns of his social philosophy.

There has been a great deal of discussion of Wollheim's work within the aesthetics journals. Mostly what has been discussed are points of detail. What remains to be explored are these broader ways in which he links aesthetic theory to philosophy of mind and social philosophy.

[*See also* Danto; Formalism; *and* Minimalism.]

BIBLIOGRAPHY

Works by Wollheim

"Babylon, Babylone." *Encounter* 18.5 (May 1962): 25–36.
Art and Its Objects. New York, 1968; 2d ed. with six supplementary essays, Cambridge and New York, 1980.
A Family Romance. New York, 1969.
Freud. London, 1971; 2d ed. London, 1991.
On Art and the Mind: Essays and Lectures. London, 1973; reprint, Cambridge, Mass., 1974.
The Thread of Life. Cambridge, Mass., 1984.
Painting as an Art. Princeton, N.J., 1987.
"Danto's Gallery of Indiscernibles." In *Danto and His Critics,* edited by Mark Rollins, pp. 28–38. Oxford and Cambridge, Mass., 1993.

Other Sources

Danto, Arthur C. "The Artworld." *The Journal of Philosophy* 61.19 October 15, 1964): 581.

DAVID CARRIER

WORDSWORTH, WILLIAM (1770–1850), English Romantic poet. Wordsworth's significance for aesthetics rests on (1) his theory of poetry, particularly as set out in his Prefaces to *Lyrical Ballads;* (2) his passion for and reflective interest in natural beauty as expressed not only in his poems but above all in his *A Guide Through the District of the Lakes in the North of England,* a work that was highly popular in its day and that has something to contribute to contemporary interest in environmental aesthetics; (3) the preoccupations manifest in his best poetry with the nature and power of the imagination and with the sublime, a heightened interest in which are bequeathed to aesthetics by the Romantic movement in poetry; and (4) what might be called Wordsworth's apology for poetry, that is, his claims for the moral seriousness of poetry.

Theory of Poetry. Wordsworth's most familiar reflections on poetry are to be found in his Preface to the *Lyrical Ballads,* a collection of poems, some written by himself and the others by Samuel Taylor Coleridge, and first published in 1798. The Preface is his and has often been reprinted (for example, in Paul Zall's edition of the *Literary Criticism of William Wordsworth*). Wordsworth's best-known proposition is that

> Poetry is the spontaneous overflow of powerful feelings: it takes its origin from emotion recollected in tranquillity: the emotion is contemplated till by a species of reaction the tranquillity gradually disappears, and an emotion, similar ["Kindred" is substituted for "similar" in the version of the Preface attached to the 1802 edition of *Lyrical Ballads* (Wordsworth, 1996, pp. 57–58)] to that which was before the subject of contemplation, is gradually produced, and does itself actually exist in the mind.
>
> (Ibid., p. 27)

"Poetry," Wordsworth observes in the Advertisement to *Lyrical Ballads, with a Few Other Poems* (1798), is "a word of very disputed meaning" (ibid., p. 10): what philosophers in our time have variously characterized as a fit subject for persuasive definition (Charles Stevenson, 1944), or as an instance of an essentially contested concept (W. B. Gallie 1955–1956). The poems in *Lyrical Ballads,* Wordsworth says, "are to be considered as experiments. They were written chiefly with a view to ascertain how far the language of conversation in the middle and lower classes of society is adapted to the purposes of poetic pleasure" (Advertisement, in Wordsworth, 1966, p. 10). Wordsworth's aim was "to make the incidents of common life interesting by tracing in them . . . the primary laws of our nature." "Low and rustic life was generally chosen [as the subjects of the poems] because in that situation . . . our elementary feelings exist in a state of greater simplicity and consequently may be more accurately contemplated and more forcibly communicated" (Preface [1800], in ibid., p. 18).

Wordsworth rejected the language of poetry that he inherited from eighteenth-century writers such as Alexander

Pope and Samuel Johnson and proposed "to myself to imitate, and, as far as possible, to adopt the very language of men" (ibid., p. 22). In the Preface to the 1802 edition, he adds the phrase: "the real language of men in a state of vivid sensation" (ibid., p. 38). The poet "is a man speaking to men: a man, it is true, endued with more lively sensibility, more enthusiasm and tenderness, who has a greater knowledge of human nature, and a more comprehensive soul, than are supposed to be common among mankind" (ibid., p. 48). Although the poet "describes and imitates passions, his situation is altogether slavish and mechanical, compared with the freedom and power of real and substantial action and suffering. So that it will be the wish of the Poet to bring his feelings near to those of the persons whose feelings he describes" (ibid., p. 49). "The Poet writes under one restriction only, namely, that of the necessity of giving immediate pleasure to a human Being possessed of that information which may be expected from him, not as a lawyer, a physician, a mariner, an astronomer or a natural philosopher, but as a Man" (ibid., p. 50). The gender expressions here may give offense today but, allowing for that, the thought is not so different from that expressed in Friedrich von Schiller's *Letters on the Aesthetic Education of Man* (again, the title may be provocative today). The idea is that it is a crucial task for the arts to speak to the whole person, many of whose mental powers will have become atrophied in the specialization demanded by the division of labor in the modern world. It is not only Schiller who deplores this; Karl Marx in his early writings identifies and analyzes it as a fundamental historical fact in the development of modern capitalism.

Zall cautions that "Wordsworth later maintained that he 'never cared a straw about the theory, and the Preface was written at the request of Mr. Coleridge out of sheer good nature'" (ibid., p. 15). It is right that we should be informed of this disclaimer but also right not to take it too seriously. For one thing, certain of Wordsworth's observations bear obvious connections with claims made in other works that have not been ejected from the history of aesthetics. This has already been suggested in the case of Schiller but it also applies to works by Edmund Burke and Joshua Reynolds. For example, Burke's distinction between a clear expression and a strong expression may profitably be compared with Wordsworth's account of what the language of poetry should be. For Burke, a clear expression "regards the understanding" and "describes a thing as it is," whereas a strong expression "belongs to the passions" and describes a thing "as it is felt." Later, Burke writes: "Uncultivated people are but ordinary observers of things, and not critical in distinguishing them; but, for that reason, they admire more, and are more affected by what they see, and therefore express themselves in a warmer and more passionate manner" (1970).

Wordsworth makes specific use of Reynolds's ideas in both editions of his Preface: "an *accurate* taste in Poetry and in all the other arts, as Sir Joshua Reynolds has observed, is an *acquired* talent, which can only be produced by thought and a long continued intercourse with the best models of composition" ([1800] Wordsworth, 1966, p. 31; [1802] ibid., p. 61). If, however, Wordsworth's theoretical views are to be accorded the same seriousness as those of other theorists in aesthetics, that requires the admission that Wordsworth is inconsistent. He invokes Reynolds's support for the view that taste in poetry is to be trained and educated, that is, improved, but also ridicules eighteenth-century talk of a taste for poetry (ibid., p. 50).

Wordsworth says that several of his friends urged him to provide "a systematic defence of the theory, upon which the poems were written," but, with an evasiveness worthy of his friend and co-contributor Coleridge, he replies: "the Reader would look coldly upon my arguments, since I might be suspected of having been principally influenced by the selfish and foolish hope of *reasoning* him into an approbation of these particular Poems" (Preface [1800], ibid., p. 16). Although this has been quoted with approval by Margaret Macdonald in a paper on the nature of arguments used in literary criticism ("Certainly, it does seem queer to suppose that anyone could be *argued* into admiring *Persuasion* or condemning *The Stag at Eve*" [Macdonald, 1959, p. 114]), Wordsworth's excuse confuses the description of poetic aim with the grounds on which a poem may be admired, which may or may not coincide. Macdonald, in turn, confuses the adducing of grounds for admiring a poem with the rhetoric that would persuade readers to admire it.

Natural Beauty. Wordsworth is himself often meticulous in giving reasons for his aesthetic judgments. In his *A Guide Through the District of the Lakes in the North of England* (in this case, we are speaking not of poems, of course, but of scenery, but the point holds good for both), there is no question of Wordsworth's trying to defend a preference for, say, native vegetation rather than plantations of foreign larch (Wordsworth, 1970, pp. 82–83), but only an attempt to get us to see the local landscape as he does. In like manner, he explains how the comparatively small size of the English lakes is favorable to the beauty of the area (ibid., p. 33) and why white is the wrong color for a house in the mountains (ibid., p. 80). The invitation to accept these judgments is one people can freely accept or not depending on how they respond to the reasons he presents for their assent or dissent.

In the *Guide*, Wordsworth seeks to adduce what one might call principles of landscape criticism, which is why the work has a continuing value transcending the usually ephemeral nature of guidebooks: "It is to be hoped . . . that this Essay may become generally serviceable, by leading to habits of more exact and considerate observation than . . . have hitherto been applied to local scenery" (ibid., p. 22). For example: "The form of the lake is most perfect when, like Derwent-water, and some of the smaller lakes, it least resembles that of a river" (ibid., p. 32). Or, because of the "craving for prospect," "which is immoderate, particularly in new settlers," their habit of placing their new houses on the "summits of naked hills in staring contrast to the snugness and privacy of the ancient houses" (ibid., p. 74) is having a deleterious effect on the landscape.

The Imagination and the Sublime. The importance of the imagination is a leading tenet of Romanticism, but there is a severe tension between a tendency, on the one hand, to regard it as a unique faculty of mind through which only access and insight into otherworldly, supersensible, or transcendental reality is to be had, and a tendency, on the other hand, to suppose "imagination" names various faculties of mind (e.g., perception, understanding, emotion) in heightened and quickened states. Notwithstanding imagination, as Wordsworth puts it, "having been our theme" of his great poem, *The Prelude* (1805 edition, book 13, line 185), it would be folly to expect a philosophically worked-out account; but, with that caveat, it can be said that Wordsworth tends to the second view of imagination:

> Imagination, which, in truth,
> Is but another name for absolute strength
> And clearest insight, amplitude of mind,
> And Reason in her most exalted mood.
> (*The Prelude*, 1805; book 13, lines 167–170)

Certainly, "imagination" for Wordsworth does not have the common connotations of illusion or the fabrication of fiction; these, one suspects owing to the influence of his friend Coleridge, he is inclined to hive off under the secondary category of fancy.

The Prelude does not, of course, offer a *theory* of the sublime in the manner of Burke or Immanuel Kant, though in fact theory is by no means absent from the poem, far from it; rather, the poem expresses sublimity. The best-known passages, not surprisingly both to do with mountains, are Wordsworth's accounts of his descent from the Alps and his ascent of Snowdon. The passages are too long to quote in full but the following should give a flavor:

> The immeasurable height
> Of woods decaying, never to be decayed,
> The stationary blasts of waterfalls,
> And everywhere along the hollow rent
> Winds thwarting winds, bewildered and forlorn,
> The torrents shooting from the clear blue sky . . .
> (Ibid., book 6, lines 556–561)

> The moon stood naked in the heavens, at height
> Immense above my head, and on the shore
> I found myself of a huge sea of mist,
> Which, meek and silent, rested at my feet.
> A hundred hills their dusky backs upheaved
> All over this still ocean . . .
> (Ibid., book 13, lines 41–46)

Wordsworth does not discourage the reader who would go to his poetry for his philosophy, for his doctrines. He is himself impatient with the artifices and contrivances of art, as already seen in his remarks on the language of poetry. Fictionality, artifice, and artistic cunning are nevertheless present in Wordsworth's poetry and the metaphysical grand statements apparently setting out a doctrine of nature that, on a first reading, seem to comprise the poem "Lines Composed a Few Miles above Tintern Abbey," on a closer reading are seen to be much more tentative and elusive.

For all that, Wordsworth is attracted to the ideal of the poet as teacher: "Every great Poet is a Teacher; I wish either to be considered as a Teacher, or as nothing," he writes in a letter (1966, p. xv). This was recognized by his early followers who treated him as leader, moralist, and sage, not primarily, it should be noted, on the subjects of art, poetry, and the other specific concerns of aesthetics but on the subjects of nature and of man, so Wordsworth can be seen in a tradition of nature philosopher-poets more familiar perhaps in the works of Ralph Waldo Emerson, Walt Whitman, and Henry Thoreau in American literature than in English. Another way to put this point is to say that Wordsworth's work, whether poetry or prose, does not sit happily within the conventional academic boundaries maintained between religion, philosophy, and poetry.

Moral Importance of Literature. Wordsworth's passionate belief in the importance of literature is recognizably in the tradition that later critics such as Matthew Arnold and F. R. Leavis also embraced when they spoke of its moral seriousness. In *Lyrical Ballads*, Wordsworth aimed to produce poetry "well adapted to interest mankind permanently, and not unimportant in the multiplicity and in the quality of its moral relations" (Preface [1800], ibid., p. 16). This tradition accordingly sees an approach to literature through the categories of aesthetics, especially those of taste and beauty, as distorting and reductive. Indeed, Wordsworth himself could be dismissive of these categories, when, for example, given his passion for poetry, he is scornful of those who speak, as philosophers and critics of his own and immediately preceding time indeed did, of a taste for literature:

> Further, it is the language of men who speak of what they do not understand; who talk of Poetry as of a matter of amusement and idle pleasure; who will converse with us as gravely about a *taste* for Poetry, as they express it, as if it were a thing as indifferent as a taste for Rope-dancing, or Frontiniac or Sherry.
> (Preface [1802], ibid., p. 50)

In Wordsworth's view, we go to poetry for teaching and for truth. As if this is not enough, "Poetry," he says in his Essay Supplementary to the Preface to *Poems* 1815, "is most just to its own divine origin when it administers the comforts and breathes the spirit of religion" (ibid., p. 162). The conjunction of truth with religion is further found in what, to borrow Richard Rorty's term, might be called Wordsworth's edificatory account of truth:

> Aristotle, I have been told, hath said, that Poetry is the most philosophic of all writing: it is so: its object is truth, not individual and local, but general, and operative; not standing upon external testimony, but carried alive into the heart by passion; truth which is its own testimony, which gives strength and divinity to the tribunal to which it appeals, and receives them from the same tribunal. Poetry is the image of man and nature.
>
> (Preface [1802], ibid., p. 50)

Wordsworth's Prefaces broaden out from an account of poetry into a more general critique of his contemporary culture, and what Wordsworth objected to in his own time has been seen by literary critics such as Leavis to have become worse since then. Wordsworth objects to the craving for excitement, a "degrading thirst after outrageous stimulation," the blunting of the "discriminating powers of the mind" that has various causes, including the "encreasing accumulation of men in cities, where the uniformity of their occupations produces a craving for extraordinary incident, which the rapid communication of intelligence [news] hourly gratifies" (Preface [1800], ibid., p. 21; [1802] ibid., p. 44). Wordsworth professes a philosophy of nature and integral to that, a critique of the cultural condition of the England of his day, which was then undergoing unprecedentedly rapid modernization. Wordsworth, then, was a writer much exercised by the experience of modernity.

The headings under which Wordsworth's contributions to aesthetics have been considered here do not, of course, encompass—nor are they intended to—the range and scope of Wordsworth's poetry, nor do they explain the devotion it aroused and still does (or, for that matter, the intense dislike that it can also cause. For instance, a poem celebrating a beautiful scene, the poem about daffodils ["I wandered lonely as a cloud"], may be picked out for especial ridicule and obloquy by those who have to study poetry at school but who develop no love for it). All this is to say that the effect of Wordsworth's poetry on the reader, whether favorable or unfavorable, is often strong, so to offer an expository account of his aesthetic ideas as if they were those of a dedicated philosopher is plainly no substitute for experiencing (itself another important notion for Wordsworth) the poetry itself.

The nineteenth-century British philosopher John Stuart Mill well catches the strong positive effect that Wordsworth could have on readers, turning them into followers. That a poet might create a following is perhaps a new development in English literature; previously, a poet was admired for talent and skill but even the greatest poets, such as William Shakespeare, Geoffrey Chaucer, and Edmund Spenser, were hardly seen by their contemporaries as spiritual advisers.

Mill, in his *Autobiography,* was careful to distinguish the question of poetic merit from the effect Wordsworth had in

transforming and redirecting his own personal experience: "The result was that I gradually, but completely, emerged from my habitual depression, and was never again subject to it. I long continued to value Wordsworth less according to his intrinsic merits, than by the measure of what he had done for me" (Mill, 1969, p. 90). The influence a poet might have as spiritual guide or counselor is distinguishable from the question of how good the poetry is as poetry. Not that we have any reason to be apologetic about the poetic value of Wordsworth's poetry. Some is very bad (e.g., certain lines in "When to the attraction of the busy world," "Peter Bell," and "Vaudrecour and Julia"), but the best poems (e.g., *The Prelude,* "Lines Composed a Few Miles above Tintern Abbey," "Michael," the sonnet "Upon Westminster Bridge," and the "Lucy" poems) hold their own as and with the finest poems in English.

Mill describes Wordsworth's restorative effect on him in chapter 5 of his *Autobiography* and pays tribute to Wordsworth's poems for their effect in resolving what he calls "a crisis in my mental history"; they offered him "a medicine for my state of mind." Mill found in Wordsworth gratification of his own "love of rural objects and natural scenery," but more deeply from the poems, "I seemed to learn what would be the perennial sources of happiness, when all the greater evils of life shall have been removed," for they "seemed to be the very culture of the feelings, which I was in quest of" (Mill, 1969, pp. 88–89.) It is an interesting thought about the nature of Wordsworth's poetry that this moving tribute to it is paid by a philosopher.

[*See also* Coleridge; Imagination; Literature, *article on* Literary Aesthetics; Poetics; Romanticism, *article on* Philosophy and Literature; *and* Sublime.]

BIBLIOGRAPHY

Works by Wordsworth

A Guide through the District of the Lakes in the North of England (5th ed., 1835). Edited by Ernest de Selincourt. London, 1970.

Literary Criticism of William Wordsworth. Edited by Paul M. Zall. Lincoln, Nebr., 1966.

The Prelude: A Parallel Text. Edited by J. C. Maxwell. Harmondsworth, England, 1971.

Other Sources

Bate, Jonathan. *Romantic Ecology: Wordsworth and the Environmental Tradition.* London and New York, 1991.

Bateson, Frederick Wilse. *Wordsworth: A Re-interpretation.* London and New York, 1956.

Burke, Edmund. *A Philosophical Enquiry into the Origin of Our Ideas of the Sublime and Beautiful.* 2d ed. London, 1759; reprint, Menston, England, 1970. See part 5, section 7, "How Words Influence the Passions."

Davies, Hunter. *William Wordsworth: A Biography.* London, 1980.

Gallie, W. B. "Essentially Contested Concepts." *Proceedings of the Aristotelian Society* 56 (1955–1956): 167–198.

Hartman, Geoffrey H. *Wordsworth's Poetry, 1787–1814.* New Haven, 1964.

Hartman, Geoffrey H. *The Unremarkable Wordsworth*. Minneapolis, 1987.

Jones, J. *The Egotistical Sublime: A History of Wordsworth's Imagination*. London, 1954.

Macdonald, Margaret. "Some Distinctive Features of Arguments Used in Criticism of the Arts." In *Aesthetics and Language*, edited by William Elton, pp. 114–130. Oxford, 1959.

Mill, John Stuart. *Autobiography*. Edited by Jack Stillinger. London, 1969.

Noyes, Russell. *Wordsworth and the Art of Landscape*. Bloomington, Ind., 1968.

Stallknecht, Newton P. *Strange Seas of Thought: Studies in William Wordsworth's Philosophy of Man and Nature*. 2d ed. Bloomington, Ind., 1958.

Stevenson, Charles L. *Ethics and Language*. New Haven, 1944. See chap. 9.

Weiskel, Thomas. *The Romantic Sublime: Studies in the Structure and Psychology of Transcendence*. Baltimore, 1976.

T. J. DIFFEY

WORK OF ART. *See* Art World; Definition of Art; Essentialism; *and* Ontology of Art.

WORRINGER, WILHELM (1881–1965), German art historian and theorist. Any assessment of Worringer's aesthetics has to begin with its reception. Although he was an academic art historian, Worringer had a greater impact in other areas than in his own field. His early works, mainly *Abstraction and Empathy* (1908) and, to a lesser extent, *Form Problems of the Gothic* (1911), exercised an uncommonly broad influence on discussions of aesthetics in the years before World War I, as well as on German Expressionist painters themselves, on writers of the period (mainly 1910–1920), on early film theory in the 1920s, on psychologists and social theorists, on later art critics such as Herbert Read, and even on American literary criticism after World War II in Joseph Frank's influential theory of "spatial form." Frank credits Worringer with a stature for aesthetics in the early twentieth century equal to Gotthold Ephraim Lessing (the author of *Laocoön* [1766]) in the eighteenth century, and Frank's use of Worringer gave another life to the latter's ideas in the second half of the twentieth century.

Nonetheless, the academic discipline of art history has been slow to consider Worringer's stature in modernism for several reasons. Worringer's scholarship departed from traditional humanism and its exaltation of Greco-Roman, Renaissance, and eighteenth-century classicism. By writing mainly about the art of so-called primitive cultures and of the Middle Ages, Worringer gave aesthetic priority to nonnaturalistic forms of representation. Also, although his studies appeared historical in topic and scope, his work addressed artistic and cultural issues of his own contemporaries—a very unconventional scholarly activism on behalf of contemporary art that at the time was not con-sidered the domain of academic scholarship. Further, in his art-historical studies, Worringer was less a systematic, historical positivist than a cultural theorist, who subordinated empirical detail to a comprehensive, but also speculative and hypothetical, "method" that seemed almost visionary in its provocative originality and its uncertain validity. Most notably perhaps, Worringer employed a simple but forceful and dramatic rhetoric, unencumbered by footnotes, that won him an audience outside the academy but suspicion within it.

Worringer's first book, *Abstraction and Empathy* (1908), was a sensation and remains his most well known, and is still in print. In it, Worringer developed the very first aesthetics for abstract or nonrepresentational art, whether it be Egyptian or African, Gothic or Baroque (or modernist), which also coincided with the earliest experiments in modern abstraction (cf. Pablo Picasso's *Demoiselles d'Avignon* of 1907); his work provided a theoretical justification and a genealogy for that tendency (in French Cubism and German Expressionism), and was duly embraced. Yet, the volume was not a history; its subtitle identifies it as *A Contribution to the Psychology of Style*, whereby formal and stylistic particularities (in any genre or medium) reflect the psychological disposition of the artist and, in turn, of the historical epoch, its "world feeling" *(Weltgefühl)*. That "world feeling" directs the artist's and epoch's "artistic volition" *(Kunstwollen)*, a concept and term borrowed from Alois Riegl. Different styles in art do not reflect progress or its lack, but simply a different "world feeling" and "artistic volition." The art of each period is thus the fullest realization of those impulses, and not a chapter in the "progress" of technical ability to copy nature. Art does not represent the external world; art presents a metaphysical disposition. Thus, Worringer's views in 1908 refute the materialist and evolutionary views of art that dominated the nineteenth century, and anticipate Expressionism, whereby *Stil* (style) in art reveals profound emotions and metaphysical depths.

Worringer's dichotomy distinguishes sharply between naturalistic and expressive tendencies in art. Naturalistic art (from the ancient Greeks to the Renaissance to nineteenth-century Realism and Impressionism) reflects, in its attempts to attain mimetic fidelity, a metaphysical disposition of existential comfort in the world, based on science and humankind's ability to understand and control nature. Such naturalistic art reveals what Worringer called "empathy" (a term adopted from Theodor Lipps) or the tautological desire to identify with what is familiar. Aestheticians such as Jakob Burckhardt (and later E. H. Gombrich) had described the history of art as a narrative of progress in mimetic depiction and equated beauty to harmony, proportion and fidelity to external appearances. In stark contrast, nonnaturalistic or abstract forms reflect primordial psychic anguish, an existential alienation from the natural world, or what Worringer famously called "spiritual agoraphobia"

(Platzangst). Abstract art in any period expresses a desire to transcend reality by transfixing the contingency and relativity of existence in timeless, static forms: in visual terms, this meant eliminating three-dimensional depth perspectives. Thus, abstract art is not representational; it expresses as a secular icon both metaphysical anxiety *(Angst)* and the urge to spiritual transcendence, an instinct for an irrational permanence beyond visible phenomena.

Worringer's second book, a study of Lucas Cranach (also 1908), expands the social dimension to his "psychology of style." Worringer goes against prevailing "genius" theories of the artist to read the "mass psyche" of the Reformation in the production of Cranach's workshop for the art market of a new German burgher class. Worringer's discussion there of the "multiple production of images" for the market may well have influenced Walter Benjamin's famous essay "The Work of Art in the Age of Mechanical Reproduction" (1936). Worringer also announced there his desire to see German art in terms of native German-Gothic traditions instead of the Greco-Roman Renaissance. The introduction to *Form Problems of the Gothic* (1911) describes his hypothetical method of art history (and his antipathy to positivism) and the text applies his general aesthetics to a specific area of nonclassical art. As in his first work, Worringer's aesthetics is based on psychological types (that influenced Carl Gustav Jung), but here also on racialist lines: "primitive," "classical," "Oriental," and Germanic "Gothic" man(kind). Worringer locates in the forms of Gothic architecture the transcendental impulse of Gothic mankind's "sublime hysteria," a "madness with method" that translates matter into the formal, constructivist expression of spiritual longing. His study figured as a disguised manifesto for German Expressionism, for which he became a leading spokesman.

Worringer's thesis countered reactionary criticism against non-German (French) influences on modern art in Germany. Indeed, Wassily Kandinsky invited him to lead the rebuttal to Carl Vinnen's nationalistic *Protest of German Artists* (1911); Worringer declined the editorship but contributed an essay, "On the Historical Development of the Most Modern Art" (1911), to the volume. Later, in an elegiac essay of 1919, "Critical Thoughts on the New Art," Worringer reflected on the yearnings and shortcomings of Expressionism, its failed attempt to spiritualize expression, and in 1921, in his *Questions about Contemporary Art,* he publicly declared its end. In his famous essay "Greatness and Decline of Expressionism" (1934), György Lukács seized on Worringer's remarks to indict the spiritual pretentions of Expressionism as an escapist mystification designed to avoid politics and accommodate reigning bourgeois ideology. Yet, Lukács, whose own early work has affinities to Worringer's, ignores the sociological dimension of Worringer's argument and the historical context of art-historical debates. In fact, Worringer argued that the Expressionist spirit had only migrated out of art and into scholarly works of critical intellect (in line with the notion of "New Objectivity" [*Neue Sachlichkeit*] in Weimar society).

By the time of his *Egyptian Art* (1927), Worringer had reversed his famous early views on "primitive" abstraction. He still engaged his historical scholarship in contemporary issues, but the parallel he draws between ancient Egypt and modern America reveals the book as a diatribe against "Americanization" and a symptom of general anxieties about social instability and change in the Weimar period. All of Worringer's work stands in relation to the thesis he developed in *Abstraction and Empathy* (1908) and elaborated on in *Form Problems of the Gothic* (1911) and in his essays. But his later scholarship never matched the suggestiveness of his early, provocative ideas on the psychological genesis of abstract art. In fact, his own career through the 1920s and then after World War II appears as only one line (and not even the most important) of the influence that extended from his early work in so many different directions.

[*See also* Abstraction; *and* Expressionism.]

BIBLIOGRAPHY

Works by Worringer

Abstraktion und Einfühlung: Ein Beitrag zur Stilpsychologie. Munich, 1908. In English as *Abstraction and Empathy: A Contribution to the Psychology of Style,* translated by Michael Bullock (New York, 1953; 4th ed., New York, 1980).
Lukas Cranach. Munich, 1908.
"Entwicklungsgeschichtliches zur modernsten Kunst." In *Im Kampf um die Kunst: Die Antwort zum "Protest deutscher Künstler,"* pp. 92–99. Munich, 1911.
Formprobleme der Gotik. Munich, 1911. In English as *Form Problems of the Gothic,* translation unattributed (New York, 1920); *Form in Gothic,* edited by Herbert Read (London, 1927; rev. ed., New York, 1964).
Die altdeutsche Buchillustration. Munich, 1912.
"Kritische Gedanken zur neuen Kunst." *Genius* 1 (1919): 221–236. Included in *Fragen und Gegenfragen.*
Künstlerische Zeitfragen. Munich, 1921. Reprinted in *Fragen und Gegenfragen.*
Die Anfänge der Tafelmalerei. Leipzig, 1924.
Ägyptische Kunst: Probleme ihrer Wertung. Munich, 1927. In English as *Egyptian Art,* authorized translation, edited by Bernhard Rackham (London, 1928).
Griechentum und Gotik: Vom Weltreich des Hellenismus. Munich, 1928.
Fragen und Gegenfragen: Schriften zum Kunstproblem. Munich, 1956.

Other Sources

Bushart, Magdalena. *Der Geist der Gotik und die expressionistische Kunst: Kunstgeschichte und Kunsttheorie, 1911–1925.* Munich, 1990.
Donahue, Neil H. *Forms of Disruption: Abstraction in Modern German Prose.* Ann Arbor, 1993.
Donahue, Neil H., ed. *Invisible Cathedrals: The Expressionist Art History of Wilhelm Worringer.* University Park, Pa., 1995.
Nachtsheim, Stephan. *Kunstphilosophie und empirische Kunstforschung, 1870–1920.* Berlin, 1984.
Perkins, Geoffrey. *Contemporary Theory of Expressionism.* Frankfurt am Main, 1974.

NEIL H. DONAHUE

WRIGHT, FRANK LLOYD (1867–1959), modern American architect. Wright's designs are more popular today, more than a century after he began his practice in 1893 and decades after his death in 1959, than they were during his lifetime. Although it is no doubt increasingly difficult to understand how Wright's designs emerged at the moment of their conception and construction, the built works that Wright left are immediately accessible to those who inhabit their precisely articulated, experientially determined spaces for living.

Born in 1867, Wright was raised in a household where the study of nature, the Unitarian faith, the ideas of American Transcendental philosophy, and the Froebel system of kindergarten training were all powerfully present. These complex yet complementary systems of thought had in common the belief that the material and spiritual worlds could not be separated, but were in fact one; that every physical thing was the consequence of, and had consequences for, spiritual thought—"All form is an effect of character," as Ralph Waldo Emerson said—and therefore that all form had moral meaning.

Wright's development as an architect involved the evolution of this moral imperative through the search for a more principled relation to historical form, for a monumentality appropriate to the young American nation, and for a systematic yet personal process of architectural design for the American house through the engagement of the landscape, the materials of construction, and the experience of inhabitation. Wright was thirty-three years of age in 1900: to be fully understood, therefore, Wright's architecture should be seen as issuing not from twentieth-century society, but from the American culture of the nineteenth century.

Toward an American Architecture. Wright's mentor and architectural father figure, Louis Sullivan, while calling attention to the absence in his own time of an appropriate American architecture, also warned against efforts to speed its arrival by transplanting historical styles onto the American continent. Any truly organic American architecture would only develop on a regional basis, he felt, with variations dependent on local climate, landscape, building methods and materials. Sullivan, together with his young apprentice Wright, searched for alternatives to what they believed to be the exhausted Western classical tradition, analyzing the ornamental patterns from Islamic and Oriental sources presented by Owen Jones in *The Grammar of Ornament*.

In an attempt to develop an indigenous American architecture, the "Chicago school," with Sullivan at its center, was established by 1890. The efforts of this group were soon overwhelmed, however, by the classical architecture dictated for the World Columbian Exposition, which opened in Chicago in 1893: uniform, academically correct, explicitly noncontextual and intended to be the same around the world. That this academically defined "tradition" was so appealing to a young America eager to establish and display its recently attained position as a global power reveals a basic aspect of the American character that Wright was to struggle against throughout his life—the belief that historical form alone is sufficient to produce architecture of significance.

Although Wright's later attacks on his academically correct contemporaries are well known, few have noted the degree to which he directly engaged the formal order underlying the architecture of classical antiquity in his own early work of the Prairie Period (1895–1915). Yet, in the first comprehensive national publication of Wright's work in 1908 when he was forty years old, Wright challenged the academic classicists' exclusive control over the interpretation of architectural history, and indicated how his own early work, with its symmetry, axial planning, hierarchical ordering from earth to sky, and attention to the nature of materials, demonstrated a more principled manner of relating to architectural history. Despite what he termed the "radical" appearance of his forms, Wright's designs were the result of exhaustive analyses of the great architecture of the past.

A Modern Monumentality. At the time Wright left Sullivan's office in 1893, an appropriate monumental form had failed to emerge in American architecture. The legacy of the steel-framed office tower, which Wright had received from Sullivan and the Chicago school, had in fact proved totally incapable of dealing with the need for monumentality in giving form to the public realm. As a manifestation of the economic determination of scale and massing, the universal planning grid, and the production of uniform interiors to be "styled" later by tenants, the Chicago frame skyscraper was a projection of private commercial interests at a scale heretofore given only to public buildings, yet totally lacking the qualities inherent in a monument. Therefore, a primary motivation for Wright's reclaiming of the buildings of antiquity was their undeniable monumentality.

Wright understood that the systematic production of universal space resulting from the office building's column grid could not give form to monumental public buildings, and this was reflected in his work as early as 1894, only a year after leaving Sullivan's office, with his project for the Monolithic Concrete Bank. Wright achieved his fully developed vision of an appropriate monumentality for public buildings ten years later with his designs for the Larkin Building of 1904 and Unity Temple of 1905.

The plans of these buildings are simple rectangles, the spaces within ordered by the exposed structural rhythm, with mezzanines surrounding and overlooking a central multiheight space, lit by high clerestory windows and skylights, and allowing no views out at eye level. On the outside, these buildings are closed, solid, and possessed a severity unlike anything else of their time, seeming to relate more to the stark rectilinearity of ancient monuments. Like Wright's later public buildings, such as the superb Johnson

Wax Building of 1936, the singularity of their central spaces, and the manner in which these are born from a fusion of their form, structure, and material, are experienced as profoundly monumental.

For Wright, the monumentality appropriate to American public spaces would inevitably take the form of introverted compounds, seen from the outside as groupings of powerful independent elements bound together by mutual purpose; a primary and secondary (service) volume with entry occurring between, leading to the low, dark, horizontal, rotating entry sequence, which compresses and then releases us into the tall, light, hidden, vertical central space—the whole admirably demonstrating Wright's mastery in orchestrating the perceptions of those inhabiting his buildings through movement, space, and light. The entire spatial and ornamental program for Wright's public buildings, from plans and massing to furniture and carpet patterns, was ordered through formal manipulations of the square and cube, which Wright considered the most perfect of geometries. Wright intended that his public buildings be experienced as sacred spaces, whatever their function, their introspective interiors flooded with transcendent light to create a morally edifying effect for those inhabiting the public place.

The Natural House. Throughout his career, the design of the American single-family house was the primary task and mission that Wright gave himself as an architect. He considered each of his house designs as a variation of an evolving ideal theme, so that each design in-formed or gave form to the next in the sequence. Wright's house designs make place through his comprehensive understanding of inhabitation, wherein site, space, and material are woven together to become the setting for the repeated rituals of daily life—his houses are places of shelter and outlook, with the fireplace as center, the horizon as edge, and the inhabitant's experience as an unfolding of space. Wright believed that the quality and integrity of spaces positively affected those who lived in them, and that a life taking place in the beneficial influence of nature would be infinitely better for it.

For Wright, it was essential that daily life be lived in direct communion with nature, and that the American house be designed as a natural place. Wright believed—as did Ralph Waldo Emerson and Henry David Thoreau—that because man was a product of nature, he was capable of learning about his own essential nature from regular and intimate contact with the natural landscape. He gave all his houses a horizontal emphasis in their form and space, believing that this grounded the house, making it a suitable foundation for the domestic life within. He began by incorporating the formative power of the landscape as the primal place of occupation—the building began with the ground on which it stood.

Wright's Prairie Period houses, such as the Robie House and the Coonley House, both of 1908, are extroverted counterparts to his introverted public buildings. The house

is anchored by the central solid fireplace mass, and the spaces open out in all directions at eye level, outriding walls and overhanging eaves layering the house into the earth, projecting its grid out into the landscape and simultaneously pulling the landscape into the house. In this way, Wright gave the entire suburban site a geometric order so that the house and site were inextricably bound to one another.

Wright believed that the house should not merely mimic or repeat or even merge with the form of the landscape, but rather that architecture clarifies and makes present the spatial and habitable qualities latent but hidden in the landform. Wright sought to construct buildings that acknowledged their influence on the site and the changes inevitably accompanying man's settlement of the landscape, with the intention that the site be a better place after construction of the house.

This is exemplified by Wright's domestic masterpiece for Edgar Kaufman, called "Fallingwater" and built outside Pittsburgh in 1935 along and over a waterfall in a heavily wooded landscape. The house draws all the profiles of the landforms to itself, resolving them within its order, so that Fallingwater appears to have grown out of the ground and into the light, making present the latent power of the boulders on which it sits above the waterfall—the same boulders that emerge from the rippling "water" of the slate living room floor to provide a place of refuge in front of the fireplace. The natural setting is so integrated into this house that in occupying it people are constantly reminded of where they are by the sound of the waterfall, the flow of space and movement inside and outside across the floors and terraces, and the views and sunlight framed by the steel windows—to inhabit Fallingwater is to engage in the most intimate communion with nature.

The year after he designed Fallingwater, Wright designed the Herbert Jacobs House of 1936, the first of his Usonian Houses, affordable homes for the emerging American middle class. Unlike the cruciform Prairie Houses, the Usonian Houses (1936–1959) were L-shaped in plan, folding inward to make a corner, anchoring their sites without completely enclosing them, so that the spatial weaving is applied to the enclosed landscape as well as interior space, and the center of the spatial composition is outside the house, in the garden. Protecting the garden as its "interior," the house presents a closed facade to the street, and the living room focuses sideways or laterally toward the garden. Wright was careful to assure that the spaces of his houses were oriented to receive sun at appropriate times during the day, insisting on a southern orientation for the living room elevation, which faced the garden; flooded with southern sun, these courts or gardens became the focus of the house and the life that went on within it.

Wright's designs emphasized the topographic, and included in that the natural landform and the history of hu-

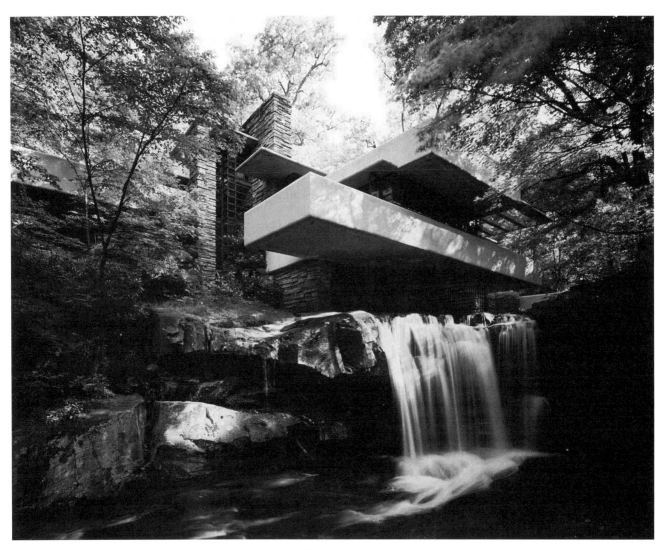

WRIGHT. Frank Lloyd Wright, *Exterior, Fallingwater House*, Bear Run, Pennsylvania. (Copyright by the Frank Lloyd Wright Foundation; photograph courtesy of Art Resource, New York; used by permission.)

man occupation of the site. In his design for Broadacre City of 1935, intended to merge city and countryside in a seamless unity, benefiting from the attributes of both, as well as the individual houses conceived as being stitched into Broadacre City's fabric, Wright's work acknowledged and made experiential the close relationship between agriculture and architecture; agriculture (to care for and cultivate the land) and architecture (to build and edify) as related activities on the earth—tending and transforming the landscape.

The Nature of Materials. The ideal of integrating space and form with the structure and materials with which it is made was primary for Wright, and he engaged in a constant search for a comprehensive order that would encompass both composition and construction, an order similar to the fusion of structure, material, form, and space that he found in his studies of nature. Essential to Wright's archi-

tecture was his understanding that the way a space is made or constructed is directly related to the way it is experienced. Construction was not simply a means to some end—it was an essential part of the final experience of life that took place within the house, and thus was to be fully integrated in the process of design.

Wright felt that this integrated understanding of structure, construction, space, and experience was capable of giving habitable form to the concepts and ideals of the American Transcendental philosophers, and he indicated that his compositions with squares and cubes were intended to connect his houses with nature, as called for in the poetry of Walt Whitman, "chanting the square deific." The square grid that underlay all of Wright's house designs operated as an essential compositional and scaling device, a measure and organizational method for construction, and a means of achieving economy—all required in his view to accomplish the integral order that resulted in the making of beautiful spaces. In synthesizing and integrating spatial and constructive grammars, Wright brought space into presence by articulating both the physical and emotional qualities that may be experienced in materials, structure, and the act of construction.

In his search for order that would be reinforced and edified in the process of construction and material realization, Wright grappled throughout his life with the one material that proved perfectly "plastic," able to be formed into any formal or structural shape: reinforced concrete. Wright was often critical of concrete's inherent lack of internal order—the type of modular order evident in the brick and standardized wood studs and boards he had used so effectively to give rhythm to his house designs. In seeking a more direct revelation of concrete's construction module, Wright developed the custom-cast concrete block, used most convincingly in the superb Freeman House of 1923. The organizing square grid operates in both plan and section, constituting a veritable knitting together of the surfaces, resulting in a fully integrated building mass that, despite its cubic form and the weight of its concrete construction, imparts an impression of being fabricated from a lightweight textile.

Wright achieved his highest level of resolution of spatial, constructive, and experiential forms in his Usonian Houses, where the horizontal (plan) grid operates at an entirely different scale than the vertical (section) layering, recognizing the fact that in inhabiting space, human beings experience horizontal dimensions (distances on the ground) very differently from vertical dimensions (distances off the ground). These houses, although physically small, feel much larger because of their asymmetrical volumes, which do not allow the inhabitant to see the entire space as a result of its wrapping around a corner and being out of sight; their horizontally layered walls, where shelves, tables, desks, seats, and storage units appear to be either pulled out of or pushed into the wooden surfaces; and the three overlapping but differing plans at floor, door top, and ceiling. Each space is literally built into the next, so that even the heating is cast into the concrete floor slab—as a result these houses feel remarkably like large pieces of furniture, with subtle articulations within the constructed spatial fabric to accommodate even the most modest of domestic events.

Intimate Possession of Every Interior. In the end, the question of Wright's importance to architecture and modern culture centers not on issues of style or form but on the aspect of expanded experiential possibilities made evident in his works. As the primary method he used to order and construct spatial experiences, Wright stated early in his career that the floor plan was of preeminent importance in his conception of architecture; the building was conceived as being generated from the plan, which gave form and order to the space within to be lived in. For Wright, the only

reason to shape space in plan was for the experience of man; architecture was first and foremost concerned with the presentation of man. Architecture gave order to man's experience, and thus made him present in the world—in space conceived and formed as being occupied; the act of inhabitation embodied.

Denying that architecture was directed toward the production of isolated sculptural objects, Wright defined buildings as the background or framework for human existence; architecture gave dignity to daily life. Wright's architecture appealed at a fundamental level to the occupant's sense of embodied presence, bodily movement, and the position of the eye. Wright's system of design was measured, scaled, and calibrated precisely by the human body and its experience, and although the geometric rigor of Wright's planning is well known, the esteem in which he held the concepts of use and comfort is not as widely understood. The intellectual and formal order of Wright's plans was balanced by the physical and spiritual engagement of the inhabitant; for Wright, concept and experience were one and the same.

Wright's designs condensed natural light in way that reflected light's complex and multivalent effect on the experience of architecture's inhabitants. Wright utilized roofs as shadow makers, and defined the place of inhabitation as the space made by shadows cast on the earth. Although Wright's house plans often projected the main rooms out so that light could enter from two or even three sides, what increased was not the interior light level but the ability to view out, to survey the landscape from within the shadowed interior. In his house designs, Wright developed a culture of light as it relates to the landscape, the creation of a sense of refuge—seeing without being seen.

Wright understood that humans inhabit architecture through movement, allowing space and material to be woven together in their experience. The dynamic spatial development of Wright's architecture originated in his understanding of inhabitation and experience as nonstatic, indivisible events, capable of being framed only by boundless space.

In his houses, Wright achieved what few if any others have in our time: the systematic production of unique places. Yet, Wright insisted that the principles on which his work was based were not invented by one man or one age, and that his work was founded on architecture understood as a discipline—a history of principled place making. Indeed, it could be argued that Wright's contribution is virtually unmatched in the twentieth century, which produced a rich assortment of new forms but few systematic conceptions that link spatial form and order to human occupation and experience. Wright's definition of architecture is exemplified in his works: each building is a celebration of man embodied in a world of his own making.

[*See also* Architecture; *and* Modernism, *article on* Modernity and Tradition in Architecture.]

BIBLIOGRAPHY

Works by Wright

Ausgeführte Bauten und Entwürfe von Frank Lloyd Wright. Berlin, 1910. Reprinted as *Drawings and Plans of Frank Lloyd Wright: The Early Period, 1893–1909* (New York, 1983) and as *Studies and Executed Buildings by Frank Lloyd Wright* (New York, 1986).
An Autobiography. New York, 1932; reprint, New York, 1977.
The Natural House. New York, 1954.
In the Cause of Architecture. Edited by Frederick Gutheim. New York, 1975. Reprint of *Architectural Record* essays, 1908–1952.
Frank Lloyd Wright: Collected Writings. 5 vols. Edited by Bruce Brooks Pfeiffer. New York, 1992–1995.

Other Sources

Alofsin, Anthony. *Frank Lloyd Wright: The Lost Years, 1910–1922.* Chicago, 1993.
Bolon, Carol R., Robert S. Nelson, and Linda Seidel, eds. *The Nature of Frank Lloyd Wright.* Chicago, 1988.
Brooks, H. Allen, ed. *Writings on Wright.* Cambridge, Mass., 1981.
Futagawa, Yokio, ed. *Frank Lloyd Wright.* 12 vols. Text by Bruce B. Pfeiffer. Tokyo, 1984–1988.
Hitchcock, Henry Russell. *In the Nature of Materials, 1887–1941: The Buildings of Frank Lloyd Wright.* New York, 1942.
Hoffmann, Donald. *Frank Lloyd Wright's Fallingwater: The House and Its History.* New York, 1978; 2d rev. ed., New York, 1993.
Levine, Neil. *The Architecture of Frank Lloyd Wright.* Princeton, N.J., 1996.
Lipman, Jonathan. *Frank Lloyd Wright and the Johnson Wax Buildings.* New York, 1986.
Manson, Grant Carpenter. *Frank Lloyd Wright to 1910: The First Golden Age.* New York, 1958.
McCarter, Robert, ed. *Frank Lloyd Wright: A Primer on Architectural Principles.* New York, 1991.
Nute, Kevin. *Frank Lloyd Wright and Japan.* New York, 1993.
Quinan, Jack. *Frank Lloyd Wright's Larkin Building: Myth and Fact.* Cambridge, Mass., 1987.
Riley, Terence, and Peter Reed, eds. *Frank Lloyd Wright: Architect.* New York, 1994.
Secrest, Meryle. *Frank Lloyd Wright.* New York, 1992.
Sergeant, John. *Frank Lloyd Wright's Usonian Houses: The Case for Organic Architecture.* New York, 1976.
Siry, Joseph M. *Unity Temple: Frank Lloyd Wright and Architecture for Liberal Religion.* Cambridge and New York, 1996.
Smith, Norris Kelly. *Frank Lloyd Wright: A Study in Architectural Content.* Englewood Cliffs, N.J., 1966.
Storrer, William Allin. *The Frank Lloyd Wright Companion.* Chicago, 1993.
Sweeney, Robert. *Frank Lloyd Wright: An Annotated Bibliography.* Los Angeles, 1978.

ROBERT MCCARTER

ZHUANGZI. *See* Daoist Aesthetics.

DIRECTORY OF CONTRIBUTORS

James S. Ackerman
Arthur Kingsley Porter Professor Emeritus of Fine Arts, Sackler Museum, Harvard University
Architecture, *article on* Italian Renaissance Aesthetics

Craig Adcock
Professor of Art History, University of Iowa
Marcel Duchamp, *article on* Survey of Art

Jan A. Aertsen
Professor of Philosophy and Director, Thomas-Institut, Universität zu Köln
Beauty, *article on* Medieval Concepts

Alexander Alberro
Assistant Professor of Art History, University of Florida, Gainesville
Conceptual Art, *historical and theoretical overview article*

Tamara Albertini
Assistant Professor of Philosophy, University of Hawaii at Manoa
Renaissance Italian Aesthetics

Daniel Albright
Richard L. Turner Professor in the Humanities, University of Rochester
Ineffability

Thomas Alexander
Associate Professor of Philosophy, Southern Illinois University
John Dewey, *article on* Theory of Expression

Philip A. Alperson
Professor of Philosophy, University of Louisville; Editor, Journal of Aesthetics and Art Criticism
Improvisation, *overview article;* Performance

Ernst van Alphen
Director of Education and Communication, Museum Boymans–Van Beuningen, Rotterdam
Morality and Aesthetics, *article on* Art, Morality, and the Holocaust

Charles Altieri
Professor of English, University of California, Berkeley
Postmodernism, *article on* Postmodern American Poetry

Douglas R. Anderson
Associate Professor of Philosophy, Pennsylvania State University
Robin George Collingwood

Richard L. Anderson
Professor of Liberal Arts, Kansas City Art Institute
Anthropology and Aesthetics

Simon Anderson
Associate Professor and Chair, Department of Art History, Theory, and Criticism, School of the Art Institute of Chicago
Anti-Art; Situationist Aesthetics

Dudley Andrew
Angelo Bertocci Professor of Critical Studies and Director, Institute for Cinema and Culture, University of Iowa
André Bazin

Keith Ansell-Pearson
Senior Lecturer in Philosophy, University of Warwick
Friedrich Wilhelm Nietzsche, *article on* Nietzsche on Art and Politics

Mark Antliff
Associate Professor of Art, Queen's University, Kingston, Canada
Henry-Louis Bergson; Politics and Aesthetics, *article on* Aestheticized Politics

David Armstrong
Professor of Classics, University of Texas, Austin
Longinus

Philip Armstrong
Visiting Lecturer, Ohio State University
Iconography and Iconology

Rudolf Arnheim
Professor Emeritus of Psychology of Art, Harvard University
Rudolf Arnheim, *article on* Dynamics of Art; Psychology of Art

Elizabeth Asmis
Professor of Classics, University of Chicago
Hellenistic Aesthetics, *article on* Philosophers and Literary Critics

George W. S. Bailey
Associate Professor of Philosophy, East Carolina University
George Dickie

George Baird
G. Ware Travelstead Professor of Architecture, Graduate School of Design, Harvard University
Semiotics, *article on* Semiotics and Architecture

Mieke Bal
Professor of the Theory of Literature and Director, Amsterdam School of Cultural Analysis, Universiteit van Amsterdam
Narrative, *article on* Narrative and the Visual and Literary Arts; Charles Sanders Peirce; Semiotics, *article on* Semiotics as a Theory of Art

Anna Balakian
Professor of Comparative Literature, New York University (deceased)
Symbolism

Michael Baldwin
Artist, Oxford, United Kingdom
Conceptual Art, *article on* History of the Unformed

Sally Banes
Marian Hannah Winter Professor of Theatre History and Dance Studies, University of Wisconsin, Madison
Postmodernism, *article on* Postmodern Dance

Stephen Bann
Professor of Modern Cultural Studies, School of Arts and Image Studies, Rutherford College, University of Kent
Victor Cousin; Walter Horatio Pater

Annette Barnes
Professor of Philosophy, University of Maryland, Baltimore County
Definition of Art; Interpretation, *article on* Analytic Interpretation

Stanley Bates
Walter Cerf Distinguished College Professor of Philosophy, Middlebury College
Leo Nikolaevich Tolstoy

Norton Batkin
Director, Graduate Program, Center for Curatorial Studies and Art in Contemporary Culture, and Associate Professor of Philosophy and Art History, Bard College
Formalism, *article on* Formalism in Analytic Aesthetics

Christine Battersby
Senior Lecturer in Philosophy, University of Warwick
Genius, *article on* Genius and Feminism

Bruce Baugh
Associate Professor of Philosophy, University College of the Cariboo, Kamloops, Canada
Rock Music

Michael Baxandall
Professor of Art History, University of California, Berkeley
Jean-Baptiste Du Bos

Gordon C. F. Bearn
Associate Professor and Chair, Department of Philosophy, Lehigh University
Kitsch

Howard S. Becker
Professor of Sociology and Music, University of Washington
Art World

Frederick Beiser
Associate Professor of Philosophy, Indiana University
Johann Georg Hamann; Johann Gottfried Herder; Johann Christoph Friedrich von Schiller; Karl Wilhelm Friedrich von Schlegel

Elizabeth Belfiore
Professor of Classical and Near Eastern Studies, University of Minnesota
Aristotle, *article on* Survey of Thought

Antonio Benítez-Rojo
Thomas B. Walton, Jr., Memorial Professor of Romance Languages, Amherst College
Caribbean Aesthetics

Maurice Berger
Senior Fellow, Vera List Center for Art and Politics, New School for Social Research
Politics and Aesthetics, *article on* Difference and Culture

Arnold Berleant
Professor Emeritus of Philosophy, Long Island University
Environmental Aesthetics

Robert Bernasconi
Moss Chair of Excellence in Philosophy, University of Memphis
Martin Heidegger, *article on* Heidegger's Displacement of the Concept of Art

J. M. Bernstein
W. Alton Jones Professor of Philosophy, Vanderbilt University
Alienation, Aesthetic

J. Duncan Berry
Independent scholar, Harwich Port, Massachusetts
Heinrich Hübsch

Monika Betzler
Assistant Professor of Philosophy, Georg-August-Universität Göttingen
Georg Simmel

Timothy Binkley
Chair, Graduate Computer Art Department, School of Visual Arts, New York
Computer Art; Digital Media, *overview article*

Inge Boer
Associate Professor of Literary Studies and Multiculturalism, Universiteit van Amsterdam
Orientalism

Ron Bontekoe
Associate Professor of Philosophy, University of Hawaii at Manoa
Paul Ricoeur; Friedrich Daniel Ernst Schleiermacher

David Bordwell
Jacques Ledoux Professor of Film Studies, University of Wisconsin, Madison
Film, *article on* Film Theory

Leon Botstein
President and Leon Levy Professor in the Arts and Humanities, Bard College; Editor, The Musical Quarterly; and Music Director, American Symphony Orchestra
Modernism, *article on* Modern Music

Curtis Bowman

Lecturer in Philosophy, University of Pennsylvania
Karl Philipp Moritz

Peggy Zeglin Brand

Assistant Professor of Philosophy and Women's Studies, Indiana University
Feminism, *article on* Feminism and Tradition; Parody; Pastiche

Richard Brilliant

A. S. Garbedian Professor in the Humanities, Art History, and Archaeology, Columbia University
Hellenistic Aesthetics, *article on* Visual Arts; Portraiture; Roman Aesthetics

Joyce Brodsky

Professor of Art, University of California, Santa Cruz
Feminism, *article on* Feminist Art History

Elisabeth Bronfen

Professor of English and American Literatures, Universität Zurich
Death and Aesthetics

Lee Brown

Associate Professor of Philosophy, Ohio State University
Jazz

Gerald L. Bruns

William P. and Hazel B. White Professor of English, University of Notre Dame
Hermeneutics

Norman Bryson

Professor of Art History, Harvard University
Semiotics, *article on* Semiotics as a Theory of Art

Peter Bürger

Professor of Linguistics and Cultural Studies, Universität Bremen
Autonomy, *article on* Critique of Autonomy; Avant Garde

Ronna Burger

Associate Professor of Philosophy, Tulane University
Aristotle, *article on* Aristole on Mimesis

Susan Bush

Associate in Research, Fairbank Center for East Asian Research, Harvard University
Chinese Aesthetics, *article on* Painting Theory and Criticism

Joseph Buttigieg

Professor of English and Fellow of the Nanovic Institute for European Studies, University of Notre Dame
Antonio Gramsci

Richard Buxton

Professor of Greek Languages and Literatures, University of Bristol
Tragedy, *article on* Greek Tragedy

Oleg V. Bychkov

Lecturer, Franciscan Institute, St. Bonaventure University
Russian Aesthetics, *article on* Religious Aesthetics

Victor V. Bychkov

Head, Department of Nonclassical Aesthetics, Institute of Philosophy, Moscow
Byzantine Aesthetics; Icon; Russian Aesthetics, *article on* Religious Aesthetics

David Cahan

Professor of History, University of Nebraska, Lincoln
Hermann von Helmholtz

Mary Ann Calo

Associate Professor of Art History, Colgate University
Bernard Berenson

Joseph Keim Campbell

Assistant Professor of Philosophy, Washington State University
Hugh Blair

Allen C. Carlson

Professor of Philosophy, University of Alberta
Landscape, *article on* Landscape Assessment; Nature, *article on* Contemporary Thought

Taylor Carman

Assistant Professor of Philosophy, Barnard College, Columbia University
Martin Heidegger, *article on* Survey of Thought

David Carrier

Professor of Philosophy, Carnegie Mellon University
Charles Baudelaire, *article on* Survey of Thought; Adrian Durham Stokes; Richard Wollheim

Joseph Carroll

Professor of English, University of Missouri, St. Louis
Matthew Arnold

Noël Carroll

Monroe C. Beardsley Professor of Philosophy, University of Wisconsin, Madison
Film, *article on* Motion Pictures; Morality and Aesthetics, *historical and conceptual overview article;* Politics and Aesthetics, *historical and conceptual overview article*

Curtis L. Carter

Professor of Aesthetics and Director, Haggerty Museum of Art, Marquette University, Milwaukee
Dadaism

Anthony Cascardi

Professor of Comparative Literature, University of California, Berkeley
Ludwig Joseph Johann Wittgenstein, *article on* Wittgenstein and Literary Theory

Allan Casebier

Professor of Communication, University of Miami, Coral Gables
Phenomenology

Terry Castle

Professor of English and Walter Haas Chair in the Humanities, Stanford University
Lesbian Aesthetics

Marcia Cavell

Occasional Associate Professor of Philosophy, University of California, Berkeley
Sigmund Freud, *article on* Freud and Literature

Mary Ann Caws

Professor of Comparative Literature, Graduate School and University Center, City University of New York
Surrealism, *article on* Surrealism and Literature

Howard Caygill

Professor of Cultural History, Goldsmiths College, University of London
Henry Home

Kermit Swiler Champa

Andrea V. Rosenthal Professor of the History of Art and Architecture, Brown University
Piet Mondrian

V. K. Chari

Adjunct Professor of English, Carleton University, Ottawa
Abhinavagupta; Indian Aesthetics, *article on* Indian Theories of Interpretation; Rasa

Michael Charlesworth

Assistant Professor of Art History, University of Texas, Austin
Uvedale Price

Mark A. Cheetham

Professor of Visual Arts, University of Western Ontario
Immanuel Kant, *article on* Kant and Art History

Thomas Christensen

Associate Professor of Music, University of Iowa
Johann Mattheson

Olivier Christin

Professor of History, Université de Lyon II
Religion and Aesthetics, *article on* Religion and Art

Margaret Cohen

Associate Professor of Comparative Literature, New York University
Walter Benjamin, *article on* Benjamin and Surrealism

Ted Cohen

Professor of Philosophy, University of Chicago
Jokes; Sports; Television, *article on* Contemporary Thought

David Cole

Professor of Law, Georgetown University Law Center
Law and Art, *article on* Government-Funded Art and the First Amendment

Frances Colpitt

Associate Professor of Art History and Criticism, University of Texas, San Antonio
Minimalism

Frances S. Connelly

Associate Professor of Art History, University of Missouri, Kansas City
Grotesque; Primitivism

David E. Cooper

Professor of Philosophy, University of Durham, United Kingdom
Romanticism, *article on* Visual Arts

Elizabeth Cornwell

Preceptor, Art History Department, Columbia University
Postcolonialism

Gregory Currie

Professor of Philosophy and Head, School of Arts, Flinders University of South Australia
Ontology of Art, *article on* Analytic Ontology

Daniel O. Dahlstrom

Professor of Philosophy, Boston University
Johann Christoph Gottsched; Edmund Gustav Albrecht Husserl; Johann Ulrich von König

Arthur C. Danto

Johnsonian Professor Emeritus of Philosophy, Columbia University
Pop Art, *article on* Aesthetics of Andy Warhol

Stephen Davies

Associate Professor of Philosophy, University of Auckland, New Zealand
Authenticity, *conceptual overview article;* Theories of Art

Whitney Davis

John Evans Professor of Art History, Northwestern University
Formalism, *article on* Formalism in Art History; Sexuality

Martine Debaisieux

Professor of French, University of Wisconsin, Madison
Nicolas Boileau-Despreaux; Charles Sorel

Mark DeBellis

Associate Professor of Music, Columbia University
Perception, *article on* Music Perception

Thierry de Duve

Elliot and Roslyn Jaffe Visiting Professor of History of Art, University of Pennsylvania
Immanuel Kant, *article on* Kant, Duchamp, and Judgment

Kelly Dennis

Assistant Professor of Art History, Theory, and Criticism, School of the Art Institute of Chicago
Performance Art, *historical overview article*

Eliot Deutsch

Professor and Chair, Department of Philosophy, University of Hawaii at Manoa
Comparative Aesthetics

Mary Devereaux

Associate Professor of Philosophy, University of California, San Diego
Autonomy, *article on* Autonomy and Its Feminist Critics

George Dickie

Professor Emeritus of Philosophy, University of Illinois, Chicago
Evaluation, *article on* Aesthetic Evaluation

T. J. Diffey
Reader in Philosophy, School of Cultural and Community Studies, University of Sussex
Essentialism, *conceptual overview article;* William Wordsworth

Jeffrey R. Di Leo
Editor in Chief, symplokē, *School of Literature, Communication, and Culture, Georgia Institute of Technology*
Text

Paul J. DiMaggio
Professor of Sociology, Princeton University
Museums, *article on* Sociological Perspectives on Museums

Edward Dimendberg
Film, Architecture, and German Departments, University of Michigan
Film, *article on* Film Noir

Randall Dipert
Professor of English and Philosophy, United States Military Academy, West Point
Artifact

Beth Ann Dobie
Assistant Professor, Division of Human Studies, Alfred University
Intention, *article on* Speech Act Theory and the Interpretation of Images

Mo Dodson
Principal Lecturer in Communications, London Guildhall University
Design

Neil H. Donahue
Associate Professor of German and Comparative Linguistics, Hofstra University
Wilhelm Worringer

Martin Donougho
Associate Professor of Philosophy, University of South Carolina
Georg Wilhelm Friedrich Hegel, *article on* Hegel on the Historicity of Art; Johann Joachim Winckelmann

Linda Dowling
Independent scholar, Princeton, New Jersey
Aestheticism

Johanna Drucker
Associate Professor of History of Art, Yale University
Modernism, *overview article*

Aruna D'Souza
Doctoral candidate, Institute of Fine Arts, New York University
Surrealism, *article on* Surrealism and the Visual Arts

Steven C. Dubin
Associate Professor of Sociology, State University of New York, Purchase
Politics and Aesthetics, *article on* Politicized Art

Daniel Dumouchel
Assistant Professor of Philosophy, Université de Montréal
Georg Friedrich Meier; Johann Georg Sulzer

Denis Dutton
Senior Lecturer in the Philosophy of Art, University of Canterbury, New Zealand
Forgery; Tribal Art

Wayne R. Dynes
Professor of Art History, Hunter College, City University of New York
Gothic Aesthetics

Marcia Muelder Eaton
Professor of Philosophy, University of Minnesota
Morality and Aesthetics, *article on* Contemporary Aesthetics and Ethics

Katherine Eggert
Assistant Professor of English, University of Colorado, Boulder
Historicism, *article on* New Historicism in Literary Theory

Richard Eldridge
Associate Professor of Philosophy, Swarthmore College
Romanticism, *article on* Philosophy and Literature

Catherine Z. Elgin
Visiting Professor of Philosophy, Princeton University
Science and Aesthetics, *article on* Contemporary Thought

Aaron H. Esman
Professor Emeritus of Clinical Psychiatry, Cornell University Medical College
Insane, Art of the

Ellen Esrock
Associate Professor of Literature, Rensselaer Polytechnic Institute
Imagery, *article on* Visual Imagery in Reading

Susan L. Feagin
Professor of Philosophy, University of Missouri, Kansas City
Drawing; Emotions, *article on* Emotions and Literature; Imagination, *article on* Contemporary Thought

Stuart Feder
Clinical Associate Professor of Psychiatry, Albert Einstein College of Medicine, New York
Sigmund Freud, *article on* Freud and Music

Rita Felski
Professor of English, University of Virginia
Feminism, *article on* Critique of Feminist Aesthetics

David Fenner
Assistant Professor of History, Philosophy, and Religious Studies, University of North Florida
Attitude, *article on* Aesthetic Attitude

Peter Fenves
Professor of German and Comparative Literature and Herman and Beulah Pearce-Miller Research Professor in Literature, Northwestern University
Johann Christian Friedrich Hölderlin

Frances Ferguson

Professor of English and the Humanities, Johns Hopkins University
Edmund Burke; Sublime, *article on* The Sublime from Burke to the Present

David H. Fisher

Professor of Philosophy and Chair, Department of Philosophy, North Central College, Illinois
Theory, History of

Christopher Fitter

Assistant Professor of English, Rutgers University
Landscape, *article on* Landscape from the Ancients to the Seventeenth Century

Lisa Florman

Assistant Professor of History of Art, Ohio State University
Pablo Picasso

Thomas R. Flynn

Samuel Candler Dobbs Professor of Philosophy, Emory University
Jean-Paul Sartre

Cheryl Foster

Assistant Professor of Philosophy, University of Rhode Island
Nature, *article on* Nature and Artistic Creation

Kenneth Frampton

Ware Professor, School of Architecture, Columbia University
Futurism

Henry Frankel

Professor of Philosophy, University of Missouri, Kansas City
Glass, *article on* Aesthetics of Glass

Susanne K. Frantz

Curator of Twentieth-Century Glass, Corning Museum of Glass
Glass, *article on* Glass Art

Francis Frascina

John Raven Professor of Visual Arts, Keele University, United Kingdom
Collage, *conceptual and historical overview article*

Cynthia Freeland

Associate Dean, College of Humanities, Fine Arts, and Communication, University of Houston
Film, *article on* Feminist Film Theory

Barbara Claire Freeman

Associate Professor of English and American Literature and Language, Harvard University
Sublime, *article on* Feminine Sublime

Eli Friedlander

Assistant Professor of Philosophy, Tel Aviv University
Opera

Michal Grover Friedlander

Assistant Professor of Musicology, Tel Aviv University
Opera

Josef Früchtl

Department of Philosophy, Westfälische Wilhelms-Universität Münster
Theodor Wiesengrund Adorno, *article on* Adorno and Mimesis

Thomas Furniss

Senior Lecturer, Department of English Studies, University of Strathclyde, Glasgow
Joseph Addison

John Gage

Reader in the History of Western Art, University of Cambridge
Synaesthesia

Claude Gandelman

Professor of French, University of Haifa, Israel (deceased)
Imagery, *article on* Reading Images

Gunter Gebauer

Professor, Institute of Philosophy, Freie Universität Berlin
Mimesis

Alexander Gelley

Professor of Comparative Literature, University of California, Irvine
Rhetoric, *article on* Exemplarity

Jeremy Gilbert-Rolfe

Chair, Graduate Program in Fine Art, Art Center College of Design, Pasadena
Contemporary Art, *article on* Aesthetics of Contemporary Art

Jonathan Gilmore

Visiting Assistant Professor of Philosophy, Barnard College, Columbia University
Arthur Coleman Danto, *article on* Danto's End of Art Thesis; Narrative, *article on* Internal Narratives of Art History; Realism, *article on* Pictorial Realism

David L. Gitomer

Associate Professor of Religious Studies, DePaul University
Indian Aesthetics, *historical and conceptual overview article*

Sima Godfrey

Associate Professor of French, University of British Columbia
Charles Baudelaire, *article on* Baudelaire and Art

David Goldblatt

Professor of Philosophy, Denison University, Granville, Ohio
Architecture, *article on* Modernism to Postmodernism

Leon Golden

Professor of Classics, Florida State University
Aristotle, *article on* Reception of Aristotle in Modernity

Alan Goldman

Professor and Chair, Department of Philosophy, University of Miami
Realism, *article on* Realism and Aesthetics; Representation, *conceptual and historical overview article*

Jennifer González

Assistant Professor of Art History, University of California, Santa Cruz
Installation Art

John Goodman
Translator and art historian, Brooklyn, New York
Denis Diderot, *article on* Diderot and the Salon

Nelson Goodman
Professor Emeritus of Philosophy, Harvard University
Nelson Goodman, *article on* Art in Action

Carol Gould
Assistant Professor of Philosophy, Florida Atlantic University
Arthur Clive Howard Bell

Timothy Gould
Professor of Philosophy, Metropolitan State College of Denver
Stanley Cavell, *article on* Survey of Thought; Ralph Waldo
Emerson; Genius, *conceptual and historical overview article*

Oleg Grabar
*Professor, School of Historical Studies, Institute for Advanced Study,
Princeton, New Jersey*
Islamic Aesthetics, *historical and conceptual overview article*

Theodore A. Gracyk
*Professor and Chair, Department of Philosophy, Moorhead State
University, Minnesota*
Immanuel Kant, *article on* Kant on Nature and Art

Jean Grondin
Professor of Philosophy, Université de Montréal
Hans-Georg Gadamer, *article on* Gadamer and the Truth of Art

Ann Hutchinson Guest
Director, Language of Dance Centre, London
Notation, *article on* Dance Notation

Yair Guttmann
Assistant Professor of Philosophy, Stanford University
Conceptual Art, *article on* Conceptual Art and Philosophy

Paul Guyer
Professor of Philosophy, University of Pennsylvania
Alexander Gottlieb Baumgarten; George Berkeley; Marcus Herz;
Karl Heinrich Heydenreich; Immanuel Kant, *article on* Survey of
Thought; Rudolph Hermann Lotze; Moses Mendelssohn

Garry Hagberg
Associate Professor of Philosophy, Bard College
Improvisation, *article on* Jazz Improvisation; Ludwig Josef Johann
Wittgenstein, *article on* Reception of Wittgenstein

Margaret A. Hagen
Professor of Psychology, Boston University
Perception, *article on* Psychology of Perception

Barry Hallen
*Fellow, W. E. B. Du Bois Institute for Afro-American Research, Harvard
University*
African Aesthetics

Stephen Halliwell
Professor of Greek, University of Saint Andrews, Scotland
Aristotle, *article on* Aristotle on Form and Unity

James R. Hamilton
Associate Professor of Philosophy, Kansas State University
Bertolt Brecht

Michele Hannoosh
Professor of French, University College London
Caricature; Ferdinand-Victor-Eugène Delacroix

Forest Hansen
Professor Emeritus of Philosophy, Lake Forest College
Susanne Knauth Langer

Karen Hanson
Professor of Philosophy, Indiana University
Fashion, *article on* Fashion and Philosophy

C. L. Hardin
Professor Emeritus of Philosophy, Syracuse University
Color, *article on* Color Science

William E. Harkins
Professor Emeritus of Slavic Languages, Columbia University
Russian Aesthetics, *articles on* Russian Formalism *and* Socialist
Realism

Karsten Harries
Professor of Philosophy, Yale University
Architecture, *modern overview article;* Martin Heidegger, *article on*
Heidegger's Confrontation with Aesthetics

Andrew Harrison
Senior Lecturer in Philosophy, University of Bristol, United Kingdom
Medium

Bernard Harrison
E. E. Erickson Professor of Philosophy, University of Utah
Literature, *article on* Literature and Cognition

Charles Harrison
*Professor of the History and Theory of Art, The Open University,
Oxford*
Conceptual Art, *article on* History of the Unformed

Joan Hart
Independent scholar, Bloomington, Indiana
Heinrich Wölfflin

Casey Haskins
*Assistant Professor of Philosophy, State University of New York,
Purchase*
Autonomy, *historical overview article;* John Dewey, *article on* Survey
of Thought

Carl R. Hausman
Professor Emeritus of Philosophy, Pennsylvania State University
Creativity, *conceptual and historical overview article;* Metaphor,
article on Metaphor and Nonverbal Arts

Deborah J. Haynes
*Director, Women's Studies Program, and Associate Professor of Fine
Arts, Washington State University*
Mikhail Mikhailovich Bakhtin

K. Michael Hays

Professor of Architectural Theory, Graduate School of Design, Harvard University
Autonomy, *article on* Autonomy and Architecture; Ludwig Mies van der Rohe

Michael Heim

Researcher in Digital Media, Art Center College of Design, Pasadena
Cyberspace; Multimedia; Virtual Reality

Hilde Hein

Professor of Philosophy, College of the Holy Cross
Law and Art, *article on* Aesthetic Concepts in Law; Museums, *article on* Museums and Aesthetics

Marjorie Heins

Director and Staff Counsel, Arts Censorship Project, American Civil Liberties Union Foundation, New York
Law and Art, *article on* Censorship

Reinhold Heller

Professor of Art History and of Germanic Studies, University of Chicago
Expressionism

James D. Herbert

Associate Professor of Art History, University of California, Irvine
Impressionism

Göran Hermerén

Chair, Department of Medical Ethics, Lunds Universitet
Qualities, Aesthetic

María Herrera

Senior Research Associate and Professor of Philosophy, Institute for Philosophical Research, Universidad Nacional Autónoma de México
Latin American Aesthetics, *article on* Latin American Aesthetics and Modernity

Daniel Herwitz

Professor and Chair, Department of Philosophy, University of Natal, Durban, South Africa
John Cage; Constructivism; Arthur Coleman Danto, *article on* Survey of Thought; Pleasure; Postmodernism, *historical and conceptual overview article*

Patricia Herzog

Visiting Assistant Professor of Philosophy, Brandeis University
Criticism, *article on* Music Criticism

Kathleen Higgins

Professor of Philosophy, University of Texas, Austin
Emotions, *historical overview article*; Friedrich Wilhelm Nietzche, *article on* Nietzsche's Literary Style

Stephen Hinton

Associate Professor and Chair, Department of Music, Stanford University
Theodor Wiesengrund Adorno, *article on* Adorno's Philosophy of Music

Harvey Hix

Professor, Department of Liberal Arts, Kansas City Art Institute
Poetics

Anne Hollander

Writer, New York
Fashion, *articles on* Dress in the World *and* La Haute Couture

Elizabeth Hollander

Doctoral candidate in English, City University of New York
Artists' Models; Oscar Wilde

John Hollander

Sterling Professor of English, Yale University
Ecphrasis

Martha Hollander

Assistant Professor of Art History, New College, Hofstra University
Baroque Aesthetics

Michael Ann Holly

Professor of Art History, University of Rochester
Erwin Panofsky

Robert C. Holub

Professor of German, University of California, Berkeley
Reception Aesthetics

Gregg Horowitz

Assistant Professor of Philosophy, Vanderbilt University
Ernst Hans Josef Gombrich

Stephen Houlgate

Professor of Philosophy, University of Warwick, United Kingdom
Georg Wilhelm Friedrich Hegel, *article on* Survey of Thought

Tom Huhn

Visiting Assistant Professor of Philosophy, Wesleyan University
Theodor Wiesengrund Adorno, *article on* Adorno and Kant

John Dixon Hunt

Professor and Chairman, Department of Landscape Architecture and Regional Planning, University of Pennsylvania
Gardens, *historical overview article*

Ian Hunter

Associate Professor in Humanities and Queen Elizabeth II Fellow, School of Humanities, Griffith University, Nathan, Australia
Cultural Studies

Ann Hurley

Professor of English, Wagner College, Staten Island, New York
Ut Pictura Poesis

Eleftherios Ikonomou

Architect, London Architectural Association
August Schmarsow

Gary Iseminger

William H. Laird Professor of Philosophy and Liberal Arts, Carleton College
Intention, *article on* Intentional Fallacy

Wolfgang Iser

Professor Emeritus of Literary Studies, Konstanz Universität; and Professor of English, University of California, Irvine
Fiction, *article on* Contemporary and Literary Account of the Fictive; Imagination, *article on* The Imaginary

Daniel Jacobson

Assistant Professor of Philosophy, College of Charleston
Philip Sidney

Dale Jacquette

Professor of Philosophy, Pennsylvania State University
Johann Wolfgang von Goethe

Christopher Janaway

Senior Lecturer in Philosophy, University of London
Plato, *article on* Survey of Thought

Richard Janko

Professor of Greek, University College London
Aristotle, *article on* Reception of Aristotle in Antiquity

I. C. Jarvie

Professor of Philosophy, University of York, Canada
Creativity, *article on* Explaining Creativity

Mark Jarzombek

Professor of Architecture, Massachusetts Institute of Technology
Leon Battista Alberti

Joan Jeffri

Director, Research Center for Arts and Culture, Columbia University; and Director, Program in Arts Administration, Teachers College, Columbia University
Artist, *article on* Sociology of the Artist

Galen A. Johnson

Professor and Chair, Department of Philosophy, University of Rhode Island
Maurice Merleau-Ponty

Jeannine Johnson

Visiting Instructor of English, Wake Forest University
New Criticism

Mark Johnson

Professor and Chair, Department of Philosophy, University of Oregon
Metaphor, *overview article*

Amelia Jones

Associate Professor of Art History, University of California, Riverside
Marcel Duchamp, *article on* En-Gendering of the Artistic Subject; Performance Art, *article on* Feminist Performance Art

Caroline A. Jones

Assistant Professor of Art History, Boston University
Abstract Expressionism

Peter Jones

Director, Institute for Advanced Studies in the Humanities, and Professor of Philosophy, University of Edinburgh
David Hume, *article on* Survey of Thought; Adam Smith

Guillemette Morel Journel

Editor, Les cahiers de la recherche architecturale, *Paris*
Le Corbusier

Deborah Jowitt

Dance Faculty, Tisch School of the Arts, New York University; Senior Dance Critic, The Village Voice
Modernism, *article on* Modern Dance

Peggy Kamuf

Professor of French and Comparative Literature, University of Southern California
Jacques Derrida, *article on* Derrida and Literature

Peter H. Karlen

Attorney, La Jolla, California
Moral Rights of Art, *article on* Moral Rights Legislation

Douglas Kellner

George F. Kneller Philosophy of Education Chair, University of California, Los Angeles
Jean Baudrillard; Fredric Jameson

Mary Kelly

Professor and Chair, Department of Art, School of the Arts and Architecture, University of California, Los Angeles
Contemporary Art, *article on* Images and Desire

Norman Kelvin

Professor of English, City College and Graduate Center, City University of New York
William Morris

Salim Kemal

Professor of Philosophy, University of Dundee, Scotland
Arab Aesthetics; Muḥammad al-Fārābī; Ibn Rushd; Ibn Sīnā; Immanuel Kant, *article on* Kant on Beauty

Grant Kester

Assistant Professor of Modern Art History and Theory, Washington State University
Raymond Williams

Peter Kivy

Professor of Philosophy, Rutgers University
Edmund Gurney

Jane Kneller

Assistant Professor of Philosophy, Colorado State University
Disinterestedness; Immanuel Kant, *article on* Feminism and Kantian Aesthetics

David Kolb

Charles A. Dana Professor of Philosophy, Bates College
Modernism, *article on* Modernity and Tradition in Architecture

Katherine Kolb

Lecturer, Department of French and Italian, University of Minnesota
Romanticism, *article on* Music

Nikolas Kompridis

Assistant Professor of Philosophy, Wilfrid Laurier University, Waterloo, Canada
Jürgen Habermas

Franz Koppe

Professor of Philosophy, Institute for Philosophy and Social Sciences, Hochschule der Künst, Berlin
Herbert Marcuse

Carolyn Korsmeyer

Associate Professor of Philosophy, State University of New York, Buffalo
Perception, *article on* Aesthetics of Perception; Taste, *article on* Modern and Recent History

Michael Krausz

Professor and Chair, Department of Philosophy, Bryn Mawr College
Interpretation, *article on* Interpretation in Art

Paul Oskar Kristeller

Woodbridge Professor Emeritus of Philosophy, Columbia University
Origins of Aesthetics, *historical and conceptual overview article*

Lucian Krukowski

Professor of Philosophy, Washington University, St. Louis
Abstraction; Formalism, *conceptual and historical overview article*

Michael Kubovy

Professor of Psychology, University of Virginia
Perspective, *article on* Psychology of Perspective

Margaret P. Kuhns

Adjunct Clinical Associate, Psychology Doctoral Program, Pace University
Sigmund Freud, *article on* Survey of Thought

Richard Kuhns

Professor Emeritus of Philosophy, Columbia University
Augustine; Sigmund Freud, *article on* Survey of Thought; Katharsis; Karl Mannheim; Tragedy, *article on* Freud on Tragedy; Donald Woods Winnicott

Peter Lamarque

Professor of Philosophy, University of Hull
Truth

George P. Landow

Professor of English and Art History, Brown University
Hypertext

Berel Lang

Professor of Philosophy, State University of New York, Albany
Marxism, *historical and conceptual overview article*; Style

Neil Larsen

Associate Professor of Spanish and Classics, University of California, Davis
Marxism, *article on* Marxism and Materialism

Thomas Leddy

Professor of Philosophy, San Jose State University
Essentialism, *article on* Anti-Essentialism

Richard Lehv

Attorney, New York
Law and Art, *article on* Trademarks and Art

Barbara Lekatsas

Professor of Comparative Literature, Hofstra University
André Breton

Jerrold Levinson

Professor of Philosophy, University of Maryland, College Park
Arthur Schopenhauer

Tamara Levitz

Associate Professor of Musicology, McGill University
Igor Fedorovich Stravinsky

Edward A. Lippman

Professor Emeritus of Music, Columbia University
Music, *historical overview article*

Rosemary Lloyd

Chair, Department of French and Italian, Indiana University, Bloomington
Stéphane Mallarmé

Patrizia Lombardo

Professor of French and Comparative Literature, Université de Genève
Hippolyte Adolphe Taine

Dominic M. McIver Lopes

Associate Professor of Philosophy, Indiana University, Kokomo
Representation, *article on* Depiction

Renée Lorraine

Professor of Music, University of Tennessee, Chattanooga
Music, *article on* Music and Feminism

Tommy Lott

Professor of Philosophy, San Jose State University
Alain Leroy Locke

Colin A. Lyas

Senior Lecturer in Philosophy, Lancaster University, United Kingdom
Benedetto Croce; Giovanni Gentile; Luigi Pareyson

Bernd Magnus

Professor of Philosophy and Humanities, University of California, Riverside
Friedrich Wilhelm Nietzsche, *article on* Survey of Thought

Rudolf Makkreel

Professor of Philosophy, Emory University
Wilhelm Dilthey; Immanuel Kant, *article on* Kant and Hermeneutics

Harry F. Mallgrave

Senior Research Fellow, Getty Research Institute for the History of Art and the Humanities
Gottfried Semper

Avishai Margalit
Professor of Philosophy, Center for Rationality and Interactive Decision Theory, Hebrew University of Jerusalem
Nelson Goodman, *article on* Survey of Thought

Joseph Margolis
Laura H. Carnell Professor of Philosophy, Temple University
Historicism, *article on* Historicism and Philosophy; Ontology of Art, *article on* Historical Ontology

Sally Markowitz
Professor of Philosophy, Willamette University
Edward Bullough

György Márkus
Professor of General Philosophy, University of Sydney
György Lukács

Richard Martin
Curator, Costume Institute, Metropolitan Museum of Art, New York
Fashion, *article on* Fashion as Art

Robert L. Martin
Professor of Philosophy and Music and Dean of Graduate Studies, Bard College
Ontology of Art, *article on* Ontology of Music

Colin Martindale
Professor of Psychology, University of Maine
Empirical Aesthetics

Joseph Masheck
Professor of Art History, Hofstra University
Rudolf Wittkower

Paul Mattick
Associate Professor of Philosophy, Adelphi University
Pierre Bourdieu, *article on* Survey of Thought; Ideology

Carol Mavor
Associate Professor of Art, University of North Carolina, Chapel Hill
Obscenity, *article on* Obscenity in Art

Gita May
Professor of French and Romance Philology, Columbia University
Jean Le Rond D'Alembert; Denis Diderot, *article on* Survey of Thought; French Aesthetics, *article on* Eighteenth-Century French Aesthetics

Patrick Maynard
Associate Professor of Philosophy, University of Western Ontario
Photography, *article on* Photography and Technology

Robert McCarter
Professor and Chair, Department of Architecture, University of Florida
Frank Lloyd Wright

Peter McCormick
Professor of Philosophy, University of Ottawa
Fiction, *historical and conceptual overview article*

Thomas McEvilley
Distinguished Lecturer in Art History, Rice University
Contemporary Art, *article on* Postmodern Transformation of Art

Indra Kagis McEwen
Faculty Lecturer, Department of Art History, McGill University
Architecture, *article on* Early Greek Aesthetics

Graham McFee
Lecturer, Chelsea School of Physical Education, Sports Science, Dance and Leisure, University of Brighton
Criticism, *article on* Dance Criticism; Dance, *article on* Contemporary Thought

Reginald McGinnis
Associate Professor of French and Italian, University of Arizona
Irony

Ralph McInerny
Professor of Philosophy, Jacques Maritain Center, University of Notre Dame
Jacques Maritain

Sheila McTighe
Assistant Professor of Art History, Barnard College, Columbia University
Nicolas Poussin

Françoise Meltzer
Chair and Professor of Comparative Literature and Professor of French and Divinity, University of Chicago
Originality, *article on* Originality in Literature

Stephen Melville
Professor of History of Art, Ohio State University
Jacques Derrida, *article on* Survey of Thought; Gaze; Clement Greenberg; Jacques Marie Lacan, *article on* Survey of Thought; Metonymy

Christoph Menke
Associate Professor of Philosophy, Graduate Faculty, New School for Social Research
Theodor Wiesengrund Adorno, *article on* Adorno's Dialectic of Appearance

Detlef Mertins
Assistant Professor of Architecture, School of Architecture and Landscape Architecture, University of Toronto
Bauhaus; Sigfried Giedion

Paul Messaris
Professor of Communications, Annenberg School of Communications, University of Pennsylvania
Film, *article on* Visual Literacy

Kerstin Mey
Lecturer in History and Theory of Art, Duncan of Jordanstone College of Art and Design, University of Dundee, Scotland
Sculpture

Christian Michel
Professor of History of Modern Art, Université de Paris X, Nanterre
Charles-Nicolas Cochin

Robin Middleton
Professor of Art History, Columbia University
Jean-Nicolas-Louis Durand

James Miller
Faculty Professor of Art, University of Western Ontario
Politics and Art, *article on* AIDS, Aesthetics, and Activism

Mara Miller
Research Fellow in Art History, Emory University
Gardens, *article on* Gardens as Art

William J. Mitchell
Professor of Architecture and Media Arts and Sciences and Dean, School of Architecture and Planning, Massachusetts Institute of Technology
Digital Media, *article on* The Postphotographic Image

Michael Mitias
Professor and Chair, Department of Philosophy, Millsaps College, Jackson, Mississippi
Mikel Dufrenne

Jeff Mitscherling
Associate Professor of Philosophy, University of Guelph, Canada
Roman Witold Ingarden

Ronald Moore
Associate Professor of Philosophy, University of Washington
Education, Aesthetic, *article on* History of Aesthetic Education; Moral Rights of Art, *historical and conceptual overview article;* Ugliness

James M. Moran
Doctoral Candidate in Critical Studies of Cinema and Television, University of Southern California
Video

Julius Moravcsik
Professor of Philosophy, Stanford University
Plato, *articles on* Plato on the Effects of Art *and* Plato and Modern Aesthetics

Robert P. Morgan
Professor of Music, Yale University
Arnold Franz Walter Schoenberg

John Morreall
Professor of Religious Studies, Univeristy of South Florida
Comics

Mary Mothersill
Professor Emerita of Philosophy, Barnard College, Columbia University
David Hume, *article on* "Of the Standard of Taste"

Keith Moxey
Professor of Art History, Barnard College, Columbia University
Canon, *article on* Politicizing the Canon in Art History

Myroslava M. Mudrak
Associate Professor in the History of Art, Ohio State University
Suprematism

Daniel Joseph Nadenicek
Director, Center for Studies in Landscape History, and Associate Professor of Landscape Architecture, Pennsylvania State University
Landscape, *article on* Landscape Architecture

Jean-Jacques Nattiez
Professor of Musicology, Université de Montréal
Semiotics, *article on* Semiology of Music

Josefine Nauckhoff
Assistant Professor of Philosophy, Wake Forest University
Archibald Alison; Thomas Reid

Alex Neill
Lecturer, Department of Moral Philosophy, University of Saint Andrews, Scotland
Tragedy, *article on* Hume on Tragedy

John Neubauer
Professor of Comparative Literature, Universiteit van Amsterdam
Novalis

Horace Newcomb
F. J. Heyne Centennial Professor in Communication, University of Texas, Austin
Television, *overview article*

H. B. Nisbet
Vice-Master, Department of Modern Languages, University of Cambridge
Gotthold Ephraim Lessing

Mignon Nixon
Lecturer in the History of American Art, Courtauld Institute of Art, University of London
Louise Bourgeois

David Novitz
Reader in Philosophy, University of Canterbury, New Zealand
Epistemology and Aesthetics

Ōhashi Ryōsuke
Professor of Philosophy and Aesthetics, Kyoto Institute of Technology
Japanese Aesthetics, *article on* Kire and Iki

Jeffrey K. Olick
Assistant Professor of Sociology, Columbia University
Popular Culture

Margaret Olin
Associate Professor of Art History, Theory and Criticism, School of the Art Institute of Chicago
Alois Riegl

Kelly Oliver
Associate Professor of Philosophy, University of Texas, Austin
Julia Kristeva

Stein Haugom Olsen

Chair Professor of Humanities and Director, School of General Education, Lingnan College, Hong Kong
Appreciation; Literature, *article on* Literary Aesthetics; Truth

Michael Orwicz

Professor of Art History, University of Connecticut, Storrs
Criticism, *article on* Art Criticism

Jerry Palmer

Professor of Communications, London Guildhall University
Design

Nickolas Pappas

Associate Professor of Philosophy, City College, City University of New York
Beauty, *article on* Classical Concepts

Esther Pasztory

Professor of Art History and Archaeology, Columbia University
Pre-Columbian Aesthetics

Thomas Pavel

Professor of Comparative Literature and Romance Languages and Literatures, Princeton University
Classicism

Geoffrey Payzant

Professor of Philosophy, University of Toronto
Eduard Hanslick

Joan Crystal Pearlman

Independent scholar, New York
Outsider Art

Max Pensky

Associate Professor of Philosophy, State University of New York, Binghamton
Walter Benjamin, *article on* Survey of Thought

Marjorie Perloff

Sadie Dernham Patek Professor of Humanities, Stanford University
Collage, *article on* Collage and Poetry; Gertrude Stein

Gloria Phares

Attorney, Paul, Hastings, Janofsky, & Walker, New York
Appropriation, *article on* Appropriation Art and Copyright Law

Carl Plantinga

Professor of Theatre Arts, Hollins College, Roanoke, Virginia
Film, *article on* Film and Documentary

Arkady Plotnitsky

Visiting Associate Professor of Literature, Duke University
Mathematics and Aesthetics; Science and Aesthetics, *conceptual and historical overview article*

Christine Poggi

Associate Professor of Art History, University of Pennsylvania
Collage, *article on* "The Pasted-Paper Revolution" Revisited

Larsen Powell

Instructor of German, Barnard College, Columbia University
Pierre Boulez

Donald Preziosi

Professor of Art History, University of California, Los Angeles
Museums, *article on* Museology

Stephen Prince

Associate Professor of Communication Studies, Virginia Polytechnic Institute and State University
Film, *article on* Film and Ideology

Jessica Prinz

Associate Professor of English, Ohio State University
Discourse

Thomas Puttfarken

Professor of History and Theory of Art, University of Essex, United Kingdom
Roger de Piles

Mel Ramsden

Artist, London
Conceptual Art, *article on* History of the Unformed

Herman Rapaport

Helen DeRoy Professor of English, Wayne State University
Jacques Marie Lacan, *article on* Visual and Literary Arts

Mary Rawlinson

Associate Professor of Philosophy, State University of New York, Stony Brook
Michel Foucault

Christopher Reed

Assistant Professor of Art History, Lake Forest College
Bloomsbury Group; Gay Aesthetics

Cedric D. Reverand II

Professor of English, University of Wyoming, Laramie
John Dryden

Michele H. Richman

Associate Professor of French, University of Pennsylvania
Georges Bataille

Aaron Ridley

Senior Lecturer in Philosophy, University of Southampton, United Kingdom
Emotions, *article on* Emotions and Music; Richard Wagner

Charles A. Riley II

Associate Professor of English, Baruch College, City University of New York; Editor in Chief, WE *magazine*
Color, *article on* Color in the Arts

Bruce Robbins

Professor of English and Comparative Literature, Rutgers University
Literature, *article on* What is Literature?

Hilary Robinson
Lecturer in the History and Theory of Art, University of Ulster at Belfast
Luce Irigaray

D. N. Rodowick
Professor of English and Visual/Cultural Studies, University of Rochester
Jacques Derrida, *article on* Derrida and Kant

Mark Rollins
Associate Professor of Philosophy, Washington University, Saint Louis
Attitude, *article on* Pictorial Attitude; Perception, *article on* Picture Perception

Holmes Rolston III
University Distinguished Professor, Colorado State University
Landscape, *article on* Landscape from the Eighteenth Century to the Present

Carlin Romano
Professor of Philosophy, Bennington College; literary critic, Philadelphia Inquirer
Umberto Eco

David Rosand
Meyer Schapiro Professor of Art History, Columbia University
Meyer Schapiro

Jason M. Rosenfeld
Adjunct Assistant Professor of Fine Arts, New York University
Joshua Reynolds

Mark Roskill
Professor of History of Modern Art, University of Massachusetts, Amherst
Cubism; Wassily Kandinsky

Stephanie Ross
Associate Professor of Philosophy, University of Missouri, Saint Louis
Picturesque

Stephen David Ross
Professor of Philosophy, State University of New York, Binghamton
Beauty, *conceptual and historical overview article*

Cynthia Rostankowski
Associate Professor of Philosophy, San Jose State University
Children's Art

Albert Rothenberg
Clinical Professor of Psychiatry, Harvard University
Creativity, *article on* Creativity and Psychology

William Rothman
Professor of Film, School of Communications, University of Miami
Stanley Cavell, *article on* Cavell and Film

Fred L. Rush, Jr.
Assistant Professor of Philosophy, University of Kansas
Georg Wilhelm Friedrich Hegel, *article on* Hegel's Conception of the End of Art; Richard Payne Knight; Jean Paul

John Paul Russo
Professor of English, University of Miami
Ivor Armstrong Richards

John Russon
Assistant Professor of Philosophy, Pennsylvania State University
Plotinus

Herman Saatkamp, Jr.
Professor, Department of Humanities in Medicine, Texas A&M University
George Santayana

Warren Sack
Research Assistant and doctoral candidate, Media Laboratory, Massachusetts Institute of Technology
Artificial Intelligence and Aesthetics

Baldine Saint Girons
Professor of Philosophy, Université de Paris X, Nanterre
Sublime, *article on* The Sublime from Longinus to Montesquieu

Yuriko Saito
Associate Professor of Liberal Arts, Rhode Island School of Design
Japanese Aesthetics, *historical overview article;* Nature, *article on* Japanese Aesthetic Appreciation of Nature

Gabriela Sakamoto
Doctoral candidate in Philosophy, University of Chicago
Representation, *article on* Resemblance

Lucia Saks
Associate Professor of Communications, Rand Afrikaans University, South Africa
Camp

David Z. Saltz
Assistant Professor of Drama, University of Georgia
Theater

Crispin Sartwell
Assistant Professor of Philosophy, University of Alabama, Tuscaloosa
Appropriation, *historical overview article;* Art for Art's Sake

David Saunders
Dean Faculty of Arts, Griffith University, Nathan, Australia
Obscenity, *article on* Aesthetics in Obscenity Law

Haun Saussy
Associate Professor of Asian Languages and Comparative Literature and Chair, Department of Asian Languages, Stanford University
Chinese Aesthetics, *historical overview article*

Barbara Savedoff
Associate Professor of Philosophy, Bernard Baruch College, City University of New York
Photography, *article on* Photography and Digital Technology

Ofelia Schutte
Professor of Philosophy, University of Florida, Gainesville
Latin American Aesthetics, *article on* Twentieth-Century Latin American Aesthetics

Mitchell Schwarzer

Associate Professor of Architectural History and Theory, California College of Arts and Crafts, San Francisco
Karl Gottlieb Wilhelm Botticher

Martin Seel

Professor of Philosophy, Justus-Liebig-Universität Giessen
Nature, *article on* Aesthetics of Nature and Ethics

Grace Seiberling

Associate Professor of Art History and Visual and Cultural Studies, University of Rochester
Art Market

David I. Seiple

Independent scholar, New York
John Dewey, *article on* Experience and the Organic Unity of Artworks

Azade Seyhan

Fairbank Professor in the Humanities, Professor of German and Comparative Literature, and Chair, Department of German, Bryn Mawr College
August Wilhelm von Schlegel

Elinor Shaffer

Visiting Fellow, All Souls College, University of Oxford
Samuel Taylor Coleridge

David Grahame Shane

Adjunct Professor of Architecture, Graduate School of Architecture, Planning, and Preservation, Columbia University
Louis Isadore Kahn

Daniel Shapiro

Attorney, New York
Law and Art, *overview article and article on* Cultural Property

Gary Shapiro

Professor of Philosophy and Tucker-Boatwright Professor in the Humanities, University of Richmond
French Aesthetics, *article on* Contemporary Painting Theory; Friedrich Wilhelm Nietzsche, *article on* Nietzsche and Visuality

Fadlou Shehadi

Professor Emeritus of Philosophy, Rutgers University
Islamic Aesthetics, *article on* Islamic Music

Bernard D. Sherman

Independent scholar, Fairfield, Iowa
Authenticity, *article on* Authenticity in Music

Richard Shiff

Professor of Art and Art History, University of Texas, Austin
Originality, *article on* Originality in the Visual Arts; Photography, *article on* Catachresis

Larry Shiner

Professor and Chair, Department of Philosophy, Sangamon State University, Springfield, Illinois
Craft; Folk Art

Roger A. Shiner

Professor Emeritus of Philosophy, University of Alberta
Law and Art, *article on* Law and Literature

Ellis Shookman

Associate Professor of German, Dartmouth College
Johann Caspar Lavater

Katy Siegel

Assistant Professor of Art, University of Memphis
Pop Art, *overview article*

Anita Silvers

Professor of Philosophy, San Francisco State University
Canon, *article on* The Canon in Aesthetics; Feminism, *overview article*

Stuart Sim

Professor of English Studies, University of Sunderland, United Kingdom
Structuralism

Barbara Herrnstein Smith

Braxton Craven Professor of Comparative Literature and English, Duke University
Evaluation, *article on* Cultural Evaluation; Value

Ralph Smith

Professor of Cultural and Educational Policy, University of Illinois, Urbana-Champaign; and Editor, Journal of Aesthetic Education
Education, Aesthetic, *article on* Contemporary Aesthetic Education

Roch C. Smith

Professor of French, University of North Carolina, Greensboro
Gaston Bachelard

John Smylie

Editorial Assistant, Journal of Philosophy, *Columbia University*
Comics

John Vignaux Smyth

Head, Department of English, Northeast Louisiana University
Irony

Joel Snyder

Professor and Chair, Department of Art History, University of Chicago
Photography, *overview article*

Robert Solomon

Professor of Philosophy, University of Texas, Austin
Emotions, *overview article*

Ruth Sonderegger

Lecturer in Philosophy, Freie Universität Berlin
Play

Priscilla Soucek

Professor of Fine Arts, Institute of Fine Arts, New York University
Islamic Aesthetics, *article on* Visual Experience in Islamic Culture

Catherine Soussloff

Associate Professor of Art History, University of California, Santa Cruz
Artist, *article on* History of the Concept of the Artist; Historicism, *article on* Historicism in Art History

John Spackman

Independent scholar, Middlebury, Vermont
Expression Theory of Art

Francis Sparshott

Professor Emeritus of Philosophy, University of Toronto
Dance, *historical and conceptual overview article*

Andreas Speer

Associate Professor of Philosophy, Thomas-Institut, Universität zu Köln
Thomas Aquinas

Ellen Handler Spitz

Lecturer on Aesthetics in Psychiatry, New York Hospital–Cornell Medical Center
Sigmund Freud, *article on* Pathography; Melanie Klein

Gayatri Chakravorty Spivak

Avalon Foundation Professor in Humanities, Columbia University
Jacques Derrida, *article on* Derrida and Deconstruction

Robert Stecker

Associate Professor of Philosophy, Central Michigan University
Relativism

Peter Steiner

Associate Professor of Slavic Literature, University of Pennsylvania
Prague School

Josef Stern

Associate Professor of Philosophy, University of Chicago
Metaphor, *article on* Metaphor and Philosophy of Language

Randall Stevenson

Reader in English Literature, University of Edinburgh
Modernism, *article on* Modern Literature

John Stopford

Visiting Lecturer in Philosophy, Universität Hannover
Politics and Aesthetics, *article on* Culture and Political Theory

Nancy S. Struever

Professor of History, Humanities Center, Johns Hopkins University
Rhetoric, *historical and conceptual overview article*

Marita Sturken

Assistant Professor of Communication, Annenberg School for Communication, University of Southern California
Monuments, *historical overview article*

David Summers

William R. Kenan, Jr., Professor of the History of Art, University of Virginia
Origins of Aesthetics, *article on* History of Aisthēsis; Metaphor, *article on* Metaphor and Art History

Kevin W. Sweeney

Associate Professor and Chair, Department of Philosophy, University of Tampa
Alexander Gerard

Jacques Taminiaux

Adelmann Professor of Philosophy, Boston College
Martin Heidegger, *article on* Philosophical Heritage in Heidegger's Concept of Art

Paul Taylor

Associate Professor of Philosophy, University of Cape Town
Intention, *overview article*

Elizabeth Telfer

Reader in Philosophy, University of Glasgow
Food

Benjamin R. Tilghman

Professor Emeritus of Philosophy, Kansas State University
Ludwig Josef Johann Wittgenstein, *article on* Survey of Thought

Marianna DeMarco Torgovnick

Professor and Chair, Department of English, Duke University
Criticism, *article on* Cultural Criticism

Dabney Townsend

Professor of Philosophy, University of Texas, Arlington
Anthony Ashley Cooper; Francis Hutcheson; Joseph Priestley; Taste, *article on* Early History

Alan Trachtenberg

Neil Grey, Jr., Professor of English and American Studies, Yale University
Photography, *article on* Daguerreotype

Zev Trachtenberg

Associate Professor of Philosophy, University of Oklahoma
Jean-Jacques Rousseau

Leo Treitler

Distinguished Professor of Music, Graduate School and University Center, City University of New York
Notation, *article on* Musical Notation

Richard Tristman

Independent scholar, New York
Canon, *historical and conceptual overview article*

Willis Truitt

Professor of Philosophy, University of South Florida
Max Raphael

Yuri Tsivian

Associate Professor of Film, University of Chicago
Sergei Mikhailovich Eisenstein

Makoto Ueda

Professor of Japanese, Stanford University
Haiku

Yayoi Uno

Assistant Professor of Music Theory, University of Colorado, Boulder
Aleatoric Processes

Julie Van Camp

Associate Professor of Philosophy, California State University, Long Beach
National Endowment of the Arts, *historical survey article and article on* Controversies; Ontology of Art, *article on* Ontology of Dance

Robert Jan van Pelt

Professor of Cultural History, University of Waterloo, Canada
Historicism, *article on* Historicism and Architecture

Michael G. Vater

Associate Professor of Philosophy, Marquette University
Friedrich Wilhelm Joseph von Schelling

Donald Verene

Charles Howard Candler Professor of Metaphysics and Moral Philosophy, Emory University
Ernst Cassirer; Giovanni Battista Vico

Ian Verstegen

Doctoral candidate in Art History, Temple University
Rudolf Arnheim, *article on* Survey of Thought

Anne Vila

Associate Professor of French, University of Wisconsin, Madison
Étienne Bonnot de Condillac; Sensibilité

Loïc Wacquant

Associate Professor of Sociology, University of California, Berkeley, and Research Associate, Center for European Sociology, Collège de France
Pierre Bourdieu, *article on* Artistic Field

Sylvia Walsh

Adjunct Professor of Philosophy, Stetson University
Søren Aabye Kierkegaard

Kenneth W. Warren

Associate Professor of English, University of Chicago
Harlem Renaissance

Samuel Weber

Professor of English and Comparative Literature, University of California, Los Angeles
Walter Benjamin, *article on* Benjamin's Writing Style

Joel Weinsheimer

Professor of English, University of Minnesota
Hans-Georg Gadamer, *article on* Gadamer and Aesthetics

Marjorie Welish

Adjunct Associate Professor of Graduate Fine Arts, Pratt Institute, New York
Donald Judd; Ad Reinhardt

Carroll William Westfall

Professor of Architectural History, University of Virginia
Historicism, *article on* Historicism and Architecture

Kenneth R. Westphal

Associate Professor of Philosophy, University of New Hampshire
Immanuel Kant, *article on* Kant on the Sublime

Samuel C. Wheeler III

Professor of Philosophy, University of Connecticut
Metaphor, *article on* Derrida and de Man on Metaphor

Cynthia White

Independent scholar, Washington, Maine
John Ruskin

Harrison Colyar White

Giddings Professor of Sociology, Columbia University
John Ruskin

James Williams

Lecturer in Philosophy, University of Dundee, Scotland
Gilles Deleuze; Jean-François Lyotard

Robert Williams

Associate Professor of History of Art and Architecture, University of California, Santa Barbara
Giorgio Vasari

Catherine Wilson

Professor of Philosophy, University of Alberta
Fiction, *article on* Epistemology of Fiction

Mary Wiseman

Professor of Philosophy, Brooklyn College, City University of New York
Roland Barthes; Poststructuralism

Nicholas Wolterstorff

Noah Porter Professor of Philosophical Theology, Yale University
Religion and Aesthetics, *overview article;* Universals

Christopher S. Wood

Associate Professor of History of Art, Yale University
Iconoclasm and Iconophobia; Perspective, *overview article*

Paul Woodruff

Professor of Philosophy, University of Texas, Austin
Plato, *articles on* Plato on Mimēsis *and* Plato's Use of Poetry

Michael J. Wreen

Associate Professor of Philosophy, Marquette University
Monroe C. Beardsley

Kathleen Wright

Professor of Philosophy, Haverford College
Hans-Georg Gadamer, *article on* Survey of Thought; Martin Heidegger, *article on* Heidegger and Hölderlin

Christoph Wulf

Professor, Institute for Sports Science, Freie Universität Berlin
Mimesis

Sylvia Wynter

Professor Emerita of Spanish and Portuguese and Afro-American Studies, Stanford University
Black Aesthetic

Robert J. Yanal

Professor of Philosophy, Wayne State University
Institutional Theory of Art

Wai-lim Yip
Professor of Chinese and Comparative Literature, University of California, San Diego
Daoist Aesthetics

James E. Young
Professor of English and Judaic Studies, University of Massachusetts, Amherst
Monuments, *article on* Twentieth-Century Countermonuments

Julian Young
Senior Lecturer in Philosophy, University of Auckland, New Zealand
Friedrich Wilhelm Nietzsche, *article on* Nietzsche, Schopenhauer, and Disinterestedness

Jan Ziolkowski
Professor of Comparative Literature and Medieval Latin and Chair, Department of Comparative Literature, Harvard University
Erick Auerbach

Vera Zolberg
Senior Lecturer in Sociology, Graduate Faculty, New School for Social Research
Sociology of Art

Günter Zöller
Professor and Chair, Department of Philosophy, University of Iowa
Joseph Beuys; Immanuel Kant, *article on* History of Kantian Aesthetics

Lambert Zuidervaart
Professor of Philosophy, Calvin College, Grand Rapids, Michigan
Theodor Wiesengrund Adorno, *article on* Survey of Thought

Marina van Zuylen
Associate Professor of French, Bard College
Difficulty, Aesthetics of

INDEX

Note: Volume numbers are printed in boldface type, followed by a colon and relevant page numbers.
Page numbers printed in boldface indicate a major discussion; those in italics refer to illustrations.

Abbate, Carolyn, **3:**322, 405
Abbt, Thomas, **2:**395
ABC (journal), **1:**223, 224
Abgeschiedenheit (Eckhart term), **2:**60
Abhinavagupta, **1:1–4**, **2:**484, 486, **4:**103, 104, 105
Abiodun, Rowland, **1:**42
Abish, Walter, **3:**287
Abramovic, Marina, **3:**468, 469, 475
Abrams, Muhal Richard, **3:**6
Abstract (Hume), **2:**426
abstract, nonobjective vs., **1:**12
Abstract Expressionism, **1:4–9**, 55, 479, **2:**307, **3:**26, 327, **4:**299–300
aleatoric processes, **1:**12, 47
art market, **1:**145
automatism, **1:**5, **3:**472
Bourgeois sculptures, **1:**302, 306
color, **1:**396
conceptual art and, **1:**441
critical interpretations, **1:**8–9, 10, **2:**215–216
Cubism and, **1:**11, 12, 383
Greenberg on, **1:**8–9, 10, 383, **2:**215–216, 335, 336
history, **1:**433, 435, 436, 441, **2:**168
as ideology, **2:**461
Lyotard on, **3:**173
Minimalism and, **3:**238, 240
originality, **1:**69
performance art and, **1:**8, **3:**467
Pop art and, **2:**282, **4:**36, 37, 38, 39, 43
Reinhardt and, **1:**6, 10, **4:**116, 118
abstraction, **1:9–12**, 433
architectural, **3:**231, 232
art evolution theories and, **4:**82
art for art's sake and, **1:**119, 120
Berenson's antipathy to, **1:**266
body depiction, **1:**303
color, **1:**396–397
Dadaist, **1:**488
formalist, **2:**215–216
Greenberg on, **2:**335
ineffability, **2:**496
Kandinsky and, **1:**6, 10, 12, **2:**496, **3:**23–26
Merleau-Ponty on, **3:**207
models, **3:**243, 247
modern dance, **3:**261
Mondrian and, **3:**266, 270, 271
postmodern reaction against, **1:**435
Reinhardt and, **4:**116–119
Romanticism comparison, **2:**46
Sartre and, **4:**214
Schapiro on, **4:**217
sculpture, **4:**258–259
Socialist Realism ban on, **4:**206
Suprematism, **1:**10, 12, **4:**336, 338

abstraction, *cont.*
Worringer as first aesthetician of, **2:**136–137, **4:**482, 483
See also Abstract Expressionism
Abstraction and Empathy (Worringer), **2:**136, 402, **4:**482, 483
Académie Française. *See* French Academy
Académie Royale de Peinture et de Sculputre (Paris), **1:**143, **3:**419, 420, **4:**74
"Academy Notes" (Ruskin), **4:**192
Acapulco (Dunn), **4:**64
Accadémia del Diségno, **1:**85, **3:**418, 431, 433
Accadèmia della Crusca, **3:**419
Accadèmia di Santo Luca, **3:**419
Acconci, Vito, **1:**434, **2:**57, **3:**469
Achugar, Hugo, **3:**114
Acker, Kathy, **2:**172
Ackerman, James S., *as contributor*, **1:**84–87
action painting. *See* Abstract Expressionism
Action Painting (Gutai), **3:**467
Act of Reading (Iser), **2:**252, 499, **4:**112
actor. *See* theater
ACT UP (AIDS Coalition to Unleash Power), **2:**283, **4:**30, 32–34
Adair, John, **1:**60
Adam, Adolphe, **4:**184
Adami, Valerio, **3:**174
Adams, Ansel, **3:**93
Adams, Henry, **2:**329
Adcock, Craig, *as contributor*, **2:**70–74
Addison, Joseph, **1:12–16**, 151, 241, **2:**292, **3:**235, 421, 442, **4:**125
cultural criticism, **1:**466
on disinterestedness, **2:**61, 63
as Du Bos influence, **2:**230
as Hume source, **2:**429
on imagination, **2:**469
influence on aesthetics theory, **3:**424, 425
music criticism, **1:**472
on nature, **2:**115, **3:**93
on pleasures of imagination, **1:**12, 13, 15–16, **2:**469, **3:**424
on sublime, **1:**14–15, **3:**30, **4:**325, 332
Adeimantus, **3:**524, 526
Adler, Judith, **1:**135
Adler, Kathleen, **2:**174
Adler, Richard, **4:**364
Adorno, Theodor Wiesengrund, **1:16–32**
on aesthetic alienation, **1:**52
on art's salvific potential, **4:**126
on artwork's social significance, **2:**461, **4:**297
avant-garde concept, **1:**185, 188

Adorno, Theodor Wiesengrund, *cont.*
and Benjamin, **1:**17, 20, 23, 258, 260
and Boulez, **1:**293, 294–295, 296
dialectic of appearance, **1:**17, 18, 19, **20–23**, **2:**349
on difficult art, **2:**44, **3:**251
on Hegel, **1:**18, 19, 24, 26, 28, **2:**361
on hermeneutics, **2:**398
on high art/mass culture relationship, **1:**383
on Holocaust representation, **3:**285–286
Jameson book on, **2:**543
and Kant, **1:**18, 24, 25, **29–32**, **3:**46, **4:**330
Lukács as influence, **3:**169
Marxist theory, **3:**185, 187, 190, **4:**386
and mimesis, **1:**18–19, **23–25**, **3:**136, 233, 234, 236
on nature, **3:**340
philosophy of music, **1:**16, 22–23, **25–29**, 55, 294, 295, 296, 473, **2:**461, **3:**67, 256, 320, **4:**386
defense of modernism, **3:**258
on jazz, **1:**17, 20, 28, **2:**46, **3:**3, 7
on opera as bourgeois, **3:**405
on Schoenberg, **4:**243–244
on Stravinsky, **4:**243, 314
on play, **3:**532, 534
reception aesthetics and, **4:**112
on Stravinsky, **1:**22, 26, 27, 28, 296, **4:**386
on sublime, **3:**40, 46, **4:**330, 331
survey of thought, **1:16–20**, 52, 54, 55, 56, 174, 218, 243, 383, **2:**198, 332, 348, **4:**14–15, 158
and theory, **4:**392
on truth in art, **4:**412
"Adrian Stokes" (Wollheim), **4:**310
advertising, **1:**32, **4:**188, 203
Bauhaus, **1:**219, 223, 224
Pop art appropriations, **1:**436
Ady, Endre, **4:**347
Aeneid (Virgil), **1:**104, 159–160, 162, **2:**69, **3:**88, 145
Aertsen, Jan A., *as contributor*, **1:**249–251
Aeschylus, **1:**96, **3:**524, 526, **4:**277, 396, 397, 398
aesthēsis. See definition of art; origins of aesthetics
Aesthetica (Baumgarten), **1:**227–228, **2:**229, **3:**203, 425
Aesthetica (Bense), **4:**271
Aesthetica in nuce (Hamann), **2:**353, 394
aesthetic attitude. *See under* attitude
aesthetic authenticity. *See* authenticity
aesthetic autonomy. *See* autonomy

"Aesthetic Concepts" (Sibley), **4:**97
aesthetic consciousness (Gadamer term), **2:**267–269
"Aesthetic Dignity of the *Fleurs du Mal, The*" (Auerbach), **1:**158
Aesthetic Dimension, The (Marcuse), **3:**180, 181
aesthetic discrimination. *See* taste
aesthetic education. *See* education, aesthetic
Aesthetic Education of Mankind (Schiller), **1:**379
Aesthetic Education Project, **2:**91
aesthetic evaluation. *See under* evaluation
aesthetic experience. *See* attitude, aesthetic; experience, aesthetic
Aesthetic Experience and Literary Hermeneutics (Jauss), **4:**113
Aesthetic Ideology (de Man), **2:**5
Aestheticism, **1:32–37**
Arnold's link with, **1:**118
Baudelaire and, **1:**186
Berenson and, **1:**265–266
Bloomsbury group and, **1:**287, 288
break with mimetic and moralistic art theories, **4:**412
gay aesthetics, **2:**280–281
"House Beautiful" ideal, **1:**34
lesbian aesthetics, **3:**141–143
Morris and, **3:**299
Pater and, **1:**33, 34, 35, 36, 118, 119, **3:**446, **4:**193, 450
Ruskin's views vs., **4:**193
sensibility of, **1:**119
vulgarization of, **1:**34–35
Wilde and, **4:**450
See also art for art's sake
Aesthetic Letters (Schiller). *See On the Aesthetic Education of Man in a Series of Letters*
Aesthetic Measure (Birkhoff), **2:**112
aesthetic perception. *See under* perception
aesthetic pleasure. *See* pleasure
Aesthetic Point of View, The (Beardsley), **1:**234, 236–237
"Aesthetic Problems of Modern Philosophy" (Cavell), **1:**352
aesthetic qualities. *See* qualities, aesthetic
"Aesthetic Rights" (Tormey), **3:**290
Aesthetics (Beardsley), **1:**233–234, **2:**130, **3:**153, **4:**421
Aesthetics (Hegel), **1:**296, 367, **2:**348, 362, 364, 365–368, **3:**194
Aesthetics (Vischer), **3:**319
Aesthetics and Psychobiology (Berlyne), **2:**112–113
Aesthetics and the Good Life (Eaton), **2:**92–93, 95
"Aesthetic Significance of the Face, The" (Simmel), **4:**290